CARD, CROSS AND JONES

CRIMINAL LAW

CARD, CROSS AND JONES

CRIMINAL LAW

Nineteenth Edition

RICHARD CARD LLB, LLM, FRSA

Emeritus Professor of Law, De Montfort University, Leicester

OXFORD
UNIVERSITY PRESS

...rsity of Oxford.
...nce in research, scholarship,
...blishing worldwide in

Oxford New York

...and Cape Town Dar es Salaam Hong Kong Karachi
Kuala Lumpur Madrid Melbourne Mexico City Nairobi
New Delhi Shanghai Taipei Toronto

With offices in

Argentina Austria Brazil Chile Czech Republic France Greece
Guatemala Hungary Italy Japan Poland Portugal Singapore
South Korea Switzerland Thailand Turkey Ukraine Vietnam

Oxford is a registered trade mark of Oxford University Press
in the UK and in certain other countries

Published in the United States
by Oxford University Press Inc., New York

© Oxford University Press 2010

First Edition 1948	Eleventh Edition 1988
Second Edition 1949	Twelfth Edition 1992
Third Edition 1953	Thirteenth Edition 1995
Fourth Edition 1959	Fourteenth Edition 1998
Fifth Edition 1964	Fifteenth Edition 2001
Sixth Edition 1968	Sixteenth Edition 2004
Seventh Edition 1972	Seventeenth Edition 2006
Eighth Edition 1976	Eighteenth Edition 2008
Ninth Edition 1980	Nineteenth Edition 2010
Tenth Edition 1984	

British Library Cataloguing in Publication Data
Data available

Library of Congress Cataloging in Publication Data
Data available

Typeset by Newgen Imaging Systems (P) Ltd, Chennai, India
Printed in Great Britain
on acid-free paper by
CPI Antony Rowe

ISBN 978-0-19-957866-5

1 3 5 7 9 10 8 6 4 2

Preface

Since the publication of the last edition of this book in 2008, Parliament has continued to be active in ways affecting the content of this edition. The Coroners and Juries Act 2009, for example, has resulted in fundamental changes to the chapter on homicide and related offences. The criminal appellate courts have also been busy, as evidenced by the numerous recent decisions referred to. Recent proposals for law reform emanating from the Law Commission are also included.

In this edition I have introduced end-of-chapter further reading lists. Further reading in respect of particular cases or specific points still appears in the footnotes in each chapter, but recommended reading of a more general nature about the contents of each chapter is now contained in the end-of-chapter reading lists.

I wish to thank all those who have assisted me in various ways. In particular, I would like to thank my wife, Rachel, for her assistance with the manuscript, and the publishers for compiling tables of cases and statutes and the index. For such imperfections that remain, I am solely responsible.

I have tried to summarise and explain the law as it was reported on 31 December 2009.

Richard Card
May 2010

Contents

Table of Statutes

Paragraph numbers in **bold** type indicate where the legislation is set out in part or in full.

International legislation

Table of Cases

1

Introduction

OVERVIEW

This chapter deals with the following introductory points:

- the characteristics of criminal offences;
- the purposes of the criminal law;
- the courts of criminal jurisdiction;
- jurisdiction;
- maximum sentences;
- the sources of the criminal law;
- the European Convention on Human Rights and the Human Rights Act 1998; and
- codification of the criminal law.

1.1 This book is concerned with the substantive criminal law of England and Wales, ie the law relating to the general principles of legal liability for an offence (otherwise known as a 'crime') and specific offences. There are around 11,000 offences at a conservative estimate. This book does not attempt to deal with all of them. It concentrates on those which are more serious in nature.[1] The law of criminal procedure and of criminal evidence is outside the scope of this book, as is that relating to the disposal of offenders, although occasionally the context requires reference to be made to parts of those areas of law.

The characteristics of criminal offences

Key points 1.1

A criminal offence is a legal wrong for which the offender is liable to be prosecuted by or in the name of the State, and if found guilty liable to be punished.

---

[1] For a discussion of a much wider range of offences see English and Card *Police Law* (11th edn, 2009).

1.2 For the purposes of the law of England and Wales, a crime is a legal wrong, whether or not it is also a tort, a breach of contract or a breach of trust. The principal legal consequence of a crime is that the offender, if he is detected and it is decided to prosecute, is prosecuted by or in the name of the State,[2] and if he is found guilty is liable to be punished.

1.3 A wrong is a breach of a rule; it may be moral or legal according to whether the rule is one of morality or law. Legal wrongs may be civil or criminal or both. The distinction between a civil wrong and a criminal wrong (a crime) depends upon that between civil and criminal law. The civil law is primarily concerned with the rights and duties of individuals among themselves, whereas the criminal law defines the duties which a person owes to society.

1.4 Civil law is not exclusively concerned with the definition of wrongs, for it embraces the law of property, which largely consists of the rules governing the methods whereby property may be transferred from one person to another, and the law of succession, which concerns the devolution of property on death. There are, however, several branches of the civil law which exist in whole or in part to provide redress for wrongs; the most important of these are contract, tort and trusts.

One purpose of the law of contract is to provide redress for breaches of legally binding agreements. The aggrieved party may claim damages as claimant in civil proceedings, and the amount which he recovers is assessed on the basis of the loss which he has sustained in consequence of the non-fulfilment of the contract.

The object of the law of tort is to provide redress for breaches of duties which are owed to persons generally and do not depend on an agreement between parties. If B assaults A, or publishes a libel concerning him, or causes him personal injuries by the negligent driving of a motor car, he commits a tort and is liable to be sued by A in civil proceedings. In these cases the claimant's damages will almost always be assessed on the basis of the loss sustained in consequence of the tort, although the detailed rules of assessment may not be the same in each case.

One purpose of the law of trusts is to provide redress for breaches of trust. A breach of trust occurs where someone who holds property as trustee for another fails to carry out the duties of his office, for example by making an improper investment or wrongfully converting the trust property to his own use. He is then civilly liable to make good the loss occasioned to those on whose behalf the property was held.

1.5 The foregoing account of civil wrongs should be sufficient to indicate the two important respects in which they differ from crimes. In each instance the wrongdoer's liability is based (with very limited exceptions) on the loss which he has occasioned, and in each the law is brought into play (and proceedings can be discontinued) at the option of the injured party. Generally speaking, no one can be obliged to sue for damages for a breach

---

[2] It is possible for a prosecution for most offences to be instituted and conducted by a private individual on behalf of the State, but this is rare. Prosecutions for some offences can only be instituted by or with the consent of the Attorney-General or the Director of Public Prosecutions (in effect the Crown Prosecution Service of which the Director is the head).

of contract, a tort, or a breach of trust. On the other hand, where a crime has been committed, the wrongdoer is liable to punishment, which is a very different thing from being ordered to compensate the victim of the wrong,[3] and as a general rule a criminal prosecution may proceed although the victim has been fully compensated and desires it to be discontinued.[4]

1.6 As already indicated, the same conduct may be both a civil wrong and a crime. There are many cases in which one who commits a tort is also guilty of a crime. Assaults and collisions between vehicles are two out of numerous examples. Where a crime is also a civil wrong, criminal and civil proceedings may usually take place concurrently and the one is normally no bar to the other.[5]

An exception of general importance to this rule is that, where criminal proceedings are taken in a magistrates' court in respect of an assault or battery by or on behalf of the party aggrieved, civil proceedings in respect of it against the defendant are barred if he obtains the magistrates' certificate of the dismissal of the complaint or undergoes the punishment inflicted upon him.[6] A certificate of dismissal must be issued if the magistrates decide that the offence is not proved, or if proved is so trifling as not to merit any punishment.

1.7 The principal criticism of the definition of a crime for the purposes of the law of England and Wales set out in para 1.2 is that it fails to indicate what types of conduct are included in the category of crimes. The answer is that a definition is not the same thing as a description; its aim is simply to draw attention to the features which distinguish that which is being defined from other things of the same kind. In any event, it is impossible to find a concise formula which will cover every kind of criminal conduct. As Lord Atkin said in 1931 in *Proprietary Articles Trade Association v A-G for Canada*,[7] 'The criminal quality of an act cannot be discerned by intuition; nor can it be discovered by reference to any standard but one: is the act prohibited with penal consequences?'

The purposes of the criminal law

1.8 Views vary as to a precise list of purposes of the criminal law but the list contained in the American Law Institute's Model Penal Code, first published in 1962,[8] commands a

---

[3] If a convicted person is ordered to pay a fine, this is paid to the State and not to the victim. However, the criminal courts do have power to order, instead of or in addition to the punishment imposed, that a convicted person pay compensation to the victim.

[4] *Smith v Dear* (1903) 88 LT 664.

[5] In many cases the exercise of the power of a court in criminal proceedings (which normally take place more speedily than civil ones) to order a convicted person to compensate his victim renders separate civil proceedings unnecessary.

[6] Offences Against the Person Act 1861, ss 44 and 45.

[7] [1931] AC 310 at 324.

[8] Proposed Official Draft, Art 1, 1.02(1). The Code has been adopted by a number of states in the USA.

good deal of support[9] since it reflects the fine balance between the punishment of offensive behaviour and the exercise of individual autonomy:

'(a) to forbid and prevent conduct that unjustifiably and inexcusably inflicts or threatens substantial harm to individual or public interests;

(b) to subject to public control persons whose conduct indicates that they are disposed to commit crimes;

(c) to safeguard conduct that is without fault from condemnation as criminal;

(d) to give warning of the nature of conduct declared to be an offence;

(e) to differentiate on reasonable grounds between serious and minor offences.'

A constant question in reading this book should be the extent to which our criminal law satisfies these purposes.

The courts of criminal jurisdiction

Key points 1.2

There are two types of courts where cases against persons accused of criminal offences are heard in the first instance. One is a magistrates' court; the other is the Crown Court. Over 95 per cent of all offences are tried summarily. The chart on the opposite page shows the outline of the structure of English trial and appellate courts of criminal jurisdiction and the following paragraphs explain this, beginning at the bottom.

Magistrates' courts

1.9 The explanation which follows is based on the law as it will be when amendments made by the Criminal Justice Act 2003 are completely in force.

Magistrates' courts have two functions in criminal matters. The first is that of a court of summary jurisdiction, which determines cases without a jury. Leaving aside the special provisions relating to defendants under 18, magistrates' courts deal with two types of offence under this jurisdiction:

- *Summary offences* These are offences which, if committed by an adult, are by statute triable only summarily (ie without a jury in a magistrates' court).[10] They comprise a

---

[9] But see Robinson 'The Modern General Part – Three Illusions' in *Criminal Law Theory* (2002) (Shute and Simester (eds)) 79 for criticism.

[10] If it is one of the handful of offences in the Criminal Justice Act 1988, s 40 an offence normally triable summarily only, may be tried on indictment in the Crown Court if it is linked with an indictable offence: see paras 7.36 and 10.111 for examples of these offences.

THE CRIMINAL COURTS IN ENGLAND AND WALES

large number of relatively minor offences, such as wilful obstruction of a constable in the execution of his duty, drink-driving offences and sexual activity in a public lavatory, as well as a host of regulatory offences.

- *Offences triable either way* These are offences, such as theft and unlawful wounding, which, if committed by an adult, are triable either in the Crown Court on indictment or summarily in a magistrates' court.

  If a defendant indicates that he intends to plead guilty to an either-way offence, the magistrates proceed straight to sentence (or commit to the Crown Court for sentence, if the magistrates consider that the Crown Court – which has greater sentencing powers – should deal with the defendant). If the defendant indicates that he intends to plead not guilty, 'allocation of trial proceedings' are held to determine whether the offence should be tried by the magistrates' court or in the Crown Court. In the light of the representations made and of any information as to the defendant's previous convictions (if any), the magistrates may decide that the case is so serious that they should not try it. If they decide that Crown Court trial is not necessary, they cannot proceed to summary trial without the defendant's consent, since he has the right to elect trial in the Crown Court. In cases of serious or complex fraud or of child abuse, these provisions can be short-circuited by the service of a notice by the Director of Public Prosecutions (or certain other people in the case of fraud), in which case the defendant must be sent to the Crown Court for trial.

The second function of a magistrates' court relates to sending the defendant to the Crown Court for trial where an offence triable only on indictment, such as murder, manslaughter, rape or robbery, is involved or where an offence triable either way is not to be tried in a magistrates' court. Sending for trial is a necessary preliminary in most cases to a trial by jury. In sending for trial proceedings, the magistrates do not consider the evidence against the defendant; they must send him for trial regardless of whether there is enough evidence on which a reasonable jury could find the defendant guilty.

1.10 A magistrates' court must normally be composed of at least two lay magistrates unless a specific exemption applies. The maximum number is three.

The jurisdiction of a magistrates' court may also be exercised by a legally qualified District Judge (Magistrates' Court) sitting alone.

Lay magistrates are not required to possess any legal qualifications: for legal advice they rely on a justices' clerk or a member of the clerk's staff who is an authorised legal adviser.

1.11 There are special provisions in respect of defendants under 18. Nearly all prosecutions of those under 18 are conducted in youth courts in less formal proceedings before a District Judge (Magistrates' Courts) or a bench of two or three lay magistrates of whom normally at least one must be a man and one a woman.

The Crown Court

1.12 The Crown Court has exclusive jurisdiction over all offences which are triable only on indictment[11] and over any offence triable either way which has been sent to it for trial. The following judges sit in the Crown Court: High Court judges, Circuit judges, Recorders (who are part-time judges) and District Judges (Magistrates' Courts).

A defendant who pleads not guilty in the Crown Court is tried by judge and jury.[12] It is for the jury to determine the facts and whether or not the defendant is guilty, but they will do so on the basis of a direction from the judge on the relevant law.

Another function which the Crown Court has is to hear appeals by a defendant from magistrates' courts. Juries are not used in these cases, but the judge sits with magistrates (the maximum number being four). Only the defendant may appeal.[13] An appeal may be against sentence or (but only if the defendant pleaded not guilty) against conviction on a point of fact or of law (or of both). An appeal to the Crown Court against conviction takes the form of a complete rehearing. Where an appeal is founded on a point of law alone it is

---

[11] The indictment is the formal legal document containing a list of the charges against a defendant in the Crown Court to which he pleads guilty or not guilty at his trial in the Crown Court.

[12] Exceptionally, under the Criminal Justice Act 2003, Pt 7 a judge may permit a trial without a jury in a case of potential or actual jury tampering.

[13] A case where a defendant has been convicted by a magistrates' court may be referred to the Crown Court by the Criminal Cases Review Commission, in which case it is treated as an appeal by the defendant against conviction and/or sentence, as appropriate.

usually thought preferable to appeal by case stated to the Queen's Bench Division of the High Court, dealt with below.

The Crown Court also deals with cases where a magistrates' court commits for sentence someone who has pleaded guilty to, or been found guilty of, an offence triable either way, on the ground that its sentencing powers are inadequate. These cases are heard by a judge sitting alone.

Appellate courts

Queen's Bench Division of the High Court

1.13 Judges in this Division hear appeals by case stated on points of law or jurisdiction from magistrates' courts and from the Crown Court when that court has heard an appeal from a magistrates' court. Either side may appeal. Cases are dealt with by the Administrative Court, which is part of the Queen's Bench Division. They are heard by a single judge or by a Divisional Court. A Divisional Court consists of two or more judges, almost invariably two, one of whom is usually a Lord Justice of Appeal, ie a member of the Court of Appeal. An appeal by case stated simply consists of hearing legal argument and a decision on that basis. There is no rehearing of the facts and witnesses.

1.14 Judges in the Queen's Bench Division also deal with claims by a 'person aggrieved' for judicial review in relation to the jurisdiction of the Crown Court other than its jurisdiction in matters relating to trials on indictment, and in relation to magistrates' courts. As in an appeal by case stated, the court simply hears legal argument and decides on that basis. It is not concerned with the correctness of the decision on its merits but with whether it was lawfully and reasonably made. Claims for judicial review are not appeals as such. Consequently, they do not appear in the chart already referred to.

Like appeals by case stated, judicial review cases are dealt with by judges sitting in the Administrative Court. Permission from a single judge is required before a claim for judicial review can be made. If it is granted, a claim for judicial review in a criminal matter may be heard by a single judge or a Divisional Court.

In cases where the facts are involved the appropriate course is to appeal by case stated, so that they can be set out in the 'case stated'.

Criminal Division of the Court of Appeal

1.15 The most important function of the Criminal Division is to hear appeals from the Crown Court by the defendant against conviction or sentence. Such appeal to the Court of Appeal may only be brought with its leave or with a certificate from the trial judge that the case is fit for appeal. In the case of an appeal against conviction the court must allow the appeal if it thinks that the conviction is unsafe; otherwise it must dismiss the appeal.

A case where there has been a conviction in the Crown Court may be referred to the Court of Appeal by the Criminal Cases Review Commission, in which case it is treated as an appeal by the defendant against conviction and/or sentence. The Court of Appeal also hears appeals by the prosecution against rulings by the trial judge in the Crown Court (for example, that there is no case to answer or that proceedings should be stayed for abuse of process).

1.16 Where a person has been acquitted on indictment of a specified serious offence, the Court of Appeal may quash the acquittal and order a retrial where new and compelling evidence of guilt comes to light.

1.17 Under the Criminal Justice Act 1972, s 36, the Attorney-General may refer to the Court of Appeal for clarification a point of law involved in a case in which the defendant was acquitted in the Crown Court. The opinion of the Court of Appeal does not affect the acquittal but provides authoritative guidance for the future. Under the Criminal Justice Act 1988, s 36, the Attorney-General can refer a sentence imposed in the Crown Court to the Court of Appeal if it appears to him unduly lenient. This power exists only in relation to offences triable only on indictment and certain serious offences triable either way. On such a reference the court may increase the severity of the sentence.

1.18 The Criminal Division usually sits in at least three and, on occasions, as many as six courts. By way of exception to the general requirement that cases before it must be heard by not less than three judges, a two-judge court may hear appeals against sentence. The court will normally consist of the Lord Chief Justice or the President of the Queen's Bench Division or a Lord Justice of Appeal plus two High Court judges, but a single Circuit judge may also sit as one of the judges of the court.

Supreme Court

1.19 Either side may appeal to the Supreme Court from a decision of the High Court (whether by a single judge or a Divisional Court) in 'a criminal cause or matter' or from a decision of the Court of Appeal (Criminal Division). The Supreme Court came into existence on 1 October 2009. It took over the appellate functions of the House of Lords.

Appeal to the Supreme Court is only possible if the necessary conditions are fulfilled and leave is granted either by the court appealed from or by the Supreme Court. The necessary conditions which must be fulfilled are:

- the court below must certify that a point of law of general public importance is involved;
- either the court below or the Supreme Court must be satisfied that the point of law is one which ought to be considered by the Supreme Court.

A point of law referred to the Court of Appeal by the Attorney-General may be further referred to the Supreme Court, and so may a point of law involved in a sentence referred to the Court of Appeal by the Attorney-General.

1.20 The Supreme Court consists of a President, Deputy President and 10 Justices of the Supreme Court, although acting judges may be appointed. Cases before the Supreme

Court are normally heard by a court consisting of five judges, headed by the President or Deputy President.

Jurisdiction

Key points 1.3

The courts of England and Wales are only concerned with conduct which is an offence against English law, or, to put it another way, with offences over which they have jurisdiction.

Generally, jurisdiction can only be exercised by the courts of England and Wales over an offence if it was committed in England or Wales (territorial jurisdiction),[14] but there are exceptions where jurisdiction can be exercised over an offence committed wholly outside England and Wales (extra-territorial jurisdiction).

A detailed examination of this matter is outside the scope of this book, but the following should be noted.

Territorial jurisdiction

1.21 Normally, the application of the normal requirement that to be an offence against English law an offence must be committed in England and Wales is easy since either all the constituent elements of an offence occur in England and Wales or they do not, and this may be true even in circumstances where there is a foreign element. In *Treacy v DPP*,[15] for instance, it was held by a majority of the House of Lords that a person who posts in England and Wales an unwarranted demand with menaces addressed to a person abroad can be convicted of blackmail because the offence is complete when the demand is posted, with the result that the offence is wholly committed in England and Wales. Similarly, in *El-Hakkaoui*,[16] it was held that a person can be convicted of possessing a firearm with intent by means thereof to endanger life, even though the intention relates to endangering life abroad, if the possession of the firearm is in England and Wales.

Partial commission in England and Wales

1.22 What is the situation where part of the constituent elements of an offence takes place in England and Wales and part abroad (including Scotland and Northern Ireland)? Until

---

[14] In construing a statute, there is a well-established presumption that, in the absence of clear and specific words to the contrary, an 'offence-creating provision' was not intended to make conduct outside the territorial limits of England and Wales an offence triable in an English and Welsh court: *Air India v Wiggins* [1980] 2 All ER 593, HL.

[15] [1971] AC 537, HL.

[16] [1975] 2 All ER 146, CA. Also see *Berry* [1985] AC 246, HL.

2004, it appeared to be the law that an offence was committed in England and Wales (and therefore subject to the jurisdiction of the English and Welsh courts) if its final constituent element (the specified consequence in the case of a result crime) occurred in England and Wales,[17] but not[18] if some earlier requisite act or occurrence occurred in England and Wales but the final constituent element occurred outside England and Wales.[19] In 2004, however, the Court of Appeal in *Smith (Wallace) (No 4)*[20] held that a court of England and Wales had jurisdiction *either* where the last constituent element occurred in England and Wales, *or* where a substantial part of the offence was committed in England and Wales and it cannot reasonably be argued that there are serious reasons of international comity (ie recognition of another state's laws) why the offence should be tried in another country.

Special rules

1.23 Jurisdiction over offences of a fraudulent or similar nature is subject to the provisions of the Criminal Justice Act 1993, Pt 1, dealt with in Chapter 12.

There are also special rules relating to jurisdiction over the inchoate offences of encouraging or assisting crime, conspiracy and attempt. These are dealt with in Chapter 14.

Territorial limits

1.24 The territorial limits of England and Wales for the purposes of the territorial jurisdiction are as follows, depending on whether or not the offence is a summary one. For the purpose of offences triable only on indictment and offences triable either way the boundary of England and Wales is, round the coast, the outer limit of territorial waters.[21] In the case of summary offences, the boundary is where the land meets the open sea according to the prevailing state of the tides, but tidal rivers, creeks and harbours within the jaws of the land also fall within that boundary.[22]

Extra-territorial jurisdiction

1.25 'Extra-territorial jurisdiction' refers to jurisdiction over an offence which has no connection at all with the territory of England and Wales. Various statutes giving effect to international conventions provide that the courts of England and Wales shall have jurisdiction over offences covered by the conventions by whomsoever and wheresoever they may be committed. One example is the Aviation Security Act 1982, s 1 of which punishes with a maximum of life imprisonment the unlawful seizure, by force or threats, of control of an aircraft while it is in flight, whether or not the aircraft is registered in the United

---

[17] *Ellis* [1899] 1 QB 230; *DPP v Stonehouse* [1978] AC 55, HL.

[18] Unless statute otherwise provided.

[19] *Harden* [1963] 1 QB 8, CCA; *Manning* [1999] QB 980, CA.

[20] [2004] EWCA Crim 631.

[21] Territorial Waters Jurisdiction Act 1878, s 2.

[22] *Keyn* (1876) 2 Ex D 63 at 168, per Lord Cockburn CJ. See also *Loose v Carlton* (1978) 41 P & CR 19 at 34; *Anderson v Alnwick DC* [1993] 3 All ER 613 at 620. Statute may provide that a summary offence can be committed in territorial waters.

Kingdom. The Aviation Security Act 1982, s 2 makes similar provision concerning acts of intentionally destroying, damaging or endangering the safety of any aircraft.

Other examples of extra-territorial jurisdiction are murder and manslaughter committed by a person within one of the categories of British citizenship in any country or territory outside the United Kingdom[23] and a long list of sexual offences against a person under 18 committed by a United Kingdom national or United Kingdom resident (or someone who is such a national or resident when the prosecution is brought) in any country or territory outside the United Kingdom.[24]

Any offence committed by a person within one of the categories of British citizenship in a foreign country outside the United Kingdom is triable in England and Wales if, at the time of the offence, he was a servant of the Crown, and was acting (or purporting to act) in the course of his employment.[25]

Jurisdiction over offences on board ships and aircraft outside the United Kingdom

1.26 The Merchant Shipping Act 1995, s 281 gives the courts of England and Wales jurisdiction for the trial of an offence charged as having been committed:

- by a person within one of the categories of British citizenship on board any United Kingdom ship on the high seas;
- by such a person in any foreign port or harbour;
- by such a person on board a foreign ship 'to which he does not belong' (ie is not a crew member); or
- by any other person on board any United Kingdom ship on the high seas.[26]

Further discussion of this and of other ship-related provisions – such as that in the Merchant Shipping Act 1995, s 282, which deals with the rules to be applied to offences against property or persons committed ashore or afloat outside the United Kingdom by persons who at the time of the offence are, or have been during the previous three months, employed on a United Kingdom ship – is beyond the scope of this book. So is the discussion of the Civil Aviation Act 1982, s 92,[27] which extends our criminal law to conduct in British-controlled aircraft or United Kingdom-bound foreign aircraft[28] while in flight outside the United Kingdom.

---

[23] Offences Against the Person Act 1861, s 9.

[24] Sexual Offences Act 2003, s 72 and Sch 2 (para 9.134).

[25] Criminal Justice Act 1948, s 31.

[26] Although the drafting of s 281 appears to limit its provisions to offences committed under the Merchant Shipping Act 1995 (MSA 1995), the Magistrates' Courts Act 1980, s 3A, and the Senior Courts Act 1981, s 46A, both inserted by the MSA 1995, Sch 13, provide that s 281 applies to other offences under the law of England and Wales as it applies in relation to offences under the MSA 1995. 'High seas' in s 281 means all oceans, seas, bays, channels, rivers, creeks and waters below low water mark and 'where great ships go', unless they are within the body of a county: *R v Liverpool JJ, ex p Molyneux* [1972] 2 QB 384, DC.

[27] As amended by the Civil Aviation (Amendment) Act 1996, s 1.

[28] In the case of a foreign aircraft the conduct must also be an offence under the law of the foreign country.

Maximum sentences

1.27 Where an offence triable in the Crown Court, whether because it is indictable only or triable either way, is referred to in this book, reference is made to the maximum term of imprisonment which can be imposed by the Crown Court on conviction before it. That term also applies to someone committed for sentence by a magistrates' court. Except in the case of murder and other offences where the sentence is fixed by law, and certain other cases, the Crown Court may fine the offender instead of, or in addition to, imprisoning him. There is no limit on the fines which the Crown Court may impose.

1.28 Where an offence triable summarily only is referred to in this book, the maximum imprisonment is set out. Many summary offences are not imprisonable. Where they are the maximum term will normally be 51 weeks when the relevant amendment to the law, made by the Criminal Justice Act 2003,[29] comes into force; currently the maximum imprisonment for a summary offence varies from offence to offence but the maximum for any offence is six months' imprisonment. On the other hand, the maximum which can be imposed by the magistrates on summary conviction for an either-way offence will be 12 months' imprisonment when the relevant provisions of the Criminal Justice Act 2003 come into force;[30] currently it is six months'.

There are also limits on the fines which magistrates may impose. The maximum fine which they may impose on conviction of most offences triable either way is a standard sum, known as the 'prescribed sum' or 'statutory maximum'. At the time of writing that sum is £5,000; the Secretary of State has power to amend the prescribed sum in the light of a change in the value of money.[31] In the case of summary offences, the maximum fine is governed by the level (on the standard scale of fines) assigned to the offence in question. The standard scale is as follows at the time of writing:[32]

Level on scale	Amount of fine
1	£200
2	£500
3	£1,000
4	£2,500
5	£5,000

[29] See the Criminal Justice Act 2003, ss 280 and 281 (not in force when this book went to press).

[30] Magistrates' Courts Act 1980, s 32 (as amended by the Criminal Justice Act 2003, s 282(1)); Criminal Justice Act 2003, s 282(2) and (3). These provisions of the Criminal Justice Act 2003 were not in force when this book went to press.

[31] Magistrates' Courts Act 1980, ss 32 and 143; Interpretation Act 1978, Sch 1. The sum currently applicable is prescribed by the Criminal Justice Act 1991, s 17.

[32] Criminal Justice Act 1982, s 37; Interpretation Act 1978, Sch 1.

There is a power to amend the amounts specified in the light of a change in the value of money.[33]

Sources

1.29 There are two main sources of English criminal law: common law and legislation. EU law is increasingly becoming an important source.

Common law

> **Key points 1.4**
>
> The common law, ie judge-made law, is the source of virtually all the general principles of criminal liability. Very few offences are now governed by the common law.

1.30 Common law is that part of English law which is not the result of legislation, ie it is the law which originated in the laws applied by the royal courts after the Norman conquest. These decisions of the judges came to be recorded and published, and in due course began to be cited in subsequent cases before the courts. This led to the development of the doctrine of precedent, under which the reported decisions of certain courts are more than just authoritative legal statements whose effect is persuasive since they can be binding (ie must be applied) in subsequent cases.

In the context of courts with criminal jurisdiction, it is the decisions of the Supreme Court (or the House of Lords), the Court of Appeal (Criminal Division), the Divisional Court of the Queen's Bench Division of the High Court and a judge sitting in the Administrative Court of that Division which have binding effect. Whether or not such a decision is binding in a particular case depends on the relative standing of the court which made the decision and the court in which that decision is subsequently cited. The reason is that the doctrine of precedent depends on the principle that the courts form a hierarchy which, in the case of courts with criminal jurisdiction, is in the following descending order: Supreme Court (or House of Lords); Court of Appeal (Criminal Division); Divisional Court of the Queen's Bench Division; a judge in the Administrative Court; Crown Court and magistrates' courts. The basic rule is that a decision by any of the courts above the Crown Court is binding on those courts below that in which it was given. On the other hand, the Supreme Court is not bound by its own decisions or those of the House of Lords, nor is a judge of the Administrative Court bound by decisions of other High Court judges, although in both cases the previous decision will normally be

---

[33] Magistrates' Courts Act 1980, s 143.

followed. In comparison, the Court of Appeal and the Divisional Court are bound by their own previous decisions, except in a number of defined exceptional circumstances.

It is not every part of the judgment of an appellate court which constitutes the 'decision' for the purposes of the doctrine of precedent but only the reasons or principles applied by the appellate court in resolving the issue before it (the ratio decidendi). Other statements on the law by the appellate court, obiter dicta (statements not necessary to the decision) as they are called, can never constitute a binding precedent, although they may be of persuasive authority for subsequent cases, their strength depending on the eminence of the court.

In terms of trial in the Crown Court, it must be borne in mind that it involves trial by jury,[34] and, subject to the defendant's right of appeal, their verdict is final. The jury are subject to the trial judge, who directs them on the relevant law. The trial judge's directions on the law do not constitute a binding precedent for the future, but are merely of persuasive authority.[35] It must be emphasised that the principles enunciated by the judge must be ascertained solely by reference to his words and without reference to the verdict of the jury, which may have been unexpected by the judge, or even contrary to his direction on the law. In cases tried in a magistrates' court, the decision of the magistrates or, on appeal, of the Crown Court[36] does not constitute a binding precedent, although an appellate decision of the Crown Court is of persuasive authority.

Reference will occasionally be made to decisions of the Judicial Committee of the Privy Council, which is the final court of appeal from the British dependent territories and certain Commonwealth countries. Except in the most exceptional circumstances, decisions of the Judicial Committee do not bind English courts but are of very strong persuasive authority. Reference will also be made to decisions by courts in Northern Ireland, the Commonwealth or the United States. Such decisions are of persuasive authority only.

Common law offences

1.31 From the twelfth to the fourteenth centuries the judges elaborated the rules relating to the more serious offences which came to be known as 'felonies'. In the fourteenth century less serious offences known later as 'misdemeanours' were similarly evolved. A few misdemeanours were subsequently created by the rulings of the judges in particular cases and by the Court of Star Chamber. After the Restoration some of the latter were developed by the judges, who always claimed the right of defining certain acts as misdemeanours, although they never attempted to do so in the case of felonies. However, in modern times statute has played a preponderant part in the criminal law. As a result, the number of offences which now exist at common law only is small. Their definition cannot be found in an Act of Parliament, but must be sought in the rulings of the judges. Prima facie, not only the definition of the offence itself but also the punishment to be awarded is contained in the common law, but several statutes prescribe specific punishments for

---

[34] For an exception, see para 1.12, n 12.

[35] Ashworth 'The Binding Effect of Crown Court Decisions' [1980] Crim LR 402.

[36] Cross and Harris *Precedent in English Law* (4th edn, 1991) 6; Ashworth, loc cit.

certain common law offences. For example, murder is an offence at common law; in no statute is there to be found a definition of it, but by reason of the wealth of judicial pronouncements it is possible to construct a comprehensive definition of the offence. The punishment for murder is, however, governed by statute; it is a mandatory sentence of life imprisonment. Manslaughter also remains an offence at common law; imprisonment for life is laid down as the maximum punishment by statute but, by way of contrast with the case of murder, a lesser sentence of imprisonment, a fine or even a conditional or absolute discharge is possible. Other examples of common law offences described in this book are public nuisance, outraging public decency and conspiracy to defraud, for the first two of which the punishment on conviction on indictment is still prescribed by the common law.

Where the punishment for a common law offence is not laid down by statute, the judge may sentence the defendant to be imprisoned for a period or fined an amount, or both, to be fixed at his discretion.[37] In theory, this could lead to some very anomalous results because, in the case of a common law offence for which no maximum punishment is provided by statute, the court could impose a longer sentence than it could in the case of a more serious offence, the punishment of which is dealt with by statute. There is, however, an overriding requirement that the punishment should not be excessive, and there is no reason to suppose that the present rule gives rise to any injustice in practice.

General principles of criminal liability

1.32 The common law remains the source of virtually all the general principles of criminal liability. Examples of such principles are the defences of insanity and duress (whether by threats or of circumstances) and the rules concerning participation in crime. These general principles apply to offences in general (although they do not always apply to every offence). In particular, when a new offence is created by legislation, it is assumed that they apply to that offence unless the contrary is indicated.

Limits on judicial law-making

> **Key points 1.5**
>
> Although the judges have the power to make law, they do not have power to create new offences or to widen existing offences so as to make punishable conduct of a type not previously punishable.

1.33 Historically, the theory underlying the development of the common law was that new cases simply illustrated the application of existing doctrine to varying facts, or, in

---

[37] *Morris* [1951] 1 KB 394, CCA, approved by the House of Lords in *Verrier v DPP* [1967] 2 AC 195, HL.

other words, that the role of the judge was to discover and declare what the law already was, not to make it.

In the last 40 years the position has changed. It has become generally recognised that judges do make law. As Lord Reid, one of the greatest judges of the twentieth century, said in 1972, 'We do not believe in fairy tales any more. So we must accept the fact that for better or worse judges do make law.'[38] The judges' power to make law is, however, limited. It does not permit the judicial extension of the criminal law by the creation of new offences or the widening of existing ones.

Until modern times, the judges did reserve the right to create new offences. However, in 1972, the House of Lords in *Knuller (Publishing, Printing and Promotions) Ltd v DPP*[39] unanimously rejected the existence of a residual power vested in the courts to create new offences. It also rejected a residual power so to widen existing offences as to make punishable conduct of a type not hitherto subject to punishment. In 2005, these points were reaffirmed in *Rimmington, Goldstein*.[40] The next year, in *Jones (Margaret)*,[41] Lord Bingham (with whose speech Lords Rodger and Carswell agreed) stated that it had become an important democratic principle in this country that it is for Parliament, and not the executive, or the judges, to decide what conduct should be treated as lying so far outside the bounds of what is acceptable in our society as to attract criminal penalties.

1.34 The judicial creation of offences is open to the following further objections:

- there is a danger that the creation of new offences under the guise of developing old law promotes uncertainty concerning the extent of the legal rule; and

- the existence of a judicial power to create new offences would contravene the principle that no one should be punished for acts which were not criminal when they were performed. The principle forms part of what is called the 'principle of legality'. It is even more important from the point of view of the liberty of the subject than other principles, such as those embodied in the doctrine that a defendant's conduct must be voluntary or in the rule that guilt must be proved beyond reasonable doubt. The principle is enshrined in the European Convention on Human Rights (ECHR), Article 7 which provides that 'No one shall be held guilty of any criminal offence on account of any act or omission which did not constitute a criminal offence... when it was committed.'

1.35 There is a fine line between widening existing offences so as to make punishable conduct of a type hitherto not punishable and the clarification and application of established offences to new circumstances within their scope. The House of Lords in *Knuller* recognised that the latter was permissible. This is a view shared by the European Court

---

[38] 'The Judge as Law Maker' (1972) 12 JSPTL 22.

[39] [1973] AC 435, HL.

[40] [2005] UKHL 63. Just as the courts have no power to create new offences, so they have no power to abolish existing offences; that is a task for Parliament: ibid.

[41] [2006] UKHL 16 at [29].

of Human Rights who have interpreted the ECHR, Article 7 as not outlawing the gradual clarification of the rules of criminal liability through judicial interpretation from case to case, provided that the resultant development is consistent with the essence of the offence and could reasonably be foreseen.[42] This may seem to be an appropriate way of resolving any tension between the principle of legality and the need for the law to develop so as to be responsive to changing social conditions, but the fact remains that the law can always be changed by Parliament and legislative changes can always be prospective, whereas judicial changes are necessarily retrospective.

The question of where the 'fine line' referred to above is to be drawn was raised by the decision in 1991 of the House of Lords in R,[43] a decision subsequently given statutory effect, that a husband could be convicted of raping his wife if he had sexual intercourse with her without her consent. This involved the abolition of the previous proposition of law, formulated in the eighteenth century, whereby a husband could not be so convicted. That proposition, which had been subjected to a number of limited exceptions in modern times, was based on the notion that a wife was a subservient chattel of her husband and by marriage gave her irrevocable consent to sexual intercourse with him. The House of Lords held that, since that notion was now clearly unacceptable, the proposition should be held no longer to be applicable. There is a strong case for saying that this decision involved an impermissible widening of the offence so as to make punishable conduct of a type not hitherto punishable, rather than simply being an application of the offence to new circumstances (the changed social position of wives) within its scope. Subsequently, the European Court of Human Rights in *SW v United Kingdom; CR v United Kingdom*[44] had to consider a complaint that the House of Lords' decision was in violation of the ECHR, Article 7. The Court held that the prima facie breach of Article 7 was justified on the ground that there was an 'evident evolution' of the law in the decisions of the English courts which was consistent with the nature of the offence and it was reasonably foreseeable to the complainants (if necessary, with legal advice) that the court might embark on the adaptation of the offence in question. This bold decision indicates that decisions which appear to change the law are unlikely to contravene Article 7, unless the development was unforeseeable. While the development in R may have been foreseeable in 1989, the date of the intercourse in question, the subsequent decision of the Court of Appeal in *C (Barry)*[45] that that development was foreseeable in 1970, so that a husband could be guilty of raping his wife then, indicated a surprising and liberal approach to the issue of foreseeability.

The House of Lords' decision in R can be contrasted with its decision in *Norris v Government of the United States of America*[46] where the House of Lords reiterated the

---

[42] *SW v United Kingdom; CR v United Kingdom* (1995) 21 EHRR 363, ECtHR; discussed by Ghandhi and James (1997) 9 CFLQ 17.

[43] [1992] 1 AC 599, HL. See Giles 'Judicial Law-Making in the Criminal Courts: The Case of Marital Rape' [1992] Crim LR 407. For another example, see *Tan* [1983] QB 1053, CA.

[44] (1996) 21 EHRR 363, ECtHR.

[45] [2004] EWCA Crim 292.

[46] [2008] UKHL 16.

importance of the principle that the courts do not have power to create new offences or to widen existing ones so as to make punishable conduct of a type not hitherto subject to punishment. The question before the House was whether an agreement for price-fixing constituted the common law offence of conspiracy to defraud, there being no previous decision which even suggested that it did unless there were aggravating elements (notably misrepresentation and deception) bringing the agreement within the existing boundaries of conspiracy to defraud. The House of Lords held that such an agreement could not constitute a conspiracy to defraud unless there were such aggravating elements; it would be wrong to extend the offence of conspiracy to defraud to cover price-fixing agreements in themselves. It distinguished *SW v United Kingdom; CR v United Kingdom*, on the ground that the extension of the law of rape in that case to cover sexual intercourse by a husband with his non-consenting, cohabiting wife was the culmination of a gradual change in the law of marital rape, which meant that the extension had been reasonably foreseeable at the time of the conduct in question, whereas it would not have been so foreseeable in respect of an extension of conspiracy to defraud to cover price-fixing agreements (such an extension only having been first suggested in an article long after the conduct in question).

1.36 The introduction by judicial decisions of new defences, or the development of existing defences to meet new circumstances, is not open to the same objections as advanced above, since this favours the defendant. In terms of new defences, Lord Mustill said this in *Kingston*,[47] where the House of Lords refused to recognise a defence of involuntary intoxication:

> 'I suspect that the recognition of a new general defence at common law [ie by judicial decision] has not happened in modern times. Nevertheless, the criminal law must not stand still, and if it is both practical and just to take this step, and if judicial decision rather than legislation is the proper medium, then the courts should not be deterred simply by the novelty of it.'

Despite Lord Mustill's first sentence, it would seem that the defence of duress of circumstances, described in Chapter 16, is a new defence recognised in modern times by judicial decision. With this it is interesting to contrast the refusal by the House of Lords in *Clegg*[48] to introduce a partial defence of excessive self-defence to murder, which would have reduced that offence to manslaughter. Lord Lloyd, with whose speech the other Law Lords agreed, said:

> 'I am not averse to judges developing law, or indeed making new law, when they can see their way clearly, even where questions of social policy are involved ... But in the present case I am in no doubt that your Lordships should abstain from law-making. The reduction of what would otherwise be murder to manslaughter in a particular class of case

---

[47] [1995] 2 AC 355 at 375.   [48] [1995] 1 AC 482, HL.

seems to me essentially a matter for decision by the legislature, and not by this House in its judicial capacity.'[49]

Parliament has now introduced a provision which will achieve such a reduction in some cases of excessive self-defence, as will be seen in Chapters 8 and 16.

1.37 In *C v DPP*,[50] where the House of Lords refused to abolish the common law rebuttable presumption that a child aged 10 to 13 was incapable of committing an offence, Lord Lowry, with whom the rest of the House of Lords agreed, stated that judicial law-making should be approached by the courts on the following basis:

> '(1) if the solution is doubtful, the judges should beware of imposing their own remedy; (2) caution should prevail if Parliament has rejected opportunities of clearing up a known difficulty or has legislated while leaving the difficulty untouched; (3) disputed matters of social policy are less suitable areas for judicial intervention than purely legal problems; (4) fundamental legal doctrines should not be lightly set aside; (5) judges should not make a change unless they can achieve finality and certainty.'

Textwriters

1.38 In criminal law, as in other branches of English law, statements in textbooks and articles in legal journals have no binding force. This means that a court is not bound to apply them in the same way as it must follow the directions contained in a statute or the principle to be inferred from a decided case.

Nevertheless, some mention should be made of certain works which are treated with great respect by the judges. To go back only so far as the seventeenth century, the writings of Sir Edward Coke (d 1634) are as important in the sphere of crime, which is dealt with in his *Third Institute*, as in other branches of the law. There is also the statement of the criminal law of a slightly later period in the unfinished *History of the Pleas of the Crown* by Sir Matthew Hale (d 1676).

In the eighteenth century, Sir Michael Foster (d 1763) left a valuable set of reports with notes and appendices entitled *Crown Law*, while Hawkins (d 1746) wrote a treatise on *Pleas of the Crown* which was used by Sir William Blackstone (d 1780) in the compilation of the fourth book of his *Commentaries*, which deals with criminal law. Finally, Sir Edward Hyde East (d 1847) published a general treatise on criminal law, known as *Pleas of the Crown*, in 1803; this book is regarded as the successor to the treatises of Coke, Hale and Foster.

All these works are regarded as of persuasive authority on the law as it stood when they were written. Several of the standard works of the nineteenth century have been re-edited and, although they are not authoritative in any strict sense of the word, some of

---

[49] [1995] 1 AC 482 at 500.   [50] [1996] AC 1 at 28. See para 15.3.

them are still relied on. They include *Stephen's Digest of the Criminal Law* and *Archbold's Pleading, Evidence and Practice in Criminal Cases*. Modern works which are frequently quoted include *Smith and Hogan's Criminal Law*, *Ashworth's Principles of Criminal Law*, *Smith's Law of Theft* and *Blackstone's Criminal Practice*.

The increasing importance of writers is shown by the following quotation from the speech of Lord Mustill in *A-G's Reference (No 3 of 1994)*:

'Before leaving this part of the appeal I would acknowledge the extensive citation by counsel of passages from learned writers, present and past. There is no space to name them all here. All have proved valuable, even if not all of the opinions expressed have been adopted. Notwithstanding the strong practical character of the criminal law it has over the years gained immeasurably from systematic analysis by scholars who have had an opportunity for research and reflection denied to those immersed in the daily life of the courts. I hope that the practice of drawing on these materials will be continued and enlarged.'[51]

Legislation

Key points 1.6

Statute is the principal source of specific offences. The source of some minor offences is to be found in subordinate legislation.

Statute

1.39 The vast majority of offences are defined and regulated by statutes, ie Acts of Parliament which have been duly passed through both Houses and received the Royal Assent. There are at least 700 indictable offences (ie offences triable in the Crown Court); the vast majority of them are regulated by statute, fewer than 20 being common law offences. All summary offences, of which there are estimated to be more than 10,000, are regulated by statute or by subordinate legislation.

1.40 Statute may create an entirely new offence. For example, before the passing of the Punishment of Incest Act 1908, it was not an offence for a man to have sexual intercourse with an adult female who was his granddaughter, daughter, sister or mother, although such incestuous intercourse had generally been regarded as morally abhorrent. The Act made such conduct criminal. This is an instance of a serious offence being created by statute and there are many others since, from time to time in the history of the criminal law, Parliament has found it necessary to punish acts which were not punished by the

---

[51] [1998] AC 245 at 262.

common law. It is in the sphere of the less morally reprehensible offences, however, that Parliament has been most active.

Particularly in modern times Parliament's response to a perceived social problem has been to make its manifestation an offence. Since 1990, for example, a range of offences has been introduced to deal with raves, collective trespasses, stalkers and keepers of dangerous dogs. It has been estimated in 2009[52] that between May 1997 and the end of 2008 the Labour Government introduced more than 3,600 criminal offences by Act of Parliament and others by statutory instrument, often for political effect in response to the latest headline in the popular press and to limited, if any, effect.

1.41 Apart from the creation of new offences by statute, it is also necessary to bear in mind, in order to have a full and proper understanding of the criminal law, that many offences which now exist by virtue of statute were originally common law offences. Many statutes have replaced common law offences and in so doing have changed the common law very considerably.

1.42 It follows from what has been said that in England we have no single criminal code such as exists in most countries. The result is that, with the exception of common law offences and those created by subordinate legislation,[53] the criminal law of England is contained in a number of statutes. The Offences Against the Person Act 1861, for example, covers a variety of offences which are broadly defined as being committed against the person, including such crimes as wounding with intent to do grievous bodily harm, administering poison, using explosives, assaults, bigamy and abortion. The Theft Act 1968 and the Criminal Damage Act 1971 cover most offences against property. The Sexual Offences Act 2003 covers all but a few sexual offences.

1.43 In addition to Acts of the kind mentioned in the last paragraph, there is a large number whose main object is to set up public services of some description, or to control certain activities such as road traffic, but which contain offences for which punishments are prescribed. They are not essentially concerned with the criminal law, but they certainly create offences and as far as they do so must be regarded as one of the sources of the criminal law. This already large category is increasing because in modern times the State has assumed the responsibility for controlling and curtailing a range of activities which previously anyone was free to undertake.

Subordinate legislation

1.44 A statute may give power to some body such as the Queen in Council, a government minister or a local authority to make regulations and prescribe for their breach.

---

[52] By the Liberal Democratic Party. The estimate appears on the Party's website at the time of writing.
[53] Para 1.44.

This method of creating minor criminal offences is of increasing importance at the present day, although it is not new. A good example is the power of the Secretary of State for Transport under the Road Traffic Acts to make regulations. Acting under this power, regulations have been made which cover a very large number of different subjects and prosecutions are regularly instituted for breach of them. Such matters as the efficiency of brakes and the use of car horns are to be found not in the Acts themselves, but in the regulations.

Subordinate legislation made under statutory powers, otherwise known as delegated legislation, is of two kinds in England. The more important kind are Orders in Council made by the Queen in Council and regulations made by Ministers. Generally, these must be made by statutory instrument and are subject to the rules governing publication and procedure contained in the Statutory Instruments Act 1946. The other kind of subordinate legislation, byelaws, are made by local authorities and certain other bodies authorised by statute and require ministerial confirmation. Although general in operation, they are restricted to the locality or undertaking to which they apply.

In Wales, subordinate legislation also includes, in addition to these two kinds, a third: Measures of the National Assembly for Wales made under the Government of Wales Act 2006, Pt 3 and Sch 5. Such Measures are made by being passed by the Assembly and approved by the Queen in Council.

EU law

1.45 Although EU legislation cannot of itself create offences punishable in England and Wales, EU law is having an increasing impact on our criminal law, for example in areas such as environmental matters, VAT evasion and carousel frauds, human trafficking and child prostitution and child pornography, as well as regulatory matters such as the use of tachographs in commercial vehicles.

In many instances where EU legislation has had an impact this has been the product of a *choice* by the UK Government to fulfil its obligation to implement a piece of EU legislation by doing this by way of criminal offences and penalties. However, developments in the last 20 years have meant that EU legislation can *require* Member States to create criminal offences and penalties, as explained below.

1.46 The Maastricht Treaty of 1992 established the 'three pillars' of the EU. Two pillars have been relevant to the criminal law: the 'first pillar' and the 'third pillar'.

The first pillar was the European Community (EC), covering a range of competences including the single market, economic and monetary union, the common agricultural and fisheries policies and environmental protection. Generally criminal law was outside the competence of the EC. However, the decision of the European Court of Justice in 2005 in *Commission of the European Communities v Council of the European*

Union[54] was to the effect that EC legislation made under the first pillar could require Member States to enact criminal offences and penalties (although it could not specify the penalty range) for breaches of EC environmental protection legislation when this was necessary to ensure that that legislation was fully effective. The applicability of this to other essential objectives of the EC was left unclear. More important for the criminal law was the third pillar, ultimately named 'Police and Judicial Co-operation in Criminal Matters' and given the objective of creating an 'area of freedom, security and justice'. Some of the EU Council's framework decisions resulting from the pursuit of this objective, which Member States were obliged to implement in their legislation by way of criminal offences and penalties, have concerned matters of substantive criminal law. For example, the EU Council's framework decision of 2003 on combating the sexual exploitation of children and child pornography required Member States to enact a number of offences criminalising child prostitution and the production, possession and distribution of child pornography, and set out minimum penalties. To the extent that English criminal law was non-compliant, provisions in the Sexual Offences Act 2003 ensured compliance with the framework decision. Under the Lisbon Treaty of 2007, which came into force on 1 December 2009, the three pillars have been dissolved and the powers under them merged. As a result, the EU has been given strengthened powers to act in respect of the matters hitherto within the third pillar because EU Council decisions in respect of them will no longer need to be unanimous, since they merely require a qualified majority. The UK does, however, have the power to opt in or out of any policies in respect of such matters.

1.47 EU legislation also has potential, which should not be ignored, as a source of defences or rules. For example, a defendant would not be liable for an offence if it conflicted with a directly applicable or effective rule[55] of EU law, which would take precedence over the offence to the extent that it was inconsistent.[56] As a further example, for the purposes of the offence of fraudulent evasion of a prohibition on importation, contrary to the Customs and Excise Management Act 1979, s 170(2), the prohibition can be one imposed by a directly effective rule of EU law.[57]

1.48 Lastly, it may be noted that domestic criminal legislation must be interpreted, so far as possible, to accord with or facilitate EU legislation which does not have direct effect.[58]

---

[54] (C-176/03) [2005] 3 CMLR 20, ECJ.

[55] A directly applicable rule is one which is part of domestic law without the need for implementation in domestic law; a directly effective rule is one which confers rights or imposes obligations in domestic law without being so implemented.

[56] See *Conegate Ltd v Customs and Excise Comrs* (C-121/85) [1987] QB 254, ECJ and DC; *Searby* [2003] EWCA Crim 1910.

[57] *Sissen* [2001] 1 WLR 902, CA, provides an example.

[58] *Pupino* Case C-105/03 [2006] QB 83, ECJ; *Dabas v Spain* [2007] UKHL 6.

European Convention on Human Rights and Fundamental Freedoms and Human Rights Act 1998

Key points 1.7

The European Convention on Human Rights and Fundamental Freedoms (ECHR), taken together with the Human Rights Act 1998, is of major importance. Their provisions have great influence over the interpretation and development of the law by the judges and over new legislation.

1.49 The criminal law can have considerable implications for the exercise of legitimate rights and freedoms. However, it was not until the Human Rights Act 1998 (HRA 1998) that the rights and freedoms guaranteed by the ECHR[59] were accorded special status under the law of England and Wales. The Convention rights are highly influential in the drafting of criminal legislation. In addition, the HRA 1998 requires judges to interpret legislation, so far as possible, in a way compatible with Convention rights and, if they cannot, the higher courts can declare that legislation incompatible with the ECHR. So far, in terms of judicial decisions, the ECHR and HRA 1998 have had more effect in respect of criminal procedure and evidence than the substantive criminal law, but there have been cases where they have been decisively influential in the latter respect. Examples are referred to at relevant points in this book.

The Convention rights

1.50 The HRA 1998 is concerned with 'the Convention rights'. The Convention rights are specified by the HRA 1998, s 1 and are set out in Sch 1.[60] They are:

- Articles 2 to 12 and 14 of the ECHR;
- Articles 1 to 3 of the First Protocol to the ECHR; and
- Article 1 of the Thirteenth Protocol to the ECHR,

as read with Articles 16 to 18 of the Convention.

1.51 The Articles listed are, in essence, the substantive rights guaranteed under the ECHR and those Protocols to it which the United Kingdom has signed and ratified. Those

---

[59] The European Convention on Human Rights was concluded in 1950.
[60] As amended by the Human Rights Act 1998 (Amendment) Order 2004.

rights which are specifically of relevance to the substantive criminal law are set out in the edited version of Sch 1 set out below:

'THE ARTICLES

PART I THE CONVENTION RIGHTS AND FREEDOMS

Article 2 Right to life

1. Everyone's right to life shall be protected by law. No one shall be deprived of his life intentionally save in the execution of a sentence of a court following his conviction of a crime for which this penalty is provided by law.

2. Deprivation of life shall not be regarded as inflicted in contravention of this Article when it results from the use of force which is no more than absolutely necessary:
    (a) in defence of any person from unlawful violence;
    (b) in order to effect a lawful arrest or to prevent the escape of a person lawfully detained;
    (c) in action lawfully taken for the purpose of quelling a riot or insurrection.

Article 3 Prohibition of torture

No one shall be subjected to torture or to inhuman or degrading treatment or punishment.

Article 4 Prohibition of slavery and forced labour

. . .

Article 5 Right to liberty and security

1. Everyone has the right to liberty and security of person. No one shall be deprived of his liberty save in the following cases and in accordance with a procedure prescribed by law:
    (a) the lawful detention of a person after conviction by a competent court;
    (b) the lawful arrest or detention of a person for non-compliance with the lawful order of a court or in order to secure the fulfilment of any obligation prescribed by law;
    (c) the lawful arrest or detention of a person effected for the purpose of bringing him before the competent legal authority on reasonable suspicion of having committed an offence or when it is reasonably considered necessary to prevent his committing an offence or fleeing after having done so;
    (d) the detention of a minor by lawful order for the purpose of educational supervision or his lawful detention for the purpose of bringing him before the competent legal authority;
    (e) the lawful detention of persons for the prevention of the spreading of infectious diseases, of persons of unsound mind, alcoholics or drug addicts or vagrants;
    (f) the lawful arrest or detention of a person to prevent his effecting an unauthorised entry into the country or of a person against whom action is being taken with a view to deportation or extradition.

. . .

Article 6 Right to a fair trial

1. In the determination of his civil rights and obligations or of any criminal charge against him, everyone is entitled to a fair and public hearing within a reasonable time by an independent and impartial tribunal established by law. . . .

2. Everyone charged with a criminal offence shall be presumed innocent until proved guilty according to law.

3. Everyone charged with a criminal offence has the following minimum rights:

   . . .

   (c) to defend himself in person or through legal assistance of his own choosing or, if he has not sufficient means to pay for legal assistance, to be given it free when the interests of justice so require;

   (d) to examine or have examined witnesses against him and to obtain the attendance and examination of witnesses on his behalf under the same conditions as witnesses against him;

   (e) to have the free assistance of an interpreter if he cannot understand or speak the language used in court.

Article 7 No punishment without law

1. No one shall be held guilty of any criminal offence on account of any act or omission which did not constitute a criminal offence under national or international law at the time when it was committed. Nor shall a heavier penalty be imposed than the one that was applicable at the time the criminal offence was committed.

2. . . .

Article 8 Right to respect for private and family life

1. Everyone has the right to respect for his private and family life, his home and his correspondence.

2. There shall be no interference by a public authority with the exercise of this right except such as is in accordance with the law and is necessary in a democratic society in the interests of national security, public safety or the economic well-being of the country, for the prevention of disorder or crime, for the protection of health or morals, or for the protection of the rights and freedoms of others.

Article 9 Freedom of thought, conscience and religion

1. Everyone has the right to freedom of thought, conscience and religion; this right includes freedom to change his religion or belief and freedom, either alone or in community with others and in public or private, to manifest his religion or belief, in worship, teaching, practice and observance.

2. Freedom to manifest one's religion or beliefs shall be subject only to such limitations as are prescribed by law and are necessary in a democratic society in the interests of public safety, for the protection of public order, health or morals, or for the protection of the rights and freedoms of others.

Article 10 *Freedom of expression*

1. Everyone has the right to freedom of expression. This right shall include freedom to hold opinions and to receive and impart information and ideas without interference by public authority and regardless of frontiers. . . .

2. The exercise of these freedoms, since it carries with it duties and responsibilities, may be subject to such formalities, conditions, restrictions or penalties as are prescribed by law and are necessary in a democratic society, in the interests of national security, territorial integrity or public safety, for the prevention of disorder or crime, for the protection of health or morals, for the protection of the reputation or rights of others, for preventing the disclosure of information received in confidence, or for maintaining the authority and impartiality of the judiciary.

Article 11 *Freedom of assembly and association*

1. Everyone has the right to freedom of peaceful assembly and to freedom of association with others, including the right to form and to join trade unions for the protection of his interests.

2. No restrictions shall be placed on the exercise of these rights other than such as are prescribed by law and are necessary in a democratic society in the interests of national security or public safety, for the prevention of disorder or crime, for the protection of health or morals or for the protection of the rights and freedoms of others. . . .

Article 12 *Right to marry*

. . .

Article 14 *Prohibition of discrimination*

The enjoyment of the rights and freedoms set forth in this Convention shall be secured without discrimination on any ground such as sex, race, colour, language, religion, political or other opinion, national or social origin, association with a national minority, property, birth or other status.

. . .

Article 16 *Restrictions on political activity of aliens*

. . .

Article 17 *Prohibition of abuse of rights*

. . .

Article 18 *Limitation on use of restrictions on rights*

. . .

PART II THE FIRST PROTOCOL

Article 1 *Protection of property*

Every natural or legal person is entitled to the peaceful enjoyment of his possessions. No one shall be deprived of his possessions except in the public interest and subject to the conditions provided for by law and by the general principles of international law. . . .

Article 2 Right to education

No person shall be denied the right to education. In the exercise of any functions which it assumes in relation to education and to teaching, the State shall respect the right of parents to ensure such education and teaching in conformity with their own religious and philosophical convictions.

Article 3 Right to free elections

...

PART III ARTICLE 1 OF THE THIRTEENTH PROTOCOL

The death penalty shall be abolished. No one shall be condemned to such penalty or be executed.'

1.52 The Convention rights have relevance across the whole range of English criminal law, for example, in relation to the fatal use of force in self-defence or the prevention of crime, and euthanasia (Article 2), parental chastisement (Article 3), the defence of insanity (Article 5), the burden of proof (Article 6(2)), consensual sexual offences (Article 8), incitement to racial or religious hatred, obscene publications and contempt of court (Article 10) and various public order offences concerning processions, assemblies and protests (Articles 10 and 11).

Application of Convention rights

1.53 The HRA 1998, s 2(1) provides that, in determining a question which has arisen in connection with a Convention right, a court must take into account the case law of the European Court of Human Rights and the European Commission of Human Rights (which were effectively merged in 1998 in a restructured European Court of Human Rights).[61] The European Court and Commission have produced a well-developed jurisprudence about the ECHR and its Protocols. The terms of s 2(1) make it clear that these decisions are not binding on an English court; they are to be taken into account along with other relevant decisions, such as those of the Privy Council or of courts in constitutional cases elsewhere in the common law world. Nevertheless, even the Supreme Court will not without good reason[62] depart from the principles laid down in a carefully considered judgment of the European Court sitting as a full court.[63] There is a right of

---

[61] The Commission decided on the admissibility of applications (ie complaints of a breach of the ECHR).

[62] A 'good reason' could be the fact that the court in question is bound by an English decision under the rules of precedent, in which case it cannot apply a contrary decision of the European Court. The ordinary rules of precedent have not been disapplied by the HRA 1998, s 2(1): *Kay v Lambeth LBC; Leeds City Council v Price* [2006] UKHL 10.

[63] *R (on the application of Anderson) v Secretary of State for the Home Dept* [2002] UKHL 46 at [18], per Lord Bingham. Also see *R (on the application of Alconbury Developments Ltd) v Secretary of State for the Environment, Transport and the Regions* [2001] UKHL 23 at [26], per Lord Slynn.

individual petition to the European Court of Human Rights, and a failure by the English courts to apply a decision of that Court could lead to an application to it.

1.54 What follows is an attempt to give a basic understanding of the structure of the Convention and its key concepts, concentrating on the Convention rights relevant to this book.

1.55 The strength of the Convention rights varies. For example, the rights in Article 2 (right to life), Article 3 (prohibition of torture or inhuman or degrading treatment) and Article 7 (no punishment without law) are absolute, permitting no interference without exception, whereas the rights set out in Articles 8–11 are qualified rights because they permit interference in specified circumstances.

1.56 Common to the analysis of a problem allegedly involving any of the Convention rights is the requirement that there must have been an interference with that right; a Convention right must have been 'engaged'. In deciding this it must be borne in mind that the European Court of Human Rights has often emphasised the importance of a broad approach to interpretation of the Convention, according full weight to the object and purpose of the ECHR, rather than a narrower, more literal approach, in order to make the rights accorded by the ECHR effective.[64] The case law of the European Court of Human Rights and the European Commission of Human Rights helps in many areas in this task of interpretation. Where there is an interference with one of the absolute rights that is the end of the matter in terms of whether there has been a breach of the ECHR.

1.57 Where a right in respect of which interference can be justified is engaged, that justification typically (see Articles 8–11) requires the following criteria to be satisfied:

- the interference must be 'prescribed by law' or 'in accordance with the law';
- any interference must have a legitimate aim; and
- the interference must be 'necessary in a democratic society' in the interests of that legitimate aim and proportionate to the pursuit of that aim.

Prescribed by law/in accordance with the law

1.58 'Lawfulness' means more than merely 'authorised' by law. The European Court of Human Rights has held that, in addition, for a rule to be 'prescribed by law' or 'in accordance with the law', it must satisfy the following, often called the 'quality of law' requirement:

- *Accessibility,* ie the law must be adequately accessible: the citizen must be able to have adequate information, in the circumstances, of the legal rules applicable in a given case.

---

[64] See *Wemhoff v Germany* (1968) 1 EHRR 55, ECtHR; *Loizidou v Turkey* (1995) 20 EHRR 99, ECtHR.

- *Foreseeability (or legal certainty)*, ie the law under which action is taken must be 'formulated with a sufficient degree of precision to enable the citizen to regulate his conduct: he must be able – if need be with appropriate advice – to foresee, to a degree that is reasonable in the circumstances, the consequences which a given action may entail'.[65] The European Court of Human Rights has held that a law which failed to describe the conduct covered by it otherwise than by reference to the standards of ordinary people did not meet the quality of law standard,[66] whereas it has been held that a law which described the behaviour covered 'by reference to its effects' did.[67]

1.59 The 'quality of law' requirement is not limited to those Articles (ie 8–11) where an interference can be justified on the ground that it is 'prescribed by law' (or 'in accordance with the law') and necessary in a democratic society for a specified purpose. It applies as well to Articles 5 (right to liberty and security) and 6 (right to a fair trial)[68] where 'prescribed by law' and 'charged with a criminal offence' respectively require that the offence (or other interference) in question must satisfy the quality of law requirement.[69]

1.60 The quality of law requirement is also relevant in determining whether there is a breach of Article 7 (no punishment without law). Article 7 is not confined to the retrospective application of the law, discussed in paras 1.34 and 1.35. According to the European Court of Human Rights in *Kokkinakis v Greece*,[70] it 'also embodies the principle that only the law can define a crime and prescribe a penalty . . . and the principle that the criminal law must not be extensively construed to the accused's detriment, for instance by analogy: it follows from this that an offence must be clearly defined in law'. So far challenges to offences based on grounds of vagueness have failed in a number of cases.[71] However, such a challenge succeeded in *Rimmington; Goldstein*,[72] where the House of Lords overruled a number of decisions on the common law offence of public nuisance on the ground that as interpreted and applied in them the offence lacked the clarity and precision which Article 7 requires. As a result the offence now seems to satisfy the requirement.

Interference for a legitimate aim

1.61 The legitimate aim of the interference referred to in Articles 8–11 must be one of the aims specified as a potential justification in the article concerned, such as the prevention of crime or disorder, or the protection of the rights and freedoms of others.

---

[65] *Sunday Times v United Kingdom* (1979) 2 EHRR 245, ECtHR (a case concerned with 'prescribed by law' in Art 10). 'Prescribed by law'/'in accordance with the law' in Arts 8, 9 and 11 are to be read in the same way: ibid, para 48; *Silver v United Kingdom* (1983) 5 EHRR 347, para 85; *Malone v United Kingdom* (1984) 7 EHRR 14, para 66; *Steel v United Kingdom* (1998) 28 EHRR 603, ECtHR.

[66] *Hashman and Harrup v United Kingdom* (2000) 30 EHRR 241, ECtHR; para 10.75.

[67] *Steel v United Kingdom* (1998) 28 EHRR 603, ECtHR.

[68] Para 1.51.

[69] See, for example, *Steel v United Kingdom* (1998) 28 EHRR 603, ECtHR (Art 5).

[70] (1993) 17 EHRR 397, ECtHR.

[71] See *Cotter* [2002] EWCA Crim 1033; *Misra and Srivastava* [2004] EWCA Crim 2375 (see para 8.120).

[72] [2005] UKHL 63.

Necessary in a democratic society

1.62 The reference to a 'democratic society' in Articles 8–11 means that regard must be had not only to the legitimate aim which the interference was intended to protect but also to the importance of the freedom in question in such a society. It is not enough that the interference is simply reasonable or desirable; there must be a 'pressing social need' for it, although it need not be indispensable.[73] According to the jurisprudence of the European Court of Human Rights, whether an interference is 'necessary in a democratic society' involves the application of the principle of 'proportionality'. 'Proportionality' requires that the interference be 'proportionate to the legitimate aim pursued'.[74] It is intended to ensure that a fair balance is struck between the relevant right of the individual and the legitimate aim(s) which the interference sought to protect. The test of proportionality was identified as follows by Lord Clyde in *De Freitas v Permanent Secretary of Ministry of Agriculture, Fisheries, Lands and Housing*:[75]

'whether: (i) the legislative objective is sufficiently important to justify limiting a fundamental right; (ii) the measures designed to meet the legislative objective are rationally connected to it, and (iii) the means used to impair the right or freedom are no more than is necessary to accomplish the objective.'

Interference with a right may be disproportionate if, for example, it applies to more cases than necessary or if it interferes more than necessary in cases where it properly applies. Where there has been a prosecution and conviction the basic issue is whether the prosecution, conviction or sentence (or any related order), taken individually or together, is or are proportionate to a legitimate aim under the relevant Article.

The proportionality of a legislative interference is judged by looking at the current effect and impact of the provision, not the position when it was enacted or came into force.[76]

Non-discriminatory

1.63 The ECHR, Article 14 prohibits discrimination in the enjoyment of the rights and freedoms guaranteed by the Convention. It has no independent existence, but complements the enjoyment of the other rights and freedoms. Thus, while discrimination in itself does not engage Article 14, discrimination in the enjoyment of one of the other rights and freedoms under the ECHR does engage Article 14 whether or not such a right or freedom is otherwise engaged.[77] Discrimination is established contrary to Article 14

[73] *Handyside v United Kingdom* (1976) 1 EHRR 737, para 49, ECtHR; *Silver v United Kingdom* (1983) 5 EHRR 347, para 85.

[74] *Handyside v United Kingdom* (1976) 1 EHRR 737, para 49, ECtHR; *Silver v United Kingdom* (1983) 5 EHRR 347, para 85.

[75] [1999] 1 AC 69 at 80. This statement was applied by Lord Steyn in *A (No 2)* [2001] UKHL 25.

[76] *Wilson v First County Trust Ltd* [2001] UKHL 40.

[77] *Inze v Austria* (1987) 10 EHRR 394, ECtHR.

where a distinction in treatment in relation to another Convention right has 'no reasonable and objective justification'.[78]

Impact of the HRA 1998

Key points 1.8

The HRA 1998 gives teeth to the Convention rights:

- by a special provision about statutory interpretation designed, so far as possible, to give effect to legislation in a way which is compatible with the Convention rights;
- by providing for certain courts to make a declaration of incompatibility if legislation cannot be interpreted so as to be compatible; and
- by making it unlawful for a public authority, such as a court, local authority or police officer to act in a way incompatible with a Convention right.

1.64 The HRA 1998 'brings home' the Convention rights. Essentially what this means is that remedies are available in courts and tribunals (hereafter simply 'courts') in England and Wales in respect of the Convention rights. This has not been achieved by the incorporation of the Convention rights into English law. Unlike directly applicable or effective EU legislation, the Convention does not automatically take priority over English law. Parliamentary sovereignty has been retained. Our domestic courts have not been given a power to disapply (ie not enforce) incompatible primary legislation (essentially Acts of Parliament),[79] but the effect of the main provisions in the Act comes close to permitting disapplication without disturbing parliamentary sovereignty. On the other hand, subordinate legislation incompatible with a Convention right can be quashed unless (leaving aside the possibility of revocation) primary legislation prevents removal of the incompatibility,[80] which it normally will.

Statutory interpretation

1.65 The HRA 1998, s 3 provides that primary legislation and subordinate legislation must, 'so far as it is possible to do so, be read and given effect in a way which is compatible with the Convention rights'.[81] The courts, where necessary, will prefer a strained but possible interpretation which is consistent with Convention rights to

---

[78] *Belgian Linguistics Case (No 2)* (1968) 1 EHRR 252, para 10.

[79] HRA 1998, s 3(2)(b).

[80] HRA 1998, s 3(2)(c).

[81] HRA 1998, s 3(1). See Lord Lester of Herne Hill 'The Art of the Possible – Interpreting Statutes under the Human Rights Act' [1998] EHRLR 665; Lord Steyn 'Incorporation and Devolution' [1998] EHRLR 153 at 155; Kavanagh 'The Elusive Divide between Interpretation and Legislation under the Human Rights Act 1998' (2004) 24 OJLS 259.

one more consistent with the statutory words themselves, by giving them a narrower meaning than their ordinary meaning (called 'reading down'). This is radically different from traditional techniques of statutory interpretation. There are, however, limits, as indicated by 'as far as possible'. A court cannot construe a statute in a way which Parliament could not conceivably have intended. Perverse interpretation or extensive redrafting is not permissible. In the rare case where the mismatch between Convention rights and the statute is this great, a competent court will have to make a declaration of incompatibility.

1.66 The effect of s 3 is illustrated by *Lambert*,[82] which was concerned with the excuse available under the Misuse of Drugs Act 1971, s 28 to a person charged with possession of a controlled drug (or certain other drugs offences). Section 28 gives the defendant an excuse 'to prove that he neither knew of nor suspected nor had reason to suspect' that the substance in question was a controlled drug. A majority (four to one) of the House of Lords held that, in order to be compatible with the presumption of innocence in the ECHR, Article 6(2), 'prove' in s 28 had to be 'read down' as imposing an evidential burden rather than a persuasive burden on the defendant, notwithstanding the apparently unequivocal nature of 'prove'.

1.67 *Ghaidan v Godin-Mendoza*[83] is the leading decision on the courts' interpretative obligation under s 3. There, the House of Lords held that the obligation under s 3 is the core remedial function under the HRA 1998, and the making of a declaration of incompatibility (described in para 1.69) is an exceptional course of last resort. The House stated that the operation of s 3 does not depend on any ambiguity in the legislative provision; it can require a provision to bear a meaning which departs from the unambiguous meaning which it would otherwise bear. However, it stated that s 3 reached its limits if a compatible interpretation would be inconsistent with a fundamental feature of the legislation; to give such an interpretation would be to cross the constitutional boundary, respect for the will of Parliament, which s 3 seeks to demarcate and preserve. The House added that, provided that boundary was not crossed, there is no need for deference to the niceties of language; the obligation under s 3 authorises (and may require) the court to insert or remove words which may change the meaning of the provision or depart from Parliament's intention in order to make the provision compatible, provided that it does not conflict with a fundamental feature of the legislation. This approach was referred to with approval by Lord Bingham in the criminal appeals in *Sheldrake v DPP; A-G's Reference (No 4 of 2002)*.[84]

1.68 A Minister of the Crown in charge of a Bill in Parliament must, before Second Reading, make a written statement about the compatibility (or otherwise) of the Bill with

---

[82] [2001] UKHL 37; for another example, see *R (on the application of Hammond) v Secretary of State for the Home Dept* [2004] EWHC 2753 (Admin).

[83] [2004] UKHL 30.

[84] [2004] UKHL 43 at [28].

the Convention rights.[85] In practice, such a statement is printed on the face of a Bill. This might be expected to provide a strong assurance that a Bill certified as compatible with Convention rights is in fact compatible but there have been instances where a Bill whose compatibility is contentious has been so certified.

Declaration of incompatibility

1.69 If a magistrates' court or the Crown Court is unable to interpret a statutory provision compatibly with a Convention right, it will have to proceed as normal. The issue of incompatibility can then be raised on appeal. A judge of the High Court, a Divisional Court, the Court of Appeal and the Supreme Court, if satisfied that a provision of primary legislation is incompatible with a Convention right, may then make a declaration of incompatibility[86] (and presumably will feel obliged to do so). They may also make such a declaration in respect of a provision of subordinate legislation which is incompatible if satisfied that (disregarding the possibility of revocation) the primary legislation prevents removal of that incompatibility.[87]

1.70 If a declaration of incompatibility is made, the validity of the provision is unaffected. The Government and Parliament are not required to take remedial action. A fast-track route for doing so via a ministerial order is provided by the HRA 1998, s 10.

Unlawful actions

1.71 It is unlawful for a public authority, such as a court, government minister or department, local authority or police officer, to act[88] in a way incompatible with a Convention right, unless:

- as the result of one or more provisions of primary legislation, the authority could not have acted differently; or
- in the case of one or more provisions of, or made under, primary legislation which cannot be read or given effect in a way which is compatible with the Convention rights, the authority was acting so as to give effect to or enforce those provisions.[89]

By the HRA 1998, s 9(1), unlawful action of this sort by a court is normally remediable only by way of appeal or judicial review.

---

[85] HRA 1998, s 19.

[86] HRA 1998, s 4(1) and (2). For declarations of incompatibility in a criminal case, see *R (on the application of Anderson) v Secretary of State for the Home Dept* [2002] UKHL 46; *R (on the application of Uttley) v Secretary of State for the Home Dept* [2003] EWCA Civ 1130.

[87] HRA 1998, s 4(3) and (4).

[88] 'Act' includes a failure to act: HRA 1998, s 6(6).

[89] HRA 1998, s 6(1)–(3).

Codification

> **Key points 1.9**
>
> Codification refers to the formulation of a branch of the law in a single set of statements, replacing and superseding all existing rules, whether derived from the common law or from legislation, in that area. Reference has already been made to the fact that English law does not contain a Criminal Code.

1.72 The main advantage of a Code containing the general principles of liability and specific offences would be enhanced accessibility, certainty, clarity and coherence of the law dealt with by it.[90] The criminal law desperately requires codification: important parts of it are obscure, uncertain, inconsistent or archaic.

At the request of the Law Commission, a group of distinguished academic lawyers prepared a report, published in 1985,[91] formulating the general principles of liability which should be contained in a Code, including a standard terminology to be used in it, together with a draft Criminal Code Bill. In the light of the support shown for the principle of codification of the criminal law, the Law Commission published a report in 1989,[92] including a revised and expanded version of the draft Criminal Code Bill. Much of this draft Code, containing some 220 clauses in all, simply restated in the standard terminology the then existing law. Parts of it, however, resolved matters of inconsistency or uncertainty under the existing law, while other parts incorporated various proposals for reform made in modern times. It became clear that a Bill as large as the Criminal Code Bill would present logistical difficulties for Parliament, and that this might increase the Government's reluctance to give parliamentary time to a Bill which offered it no political or strategic advantage. For this reason, the Law Commission decided to put forward a number of shorter draft Bills dealing with discrete areas of law as a way of making progress on the codification of the criminal law. The plan was that, when enacted, these Bills would eventually be consolidated into a Criminal Code Act. However, despite a number of Law Commission reports since 1993 implementing this strategy, successive governments have dragged their feet in terms of giving effect to them by introducing Bills in Parliament.

1.73 Clearly, codification of the substantive criminal law has been a low priority for governments. Nevertheless, in 2001, after discussion with the relevant government departments, it was agreed that the Law Commission would review and revise the draft Criminal

---

[90] But see de Burca and Gardner 'The Codification of the Criminal Law' (1990) 10 OJLS 559 as to what could be achieved in these respects.

[91] *Codification of the Criminal Law: A Report to the Law Commission* (1985), Law Com No 143.

[92] Law Commission *A Criminal Code for England and Wales* (1989), Law Com No 177.

Code Bill of 1989.[93] In a White Paper, *Justice for All*,[94] published in 2002, the Government confirmed its intention to codify the criminal law but made no further progress.

The Law Commission announced in 2008 that it had removed the codification project from its current *Tenth Programme of Law Reform* because of the increasing difficulty of the task due to 'the complexity of the common law, the increased pace of legislation, layers of legislation on a topic being placed one on another with bewildering speed, and the influence of European legislation'. Instead the Commission's current strategy is to focus on specific projects to reform and simplify the criminal law, although it aims to return to the codification of that law at some time in the future.[95]

FURTHER READING

Alldridge 'Making Criminal Law Known' in *Criminal Law Theory: Doctrines of the General Part* (2002) (Shute and Simester (eds)) 103

Cross and Harris *Precedent in English Law* (4th edn, 1991)

Duff 'Rule Violations and Wrong Doings' in *Criminal Law Theory: Doctrines of the General Part* (2002) (Shute and Simester (eds)) 47

Emmerson, Ashworth and Macdonald *Human Rights and Criminal Justice* (2nd edn, 2007)

Hirst *Jurisdiction and Ambit of the Criminal Law* (2003)

Lamond 'What is a Crime?' (2007) 27 OJLS 609

Peers *EU Justice and Home Affairs Law* (2nd edn, 2006) Ch 8

Ward and Akhtar *Walker and Walker's English Legal System* (10th edn, 2008) Pts I and IV

Williams 'The Definition of Crime' (1955) 8 *Current Legal Problems* 107

---

[93] See Law Commission *Annual Report 2004/05*, para 5.2.
[94] Cm 5563.
[95] *Tenth Programme of Law Reform* Law Com No 311, paras 1.2–1.6.

2

Criminal liability 1: *actus reus*

OVERVIEW

Liability for an offence requires that the defendant's outward conduct satisfies the requirements of that offence and that he had the appropriate legally blameworthy state of mind. This chapter concentrates on the former point.

Actus reus and *mens rea*

2.1 A cardinal principle of criminal law is embodied in the maxim *actus non facit reum, nisi mens sit rea*. In *Haughton v Smith*,[1] Lord Hailsham LC stated that 'the phrase means "an act does not make a man guilty of a crime, unless his mind is also guilty"'. He continued: 'It is thus not the actus which is reus [ie guilty] but the man and his mind respectively...it is as well to record this as it has frequently led to confusion.'

In this and the next chapter it is proposed to deal generally with what must be proved in order to secure a conviction, although it may be that the defendant can avoid conviction by relying on a defence. Two points are involved: first, the outward conduct which must be proved against the defendant (which is customarily known as the *actus reus*, despite objections of the type voiced by Lord Hailsham); and secondly, the state of mind which he must be proved to have had at the time of the relevant conduct (customarily known as the *mens rea*). Although the opinion has been expressed by at least two former members of the House of Lords[2] that it would be conducive to clarity of analysis of the ingredients of an offence to avoid these Latin tags and to replace them with the terms 'prohibited conduct' and 'state of mind', they continue to be used by the judges.[3]

2.2 It is convenient to begin with a few general observations before analysing the expressions *actus reus* and *mens rea*. The maxim *actus non facit reum, nisi mens sit rea* has not

---

[1] [1975] AC 476 at 491.

[2] *Miller* [1983] 2 AC 161 at 174, per Lord Diplock; *Courtie* [1984] AC 463 at 491–492, per Lord Diplock. Also see *Shivpuri* [1987] AC 1 at 11, per Lord Hailsham LC.

[3] See, for example, *Reid* [1992] 3 All ER 673, HL; *Vehicle Inspectorate v Nuttall* [1999] 3 All ER 833, HL; *B v DPP* [2000] 2 AC 428, HL; *Antoine* [2001] 1 AC 340, HL.

escaped criticism. When commenting on a similar phrase, *non est reus nisi mens sit rea*, Stephen J said:

> 'though this phrase is in common use, I think it most unfortunate, and not only likely to mislead, but actually misleading, on the following grounds. It naturally suggests that, apart from all particular definitions of crimes, such a thing exists as a *"mens rea"*, or "guilty mind", which is always expressly or by implication involved in every definition. This is obviously not the case, for the mental elements of different crimes differ widely.'[4]

This remains true today. *Mens rea* means in murder an intention unlawfully to kill or cause grievous bodily harm; in theft that the defendant acted 'dishonestly' and with the intention of permanently depriving another of the property; and in criminal damage an intention to damage property belonging to another, or recklessness as to whether any such property would be damaged.

The maxim can also be criticised in that *mens rea* is not always required for criminal liability; in many offences a person can be convicted despite the fact of his blameless inadvertence as to a particular element of the *actus reus*, and in some despite his blameless inadvertence as to all such elements.[5]

Notwithstanding these strictures, the significance of the maxim has been stressed in a number of judgments, where it has been held by the House of Lords and other courts that, unless a statute either by clear words or by necessary implication rules out *mens rea* as a constituent part of a crime, a court should not find a person guilty of an offence against the criminal law unless he has a guilty mind.[6]

The maxim is also important, in that it reminds us that, save in exceptional offences where no *mens rea* is required, the commission of the *actus reus* is not in itself criminal but only becomes so if committed with the requisite *mens rea*.

2.3 Most people would agree that, as a general rule, the infliction of punishment is only justified when the defendant was at fault.

The requirement of *mens rea* is thus designed to give effect to the idea of just punishment. For those who believe that everyone who does an act prohibited by the criminal law should be liable to therapeutic treatment rather than punishment, the state of mind with which an act is done is a relevant consideration only when the method of treatment falls to be determined. A leading exponent of these beliefs was the eminent social scientist, Baroness Wootton, who argued in favour of the abolition of the requirement of *mens rea*, stating:

> 'If...the primary function of the courts is conceived as the prevention of forbidden acts, there is little cause to be disturbed by the multiplication of offences of strict liability. If the law says that certain things are not to be done, it is illogical to confine this prohibition

---

[4] *Tolson* (1889) 23 QBD 168 at 187.
[5] See Ch 6.
[6] Eg *Sweet v Parsley* [1970] AC 132, HL; *B v DPP* [2000] 2 AC 428, HL; *K* [2001] UKHL 41.

> to occasions on which they are done from malice aforethought; for at least the material consequences of an action, and the reasons for prohibiting it, are the same whether it is the result of sinister malicious plotting, of negligence or of sheer accident.[7]

The holders of such beliefs have not supplied a blueprint of the practical means of giving effect to their views.

Nonetheless, the fact that the requirement that an *actus reus* should always be proved is even more important than the requirement of *mens rea*. Evil intentions only become sufficiently dangerous to society to merit punishment when the agent has gone a considerable distance towards carrying them out. Even the most diehard believers in punishment concede that a system of law according to which wishes were equivalent to deeds would be even less satisfactory than one which punished deeds without considering the mental state of the doer. As Stephen J put it:

> 'The reasons for imposing this great leading restriction upon the law are obvious. If it were not so restricted it would be utterly intolerable; all mankind would be criminals and most of their lives would be passed in trying and punishing each other for offences which could never be proved.'[8]

2.4 Not only does the maxim *actus non facit reum, nisi mens sit rea* serve the important purpose of stressing two basic requirements of criminal liability, but it also suggests a useful framework for the analysis of the definition of specific offences. This task is undertaken in Chapters 7 to 14 and the discussion is generally divided into a consideration of the *actus reus* and *mens rea* required in each case. It is, however, most important that the maxim should not be allowed to become the master rather than the tool of the criminal lawyer. A perfectly coherent account of the criminal law could be given without it. Sometimes, as in the case of conspiracy, it is not easy to split an offence into its *actus reus* and *mens rea*.

Time is occasionally wasted by the consideration of pointless questions concerning the heading under which certain undeniable requisites of criminal liability should be discussed. Thus, there is no doubt that, even when the defendant is sane, automatism is generally a defence. This means that, if there is sufficient evidence that, because of non-insane automatism, the defendant did not know what he was doing at the material time, the prosecution will fail unless it can satisfy the jury that the defendant did know what he was doing. No useful purpose is served by considering whether the requirement that the defendant must generally have acted voluntarily, ie when not in a state of automatism, relates to *actus reus* or *mens rea* or to neither. There can, however, be exceptional cases where the application of a rule depends on the classification of the elements of an offence.[9]

---

[7] *Crime and the Criminal Law* (2nd edn, 1981) 46.

[8] Stephen *History of the Criminal Law* Vol II (1883), 78.

[9] See paras 5.18 and 17.25.

Actus reus

> **Key points 2.1**
>
> The expression *actus reus* can be summarised as meaning an act (or sometimes an omission or state of affairs) *indicated in the definition of the offence* charged together with:
>
> - any consequences of that act, and
> - any surrounding circumstances (other than references to the *mens rea*[10] required on the part of the defendant, or to any excuse[11]),
>
> which are indicated by that definition.

2.5 It is necessary to refer to the definition of the offence charged in order to ascertain the precise nature of the prohibited conduct. The *actus reus* is every part of the definition of an offence other than references to the *mens rea* required or to any excuse. Even the most cursory consideration of the different offences makes it plain that, if the phrase '*actus reus*' is to be used as a description of the requisite external conduct, it must be given a far wider meaning than 'criminal act'. One reason is that an omission to act or the mere existence of a state of affairs may suffice, no act on the defendant's part being required. Another reason is that rarely is a mere act sufficient to constitute the *actus reus* of an offence.[12] The definitions of offences often specify surrounding circumstances, such as time or place, which are essential to render the act criminal. Sometimes the definition requires a consequence to result from the act, such as the consequence of the death of another human being in murder, as an essential element in making it criminal.

Acts, omissions and states of affairs

Acts

2.6 An act (ie the doing of something) is the most common basis of criminal liability. Of course, the nature of the requisite act varies from offence to offence. The definitions of

---

[10] As was recognised in *R (on the application of Young) v Central Criminal Court* [2002] EWHC 548 (Admin), sometimes an element of the *actus reus* may involve a mental element as well as a physical element. For example, whether an article is an offensive weapon for the purposes of the Prevention of Crime Act 1953, s 1 may depend on whether the defendant intends to use it to cause injury. Likewise, there are a number of offences of possessing a specified article. Possession of something cannot begin until the person with control of it is aware that it is under his control: *Lockyer v Gibb* [1967] 2 QB 243, DC; *Ashton-Rickardt* [1978] 1 All ER 173, CA. In addition, whether something is 'sexual' for the purposes of all but one of the offences under the Sexual Offences Act 2003 sometimes depends on the defendant's purpose: para 9.8. Also see para 2.24.

[11] See, further, paras 2.20–2.26.

[12] For examples of offences where the *actus reus* consists simply of an act, see the offences of encouragement or assistance of crime, conspiracy and attempt: Ch 14. Other examples are the offence of unlawful harassment of a residential occupier, contrary to the Protection from Eviction Act 1977, s 1(3) (see para 2.9), and the offence of encouragement or assistance of suicide (see paras 8.44–8.52).

some offences indicate the requisite act precisely, so that in rape an act of vaginal, anal or oral penetration by a penis is required, and in causing death by dangerous driving an act of driving. However, the relevant act is specified less precisely in the definitions of other offences, particularly where they use words which comprise two concepts, that of an act and that of a consequence flowing from it. For example, the common law definitions of murder and manslaughter simply require the 'killing' of another. Where the act is left undefined in this way, any act which results in the death of another will suffice. Thus, murder can be committed by an act of shooting or hitting or strangling or planting a bomb or poisoning or by any other of the many ways which men and women have devised for killing each other. Likewise, there are a number of statutory offences involving the 'obstruction' of various types of public officer; such an offence can be committed by any act which results in the 'obstruction' of an officer of the appropriate type.

Omissions

Key points 2.2

An omission to act can suffice for criminal liability in two cases:

- where the definition of an offence is expressed in terms which refer to an omission;

- in other offences, unless otherwise precluded, where the defendant was under a legal duty to act and omitted to fulfil that duty.

2.7 An omission to act (ie failure to do something) is a less common basis of criminal liability than a positive act. Historically, the criminal law has been concerned essentially with prohibiting (and punishing) positive actions rather than with imposing duties to act (and punishing failure to do so). In recent times, however, it has increasingly concerned itself with failures to act.

It has to be admitted that the distinction between an act and an omission can be a fine one, and the distinction in terms of culpability can sometimes be an even finer one, but the courts continue to draw it. The results of the distinction are significant.[13]

Express offences of omission

2.8 An obvious instance where an omission to act can give rise to liability is where the definition of an offence actually specifies an omission to act. Examples are the offence of wilful neglect, by a person with responsibility for it, of a child in a manner likely to cause it unnecessary suffering or injury to health,[14] the offence of dishonestly retaining a wrongful credit,[15] the offence of failing without reasonable excuse to provide information required

---

[13] See, for example, the effect of the distinction in relation to euthanasia: para 2.15, and in relation to obstruction of a constable: para 7.70.

[14] Contrary to the Children and Young Persons Act 1933, s 1(1).

[15] Contrary to the Theft Act 1968, s 24A.

under the Gas Act 1986,[16] the offence of failing to accord precedence to a pedestrian on a 'zebra' pedestrian crossing,[17] and the offence of failing to report a motor accident.[18] In *Greener*,[19] the Divisional Court held that the verb 'allow' in the offence which is committed under the Dangerous Dogs Act 1991, s 3(3) by the owner of a dog who allows it to enter a non-public place where it is not permitted to be, if (while there) it injures someone, included failing to take adequate precautions to prevent the dog entering such a place, as well as taking a positive step which resulted in it doing so. This shows that an offence can be expressly an offence of omission in the alternative to an act.

Apart from the common law offences of misprision of treason (a failure to report a treason) and of refusing a police officer's request for assistance in preserving the public peace,[20] neither of which appears to have been charged in modern times, express offences of omission are statutory. Such offences are increasingly common in modern statutes; generally they are minor in nature.

Other offences

2.9 Leaving aside offences which by their express definition are (or may be) committed by an omission, the issue of when an omission to act can give rise to criminal liability can be explained as follows. The starting point is to note that the issue relates to offences whose definition employs an active verb (otherwise the offence would expressly be an omission offence or a state of affairs offence, described later) and that the determination of the issue involves in part the construction of that verb. In the case of some offences it is impossible to imagine their commission by an omission; examples are rape, offences involving driving, and the offences of robbery and burglary. In addition, the words used in the definition of an offence may indicate that it may only be committed by an act. For example, in *Ahmad*,[21] where the offence of harassment in question, provided by the Protection from Eviction Act 1977, s 1(3), requires a defendant landlord to do acts[22] likely to interfere with the peace or comfort of a residential occupier with intent to cause him to give up occupation, it was held that a landlord was not guilty where he failed to rectify a serious defect on the premises with the requisite intent. Likewise, although the verb 'cause' may be construed to include causing by omission in the alternative to an act if the principles in para 2.10 are satisfied, this construction will not be accorded if the statute specifies a verb like 'permit', which clearly includes a failure to act, as an alternative to

---

[16] Contrary to the Gas Act 1986, s 38(2).

[17] Contrary to the Zebra, Pelican and Puffin Pedestrian Crossings Regulations and General Directions 1997 and Road Traffic Regulation Act 1984, s 25(5).

[18] Contrary to the Road Traffic Act 1988, s 170.

[19] (1996) 160 JP 265, DC.

[20] As to these offences, see *Sykes v DPP* [1962] AC 528, HL, and *Brown* (1841) Car & M 314, respectively. Also see Nicholson 'The Citizen's Duty to Assist the Police' [1993] Crim LR 611.

[21] (1986) 84 Cr App Rep 64, CA. Also see *DPP v Waite* (1996) 160 JP 726, DC (offence of unauthorised use of a receiver with intent to obtain information, contrary to the Wireless Telegraphy Act 1949, s 5(b)(i) (repealed and re-enacted in Wireless Telegraphy Act 2006, s 48(1)(a)), requires proof of an act, normally provided by the deliberate tuning in to the wavelength).

[22] A single act suffices: *Polycarpou* (1978) 9 HLR 129, CA.

'cause'. For example, it has been held that the offence of causing polluting matter to enter controlled waters, contrary to the Water Resources Act 1991, s 85(1), is limited to causing by a positive act, because s 85(1) provides an alternative offence of knowingly permitting polluting matter to enter such waters.[23]

2.10 Apart from offences which cannot conceivably be committed by an omission, and any others whose definitions indicate that they are incapable of commission by an omission, the situation is that, while an offence whose definition employs an active verb (eg 'kill' or 'obstruct') may ordinarily require an act on the part of the defendant, it can also in principle be committed by an omission to act, provided the defendant was under a duty to act recognised by the criminal law and failed to fulfil it.[24] 'In principle' is used deliberately, since there is nothing to stop a court, when an offence is first construed authoritatively, from giving the active verb in the definition a narrow construction so as to require an act on the defendant's part.

Whereas some continental Codes provide a general duty on all persons to assist others in peril according to their abilities, breach of which is a specific offence in its own right, our criminal law does not impose a general duty to act to save other people or property from harm, even if this could be done without any risk or inconvenience. For example, a stranger who stands by and watches a child drown in a shallow pool when he could easily rescue it commits no offence, because he is not under a legal duty to rescue it.

How may a legal duty to act arise?

Key points 2.3

Duties to act recognised by the criminal law may arise under statute, but more commonly in the present type of case they arise under the common law. The common law has developed particularly in this respect in relation to a duty to act to save another from physical harm, and it is on this duty that the following text concentrates.

The duty to save others from physical harm can arise:

- under a contract;
- through the holding of a public office;
- through parenthood (and perhaps other close relationships); or
- through the voluntary undertaking of care for someone unable to care for himself.

---

[23] *Environment Agency (formerly National Rivers Authority) v Empress Car Co (Abertillery) Ltd* [1999] 2 AC 22, HL.

[24] Examples of offences which can be committed by a failure to fulfil such a duty are murder and manslaughter (Ch 8) and the offence of obstructing a constable in the execution of his duty (para 7.70).

It is for the judge to determine whether such a duty could exist on the facts and, if they could, to direct the jury on what would be required to establish that it existed; it is for the jury to determine whether the requisite facts to establish the duty are proved: see *Evans (Gemma)* [2009] EWCA Crim 650 at [39].

2.11 The following examples of a common law duty to act to save another from physical harm can be derived from the cases, most of which were concerned with the offence of manslaughter:

- **A duty to act to save another from harm may arise under a contract, at least where the failure to fulfil a contractual obligation is likely to endanger the lives of others, and maybe in other cases.** A duty recognised by the criminal law which arises under a contract can be owed to third parties to it to whom the contractual obligation is not owed. In *Pittwood*,[25] for example, D, a level-crossing keeper, failed in breach of his contract of employment to close the gate when a train was approaching with the result that someone was killed on the crossing. D was convicted of manslaughter after Wright J had held that a person might incur criminal liability from failure to perform a duty arising out of a contract and that that duty could be owed to road users even though the contractual obligation was only owed to the railway company. A common example of a contractual duty is that of a doctor to care for his patients which is owed under a contract with a patient or the medical insurance company in the case of a private patient, or under a contract with the relevant NHS body in the case of a NHS patient.

- **A person is under a duty to act to save another from harm if he holds a public office which requires him to do so.** For example, in *Curtis*,[26] a relieving officer of a local authority was held liable for manslaughter when he had failed to provide medical assistance for a destitute person. Likewise, in *Dytham*,[27] where a uniformed police officer had failed to intervene when he saw a man being kicked to death some 30 yards away, it was held that he could be convicted of the common law offence of misconduct in a public office.

- **A parent is under a duty to his young child to save it from harm.** Consequently, a parent who fails to feed his or her young child with the result that it dies can be convicted of murder or manslaughter, depending on his or her state of mind.[28] Presumably, a child over the age of criminal responsibility (ie 10) owes a corresponding duty to his or her parents,[29] and other close relationships (eg husband and wife) possibly involve a similar duty.[30]

- **A person who voluntarily undertakes the care of another who is unable to care for himself owes a duty to that person to save him from harm.** The undertaking of care may be done by some express (or overt) act, as in *Nicholls*,[31] where D received into her home her young grandchild after the death of its mother. On an indictment for manslaughter by neglect, Brett J directed the jury that, if a person chooses to

---

[25] (1902) 19 TLR 37. See Harrison 'Manslaughter by Breach of Employment Contract' (1992) 21ILJ 31.

[26] (1885) 15 Cox CC 746.   [27] [1979] QB 722, CA.

[28] *Gibbins and Proctor* (1918) 82 JP 287, CCA (father). There can be no doubt that a guardian is likewise under a duty.

[29] Smith and Hogan *Criminal Law* (12th edn, 2008) (Ormerod (ed)) 66. If such a duty exists a boy of 14 would, for example, owe a duty to take steps to save his mother if he found her drowning in a shallow pool: ibid.

[30] In *Evans (Gemma)* [2009] EWCA Crim 650 at [20] the Court of Appeal accepted that the defendant did not owe her half-sister such a duty.

[31] (1874) 13 Cox CC 75.

undertake the care of a person who is helpless either from infancy, mental illness or other infirmity, he is bound to execute that responsibility and, if (with the necessary *mens rea*) he allows him to die, he is guilty of manslaughter.

The Court of Appeal's decision in *Stone and Dobinson*[32] shows that a voluntary undertaking of care may be implied from the defendant's conduct generally towards the victim of his neglect, in which case a duty to act will arise. The importance of this is that it is possible for a duty to a helpless person to arise where the defendant and the victim of the neglect were initially in a relationship, for example as members of the same household, where each was able to look after him or herself but where the victim has subsequently become helpless through mental or physical illness and become dependent on the defendant for care. In such a case it cannot be said that the defendant has undertaken the care of the victim by any express (or overt) act, such as the act of receiving the grandchild into the home in *Nicholls*. In *Stone and Dobinson*, D1's sister came to live with D1 and his partner (D2) in 1972. At the time she was able to look after herself but later, being morbidly anxious about putting on weight, she denied herself proper meals and by July 1975 became unable or unwilling to leave her bed. D1 and D2 made ineffectual efforts to get a doctor and D2 undertook the task of trying to wash the sister and of taking such food to her as she required, but they made no effort to contact the social services or similar agencies. The sister was found dead in bed in an emaciated and filthy condition in August 1975. The Court of Appeal dismissed appeals by D1 and D2 against convictions for manslaughter. On the question of whether D1 and D2 had been under a duty to care for the sister, it held that there was evidence on which the jury could conclude that, by mid-July 1975, when the sister had become helplessly infirm, D1 and D2 were under a legal duty to summon help or care for her themselves. This evidence was that D1 and D2 were aware of the sister's poor condition and had attempted to get a doctor, and (in D1's case) that the victim was his sister and occupied a room in his house, and (in D2's case) that she had tried to wash her and provide food. From this the undertaking of a duty to act could be inferred. Clearly, very little is needed for such an undertaking to be inferred.

When does a duty to act come to an end?

2.12 A duty to act for another of the type referred to in para 2.11 will be extinguished if, and when, the relationship giving rise to it ends.

In addition, a mentally competent adult can release someone (B) who owes him a duty, either before or at the time that the duty would otherwise require action, even if it is contrary to his (A's) best interests.[33]

---

[32] [1977] QB 354, CA. Also see *Gibbins and Proctor* (1918) 82 JP 287, CCA (partner of father failed to feed his children with fatal consequences and with *mens rea* for murder; held guilty of murder since, by taking money to buy food, she had assumed a duty towards the child).

[33] *Re T* [1993] Fam 95, CA; *Re C* [1994] 1 All ER 819; *Airedale National Health Service Trust v Bland* [1993] AC 789 at 857, 864, 882–883 and 891, per Lords Keith, Goff, Browne-Wilkinson and Mustill; *St George's Healthcare NHS Trust v S* [1998] 3 All ER 673, CA.

Thus, for example, if a mentally competent adult refuses all nutrition (as in the case of a hunger-striking prisoner or a person who wishes to commit suicide) those caring for him must respect his wishes, whether his reasons are rational or irrational.[34] The right of a mentally competent adult to self-determination prevails over any countervailing interest of the State.[35]

Likewise, a mentally competent adult,[36] who has been informed of the consequences of a refusal, may give an advance refusal of specified treatment should he lack the capacity to consent to that treatment at a later date. The source of this principle was the common law[37] but it is now dealt with by the Mental Capacity Act 2005, ss 24–26. Under these provisions an advance refusal of treatment need not be in writing, unless it is an advance refusal of life-sustaining treatment in which case it must be in writing and signed by the person making it in the presence of a witness. Thus, if a mentally competent adult hospital patient who has suffered a number of heart attacks instructs the hospital in the prescribed written form that next time he suffers a heart attack he does not want specified resuscitatory treatment, the medical staff will be released from their duty to provide that treatment when the next heart attack occurs if the patient then lacks capacity to give or refuse consent to the treatment. Indeed, the Mental Capacity Act 2005, s 24 provides that if there is a valid advance refusal of the treatment in question that treatment must not be carried out; if a doctor carries it out against the patient's wishes he commits a battery, or a more serious offence against the person, depending on what harm, if any, is caused,[38] just as would someone who force-fed a hunger-striker or the like.

A special situation

Key points 2.4

Where the defendant does an act which puts a person or property in danger, he becomes under a legal duty to take such steps as lie within his power to try to counteract the danger before it materialises.

2.13 In one situation liability may be based on an omission to act even if the offence is one which has been judicially construed as generally incapable of commission by

---

[34] *Secretary of State for the Home Dept v Robb* [1995] Fam 127.

[35] *Secretary of State for the Home Dept v Robb* above.

[36] Ie someone who has reached 18 who does not lack 'capacity' under the Mental Capacity Act 2005, s 2. A person lacks 'capacity' under s 2 if at the material time he is unable to make a decision for himself in relation to the particular matter because of an impairment of, or a disturbance in, the functioning of the mind or brain. It does not matter whether the impairment or disturbance is permanent or temporary.

[37] *Re T* [1993] Fam 95; *Airedale National Health Service Trust v Bland* [1993] AC 789 at 881–882, 891–892, per Lords Browne-Wilkinson and Mustill; *Re AK* [2001] 1 FLR 129. There is no corollary, ie that an adult of sound mind can insist on receiving a particular medical treatment: *R (on the application of Burke) v General Medical Council* [2005] EWCA Civ 1003 at [31].

[38] *Re T* above; *Airedale National Health Service Trust v Bland* above; *Re AK* above; *Re B* (consent to treatment: capacity) [2002] EWHC 429 (Fam); see further as to consent para 7.2.

an omission,[39] although not where the express terms of the offence clearly require an act.[40] This is the situation where the defendant does an act which puts a person or property in danger. In such a case he becomes under a legal duty to take such steps as lie within his power to try to counteract the danger before it materialises. The leading authority for this principle is *Miller*,[41] where D had been convicted of arson (contrary to the Criminal Damage Act 1971, s 1(1) and (3)) in relation to V's house. D had claimed that he had started the fire accidentally, having fallen asleep while smoking a cigarette. On his own admission he had woken up before the house was damaged and discovered that he had set his mattress on fire but had simply gone to another room to resume his slumbers. Dismissing D's appeal against conviction, Lord Diplock giving the opinion of the House of Lords, and speaking in the context of the offence of arson, said that he could see:

'no rational ground for excluding from conduct capable of giving rise to criminal liability, conduct which consists of failing to take measures that lie within one's power to counteract a danger that one has oneself created, if at the time of such conduct one's state of mind[42] is such as constitutes a necessary ingredient of the offence.... I cannot see any good reason why, so far as liability under criminal law is concerned, it should matter at what point of time before the resultant damage is complete a person becomes aware[43] that he has done a physical act which, whether or not he appreciated that it would at the time when he did it, does in fact create a risk that property of another will be damaged: provided that at the moment of awareness, it lies within his power to take steps... to prevent or minimise the damage to the property at risk.'[44]

The principle is important where the defendant inadvertently creates the situation of danger, and therefore does not have the necessary *mens rea* at the time of his act, but becomes aware of the train of events caused by his act before the resulting harm is complete. If, in such a case, he then has the relevant *mens rea*, he will be criminally liable. For further discussion on this point, see para 3.68.

Extent of duty to act

2.14 A general point which may be made about the extent of a duty arising under the common law is that its extent varies depending on the circumstances and the nature of the duty. For example, a person who owes a duty of care towards a person who is helpless must take steps to care for him, such as summoning medical help or providing food.[45] Someone

---

[39] See para 7.47.

[40] *Ahmad* (1986) 84 Cr App Rep 64, CA

[41] [1983] 2 AC 161, HL. For examples of the application of this principle in respect of battery and of manslaughter by gross negligence see paras 7.48, 7.49 and 8.123.

[42] Including negligence (as in the case of an offence such as gross negligence manslaughter): *Evans (Gemma)* [2009] EWCA Crim 650 at [24].

[43] Or, in the case of an offence where negligence suffices, ought reasonably to be aware: *Evans (Gemma)* [2009] EWCA Crim 650 at [31].

[44] [1983] 2 AC 161 at 176.

[45] *Stone and Dobinson* [1977] QB 354, CA.

like Miller must take such steps as lie within his power to counteract the danger he has accidentally created, either by trying to put out the fire himself or by calling out the fire brigade. If there are no steps which he could take his omission is not culpable.[46] As yet there is no clear authority on how much of a risk a person under a duty to act can be expected to run in order to perform that duty, but **there can be no doubt that a common law duty requires reasonable steps to be taken to perform it** (reasonableness being assessed in the light of the circumstances, including the defendant's age and other relevant characteristics, and any risks to the defendant or others involved, but excluding inconvenience or expense).

2.15 Further clarification on the extent of a duty to care for another is provided by *Airedale National Health Service Trust v Bland*.[47] B had been crushed in the Hillsborough Stadium disaster. He never recovered consciousness. He remained in a hospital in a persistent vegetative state (PVS), with no prospect of recovery or improvement. He was kept alive by a life support system and fed by a nasogastric drip, since he could not swallow. It was known that the withdrawal of this artificial feeding would cause death by starvation within a few weeks. The Trust applied for a declaration that its doctors might lawfully discontinue all life-saving treatment, including the artificial feeding.

The House of Lords granted the declaration, holding that a doctor would not be behaving unlawfully in discontinuing this treatment, including the artificial feeding. The House regarded the withdrawal of the treatment and feeding as an omission, and not as an act. It was probably right to do so, despite the fact that the withdrawal of feeding involved the act of removing the nasogastric drip from B. Because an omission was involved, the crucial question was whether the doctors would be in breach of their duty to treat B by withdrawing treatment and feeding. **The House held that a doctor's duty is to act in the best interests of the patient. It held that, where a patient is incapable of communicating, life-preserving treatment can be discontinued if responsible and competent medical opinion is of the view that its continuation is not in the patient's interests because it is futile and cannot confer any benefit on him; in such a case discontinuation of life-preserving treatment will not involve a breach of the doctor's duty.** The House emphasised that the question is not whether the withdrawal is in the patient's best interests, but whether the artificial prolongation of life is, and that it is not in the patient's best interest to prolong life where there is no hope of any improvement in his condition.

Similar principles applied, it held, to the initial decision to put a patient on a life support machine.

The House held that, where doctors decide to end life support treatment, the opinion of the Family Division of the High Court should, as a matter of practice, be sought, although with the passage of time a body of experience and practice might build up which would enable the President of that Division to relax the requirement.

The House emphasised that euthanasia by means of a positive act to end a patient's life, such as administering a lethal drug, remains unlawful. It is for this reason that the House considered it necessary to approach the issue before it from the viewpoint of an omission.

---

[46] *Tilley* [2009] EWCA Crim 1426.   [47] [1993] AC 789, HL.

The distinction drawn by the House between an act and an omission is dubious in moral terms, as Lords Lowry, Browne-Wilkinson and Mustill recognised in *Bland*.[48] Arguably, euthanasia by a fast-acting drug is less deserving of punishment than a slow death by starvation in consequence of a failure to feed.

The principles set out in *Bland* in respect of withdrawing treatment from a patient were held not to be contrary to the ECHR by Butler-Sloss P in *NHS Trust A v M; NHS Trust B v H*.[49] Her Ladyship held that an omission to provide medical treatment by a medical team would only be incompatible with Article 2 (right to life) if the circumstances were such as to impose an obligation on the State to prolong a person's life, and there was not such an obligation in the case of a patient; Article 2 only imposed an obligation not to be killed by an act, and did not cover omissions. Her Ladyship added that Article 3 (prohibition of inhuman or degrading treatment), which – she held – requires the victim to be aware of such treatment, does not apply to protect an insensate patient against the withdrawal of treatment. Indeed, it has been suggested in another High Court case that Article 3 could require the withdrawal of treatment from a patient close to death who was suffering an intolerable level of pain.[50]

States of affairs

2.16 Sometimes the definition of an offence simply requires the occurrence of a specified state of affairs in which the defendant is involved, no act or omission on his part being required. All offences where a mere state of affairs is sufficient are statutory. One example is provided by the Prevention of Crime Act 1953, s 1, whereby a person is guilty of an offence if he has with him in any public place any offensive weapon without lawful authority or reasonable excuse; another is provided by the Licensing Act 1872, s 12, whereby it is an offence to be found drunk in a public place. A third example is provided by the Road Traffic Act 1988, s 4, whereby it is an offence to be in charge of a mechanically propelled vehicle on a road or other public place when unfit to drive through drink or drugs. A last example is provided by the Fraud Act 2006, s 6, whereby it is an offence to have in one's possession or under one's control any article for use in the course of or in connection with any fraud.

Consequences and circumstances

Consequences

2.17 The defendant's act or omission may be required to cause a particular consequence. In murder and manslaughter it must be proved that the defendant's act or omission

---

[48] [1993] AC 789, 881–882, 887, per Lords Browne-Wilkinson and Mustill.
[49] [2001] Fam 348.
[50] *A NHS Trust v D* [2000] 2 FCR 577.

resulted in the unlawful killing of a human being,[51] and in criminal damage, contrary to the Criminal Damage Act 1971, s 1(1), it must be proved that property belonging to another was destroyed or damaged as the result of the defendant's behaviour.[52] The rules relating to the issue of causation are dealt with in paras 2.28 to 2.57.

Offences requiring a consequence to result from the defendant's act or omission are referred to as 'result crimes' and other offences as 'conduct crimes'.[53]

Circumstances

2.18 The circumstances in which the act, omission or state of affairs may be required to occur vary widely from offence to offence. The sexual intercourse in the offences of sex with an adult relative must be with someone who is a relative of a prescribed type;[54] the act of entry in burglary must be as a trespasser,[55] and bigamy can be perpetrated only by a person who is already married.[56]

2.19 Sometimes a circumstance of the *actus reus* is framed in negative terms, as in the case of the statutory offences of using a motor vehicle on a road or other public place *without insurance*[57] and of carrying on a business of tattooing, semi-permanent skin colouring, cosmetic piercing or electrolysis *without being registered* by the local authority.[58] Such phrases are requisite circumstances of the *actus reus* because they are an essential element in making the conduct criminal; it is, for example, no offence to use a motor vehicle on a road, but it becomes so if there is no insurance in effect. Likewise, there is no offence of carrying on a business of tattooing but it becomes an offence if it is not registered. Negatively drafted phrases of the present type must be distinguished from references in a statute to some matter which provides an excuse (ie a defence) to conduct which tends to criminality in its own right, an example being the phrase 'without lawful excuse' in respect of the offence of criminal damage to property belonging to another.[59] Deciding which side of the line a phrase falls can give rise to fine distinctions. For example, in an offence of 'knowingly making a record *without the written consent of the performers*' it was held that the words italicised were part of the *actus reus* of the offence,[60] whereas in an offence of knowingly delivering intoxicating liquor to a child under 14 *except in a vessel sealed in the prescribed manner* the italicised words indicated an excuse.[61]

[51] Key Points 8.1.

[52] Para 13.4.

[53] See, for example, *Treacy v DPP* [1971] AC 537 at 560, per Lord Diplock; *Berry* [1985] AC 246 at 254, per Lord Roskill; *Steer* [1986] 3 All ER 611, CA; *A-G's Reference (No 3 of 2003)* [2004] EWCA Crim 868. 'Conduct crime' would seem to be an inappropriate term to describe offences based on an omission or a state of affairs.

[54] Sexual Offences Act 2003, ss 64 and 65; paras 9.102 and 9.103.

[55] Theft Act 1968, s 9; para 11.2.

[56] Offences Against the Person Act 1861, s 57.

[57] Road Traffic Act 1988, s 143.

[58] Local Government (Miscellaneous Provisions) Act 1982, s 15. This offence only applies in the area of a local authority which has adopted the relevant provisions.

[59] Criminal Damage Act 1971, s 1.

[60] *Gaumont British Distributors Ltd v Henry* [1939] 2 KB 711, DC; para 6.12.

[61] *Brooks v Mason* [1902] 2 KB 743, DC; para 6.12.

Are justifications or excuses part of the *actus reus*?

Key points 2.5

Justifications referred to by the definition of an offence are part of its *actus reus*; excuses referred to in the definition are not.

2.20 The definitions of many offences refer to justifications or to excuses. Sometimes, the reference is to a justification or excuse specifically provided for the offence charged, which may be defined in detail. In other definitions, reference is made to a number of general justifications or excuses and is made by one word or phrase.

Although it has been said that the criminal law does not make any clear-cut distinction between a justification and an excuse,[62] **a justification differs from an excuse in that it renders the defendant's conduct lawful, whereas an excuse simply excuses a defendant from liability for conduct which is nevertheless unlawful.**

Justifications

2.21 Examples of justifications are the 'public and private defences' of prevention of crime, self-defence and related 'defences'.[63] 'Defences' has been placed in inverted commas because, as has been indicated in the Court of Appeal,[64] none of these justifications is properly to be regarded as a defence; instead, they are matters which, if they are raised, the prosecution must disprove as an essential part of the prosecution case before a guilty verdict is possible. In the definitions of murder and other offences against the person there appear the words 'unlawful' or 'unlawfully', which indicate that no offence is committed if one of these justifications exists, as where D kills V in lawful self-defence. This being so, it would certainly be odd to say that, for example, a person who kills another in lawful self-defence has committed the *actus reus* of murder. It is clear from modern cases, particularly *Gladstone Williams*[65] and *Beckford v R*,[66] that references to these and other justifications in the definition of an offence are to an element of its *actus reus*, being part of its prescribed consequence. While a defendant does not have to prove a justification, the prosecution does not have to disprove it (and thereby prove the element of unlawfulness) unless there is sufficient evidence – normally from the defendant – to raise it.[67] This is an exceptional situation where a defendant has even an evidential burden in relation to an element of the *actus reus* of an offence.

---

[62] *Re A (conjoined twins: surgical separation)* [2001] Fam 147 at 237, per Brooke LJ.
[63] These are described in detail in paras 16.1–16.35. For other examples, see para 7.51.
[64] *Wheeler* [1967] 3 All ER 829 at 830; *Abraham* [1973] 3 All ER 694 at 696.
[65] (1984) 78 Cr App Rep 276, CA; para 5.7.
[66] [1988] AC 130, PC; para 5.7.
[67] Paras 4.10 and 4.11.

The public and private defences are general defences. They apply not only to offences whose definition refers to them but also to offences which do not. In the case of the latter type of offence these justifications are not part of the *actus reus*.

2.22 Another example of a justification is consent. In the definition of rape and a number of other sexual offences the defendant's conduct is expressly required to be without the victim's consent. In these offences, 'without consent' is an essential element in making the conduct criminal and is clearly part of the *actus reus*.[68]

2.23 In a number of non-fatal offences against the person in whose definition 'unlawful' or 'unlawfully' appears, the presence of a valid consent can render lawful what would otherwise be unlawful. As with the elements of justification mentioned above, a defendant will not act 'unlawfully' (nor will what he does be 'unlawful') if he acts with a valid consent from the victim. As with those elements of justification, the defendant has an evidential burden in respect of the issue of consent. The relevance of consent in these respects is dealt with in Chapter 7.

In *Kimber*,[69] a case concerned with the repealed offence of indecent assault on a woman, which required proof of an assault or a battery in circumstances of indecency, the Court of Appeal took the view, as part of the ratio decidendi in that case, that absence of consent, where it was relevant to liability, was an element of the *actus reus* of a non-fatal offence against the person.[70] This must be correct: it would be odd to treat consent as a justification differently from other elements of justification or from the situations where 'without consent' appears in the definition of the offence. For this reason it is surprising that in an obiter dictum in *Brown*,[71] where none of their Lordships referred to *Kimber*, Lord Jauncey, without deciding the point, preferred the view that (a valid) consent was a defence, as opposed to the absence of consent being an element of the *actus reus* of an offence.[72] In *Brown* Lord Templeman, obiter, treated (a valid) consent as a 'defence' but he did not say that the absence of consent was not an element of the *actus reus* of an offence; he may simply have been using 'defence' in the way that term is loosely used in relation to self-defence and the like. Lord Lowry also referred obiter to consent as a 'defence', but he must have been using that term in its loose sense and regarded the absence of consent as an element of the *actus reus* of an offence, because he referred with approval to the definition of common assault in the draft Criminal Code Bill, which treats the absence of consent as an element of the *actus reus*. Lords Mustill and Slynn were clearly of the view obiter that the absence of (a valid) consent was an element of the *actus reus*, and

---

[68] *Olugboja* [1981] 3 All ER 443 at 444.

[69] [1983] 3 All ER 316, CA; para 5.7.

[70] The same view was taken by the Court of Criminal Appeal in *May* [1912] 3 KB 572 at 575 and by the Court of Appeal in *A-G's Reference (No 6 of 1980)* [1981] QB 715 at 718.

[71] [1994] 1 AC 212, HL; para 7.3. *Brown* was concerned with offences under the Offences Against the Person Act 1861, ss 20 and 47.

[72] In an extempore judgment, the Divisional Court in *CPS v Shabbir* [2009] EWHC 2754 (Admin) appears in a single-sentence statement to have taken the same view.

not simply a defence. It is submitted that, overall, there is nothing in these obiter dicta in *Brown* to affect the view taken as part of the ratio decidendi in *Kimber*.

Subsequent to *Brown*, in *K*,[73] a case concerned with indecent assault on a woman, Lord Hobhouse took the same view as that taken in *Kimber*. In *Barnes*,[74] another later case, the Court of Appeal appears to have taken the same view as in *Kimber*, stating that it is a requirement of the offences under the Offences Against the Person Act 1861, ss 18 and 20, referred to in paras 7.76 to 7.95, that the conduct itself should be unlawful and that where the offending act is done with the victim's (valid) consent, the defendant is not guilty of such an offence because his conduct is not unlawful.

What if the defendant is unaware that a justification exists?

2.24 The principle that a reference to justifications in the definition of an offence is part of its *actus reus* does not necessarily mean that a person who acts in circumstances justifying his conduct, but without realising that they exist, does not commit the *actus reus* of such an offence. The reason is that all that 'unlawfully' or some other word in the definition referring to justification does is to make it clear that the offence is not committed if a relevant justification applies on the facts. Such a word says nothing about the nature of the element of justification, and it may be that the element is only available if the defendant knew of the facts which justified his conduct (or believed that they existed). Authority that this is the position in law is provided by the decision in the old case of *Dadson*,[75] where D, a constable, was employed to guard a copse from which wood had been stolen. He saw V come out carrying wood, which he was stealing. V refused to stop and D shot him in the leg in order to stop him and arrest him. At the time, it was assumed that it was lawful to shoot an escaping felon in order to arrest him. The theft of the wood was not itself a felony, but V was committing a felony because (unknown to D) he had repeatedly been convicted of stealing wood. It was held that D had rightly been convicted of unlawfully wounding V with intent to do him grievous bodily harm since there was no justification for it, D being ignorant of the facts making V a felon. In relation to a case where a constable makes an arrest in ignorance of facts entitling him to make it, the solution remains the same as in *Dadson* because the Police and Criminal Evidence Act 1984, s 28(3) states that an arrest is only lawful if the person arrested is informed of the ground of the arrest at the time or as soon as practicable thereafter. As the Divisional Court in *Chapman v DPP*[76] pointed out, this means that if a person is unaware of the facts justifying the arrest he cannot comply with s 28(3) and the arrest will be unlawful, as will force used in effecting it.

However, it may be that the approach taken in *Dadson* no longer represents the law, outside the case where, unknown to the defendant, he was entitled to make an arrest.

---

[73] [2001] UKHL 41.

[74] [2004] EWCA Crim 3246.

[75] (1850) 3 Car & Kir 148. Also see *Thain* [1985] NI 457, NICA, and Christopher 'Unknowing Justification and the Logical Necessity of the *Dadson* Principle in Self-Defence' (1995) 15 OJLS 229.

[76] (1988) 89 Cr App Rep 190, DC.

This is because of the Court of Appeal's decision in *McKoy*.[77] In that case, D used force to escape from restraint by a police officer, mistakenly believing that he was being lawfully arrested when in fact the restraint (imprisonment) was unlawful. Allowing D's appeal against conviction for two offences, one of which was assault occasioning actual bodily harm, the Court of Appeal held that the fact that D mistakenly believed he was being lawfully arrested did not affect his entitlement to use reasonable force to resist the unlawful arrest. This decision would have been a stronger one had *Dadson* been referred to by the Court.

In practice, the point is not as important as it may seem. The reason is that, if (apart from the arrest type of case) a person who acts under circumstances of justification of which he is ignorant does not commit the *actus reus* of an offence requiring him by its definition to act 'unlawfully' or otherwise without justification, he may nevertheless be guilty of an attempt to commit that offence[78] if it is an indictable one (ie one triable only on indictment or one triable either way).[79] This is because the Criminal Attempts Act 1981, s 1(3) provides that, on a charge of attempt, the defendant is to be treated as if the facts were as he believed them to be.[80]

Excuses

2.25 The definitions of many more offences refer to excuses (ie defences which excuse a defendant from liability for conduct which is otherwise criminal) than refer to elements of justification.

It is a matter of dispute[81] whether or not an excuse which is referred to by the definition of an offence is part of its *actus reus*. The arguments on both sides are fairly evenly balanced but the view taken in this book is that under the law as it now stands matters of excuse referred to in the definition of an offence are not part of its *actus reus*. That is why it was stated in Key Points 2.1 that the circumstances of an *actus reus* do not include excuses to which the definition of an offence refers.

2.26 For the sake of completeness it should be noted that many excuses are not contained in the definition but are found elsewhere. An example is the defence of publication for the public good provided by the Obscene Publications Act 1959, s 4(1) in respect of the offences of publishing an obscene article and of having such an article for publication for gain, contrary to the Obscene Publications Act 1959, s 2(1). By way of further example, murder is defined by the common law, but the Homicide Act 1957, s 2 provides the defence to a murder charge of diminished responsibility.

---

[77] [2002] EWCA Crim 1628, CA.

[78] Hogan 'The *Dadson* Principle' [1989] Crim LR 679.

[79] Or a summary offence to which the Criminal Attempts Act 1981 applies; see para 14.142.

[80] Para 14.131.

[81] See Lanham '*Larsonneur* Revisited' [1976] Crim LR 276; Smith 'On Actus Reus and Mens Rea' in *Reshaping the Criminal Law* (1978) (Glazebrook (ed)) 95; Williams 'Offences and Defences' (1982) 2 LS 233; Campbell 'Offence and Defence' in *Criminal Law and Criminal Justice* (1987) (Dennis (ed)), esp at 80–81.

The excuses just mentioned are specific defences, in that they are limited to one offence or to a narrow range of offences. There are, in addition, three general defences described in Chapter 16 which operate as excuses: duress by threats, marital coercion and duress of circumstances.

It follows from the view that excuses which are part of the definition of an offence are not part of its *actus reus* that these non-definitional excuses, whether specific or general, are clearly not part of the *actus reus* of an offence in a negative sense (eg 'otherwise than under duress'). In terms of the defence of duress by threats, for example, *DPP for Northern Ireland v Lynch*[82] can be cited in support. According to the House of Lords in that case that defence is something superimposed on the other ingredients of an offence, the *actus reus* and the *mens rea,* which by themselves would constitute the offence.

Whole of *actus reus* must be satisfied

2.27 There can be no criminal liability unless the whole *actus reus* is satisfied. A person who had the *mens rea* for an offence cannot be convicted of that offence if he has not committed its *actus reus*. In *White,*[83] for instance, the defendant put potassium cyanide in his mother's drink, intending to kill her. Shortly afterwards the mother was found dead with the glass, partly full, beside her. The medical evidence was that she had died from a heart attack, and not from poisoning, and that the quantity of potassium cyanide administered was insufficient to cause her death. The defendant was acquitted of murder (but convicted of attempted murder) because, although the intended consequence – death – had occurred, it had not been caused by his conduct and thus an element of the *actus reus* of murder was missing. Similarly, one who handles goods, mistakenly believing that they are stolen goods, cannot be convicted of handling stolen goods (but only of attempted handling)[84] since the necessary circumstance that the goods are stolen is absent.

Causation

Key points 2.6

Where the *actus reus* of an offence requires a consequence to result from the defendant's conduct, the prosecution must prove:

- that the defendant's conduct was a factual cause of that consequence (factual causation); and

- that the consequence is legally attributable to the defendant's conduct (legal causation).

---

82 [1975] AC 653, HL.   83 [1910] 2 KB 124, CCA.   84 Para 14.133.

2.28 For the purposes of causation, 'cause' simply means 'accelerate'. Thus, it is no defence, in itself, in offences of homicide that the victim was already dying from some mortal illness if the defendant's conduct has accelerated death.[85]

Factual causation

2.29 The defendant's conduct is not a factual cause of the specified consequence unless that consequence would not have occurred, when and as it did, but for that conduct; this is often described as the 'but for' test.

Application of the 'but for' test indicates whether or not the specified consequence can be attributed to the defendant's conduct as a matter of fact. If it can be, the question of whether that death can be attributed to him for the purposes of legal liability depends on whether or not his conduct is a legal cause of the specified consequence; only if it is (and this depends on the principles set out in paras 2.31 to 2.56) can that consequence be attributed to him for that purpose.

All this can be illustrated as follows:

- D stabs V. X subsequently decapitates V.
- as in *White*, D administers a poison to V. Before it can take effect V dies of a heart attack induced by natural causes.

In neither of these cases is D's conduct a factual cause of death because it cannot be said that the death *would* not have occurred, when and as it did, but for it.[86] Contrast the following:

- D stabs V who is later stabbed by X. V dies from the effects of both wounds.
- D stabs V who receives emergency treatment in hospital from which he dies.

In these two cases the death would not have occurred, when and as it did, but for D's conduct, which is therefore a factual cause of death. However, whether V's death in these cases is attributable to D for the purposes of liability (ie whether D's conduct is a legal cause of V's death) depends on the principles of legal causation set out below.

2.30 As part of the 'but for' test, there will be no factual causation if the defendant was unable to prevent the consequence occurring. This is shown by *Dalloway*[87] where D was driving a cart when a young child ran into the road a few yards in front of the horse. The child was hit by one of the wheels and killed. At the time D was driving the cart carelessly because the reins were not in his hands. The jury were directed that if D could have

---

[85] *Dyson* [1908] 2 KB 454, CCA; *Adams* [1957] Crim LR 365; *Re A (conjoined twins: surgical separation)* [2001] Fam 147 at 199, per Ward LJ. See paras 2.32 and 3.23 in respect of the liability of doctors who hasten death by medical treatment designed to relieve pain.

[86] See *White* [1910] 2 KB 124 (para 2.27) in relation to the second example.

[87] (1847) 2 Cox CC 273.

avoided killing the child if he had hold of the reins, he was guilty of manslaughter, but if he could not have done so by the use of the reins, he was not guilty.

Legal causation

2.31 In the following paragraphs there is a set of principles relating to legal causation, which have mainly been established in homicide cases but which are equally applicable to other types of offence.

It would be wrong to assume that those principles always apply whenever legal causation is in issue in other types of offence. In *Kennedy (No 2),* Lord Bingham giving the opinion of the House of Lords stated that:

> 'Questions of causation frequently arise in many areas of the law, but causation is not a single, unvarying concept to be mechanically applied without regard to the context[88] in which the question arises.'[89]

The same point had previously been made by Lord Hoffman, with whose speech three other Law Lords agreed, in *Environment Agency (formerly National Rivers Authority) v Empress Car Co (Abertillery) Ltd.*[90] This is a fair point to make but it would be wrong to assume from it that there are many contexts in the criminal law in which the principles of legal causation applicable to homicide do not apply to an offence where the defendant's conduct is required to have caused a specified consequence. That said, it has to be admitted that the nature of an offence may be such that many of those principles are irrelevant.

In para 2.44, reference is made to a different context where a different principle applies from that which applies under the set of principles referred to above.

More than negligible contribution

2.32 Courts have often said that a specified consequence can only be attributed to the defendant (ie his conduct will be a legal cause of it) if his conduct was a substantial cause of it.[91] 'Substantial' in this context does not mean 'principal' or 'predominant'; it merely means that the defendant's contribution to the consequence must be more than a minute or negligible contribution (which would be ignored anyway under the general

---

[88] Ie the purpose and scope of the rule in question.

[89] [2007] UKHL 38 at [15].

[90] [1999] 2 AC 22, HL.

[91] See, for example, *Smith* [1959] 2 QB 35, Courts-Martial Appeal Court (renamed the Court Martial Appeal Court by the Armed Forces Act 2006, s 272; this court's powers correspond in general with those of the Court of Appeal (Criminal Division), as does its composition); *Hennigan* [1971] 3 All ER 133, CA; *Cato* [1976] 1 All ER 260, CA; *Notman* [1994] Crim LR 518, CA.

de minimis principle).[92] A useful way of explaining the word 'substantial' is to say that it requires 'more than a slight or a trifling' contribution to the consequence.[93]

The present principle provides an explanation for a statement by Devlin J, as he then was, in *Adams*.[94] Dealing with the situation where a doctor administered drugs, which would shorten life, in order to ease severe pain, he said:

> 'If life were cut short by weeks or months it was just as much murder as if it were cut short by years. But that does not mean that a doctor aiding the sick or dying has to calculate in minutes or hours, or perhaps in days or weeks, the effect on the patient's life of the medicines which he administers. If the first purpose of medicine – the restoration of life – can no longer be achieved, there is still much for the doctor to do, and he is entitled to do all that is proper and necessary to relieve pain and suffering even if measures he takes may incidentally shorten life.'

The distinction between shortening life by 'weeks or months' and 'by minutes or hours' is that the former involves a more than negligible acceleration of death, whereas the latter does not. The possible equation of shortening life by days or weeks with shortening it by minutes or hours would seem to be generous and is of doubtful validity. Such a shortening would seem to be a more than negligible acceleration of death, particularly where it is by weeks. Even with a liberal application, a defence based on causation for doctors in the present situation has a very limited scope. The application of the doctrine of 'double effect', referred to in paras 3.22 and 3.23, provides a more generous defence.

Key points 2.7

In the event of one of the situations outlined below being involved, additional principles of legal causation specific to it come into operation.

Contributions by third parties

2.33 As already indicated, **the defendant's conduct need not be the sole, or even the main, cause of the specified consequence.[95] Thus, even though a third party has substantially contributed to someone's death, the death can be legally attributed to the defendant if the defendant's act is also a substantial cause.** It is not the function of the jury to evaluate competing causes or to choose which is dominant.[96] In *Benge*,[97] D, a

---

[92] *Hennigan* [1971] 3 All ER 133, CA; *Cato* [1976] 1 All ER 260, CA.

[93] *Kimsey* [1996] Crim LR 35, CA.

[94] [1957] Crim LR 365.

[95] *Smith* [1959] 2 QB 35, C-MAC (see para 2.32, n 91); *Pagett* (1983) 76 Cr App Rep 279 at 288; *Cheshire* [1991] 3 All ER 670, CA.

[96] *Cheshire* [1991] 3 All ER 670, CA.

[97] (1865) 4 F & F 504.

foreman platelayer, misread the timetable so that the track was up when a train arrived. D had placed a signalman with a flag up the line but only half as far as he should have been sent under the company's rules, and the engine driver, who was not keeping a very sharp lookout, did not see the signal in time to stop. The resulting accident caused several deaths. If the signalman had gone the proper distance and the driver had been keeping a proper lookout there would not have been an accident, but D was convicted of manslaughter after the judge had ruled that, if D's conduct was a substantial cause of the accident, it was irrelevant that the conduct of others had contributed to it. Of course, in a case like this the other railwaymen could also be convicted of homicide in relation to the same death if their contribution was also substantial, and this would be possible whether or not they were acting in combination.

Victim's contributory negligence

2.34 Unless it is so gross as to prevent the defendant's act being a substantial cause, the contributory negligence of the victim is no defence. In *Longbottom*,[98] the victim, who was deaf, was walking in the middle of the highway and was run over by D, who was driving too fast. It was held that D could be convicted of manslaughter notwithstanding any contributory negligence on the part of the victim in walking as he had done.

Cases where the victim contributes to the specified consequence by an intervening act are dealt with below.

Pre-existing conditions in the victim

2.35 The existence of a medical condition which rendered the victim more susceptible to death or injury, eg haemophilia, does not prevent legal attribution of that consequence to the defendant. The defendant must take his victim as he finds him. In *Hayward*,[99] D arrived home in a state of agitation, saying that he was 'going to give his wife something' when she came home. On her arrival there was an altercation and the wife ran into the road, closely pursued by D who was making violent threats towards her. The wife fell down in the road and was found to be dead when she was picked up. The medical evidence was that the wife was in good health apart from a persistent thymus gland, but that in this condition death might result from a combination of fright and physical exertion. The jury were directed that the wife's susceptibility to death, whether D knew of it or not, was irrelevant if they were satisfied that her death was accelerated by his threats of violence. The judge directed the jury that proof of actual physical violence was unnecessary, since death from fright alone, caused by an illegal act, such as a threat of violence, was enough.

---

[98] (1849) 13 JP 270. Also see *Swindall and Osborne* (1846) 2 Car & Kir 230.
[99] (1908) 21 Cox CC 692.

2.36 The rule that the defendant must take his victim as he finds him is not limited to physical conditions. It was established in *Blaue*[100] that it also applies to the 'whole person' and therefore applies to mental conditions and, even, to the victim's religion. In *Blaue*, the deceased girl, who had been stabbed by D, was a Jehovah's Witness and consequently refused to have a blood transfusion which was required before surgery and which might have saved her life. The Court of Appeal held that a victim's refusal to have medical treatment could not provide a defence. In such a case the defendant would be liable if his act was still an operating and substantial cause of death. D was liable because the physical cause of death was the bleeding in the pleural cavity arising from the penetration of the lung. This was not brought about by any decision of the girl, but by the stab wound. Rejecting an argument that the victim's refusal had been unreasonable and prevented the death being legally attributable to the defendant, the Court of Appeal said:

> 'It has long been the policy of the law that those who use violence on other people must take their victims as they find them. This in our judgment means the whole man, not just the physical man. It does not lie in the mouth of the assailant to say that his victim's religious beliefs which inhibited him from accepting certain kinds of treatment were unreasonable. The question for decision is what caused the death. The answer is the stab wound.'[101]

Under the law of tort, the victim's refusal of a transfusion would have broken the chain of causation (ie prevented legal attribution of the death) if it was not reasonably foreseeable, but the Court of Appeal refused to adopt such a test for the criminal law, adopting the argument that the criminal law is concerned with the maintenance of law and order and the protection of the public generally. It has been observed[102] that this argument ignores the fact that the defendant in *Blaue* could in any event have been convicted of the serious crime of wounding with intent and the need for public protection could have been served by a conviction and sentence for that offence as much as it is in a conviction and sentence for manslaughter. On the other hand, it could be said that once one accepts the rule that the defendant must take his victim as he finds him there is no valid distinction between a physical condition making the victim susceptible to death and a religious conviction which makes it impossible for the victim to permit steps to be taken to save his life.

Intervening causes

2.37 An intervening act or event (ie an act or event occurring after the defendant's conduct) may break the chain of causation. Whether or not it does so depends on the application of the relevant legal principle referred to below.

---

[100] [1975] 3 All ER 446, CA.
[101] [1975] 3 All ER 446 at 450.
[102] Williams 'Criminal Law – Causation' (1976) 35 CLJ 15.

Intervening natural events

2.38 The occurrence of an independent intervening natural event causing the speci-fied consequence, which would not have had that effect but for the defendant's act, will not prevent the legal attribution of the consequence to the defendant if the type of event (as opposed to the details of the particular event) was reasonably foreseeable in the ordinary course of things; in such a case the specified consequence is said to be a 'natural' consequence of the defendant's act.[103] Thus, if D injures V and leaves him lying incapacitated on the ground, it is immaterial that V dies of exposure when the tempera-ture drops that night. The same would be so, as in the New Zealand case of *Hart*,[104] if D injures V and leaves V incapacitated on the beach below the high water line, and V is drowned by the incoming tide. Conversely, the death would not be attributable to D if V was killed by an unlikely event such as an earthquake or a lightning strike.

The law is not dissimilar in a context far removed from that of offences against the person, viz a strict liability[105] offence based on a duty to guard against natural events. In *Environment Agency (formerly National Rivers Authority) v Empress Car Co (Abertillery) Ltd*,[106] Lord Hoffmann (with whose speech three other Law Lords agreed) said that in such an offence an intervening natural event only prevents legal attribution if its occur-rence is abnormal and extraordinary rather than a normal fact of life. Lord Hoffmann thought that an event could be a normal fact of life 'if it was in the general run of things a matter of ordinary occurrence, even if it was not foreseeable that it would happen to that particular defendant, or take that particular form'. There is no real difference between Lord Hoffmann's test and that above because whether an event is in the general run of things must depend on whether the event is of a type which is reasonably foreseeable. The point that Lord Hoffmann was making seems simply to have been that the details of the particular event need not have been foreseeable.

It would seem that a specified consequence can be legally attributed to the defendant's conduct notwithstanding that it was caused by an unforeseeable intervening occurrence, if that occurrence was dependent on (ie caused by) his conduct. For example, if D intend-ing to kill V, throws a fire bomb at V, and V is killed not by being burnt to death but by an explosion when the bomb misses him and ignites a gas leak, V's death is legally attrib-utable to D.

Intervening acts by the victim or a third party

2.39 This heading relates to cases where, although the required consequence would not have occurred without the defendant's act, an intervening act by the victim or a third party contributed to it. In the case of an intervening act, whether by a third party or by the victim, the situation is complicated by the fact that, while there are principles which

---

[103] Perkins *Criminal Law* (2nd edn) 722–723; *Hallett v R* [1969] SASR 141, S Australian Supreme Ct.
[104] [1986] 2 NZLR 408, NZCA.
[105] Para 6.1.
[106] [1999] 2 AC 22, HL.

apply to intervening acts in general by a third party or by a victim, they give way to other principles which apply to specific types of intervening acts:

- where the victim neglects treatment or maltreats himself;
- where the victim dies or injures himself in trying to escape; and
- where intervening medical treatment contributes to the victim's death or injury.

Leaving aside these special cases, which are dealt with later, the position is as follows.

Where the defendant's act is an immediate cause

2.40 Where the defendant's act is an immediate cause (as well as a substantial cause) of the consequence, that result is attributable legally to him even though the later act of a victim or a third party was also a cause of it.

Suppose D stabs V and shortly afterwards E stabs V. V dies from the cumulative effect of the two wounds, the second merely aggravating the effect of the first. The death can be attributed to both D and E, whether or not they were acting in combination and whether or not either wound was mortal in itself. Support for this principle can be found in *Malcherek; Steel*.[107] Both of these consolidated appeals concerned defendants who had injured their victims so severely that they suffered irreversible brain damage. Both victims were put on life-support machines. In both cases the machines were turned off after doctors diagnosed brain stem death, although they had not carried out all the relevant tests. The victims were declared dead soon afterwards. Both defendants were convicted of murder after the trial judge in each case withdrew the issue of causation from the jury on the basis that there was no evidence that the defendant had not caused the death of his victim. The question in each case for the Court of Appeal, who proceeded on the basis that the victims died at the latest soon after the machines were turned off, was whether the judge had been correct in doing so because there was evidence on which the jury could have found that the cause of death was the switching off of the machines. Dismissing the appeals, the Court of Appeal said that this evidence was immaterial. Even if the switching off had also been a cause of death, this would not have altered the fact that the defendants' actions were a substantial and operating cause of death.

Where the defendant's act is not an immediate cause

2.41 Where the defendant's act is not an immediate cause of the required consequence but nevertheless contributes to it, by providing the setting for an intervening act by someone else which is the immediate cause of the consequence, the situation is as follows.

---

[107] [1981] 2 All ER 422, CA.

According to the leading academic work on causation, Hart and Honoré's *Causation in the Law*:

> 'The free, deliberate and informed intervention of a second person, who intends to exploit the situation created by the first, but is not acting in concert with him, is normally held to relieve the first actor of criminal responsibility.'[108]

The 'first person/actor' is, of course, the defendant in question; the 'second person' may be the victim or a third party. The meaning of 'not acting in concert with him [the first person]' is not explained, but it is submitted that it must be meant to refer to cases where the first person would not be liable as an accomplice (eg an aider or abettor) to an offence perpetrated by a second person. Otherwise the well-established rules about secondary liability[109] would be greatly limited in their operation, something which Hart and Honoré did not intend.

Under Hart and Honoré's principle, an intervening act by the victim or a third party which is the immediate cause of the consequence breaks the chain of causation from the defendant's act if it is free, deliberate and informed; an intervening act which breaks the chain of causation is sometimes referred to as a *novus actus interveniens*. On the other hand, if the intervening act by the victim or a third party *is not* a free one, or *is not* a deliberate act, or *is not* an informed act, the chain of causation from the defendant's act is not broken. By way of example, an intervening act is not a 'free' one if done under compulsion or duress or in self-defence; it is not 'deliberate' if it is done instinctively or in blind panic, and it is not 'informed' if the intervening actor does not appreciate the situation in which he acts (for example, because of mistake or youth or mental incapacity).

Hart and Honoré's statement of principle received qualified approval from the Court of Appeal in *Pagett*.[110] In *Pagett*, D, in order to resist arrest, held a girl in front of him as a shield and fired at armed policemen who fired back instinctively and killed the girl. Dismissing an appeal against a conviction for manslaughter, the Court of Appeal held that, if a reasonable act of self-defence, or in the execution of duty, by a third party against an act by a defendant causes the death of the victim, the causal link between the defendant's act and the victim's death is not broken. Clearly, the policemen's instinctive act of firing back was neither free nor a deliberate one. Referring to Hart and Honoré's principle, Robert Goff LJ (as he then was) stated: 'We resist the temptation of expressing the judicial opinion whether we find ourselves in complete agreement with that definition; though we certainly consider it to be broadly correct and supported by authority.'[111]

---

[108] (2nd edn, 1985) 326. For a critique of Hart and Honoré's analysis, see Jones 'Causation, Homicide and the Supply of Drugs' (2006) 26 LS 139.

[109] These rules are set out in Ch 17.

[110] (1983) 76 Cr App Rep 279, CA.

[111] (1983) 76 Cr App Rep 279 at 289.

In *Latif and Shahzad*,[112] the House of Lords was less hesitant and gave Hart and Honoré's principle unqualified approval. *Latif and Shahzad* concerned a charge against S of being concerned in the importation of a controlled drug, contrary to the Customs and Excise Management Act 1979, s 170(2). S delivered the drugs abroad to an intermediary for importation to England. The intermediary had alerted the authorities and the drug was transported to this country by a customs officer in order to entrap S. The officer's acts were obviously deliberate, free and informed. The House of Lords held that the officer's intervention prevented the importation being legally attributed to S; the most that he was guilty of was attempting to commit the offence in question. Lord Steyn, with whose reasons the other Law Lords agreed, adopted Hart and Honoré's principle, saying: 'The general principle is that the free, deliberate and informed intervention of a second person who intends to exploit the situation created by the first, but is not acting in concert with him, is held to relieve the first actor of criminal responsibility.'[113]

2.42 The general applicability of the Hart and Honoré principle was subsequently put in doubt by Court of Appeal decisions in *Rogers (Stephen)*[114] and *Kennedy (No 2)*.[115] In these cases the Court of Appeal held that a person (D) who held a tourniquet while the victim self-injected heroin with fatal effect (*Rogers (Stephen)*), or who supplied heroin to the victim for immediate self-injection and the victim did so with fatal effect (*Kennedy (No 2)*), could be convicted of constructive manslaughter (which requires death to have been caused by a criminal and dangerous act).[116] The basis for each decision was that the death had resulted from an offence under the Offences Against the Person Act 1861, s 23 which penalises the administering of a noxious thing or causing it to be administered or taken. Self-injectors do not commit an offence under s 23, so D was not liable in either case as an accomplice to a s 23 offence. The only way in which D could be convicted in either case was as a perpetrator of it. The Court of Appeal in both cases held that D had perpetrated the offence of administration under s 23 because in *Rogers (Stephen)* D had played a part in the mechanics of the injection and in *Kennedy (No 2)* D had been involved in a joint activity with the self-injector, and that as the death in each case had resulted from this administration D was responsible for the death and guilty of manslaughter. When *Kennedy (No 2)* was appealed to the House of Lords in 2007 the House held that both decisions were wrong. The House allowed the appeal in *Kennedy (No 2)* and overruled *Rogers (Stephen)*.

2.43 The House of Lords in *Kennedy (No 2)*[117] reaffirmed the status of the Hart and Honoré principle as 'fundamental and not controversial'.[118] The prosecution had conceded that, if it could not show that D had committed the offence of administering a noxious thing, contrary to s 23, it could not hope to show an offence of causing it to be administered or taken. The House of Lords held that this concession had been rightly

---

[112] [1996] 1 All ER 353, HL.   [113] [1996] 1 All ER 353 at 364.
[114] [2003] EWCA Crim 945.   [115] [2005] EWCA Crim 685.
[116] Paras 8.97–8.118.   [117] [2007] UKHL 38.   [118] [2007] UKHL 38 at [14].

made. Referring to the statement of Hart and Honoré quoted above, Lord Bingham, giving the opinion of the House, said:

> 'The criminal law generally assumes the existence of free will. The law recognises certain exceptions, in the case of the young, those who for any reason are not fully responsible for their actions, and the vulnerable, and it acknowledges situations of duress and necessity, as also of deception and mistake. But, generally speaking, informed adults of sound mind are treated as autonomous beings able to make their own decisions how they will act, and none of the exceptions is relied on as possibly applicable in this case. Thus D is not to be treated as causing V to act in a certain way if V makes a voluntary and informed decision to act in that way rather than another...
>
> ... The finding that the deceased freely and voluntarily administered the injection to himself, knowing what it was, is fatal to any contention that the appellant caused the heroin to be administered to the deceased or taken by him.'[119]

This left the argument that D had administered the injection to the deceased. The House held that he had not. It held that where the defendant supplied the heroin and prepared the syringe, but the deceased had a choice whether to self-inject, and did so, ie did so freely and voluntarily, knowing what he was doing, it was the deceased's act of administration. Having referred to *Rogers (Stephen)*, Lord Bingham went on to say:

> '...the crucial question is not whether the defendant facilitated or contributed to the administration of the noxious thing but whether he went further and administered it. What matters, in a case such as *R v Rogers* and the present, is whether the injection itself was the result of a voluntary and informed decision by the person injecting himself. In *R v Rogers*, as in the present case, it was. That case was, therefore, wrongly decided.'[120]

Because D had not committed an offence under s 23 (nor any other criminal and dangerous act), there was no basis for a conviction for constructive manslaughter, and D's conviction for it was quashed.

2.44 As pointed out in para 2.31, the principles of causation developed in relation to offences against the person do not necessarily apply in other contexts. This is shown by reference to the decision in 1998 of the House of Lords in *Environment Agency (formerly National Rivers Authority) v Empress Car Co (Abertillery) Ltd* [121] in respect of the offence of causing polluting matter to enter controlled water, contrary to the Water Resources Act 1991, s 85(1). In that case, D Ltd kept diesel in a tank in their yard. An unknown person entered the yard and opened the tank's tap. As a result the contents of the tank escaped down a storm drain into a river. There was nothing in *Empress Car* to suggest that the act of the third party was anything other than a free, deliberate and informed one. Thus, according to the Hart and Honoré principle, the pollution should not have been legally

---

[119] [2007] UKHL 38 at [14].   [120] [2007] UKHL 38 at [20]. See also para 7.117.
[121] [1999] 2 AC 22, HL.

attributable to D Ltd. Nevertheless, D Ltd were convicted. D Ltd appealed ultimately to the House of Lords contending, inter alia, that, as the tap had been opened by a stranger, the pollution of the river could not be legally attributable to D Ltd. The House of Lords, without reference to *Pagett* or *Latif and Shahzad*,[122] rejected that argument. As will be seen, it held that the same test applied in the case of an intervening act by the third party as has traditionally applied in the case of an intervening natural event.

Lord Hoffmann stated that whether or not to attribute to the defendant a consequence immediately caused by a third party or natural event depended on the nature and scope (ie the context) of the rule in relation to which the question of causation was being asked. Lord Hoffmann continued that if the rule imposed on D strict liability for the deliberate acts of third parties or natural events, an intervening third party act or an intervening event would not prevent attribution of the consequence to the conduct unless that act or event was extraordinary, rather than a normal fact of life. Lord Hoffmann stated:

> 'If the defendant did something which produced a situation in which the polluting matter could escape but a necessary condition of the actual escape which happened was also the act of a third party or a natural event, the justices should consider whether that act or event should be regarded as a normal fact of life or something extraordinary. If it was in the general run of things a matter of ordinary occurrence, it will not negative the causal effect of the defendant's acts, even if it was not foreseeable that it would happen to that particular defendant or take that particular form. If it can be regarded as something extraordinary, it will be open to the justices to hold that the defendant did not cause the pollution.'[123]

Applying these principles, the House of Lords held, there was ample evidence to entitle a finding that D Ltd had caused the pollution.

A telling criticism of the decision in *Empress Car* has been made as follows:

> 'There is something almost perverse about reasoning which concludes that D should be responsible for a result which he did not cause simply because the act of vandalism by which it was caused was not so extraordinary as to be unforeseeable. There is a major difference between a natural event and the action of a third party: the act of the third party is "free, deliberate and informed". In the instant case it was also malicious. In such a case D's liability ends up depending on the choices and actions of others rather than his own choices and actions.'[124]

As explained in para 2.38, the formulation stated in *Empress Car* involves a test of whether the *type* of intervening act, rather than the particular one, was reasonably foreseeable. The formulation is obviously a narrower ground of exemption than the Hart and Honoré principle applied by the House of Lords in *Latif and Shahzad* and endorsed by it in *Kennedy (No 2)*.

---

[122] Para 2.41.   [123] [1999] 2 AC 22 at 36.
[124] Allen *Textbook on Criminal Law* (10th edn, 2009) 44.

It must be emphasised that *Empress Car* does not lay down a general rule about causation in the criminal law but is limited to the context described above.[125] Any doubt on this matter was settled by *Kennedy (No 2)* where the unanimous opinion of the House of Lords was to the effect that:

'The House [in *Empress Car*] was not in that decision purporting to lay down general rules governing causation in criminal law. It was construing, with reference to the facts of the case before it, a statutory provision imposing strict criminal liability on those who cause pollution of controlled waters. Lord Hoffman made clear that common sense answers to questions of causation will differ according to the purpose for which the question is asked; that one cannot give a common sense answer to a question of causation for the purpose of attributing responsibility under some rule without knowing the purpose and scope of the rule; that strict liability was imposed in the interests of protecting controlled waters; and that in the situation under consideration the act of the defendant could properly be held to have caused the pollution even though an ordinary act of a third party was the immediate cause of the diesel oil flowing into the river. It is worth underlining that the relevant question was the cause of the pollution, not the cause of the third party's act.

The committee [ie the Appellate Committee of the House of Lords] would not wish to throw any doubt on the correctness of the *Empress Car* case. But the reasoning in that case cannot be applied to the wholly different context of causing a noxious thing to be administered to or taken by another person contrary to section 23 of the 1861 Act.'[126]

Victim's neglect of treatment or maltreatment of self

2.45 If, following the defendant's act, the victim neglects or maltreats himself this does not prevent his subsequent death being legally attributable to the defendant if the defendant's act is a substantial and operating cause of the death.

2.46 In *Wall*,[127] the governor of a colony was charged with the murder of a soldier whom he had sentenced to an illegal flogging. It was argued that the victim might not have died if he had refrained from drinking spirits while in hospital in consequence of the blows he had received. The jury convicted the governor of murder after the judge had directed them that:

'There is no apology for a man if he puts another in so dangerous and hazardous a situation by his treatment of him, that some degree of unskilfulness and mistaken treatment of himself may possibly accelerate the fatal catastrophe.'

[125] *Empress Car* was applied a year after the House of Lords' decision in *Kennedy (No 2)* in *L* [2008] EWCA Crim 1970 in respect of the same offence as was in issue in *Empress Car*.

[126] [2007] UKHL 38 at [15]. As a result, the House of Lords in *Kennedy (No 2)* held that in *Finlay* [2003] EWCA Crim 3868 the Court of Appeal had been wrong to apply *Empress Car* in a case whose facts were similar to those in *Kennedy (No 2)*. See also *Finlay (deceased)* [2009] EWCA Crim 1493 where the Court of Appeal held that, in the light of the decision in *Kennedy (No 2)*, the defendant's conviction in *Finlay* had been wrong.

[127] (1802) 28 State Tr 51.

A case involving refusal of treatment by the victim is *Holland*.[128] D deliberately inflicted some wounds on V. One of these caused blood poisoning in a finger, and V was advised to have it amputated. Had V done so, his surgeon stated, his life would probably have been saved. However, lockjaw set in and death ensued. The jury were directed that it made no difference whether the wound was instantly mortal of its own nature, or became the cause of death only by reason of V's not having adopted the best mode of treatment. A verdict of guilty of murder was returned.

2.47 The dictum of the judge in *Wall* cited above did not preclude the possibility that the victim's neglect of treatment or maltreatment of himself might prevent legal attribution to the defendant if it was unreasonable.

In the last century it was argued that a direction of the type in *Holland* might have become incorrect because, medical science having advanced greatly since 1841, a refusal of an operation might be regarded as unreasonable, and might therefore prevent legal attribution to the defendant. However, such an argument was rejected in 1975 by the Court of Appeal in *Blaue*.[129]

That the law remains unchanged in relation to the victim's maltreatment of himself was confirmed by the Court of Appeal in *Dear*,[130] a case where the victim had either maltreated himself or neglected treatment. D, who had heard that V had sexually interfered with his daughter, slashed him repeatedly with a knife. V died two days later as a result of the wounds. D argued that the chain of causation was broken between his actions and the death because V had committed suicide either by reopening his wounds or, the wounds having reopened themselves, by failing to staunch the consequent blood flow. It was argued that the suicide would have broken the chain of causation (ie prevented legal attribution of the death to D). Dismissing D's appeal against conviction for murder, the Court of Appeal agreed with the trial judge's direction that, if V had reopened his wounds or failed to stop the bleeding because of the fact of the attack (which had horrifically disfigured him), the question for them was whether the injuries inflicted by D were an operating and substantial cause of death. The Court stated that, if the wounds were an operating and substantial cause of death, it was irrelevant whether V had treated himself with mere negligence or gross neglect. The Court appears to have treated it as immaterial whether or not the victim's conduct in the present type of case was unforeseeable, which may be contrasted with the rule in para 2.48 which applies where a victim injures himself in trying to escape, but is consistent with the rule in para 2.35 which applies where the victim has a medical condition rendering him susceptible to death or injury.

In *Dear*, the Court of Appeal accepted that, if V had reopened his wounds because of shame over what he had done or some other reason unrelated to D's conduct, there would not have been a causal link between D's acts and V's death. D's acts would not have been a factual cause of death because it could not have been said that V would not have killed himself but for the injuries inflicted by D.

---

[128] (1841) 2 Mood & R 351; for a full account of the facts see [1957] Crim LR 702.
[129] [1975] 3 All ER 446, CA.   [130] [1996] Crim LR 595, CA; the above is based on the transcript.

Where the victim dies or injures himself in trying to escape

2.48 If the defendant puts the victim in fear of harm and the victim brings about his own death or injures himself in trying to escape, the victim's death or injury can be attributed legally to the defendant, provided that the victim's reaction was likely (ie within the range of responses reasonably foreseeable as possible by a victim placed in the situation in which the victim was).[131] An example of the present rule is provided by *Roberts*,[132] where D had tried to remove the coat of a girl in a moving car, indicating that he meant to take liberties with her against her will. The girl jumped out of the car and was injured. D appealed against conviction for assault occasioning actual bodily harm on the ground that the jury were not directed to consider whether he foresaw that she would jump and suffer injury. The Court of Appeal rejected this, saying that the only issue was one of causation; the question was whether the victim's actions were the natural result of D's conduct, in the sense that they were something that could reasonably have been foreseen as the consequence of what D was saying and doing.

Although this test has been described as being applied on the basis of what a reasonable person 'in the [defendant's] shoes' would have foreseen,[133] that reasonable person is not endowed with the defendant's age or sex[134] or any other of his characteristics.

The rationale for having an objective test was explained in *Marjoram*[135] where the Court of Appeal rejected the argument of the defendant, aged 16, that the reasonable person for the present purpose should be the same age and sex as the defendant. It stated that, in the present type of situation, the law was concerned with the effect of the defendant's conduct on the victim's mind. If the test were other than objective, one co-defendant might be held not to have caused an injury, because he did not foresee the victim's reaction; whereas another co-defendant, who did exactly the same thing, might be held to have caused it because he foresaw it. That, it said, would be an absurd position.

The victim's reaction will not be likely if his fear of harm is an unreasonable one or, if his fear is reasonable, he does something daft in trying to escape.[136] In deciding whether the victim's response was likely the jury should bear in mind 'any particular characteristics of *the victim* and the fact that in the agony of the moment he may act without thought and deliberation'.[137]

2.49 It may be that the present principle provides the answer to the question of causation posed in a different type of case, that where physical or sexual abuse suffered at the hands of the defendant triggers a decision by the victim to commit suicide, which the victim succeeds in doing. In *Dhaliwal*,[138] the Court of Appeal recognised that if a defendant's unlawful conduct causes a psychiatric illness, with resulting suicide, the defendant is not excluded from liability for manslaughter, 'subject always to the law of causation'. The

---

[131] *Roberts* (1971) 56 Cr App Rep 95, CA; *Mackie* (1973) 57 Cr App Rep 453, CA; *Williams* [1992] 2 All ER 183, CA; *Corbett* [1996] Crim LR 594, CA.

[132] (1972) 56 Cr App Rep 95, CA.   [133] *Williams* [1992] 2 All ER 183 at 191.

[134] *Marjoram* [2000] Crim LR 372, CA.   [135] [2000] Crim LR 372, CA.

[136] *Williams* [1992] 2 All ER 183 at 191.   [137] Ibid. Italics supplied.

[138] [2006] EWCA Crim 1139.

Court decided the case on another point and did not need to deal with the law of causation. The defendant's conduct clearly constituted a factual cause of death, but the applicable principle of legal attribution is undecided.[139]

An argument in favour of saying that the present principle is applicable is that the victim who commits suicide is in a sense trying to escape the defendant (or, at least, the consequences of the abuse). An argument against is that a person who commits suicide necessarily aims to kill himself, whereas a person who kills himself in trying to escape an attack does not. This may be regarded as an important distinction. If the present principle is applied, the question will be whether the victim's actions in committing suicide were within the range of responses reasonably foreseeable as possible by someone in the victim's situation, taking into account the victim's characteristics; if it was, the chain of causation will not be broken and the death will be attributable to the defendant.

If the present principle is inapplicable to the situation in *Dhaliwal*, one must presumably fall back on the general rule about intervening acts by the victim referred to in para 2.41, whereby the victim's intervening act resulting in his suicide will break the chain of causation from the defendant's conduct to the victim's death unless the victim's intervening act was not deliberate, free or informed. An act done to commit suicide would clearly seem to be deliberate and informed, but (depending on the degree of trauma suffered by the victim) it could be found not to be free in certain cases; if so the chain of causation would not be broken.

Depending on the facts, each of these two tests is liable to produce a different answer to the question 'is causation proved?' in the *Dhaliwal* type of case.[140]

Intervening medical treatment

2.50 The fact that the victim subsequently receives medical treatment (whether a surgical operation or the administration of drugs) for his injury, which kills him, will not excuse the person who injured him if that treatment is not negligent (ie if it is given with the care and skill of a competent medical practitioner).[141]

2.51 Even if the treatment is negligent it is only in the most exceptional case that it will break the chain of causation between the act which caused the injury and the death.

In *Smith*,[142] a person who had been stabbed by D in a barrack-room brawl was twice dropped on the way to hospital and when he got there he was given treatment which was 'thoroughly bad' and might have affected his chances of recovery. He died some two hours after being stabbed. The Courts-Martial Appeal Court held that these events

---

[139] The psychiatric illness could not be regarded as an operating cause of death, which distinguishes the present type of case from that in *Dear* discussed in para 2.47.

[140] See, further, paras 8.97–8.118, as to liability for manslaughter in respect of the type of case discussed above.

[141] *Cheshire* [1991] 3 All ER 670 at 674.

[142] [1959] 2 QB 35, C-MAC (see para 2.32, n 91, in relation to this court).

did not break the chain of causation between the stabbing and the death. Delivering the Court's judgment, Lord Parker CJ said:

> 'It seems to this court that if at the time of death the original wound is still an operating cause and a substantial cause, then the death can properly be said to be the result of the wound, albeit that some other cause of death is also operating.[143] Only if it can be said that the original wound is merely the setting in which another cause operates can it be said that the death did not result from the wound. Putting it another way, only if the second cause is so overwhelming as to make the original wound merely part of the history can it be said that the death does not flow from the wound.'[144]

2.52 The first sentence in the above dictum shows that, if at the time of death the original wound is still an operating cause and a substantial cause, the death is legally attributable to the defendant, albeit that some other cause of the death is also operating. The facts in *Smith* clearly fell within the first sentence of this dictum, since D's act was an operating and substantial cause of death.

2.53 The second two sentences in Lord Parker's statement are concerned with the situation where the wound or injury caused by the defendant's act is not an operating cause of death because the original wound or injury is not (or is no longer) life-threatening and the deceased dies not from the wound or injury caused by the defendant but from treatment given for it. In *Jordan*,[145] where the defendant had stabbed the deceased, it was held that the death could not be attributed to the defendant in the light of fresh evidence that it had been caused by the administration of terramycin after the deceased had shown he was intolerant to it (which was described as 'palpably wrong' treatment) and when his wound was nearly healed.

Jordan was distinguished in *Smith* and in *Blaue*[146] as 'a very particular case depending on its exact facts', although in *Blaue* the Court of Appeal thought *Jordan* was probably rightly decided on its facts.

Further explanation of the current law which applies where the wound or injury inflicted by the defendant is not an operating cause of death was given by the Court of Appeal in *Cheshire*,[147] where it was emphasised that it will only be in the most extraordinary and unusual case that negligent medical treatment, however gross the negligence, for wounds or injuries caused to the victim by the defendant can break the chain of causation from his conduct. The Court held that the chain of causation would not be broken unless the negligent treatment was 'so independent' of the defendant's conduct and

---

[143] In such a case the doctor giving the treatment could also be said to satisfy the requirements of causation. If the medical treatment was grossly negligent the doctor might be convicted of manslaughter, although a prosecution would be unlikely.

[144] [1959] 2 QB 35 at 42–43.

[145] (1956) 40 Cr App Rep 152, CCA.

[146] [1975] 3 All ER 446, CA.

[147] [1991] 3 All ER 670, CA. Also see *Mellor* [1996] 2 Cr App Rep 245, CA.

in itself 'so potent' as to render the contribution to death of the defendant's conduct insignificant. It is the consequences of the treatment, said the Court, rather than possible degrees of fault attached to it, which are the essential issues. A problem with this is that the Court did not explain what was meant by 'so independent of [the defendant's] acts' and 'so potent'.

The operation of these statements can be demonstrated by reference to the facts of *Cheshire*. In the course of an argument in a fish and chip shop, D shot V in the leg and stomach, seriously wounding him. After an operation, V developed respiratory problems and a tracheotomy tube was inserted to assist his breathing. V died in hospital over two months after the shooting; the immediate cause of death was a narrowing of the windpipe where the tracheotomy tube had been inserted, such a condition being a rare but not unknown complication arising out of a tracheotomy. V had complained of further breathing difficulties and suffered a chest infection after the tracheotomy. At D's trial for murder, there was evidence that V's wounds no longer threatened his life at the time of his death and that his death was caused by the negligence of the hospital staff in failing to diagnose and treat V's respiratory condition. The trial judge directed the jury to consider the degree of fault in the medical treatment (rather than its practical consequences) in deciding whether or not the death was to be legally attributed to D.

Dismissing D's appeal against conviction for murder, the Court of Appeal held that, while the judge had misdirected the jury, there had been no miscarriage of justice because, even if more experienced doctors than those who attended V would have recognised the rare complication in time to have prevented V's death, that complication was a direct consequence of D's acts, which remained a significant cause of death. It was inconceivable that a jury properly directed (ie along the lines indicated in the Court's judgment above) would have found otherwise.

2.54 The upshot of these cases is that negligent medical treatment for the original injury which brings about death will only prevent legal attribution to the defendant if the original wound is no longer an operating cause of death and the negligent treatment is so independent of the defendant's conduct and in itself so potent as to render the contribution of the defendant's conduct insignificant. It will be extremely rare that negligent medical treatment will satisfy this test. If (as in *Cheshire*) the negligent treatment consists solely of a failure to diagnose and give a treatment which would have been effectual it seems inconceivable that the test could be satisfied. Examples of extreme cases where the test might be satisfied are where the doctor misreads his notes and performs an operation that is not required or where medical staff give a manifest overdose of drugs or continue (as in *Jordan*) to give drugs to which the victim has shown himself intolerant. It must not be forgotten that, whether or not the negligent treatment breaks the chain of causation, the death can also be legally attributed to the person giving the fatal medical treatment; if that person is grossly negligent he can be convicted of involuntary manslaughter.

2.55 In *Jordan* and *Cheshire*, it was the medical treatment, not the injury, which was alleged to be the immediate cause of death. The same principles apply where the injury prevents medical treatment for a pre-existing condition, which would have saved the victim's life. In *McKechnie*,[148] the injuries inflicted by D prevented the victim being treated for a duodenal ulcer (since the doctors thought he might die under anaesthetic). The ulcer burst and the victim died. Dismissing D's appeal against a conviction for manslaughter by reason of provocation, the Court of Appeal held that only an 'extraordinary and unusual' medical decision that life-saving treatment was impossible would break the chain of causation.

Omissions

2.56 Doubts have sometimes been cast[149] as to how one can say that an omission can cause death or some other specified consequence, because a failure to act when one is under a legal duty to do so, eg to save one's young child from drowning, does not initiate the causal process but is simply a failure to prevent other factors bringing about that harm.

This has not, however, prevented the convictions for homicide or other result crimes of those whose wrongdoing has simply consisted of a failure to prevent the harm in breach of a legal duty to do so, as the cases cited in para 2.11 show. **Provided that if D had fulfilled his legal duty to act he would have prevented the consequence, the consequence is factually and legally attributable to him (subject to any of the general principles of legal causation); if he could not have prevented the consequence it is not.** Thus, if D fails to get medical attention for his sick child and the child dies, the death can be attributed to D if the child *would* have survived if it had received medical attention, but not if it *might have* survived.[150] What distinguishes D from anyone else who stands by and fails to get the medical attention is that, while their omissions will also satisfy the 'but for' test and are therefore a factual cause of death, the absence of a legal duty to act on their part means that the death cannot be legally attributable to them and therefore their omission to act is not a legal cause of death.

Causation: the function of judge and jury

2.57 This was dealt with by the Court of Appeal in *Pagett*,[151] where, in line with the normal well-established principle, it was held that **it is for the judge to direct the jury on the relevant principles relating to causation, and then to leave it to the jury to decide,**

---

[148] (1991) 94 Cr App Rep 51.

[149] See, for example, Hogan 'Omissions and the Duty Myth' in *Criminal Law: Essays in Honour of JC Smith* (1987) (Smith (ed)) 85 at 88.

[150] *Morby* (1882) 8 QBD 571, CCR. The Draft Criminal Code Bill, cl 17(1)(b) provides a wider test, viz: 'a person causes a result which is an element of an offence when…(b) he omits to do an act which might prevent its occurrence and which he is under a duty to do according to the law relating to the offence' (Law Commission: *A Criminal Code for England and Wales* (1989), Law Com No 177; see para 1.72). See Williams 'What should the Code do about Omissions?' (1987) 7 LS 92 at 106–107.

[151] (1983) 76 Cr App Rep 279, CA.

in the light of those principles on which they are bound to act, whether or not the relevant causal link has been established. In *Pagett*, it was stated that it is rarely necessary to give the jury any direction on causation as such, because that issue is usually not in dispute. Indeed, it was held in *Blaue*[152] that 'where there is no conflict in the evidence and all the jury has to do is to apply the law to the admitted facts, the judge is entitled to tell the jury what the result of that application will be'. However, although the judge may direct the jury that they must acquit the defendant because there is insufficient evidence that the requirement of causation is satisfied, *Pagett* shows that the reverse is not true. The judge cannot withdraw the issue of causation from the jury on the ground that the only reasonable conclusion is that the requirements of causation are satisfied. This is so despite the Court of Appeal's acceptance in the earlier case of *Malcherek; Steel*[153] of the judge's power to do so on such a ground.

In *Pagett*, the Court of Appeal held that, where a direction on causation is necessary, it is usually enough to direct the jury simply that in law the defendant's act or omission need not be the sole cause, or even the main cause, of the relevant consequence, it being enough that it contributed substantially to that result. Occasionally, however, a specific issue of legal attribution may arise. Where such a specific issue of causation arises, the judge should also direct the jury in terms of the specific principles of legal causation which apply to that issue. Robert Goff LJ (as he then was) giving the judgment of the Court in *Pagett*, continued:

> 'It would then fall to the jury to decide the relevant factual issues which, identified with reference to those legal principles, will lead to the conclusion whether or not the prosecution have established [the relevant causal link].'[154]

FURTHER READING

Alexander 'Criminal Liability for Omissions' in *Criminal Law Theory: Doctrines of the General Part* (2002) (Shute and Simester (eds)) 121

Ashworth 'The Scope of Criminal Liability for Omissions' (1989) 105 LQR 424

Beynon 'Causation, Omissions and Complicity' [1987] Crim LR 539

Finnis 'Bland: Crossing the Rubicon?' (1993) 109 LQR 329

Gross 'A Note on Omissions' (1984) 4 LS 308

Hart and Honoré *Causation in the Law* (2nd edn, 1985) Chs XII–XIV

Hogan 'Omissions and the Duty Myth' in *Criminal Law: Essays in Honour of J C Smith* (1987) (Smith (ed)) 85

Keown 'Restoring Moral and Intellectual Shape to the Law after *Bland*' (1997) 113 LQR 481

---

[152] [1975] 3 All ER 446 at 450.   [153] Para 2.40.   [154] (1983) 76 Cr App Rep 279 at 290.

Lynch 'The Mental Element in the *Actus Reus*' (1982) 98 LQR 109

Nkrumah '*R v Kennedy* Revisited' (2008) 72 JCL 117

Norrie 'A Critique of Criminal Causation' (1991) 54 MLR 685

Price 'What Shape to Euthanasia after *Bland*? Historical, Contemporary and Futuristic Paradigms' (2009) 125 LQR 142

Robinson 'Should the Criminal Law Abandon the *Actus Reus/Mens Rea* Distinction?' in *Action and Value in Criminal Law* (1993) (Shute, Gardner and Horder (eds)) 187

Simester 'Why Omissions are Special' (1995) 15 LS 311

JC Smith 'Liability for Omissions in the Criminal Law' (1984) 4 LS 88

JC Smith *Justification and Excuse in Criminal Law* (1989) Ch 2

Stannard 'Medical Treatment and the Chain of Causation' (1993) 57 JCL 88

Williams 'The Theory of Excuses' [1982] Crim LR 732

Williams 'Criminal Omissions: The Conventional View' (1991) 107 LQR 86

3

Criminal liability 2: *mens rea*

OVERVIEW

The term *'mens rea'* refers to the state of mind expressly or impliedly required by the definition of the offence charged. Typical instances are intention, recklessness and knowledge. These are explained in this chapter, as is negligence.

Mens rea

3.1 Despite occasional judicial utterances to the contrary,[1] it is clear from the application of *mens rea* in the courts that **mens rea has nothing necessarily to do with notions of an evil mind, moral fault or knowledge of the wrongfulness of the conduct**. The fact that the defendant was not morally at fault is not in itself a defence,[2] nor is the fact that the defendant was ignorant that his conduct constituted an offence,[3] nor generally is the fact that the defendant did not consider his conduct to be immoral or know that it was regarded as immoral by the bulk of society.[4] Moreover, it is generally irrelevant to liability whether the defendant acted with a 'good' or 'bad' motive.[5]

3.2 The expression *'mens rea'* refers to the state of mind expressly or impliedly required by the definition of the offence charged. This varies from offence to offence, but typical instances are intention, recklessness and knowledge. In the course of our examination of typical states of mind it will be necessary to refer to negligence, although it can hardly be said to be a state of mind because it is concerned with whether a reasonable person would have realised the risk in question.

3.3 In modern times, the courts, particularly the House of Lords, have indicated a preference for judging a defendant on the basis of what he intended or knew and so on, rather

---

[1] See, for example, *Sherras v de Rutzen* [1895] 1 QB 918 at 921, per Wright J; *Sweet v Parsley* [1970] AC 132 at 152, per Lord Morris.

[2] *Yip Chiu-cheung v R* [1995] 1 AC 111, especially at 117–118; *Kingston* [1995] 2 AC 355 at 364–366, per Lord Mustill; *Dodman* [1998] 2 Cr App Rep 338, CMAC (as to this court, see para 2.32, n 91).

[3] Para 3.73.   [4] Para 3.85.   [5] Para 3.70.

than on the basis of what a reasonable person would have realised.[6] This was described in *G* by Lord Steyn as a 'shift...towards adopting a subjective approach'.[7] While the 'subjectivists' are overall winning the battle with the 'objectivists' in terms of this development of the law by the judges, the battle is not going so well for them in Parliament, as the objective[8] terms of the vast majority of offences in the Sexual Offences Act 2003[9] indicate.

3.4 The *mens rea* required for an offence normally relates to the consequences or circumstances, or both, required for the *actus reus* of the offence charged.

Intention

Key points 3.1

A person intends a consequence of his act (or omission) if he acts (or fails to act) with the aim or purpose of thereby bringing about that consequence. In addition, if a person foresees that a consequence is virtually certain to result from his conduct, although it is not his aim or purpose to achieve it, he can be found to have intended that consequence.

Sometimes the intention required by the definition of an offence relates not to a consequence of the defendant's conduct, but to something ulterior to it, which does not have to be brought about. Such an intention is known as an 'ulterior intention'.

3.5 Where the definition of the *actus reus* of the offence charged requires the defendant's conduct to produce a particular consequence, he has a sufficient mental state as to that consequence if he intends his act (or omission) to produce that consequence. In many offences where the defendant's conduct is required to produce a particular consequence, liability can be based either on his intention or his recklessness as to that consequence being produced by his act (or omission). However, in the definitions of some offences liability can be based only on intention and it is in these that the question of what is meant in law by intention is of crucial importance.

Like the other concepts of *mens rea* referred to in this chapter, 'intention' is not defined as a general concept by any statute and its meaning must therefore be derived from judicial decisions.[10] Intention is something quite distinct from motive (ie a person's reason

---

[6] Eg *DPP v Morgan* [1976] AC 182, HL; *B v DPP* [2000] 2 AC 428, HL; *K* [2001] UKHL 41; *G* [2003] UKHL 50.

[7] [2003] UKHL 50 at [55].

[8] Ie terms which are judged by reference to whether or not a reasonable person would have believed something or had some other state of mind.

[9] Ch 9.

[10] It is possible, but extremely rare, for a statute to set out the meaning of a *mens rea* term for the purposes of an offence under it. The Identity Card Act 2006, s 29(2) provides an example in respect of 'intention' for the purposes of s 29.

for acting as he did) or desire;[11] if D kills V with great regret (but seeing no other way) in order to take V's money, his intention is to kill V but his motive is to take the money, and it is irrelevant that D did not desire V's death.

3.6 In terms of moral philosophy, there are two types of intention with regard to prohibited consequences, 'direct' intention and 'oblique' intention, whereby a person directly intends a consequence if he has decided to achieve it and a person obliquely intends to achieve it if he realises that it is likely to result as a side-effect of achieving his aim of achieving some other consequence.[12]

The following paragraphs consider the extent to which the criminal law replicates this view.

Direct intention

3.7 Direct intention is undoubtedly 'intention' for the purposes of the criminal law. 'Intention' was defined by the Court of Appeal in *Mohan*[13] as: 'a decision to bring about, insofar as it lies within the accused's power, [a particular consequence], no matter whether the accused desired that consequence of his act or not'. As the Court recognised,[14] **this can be described more briefly as the defendant's 'aim' or 'purpose'.** The definition in *Mohan*, which refers, of course, to direct intention, could be described as a commonsense definition, since it probably accords with most people's idea of what constitutes intention, as well as being the relevant meaning given by the dictionaries.[15] As the Court of Appeal stated in *Walker and Hayles*,[16] 'It has never been suggested that a man does not intend what he is trying to achieve'. Provided that he has decided to bring about a particular consequence, insofar as it lies within his power, a person acts with a direct intention in relation to it even though he believes he is unlikely to succeed in bringing it about. For example, a person has a direct intention to kill if he fires at someone whom he believes to be outside the normal range of his gun in an endeavour to kill him.

3.8 It follows, from the reference in the definition in *Mohan* to the fact that it is irrelevant that the defendant did not desire a consequence which he had decided to bring about, that a person can be said to act with a direct intention to cause a particular consequence, even though it is not desired in itself, if it is the means (ie a condition precedent) to the achievement of a desired objective and he decides to cause that consequence, insofar as it lies within his power. Not only is this implicit in that definition, but also support for it

[11] *Moloney* [1985] AC 905 at 926, per Lord Bridge with whose speech the rest of the Law Lords agreed.

[12] See, for example, Bentham *Principles of Morals and Legislation* (1948) (Harrison (ed)) 207.

[13] [1976] QB 1 at 11. This statement in *Mohan* was endorsed in *Pearman* (1984) 80 Cr App Rep 259, CA. It had a precursor in a similar statement by Asquith LJ in a civil case, *Cunliffe v Goodman* [1950] 2 KB 237 at 253, which was approved by Lord Hailsham in *Hyam v DPP* [1975] AC 55 at 74.

[14] [1976] QB 1 at 8.

[15] See, eg *Shorter Oxford English Dictionary; Chambers Twentieth Century Dictionary*. In *Re A (conjoined twins: surgical separation)* [2001] Fam 147 at 256, 'purpose' was regarded as the 'natural and ordinary' meaning of 'intention' by Robert Walker LJ.

[16] (1989) 90 Cr App Rep 226 at 230.

can be found in the speech of Lord Hailsham in *Hyam v DPP*,[17] decided by the House of Lords a year before *Mohan*. Lord Hailsham, adopting a definition of intention very similar to that in *Mohan*, stated that it should be held to include 'the means as well as the end' (ie that a person who has decided to bring about a consequence as a means to a desired end or objective falls within the definition of direct intention in relation to that consequence). Suppose that a person is charged with an offence which requires him to intend to cause economic loss to another, and that the defendant admittedly acted to make a gain for himself by depriving another of something. It is no defence for him to say that, since his desired objective was to make a gain for himself, he did not intend to cause economic loss. Likewise, if X shoots at, and kills, an attacker with the objective of saving his (X's) life, he will directly intend the attacker's death if he has decided to bring it about in order to save his own life.

The case law, however, is not wholly in accord with the principle just stated. In *Steane*,[18] D made broadcasts in Germany during the Second World War in order to save his family from a concentration camp. It was held on appeal that the broadcasts were not made 'with intent to assist the enemy', even though D knew that his desired objective of saving his family could only be achieved by doing acts assisting the enemy. This decision perverted the concept of intention so as to excuse a defendant who was deserving. As we shall see in Chapter 16, there may have been a more acceptable basis for Steane not being guilty, namely the defence of duress by threats. Hard cases can make bad law and it is submitted that *Steane* should not be allowed to cast doubt on the statements concerning intention in the previous paragraph. It is inconceivable that the Court would have reached the same conclusion if Steane had broadcast in order to obtain a packet of cigarettes.

Oblique intention

The case law before *Woollin*

3.9 Before the House of Lords' decision in *Moloney*,[19] the general understanding from the cases was that, for the purposes of most offences, a person would intend a consequence of his conduct which he did not aim to achieve if he obliquely intended it, in that he foresaw that that consequence was virtually certain to result as a side-effect from achieving something which he did aim to achieve.[20] Thus, if F, who wished to collect the insurance money on an air cargo, put a time bomb on an aircraft to blow it up in flight, realising that it was almost inevitable that those on board would be killed by the explosion, he was regarded as having intended those deaths, even though he wished those on board no harm and would have been delighted if they had survived.[21]

Indeed, before *Moloney*, the balance of judicial statements also supported the view that, for the purpose of murder and some other offences, a person who foresaw a consequence

---

[17] [1975] AC 55 at 74.   [18] [1947] KB 997, CCA.   [19] [1985] AC 905, HL.
[20] Eg *Williams v Bayley* (1866) LR 1 HL 200 at 221; *Serné* (1887) 16 Cox CC 311 at 313, per Stephen J.
[21] See *Hyam v DPP* [1975] AC 55 at 74, per Lord Hailsham, LC.

as a highly probable (or, perhaps, even probable)[22] consequence of his act intended it, although he did not aim to produce it.

3.10 The House of Lords in *Moloney*[23] decided, and affirmed in *Hancock and Shankland*,[24] that foresight, even of virtual certainty, is not intention in a legal sense or the equivalent of it. As a result, the authority to the contrary was impliedly overruled.

In *Moloney*, the House of Lords held that the *mens rea* for murder was an intention to kill or do serious bodily harm, and that foresight of death or serious bodily harm was neither intention as to such a consequence nor the equivalent of intention. On the other hand, the House of Lords held, the jury should be told that, if it was proved that the defendant foresaw a consequence of his act, they were entitled (but not obliged) to infer that the defendant intended it. Thus, although foresight was not itself intention, intention could be inferred from it. This raised the question of the degree of risk of the consequence which had to be foreseen before it could be inferred that the defendant intended it. Lord Bridge, giving the lead judgment (with which the other Law Lords agreed), was ambiguous, speaking at different points in terms of 'moral certainty' (ie virtual certainty), of 'probability little short of overwhelming' (which is not very different, if at all) and of what appears to be high probability (which is different).

It seems that Lord Bridge in reality opted for 'moral certainty'. However, in a passage at the end of his speech which was clearly meant to embody the principles in it, Lord Bridge said that, when elaboration was required about intention (ie in a case where the evidence suggests that it was not the defendant's aim or purpose to bring about the consequence which must be intended), two questions had to be asked:

> 'First, was death or really serious injury in a murder case (or whatever relevant consequence must be proved to have been intended in any other case) a natural consequence of the defendant's voluntary act? Secondly, did the defendant foresee that consequence as being a natural consequence of his act? The jury should then be told that if they answer yes to both questions it is a proper inference for them to draw that he intended that consequence.'[25]

This passage was ambiguous: what did 'natural consequence' mean? 'Natural' can mean 'causally connected to an act', whether a morally (ie virtually) certain consequence or not. Alternatively, it can mean a morally certain consequence. It seems from an earlier passage in his speech that this is what Lord Bridge meant to require, ie that the consequence must have been virtually certain and foreseen as virtually certain before it could be inferred that the defendant intended it.

The passage quoted above was particularly likely to cause confusion, and so it proved in *Hancock and Shankland*, another murder case, where V, a taxi-driver taking a miner to work during a miners' strike, was killed when two lumps of concrete projected from

---

[22] See the differing views of Lords Hailsham and Diplock and Viscount Dilhorne in *Hyam v DPP* [1975] AC 55, HL.

[23] [1985] AC 905, HL.   [24] [1986] AC 455, HL.   [25] [1985] AC 905 at 929.

a bridge by the defendant strikers hit his car as it passed under the bridge. At their trial for murder, the defendants said that they had intended simply to block the road and stop the passenger going to work but not to kill or do serious harm to anyone. The trial judge directed the jury in terms of the statement in *Moloney* by Lord Bridge quoted above, without explaining that 'natural' did not simply mean 'causally connected'. The defendants were convicted of murder but appealed successfully to the Court of Appeal. Rejecting an appeal by the prosecution, the House of Lords held that the judge had misdirected the jury by failing to explain to them what was meant by the 'natural' consequence which must be foreseen before an intention to kill or cause grievous bodily harm could be inferred. However, the water was muddied somewhat by Lord Scarman, with whom the other Law Lords agreed, who said that Lord Bridge had included *probability* in the meaning which he attributed to 'natural'. He thought that, where the jury were directed about inferring intention from foresight, they should be directed as to the relevance of probability but he did not clearly state the matter in terms of any particular level of probability. This left unclear how a judge was to direct a jury.

3.11 The statements in *Moloney* and *Hancock and Shankland* were the subject of further exposition by the Court of Appeal in *Nedrick*.[26] In *Nedrick* D poured paraffin through the letterbox of X, against whom he had a grudge, and set fire to it. A child died in the resulting blaze. D was convicted of murder after the judge had directed the jury in terms equating foresight with intent. The Court of Appeal allowed his appeal and substituted a conviction for manslaughter. Purporting to crystallise *Moloney* and *Hancock*, it endorsed the view that foresight of virtual certainty was required in order for the jury to be entitled to infer intention. In what was regarded by the House of Lords in *Woollin* as the model direction it said:

> 'Where the charge is murder and in the rare case where [it is necessary to direct the jury on the matter], the jury should be directed that they are not entitled to infer the necessary intention unless they feel sure that death or serious bodily harm was a virtual certainty (barring some unforeseen intervention) as a result of the defendant's actions and that the defendant appreciated that such was the case... The decision is one for the jury to be reached on a consideration of all the evidence.'[27]

The law as it now is after *Woollin*

3.12 *Nedrick model direction approved*   In *Woollin*,[28] the House of Lords approved the model direction in *Nedrick*, with one change. D had lost his cool when his baby son choked on his food and he had thrown him four or five feet across a room. The baby died as a result and D was charged with murder. D said that he had not thought that he would kill the baby, nor had he intended to. For some unexplained reason the prosecution case was not that D had the aim or purpose to kill the baby or cause it serious bodily harm, but

---

[26] [1986] 3 All ER 1, CA.   [27] [1986] 3 All ER 1 at 4.   [28] [1999] 1 AC 82, HL.

that he must have realised that what he was doing was virtually certain to cause the baby serious bodily harm. The judge directed the jury that it was open to them to find that D had the necessary intent to cause serious bodily harm if they were satisfied that he must have realised when he threw the child that there was a substantial risk that he would cause serious bodily harm. D, having appealed unsuccessfully against conviction to the Court of Appeal on the ground that this was a misdirection because the judge had not directed the jury in accordance with *Nedrick*, appealed to the House of Lords.

The House of Lords allowed D's appeal against his conviction for murder and substituted a conviction for manslaughter. It held that the Court of Appeal had been wrong to hold that 'virtual certainty' should be confined to cases where the evidence of intent is limited to the admitted actions of the defendant and the consequences of those actions and was not obligatory where there was other evidence to be considered. There was no such distinction. The use of 'substantial risk' blurred the line between intention and recklessness and enlarged the scope of murder; if in either type of case it was necessary to give a direction in terms of foresight, the direction should be in accordance with the model direction in *Nedrick* set out in para 3.11, described by Lord Steyn as a 'tried and tested formula' which trial judges ought to continue to use. However, both Lord Steyn and Lord Hope, who gave the only substantive speeches, thought that in the model direction 'to find' should be substituted for 'to infer' for the sake of clarity.

As indicated in *Nedrick*, it is rarely necessary to direct the jury in terms of the model direction in that case as modified in *Woollin*. It is needed, however, where the defendant denies that he aimed to achieve the consequence which has to be intended,[29] or where, on the facts, and having regard to the way the case has been presented, further explanation is required to avoid misunderstanding.[30]

3.13 *Additional need for consequence actually to be virtually certain*   The model direction in *Nedrick* approved by the House of Lords in *Woollin* contains an additional precondition (to that of foresight of virtual certainty) to the entitlement to find that the defendant intended death or serious bodily harm (in the case of murder). **This is that death or serious bodily harm was actually a virtual certainty as a result of the defendant's actions.** Whether or not it was must be determined by asking whether a reasonable person would have foreseen death or serious bodily harm as virtually certain to result from the defendant's actions. It is not clear why this precondition, which can be traced back to *Moloney*, was thought necessary. If there is evidence that, although the relevant consequence would not have been foreseen by a reasonable person as virtually certain, D foresaw it as virtually certain, there is no reason in principle why a finding of intent should not be made. D's state of mind is the same as it would have been if the consequence had objectively been virtually certain.

3.14 Woollin *not limited to murder*   Although *Woollin*, like *Moloney*, *Hancock and Shankland* and *Nedrick*, was concerned with murder, and although Lord Steyn, giving the lead judgment, recognised that intent does not necessarily have the same meaning in every context of criminal law, the approach taken in *Woollin* is not limited to murder.

---

[29] *MD* [2004] EWCA Crim 1391; *Phillips* [2004] EWCA Crim 112.
[30] *Allen* [2005] EWCA Crim 1344.

The approach commenced in *Moloney* and now explained in *Woollin* has been taken in respect of other offences.[31] It would be extremely odd if the House of Lords' emphatic decision in terms of 'virtual certainty' (actual and foreseen) as the threshold degree of risk before intention can be found from foresight, and its concern not to blur the distinction between intention and recklessness, were held not to be equally applicable to other offences. In other offences, *Woollin* is applied on the basis of whether the consequence (whatever it is) which must be intended was actually virtually certain to result from the defendant's conduct and was foreseen by him as virtually certain to result.

3.15 *Woollin not limited to cases where consequence foreseen as virtually certain side-effect of achieving consequence defendant aims to achieve* The principles in *Woollin* usually come into operation where, although the defendant's purpose was to bring about some consequence other than that which must be intended, he realised that the consequence which must be intended was virtually certain to result as a side-effect of achieving his purpose. However, those principles are not limited to that situation. It seems that they can also apply where the defendant acted without any purpose to bring about a consequence. In *Woollin* the prosecution did not allege that the defendant acted with the purpose of killing or seriously injuring the child (direct intent) and, if he did not act with that purpose, it would appear that he did not act with any purpose to bring about anything but acted simply in mindless anger. Nevertheless, the House of Lords in *Woollin* did not dispute that the principles endorsed by it were applicable in such a situation.

3.16 *Must intention be found from foresight of virtual certainty, or is it just that it may be found?* *Moloney* and *Hancock and Shankland* clearly established that foresight of virtual certainty did not constitute intention but was only evidence from which the jury could infer intention. Lord Lane, who delivered the Court of Appeal's judgment in *Nedrick*, stated extra-judicially[32] that he agreed with the definition of 'intention' in the draft Criminal Code Bill[33] whereby a person would act intentionally with respect to a result when he acted either in order to bring it about or being aware that it would occur in the ordinary course of events, ie such foresight would be intent as opposed to intent being found from it. His Lordship added that this expressed clearly what, because of the constraints of precedent, ie *Moloney* and *Hancock and Shankland*, the Court of Appeal had 'failed properly to explain'. No doubt in an effort to get as close to stating that foresight of certainty *constituted* intention as it could the Court of Appeal stated that:

> 'Where a man realises that it is for all practical purposes inevitable that his actions will result in death or serious bodily harm, the inference may be irresistible that he intended that result, however little he may have desired or wished it to happen.'[34]

---

[31] Eg *Bryson* [1985] Crim LR 669, CA (wounding with intent); *Walker and Hayles* (1989) 90 Cr App Rep 226, CA (attempt; note the reference in this case to a 'very high degree of probability' is now wrong).

[32] HL Paper 78–1 (1989).   [33] Para 3.20.

[34] [1986] 3 All ER 1 at 4. A similar point was made by Lords Hailsham and Bridge in *Moloney* [1985] AC 905 at 913 and 920.

These words were not part of the statement approved by the House of Lords in *Woollin* as forming the model direction in *Nedrick*.

3.17 *Woollin* **is open to at least**[35] **two interpretations. The first is that on proof of foresight of virtual certainty as to a consequence a jury** *may* **find some unspecified type of intention other than direct intention.** This derives support in terms of the cases culminating in the *Nedrick* model direction and from the fact that, even as amended, that direction still speaks of an *entitlement* to find intention as opposed to stating that foresight of virtual certainty *is* intention.

This was the interpretation given to *Woollin* by the Court of Appeal in *Matthews and Alleyne*,[36] where the defendants had been charged with murder. The prosecution case was that the victim (who had told the defendants that he could not swim) had drowned after they had pushed him off a bridge and that the defendants had intended to kill him. The trial judge directed the jury that an intent to kill would only be proved against a defendant if the prosecution proved that at the material time *either* he had a 'specific intention' (direct intention) to kill *or* that the victim's death was a virtual certainty (barring an attempt to save him) and he appreciated that this was the case (and did not intend to save the victim and realised that no one else intended to do so). The jury convicted both the defendants of murder. They appealed against conviction, arguing that the second alternative in the judge's direction indicated that it was a rule of law that if it was satisfied the defendant would have intended to kill (ie the jury must find an intent to kill) whereas in truth foresight of virtual certainty etc of death merely gave rise to a rule of evidence (ie the jury might find intention proved).

The Court of Appeal stated that the judge had been wrong in stating in the second alternative that an appreciation of a virtual certainty of a consequence constituted intention as to it: 'the law has not yet reached a *definition* of intent in murder in terms of appreciation of a virtual certainty'.[37] Such a conclusion, said the Court of Appeal, would be inconsistent with the approved model direction which is in terms of 'not entitled to find the necessary intention unless…'. Foresight of virtual certainty was merely evidence on which the jury might find intention. Ultimately, however, the Court of Appeal dismissed the appeals against conviction. It held that, if the jury were sure that the victim's death had been virtually certain to result and that the defendants appreciated this and had no intention of the victim being saved, it was impossible that the jury would not have found that the defendants intended the victim to die. The convictions were not unsafe.

The problem with this interpretation of *Woollin* is that (like the decision in *Moloney*) it gives rise to a conundrum. If foresight of virtual certainty in itself is not intention, and the defendant did not act with what is established in law as intention (ie he had not aimed to achieve the particular consequence), how can it be found from foresight of consequence on his part that he intended it, when any additional type of 'intention' is left undefined by the law? The courts have not stated what the mystery ingredient is that can be found

---

[35] For another interpretation see Simester and Shute [2000] Crim LR 204 (letter).
[36] [2003] EWCA Crim 192.   [37] [2003] EWCA Crim 192 at [43].

from foresight so as to convert foresight (which is not intention, according to cases like *Moloney* and *Matthews and Alleyne*) into intention. The only obvious ingredients are:

- aim or purpose on the defendant's part, but that, of course, will have been ruled out – otherwise one would not be concerned with the present point; and
- motive or desire on the defendant's part, but in *Moloney* the House of Lords said that intention is something quite distinct from motive or desire.

Until the courts tell us what the mystery ingredient is, the proposition that intent can be found from foresight must be regarded with scepticism as a matter of principle.[38]

Another defect is that giving the jury discretion – 'moral elbow room'[39] – to find that a person who foresaw a consequence as virtually certain intended that consequence is liable to lead to inconsistent verdicts on essentially the same facts.

3.18 A second interpretation of *Woollin* is that proof of foresight of virtual certainty is proof of intention (oblique intention) itself, ie that foresight of virtual certainty is itself a species of intention. At first sight this seems difficult to accept. After all, in *Woollin* the House of Lords did not purport to overrule *Moloney* or *Hancock and Shankland* and expressly applied *Nedrick*. Nevertheless, Lord Steyn, giving the lead judgment, provides indications of a new interpretation of *Moloney* (on which case, of course, the other two cases were based) because on two occasions he refers to a statement by Lord Bridge that 'the probability of the consequence taken to have been foreseen must be little short of overwhelming before it will suffice to establish the necessary intent'. On each occasion, Lord Steyn emphasised the words 'to establish'.[40] Elsewhere, Lord Steyn referred to *Moloney* adopting a 'test of what may constitute intention which is similar to the "virtual certainty test" in *Nedrick*'.[41] Later, referring to *Nedrick*, he said that: 'The effect of the critical direction [in *Nedrick*, approved in *Woollin*] is that a result foreseen as virtually certain is an intended result'.[42] Although the substitution of 'find' in the *Nedrick* model direction in itself supports this interpretation, that support is weakened by the reference to foresight of virtual certainty giving rise to an 'entitlement' to find intention rather than an obligation to do so.

It is submitted that the second interpretation of *Woollin* commands the most support in that case, whatever the problems of reconciling it with the previous case law. In returning the law full circle to approximately where it was before *Moloney* (leaving aside Lord Steyn's interpretation of that case) it avoids the intellectual difficulties of the first interpretation and provides certainty of definition.

---

[38] Norrie 'After *Woollin*' [1999] Crim LR 532 has argued that a moral threshold must be passed before the jury, having found that the defendant foresaw a prohibited consequence as virtually certain to result, should attribute to him an intention to cause it. On this argument, the jury's entitlement to find intention from proof of such foresight would depend on the wickedness (or otherwise) of his motives. For an objection to this see Simester and Shute [2000] Crim LR 204 at 205.

[39] Horder 'Intention in the Criminal Law – A Rejoinder' (1995) 58 MLR 678 at 688.

[40] [1999] 1 AC 82 at 91 and 93.   [41] [1999] 1 AC 82 at 91.   [42] [1999] 1 AC 82 at 93.

The second interpretation is supported by reference to *Re A (conjoined twins: surgical separation)*[43] where the Civil Division of the Court of Appeal was concerned with the legality of separating conjoined ('Siamese') twins, who were otherwise doomed to die, probably within three to six months, in order to save the stronger twin, when it was known that the proposed operation would result in the death of the weaker one. Dealing with the issue of whether the doctors would intend to kill or do serious bodily harm to Mary (the twin who would die), Ward LJ stated:

> '*Woollin* is binding upon us... The test I have to set myself is that established by that case. I have to ask myself whether I am satisfied that the doctors recognise that death or serious harm will be virtually certain (barring some unforeseen intervention) to result from carrying out this operation. If so, the doctors intend to kill or to do that serious harm even though they may not have any desire to achieve that result. It is common ground that they appreciate that death to Mary would result from the severance of the common aorta. Unpalatable though it may be to stigmatise the doctors with "murderous intent", that is what in law they will have if they perform the operation and Mary dies as a result.'[44]

Brooke and Robert Walker LJJ regarded *Woollin* in the same way, although (as noted in para 3.24) Robert Walker LJ thought that its application was excluded on the facts.

Re A was not referred to by the Court of Appeal in *Matthews and Alleyne*.

3.19 In practical terms, it is unlikely in most cases that a jury would decline to find intent from proof of foresight of virtual certainty if the first interpretation is correct. In *Matthews and Alleyne*,[45] the Court of Appeal stated that there was very little to choose between the two interpretations. However, there can be hard cases where the jury might not wish to find intent from proof of foresight of virtual certainty. An example would be where D has no real choice in an emergency in which A will inevitably die if he acts one way and B will inevitably die if he acts in the only other possible way, as D realises, and D acts in the way which brings about A's death. Consequently, the issue of which interpretation is correct is an important one. **The issue will not be resolved until the Supreme Court (or Parliament) has the opportunity to do so. Until then, it is likely that the courts will follow the decision of the Criminal Division of the Court of Appeal in *Matthews and Alleyne* where, unlike *Re A*, the issue was the fundamental issue in the appeal.**

3.20 Proposals for statutory guidance about intention have been made on a number of occasions in modern times. For example, cl 14 of the draft Offences Against the Person Bill of 1998 contains a definition of 'intention'[46] as to consequence in relation to the non-fatal offences contained in the draft Bill which is similar to that in cl 18 of the draft Criminal Code Bill which provided that a person would act '"intentionally" with respect

---

[43] [2001] Fam 147, CA.   [44] [2001] Fam 147 at 198–9.   [45] [2003] EWCA Crim 192 at [45].

[46] This definition is a reformulation of the definition contained in cl 1 of the Law Commission's draft Criminal Law Bill: see *Legislating the Criminal Code: Offences against the Person and General Defences* (1993), Law Com No 218; see para 7.131.

to a result when he acts either in order to bring it about or being aware that it will occur in the ordinary course of events'. However, cl 14 differs in one important respect, as the italicised words below indicate. Clause 14 provides that for the purpose of the provisions in the Bill relating to non-fatal offences a person acts:

> '(a) intentionally with respect to a result when:
> (i) it is his purpose to cause it; or
> (ii) although it is not his purpose to cause it, he knows that it would occur in the ordinary course of events *if he were to succeed in his purpose of causing some other result;...*'

This formulation would bring certainty to the meaning of intention but it would not cover the type of intention described in para 3.15.

3.21 In its report, *Murder, Manslaughter and Infanticide*,[47] published in 2006, the Law Commission recommended that the existing law governing the meaning of intention is codified as follows:

> '(1) A person should be taken to intend a result if he or she acts in order to bring it about.
> (2) In cases where the judge believes that justice may not be done unless an expanded understanding of intention is given, the jury should be directed as follows: an intention to bring about a result may be found if it is shown that the defendant thought that the result was a virtually certain consequence of his or her action.'

Clause (2) would perpetuate the lack of certainty about the meaning of 'intention'. The Commission stated that the present law is not difficult for juries to apply and that it is better to give juries some discretion in determining the limits of murder than to try to constrain their decision-making by complex legal rules about the definition of intention.

Doctrine of double effect

3.22 The speeches in *Woollin* do not deal expressly with the situation where someone acts for a good purpose which he knows cannot be achieved without also having a bad consequence. This raises what has been called in moral philosophy the doctrine of double effect. Two classes of double effect, at least, can be distinguished.

3.23 The first class of double effect is where the good purpose and the foreseen (but undesired) bad consequence both relate to the same individual, as where a doctor, in the best interests of the patient, administers pain-killing drugs in appropriate quantities for the purpose of relieving that patient's pain, but realising that an incidental effect of doing so will be to hasten death.

---

[47] Law Commission Report No 304, paras 3.9–3.27.

There is some authority that in law, as well as in moral philosophy, there is a doctrine of double effect which makes such conduct permissible if it is in the interests of the victim.[48] This appears to have been recognised as part of our law by Lord Donaldson MR in *Re J* and by Lord Goff in *Airedale National Health Service Trust v Bland*. In *Re J*, Lord Donaldson identified the relevant principle as follows:

> 'What doctors and the courts have to decide is whether, in the best interests of the child patient, a particular decision as to medical treatment should be taken which as a side effect will render death more or less likely. This is not a matter of semantics. It is fundamental. At the other end of the age spectrum, the use of drugs to reduce pain will often be fully justified, notwithstanding that this will hasten the moment of death. What can never be justified is the use of drugs or surgical procedures with the primary purpose of doing so.'[49]

In *Airedale National Health Service Trust v Bland*, Lord Goff said this when describing the doctor's duty to act in the best interests of his patient:

> 'It is this principle too which, in my opinion, underlies the established rule that a doctor may, when caring for a patient who is, for example, dying of cancer, lawfully administer pain-killing drugs despite the fact that he knows that an incidental effect of that application will be to abbreviate the patient's life. Such a decision may properly be made as part of the care of the living patient, in his best interests; and, on this basis, the treatment will be lawful. Moreover, where the doctor's treatment of his patient is lawful, the patient's death will be regarded in law as exclusively caused by the injury or disease to which his condition is attributable.'[50]

Similar language to that of Lord Donaldson MR was used by Ognall J in his summing-up to the jury in *Cox*,[51] a case where a doctor administered potassium chloride to a dying patient who was in extreme pain. The dose had the inevitable effect of killing the patient, but would have alleviated her pain in the short period of remaining life. Ognall J indicated that what mattered was the doctor's 'primary purpose'.

In *Re A (conjoined twins: surgical separation)*,[52] Ward LJ thought that the doctrine of double effect might be 'difficult to reconcile with *Woollin*', but recognised that it enjoyed some judicial approval. Brooke LJ did not consider it necessary to decide whether the correct analysis of the doctrine of double effect was that it negated intention (or causation) or that it simply rendered non-culpable the intention to kill and non-blameworthy the causing of death because the law permits the doctor to do the act in question. Neither judge considered it necessary to go any further because in their view (correctly, it is submitted)

---

[48] For criticism of the doctrine of double effect, see Price 'Euthanasia, Pain Relief and Double Effect' (1997) 17 LS 323. For argument that utilisation of a redefined defence of necessity would be a better way of dealing with euthanasia in a medical context than the doctrine of double effect, see Ost 'Euthanasia and the Defence of Necessity: Advocating a More Appropriate Legal Response' [2005] Crim LR 355.

[49] [1991] Fam 33 at 46.   [50] [1993] AC 789 at 867.

[51] (1992) 12 BMLR 38.   [52] [2001] Fam 147, CA.

it could not be said that the surgeons would be acting for the purpose of benefiting Mary, the weaker twin. It remains to be seen how far beyond the doctor–patient relationship the courts are prepared to extend the law relating to the present class of double effect.[53]

3.24 The second class of double effect is where the good purpose relates to A but it cannot be achieved without having a foreseen (but undesired) consequence for B. The judgments of Ward and Brooke LJJ in *Re A (conjoined twins: surgical separation)* indicate that they did not consider that the doctrine of double effect is recognised in law in such a case. On the other hand, Robert Walker LJ appears to have taken the opposite view, which cannot be regarded as representing the law. He said:

> 'The proposed operation would not be unlawful. It would involve the positive act of invasive surgery and Mary's death would be foreseen as an inevitable consequence of an operation which is intended, and is necessary, to save Jodie [the stronger twin]'s life. But Mary's death would not be the purpose or intention of the surgery, and she would die because tragically her body, on its own, is not and never has been viable.'[54]

Ulterior intention

3.25 This type of intention is alternatively known as 'further intention'. These terms are used to describe an **intention on the part of the defendant which does not relate to a consequence of his conduct required to result by the definition of the *actus reus* of the offence charged, but relates instead to something ulterior to it (ie something beyond it).** Where the definition of an offence requires an ulterior intent as to a particular thing, the offence cannot be committed unless that thing is intended; recklessness, as opposed to intention, as to the further thing occurring is insufficient.[55] Since the ulterior thing is not a requisite of the *actus reus*, it is irrelevant that it never occurs.

3.26 Certain acts which would not otherwise be criminal are made criminal if the *actus reus* is performed with intent to do something ulterior to it. For example, it is normally not an offence to enter a building as a trespasser, but, by the Theft Act 1968, s 9, a person who does so with intent to steal anything in the building is guilty of burglary. Consequently, if D enters a house, intending to steal jewellery there, he is guilty of burglary, and the fact that he is arrested a split second later and never steals anything is irrelevant. Sometimes the criminal law punishes what would otherwise be a comparatively minor offence with much greater severity if it was committed with the ulterior intent of perpetrating a more serious offence. For example, the offence of common assault is punishable with a very modest period of imprisonment, but the offence of assault with intent

---

[53] Contrast the views expressed by Arlidge 'The Trial of Dr David Moor' [2000] Crim LR 31 and Smith 'A Comment on Moor's Case' ibid 41 with Cooper 'Summing Up Intention' (2000) 150 NLJ 1258. See also Goss 'A Postscript to the Trial of Dr David Moor' [2000] Crim LR 568.

[54] [2001] Fam 147 at 259.   [55] *Belfon* [1976] 3 All ER 46, CA.

to rob is punishable with imprisonment for life. In these and the fairly numerous similar cases, it must be proved that, when he did the prohibited act, the defendant's purpose was to commit the further act or offence. Reference to finding intent from foresight of virtual certainty would be meaningless and confusing.

3.27 Sometimes the ulterior intent relates to an intended consequence of the prohibited act committed by the defendant which is not required to have been achieved. The offence of harassment of a residential occupier provides an example. By the Protection from Eviction Act 1977, s 1(3), it is an offence for a landlord to do acts likely to interfere with the peace or comfort of a residential occupier if he does so with intent to cause the residential occupier to give up the occupation of the premises. Another example is the offence of sending letters etc with intent to cause distress or anxiety, contrary to the Malicious Communications Act 1988, s 1(1). This provides that a person who sends to another a letter, electronic communication or other article conveying an indecent or grossly offensive message, a threat, or information which is false (to the offender's knowledge or belief), or who sends an indecent or grossly offensive article or electronic communication, is guilty of an offence if his purpose or one of his purposes in sending it is to cause distress or anxiety to the recipient or to someone to whom he intends it to be communicated.

Offences where only direct intent suffices

3.28 In some offences, only direct intention suffices as intention. Among these are those offences which expressly require the defendant to act with a specified purpose, such as an offence under the Malicious Communications Act 1988, s 1 referred to above.

3.29 In addition, in the case of some other offences requiring 'intention', their wording and/or nature may be such that only direct intention as to a particular element can meaningfully be required. Examples are the inchoate offences of intentionally encouraging or assisting an offence, statutory conspiracy and attempt, described in Chapter 14. Alternatively, an offence may have been held to require a direct intent. The common law offence of treason (at least in the form of treason by adhering to the Queen's enemies) is an example of such an offence.[56] So, it seems, is the offence of assisting offenders.[57]

Sometimes, as seen in para 3.26, the use of the words 'with intent to...' in a statutory definition of an offence is in a context where only a direct intention can meaningfully be said to be possible. In such a case it is appropriate to say that the offence requires such an intention.

Specific intent and basic intent

3.30 'Specific intent' is used frequently in the reports and should be treated with caution since, although it does not connote an additional species of intention, it can bear four different meanings which are not mutually exclusive:

---

[56] *Ahlers* [1915] 1 KB 616, CCA. Also see *Sinnasamy Selvanayagam v R* [1951] AC 83, PC; *Steane* [1947] KB 997, CCA, para 3.8 (the decision in which necessarily ruled out foresight of virtual certainty of assisting the enemy as sufficient to establish the intent to assist the enemy required for the offence in question).

[57] Para 17.85.

- the intention which must be proved to secure a conviction for a particular offence for which intention is the only state of mind specified in relation to an element;[58]
- a direct intention;[59]
- an ulterior intention or other form of ulterior *mens rea*;[60] and
- a state of mind, required for particular offences only, in relation to which the defendant may successfully plead its absence by relying on evidence of voluntary intoxication.[61]

3.31 Some judges have added to the confusion by introducing the term 'basic intent'. A 'basic intent' is not another type of intent and, surprisingly, it is not limited to intention at all. 'Basic intent' bears at least three meanings which are not mutually exclusive:

- in the words of Lord Simon in *DPP v Morgan*:[62] 'By "crimes of basic intent" I mean those crimes whose definition expresses (or, more often, implies) a *mens rea* [whether intention, or recklessness or knowledge which are discussed later] which does not go beyond the *actus reus*';
- a state of mind in respect of whose absence evidence of the defendant's voluntary intoxication is irrelevant;[63] and
- an intent to do the act required for the *actus reus*, ie a deliberate or voluntary act.[64]

The variety of meanings of 'specific intent' and 'basic intent' means that, when confronted with one of these terms, the reader must stop and consider what meaning or meanings it bears in the particular context.

Recklessness

Key points 3.2

A person may be reckless as to a consequence or circumstance.
A person is reckless:

- as to a circumstance if he is aware of a risk that it exists or will exist;
- as to a consequence if he is aware of a risk that it will occur,

and, in the circumstances known to him, it is unreasonable to take the risk.

---

[58] *Mohan* [1976] QB 1, CA; *Moloney* [1985] AC 905, HL; *Hancock and Shankland* [1986] AC 455, HL.
[59] Paras 15.86 and 15.87.
[60] Paras 15.86 and 15.87.
[61] Paras 15.70–15.73.
[62] [1976] AC 182 at 216.
[63] Paras 15.74–15.78.
[64] *James* [1997] 34 LS Gaz R 27, CA. On a literal interpretation, the House of Lords in *DPP v Newbury* [1977] AC 500, used 'basic intent' in this sense; see paras 8.102–8.104.

3.32 In many offences 'recklessness' on the part of the defendant, as to a risk of his act (or omission) resulting in the consequence required for the *actus reus* or as to a risk that a circumstance required for the *actus reus* exists or will exist, suffices for criminal liability as an alternative to some other mental state such as intention or knowledge. Sometimes the definition of an offence may require that the defendant is reckless as to the risk of a consequence occurring which is not required for the *actus reus* of the offence. For example a person is guilty of an offence, contrary to the Criminal Damage Act 1971, s 1(2) if he intentionally or recklessly damages property and is reckless as to the risk of endangering the life of another thereby; life does not actually have to be endangered.

3.33 Recklessness means the taking of an unreasonable risk of which the risk-taker is aware. In *G*,[65] Lord Bingham, giving the principal speech in the House of Lords, referred with approval to the definition of recklessness contained in the draft Criminal Code Bill, clause 18(c), viz that a person acts:

'"recklessly" with respect to:

(i) a circumstance when he is aware of a risk that it exists or will exist;
(ii) a result when he is aware of a risk that it will occur,

and it is, in the circumstances known to him, unreasonable to take the risk.'[66]

Recklessness of this type is sometimes called subjective recklessness. Provided that it is proved that the defendant was aware of a risk of a relevant circumstance or result, it is irrelevant that for some reason, such as bad temper, he chose to disregard the risk or to put it to the back of his mind or to close his mind to it,[67] not caring whether the risk materialised or not.[68] Indeed, although it is normally the case that a person who consciously takes an unreasonable risk does not care whether or not it materialises, it is not necessary that this should be so. A person who consciously takes an unreasonable risk which he hopes will not materialise is also reckless.

For recklessness the material risk, ie the risk which must be foreseen or realised, need merely be foreseen or realised as a possible risk;[69] it does not have to be an obvious and

---

[65] [2003] UKHL 50.

[66] An earlier authority for this definition of recklessness, in respect of a consequence (result), is *Stephenson* [1979] QB 695, CA. It will be noted that the frequently cited *Cunningham* [1957] 2 QB 396, CCA does not contain a complete definition of the present type of recklessness because it does not refer to the requirement that the risk be unreasonable.

[67] A person cannot close his mind to a risk unless he first realises that there is a risk: *Comr of Metropolitan Police v Caldwell* [1982] AC 341 at 358, per Lord Edmund-Davies; *G* [2003] UKHL 50 at [32], [58], per Lords Bingham and Steyn.

[68] *Stephenson* [1979] QB 695, CA; *Comr of Metropolitan Police v Caldwell* [1982] AC 341 at 358, per Lord Edmund-Davies; *G* [2003] UKHL 50 at [32], [58], per Lords Bingham and Steyn; *Booth v CPS* [2006] EWHC 192 (Admin).

[69] By way of exception, in involuntary manslaughter the relevant risk must be foreseen as highly probable: see *Lidar* [2000] 4 Archbold News 3, CA; para 8.131.

significant risk.[70] If the degree of risk foreseen is one of virtual certainty, the defendant can be found to have intended the consequence in question, as explained above. In such a case, there will be to that extent an overlap between intention and recklessness.

Provided that the defendant foresees or realises the material risk, it is irrelevant that that risk is not the only or foremost risk in his mind when he takes it.[71]

3.34 All that can be said by way of generalisation about the requirement that the risk must have been an unreasonable one to take is that it has to be judged objectively (ie by reference to the standards of a reasonable person) and that it raises a variety of questions to be answered by the jury if it is in issue in the Crown Court. How great was the risk? How beneficial to society or to the victim was the object which the defendant was seeking to achieve? Every surgeon foresees the risk of the death of the patient upon whom he is operating but, unless he takes an unreasonable risk, he cannot be regarded as being reckless as to the patient's death. As stated above, the unreasonableness of taking a risk must be assessed in the light of the circumstances known to the defendant.

3.35 For just over 20 years, recklessness could also consist of a failure to think about an obvious risk in the case of offences of criminal damage and possibly a few other statutory offences in whose definition recklessness was specified as *mens rea*. This type of recklessness, called objective recklessness or *Caldwell* recklessness after the case, *Comr of Metropolitan Police v Caldwell*,[72] in which it was recognised, was widely criticised,[73] in particular because the risk had to be obvious to a reasonable person who was not endowed with the defendant's characteristics (and did not have to be obvious to the defendant), and because failing to think about a risk (inadvertent risk-taking) would seem less culpable than advertent risk-taking and can hardly be described as *mens rea*, a state of mind; it is quite the contrary – the absence of a state of mind.

Caldwell was overruled in 2003 by the House of Lords in *G*,[74] where the House of Lords held that 'reckless' in the Criminal Damage Act 1971, s 1 should be assessed in the subjective sense referred to in para 3.33, as it had been before *Caldwell*. In *G*, the defendants, two boys aged 11 and 12, entered the back yard of a shop. They found some newspapers. They set fire to some of them and threw them under a wheelie-bin. The newspapers set fire to the wheelie-bin and the fire spread to the shop and then to adjoining commercial buildings, causing about £1m worth of damage. It was accepted that neither boy appreciated that there was any risk of the fire spreading in the way it eventually did. The boys were charged with arson, ie causing damage by fire, to the commercial buildings, 'being reckless whether such property would be damaged', contrary to the Criminal Damage Act 1971, s 1(1) and (3).

The trial judge directed the jury in terms of *Caldwell* recklessness, telling them that, in the alternative to awareness that there was some risk of building damage involved, the

---

[70] *Brady* [2006] EWCA Crim 2413.
[71] *Booth v CPS* [2006] EWHC 192 (Admin).   [72] [1982] AC 341, HL.
[73] See the 15th edition of this book.
[74] [2003] UKHL 50. See Kimel 'Inadvertent Recklessness in the Criminal Law' (2004) 120 LQR 548.

defendants would be guilty if they had not thought about the possibility of that risk and that risk would have been obvious to a reasonable bystander.[75] He also directed the jury that the reasonable bystander was 'an adult... [N]o allowance is made by the law for the youth of these boys or their lack of maturity or their inability... to assess what was going on'. The boys were convicted. The Court of Appeal, bound by *Caldwell*, dismissed their appeals. They appealed to the House of Lords.

The House of Lords unanimously allowed the boys' appeals. It held that the House of Lords in *Caldwell* had misinterpreted the law for the following reasons. It was a principle of the criminal law that conviction of serious crime should depend on proof that the defendant's conduct was accompanied by a culpable state of mind. It was not clearly culpable to be doing something involving a risk of injury to another if, for reasons other than self-induced intoxication, one did not perceive such a risk. Moreover, the facts of the case illustrated the unfairness which *Caldwell* could cause. The House of Lords also noted the criticism of *Caldwell*, which had been expressed by judges, practitioners and academics, that *Caldwell* recklessness involved a misinterpretation of Parliament's intention. In inserting 'reckless' in the statute, Parliament had been implementing a Law Commission report which made plain that 'reckless' in the Act was intended to refer to a requirement of foresight by the defendant of a risk of damage.

3.36 Although it is, strictly, limited to the meaning of recklessness in the Criminal Damage Act 1971, **there can be no doubt that the decision in G also applies to recklessness in the context of any other offence for which recklessness is sufficient *mens rea*.** *G* has been applied by the Court of Appeal outside the Criminal Damage Act 1971,[76] and the Court of Appeal has stated obiter that, since *G*, 'recklessness' bears the meaning approved in that case.[77] It would, of course, be possible for a statute to give the term a different meaning in respect of a particular offence.

General points concerning intention or recklessness as to a consequence

Correspondence principle

3.37 Generally, the defendant must intend, or be reckless as to, the consequence of the *actus reus* of the offence in question as it is described in the definition of the offence, eg

---

[75] The boys must surely have appreciated that throwing lighted newspapers under a wheelie-bin might damage it. If so, they could certainly have been convicted of criminal damage to the wheelie-bin and another wheelie-bin by the fire en route to the shop and other buildings. On this basis, if they had been appropriately charged, a properly directed jury could have convicted them of the criminal damage by fire to the buildings, because they would have had the necessary *mens rea* (recklessness as to the risk of their act of throwing the lighted newspapers resulting in damaging by fire property belonging to another), as explained in para 3.38. This point was not, however, adverted to by the trial judge or on appeal.

[76] It was applied by the Court of Appeal in *A-G's Reference (No 3 of 2003)* [2004] EWCA Crim 868 in the context of the common law offence of wilful misconduct in a public office.

[77] *Heard* [2007] EWCA Crim 125.

the destruction of or damage to property belonging to another in the offence of criminal damage.[78] This is called the correspondence principle. However, as Lord Ackner (with whose speech the other Law Lords agreed) observed in *Savage; DPP v Parmenter*,[79] there is no hard and fast principle to this effect. **There are some exceptional offences where intention or recklessness, or in some cases only intention, in relation to something less than the actual consequence required for their *actus reus* suffices.** For example, in the offences under the Offences Against the Person Act 1861, s 20 of unlawfully and maliciously wounding another and of unlawfully and maliciously inflicting grievous bodily harm on another, the defendant has sufficient *mens rea* if he merely intended or was reckless as to some unlawful physical harm to a person, albeit of a minor nature: he need not have foreseen that his act might cause physical harm of the gravity described in the statute, ie a wound or grievous bodily harm.[80] Another example, already referred to, is murder where the *mens rea* consists of an intention unlawfully to kill or do grievous bodily harm to another human being.[81]

'Transferred malice'

3.38 Provided the defendant acted intentionally or recklessly in the way required by the definition of the offence charged, it is irrelevant that the actual object (whether person or property) was unintended or unforeseen. For example, if the defendant does something intending that it should damage X's property, or being reckless as to this occurring, and quite unforeseeably V's property is damaged instead, the defendant can be convicted of criminal damage, contrary to the Criminal Damage Act 1971, s 1(1), since the *mens rea* for that offence is intention or recklessness as to damaging property belonging to another, and the defendant acted with such intention or recklessness. This is a simple application of the wording of the *mens rea* requirement of the offence. The general practice of writers to dignify it by calling it the doctrine of 'transferred malice', 'transferred intention' or 'transferred fault' seems unnecessary and, in the case of the first two terms, inaccurate (since the 'doctrine' is not limited to 'malice' or intention). The doctrine was affirmed, albeit unenthusiastically, by the House of Lords in *A-G's Reference (No 3 of 1994)*,[82] although it was held inapplicable to the facts subject to the reference. Since it obscures the simple application of the *mens rea* requirement, the doctrine is liable to lead to developments inconsistent with that requirement, as is shown by the decision of the House of Lords in *A-G's Reference (No 3 of 1994)*, discussed below.

Latimer[83] provides an example of the operation of the present point. D aimed a blow at X which glanced off him and struck V who was standing beside X, wounding her severely. It was held that D could be convicted of maliciously wounding V because he had an intent to injure and it was irrelevant that he had not intended to injure V.

3.39 By way of contrast, and not surprisingly, the defendant cannot be convicted if he acted with the *mens rea* for one offence but unexpectedly commits the *actus reus* of

---

[78] See, for example, *Smith (David)* [1974] QB 354, CA; para 3.81.   [79] [1992] 1 AC 699, HL.
[80] Para 7.87.   [81] Para 8.24. For further examples, see paras 7.62, 8.97–8.118 and 8.131.
[82] [1998] AC 245, HL.   [83] (1886) 17 QBD 359, CCR.

another offence, unless the offence is one where recklessness suffices and he is proved to have been reckless as to the risk of the type of harm which he actually caused. This is shown by *Pembliton*,[84] where D, who had been fighting with persons in the street, threw a stone at them, which missed but went through the window of a nearby public house. His conviction for maliciously damaging the window was quashed because he had acted with intent to injure persons and not with intent to injure property. The Court for Crown Cases Reserved pointed out that, if the jury had found the defendant had been reckless as to the risk of the window being broken, the conviction would have been upheld, because recklessness was sufficient for the offence in question.

3.40 In *A-G's Reference (No 3 of 1994)*,[85] the House of Lords limited the simple application of the requirement of *mens rea* described above, on the basis of what was (it is submitted) a mistaken understanding of the doctrine of transferred malice. It held that that doctrine could not apply in a case of murder where an unintended victim was not in being at the time of the relevant act. In *A-G's Reference (No 3 of 1994)*, D stabbed a pregnant woman, intending to do her serious bodily harm. He intended to do serious harm only to the woman. As a result of the attack, the woman went into premature labour and her child, although born alive, subsequently died owing to its prematurity. D had clearly committed the *actus reus* of an offence of homicide, but the House of Lords held that he was not guilty of murder. Its reason was that the doctrine of transferred malice could not apply because the effect of the doctrine was that the intended victim and the actual victim were treated as if they were one, as if the latter had been the intended victim from the start. Since a foetus cannot be the victim of murder,[86] it was impossible, the House held, to treat the intended victim and the actual victim as one, as if the latter had been the intended victim from the start. Strangely, the House of Lords held that D could have been convicted of involuntary manslaughter[87] of the child. Its reason was that D had the necessary *mens rea* for constructive manslaughter, one type of involuntary manslaughter, when he stabbed the mother and, although the child was a foetus then, the requisite *mens rea* was established, because, when she became a living person, the child could be regarded as within the scope of the *mens rea* which D had when he stabbed her mother. *A-G's Reference (No 3 of 1994)* is discussed further in Chapter 8.

Consequence occurring in unexpected manner

3.41 It is irrelevant, as far as the question of *mens rea* is concerned, that the consequence in relation to which the defendant acted intentionally or recklessly occurred in an unexpected manner.[88] If D, intending to cause V really serious harm, throws a petrol bomb at him, it is irrelevant that V is not injured by being burnt but is injured by an explosion caused when the bomb misses him and ignites a gas leak.

---

[84] (1874) LR 2 CCR 119, CCR.   [85] [1998] AC 245, HL.
[86] Para 8.7.   [87] Para 8.110.
[88] *A-G's Reference (No 3 of 1994)* [1996] QB 581, CA; this point was not dealt with in the speeches of the House of Lords in the subsequent appeal, [1998] AC 245.

Knowledge

Key points 3.3

'Knowledge' refers to a state of mind relating to a circumstance of an act, omission or state of affairs.

Mental states other than 'actual knowledge' can suffice where the definition of an offence requires the defendant to 'know' something.

3.42 Knowledge of the circumstances by virtue of which an act or omission or state of affairs is criminal (ie those specified for the *actus reus*) is expressly required in the case of many statutory offences on account of the inclusion of some such word as 'knowingly' in the definition. However, the use of 'knowingly' or the like is not essential since, even when no appropriate word appears in the definition, a requirement of knowledge is frequently implied by the courts, as explained in Chapter 6. In *Sweet v Parsley*,[89] for example, the House of Lords held that a person could not be guilty of 'being concerned in the management of premises used for the purpose of smoking cannabis' (an offence which has subsequently been modified) in the absence of proof of knowledge of such use.

Actual knowledge

3.43 A person knows that a surrounding circumstance exists if he is certain that it exists. This state of mind is known as 'actual knowledge'.[90] Actual knowledge is the equivalent of intention in that if the defendant acts, certain that a circumstance exists, he can be said to act intentionally in respect of it. If this is all that 'knowledge' meant it would often be difficult to prove it. There will be many cases where the defendant is not absolutely certain about a surrounding circumstance, although he has no substantial doubt about its existence or, at least, realises the risk that it may exist.

From the point of view of the enforcement of the criminal law it is therefore a good thing that knowledge also normally[91] includes the case where a defendant is virtually certain about a surrounding circumstance or is wilfully blind about it, even where the statute uses the word 'knowingly'.

Belief

3.44 The state of mind of someone who is virtually certain about something can be described as 'belief'.[92] According to the Court of Appeal in *Hall*:

---

[89] [1970] AC 132, HL.

[90] *Roper v Taylor's Central Garages (Exeter) Ltd* [1951] 2 TLR 284 at 288–289, per Devlin J.

[91] For exceptions, see para 3.46.

[92] It was recognised in *Dunne* (1998) 162 JP 399, CA, that someone who believes that something exists can be said to act 'knowingly' in relation to it.

'Belief, of course, is something short of knowledge. It may be said to be the state of mind of a person who says to himself: "I cannot say I know for certain that these goods are stolen, but there can be no other reasonable conclusion in the light of all the circumstances, in the light of all that I have heard and seen".'[93]

'Believe' is a particularly useful word to cover the situation, relevant in conspiracy or attempt, where a circumstance does not actually exist. One cannot be said to 'know' that a non-existent circumstance exists but one can believe it. If foresight of the virtual certainty of a consequence is in itself intention in respect of it, a person who is virtually certain of a circumstance in which he is acting could by way of parity be said to act intentionally in relation to it.

'Belief' is discussed further in para 11.51.

Wilful blindness

3.45 **Wilful blindness has been variously described by the judges. It has been said to exist where the defendant shuts his eyes to the obvious or refrains from inquiry because he suspects the truth but does not want his suspicion confirmed,[94] or to exist where a person *deliberately* refrains from making enquiries, the results of which he may not care to have.[95]** Wilful blindness is a species of recklessness with reference to surrounding circumstances, and it is often called connivance.[96] The first reported instance of the recognition of wilful blindness is *Sleep*,[97] where several members of the Court for Crown Cases Reserved would clearly have been prepared to treat it as a basis for liability. In a more modern case, the House of Lords in *Westminster City Council v Croyalgrange Ltd*,[98] held that a person could be convicted of the statutory offence of knowingly permitting the use of premises as a sex establishment contrary to a prohibition of their use otherwise than with a licence if he actually knew of their use as a sex establishment without a licence or was wilfully blind as to this. Lord Bridge, with whose speech the other Law Lords agreed, said:

'[I]t is always open to the tribunal of fact, when knowledge on the part of a defendant is required to be proved, to base a finding of knowledge on evidence that the defendant had deliberately shut his eyes to the obvious or refrained from inquiry because he suspected the truth but did not want to have his suspicion confirmed.'[99]

As seen in the next paragraph, Lord Bridge's use of the word 'always' was not strictly accurate. There are exceptional cases where 'knowledge' does not include wilful blindness.

---

[93] (1985) 81 Cr App Rep 260 at 264.
[94] *Westminster City Council v Croyalgrange* [1986] 2 All ER 353, HL.
[95] *Roper v Taylor's Central Garages (Exeter) Ltd* [1951] 2 TLR 284 at 288–289, per Devlin J.
[96] Edwards *Mens Rea in Statutory Offences* (1955) 203; see also *Somerset v Hart* (1884) 12 QBD 360, DC; *Ross v Moss* [1965] 2 QB 396, DC; *Vehicle Inspectorate v Nuttall* [1999] 3 All ER 833 at 840, per Lord Steyn.
[97] (1861) Le & Ca 44.   [98] [1986] 2 All ER 353, HL.   [99] [1986] 2 All ER 353 at 359.

Instances where 'knowledge' has restricted meaning

3.46 Some offences require the defendant to know or believe something. For example, the offences of handling stolen goods, of assisting offenders and of copying a false instrument require the defendant to know or believe, respectively, that the goods are stolen, that the person assisted has committed a relevant offence and that the 'instrument' is false.[100] The importance of 'belief' being required in the alternative to 'knowledge' is to limit 'knowledge' to cases where the defendant is certain of the relevant circumstance. While 'believe' covers the case where the defendant is virtually certain of a circumstance, it has been held that the effect of the use of 'knowledge or belief' is to exclude wilful blindness from being sufficient.[101] However, it has also been held that knowledge or belief may be inferred from wilful blindness,[102] which is somewhat difficult to understand if the suspicion involved in wilful blindness is not enough for belief. What is it which is inferable from wilful blindness which constitutes 'belief'? The courts have not supplied the answer.

Sometimes a requirement of 'belief' is expressed in the negative in respect of a particular offence. For example, the Perjury Act 1911, s 1(1) provides that a person is guilty of perjury if he makes the material statement in question 'without belief' in its truth.

3.47 Some offences require the defendant to know or be reckless about a particular circumstance. For example, there are a large number of statutory offences which consist of making a statement which, as the defendant knows, or as to which he is reckless, is false in a material particular in a specified respect.[103] The concept of 'recklessness' has already been discussed. In offences such as these, the effect of the alternative of recklessness is to remove wilful blindness from the normal meaning of 'knowledge', because wilful blindness is a species of recklessness, so that only being certain or virtually certain as to the relevant matter constitutes 'knowledge' as to it.

3.48 Some offences require the defendant to know or suspect something. Examples are the various money laundering offences under the Proceeds of Crime Act 2002, ss 327–329,[104] which require the defendant to have known or suspected specified facts. 'Suspicion' was defined for the first time in the context of a criminal offence in *Da Silva*.[105] In *Da Silva*, the defendant had been convicted of the offence of assisting another to retain the benefit of criminal conduct, knowing or suspecting that the other person was or had been engaged in criminal conduct, contrary to the Criminal Justice Act 1988, s 93A, which was repealed and replaced by the Proceeds of Crime Act 2002. The Court of Appeal held that in that context **the essential element of 'suspect' and its affiliates is that the**

---

[100] See paras 11.51 and 12.60. For a more recent example, see the Communications Act 2003, s 126(2).

[101] *Griffiths* (1974) 60 Cr App Rep 14, CA; *Moys* (1984) 79 Cr App Rep 72, CA.

[102] *Griffiths* (1974) 60 Cr App Rep 14, CA; *Moys* (1984) 79 Cr App Rep 72, CA; *Forsyth* [1997] 2 Cr App Rep 299, CA; *Sheriff, Ali and others* [2008] EWCA Crim 2653.

[103] Modern examples are provided by the Electricity Act 1989, s 59(1), the Railways Act 1993, s 146(1), the Broadcasting Act 1996, s 144(1), and the Identity Cards Act 2006, s 28(2).

[104] Together with the Proceeds of Crime Act 2002, s 340(3).

[105] [2006] EWCA Crim 1654.

defendant must think that there is a possibility, which is more than fanciful, that the relevant fact exists;[106] a vague feeling of unease would not suffice. The Court of Appeal added that, where there is reason to suppose that the defendant had entertained a suspicion but on further thought honestly dismissed it from his mind as being unworthy or contrary to the evidence or as being outweighed by other considerations (or in similar cases), the judge should also direct the jury that the suspicion must be of a settled nature.

'Suspicion' differs from 'wilful blindness'. It can exist even though there is no element of shutting one's eyes to the obvious or failing to make enquiries because one does not want to know the result. 'Suspicion' does not amount to knowledge.[107] The use of 'suspicion' in the alternative to 'knowing' clearly limits the latter term to the case where the defendant is certain or virtually certain about a circumstance.

How much must be known etc?

3.49 Where the definition of an offence requires that the defendant should knowingly commit the offence, 'knowledge' is normally required as to all the circumstances of the *actus reus* prescribed by that definition. This is another application of the correspondence principle referred to in para 3.37. In *Westminster City Council v Croyalgrange*,[108] for example, Robert Goff LJ (as he then was) referred to 'the ordinary principle that, where it is required that an offence should be knowingly committed, the requisite knowledge must embrace all the elements of the offence', a view affirmed by the House of Lords. We return to this matter in para 6.12.

3.50 Knowledge need extend only to a circumstance as it is prescribed in the definition of the offence in question.[109] Thus, on a charge of handling stolen goods, knowing or believing that they are stolen, contrary to the Theft Act 1968, s 22, it would be irrelevant that a handler who knew that the ring handled was stolen believed it contained imitation stones whereas in fact they were diamonds. Likewise, on a charge of, being the occupier, knowingly permitting premises to be used for the supply of a controlled drug, contrary to the Misuse of Drugs Act 1971, s 8, it would be irrelevant that the defendant occupier believed that heroin (a controlled drug) was being supplied whereas in fact it was cocaine (another controlled drug) which was being supplied.[110]

In a few offences, knowledge of something less than the specified circumstances suffices, as is shown by decisions relating to the Customs and Excise Management Act 1979, s 170(2), under which there are various offences[111] of being knowingly concerned in the

---

[106] It does not matter whether there are reasonable grounds for a suspicion: *Da Silva* [2006] EWCA Crim 1654.

[107] See, for example, *Saik* [2006] UKHL 18 at [32], [78] and [120], per Lords Nicholls, Hope and Brown.

[108] [1985] 1 All ER 740 at 744; affd [1986] 2 All ER 353, HL.

[109] *McCullum* (1973) 57 Cr App Rep 645, CA.

[110] *Bett* [1999] 1 All ER 600, CA.

[111] This is the effect of the rule laid down in *Courtie* [1984] AC 463, HL, whereby, if a greater maximum punishment can be imposed if a particular factual ingredient can be established than if it is not, two or more distinct

fraudulent evasion or attempt at evasion of a prohibition on the importation of various types of goods. For example, it is an offence, punishable with a maximum of life imprisonment, for a person knowingly to be concerned in the fraudulent evasion of the prohibition on the importation of a Class A controlled drug, and it is also an offence – a separate offence – knowingly to be concerned in the fraudulent evasion of the prohibition on the importation of obscene material (for which offence the maximum imprisonment is seven years). There is clear authority that, provided a person knows that the thing in question is something which is a prohibited good, he has sufficient *mens rea* in this respect, even if he was mistaken as to its precise nature.[112] Thus, for example, a person who has been concerned in the evasion of the prohibition on the importation of a Class A controlled drug can be convicted of the former of the two offences just mentioned even if he thought that the article in question (which was in a sack) was obscene material, because he will have known that it was a prohibited good, and even though on his understanding of the facts he was committing the latter, less serious offence.

Negligence

Key points 3.4

A person is negligent if his conduct in relation to a risk, of which a reasonable person would have been aware, falls below the standard which would be expected of a reasonable person in the light of that risk.

3.51 Negligence suffices for criminal liability in more offences than is commonly realised. For example, a survey published in 1996 of 540 offences triable in the Crown Court revealed that in 23 of them negligence was their principal *mens rea* element, or one of their *mens rea* elements.[113] That number has now been increased substantially by the Sexual Offences Act 2003 referred to below. The number is undoubtedly even higher in the case of offences triable only in a magistrates' court.

offences presumptively exist. In *Shivpuri* [1987] AC 1, HL, Lord Bridge, with whom the other Law Lords agreed, expressly regarded the *Courtie* principle as applicable to s 170(2). In contrast, in *Latif and Shahzad* [1996] 1 All ER 353, the House of Lords held that there is one offence under s 170(2), which can be committed in two different ways, by an evasion or by an attempt at evasion. This decision, made without reference to *Courtie*, can be reconciled with *Courtie* on the ground that the House of Lords in *Latif and Shahzad* merely recognised that, in respect of a relevant type of prohibited good, there is one offence of evading or attempting to evade a prohibition on import (which was material to the case), and did not mean – in respect of all prohibited goods – that there was one offence of evading or attempting to evade a prohibition on their import (which was not material to the case). The House of Lords did not avert to this issue in its later decision in *Forbes*, n 112 below (although in passing Lord Hutton referred to 'the offence created by s 170(2)').

[112] *Hussain* [1969] 2 QB 567, CA; *Hennessey* (1978) 68 Cr App Rep 419, CA; *Shivpuri* [1987] AC 1, HL; *Forbes* [2001] UKHL 40.

[113] Ashworth and Blake 'The Presumption of Innocence in English Criminal Law' [1996] Crim LR 306.

Negligence as to consequence

3.52 The risk in question as to which the defendant is required to be negligent may concern a consequence of his conduct or a circumstance in relation to which his conduct occurs. **A defendant is negligent as to a consequence of an act or omission on his part if:**

- the risk of it occurring would have been foreseen by a reasonable person; *and*
- the defendant *either* fails to foresee the risk and to take steps to avoid it *or*, having foreseen it, fails to take steps to avoid it or takes steps which fall below the standard of conduct which would be expected of a reasonable person in the light of that risk.

3.53 Negligence as to a consequence required to result from the defendant's conduct very rarely suffices for criminal liability. An example is provided by the offence of putting people in fear of violence, contrary to the Protection from Harassment Act 1997, s 4(1).[114] Section 4(1) provides that a person whose course of conduct causes another person to fear, on at least two occasions, that violence will be used against him is guilty of an offence if he knows or ought to know that his course of conduct will cause the other so to fear on each of those occasions.[115] The only common law offences where negligence as to consequence suffices seem to be involuntary manslaughter (provided the negligence is gross)[116] and public nuisance.[117]

3.54 In some statutory offences liability is based on the fact that there is a reasonably foreseeable risk that some consequence may result from the defendant's conduct, although that consequence need not be proved actually to have resulted. Examples are provided by a number of offences where the word 'likely' is used in relation to such a risk. For instance, the Public Order Act 1986, s 5 makes it an offence to use threatening, abusive or insulting words or behaviour or disorderly behaviour within the hearing or sight of a person likely to be harassed, alarmed or distressed thereby. Other examples are offences where the defendant's conduct is required to be 'calculated' to cause a particular consequence (eg to deceive). 'Calculated' has been interpreted as meaning 'likely'.[118] 'Likely' bears an objective meaning, although whether the reasonably foreseeable risk must be a probable risk or a lower degree of risk, such as a real risk that should not be ignored, varies depending on the particular context of the statutory words.[119]

---

[114] For another modern example of an offence where negligence as to consequence suffices, see the Water Industry Act 1991, s 73(1).

[115] Para 7.146. Also see the offence under the Protection from Harassment Act 1997, s 2; para 7.145.

[116] Para 8.119.

[117] *Shorrock* [1994] QB 279, CA; approved in *Rimmington; Goldstein* [2005] UKHL 63. For the definition of public nuisance, see para 6.9.

[118] *Turner v Shearer* (1972) 116 Sol Jo 800, DC; *Davison* [1972] Crim LR 786, CA.

[119] *Whitehouse* (1999) Times, 10 December, CA.

Negligence as to circumstance

3.55 A defendant is negligent as to a circumstance relevant to his conduct if he ought to have been aware of its existence because a reasonable person would have thought about the risk that it might exist and would have found out that it did. Negligence as to a circumstance is otherwise known, rather misleadingly (because it does not constitute 'knowledge' in criminal law),[120] as constructive knowledge.[121] Negligence as to circumstance is 'a conception which, generally speaking, has no place in the criminal law'.[122] It suffices, however, for liability in statutory offences in two cases:

- where the statute expressly uses words connoting negligence;
- where appellate judges have implied into a statutory offence words connoting negligence.

Express provision

3.56 Negligence as to circumstance suffices in statutory offences by whose definition the defendant can be convicted on the ground that he had 'reasonable cause to believe', 'reason to believe' or 'reason to suspect', or that he 'could reasonably be expected to know' or 'ought to know' that a circumstance existed or did 'not reasonably believe' that it did not. The Sexual Offences Act 2003 introduced a wide range of offences, described in Chapter 9, where negligence as to a circumstance suffices for liability. Other examples are to be found in various statutes. For example, under the Official Secrets Act 1989, s 5(2), a person who has come into possession, in one of certain ways, of information protected against disclosure by the Act is guilty of an offence if he discloses it without lawful authority, knowing, or having reasonable cause to believe, that it is protected against disclosure by the Act and that it has come into his possession in one of those ways. Likewise, under the Firearms Act 1968, s 25, it is an offence for a person to sell any firearm or ammunition to another person whom he knows or has reasonable cause for believing to be drunk or of unsound mind.

3.57 In *Saik*,[123] the House of Lords held that 'reasonable grounds to suspect that any property is...or represents another person's proceeds of criminal conduct' in the Criminal Justice Act 1988, s 93C(2) (repealed by the Proceeds of Crime Act 2002) included a requirement that the defendant had actual suspicion as well as a requirement that there were reasonable grounds for the suspicion, so that the test was not a purely objective one.

---

[120] *Roper v Taylor's Central Garages (Exeter) Ltd* [1951] 2 TLR 284 at 288–289, per Devlin J. Thus, it cannot suffice where a statute uses the word 'knowingly' in its definition: *Flintshire CC v Reynolds* [2006] EWHC 195 (Admin).

[121] *Roper v Taylor's Central Garages (Exeter) Ltd* [1951] 2 TLR 284 at 288–289, per Devlin J.

[122] *Roper v Taylor's Central Garages (Exeter) Ltd* [1951] 2 TLR 284 at 288–289, per Devlin J.

[123] [2006] UKHL 18.

Section 93C(2) provided:

> 'A person is guilty of an offence if, knowing or *having reasonable grounds to suspect* that any property is, or in whole or in part directly or indirectly represents, another person's proceeds of criminal conduct, he –
>
> (a) conceals or disguises that property; or
>
> (b) converts or transfers that property or removes it from the jurisdiction,
>
> *for the purpose of assisting* any person to avoid prosecution for an offence to which this Part of this Act applies or the making or enforcement in his case of a confiscation order.'[124]

It would be unwise to assume that the decision on the above point is of general application. It would place a major limitation on any offence to which it applied because a person who has reasonable grounds for suspicion about a material fact may well not suspect it because of inexperience or foolishness. Only two members of the House of Lords dealt with the issue in detail. Lord Hope, referring to a case[125] relating to a statutory power of arrest on reasonable grounds for suspecting that a person was concerned in acts of terrorism, where he had held that the test was partly subjective and partly objective, opined that the words used in s 93C(2) could be analysed in the same way. Lord Brown based his conclusion on the view that the defendant could not have acted with the required purpose of assisting a person to avoid prosecution unless subjectively he either actually knew or suspected the property to be 'hot'. Thus, it was necessarily implicit in s 93C(2) that not only must the defendant have reasonable grounds to suspect that the property was 'hot' but that he also did suspect it. Although Lord Hope's reasoning is of potentially general application to 'reason to suspect' or 'reasonable grounds to suspect' or like terms when they are *mens rea* requirements, Lord Brown's is limited to the particular wording of s 93C(2) (ie the illogicality which would arise if, in s 93C(2), 'reasonable grounds to suspect' the 'hotness' of the property was a purely objective requirement while at the same time s 93C(2) required a purpose to assist a person to avoid prosecution).

Judicial implication

3.58 **Negligence as to circumstance will suffice where a phrase of the type referred to in para 3.56 has been introduced into the offence by judicial interpretation of its definition. There are a few instances where this has been done,[126] but the making of such an implication has been deplored.[127]** The emphasis on a subjective approach to criminal liability by the House of Lords in *B v DPP*[128] and *G* (2003)[129] makes it most unlikely that such an implication would now be made or would survive an appeal.

---

[124] Italics supplied.
[125] *O'Hara v Chief Constable of the Royal Ulster Constabulary* [1997] AC 286, HL.
[126] *Browning v J W H Watson (Rochester) Ltd* [1953] 2 All ER 775, DC.
[127] *Gray's Haulage Co Ltd v Arnold* [1966] 1 All ER 896, DC.
[128] [2000] 2 AC 428, HL.
[129] [2003] UKHL 50.

Are the defendant's mental and other capacities relevant?

3.59 Unqualified, phrases such as 'reasonable cause to believe', 'reason to believe' or 'reason to suspect', when used to describe the *mens rea* for an offence, undoubtedly postulate a wholly objective test.[130] A case apparently to the contrary, *Hudson*,[131] contains a dictum that not only must there be an objective 'reason to suspect' but also the defendant himself, taking into account his mental and other capacities, ought to have suspected. However, this dictum has not been followed in any other case.

It is, of course, possible for Parliament to provide for a subjective element. This has been done, for example, by the Sexual Offences Act 2003 in respect of the negligence element in the non-consensual offences under ss 1–4 of that Act where account must be taken of all the circumstances (including, it seems, the defendant's characteristics which affect his perception of the relevant risk).[132]

Negligence as to the very essence of an offence

3.60 In most offences where negligence suffices for liability it only does so in relation to a particular element, normally a circumstance of the *actus reus* of the offence, intention, recklessness or knowledge normally being required as to any other elements. In such offences the *actus reus* is established without reference to the defendant's negligence.

However, in a very limited number of offences, of which manslaughter by gross negligence, corporate manslaughter, careless driving, causing death by careless driving, dangerous driving and causing death by dangerous driving are the most obvious examples,[133] negligence is the very essence of the offence, in that whether or not the defendant's conduct constitutes the *actus reus* of the offence depends on whether it can be described as negligent. A person is guilty of driving without due care and attention, for example, if (and only if) the way he drives falls below what would be expected of a competent and careful driver in the circumstances.[134] In this case the nature of the reasonably foreseeable risk is not specified; the matter is at large, in that the question is whether the defendant driver fell below the requisite standard in the light of any foreseeable and unjustifiable risk. A person is guilty of dangerous driving, on the other hand, if the standard of his driving falls far below the standard which would be expected of a competent and careful driver and it would be obvious to such a driver that driving in the way in question creates a danger of injury to any person or of serious damage to property.[135]

In *Loukes*,[136] the Court of Appeal held that in offences of dangerous driving, the offence simply consists of the commission of the *actus reus*, and *mens rea* plays no part in the commission of the offence. No doubt it would have held the same in respect of careless driving or any other offence whose very essence is negligence. The practical effects of the

---

[130] See, for example, *Young* [1984] 2 All ER 164, C-MAC; as to this court, see para 2.32, n 91.
[131] [1966] 1 QB 448, CCA.   [132] Para 9.29.   [133] Paras 8.119, 8.143, 8.172 and 8.164.
[134] Para 8.173.   [135] Paras 8.166 and 8.168.   [136] [1996] 1 Cr App Rep 444, CA.

classification of all elements of an offence as part of its *actus reus*, so that there are no *mens rea* elements, has important practical consequences, as seen in paras 15.35 and 17.25.

Other points about negligence

Degrees of negligence

3.61 As a comparison of the definitions of careless driving and dangerous driving shows, there can be degrees of negligence. Dangerous driving requires a higher degree of negligence, usually called gross negligence, than careless driving because the defendant must fall far below the standard of a reasonable person in relation to a risk to a person or serious damage to property, and not simply below it. In manslaughter by gross negligence, the gross negligence must be in relation to the risk of death.[137]

Distinction between negligence and intention etc

3.62 Negligence is distinguishable from intention, recklessness and knowledge, since it does not require the defendant to foresee or be aware of the risk in question; evidence of the defendant's state of mind is not a prerequisite to a finding of negligence.[138]

Of course, where negligence suffices for an offence it is no defence for the defendant to claim that he was not negligent as to the risk in question but acted intentionally in relation to it. Where an offence can be committed negligently in some respect, this simply means that the prosecution does not need to prove any intention or the like on the part of the defendant in that respect; it does not mean that he cannot commit the offence if he actually has that state of mind.

Is negligence a species of *mens rea?*

3.63 At the start of this chapter it was stated that *mens rea* means the state of mind expressly or impliedly required by the definition of the offence charged. Negligence cannot properly be described as a state of mind, since it can exist where there is the absence of a state of mind. For this reason, negligence cannot strictly be described as a species of *mens rea*, despite the fact that it has on occasions been so described by judges.[139] Nevertheless, for convenience, whenever the term '*mens rea*' is used in a general sense in this book the reference to it should be understood as including negligence (except where negligence is of the very essence of the offence),[140] unless the context indicates the contrary. The replacement of the term '*mens rea*' by that of 'fault element' in the draft Criminal Code has much to commend it.

3.64 The question of the inclusion of negligence under the head of *mens rea* also raises the question of whether it should be a sufficient fault element for criminal

---

[137] Paras 8.126, 8.166–8.169 and 8.173.

[138] *A-G's Reference (No 2 of 1999)* [2000] QB 796 at 809 (manslaughter by gross negligence).

[139] Eg Lord Rodger in *Rimmington; Goldstein* [2005] UKHL 63 at [56].

[140] Para 3.60.

liability. Negligence involves fault, but usually it is less blameworthy than the fault displayed by people who intend, or are aware of the risk of, their wrongdoing. Neither Parliament nor the courts appear so far to have considered fully the answer to the question: 'When is it proper to punish a person because he has failed to match up to the standard expected of a reasonable person?' It would be easier to accept negligence as a basis of liability if it was always the case that a defendant could only be liable on that ground if he could, given his mental ability, skill and experience, have avoided being negligent.

Contemporaneity

> **Key points 3.5**
>
> It is a cardinal rule that the defendant's *mens rea* must exist at the time of the relevant act, omission or state of affairs on his part.[141] This rule is mitigated or avoided in two ways.

3.65 A person cannot be convicted of an offence if he only acquires the relevant *mens rea* after the culpable act, omission or state of affairs on his part has ceased. Provided that the defendant had the necessary *mens rea* at the time of his act or omission, he may be convicted of the offence in question even though (for example, because of repentance or because he is asleep) he lacks that *mens rea* when a consequence required for the *actus reus* occurs.[142] In addition, in the case of conduct which is clearly continuing in nature, as is almost invariably so in the case of a state of affairs and can happen in the case of an omission or an act, it is irrelevant that the defendant lacked *mens rea* at the inception of the conduct provided that he has the *mens rea* at some time during its continuance, as where he realises the true situation before his conduct is complete.

3.66 The requirement of contemporaneity can give rise to problems in the case of offences which are normally based on some act on the part of the defendant because an act is usually momentary, as opposed to continuing, in nature, in which case the time span in which any accompanying *mens rea* must exist is limited. **The courts have postulated two different ways in which the difficulties which this could cause can be mitigated or avoided.**

3.67 The first, which is illustrated by *Fagan v Metropolitan Police Comr*,[143] is that **where an act can be regarded as a continuing one it is enough if *mens rea* exists at some stage during its continuance** and that, in deciding whether an act is continuing,

---

[141] *Fowler v Padget* (1798) 7 Term Rep 509, per Lord Kenyon CJ. It is, of course, possible for a statute to make an exception to this rule, as is shown by the Fraud Act 2006, s 11; see para 12.42.

[142] *Jakeman* (1982) 76 Cr App Rep 223, CA.

[143] [1969] 1 QB 439, DC.

a liberal approach should be taken. In *Fagan,* a motorist, having been asked by a police officer to draw into the kerb, drove his car onto the officer's foot. The officer requested him to drive off his foot but the motorist refused to do so for some little time thereafter. The question was whether the motorist's conduct amounted to a battery, since it had not been proved that the original driving onto the foot had been accompanied by the relevant *mens rea.* The majority of the Divisional Court held that the motorist's conduct did amount to a battery because the driving of the car onto the officer's foot and allowing it to remain there could be treated as a continuing act of application of force, with the result that the motorist's act was not spent and complete by the time his *mens rea* began, as would have been the case if the driving onto the foot had been treated as a single complete act. His *mens rea* could therefore be superimposed on his existing continuing act.

3.68 The type of solution adopted in *Fagan* is clearly sensible where the defendant's act is truly continuing. However, the actual application of the approach in *Fagan* in a particular case may be open to the objection that it may involve (as it did in that case) a certain degree of artificiality in finding a continuing act. For these reasons the approach which was preferred and adopted by the House of Lords in *Miller,*[144] whose facts were set out in para 2.13, is better. As was stated, the rule adopted by the House of Lords is that, **where a person inadvertently and without the appropriate *mens rea* does an act which puts a person or property in danger, but before the resulting harm is complete he becomes aware**[145] **of the train of events caused by his act, he is under a duty to take such steps as lie within his power to try to prevent or reduce the risk of harm. Consequently if, before the harm resulting from his act is complete, he realises what he has done and fails to take such steps to prevent or reduce the risk, and provided he then has the relevant *mens rea*, he will be criminally liable because his *mens rea* will be contemporaneous with his culpable omission to act.**

The adoption in *Miller* by the House of Lords of what may be called the 'duty theory' in preference to the theory adopted in *Fagan* means that the latter is now unlikely to be utilised, unless the act is truly of a continuing character or unless the offence is one which by its express terms can only be committed by an act.

3.69 The rules discussed in paras 3.67 and 3.68 are not, of course, exceptions to the requirement of contemporaneity but are methods of satisfying it. There are, however, exceptions to the requirement of contemporaneity in two types of situation which are dealt with later.[146]

---

[144] [1983] 2 AC 161, HL. See Sullivan 'Cause and Contemporaneity of *Actus Reus* and *Mens Rea*' (1993) 12 CLJ 487.

[145] Or, in the case of an offence where negligence suffices, ought reasonably to be aware: *Evans (Gemma)* [2009] EWCA Crim 650 at [31].

[146] Paras 8.33 and 15.100.

> **Key points 3.6**
>
> In the rest of this chapter the relevance to liability of the defendant's motive, ignorance or mistake of law or ignorance of morals is considered. It will be seen that generally these things are irrelevant to liability, but there are exceptions in each case.

Motive

3.70 A person's motive is his reason for acting as he did. Thus A's motive for killing B may be financial gain, and C's motive for stealing may be his wish to feed his starving children. **The general rule is that the defendant's motives, good or bad, are irrelevant to his criminal liability, although they may affect the punishment imposed.** In *Sharpe*,[147] where D, motivated by affection for his mother and religious duty, had removed her corpse from a grave in a cemetery belonging to Protestant Dissenters in order to bury it with the body of his recently deceased father in a churchyard, it was held that D's motives, however estimable they might be, did not provide a defence to a charge of removing a corpse without lawful authority. However, D's 'good' motives were reflected in the punishment awarded, a fine of one shilling (5p) being imposed. More recently, in *A-G's Reference (No 1 of 2002)*,[148] the Court of Appeal held that a police officer who presented false evidence in the hope of securing the conviction of someone whom she believed to be guilty of burglary could be convicted of the offence of perverting the course of justice. She would have committed the *actus reus* of that offence with the relevant *mens rea*. It was irrelevant that her motive would have been to achieve a just result. In another modern case, *A-G v Scotcher*,[149] the House of Lords held that it was no defence to a contempt of court, committed by a juror who disclosed to a third party particulars about the jury's deliberations and criticised them, that the defendant had been motivated by a desire to expose a perceived miscarriage of justice.

3.71 Intention, whether relating to a consequence required for the *actus reus* or ulterior to it, is clearly distinguishable from motive.[150] A person's intention has been defined by the Privy Council as his immediate purpose, and his motive as his underlying purpose.[151]

An illustration of the distinction between intention and motive is provided by *Smith*.[152] D was charged with corruptly offering a gift to the mayor of a borough. He had handed an IOU to his agent with the intention that it should be given to the mayor to induce him to promote the sale of land by the borough council to D; the agent had then given the IOU

---

[147] (1857) 26 LJMC 47. For more recent authorities, see *Chandler v DPP* [1964] AC 763, HL; *Hills v Ellis* [1983] QB 680, DC; *X* [1994] Crim LR 827, CA.

[148] [2003] Crim LR 410, CA.   [149] [2005] UKHL 36.

[150] *A-G's Reference (No 1 of 2002)* [2002] EWCA Crim 2392.

[151] *Wai Yu-tsang v R* [1992] 1 AC 269 at 280.

[152] [1960] 2 QB 423, CCA.

to the mayor. D did not intend to go through with the transaction, his reason for causing the offer to be made being his desire to expose what he believed to be the corrupt habits of those connected with the local administration. It was held that 'corruptly' in the definition of the relevant offence meant 'with intent that the donee should enter into a corrupt bargain' and that, even though his motive was not corrupt, D was guilty of the offence since he had offered the money with that requisite ulterior intent.

3.72 Exceptionally, a defendant's motive may be relevant to his liability because the definition of the offence expressly so provides. Examples are the various racially or religiously aggravated offences described later in this book.[153]

Ignorance or mistake of law

3.73 It should be clear by now that *mens rea* does not mean that the defendant must have been aware of the illegality of his conduct.[154] **Ignorance or mistake of law is usually no defence, although it may mitigate the punishment imposed.**[155] It is no defence, for example, for someone charged with the offence of beating a rug in a street, contrary to the Town Police Clauses Act 1847, s 28, to say that he did not know that such conduct was criminal.

3.74 Another aspect of the general rule that ignorance or mistake of law is no defence is that a person, who makes a mistake of criminal law and consequently uses reasonable force to prevent what he mistakenly believes constitutes an offence, cannot rely on the defence of reasonable force in the prevention of crime.[156]

3.75 Sometimes ignorance or mistake of the criminal law prevents a defendant realising that an element of the *actus reus* exists or may exist. An example is where D who handles goods given to him by X, not knowing the intricacies of the law of theft, does not realise that the goods were stolen by X, although he knows how X acquired them; it would be possible to convict D of handling stolen goods, the *mens rea* for which requires that D should know or believe the goods are stolen. Another example would be where D, not knowing that the relevant law requires a particular activity to be licensed, carries it out without a licence; D can be convicted of an offence of carrying out the relevant activity without a licence, with knowledge of the material circumstances. In such cases D will be aware of the factual situation which constitutes the element in question, albeit he does not realise its legal significance, and will therefore have the relevant form of *mens rea* as to it.[157]

---

[153] Paras 7.96, 7.152 and 13.26.

[154] For modern recognition of this, see *Official Solicitor v News Group Newspapers Ltd* [1994] 2 FLR 174; *Reading Borough Council v Ahmad* (1999) 163 JP 451, DC. See also *Broad* [1997] Crim LR 666, CA; para 14.72.

[155] See, for example, *Paul v Minister of Posts and Telecommunications* [1973] RTR 245, DC.

[156] *Albert v Lavin* [1982] AC 546, HL; *Baker and Wilkins* [1997] Crim LR 497, CA.

[157] *A-G's Reference (No 1 of 1995)* [1996] 4 All ER 21, CA.

Rationale

3.76 Various reasons have been given for the rule that ignorance or mistake of law is usually no defence. First, it is said that everyone knows the law, but this is palpably untrue. Secondly, it can be argued that it is a duty of citizenship to know the law.[158] Thirdly, it is said that it would be difficult to prove that the defendant knew the law; if this were the real reason for the rule, ignorance of the law should be a defence when it can be clearly proved. However, it has been held that a person who was on the high seas, in circumstances in which he could not have been informed of the contents of a recent statute, might be convicted of contravening it.[159] The best reason for the rule is expediency:

> 'Every man must be taken to be cognisant of the law, otherwise there is no knowing of the extent to which the excuse of ignorance might be carried. It would be urged in almost every case.'[160]

Even a foreigner who proves that he mistakenly believed his conduct to be lawful because it is lawful in his homeland is not exempt from criminal liability in England and Wales.[161]

3.77 The rule that ignorance or mistake of law is no excuse (which is applied more strictly in England and Wales than in many other countries) is only rendered compatible with most people's idea of justice by the facts that many offences are also moral wrongs and that even when this is not so the ordinary member of the public or, at least, the ordinary member of the class most affected (as motorists are affected by traffic legislation) normally has a rough idea of the provisions of the criminal law.

The rule is liable to be particularly harsh where a person has reasonably relied on the advice of a lawyer or someone in authority that a proposed course of action is not criminal. It has been suggested that a person should have a defence to a charge concerning that action in such circumstances,[162] as is the position under French law.[163]

Stay of proceedings

Erroneous legal advice by prosecuting body

3.78 Where the erroneous legal advice has been given by an official in the organisation which prosecutes the defendant, a court has power to stay the prosecution as an

---

[158] See Ashworth *Principles of Criminal Law* (6th edn, 2006) 220–221.

[159] *Bailey* (1800) Russ & Ry 1, CCR.

[160] *Bilbie v Lumley* (1802) 2 East 469.

[161] *Esop* (1836) 7 C & P 456.

[162] Ashworth 'Excusable Mistake of Law' [1974] Crim LR 652. See also the note by JC Smith [1988] Crim LR 138, Williams 'The Draft Code and Reliance on Official Statements' (1989) 9 LS 177 and Ashworth 'Testing Fidelity to Legal Values: Official Involvement and Criminal Justice' (2000) 63 MLR 633, esp at 635–642.

[163] French Criminal Code 1992, art 122–123; discussed by Kirsch (1999) 16 *Amicus Curiae* 25.

abuse of process if in the light of the defendant's reliance on it the prosecution is unfair. This was established by the Divisional Court in *Postermobile plc v Brent London Borough Council*,[164] where D, having been wrongly advised by members of the council's planning department that certain advertisements did not in law require planning consent, erected the advertisements without such consent. The council prosecuted him. The Divisional Court held that the prosecution was an abuse of process, as it would be unfair for D to be tried, and should be stayed. It would seem that a stay can only be ordered if the defendant has justifiably relied on the advice. As Schiemann LJ said in *Postermobile*: 'it is not as though [D] had requested planning advice from one of the council's gardeners'. It must be emphasised that the power to stay proceedings does not mean that the defendant has a defence in the present type of case. Unless a prosecution is stayed, reasonable reliance on erroneous legal advice by the prosecuting body can only be reflected in mitigation of the sentence imposed.[165]

Non-publication of law

3.79 It would seem that proceedings can also be stayed in the unlikely case that the State has not made a new offence known or ascertainable. This is because of ECHR, Article 7, which, as the Court of Appeal stated in *Misra and Srivastava*:

> 'sustains [the] contention that a criminal offence must be clearly defined in law, and represents the operation of "the principle of legal certainty"[166] .... The principle enables each community to regulate itself "with reference to the norms prevailing in the society in which they live. That generally entails that the law must be adequately accessible – an individual must have an indication of the legal rules applicable in a given case – and he must be able[167] to foresee the consequences of his actions, in particular to be able to avoid incurring the sanction of the criminal law".'[168]

Consistent with the principle of legal certainty (or foreseeability), the Privy Council indicated in *Christian v R*[169] that ignorance of the law resulting from the non-publication of a law, which law could not reasonably have been known to exist, might be a ground for the exercise of the power to stay proceedings for contravention of the law as an abuse of process, although it accepted that in the case before it the court had been right not to stay the particular proceedings because the defendants were aware that their conduct was contrary to the criminal law despite the non-publication of the law in question.

---

164 (1997) Times, 8 December, DC; see [1998] Crim LR 435.

165 *Surrey County Council v Battersby* [1965] 2 QB 194, DC. See also *Arrowsmith* [1975] QB 678, CA.

166 Para 1.58.

167 With legal advice, if necessary.

168 [2004] EWCA Crim 2375 at [30]. These words were approved by Lord Bingham in *Rimmington; Goldstein* [2005] UKHL 63 at [33]. The words quoted at the end of the quotation come from the European Court of Human Rights' decision in *SW v United Kingdom; CR v United Kingdom* (1996) 21 EHRR 363 at [30].

169 [2006] UKPC 47; discussed by Power 'Pitcairn Island: Sexual offending, Cultural Differences and Ignorance of the Law' [2007] Crim LR 609.

Exceptions

Statutory instruments

3.80 By way of exception to the general rule, the Statutory Instruments Act 1946, s 3 provides that it is a defence for a person charged with an offence under a statutory instrument[170] to prove that it had not been issued by or under the authority of the Stationery Office at the date of the alleged offence, unless it is proved that at that date reasonable steps had been taken to bring the purport of the instrument to the notice of the public, or of persons likely to be affected by it, or of the defendant. This provides better protection in the case of statutory instruments than is available under the power to stay referred to in para 3.79.

Lack of mens rea *due to ignorance or mistake of civil law*

3.81 As a further exception to the general rule, ignorance or mistake of the *civil law* does provide a defence where it precludes the defendant from having the *mens rea* required for the offence charged,[171] as opposed simply to causing him to be ignorant that what he knows he is doing constitutes an offence. This is shown by *Smith (David)*.[172] D, a tenant, installed stereo wiring in his flat. With the landlord's permission he covered the wiring with panels and other materials. When the tenancy was terminated, D removed the wiring. In doing so, he damaged the panels and other materials. Unknown to D, by operation of the civil law, the panels and other materials had become part of the flat, and so belonged to the landlord, when they were installed. Allowing D's appeal against a conviction for criminal damage to the panels and other materials, contrary to the Criminal Damage Act 1971, s 1(1), the Court of Appeal held that a person could not be convicted of intentionally or recklessly damaging property belonging to another (the *mens rea* for criminal damage) if, because of a mistake of civil law, he believed that it belonged to him. Likewise, it has been held that a person who acts as an auditor for a company, in ignorance of a statutory provision whereby he is disqualified in the circumstances in question, cannot be convicted of the statutory offence of acting as an auditor 'knowing that he is disqualified'.[173] A problem with the present exception is determining when a mistake relates to the civil law. In *Grant v Borg*,[174] the House of Lords held that a person who was a visitor to this country could be convicted of the offence of knowingly remaining without leave despite wrongly believing that his leave had not expired because of a mistake of law; the question of whether one has leave to remain would seem to be one of civil, rather than criminal law. Someone who makes a mistake about the arrest powers of a police officer makes a mistake of criminal law.[175]

---

[170] Para 1.44.   [171] As to mistake negativing *mens rea*, see paras 5.5–5.11.
[172] [1974] QB 354, CA.   [173] *Secretary of State for Trade and Industry v Hart* [1982] 1 All ER 817, DC.
[174] [1982] 2 All ER 257, HL.   [175] *Bentley* (1850) 4 Cox CC 406. See para 16.35.

3.82 Some offences contain mental elements which expressly envisage the defence of mistake of civil law.[176] For example, in the offence of theft, where the defendant's appropriation of another's property must be proved to have been dishonest, the Theft Act 1968, s 2(1) provides that an appropriation is not to be regarded as dishonest if the appropriator believed that he had in law the right to deprive the other of it.[177]

Other exceptions

3.83 For another case where ignorance or mistake of law may be relevant to criminal liability, the reader is referred to para 15.27.

Of course, it is open to a piece of legislation to provide expressly that ignorance or mistake as to a matter of law is a defence, but such cases are likely to be rare.

Mistaken belief that conduct is criminal

3.84 A mistake of law cannot render a defendant criminally liable. For example, if a man has intercourse with a girl of 17, mistakenly believing that it is an offence to have sexual intercourse with a girl under 18, he cannot be convicted of a substantive offence because, contrary to his belief, he has not committed the *actus reus* of an offence, nor can he be convicted of an attempt.[178]

Moreover, even if a defendant has committed the *actus reus* of an offence, he is to be judged (in terms of any requisite *mens rea*) on the facts as he believed them to be, regardless of his understanding of their implications in criminal law. This was held by the House of Lords in *Taaffe*,[179] where D had mistakenly believed that he was bringing currency into the country and that such importation was prohibited. In fact, he had been bringing in cannabis resin, the importation of which was prohibited. The House of Lords held that D was not guilty of the relevant offence (under the Customs and Excise Management Act 1979, s 170(2)) of being knowingly concerned in the fraudulent evasion of the prohibition on the importation of a controlled drug. Its reason was that, although only knowledge that the importation of the article was prohibited was required, on the facts as D believed them to be the article was not prohibited goods and it was irrelevant that he thought that the currency was the subject of a prohibition on its importation. Nor would D have been guilty of an attempt to commit the above offence.

Ignorance of morals

3.85 The fact that the defendant did not personally consider his conduct to be immoral or know that it was regarded as immoral by the bulk of society is generally irrelevant to

---

[176] Or a mistake of criminal law, as, for example, in the case of the offence under the Official Secrets Act 1989, s 5(2), referred to in para 3.56.

[177] Para 10.70.   [178] Para 14.137.   [179] [1984] AC 539, HL.

his criminal liability. The principal exceptional cases where it is relevant that the defendant was unaware of the moral turpitude of his conduct relate to the various offences of dishonesty under the Theft Acts 1968 and 1978, the offences of fraud and obtaining services dishonestly under the Fraud Act 2006 and the offence of blackmail.[180]

FURTHER READING

Ashworth 'Transferred Malice and Punishment for Unforeseen Consequences' in *Reshaping the Criminal Law* (1978) (Glazebrook (ed)) 77

Buzzard 'Intent' [1978] Crim LR 5

Duff 'The Politics of Intention: A Response to Norrie' [1990] Crim LR 637

Duff *Answering for Crime* (2007) Ch 3

Lord Goff 'The Mental Element in the Crime of Murder' (1988) 104 LQR 30

Hart *Punishment and Responsibility* (2nd edn, 2008, Introduction (by J Gardner), Chs 2, 5 and 6

Horder 'A Critique of the Correspondence Principle in Criminal Law' [1995] Crim LR 759

Horder 'Intention in the Criminal Law – A Rejoinder' (1995) 58 MLR 678

Horder 'Questioning the Correspondence Principle – A Reply' [1999] Crim LR 206

Horder 'On the Irrelevance of Motive in Criminal Law' in *Oxford Essays in Jurisprudence* (4th series, 2000) (Horder (ed)) 173

Horder 'Transferred Malice and the Remoteness of Unexpected Outcomes from Intention' [2006] Crim LR 383

Kaveny 'Inferring Intention from Foresight' (2004) 120 LQR 81

Kugler *Direct and Oblique Intent in the Criminal Law* (2002)

Lacey 'A Clear Concept of Intention' (1993) 56 MLR 621

Lacey 'In(de)terminable Intentions' (1995) 58 MLR 692

Marston 'Contemporaneity of Act and Intention' (1970) 86 LQR 208

Matthews 'Ignorance of the Law is No Excuse?' (1983) 3 LS 174

Mitchell 'In Defence of a Principle of Correspondence' [1999] Crim LR 195

Norrie 'Oblique Intention and Legal Politics' [1989] Crim LR 793

Norrie 'Intention: More Loose Talk' [1990] Crim LR 642

Pedain 'Intention and the Terrorist Example' [2003] Crim LR 579

Shute 'Knowledge and Belief in the Criminal Law' in *Criminal Law: Doctrines of the General Part* (2002) (Shute and Simester (eds)) 184

Simester 'Moral Certainty and the Boundaries of Intention' (1996) 16 OJLS 445

Simester 'Can Negligence be Culpable?' in *Oxford Essays in Jurisprudence* (4th series, 2000) (Horder (ed)) 85

ATH Smith 'Error and Mistake of Law in Anglo-American Criminal Law' (1985) 14 Anglo-American LR 3

JC Smith 'Intention in Criminal Law' (1974) 27 *Current Legal Problems* 93

JC Smith '"Intent": A Reply' [1978] Crim LR 14

---

[180] Chs 10, 11 and 12.

Sullivan 'Knowledge, Belief and Culpability' in *Criminal Law: Doctrines of the General Part* (2002) (Shute and Simester (eds)) 207

Tadros *Criminal Responsibility* (2005) Ch 8

Williams 'Convictions and Fair Labelling' (1983) 42 CLJ 85

Williams 'Oblique Intent' (1987) 46 CLJ 417

Williams 'The Mens Rea for Murder – Leave it Alone' (1989) 105 LQR 387

Wilson 'Doctrinal Rationality after *Woollin*' (1999) 62 MLR 448

4

Proof

OVERVIEW

This chapter is concerned with an outline of:

- the burden of proof and the burden of adducing evidence;
- the use of presumptions as an aid to proof; and
- proof of a state of mind.

The two burdens

Key points 4.1

The general rule is that the prosecution must prove the guilt of the defendant beyond reasonable doubt. This rule is reinforced by the presumption of innocence under the ECHR, Article 6(2).[1] The general rule means that the prosecution has the burden of proving beyond reasonable doubt that the defendant has committed the *actus reus* of an offence with the *mens rea* required for it, but the burden of adducing sufficient evidence to raise an issue may be borne by the defendant. Very exceptionally, the defendant may have the burden of disproving an element of the offence.

In relation to excuses, the defendant has the burden of adducing sufficient evidence to raise an excuse; if he does so it is, in principle, then for the prosecution to disprove the alleged excuse beyond reasonable doubt. There are, however, exceptions whereby the defendant not only has the burden of adducing sufficient evidence to raise an excuse but also has the burden of proving it on the balance of probabilities. This may be held in a particular context to be incompatible with the presumption of innocence under the ECHR, Article 6(2).

4.1 The burden of proof is sometimes described as the 'persuasive burden' (or 'legal burden'), while the burden of adducing evidence is sometimes described as the 'evidential burden'.

---

[1] See para 4.8.

4.2 Although the great majority of criminal cases are tried before magistrates, and therefore without a jury, it is convenient for the student to think in terms of a trial by judge and jury when considering the following paragraphs. All questions of fact have to be determined by the jury, but the judge exercises a considerable degree of control in two ways in particular. One concerns the judge's power to withdraw a case from the jury, usually on the submission of the defence, on the ground that there is no case for the defendant to answer on the prosecution's evidence. This may be because no evidence that the offence alleged to have been committed by the defendant has been produced by the prosecution, or because, where some evidence has been produced, that evidence (taken at its highest) is such that a reasonable jury properly directed could not properly convict on it.[2] A judge has no power to rule that there is no case to answer until the conclusion of the prosecution's evidence.[3] If the judge rules that there is no case to answer, the judge must direct the jury to return a verdict of not guilty and the case is at an end. The other way in which the judge exercises control is by means of his summing up, where the judge can withdraw from the jury an issue raised by way of defence if there is insufficient evidence in law to support it.

However strong the evidence is in respect of a matter which the prosecution must prove, or however weak the evidence on a point which the defence must prove, the judge is never entitled to direct the jury to return a verdict of guilty.[4]

The burden of proof

4.3 The party who bears the persuasive burden of proof on a given issue will lose on that issue if, after reviewing all the evidence, the jury or magistrates entertain the appropriate degree of doubt whether the proposition in question has been established. As the prosecution bears the burden of proving most issues in a criminal case beyond reasonable doubt, it is generally true to say that the guilt of the defendant must be established beyond reasonable doubt. The judges are currently advised to translate 'proof beyond reasonable doubt' to juries by directing them that they must be sure of the defendant's guilt and that nothing less will do.[5]

As far as most criminal charges were concerned, it had been the recognised position for a long time that as a rule the prosecution must prove the defendant's guilt beyond reasonable doubt. However, before 1935 there was believed to be an exception in the case of murder. It was thought that, if the deceased was shown to have met his death as a result of the conduct of the defendant, it was incumbent on the defendant to satisfy the jury of his innocence, or of the existence of a mitigating circumstance, such as provocation, which would justify a verdict of manslaughter.

---

[2] *Galbraith* [1981] 2 All ER 1060, CA.   [3] *N Ltd* [2008] EWCA Crim 1223.
[4] *Wang* [2005] UKHL 9.
[5] Judicial Studies Board, Crown Court Bench Book, Specimen Direction No 2B.

There were several authorities which seemed to support this view concerning the law of murder, but they were overruled or explained on other grounds by the House of Lords in *Woolmington v DPP*,[6] where Viscount Sankey LC made the following classic statement:

> 'If it is proved that the conscious act of the prisoner killed a man and nothing else appears in the case, there is evidence upon which the jury may, not must, find him guilty of murder. It is difficult to conceive so bare and meagre a case, but that does not mean that the onus is not still on the prosecution…Throughout the web of the English criminal law one golden thread is always to be seen, that it is the duty of the prosecution to prove the prisoner's guilt…If, at the end of and on the whole of the case, there is a reasonable doubt, created by the evidence given by either the prosecution or the prisoner, as to whether the prisoner killed the deceased with a malicious intention, the prosecution has not made out the case and the prisoner is entitled to an acquittal. No matter what the charge or where the trial, the principle that the prosecution must prove the guilt of the prisoner is part of the common law of England and no attempt to whittle it down can be entertained.'[7]

4.4 In principle, the general rule that the prosecution must prove the defendant's guilt beyond reasonable doubt means not only that it must prove beyond reasonable doubt that the defendant committed the *actus reus* of an offence with the *mens rea* required for that offence, but also that it must negative any excuse (ie a defence which excuses a defendant from liability for conduct which is otherwise criminal) raised by the defendant. For example, the burden of negativing a plea of duress,[8] or is borne by the prosecution. In addition, the burden of negativing automatism,[9] when it is not caused by insanity, is likewise borne by the prosecution.[10]

Burden of proof on defendant

4.5 The general rule that the prosecution must prove the defendant's guilt beyond reasonable doubt is weakened by the fact that in many offences the defendant has the persuasive burden of proving something, normally an excuse. In *Woolmington v DPP*, Viscount Sankey LC, having referred to the general duty of the prosecution to prove the defendant's guilt, went on to note that it has always been possible for Parliament to transfer the onus of proof of some matter to the defendant; such a provision is known as a 'reverse onus provision'. When the defendant bears the burden of proof, the burden borne by him is lighter than that borne by the prosecution on the issues on which it has to prove guilt, for the defendant has only to prove the exculpating facts on the balance of probabilities, not beyond reasonable doubt.[11] He will succeed in doing this if the jury are satisfied that it is more likely than not (or more probable than not) that the relevant facts are made

---

[6] [1935] AC 462, HL.   [7] [1935] AC 462 at 481–482.
[8] *Gill* [1963] 2 All ER 688, CCA; *Bone* [1968] 2 All ER 644, CA.   [9] Para 15.50.
[10] *Bratty v A-G for Northern Ireland* [1963] AC 386, HL; *Stripp* (1978) 69 Cr App Rep 318, CA.
[11] *Sodeman v R* [1936] 2 All ER 1138, PC; *Carr-Briant* [1943] KB 607, CCA.

out.[12] He will not succeed if the jury merely conclude that it is as likely as not that the facts existed. Where an issue is raised in respect of which the defendant has the burden of proof, the issue is not automatically left to the jury; it is only left to them if there is evidence, however weak, on which (if it is accepted and not contradicted) a jury could find the matter proved.[13] If the issue is left to the jury, it is then up to the defence to prove it as explained above.

4.6 The prosecution must always prove the facts in respect of which it bears the burden of proof (or they must be formally admitted) before the defendant can be required to discharge a burden of proof imposed on him in respect of an excuse or other matter. It follows that, even if the defendant fails to discharge a burden of proof placed upon him, he must still be acquitted if the prosecution fails to satisfy the jury beyond reasonable doubt as to the facts which it must prove which give rise to the imposition of the defendant's burden. For example, in *Gatland v Comr of Metropolitan Police*,[14] D was charged with depositing, without lawful authority or excuse, a skip on the highway whereby a user of the highway was endangered, contrary to the Highways Act 1959, s 140(1) (now the Highways Act 1980, s 161(1)). D failed to prove any lawful authority or excuse for his actions, as the Divisional Court held was required by statute, but it was held by the Divisional Court that D could not be convicted of the offence because the prosecution had not proved that the presence of the skip on the highway caused any highway-user to be endangered.

When is the burden of proof on the defendant?

4.7 The defendant bears the burden of proof in the following situations:

- *Defence of insanity*[15] This is the only common law exception to *Woolmington* in relation to an excuse. In *Woolmington* itself, it was confirmed that a defendant who raises the defence of insanity has the burden of proving it.

- *Express statutory provision* It has been common for a statute to provide that it shall be for the defence to prove certain facts.[16] For example, a person charged with sexual activity with a child family member aged 16 or over under the Sexual Offences Act 2003, s 25 has an excuse if he proves that he was lawfully married to, or the civil partner of, the other person at the time.

- *Implied statutory provision* Even if a statute does not expressly place on the defendant the persuasive burden of proving a particular matter, the statutory provision may, on its true construction, place that burden on him. A statutory provision will have this effect if, on its true construction, it contains any exception, exemption, proviso,

---

[12] *Miller v Minister of Pensions* [1947] 2 All ER 372 at 373–374.
[13] See para 4.10.   [14] [1968] 2 QB 279, DC.   [15] See para 15.18.
[16] A survey published in 1996 indicated that 40 per cent of offences triable in the Crown Court appeared to place the onus on the defendant of proving a particular fact: Ashworth and Blake 'The Presumption of Innocence in English Criminal Law' [1996] Crim LR 306.

excuse or qualification, whether or not it accompanies the description of the offence in the enactment creating the offence. The detail concerning this exception is outside the scope of this book; reference should be made to a work on the Law of Evidence.

- *Presumptions of law against defendant rebuttable by persuasive proof to the contrary.* Sometimes a thing is presumed against the defendant unless he rebuts the presumption by proof to the contrary. This type of reverse onus provision is dealt with in para 4.14.

Compatibility with ECHR, Article 6(2)

4.8 Putting the burden of proving an issue on the defendant is open to the grave objection that, assuming that the prosecution has discharged its burden of proof, a magistrates' court or jury may have to convict the defendant although it thinks it as likely as not that he had an excuse or is otherwise not guilty.

The position concerning provisions which apparently place a persuasive (as opposed to an evidential)[17] burden on the defendant is complicated by the fact that they may be incompatible with the ECHR, Article 6(2), which provides: 'Everyone charged with a criminal offence shall be presumed innocent until proved guilty according to law.' Article 6(2) does not, however, create an absolute rule.[18] There can be circumstances where the imposition of a burden of proof on the defendant is permissible under the ECHR.[19] The question of compatibility of an express or implied reverse onus provision has to be decided by the courts and if a court finds that such a provision is incompatible with Article 6(2) it is required by the Human Rights Act 1998, s 3,[20] wherever possible, to 'read down' that provision so as to impose only an evidential burden, even where Parliament appears clearly to have intended to impose a persuasive burden on the defendant.[21] An explanation of how the courts decide whether the imposition of a reverse onus provision is compatible with the ECHR is outside the scope of this book; reference should be made to a work on the Law of Evidence.

The burden of adducing evidence

4.9 The prosecution must adduce prima facie evidence of the defendant's guilt, for otherwise there is no case to answer and the judge directs an acquittal. This means only that the prosecution must adduce sufficient evidence of the *actus reus* and *mens rea* mentioned

---

[17] Placing an evidential burden on the defendant does not ordinarily contravene the ECHR, Art 6(2): *Lingens v Austria* 26 DR 171 (1981), EComHR; *Lambert* [2001] UKHL 37; *A-G's Reference (No 1 of 2004); Edwards; Denton; Jackson; Hendley; Crowley* [2004] EWCA Crim 1025.

[18] *Salabiaku v France* (1988) 13 EHRR 379, ECtHR; *Brown v Stott* [2003] 1 AC 681, PC.

[19] *DPP, ex p Kebiline* [2000] 2 AC 326, HL; *Lambert* [2001] UKHL 37; *Johnstone* [2003] UKHL 28; *A-G's Reference (No 1 of 2004); Edwards; Denton; Jackson; Hendley; Crowley* [2004] EWCA Crim 1025; *Sheldrake v DPP* [2004] UKHL 43.

[20] Para 1.65.   [21] See the cases cited in n 19.

in the definition of the offence charged. There are rare exceptions to this where a statute expressly or impliedly requires the defendant to disprove a particular element of the *actus reus* or *mens rea* of the offence or requires the prosecution to prove that such an element is satisfied only if sufficient evidence to the contrary has been adduced by the defendant or other witness.

4.10 It is not necessary for the prosecution to negative every type of defence that might be available to the defendant. In the words of Devlin J (as he then was):

> 'It would be quite unreasonable to allow the defence to submit at the end of the prosecution's case that the Crown had not proved affirmatively and beyond reasonable doubt that the defendant was at the time of the crime sober, or not sleepwalking or not in a trance or blackout.'[22]

It follows that it is normally incumbent on the defendant to adduce sufficient evidence to raise a particular defence and (where he does not have the burden of proving this defence) he satisfies this burden if there is evidence, however weak,[23] which (if believed and not contradicted) could result in the jury determining that the defence was available.[24] If the defendant does this, the judge must leave the issue to the jury. Unless the defence is one which the defendant must prove (see paras 4.5 to 4.7), the judge must direct the jury that the defence must succeed (and the defendant be acquitted) unless the Crown disproves one or more elements of it beyond reasonable doubt.[25]

For example, at a trial for murder the prosecution must dispel all reasonable doubt on the question of non-insane automatism for otherwise a verdict of not guilty must be returned, but this duty of the prosecution only arises if there is evidence to raise the issue that the defendant was a non-insane automaton at the material time. If there is no such evidence, the judge must not leave the defence of non-insane automatism to the jury. On the other hand, if there is such evidence the judge must leave that excuse to the jury, even though the defendant has not specifically raised it as an excuse.

4.11 It is common practice to speak of the defendant's burden of adducing evidence, but it should never be forgotten that the burden may have been discharged for the defendant by the evidence of a witness for the prosecution or of a co-defendant.[26]

---

[22] *Hill v Baxter* [1958] 1 QB 277 at 284, per Devlin J.

[23] *Dinnick* (1909) 3 Cr App Rep 77, CCA; *Rossiter* [1994] 2 All ER 752, CA; *Bane* [1994] Crim LR 134, CA.

[24] *Lee Chun-Chuen v R* [1963] AC 220, PC; *Bratty v A-G for Northern Ireland* [1963] AC 386 at 416–417, per Lord Morris; *Jayasena v R* [1970] AC 618 at 623, PC. See also *Galbraith* [1981] 2 All ER 1060, CA.

[25] *Abraham* [1973] 3 All ER 694 at 697–698; *Moore* [1986] Crim LR 552, CA. Statements in *Moore* that it is enough if some of the jury are satisfied beyond reasonable doubt that one element is not made out, while the rest are so satisfied that another element is not made out, must be regarded as wrong.

[26] *Bullard v R* [1957] AC 635, PC; *Rolle v R* [1965] 3 All ER 582, PC.

Presumptions

> **Key points 4.2**
>
> Proof may be aided by the use of presumptions. A presumption is the product of a rule according to which on proof of one fact the jury must or may find that some other fact (often called the 'presumed fact') exists. The 'must' or 'may' in the last sentence gives the clue to the classification of presumptions into presumptions of law and presumptions of fact.

Presumptions of law

4.12 When the jury must find that the presumed fact exists, the presumption is a presumption of law. There are two kinds of presumption of law, rebuttable and irrebuttable (otherwise called 'conclusive').

4.13 When a presumption of law is irrebuttable, no evidence can be received to contradict the presumed fact. An example of an irrebuttable presumption of law is provided by the rule[27] that a child under 10 is incapable of committing an offence. Here the presumption operates to prevent criminal liability. Sometimes an irrebuttable presumption can operate against a defendant; examples are certain conclusive presumptions which can arise about absence of consent and lack of reasonable belief in consent for the purposes of rape and certain other sexual offences, in the situations specified by the Sexual Offences Act 2003, s 76.[28] Irrebuttable presumptions of law are rules of substantive law, rather than of evidence.

4.14 Where there is a rebuttable presumption of law, the jury must find that the presumed fact exists unless sufficient evidence to the contrary is adduced. The amount of evidence required in rebuttal varies, since a rebuttable presumption of law may be of a 'persuasive' or 'evidential' type. Where it is of the persuasive type, it can only be rebutted by disproving the presumed fact to the appropriate standard of proof. On the other hand, where it is of the evidential type, it can be rebutted by the introduction of evidence sufficient to raise a doubt about the presumed fact, in which case the fact will be decided according to the applicable rules relating to the burden and standard of proof.

An example of a persuasive rebuttable presumption of law is provided by the Criminal Justice and Public Order Act 1994, s 51. Section 51(1), as amended, provides:

> 'A person commits an offence if –
>
> (a) he does an act which intimidates, and is intended to intimidate, another person (the "victim");

---

[27] Para 15.1.   [28] Para 9.33.

(b) he does the act knowing or believing that the victim is assisting in the investigation of an offence or is a witness or potential witness or a juror or potential juror in
proceedings for an offence; and

(c) he does it intending thereby to cause the investigation or the course of justice to be
obstructed, perverted or interfered with.'

Section 51(7) provides that, if s 51(1)(a) and (b) are proved by the prosecution, a defendant
is to be presumed to have acted with the intention required by s 51(1)(c), unless the contrary is proved. Section 51(7) of the 1994 Act has been held not to be incompatible with
Article 6(2) in placing the persuasive burden on the defendant.[29]

An example of an evidential rebuttable presumption of law is provided by the rebuttable presumption of the absence of consent and of reasonable belief in consent for the
purposes of rape and certain other sexual offences, in the situations specified by the
Sexual Offences Act 2003, s 75.[30]

Presumptions of fact

4.15 When the jury may find that the presumed fact exists on proof of some other fact,
the presumption is one of fact. Presumptions (or inferences) of fact play a very important part in the administration of the criminal law, because they are frequently the only
means by which the state of the defendant's mind can be proved, as will be seen.

Proof of a state of mind

Key points 4.3

Proof of the defendant's state of mind at the material time is aided by reference to various
factors. Among them is the fact that, in the absence of a credible explanation, it may be
inferred that the defendant intended or foresaw the likely consequences of his conduct
but a court or jury is never legally bound to make such an inference.

4.16 The extent to which it is possible to prove the past state of the defendant's mind is
apt to trouble the student. Regard must be had to the statements of the defendant at the
time, or at a later date, or in the course of his testimony. If the statements out of court
amount to admissions, great weight is attached to them on the assumption that what

---

[29] *A-G's Reference (No 1 of 2004); Edwards; Denton; Jackson; Hendley; Crowley* [2004] EWCA Crim 1025.
[30] Paras 9.31 and 9.32.

people say adverse to their case is probably true. The presence or absence of motive is another important consideration.

4.17 Regard must also be had to the conduct and circumstances of the defendant. Proof of the mere doing by him of the prohibited act can justify an inference that he did it voluntarily, with knowledge of the surrounding circumstances, and, where relevant, with intent or foresight as to its normal consequences, although it must never be forgotten that this is only an inference, and the jury may well conclude that it is not warranted on the particular facts of the case. As Lord Brightman said in *Westminster City Council v Croyalgrange Ltd*:[31]

> 'But although…knowledge is an ingredient of [this] offence, and although the onus of establishing all the ingredients of the offence must lie on the prosecution, this does not impose on the prosecution an undue burden; if (1) all the other ingredients of the offence are proven, (2) the defendant chooses not to give evidence of his absence of knowledge and (3) there are no circumstances which sufficiently suggest absence of knowledge, the court may properly infer without direct evidence that the defendant did indeed possess the requisite knowledge.'

This is a matter of common sense, because people generally are aware of the circumstances in which they act, and they generally do foresee that what does result from their conduct will result from it. If a credible explanation is offered, the jury must consider the evidence as a whole and, if they entertain any reasonable doubt, the general rule that the prosecution has the burden of proof obliges them to give the defendant the benefit of that doubt. If the defendant does not offer a credible explanation the inference will usually be drawn. This point is implicit in the following statement by Lord Steyn in *B v DPP*,[32] where the House of Lords held that an offence contrary to the subsequently repealed[33] Indecency with Children Act 1960 required proof that the defendant did not believe the child was 14 or over (which was then the age limit for the offence). Lord Steyn said:

> '…recklessness or indifference as to the existence of the prohibited circumstance would be sufficient for guilt. And in practice the Crown would only have to shoulder the burden of proving that the defendant was aware of the age of the victim if there was some evidential material before the jury or magistrates suggesting the possibility of an honest belief that the child was over 14.'

4.18 Certain acts are known to be likely to produce particular consequences frequently spoken of as the 'natural and probable' consequences of those acts. This fact, coupled with the fact that people usually do foresee the normal consequences of their conduct, has led people to talk of a presumption (or inference) that everyone intends or foresees the natural and probable consequences of his conscious acts. Such talk is harmless provided

---

[31] [1986] 2 All ER 353 at 359. A similar statement was made by Lord Bridge ibid, at 358.
[32] [2000] 2 AC 428 at 477.   [33] By the Sexual Offences Act 2003.

it is always remembered that the presumption is one of fact. If this point is forgotten, it is fatally easy to suggest that, once a particular act is proved against him, the defendant must as a matter of law adduce evidence to disprove that he intended or foresaw the natural and probable consequences of that act; it may even come to be suggested that the defendant bears the burden of disproving such an intention or foresight.

That the presumption is one of fact is made clear by the Criminal Justice Act 1967, s 8, which states:

> 'A court or jury in determining whether a person has committed an offence (a) shall not be bound in law to infer that he intended or foresaw a result of his actions by reason only of its being a natural and probable consequence of those actions, but (b) shall decide whether he did intend or foresee that result by reference to all the evidence, drawing such inferences from the evidence as appear proper in the circumstances.'

It must be borne in mind constantly that this provision is not concerned with when intention or foresight is required for criminal liability but with how it is proved if required.[34]

Thus, although foresight of the consequences of an act does not necessarily imply the existence of intention, it may be a factor from which, when considered together with all the other evidence, the jury may infer that the defendant had the alleged intention.[35] The probability of the result is another factor, and an important one, for the jury to consider when deciding whether the result was intended.[36] As a matter of evidence, the greater the probability of a consequence, the more likely it is that the consequence was foreseen and, if that consequence was foreseen, the more likely it is that the consequence was also intended.[37] A similar point can be made about proof of recklessness as to the consequences of an act.

FURTHER READING

Munday *Evidence* (2009) Ch 2

---

[34] See, for example, the speeches of Lords Diplock, Dilhorne and Edmund-Davies in *Lemon* [1979] AC 617 at 637, 642 and 656.

[35] *Hancock and Shankland* [1986] AC 455, HL.

[36] *Hancock and Shankland* [1986] AC 455, HL.

[37] *Hancock and Shankland* [1986] AC 455, HL.

5

Mistake and related matters

OVERVIEW

This chapter deals with the situation where there is evidence that the defendant lacks the *mens rea* for an offence because of accident, ignorance or mistake.

The chapter concludes by dealing with the law which applies where the defendant makes a mistake which does not prevent the defendant having the *mens rea* for an offence but leads to the defendant mistakenly believing that circumstances exist which would provide an excuse.

5.1 In this chapter, it must be remembered that the jury's role is undertaken by the magistrates in a summary trial, as well as that of the judge.

This chapter is concerned with cases in which there is no doubt that the conduct of the defendant satisfied the requirements of the *actus reus* of an offence. The question at issue in the first part of the chapter is whether the prosecution can prove that he had the necessary *mens rea*. As seen, the normal inference from the defendant's conduct and its surrounding circumstances is that he had the necessary state of mind as to any circumstances or consequences prescribed for the *actus reus*. The jury are very likely to make that inference unless there is evidence that the defendant lacked that state of mind. Amongst such evidence is evidence of accident, ignorance or mistake. Unless there is evidence from whatever source such that there is room for the possibility of accident, ignorance or mistake, the judge does not have to direct the jury on the legal effect of an accident, ignorance or a mistake and the prosecution does not have to prove that the defendant did not act by accident, in ignorance or under a mistake.[1]

For convenience, the situation where the defendant had the necessary *mens rea* but mistakenly believed that he was acting in circumstances which would provide him with an excuse will also be discussed.

Accident

5.2 'Accident' is a word which has several shades of meaning but, when we speak of a *consequence* as accidental in a case where the conscious conduct of the defendant constitutes

---

[1] See, for example, *Adkins* [2000] 2 All ER 185, CA.

the *actus reus* of the crime charged, the allegation always is that the defendant did not intend to produce the prohibited consequence. A person does not intend an accidental consequence of his conduct.

The typical instance is one in which someone, who was conscious of, and in control of, his bodily movements and aware of all relevant circumstances, did not foresee that his conduct would have the prohibited consequence. The defendant aims a bullet at a bull's-eye target, but owing to the presence of a high wind or the fact that he is a poor shot he hits a house pigeon. In either event, he is said to have killed the bird accidentally.[2]

When the prohibited consequence occurs in a way which would be described as accidental because it was unintended, a defendant can be convicted of an offence in which liability may be based on recklessness or negligence if he has been reckless or negligent as to the risk of that consequence; an accident caused by reckless or negligent conduct cannot constitute a defence to a charge of such an offence.

Ignorance

5.3 The defendant's ignorance of something prevents him being criminally liable if it results in the defendant lacking the intention, recklessness, knowledge or other subjective mental element which is expressly or impliedly required by the definition of the offence charged. It is most exceptional for ignorance of law to have this effect, as opposed simply to causing the defendant to be unaware that what he is doing is criminal.[3]

Lack of intention, recklessness or knowledge etc caused by simple ignorance (ie where the defendant's mind is a complete blank as to a particular matter) is comparatively rare, because lack of a subjective mental element is normally connected with a mistake, in that the defendant has thought about the possible existence of the matter but wrongly concluded that it does not exist.

Mistake

Key points 5.1

Mistakes of two types are relevant to the criminal liability of a defendant:

- a mistake which prevents the defendant having the *mens rea* for an offence (mistake negativing *mens rea*) prevents him being liable for it. Except where the *mens rea* consists of negligence the mistake need not be reasonable; and

- a mistake which relates to an excuse can absolve the defendant, but in the case of most excuses the mistake must be reasonable.

---

[2] *Horton v Gwynne* [1921] 2 KB 661, DC.   [3] See paras 3.73–3.75 and 3.81–3.83.

5.4 Where there is evidence that a defendant acted under a mistake it is of vital importance to classify the matter to which the mistake relates. In particular, it is vital to determine whether the alleged mistake negatives the *mens rea* required for the offence charged or whether (although it does not have that effect) it relates to facts which, if true, would have given rise to an excuse (ie a defence which excuses a defendant from liability for conduct which is otherwise criminal).

If the alleged mistake has neither effect, it is immaterial and cannot affect the defendant's liability.[4] For example, as said in para 3.50, if D handles a diamond ring, knowing that it is stolen, it would be irrelevant that he believed the ring only contained imitation stones. Likewise, if D shoots at (and kills) someone, intending unlawfully to kill him but mistakenly believing it is X whereas it is in fact V, he can be convicted of murder. In both cases, D's mistake is immaterial because it does not prevent him having the *mens rea* for the offence and it does not relate to a matter of excuse. A mistake of law will rarely have either effect, because usually its sole effect is to cause the defendant to be unaware that he is committing an offence.[5]

The effect of the above rules is that where an offence is one of strict liability as to an element of its *actus reus*, ie no *mens rea* is required as to that element, a mistaken belief, however reasonable, in respect of that element is immaterial and cannot excuse.

Mistake negativing *mens rea*

Mistakes negativing *mens rea* (other than negligence)

5.5 A defendant cannot be convicted of an offence if, because of a mistake, he lacked the intention, recklessness, knowledge, absence of belief or similar state of mind which the prosecution is required to prove. The law does not require the mistake to be reasonable.

When there is evidence that the defendant acted under a mistaken belief of the present type, the mistake must be left to the jury and the jury must acquit the defendant unless the prosecution prove beyond reasonable doubt that the defendant was not mistaken in the alleged way and that he had the state of mind required for the offence.[6]

5.6 The rule that a mistake negativing a state of mind which the prosecution must prove need not be reasonable was clearly implied in relation to mistakes negativing intention or recklessness as to consequences by the Criminal Justice Act 1967, s 8,[7] and it was affirmed

---

[4] Subject to the very limited rule in *Tolson*; paras 5.12–5.13.

[5] See paras 3.73–3.75 and 3.81–3.83.

[6] See, for example, *Westminster City Council v Croyalgrange Ltd* [1986] 2 All ER 353, HL; *B v DPP* [2000] 2 AC 428, HL.

[7] See para 4.18.

in relation to mistakes negativing the requisite state of mind, whatever its description, by the majority of the House of Lords in *DPP v Morgan*.[8]

In *Morgan*, which was concerned with the common law offence of rape, the majority held that, since he would lack the *mens rea* which had to be proved by the prosecution, a defendant could not be convicted if he believed (albeit unreasonably) that the woman was consenting. As Lord Hailsham said:

'Once one has accepted...that the prohibited act in rape is non-consensual sexual intercourse, and that the guilty state of mind is an intention to commit it, it seems to me to follow as a matter of inexorable logic that there is no room either for a "defence" of honest[9] belief or mistake, or of a defence of honest and reasonable belief or mistake. Either the prosecution proves that the accused had the requisite intention, or it does not. In the former case it succeeds, and in the latter it fails.'[10]

5.7 In some subsequent cases, there were obiter dicta to the effect that the decision in *DPP v Morgan* was confined (and intended to be confined) to the common law offence of rape,[11] but this view was not accepted by the Court of Appeal in *Kimber*[12] nor in *Gladstone Williams*;[13] in these cases the principle endorsed in *Morgan* was applied to two different offences of assault.

In *Kimber*, which was concerned with the statutory offence (since repealed)[14] of indecent assault on a woman, D had alleged that the woman had consented to his actions. The Court of Appeal held that, since the *mens rea* required for the offence of indecent assault on a woman was intentionally causing the woman to apprehend immediate, or to sustain, unlawful personal violence, and since violence would not be unlawful if the woman had consented to it, a defendant was entitled to be acquitted if because of his mistaken belief in consent he did not intend to lay hands on the woman without her consent, whether or not his mistake was reasonable.

Gladstone Williams was concerned with the statutory offence of assault occasioning actual bodily harm. V saw a youth seizing a woman's handbag. V chased and caught the youth and knocked him to the ground. D, who had only seen the later stages of the incident, was told by V that he was arresting the youth for mugging and that he was a policeman (which he was not). D asked V for his warrant card. When V could not produce it, a struggle ensued, during which D punched V and injured V's face. V was entitled

---

8 [1976] AC 182, HL. See also *Smith (David)* [1974] QB 354, CA.

9 The word 'honest' may be useful emphasis but in fact adds nothing: *Albert v Lavin* [1981] 1 All ER 628 at 633, per Hodgson J.

10 [1976] AC 182 at 214. The *mens rea* for the offence of rape, contrary to the Sexual Offences Act 2003, s 1, is different from that for the common law offence of rape (which has been abolished) and a mistaken belief in consent must now be reasonable to excuse someone charged with rape: see paras 9.9 and 9.24 (and 5.11).

11 *Phekoo* [1981] 3 All ER 84, CA; *Barrett and Barrett* (1980) 72 Cr App Rep 212, CA.

12 [1983] 3 All ER 316, CA. Also see *Jones* (1986) 83 Cr App Rep 375, CA, and *Blackburn v Bowering* [1994] 3 All ER 380, CA.

13 (1984) 78 Cr App Rep 276, CA.   14 By the Sexual Offences Act 2003.

to arrest the youth and therefore his use of reasonable force against the youth was lawful. Although it is lawful to use reasonable force in self-defence or the prevention of crime, a person is not entitled to use force against someone using lawful force and therefore D's use of force was unlawful. At his trial for assault occasioning actual bodily harm, D said that he had acted under the honest but mistaken belief that V was unlawfully attacking the youth and that he must use force against V in order to protect the youth. The trial judge directed the jury that D could have an excuse if he had a belief based on reasonable grounds that V was acting unlawfully. The Court of Appeal held that that direction was wrong. It said that a person who mistakenly believed that he had to act in self-defence or in the prevention of crime had to be judged on the facts as he believed them to be, reasonably or not. Consequently, if, on the facts as he mistakenly believed them to be, reasonably or not, he was entitled to use reasonable force in self-defence or the prevention of crime, he would lack the necessary *mens rea* for the offence charged. The reason was that that *mens rea* was not simply an intent to apply force to another; instead, it was an intention to apply unlawful force to another[15] (and, on the facts as D understood them, the force which he intended to apply would not be unlawful).

The statement of law in *Gladstone Williams* may have been an obiter dictum, since the conviction had to be quashed because of a misdirection concerning the onus of proof, but it has been applied or referred to with approval in a number of cases.[16] In particular, it was followed by the Privy Council in *Beckford v R*,[17] where it was held that an essential element of the offence of murder was that the violence used by the defendant was unlawful and that a mistaken belief (albeit unreasonable) in facts which – if true – would justify self-defence would negative the *mens rea* for murder (provided that the force was reasonable on the facts believed to exist) because it would negative the requisite intent *unlawfully* to kill or cause grievous bodily harm.

Subsequently, the House of Lords in *B v DPP*[18] and in *K*[19] endorsed the principle in *Morgan* and the subsequent cases as a general principle.

5.8 It follows from the general application of the principle in *DPP v Morgan* and subsequent cases that, for example, on a charge of murder by shooting, the defendant's evidence that he believed the gun with which he shot the deceased to be unloaded must be left to the jury, however weak that evidence may be, and that the jury must be directed to acquit the defendant of murder if they are not sure that he knew it was loaded, even if they think that his alleged belief was grossly unreasonable, since the prosecution will have failed to prove that he had the *mens rea* for murder. (The defendant could, however, be convicted of involuntary manslaughter by gross negligence, even though his alleged

---

[15] This formulation sufficed for the purposes of the Court of Appeal's decision. See further paras 7.53 and 7.62.

[16] *Jackson* [1985] RTR 257, CA; *Fisher* [1987] Crim LR 334, CA; *Asbury* [1986] Crim LR 258, CA; *Owino* [1996] 2 Cr App Rep 128, CA; para 16.14.

[17] [1988] AC 130, PC. See also *Blackburn v Bowering* [1994] 3 All ER 380; *Faraj* [2007] EWCA Crim 1033.

[18] [2000] 2 AC 428, HL (para 6.16).

[19] [2001] UKHL 41 (para 6.16).

mistake is not disproved, if the prosecution satisfied the jury beyond reasonable doubt that he was grossly negligent in acting as he did.[20])

5.9 The fact that in the present context the defendant's mistaken belief is not required as a matter of law to be a reasonable one does not mean that the reasonableness of a mistake is entirely irrelevant. As was recognised in *DPP v Morgan*, in *Gladstone Williams*, in *Beckford v R* and in *K*, the reasonableness of the defendant's alleged mistake is of considerable evidential significance, because the more reasonable the mistake the more likely it is that the jury (or magistrates) will accept his story that he was acting under a mistake.

5.10 Special rules apply where the defendant's mistake was attended by intoxication; they are discussed in Chapter 15.

Mistakes in offences where negligence suffices

5.11 Where, because of a mistake, the defendant does not realise a risk in relation to which proof of negligence suffices, his mistake must have been a reasonable one in order to negative negligence. The reason is that a person who acts under a mistaken belief which is not based on reasonable grounds is necessarily negligent, because a reasonable person would not, by definition, have made the mistake and would have realised the risk. For example, even if he has thought about the matter but wrongly concluded that his customer is sober, a person can be convicted of the statutory offence of selling a firearm to a person whom he knows or has reasonable cause to believe to be drunk[21] unless his mistaken belief was based on reasonable grounds.

The *Tolson* rule

5.12 Mention must be made of a special rule, which is now only applicable to bigamy.

The leading authority for this special rule is *Tolson*.[22] D married for a second time within seven years of the disappearance of her first husband from whom she had not been divorced. She was charged with bigamy, contrary to the Offences Against the Person Act 1861, s 57, which is committed by a person who 'being married, shall marry any other person during the life of the former [sic] husband or wife'. Section 57 does not specify any requirement of intention, recklessness or knowledge but subsequent to *Tolson* it has been held that it requires an intent simply to go through the second ceremony.[23] D was found by the jury to have believed on reasonable grounds and in good faith that her first husband was dead, and her conviction was quashed by a majority decision of the Court for Crown Cases Reserved on the ground that a reasonable belief in such a fact would excuse a defendant. In accordance with *Tolson*, it has subsequently been held that a mistaken

---

[20] *Lamb* [1967] 2 QB 981, CA. As to gross negligence, see paras 8.125–8.128.
[21] Para 3.56.   [22] (1899) 23 QBD 168, CCR.
[23] *DPP v Morgan* [1976] AC 182 at 238, per Lord Fraser.

belief on the part of someone charged with bigamy that his first marriage was void or had been dissolved (and therefore that he was not married) is an excuse provided that the mistake was reasonable.[24] This means that negligence suffices as to the element of 'being married' in bigamy. *Tolson* was distinguished by the majority of the House of Lords in *DPP v Morgan* on the ground that the mistake in question did not relate to the issue of whether Mrs Tolson had the necessary *mens rea* required for bigamy.

5.13 In *Sweet v Parsley*,[25] Lord Diplock stated that *Tolson* laid down:

> '…as a general principle of construction of any enactment, which creates a criminal offence, that, even where the words used to describe the prohibited conduct [ie the *actus reus*] would not in any other context connote the necessity for any particular mental element, they are nevertheless to be read as subject to the implication that a necessary element in the offence is the absence of a belief, held honestly and *upon reasonable grounds*, in the existence of facts which, if true, would make the act innocent.'

On this view, the rule in *Tolson* was potentially of widespread application: it would have applied to any offence whose definition did not contain a word connoting the need for *mens rea* as to an element of its *actus reus*, and which was not interpreted as being one of strict liability.

Lord Diplock's statement became increasingly doubtful after the decision in *DPP v Morgan* and its endorsement as a general principle by a succession of cases. Ultimately, in *B v DPP*,[26] the House of Lords held that Lord Diplock's dictum should be read in future as though the reference to reasonable grounds was omitted.

As a result, it is no longer permissible to interpret an offence of the type referred to by Lord Diplock according to the *Tolson* rule. It appears that *Tolson* has not been applied in a reported decision after the decision in *DPP v Morgan* became generalised. Although not yet overruled, the application of the *Tolson* rule to bigamy must now be open to doubt. In the light of the modern emphasis on subjectivism in the criminal law in *B v DPP* and *K*[27] and *G* (2003),[28] it is unlikely that the application of the *Tolson* rule in bigamy would survive reconsideration.

Mistake relating to an excuse

Excuses framed in terms of defendant's own belief

5.14 In a small number of excuses contained in the definition of statutory offences, particularly modern ones, statute makes it clear that the excuse is determined by reference to the defendant's own belief in a situation. For example, under the Criminal Damage Act

---

[24] *King* [1964] 1 QB 285, CCA; *Gould* [1968] 2 QB 65, CA.   [25] [1970] AC 132 at 163.
[26] [2000] 2 AC 428, HL.   [27] [2001] UKHL 41.   [28] [2003] UKHL 50.

1971, s 1(1) it is an offence intentionally or recklessly to destroy or damage another's property 'without lawful excuse'. The Criminal Damage Act 1971, s 5 provides, inter alia, that a person is to be treated as having a lawful excuse if, at the material time, he believed that the person whom he believed to be entitled to consent to the destruction or damage had so consented to it or would have so consented if he had known of the destruction or damage and its circumstances.[29] Where there is this type of excuse **it is no bar to the excuse succeeding that the belief was based on unreasonable grounds**.[30]

Other excuses

5.15 Other excuses are framed in terms of the defendant's reasonable belief (or reasonable suspicion) in a factual situation. The excuse in the Misuse of Drugs Act 1971, s 28 referred to in para 6.47 is an example. In such cases, a mere mistaken belief is obviously insufficient; the belief must be reasonable.

5.16 For the reason given below the same appears to be true in the case of a specific statutory excuse framed in terms simply of a factual situation which operates to absolve a defendant, with no reference to the defendant's state of mind as to it, unless it has been held that not even a reasonable mistake as to the excuse can absolve.

5.17 The law has become increasingly complex in relation to general defences. In *DPP v Morgan*,[31] the House of Lords was concerned with mistakes negativing the *mens rea* required as to an element of the *actus reus*. The House of Lords did not overrule the pre-existing traditional rule that a mistake as to a matter of excuse (ie a mistaken belief in facts which if true would bring the case within an excuse) had to be reasonable; in fact, in their speeches their Lordships accepted the requirement of reasonableness in relation to mistaken belief in facts which, if true, would constitute an excuse.

5.18 The traditional rule does not offend the 'inexorable logic' to which Lord Hailsham referred in *DPP v Morgan*[32] because the type of mistake covered by it does not prevent the defendant having the *mens rea* for the offence charged. However, it cannot be denied that fine distinctions can be involved in classifying that to which an alleged mistake relates. For example, at the time that *Morgan* was decided, self-defence and the other 'defences' which justify (render lawful) conduct, were not regarded as part of the *actus reus* of an offence against the person as to which the defendant had to have *mens rea*. *Morgan* did not disturb the rule that, for example, in cases of self-defence any mistake about the circumstances had to be reasonable.[33] In *Albert v Lavin*,[34] decided six years after *Morgan*

---

[29] For another example, see para 10.118.

[30] The Criminal Damage Act 1971, s 5(3) confirms this; see para 13.9, n 36.

[31] [1976] AC 182, HL.

[32] See para 5.6.

[33] See, for example, *Rose* (1884) 15 Cox CC 540; *Chisam* (1963) 47 Cr App Rep 130, CCA.

[34] [1981] 1 All ER 628, DC. On appeal to the House of Lords [1982] AC 546, the House did not find it necessary to discuss the present issue.

the Divisional Court proceeded on the basis that the requisite *mens rea* for an assault was an intention to apply force to another without his consent and held that a defendant who, with such a state of mind, had hit someone mistakenly believing that he was acting in self-defence could be convicted of an offence involving an assault, unless his mistaken belief was reasonable. The Court's reason was that the mistake related to a matter of defence (and therefore had to be reasonable), as opposed to a 'definitional element' (ie part of the *actus reus*) of the offence in relation to which the defendant had to have subjective *mens rea*. On the other hand, the law is now different as a result of *Gladstone Williams*,[35] where the decision in *Albert v Lavin* was disapproved, simply because the element of unlawfulness was classified in *Gladstone Williams* as a definitional element of the offence in relation to which a defendant must have the required state of mind. Once the Court of Appeal in *Gladstone Williams* had held that the *mens rea* for an assault was an intention to apply *unlawful* force, it would have been inconsistent (and contrary to *Morgan*) for it to have required a mistaken belief that one was acting in self-defence or the like to be reasonable, since such a mistake would negative the state of mind required.[36] This brings us back to the point made earlier about the importance of classifying that to which an alleged mistake relates.

5.19 In *Graham*,[37] decided seven years after *DPP v Morgan*, the Court of Appeal held that for the excuse of duress by threats to succeed the defendant's belief that he was being subjected to duress must have been reasonable. Subsequently, the House of Lords in *Howe*[38] and *Hasan*[39] and the Court of Appeal in a number of cases[40] defined the excuses of duress by threats and duress of circumstances in terms which endorse the approach in *Graham*. In principle, as affirmed in *Morgan*, the same approach applies to mistakes relating to other excuses where the mistake does not prevent the defendant having the *mens rea* for the offence in question.

Basis of requirement of reasonable mistake

5.20 The rule that a mistake as to a matter of excuse must be reasonable in order to excuse seems to be based on judicial policy. Its effect is to convict a person on the grounds of his negligence.[41] So far the courts have not given any adequate explanation as to why the rule is as it is. In particular they have not explained why a person who unreasonably believes that circumstances exist which would excuse him is any more deserving of criminal liability than one whose mistake is reasonable, when a similar distinction is not drawn in relation to mistakes negativing the intent, recklessness, knowledge or

---

[35] (1984) 78 Cr App Rep 276, CA. Also see *Beckford v R* [1988] AC 130, PC.
[36] See, further, para 16.14.
[37] [1982] 1 All ER 801, CA.
[38] [1987] AC 417, HL.
[39] [2005] UKHL 22.
[40] Eg *Conway* [1989] QB 290, CA; *Martin (Colin)* [1989] 1 All ER 652, CA.
[41] Paras 3.51–3.64.

similar state of mind which the prosecution must prove in order to prove the *mens rea* of an offence.

Anomalous results

5.21 The different approach to material mistakes negativing intent, recklessness, knowledge and similar states of mind which the prosecution must prove and the present type of mistake can give rise to anomalous results. Suppose that D, unreasonably mistakenly believing that he is being threatened with serious harm by X unless he commits an offence, commits that offence; D cannot succeed with a plea of duress by threats because, as stated above, an excuse of duress operates on the basis of the facts as D reasonably believed them to be; its requirements are not applied on the basis of facts as they are unreasonably mistakenly believed to be.[42] Suppose, instead, that D, acting under the same unreasonable mistake, hits X, D can succeed in a plea of self-defence because that defence is applied on the basis of the facts as D thought they were regardless of whether he made an unreasonable mistake.[43] There is force in the argument that making the law of mistake depend on whether or not the mistake relates to an element of the *actus reus* or to an excuse places legalism above substantive moral assessment. The distinction between types of mistake would not survive if ever the draft Criminal Code Bill was enacted.[44] Clause 41 provides that someone who acts in the belief that a circumstance exists has any excuse which he would have if it did exist; a reasonable belief is not required.

Prospects of the traditional rule

5.22 There have been indications that the traditional requirement that a mistaken belief in a matter of excuse must be reasonable is unlikely to survive much longer. Arguments of the type just made are highly persuasive. Moreover, the courts have already whittled down the rule's application. Mention has already been made of the change relating to mistaken belief in consent, self-defence and so on[45] (the change in the definition of the relevant *mens rea* was doubtless driven by a wish to escape the requirement of reasonableness of the mistake) and of the increasing judicial preference for a subjective basis of liability.[46] In addition, in *Letenock*[47] and *Wardrope*,[48] it was stated in relation to the defence of provocation, abolished by the Coroners and Justice Act 2009, s 56(1), that if someone charged with murder mistakenly believed in his drunken condition that he was being provoked he was to be judged on the facts as he mistakenly believed them to be. Clearly, a drunken mistake cannot be said to be a reasonable one.

---

[42] See, further, paras 16.43 and 16.73.

[43] See Elliott 'Necessity, Duress and Self-defence' [1989] Crim LR 611.

[44] Para 1.72.

[45] Para 5.18. The situation is the same in respect of a claim of mistaken belief in self-defence in an offence whose *mens rea* does not refer to an element of lawfulness: paras 16.14–16.18.

[46] Para 3.3.

[47] (1917) 12 Cr App Rep 221, CCA.

[48] [1960] Crim LR 770.

5.23 Even in the context of the two excuses of duress there were clear signs that the judges favoured dispensing with the requirement that a mistake be reasonable. In two more recent cases than *Howe* on the point the appellate courts held that these defences were to be judged on the facts as the defendant believed them to be, whether reasonably or not. In *DPP v Rogers*[49] the Divisional Court stated this in relation to duress of circumstances, although it based this statement on a false assumption that the existing law was accurately defined by a proposal, framed in terms of the defendant's belief, in a Law Commission report. In *Martin (David Paul)*,[50] the Court of Appeal held that the defence of duress by threats was to be judged on the facts as the defendant believed them to be, reasonably or not, but this was based on a misunderstanding of the previous case law. Despite these flaws, the readiness of the appeal courts in *DPP v Rogers* and *Martin (David Paul)* to embrace a subjective approach to the issue of mistake as to duress suggested that when the question next arose in the House of Lords the House would depart from the approach laid down in *Howe*. Such a suggestion was, however, dismissed by the House of Lords in *Hasan*,[51] where the trial judge had directed the jury along the lines adopted in *DPP v Rogers* and *Martin (David Paul)*. The House of Lords held that this was incorrect. Lord Bingham giving the leading judgment, whose reasoning was approved by Lords Steyn, Rodger and Brown, said this about the judge's direction that the question was what the defendant 'genuinely believed':

> 'But the words used in *Graham* and approved in *Howe* were "he reasonably believed". It is, of course, essential that the defendant should genuinely, ie actually, believe in the efficacy of the threat by which he claims to have been compelled. But there is no warrant for relaxing the requirement that the belief must be reasonable as well as genuine'.[52]

5.24 The law relating to the effect of an alleged mistake on criminal liability can be summarised as follows in the table below.

Type of mistake	Effect of mistake	
	General rule	Exception
Mistake negativing *mens rea*	Defendant *not guilty, even* if mistake is unreasonable	Where *mens rea* in question is *negligence*, defendant *not guilty only* if mistake is *reasonable*
Mistake not negativing *mens rea* but relating to an excuse	Defendant *not guilty only* if mistake is *reasonable*	If defence is framed in terms of defendant's own belief, *defendant is not guilty, even if* mistake is *unreasonable*
Mistake of some other type, eg relating to an element of an *actus reus* as to which *mens rea* is not required	Mistake is immaterial *and cannot excuse the defendant*	

[49] [1998] Crim LR 202, DC.   [50] [2000] 2 Cr App Rep 42, CA.
[51] [2005] UKHL 22.   [52] [2005] UKHL 22, at [23].

FURTHER READING

Horder 'Cognition, Emotion and Criminal Culpability' (1990) 106 LQR 469

Simester 'Mistakes in Defence' (1992) 12 OJLS 295

Tur 'Subjectivism and Objectivism: Towards Synthesis' in *Action and Value in Criminal Law* (1993) (Shute, Gardner and Horder (eds)) 213

6

Strict liability

OVERVIEW

This chapter deals principally with:

- the meaning of strict liability;
- the distinction between strict liability and absolute liability;
- strict liability and the presumption of innocence under ECHR, Article 6(2);
- offences of strict liability at common law;
- statutory offences of strict liability, and how it is determined whether a statutory offence is one of strict liability;
- the justification for strict liability; and
- the reduction of the operation of strict liability in the criminal law.

The meaning of strict liability

> **Key points 6.1**
>
> An offence is one of strict liability if *mens rea* is not required in respect of one or more elements of the *actus reus* of that offence.

6.1 It was stated in para 2.3 that, although the argument has been made that the state of mind with which a person acts should be irrelevant to his criminal liability (as opposed to whether and how he should be dealt with on conviction), this does not represent the law.

In many[1] offences, particularly regulatory ones, however, the defendant may be convicted even though his conduct was not intentional, knowing, reckless or negligent with reference to a requisite element of the offence charged. In such cases, a person is liable to

---

[1] In *JUSTICE, Breaking the Rules* (1980), a Committee of Justice reported that just over half of the then 7,200 offences in *Stone's Justices' Manual* were offences of strict liability. See also Ashworth and Blake 'The Presumption of Innocence in English Criminal Law' [1997] Crim LR 306.

punishment in the absence of any fault on his part in respect of the element(s) in question and is said to be under strict liability[2] (of which there are many critics).

6.2 Most cases of strict liability are ones in which it has been held that ignorance or mistake, however reasonable, in relation to a particular element of the *actus reus* of an offence is no excuse, since no *mens rea* is required as to that element, although it is required in relation to one or more other elements. This can be shown by reference to *Prince*[3] and *Hibbert*.[4] In *Prince*, the charge was one of taking an unmarried girl under the age of 16 out of the possession of her father against his will, contrary to the Offences Against the Person Act 1861, s 55 (an offence which no longer exists). Prince knew that the girl was in the custody of her father, but he believed, on reasonable grounds, that she was 18. Had this been so, the offence would not have been committed; but Prince was held by the Court for Crown Cases Reserved to have been rightly convicted since knowledge that the girl was under 16 was not required. The Court clearly took the view that knowledge that the girl was in the possession of her father was required to be proved, proof of which knowledge was not disputed. *Prince* is distinguishable on this ground from *Hibbert*, where Hibbert's conviction for an offence under the same section was quashed, because Hibbert did not know that the girl he abducted was in anybody's possession. The jury appear to have found that he did not know that she was in anybody's guardianship.

6.3 There have, however, also been isolated instances in which the courts have held that an offence does not require any *mens rea*. An example relates to the offence of driving with excess alcohol, contrary to the Road Traffic Act 1988, s 5, which was stated in *DPP v H*[5] not to require proof of any *mens rea*. Another example is provided by *Bezzina*,[6] dealt with in para 6.42.

6.4 Quite inexplicably, the Court of Appeal in *Sandhu*[7] held that strict liability as to an element or elements of an *actus reus* does not simply mean that proof of *mens rea* in that respect is not required but that the prosecution must not prove it or seek to prove it. It quashed D's conviction for the strict liability offence of causing unauthorised alterations to a listed building on grounds that the evidence in respect of *mens rea* was inadmissible and prejudicial to the interests of the defendant. The result is that, where the prosecution has evidence of *mens rea* as to a strict liability element of the *actus reus*, it should not

---

[2] *Lemon* [1979] AC 617 at 656, per Lord Edmund-Davies (contrast at 639–640, 657, and 662, per Viscount Dilhorne, Lord Russell and Lord Scarman); *K* [2002] 1 AC 462 at [18], per Lord Bingham. Oddly, offences involving dangerous driving were described as strict liability offences in *Loukes* [1996] 1 Cr App Rep 444, CA; *Roberts and George* [1997] RTR 462, CA, despite the fact that they require proof of negligence, on the ground that that fault element is part of the *actus reus* and not a separate element of *mens rea*. The court in both cases described such offences as 'absolute' (as to which term, see para 6.5), but it must have meant that they were ones of strict liability because some, if not all, of the general defences in the criminal law are open to a person charged with an offence involving dangerous driving.

[3] (1875) LR 2 CCR 154, CCR.   [4] (1869) LR 1 CCR 184, CCR.

[5] [1997] 1 WLR 1406, DC. See also *Harrison and Francis* [1996] 1 Cr App Rep 138, CA.

[6] [1994] 3 All ER 964, CA.   [7] [1997] Crim LR 288, CA.

adduce it. This seems an artificial and unnecessary limitation, especially as evidence of fault will be relevant at the sentencing stage.

Strict liability and absolute liability distinguished

Key points 6.2

'Strict liability' refers to liability despite the absence of any *mens rea* in relation to one or more elements of the *actus reus* of an offence. 'Absolute liability' refers to liability despite the absence of any *mens rea* in relation to the elements of the *actus reus* and without the availability of any defence other than that the defendant is under 10 (the age of criminal responsibility).

6.5 Strict liability is sometimes spoken of as 'absolute liability' and the corresponding expressions of 'absolute prohibition' and 'absolute offence' are occasionally used.[8] Such statements involve a confusion between strict liability and absolute liability, a concept which generally has no part in the criminal law. 'Absolute liability' refers to liability despite the absence of any *mens rea* in relation to the *actus reus* and without the availability of any defence such as duress by threats or circumstances, compulsion, automatism or insanity, other than the fact that the defendant is under 10 (in which case he is irrebuttably presumed incapable of crime). Absolute liability is a concept which offends any idea of justice. In an Australian case it has been criticised as a 'throwback to a highly primitive form of concept'.[9]

6.6 The nature of the judicial process means that it is difficult to be certain which offences, if any, are ones of absolute liability in the proper sense of the term. However, the wording of a small number of offences would seem to indicate that they are ones of absolute liability. Certainly, the wording of some so-called 'status offences' or 'situational offences', such as that in issue in *Larsonneur*,[10] may lead to such a conclusion.

In *Larsonneur*, D, an alien who had not got leave to land in the United Kingdom was deported from Ireland. She was brought to Holyhead in the custody of the Irish police, was handed over to the police there, and was 'found', still in custody, in a cell at Holyhead. She was convicted of an offence under orders made under the Aliens Restriction Acts, according to which it was an offence for an alien, to whom leave to land in the United

---

[8] For modern examples, see *Loukes* [1996] 1 Cr App Rep 444, CA; *Roberts and George* [1997] RTR 462, CA; para 6.1, n 2. Also see Lord Reid's statement in *Sweet v Parsley*, para 6.15.

[9] *Mayer v Marchant* (1973) 5 SASR 567 at 585, per Zelling J.

[10] (1933) 149 LT 542, CCA. For a defence of this decision on the basis that the case involved the prior fault of the defendant, since she was the author of her own misfortune, see Lanham 'Larsonneur Revisited' [1976] Crim LR 276. Prior fault was not relied on by the Court of Criminal Appeal as a ground of its decision. For another defence of *Larsonneur* see Doegar 'Strict Liability in Criminal Law and *Larsonneur* Reassessed' [1998] Crim LR 791, but see the persuasive response at [1999] Crim LR 100 by JC Smith. See also the response by Lanham at [1999] Crim LR 683.

Kingdom had been refused, to be found in any place within the United Kingdom.[11] D appealed unsuccessfully against conviction. Normally, someone is not guilty of an offence if the event is involuntary on his part, but the Court of Criminal Appeal took the view that D came precisely within the wording of the relevant order and that the circumstances of her entry and confinement were 'perfectly immaterial'. This decision has rightly been criticised as the 'acme of strict injustice'.[12] It is a matter of speculation whether Larsonneur might not equally have been held guilty if she had been brought to Holyhead unconscious and been 'found' in that state, or had been parachuted from an aeroplane against her will.

In *Winzar v Chief Constable of Kent*,[13] the Divisional Court evinced the same attitude as in *Larsonneur*. D was taken to hospital on a stretcher. The doctor discovered that D was drunk and D was told to leave. Later, D was seen slumped on a seat in a corridor. The police were called and they removed him to their car on the highway. D's conviction of the offence, under the Licensing Act 1872, s 12, of being found drunk in a highway was affirmed by the Divisional Court. Such cases are most exceptional, because very few offences are defined in the same way as those with which Larsonneur and Winzar were charged, ie in terms of 'being found'.

6.7 Apart from rare offences of the type just referred to in para 6.6, the general defences of the criminal law[14] are normally available to a person accused of an offence of strict liability.[15] It is very doubtful, to say the least, whether there are any offences, except those whose wording is similar to that of the offences in *Larsonneur* and in *Winzar v Chief Constable of Kent*, to which the general defences such as duress by threat or of circumstances, compulsion and non-insane automatism would not apply.[16]

It had been thought that it was very doubtful whether, apart from rare offences of the type just referred to, there were any offences to which the defence of insanity did not apply. However, in *DPP v H*[17] the Divisional Court held that the defence of insanity could only apply in a case where *mens rea* was in issue and therefore that it could not apply to a strict liability offence for which no *mens rea* was required. Thus, it held, the defence of insanity was not available on a charge of driving with excess alcohol, contrary to the Road Traffic Act 1988, s 5. For criticism of this decision, see para 15.35.

---

[11] This offence has since been repealed.

[12] Hall *General Principles of Criminal Law* (2nd edn, 1960) 329, n 14.

[13] (1983) Times, 28 March, DC.

[14] See Chs 15 and 16.

[15] For example, the general defences of involuntary conduct and of duress are available on a charge of committing a strict liability offence: *Leicester v Pearson* [1952] 2 QB 668, DC (para 15.54 (involuntary conduct)); *Eden District Council v Braid* [1999] RTR 329, DC (duress by threats); *Martin (Colin)* [1989] 1 All ER 652, CA (para 16.71 (duress of circumstances)).

[16] As to these defences, see Chs 15 and 16.

[17] [1997] 1 WLR 1406, DC.

Strict liability and the presumption of innocence

> **Key points 6.3**
>
> Strict liability does not infringe the presumption of innocence under ECHR, Article 6(2).

6.8 As explained in Chapter 4,[18] the presumption of innocence contained in ECHR, Article 6(2) may be contravened where the persuasive burden is imposed on the defendant to prove the absence of *mens rea*. On the other hand, Article 6(2) is not contravened where no *mens rea* is required as to all or some of the elements of an offence (ie strict liability).

The starting point is *Salabiaku v France*,[19] where the European Court of Human Rights stated that:

> '[I]n principle the Contracting States remain free to apply the criminal law to an act where it is not carried out in the normal exercise of one of the rights protected under the Convention and, accordingly, to define the constituent elements of the resulting offence. In particular, and *in principle* the Contracting States may, *under certain conditions*, pen-alise a simple or objective fact as such, irrespective of whether it results from criminal intent or from negligence'.[20]

The Court did not specify what those conditions are.

Salabiaku v France has been referred to on a number of occasions by English appellate courts. They have held that Article 6(2) is restricted to the fairness of the trial in pro-cedural terms and not with the fairness of the substantive law, with the result that strict liability does not infringe Article 6(2).

In *Barnfather v Islington Education Authority*,[21] for example, the Divisional Court held that the fact that an offence was one of strict liability was not incompatible with Article 6(2) because Article 6(2) provided a criterion against which only procedural (including evidential) matters could be tested and not the substantive requirements of an offence.[22]

More recently, *Salabiaku* was referred to in *G*,[23] where the House of Lords unani-mously held that construing the Sexual Offences Act 2003, s 5 (rape of a child under 13)[24] as an offence of strict liability did not infringe the right to a fair trial under Article 6(1) or the presumption of innocence under Article 6(2) because Article 6 was not concerned

---

[18] Para 4.8.   [19] (1988) 13 EHRR 379, ECtHR.

[20] (1988) 13 EHRR 379 at [27], ECtHR.

[21] [2003] EWHC 418 (Admin).

[22] In *Muhamad* [2002] EWCA Crim 1856, the Court of Appeal, having referred to *Salabiaku*, held that offences of strict liability were not in themselves objectionable under the ECHR.

[23] [2008] UKHL 37. See also *Deyemi and Edwards* [2007] EWCA Crim 2060, CA.

[24] Para 9.36.

with the substantive law but with the fairness of the procedure, and strict liability did not affect procedural fairness. Lord Hope explained the passage from *Salabiaku* quoted above as follows:

'It contains a clear affirmation of the principle that the contracting States are free to apply the criminal law to any act, so long as it is not one which is carried out in the exercise of one of the rights protected under the [ECHR]. Accordingly they are free to define the constituent elements of the offence that results from that act. So when the court said in the next sentence that the contracting States may "under certain conditions" penalise a simple or objective fact as such, irrespective of whether it results from criminal intent or negligence, it was reaffirming the same principle. As in the previous sentence, the certain conditions that are referred to indicate that objection could be taken if the offence was incompatible with other articles of the [ECHR]. But they have no wider significance... The substantive content of the criminal law does not raise issues of the kind to which [Article 6] is directed.'[25]

Offences of strict liability

Key points 6.4

There are very few common law offences of strict liability. For the most part it is in statutory offences that strict liability in criminal cases is imposed, normally as the result of the courts' interpretation of the particular statute.

Strict liability at common law

6.9 The list of these offences only includes the following.

- *Public nuisance* Although liability for committing the ancient offence of public nuisance depends on proof of negligence,[26] a person may be vicariously liable for such an offence committed on his property or on the highway by his employee, even if the latter was disobeying orders.[27] In such a case the employer is said to be strictly liable because he can be convicted even if he was reasonably unaware of the employee's conduct.

  A public nuisance is an act not warranted by law, or an omission to discharge a legal duty, whose effect is to endanger the life, health, property or comfort of the

---

[25] [2008] UKHL 37, at [28] and [29].
[26] *Shorrock* [1994] QB 279, CA: *Rimmington; Goldstein* [2005] UKHL 63.
[27] *Stephens* (1866) LR 1 QB 702, CCR.

public, or to obstruct the public in the exercise or enjoyment of rights common to all members of the public.[28] Typical examples are the obstruction of the highway or the emission of noise or smells from a factory in such a way as to cause serious inconvenience to the neighbourhood. Many instances of public nuisance now also constitute statutory offences with limited maximum sentences, and often with time limitations on prosecutions and defences unavailable on a charge of public nuisance. In 2005, the House of Lords held that, ordinarily, conduct falling within a statutory offence and under public nuisance should no longer be prosecuted as the common law offence of public nuisance.[29]

- *Outraging public decency* This offence requires proof of conduct of such a lewd, obscene or disgusting nature as to result in an outrage to public decency.[30] It does not have to be proved that the defendant intended his conduct to have the effect of outraging public decency or was reckless as to the risk of this effect (or, indeed, that he had any type of *mens rea* as to this).[31]

- *Criminal contempt of court* Subject to various limitations, liability for contempt in relation to publications which interfere with the course of justice in particular proceedings is strict.[32]

Strict liability in statutory offences

Key points 6.5

Strict liability in statutory offences normally results from the courts' refusal to read into a provision which does not contain a *mens rea* term in respect of an element of the *actus reus* a requirement that *mens rea* in relation to it is required.

6.10 Most of the statutory offences of strict liability are 'regulatory offences' which arise under the regulatory legislation controlling such matters as the sale of food and other types of trading activity, health and safety at work, pollution and other public welfare matters, which are usually investigated and prosecuted by a regulatory authority rather than the police and the Crown Prosecution Service.[33] Similarly, many of the offences in statutes regulating road traffic have also been held to be of strict liability. Offences

---

[28] *Rimmington; Goldstein* [2005] UKHL 63.   [29] *Rimmington; Goldstein* [2005] UKHL 63.
[30] See further para 14.98.   [31] *Gibson and Sylveire* [1990] 2 QB 619, CA.
[32] Contempt of Court Act 1981, s 1.
[33] Research has shown that prosecution for a regulatory offence is usually a weapon of last resort against persistent offenders against a regulatory offence because the preference of regulatory authorities is to seek compliance by advice and persuasion: Richardson 'Strict Liability for Regulatory Offences' [1987] Crim LR 295. See also para 6.45.

of the above types do not normally involve any inherently immoral conduct. The conduct subject to them is criminal simply because it is prohibited, and the offences are known as *mala prohibita*. People who are convicted of them are not normally regarded as criminals. It must be emphasised, however, that strict liability can arise even in respect of offences described as 'real crimes', ie crimes dealing with things which are inherently immoral (*mala in se*).

6.11 When enacting statutory offences, Parliament often stipulates a requirement of *mens rea* as to the elements of the *actus reus*. However, although it is almost unknown for a statutory provision expressly to state that *mens rea* is not required as to such an element,[34] it has been common for Parliament simply to define the prohibited conduct without any reference to the *mens rea* in relation to an element. Strict liability in statutory offences normally results from the courts' refusal to read into a statutory provision which does not use a word like 'intentionally', 'recklessly' or 'knowingly' in relation to an element of the *actus reus* of a particular offence a requirement of *mens rea* in relation to it.

6.12 Where the statutory definition of an offence expressly requires the defendant to have acted 'knowingly', knowledge is normally required as to all the circumstances of the *actus reus* prescribed by that definition.[35] Thus, in relation to the statutory offence of knowingly permitting the use of premises as a sex establishment without a licence, the House of Lords held in *Westminster City Council v Croyalgrange Ltd*[36] that the defendant must have knowledge not only of the premises' use as a sex establishment but also that that use is without a licence. Likewise, in *Hallam*,[37] the Court of Criminal Appeal held that the offence of knowingly having possession of any explosive substance, contrary to the Explosive Substances Act 1883, s 4, requires proof that the defendant knew not only that he possessed a substance but also that the substance was an explosive. Lastly, in *Gaumont British Distributors Ltd v Henry*,[38] the Divisional Court held that, in order to be guilty of the statutory offence of knowingly making a record without the consent in writing of the performers, the defendant had to know of the absence of consent as well as of the making. These cases can be distinguished from *Brooks v Mason*,[39] where the Divisional Court held that a person could be convicted of the statutory offence of knowingly delivering intoxicating liquor to a child under 14 except in a vessel sealed in the prescribed manner, even though he lacked knowledge that the vessel was not so sealed, apparently because the exception specified a matter of excuse (as opposed to being an element of the *actus reus* of the offence). It is unfortunate that whether or not *mens rea* is required as to a matter should turn on such a fine distinction.

---

[34] A modern example of where this has been done is the Sexual Offences Act 2003, s 53A (added by the Policing and Crime Act 2009, s 14 which provides, in relation to the offence of paying for the sexual services of a prostitute (B) who has been subjected by a third party to exploitative conduct (ie coercion or deception) likely to induce B to provide the sexual services, that it is irrelevant whether the defendant is, or ought to be aware, that the third party has engaged in exploitative conduct.

[35] Subject to what is said in para 3.50.

[36] [1986] 2 All ER 353, HL.   [37] [1957] 1 QB 569, CCA.

[38] [1939] 2 KB 711, DC.   [39] [1902] 2 KB 743, DC.

6.13 Some statutory offences are made subject by their parent statute to a defence whereby a defendant is not guilty if he proves that he neither believed, nor suspected, nor had reason to suspect that one or more of the specified elements of the offence existed, or whereby he proves some other defence of a 'no *mens rea*' type.[40] Where such a defence is provided in relation to a particular offence, its effect is to make it clear that the defendant can be convicted even though no *mens rea* as to the specified element or elements to which the defence applies is proved by the prosecution.

Presumption that *mens rea* is required

> **Key points 6.6**
>
> The absence of an express requirement of *mens rea* does not automatically mean that the offence is one of strict liability, since it is rebuttably presumed that *mens rea* is required.

6.14 It was stated by Lords Diplock and Fraser in *Sheppard*[41] in 1980 that in relatively recent years the climate of judicial opinion had grown less favourable to the recognition of strict liability offences.

6.15 In particular, the decision of the House of Lords in 1969 in *Sweet v Parsley*[42] indicated a significant shift in the judicial approach to statutory offences which do not clearly require *mens rea* by categorically reaffirming a principle which had increasingly appeared to be of little importance. This is the principle that, in interpreting a statutory provision which is silent on the point, there is a presumption that *mens rea* is required, unless this is rebutted by clear evidence that Parliament intended the contrary. In *Sweet v Parsley* the House of Lords, reversing the Divisional Court and overruling previous decisions of that court, held that a person could not be convicted of the offence of 'being concerned in the management of premises used for the purpose of smoking cannabis' in the absence of knowledge of such use, the presumption that *mens rea* was required not having been rebutted. (Parliament subsequently made the requirement of knowledge doubly sure by inserting the word 'knowingly' in the definition of the corresponding offence in the Misuse of Drugs Act 1971, which replaced the previous provision.)

In a passage regarded as an authoritative and accurate statement of the law, Lord Reid said this about the interpretation of a statutory provision and whether it required *mens rea*:

'Our first duty is to consider the words of the Act; if they show a clear intention to create an absolute offence,[43] that is the end of the matter. But such cases are very rare. Sometimes the words of the section which creates a particular offence make it clear that *mens rea* is

---

[40] See paras 6.46 and 6.47.   [41] [1981] AC 394, HL; para 6.30.
[42] [1970] AC 132, HL.   [43] In this context this means a strict liability offence; see para 6.5.

required in one form or another. Such cases are quite frequent. But in a very large number of cases there is no clear indication either way. In such cases there has for centuries been a presumption that Parliament did not intend to make criminals of persons who were in no way blameworthy in what they did. That means that, whenever a section is silent as to *mens rea*, there is a presumption that, in order to give effect to the will of Parliament, we must read in words appropriate to require *mens rea*...

[I]t is firmly established by a host of authorities that *mens rea* is an essential ingredient of every offence unless some reason can be found for holding that that is not necessary.... In the absence of a clear indication in the Act that an offence is intended to be an absolute offence, it is necessary to go outside the Act and examine all relevant circumstances in order to establish that this must have been the intention of Parliament.'[44]

6.16 The presumption that *mens rea* is required was again affirmed in 1984 by the Privy Council in *Gammon (Hong Kong) Ltd v A-G of Hong Kong*,[45] although on that occasion it was found to be rebutted. The defendants were charged with diverging in a material way from approved building plans, contrary to the Hong Kong Building Ordinance. They claimed that they were not guilty because they did not know that the divergence from the plans was a material one. Applying the approach set out in para 6.23 and subsequent paragraphs, the Privy Council held that the presumption that *mens rea* was required was rebutted in relation to the alleged need to prove knowledge of the materiality of the divergence.

In 2000, in *B v DPP*,[46] the House of Lords, reversing the Divisional Court, expressed the presumption in terms which gave further strength to it. It held that a person could not be convicted of an offence under the subsequently repealed[47] Indecency with Children Act 1960, s 1(1) (gross indecency with or towards a child under 14, or incitement of a child under 14 to such an act) unless the prosecution proved the absence of a genuine belief on his part that the child was 14 or over. Section 1(1) did not expressly rule out *mens rea* as a constituent element of the offence; it simply made no reference one way or the other to any mental element in respect of the victim's age. The House of Lords could not find, in the statutory context or otherwise, any necessary implication to rebut the presumption that *mens rea* was required as to the fact that the victim was under 14.

The strength of the presumption was reaffirmed in 2001 by the House of Lords in *K*[48] in respect of the now-repealed[49] offence of indecent assault on a female contrary to the Sexual Offences Act 1956, s 14. This section provided that a girl under 16 or a mentally defective woman could not consent to the indecency so as to prevent there being an indecent assault but that a defendant would not be guilty (in the case of a girl under 16) if he reasonably believed that he was married to the girl or (if a woman was a defective) he did not know or have reason to suspect that she was a defective. Section 14 made no provision for the case where the defendant was ignorant that a girl was under 16. The House of Lords held that the words of the section did not exclude by necessary implication the

---

[44] [1970] AC 132 at 148–149.
[45] [1985] AC 1, PC.
[46] [2000] 2 AC 428, HL.
[47] By the Sexual Offences Act 2003.
[48] [2001] UKHL 41.
[49] By the Sexual Offences Act 2003.

presumption of *mens rea* as to the girl's age. Lord Steyn stated that the applicability of the presumption was not dependent on finding an ambiguity in the text; the presumption operated to supplement the text.[50]

6.17 The first nine lines of the quotation from Lord Reid's speech in *Sweet v Parsley*, set out in para 6.15, were considered by Lord Bingham in *DPP v Collins*.[51] In that case, the House of Lords was concerned with the offence under the Communications Act 2003, s 127(1)(a), which provides that a person is guilty of any offence if he 'sends by means of a public electronic communications network a message or other matter that is grossly offensive or of an indecent, obscene or menacing character'. Lord Bingham, with whom the other Law Lords agreed, held that the above nine lines were relevant to the offence before the House, because Parliament could not have intended to criminalise the conduct of a person using language which was, for reasons unknown to him, grossly offensive to those to whom it related or which was thought by the person, however unreasonably, to represent a polite or acceptable usage. Lord Bingham therefore concluded, as part of his reasons for determining the appeal, that, in addition to an intention to send the message in question, the defendant must intend his words to be grossly offensive to those to whom they relate, or be aware that they may be taken to be so.

What is the mens rea that is presumed to be required?

6.18 Where a *mens rea* requirement is read in under the presumption that *mens rea* is required, it will be a subjective mental element of some kind, eg intention or recklessness as to a consequence-element or knowledge or recklessness as to a circumstance-element.[52] It should not be read in that negligence is sufficient.[53]

Does Parliament really have an intention in respect of mens rea?

6.19 The presumption that *mens rea* is required is one of the rules of statutory interpretation, rules whose purpose is rather inaccurately said to be to discover Parliament's intention. In *K*,[54] Lord Millett, in holding that the presumption of *mens rea* was not rebutted, stated that he did so 'without reluctance but with some misgiving, for I have little doubt that we shall be failing to give effect to the intention of Parliament'.[55] In truth, the presumption that Parliament intended *mens rea* to be required is a somewhat artificial rule. Lord Devlin, one of the great judges of modern times, wrote in respect of strict liability:

> 'The fact is that Parliament has no intention whatever of troubling itself about *mens rea*. If it had, the thing would have been settled long ago. All that Parliament would have to do would be to use express words that left no room for implication. One is driven to the

---

[50] [2001] UKHL 41.   [51] [2006] UKHL 40.   [52] Ch 3.
[53] *Gray's Haulage Co Ltd v Arnold Ltd* [1966] 1 All ER 896, DC (para 3.58); *B v DPP* [2000] 2 AC 428, HL (see para 5.13).
[54] [2001] UKHL 41.   [55] [2001] UKHL 41 at [41].

> conclusion that the reason why Parliament has never done that is that it prefers to leave the point to the judges and does not want to legislate about it.'[56]

Attention paid to the presumption by the courts

6.20 Despite what was said by the House of Lords in *Sweet v Parsley*, by Lords Diplock and Fraser in *Sheppard*, by Lord Scarman on behalf of the Privy Council in *Gammon* and by the House of Lords in *B v DPP* and in *K*, it would be wrong to leave the reader with the impression that there has been a massive reduction in recent years in the number of occasions on which the courts have held that an offence is one of strict liability. *Sweet v Parsley* was concerned with a drugs offence, and, as *B v DPP* and *K* indicate, the shift of approach has clearly been maintained in relation to the more serious types of offence. In *Phekoo*,[57] for instance, the Court of Appeal held that the offence of harassment of a residential occupier (contrary to the Protection from Eviction Act 1977, s 1(3)) was not one of strict liability as to the fact that the person harassed was a residential occupier, and in *Sheppard*[58] the House of Lords, overruling well-established decisions to the opposite effect, held that the offence of wilful neglect of a child in a manner likely to cause him unnecessary suffering or injury to health was not one of strict liability as to the risk of suffering or injury to health.

However, as far as regulatory offences are concerned, the change of attitude towards strict liability revealed in *Sweet v Parsley* has had less effect. On a considerable number of subsequent occasions in the 40 years after *Sweet v Parsley*, appellate courts, including the House of Lords in *Alphacell Ltd v Woodward*[59] and *Wings Ltd v Ellis*,[60] have paid little or no regard to the weight of this presumption in holding that, on the true interpretation of a statutory offence, Parliament intended to rule out the need for *mens rea* in relation to an element of its *actus reus*.

6.21 Despite the fact that the suggestion in the decision in *Sweet v Parsley* that any further expansion of strict liability would be closely scrutinised and confined within narrow limits has not wholly borne fruit, it nevertheless remains true that the general approach reaffirmed in *Sweet v Parsley*, and equally emphatically in *Gammon (Hong Kong) Ltd v A-G of Hong Kong*, and given even greater force in *B v DPP* and *K*, remains the correct approach to the interpretation of whether a statutory provision imposes strict liability. It still remains to be seen whether the powerful reaffirmation of this approach in *B v DPP* and *K* leads to the courts in practice giving greater weight to the presumption. *B v DPP*

---

[56] *Samples of Lawmaking* (1962).

[57] [1981] 3 All ER 84, CA. The terms of the offence were amended by the Housing Act 1988, s 29.

[58] [1981] AC 394, HL.

[59] [1972] AC 824, HL; para 6.37.

[60] [1985] AC 272, HL. The House of Lords held that the offence under the Trade Descriptions Act 1968, s 14(1)(a) (since repealed), whereby a person commits an offence if he makes a statement 'which he knows to be false' was an offence of strict liability as to the making of the statement (but not as to its falsity).

and *K* raised hopes that the courts would give greater weight to the presumption and would also review decisions imposing strict liability.

The Court of Appeal's decision in *Muhamad*[61] one year after *K* does not excite optimism in the first respect in relation to offences which might be regarded as regulatory. D, charged with materially contributing to his insolvency by gambling, contrary to the Insolvency Act 1986, s 362(1), argued that the offence required *mens rea*, viz that he knew or was reckless as to whether his act of gambling would materially contribute to his insolvency. The Court of Appeal rejected this argument; the offence was one of strict liability in this respect. It doubted that the offence was truly criminal (despite the maximum sentence of two years' imprisonment), and it held that the language of the statute (other offences in the statute specifically requiring *mens rea* generally carried a maximum of 10 years' imprisonment), the maximum sentence and social concern provided support for the rebuttal of the presumption. In addition, making the offence one of strict liability would promote the objects of the statute by encouraging greater vigilance to prevent gambling which would or might contribute to insolvency.

The Court of Appeal's decision in *Matudi*[62] soon afterwards is to like effect. On a charge of importing animal products without border inspection, contrary to the Products of Animal Origin (Import and Export) Regulations 1996, regs 21 and 37 (which made breach of reg 21 an offence), D's defence was that he had no idea that the items contained meat (ie animal products) because they were only supposed to contain vegetables. The Court of Appeal held that it was compellingly clear that Parliament had not intended *mens rea* to be a requirement of an offence under reg 21. The wording of reg 21 itself gave no indication of whether it required *mens rea* or created a strict liability offence, whereas the wording of other offences in the Regulations expressly made a requirement of knowledge. Moreover, the unmonitored importation of animal products was of public concern as it created significant dangers to public and animal health, which could also have serious economic consequences. The greater the social risk, the more likely that the court would infer an intention to create a strict liability offence. The imposition of strict liability, the Court of Appeal added, was effective in promoting the objectives of the legislation as it deterred importers from bypassing the provisions of the Regulations and encouraged the use of reputable suppliers.

6.22 *Muhamad* and *Matudi* were both cases where the statutory provisions in question had not been the subject of an authoritative interpretation. In *Deyemi and Edwards*,[63] decided in 2007, the Court of Appeal regarded itself as unable to revisit, in the light of the emphatic statements in *B v DPP* and *K*, the interpretation of a provision which had already been interpreted in a decision binding on the court. In *Deyemi and Edwards* D1 and D2 had pleaded guilty to the possession of a prohibited weapon (a stun gun) contrary to the Firearms Act 1968, s 5 after the judge had ruled that the offence was one of strict liability. They did not know that the article was a stun gun and were each given a conditional discharge. Their appeals against conviction were rejected by the Court of Appeal. The Court

---

[61] [2002] EWCA Crim 1856.   [62] [2003] EWCA Crim 697.   [63] [2007] EWCA Crim 2060.

recognised the importance of *B v DPP* and *K* but held that it was bound by its decision in 1990 in *Bradish*[64] that the offence under s 5 was one of strict liability as to the nature of the thing possessed. It stated that its conclusion as to the binding effect of *Bradish* meant, at least for the Court of Appeal, that the decisions in *B v DPP* and *K* did not assist. The Court went on to say: 'Each of [those decisions] is concerned with the proper meaning to be attributed to the statutory provisions in question; the statutory provisions with which we are concerned have been construed by decisions binding on us'.[65] Thus, unless an existing interpretation of an offence is not binding on the court under the rules of precedent, the effect of *B v DPP* and *K* is limited to provisions which have not yet been interpreted by an appellate court. Hopes that *B v DPP* and *K* would lead a review by the courts of decisions imposing strict liability have therefore been dashed.

Rebutting the presumption

> **Key points 6.7**
>
> The presumption that *mens rea* is required can be rebutted by clear words in the statute or by necessary implication.

6.23 In *Sweet v Parsley* the House of Lords held that clear evidence to the contrary was required before the presumption that *mens rea* was required could be rebutted. Further guidance was given in *Gammon (Hong Kong) Ltd v A-G of Hong Kong* where Lord Scarman, giving the opinion of the Privy Council, said:

> 'In their Lordships' opinion, the law relevant to this appeal may be stated in the following propositions... (1) there is a presumption of law that *mens rea* is required before a person can be held guilty of a criminal offence; (2) the presumption is particularly strong where the offence is "truly criminal" in character; (3) the presumption applies to statutory offences, and can be displaced only if this is clearly or by necessary implication the effect of the statute; (4) the only situation in which the presumption can be displaced is where the statute is concerned with an issue of social concern; public safety is such an issue; (5) even where a statute is concerned with such an issue, the presumption of *mens rea* stands unless it can also be shown that the creation of strict liability will be effective to promote the objects of the statute by encouraging greater vigilance to prevent the commission of the prohibited act.'[66]

6.24 The requirement that the presumption can only be rebutted by clear words (ie express provision) or 'necessary implication' was emphasised and strengthened by the House of

---

[64] [1990] 1 QB 981, CA.   [65] [2007] EWCA Crim 2060 at [25].

[66] [1985] AC 1 at 14. This was applied, for example, in *Wings Ltd v Ellis* [1985] AC 272, HL; *Wells Street Metropolitan Stipendiary Magistrate, ex p Westminster City Council* [1986] 3 All ER 4, DC; *Blake* [1997] 1 All ER 963, CA.

Lords in *B v DPP*.[67] As Lord Hutton (with whom Lords Mackay and Steyn agreed) stated, 'the test is not whether it is a reasonable implication that the statute rules out *mens rea* as a constituent part of the crime – the test is whether it is a *necessary* implication'.[68] Lord Nicholls (with whom Lords Irvine and Mackay agreed) took an equally tough approach in giving the leading speech: '"Necessary implication" connotes an implication which is compellingly clear.'[69] In *K*, Lord Steyn held that: 'In the present case a compellingly clear implication can only be established if the supplementation of the text by reading in words appropriate to require *mens rea* results in an internal inconsistency of the text.'[70] In *B v DPP*, Lord Steyn regarded the presumption that *mens rea* is required, unless Parliament has expressly or by necessary implication indicated the contrary, as a constitutional principle. He quoted with approval Lord Hoffmann's statement in *Secretary of State for the Home Department, ex p Simms*:

> 'But the principle of legality means that Parliament must squarely confront what it is doing and accept the political cost. Fundamental rights cannot be overridden by general or ambiguous words. This is because there is too great a risk that the full implications of their unqualified meaning may have passed unnoticed in the democratic process. In the absence of express language or necessary implication to the contrary, the courts therefore presume that even the most general words were intended to be subject to the basic rights of the individual.'[71]

Lord Steyn then said: 'In other words, in the absence of express words or a truly necessary implication, Parliament must be presumed to legislate on the assumption that the principle of legality will supplement the text.'[72] If the presumption of *mens rea* is regarded as a constitutional principle its rebuttal will be made even more difficult.

6.25 From *B v DPP* and *K* the Court of Appeal in *Kumar* concluded:

> '[F]irstly that in all statutory offences whenever a section is silent as to *mens rea* there is a presumption that the mental element is an essential ingredient of the offence. Secondly, in the absence of express statutory provision the presumption of the mental element can only be excluded if the necessary implication is "compellingly clear", "truly necessary" and free from ambiguity. Further, the presumption must not involve an internal inconsistency.'[73]

6.26 In deciding whether the effect of the statutory provision is 'by necessary implication' to rebut the presumption that *mens rea* is required in respect of the elements of the offence, the court can look at the words of the statute and various extrinsic factors (such

---

[67] [2000] 2 AC 428, HL. [68] [2000] 2 AC 428 at 481. [69] [2000] 2 AC 428 at 464.
[70] [2001] UKHL 41 at [33]. [71] [2000] 2 AC 115 at 131.
[72] [2000] 2 AC 428 at 470. [73] [2004] EWCA Crim 3207 at [25].

as the nature of the offence and the mischief sought to be prevented) and must consider whether strict liability would promote the object of the provision.[74]

6.27 Lord Scarman's fourth proposition in *Gammon*, that the presumption can only be displaced where the statute is concerned with an issue of social concern (public safety in that case), is of little significance. It is hard to think of many statutes containing criminal offences which are not concerned with such an issue. Subsequent cases indicate that the courts have not spent much time considering the matter, and have held, for instance, that Acts relating to town and country planning,[75] broadcasting[76] and the National Lottery[77] dealt with issues of social concern. There are, of course, many offences in statutes dealing with matters of social concern which are not strict liability: rape and theft are obvious examples. Lord Scarman's last proposition in *Gammon* (presumption that *mens rea* required not rebutted unless strict liability would aid enforcement of the law) is also, generally, easily satisfied, as shown in para 6.42. It is unfortunate that courts, having found Lord Scarman's fourth and last requirements satisfied, have often given too much weight to them in finding the presumption of *mens rea* rebutted;[78] satisfaction of these requirements only means that an offence *may* be one of strict liability, not that it must be.

Words of the statute

6.28 Certain words which commonly appear in statutory offences have been considered by appellate courts on a sufficient number of occasions as to indicate whether they are likely to be held to support or rebut the presumption that *mens rea* is required in a particular offence. Examples of such words are as follows:

'Permitting' or 'suffering'

6.29 There is a substantial number of statutory offences of 'permitting' or 'suffering' (which terms have been held to be synonymous).[79]

'Permit' has been held by the House of Lords in *Vehicle Inspectorate v Nuttall*[80] to be capable of having at least two types of meaning, a narrow meaning, 'allow', 'agree to' or 'authorise', and a wider one, 'fail to take reasonable steps to prevent', its meaning in any particular offence depending on its context. No guidance was given as to how a court is to approach the question of context.

---

[74] *Sweet v Parsley* [1970] AC 132 at 163, per Lord Diplock; *Gammon (Hong Kong) Ltd v A-G of Hong Kong* [1985] AC 1, PC; *Wings Ltd v Ellis* [1985] AC 272, HL.

[75] *Wells Street Metropolitan Stipendiary Magistrate, ex p Westminster City Council* [1986] 3 All ER 4, DC.

[76] *Blake* [1997] 1 All ER 963, CA.

[77] *Harrow London Borough Council v Shah* [1999] 3 All ER 302, DC.

[78] See, for example, *Blake* [1997] 1 All ER 963, CA.

[79] *Somerset v Wade* [1894] 1 QB 574, DC; *Ferguson v Weaving* [1951] 1 KB 814, DC.

[80] [1999] 3 All ER 833, HL.

It has been stated by the Divisional Court that 'It is of the very essence of the offence of permitting someone to do something that there should be knowledge.'[81] Consistent with this, it has been held, for example, on a charge of committing the statutory offence of permitting a motor vehicle to be used in breach of the Construction and Use Regulations or of permitting an employee to drive in excess of lawful hours, that liability depended on proof that the defendant knew about the contravention in question.[82]

The courts have not always taken the same approach. It has been held that the statutory offences of permitting another to use a motor vehicle on a road without insurance, or permitting another to drive on a road without a driving licence, are strict liability offences in respect of the uninsured use or lack of a licence.[83] Likewise, it has been held that the statutory offence of permitting an animal to be carried so as to be likely to cause unnecessary suffering is one of strict liability as to this risk.[84] These cases are, however, isolated exceptions to a general rule that 'permit' or 'suffer' are to be interpreted as requiring *mens rea*. In *Vehicle Inspectorate v Nuttall*[85] the House of Lords (or at least a majority of it) held that, on a charge of the statutory offence of permitting a driver to contravene rules restricting driving hours, 'knowledge' is required, so that at the very least recklessness in the sense of not caring whether a contravention occurred is necessary. The House added, however, that if an employer failed in his legal duty to check tachograph records, this amounted to a prima facie case of recklessness. Lord Hobhouse said: 'On the authorities, as cited by Lord Steyn, a reckless state of mind suffices.' He went on to say, however, that:

> 'The commission of the offence does not *in practice* depend upon any particular subjective state of mind or any particular knowledge of the employer. It is part of his duty to see that he is informed of the relevant facts.... Absent any special factor such as accident or innocent mistake of fact..., he will not be able to escape criminal responsibility for his acts and omissions, nor will he be able to rebut the case made against him.'[86]

The speeches in *Vehicle Inspectorate v Nuttall* are not noteworthy for their clarity but the Divisional Court in *Yorkshire Traction Co Ltd v Vehicle Inspectorate*[87] subsequently confirmed that the offence in question in *Nuttall* was not one of strict liability and required 'knowledge'.

---

[81] *Gray's Haulage Co Ltd v Arnold Ltd* [1966] 1 All ER 896 at 898, per Lord Parker CJ with whom the other judge, Winn LJ, entirely agreed. As in other contexts, knowledge in this context includes wilful blindness: *Gray's Haulage Co Ltd v Arnold Ltd* [1966] 1 All ER 896 at 898, per Lord Parker CJ. Also see *James & Son Ltd v Smee* [1955] 1 QB 78, DC; *Vehicle Inspectorate v Nuttall* [1999] 3 All ER 833 at 840, per Lord Steyn.

[82] *James & Son Ltd v Smee* [1955] 1 QB 78, DC; *Gray's Haulage Co Ltd v Arnold Ltd* [1966] 1 All ER 896, DC.

[83] *Lyons v May* [1948] 2 All ER 1062, DC.

[84] *Cheshire County Council v Alan Helliwell & Sons (Bolton) Ltd* (1991) 155 JP 425, DC; *Greener v DPP* (1996) 160 JP 265, DC.

[85] [1999] 3 All ER 833, HL. 'Permit' was held to bear the wider meaning referred to above.

[86] [1999] 3 All ER 833 at 844–845.

[87] [2001] RTR 518, DC.

'Wilfully'

6.30 The appearance of the adverb 'wilfully' in a statutory offence might be thought clearly to indicate a requirement of *mens rea* as to all the elements of its *actus reus*, but the courts have not always been willing to accept such an indication.[88] Some cases have appeared to hold that 'wilfully' requires no more than proof of a voluntary act, in which case it added nothing to the general principle that such an act is required. In *Cotterill v Penn*,[89] for example, the Divisional Court held that the offence of unlawfully and wilfully killing a house pigeon, contrary to the Larceny Act 1861, s 23 (which has since been repealed), merely required that the defendant should intend to do the act forbidden, which was that of shooting at the bird in that case, and did not also require that he should realise that what he was shooting at was a house pigeon, so that a belief that it was a wild pigeon was immaterial.[90] In other cases the approach has been to interpret 'wilfully' so as to require *mens rea* as to all the elements of the *actus reus*.[91]

A particularly important decision is that of the House of Lords in 1980 in *Sheppard*[92] which was concerned with the Children and Young Persons Act 1933, s 1. This makes it an offence where someone having the responsibility for a child or young person under 16 'wilfully assaults, ill-treats, neglects, abandons or exposes him...in a manner likely to cause unnecessary suffering or injury to health'. By a majority of three to two, the House of Lords, overruling previous decisions to the contrary, held that in the offence of wilfully neglecting under s 1 there was an element of *mens rea* as to the relevant risk and that the term meant 'intentionally or recklessly' as to the risk of causing unnecessary suffering or injury to health. Dealing with the case, where the charge involved failure to provide adequate medical aid, the requirement of wilfulness could only be satisfied (a) where the defendant was aware the child's health might be at risk if it was not provided with medical aid, or (b) where he was unaware of this risk because he did not care whether the child's health was at risk or not. Part (b) seemed to suggest that it referred to objective (ie *Caldwell*)[93] recklessness, but in *A-G's Reference (No 3 of 2003)*[94] it was held that the approach to recklessness in *G*[95] could be incorporated into a direction on wilfulness under the test in *Sheppard*. It held that there was no material difference between the two cases; the alternative test in *Sheppard* (unawareness due to not caring) was, like the first, one of subjective recklessness as in *G*. In *Sheppard* two of the Law Lords in the majority, Lords Diplock and Keith, noted that 'wilfully' qualifies all five verbs in s 1 – 'assaults, ill-treats, neglects, abandons or exposes'. In *D*[96] the Court of Appeal confirmed that the term bore the same meaning in respect of each of these verbs.

---

[88] Andrews 'Wilfulness: A Lesson in Ambiguity' (1981) 1 LS 303. [89] [1936] 1 KB 53, DC.

[90] For further examples see *Arrowsmith v Jenkins* [1963] 2 QB 561, DC; *Maidstone Borough Council v Mortimer* [1980] 3 All ER 552, DC; *Millward* [1985] QB 519, CA.

[91] See, for example, *Eaton v Cobb* [1950] 1 All ER 1016, DC; *Bullock v Turnbull* [1952] 2 Lloyd's Rep 303, DC; *Gittins* [1982] RTR 363, CA; *Hills and Ellis* [1983] QB 680 (para 7.72).

[92] [1981] AC 394, HL.   [93] Para 3.35.   [94] [2004] EWCA Crim 868.

[95] [2003] UKHL 50 (para 3.33).   [96] [2008] EWCA Crim 2360.

In the light of *Sheppard, A-G's Reference (No 3 of 2003)* and *D*, cases which have apparently held that 'wilfully' simply requires a voluntary act in the context of particular statutory offences are unlikely to be followed.

'Cause'

6.31 Some statutory offences are framed in terms of causing something to happen (eg the pollution of controlled waters) or of causing someone to do something (eg to use a defective motor vehicle which is mechanically dangerous).

Where a statutory offence is defined simply in terms of causing something to happen, the courts have traditionally been very likely to interpret it as an offence of strict liability as to the occurrence of that thing. An example is provided by *Alphacell Ltd v Woodward*,[97] whose facts are set out in para 6.37. On the other hand, where the offence is defined in terms of causing someone else to do something, 'cause'[98] has been interpreted as requiring *mens rea* as to the thing being done.[99]

Wording of other offences in statute

6.32 Another way in which the wording of the statute can be important is that the appearance in the definition of other offences in the statute (or, indeed, in another statute to which it may be regarded as an appendix),[100] but not in the definition of the offence in question, of words such as 'knowingly' is likely to lead to a finding that *mens rea* is not required in relation to an element or elements of the offence in question. This is a significant point because it is common for different provisions, or even different offences in the same provision, to be expressed in a way which expressly requires full *mens rea* for one but not for another. However, as Lord Reid stated in *Sweet v Parsley*:

> 'It is also firmly established that the fact that other sections of the Act expressly require *mens rea*, for example because they contain the word "knowingly", is not in itself sufficient to justify a decision that a section which is silent as to *mens rea* creates an absolute offence.'[101]

This point is illustrated by a comparison of the cases set out below.

---

[97] [1972] AC 824, HL.

[98] D 'causes' someone else to do something if it is done on the actual authority, express or implied, of D or in consequence of D exerting some influence on the acts of the other person: *A-G of Hong Kong v Tse Hung-Lit* [1986] AC 876, PC.

[99] *Lovelace v DPP* [1954] 3 All ER 481, DC; *Ross Hillman Ltd v Bond* [1974] QB 435, DC. Contrast *Sopp v Long* [1970] 1 QB 518, DC.

[100] In *B v DPP* [2000] 2 AC 428, the House of Lords, in considering whether the offence of inciting a child to commit an act of gross indecency, contrary to the Indecency with Children Act 1960 (since repealed by the Sexual Offences Act 2003 (SOA 2003)), which did not contain a word such as 'knowingly', was an offence of strict liability, considered the wording of other sexual offences under the Sexual Offences Act 1956 (repealed by SOA 2003). However, it concluded that a comparison of the wording of the offences did not give rise to a necessary implication that the presumption of *mens rea* was rebutted in respect of the 1960 Act.

[101] [1970] AC 132 at 149. More recently the point was made by the Court of Appeal in *Muhamad* [2002] EWCA Crim 1856 at [18].

6.33 A famous case in the present context is *Cundy v Le Cocq*,[102] which concerned the offence under the Licensing Act 1872, s 13 (since repealed) of sale by a publican of liquor to a drunken person. It was held that the defendant licensee's belief, even if founded on reasonable grounds, in the sobriety of his customer was no defence. This conclusion was reached in the light of the general scope of the Act, which was for the repression of drunkenness, and of a comparison of the various sections in the relevant part of the Act, some of which, unlike the section in question, contained the word 'knowingly'.

The same conclusion as in *Cundy v Le Cocq* was reached by the Divisional Court in *Neville v Mavroghenis*,[103] where contrasting provisions actually appeared in two limbs of the same subsection, the offence in one limb requiring the defendant to have acted 'knowingly' and the offence in the other containing no such word; it was held that the offence in the latter limb was one of strict liability.

Another decision to like effect is *Pharmaceutical Society of Great Britain v Storkwain Ltd*,[104] which was concerned with the offence of supplying specified medicinal products except in accordance with a prescription by an appropriate practitioner, contrary to the Medicines Act 1968, s 58(2)(a). The House of Lords relied principally on the fact that other offence-creating provisions in the Act expressly required *mens rea* in holding that the presumption that *mens rea* was required was rebutted in relation to s 58(2)(a), which did not make such express provision. Consequently, it upheld convictions under s 58(2)(a) of retail pharmacists who had supplied drugs after being given forged prescriptions which they believed to be genuine.

More recently, the presumption that a criminal statute requires *mens rea* was held by the Court of Appeal in 2006 in *G*[105] to be rebutted by necessary implication in respect of the Sexual Offences Act 2003, s 5 (rape of a child under 13)[106] in relation to the child's age. The Court of Appeal held that:

'Such an implication arises in respect of s 5...from the contrast between the express references to reasonable belief that a child is 16 or over in, for instance, s 9, and the absence of any such reference in relation to children under 13. Thus, on its actual meaning, s 5 creates an offence even if the defendant reasonably believes that the child was 13 or over.'[107]

This issue was not argued when the case was unsuccessfully appealed to the House of Lords.[108] The argument before the House concerned whether:

---

[102] (1884) 13 QBD 207, DC.

[103] [1984] Crim LR 42, DC. Also see *Kirkland v Robinson* (1986) 151 JP 377, DC.

[104] [1986] 2 All ER 635, HL; see Jackson '*Storkwain*: A Case Study in Strict Liability and Self-regulation' [1991] Crim LR 892.

[105] [2006] EWCA Crim 821.   [106] Para 9.35.

[107] [2006] EWCA Crim 821 at [17].

[108] [2008] UKHL 37. The speeches in the House, however, confirmed that the offence was one of strict liability as to the age of the child. See, in particular, Lord Hoffmann at [3], Baroness Hale at [46] and Lord Mance at [71].

- to hold that s 5 imposes strict liability as to the child's age breaches the defendant's rights under ECHR, Article 6(1) and/or (2) (right to fair trial and presumption of innocence); and

- it is compatible with a child defendant's rights under Article 8 (right to private life) to convict him of the offence under s 5 where the agreed basis of his appeal established that the defendant's offence fell properly within a less serious offence under s 13.

As said earlier, the House answered 'no' on the first point.[109] A majority (3–2) also answered 'no' on the second.[110]

6.34 By way of comparison, reference may be made to *Sherras v De Rutzen*,[111] where a licensee had supplied liquor to a police officer who was on duty, contrary to the Licensing Act 1872, s 16(2) (since repealed). The licensee reasonably believed that the officer was off duty because he had removed his armlet which at that time, to the knowledge of the licensee, was worn by police officers in the locality when on duty. The licensee was convicted by the magistrates but his conviction was quashed on appeal, the Divisional Court holding that the licensee could not be convicted if he did not know that the police officer was on duty, even though the definition in s 16(1) of another offence contained the word 'knowingly' and s 16(2) did not. One of the two judges, Day J, thought that the only effect of the presence of 'knowingly' in s 16(1) and its absence in s 16(2) was to shift the burden of proof on the issue of knowledge to the defendant (ie the defendant had to prove that he did not know). Day J's approach has, however, not been generally adopted.

The approach taken by the Divisional Court in *Sherras v De Rutzen* was taken in modern times by the Court of Appeal in *Berry (No 3)*[112] which was concerned with the Explosive Substances Act 1883, s 4(1). Section 4(1) provides that any person who 'makes or knowingly has in his possession or under his control' any explosive substance (including any apparatus or part of an apparatus for causing an explosion) commits an offence punishable with up to 14 years' imprisonment. The Court held that, although 'knowingly' only qualified the second and third categories of offence, the first category must be interpreted as requiring proof by the prosecution that an alleged 'maker' acted with knowledge that the substance was an explosive substance.

6.35 There is a further qualification to the approach taken in cases like *Cundy v Le Cocq, Neville v Mavroghenis, Storkwain* and *G*. According to Lord Steyn in *B v DPP*,[113] the argument that comparisons or contrasts can be drawn between different provisions in a statute (or between a parent statute and a statute to which it is an appendix) is considerably weakened where the statute contains a motley of offences of diverse origins, gathered together by the statute with little or no change in their phraseology and with no clear or coherent pattern or consistent theme.

---

[109] See para 6.8.   [110] See para 9.36.   [111] [1895] 1 QB 918, DC.

[112] [1994] 2 All ER 913, CA.

[113] [2000] 2 AC 428 at 473. Also see Lords Nicholls and Hutton [2000] 2 AC 428 at 465 and 481 for a similar approach.

Extrinsic factors

6.36 Where no clear indication as to the need for *mens rea* or otherwise is given by the words of the statute, the courts can go outside the Act and examine all the relevant circumstances to determine whether, by necessary implication, Parliament intended to displace the need for *mens rea*. In *K*, Lord Steyn stated that the presumption 'can only be displaced by *specific language*, ie an express provision or a necessary implication [from that language]'.[114] However, his fellow Law Lords did not comment on this and, as reference to *Muhamad* and to *Matudi* in para 6.21 shows, extrinsic factors are not yet excluded from being taken into account. Some of these factors are discussed in the following paragraphs.

The subject matter of the enactment

6.37 An offence is more likely to be construed as one of strict liability if it falls within the three classes enumerated by Wright J in *Sherras v De Rutzen*:[115]

> 'Apart from isolated and extreme cases [such as *Prince*], the principal classes of exceptions [to the general rule that *mens rea* is required] may perhaps be reduced to three. One is a class of acts which...are not criminal in any real sense, but are acts which in the public interest are prohibited under a penalty. Several such instances are to be found in the decisions on the Revenue Statutes, eg *A-G v Lockwood*,[116] where the innocent possession of liquorice by a beer retailer was held to be an offence. So under the Adulteration Acts, *Woodrow*[117] as to innocent possession of adulterated tobacco; *Fitzpatrick v Kelly*[118] and *Roberts v Egerton*[119] as to the sale of adulterated food...to the same head may be referred *Bishop*[120] where a person was held rightly convicted of receiving lunatics in an unlicensed house, although the jury found that he honestly and on reasonable grounds believed that they were not lunatics. Another class comprehends some, and perhaps all, public nuisances[121]...Lastly, there may be cases in which, although the proceeding is criminal in form, it is really only a summary mode of enforcing a civil right: see per Williams and Willes JJ in *Morden v Porter*,[122] as to unintentional trespass in pursuit of game...But except in such cases as these, there must in general be guilty knowledge on the part of the defendant...'

This dictum was referred to by the House of Lords in *Alphacell Ltd v Woodward*,[123] where the defendant company, whose settling tanks overflowed into a river, was held to have been rightly convicted of causing polluted matter to enter a river contrary to the Rivers (Prevention of Pollution) Act 1951, s 2 (which offence, as amended, is now contained in the Water Resources Act 1991, s 85), despite the fact that there was no evidence that it knew

---

[114] [2001] UKHL 41 at [32]. Italics supplied.   [115] [1895] 1 QB 918 at 921.
[116] (1842) 9 M & W 378.   [117] (1846) 15 M & W 404.
[118] (1873) LR 8 QB 337.   [119] (1874) LR 9 QB 494.
[120] (1880) 5 QBD 259.   [121] This refers to statutory offences in the nature of a public nuisance.
[122] (1860) 7 CBNS 641.   [123] [1972] AC 824, HL.

that pollution was taking place from its settling tanks or had been in any way negligent. In construing the offence as one of strict liability, Viscount Dilhorne and Lord Salmon regarded the statute as dealing with acts falling within the first class, ie acts which 'are not criminal in any real sense, but are acts which in the public interest are prohibited under a penalty', while Lord Pearson thought that the offence fell within the second class enumerated, saying '*mens rea* is generally not a necessary ingredient in an offence of this kind, which is in the nature of a public nuisance'.[124]

6.38 The first of Wright J's three classes is particularly important since it covers many statutes regulating particular activities involving potential danger to public health or safety which a person may choose to undertake, such as those relating to the sale of food, pollution, dangerous substances and the condition and use of vehicles. The fact that an offence is not truly criminal (ie falls within the category of *mala prohibita*, and not *mala in se*) has often been given by a court as a reason (or one of the reasons) for concluding that it is one of strict liability.[125] In contrast, as Lord Scarman said in the *Gammon* case, the presumption of *mens rea* is particularly strong where the offence is 'truly criminal' in character.[126] This prompts one to ask what the criteria of 'true criminality' are. The courts have yet to supply an answer. Indeed, they do not appear to share a consistent approach. In three modern cases, in which the offences in question were punishable with a maximum of two years' imprisonment, one Divisional Court said that because the offence was imprisonable it was 'truly criminal' in character,[127] while another Divisional Court said that the offence was 'not truly criminal' despite the severity of the maximum punishment.[128] In the third case, decided in 2002, the Court of Appeal doubted that an offence punishable with two years' imprisonment was 'truly criminal'.[129]

The mischief of the crime

6.39 Where an offence is aimed at the prevention of some particularly serious social danger, such as inflation or pollution, this may persuade the court that the need for *mens rea* is displaced. This is illustrated by *St Margaret's Trust Ltd*[130] where the defendant finance company was charged with offences against the Hire-Purchase and Credit Sales Agreements (Control) Order 1956, subsequently revoked, Article 1 of which prohibited a person from disposing of any goods in pursuance of a hire-purchase agreement unless 50 per cent of the cash price had been paid. This requirement was not satisfied in the case of a number of hire-purchase transactions relating to motor cars because, although the company had acted innocently, it had been misled as to the true cash price and had been informed that the requisite 50 per cent had been paid. The Court of Criminal Appeal

---

[124] [1972] AC 824 at 842.
[125] See, for example, *Chilvers v Rayner* [1984] 1 All ER 843 at 847, per Robert Goff LJ.
[126] Para 6.23.
[127] *Blake* [1997] 1 All ER 963 at 968; para 6.42.
[128] *Harrow London Borough Council v Shah* [1999] 3 All ER 302 at 306.
[129] *Muhamad* [2002] EWCA Crim 1856; para 6.21.
[130] [1958] 2 All ER 289, CCA. Also see *Howells* [1977] QB 614, CA.

dismissed the company's appeal against conviction, holding that the offence was one of strict liability. Donovan J had this to say about the mischief of the offence:

> 'The object of the order was to help to defend the currency against the peril of inflation which, if unchecked, would bring disaster on the country. There is no need to elaborate this. The present generation has witnessed the collapse of the currency in other countries and the consequent chaos, misery and widespread ruin. It would not be at all surprising if Parliament, determined to prevent similar calamities here, enacted measures which it intended to be absolute prohibitions of acts which might increase the risk in however small a degree. Indeed, that would be the natural expectation. There would be little point in enacting that no one should breach the defences against a flood, and at the same time excusing anyone who did it innocently. For these reasons we think that art 1 of the order should receive a literal construction [under which *mens rea* was not required].'[131]

A more recent example of this factor being relied on by a court is *Matudi*, referred to in para 6.21.

It must not be forgotten, however, that the presence of a grave social danger is not alone enough to rebut the presumption that *mens rea* is required.[132] In addition, it can conflict with the next factor.

The seriousness of the offence

6.40 In *B v DPP*,[133] Lord Nicholls stated:

> 'The more serious the offence, the greater is the weight to be attached to the presumption [that *mens rea* is required], because the more severe is the punishment and the graver the stigma which accompany a conviction'.

The offence in *B v DPP* was punishable with 10 years' imprisonment, and a conviction for it carried an undoubted stigma. These factors reinforced, rather than negatived, the application of the presumption in that case.

On occasions, however, the courts have construed offences carrying a lengthy maximum term of imprisonment as not requiring *mens rea*. In *Warner v Comr of Metropolitan Police*[134] a pre-*Sweet v Parsley* case, the offence of unauthorised possession of drugs was held not to require proof that the defendant knew that what he was in possession of was a drug, despite the fact that the offence in question was punishable with a maximum of two years' imprisonment, and could, if the drug had been of a different type, have been punished with a maximum of 10 years'. (The law on this subject has

---

[131] [1958] 2 All ER 289 at 293.

[132] See *Lim Chin Aik v R* [1963] AC 160 at 174; para 6.41.

[133] [2000] 2 AC 428 at 464. The seriousness of the offence is one way in which an offence can be said to be of 'truly criminal' character. Also see Lord Steyn ibid at 472, and *Sweet v Parsley* [1970] AC 132 at 149 and 156, per Lords Reid and Pearce. Contrast para 6.38, nn 127–129.

[134] [1969] 2 AC 256, HL.

been changed since *Warner*.)[135] Similarly, in the post-*Sweet v Parsley* (but pre-*B v DPP*) cases of *Howells*,[136] *Bradish*[137] and *Harrison and Francis*[138] the offences of possessing a firearm without a certificate (*Howells*), of possessing a prohibited weapon (*Bradish*), and of having a loaded firearm in a public place (*Harrison*) were held to be ones of strict liability as to their circumstances that the article possessed was respectively a firearm, a prohibited weapon, or a loaded shotgun (or, indeed, a firearm at all), although the maximum punishment on conviction on indictment for these offences was respectively three (or in some cases five)[139] years' imprisonment, five years'[140] and seven years'. In *Gammon v A-G of Hong Kong*,[141] the maximum imprisonment was three years, and the offences of which the defendant in *Pharmaceutical Society of Great Britain v Storkwain Ltd*[142] and in *Brockley*, referred to in para 6.42, were convicted were punishable with two years' imprisonment. All three cases were decided after *Sweet v Parsley* but before *B v DPP*. Since the decisions in *B v DPP* and *K*, the Court of Appeal in *Muhamad*,[143] has held that the offence of materially contributing to one's insolvency by gambling was 'not a particularly serious' offence, and was one of strict liability, despite the fact that it is punishable with two years' imprisonment.

Whether strict liability would assist the enforcement of the law

6.41 In *Gammon (Hong Kong) Ltd v A-G of Hong Kong*,[144] Lord Scarman, giving the Privy Council's opinion, said that, even where a statute is concerned with an issue of social concern, the presumption of *mens rea* stands unless it can be shown that strict liability will be effective to promote the objects of the statute by encouraging greater vigilance to prevent the commission of the prohibited act.

This point was initially developed by Devlin J in *Reynolds v GH Austin & Sons Ltd*[145] and by the Privy Council in *Lim Chin Aik v R*.[146]

In *Reynolds v GH Austin & Sons Ltd*, D Ltd, a private hire coach company, contracted to take members of a women's guild on a trip to the seaside. Six seats on the coach remained unbooked and the organiser of the trip advertised tickets for them to the general public. The effect of doing so was that the use of the coach to carry the passengers on the trip would be as an 'express carriage', which would require a road service licence to be held by D Ltd. D Ltd did not have such a licence and, being unaware of the advertisement (and hence of the need for one), performed the contract. D Ltd was charged with using the coach as an express carriage without a road service licence, contrary to the Road Traffic

---

135 Para 6.47. 136 [1977] QB 614, CA. See also *Hussain* [1981] 2 All ER 287, CA.
137 [1990] 1 QB 981, CA. 138 [1996] 1 Cr App Rep 138, CA.
139 Now five years' or – in some cases – seven. 140 Now 10 years'.
141 Para 6.16. 142 Para 6.33. 143 Para 6.21.
144 Para 6.23. 145 [1951] 2 KB 135, DC. 146 [1963] AC 160, PC.

Act 1930, s 72 (since repealed). The Divisional Court held that the offence was not one of strict liability. Devlin J (as he then was) stated:

> 'If a man is punished because of an act done by another, whom he cannot reasonably be expected to influence or control, the law is engaged, not in punishing thoughtlessness or inefficiency and thereby promoting the welfare of the community, but in pouncing on the most convenient victim. Without the authority of express words, I am not willing to conclude that Parliament can intend what would seem to the ordinary man to be the useless and unjust infliction of a penalty.... I think it a safe general principle to follow (I state it negatively, since that is sufficient for the purposes of this case), that where the punishment of an individual will not promote the observance of the law either by that individual or by others whose conduct he may reasonably be expected to influence, then, in the absence of clear and express words, such punishment is not intended.'[147]

In *Lim Chin Aik v R*, a case concerned with Singapore immigration regulations, the Privy Council observed that, in considering whether the presumption that *mens rea* was required was rebutted, it is 'not enough merely to label the statute before the court as one dealing with a grave social evil, and from that to infer that strict liability was intended'.[148] It is also necessary to inquire whether putting the defendant under strict liability will assist the enforcement of the law. There must be something he could do

> 'directly or indirectly, by supervision or inspection, by improvement of his business methods or by exhorting those whom he may be expected to influence or control, which will promote the observance of the regulations... Where it can be shown that the imposition of strict liability would result in the prosecution and conviction of a class of persons whose conduct would not in any way affect the observance of the law, their Lordships consider that, even where the statute is dealing with a grave social evil, strict liability is not likely to be intended.'[149]

Lim Chin Aik had been convicted under a Singapore Immigration Ordinance which made it an offence for someone prohibited from entering Singapore to enter or remain there. He had been prohibited from entering Singapore, but the prohibition had not been published or made known to him. The Privy Council advised that his conviction should be quashed on account of the futility of imposing punishment in such a case.

6.42 These decisions can be contrasted with those in the following three cases. In *Brockley*[150] where the Court of Appeal dismissed D's appeal against conviction for acting as a company director when an undischarged bankrupt, contrary to the Company Directors Disqualification Act 1986, s 11, the Court of Appeal held that the trial judge had been correct to rule that the offence was one of strict liability as to the 'undischarged

---

[147] [1951] 2 KB 135 at 149–150.   [148] [1963] AC 160 at 174.

[149] [1963] AC 160 at 174.

[150] (1993) 99 Cr App Rep 385, CA. Also see *Wells Street Metropolitan Stipendiary Magistrate, ex p Westminster City Council* [1986] 3 All ER 4, DC.

bankrupt element'; consequently, it was irrelevant that D might have believed that he had been discharged. The Court stated that it was clear that strict liability would be effective to promote the objects of the statute by ensuring greater vigilance to prevent the commission of the prohibited act; it would oblige bankrupts to ensure that their bankruptcy had in fact been discharged before they engaged in any of the prohibited activities in relation to a company.

The second decision is *Blake*[151] where the Court of Appeal, in holding that the offence of establishing or using any station, or using apparatus, for wireless telegraphy without a licence, contrary to the Wireless Telegraphy Act 1949, s 1(1) (since repealed),[152] was one of strict liability as to the lack of a licence, stated that the imposition of strict liability would encourage greater vigilance on the part of those establishing or using a station, or using equipment, to avoid committing the offence, eg in the case of users by carefully checking whether they were on the air.

The third decision is *Bezzina*[153] which was concerned with the offence under the Dangerous Dogs Act 1991, s 3(1), whereby, if a dog is dangerously out of control in a public place, its owner or handler is guilty of an offence. Dismissing appeals against conviction, the Court of Appeal held that the presumption that *mens rea* was required for this offence was rebutted and that no *mens rea* need be proved on the part of the owner or handler. It had no doubt that strict liability would be effective to promote the objects of the Dangerous Dogs Act 1991 by encouraging greater vigilance among dog owners or handlers to prevent the offence being committed.

These three cases indicate that with isolated exceptions the present requirement will normally be easily satisfied. It must be emphasised that its satisfaction does not automatically rebut the presumption that *mens rea* is required.

The justification for strict liability

Key points 6.8

The arguments for and against strict liability commonly put forward centre on the effective enforcement of the law and the maintenance of standards.

6.43 One justification for strict liability is that the commission of many regulatory offences is very harmful to the public and, it being very difficult to prove that the defendant had acted with *mens rea* as to all the elements of the *actus reus*, such offences would often go unpunished and the legislation rendered nugatory.[154] Again, it is sometimes said

---

[151] [1997] 1 All ER 963, CA.

[152] A corresponding offence is now contained in the Wireless Telegraphy Act 2006, ss 8(1), 35(1).

[153] [1994] 3 All ER 964, CA. Also see *Muhamad* [2002] EWCA Crim 1856 and *Matudi* [2003] EWCA Crim 697; para 6.21.

[154] *Alphacell Ltd v Woodward* [1972] AC 824 at 839 and 848, per Viscount Dilhorne and Lord Salmon.

that too many bogus defences would succeed if excusable ignorance or mistake were always accepted as defences. It is also argued that the great pressure of work upon the minor criminal courts nowadays makes it impractical to inquire into *mens rea* in each prosecution for a regulatory offence.[155] Moreover, it is urged that the imposition of strict liability does something towards ensuring that the controllers of business organisations do everything possible to see that important regulatory legislation is carried out.[156] Repeated convictions may discourage or oblige the incompetent to refrain from certain undertakings and ensure that the competent stay competent.

6.44 There are many who remain unconvinced by these arguments[157]and who reply that the fact that the prosecution may find proof of *mens rea* as to a particular element or elements of the *actus reus* difficult is of itself no reason for depriving the defendant of his customary safeguards.[158] They argue, in any event, that it does not follow that, even if proof of *mens rea* is impossible in certain types of cases, the only solution is to go to the other extreme by denying that the defendant's mental state is relevant to the question of responsibility, since there are other possibilities such as a defence of no negligence. They add that it is improper to jettison the requirement of *mens rea* simply to facilitate the flow of judicial business, that the courts' time is taken up anyway by considerations of *mens rea* in determining sentence, particularly because, if the defendant's state of mind is a matter of dispute, there will have to be a post-conviction hearing to determine this, and that it is not a satisfactory answer to say that it is always possible to subject the offender to a small fine (or even to grant him an absolute discharge), since the 'mere' stigma of a conviction may have serious consequences for the defendant. For example, it may lead to loss of a professional status. In addition, critics of strict liability point out that strict liability is particularly unjust where defendants have taken *all* reasonable precautions to avoid infringing regulatory legislation and therefore cannot reasonably be expected to take further steps to improve their systems. It serves no useful purpose, and may either discourage efficient operators from continuing to trade etc or may encourage them to take precautionary steps which go beyond the reasonable (with consequent costs which will be passed on to the consumer). It is questionable, however, whether the imposition of strict liability results in higher standards of care. In a case before the Supreme Court of Canada, it was observed that:

> 'There is no evidence that a higher standard of care results from [strict] liability. If a person is already taking every reasonable precautionary measure, is he likely to take additional measures, knowing that however much care he takes, it will not serve as a defence

---

[155] Sayre 'Public Welfare Offences' (1933) 33 Columbia Law Review at 69.

[156] *Alphacell Ltd v Woodward* [1972] AC 824 at 848, per Lord Salmon.

[157] For instance, Howard *Strict Responsibility* (1963) 9–28.

[158] See *Thomas v R* (1937) 59 CLR 279 at 309, per Sir Owen Dixon, for a statement to this effect by one of the great judges of the twentieth century.

in the event of breach? If he has exercised care and skill, will conviction have a deterrent effect upon him or others?'[159]

6.45 There is much to be said for removing regulatory offences from the scope of the criminal law and leaving them to be dealt with by administrative remedies. Such a system would leave our criminal courts free to deal with 'real' criminal offences, most of which do not involve strict liability. It would greatly reduce the criticisms made of strict liability in the criminal law.

The Regulatory Enforcement and Sanctions Act 2008, Part 3 (ss 36–65)[160] goes some way to achieving this. It provides a range of civil administrative sanctions which can be imposed by the regulator of a regulated activity in respect of which the regulatory offence of a specified type was committed. Schedule 5 to the Act specifies the regulators who will be allowed to use these sanctions if granted the relevant power to do so. The implementation of this new scheme depends on subordinate legislation which had not been made when this book went to press. Where they are available the civil administrative sanctions will not replace the criminal sanction of a prosecution and conviction in the courts, but it is intended that a prosecution would only be instituted where the breach in question was a serious one. The civil administrative sanctions will be appropriate for cases where advice and persuasion to comply have failed or would otherwise be inadequate.

Under Part 3 of the Act, a regulator can impose the following civil administrative sanctions where the offence is specified by a government minister in respect of the particular sanction:

- a fixed monetary penalty; ie a penalty of an amount prescribed by subordinate legislation;
- one or more of the following discretionary requirements, viz:
  (a) a variable monetary penalty, ie a penalty of an amount determined by the regulator;
  (b) a compliance notice, ie a requirement that steps specified by the regulator be taken to secure that the offence does not continue or recur;
  (c) a restoration notice, ie a requirement by the regulator to restore the position as it would have been if the offence had not been committed;
- a stop notice, which requires the offender to cease the offending activity until he has taken the steps specified in the notice;
- an enforcement undertaking, ie an undertaking to take such action as may be specified in the undertaking within such period as may be specified in it.

When implemented these provisions will be a welcome addition to the powers of regulatory enforcement.

[159] *City of Sault Ste Marie* (1978) 85 DLR (3d) 161 at 171, per Dickson J.
[160] The provisions of Part 3 of the Act are based on the Final Report of the *Macrory Review of Regulatory Penalties* (2006).

Reducing operation of strict liability in the criminal law

Key points 6.9

The injustice involved in strict liability is increasingly being mitigated in statutory offences by the provision of various types of defences.

Statutory defences

6.46 In a limited number of offences, mostly concerned with financial or commercial matters, a defence of 'no intention' is provided. For example, in the offence of destruction by an officer of a company of company documents, contrary to the Companies Act 1985, s 450, a defendant has a defence if he proves that he had no intention to conceal the company's state of affairs or to defeat the law. However, by far the most common statutory defences are 'no negligence' defences.

Although most statutory defences of these types expressly require the defendant to prove them, a particular provision may be interpreted as merely imposing an evidential burden rather than a persuasive one. Exceptionally, the statute expressly states that the defendant merely bears an evidential burden in respect of such a defence: an example is provided by the Tobacco Advertising and Promotion Act 2002, s 17, in respect of no negligence defences (under s 5) to specified offences under that Act.

6.47 One type of 'no negligence' defence is one whereby a burden is placed on the defendant of proving that he had no knowledge of, and was not negligent as to, a particular element of the offence. An example is provided by the Misuse of Drugs Act 1971, s 28, which applies to offences of possession of a controlled drug and certain other drugs-related offences. The section provides that the defendant shall be acquitted if he proves[161] that he neither believed, nor suspected, nor had reason to suspect, that the substance involved was a controlled drug.[162]

Another type of a 'no negligence' defence is the Trade Descriptions Act 1968, s 24(1), which provides the defendant with a defence if he proves that the commission of an offence under the Act was due to a mistake, or to reliance on information supplied to him or to the act or default of another person, an accident or some other cause beyond his control, and that he exercised due diligence to avoid committing the offence in question.[163]

A third type of a 'no negligence' defence is provided by the Weights and Measures Act 1985, s 34,[164] which provides that it is a defence for a person charged with an offence

---

[161] In *Lambert* [2001] UKHL 37, 'proves' in s 28 was interpreted, obiter, as simply requiring the defendant to adduce evidence (as opposed to prove on the balance of probabilities) so as to comply with the ECHR, Art 6(2).

[162] For another example, see para 18.30.

[163] For a similar example, see the Video Recordings Act 1984, s 14A.

[164] Similar examples of this provision are provided by the Building Societies Act 1986, s 112(4); Consumer Protection Act 1987, s 39; Food Safety Act 1990, s 21; and Property Misdescriptions Act 1991, s 2(1).

under Pt IV of the Act to prove that he took all reasonable precautions and exercised all due diligence to avoid the commission of the offence.[165]

6.48 It must be emphasised that there is no general 'no intention' or 'no negligence' defence. Instead, a statutory offence is only subject to such a defence if the statute in question expressly creates it and applies it to that offence.

In comparison, the courts in Australia and Canada have developed a general no-negligence defence to offences which do not require proof of *mens rea* as to one or more elements of the *actus reus*, the persuasive burden of proving which is borne by the defendant.[166] Although such a defence found some favour with three Law Lords in *Sweet v Parsley*,[167] it has yet to be implied by our courts into a statutory offence. Likewise, our courts have not adopted another possibility referred to by Lord Reid in *Sweet v Parsley*: the substitution of a requirement for negligence to be proved instead of subjective *mens rea* when a statutory offence was silent as to the need for *mens rea*.[168] Indeed, a variation on this, preferred by Lord Diplock in *Sweet v Parsley*,[169] the implication of a defence of reasonable mistake under the so-called *Tolson* rule, has been expressly rejected by the House of Lords in *B v DPP*,[170] as explained in para 5.13.

FURTHER READING

Brett 'Strict Responsibility: Possible Solutions' (1974) 37 MLR 417

Horder 'Strict Liability, Statutory Construction and the Spirit of Liberty' (2002) 118 LQR 459

Leigh *Strict and Vicarious Liability* (1982)

Manchester 'Knowledge, Due Diligence and Strict Liability in Statutory Offences' [2006] Crim LR 213

Paulus 'Strict Liability for Public Welfare Offences' (1978) 20 Crim LQ 445

Richardson 'Strict Liability for Regulating Crime: the Empirical Research' [1987] Crim LR 295

Sayre 'Public Welfare Offences' (1933) 33 Columbia LR 55

Simester (ed) *Appraising Strict Liability* (2005)

JC Smith 'Responsibility in Criminal Law' in *Barbara Wootton, Essays in Her Honour* (1986) (Bean and Whynes (eds)) 141

Smith and Pearson 'The Value of Strict Liability' [1969] Crim LR 5

---

[165] For an account of difficulties which may be faced in relying on a 'no negligence' defence, see Cotter 'Due Diligence: the Disappearing Defence' (1992) 142 NLJ 133 and 170.

[166] *Maher v Musson* (1934) 52 CLR 100, HC of Australia; *Proudman v Dayman* (1941) 67 CLR 536, HC of Australia; *City of Sault Ste Marie* (1978) 85 DLR (3d) 161, SC of Canada.

[167] [1970] AC 132 at 150 and 158, per Lords Reid and Pearce.

[168] [1970] AC 132 at 150.

[169] [1970] AC 132 at 163–164.

[170] [2000] 2 AC 428, HL.

7

Non-fatal offences against the person

OVERVIEW

The various kinds of offence against the person, non-fatal, fatal and sexual, are considered in this and the next two chapters. This chapter commences with an examination of the relevance of the victim's consent to the liability for a non-fatal offence against the person. It then deals with the following non-fatal offences against the person:

- assault and battery;
- assault occasioning actual bodily harm and other aggravated assaults;
- offences of wounding or inflicting or causing grievous bodily harm;
- offences relating to administering poison or the like;
- racially or religiously aggravated assaults; and
- offences requiring a course of conduct which amounts to harassment or which puts a person in fear of violence.

The Offences Against the Person Act 1861 (OAPA 1861) deals in detail with most offences against the person which are not fatal but provision is also made by a number of other statutes referred to in this chapter: the Police Act 1996, the Protection from Harassment Act 1997 and the Crime and Disorder Act 1998.

Consent

Introduction

7.1 Many offences against the person, such as common assault and battery, cannot be committed if the victim gives a valid consent. On the other hand, if a mentally competent adult refuses consent to what is done, an offence against the person will be committed (unless some other excuse is available, as it may be if the refusal relates to medical treatment and the person refusing is compulsorily detained in a mental hospital under statute for such treatment[1]). Thus, if an adult patient[2] who is mentally competent refuses to consent to medical treatment, a doctor will commit an offence against the person if he performs the treatment on the patient.[3] This is so however unreasonable or dangerous the refusal is, provided that it was freely and independently made, even where the refusal might lead to the patient's death.[4]

7.2 An offence against the person can be committed, despite the fact that the victim is mentally competent and consents to what is done, if that consent is invalid. While one can validly consent to an application of force which does not cause 'actual bodily harm', or in some cases even if it does, no one can lawfully consent to his own death at the hands of another.[5] Although suicide is no longer an offence, euthanasia at the victim's request still is. However excellent his motives may be, someone who by some positive act kills another at that other's request is guilty of murder unless he acted in pursuance of a suicide pact, in which case his offence is manslaughter.[6] On the other hand, as mentioned in para 2.12, a doctor or someone else with care of an adult who is mentally competent does not commit an offence if, at the request of that adult, he fails to look after him and thereby allows him to die or suffer other harm. The reason is that his duty to act has been extinguished by the other's request.

Key points 7.1

Consent can validly be given to an act which does not cause actual bodily harm.

Consent cannot validly be given if an act causes actual bodily harm which the defendant intended or foresaw unless the case falls within one of a number of recognised exceptions or a new exception is recognised on public interest grounds.

Validity of consent to actual bodily harm: the general rule

7.3 In *A-G's Reference (No 6 of 1980)*[7] the Court of Appeal stated that, generally, **a person's consent is irrelevant and cannot prevent criminal liability for an offence if actual bodily harm was 'intended and/or caused'.** 'Actual bodily harm' means an injury which is not so trivial as to be wholly insignificant; it is explained further in paras 7.58–7.60.

The statement in *A-G's Reference (No 6 of 1980)* was based on the view that 'it is not in the public interest that people should try to cause or should cause each other actual

---

[1] Mental Health Act 1983, s 63.   [2] As to children, see para 7.26.
[3] Para 2.12.
[4] *St George's Healthcare NHS Trust v S* [1998] 3 All ER 673, CA. Also see *Airedale National Health Service Trust v Bland* [1993] AC 789 at 891, per Lord Mustill.
[5] *Young* (1838) 8 C & P 644; *Cuddy* (1843) 1 Car & Kir 210.   [6] Para 8.42.
[7] [1981] QB 715, CA.

bodily harm for no good reason'. In some cases there may be a good reason, and the Court of Appeal was at pains to emphasise that the rule did not affect the accepted legality of certain situations, referred to below, in which the consent of the victim is legally relevant and renders the conduct in question lawful.

The Court of Appeal's views were approved, applied and developed by the majority of the House of Lords in *Brown*[8] which is the leading case in this area. In *Brown*,[9] the defendants belonged to a group of sado-masochistic homosexuals who willingly participated in acts of violence against each other, including genital torture by the insertion of fish-hooks through the penis, for the sexual pleasure engendered in the giving and receiving of pain. The passive partner in each case consented to what was done and the bodily harm suffered was not permanent. The activities took place in private. They were video-recorded, the videotapes being distributed only among the group. The defendants were convicted of assault occasioning actual bodily harm and unlawful wounding, contrary to the OAPA 1861, ss 47 and 20 respectively. Their convictions were upheld by the Court of Appeal. The defendants appealed to the House of Lords, contending that a person could not be guilty of offences under the OAPA 1861, ss 47 and 20 in respect of acts carried out in private with the victim's consent.

By a majority of three to two, the House of Lords dismissed the appeals.

It held that, since actual bodily harm was intended and caused, consent was irrelevant unless it could find that it was in the public interest to permit the intentional causing of actual bodily harm in the course of sado-masochistic practices, and there were several good reasons why it should not do so.[10] First, it was only luck that the participants had not suffered any serious harm or infections. Second, there was a risk of spreading diseases such as AIDS. Third, there was the danger that young people could be drawn into the unnatural practices.

7.4 Three of the defendants in *Brown* unsuccessfully complained to the European Court of Human Rights that their convictions constituted an unjustified intrusion into their right to respect for their private lives under ECHR, Article 8. In *Laskey, Jaggard and Brown v United Kingdom*,[11] the name of the case before the European Court of Human Rights, the Court held that, while Article 8 was engaged, the interference with the right to respect for private life was justified under Article 8(2) because it was necessary in a democratic society for the protection of health and, possibly, of morals. It held that, in the first instance, it was within the competence of each State, including its courts, to determine

---

8 [1994] 1 AC 212, HL.

9 For discussion of *Brown*, see Mullender 'Sado-Masochism, Criminal Law and Adjudicative Method: *R v Brown* in the House of Lords' (1993) 44 NILQ 380; Giles '*R v Brown*: Consensual Harm and the Public Interest' (1994) 57 MLR 101; Allen 'Consent and Assault' (1994) 58 JCL 183.

10 The same view was taken about the validity of consent in an earlier case involving heterosexual sado-masochism, *Donovan* [1934] 2 KB 498, CCA, where D beat a 17-year-old girl with her consent for the purposes of sexual gratification: the Court held her consent would be invalid if the blows were intended or likely to cause bodily harm.

11 (1997) 24 EHRR 39, ECtHR.

the degree of physical harm which should be tolerated where a victim consented. Because the harm inflicted was not insignificant, even though no hospital treatment was required, and because public health considerations were also in issue, the applicants' behaviour did not form part of their private sexual behaviour which it was not the State's function to regulate.

7.5 The statement in *A-G's Reference (No 6 of 1980)*, approved in *Brown*, about consent being invalid if actual bodily harm is 'intended *and/or* caused' has been problematic. **One thing is clear, however, and this is that under the statement a valid consent to conduct cannot generally be given to an act where, as in *Brown*, the defendant intentionally causes actual bodily harm (or worse).**

7.6 One difficulty with the statement is that it suggested that consent was invalid if actual bodily harm (or worse) was intended but did not actually result. On this basis, if the dominant partner in a sado-masochistic partnership has only landed a few harmless blows and is then stopped before he can cause the intended actual bodily harm, his partner's consent will not prevent him being liable for a battery. This would be consistent with suggestions in dicta in two appeal court decisions.[12] On the other hand, in *Brown* the majority of the House of Lords were of the view that consent was a defence to a charge of common assault (a term which covers the offences of assault and battery, which do not require actual bodily harm to be caused). More importantly, in *Barnes*,[13] the Court of Appeal stated, obiter, that: 'When no bodily harm is caused, the consent of the victim is always a defence to a charge.'[14] On this basis, the law now seems to be that **if the defendant intends to cause the victim actual bodily harm, but does not cause it, the victim's consent is valid.**

7.7 Another difficulty with the reference to actual bodily harm being 'intended *and/or* caused' arose where the victim consented to the defendant's act and that act unintentionally and unexpectedly caused actual bodily harm (or worse). Read literally, the wording of the phrase seemed to mean that it is irrelevant that actual bodily harm was unintended, unforeseen or even unforeseeable by the defendant; the victim's consent would be invalid. However, as explained below, the courts have found a way round such an unreasonable outcome.

Initially, it seemed that the victim's consent to conduct which caused unintended actual bodily harm was only invalid if such harm was objectively likely. This supposition was based on *Boyea*,[15] where D had engaged in vigorous sexual activity with a woman. During it he caused her harm by inserting his hand into her vagina and twisting it. His conviction for indecent assault was affirmed on the ground that D was guilty of an assault because his conduct was likely to cause actual bodily harm, even if D did not intend or foresee that harm was likely to be caused. This suggested that if the defendant's conduct

---

[12] *Donovan* [1934] 2 KB 498, CCA; *Boyea* (1992) 156 JP 505, CA. [13] [2004] EWCA Crim 3246.
[14] [2004] EWCA Crim 3246 at [7]. [15] (1992) 156 JP 505, CA.

was objectively likely to cause actual bodily harm, consent to it was invalid, even if the defendant did not intend or foresee it.

The Crown Court ruling of Judge J (as he then was) in *Slingsby*[16] went further because it provided authority that, where unintended actual bodily harm occurred, the victim's consent to the defendant's conduct was only invalid if the risk of such harm was foreseen. In *Slingsby*, D and the victim also engaged in vigorous sexual activity, involving D penetrating V's vagina and rectum with his hand. V consented to this use of force. V suffered cuts from D's signet ring, and subsequently died from septicaemia. At D's trial for manslaughter by an unlawful and dangerous act, Judge J ruled that, as V's injury had not been anticipated by D or V, it would be contrary to principle to treat as an unlawful act conduct which would not otherwise constitute an 'assault' simply because injury occurred. Consequently, this was not a case where a consent was invalid under the rule in *A-G's Reference (No 6 of 1980)*, and V had given a valid consent to the force involved: there was therefore no unlawful act for the purposes of manslaughter.

The approach in *Slingsby* was applied by the Court of Appeal in *Meachen*,[17] another case where, according to D, unforeseen actual bodily harm had been caused to V in the course of consensual sexual activity. Quashing D's convictions for inflicting grievous bodily harm and indecent assault, the Court of Appeal held that the trial judge had been wrong not to direct the jury that V's consent could excuse D in these circumstances. It concluded that if the defendant did not intend, or foresee the risk of, actual bodily harm, and the victim consented to the acts done from which such harm unexpectedly results, the victim's consent to those acts is valid. Following a dictum in *Dica*,[18] discussed later, it regarded *Boyea* as having been decided on the basis that the victim had not in fact consented and that therefore the issue which arose in *Slingsby* and in *Meachen* was not before the court in *Boyea*.

Thus, despite the statement with which this discussion began, the law relating to when a valid consent to the defendant's conduct can be given for the purposes of the law relating to non-fatal offences against the person can be summarised as follows:

ABH intended or foreseen as risk *but not* caused:	Consent valid
ABH intended or foreseen as risk *and* caused:	Consent invalid unless case falls within an exception
ABH caused but *not* intended or foreseen as risk:	Consent valid

---

[16] [1995] Crim LR 570, Crown Ct. What follows is based on the transcript of the judge's ruling cited in *Meachen* [2006] EWCA Crim 2414 at [39].

[17] [2006] EWCA Crim 2414.   [18] [2004] EWCA Crim 1103 at [44].

Exceptions to the general rule

Key points 7.2

Recognised exceptions to the general rule that consent cannot validly be given to an act which causes actual bodily harm (or worse) as intended or foreseen as a risk are in the cases of:

- properly conducted games or sports;
- reasonable surgical interference;
- tattooing, ear piercing and personal adornment;
- horseplay;
- dangerous exhibitions;
- religious mortification; and
- consensual non-violent sexual conduct carrying the risk of the transmission of disease.

Further exceptions may be recognised by the courts.

7.8 As the House of Lords recognised in *A-G's Reference (No 6 of 1980)* and in *Brown*, there may be 'good reason' for the infliction of actual bodily harm, in which case a valid consent to it may be given by way of exception to the general rule. The exceptional cases where a person may validly consent to actual bodily harm are situations where the law considers that the public interest requires the exception. In other words, like the general rule, the exceptions are based on public policy and have no separate jurisprudential basis for each of the contexts in which they apply.[19] This means that changing public attitudes can affect the number and extent of exceptions.[20] In respect of two of the exceptional cases that have been recognised, a properly conducted game or sport and reasonable surgical interference,[21] what is a 'properly conducted game or sport' or 'reasonable surgical interference' itself turns on the public interest.

Properly conducted games or sports

7.9 A participant in a sport, such as a football, rugby or cricket match, impliedly and validly consents to conduct which carries the risk of such accidental actual bodily harm, even serious harm, as can reasonably be expected during the match because these are

---

[19] This was recognised by the Court of Appeal in *Barnes* [2004] EWCA Crim 3246 at [11].

[20] This was also recognised in *Barnes* [2004] EWCA Crim 3246 at [11].

[21] These two exceptions were recognised in *A-G's Reference (No 6 of 1980)* [1981] QB 715, CA, and *Brown* [1994] 1 AC 212, HL.

regarded as properly conducted sports; if such harm is caused the valid consent prevents it being criminal.[22] On the other hand, the participant does not consent to conduct which cannot reasonably be expected and, anyway, he cannot validly consent to the intentional infliction of actual bodily harm. A footballer, rugby player or cricketer, for example, does not, and could not, consent to being intentionally punched or kicked.[23]

In *Barnes*,[24] the Court of Appeal gave the following guidance on whether or not the risk of what has occurred could reasonably be expected. The fact that the play is within the rules of the game gives a firm indication that what has happened is not criminal. In judging whether conduct is criminal or not, it must be remembered that, in highly competitive sports, conduct outside the rules can be expected to occur in the heat of the moment, and even if the conduct justifies a sending off, it still may not reach the threshold level required for it to be criminal. That level is an objective one and does not depend upon the views of individual players. The type of the sport, the level at which it is played, the nature of the act, the degree of force used, the extent of the risk of injury and the state of mind of the defendant are all likely to be relevant in determining whether the defendant's actions go beyond the threshold. Whether conduct reaches the required level depends on all the circumstances. However, there will be cases that fall within a 'grey area', and then the jury will have to make its own determination as to which side of the line the case falls.

7.10 Apart from boxing under the Queensberry Rules and martial arts, it is difficult to think of a game or sport where the participants consent to intentional actual bodily harm which would be regarded as properly conducted. For example, a prize fight (a fight with bare fists until one participant is unable to continue) is not regarded as a properly conducted sport, whereas boxing and wrestling are, because the serious physical risks which attach to the former are against the public interest,[25] while the latter are 'manly diversions, they intend to give strength, skill and activity, and may fit people for defence, public as well as personal, in time of need'.[26] The consent in boxing is only to intentional harm within the rules; a boxer does not consent to being intentionally harmed by, for example, a blow delivered between rounds.

In *Brown*, there were obiter dicta by four Law Lords indicating that they were clearly of the opinion that boxing is lawful. Lord Mustill thought that it was impossible 'to arrive at an intellectually satisfying account of the apparent immunity of professional boxing from the criminal process'. He suggested that this was a 'special situation which for the time being stands outside the ordinary law of violence because society chooses to tolerate it'.[27]

---

[22] *Coney* (1882) 8 QBD 534, CCR; *Barnes* [2004] EWCA Crim 3246.

[23] *Bradshaw* (1878) 14 Cox CC 83; *Barnes* [2004] EWCA Crim 3246 at [14].

[24] [2004] EWCA Crim 3246. See also *Bradshaw* (1878) 14 Cox CC 83; *Moore* (1898) 14 TLR 229.

[25] *Coney* (1882) 8 QBD 534 at 537, per Cave J.   [26] Foster *Crown Law* (3rd edn, 1792) 259.

[27] [1994] 1 AC 212 at 265. The Law Commission's view is that the continued legality of boxing should be considered by Parliament: *Consent and Offences against the Person* (1994), Law Com Consultation Paper No 134, paras 6.22 and 6.23; *Consent in the Criminal Law* (1995), Law Com Consultation Paper No 139, para 12.38. Subsequent attempts in Parliament to outlaw boxing have failed at an early stage: see (1995) 145 NLJ 1851.

Reasonable surgical interference

7.11 A valid consent can be given to actual bodily harm caused by reasonable surgical interference. It may seem odd to refer to surgical interference causing 'actual bodily harm' since benefit rather than harm will normally be its purpose. However, surgical interference will often involve permanent harm to the body (as in the case of an amputation) or a short-term wound or other harm to the body.

7.12 The question whether a surgical operation is 'reasonable surgical interference' is answered in the case of female circumcision by legislation which declares that it is unlawful[28] (and therefore not reasonable surgical interference) save in specified circumstances.

In other cases, the question whether a surgical operation is 'reasonable surgical interference' clearly admits only of the answer 'yes' where it is performed for therapeutic reasons. It appears, for example, that a sex-change operation[29] performed for genuine therapeutic reasons is not open to legal objection.

On the other hand, the answer may be different in some cases where an operation is performed for non-therapeutic reasons. A prime example of such an operation is one involving the mutilation of the body in accordance with religious or tribal ritual or custom, or in order to secure a discharge from military service. Operations which *may* not be performed for therapeutic reasons include sterilisation and cosmetic surgery. Whether a non-therapeutic operation is contrary to the public interest in this area may give rise to differences of opinion, and opinions may change with the times. For example, in *Bravery v Bravery*,[30] a civil case decided in 1954, Denning LJ held that a sterilisation operation performed on a man for non-eugenic reasons (to enable him to enjoy sexual intercourse without the risk of becoming a father) would be unlawful as being injurious to the public interest, whereas the other two Lords Justices expressly dissociated themselves from this view, saying that they were not prepared 'in the present case' to hold that such operations were injurious to the public interest. There can be no doubt that a sterilisation operation for such a purpose would now be held to be reasonable surgical interference so that a valid consent could be given to it.[31] The same is no doubt true about a cosmetic operation, except presumably for a cosmetic operation performed for some purpose contrary to the public interest, eg to enable a criminal to avoid detection. In addition, ritual male circumcision has been held to be an interference to which consent can validly be given.[32] On the other hand, for example, the surgical mutilation of someone in order to secure his discharge from military service or to enable him better to beg would seem to be against the

---

[28] Female Genital Mutilation Act 2003, s 1. Contravention of the statute is in itself an offence, quite apart from invalidating any consent on the part of the 'patient'.

[29] *Corbett v Corbett* [1971] P 83 at 99.   [30] [1954] 3 All ER 59, CA.

[31] In *Dica* [2004] EWCA Crim 1103 at [41] the Court of Appeal, obiter, described Denning LJ's approach as dated.

[32] *Brown* [1994] 1 AC 212 at 231, per Lord Templeman; *Re J* [2000] 1 FCR 307, CA.

public interest, and therefore not reasonable surgical interference, in which case a valid consent could not be given to it.[33]

Tattooing, ear piercing and personal adornment

7.13 These activities can be regarded as involving actual bodily harm. In *Brown*,[34] Lord Templeman and Lord Slynn (in his dissenting speech) regarded tattooing and ear piercing as activities to which a valid consent could be given. However, whether or not a consent to being tattooed or ear pierced is valid depends on an evaluation in public interest terms of the circumstances,[35] such as who carries out the procedure (an amateur or professional?) and the way in which the procedure is carried out (eg is adequately sterilised equipment or material used to prevent the spread of hepatitis, HIV and so on?). Tattooing of someone under 18 (otherwise than by a doctor for medical reasons) is an offence under the Tattooing of Minors Act 1969. There can be no doubt that contravention of the statute would invalidate any consent on the part of the minor.

In *Wilson*, dealt with in para 7.20, the Court of Appeal regarded branding as not logically different from tattooing. However, it is clear from that decision that whether or not a consent to being branded is valid likewise depends on the circumstances.

7.14 Forms of cosmetic body piercing other than ear piercing, such as navel, nipple, lip or tongue piercing done for the purposes of adornment, rather than sado-masochism (see *Brown*), do not appear to have been the subject of judicial consideration in our courts so far. It is submitted that, in determining whether a consent to such piercing for the purposes of adornment is valid, the court should look at the type of circumstances mentioned in para 7.13, as well as any potential long-term damage. Tongue piercing, for example, can interfere with speech and result in chipping to teeth (from impact from the stud) and recessed gums, and any form of body piercing described here can damage nerve ends. *Wilson* suggests that, when the point arises, the courts will regard these types of piercing as akin to ear piercing and tattooing if they are carried out in appropriate circumstances.[36]

Horseplay

7.15 Another exception, recognised by the Court of Appeal in *Jones*,[37] but not referred to in *Brown* (except by Lord Mustill), is that, **if a person is caused actual bodily harm by rough and undisciplined horseplay which is not intended to cause injury,**

---

[33] There is old persuasive authority in support: Coke 1 *Institutes* 127a and 127b, Hawkins 1 *Pleas of the Crown* 108, Stephen *Digest of Criminal Law* (3rd edn) 142.

[34] [1994] 1 AC 212 at 231 and 277.

[35] This statement is in line with the approach taken in *Wilson*, discussed in para 7.20.

[36] The Local Government (Miscellaneous Provisions) Act 1982, s 15, referred to in para 2.19, assumes that cosmetic piercing can be legally performed with consent with a licence, but whether it is in such a case remains dependent on the circumstances.

[37] (1986) 83 Cr App Rep 375, CA.

his consent to run the risk of it is legally relevant and prevents the conduct being unlawful. In that case, boys who had been tossed in the air by others were accidentally injured when the others failed to catch them. The trial judge did not leave the issue of consent to the jury on the ground that it was irrelevant. The Court of Appeal held that he had been wrong: if the boys had consented that consent would have been valid and relevant. In *Aitken*,[38] discussed in para 15.77, the Courts-Martial Appeal Court assumed that the victim's consent would have provided a defence to horseplay which gave rise a risk of serious bodily harm. Where the risk is of serious bodily harm and is reasonably foreseeable (as it was in *Aitken*), it is difficult to see why the public interest test is satisfied.

Dangerous exhibitions

7.16 Another exception which has been recognised is that a person who takes part in a dangerous exhibition can give a valid consent to the risk of being unintentionally harmed.[39]

Religious mortification

7.17 In *Brown*,[40] Lord Mustill recognised that a valid consent could be given to religious mortification, ie the infliction of pain on a penitent with his consent as part of his religious repentance.

Consensual non-violent sexual conduct carrying the risk of transmission of disease

7.18 A further exception, recognised by the Court of Appeal in *Dica* in 2004,[41] is that **someone can validly consent to run the known risk of infection, as well as all the other risks inherent in, and possible consequences of, sexual intercourse, just as he can validly consent to run the risks inherent in other aspects of everyday life.** Thus, as the Court recognised, if D, who has a serious sexual disease, has sexual intercourse with V who knows of D's disease but nevertheless consents to run the risk of contracting it and have the intercourse, and V becomes infected and suffers grievous bodily harm in consequence, V will have given a valid consent to the risk of being infected

---

[38] [1992] 1 WLR 1006, C-MAC (as to this court see para 2.32, n 91). Also see *Richardson and Irwin* [1999] 1 Cr App Rep 392, CA.

[39] *A-G's Reference (No 6 of 1980)* [1981] QB 715, CA.   [40] [1994] 1 AC 212 at 267.

[41] [2004] EWCA Crim 1103 at [47]–[50]. The Court distinguished *Brown* (para 7.3) on the ground that it involved serious violence and the intentional infliction of serious injury. It stated, obiter, that, in the case of the intentional transmission of serious disease, the consent of the infected party would be no defence: see [46] and [58]. For another issue in *Dica*, see para 7.32. For commendation of the Court of Appeal's decision in *Dica*, see JR Spencer 'Retrial for Reckless Infection' (2004) 154 NLJ 762; for criticism, see Weait '*Dica*: Knowledge, Consent and the Transmission of HIV' (2004) 154 NLJ 826.

and suffering grievous bodily harm. The Court of Appeal distinguished *Brown* in the following terms:

> 'In our judgment the impact of the authorities dealing with sexual gratification can too readily be misunderstood. It does not follow from them, and they do not suggest, that consensual acts of sexual intercourse are unlawful merely because there may be a known risk to the health of one or other participants. These participants are not intent on spreading or becoming infected with disease through sexual intercourse. They are not indulging in serious violence for the purposes of sexual gratification. They are simply prepared, knowingly, to run the risk – not the certainty – of infection, as well as all the other risks inherent in and possible consequences of sexual intercourse, such as, and despite the most careful precautions, an unintended pregnancy.'[42]

As indicated in *Dica*, and confirmed by the Court of Appeal in *Konzani*,[43] to be valid the consent must be an informed consent, which it will not be if D has concealed his disease (unless V knows of it through another source).

Further exceptions

7.19 According to the approach of the Court of Appeal in *A-G's Reference (No 6 of 1980)*[44] and of the majority of the House of Lords in *Brown*,[45] consent to actual bodily harm will be invalid unless there is held to be good reason (ie to be in the public interest) for the activity in question.

The approach of the majority in *Brown* may be contrasted with that of Lord Mustill,[46] one of the minority in *Brown*, to the effect that a consent to an act which caused actual bodily harm would be valid unless there was good reason to stop the activity in question. This more liberal approach would result in the recognition of a wider range of activities in which a valid consent to intentional bodily harm could be given.

7.20 Lord Mustill's approach was taken by the Court of Appeal in *Wilson*,[47] although the Court thought that it was taking the approach of the majority. In *Wilson*, D burned his initials on his wife's buttocks with a hot knife. He did so with her consent and at her instigation. D was convicted of an assault occasioning actual bodily harm. The Court of Appeal allowed his appeal against conviction. It stated that there was no evidence that the method of branding adopted by D was more dangerous than tattooing and that there was no logical difference between it and tattooing. Having asked the question whether the public interest demanded that D's activity should be criminal, it concluded that it was not

---

[42] [2004] EWCA Crim 1103 at [47].

[43] [2005] EWCA Crim 706, discussed by Weait 'Knowledge, Autonomy and Consent: *R v Konzani*' [2005] Crim LR 763.

[44] [1981] QB 715, CA.   [45] [1994] 1 AC 212, HL.

[46] In *Barnes* [2004] EWCA Crim 3246 at [9], the Court of Appeal considered that Lord Mustill's analysis of the case law was of the highest authority.

[47] [1997] QB 47, CA. See Roberts 'Consent to Injury: How Far Can You Go?' (1997) 113 LQR 27.

in the public interest that the consensual activity of branding carried out between husband and wife in the privacy of the matrimonial home should be criminal where there was no aggressive intent. Consequently, the wife's consent to the branding was a valid one.

The Court of Appeal considered that the case before it could be distinguished from *Brown* in the following ways, none of which is very convincing as a ground of distinction:

- Mrs Wilson had not only consented to the branding but had instigated it. (It is hard to see why this should be relevant);

- there was no 'aggressive intent' in *Wilson*. (Given that it was done with consent, what was done in *Brown* could hardly be said to have been done with 'aggressive intent');

- *Brown* was a case about sado-masochism, unlike *Wilson*. (But why should the fact that something is done in private for a sexual motive as opposed to the motive in *Wilson* make a difference?);

- what was done in *Wilson* was not logically different from tattooing;

- *Wilson* involved consensual activity between a husband and wife in the privacy of their own home.

The Court of Appeal's reference to the circumstances of the case raises interesting speculation in terms of the public interest: what if the couple had not been married, and what if a homosexual man brands his casual male partner, for example?

The Court of Appeal said in *Wilson* that in the area of consent the law should develop on a case-by-case basis, rather than upon general propositions. This is an unsatisfactory approach in the light of the vagueness of the public interest and the consequent variability in the application of that concept. It makes it difficult to predict the result of a case.

7.21 The preference of the courts to develop the law on a case-by-case basis, rather than through developing general propositions, was shown again by the Court of Appeal in *Emmett*,[48] another sado-masochism case. D and the woman with whom he was cohabiting, and whom he had married by the time of the trial, were apparently involved in an energetic and very physical sexual relationship. On one occasion, D had tied a plastic bag over the woman's head during sexual activity. As a result she had suffered restriction of oxygen to the brain. During the next day her eyes had become increasingly bloodshot. Her doctor diagnosed a subconjunctival haemorrhage in both eyes. No treatment was necessary. If D had allowed the restriction of oxygen to have gone on for too long brain damage and ultimately death might have resulted. On a second occasion, D poured lighter fuel on the woman's breasts and set light to it. According to D, the woman then panicked, so he could not extinguish the flames immediately. As a result she suffered a burn measuring 6cm × 4cm; contrary to early expectations, a skin graft was not required. Neither of these incidents was reported by the woman. The doctor reported them. D was charged with assault occasioning actual bodily harm in respect of both incidents. He alleged that the woman had consented to what was done on both occasions. He was convicted by the

---

[48] (1999) *Times*, 15 October, CA. This is a brief report. See the transcript for a full report.

jury in respect of the first incident on the judge's direction that the woman's consent on that occasion was invalid, and in the light of that direction he pleaded guilty in respect of the second.

The Court of Appeal dismissed D's appeals against conviction. D did not intend to cause the woman bodily harm; he had simply taken a risk of it on both occasions when harm had resulted, aware of the dangers. Nevertheless, the Court of Appeal, applying the approach of the majority in *Brown*, held that the trial judge had been correct to conclude that consent was no defence. It distinguished *Wilson* on the ground that the 'actual or potential damage to which the woman was exposed' in *Emmett* 'plainly went beyond that which was established in *Wilson*... This was not tattooing'. The Court expressed a reluctance to say where the line should be drawn on the ground that it was plain that the activities involved went well beyond that line wherever it was drawn.

Further points

7.22 One consequence of the legal rules just described is that it is not unlawful for one man intentionally to cause actual bodily harm to the other participant during the ordinary course of a boxing match, whereas blows given for the purposes of sexual gratification during a sado-masochistic homosexual flagellation session or given during a fist-fight by two men who are 'settling a score' are unlawful, even though the bodily harm intended and resulting may well be less serious than in the case of the boxing match.

7.23 *Brown* and the other cases referred to above raise in an acute form the question of the extent to which mentally competent adults should be able to consent to what is done to their bodies in private when there has been no external impact; they raise the question of the weight to be given to paternalism on the one hand, and personal autonomy on the other. The balance between these two concepts comes down firmly in favour of paternalism. The conduct in *Brown* would be found to be repulsive by the vast majority of the population, but – even though interference may be justifiable under the ECHR – should that be enough to justify interfering with the sexual autonomy and privacy of those involved by making it criminal?

7.24 In 1995,[49] the Law Commission provisionally proposed that the intentional or reckless causing of *seriously disabling injury* should continue to be criminal, even if the person injured consents to such injury or to the risk of such injury.[50] A 'seriously disabling injury' was defined as one which 'causes serious distress and involves the loss of a bodily member or organ or permanent bodily injury or permanent functional impairment, or serious or permanent disfigurement, or severe and prolonged pain, or serious impairment of health or prolonged unconsciousness'. The victim's consent would be invalid here because such harm is contrary to his interests.

---

[49] *Consent in the Criminal Law*, Law Com Consultation Paper, No 139.

[50] The proposal would not affect the statutory limitations on female circumcision and the tattooing of minors (although the Commission sought views on the age limit). A valid consent could be given to any degree of seriously disabling injury if it was caused during the course of proper medical treatment or care. There would be similar exceptions for injuries caused in the course of properly approved medical research.

Where the injury failed to meet the test of seriously disabling injury, a valid consent could be given (except in the case of fighting otherwise than in the course of a recognised sport), and no offence committed, except that someone under 18 could not validly consent to intentional injuries caused for sexual, religious or spiritual purposes (and possibly in certain other cases, such as below-the-neck body piercing).

A possible defect with this proposal is that it draws the level of the harm to which someone can consent at a high point, well beyond minor harm, and that it seems to ignore the fact that personal injury prognosis often cannot be evaluated quickly or easily. On the other hand, if one accepts that the Commission is right to propose drawing the line as it has, the proposal can be criticised on the ground that the definition of serious bodily harm ignores whether or not the injury is remediable by surgery or otherwise.

The adoption of the above proposal would redress to some extent the balance between paternalism and personal autonomy, but the balance would still come down in favour of the former.[51]

Apparent consent invalid[52]

Key points 7.3

Sometimes a person may appear to consent to conduct to which a valid consent can be given under the above rules but his consent is invalidated because:

- he lacks the capacity to consent on grounds of his youth, intoxication or mental incompetence;
- he gives the consent under duress; or
- he gives the consent under a mistake which invalidates it.

Lack of capacity

7.25 An apparent consent is invalid where the person giving it is so young, intoxicated or mentally disordered or retarded that his knowledge or understanding is such that he is unable to make a rational decision whether or not to consent.[53] However, the act will nevertheless be lawful in such a case if the physical contact is generally acceptable in the ordinary conduct of daily life.[54]

---

[51] For different evaluations of what was proposed in the consultation paper, see Ashworth 'The Revisiting of Consent' [1996] Crim LR 73; Shute 'Something Old, Something New, Something Borrowed: Three Aspects of the Project' [1996] Crim LR 684; Ormerod and Gunn 'Consent – A Second Bash' [1996] Crim LR 694 and Roberts 'The Philosophical Foundations of Consent in the Criminal Law' (1997) 17 OJLS 389.

[52] This issue arises most commonly in respect of sexual offences under the Sexual Offences Act 2003 and is dealt with in Ch 9 in relation to them. The Sexual Offences Act 2003 contains special provisions.

[53] *Burrell v Harmer* [1967] Crim LR 169, DC; *Howard* [1965] 3 All ER 684, CCA; *Lang* (1975) 62 Cr App Rep 50, CA.

[54] See para 7.34.

7.26 Consent can generally be given on behalf of a child by a person with parental responsibility for it.[55] In respect of surgical, medical or dental treatment a minor of 16 or 17 can, by statute,[56] give a valid consent. The House of Lords in *Gillick v West Norfolk and Wisbech Area Health Authority*[57] held that a minor under 16 can also give a valid consent to treatment if he has sufficient maturity and understanding to understand what is involved. However, the wishes of a competent minor under 16 can be overridden by consent being given by someone with parental responsibility or by a civil court exercising its wardship over children.[58]

A court can overrule a giving or refusal of consent by someone with parental responsibility.[59]

Duress

7.27 The victim's apparent consent may be invalid if it has been procured by an express or implied threat. In *Day*,[60] D was charged, inter alia, with an assault on a girl of nine. The girl had not resisted his conduct and it was argued that, since she had submitted to his acts, she must be taken to have consented and that therefore D was not guilty. The jury were directed that if the girl had submitted to D's acts out of fear there would have been no real consent on her part and they would be without her consent. What constitutes sufficient duress remains undecided. Clearly, a threat of violence does and so would a threat of imprisonment. Probably any pressure which the victim cannot reasonably be expected to withstand from the particular defendant will suffice for duress.

Mistake

Mistake as to nature of act or defendant's identity

7.28 There is no valid consent if a person, apparently consenting, is induced to do so by a mistake, whether induced by the defendant's deception or self-induced,[61] as to the nature of the act or as to the identity of the defendant.[62] For example, if V consents in the dark to being embraced by D, having been fooled by D into thinking that he is X, her boyfriend, there is no valid consent by V to being touched by D. V's mistake as to D's identity invalidates her apparent consent. A mistake as to the nature of an act is one which relates to the essence of the act. The purpose with which an act is done clearly goes to the essence of an act and it is submitted that, whether or not it can be said to involve a mistake as to the nature of the act, a mistake as to its purpose is not a valid consent.

---

[55] See Cretney, Masson and Bailey-Harris *Principles of Family Law* (8th edn, 2009) 542.
[56] Family Law Reform Act 1969, s 8.   [57] [1986] AC 112, HL.
[58] *Re W (a minor) (medical treatment: court's jurisdiction)* [1993] Fam 64, CA.
[59] *Re B* [1990] 3 All ER 927, CA.   [60] (1841) 9 C & P 722.
[61] *Richardson* [1999] QB 444 at 450. If the defendant is unaware of a self-induced mistake he will lack the *mens rea* for the assault or other non-fatal offence in question: *Tabassum* [2000] 2 Cr App Rep 328, CA.
[62] *Case* (1850) 4 Cox CC 220; *Williams* [1923] 1 KB 340, CCA.

Mistake as to collateral matter

7.29 Until fairly recently, the courts have been consistent in stating that, provided that the victim knew the nature of the act and the identity of who was doing it, it was irrelevant that he was mistaken about a collateral detail relating to the act.

Thus, it was held that no assault had occurred in *Clarence*[63] where D had intercourse with his wife, knowing that he had venereal disease, and thereby infected her. The wife did not know of D's disease. D was convicted of inflicting grievous bodily harm, contrary to the OAPA 1861, s 20, an offence which was then regarded as requiring the grievous bodily harm to result from an 'assault' (ie assault or battery). It was argued that D's concealment of his condition amounted to a fraud which negatived his wife's consent to the intercourse and thus rendered the bodily contact an 'assault'. It was held that even if D's conduct did amount to a fraud it would not vitiate the wife's consent to the sexual intercourse because she understood the nature of the act; her ignorance of D's disease was not enough. Similarly, in *Richardson*,[64] it was held that there was no assault occasioning actual bodily harm on patients by a dentist who had given them dental treatment while suspended from practice (which suspension she had not disclosed to them). The Court of Appeal held that the 'identity' of a person did not include his qualifications or attributes. The mistake had not been about the identity of the defendant (ie who she was) but about what she was.

7.30 In *Tabassum*,[65] the Court of Appeal adopted a more liberal approach than that set out above. **It held that, in addition to a mistake as to identity, a mistake as to the nature or *quality* of an act would vitiate an apparent consent.** In that case, three women, who had been asked by D to participate in what he said was a breast cancer survey to enable him to prepare a software package for sale to doctors, consented to D feeling their naked breasts (in two cases) and to putting a stethoscope under her bra (in the third case). All three women gave their consent, wrongly believing that D had either medical qualifications or relevant training (as he had alleged). None of the women would have allowed D to touch her if she had known the truth. D was convicted on three counts of indecent assault on a woman, contrary to the Sexual Offences Act 1956, an offence now replaced by offences of sexual assault under the Sexual Offences Act 2003. The Court of Appeal dismissed D's appeal against these convictions. There was no true consent, it held, because the women 'were consenting to touching for medical purposes not to indecent behaviour, that is there was consent to the nature of the act but not its quality'.

The actual decision in *Tabassum* is acceptable because the women's mistake related to the purpose of the acts in question. The problem with the case is the reference to the fact that a mistake as to 'quality' can vitiate consent. The Court of Appeal in *Tabassum* does not appear to have realised that it was extending the range of cases in which mistake can invalidate consent to bodily contact. It is doubtful whether the approach taken by it would survive an appeal to the House of Lords. In the later case of *Dica*,[66] where a

---

[63] (1888) 22 QBD 23, CCR.   [64] [1999] QB 444.   [65] [2000] 2 Cr App Rep 328, CA.
[66] [2004] EWCA Crim 1103.

HIV-infected man had sexual intercourse with two women, the Court of Appeal stated that, if the man had concealed his disease, the women would have consented to the bodily contact involved for the purpose of negating the offence of rape. There is a strong case for saying that the women would have been mistaken as to the quality of the act of bodily contact.

7.31 A difficulty with the decision in *Tabassum* is what constitutes the 'quality' of an act.

The Court of Appeal in *Tabassum* distinguished *Clarence* on the ground that in *Clarence* the wife consented to the sexual intercourse knowing both the nature and quality of her husband's act despite the 'additional unexpected consequences of infection'. It is admittedly true that a consequence of an act is not appropriately described as a 'quality' of it, a term which seems to refer to something co-existing with the act. It is, however, difficult to accept that the wife's ignorance of her husband's sexual disease did not result in a mistake on her part as to the quality of the act of sexual intercourse.

Likewise, the Court of Appeal in *Tabassum* distinguished *Linekar*,[67] where it was held that a prostitute who had been tricked by D's false pretence that he would pay her for having sex with him had validly consented to the intercourse and that D was therefore not guilty of rape contrary to the Sexual Offences Act 1956, s 1 (since repealed). The Court of Appeal in *Tabassum* held that 'the additional unexpected consequence' of non-payment did not detract from the prostitute's consent.

On the other hand, it may be that the Court of Appeal in *Tabassum* thought that *Richardson* did involve a mistake of quality because it noted that that case had proceeded solely by reference to whether there was a mistake of identity, and not on whether there was a mistake as to the nature or quality of the act in question.

Clearly, if *Tabassum* is correct, the law will need to be developed further by the courts if we are to be able to understand what makes something a 'quality' of an act for present purposes.

Risk of transmission of disease

7.32 A criticism of the decision in *Clarence* is that, while it may have been correct in terms of the issue of consent as to the bodily contact involved, it did not address the issue of consent as to the grievous bodily harm resulting from the sexual intercourse by way of a sexually transmitted disease. There is obviously a significant difference in answer (where someone (V) has consented to sexual intercourse in ignorance of the other party's sexually transmitted disease) between the question 'Did V consent to sexual intercourse?' and the question 'Did V consent to the risk of being infected and suffering grievous bodily harm in consequence?'. **While someone who is ignorant of the disease may consent to the intercourse (bodily contact), it does not mean that that person has consented to**

---

[67] [1995] QB 250, CA.

run the risk of grievous bodily harm. This point was recognised by the Court of Appeal in *Dica*.[68]

The matter was considered further in *Konzani*,[69] where D who had the HIV virus had sexual intercourse with three women, concealing his disease from them. All three women were infected with the virus as a result of the intercourse. Upholding D's convictions for inflicting grievous bodily harm on the women, contrary to the OAPA 1861, s 20, the Court of Appeal said that it was implicit from the reasoning in *Dica*, and confirmed by observations in *Barnes*,[70] that **for a sexual partner's consent to the risks of contracting the HIV virus to be valid that partner's consent must be an informed consent.** It added that concealment by D of the fact that he is suffering from the HIV virus almost inevitably means that D's sexual partner is deceived. The sexual partner is not properly informed, and the sexual partner cannot give an informed consent to something if ignorant of it. It would only be in rare circumstances, the Court stated, that there could be an informed consent by a sexual partner from whom the defendant had concealed his HIV virus; an example would be where the sexual partner had known the defendant while he was being treated in the hospital for the HIV virus.

Implied consent

7.33 Consent may be express or implied. One impliedly consents to the risk of accidental bodily contact in ordinary activities in the street, in queues or on buses, to name a few places. Likewise, one impliedly consents to a person seizing one's hand to shake it in friendship or to having one's back slapped (within reason) in congratulation.[71]

Of course, consent cannot be implied if it is clear, by words or conduct, that the victim is positively not consenting or would refuse consent if asked.

7.34 A drawback with the concept of implied consent is that consent cannot be implied if the victim is mentally incapable, on grounds of youth or mental incompetence, of giving consent.[72] For this reason, a test put forward by Lord Goff (Robert Goff LJ, as he then was), when giving the judgment of the Divisional Court in *Collins v Wilcock*, has much to commend it. His Lordship said:

> 'Generally speaking, consent is a defence to battery; and most of the physical contacts of ordinary life are not actionable because they are impliedly consented to by all who move in society and expose themselves to the risk of bodily contact. So nobody can complain of the jostling which is inevitable from his presence in, for example, a supermarket, an

---

[68] [2004] EWCA Crim 1103. For criticism see Weait 'Criminal Law and the Sexual Transmission of HIV: *R v Dica*' (2005) 68 MLR 121.

[69] [2005] EWCA Crim 706. For criticism see Weait 'Knowledge, Autonomy and Consent: *R v Konzani*' [2005] Crim LR 763.

[70] [2004] EWCA Crim 3246.

[71] *Cole v Turner* (1704) 6 Mod Rep 149; *Collins v Wilcock* [1984] 3 All ER 374 at 378.

[72] For recognition of this, see *T v T* [1988] Fam 52 at 62.

> underground station or a busy street; nor can a person who attends a party complain if his hand is seized in friendship, or even if his back is (within reason) slapped ... Although such cases are regarded as examples of implied consent, it is more common nowadays to treat them as falling within a general exception embracing all physical contact which is generally acceptable in the ordinary conduct of daily life.[73] Among such forms of conduct ... is touching a person for the purpose of engaging his attention, though of course using no greater degree of physical contact than is reasonably necessary in the circumstances for that purpose.'[74]

Lord Goff repeated this view in *Re F.*[75] Lord Goff's test of 'social acceptability' has the effect of widening the range of cases in which force is not unlawful in other ways beyond that cited above. For example, it can cover a second touching of someone who has not indicated a consent. In *Collins v Wilcock*, Lord Goff said:

> 'We do not say that more than one touch is never permitted; for example, the lost or distressed may surely be permitted a second touch, or possibly even more, on a reluctant or impervious sleeve, as may a person who is acting reasonably in the execution of a duty. In each case the test must be whether the physical conduct so persisted in has in the circumstances gone beyond generally acceptable standards of conduct; and the answer to that question will depend on the facts of the particular case.'[76]

Lord Goff's 'social acceptability' test was applied by the Divisional Court in *McMillan v Crown Prosecution Service*,[77] where it was held that physical contact for the purposes of steadying a drunken person fell within the bounds of what was generally acceptable in the ordinary conduct of daily life.

Whether the physical contact goes beyond what is acceptable in the ordinary conduct of daily life is for the jury or magistrates,[78] as the case may be.

Assault and battery

Key points 7.4

Assault and battery are separate offences.

- A person is guilty of an assault if he intentionally or recklessly causes another person to apprehend the application to his body of immediate, unlawful force.

- A person is guilty of battery if he intentionally or recklessly applies unlawful force to the body of another person.

---

[73] Surgical operations and medical treatment do not fall within this phrase: *T v T* [1988] Fam 52 at 66; *Re F* [1990] 2 AC 1 at 73, per Lord Goff.
[74] [1984] 3 All ER 374 at 378.   [75] [1990] 2 AC 1 at 72.   [76] [1984] 3 All ER 374 at 378.
[77] [2008] EWHC 1457 (Admin), DC.   [78] *Mepstead v DPP* (1995) 160 JP 475, DC.

7.35 Assault and battery are the most minor offences in a scale of non-fatal offences, of which the most serious are wounding or causing grievous bodily harm with intent.

Assault and battery were originally common law offences, triable only on indictment as common assault. However, according to *DPP v Taylor; DPP v Little*,[79] since 1861 assault and battery have been statutory offences. A contrary view, viz that battery (and, by implication, assault) remains a common law offence, was taken in *Haystead v Chief Constable of Derbyshire*,[80] where *DPP v Taylor; DPP v Little* was not referred to by the Court. There is much to be said for this view. The definition of the two offences is provided by the common law; all that statute, currently the Criminal Justice Act 1988, s 39, does is to provide for their mode of trial and maximum sentence. However, the view in *DPP v Taylor; DPP v Little* forms part of the ratio decidendi, whereas the statement in *Haystead v Chief Constable of Derbyshire* was only obiter.

7.36 By the Criminal Justice Act 1988, s 39, assault and battery (described by the section as 'common assault and battery' but generally described simply, and misleadingly, as 'common assault')[81] are purely summary offences. The maximum punishment is six months' imprisonment (51 weeks' when the Criminal Justice Act 2003, s 281(4) and (5) is in force) or a fine not exceeding level 5 on the standard scale or both. However, by the Criminal Justice Act 1988, s 40(1), a count charging a person with assault (or a count charging battery) may be included in an indictment if the charge:

- is founded on the same facts or evidence as a count charging an indictable offence; or

- is part of a series of offences of the same or similar character as an indictable offence which is also charged,

but only if (in either case) the facts or evidence relating to the offence were disclosed in material served on a person sent for trial for the indictable offence.

If a count for assault or for battery is included in an indictment under s 40 of the 1988 Act, the maximum punishment available on conviction is limited to the maximum for the offence available in a magistrates' court.[82]

7.37 Assault and battery are separate offences, and for that reason a conviction of 'assault and battery' or of 'assault or battery' will be quashed because a person cannot be convicted of more than one offence or of alternative offences in one information or written charge.[83]

A person is guilty of an assault if he intentionally or recklessly causes another person to apprehend the application to his body of immediate, unlawful force; for this reason the assault is sometimes referred to as 'psychic assault'. A person is guilty of battery if he intentionally or recklessly applies unlawful force to the body of another person.[84]

---

[79] [1992] QB 645, DC.   [80] [2000] 3 All ER 890, DC.

[81] They are so described, for example, in the Criminal Justice Act 1988, s 40, as recognised by the Court of Appeal in *Lynsey* [1995] 3 All ER 654.

[82] Criminal Justice Act 1988, s 40(2).

[83] *Jones v Sherwood* [1942] 1 KB 127, DC; *DPP v Taylor; DPP v Little* [1992] QB 645, DC.

[84] *Fagan v Metropolitan Police Comr* [1969] 1 QB 439, DC; *Venna* [1976] QB 421, CA; *Kimber* [1983] 3 All ER 316, CA; *Savage; DPP v Parmenter* [1992] 1 AC 699, HL; *Ireland; Burstow* [1998] AC 147, HL.

A battery generally includes an assault but this is not always so. Someone who hit another without having previously caused him to fear that unlawful force was about to be used against him, for example, because he had crept up behind him or because the victim was asleep, would commit battery even though no assault had been committed.

Actus reus of assault

7.38 The *actus reus* of assault is causing[85] the victim to apprehend the immediate application of unlawful force to his body; for what constitutes 'force to the body', see para 7.44. A mere omission to act which creates such an apprehension is generally not enough.[86] The only exception is where the defendant has created a dangerous situation (even inadvertently) in which case he is under a duty to take such steps as lie within his power to counteract the danger, and a failure (with the appropriate *mens rea*) to do so can suffice if it results in the necessary apprehension.[87]

An assault can be committed by words alone if they cause the necessary apprehension. Until 1997 it was a moot point whether they could, but the matter was resolved in the decision of the House of Lords in respect of one of the consolidated appeals in *Ireland; Burstow*[88] where the same view was taken as had been taken earlier in that year by the Court of Appeal in *Constanza*,[89] viz that mere words alone can suffice for an assault. In both cases the view was also taken that an assault can be committed even though the victim cannot see the defendant, as where a threat is made in total darkness or over the telephone. Even silence can suffice if it has the necessary result, as it can in the case of a 'silent telephone call'.[90] In *Constanza*, the Court of Appeal stressed that what is important for the prosecution to prove is what is in the victim's mind:

'how it got there, whether by seeing an action or hearing a threat and whether that threat was conveyed verbally through words spoken either directly in the presence of the [victim] or over the telephone or whether the fear was aroused through something written whether it be a letter or fax seems to us wholly irrelevant'.[91]

These words indicate the width of the offence of assault, many applications of which are also covered by various public order offences and the offences under the Protection from Harassment Act 1997.[92]

---

[85] The rules of causation are described in paras 2.28–2.57.

[86] *Fagan v Metropolitan Police Comr* [1969] 1 QB 439, DC.

[87] *Miller* [1983] 2 AC 161, HL; para 2.13. See *DPP v Santana-Bermudez* [2003] EWHC 2908 (Admin), DC; para 7.49.

[88] [1998] AC 147, HL.   [89] [1997] 2 Cr App Rep 492, CA.

[90] *Ireland; Burstow* [1998] AC 147, HL; see especially at 166, per Lord Hope.

[91] [1997] 2 Cr App Rep 492 at 495.   [92] See paras 7.145 and 7.146.

Apprehension of immediate application of force

7.39 The requirement that the immediate application of force must be apprehended means that:

- pointing an unloaded gun or an imitation gun at one who is unaware of its harmlessness may amount to an assault;[93]

- inviting another to touch the invitor cannot amount to an assault on the invitee;[94] and

- someone may be guilty of this offence if he shakes his fist at another in a threatening manner, although he thereafter is prevented from touching him.[95]

The question is not whether the victim is immediately put in fear, but whether the defendant's conduct causes the victim to fear immediate unlawful force. Clearly, if the circumstances are such that there cannot possibly be any fear that the threats will be carried out immediately, as where a person on a rapidly moving train shakes his fist at someone who is standing on a station platform, there is no assault. Moreover, the threatening gesture may be accompanied by words indicating that there is no intention to carry it out, as in the old case of *Tuberville v Savage*.[96] There, a man put his hand menacingly upon his sword but said 'If it were not assize time I'd run you through the body'; it was held that an assault had not been committed.

7.40 **The importance of the requirement that** *immediate* **unlawful force must be apprehended is reduced by the fact that the courts have taken a generous view of what is 'immediate'.** For example, in *Smith v Chief Superintendent, Woking Police Station*,[97] it was held that it had been open to magistrates to infer that a woman, who had been frightened (as he had intended) by seeing the defendant looking at her through the window of her bed-sitting room at 11pm, had apprehended the immediate application of force.

In this case there was physical proximity between the defendant and the woman such that she could have feared that he would then and there apply force to her. More extreme examples are provided by two later cases involving 'stalking': *Constanza*[98] and *Ireland; Burstow*[99] (where two consolidated appeals were heard, one relating to the aggravated offence of assault occasioning actual bodily harm). In both cases the female victims suffered psychiatric harm: in *Constanza* as a result of repeated telephone calls, in some of which D spoke and in others he kept silent, of over 800 letters and of other unusual behaviour by him; and in *Ireland; Burstow* as a result of repeated telephone calls in which Ireland remained silent. In both cases the defendants were convicted of assault

---

[93] *St George* (1840) 9 C & P 483; *Logdon v DPP* [1976] Crim LR 121, DC; cf *James* (1844) 1 Car & Kir 530; *Kwaku Mensah v R* [1946] AC 83, PC.

[94] *Fairclough v Whipp* [1951] 2 All ER 834, DC.   [95] *Stephens v Myers* (1830) 4 C & P 349.

[96] (1669) 1 Mod Rep 3.

[97] (1983) 76 Cr App Rep 234, DC. Also see *Logdon v DPP* [1976] Crim LR 121, DC.

[98] [1997] 2 Cr App Rep 492, CA.

[99] [1998] AC 147, HL. See Ormerod and Gunn 'In Defence of *Ireland*' [1997] 3 Web JCLI; Gardner 'Stalking' (1998) 114 LQR 33.

occasioning actual bodily harm, contrary to the OAPA 1861, s 47, and appealed against their convictions. Their appeals were dismissed respectively by the Court of Appeal and House of Lords.

7.41 In *Constanza*, where the indictment indicated that the assault relied on was constituted by the last letter, the Court of Appeal held that the judge was entitled to leave to the jury the question whether or not the woman had a fear of immediate violence, and that the jury were entitled to find that she had. It emphasised that D, who was known to the woman, lived near her and she thought that something could happen at any time. In a curious statement, the Court of Appeal, albeit accepting the requirement of the apprehension of immediate force, said that it was enough if the prosecution proved a fear of force 'at some time not excluding the immediate future'. This rather ambiguous statement cannot mean that a fear of force some time in the distant future can suffice, because this would deprive 'immediate' of any meaning. Instead, it must mean that **it is enough that the victim fears force at some time in the future, including the immediate future**.[100]

7.42 In *Ireland; Burstow*, Ireland had pleaded guilty and therefore, as Lords Slynn and Hope pointed out, the question as to how the concept of immediacy is to be applied, and whether it was satisfied in Ireland's case, did not arise for decision by the House of Lords. Nevertheless, Lord Steyn, with whose speech the other Law Lords agreed, rejected the submission that a telephone caller, even a silent one, can never be guilty of an assault. Lord Steyn said:

> 'The answer to this question [may a silent caller be guilty of an assault?] seems to me to be "Yes, depending on the facts"... After all, there is no reason why a telephone caller who says to a woman in a menacing way "I will be at your door in a minute or two" may not be guilty of an assault if he causes his victim to apprehend immediate personal violence. Take now the case of the silent caller. He intends by his silence to cause fear and he is so understood. The victim is assailed by uncertainty about his intentions. Fear may dominate her emotions, and it may be the fear that the caller's arrival at her door may be imminent. She may fear the *possibility* of immediate personal violence. As a matter of law the caller may be guilty of an assault: whether he is or not will depend on the circumstance and in particular on the impact of the caller's potentially menacing call or calls on the victim.'[101]

It is submitted that *Constanza* and *Ireland; Burstow* went too far in their liberal interpretation of the concept of apprehending immediate force. The dictionary definition of 'immediate' suggests that what must be apprehended is the application of force without delay, as where the victim flinches at, or seeks to dodge, the force which he apprehends as the result of the defendant's act. What was said on the point in the two decisions seems

---

[100] See commentary by Professor Sir John Smith in [1997] Crim LR 576 at 577.
[101] [1998] AC 147 at 162.

to equate 'immediate' with 'imminent', ie 'liable to happen soon', a less stringent test.[102] Indeed, in his speech in *Ireland; Burstow* Lord Steyn twice referred to the issue in terms of whether the defendant had caused the victim to apprehend an imminent application of force. In fact, on the second occasion, he thought that a fear of the possibility of imminent force would suffice.

7.43 The view taken in *Constanza* and by Lord Steyn in *Ireland; Burstow* was doubtless influenced by a desire that the criminal law should punish 'stalkers'. With this all would agree, but achieving this result by the extension of assault is questionable. A number of offences can cover stalking, and by the time that *Ireland; Burstow* was decided by the House of Lords an offence primarily designed to deal with stalking was in force under the Protection from Harassment Act 1997.[103] Cases of stalking are now generally dealt with under the 1997 Act, but the views expressed in the above two cases are of general application. One may question the appropriateness of the courts, as opposed to Parliament, enlarging the extent of criminal liability in respect of the making of threats to the person.

Actus reus of battery

7.44 The *actus reus* of battery is causing[104] **the application of unlawful force to the body of another.**

The application of 'force' means the application of 'strength, energy or violence, as an attribute of physical action or movement.'[105] **The slightest degree of force, even mere touching, will suffice.**[106] Blackstone justified this by saying that the law cannot distinguish between criminal and non-criminal violence and therefore prohibits the lowest degree of it.[107] It is not necessary that the victim should feel the force through his clothes: a touching of a person's clothes is the equivalent of touching him.[108] In some cases the courts have used the term 'violence' instead of 'force' in describing the offences of assault and battery,[109] but this does not indicate any difference in degree in what is required. The force applied does not have to be personal contact. Consequently, for example, throwing water (or swinging a weapon) at someone[110] can be a battery if the water (or weapon) hits him.[111]

---

[102] 'Imminent' is used in the definition of 'assault' in the draft Offences against the Person Bill (see para 7.132).

[103] Para 7.145.

[104] The rules of causation are described in paras 2.28–2.57.

[105] *Shorter Oxford English Dictionary*. This was the meaning given to 'force' in relation to the statutory power to enter premises by force to arrest someone in *Swales v Cox* [1981] QB 849, DC.

[106] *Cole v Turner* (1704) 6 Mod Rep 149.

[107] Blackstone 4 *Commentaries* (1769) 217, referring to 3 *Commentaries* (1768) 120.

[108] *Thomas* (1985) 81 Cr App Rep 331 at 334.

[109] Eg *Fagan v Metropolitan Police Comr* [1969] 1 QB 439; *Kimber* [1983] 3 All ER 316, CA; *Savage*; *DPP v Parmenter* [1992] 1 AC 699, HL.

[110] *Pursell v Horn* (1838) 8 Ad & El 602.

[111] If the water or weapon misses, there could be an assault.

Without the application, however, of some force there cannot be a battery. Thus, it has been held that a person who put Spanish fly (a toxic substance, sometimes taken as an aphrodisiac) into the guests' beer at a wedding reception was not guilty of a battery.[112] (Such conduct could, however, result in a conviction for the offence of causing a noxious thing to be taken with intent to injure, aggrieve or annoy, contrary to the OAPA 1861, s 24.) Likewise, causing someone psychiatric harm by a threat does not constitute a battery[113] because it does not involve the application of any (physical) force to the victim, although – depending on the circumstances (see paras 7.40–7.42) – it may constitute an assault. Similarly, the use of force merely to pull away from another does not constitute a battery.[114]

Direct or indirect application

7.45 The force may be applied *directly*, which requires that the assailant has direct physical contact with the victim, for example, hitting the victim with a fist or cosh, or throwing a stone at him, or treading or driving on to his foot,[115] or *indirectly*.

7.46 Force will be applied indirectly for this purpose where the defendant creates an obstruction or places an object or does something else which results in force being applied to the victim when the victim (unaware of what the defendant has done) does an act, as where the victim falls into a hole which the defendant has dug,[116] or where the victim is hit by a bucket of water, placed by the defendant on top of a door as a 'booby trap', when he opens the door, or where the defendant causes a theatre audience to panic and rush down an unlighted staircase across whose exit doorway he has placed an iron bar and against which those at the front of the crowd are injured.[117]

DPP v K[118] provides a modern authority that a battery can be committed by an indirect application of force. D, a schoolboy had been carrying out an experiment using sulphuric acid during a chemistry class. He was given permission to go to the toilet to wash some acid off his hand. He surreptitiously took with him a test tube of the acid to test its reaction on toilet paper. While he was in the toilet he heard some footsteps in the corridor. In a panic he poured the acid into a hot air drier to conceal it. He then returned to class, intending to remove the acid from the drier and to wash it out. Before he could do so, another pupil used the drier and had acid squirted in his face; he was permanently scarred. The Divisional Court held that D was guilty of assault occasioning actual bodily harm, contrary to the OAPA 1861, s 47.[119] It had no doubt that, if a defendant placed acid in a machine and the acid was ejected on to the next user of the machine, the defendant

---

[112] *Walkden* (1845) 1 Cox CC 282.   [113] *Ireland; Burstow* [1998] AC 147 at 161, per Lord Steyn.

[114] *Sherriff* [1969] Crim LR 260, CA.   [115] *Fagan v Metropolitan Police Comr* [1969] 1 QB 439, DC.

[116] This last example was given by Stephen J in *Clarence* (1888) 22 QBD 23, CCR.

[117] Stephen J in *Clarence* (1888) 22 QBD 23, CCR, referring to *Martin* (1881) 8 QBD 54, CCR (this case concerned an offence of inflicting grievous bodily harm, contrary to the OAPA 1861, s 20, which at the time required proof of an assault or battery (see para 7.82)). Contrast the view taken of *Martin* in *Clarence*, per Hawkins J (dissenting).

[118] [1990] 1 All ER 331, DC.   [119] Para 7.56.

(provided that he had the appropriate *mens rea* at the time of his act) would commit a battery on the next user just as if the defendant had himself switched on the machine.

A more recent affirmation that there can be a battery by the indirect application of force is provided by a statement to that effect in *Haystead v Chief Constable of Derbyshire*.[120] The statement was, however, obiter because on the facts there was a direct application of force. D hit a woman who was holding a baby, causing her to drop the baby onto the floor. The Divisional Court dismissed D's appeal against conviction for a battery on the baby. There was a clear causal link[121] between D's act and the consequence that force was applied to the baby when it hit the floor, and the Divisional Court saw no difference in logic or good sense in terms of *actus reus* between the facts of this case and one where D might have used a weapon to fell the baby to the floor.

It has been argued[122] that the decisions in favour of battery by an indirect application of force are impliedly inconsistent with the decision of the House of Lords in *Wilson*[123] but that case was not concerned with defining what constitutes a battery.[124]

Can a battery be committed by an omission to act?

7.47 In *Fagan v Metropolitan Police Comr*,[125] the Divisional Court was adamant that a mere omission to act which results in force to another, eg failing to stop a baby from falling from a height to the floor or failing to remove an obstruction in a darkened corridor, over which P trips, will not suffice. However, the decisions of the Divisional Court in *DPP v K*[126] and *DPP v Santana-Bermudez*[127] indicate that **liability may be based on an omission (with the appropriate *mens rea*) to take such steps as lie within his power to counteract a dangerous situation created (even if inadvertently) by the defendant himself.** This is an application of the principle in *Miller*, discussed in para 2.13.

7.48 In *DPP v K*, the Divisional Court recognised that if the defendant had lacked the appropriate *mens rea* at the time of his act, but realised the risk before the victim was hit by the acid, liability for battery could be based on an omission (with *mens rea*) to rectify the inadvertently created dangerous situation.

7.49 In *DPP v Santana-Bermudez*, a police officer, V, approached D and told him that she intended to carry out a full body search. She asked him to turn out his pockets. He did so and produced some syringes without needles. V asked D if he had any needles on him and he replied 'No'. When V searched one of D's pockets her finger was pierced by a hypodermic needle, at which D smirked. D was convicted by a magistrates' court of assault

120 [2000] 3 All ER 890, DC

121 The woman's involuntary dropping of the child would not have broken the causal link: para 2.41.

122 Hirst 'Assault, Battery and Indirect Violence' [1999] Crim LR 557.

123 [1984] AC 242, HL (para 7.82).

124 The case decided that 'inflict' in the OAPA 1861, s 20, does not necessarily require an assault but that an allegation in an indictment of 'inflicting grievous bodily harm' contrary to s 20 may do so for the purpose of provisions relating to alternative verdicts.

125 [1969] 1 QB 439, DC.   126 [1990] 1 All ER 331, DC.   127 [2003] EWHC 2908 (Admin), DC.

occasioning actual bodily harm but appealed successfully to the Crown Court, which ruled that there was no case to answer because an omission to act could not amount to an assault or battery. On an appeal to the Divisional Court by the prosecution, the only question was whether the Crown Court had been correct in law in concluding that there was no evidence that D had committed the *actus reus* of an assault or battery.

The Divisional Court allowed the appeal. Applying *Miller* and *DPP v K*, it held that where someone (by act or word or a combination of the two) creates a danger and thereby exposes someone to a reasonably foreseeable risk of injury which materialises, there is an evidential basis for the *actus reus* of an assault occasioning actual bodily harm (and therefore for the assault or battery required for such an offence). The offence would be committed if the defendant had the necessary *mens rea* at the time of the failure to counteract the danger. On the facts of the case, the Divisional Court held, D, by giving V a dishonest assurance about the contents of his pockets, thereby exposed her to a reasonably foreseeable risk of the injury which materialised. Clearly, D had failed to counteract a danger, which his assurance had created, by not warning V not to put her hand in the pocket.

7.50 In the light of the emphatic statement in *Fagan* that a mere omission will not suffice for a battery, it would seem that an omission to fulfil a legal duty other than that arising under the *Miller* principle cannot constitute a battery if force to another results from it.[128] This is not easy to understand in the light of the fact that, if someone died from the force in such a case, the person who had failed to act in breach of duty could be convicted of murder or manslaughter if his omission to act was accompanied by the *mens rea* for one of those offences.

Unlawful force

7.51 A threat or use of force cannot constitute an assault or a battery if the force threatened or used is lawful. It will be lawful if one of the following justifications apply:

- the victim validly consents to it;[129]
- the defendant threatens or uses reasonable force in public or private defence, as where he threatens or uses reasonable force in self-defence, the defence of another or of property, the prevention of crime or the furtherance of lawful arrest;[130]
- the defendant's conduct is justified by the principle of necessity;[131]
- the defendant is acting under statutory authority to use the force; or
- the defendant is acting in the exercise of the power to use force to discipline a child.

---

[128] Contrast the view of Harrison and Bell 'Assaulting our Common Sense' (1990) 53 MLR 518 at 522–523.
[129] Paras 7.2–7.34.
[130] Or in any other of the circumstances referred to in para 16.1. See further paras 16.2–16.35.
[131] Paras 16.84–16.96.

A defendant does not have to prove that the force used or threatened was lawful on one of these grounds. Instead, if, but only if, there is evidence that it may have been, the defendant must be acquitted unless the prosecution proves beyond reasonable doubt that the force was not lawful under the relevant rules of law.[132]

7.52 Parents[133] and other persons in loco parentis are entitled as a disciplinary measure[134] to apply a reasonable degree of force to their children or charges old enough to understand its purpose.[135] However, this power is severely limited by the Children Act 2004, s 58(1) and (2), which provides that, in relation to the following offences:

(a) wounding, or causing grievous bodily harm with intent, or unlawful wounding or infliction of grievous bodily harm;[136]

(b) assault occasioning actual bodily harm;[137]

(c) cruelty to a person under 16,[138]

battery[139] of a child cannot be justified on the ground that it constituted reasonable punishment. In addition, battery of a child causing actual bodily harm[140] cannot be justified in any civil proceedings on the ground that it constituted reasonable punishment.[141] The result of these provisions is that, for the purposes of both criminal law and civil law, the justification of reasonable chastisement is not available if the physical punishment results in actual bodily harm but is available if such harm is not caused, as in the case of transient and trifling harm resulting from a moderate slap.

A teacher or other member of staff at a school is no longer entitled by virtue of his position as such to apply corporal punishment as a disciplinary measure.[142]

---

[132] Para 16.12; *May* [1912] 3 KB 572 at 575, per Lord Alverstone CJ; *Smith* [1985] LS Gaz R 198, CA. If the issue of consent is raised, lack of consent may be inferred from evidence other than that given by the victim: *CPS v Shabbir* [2009] EWHC 2754 (Admin), DC.

[133] A father who was not married to the mother at the time of the child's birth is not a 'parent' for this purpose, unless he has subsequently acquired parental responsibility (ie parental rights, duties etc) and not ceased to have it: Children Act 1989, s 2.

[134] *Cleary v Booth* [1893] 1 QB 465; *Donovan* [1934] 2 KB 498 at 509; *Mackie* (1973) 57 Cr App Rep 453, CA.

[135] *Griffin* (1869) 11 Cox CC 402. When considering the question of reasonableness a jury or magistrates' court must consider: the nature and context of the defendant's behaviour; the duration of the behaviour; the physical and mental consequences for the child; the child's age and personal characteristics, and the defendant's reasons for administering the punishment: *H (assault of child: reasonable chastisement)* [2001] EWCA Crim 1024, decided before the Children Act 2004, s 58, relying on factors identified in *A v United Kingdom* (1998) 27 EHRR 611, ECtHR.

[136] Ie an offence under the OAPA 1861, s 18 or s 20; see paras 7.91 and 7.76 respectively.

[137] Ie an offence under the OAPA 1861, s 47; see para 7.56.

[138] Ie an offence under the Children and Young Persons Act 1933, s 1.

[139] See para 7.37.

[140] 'Actual bodily harm' has the same meaning as it has for the purposes of the OAPA 1861, s 47; see paras 7.58–7.60.

[141] Children Act 2004, s 58(3).

[142] Education Act 1996, s 548, as substituted by the School Standards and Framework Act 1998. A teacher acting in some other capacity, such as the child's parent, is not subject to this prohibition: *R (on the application of Williamson and others) v Secretary of State for Education and Employment* [2005] UKHL 15. The phrase

The prohibition on corporal punishment by teachers does not affect the power of members of staff of a school to use reasonable force to restrain a pupil from:

- committing an offence or continuing to do so;
- causing or continuing to cause personal injury or damage to property,
- or behaving or continuing to behave in a way prejudicial to good order and discipline at the school or among its pupils.

This power, originally based on the common law, is now conferred by the Education and Inspections Act 2006, s 93.[143] The power under s 93 may be exercised only where the member of staff and the pupil are on school premises or are elsewhere and the member of staff has lawful control or charge of the pupil. It permits teachers and other members of staff to use reasonable force to break up playground fights or to quell classroom disruption or disruption on a school trip, for example, but it expressly does not authorise anything to be done in relation to a pupil which constitutes corporal punishment.

Mens rea in assault and battery

7.53 An intention to injure is not required, nor need the defendant act with any sort of hostile state of mind. Instead what must be proved is that the defendant:

- in the case of an assault, intended to cause another person to apprehend the immediate application to his body of unlawful force, or was reckless as to whether another person might so apprehend;[144]
- in the case of a battery, intended to apply unlawful force to the body of another person, or was reckless as to whether such force might be applied.[145]

'by virtue of his position' in s 548 includes the case where a teacher has been expressly authorised by parents to administer corporal punishment: *R (on the application of Williamson and others) v Secretary of State for Education and Employment*. The present state of the law is the culmination of a move away from a common law position where teachers were legally entitled by virtue of their position to administer reasonable corporal punishment as a disciplinary measure. The complete removal of this entitlement means that the law is now consistent in this respect with the ECHR, Art 3. Section 548 does not violate the rights of a parent or teacher to manifest a religious belief (ECHR, Art 9), or the right of a parent to expect that education conforms with his religious and philosophical convictions (ECHR First Protocol, Art 2); the interference by s 548 with those rights is prescribed by primary legislation in clear terms, pursues a legitimate aim and is appropriate and not disproportionate in achieving that aim; accordingly Parliament was entitled to conclude that overall all corporal punishment of children at school was undesirable and unnecessary, and that other means of discipline were available and preferable: *R (on the application of Williamson and others) v Secretary of State for Education and Employment*.

143 This provision is not yet in force in Wales, where an essentially similar provision will remain in force until s 93 is brought into force in respect of Wales. The Education and Inspections Act 2006, s 165 (not yet in force in Wales) inserts a provision (s 85C) in the Further and Higher Education Act 1992 corresponding to s 93 in respect of a member of staff of an institution within the further education sector.

144 *Fagan v Metropolitan Police Comr* [1969] 1 QB 439; *Venna* [1976] QB 421, CA; *Kimber* [1983] 3 All ER 316, CA.

145 *Venna* [1976] QB 421, CA; *Kimber* [1983] 3 All ER 316, CA; *Gladstone Williams* [1987] 3 All ER 411, CA; *D v DPP* [2005] EWHC 967 (Admin), DC.

It follows, for example, that if A lays hands on B, whom he wrongly believes is consenting (ie validly consenting) to a piece of horseplay, A must be acquitted of committing an assault or a battery.[146] In relation to a battery, the reason is that, while A intends to apply force to B, he does not (because of his mistake as to B's consent) intend to apply unlawful force to B, nor is he reckless as to this.[147] (Similar reasoning applies in relation to an assault.) The same would be true if G hit H, wrongly believing that he must do so in self-defence, provided his force was reasonable on the facts as he believed them.[148] On the other hand, if X, a sexual pervert, beats Y severely and causes actual bodily harm, wrongly believing that Y is consenting, he can be convicted because, even if Y had consented, the consent would have been invalid and therefore X would not merely have intended to apply force but would have intended to apply force which was unlawful on the facts as he understood them.

Element of hostility

7.54 It was said in para 7.53 that there is no need for a hostile state of mind. An embrace by a rejected lover may be a battery.[149] This is true despite its apparent contradiction in the civil case of *Wilson v Pringle*[150] where the Court of Appeal held that for a battery 'touching must be proved to be a hostile touching'. However, it seems that this does not require a hostile state of mind, since the Court of Appeal said that 'hostile':

> 'cannot be equated with ill-will or malevolence. It cannot be governed by the obvious intention shown in acts like punching, stabbing or shooting. It cannot be governed solely by an expressed intention, although that may be strong evidence. But the element of hostility...must be a question of fact.'[151]

Unfortunately, having said what 'hostility' does not mean, the Court of Appeal said little about what it does mean. Indeed, it provided only one example of its meaning, stating that in *Collins v Wilcock*,[152] where a police officer touched a woman, intending simply to restrain her temporarily, there was a hostile touching because the officer was acting unlawfully, having no power to restrain her.

In *Brown*,[153] the majority of the House of Lords seem to have accepted that 'hostility' is required for a battery, but the interpretation which they gave to it, that if an act was unlawful it was hostile, is circular and adds nothing to the law.

---

[146] *Jones* (1986) 83 Cr App Rep 375, CA; *Aitken* [1992] 1 WLR 1006, C-MAC (as to this court see para 2.32, n 91); *Boyea* (1992) 156 JP 505, CA; *Tabassum* [2000] 2 Cr App Rep 328, CA.

[147] *Kimber* [1983] 3 All ER 316, CA; *K* [2001] UKHL 41.

[148] *Gladstone Williams* (1984) 78 Cr App Rep 276, CA.

[149] Depending on the facts, it may also constitute a sexual assault, para 9.45.

[150] [1986] 2 All ER 440, CA.   [151] [1986] 2 All ER 440 at 447–448.   [152] [1984] 3 All ER 374, DC.

[153] [1994] 1 AC 212, HL.

In *Re F*,[154] Lord Goff doubted that it was correct that a touching had to be hostile for it to amount to a battery, and in *Faulkner v Talbot*[155] Lord Lane CJ denied the need for hostility.

In the light of the above, the reference in *Wilson v Pringle* to hostility is redundant and is merely another way of saying that the use of force must be unlawful.

Aggravated assaults

> **Key points 7.5**
>
> There are several statutory offences of assault which by virtue of defined aggravating elements are generally subject to higher penalties than common assault and battery. Common offences of aggravated assault include assault occasioning actual bodily harm, assault with intent to resist arrest and assault on a constable in the execution of his duty.

7.55 'Assault' in offences of aggravated assault is not limited to an assault in its strict sense but also includes a battery.[156] It follows from the fact that assault and battery are separate offences that each offence of 'aggravated assault' involves two separate offences: aggravated assault in its strict sense and aggravated battery. For convenience, 'aggravated assault' will be used to describe both types of offence.

Offences of assault occasioning actual bodily harm

7.56 These are governed by the Offences Against the Person Act 1861 (OAPA 1861), s 47, which simply makes it an offence to commit 'any assault occasioning actual bodily harm'. These offences are triable either way[157] and punishable with a maximum of five years' imprisonment on conviction on indictment.

Actus reus

7.57 The prosecution must prove the commission of the *actus reus* of an assault or battery, as the case may be, and that that assault or battery caused[158] actual bodily harm.

---

154 [1990] 2 AC 1 at 73. See also *Collins v Wilcock* [1984] 3 All ER 374 at 378, per Robert Goff LJ.

155 [1981] 3 All ER 468 at 471. In *T v T* [1988] Fam 52, Wood J did not regard a requirement of a hostile act with favour.

156 *DPP v Taylor; DPP v Little* [1992] QB 645, DC. Cf *Notman* [1994] Crim LR 518, CA, and commentary.

157 Magistrates' Courts Act 1980, s 17(1) and Sch 1.

158 The rules of causation are described in paras 2.28–2.57.

Actual bodily harm

7.58 In *Donovan*,[159] the Court of Criminal Appeal stated that:

> '"bodily harm" has its ordinary meaning and includes any hurt or injury calculated to interfere with health or comfort of the victim. Such hurt or injury need not be permanent but must, no doubt, be more than merely transient and trifling.'[160]

The essence of the first of these two sentences was given by way of definition of actual bodily harm by Lynskey J in *Miller*.[161] The effect of the second sentence in the quotation from *Donovan* is to exclude from being actual bodily harm, harm which is both transient *and* trifling, and not simply harm which is transient *or* trifling.[162]

7.59 The meaning of 'actual bodily harm' was explained further by the Court of Appeal in *Chan-Fook*.[163] **The Court held that 'harm' is a synonym for 'injury' (so that it would not be enough that the victim's health or comfort had been interfered with, if no injury had been caused), and that 'actual' indicates that the injury should not be so trivial as to be wholly insignificant (although there was no need for it to be permanent). The Court of Appeal also held that 'bodily harm' is not limited to harm to the skin, flesh and bones of the victim. The body of the victim includes all parts of his body, including his organs, his nervous system and his brain. Bodily harm, therefore, it held, includes injury to any of those parts of his body responsible for his mental or other faculties. Accordingly, it held, 'actual bodily harm' is capable of including an identifiable psychiatric injury, brought about by psychological factors, ie a medically recognised illness (such as post-traumatic stress disorder, or battered wife syndrome, or reactive depression), but not panic or a hysterical or nervous condition.**[164] The Court of Appeal stated that, where psychiatric injury was alleged but not admitted by the defence, the question whether or not the assault occasioned psychiatric injury should not be left to the jury in the absence of expert evidence.[165] In *Ireland; Burstow*,[166] the House of Lords held that *Chan-Fook* was correctly decided; psychiatric injury could amount to actual bodily harm. Lord Steyn, with whose speech the other Law Lords agreed, said that the OAPA 1861 had to be interpreted in the light of the current scientific appreciation of the link between the body and psychiatric injury.[167]

In *Dhaliwal*,[168] the Court of Appeal, applying the statements in *Chan-Fook* and *Ireland; Burstow*, declined to hold that a psychological injury not amounting to an identifiable psychiatric injury could constitute bodily harm. It stated that the distinction, between an identifiable psychiatric injury and any other psychological condition, drawn in respect

---

[159] [1934] 2 KB 498, CCA.   [160] [1934] 2 KB 498 at 509.   [161] [1954] 2 QB 282 at 292.
[162] *T v DPP* [2003] EWHC 266 (Admin), Maurice Kay J.   [163] [1994] 2 All ER 552, CA.
[164] Lynskey J's statement in *Miller*, n 161, that an hysterical or nervous condition was within the definition of actual bodily harm does not therefore represent the law today.
[165] Also see *Morris* [1998] 1 Cr App Rep 386, CA.   [166] [1998] AC 147, HL.
[167] [1998] AC 147 at 158.   [168] [2006] EWCA Crim 1139 (reported as *D*).

of the criminal law was consistent with the civil law in respect of claims for damages for personal injury. It considered that to extend 'bodily harm' to cover a medically diagnosed psychological condition not resulting in an identifiable psychiatric injury, as the prosecution had argued, would introduce an element of uncertainty about the true ambit of the relevant legal principle to which the concept of 'bodily harm' in the OAPA 1861 applied. This would be compounded by the inevitable problems of conflicting medical opinion in a developing area.

7.60 Further clarification of 'actual bodily harm' has been given in two subsequent cases.

In *T v DPP*,[169] it was held by Maurice Kay J, as he then was, that loss of consciousness falls within the meaning of 'harm', because it involves an injurious impairment to the victim's sensory functions. His Lordship added that it was axiomatic that, even though the loss of consciousness was momentary, the bodily harm was 'actual'.

In *DPP v Smith (Michael)*,[170] the Divisional Court held that 'harm' is not limited to 'injury' but extends to 'hurt' or 'damage' and that 'bodily' meant 'concerned with the body' in the sense defined in *Chan Fook*. It followed, it said, that physical pain consequent on an assault is not a requirement. It concluded that a person's hair is an attribute and part of the human body, and that therefore the actions of the defendant in cutting off a substantial part of his former girlfriend's hair (her pony tail) without her consent were capable of amounting to an assault occasioning actual bodily harm. This does not mean that any cutting of hair will always amount to actual bodily harm; a substantial amount would have to be cut for there to be actual (as opposed to trivial) bodily harm.

7.61 The test of 'actual bodily harm' sets a low threshold for an offence under the OAPA 1861, s 47, given that it carries a maximum of five years' imprisonment. In practice charges of a s 47 offence may be inhibited in marginal cases by the Charging Standard for s 47,[171] agreed by the police and the Crown Prosecution Service, which does not, however, have any legal force. The Charging Standard states that s 47 should be charged where there is loss or breaking of a tooth, temporary loss of sensory function, extensive or multiple bruising, displaced broken nose, minor fractures, minor, but not merely superficial, cuts probably requiring medical attention (eg stitches), and psychiatric injury. The Charging Standard also states that although any injury that is more than transient or trifling can be classified as actual bodily harm, the appropriate charge will normally be contrary to the Criminal Justice Act 1988, s 39 (assault or battery) where injuries amount to no more than the following – grazes, scratches, abrasions, minor bruising, swelling, reddening of the skin, superficial cuts or a 'black eye'.

---

[169] [2003] EWHC 266 (Admin), Admin Ct.   [170] [2006] EWHC 94 (Admin), DC.

[171] Crown Prosecution Service *Charging Standards* available at http://www.cps.gov.uk/legal/. The aim of the Standards is to improve fairness to defendants, through greater uniformity of approach to charging, and to make the criminal justice system more efficient by ensuring that appropriate charges are laid at the start of the process. It is difficult to assess its practical effect.

Mens rea

7.62 Although the defendant's assault or battery must have been causally related to the actual bodily harm, **the *mens rea* required to be proved is simply that for assault or battery, as the case may be, and bodily harm to another does not have to have been intended or foreseen as a risk by the defendant.** Authority for this proposition of law was originally provided by the decision of the Court of Appeal in *Roberts*,[172] whose facts are set out in para 2.48. Rejecting an argument that the jury should have been directed to consider whether the defendant foresaw that the victim would suffer injury, the Court of Appeal said that the only issue was one of causation.

The view taken by the Court of Appeal in *Roberts* was confirmed by the House of Lords in 1991 in the consolidated appeals in *Savage; DPP v Parmenter*.[173] In *Savage*, D committed a battery on V, a former girlfriend of D's husband, when she threw a pint of beer over her. Not only was V soaked, but she was also cut by a piece of flying glass, because D had let go of the glass and it had shattered. It was not clear whether D had deliberately thrown the glass or whether it had accidentally slipped from her grasp. D was charged with unlawfully and maliciously wounding V, contrary to the OAPA 1861, s 20. The jury convicted D, but her conviction was quashed on appeal by the Court of Appeal because of a misdirection as to the meaning of the word 'maliciously'. The Court of Appeal, however, substituted a verdict of guilty of assault occasioning actual bodily harm. Before the House of Lords it was not disputed that D had committed a battery on V and that that battery had occasioned actual bodily harm. However, the trial judge had not directed the jury that they had to find that D foresaw the risk that some bodily harm would result from what she did, and therefore it was not clear what view the jury had formed on that issue of foresight. The question for the House of Lords was whether a s 47 offence had been established on the basis that it had been proved that actual bodily harm had been occasioned by the battery, or whether such an offence would only have been established if foresight as to the risk of bodily harm resulting from the battery had also been proved. The House of Lords, approving *Roberts*, answered 'yes' to the first alternative; the prosecution did not have to prove that a person charged with an offence under s 47 intended to cause some actual bodily harm or was reckless as to whether such harm would be caused. The policy behind this lack of correspondence between the consequence which the defendant must have occasioned in order to commit the *actus reus* and the *mens rea* which must be proved was not explained by the House of Lords.

Offences of assault with intent to resist arrest

7.63 The OAPA 1861, s 38 makes it an offence for someone to 'assault any person with intent to resist or prevent the lawful apprehension or detainer of himself or of any other

---

[172] (1971) 56 Cr App Rep 95, CA.
[173] [1992] 1 AC 699, HL. The decision to the contrary in *Spratt* [1991] 2 All ER 210, CA, was overruled.

person for any offence'. An offence under s 38 is triable either way[174] and punishable with a maximum of two years' imprisonment. **The defendant must be proved to have committed the *actus reus* of an assault or battery, as the case may be, with the appropriate *mens rea* for that offence and with the requisite intent to resist or prevent the lawful apprehension or detainer of himself or another.**

7.64 The lawful arrest which the defendant must intend to resist or prevent is required to be for an offence. Consequently, it is not an offence under s 38 to assault someone with intent to resist an arrest for a breach of the peace[175] or in civil process, although if a wound or really serious harm results there could be a conviction for the major offence under the OAPA 1861, s 18.[176]

A defendant will intend to resist lawful arrest if the arrest is lawful and, knowing that the victim of the assault is trying to arrest him, he intends to resist that arrest.[177] The fact that he is mistaken as to the arrester's power (ie authority) to arrest him, so that he thinks the arrest is unlawful, is a mistake of criminal law and irrelevant.[178] So, it has been held,[179] is a mistaken belief which leads the defendant to think that the facts do not satisfy the requirements for a lawful arrest, as where he knows or believes he has not committed an offence.[180] Although there are sound policy grounds for not permitting those who are lawfully arrested, but who think they are innocent, to challenge the arrest by a threat or use of force, it is doubtful that the mistake in this type of case is one of law. It looks like a mistake of fact, whose effect is that the defendant does not intend to resist lawful arrest.

On the other hand, if – because of a mistake as to the victim's capacity (eg a mistaken belief that he is not a police constable) or conduct – the defendant does not know that he is being arrested, for example because he thinks he is being attacked by a thug, he will lack the intent to resist a lawful arrest. Here, the mistake is one of fact which prevents him knowing that he is being arrested.[181] If, however, on the facts as he believes them to be, his force (actual or threatened) is unreasonable, he may be convicted of assault, battery, assault occasioning actual bodily harm or affray[182] (as the circumstances warrant).[183]

---

[174] Magistrates' Courts Act 1980, s 17(1) and Sch 1.

[175] A breach of the peace is not in itself an offence under English law: *Davies v Griffiths* [1937] 2 All ER 671, DC; *Williamson v Chief Constable of the West Midlands* [2003] EWCA Civ 337.

[176] See paras 7.91–7.95.   [177] *Lee* [2001] 1 Cr App Rep 293, CA.

[178] *Fennell* [1971] 1 QB 428, CA.   [179] *Lee* [2001] 1 Cr App Rep 293, CA.

[180] See further para 16.35.

[181] *Brightling* [1991] Crim LR 364, CA; *Lee* [2001] 1 Cr App Rep 293, CA.

[182] A person is guilty of affray if he uses or threatens unlawful violence towards another and his conduct is such as would cause a person of reasonable firmness present at the scene to fear for his personal safety: Public Order Act 1986, s 3(1). The offence is triable either way and punishable on conviction on indictment with a maximum of three years' imprisonment: s 3(2).

[183] See *Fennell* [1971] 1 QB 428, CA.

Offences of assault on a constable in the execution of his duty

7.65 These offences are provided by the Police Act 1996, s 89(1), which re-enacted an earlier identical offence. Under s 89(1):

'Any person who assaults a constable in the execution of his duty, or a person assisting a constable in the execution of his duty, shall be guilty of an offence'.

An offence under s 89(1) is triable only summarily and currently punishable with a maximum of six months' imprisonment (51 weeks' when the Criminal Justice Act 2003, s 281(4) and (5) is in force) or a fine not exceeding level 5 on the standard scale or both.[184]

Actus reus

7.66 Proof of the *actus reus* requires proof of the *actus reus* of assault, or of battery, as appropriate, and that the victim was a constable acting in the execution of his duty (or someone assisting such a constable).

A 'constable' is anyone holding the office of constable, whatever his rank in his force.[185]

7.67 To be acting in the execution of his duty a constable need not be doing something which he is compelled by law to do,[186] but his conduct must fall within the general scope of a duty imposed on him by law (such as his duties to protect life and property, to keep the peace, to prevent and investigate crime and to prevent obstruction of the highway) and he must not be acting unlawfully at the time.[187] The test as to whether a constable is acting lawfully is objective, with the result that the legality of his conduct is judged on the facts as they actually were and not on the facts as the constable mistakenly believed them to be.[188]

It frequently happens that a constable performing one of his duties does something to a person or his property, such as detaining him or entering his house without consent to search it, which would be unlawful unless authorised by a positive legal power. In such

---

[184] Police Act 1996, s 89(1).

[185] By the Police Act 1996, s 89(3), s 89(1) also applies to a Northern Irish or Scots constable when he is executing a warrant or otherwise acting in England or Wales under a statutory power to do so. Section 89(1) also applies to a constable of the British Transport Police Force in the same way as it applies to other constables in England and Wales (Railways and Transport Safety Act 2003, s 68(1)). A person carrying out surveillance in England and Wales under the Regulation of Investigatory Powers Act 2000, s 76A is treated as if he were acting as a constable in the execution of his duty: Crime (International Co-operation) Act 2003, s 84(1). See also the Energy Act 2004, s 68(1).

[186] *Coffin v Smith* (1980) 71 Cr App Rep 221, DC.

[187] *Waterfield and Lynn* [1964] 1 QB 164, CA; *Rice v Connolly* [1966] 2 QB 414 at 419; *Ludlow v Burgess* [1971] Crim LR 238, DC; *Pedro v Diss* [1981] 2 All ER 59, DC; *Edwards v DPP* (1993) 97 Cr App Rep 301, DC.

[188] *Kerr v DPP* (1994) 158 JP 1048, DC.

a case, the question arises whether he has such a power (either at common law or under a statute) and, if he has, whether he has exercised it correctly and without exceeding it; if his conduct does not fall within the proper execution of a power he is not acting in the execution of his duty.[189] For example, as a constable has no power physically to detain a person for questioning without making an arrest, he will be acting unlawfully[190] and therefore not in the execution of his duty if he does so.[191] On the other hand, since physical contact which is generally acceptable in the ordinary conduct of everyday life is not unlawful,[192] taking hold of a person's arm or tapping him on the shoulder not in order to detain him, but to speak to him or draw something to his attention, does not take a constable outside the execution of his duty because his act is not unlawful.[193] Turning to cases where a constable does have a relevant power but fails to exercise it correctly, an arrest without warrant in circumstances where the constable has such a power is nevertheless unlawful, generally speaking, if he does not inform the person of his reasons,[194] and the same is true if he exercises a power of search without giving his reasons.[195]

If a constable purports to exercise some power which he does not possess or makes an improper use of one of his powers and therefore is not acting in the execution of his duty, the threat or use of force against him, for example to escape an unlawful detention for questioning, is not an assault on him in the execution of his duty.[196] However, if force is used or threatened in order to escape, which is unreasonable on the facts as the defendant believes them to be, the defendant may be convicted of assault, battery, assault occasioning actual bodily harm or affray (as the circumstances warrant).[197]

7.68 The reference to 'a person assisting a constable in the execution of his duty' includes reference to any person who is neither a constable nor in the company of a constable but who is a member of a joint investigation team (ie an investigation team established under an international framework) led by a member of a police force.[198]

Mens rea

7.69 It must be proved that the defendant had the *mens rea* for assault or battery, as the case may be. It is unnecessary for the prosecution to prove that the defendant knew that

---

[189] *Waterfield and Lynn* [1964] 1 QB 164, CCA.   [190] He will be committing a battery.

[191] *Kenlin v Gardiner* [1967] 2 QB 510, DC; *Collins v Wilcock* [1984] 3 All ER 374, DC. Where a constable physically detains a person, but does not at that time intend or purport to arrest him, he is acting unlawfully, even if an arrest would have been justified: *Wood v DPP* [2008] EWHC 1056 (Admin).

[192] *Collins v Wilcock* [1984] 3 All ER 374, DC; para 7.34.

[193] *Donnelly v Jackman* [1970] 1 All ER 987, DC; *Collins v Wilcock* [1984] 3 All ER 374, DC; *Mepstead v DPP* (1995) 160 JP 475, DC; cf *Bentley v Brudzinski* [1982] Crim LR 825, DC.

[194] Police and Criminal Evidence Act 1984, s 28(3).

[195] *McBean v Parker* [1983] Crim LR 399, DC; *Brazil v Chief Constable of Surrey* [1983] 3 All ER 537, DC.

[196] *Kenlin v Gardiner* [1967] 2 QB 510, DC; *Pedro v Diss* [1981] 2 All ER 59 at 64.

[197] *Purdy* [1975] QB 288, CA. As to affray, see para 7.64, n 182.

[198] Police Act 1996, s 89(4), inserted by the Police Reform Act 2002, s 104; amended by the Serious Organised Crime and Police Act 2005, Sch 4.

his victim was a constable acting in the execution of his duty.[199] Suppose, however, that the defendant, not knowing that his victim is a constable, and thinking that he must act in self-defence, applies force to a constable, who is exercising one of his powers, and that force would be reasonable if the victim had not been a constable (because he would not have the power in question). In this situation, the defendant does not commit an offence under the Police Act 1996, s 89(1). The reason is that he lacks the *mens rea* required for the assault (ie battery), since he neither intends, nor is he reckless as to, the application of *unlawful* force to his victim.[200] (This is important because in many cases where some-one assaults a constable in the execution of his duty, not knowing that the victim is a constable, that person may think that he is being attacked.) On the other hand, if the defendant knows that his victim is a constable but mistakenly believes that the constable is acting in excess of his powers, he is not excused; it has been held that his mistake is not one of fact but one of criminal law relating to the powers of the constable.[201] As indicated in para 7.64, while this is undoubtedly correct where the mistake relates to the powers of a constable, the correctness of this is open to doubt where the mistake about the excess of the constable's powers is based on a mistaken belief that the facts do not satisfy the requirements for the exercise of the power.

Related offences of wilful obstruction or resistance of constable in the execution of his duty

7.70 Under the Police Act 1996, s 89(2), which re-enacted an earlier identical provision:

> 'A person who resists or wilfully obstructs a constable in the execution of his duty, or a person assisting a constable in the execution of his duty, shall be guilty of an offence'.

An offence under s 89(2) is triable only summarily and punishable by a maximum of one month's imprisonment[202] or a fine not exceeding level 3 on the standard scale or both. **These offences are mentioned for the sake of completeness. They do not require any-thing in the nature of an assault or battery.**

Wilful obstruction

7.71 In general, any conduct which actually prevents a constable from carrying out his duty or makes it more difficult for him to do so amounts to obstructing him.[203]

---

[199] *Forbes and Webb* (1865) 10 Cox CC 362; *Maxwell and Clanchy* (1909) 2 Cr App Rep 26; *McBride v Turnock* [1964] Crim LR 456, DC; *Kenlin v Gardiner* [1967] 2 QB 510, DC; Howard 'Assaulting Policemen in the Execution of their Duty' (1963) 79 LQR 247.

[200] *Blackburn v Bowering* [1994] 3 All ER 380, CA. See Fairweather and Levy 'Assaults on the Police: A Case of Mistaken Identity' [1994] Crim LR 817.

[201] *Fennell* [1971] 1 QB 428, CA.

[202] This will be increased to 51 weeks' imprisonment when the Criminal Justice Act 2003, s 280(2) and Sch 26 are in force.

[203] *Hinchcliffe v Sheldon* [1955] 3 All ER 406, DC; *Rice v Connolly* [1966] 2 QB 414, DC; *Lewis v Cox* [1985] QB 509, DC.

Where a positive act has this effect it constitutes an obstruction, even though it is not unlawful independently of its operation as an obstruction. Thus, a person who consumes alcohol in order to frustrate a breath test under the Road Traffic Act 1988 may be convicted of the present offence.[204] Other examples of obstruction are hampering a constable in making an arrest or in interviewing a witness or suspect, hampering a constable in finding drugs by telling the constable a false story,[205] running away with intent to avoid arrest when approached for questioning by the police,[206] refusing to remove an obstruction from the highway when lawfully required to do so by a constable,[207] and refusing to open a door when lawfully required to do so by a constable seeking to exercise a power of entry.[208]

It amounts to an obstruction to give a warning to someone who is already committing an offence[209] or who is likely to commit an offence.[210] On the other hand, it is not an obstruction where a warning is given to a person who is not committing an offence or likely to do so in order to discourage him from doing so.[211] It follows that an obstruction cannot be proved where the defendant has warned other drivers of a speed trap if it cannot be proved that those warned were either exceeding the speed limit or likely to do so at the location of the speed trap.[212]

7.72 The requirement of 'wilfulness' has been interpreted to mean that the defendant's conduct which resulted in the obstruction must have been deliberate and intended by him to bring about a state of affairs which, regarded objectively, prevented or made it more difficult for the constable to carry out his duty, whether or not the defendant appreciated that that state of affairs would have that effect or that it would in law amount to an obstruction.[213] Thus, to do something deliberately which in fact makes it more difficult for a constable to carry out his duties is not enough; there must be an intention that the deliberate conduct should result in that state of affairs. There is no need for any hostility towards the constable,[214] nor need the conduct be 'aimed at' him.[215]

The above is well illustrated by *Hills v Ellis*[216] where D intervened in a lawful arrest by a constable in order to draw his attention to the fact that, as D believed, he was arresting the wrong man. The Divisional Court held that as D's deliberate conduct had resulted in

---

[204] *Dibble v Ingleton* [1972] 1 QB 480, DC.

[205] *Rice v Connolly* [1966] 2 QB 414 at 420, per Lord Parker CJ.

[206] *Sekfali v DPP* [2006] EWHC 894 (Admin), DC.   [207] See *Tynan v Balmer* [1967] 1 QB 91, DC.

[208] *Lunt v DPP* [1993] Crim LR 534, DC.

[209] *Betts v Stevens* [1910] 1 KB 1, DC; *DPP v Glendinning* [2005] EWHC 2333 (Admin), DC.

[210] *Green v Moore* [1982] QB 1044, DC; *DPP v Glendinning* [2005] EWHC 2333 (Admin), DC.

[211] *Bastable v Little* [1907] 1 KB 59, DC; *Green v Moore* [1982] QB 1044; *DPP v Glendinning* [2005] EWHC 2333 (Admin), DC.

[212] See the cases cited at nn 209 and 210.

[213] *Hills v Ellis* [1983] QB 680, DC; *Moore v Green* [1983] 1 All ER 663, DC.

[214] *Hills v Ellis* [1983] QB 680, DC. Also see *Moore v Green* [1983] 1 All ER 663, DC.

[215] *Lewis v Cox* [1985] QB 509, DC (not following a statement to the contrary by Griffiths LJ in *Hills v Ellis* [1983] QB 680 at 685, DC).

[216] [1983] QB 680, DC. Also see *Lewis v Cox* [1985] QB 509, DC.

a situation which made it more difficult for the constable to carry out his duty, and as D had intended that situation, D was guilty of wilful obstruction, despite the fact that he was actuated by good motives and not by hostility towards the constable.

Unlike the offence of assaulting a constable in the execution of his duty,[217] there cannot be a conviction for wilful obstruction unless the defendant knew or believed that that person was a constable.[218] It remains to be decided whether a defendant must also know or believe (leaving aside any mistake of law) that the constable was acting in the execution of his duty.

7.73 In *Rice v Connolly*,[219] it was held that **'wilfully' meant not only 'intentionally' but also 'without lawful excuse'**. This is rather surprising since 'wilfully' seems to refer to the defendant's state of mind, whereas the question of 'lawful excuse' generally relates to factual matters surrounding conduct which excuse it.

The requirement that the obstruction must be without lawful excuse means that, unless a constable has a legal right to require a person to do something (and thereby to impose a legal duty on him to do it), a failure by that person to do the thing when requested by the constable cannot constitute a wilful obstruction because, although it makes it more difficult for the constable to carry out his duties, there will be a lawful excuse for that failure. Thus, as there is no general legal duty to assist the police (eg by answering questions put by a constable); a mere refusal to answer such questions is not a wilful obstruction[220] (unless a special duty to answer exists in the circumstances). Nor, according to the Divisional Court in *Green v DPP*,[221] is it a wilful obstruction to advise someone else not to answer police questions, even if that advice is given in an abusive way.

Resistance

7.74 The wide meaning given to 'obstruction' probably renders 'resistance' otiose, since anyone who resists seems to obstruct (although the converse is not true). However, 'resisting' is a more appropriate word in certain cases, such as where a person arrested by a constable tears himself away.

The resistance is not required to be wilful. There can be no doubt that an intent to resist must be proved, but it remains to be seen what *mens rea*, if any, is required as to the fact that the person resisted is a constable. Analogy with the offence of obstructing a constable suggests that a person must know or believe that the person resisted is a constable, although it is uncertain whether he must also know or believe (leaving aside any mistake of law) that the constable is acting in the execution of his duty.

---

[217] Para 7.65.

[218] *Ostler v Elliott* [1980] Crim LR 584, DC. This point is not clear from this brief report but appears in the transcript.

[219] [1966] 2 QB 414, DC.

[220] *Rice v Connolly* [1966] 2 QB 414, DC; *Sekfali v DPP* [2006] EWHC 894 (Admin), DC.

[221] (1991) 155 JP 816, DC.

Other offences of aggravated assault

7.75 Other offences of aggravated assault include:

- assault with intent to rob;[222] and
- racially or religiously aggravated assault.[223]

Although it is not strictly an aggravated assault, an assault or battery which would cause a person of reasonable firmness present at the scene to fear for his personal safety can amount to the more serious offence of affray.[224]

The offences of assault by penetration and sexual assault under the Sexual Offences Act 2003[225] are not true offences of aggravated assault because, despite their names, they require a touching and therefore cannot be committed by an 'assault' alone in the strict sense of that term.

Wounding and grievous bodily harm

Key points 7.6

The offences under the Offences Against the Person Act 1861 (OAPA 1861), ss 18 and 20 discussed below deal with cases where someone has been wounded or suffered grievous bodily harm as a result of the defendant's conduct. Apart from specifying different *mens rea* requirements, the two sections are virtually identical.

Section 20

7.76 The OAPA 1861, s 20 provides that:

'Whosoever shall unlawfully and maliciously wound or inflict any grievous bodily harm upon any other person, either with or without any weapon or instrument, shall be guilty of [an offence] ...'.

The phrase 'either with or without any weapon or instrument' adds nothing to the definition but was presumably added for the avoidance of doubt. An offence under s 20 is triable either way[226] and punishable on conviction on indictment with a maximum of five years' imprisonment.[227] The fact that the maximum punishment is the same as for an assault

---

[222] Theft Act 1968, s 8(2); para 10.99.   [223] Crime and Disorder Act 1998, s 29(1)(b) and (c); para 7.97.
[224] See para 7.64, n 182.   [225] Paras 9.39–9.49.
[226] Magistrates' Courts Act 1980, s 17(1) and Sch 1.   [227] OAPA 1861, s 20.

occasioning actual bodily harm under s 47 fails to reflect the greater seriousness of an offence under s 20.

Actus reus

7.77 Section 20 creates two offences. The *actus reus* of one is an act resulting in the unlawful infliction of grievous bodily harm on him, and of the other an act resulting in the unlawful wounding of another.[228]

Inflicting grievous bodily harm

7.78 *Grievous bodily harm* 'Grievous bodily harm' was defined by the House of Lords in *DPP v Smith*.[229] Lord Kilmuir LC, giving the only reasoned speech (with which the other Law Lords agreed), said that **'grievous bodily harm' is to be given its natural meaning and that 'grievous' means 'really serious'.** 'Really' seems to mean no more than that the harm must actually be serious. In *Saunders*[230] (a case of a fractured nose and cuts to the head) the Court of Appeal held that there was no need for the judge in his direction to refer the jury to 'really' in conjunction with 'serious bodily harm'. Other Court of Appeal decisions have also held that it is not a misdirection to fail to refer the jury to the word 'really'.[231] In the later case of *Janjua and Choudhury*,[232] the Court of Appeal held that, on the facts of the case (deep stab wounds with a knife with a five-and-a-half-inch blade), the omission by the judge of 'really' before 'serious' was not material. However, it went on to say that there could be circumstances where a judge would think it right to use 'really' before 'serious', although this was not required in every case. It added that it was a matter for the judge in the light of the facts of the case to decide whether to use 'really' before 'serious'.

7.79 As in the case of 'actual bodily harm',[233] 'bodily harm' includes an identifiable psychiatric injury. This was finally settled in 1997 by the House of Lords in *Ireland; Burstow*.[234] It also includes lack of consciousness.[235]

7.80 Whether harm is grievous is a question for the jury in the Crown Court. It must be judged objectively, according to the ordinary standards of usage and experience, not subjectively from the standpoint of how the victim would describe it.[236] Although the

---

[228] As to whether an omission to act can suffice instead of an act, see para 7.84. The rules of causation are described in paras 2.28–2.57.

[229] [1961] AC 290, HL.   [230] [1985] Crim LR 230, CA.

[231] *Bryan* (1984) unreported, CA; *McMillan* (1984) unreported, CA; *Doyle* [2004] EWCA Crim 2714.

[232] [1999] 1 Cr App Rep 91, CA; discussed by Beaumont 'The Reality of Really Serious Harm' [1998] 10 Archbold News 4.

[233] Para 7.59.

[234] [1998] AC 147, HL. As in the case of an assault occasioning actual bodily harm, where really serious psychiatric injury is alleged but not admitted by the defence, the question whether or not the defendant caused such injury should not be left to the jury in the absence of expert evidence (see para 7.59).

[235] See *T v DPP* [2003] EWHC 266 (Admin), Maurice Kay J.

[236] *Brown and Stratton* [1998] Crim LR 485, CA.

test of whether bodily harm is grievous is objective, in deciding whether or not the harm is serious regard must be had to the effect of the injury on the particular victim, taking account of the victim's age, health and any other particular factors.[237] Injuries to a six-foot adult in good health may be less serious than the same injuries to, for instance, an elderly or unwell person, or to someone physically or psychiatrically vulnerable, or very young.[238] Where the defendant has caused a number of injuries to the victim, whether there is grievous bodily harm can be judged by looking at the totality of those injuries; injuries which individually are not serious can amount to serious harm when aggregated.[239]

7.81 The ambit of grievous bodily harm is potentially wide; harm need not be lifethreatening or permanent or have lasting consequences or even require treatment.[240] The Charging Standard[241] for inflicting grievous bodily harm contrary to s 20, however, refers to the following as examples of grievous bodily harm: injuries resulting in permanent disability or permanent loss of sensory function; injuries resulting in nonminor permanent visible disfigurement, broken or displaced limbs or bones (including fractured skull); compound fractures, broken cheek bone, jaw, ribs etc; injuries which cause substantial loss of blood; injuries resulting in lengthy treatment or incapacity; and psychiatric injury.

7.82 *Inflicting* Until relatively recently the courts have taken a restricted view of how grievous bodily harm could be 'inflicted' for the purposes of the OAPA 1861, s 20.

In a number of cases, including the particularly well-known decision in *Clarence*,[242] the courts held that grievous bodily harm was not inflicted for the purposes of s 20 unless it was caused by an 'assault', ie an assault or battery. In *Clarence*, D, as already mentioned, knowing that he had venereal disease but concealing this fact from her, had intercourse with his wife as a result of which she contracted that disease. The majority of the Court for Crown Cases Reserved held that D could not be convicted of unlawfully inflicting grievous bodily harm on his wife because 'inflict' implied the need for an assault and, since the wife had consented to the bodily contact involved, there had been no assault.

In 1983, the House of Lords in *Wilson*[243] declined to take this narrow approach and held that there could be an infliction of grievous bodily harm contrary to s 20 without an 'assault'. *Wilson*, however, seemed to leave 'inflict' with a restricted meaning because it quoted with apparent approval a passage in the Australian decision in *Salisbury*[244] which

---

[237] *Bollom* [2003] EWCA Crim 2846.   [238] *Bollom* [2003] EWCA Crim 2846.

[239] *Birmingham* [2002] EWCA Crim 2608.   [240] *Bollom* [2003] EWCA Crim 2846.

[241] Crown Prosecution Service *Charging Standards* (see n 171). A Charging Standard has no legal force: see para 7.61.

[242] (1888) 22 QBD 23, CCR; para 7.29. Also see *Taylor* (1869) LR 1 CCR 194, CCR; *Beasley* (1981) 73 Cr App Rep 44, CA.

[243] [1984] AC 242, HL.

[244] [1976] VR 452, 76 Cr App Rep 261n, SC of Victoria. In this case an Australian offence practically identical to s 20 was considered and the English cases on s 20 examined.

stated that 'inflict' required the grievous bodily harm to result from force being violently applied to the body of the victim.

7.83 It is now clear from the decision of the House of Lords in the consolidated appeals in *Ireland; Burstow*[245] that **the application of force is not required for 'infliction'.** In *Burstow* the question of law of general public importance which had been certified by the Court of Appeal for consideration by the House of Lords was: 'Whether an offence of inflicting grievous bodily harm under s 20 can be committed where no physical violence is applied directly or indirectly to the body of the victim.' The House of Lords' answer was in the affirmative. As a result, *Clarence* must now be regarded as wrongly decided on the meaning of 'inflict' in s 20, although the House did not expressly overrule it.

The facts of *Burstow* were that Burstow, refusing to accept that his social relationship with a woman had come to an end, had pestered her in various ways and had been dealt with for this on more than one occasion by the courts, and this had culminated in his imprisonment. On his release, Burstow continued to pester the woman. During the period February to July 1995 (which formed the basis of the charge) his conduct included telephone calls (some silent, and some abusive), letters and photographs and frequent, and unnecessary, visits to the woman's home and to her workplace and distributing offensive cards in the street where she lived. He also sent the woman a note which was intended to be menacing, and was so understood. The woman was badly affected by this campaign of harassment. As a result she suffered a severe psychiatric injury. Burstow was convicted of inflicting grievous bodily harm, contrary to s 20. He appealed unsuccessfully against conviction to the Court of Appeal, and thence to the House of Lords.

Dismissing the appeal, the House held that the contextual interpretation of 'inflict' could embrace the idea of one person inflicting serious psychiatric injury on another, and that (as already stated) 'inflict' did not require any physical force to be applied to the victim.

As a result of this decision, there can be no doubt that any act which causes grievous bodily harm constitutes inflicting such harm. Thus, causing someone to suffer grievous bodily harm by infecting him with a disease now constitutes an infliction of that harm for the purposes of s 20,[246] and so does causing someone grievous bodily harm by giving him poison (although a prosecution for administering, or causing to be administered or taken, a poison, or other destructive or noxious thing, so as thereby to endanger life or thereby to inflict grievous bodily harm, contrary to the OAPA 1861, s 23, would be more appropriate).

7.84 The decision in *Burstow* is not without its difficulties. First, the speeches in the House of Lords gave no weight to the apparent approval in *Wilson* of the passage in *Salisbury*

---

[245] [1998] AC 147, HL. See S Gardner 'Stalking' (1998) 114 LQR 33.

[246] *Dica* [2004] EWCA Crim 1103. The Court confirmed that the reasoning which led the majority in *Clarence* to hold that there could not be a conviction under s 20 on the facts of that case has no continuing application. The infliction will not be unlawful if the victim has given an informed consent to the risk of being infected: para 7.18.

referred to above. This is not a major defect because, as the trial judge in *Burstow*[247] stated, the quotation of that passage did not necessarily mean that the House in *Wilson* accepted it and, anyway, even if it had, that approval would have been an obiter dictum, whereas the statement that there can be an 'infliction' without an assault was part of the ratio decidendi of *Wilson*.

A second difficulty is whether, after *Ireland; Burstow*, an omission to act which results in grievous bodily harm can amount to 'inflicting' grievous bodily harm and therefore liability under s 20, assuming that there was a legal duty to prevent the harm. In such a case, the failure to act can be said to 'cause' the grievous bodily harm (as required in the OAPA 1861, s 18), and in the absence of any authority on the point a failure to act doubtless suffices for liability for that offence. In *Ireland; Burstow*, Lord Hope[248] stated that 'for all practical purposes there is, in my opinion, no practical difference between ["cause" and "inflict"]'. In contrast, Lord Steyn[249] was of the view that the two terms were not synonymous. He did not explain why, but a good reason would be that one cannot inflict grievous bodily harm by an omission. The natural meaning of 'inflict' would seem to imply the need for some sort of act.

Wounding

7.85 To constitute a wound, the inner and outer skin must actually be broken.[250] A bruise or internal rupturing of blood vessels alone is not sufficient,[251] nor is a broken bone alone.[252] The wound need not be serious; a minor cut of both layers of skin will do. The threshold for a wound is therefore lower than for grievous bodily harm. Where only a minor wound is caused a prosecution for an offence under the OAPA 1861, s 47[253] would be more appropriate than under s 20.[254]

It was thought that there could not be a wounding unless the wound resulted from an 'assault'[255] in the sense of an assault or battery.[256] The decision in *Wilson* did not, strictly, affect this, although it suggested that there could be a wounding even though there was no assault, provided that the defendant did something deliberately which directly resulted in force being applied violently to the victim's body so that he was wounded. In *Savage; DPP v Parmenter*,[257] the Court of Appeal was of the opinion that, although almost inevitably a wounding would result from an assault, it would not do so if the facts were 'quite

---

[247] [1996] Crim LR 331, Crown Ct.   [248] [1998] AC 147 at 160.
[249] [1998] AC 147 at 164.
[250] *M'Loughlin* (1838) 8 C & P 635; *C (a minor) v Eisenhower* [1984] QB 331, DC. In *Waltham* (1849) 3 Cox CC 442, the lining membrane of the victim's urethra was ruptured and bled. There was evidence that the membrane is precisely the same in nature as the membrane which lines the cheek and the external and inner and outer skin of the lip. It was held that there had been a wound.
[251] *C (a minor) v Eisenhower* [1984] QB 331, DC.   [252] *M'Loughlin* (1838) 8 C & P 635.
[253] See paras 7.56–7.62.   [254] Crown Prosecution Service *Charging Standards* (see n 171).
[255] *Taylor* (1869) LR 1 CCR 194, CCR.   [256] *Beasley* (1981) 73 Cr App Rep 44, CA.
[257] (1990) 91 Cr App Rep 317, CA.

extraordinary'. On appeal, Lord Ackner, with whose speech the other Law Lords agreed, was of the same opinion as the Court of Appeal.[258]

Unlawfully

7.86 The reference to 'unlawfully' in the definition of the offences is simply a reference to the fact that a person cannot be convicted of an offence under s 20 if his conduct is legally justified, eg because he is using reasonable force in self-defence or to prevent crime or effect a lawful arrest,[259] or because the victim has given a valid consent to being wounded or caused grievous bodily harm (or to the risk of this occurring). In such a case the wounding or grievous bodily harm will be lawful, not unlawful.

Mens rea

7.87 The *mens rea* required for both offences is comprised by the word 'maliciously', which does not connote spite or ill-will.[260] It was confirmed by the House of Lords in 1991 in *Savage; DPP v Parmenter*[261] that, in order to prove that the defendant acted maliciously, it is sufficient to prove that he intended his act to result in some unlawful[262] bodily harm[263] to some other person, albeit of a minor nature, or was reckless as to the risk that his act might[264] result in such harm.

7.88 Thus, for no articulated policy reason, and contrary to the normal rule that *mens rea* as to a consequence of conduct must correspond with the consequence as defined for the *actus reus*,[265] it is not necessary to prove that the defendant intended, or was reckless as to, the infliction of a wound or grievous bodily harm.[266] On the other hand, it is not enough to prove that the defendant ought to have foreseen the risk of bodily harm to another; he must be proved actually to have foreseen the risk of such harm.[267]

The fact that intent or foresight as to something less than the degree of harm required for the *actus reus* of the offence charged suffices is a matter of criticism. (So is the analogous rule referred to in para 7.62 in respect of the *mens rea* required for offences of assault occasioning actual bodily harm.) Nevertheless, despite the low level of the *mens*

---

[258] *Savage; DPP v Parmenter* [1992] 1 AC 699, HL. There is no authority on whether there can be a 'wounding' by omission.

[259] Ch 16.   [260] *Cunningham* [1957] 2 QB 396, CCA.

[261] [1992] 1 AC 699, HL.   [262] *Jones* (1986) 83 Cr App Rep 375, CA.

[263] As defined in para 7.59.

[264] It was affirmed in *Rushworth* (1992) 95 Cr App Rep 252, CA, that it need only be foreseen that harm might (as opposed to would) result. To require foresight that harm would result, where it was not the defendant's purpose (ie direct intent) to cause it, would greatly limit the scope of s 20.

[265] Para 3.37.

[266] *Savage; DPP v Parmenter* [1992] 1 AC 699, HL. For earlier authority, see, for example, *Mowatt* [1968] 1 QB 421, CA; *Flack v Hunt* [1980] Crim LR 44, DC; *Sullivan* [1981] Crim LR 46, CA.

[267] Confirmed in *Savage; DPP v Parmenter* [1992] 1 AC 699, HL.

rea requirement, it may often be difficult to satisfy it where the defendant's conduct only causes serious psychiatric injury.

7.89 The fact that recklessness as to the risk of causing some unlawful bodily harm to another suffices for s 20 means that if D, knowing that he has (or may have)[268] the HIV virus or some other serious sexually transmitted disease, and therefore aware of the risk of infecting her, has intercourse with V who consents to the intercourse in ignorance of D's disease, as D knows, D will be guilty of the present offence if V becomes infected with the disease and suffers grievous bodily harm in consequence.[269]

7.90 Because the defendant must have been aware that his act might cause some *unlawful* bodily harm, a defendant who mistakenly believes, for example, that he is acting in self-defence, or that his victim has consented to the horseplay which seriously injures him accidentally, is not guilty of the present offence if he wounds or inflicts grievous bodily harm on his victim.[270] Likewise, a man who mistakenly believes that his sexual partner is aware that he has the HIV virus is not guilty of an offence under s 20 because he will not have been reckless as to the risk that his partner is not consenting to the risk of infection by the virus. However, as the Court of Appeal pointed out in *Konzani*,[271] where a defendant who knows that he is suffering from the HIV virus deliberately conceals it from a sexual partner, his silence is incongruous with a genuine belief that there was an informed consent to the risk of contracting the disease. The Court of Appeal nevertheless recognised that there could be rare exceptions, as where the sexual partner knew the defendant while he was in hospital being treated for the HIV virus or where the defendant believed that his new sexual partner had been told of his disease by someone who knew them both.

Section 18

7.91 The OAPA 1861, s 18[272] provides:

> 'Whosoever shall unlawfully and maliciously by any means whatsoever wound or cause any grievous bodily harm to any person, with intent to do some grievous bodily harm to

---

[268] There is no direct authority in the Court of Appeal decisions, *Dica* [2004] EWCA Crim 1103 and *Konzani* [2004] EWCA Crim 706, where convictions under s 20 for infecting someone with the HIV virus were upheld, as to whether it would suffice that D knows that he may have HIV etc, but in principle there is no reason why it should not. For a discussion of this matter see Ryan 'Reckless Transmission of HIV: Knowledge and Culpability' [2006] Crim LR 981. The author concludes that this is the present position in law, ie that wilful blindness to one's HIV status is sufficient. In the article the author examines (1) whether actual knowledge of HIV positive status is (or should be) necessary in order to impose liability under the OAPA 1861, s 20 for the reckless transmission of HIV, and (2) whether actual knowledge of the risks of transmission of HIV is (or should be) required for such liability.

[269] *Dica* [2004] EWCA Crim 1103. See Weait 'Criminal Law and the Sexual Transmission of HIV: *R v Dica*' (2005) 68 MLR 121 at 129 et seq.

[270] *Jones* (1986) 83 Cr App Rep 375, CA; *Aitken* [1992] 1 WLR 1006, C-MAC (as to this court, see para 2.32, n 91).

[271] [2005] EWCA Crim 706.

[272] As amended by the Criminal Law Act 1967, ss 10(2) and 12(5) and Sch 3.

any person, or with intent to resist or prevent the lawful apprehension or detainer of any person, shall be guilty [of an offence] . . .'.

There are two offences under s 18: wounding with intent to do grievous bodily harm or to resist etc lawful apprehension and causing grievous bodily harm with one of these intents. Because the two types of intent do not create separate offences; a count charging wounding (or one charging causing grievous bodily harm) is not bad for duplicity if it specifies both intents in the alternative.[273] An offence under s 18 is triable only on indictment and punishable with a maximum of life imprisonment.[274]

Actus reus

7.92 'Wound' and 'grievous bodily harm' mean the same as in s 20. Section 18 speaks of 'causing[275] by any means whatsoever', as opposed to 'inflicting', grievous bodily harm. As seen above, the two terms are identical, save that 'cause' doubtless covers, and 'inflict' may not, the case where a person deliberately fails to do something which he is under a legal duty to do and thereby grievous bodily harm is caused to another. Otherwise the *actus reus* of the offences under s 18 is identical to the corresponding *actus reus* under s 20.

Mens rea

Intent to do some grievous bodily harm or to resist etc lawful apprehension

7.93 The OAPA 1861, s 18 differs significantly from the s 20 offences in relation to its *mens rea* because the prosecution must prove that the defendant had the intent to do (unlawful) grievous bodily harm or to resist or prevent the lawful apprehension (ie arrest) or detainer of himself or another.

While a person who causes grievous bodily harm by means of a practical joke will be guilty of an offence under s 20 if he merely foresaw the risk of some harm, he cannot be convicted of an offence under s 18 on account of the absence of an intention to do grievous bodily harm. 'Intention' bears its normal meaning, outlined in Chapter 3, so that it is irrelevant whether or not the defendant desired to cause grievous bodily harm or to resist or prevent arrest.[276] The requirement of an intent to cause grievous bodily harm does not mean that the defendant himself should regard his intended consequence as grievous (ie serious) bodily harm. Provided that, in the view of the jury, his intended consequence amounts to grievous bodily harm he will have an intent to cause such harm. Thus, if the jury decides that D intended to break V's wrist and that a broken wrist is serious bodily harm, it is irrelevant that D did not think that a broken wrist was serious harm; the necessary intent will have been proved.

---

[273] *Naismith* [1961] 2 All ER 735, C-MAC (as to this court, see para 2.32, n 91).
[274] OAPA 1861, s 18.   [275] The rules of causation are described in paras 2.28–2.57.
[276] *Bryson* [1985] Crim LR 669, CA; *Purcell* (1986) 83 Cr App Rep 45, CA.

In cases of harassment and the like where really serious psychiatric injury is caused, but not any physical bodily harm, it will normally be difficult to prove an intent to cause grievous bodily harm in the absence of evidence of a clear determination to bring it about or of knowledge of a special susceptibility to serious psychiatric injury on the part of the defendant.

7.94 Unlike the corresponding intent under the OAPA 1861, s 38 referred to in para 7.64, the intent to resist lawful arrest need not relate to an arrest for an offence, so that an intent to resist a lawful arrest for a breach of the peace or in civil process suffices. Otherwise what is said there is equally applicable here, except that it is an open question whether a mistaken belief of law which led to the belief that an arrest for a breach of the peace or in civil process was unlawful could in itself negative the necessary intent. A mistake as to a civil power of arrest cannot be described as a mistake of criminal law and normally a mistake of civil law does excuse the defendant if it prevents him having the specified *mens rea*.[277]

Maliciously

7.95 Section 18 requires the defendant to wound or cause grievous bodily harm 'maliciously'. **'Maliciously', however, is redundant in s 18 where the defendant has the intent to do grievous bodily harm, but probably not where the defendant does not have that intent and only intends to resist etc lawful apprehension or detainer.** The reason why 'maliciously' is redundant in the former case is that causing grievous bodily harm or wounding with intent to do grievous bodily harm must, given the nature of the requisite intent, include foresight of the possibility of some physical harm which, as stated in para 7.87, is the meaning to be attached to 'maliciously' in s 20. On the other hand, it is possible to attach some force to the word 'maliciously' in s 18 when the alleged intent is to resist or prevent lawful apprehension or detainer. If D gently seizes a policeman's jacket, or even gently trips him up, in order to prevent him giving instant chase to X, an escaping criminal, D would undoubtedly have acted with intent to prevent X's apprehension, but, if the policeman suffered serious injury wholly unforeseen by D, D would not have acted 'maliciously', ie with foresight of the risk of some bodily harm to the policeman. It is submitted that that meaning should be given to 'maliciously' in this context, since it would seem unduly harsh to convict a person of the serious offence under s 18 where he accidentally but seriously injured another in trying to resist or prevent a lawful arrest.[278] It was said in *Mowatt*[279] that '"maliciously" adds nothing' in s 18, but the case was concerned with a charge of wounding with intent to do grievous bodily harm.[280]

---

[277] Para 3.81.

[278] Such a person could, of course, be convicted of one or more of the offences already discussed in this chapter, the particular offence(s) depending on the facts of the case.

[279] [1968] 1 QB 421, CA.

[280] It seems to have been assumed in *Morrison* (1988) 89 Cr App Rep 17, CA, that 'maliciously' in the context of a charge under s 18 involving an intent to resist etc arrest does bear some meaning, that given to it in relation to s 20.

'Racially or religiously aggravated assaults'

> **Key points 7.7**
>
> A person is guilty of an offence of racially or religiously aggravated assault if he commits:
>
> - an offence under the OAPA 1861, s 20;
> - an offence under the OAPA 1861, s 47; or
> - common assault,
>
> which is 'racially or religiously aggravated'.

7.96 A substantial increase in incidents of racial violence and harassment led to a number of racially aggravated offences being introduced by the Crime and Disorder Act 1998 (CDA 1998). These offences were extended to deal with religious aggravation as well by the Anti-terrorism, Crime and Security Act 2001.

All the racially or religiously aggravated offences in the CDA 1998 are based, as aggravated versions carrying a higher maximum punishment, on pre-existing offences.[281] In all other offences, racial or religious aggravation is a factor aggravating the seriousness of the offence (and thus the sentence).[282] It is questionable whether the various racially or religiously aggravated offences are necessary. Would it not have been enough simply to leave the matter as an aggravating factor in determining sentence in every case?

7.97 Racially or religiously aggravated assaults are governed by the CDA 1998, s 29. Section 29(1) provides that:

> 'A person is guilty of an offence under this section if he commits –
>
> (a) an offence under section 20 of the Offences Against the Person Act 1861 (malicious wounding or grievous bodily harm);
>
> (b) an offence under section 47 of that Act (actual bodily harm); or
>
> (c) common assault,
>
> which is racially or religiously aggravated for the purposes of this section.'

Section 29(1) does not create one offence which can be committed in various ways but a number of separate ones. Given that an offence under the Offences Against the Person Act 1861, s 20 does not require an assault or battery, the marginal note to s 29 (which describes the offences covered by the section as 'assaults') is not strictly accurate.

---

[281] For the other offences dealt with in this book, see paras 7.152 and 13.26. There are also racially and religiously aggravated public order offences under CDA 1998, outside the scope of this book.

[282] Criminal Justice Act 2003, s 145.

A racially or religiously aggravated offence under the Offences Against the Person Act 1861, s 20 or s 47 is triable either way; the maximum imprisonment on conviction on indictment is seven years (as opposed to five for the 'simple' offence).[283]

It is submitted that, as in the case of 'common assault' in other contexts, a common assault in s 29 can be committed either by an assault or by a battery. An offence of racially or religiously aggravated common assault is a significantly more serious one than a 'simple' common assault. It is triable either way and punishable on conviction on indictment with a maximum of two years' imprisonment.[284] The increase in the maximum term of imprisonment for what will normally be a threat or push which has caused no harm is significant. Apparently two years was chosen on the ground that this is the normal lowest maximum specified for either-way offences.

Definition of racial or religious aggravation

7.98 On a charge of an offence under the CDA 1998, s 29 the prosecution must prove that the defendant has committed one of the relevant specified basic offences and that it (the offence) was racially or religiously aggravated. Sometimes one of the offences will be both racially and religiously aggravated.

The CDA 1998, s 28(1) provides that, for the purposes of the various racially and religiously aggravated offences under the Act:

> 'An offence is racially or religiously aggravated . . . if:
>
> (a) at the time of committing the offence, or immediately before or after doing so, the offender demonstrates towards the victim of the offence hostility based on the victim's membership of (or presumed membership of) a racial or religious group; or
>
> (b) the offence is motivated (wholly or partly) by hostility towards members of a racial or religious group based on their membership of that group.'

'Racial or religious aggravation' can exist notwithstanding that the defendant is of the same racial or religious group as the object of the offence.[285]

Racial group

7.99 The CDA 1998, s 28(4) provides that, for the purposes of s 28, '"racial group" means a group of persons defined by reference to race, colour, nationality (including citizenship) or ethnic or national origins'. The wording of the definition must be given a broad, non-technical interpretation.[286] Most of the terms used in the definition have a fairly clear meaning, but the following does need to be made clear.

First, the group of persons must be defined by reference to colour, race, nationality or ethnic or national origins. Sikhs, for example, are not a group defined by reference to

---

[283] CDA 1998, s 29(2).   [284] CDA 1998, s 29(3).   [285] *White* [2001] EWCA Crim 216.
[286] *White* [2001] EWCA Crim 216; *Rogers (Philip)* [2007] UKHL 8.

colour or race or nationality, but (as will be seen) they are a group defined by reference to their ethnic origins.

Second, applying the broad, non-technical approach referred to above, a group of people will be a racial group defined by reference to *race* if, in ordinary speech, those people would be regarded as belonging to a named race.[287] In *White*,[288] for example, it was held that 'African' described a racial group defined by reference to race because in ordinary language 'African' denotes a limited group of people regarded as of common stock and as one of the major divisions of humankind having distinct physical features in common; it 'denotes a person characteristic of the blacks in Africa'. This was said to be so despite the fact that *strictly* 'African' is capable of covering Egyptians and White South Africans who would *not commonly* be described as 'Africans'. This broad, non-technical approach was confirmed and taken further in *Rogers (Philip)*,[289] where the victims of the words 'bloody foreigners' were Spanish. The House of Lords held that these words were capable of satisfying the requirements of s 28(1)(a). It held that people who are not of British origin constitute a racial group for the purposes of the definition of 'racial group' in the CDA 1998, s 28(1). Thus, a racial group can be defined exclusively by reference to what its members are not in terms of race, colour, nationality, or ethnic or national origins, eg non-British or non-White, as well as inclusively by reference to what they are in such terms, eg Spanish or black. The broad non-technical approach confirmed in *Rogers (Philip)* was justified by Baroness Hale, delivering the unanimous decision of the House, as follows:

'This flexible, non-technical approach makes sense, not only as a matter of language, but also in policy terms. The mischiefs attacked by the aggravated versions of these offences are racism and xenophobia. Their essence is the denial of equal respect and dignity to people who are seen as 'other'. This is more deeply hurtful, damaging and disrespectful to the victims than the simple versions of these offences. It is also more damaging to the community as a whole, by denying acceptance to members of certain groups not for their own sake, but for the sake of something they can do nothing about. This is just as true if the group is defined exclusively as if it is defined inclusively.

...Fine distinctions depending upon the particular words used would bring the law into disrepute.'[290]

Third, the term 'ethnic' is construed relatively widely and, although a cultural or religious group is not per se defined by reference to its ethnic origins, 'ethnic' is used in a sense wider than the strictly racial or biological. This was held by the House of Lords in *Mandla v Dowell Lee*,[291] where Lord Fraser, with whose speech the other Law Lords

---

[287] *White* [2001] EWCA Crim 216.

[288] [2001] EWCA Crim 216. The Court accepted that 'African' did not refer to a racial group defined by reference to ethnic origins.

[289] [2007] UKHL 8.   [290] [2007] UKHL 8 at [12]–[13].   [291] [1983] 2 AC 548, HL.

agreed, said this about the concept of an ethnic group in the identical definition of racial group in the Race Relations Act 1976:

'For a group to constitute an ethnic group in the sense of the Race Relations Act 1976, it must, in my opinion, regard itself, and be regarded by others, as a distinct community by virtue of certain characteristics. Some of these characteristics are essential; others are not essential but one or more of them will commonly be found and will help to distinguish the group from the surrounding community. The conditions which appear to me to be essential are these: (1) a long shared history, of which the group is conscious as distinguishing it from other groups, and the memory of which it keeps alive; (2) a cultural tradition of its own, including family and social customs and manners, often but not necessarily associated with religious observance. In addition to these two essential characteristics the following characteristics are, in my opinion, relevant: (3) either a common geographical origin, or descent from a small number of common ancestors; (4) a common language, not necessarily peculiar to the group; (5) a common literature peculiar to the group; (6) a common religion different from that of neighbouring groups or from the general community surrounding it; (7) being a minority or being an oppressed or a dominant group within a larger community, for example a conquered people...and their conquerors might both be ethnic groups.'[292]

Pursuant to the above dictum, it is clear that Sikhs (as the House held in *Mandla*) and Romany gypsies are groups defined by reference to their ethnic origins.[293] On the other hand, tinkers or travellers are not.

Religious group

7.100 The CDA 1998, s 28(5) provides that, for the purposes of s 28, '"religious group" means a group of persons defined by reference to religious belief or lack of religious belief'. 'Religious belief' is not defined. It is, however, clear, for example, that Sikhs, Muslims and Rastafarians are religious groups, although the last two are not racial groups.[294]

As can be seen from the references to Sikhs, it is possible for a group to be both a racial and a religious one.

Two types of racial or religious aggravation

7.101 Under the CDA 1998, s 28(1), there are two types of racial or religious aggravation, the first based on the *demonstration towards the victim of hostility based on*

---

[292] [1983] 2 AC 548 at 562.

[293] *Commission for Racial Equality v Dutton* [1989] QB 783, CA. As to the Jewish ethnic group and membership of it, see *R (on the application of E) v Governing Body of JFS* [2009] UKSC 15.

[294] *Malik v Bartram Personnel Group* (1990), an Employment Tribunal decision, No 4343/90 (in respect of Muslims); *Crown Suppliers (Property Services Agency) v Dawkins* [1993] ICR 517, CA (in respect of Rastafarians).

the victim's membership or presumed membership of a racial or religious group and the second based on *motivation by hostility towards members of a racial or religious group based on their membership of that group.* The first type is 'concerned with the outward manifestation of racial or religious hostility, the other with the inner motivation of the offender'.[295]

Both types of racial or religious aggravation refer to the concept of membership of a racial or religious group, which is not always an easy one to apply where a racial group is identified by reference to its ethnic or national origins.

Clearly, a religious group includes converts and excludes those who have abandoned the religion. The same is true, according to Lord Fraser of Tullybelton, obiter, in *Mandla v Dowell Lee*[296] in the case of an ethnic group. He said: 'Provided a person who joins the group [eg by marriage] feels him or herself to be a member of it, and is accepted by other members, he is…a member'.

The importance of the precise meaning of 'membership' in s 28(1)(a) is lessened by s 28(2)(a), which provides that in s 28(1)(a) 'membership' in relation to a racial or religious group includes association with members of that group. Thus, a person who has not converted to a religious or ethnic group but is the spouse or adopted child of a member of the group and thereby in association with that member and members of his family etc who are members of the group is a member of the group. Consequently, if a white woman who is married to a Pakistani is attacked or abused because of her association with Pakistanis the offence will be racially aggravated.

7.102 *Demonstration of hostility based on victim's membership etc of a racial or religious group* The first alternative meaning of 'racially or religiously aggravated' is contained in the CDA 1998, s 28(1)(a). **This requires that 'at the time of committing the offence, or immediately before or after doing so, the offender demonstrates towards the victim hostility based on the victim's membership or presumed membership of a racial or religious group'.**

7.103 Unlike s 28(1)(b), s 28(1)(a) does not require the offence committed by the defendant to be motivated by racial or religious hostility.[297] In *DPP v Woods*[298] D assaulted a club doorman (V) who refused to admit D's friend. D also called V a 'black bastard' a few moments before he hit V. The magistrates found that D's hostility arose from his frustration and annoyance as a result of his friend being denied entry and was not based on V's membership of a racial group; they believed that he would have abused anyone in V's shoes by reference to an obvious physical characteristic that that individual had. Accordingly they found that the battery was not racially aggravated. Maurice Kay J allowed the prosecution's appeal. He held that s 28(1)(a) did not apply solely to cases where an offender's only motivation was racial malevolence. It extended to cases where there was a racially neutral gravamen but in which hostility was demonstrated towards the victim based on

---

[295] *Rogers (Philip)* [2007] UKHL 8 at [6], per Baroness Hale.   [296] [1983] 2 AC 548 at 562.
[297] *DPP v Woods* [2002] EWHC 85 (Admin), Maurice Kay J; *DPP v Green* [2004] EWHC 1225 (Admin), DC.
[298] [2002] EWHC 85 (Admin).

his membership of a racial group.[299] The fact that D would have abused anyone who had been in V's position by reference to an obvious physical characteristic was an irrelevant consideration.

7.104 For the test under s 28(1)(a) to be satisfied, the defendant must have formed the view that the victim was a member of a racial or religious group and the defendant must have done or said something which demonstrated hostility towards the victim based on that membership. Such demonstrations will normally be made by words, but they can be made in other ways, eg by the wearing of swastikas.[300] Words used need not expressly identify the racial or religious group to which the victim belongs nor explicitly demonstrate racial or religious hostility. In *A-G's Reference (No 4 of 2004)*,[301] the victim was Indian and brown-skinned. He was called an 'immigrant doctor' by the defendant immediately before the defendant assaulted him. The Court of Appeal held that it was open to the jury to conclude that the defendant had identified her victim as falling within the racial groups of Indian and brown-skinned and that the use of 'immigrant' demonstrated hostility based on the victim's membership of such groups. Reference may also be made to *Johnson v DPP*,[302] where D, who was black, had said to two white parking attendants during an argument 'why don't you get up [a white area] with your white uncles and aunties?'. The Divisional Court held that it was reasonably open to the magistrates' court to conclude that these words demonstrated racial hostility, at least in part.

7.105 The requirement that such hostility must be demonstrated at the time of, or immediately before or after, the offence means that there must be some evidence of an overt demonstration of what could be found to be racial or religious hostility during that period. The fact that the victim was unconcerned by the hostility demonstrated is irrelevant.[303]

7.106 Section 28(1)(a) does not require the hostility demonstrated to be based only on the victim's membership of a racial or religious group, or even principally on it; this is confirmed by s 28(3) referred to in para 7.113. Thus, in *DPP v M (A Minor)*,[304] the fact that the hostility demonstrated was based more on a dispute over food at a kebab shop than on racial hostility did not prevent racial aggravation being proved under s 28(1)(a). Another example is provided by *Johnson v DPP*,[305] where it was held that it was irrelevant that the defendant's hostility was based partly on the victims' membership of a racial group and partly on hostility towards parking attendants generally or by reason of their duties as parking attendants. However, the more incidental the words or other conduct with a racial or religious content, the more difficult it will be to prove that the defendant has demonstrated racial or religious hostility. In this context it must be emphasised that

---

[299] Or, of course, religious group.   [300] *Rogers (Philip)* [2007] UKHL 8 at [13], per Baroness Hale.
[301] [2005] EWCA Crim 889.   [302] [2008] EWHC 509 (Admin), DC.
[303] *DPP v Woods* [2002] EWHC 85 (Admin), Maurice Kay J.
[304] [2004] EWHC 1453 (Admin), DC.
[305] [2008] EWHC 509 (Admin), DC. See also *Kendall v South East Magistrates' Court* [2008] EWHC 1848 (Admin), DC; *Rogers (Philip)* [2007] UKHL 8 at [11], per Baroness Hale.

it is not enough simply to refer, for example, to the victim's race or religion; the defendant must be proved to have demonstrated 'hostility'.

7.107 In relation to the requirement that the hostility must be demonstrated at the time of committing the offence, or immediately before or after doing so, reference can be made to case law on the offence of robbery, which requires a use or threat of force 'immediately before or at the time of' the stealing.[306] It has been held for the purposes of that offence that 'the time' of the stealing is not limited to the period (possibly a split second of time) during which the material act with *mens rea* of theft occurs, and that 'the time' of the stealing lasts as long as the theft can be said to be still in progress in commonsense terms, ie so long as the defendant is 'on the job'.

The word 'immediately' in s 28(1)(a) qualifies 'after' as well as 'before'; s 28(1)(a) strikes at words uttered or acts done in the immediate context of the basic substantive offence.[307] Thus, it was held in *Parry v DPP*[308] that a racially aggravated offence was not made out where the defendant demonstrated racial hostility to the victim only 20 minutes after committing the basic offence, while being questioned by the police. The victim, however, does not need to be in the defendant's presence at the time of the demonstration of racial hostility.[309]

Words used at a time not immediately before the basic offence is committed can colour the defendant's behaviour at the time of the offence and justify the conclusion that the defendant demonstrated racial or religious hostility at the time of the offence. In *Babbs*,[310] D had described V and his companion as 'foreign fuckers' and during a second confrontation 15 minutes later assaulted V; the Court of Appeal held that the jury were entitled to find that racial hostility had been demonstrated at the material time.

7.108 Sometimes hostility may be demonstrated towards someone in the mistaken belief that he is a member of a racial or religious group, as where a Bangladeshi (or atheist) is the victim of hostility intended to be directed at a Pakistani (or a Catholic). In such a case the offence will be racially or religiously aggravated because s 28(2)(b) provides that the reference to 'presumed membership' in s 28(1)(a) means presumed by the offender. Similarly, if a racist threatens a white woman whom he mistakenly believes is associated with a Pakistani and his family, and the hostility he demonstrates is based on that association, his offence is racially aggravated because of the definition of 'membership' and 'presumed membership'.

7.109 *Motivation by hostility towards members of a racial or religious group based on their membership of that group* The second alternative meaning of 'racially or religiously aggravated' is contained in the CDA 1998, s 28(1)(b). **This requires that 'the offence is motivated (wholly or partly) by hostility towards members of a racial or religious group based on their membership of that group'.** It has the effect in relation to the

---

[306] Para 10.103.   [307] *Parry v DPP* [2004] EWHC 3112 (Admin), DC.
[308] [2004] EWHC 3112 (Admin), DC.   [309] *Parry v DPP* [2004] EWHC 3112 (Admin).
[310] [2007] EWCA Crim 2737.

specified offences of making motive relevant to criminal liability, something which is exceptional.[311]

7.110 It should be noted that the offence need not be motivated wholly by hostility towards members of a racial or religious group based on their membership of that group, nor need it be principally so motivated. However, where it is partly so motivated – particularly where the racial or religious motivation is subordinate to other motives – it will be particularly difficult to prove the necessary motivation.

7.111 Section 28(1)(b) does not require the defendant to be motivated by racial or religious hostility towards the victim of the offence but 'merely' by hostility 'towards members of a racial or religious group'. Hostility towards one member of a racial or religious group based on his membership of that group is sufficient to qualify under s 29(1)(b) so long as it forms part of the motivation for the conduct. Normally the victim will be a member of that group (and thus included within the ambit of that hostility) or at least be associated with it but this is not a requirement of s 28(1)(b). A person who, motivated by hostility towards members of the Jewish religious community, attacked a bricklayer whom he knew was not Jewish who was working on the building of a synagogue would fall foul of s 28(1)(b), for example. It is for this reason that it was not necessary to extend to s 28(1)(b) the provision that membership of a racial or religious group includes association with it.

7.112 Proof of motivation by hostility towards members of a racial or religious group based on their membership of that group under s 28(1)(b) can be established by evidence relating to what the defendant may have said or done on other occasions.[312]

7.113 What was said in para 7.110 is reinforced by the CDA 1998, s 28(3) which also makes a similar provision in respect of racial or religious aggravation within s 28(1)(a). Section 28(3) provides that:

> 'It is immaterial for the purposes of paragraph (a) or (b) of [s 28(1)] whether or not the offender's hostility is also based, to any extent, on any other factor not mentioned in that paragraph.'

Administering poison etc

Key points 7.8

The OAPA 1861, ss 23 and 24 provide offences specifically dealing with 'poisoning':

- administering etc poison or other destructive or noxious thing and thereby endangering life or inflicting grievous bodily harm;
- administering etc such a substance with intent to injure, aggrieve or annoy.

---

[311] Para 3.70.   [312] *RG v DPP; LT v DPP* [2004] EWHC 183 (Admin), DC.

7.114 The OAPA 1861, s 23 provides:

> 'Whosoever shall unlawfully and maliciously administer to or cause to be administered to or taken by any other person any poison or other destructive or noxious thing, so as thereby to endanger the life of such person, or so as thereby to inflict upon such person any grievous bodily harm, shall be guilty of [an offence]...'.

An offence under s 23 is triable only on indictment and punishable with a maximum of 10 years' imprisonment.[313]

The OAPA 1861, s 24 provides:

> 'Whosoever shall unlawfully and maliciously administer to or cause to be administered to or taken by any other person any poison or other destructive or noxious thing, with intent to injure, aggrieve, or annoy such person, shall be guilty of [an offence]...'.

An offence under s 24 is less serious than that under s 23 since, although it is triable only on indictment, its maximum punishment is five years' imprisonment.[314]

In *Kennedy (No 2)*,[315] the House of Lords held that s 23 creates three distinct offences whose bases are:

- administering a poison etc;
- causing a poison etc to be administered to another person;
- causing a poison etc to be taken by another person.

The same is obviously true in respect of s 24.

The distinction between the wording of the two sections is that s 23 requires grievous bodily harm actually to result (the defendant's intention being irrelevant) and that s 24 requires the defendant to intend to injure, aggrieve or annoy the person to whom the poison etc is administered etc (whether or not anything results from what he has done).

Administer, or cause to be administered or taken

7.115 The meaning of these terms is a matter for the judge in the Crown Court and is not to be left to the jury as a question of fact.[316] In *Kennedy (No 2)*,[317] a case where s 23 was in issue, the House of Lords provided guidance about these terms which is equally applicable to s 24.

Administer

7.116 In *Kennedy (No 2)*, the House of Lords held that the offence of **administration under s 23 'is committed where D administers the noxious thing directly to V, as by**

---

[313] OAPA 1861, s 23.   [314] OAPA 1861, s 24.   [315] [2007] UKHL 38 at [9].
[316] *Gillard* (1988) 87 Cr App Rep 189 at 194.   [317] [2007] UKHL 38.

injecting V with the noxious thing, holding a glass containing the noxious thing to V's lips, or (as in *Gillard*[318]) spraying the noxious thing in V's face'.[319] There is no necessity when 'administer' is in issue to postulate any form of entry into the victim's body, whether through any orifice or through absorption.[320]

7.117 For a few years it was the law that someone who participated in the self-injection of a drug by another person (V), by holding a tourniquet while V did so (*Rogers (Stephen)*)[321] or by handing V the syringe for immediate voluntary and informed self-injection by V (*Kennedy (No 2)*),[322] administered the drug to V. These actions were held by the Court of Appeal to be 'administration' on the ground that in the former case the defendant had played a part in the mechanics of the injection and that in the latter case he had been involved in a joint activity with V, the self-injector. These decisions raised major problems in respect of the previous law of causation which, as under the current law, regarded the chain of causation from holding the tourniquet or providing the drug, as broken by the self-injector's free, deliberate and informed act of self-injection.

Fortunately those decisions were overruled by the House of Lords in *Kennedy (No 2)*. The House held that, although it was possible to imagine factual scenarios in which two people could properly be regarded as acting together to administer an injection, where D supplies a drug to V who, knowing the facts, and by choice, ie freely and voluntarily, self-injects it, D does not jointly administer it.[323] The House also considered that a person who holds a tourniquet around another's arm so as to raise a vein is not engaged in joint administration. It stated that:

> 'There is, clearly, a difficult borderline between contributory acts which may properly be regarded as administering a noxious thing and acts which may not. But the crucial question is not whether the defendant facilitated or contributed to administration of the noxious thing but whether he went further and administered it. What matters, in a case such as *R v Rogers* and the present, is whether the injection itself was the result of a voluntary and informed decision by the person injecting himself. In *R v Rogers*, as in the present case, it was.[324] That case was, therefore, wrongly decided.'[325]

The House of Lords did not give an example of the 'imaginable factual scenarios' in which two people could properly be regarded as acting together to administer an injection. A case which may fall on the 'administration' side of the 'difficult borderline' referred to by the House of Lords was suggested by the Court of Appeal in *Burgess; Byram*, although

---

[318] (1988) 87 Cr App Rep 189, CA.   [319] [2007] UKHL 38 at [10].

[320] *Gillard* (1988) 87 Cr App Rep 189, CA; *Walford* (1899) 34 L Jo 116, per Wills J. The contrary view, that a thing is not administered until it is ingested, taken by trial judges in *Cadman* (1825) Carrington's Supplement 237 and *Harley* (1830) 4 C & P 369, would seem to be wrong.

[321] [2003] EWCA Crim 945.   [322] [2005] EWCA Crim 685.   [323] [2007] UKHL 38 at [24].

[324] See paras 2.42 and 2.43.   [325] [2007] UKHL 38 at [20].

the decision in that case was on a different factual basis on which the defendant had pleaded guilty. The Court of Appeal said:

'If a defendant may be convicted on the basis that the fatal dose was jointly administered, then it follows that he is not automatically entitled to be acquitted if the deceased rather than the defendant physically operated the plunger on the syringe and caused the drug to enter his body. In the present case there was evidence which might reasonably have lead a jury to conclude that this appellant had indeed jointly participated in the administration of the fatal dose of heroin. From the interviews as they developed, it emerged that he supplied the deceased with the heroin, which he, the appellant, drew into the syringe. He did not hand the syringe to the deceased but he took it and the needle to the deceased's arm, where he found an appropriate vein. He laid the tip of the needle against the skin of the deceased above that vein. It is not clear from the interview that he ever in fact let go of the syringe, but on his account the deceased depressed the plunger. Having done so, the appellant assisted in the physical withdrawal of the plunger from the deceased's arm.'[326]

Cause to be administered

7.118 In *Kennedy (No 2)*, the House of Lords held that the **'causing to be administered' offence under s 23 'is typically committed where D does not directly administer the noxious thing to V but causes an innocent third party TP to administer it to V. If D,** knowing a syringe to be filled with poison, instructs TP to inject V, TP believing the syringe to contain a legitimate therapeutic substance, D would commit the offence'.[327] If TP had known the true nature of the substance and acted with the necessary *mens rea*, TP would be guilty of the administration offence as its perpetrator and D would be guilty of it as an accomplice.

Cause to be taken

7.119 In *Kennedy (No 2)*, the House of Lords held that the **'causing to be taken' offence under s 23 'covers the situation where the noxious thing is not administered to V but taken by him, provided D causes the noxious thing to be taken by V and V does not make a voluntary and informed decision to take it.** If D puts a noxious thing in food which V is about to eat and V, ignorant of the presence of the noxious thing, eats it D commits the offence'.[328] In *Gillard*,[329] the Court of Appeal stated that 'taking', for the purposes of 'causing to be taken' in s 24, requires ingestion into the digestive system.

---

[326] [2008] EWCA Crim 516 at [12].   [327] [2007] UKHL 38 at [11].
[328] [2007] UKHL 38 at [12].   [329] (1988) 87 Cr App Rep 189 at 193–194.

Poison or other destructive or noxious thing

7.120 For the purposes of the offence of administering a poison or other noxious substance with intent to procure a miscarriage, contrary to the OAPA 1861, s 58, **'poison' has been said to mean a recognised poison, and it has been stated in the same case that if the thing administered is a recognised poison the offence may be committed, even though the quantity given is so small as to be incapable of doing harm.**[330] This must be equally applicable to the offences under ss 23 and 24.

7.121 **'Noxious thing' means something different in quality from, and of less importance than, poison or other destructive thing, which is 'noxious' in the dosage in which it was administered, even though it is innocuous in small quantities.**[331] The leading authority is the decision of the Court of Appeal in *Marcus*.[332] The Court held that, since the offence under s 24 involved an intent to injure, aggrieve or annoy, the concept of 'noxious thing' in s 24 involved not only the quality or nature of the substance but also the quantity administered. A substance which might be harmless in small quantities could therefore be noxious for the purposes of s 24 if the quantity administered was sufficient to injure, annoy or aggrieve. The Court added that the meaning of 'noxious' was not limited to substances which caused injury to bodily health. Referring to the definition of 'noxious' in the *Shorter Oxford English Dictionary*: 'injurious, hurtful, harmful, unwholesome', the Court stated that the meaning of 'noxious' was clearly very wide.

Whether 'noxious' in s 23 is, as in s 24, not limited to substances which cause injury to bodily health is open to debate in the light of the fact that the Court of Appeal in *Marcus*[333] was clearly addressing the meaning of that term in the context of s 24 and was influenced by the requirement that s 24 involves an intent to injure, annoy or aggrieve. The point is, however, somewhat academic because, unless the substance is administered in a sufficient quantity to be harmful, it is difficult to see how grievous bodily harm could be inflicted by it or life endangered by it, as required by s 23.

In *Cato*,[334] where s 23 was in issue, it was held that heroin is always a noxious thing – even if administered to a person with high tolerance, and therefore unlikely to suffer any particular harm. The Court of Appeal based this conclusion on the fact that heroin is liable to cause injury in common use. Ecstasy has likewise been held to be a noxious thing.[335]

7.122 It has been argued[336] that bodily fluids containing HIV are 'noxious things' and that their transmission through sexual activity can amount to an 'administration' of it. However, a charge under the OAPA 1861, s 20 is more likely in such a case.

---

[330] *Cramp* (1880) 5 QBD 307 at 309–310, per Field J; see also Stephen J, at 310. See also *Hennah* (1877) 13 Cox CC 547 at 549, per Lord Cockburn CJ.

[331] *Marcus* [1981] 2 All ER 833, CA, following *Hennah* (1877) 13 Cox CC 547 and *Cramp* (1880) 5 QBD 307.

[332] [1981] 2 All ER 833 at 837.   [333] [1981] 2 All ER 833, CA.   [334] [1976] 1 All ER 260, CA.

[335] *Gantz* [2004] EWCA Crim 2862.

[336] Ormerod and Gunn 'Criminal Liability for the Transmission of HIV' [1996] Web JCLI.

Unlawfully

7.123 An administration etc will not be unlawful if the victim has given a valid consent. In accordance with the principles discussed earlier in this chapter, the victim's consent will not be valid where the administration is intended to cause actual bodily harm (or the risk of such harm was foreseen) and its administration is not in the public interest. It was held in *Cato*, for example, that a valid consent cannot be given to the administration of heroin or other dangerous drug unless the administration is done for bona fide medical reasons.

Section 23

Actus reus

7.124 The *actus reus* for the offence under the OAPA 1861, s 23 requires the defendant unlawfully to administer to, or cause to be administered to or taken by, another person any poison or other destructive or noxious thing so as thereby to endanger the life of the person to whom it is administered etc, or so as to inflict upon him any grievous bodily harm. For convenience, 'poison or other destructive or noxious thing' is referred to hereafter simply as 'noxious thing'.

7.125 It would seem that the endangerment of life or infliction of grievous bodily harm must result from the noxious thing itself and not from any condition caused by it. Therefore, if the administration of a substance causes the victim to fall asleep while working machinery and he is injured as a result, an offence would not be committed.

Mens rea

7.126 The only *mens rea* required for s 23 is that the defendant should have maliciously administered etc the poison etc. In *Cunningham*,[337] a case under s 23, the Court of Criminal Appeal held that this means that the defendant must act with intent or recklessness, but only as to the administration, or causing to be administered or taken, of a noxious thing, which states of mind the defendant will not have if he does not know that the thing is noxious. Almost certainly, a person who intends, or is reckless as to, the administration etc of a noxious thing will foresee the risk of injury. In *Cunningham* the Court was of the opinion that the jury should have been told that the defendant must have foreseen that someone might be caused injury by the noxious thing.[338]

7.127 It was confirmed by the Court of Appeal in *Cato* that no *mens rea* is required as to endangering life or the infliction of grievous bodily harm.

---

[337] *Cunningham* [1957] 2 QB 396, CCA.
[338] Spite or ill-will is not required: *Cunningham* [1957] 2 QB 396, CCA.

Section 24

Actus reus

7.128 The *actus reus* of an offence under the OAPA 1861, s 24 is the same as that under s 23 except that it does not require the administration etc to result in endangering life or inflicting grievous bodily harm.

Mens rea

Maliciously

7.129 The OAPA 1861, s 24 requires the defendant maliciously to have administered etc the noxious thing. 'Maliciously' has the same meaning as in s 23. Where the defendant acts with an ulterior intent to injure (below), 'maliciously' is redundant.

Ulterior intent

7.130 Section 24 also requires the defendant in addition to act with intent to injure, aggrieve or annoy. In *Hill*,[339] the House of Lords held that an intent to injure depends not only on the effect which the defendant intends to produce but also on whether his purpose is a 'good' or 'bad' one. In *Hill*, D administered slimming tablets to two boys, aged 11 and 13, telling them that they would make them feel cheerful and happy. Both boys suffered from vomiting and diarrhoea the next day. On arrest D admitted that he was a homosexual interested in young boys. The House of Lords upheld D's conviction under s 24. Lord Griffiths, giving the opinion of the House of Lords said:

> 'The defence conceded that the tablets were a noxious thing and that [D] had unlawfully administered them to the boys. In these circumstances the only issue that the jury had to determine was whether he did so with the intent to injure them...Here was a man who admitted being sexually attracted to young boys plying them with a drug which he knew would overstimulate and excite them and doing so with reckless disregard for what might be the safe dosage, and, in fact, giving them a gross overdosage. The only reasonable inference to draw from such conduct was an intention that the drug should injure the boys in the sense of causing harm to the metabolism of their bodies by overstimulation with the motive of either ingratiating himself with them or, more probably, rendering them susceptible to homosexual advances.'[340]

A different view would no doubt have been taken if someone slipped stimulants into another's tea, with similar effect, in order to help him complete a sponsored race for charity.

---

[339] (1986) 83 Cr App Rep 386, HL.
[340] (1986) 83 Cr App Rep 386 at 388.

Draft Offences Against the Person Bill

7.131 Even after the clarification of the law by the House of Lords in the 1990s, the law on non-fatal offences against the person is open to serious criticism in that it does not deal adequately with modern situations, and through its unclear and outdated language is liable to continue to create scope for legal argument with cases having to go to the House of Lords at considerable public expense. The state of this area of the law was strongly criticised in 1993 by the Law Commission in the report in which it promulgated the draft Criminal Law Bill containing provisions to reform the law relating to non-fatal offences.[341] The appellate courts have also agreed and called for reform.[342] The Government partially accepted the Law Commission's reform proposals in 1997 and announced that it proposed to introduce legislation to reform the law of non-fatal offences. A consultation paper[343] was published in 1998 as the first stage in the process. The Government's reaction to the responses to the consultation is still awaited. It looks increasingly likely that it never will be published.

The consultation paper contains a draft Offences Against the Person Bill whose provisions are based on the draft Criminal Law Bill, although there are some significant differences. In particular, the draft Offences Against the Person Bill does not contain provisions defining general defences such as duress by threats and self-defence; it simply provides that all existing defences shall continue to apply to its offences. Because the Law Commission had not completed its study of the issue of consent, the draft Offences Against the Person Bill does not deal with that issue, which would continue to be dealt with under the rules described at the start of this chapter if the draft Bill is ever enacted.[344]

7.132 Under the draft Offences Against the Person Bill the law relating to common assault and battery would be replaced by the following provision (cl 4), which would create a single offence of assault:

'(1) A person is guilty of an offence if –
  (a) he intentionally or recklessly applies force to or causes an impact on the body of another, or
  (b) he intentionally or recklessly causes the other to believe that any such force or impact is imminent.

---

[341] Law Commission: *Legislating the Criminal Code: Offences against the Person and General Principles* (1993), Law Com No 218.

[342] See, for example, *Lynsey* [1995] 3 All ER 654 at 654–655; *Mandair* [1995] 1 AC 208 at 221, per Lord Mustill.

[343] Home Office: *Violence: Reforming the Offences against the Person Act 1861*. See Professor Sir John Smith [1998] Crim LR 317.

[344] For a discussion of the Law Commission's proposals see Clarkson [1994] Crim LR 324, and J Gardner (1994) 53 CLJ 502.

> (2) No such offence is committed if the force or impact, not being intended or likely to cause injury, is in the circumstances such as is generally acceptable in the ordinary conduct of daily life and the defendant does not know or believe that it is in fact unacceptable to the other person.'

Like the existing offences of common assault and battery, the offence would be a purely summary one.

For the sake of completeness, cl 5 of the draft Bill replicates the offence of assaulting a constable in the execution of his duty. Under the corresponding provision in the draft Criminal Law Bill it would have to be proved that the defendant knew or was reckless as to whether his victim was a constable. This requirement does not appear in cl 5, because the Government did not wish to reduce the protection given to the police.

By cl 7, there would continue to be an offence of assault with intent to resist lawful arrest, triable and punishable in the same way as the existing offence. Clause 6 adds a more serious offence, triable only on indictment and punishable with a maximum of life imprisonment, of causing serious injury with intent to resist arrest. What is said about 'injury' in para 7.133 also applies here.

The draft Bill preceded the introduction of the offences of racially or religiously aggravated assault and therefore does not refer to them.

7.133 Clauses 1, 2 and 3 of the draft Offences Against the Person Bill would replace the Offences Against the Person Act 1861, ss 18, 20 and 47 with three new offences. The substance of the three offences would be:

- Intentionally causing serious injury to another. This would be triable only on indictment and punishable with a maximum of life imprisonment. It would cover most cases at present falling within the Offences Against the Person Act 1861, s 18. As in the case of the next proposed offence, the distinction between wounding and grievous bodily harm would disappear.

- Recklessly causing serious injury to another. This either-way offence would be punishable with up to seven years' imprisonment. It would replace the Offences Against the Person Act 1861, s 20, but the mental element would be stricter, since the defendant would have to be aware that he was taking the risk of causing serious injury and persist in taking it.

- Intentionally or recklessly causing injury to another. This either-way offence would replace the Offences Against the Person Act 1861, s 47. It would be punishable with a maximum of five years' imprisonment.

'Injury' is defined by cl 15 as meaning physical injury or mental injury. 'Physical injury' includes pain, unconsciousness and any other impairment of a person's physical condition. 'Mental injury' includes any impairment of a person's mental health. Except in relation to the offence of intentionally causing serious injury, 'injury' does not include anything caused by disease. Thus, a person who transmits a disease would only commit an offence under the draft Bill if the disease causes serious injury and he intends to cause serious injury.[345]

The draft Bill provides that a person would commit the offence of intentionally causing serious injury if he omitted to do an act which he had a common law duty to do, the omission resulted in serious injury and he intended it to have that result. On the other hand, an omission would not suffice for any of the other proposed offences described above. This is in line with the approach taken in the draft Criminal Law Bill, which was based on a policy of only punishing omissions in the case of the more serious offences.[346]

The main reason why the draft Offences Against the Person Bill contains separate offences of intentionally causing serious injury and recklessly causing serious injury is that there is a moral and psychological distinction between the two offences which it is appropriate for the criminal law to reflect. On the other hand, the moral distinction between intention and recklessness is not an easy one for the police, magistrates and juries to make, and, with regard to acts of violence amounting to injury but not serious injury, it was thought that the law need not be altered to require the distinction in mental element to be made in every case (which would be necessary if there were two separate offences of causing injury).[347]

7.134 Clause 11 of the draft Offences Against the Person Bill would replace the offences under the OAPA 1861, ss 23 and 24 (poisoning etc). Under cl 11 it would be an offence, punishable with a maximum of five years' imprisonment, if a person, 'knowing that a substance was capable of causing injury', administered it to another or caused it to be taken by him and (in either case) did so intentionally or recklessly, and it was unreasonable to administer the substance or cause it to be taken having regard to the circumstances as he knew or believed them to be.

7.135 If enacted, the provisions in the draft Offences Against the Person Bill would simplify and modernise the law of non-fatal offences against the person. It is to be regretted that they have not yet been enacted.

Protection from Harassment Act 1997

> **Key points 7.9**
>
> The Protection from Harassment Act 1997 penalises those who pursue a course of conduct which amounts to harassment or causes the victim to fear violence.

---

[345] Contrast the position under the existing law described earlier in this chapter; see in particular para 7.89. The Government did not consider that such conduct would fall within cl 11 (para 7.134).

[346] Law Commission: *Legislating the Criminal Code: Offences against the Person and General Principles* (1993), para 11.2.

[347] This was the reasoning of the Criminal Law Revision Committee (14th Report (1980), Cmnd 7844) whose report provided the basis for the Law Commission's recommendations.

7.136 This Act was initially passed to deal with the problem of 'stalkers' but the Act is not confined to them. As well as an offence of harassment, which centres on breach of one or other of two prohibitions of harassment contained in s 1 of the Act, the Act also provides a more serious offence of putting people in fear of violence.

Prohibitions of harassment

7.137 The first prohibition is concerned with the harassment of another person, no ulterior intent being specified. It is framed as follows by the Protection from Harassment Act 1997 (PHA 1997), s 1(1):

'A person must not pursue a course of conduct –

(a) which amounts to harassment of another, and

(b) which he knows or ought to know amounts to harassment of the other.'

The second prohibition of harassment is concerned with the harassment of two or more persons and the ulterior intent to prevent lawful conduct. It is contained in PHA 1997, s 1(1A) (inserted by the Serious Organised Crime and Police Act 2005, s 125):

'A person must not pursue a course of conduct –

(a) which involves harassment of two or more persons, and

(b) which he knows or ought to know involves harassment of those persons, and

(c) by which he intends to persuade any person (whether or not one of those mentioned above) –
    (i) not to do something that he is entitled or required to do, or
    (ii) to do something that he is not under any obligation to do.'

References in the PHA 1997 to a person, in the context of the *harassment* of a person, are references to a person who is an individual.[348] Thus, the complainant cannot be a company or other corporate body. Conduct includes speech.[349]

Course of conduct

7.138 By PHA 1997, s 7(3),[350] a 'course of conduct' must involve:

'(a) in the case of conduct in relation to a single person (see s 1(1)), conduct on at least two occasions in relation to that person, or

(b) in the case of conduct in relation to two or more persons (see s 1(1A)), conduct on at least one occasion in relation to each of those persons.'

---

[348] PHA 1997, s 7(5) (inserted by the Serious Organised Crime and Police Act 2005, s 125). This provision ousts the normal meaning of 'person' under the Interpretation Act 1978, s 5 and Sch 1, whereby unless the contrary intention appears 'person' includes a corporate body.

[349] PHA 1997, s 7(4).   [350] As amended by the Serious Organised Crime and Police Act 2005, s 125.

This is true of 'course of conduct' whenever it appears in the following provisions. It is not simply a matter of counting the number of incidents. There must be a sufficient connection between the acts in type and context as to justify the conclusion that they amount to a *course* of conduct,[351] taking into account all the circumstances. The fewer the incidents and the wider apart they were spread the less likely it is that a finding of harassment can reasonably be made.[352] Nevertheless, the Divisional Court has stated, obiter, that incidents as far apart as a year could constitute a course of conduct, for example a threat made once a year on a person's birthday.[353] At the other extreme, the Divisional Court held in one case that a finding by magistrates that three separate and distinct phone calls to a former partner within the space of five minutes constituted a course of conduct was not irrational; the time interval between the calls was only one factor to be taken into account.[354] Likewise, where D followed V and tried to stop her entering a shop, and then confronted her when she left the shop shortly afterwards, the Divisional Court held that this was capable of amounting to conduct on two separate occasions and thus to a course of conduct.[355] The incidents do not have to be similar in nature but it may be more difficult to prove a course of conduct if they are different. It will be particularly difficult to establish a course of conduct if the parties have been reconciled during a part of the period.[356]

If an individual is continually abusive to someone who makes telephone calls to him or comes within his vicinity, that will amount to a course of conduct, even if the victim has chosen to make the telephone calls or come within his vicinity.[357]

Harassment

7.139 The PHA 1997, s 1(1) requires the defendant's course of conduct to amount to harassment of another, and s 1(1A) requires it to involve harassment of two or more persons. Conduct which begins innocuously may become harassment by reason of the manner and frequency with which it is repeated.[358] Section 7(2) provides that **the reference to harassment of a person here, and elsewhere in the Act, includes alarming that person or causing that person distress.** This has been treated as a non-exhaustive definition, so that there could be other ways of 'harassing' someone.[359]

---

[351] *Lau v DPP* [2000] 1 FLR 799, DC; *Patel* [2004] EWCA Crim 3284.

[352] *Lau v DPP* [2000] 1 FLR 799, DC; *Patel* [2004] EWCA Crim 3284.

[353] *Lau v DPP* [2000] 1 FLR 799, DC.   [354] *Kelly v DPP* [2002] EWHC Admin 1428, DC.

[355] *Wass v DPP* (2000) unreported, DC. See also *Buckley and Smith v DPP* [2008] EWHC 136 (Admin), DC.

[356] *H (Gavin Spence)* [2001] 1 FLR 580, CA.   [357] *James v CPS* [2009] EWHC 2925 (Admin) DC.

[358] *DPP v Hardy* [2008] EWHC 2874 (Admin). In this case, D made a telephone call to find out why his partner had not got a job. When D did not receive an explanation, he made a further 95 telephone calls in 90 minutes, setting the telephone to automatic redial, during the course of which he stated that he was 'set for the night'. The Divisional Court held that this conduct was capable of constituting harassment for the purposes of PHA 1997.

[359] *DPP v Ramsdale* [2001] EWHC Admin 106, DC.

7.140 Although the PHA 1997, s 1(1) refers to 'harassment of another', it was recognised by the Divisional Court in *DPP v Dunn*[360] that this does not mean that a breach of the prohibition of harassment under s 1(1) cannot be committed where two or more individuals are subjected to a course of conduct amounting to harassment. The reason is that there is nothing in the Act to indicate a contrary intention to oust the normal rule under the Interpretation Act 1978, s 6 that words in the singular in a statute should be read as including their plural forms. Thus, more than one person can be named as a complainant in one charge under s 2, referred to in para 7.145, alleging a breach of the prohibition of harassment under s 1(1). Moreover, it was held in *DPP v Dunn*, it is not inappropriate to include more than one complainant in a charge alleging a course of conduct amounting to harassment, even though only one of the complainants might have been present during any one incident of harassment relied on, if they were members of a 'close knit definable group' and the conduct complained of was clearly aimed at both (or all) of them on each occasion. Bell J left open for future decision what the situation would be if a large number of victims were specified in the charge, not every one of whom was present at the time of the harassment. In *DPP v Dunn*, the complainants were a married couple living together in the same property, who were engaged in a boundary dispute with the defendant (their neighbour). The Divisional Court held that there was sufficient nexus between them to constitute a close-knit definable group. On the other hand, in *DPP v Dziurzynski*,[361] the Divisional Court held that 60 employees of a company, not all of whom were present on the two occasions referred to in the charge and none of whom were present on both, did not constitute a close knit and definable group. Despite the addition of s 1(1A) the above case law remains important in respect of s 1(1) where the intention in s 1(1A)(c) cannot be proved.

7.141 Before the PHA 1997, s 7(3A), was added by the Criminal Justice and Police Act 2001, proving a course of conduct was difficult where the defendant used other people to take part in the harassment. This problem has been dealt with by s 7(3A), which provides that a person's (X's) conduct on any occasion which is aided, abetted, counselled or procured by another (Y) is taken:

(a) also to be on that occasion the conduct of Y; and

(b) to be conduct in relation to which Y's knowledge and purpose (and what Y ought to have known) are the same as they were in relation to what was contemplated or reasonably foreseeable at the time of the aiding, abetting etc.

This means in relation to the wording of s 1(1) or 1(1A) that there can be a breach of the prohibition on harassment thereunder by Y if, for example, on one occasion the harassing conduct is by X aided and abetted by Y and on the second occasion it is by Y himself provided that the two pieces of conduct can be regarded as a 'course' and that (b) is satisfied.

---

[360] [2001] 1 Cr App Rep 352, DC.   [361] [2002] EWHC 1380 (Admin), DC.

Know or ought to know

7.142 Because it is enough that the defendant ought to know that his conduct amounts to or involves harassment, it is no defence that he did not know that his conduct would amount to or involve harassment, if a reasonable person would know that it does. 'Knowledge' bears its ordinary meaning.[362] The objective nature of 'ought to know' in the PHA 1997, s 1(1)(b) and s 1(1A)(b) is given a subjective aspect by s 1(2),[363] which provides that **the person whose course of conduct is in question ought to know that it amounts to or involves harassment of another if a reasonable person in possession of the same information would think the course of conduct amounted to or involved harassment of the other.** It was held in *Colohan*[364] that the 'reasonable person' in this context is, however, a hypothetical reasonable person; he is not endowed with the defendant's standards or characteristics. Thus, D's schizophrenia could not be taken into account in deciding whether a reasonable person would think that D's conduct amounted to harassment.

Conduct covered

7.143 The breadth of the prohibitions of harassment means that they apply to a wide range of activities. Conduct involved in disputes between neighbours (as in *DPP v Dunn*) or in industrial disputes, racial harassment, protests of various kinds, the activities of the 'paparazzi', the sending of a series of threatening letters demanding payment of a debt[365] and the publication of press articles calculated to incite hatred or contempt of the victim[366] are all liable to amount to a breach of the prohibition of harassment in the PHA 1997, s 1(1). In *Howlett v Holding*,[367] a civil case, Eady J held that the instigation at various times of secret surveillance of a woman of which she was aware (although she did not know exactly when it was taking place) constituted a course of conduct amounting to a breach of the prohibition of harassment under the PHA 1997, s 1(1), because she was caused distress by her awareness that the secret surveillance was taking place, or was likely to take place at any moment. Although the PHA 1997, s 1(1A) was introduced to deal with the particular problem of the harassment by animal rights protesters of people connected with organisations engaged in the use of animals for scientific research with intent to cause the cessation of such use, it is not limited to such conduct. On the other hand, in another civil case, a High Court judge has held that s 1 should be given a restrictive interpretation, so as not to cover conduct involved in the conduct of litigation by a claimant.[368]

---

[362] Para 3.43.   [363] As amended by the Serious Organised Crime and Police Act 2005, s 125.

[364] [2001] EWCA Crim 1251 (reported as *C*).

[365] *Ferguson v British Gas Trading Ltd* [2009] EWCA Civ 46.

[366] In *Thomas v News Group Newspapers Ltd* [2001] EWCA Civ 1233, a civil case, it was held that the publication of articles and letters in *The Sun* newspaper calculated to incite racial hatred of an individual was a course of conduct capable of amounting to harassment.

[367] [2006] EWHC 41 (QB).   [368] *Tuppen v Microsoft Corpn Ltd* (2000) Times, 15 November.

The width of the prohibitions of harassment means that in some types of case a prosecution for breach of the prohibition may be open to objection under the ECHR, Arts 10 (freedom of expression) and 11 (freedom of peaceful assembly and association).[369]

Defences

7.144 The prohibitions of harassment in the PHA 1997, s 1(1) and s 1(1A) do not apply to a course of conduct if the person who pursued it shows:[370]

> '(a) that it was pursued for the purpose of preventing or detecting crime [eg by a police officer];
>
> (b) that it was pursued under any enactment or rule of law or to comply with any condition or requirement imposed by any person under any enactment [eg by a court bailiff]; or
>
> (c) that in the particular circumstances the pursuit of the course of conduct was reasonable.'[371]

In *Howlett v Holding*,[372] Eady J thought that the defence relating to the prevention or detection of crime was framed with law enforcement agencies in mind. He added that, even if a private individual was entitled to avail himself of it, he would have to show that there was, objectively judged, some rational basis for the conduct to be undertaken to prevent or detect crime.

The last defence involves an objective test, and therefore D's characteristics must be ignored in determining whether his course of conduct was reasonable.[373] It is an important, albeit vague, curb on the width of the prohibition of harassment. Eady J stated in another civil case, *Huntingdon Life Sciences Ltd v Curtin*,[374] that the PHA 1997 was not intended by Parliament to be used to clamp down on the discussion of matters of public interest or upon the rights of public protest and public demonstration which was so much part of our democratic tradition, and that he had little doubt that the courts would resist any wide interpretation of the Act.

In *DPP v Moseley*,[375] Collins J stated that in determining whether conduct was reasonable a court had to balance the interests of the victim against the purpose and nature of the course of conduct pursued, including the right to peaceful protest. However, the Divisional Court agreed in that case that, if the course of conduct in question

---

[369] The exercise by an individual of his right under ECHR, Art 10 or 11 is capable of amounting to a breach of the prohibition of harassment if all the necessary ingredients are satisfied and the effect on the victim is out of all proportion to the value to be attached to the exercise of that right by the chosen method: *Howlett v Holding* [2006] EWHC 41 (QB).

[370] In *Thomas v News Group Newspapers Ltd* above, a civil case, the Court of Appeal stated that the persuasive burden of proof was on the defendant.

[371] PHA 1997, s 1(3) (as amended by the Serious Organised Crime and Police Act 2005, s 125).

[372] [2006] EWHC 41 (QB).   [373] *Colohan* [2001] EWCA Crim 1251.

[374] (1997) Times, 11 December.   [375] (1999) Times, 23 June, DC.

involved breach of an injunction, it could not be reasonable conduct, at least unless the circumstances were very special.

In determining whether the defence of reasonable conduct applies, a court must also have regard to the ECHR, Article 10(2) and 11(2), which set out the grounds on which the freedom of expression and freedom of peaceful assembly and association, respectively, may be interfered with.

Offence of harassment

7.145 The Protection from Harassment Act 1997, s 2(1)[376] makes it an offence to pursue a course of conduct in breach of the prohibition on harassment in s 1 or s 1(1A). The offence is summary only, and currently punishable with six months' imprisonment (51 weeks' when the Criminal Justice Act 2003, s 281(4) and (5) is in force) or a fine not exceeding level 5 on the standard scale or both.[377] This penalty may be inadequate where the victim suffers serious psychiatric injury.[378] In such a case it may be possible to secure a conviction for an offence under s 4 (below) or for one of the offences under the Offences Against the Person Act 1861 discussed earlier in this chapter.

Because the offence is summary only, it is not an offence to attempt to commit it.[379] Thus, no case of an apprehended breach of the prohibition on harassment can result in a conviction for attempting to commit a s 2 offence.

Offence of putting people in fear of violence

7.146 The Protection from Harassment Act 1997, s 4(1) provides a more serious offence, which does not centre on a course of conduct in breach of the prohibition on harassment, but on a course of conduct putting people in fear of violence.

Section 4(1) provides that:

> 'A person whose course of conduct causes another to fear, on at least two occasions, that violence will be used against him is guilty of an offence if he knows or ought to know that his course of conduct will cause the other so to fear on each of those occasions.'

It will be noted that the fear of violence need not be of 'immediate' violence, even in the watered-down sense accorded to that term elsewhere in the criminal law.[380] The victim, however, must fear that violence *will* be used against *him*; a fear that violence may be used will not suffice, nor will a fear of violence against a third party.[381] This may make it difficult, for example, to get a conviction against a silent telephone caller who on at least

---

[376] As amended by the Serious Organised Crime and Police Act 2005, s 125.
[377] PHA 1997, s 2(2).   [378] As Lord Steyn observed in *Ireland; Burstow* [1998] AC 147 at 153.
[379] Criminal Attempts Act 1981, s 1(1) and (4).   [380] Paras 7.40–7.42.
[381] *Henley* [2000] Crim LR 582, CA.

two occasions causes the victim to fear violence, because the victim may only be caused to fear the potential, as opposed to definite, use of violence.[382]

7.147 The provisions relating to the s 4 offence are markedly similar to the provisions relating to the prohibition of harassment, in that:

- there must be a 'course of conduct'; 'conduct' includes 'speech';[383] However, for the purposes of s 4, the course of conduct must cause another person to fear, on at least two occasions, that violence will be used against him;

- the objective nature of 'ought to know' is given a subjective aspect by s 4(2), which provides that the person whose course of conduct is in question ought to know that it will cause another to fear that violence will be used against him on any occasion if a reasonable person in possession of the same information would think the course of conduct would cause the other so to fear on that occasion;

- it is a defence for the defendant to show that:
  - his course of conduct was pursued for the purpose of preventing or detecting crime,
  - his course of conduct was pursued under any enactment or rule of law or to comply with any condition or requirement imposed by any person under any enactment, or
  - the pursuit of his course of conduct was reasonable for the *protection of himself or another or for the protection of his or another's property*;[384] and

- a person's (X's) conduct on any occasion which is aided, abetted, counselled or procured by another (Y) is taken also to be the conduct of Y, and X's conduct is taken to be conduct in relation to which Y's knowledge and purpose (and what Y ought to have known) are the same as they were in relation to what was contemplated or reasonably foreseeable at the time of the aiding, abetting etc.[385]

7.148 The distinguishing feature between the offence under s 4 and that under s 2 is, of course, that the course of conduct must cause another to fear that *violence* will be used *against him*. It is not enough that on one occasion A fears violence against himself (but B does not) and that on another occasion B fears such violence (but A does not).[386] This is so even if A and B form a 'close knit and identifiable group',[387] although in such a case there could be a conviction under s 2 for breach of the prohibition of harassment if the conduct (eg abuse) on both occasions was aimed at both of them.[388] Direct evidence from the victim that he was caused to fear such violence is not essential, because a court may infer such fear if there is other evidence entitling it to do so, but without direct evidence from the victim proof may be difficult.[389]

---

[382] This point was made by Lord Steyn in *Ireland; Burstow* [1998] AC 147 at 162.
[383] PHA 1997, s 7(4).   [384] PHA 1997, s 4(3).   [385] PHA 1997, s 7(3A).
[386] *Caurti v DPP* [2001] EWHC Admin 867, DC.   [387] *Caurti v DPP* [2001] EWHC Admin 867, DC.
[388] Para 7.140.   [389] *R (a child) v DPP* [2001] EWHC Admin 17, DC.

7.149 Fear of violence only against property is not enough. On the other hand, the fact that the defendant's words or conduct were directed ostensibly against property or a third party does not prevent proof of an offence under s 4; if they cause the victim to fear, on at least two occasions, that violence will be used against him and the defendant knows or ought to know that his conduct will cause the victim so to fear on each of those occasions, the defendant is guilty of that offence.[390]

7.150 The prosecution does not have to prove that the violence feared was unlawful violence, but under the third defence referred to above it will be a defence, in effect, for the defendant to show that the violence feared was not unlawful violence.

7.151 The offence under s 4 is an either-way offence. A person guilty of it is liable on conviction on indictment to imprisonment for a term not exceeding five years.[391] Given that the prohibited conduct is not required to result in psychiatric injury, and that the defendant is not required to have intended that the victim would fear violence, this is a surprisingly high maximum.

Racially or religiously aggravated harassment

7.152 The Crime and Disorder Act 1998 (CDA 1998), s 32(1), as amended by the Anti-terrorism, Crime and Security Act 2001, provides that:

'A person is guilty of an offence under this section if he commits –

(a) an offence under s 2 of the Protection from Harassment Act 1997 (offence of harassment); or

(b) an offence under s 4 of that Act (putting people in fear of violence),

which is racially or religiously aggravated for the purposes of this section.'

Section 32(1) does not create one offence which can be committed in more than one way; it creates two separate racially or religiously aggravated offences which are offences in their own right.

7.153 On a charge of either of these aggravated offences the prosecution must prove that the defendant has committed the relevant specified basic offence (set out above) and that it was racially or religiously aggravated (as defined in para 7.98).

7.154 The aggravated offences within the CDA 1998 both have higher maximum sentences than the basic offence to which they refer. An aggravated offence within the CDA 1998, s 32(1)(a) is triable either way[392] and on conviction on indictment is punishable

---

[390] *R (a child) v DPP* [2001] EWHC Admin 17, DC.   [391] PHA 1997, s 4(4).

[392] This can be contrasted with the basic offence under the PHA 1997, s 2, which is only triable summarily.

with a maximum term of imprisonment of two years. The maximum imprisonment on conviction on indictment for the aggravated offence within the CDA 1998, s 32(1)(b), which is also triable either way, is seven years.[393]

FURTHER READING

Addison and Lawson-Cruttenden *Harassment Law and Practice* (1998)

Allen 'Consent and Assault' (1994) 58 JCL 193

Bamforth 'Sado-Masochism and Consent' [1994] Crim LR 661

Cooper and Read 'Informed Consent and the Transmission of Disease: *Dadson* Revivified' (2007) 71 JCL 461

Edge 'Extending Hate Crime to Religion' (2003) 8 J Civ Lib 5

Elliott and de Than 'The Case for a Rational Reconstruction of Consent in Criminal Law' (2007) 70 MLR 225

Finch *The Criminalisation of Stalking* (2001)

Finch 'Stalking the Perfect Stalking Law: An Evaluation of the Efficacy of the Protection from Harassment Act 1997' [2002] Crim LR 703

J Gardner 'Rationality and the Rule of Law in Offences against the Person' in *Offences and Defences* (2007) (J Gardner (ed)) Ch 2

Gibbons 'The Offence of Obstruction' [1983] Crim LR 21

Gunn and Ormerod 'The Legality of Boxing' (1995) 15 LS 181

Hare '*R v Savage, DPP v Parmenter* – A Compelling Case for the Code' (1993) 56 MLR 74

Horder 'Reconsidering Psychic Assault' [1998] Crim LR 392

Horder 'Re-thinking Non-fatal Offences against the Person' (1994) 14 OJLS 392

Idriss 'Religion and the Anti-terrorism, Crime and Security Act 2001' [2002] Crim LR 890

Keating 'Protecting or Punishing Children: Physical Punishment, Human Rights and English Law Reform' (2006) 26 LS 394

Lidstone 'The Offence of Obstruction' [1983] Crim LR 29

McCutcheon 'Sports, Violence, Consent and the Criminal Law' (1994) 45 NILQ 267

Malik 'Racist Crime: Racially Aggravated Offences in the Crime and Disorder Act 1998 Part II' (1998) 62 MLR 409

Ormerod and Gunn 'Criminal Liability for the Transmission of HIV' [1996] 1 Web JCLI

Ormerod and Gunn 'In Defence of Ireland' [1997] 3 Web JCLI

Roberts 'The Philosophical Foundations of Consent in the Criminal Law' (1997) 17 OJLS 389

Rogers 'A Criminal Lawyer's Response to Chastisement' [2003] Crim LR 98

Ryan 'Reckless Transmission of HIV: Knowledge and Culpability' [2006] Crim LR 981

Skegg 'Medical Procedures and the Crime of Battery' [1974] Crim LR 693

Wells 'Stalking: the Criminal Law Response' [1997] Crim LR 463

Williams 'Force, Injury and Serious Injury' (1990) 140 NLJ 1227

---

[393] CDA 1998, s 32(3) and (4).

8

Homicide and related offences

OVERVIEW

The offences of murder, manslaughter and infanticide are dealt with in the first part, the major part, of this chapter. Corporate manslaughter and various offences of causing death by driving are then dealt with. The chapter concludes by dealing with a number of other offences related to homicide.

Introduction

8.1 Homicide may be lawful or unlawful. An example of lawful homicide is killing by using reasonable force in self-defence.[1] If the homicide is unlawful, it may be:

- murder;
- manslaughter (of which there are two generic types: voluntary manslaughter and involuntary manslaughter);
- infanticide;
- corporate manslaughter;
- causing death by dangerous driving;
- causing death by careless, or inconsiderate, driving;
- causing death by careless, or inconsiderate, driving when under the influence of drink or drugs; or
- causing death by driving when unlicensed, disqualified or uninsured.

8.2 Murder and manslaughter are common law offences. The others are statutory.

---

[1] See further as to lawful homicide, para 8.16.

Murder, manslaughter and infanticide

Key points 8.1

The *actus reus* for murder is unlawfully killing a human being under the Queen's peace. Essentially, this is also the *actus reus* required for manslaughter and infanticide except that two types of involuntary manslaughter require additional elements to be proved, as does infanticide.

Quite apart from these distinctions, murder, involuntary manslaughter and infanticide are distinguished by the fact that the fault element which the last two offences require is less than the *mens rea* for murder. A person who would otherwise be guilty of murder has his liability reduced to voluntary manslaughter if one of three mitigating defences is available on the facts.

8.3 According to Coke, 'murder is when a man of sound memory, and of the age of discretion, unlawfully killeth within any county of the realm any reasonable creature *in rerum natura* under the King's peace, with malice aforethought…'.[2] The reference to a 'man of sound memory, and of the age of discretion' excludes those who are legally insane or under the age of criminal responsibility, matters dealt with in Chapter 15. The reference to a killing 'in any county of the realm' is no longer accurate because by way of exceptions to the general rule that our courts only have jurisdiction over offences committed in England and Wales:[3]

- a British citizen[4] who commits murder or manslaughter in any country or territory outside the United Kingdom is subject to the jurisdiction of our courts;[5] and

- proceedings for murder or manslaughter may be brought against a person irrespective of his nationality at the time of the alleged offence if it was committed as a war crime in Germany or German occupied territory during the Second World War, provided that on or after 8 March 1991 he was or has become a British citizen or resident in the United Kingdom, the Isle of Man or the Channel Islands.[6] Only one of the very few prosecutions on this basis has been successful. Human mortality means that it will soon become irrelevant. The death of suspects or the insufficiency of evidence have been the reasons for the paucity of prosecutions.

---

[2] 3 *Institutes* 47. Coke's definition is given as amended by the Law Reform (Year and A Day Rule) Act 1996: para 8.15.

[3] Para 1.21. As to offences on ships or aircraft, see para 1.26.

[4] Or a British Overseas citizen, citizen of British Overseas Territories or British National (Overseas): see the British Nationality Act 1948, s 3(1), the British Nationality Act 1981, s 51, and the Hong Kong (British Nationality) Order 1986.

[5] This is the effect of the Offences Against the Person Act 1861, s 9, and the British Nationality Act 1948, s 3.

[6] War Crimes Act 1991, s 1. A prosecution may only be instituted by or with the consent of the Attorney-General. For criticism of the War Crimes Act 1991, see (1997) 147 NLJ 81.

8.4 In modern language, the *actus reus* of murder which can now be derived from Coke's words is unlawfully killing a human being under the Queen's peace. Essentially, this is also the *actus reus* for manslaughter and infanticide but there are the following variations. The *actus reus* of constructive manslaughter (a form of involuntary manslaughter) also requires proof that the killing was caused by an unlawful and dangerous act. The *actus reus* of manslaughter by gross negligence (another form of involuntary manslaughter) also requires proof that the defendant's conduct fell so far below the standard to be expected of a reasonable person as to be judged criminal. Where infanticide is charged, its *actus reus* also requires proof that the victim was under 12 months old and that the defendant mother's mind was mentally disturbed consequent on its birth.

Common elements of murder, manslaughter and infanticide

The victim

8.5 Before any question of a person's liability for homicide can arise, it must be established that he killed a 'reasonable creature *in rerum natura*'. On rare occasions the offspring of human parentage may be so deformed as to be unrecognisable as a human being, or barely so recognisable. Such offspring are usually a freak of nature, but they can result from radiation or the use of drugs. They may be anencephalic (ie lacking all or most of the cerebral hemispheres but capable of breathing). Sometimes they belong to the fish stage of development with gills, webbed arms and feet and sightless eyes. Such 'monsters' are usually stillborn, but some do survive for a short period ranging from minutes to days or, even, a couple of weeks. If a person kills such a being the question may arise whether he has committed an offence of homicide. Although at one time a 'monster' may not have been protected by the law,[7] it is now clear that a 'reasonable creature' means a person (ie a human being) however deformed or disabled.[8] In *Re A (conjoined twins: surgical separation)*,[9] conjoined (ie Siamese) twins, each with a brain (although one was so undeveloped as to be practically useless) and nearly complete bodies, were regarded by the Court of Appeal as separate persons in the eyes of the law.

8.6 The issues of when life begins and ends for the purposes of the law are clearly relevant to homicide. It is not homicide to destroy a baby who is not yet born alive, nor to cause it to be stillborn,[10] or to destroy the corpse of a person already dead.

---

[7] Williams *The Sanctity of Life and the Criminal Law* (1958) 31–35.

[8] *Rance v Mid-Downs Health Authority* [1991] 1 QB 587 at 621, per Brooke J; *Re A (conjoined twins: surgical separation)* [2001] Fam 147, CA.

[9] [2001] Fam 147, CA.

[10] Coke 3 *Institutes* 50; Blackstone 4 *Commentaries* 198. This point was recognised in *A-G's Reference (No 3 of 1994)* [1998] AC 245 at 254 and 267, per Lords Mustill and Hope.

When life begins

8.7 The law states that a child is born alive when two requirements are satisfied:

- the whole body of the child must have emerged into the world;[11] and
- thereafter the child must have breathed and lived by reason of its breathing through its own lungs, without deriving any of its living or power of living through any connection with its mother.[12] This latter requirement is subject to the qualification, in the case of conjoined twins where one of them (X) has impaired lungs and cannot breathe but depends on the breathing of the other (Y), that X is a life in being as well as Y.[13]

An Australian court has held that the common law does not require that unassisted breathing is required before a baby can be said to be born alive, and that live birth for the purposes of the 'born alive' rule could be proved by many different overt acts including crying, breathing and the presence of a heart beat;[14] this has not yet been considered by our courts and does not yet represent English law on the matter.

Provided both requirements are satisfied a child is born alive regardless of whether the umbilical cord has been severed.[15] There is no requirement that the child should be viable, ie capable of sustained survival.

8.8 Although the destruction of an unborn child cannot amount to an offence of homicide (or, indeed, any other offence against the person, since such a child is not a 'person' in law),[16] the wilful destruction of a child capable of being born alive before it is born alive may amount to the offence of child destruction, while the intentional procuring of a miscarriage may constitute the offence of abortion.[17]

8.9 If a child is born alive, and dies wholly or partly because of antenatal injuries to the mother or child, the person who inflicted them cannot be convicted of murder[18] but may be convicted of manslaughter.[19] This includes the case where the antenatal injuries result in a premature birth which fatally affects the child's ability to withstand the ordinary perils of infancy.[20]

---

[11] *Poulton* (1832) 5 C & P 329.

[12] *Enoch* (1833) 5 C & P 539; *Handley* (1874) 13 Cox CC 79; *C v S* [1988] QB 135, CA; *Rance v Mid-Downs Health Authority* [1991] 1 QB 587.

[13] *Re A (conjoined twins: surgical separation)* [2001] Fam 147, CA.

[14] *Iby* [2005] NSWCCA 178, [2005] Crim LR 742.

[15] *Reeves* (1839) 9 C & P 25.

[16] *Tait* [1990] 1 QB 290, CA.

[17] Paras 8.192–8.206.

[18] Paras 8.30 and 8.31.

[19] *A-G's Reference (No 3 of 1994)* [1998] AC 245, HL. Lord Mustill made rather heavy weather of this, in respect of murder: [1998] AC 245 at 264.

[20] *A-G's Reference (No 3 of 1994)* [1998] AC 245, HL.

When life ends

8.10 Medical science recognises that death is not instantaneous but is a continuing process, since different parts of the body die at different times. At one time, the medical view was that death occurred when the heart stopped beating and breathing ended. This was not very satisfactory since these symptoms can occur in conditions like barbiturate overdosage, drowning and hypothermia, from all of which recovery is possible. The concept of 'heart death' was established before the technology was developed whereby heart beats and breathing can be artificially maintained by ventilating a body on a respirator. Because of the medical dilemma of determining when a respirator may be switched off in the case of comatose and unresponsive patients, the Conference of Royal Medical Colleges and their Faculties of the United Kingdom adopted in 1976 the concept of 'brain stem death' as the determinant of death.[21] This occurs where irremediable structural brain damage is diagnosed by tests establishing that none of the vital centres of the brain stem is still functioning. In 1995, a Working Group of the Royal College of Physicians, stating that 'brain stem death is equivalent to the death of the individual', agreed the following definition of 'death': 'The irreversible loss of the capacity for consciousness, combined with irreversible loss of the capacity to breathe.'[22] This definition was repeated in a Code published by the Academy of Medical Royal Colleges in 2008.[23] A patient in a 'persistent vegetative state' is not suffering from 'brain stem death' since in this condition only the higher brain is destroyed; such a patient can breathe unaided and has reflex actions to sound and light, but he has no awareness of his environment and no swallowing reflex (so that he has to be fed nasogastrically).

8.11 In *Airedale National Health Service Trust v Bland*,[24] Lords Keith, Goff and Browne-Wilkinson were of the opinion, obiter, that 'brain stem death' is the legal definition of death,[25] although the matter was not disputed before them.

Under the Queen's peace

8.12 Any human being can be the victim of murder, manslaughter or infanticide with the exception of persons who are not 'under the Queen's peace', ie alien enemies killed in the actual heat and exercise of war and, perhaps, rebels who are at the time actually

---

[21] [1976] 2 British Medical Journal 1187. For a discussion of the question of 'death' and the timing of death in law, see Price (1997) 23 Journal of Medical Ethics 170; Dickens 'Death' in *Principles of Medical Law* (2nd edn, 2004) (Grubb (ed)) 1133.

[22] Royal College of Physicians' Working Group 'Criteria for the diagnosis of brain stem death' (1995) 29 Journal of the Royal College of Physicians 381.

[23] *A Code for the Diagnosis and Confirmation of Death*; discussed by Burns 'How Certain is Death?' (2009) 159 NLJ 459.

[24] [1993] AC 789 at 856, 863 and 878. See also *Re A* [1992] 3 Med LR 303.

[25] The same view was taken in *Mail Newspapers plc v Express Newspapers plc* [1987] FSR 90 and in *Re A* [1992] 3 Med LR 303.

engaged in hostile operations against the Crown.[26] The deliberate and unjustified shooting of prisoners of war amounts to murder.[27]

The killing

8.13 Murder, manslaughter and infanticide may be punishable even if the death is the outcome of an omission to act, rather than a positive act, provided the omission consists of a failure to perform a duty to act recognised by the criminal law. As was explained in Chapter 2, duties to act can be imposed by the common law or by statute. However, up to the present, the law has been slow to impose duties to do positive acts. Almost all the prosecutions for homicide by omission have been prosecutions for manslaughter, but if a person who is under a legal duty to act (as where a parent is under a duty to provide food for his or her helpless child) omits to perform that duty intending thereby to cause death (and death does result), that person can be convicted of murder.[28] Proving the necessary intent in such a case is not easy. The possibility of infanticide by omission is expressly contemplated by the Infanticide Act 1938.[29]

8.14 The prosecution must prove that the defendant's act (or omission, if he was under a legal duty to act) resulted in the victim's death. The rules of causation were explained in paras 2.28 to 2.57.

8.15 At common law, the death with which it was sought to charge the defendant had to be shown to have occurred within a year and a day of the infliction of the injury by which it is alleged to have been caused.[30] This rule evolved, latterly as an irrebuttable presumption of law about causation, because of the difficulty in proving that an injury outside the period did cause the death in question. It is now possible to diagnose the cause of death even though it occurred a substantial time afterwards, and it became a matter of concern that the rule allowed a person to escape liability for a homicide which he was scientifically shown to have caused. The rule meant that a person who severely injured another escaped any criminal liability for homicide if his victim was kept alive, say in a coma, for more than a year and a day before dying as a result of his injuries, although he could be convicted of a non-fatal offence, such as attempted murder or an offence under the Offences Against the Person Act 1861, ss 18 or 20. This, however, hardly reflected the gravity of what had occurred (and, leaving aside attempted murder or an offence under s 18 or a few other offences, the maximum punishment was below that available for homicide).

---

[26] Hale *Pleas of the Crown* Vol I, 433; *Page* [1954] 1 QB 170, C-MAC (as to this court, see para 2.32, n 91).

[27] *Maria v Hall* (1807) 1 Taunt 33 at 36. It has been argued by Hirst 'Murder under the Queen's Peace' [2008] Crim LR 541 that the 'Queen's peace' element does not bear the sense in the text, in which it has traditionally been understood. He argues that it is simply a reference to the fact that the killing must be by a person to whom, and in circumstances to which, the English law of murder applies.

[28] *Gibbins and Proctor* (1918) 82 JP 287, CCA.

[29] Para 8.135.

[30] Coke 3 *Institutes* 47; *Dyson* [1908] 2 KB 454, CCA; *Inner West London Coroner, ex p De Luca* [1989] QB 249, CA.

Moreover, where a victim of gross negligence died more than a year and a day later, the perpetrator might have escaped criminal liability completely, since there is no general non-fatal offence based on negligence.

In 1995, the Law Commission proposed the abolition of the year and a day rule without any replacement.[31] This proposal was put into effect by the Law Reform (Year and A Day Rule) Act 1996, s 1, which abolished the year and a day rule in respect of offences involving death and of suicide. This abolition, however, does not affect the continued application of the rule where the act or omission (or the last act or omission) which caused death occurred before 17 June 1996,[32] the day of Royal Assent.

Section 2(1) and (2) provides that proceedings may only be instituted in respect of a 'fatal offence'[33] by or with the consent of the Attorney-General:

(a) where the injury alleged to have caused the death was sustained more than three years before the death occurred; or

(b) where the defendant has previously been convicted of an offence committed in circumstances alleged to be connected with the death.

The purpose of (a) 'is to protect a proposed defendant from prosecutions being brought after a substantial interval of time, when his memory might not be reliable, and when other evidence might have disappeared'.[34] This factor has not been thought to require the Attorney-General's consent to a prosecution for other offences, and it is questionable whether it should in respect of fatal offences. A similar comment can be made in respect of (b), which is widely drafted.

Unlawful killing

8.16 The killing of another is unlawful unless it falls within one of the following categories of lawful homicide:

- *Public or private defence* Here the defendant kills by using reasonable force in self-defence, in prevention of crime or in certain other similar situations. This is explained in paras 16.1 to 16.35.[35]

- *Misadventure* Death is caused by misadventure where it results, by an accident not involving gross negligence, from the doing of a lawful act. An obvious instance is

---

[31] *Legislating the Criminal Code: The Year and a Day Rule*, Law Com No 230.

[32] Law Reform (Year and A Day Rule) Act 1996, s 3(2).

[33] Ie murder, manslaughter, infanticide or any other offence of which an element is causing a person's death, encouraging or assisting suicide in connection with the death of a person, or an offence contrary to the Domestic Violence, Crime and Victims Act 2004, s 5 (causing or allowing the death of a child or vulnerable adult): Law Reform (Year and A Day Rule) Act 1996, s 2(3) (as amended by the Domestic Violence, Crime and Victims Act 2004, Schs 10 and 11; the Coroners and Justice Act 2009, Sch 21).

[34] *Legislating the Criminal Code: The Year and a Day Rule*, para 5.28.

[35] In the very rare situation where a killing is justified by necessity (see para 16.95) the killing will also be lawful.

where death results from a lawful operation carried out with due care by a surgeon. Another example is death resulting from lawful acts done in the course of lawful games, such as football and boxing.[36]

Murder

Key points 8.2

Murder consists of unlawful homicide with malice aforethought.
Malice aforethought consists of intention on the part of the defendant:

- unlawfully to kill another human being; or

- unlawfully to cause grievous bodily harm to another human being.

8.17 The only punishment for murder is imprisonment for life. It is triable only on indictment.

8.18 There is no exception to the mandatory life sentence for murder, even in the case of 'mercy killings' (ie where someone actively brings another's life to an end to avoid his further suffering and with that person's consent). However, verdicts of murder have quite commonly been avoided where long-term carers have caused the death by a conviction of manslaughter on grounds of diminished responsibility. Strictly, such cases may not have satisfied all the requirements of the defence[37] but this problem has been swept under the carpet by the prosecution's acceptance of a plea of guilty of manslaughter on grounds of diminished responsibility. The amendment of diminished responsibility by the Coroners and Justice Act 2009, s 52 could make the prosecution less prepared to accept such a plea.

8.19 Murder was a purely capital offence (ie the only sentence was death) until the law was modified by the Homicide Act 1957, which drew a distinction between capital and non-capital murder. Capital murder included murders done in the course or furtherance of theft; by shooting or causing an explosion; in resisting, avoiding or preventing lawful arrest, and murders of police officers acting in the execution of their duty. Non-capital murder was punished with life imprisonment. The distinction between capital and non-capital murder did not prove satisfactory.

8.20 The death penalty for murder was abolished by the Murder (Abolition of Death Penalty) Act 1965, under which the only sentence for murder is imprisonment for life. Where the convicted murderer was under 18 at the time of the offence, he is ordered to

---

[36] Paras 7.8–7.21.   [37] See para 8.57.

be detained during Her Majesty's pleasure, in effect a mandatory life sentence, instead of being sentenced to life imprisonment.[38] There have been various attempts in Parliament to restore the death penalty for murder, in some cases at least, but they have all been unsuccessful. The ratification by the United Kingdom of Article 1 of the Thirteenth Protocol to the ECHR, a Convention right under the Human Rights Act 1998, which prohibits the death penalty, means that the death penalty could only be re-introduced by amending the Human Rights Act 1998.

8.21 A mandatory sentence of life imprisonment does not necessarily mean that the offender has to remain in prison for the rest of his life, but it does mean that the sentence of imprisonment is not for a fixed period at the outset. However, unless the trial judge decides not to do so, because of the seriousness of the murder or of the murder and an associated offence or offences, he must specify a minimum term to be served in custody which he considers appropriate, taking into account the seriousness of the murder (and any associated offence(s)) and any period of remand in custody or on bail subject to a curfew condition for nine or more hours a day and to an electronic monitoring condition.[39] The offender must be released on licence, once that term has been served, if the Parole Board has recommended that continued confinement is no longer necessary for public protection. It will be noted that the judge only has power to specify a minimum term, not a maximum term. The rules are essentially the same in relation to someone convicted of a murder committed while under 18 who has been ordered to be detained during Her Majesty's pleasure. The mandatory life sentence in itself has been held by the House of Lords not to be incompatible with the ECHR, Articles 3 (prohibition of inhuman or degrading treatment) or 5 (right to liberty) on the ground that the operation in practice of an indeterminate sentence for murder does not constitute an arbitrary and disproportionate punishment.[40]

8.22 It can be argued that the mandatory life sentence for murder is necessary for the purposes of prevention and deterrence, and also in order to maintain the stigma attached to murder and to reassure the public as to the gravity of the offence. The mandatory sentence can also be supported by the argument that at the time of sentence neither the judge nor the Court of Appeal can have the foresight to know when the murderer can be released compatibly with the safety of society. On the other hand, murders can vary greatly in their gravity, and so can murderers in their dangerousness. Many people would agree, for example, that committing murder by intentionally killing under extreme duress[41] is less heinous, and the offender less dangerous, than where someone makes a cold-blooded attempt to kill someone which fails but leaves the victim completely paralysed for life. Many would doubtless also agree that the intentional killer under duress may be less dangerous than an intentional killer whose liability is reduced on grounds of

---

[38] Powers of Criminal Courts (Sentencing) Act 2000, s 90.
[39] Criminal Justice Act 2003, s 269.
[40] *Lichniak; Pyrah* [2002] UKHL 47.
[41] Duress is not a defence to murder (paras 16.53–16.57 and 16.80).

diminished responsibility to manslaughter. Nevertheless, a convicted murderer has to be given a life sentence whereas the person convicted of attempted murder or manslaughter may be given any sentence at the judge's discretion up to a maximum of life. A similar point in terms of heinousness may be made in respect of the convicted murderer whose liability is based on a serious injury, not intended to cause more than serious harm, which would not have proved fatal if the hospital to which the victim was taken had provided treatment. The mandatory life sentence may also be criticised on the ground that a jury, knowing of it and considering it too severe a sentence, may decide to acquit a defendant whom they consider guilty of murder in order to avoid it.

8.23 The arguments in favour of the mandatory life sentence are unconvincing. In 1989 a Select Committee of the House of Lords (the Nathan Committee)[42] recommended that the mandatory sentence be abolished and replaced by a maximum sentence of life imprisonment, which would permit the judge, as in other offences, to impose a lower sentence if that was appropriate in the circumstances. The same recommendation was made in 1993 by a committee chaired by a former Lord Chief Justice.[43] On neither occasion, did this recommendation receive government support. It seems unlikely that the mandatory life sentence for murder will be abolished in the foreseeable future. When the Government asked the Law Commission in 2005 to review the law of murder[44] the request was prefaced by a commitment to the mandatory life sentence.

Malice aforethought

8.24 Malice aforethought consists of intention on the part of the defendant:

- unlawfully to kill another human being; or
- unlawfully to cause grievous bodily harm to another human being.[45]

Nothing less, such as recklessness as to death, suffices.[46] Malice aforethought does not imply either premeditation or ill-will. The sudden intentional killing of one's nearest and dearest is no less murder than the cunningly contrived assassination of a deadly enemy. Malice aforethought is thus a misleading term of art and the abolition of that term would improve the precision and lucidity of the law of murder.[47]

8.25 Before the Homicide Act 1957 came into force, there were three kinds of malice aforethought. It might have been 'express', 'implied' or 'constructive'. Constructive malice aforethought was abolished by the Homicide Act 1957, s 1, but malice aforethought

---

[42] *Report of the Select Committee on Murder and Life Imprisonment* (Session 1988–89) HL Paper 78-1.

[43] *Lane Committee on the Penalty for Homicide* (Prison Reform Trust).

[44] See para 8.38.

[45] For a modern authority that murder is an offence requiring intention, see *Moloney* [1985] AC 905, HL.

[46] *Leung Kam Kwok v R* (1984) 81 Cr App Rep 83, PC.

[47] Stephen *History of the Criminal Law* Vol III, 83; *Hyam v DPP* [1975] AC 55 at 66, per Lord Hailsham LC; *A-G's Reference (No 3 of 1994)* [1998] AC 245 at 250, per Lord Mustill.

may still be express or implied. Although the terms 'express malice' and 'implied malice' had not been used in any consistent sense by the courts prior to that Act coming into force, the judgment soon afterwards of the Court of Criminal Appeal in *Vickers*,[48] which has been endorsed by the House of Lords on three subsequent occasions,[49] made it clear that 'express malice' means an intention to kill and 'implied malice' an intention to cause grievous bodily harm.

There were two types of constructive malice aforethought, for it was murder to cause death in furtherance of a felony[50] or when resisting lawful arrest, even though the defendant might not have intended to kill or to cause grievous bodily harm, provided the defendant had the *mens rea* for the felony or (as the case might have been) intended to resist lawful arrest. Consequently, the doctrine was capable of operating very harshly, for it meant that someone would be technically guilty of murder if, when committing robbery or trying to resist lawful arrest, he gave his victim a slight push which happened to prove fatal through an unforeseen contingency such as a heart attack.

Intention unlawfully to kill, or cause grievous bodily harm to, another human being

8.26 That the defendant must intend *unlawfully*[51] to kill or cause grievous bodily harm to another human being was implicit in the Court of Appeal's decision in *Gladstone Williams*[52] and put beyond doubt by the decision of the Privy Council in *Beckford v R*,[53] where the Privy Council held that a person could not be convicted of murder, even if he intentionally killed someone, if he did so in a mistaken belief in facts which, if true, would justify him in using reasonable force in self-defence and he had not exceeded such force, because he would not have intended unlawfully to kill his victim.[54]

Intention unlawfully to kill another human being

8.27 Not surprisingly there is uncontradicted authority[55] to support the proposition that an intention unlawfully to kill another human being constitutes malice aforethought.

---

[48] [1957] 2 QB 664, CCA.

[49] *DPP v Smith* [1961] AC 290, HL; *Hyam v DPP* [1975] AC 55, HL (Lords Diplock and Kilbrandon dissenting); *Cunningham* [1982] AC 566, HL. For criticism of these terms, see *Cunningham* [1982] AC 566 at 576, per Lord Hailsham LC.

[50] Until the Criminal Law Act 1967, there were distinctions between offences classified as felonies and misdemeanours. This was one of them.

[51] For the meaning of 'unlawfully', see para 8.16. Doubtless, a soldier who intentionally killed someone, mistakenly believing that his victim was a person who would be outside the Queen's peace (para 8.12), would also not intend unlawfully to kill.

[52] (1984) 78 Cr App Rep 276, CA; para 5.7.

[53] [1988] AC 130, PC.

[54] Such a person would not be guilty of manslaughter or any other offence against the person: see Ch 16.

[55] *Moloney* [1985] AC 905, HL, can now be regarded as the leading authority.

Intention unlawfully to cause grievous bodily harm to another human being

8.28 'Grievous bodily harm' was defined by the House of Lords in *DPP v Smith*.[56] Lord Kilmuir, giving the only reasoned speech (with which the other Law Lords agreed), said that **'grievous bodily harm' is to be given its natural meaning and that 'grievous' means 'really serious'.** 'Really' seems to mean no more than that the harm must actually be serious.[57] In relation to intent to cause grievous bodily harm, if the defendant is proved to have intended to cause bodily harm and that harm is regarded as really serious (ie grievous) by the jury, it is irrelevant that the defendant did not so regard it.[58]

It was only in 1981 in *Cunningham*[59] that it was settled beyond doubt by the House of Lords that an intention to cause grievous bodily harm to another constitutes malice aforethought.

In *Rahman*, Lord Bingham explained the rationale behind this type of malice aforethought as follows:

'The rationale of that principle plainly is that if a person unlawfully assaults another with intent to cause him really serious injury, and death results, he should be held criminally responsible for that fatality, even though he did not intend it. If he had not embarked on a course of deliberate violence, the fatality would not have occurred. This rationale may lack logical purity, but it is underpinned by a quality of earthy realism.'[60]

8.29 The result of the present rule is that a defendant who only intended to cause grievous bodily harm and did not foresee death even as a remote possibility, and who could only have been guilty of unlawfully causing grievous bodily harm with intent, contrary to the Offences Against the Person Act 1861, s 18, if death had not unexpectedly resulted, is guilty of murder and subject to the mandatory life sentence. On the other hand, a defendant who lacked that intent but realised that there was a probability (but not a virtual certainty) that death might result from his conduct but was indifferent to that risk cannot be so convicted. The former state of mind does not fall within the popular conception of murder and is a conspicuous exception to the normal rule that *mens rea* should correspond to the consequence of the *actus reus*.[61] On the other hand, the latter state of mind may well fall within the popular conception of murder.

Antenatal injury to child or mother: malice aforethought

8.30 **Inflicting an injury on a foetus, which is intended to destroy it in the womb but which results in the child being born alive and then dying, cannot constitute murder,**

[56] [1961] AC 290, HL.   [57] See para 7.78.   [58] See para 7.93.
[59] [1982] AC 566, HL.   [60] [2008] UKHL 45 at [25].
[61] *A-G's Reference (No 3 of 1994)* [1998] AC 245 at 250, per Lord Mustill; *Powell and Daniels; English* [1999] 1 AC 1 at 12 and 15, per Lords Mustill and Steyn.

although it will constitute involuntary manslaughter.[62] True, the *actus reus* of homicide is committed but the person who commits it does not act with intent to kill or do grievous bodily harm to a human being.[63]

8.31 What if the defendant had acted instead with intent to do grievous bodily harm to the mother, and with no intent to injure the foetus or the child it would become? Can he be convicted of murder? The answer 'no' is provided by the decision of the House of Lords in *A-G's Reference (No 3 of 1994)*;[64] the House held that he could, however, be convicted of involuntary manslaughter.

D had stabbed a woman who was between 22 and 24 weeks pregnant. On his own admission D intended to do the woman grievous bodily harm but there was no evidence that he intended to destroy the foetus or to cause injury to the woman which would cause harm to the baby after it was born. The woman went into labour 17 days later and a baby was born alive but grossly premature. D pleaded guilty to wounding the woman with intent to cause her grievous bodily harm, and was sentenced to four years' imprisonment. Subsequently, the baby died from broncho-pulmonary dysplasia consequent on the effects of its premature birth. D was then charged with the murder of the baby. He pleaded not guilty. The trial judge ruled that there could be no conviction for murder or manslaughter on these facts, and directed the jury to acquit D.

The Attorney-General referred the following points of law to the Court of Appeal, whence the case was referred to the House of Lords:

'1. Subject to the proof by the prosecution of the requisite intent in either case: whether the crimes of murder or manslaughter can be committed where unlawful injury is deliberately inflicted: (i) to a child in utero (ii) to a mother carrying a child in utero where the child is subsequently born alive, enjoys an existence independent of the mother, thereafter dies and the injuries inflicted while in utero either caused or made a substantial contribution to the death.

2. Whether the fact that the death of the child is caused solely as a consequence of injury to the mother rather than as a consequence of direct injury to the foetus can negative any liability for murder or manslaughter in the circumstances set out in question 1.'

The House of Lords declined to answer part (i) of point 1 because it did not arise on the facts of the case. Its answer to part (ii) of point 1 was 'no' in respect of murder, but 'yes' in

[62] Paras 8.95–8.134.

[63] In *West* (1848) 2 Car & Kir 784, it was held that there could be a conviction for murder on these facts but this decision depended on the application of the doctrine of constructive malice aforethought abolished by the Homicide Act 1957; para 8.25. The House of Lords declined to rule on the correctness or otherwise of *West* in *A-G's Reference (No 3 of 1994)* [1998] AC 245 on the ground that the question did not arise on the facts of the reference, but it is submitted that when the question does arise for a judicial ruling the answer will be as set out above. For support for this, see an obiter dictum by the Court of Appeal in *A-G's Reference (No 3 of 1994)* [1996] QB 581 at 594.

[64] [1998] AC 245, HL.

respect of manslaughter. Its answer to point 2 was that in relation to murder the point was superseded by its answer to point 1 and 'no' in relation to manslaughter.

The question of liability for manslaughter is dealt with in para 8.110. We are concerned here with why the House of Lords considered that the *mens rea* for murder was not satisfied on the facts, although the *actus reus* was.

Disagreeing with the Court of Appeal, the House of Lords held that the foetus could not be identified with the mother. Consequently, an intention to cause grievous bodily harm to the mother was not equivalent to an intent to cause grievous bodily harm to the foetus, since when the foetus – if born alive – becomes a life in being it is a separate organism from the mother.

The House of Lords also rejected an argument that an intent to do grievous bodily harm to the mother could be added to the contemporaneous train of events from D's acts resulting in the death of the baby. It regarded such an argument as involving an extension of the law. While it acknowledged that it had to accept that an intention to do grievous bodily harm was malice aforethought, it was not prepared to apply it to what it regarded as a new situation, where the actual victim was not alive at the time of the conduct in question and died not of an injury inflicted on it but as a result of premature birth brought about by an injury to its mother. In particular, it did not think that the offence of murder could be extended in such a case by using the doctrine of 'transferred malice (or intent)'.[65] Lord Mustill, with whose speech the other Law Lords agreed, said that to do so would require a double transfer of intent: 'first from the mother to the foetus and then from the foetus to the child as yet unborn. Then one would have to deploy the fiction (or at least the doctrine) which converts an intention to commit serious harm into the *mens rea* of murder. For me, this is too much.'[66] His Lordship also gave another reason:

> 'The effect of transferred malice, as I understand it, is that the intended victim and the actual victim are treated as if they were one, so that what was intended to happen to the first person (but did not happen) is added to what actually did happen to the second person (but was not intended to happen), with the result that what was intended and what happened are married to make a notionally intended and actually consummated crime. The cases are treated as if the actual victim had been the intended victim from the start. To make any sense of this process there must, as it seems to me, be some compatibility between the original intention and the actual occurrence and this is, indeed, what one finds in the cases. There is no such compatibility here. The defendant intended to commit and did commit an immediate crime of violence to the mother. He committed no relevant violence to the foetus, which was not a person, and intended no harm to the foetus or to the human person which it would become. If fictions are useful, as they can be, they are only damaged by straining them beyond their limits. I would not overstrain the idea of transferred malice by trying to make it fit the present case.'[67]

This decision is open to criticism in that it involves a misunderstanding of the requirement of *mens rea*: *mens rea* for murder is an intent unlawfully to kill or do grievous bodily

---

[65] Para 3.38.   [66] [1998] AC 245 at 262.   [67] [1998] AC 245 at 262.

harm to another person, and not an intent to bring about such a consequence in relation to a particular person. As previously explained, the doctrine of transferred malice is simply a recognition that the *mens rea* of an offence is framed in a way non-specific to the victim.[68] As already indicated, the defendant in a case like *A-G's Reference (No 3 of 1994)* can be convicted of manslaughter. This adds to the oddity of the decision. If not murder, why manslaughter? To which, one may add: 'Why only manslaughter, if the defendant has killed with the *mens rea* for murder?'

8.32 In *A-G's Reference (No 3 of 1994)*, the House of Lords did not directly deal with the situation where the defendant injured a pregnant woman (but not her foetus), intending to kill her, and the foetus is born prematurely as a result of the mother's injury and dies in consequence of the premature birth. This situation is not caught by the House of Lords' reluctance to extend intent to do grievous bodily harm as a species of malice aforethought, but it is open to the same arguments against double transfer of intent and about the effect of 'transferred malice' put forward by Lord Mustill.

The requirement of contemporaneity: an exception

8.33 Generally, the intent unlawfully to kill or cause grievous bodily harm must exist at the time of the defendant's act which caused death.[69] However, if death is caused by one act in a series of acts, it is irrelevant that the defendant lacked the necessary intent for murder when that act was done, if he had that intent when an earlier act in the series was done. In *Thabo Meli v R*,[70] the defendants planned to kill the deceased in a hut and thereafter to roll his body over a cliff so that it might appear to be a case of accidental death. The deceased was rendered unconscious by a blow in the hut and, believing him to be dead, the defendants rolled him over the cliff. There was medical evidence that the deceased was not killed by the injuries received in the hut, but died from exposure where he had been left at the bottom of the cliff. It was contended that the defendants were not guilty of murder because, while the first act was accompanied by the *mens rea* for murder, it was not the cause of death;[71] and because the second act, while it was the cause of death, was not accompanied by the *mens rea* for murder, the defendants believing their victim to be dead already. The Privy Council rejected this argument, holding that the two acts formed part of a series which could not be divided up. Accordingly, the defendants were guilty of murder, and not of attempted murder or culpable homicide (manslaughter) as would have been the case if the rejected argument had prevailed.

8.34 The advice of the Privy Council suggests that its decision might have been different if the act done with intent to kill and the actual act which caused death had not formed

---

[68] Para 3.38.   [69] Para 3.65.

[70] [1954] 1 All ER 373, PC. Also see *Moore and Dorn* [1975] Crim LR 229, CA.

[71] Arguably, there was still a causal link between the first act (the blow) and the death: Marston 'Contemporaneity of Act and Intention in Crimes' (1970) 86 LQR 208 at 218–219; *McKinnon* [1980] 2 NZLR 31 at 36–37. The Privy Council, however, did not consider this point.

part of a preconceived plan. However, **the decision of the Court of Criminal Appeal in** **Church,[72] which established that** *Thabo Meli* **also applies to manslaughter, shows that it** **applies where the act which caused death was not part of a plan, being quite unforeseen** **at the time of the act done with** ***mens rea***. In *Church*, D had a sudden fight with a woman (V) and rendered her unconscious. Then, having tried for about half-an-hour to revive V and believing that V was dead, D threw V's body into a nearby river, where V drowned. His conviction for manslaughter was upheld on appeal on the basis that his conduct constituted a series of acts which culminated in V's death.

The approach in *Church* was approved by the Court of Appeal in *Le Brun*.[73] D and his wife (V) had had an argument as they were walking home one night. D knocked V unconscious. He then tried to drag V away from the scene, but V slipped from his grasp and hit her head on the pavement; as a result V suffered a fractured skull from which she died. There was no antecedent plan. On appeal against conviction for manslaughter, the Court of Appeal held that the judge had been correct to tell the jury to convict D of murder or manslaughter, depending on the intent with which he knocked V unconscious, if he accidentally dropped her while trying to drag her home against her wishes or to conceal what he had done.

8.35 The above principle raises the question of when an act can be said to be part of a series. There must of course be some proximity in time but *Church* shows that the time span need not be very short. In *Le Brun,* there is a suggestion that for the purposes of the present principle an act done while trying to help the victim or to take his supposedly dead body to the police, as opposed to an act to conceal the original act or to further the unlawful activity, will not form part of a series with the first act. Applying *Church*, the Court held that, where the non-fatal act done with *mens rea* and the eventual act causing death are parts of the same sequence of events, the fact that there is an interval of time between the two does not serve to exonerate the defendant. It stated that this was certainly so where a defendant's subsequent actions which caused death, after the initial unlawful blow, were designed to conceal the commission of the original assault.

8.36 The above decisions seem to be right, although it will often be difficult to decide whether the defendant's acts form a series.

It remains to be seen whether these decisions apply to offences other than murder and manslaughter. Probably they will be held to do so when the occasion arises.

Two or more acts: impossibility of proving which one was fatal

8.37 What if one of two or more acts by the defendant caused death but it is impossible to prove which one? It was held by the Court of Appeal in *A-G's Reference (No 4 of 1980)*,[74] which was concerned with involuntary manslaughter, that there can be a conviction for that offence if each act was accompanied by a sufficient state of mind or fault element (hereafter simply referred to as *mens rea*) for that offence.

---

[72] [1966] 1 QB 59, CCA.

[73] [1992] QB 61, CA; discussed by Sullivan 'Cause and Contemporaneity of *Actus Reus* and *Mens Rea*' (1993) 52 CLJ 487.

[74] [1981] 2 All ER 617, CA.

Thus, to adopt the facts in that reference, if D pushes V downstairs and then, thinking that V is dead, cuts her throat preparatory to dismembering her body, and it is not proved which of these acts caused her death, D can be convicted of involuntary manslaughter if the jury are satisfied that, whichever act killed V, each of them was accompanied by a sufficient *mens rea* to establish involuntary manslaughter. Such a principle is equally applicable on a charge of murder if each act is proved to have been accompanied by malice aforethought.

The Court of Appeal held that if it was not proved that each act was accompanied by a sufficient state of mind, the jury should acquit of manslaughter. This is open to doubt where the defendant had the requisite *mens rea* when he committed the first act in a series of acts; it would not matter in such a situation whether the first act caused death (in which case he would be guilty under the normal rules of liability) or not (in which case he would be caught by the principle in *Thabo Meli* and *Church*).

Reform

8.38 In 2005, the Home Office asked the Law Commission to review the law of murder, other than the mandatory life sentence. The Law Commission published *Murder, Manslaughter and Infanticide,* its report, in 2006.[75] Its recommendations circumvent the difficulty of the mandatory life sentence to some extent by proposing the introduction of a three-tier ladder of general homicide offences to reflect different degrees of culpability and proposing that that sentence should only apply to the most serious, 'first degree murder'.

There would be two degrees of murder. 'First degree murder' would encompass:

> '(1) intentional[76] killings, *and*
>
> (2) killings with the intent to cause serious injury where the killer was aware that his or her conduct involved a serious risk of causing death.'[77]

The Commission rightly regarded the worst cases of reckless killing as morally equivalent to intentional killing.

'Second degree murder' would encompass:

> '(1) killings intended to cause serious injury; or
>
> (2) killings intended to cause injury or fear or risk of injury where the killer was aware that his or her conduct involved a serious risk of causing death; or

---

[75] Law Com No 304. For previous recommendations for the reform of the law of murder see 14th Report of the Criminal Law Revision Committee: *Offences against the Person* (1980) Cmnd 7844, paras 14–31, adopted in the draft Criminal Code Bill cl 54: Law Commission: *A Criminal Code for England and Wales* (1989), Law Com No 177; see para 1.72.

[76] See para 3.21.

[77] Law Com No 304, para 2.69. For the Law Commission's discussion of first and second degree murder and the three-tier structure, see Part 2, and Appendix A, paras A.5–A.15, of the Report.

> (3) killings intended to kill or to cause serious injury where the killer was aware that his or her conduct involved a serious risk of causing death but successfully pleads provocation, diminished responsibility or that he or she killed pursuant to a suicide pact.'[78]

Second degree murder would be punishable with a maximum of life imprisonment.

Below the two degrees of murder there would be the third tier on the ladder of general homicide offences: a redefined offence of manslaughter.[79]

The review undertaken by the Law Commission was intended to be the first stage of a review of homicide law, with the second stage to be undertaken by the Government.

Murder, Manslaughter and Infanticide: Proposals for Reform of the Law,[80] the Government's first (and so far only) consultation paper emanating from the second stage of the review of the law of murder, was published in 2008. It made proposals relating to partial defences and infanticide (both now enacted by the Coroners and Justice Act 2009) and to complicity in homicide but these were based on the existing structure: a single common law offence of murder, with its present elements and a mandatory penalty of life imprisonment. One cannot now be confident that the three-tier ladder structure recommended by the Law Commission will be considered further by the Government. The consultation paper simply said that it might be.

Manslaughter

Key points 8.3

There are two generic types of manslaughter – voluntary and involuntary. Corporate manslaughter is a separate offence and is dealt with later.

A person is guilty of *voluntary manslaughter* where, although he has killed with malice aforethought, he has a partial defence which mitigates the gravity of his offence. Partial defences are the defences of:

- suicide pact;
- diminished responsibility;
- until its abolition takes effect on 4 October 2010, provocation; or
- as from that date, loss of control.

Involuntary manslaughter is an unlawful killing where the defendant does not intend to kill or cause grievous bodily harm to another human being[81] but some other, less blameworthy, fault element is proved.

---

[78] Law Com No 304, para 2.70. [79] See para 8.134.
[80] Ministry of Justice, Consultation Paper 19/08. [81] *Taylor* (1834) 2 Lew CC 215.

8.39 The maximum punishment for manslaughter is imprisonment for life.[82]

8.40 The rationale behind voluntary manslaughter is that it provides a way in the circumstances just described to avoid the mandatory sentence for murder. It is arguable that if the mandatory sentence for murder was abolished, there would be no justification for having distinct offences of murder and voluntary manslaughter. Under the recommendations of the Law Commission referred to in para 8.38, voluntary manslaughter would cease to exist as a type of manslaughter and would become part of second degree murder.

8.41 A person cannot be charged with voluntary manslaughter. A verdict of voluntary manslaughter is only possible by means of a successful plea of one of the three mitigating circumstances by way of defence to a murder charge. An offence of involuntary manslaughter, on the other hand, can be charged in its own right; alternatively a verdict of guilty of such an offence may be returned at a murder trial where the prosecution fails to prove the *mens rea* for murder.[83] Like a murder charge, a charge of involuntary manslaughter may only be tried on indictment.

Voluntary manslaughter

Suicide pacts

8.42 It is not murder intentionally to kill a person in pursuance of a suicide pact. A 'suicide pact' means a common agreement between two or more persons whose object is the death of all of them, whether or not each is to take his own life.[84]

At common law, a survivor of such a pact which had been put into partial effect was guilty of murder, but the Homicide Act 1957, s 4(1)[85] now provides that:

> 'It shall be manslaughter, and shall not be murder, for a person acting in pursuance of a suicide pact between him and another to kill the other or be a party to the other being killed by a third person.'

On a charge of murder the persuasive burden of proving that he was acting pursuant to a suicide pact between him and the other is borne by the defendant.[86] This has been held not to be incompatible with the ECHR, Article 6(2).[87]

Prosecutions for an offence under the Homicide Act 1957, s 4 are rare.

---

[82] Offences Against the Person Act 1861, s 5.
[83] Criminal Law Act 1967, s 6(2). See also *Saunders* [1988] AC 148, HL.
[84] Homicide Act 1957, s 4(3).
[85] As amended by the Suicide Act 1961, s 3(2), Sch 2.
[86] Homicide Act 1957, s 4(2).
[87] *A-G's Reference (No 1 of 2004); Edwards; Denton; Jackson; Hendley; Crowley* [2004] EWCA Crim 1025; para 4.8.

8.43 Although the Homicide Act 1957, s 4 was intended to be a compassionate measure to reduce an intentional killing below murder, it can theoretically cover cases which are not deserving of compassion, as where D, the leader of a religious cult, persuades its members to meet to commit suicide together. At the meeting he hands each of them an instantly lethal poison which they all take with the exception of D who loses his nerve at the last moment. For this reason, the Law Commission's provisional proposal in 2005[88] that the defence of suicide pact should be repealed, leaving deserving cases of killing pursuant to a suicide pact to be covered by a reformed defence of diminished responsibility, had much to commend it, although a rational and deserving person who can currently rely successfully on the Homicide Act 1957, s 4 would have been unable to succeed with a defence of diminished responsibility. In its subsequent report, *Murder, Manslaughter and Infanticide*,[89] the Law Commission recommended that s 4 should be retained, pending the outcome of a public consultation on whether and, if so, to what extent the law should recognise either an offence of 'mercy' killing or a partial defence of 'mercy' killing (which it recommended should take place). Such a consultation has not yet occurred.

Encouraging or assisting suicide

8.44 It is convenient here to describe the related offence of encouraging or assisting suicide. At common law, a person who aided, abetted, counselled or procured another to kill himself was guilty of murder as an accomplice, because suicide was self-murder. Under the Homicide Act 1957, s 4, as originally enacted, the liability of one who aided, abetted etc the suicide of another was reduced to manslaughter, provided that he had agreed to die also. However, when the Suicide Act 1961 (SA 1961), s 1 abolished criminal liability for suicide (and therefore for attempted suicide, since there was no longer an offence which could be attempted), s 2(1) of that Act created a lesser offence of aiding, abetting, counselling or procuring suicide.

In 2008 a report to the Prime Minister by a leading child psychologist stated that there was some confusion about how this offence applied to websites promoting suicide. It recommended an investigation of the matter to see if it could be usefully clarified.[90] As a result of a Government review, the Coroners and Justice Act 2009, s 59 amended the SA 1961. In particular, it substituted s 2(1)–(1C) for s 2(1) so as to replace the offence of aiding, abetting, counselling or procuring suicide with that of encouraging or assisting suicide, which is intended to provide reassurance that criminal liability for such activity applies as much to the Internet as to off-line.[91] The wording of the new offence takes into account the view of the Law Commission in 2006 that there was a strong case for updating the language of s 2.[92]

---

[88] Law Commission Consultation Paper No 177: *A New Homicide Act for England and Wales?* paras 8.1–8.38, 8.68–8.94.

[89] Law Com Report No 304 (2006), paras 7.38–7.39, 7.50.

[90] Byron Report *Safer Children in a Digital World* para 3.126.

[91] Hansard (House of Commons) vol 479 col 142 WS.

[92] *Inchoate Liability for Assisting or Encouraging Crime* Law Com No 300, Appendix B, para 8.28.

The offence

8.45 As substituted, the SA 1961, s 2(1) provides:

> '(1) A person ("D") commits an offence if –
>
>   (a) D does an act capable of encouraging or assisting the suicide or attempted suicide of another person, and
>
>   (b) D's act was intended to encourage or assist suicide or an attempt at suicide.'

The offence is triable only on indictment and punishable with a maximum of 14 years' imprisonment.[93] If, on a trial for murder or manslaughter, it is proved that the deceased person committed suicide, and the defendant committed an offence under s 2(1) in relation to that suicide, there may be a conviction for the offence under s 2(1).[94]

8.46 It will be noted that an act is required on D's part; an omission which has the capability referred to does not suffice.

Section 2A[95] elaborates on what constitutes an 'act capable of encouraging or assisting the suicide or attempted suicide of another person'. It provides that:

- if D arranges for D2 to do an act that is capable of encouraging or assisting the suicide or attempted suicide of another person and D2 does that act, D is also to be treated as having done it. Thus, if D tells D2 to assist in the commission of suicide by T, and D2 does so, D is treated as having done the act of assistance done by D2. Both of them can be convicted of an offence of encouraging or assisting crime. If D2 does not do as he was told by D, neither of them can be. The reason for this provision is not obvious because D can be convicted of an offence under s 2 under the rules relating to secondary liability if D2 carries out the arranged act;
- where the facts are such that an act is not capable of encouraging or assisting suicide or attempted suicide, it is to be treated as so capable:
  - if the act would have been so capable had the facts been as D believed them to be at the time of the act (as where D wrongly believes that the harmless drugs which he supplies to assist another's suicide are lethal); or
  - had subsequent events happened in the manner D believed they would happen (as where D posts a lethal drug to another to assist the other's suicide but this is lost in the post); or
  - both;
- a reference to a person (P) doing an act that is capable of encouraging the suicide or attempted suicide of another person includes a reference to P doing so by threatening another person or otherwise putting pressure on another person to commit or attempt suicide.

---

[93] SA 1961, s 2(1C). The Law Reform (Year and a Day Rule) Act 1996 applies to encouraging or assisting suicide in connection with the death of a person: see para 8.15, n 33.

[94] SA 1961, s 2(2), amended by the Coroners and Justice Act 2009, s 59.

[95] The SA 1961, ss 2A and 2B were added by the Coroners and Justice Act 2009, s 59.

By s 2B, a reference in the SA 1961 to an act 'includes a reference to a course of conduct, and a reference to doing an act is to be read accordingly'.

Section 2(1A) provides that the person referred to in the SA 1961, s 2(1)(a) need not be a specific person (or class of persons) known to, or identified by, D. Thus, provided the necessary *mens rea* can be proved, a person who posts information about how to commit suicide to a suicide chat room may be convicted of the present offence. By s 2(1B), D may commit an offence under s 2 whether or not a suicide, or an attempt at suicide, occurs; it may be difficult, for example, in the case of information posted to a suicide chat room to prove that any reader committed suicide or attempted to do so.

8.47 There is no intrinsic reason why the term 'suicide' in the SA 1961, s 2(1) should not cover a person's intentional killing of himself by a refusal to have medical treatment, but it has been stated in the House of Lords that there is no question of that person having committed suicide.[96] By analogy, a person who intentionally brings about his death by some other omission does not commit suicide, and therefore someone who encourages or assists him in this does not do an act capable of encouraging or assisting suicide.[97]

Even if it could be said that a mentally competent patient or the like who kills himself by refusing nutrition or medical treatment does commit suicide, a doctor or the like who did not give treatment etc which might have saved or prolonged life – in response to the refusal – would not do an *act* capable of encouraging or assisting suicide, and in any event his omission would not be culpable because he would be released from his duty to do so by the competent refusal.[98]

Jurisdiction

8.48 Because the offence under s 2(1) is a 'conduct' crime, ie doing an act capable of encouraging or assisting suicide or attempted suicide, if D in England and Wales does an act capable of encouraging or assisting someone to commit suicide abroad D commits an offence under s 2(1). On the other hand, under the general rules of jurisdiction,[99] and subject to a special rule for information service providers established in England and Wales described in the next paragraph, D would not commit that offence if his relevant conduct occurred wholly abroad. It is a moot point whether an act done abroad by D which is capable of encouraging or assisting suicide (eg sending an encouraging e-mail or the means for suicide) can suffice if the encouragement or assistance (eg the e-mail or parcel) is received in England and Wales. It would seem that it could if the act of encouragement or assistance could be described as a continuing one and continued in England or Wales.[100]

---

[96] *Airedale NHS Trust v Bland* [1993] AC 789 at 864, per Lord Goff.

[97] For a discussion of the issues, see Alldridge 'Let Me Die – My Mother Insists' (1992) 142 NLJ 1691.

[98] Para 2.12. Indeed, if the doctor etc forced food on the patient or continued treatment after such a refusal he would commit a battery on the patient: see para 2.12.

[99] Para 1.21.

[100] See *Baxter* [1972] 1 QB 1, CA; Hirst 'Assisted Suicide after *Purdy*: The Unresolved Issue' [2009] Crim LR 870 at 875–876.

Information service providers

8.49 In order to ensure that the SA 1961, s 2 is compatible with the UK's obligations under the EU's E-Commerce Directive, Sch 12 to the Coroners and Justice Act 2009 makes special provision in connection with the operation of the SA 1961 (as amended) in relation to persons providing 'information society services', otherwise known as 'service providers'.

A service provider established in England and Wales can also be liable under the SA 1961, s 2(1) for doing an act in another European Economic Area State which is capable of encouraging or assisting the suicide or attempted suicide of another person.

A service provider established in an EEA State other than the UK may not be prosecuted for an offence under s 2(1) unless this is necessary for the 'public interest objective' (ie the pursuit of public policy), relates to a service that prejudices that objective (or seriously and gravely risks doing so), and is proportionate to that objective.

A service provider cannot be guilty of an offence under s 2(1) where the service provider is acting as a mere conduit for the information in question or where it is simply involved in caching or hosting information.

The details of Sch 12 to the 2009 Act are outside the scope of this book.

Prosecution

8.50 The offence under the SA 1961, s 2(1) covers a wide range of cases, from the greedy son who urges a parent to commit suicide so that he can inherit the parent's estate to the distraught husband who, at her request, helps his terminally ill wife to kill herself to end her pain and misery.

8.51 The original offence under the SA 1961, s 2(1) of aiding or abetting suicide was thought to be necessary to plug what would otherwise be an unacceptable gap in the law resulting from the abolition of the crimes of suicide and attempted suicide, since it was thought that there might be good reasons for punishing someone who encouraged or assisted someone to commit suicide. This remains the rationale of the offence. Prosecutions for an offence under the original s 2(1) were rare. By s 2(4), a prosecution for an offence under s 2(1) may only be instituted by or with the consent of the Director of Public Prosecutions.[101]

8.52 The offence clearly inhibits the exercise of the right to self-determination by those who wish to commit suicide by prohibiting others from encouraging or assisting them to do so. The original s 2(1) was held not incompatible with a person's rights under the ECHR. The only right which was engaged was Article 8 (right to respect for private life) which applies to a person's choice as to how to pass the closing moments of life, but s 2(1) was held to be justifiable under Article 8(2) in regulating suicide for the protection of public morals.[102] This decision is equally applicable to the new s 2(1).

---

[101] SA 1961, s 2(4).

[102] *Pretty v United Kingdom* (2002) 35 EHRLR 1, ECtHR. The House of Lords in *R (on the application of Pretty) v DPP* [2001] UKHL 61 had previously held that Article 8 was not engaged. The House of Lords in *R (on the application of Purdy) v DPP* [2009] UKHL 45 declined to follow its decision in *Pretty* and applied the decision of the European Court of Human Rights in that case.

In 2009, the Director of Public Prosecutions was required by the House of Lords[103] to promulgate an offence-specific policy identifying the facts and circumstances which he would have taken into account in deciding whether or not to consent to a prosecution for assisting suicide contrary to the original s 2(1) where the assisted suicide was in a country where assisted suicide was lawful. Without such a statement, said the House of Lords, the requirement under Article 8(2) that the interference with the Article 8 right be 'in accordance with law' would not be satisfied because that phrase involves the requirements that 'the law' (a term which included the Code for Crown Prosecutors) should be accessible and should be formulated with sufficient precision to enable the individual, if need be with appropriate advice, to regulate his conduct.

The Director complied with this requirement by issuing the *Policy for Prosecutors in Respect of Cases of Encouraging or Assisting Suicide*[104] which relates to all cases of assisted suicide. Although each case is to be considered on its own facts and merits, the *Policy* outlines 16 public interest factors in favour of a prosecution and six public interest factors against a prosecution.

Diminished responsibility

Key points 8.4

A defendant who would otherwise be guilty of murder (whether as a perpetrator or an accomplice) has a partial defence if he proves the defence of diminished responsibility. If the defendant does so his liability is reduced to manslaughter.

Where at a murder trial the defendant pleads insanity, the prosecution may adduce or elicit evidence that the defendant was suffering from diminished responsibility, in which case the prosecution must prove the requirements of the defence.

The defence of diminished responsibility is governed by the Homicide Act 1957, s 2. The original s 2(1) of that Act is substituted by a new s 2(1), (1A) and (1B) by the Coroners and Justice Act 2009, s 52. *This substitution comes into force on 4 October 2010. The following discussion concentrates on the defence as it will be after that substitution is effective. Until then a fuller description of the defence in its original form will appear on the companion website of this book.*

Introduction

8.53 The concept of diminished responsibility, which had been known to Scots law for some time, was introduced into English law by the Homicide Act 1957 (HA 1957), s 2. The partial defence of diminished responsibility is quite different from that of insanity dealt

---

[103] *R (on the application of Purdy) v DPP* [2009] UKHL 45.
[104] Available on the Crown Prosecution Service's website.

with in Chapter 15. Insanity covered by the *M'Naghten Rules*[105] is a complete defence to most offences and leads to an acquittal. Diminished responsibility, on the other hand, is merely a mitigating factor limited to charges of murder. It applies only where the defendant would otherwise be guilty of murder because the *actus reus* and *mens rea* of that offence have been proved or admitted.[106] If successfully pleaded, it reduces the liability of someone who but for s 2 would be liable to be convicted of murder (and given the mandatory life sentence) to manslaughter.[107] This means that the court has a discretion in the matter of punishment which may vary from imprisonment for life to an absolute discharge; where considered appropriate, a hospital order (with or without restriction of time), a hospital direction and a limitation direction (which can only be made if the offender is suffering from psychopathic disorder and is sentenced to imprisonment), or a guardianship order, may be made under the Mental Health Act 1983.

8.54 A defence of diminished responsibility is not required for other offences because they do not carry a fixed penalty, so that the judge has a discretion as to the punishment imposed. In *Campbell*,[108] Sedley J, as he then was, rejected an argument that diminished responsibility could be a defence on a charge of attempted murder.

8.55 The terms of the defence of diminished responsibility are less strict than those of insanity. For this reason, it has historically been pleaded successfully far more often than insanity in murder cases. However, there has been a significant decline in the figures in recent years. For example, whereas in the five-year period 1992–1996 the average number of cases a year in which diminished responsibility was successfully pleaded was 63, that figure had fallen to 35 in the five-year period 1998/1999–2002/2003. Indeed in the last two years in that period the numbers fell to 15 and 5 respectively.[109]

8.56 Among the reasons why it is appropriate that there should be a partial defence of diminished responsibility which gives the judge a discretion in passing sentence are:

- the need to enable jurors to convict a defendant of a homicide offence in cases where, if the only conviction available to them was for murder, they might otherwise (perversely) acquit altogether;
- the fact that in some cases diminished responsibility may be the only defence to murder available to an abused woman who kills her partner.

Quite apart from arguments based on the existence of the mandatory sentence for murder, the existence of the defence of diminished responsibility can be supported on the ground of the importance of 'fair and just labelling', ie that it is unjust to label as murderers those not fully responsible for their actions.

---

[105] (1843) 10 Cl & Fin 200.
[106] *Antoine* [2001] 1 AC 340, HL.
[107] Homicide Act 1957, s 2(3).
[108] [1997] Crim LR 495, Crown Ct. Also see para 14.109.
[109] Home Office Statistical Bulletin 01/04.

8.57 As originally enacted, the HA 1957, s 2(1) provided that a person who killed or was a party to the killing was not to be convicted of murder if:

- he was suffering from an abnormality of mind;
- the abnormality of mind was due to a condition of arrested or retarded development of mind or any inherent causes or induced by disease or injury; and
- the abnormality of mind was such as to have substantially impaired his mental responsibility for his acts or omissions in killing or being a party to the killing.

8.58 In its original form s 2(1) was unsatisfactory. 'Abnormality of mind' and 'substantial impairment of mental responsibility' were imprecise terms which created problems for judges and juries. 'Abnormality of mind' was not a psychiatric term, which caused problems for medical expert witnesses (whose evidence is crucial to the legal viability of a plea of diminished responsibility), so its meaning had to be developed by the courts on a case–by–case basis. Moreover, diagnostic practice in diminished responsibility cases had developed beyond identification of the fixed range of permissible causes of mental abnormality stipulated by the definition. In addition, the specified permissible causes never had an agreed psychiatric meaning. Attempting to specify the causes of mental disorders is irrelevant and misleading; in fact there are almost always multiple causes stemming from the interaction between genetic vulnerability and life events.[110] Section 2 as enacted did not explain what was involved in a 'substantial impairment of mental responsibility'. The implication was that the effects of the abnormality of mind must significantly reduce the defendant's culpability, but s 2 did not make this clear, nor indicate how the effects of an abnormality could reduce culpability for what would otherwise be murder.

8.59 Points such as these were noted in the various reports[111] in the last 35 years in which proposals for the reform of diminished responsibility have been made.

In its consultation paper, *Murder, Manslaughter and Infanticide: Proposals for Reform of the Law*,[112] the Government proposed the replacement of the existing partial defence of diminished responsibility with a new defence whose terms owe much to the recommendations of the Law Commission in 2006,[113] although they departed from them in some aspects. The Government's proposals were enacted with some structural changes by the Coroners and Justice Act 2009, s 52. As will be indicated, these changes may have the effect of narrowing the defence of diminished responsibility, and thereby reducing its utility as a way round the mandatory sentence for murder.

---

[110] *Murder, Manslaughter and Infanticide* Law Com No 304, para 5.111.

[111] *Report of the Committee on Mentally Abnormal Offenders* (1975), Cmnd 6244, paras 19.1–19.21; Law Commission: *Partial Defences to Murder* (2004), Law Com No 290, paras 5.1–5.105; Law Commission: *Murder, Manslaughter and Infanticide* (2006), Law Com No 304, paras 5.83–5.142.

[112] Ministry of Justice Consultation Paper 19/08.

[113] *Murder, Manslaughter and Infanticide* Law Com No 304.

Requirements of the defence

8.60 The Coroners and Justice Act 2009, s 52 provides that the Homicide Act 1957, s 2(1) is substituted by s 2(1), (1A) and (1B). Section 2(1) and (1A) provides:

'(1) A person ("D") who kills or is a party to the killing of another is not to be convicted of murder if D was suffering from an abnormality of mental functioning which –
  (a) arose from a recognised medical condition,
  (b) substantially impaired D's ability to do one or more of the things mentioned in subsection (1A), and
  (c) provides an explanation for D's acts and omissions in doing or being a party to the killing.

(1A) Those things are –
  (a) to understand the nature of D's conduct;
  (b) to form a rational judgement;
  (c) to exercise self-control.'

8.61 The wording of the HA 1957, s 2(1) can be broken down into four requirements which by s 2(2) the defendant has the persuasive burden of proving. It has been held that placing the burden of proof on the defendant does not breach the presumption of innocence in the ECHR, Article 6(2) because someone charged with murder is not required to prove anything unless he seeks to rely on s 2, and if he can take advantage of s 2 it is to his benefit.[114] The burden of proof is discharged by proof on the balance of probabilities.[115]

The Court of Appeal in *Campbell*[116] held, obiter, that the wording of the Homicide Act 1957, s 2(2) is such that **only the defendant can raise the defence of diminished responsibility.** The result is that, if there is prima facie evidence of the requirements of diminished responsibility, the judge cannot leave that defence to the jury without the defendant's consent.

There is one exception to the imposition of the burden of proof on the defendant and to the rule that only the defendant can raise the defence of diminished responsibility. It is provided by the Criminal Procedure (Insanity) Act 1964, s 6. Section 6 provides that, **where, at a murder trial, the defendant contends that he was insane under the *M'Naghten Rules*, the prosecution may adduce or elicit evidence that he was suffering from diminished responsibility. In such a case, it is for the prosecution to prove the requirements of diminished responsibility beyond reasonable doubt.**[117]

Abnormality of mental functioning

8.62 The first of the four requirements for diminished responsibility is that the defendant must have been suffering from an 'abnormality of mental functioning' at the

---

[114] *Lambert, Ali and Jordan* [2002] QB 1112, CA; *McQuade* [2005] NICA 2, [2005] NI 331, NICA.
[115] *Dunbar* [1958] 1 QB 1, CCA.
[116] (1986) 84 Cr App Rep 255, CA. Also see *Kooken* (1981) 74 Cr App Rep 30, CA.
[117] *Grant* [1960] Crim LR 424.

material time. 'Mental functioning' is a term preferred to 'mind' by psychiatrists.[118] In respect of the original version s 2(1), the Court of Criminal Appeal in *Byrne*[119] held that '*abnormality* of mind' meant a state of mind *so different from that of an ordinary person that the reasonable man would term it abnormal*. It is submitted that 'abnormality' should be understood in the sense of the words italicised in respect of the new requirement of abnormality of mental functioning.

Recognised medical condition

8.63 The second requirement for diminished responsibility is that the abnormality of mental functioning must arise from a recognised medical condition.[120] Thus, the defence is no longer governed by a fixed and out-of-date set of causes from which the mental abnormality must stem.

The reference to 'recognised medical condition' is intended to ensure that a successful plea of diminished responsibility is grounded on a valid medical diagnosis. It will encourage medical expert evidence in terms of one or two of the accepted international classificatory systems of mental conditions,[121] which will avoid medical expert witnesses giving idiosyncratic diagnoses as the basis for a plea of diminished responsibility.[122] Psychotic disorders are recognised medical conditions, for instance, and so are neurotic disorders. An example of the latter would be post-traumatic disorder suffered by a woman due to violent abuse suffered over many years. The present requirement contributes to making the new version stricter than the original.

8.64 The HA 1957, s 2(1), as substituted, does not incorporate the Law Commission's recommendation[123] that the definition of diminished responsibility should include abnormality of mental functioning arising from developmental immaturity in a defendant under 18, as an alternative cause of impairment to that of abnormality of mental functioning arising from a recognised medical condition. This alternative was designed to address the difficulty of distinguishing between mental conditions and differing stages of maturity where juveniles are concerned and to respond to the Commission's view that it was unrealistic and unfair to assume that all children above the age of legal responsibility (10) who kill with malice aforethought must have had the kind of developed sense of judgement, control and understanding that makes a murder conviction right. The Government decided against implementing this recommendation. It was not persuaded that the absence of a provision along the lines recommended was causing significant problems in practice, and it thought that there was a risk that such a provision would

---

[118] *Murder, Manslaughter and Infanticide* (2006) Law Com No 304, para 5.114.

[119] [1960] 2 QB 396, CCA.

[120] HA 1957, s 2(1)(a).

[121] The World Health Organisation *International Classification of Diseases* (ICD-10) and the American Psychiatric Association *Diagnostic and Statistical Manual of Mental Disorders* (DSM-IV).

[122] *Murder, Manslaughter and Infanticide* Law Com No 304, paras 5.114, 5.116.

[123] *Murder, Manslaughter and Infanticide* Law Com No 304, paras 5.125–5.131.

open up the defence too widely and catch inappropriate cases.[124] In any event, it argued, the accepted classificatory systems cover conditions such as learning disabilities and autistic spectrum disorders which can be particularly relevant in the context of those under 18, so that those who have such conditions have the opportunity to run the defence of diminished responsibility. Because developmental immaturity is not in itself an alternative to a recognised medical condition it would seem that the following scenario given by the Law Commission[125] falls outside the defence:

'A boy aged 10 who has been left to play very violent video games for hours on end for much of his life, loses his temper and kills another child when the child attempts to take a game from him. When interviewed, he shows no real understanding that, when a person is killed they cannot simply be later revived, as happens in the games he has been continually playing.'

The boy certainly has an impaired capacity to understand the nature of his conduct arising from an abnormality of mental functioning and this may be regarded as an explanation for his conduct but his abnormality of mental functioning arises from developmental immaturity and not from a recognised medical condition.

Substantial impairment of D's ability

8.65 The third requirement is that the abnormality of mental functioning arising from a recognised medical condition must have substantially impaired D's ability to do one or more of the following:

- to understand the nature of D's conduct;
- to form a rational judgement;
- to exercise self-control.[126]

This makes it clearer than the original version of s 2(1) which aspects of a defendant's mental functioning must be affected in order for the defence to succeed.

Because D's ability in one or more of these respects must have been impaired substantially, D is not required to have been deprived of such ability. By analogy with the original version of s 2(1) which also employed the concept of 'substantial impairment' (although in a different context), it would seem that 'substantial' means that the impairment of D's ability in one of the relevant respects need not be 'total' but it must be more than 'trivial' or 'minimal'. 'Substantial' means something in between.[127]

As can be seen from the above list, substantially impaired self-control, though irrelevant to the defence of insanity under the *M'Naghten Rules*[128] as construed in this country, is highly relevant to the question whether the defendant was suffering from diminished

---

[124] *Murder, Manslaughter and Infanticide: Proposals for Reform of the Law* Ministry of Justice Consultation Paper 19/08, para 53.

[125] Law Com No 304, para 5.121.   [126] HA 1957, s 2(1)(b), (1A).

[127] *Lloyd* [1967] 1 QB 175, CCA; *Egan* [1992] 4 All ER 470, CA.   [128] (1843) 10 Cl & Fin 200.

responsibility; and, unlike the defence of insanity, the defendant may rely on the defence although he knew what he was doing and knew that it was wrong.

The following scenarios based with some amendment on those given by the Law Commission[129] are examples of facts where a plea of diminished responsibility would be capable of success:

Substantially impaired mental capacity to 'understand the nature of his or her conduct' A man, aged 30, *with learning difficulties* who has been left to play very violent video games for hours on end for much of his life, loses his temper and kills a child when the child attempts to take a game from him. When interviewed, he shows no real understanding that, when a person is killed they cannot simply be later revived, as happens in the games he has been continually playing.

Substantially impaired capacity to 'form a rational judgement':

- a woman suffering from post-traumatic stress disorder, consequent upon violent abuse suffered at her husband's hands, comes to believe that only burning her husband to death will rid the world of his sins;

- a boy with learning difficulties believes that he must follow his older brother's instructions, even when they involve taking part in a killing. He says, 'I wouldn't dream of disobeying my brother and he would never tell me to do something if it was really wrong';

- a depressed man who has been caring for many years for a terminally ill spouse, kills her, at her request. He says that he had found it progressively more difficult to stop her repeated requests dominating his thoughts to the exclusion of all else, so that 'I felt I would never think straight again until I had given her what she wanted'.

Substantially impaired capacity to 'control him or herself' A man who suffers from schizophrenia says that sometimes the devil takes control of him and implants in him a desire to kill, a desire that must be acted on before the devil will go away.

Explanation for D's acts and omissions

8.66 There must be some connection between the abnormality of mental functioning and the killing. The abnormality of mental functioning must provide *an* explanation for D's acts and omissions in doing or being a party to the killing.[130] By HA 1957, s 2(1B), 'an abnormality of mental functioning provides an explanation for D's conduct if it causes, or is a significant contributory factor in causing, D to carry out that conduct'. This means that abnormality of mental functioning need not be the sole cause of the defendant's conduct. It would be impractical to require it to be. As the Government stated in its consultation paper:

'It is rare that a person's actions will be driven solely from within to such an extent that they would not otherwise have committed the offence, regardless of the influence of

---

[129] *Murder, Manslaughter and Infanticide* Law Com No 304, para 5.121.   [130] HA 1957, s 2(1)(c).

external circumstances, and a strict causation requirement of this kind would limit the availability of the partial defence too much.'[131]

Thus, for example, the fact that other explanations or causes were also operative does not in itself negative the defence of diminished responsibility. Proof of the necessary link may be difficult, if not impossible, from the psychiatric point of view.[132]

This requirement is another reason why the new s 2(1) is liable to make the defence of diminished responsibility stricter than its predecessor.

Where drink or drugs are involved

8.67 An abnormality of mental functioning which arises from intoxication through drink or drugs is outside the defence of diminished responsibility because it does not arise from a recognised medical condition.

8.68 Where the defendant was suffering from abnormality of mental functioning arising from two or more conditions, one of which is a recognised medical condition and the other of which is intoxication, the defendant is not deprived of the defence of diminished responsibility merely because he would not (or might not) have killed if he had not been intoxicated. This was held by the House of Lords in *Dietschmann*[133] in relation to the defence of diminished responsibility under the original HA 1957, s 2(1) and the same is no doubt true in respect of the substituted s 2(1). It would appear by analogy from *Dietschmann* that, if the jury take the view that D's abnormality of mental functioning arising from a recognised mental condition and D's intoxication played a part in impairing D's ability in one of the ways specified in s 2(1A) and that D might not have killed if he had not taken drink or drugs, they must decide whether, despite the drink or drugs, his ability in the specified respect was substantially impaired by the abnormality of mental functioning arising from a medical condition and whether this provided an explanation for his acts in doing or being a party to the killing. If they are so satisfied they must find the defence proved; if they are not so satisfied the defence fails.

Such an approach is not an easy one for the jury to apply but it does recognise that there is a moral difference between an intoxicated person with an abnormality of mental functioning arising from a recognised medical condition who kills and a killer who is simply intoxicated. It will be noted that the question of whether one of the competing causes is the immediate cause of the defendant's mental state is irrelevant, a different approach from that taken in relation to the defence of insanity and non-insane automatism dealt with in Chapter 15.

8.69 What about the case where the defendant suffers from alcoholism (alcohol dependence syndrome, a recognised medical condition) and bases a plea of diminished responsibility on this? In such a case, whether or not brain damage has occurred, the jury must

---

[131] *Murder, Manslaughter and Infanticide: Proposals for Reform of the Law* Ministry of Justice Consultation Paper 19/08, para 51.
[132] See Baroness Murphy HL Deb, vol 712 cols 177 and 180.
[133] [2003] UKHL 10. See also *Hendy* [2006] EWCA Crim 819.

decide whether the defendant was suffering from an abnormality of mental functioning. This decision depends on their findings about the extent and nature of the syndrome and, it seems (by analogy with the case law on the original HA 1957, s 2(1)), whether the defendant's consumption of alcohol before the killing is fairly to be regarded as the involuntary result of an irresistible compulsion to drink. If he was not suffering from an abnormality of mental functioning, diminished responsibility will fail. If, on the other hand, he was, the jury must then consider whether the defendant's ability to do one or more of the things specified in s 2(1A) at the material time was substantially impaired as a result and whether this provides an explanation for his acts or omissions in doing or being a party to the killing.[134] Until the matter comes before the appellate courts the factors which may be relevant in the latter respect are uncertain but it is submitted that the extent to which the defendant was able to choose when and what to drink would be highly relevant, just as it was in relation to the different issue of substantial impairment of mental responsibility under the original s 2(1).[135]

Function of jury

8.70 Although, unlike the defence of insanity, there is no statutory requirement of medical evidence, medical evidence in support of the defence of diminished responsibility is 'a practical necessity if the defence is to begin to run at all'.[136]

Whether or not the requirements of the defence are established is for the jury to decide.[137] It would seem that, as with the original version of the HA 1957, s 2(1), the jury should approach these issues in a broad, commonsense way,[138] taking into account not only the medical evidence but all the evidence, including the acts or statements of the defendant and his demeanour.[139] The medical evidence is important but the jury are not bound to accept it, even though it is unanimous, if there is other material before them which, in their opinion, conflicts with and outweighs it.[140] In *Eifinger*, decided under the original s 2(1),[141] D had been convicted of murder despite the fact that the medical evidence was that, at the time of the killing, D was suffering from a depressive illness amounting to an abnormality of mind. Dismissing D's appeal against conviction, the Court of Appeal held that the jury were entitled to evaluate the medical evidence along with all the defendant's evidence in the light of all the surrounding circumstances and

---

[134] *Stewart* [2009] EWCA Crim 593.

[135] *Stewart* [2009] EWCA Crim 593.

[136] *Dix* (1981) 74 Cr App Rep 306 at 311.

[137] This was the position in relation to the original s 2(1): *Byrne* [1960] 2 QB 396 at 402–403; and there is no reason to doubt that it continues to be the case. The aetiology of the abnormality of mental functioning (ie whether it arose from a recognised medical condition) would seem to be a matter to be determined on medical evidence, as it was in respect of the issue of whether abnormality of mind was due to a permissible cause in respect of the original s 2(1).

[138] *Walton v R* [1978] AC 788, PC; *Stewart* [2009] EWCA Crim 593.

[139] *Byrne* [1960] 2 QB 396 at 402–403.

[140] *Byrne* [1960] 2 QB 396 at 403; *Walton v R* [1978] AC 788, PC; *Sanders* (1991) 93 Cr App Rep 245, CA; *Salmon* [2005] 3 Archbold News 2, CA.

[141] [2001] EWCA Crim 1855, CA.

come to a conclusion about whether the medical evidence was reliable and accurate, particularly as it was based on what D had told the psychiatrists concerned.

The jury must, however, found their verdict on the evidence, and, if medical evidence in support of the defence is clear, unanimous and unchallenged and there is no other evidence which would justify the jury in rejecting the medical evidence, the jury are bound to accept the medical evidence and a verdict against the defendant (ie of murder) contrary to the medical evidence will be set aside on appeal.[142] Sometimes the jury are faced with the difficult task of weighing conflicting medical evidence.[143]

General

8.71 The judge may accept a plea of not guilty of murder but guilty of manslaughter on grounds of diminished responsibility, in which case a verdict from the jury will not be required, but this should only be done where there is clear and undisputed medical evidence of diminished responsibility.[144] In practice, the prosecution often concedes the issue of diminished responsibility at the outset and the acceptance of such a plea by the judge is common.[145] If it happens, it means that medical evidence that the defendant was suffering from a recognised medical condition such as substantially to impair his ability, as specified in s 2(1) and (1A) will not be tested, and that, provided medical witnesses are willing to give a sympathetic diagnosis to the defendant's condition in order to get round the mandatory sentence for murder, what may be no more than an ordinary reaction to a stressful situation may result in a conviction for manslaughter on a murder charge. Diagnoses such as reactive depression or post-traumatic stress disorder or dissociation are apt, if not probed too closely, to cover such a reaction. In this way, a condition whose cause is external to the defendant, having been diagnosed as a psychiatric disorder, can be viewed as satisfying s 2(1). For example, in respect of the original s 2(1), it has not been uncommon where someone is charged with murder on the basis of the mercy-killing of a terminally ill relative or friend that the expert witnesses have offered the diagnosis that the defendant was suffering from 'reactive depression' or other vague condition brought about by the situation in question. Other instances of cases where it has not been infrequent for medical witnesses to put a sympathetic gloss on ordinary reactions to stress are those where a killing is induced by stress arising from domestic disputes or anti-social neighbours. It may be that the new, more tightly drafted definition of diminished responsibility will result in the prosecution being more sceptical about claims to

---

[142] *Matheson* [1958] 2 All ER 87, CCA; *Bailey* (1977) 66 Cr App Rep 31n, CCA; *Vernege* [1982] 1 WLR 293, CA; *Sanders* (1991) 93 Cr App Rep 245, CA.

[143] *Jennion* [1962] 1 All ER 689, CCA.

[144] *Cox* [1968] 1 All ER 386, CA; *Vinagre* (1979) 69 Cr App Rep 104, CA.

[145] See Dell 'Diminished Responsibility Reconsidered' [1982] Crim LR 809. A research study conducted for the Law Commission indicated that of the 157 cases studied the prosecution conceded a diminished responsibility plea in 77.1 per cent of them: Law Commission: *Partial Defences to Murder* (2004) Law Com No 290, para 5.34, Appendix B. In the period 1986–1988, the prosecution only refused to concede such a plea in 9.2 per cent of cases where it was offered: House of Lords *Report of the Select Committee on Murder and Life Imprisonment, Vol II – Oral Evidence, Part I* (1988–1989) 115. Where a diminished responsibility plea is not accepted and goes to trial, it fails in about 60 per cent of cases: Dell *Murder into Manslaughter* (1984).

the defence and consequently to be less prepared to concede pleas of diminished responsibility. As the Law Commission said:

> 'It is possible to imagine, for example, a sceptical view being more commonly taken of claims by jealous husbands, who have killed their wives or children, that their capacity to form a rational judgement was substantially impaired by clinically recognised depression. Prosecutors may well think it right to show a much greater readiness to test claims of this kind before the jury than they might show in a case where, for example, a child assessed before trial as severely subnormal has become involved in a killing at the urging of his domineering father. We take no stance on this issue ourselves.'[146]

If the prosecution does not concede the issue, the judge should accept a plea of not guilty of murder but guilty of manslaughter on the grounds of diminished responsibility at the close of evidence only in very exceptional cases.[147]

8.72 Although there will be cases where the defence of diminished responsibility may overlap with the defence of loss of control (a more attractive defence since the defendant does not have to prove it), the two defences are different in important respects. This can be seen by comparing the requirements of diminished responsibility set out above with those of the loss of control defence set out in paras 8.73 to 8.94. One obvious difference is that, unlike loss of control, the defence of diminished responsibility does not depend on facts external to the defendant.

Loss of control

> **Key points 8.5**
>
> While evidence of loss of control on the defendant's part is something which the jury must take into account at a murder trial, along with all the other circumstances, in deciding whether a party to the killing had the necessary *mens rea*,[148] the defence of loss of control is concerned with the situation where a party had that *mens rea* but acted under a loss of self-control.
>
> The partial defence of loss of control is governed by the Coroners and Justice Act 2009, ss 54 and 55 which replace the common law partial defence of provocation. *The abolition of the common law defence and its replacement by the new defence comes into force on 4 October 2010. The following discussion concentrates on the law as it will be when the defence of loss of control is in force. Until its abolition comes into force the defence of provocation will be described in more detail on the companion website to this book.*

---

[146] *Murder, Manslaughter and Infanticide* Law Com No 304, para 5.141.

[147] *Khan (Danwood)* [2009] EWCA Crim 1569. The judge must be satisfied that, on the evidence (including the medical evidence), no reasonable jury could fail to conclude that the defendant had proved the essential requirements of the defence: *Khan (Danwood)*.

[148] Criminal Justice Act 1967, s 8; *Ives* [1970] 1 QB 208, CA.

The defects with the defence of provocation

8.73 The test of whether the defence of provocation was entitled to succeed was a dual one. The alleged provocative conduct:

- had to cause in the defendant a sudden and temporary loss of self-control (the subjective test); and
- had to be 'enough to make a reasonable person do as the defendant did', ie enough to cause a reasonable person to suffer such a loss of self-control and, having lost self-control, to do as the defendant did (the objective test). This test was applied on the basis of a person with the powers of self-control of an ordinary person of the defendant's age and sex, disregarding any characteristics of the defendant which might affect the defendant's powers of self-control.

8.74 At the time of its abolition there were the following problems with the defence of provocation:

- *lack of judicial control* If there was any evidence – however trivial (eg the crying of a baby, the announcement by a wife that she was quitting, the innocent conduct of an ex-partner or a failure to cook the defendant's steak medium rare as ordered)[149] – that the defendant was provoked to lose self-control, the judge had to leave the defence to the jury no matter how unlikely it was that the defence would succeed. This did not necessarily serve the interests of the defendant because, despite the evidence of loss of self-control, the defendant might have been seeking a complete acquittal on other grounds (eg self-defence) and not have wanted the jury's attention to this to be diverted by consideration of the defence of provocation;
- *sudden and temporary loss of self-control* The concept of loss of self-control lacks clarity or a clear foundation in psychology. The requirement of a sudden loss of self-control tended to favour the typical reactions of men to provocation, namely to lose their temper and respond violently; the typical reactions of women to provocation are more likely to take the form of anger, fear, frustration and a sense of desperation.[150] Because women typically have this 'slow burn' reaction it could be difficult or impossible for the defence of provocation to succeed in domestic abuse cases, for example. This was not always the case because 'sudden' had been interpreted so as not to mean 'immediate' but it was still necessary that when the loss of self-control occurred it was abrupt. This could present problems for some women defendants whose cases were deserving. In such a case, no other defence was available unless the woman satisfied the requirements of diminished responsibility or there was a fear of imminent attack;[151]

---

[149] An example given by the Law Commission *Murder, Manslaughter and Infanticide* (2006) Law Com No 304, para 1.47.

[150] Law Com No 304, para 5.18.

[151] Self-defence would not be available unless there was a fear of imminent attack and the force used would have to be reasonable: para 16.8.

- *over-reaction to fear of serious violence* Neither provocation nor any other defence was available to the householder who had killed by over-reacting when in fear of serious violence at the hands of a burglar.[152]

The new defence of loss of control

8.75 It was in response to these problems that the partial defence of provocation was abolished by the Coroners and Justice Act 2009 (C&JA 2009), s 56(1), and replaced by the partial defence of loss of control enacted by ss 54 and 55.

8.76 These provisions have their foundations in recommendations made in 2004 by the Law Commission as part of a review of partial defences to murder in general.[153] In its report in 2006, *Murder, Manslaughter and Infanticide*,[154] the Law Commission saw no compelling reason to depart from its 2004 recommendations, although its recommendations differ from them in a few ways. Both sets of recommendations involved the radical reform of the defence of provocation. In particular:

- the defence would cease to be based on the idea that the defendant's culpability is reduced simply because of a loss of self-control by the defendant. Loss of self-control would no longer have been a requirement for the defence;
- there would be a two-limbed test under which provocation could be pleaded if there was:
  - a fear of serious violence; or
  - gross provocation (ie words or conduct which caused the defendant to have a justifiable sense of being seriously wronged); or
  - both;
- the judge would not be required to leave the defence to the jury unless there was evidence on which a reasonable jury properly directed could conclude that it might apply.

The Law Commission's recommendations were taken forward, with some important amendments, by the Government in its consultation paper, *Murder, Manslaughter and Infanticide: Proposals for Reform of the Law*, referred to in para 8.38. The Government's consultation paper proposed the abolition of the defence of provocation and its replacement by what it described as two new partial defences (better viewed as two limbs of the same defence), both of which would require a loss of self-control and have an objective element, to cover:

- killing in response to a fear of serious violence; and
- killing in response to words and conduct which amounted to an exceptional happening and caused the defendant to have a justifiable sense of being seriously wronged,

---

[152] Excessive self-defence is not a defence (partial or otherwise) to murder under the rules relating to that defence: see para 16.33.

[153] *Law Commission: Partial Defences to Murder* (2004), Law Com No 290.

[154] Law Commission Report No 304. See paras 5.1–5.82 of the Report.

which could be run separately or in parallel. With some amendments, the Government's proposals in its consultation paper are now contained in a somewhat complex form in the C&JA 2009, ss 54 and 55.

Requirements of defence of loss of control

8.77 The C&JA 2009, s 54(1) provides:

> 'Where a person ("D") kills or is a party to the killing of another ("V"), D is not to be convicted of murder if:
>
> (a) D's acts and omissions in doing or being a party to the killing resulted from D's loss of self-control,
>
> (b) the loss of self-control had a qualifying trigger, and
>
> (c) a person of D's sex and age, with a normal degree of tolerance and self-restraint and in the circumstances of D, might have reacted in the same or in a similar way to D.'

A person who, but for the defence of loss of control, would be liable to be convicted of murder is liable instead to be convicted of manslaughter.[155] The defence does not apply to other offences, not even attempted murder.[156] The reason is that in other offences the judge has a sentencing discretion which makes it possible to reflect the loss of control in the sentence itself.

8.78 The fact that one party to a killing is by virtue of the defence of loss of control not liable to be convicted of murder does not affect the question whether the killing amounted to murder in the case of any other party to it.[157]

8.79 Under s 54(4) the defence does not apply if, in doing or being a party to the killing, D acted in a considered desire for revenge.

Loss of self-control

8.80 The requirement that D's acts and omissions in doing or being a party to the killing of V must have resulted from D's loss of self-control represents the principal difference between the new defence and the Law Commission's recommendations for a reformed defence of provocation. The Law Commission presented powerful arguments against the retention of the concept of self-control on the grounds that it was unnecessary and undesirable.[158] The Government, however, remained

> 'concerned that there is a risk of the partial defence being used inappropriately, for example in cold-blooded gang-related or "honour" killings. Even in cases which are less obviously unsympathetic, there is still a fundamental problem about providing a partial

---

[155] C&JA 2009, s 54(7).   [156] See para 14.109.   [157] C&JA 2009, s 54(8).
[158] *Partial Defences to Murder* Law Com No 290, paras 3.28–3.30, 3.135–3.137.

> defence in situations where a defendant has killed while basically in full possession of his or her senses, even if he or she is frightened, other than in a situation which is complete self-defence.'[159]

It is hard to see how cold-blooded gang-related or 'honour killings' would satisfy the other requirements of the defence. An 'honour killing', for example, would seem to fall foul of the bar (above) that the killing was done in a considered desire for revenge. It is regrettable that the Government took this view.

8.81 The C&JA 2009, s 54(2) makes explicit what is implicit in s 54(1)(a): that it does not matter whether or not the loss of self-control was sudden, which raises the interesting question whether there can be a loss of self-control which is not abrupt. Nevertheless, although s 54(2) 'softens' the requirement and permits it to be satisfied where the defendant's loss of self-control has been delayed or builds up gradually (as in the 'slow burn' reaction typical of women), the requirement of loss of self-control is liable to exclude cases deserving of relief from the mandatory sentence of murder. It seems wrong, for example, to exclude the battered woman who, because of fear of serious violence in a future confrontation, uses excessive force against her abusive partner simply because there is no evidence of loss of self-control. Indeed, the application of the concept of 'loss of self-control' to cases where the defendant acts under fear of serious violence seems problematic. It would have been preferable to have omitted the reference to self-control and to have left undeserving cases to be dealt with via the judge's duty to withdraw cases from the jury if there is insufficient evidence of the other requirements of the defence.

8.82 The longer the delay between the alleged trigger and the alleged loss of self-control, the more likely it is that an aspect of the defence is not satisfied, eg because the defendant was acting in a considered desire for revenge or had not lost self-control.

8.83 Another problem with the requirement of loss of self-control is the meaning of that term. As pointed out above, it lacks clarity (as well as a clear foundation in psychology). According to Devlin J in *Duffy*,[160] in the context of the defence of provocation, the defendant must be rendered so subject to passion as to make him or her for the moment not master of his or her mind. This statement was subsequently reaffirmed by the Court of Appeal.[161] Even under this strict test, it is not necessary, however, that there should be a complete loss of control to the extent that the defendant does not know what he is doing.[162] It would completely defeat the defence otherwise; a killer who does not know what he is doing would lack the *mens rea* for murder, and the defence of loss of control only comes into play as a defence where the defendant admits that he had the *mens rea* for murder or is proved to have had it. It was not clear under the law on provocation, nor is it clear in

---

[159] Ministry of Justice Consultation Paper No 19/08, para 36.
[160] [1949] 1 All ER 932n.
[161] Eg *Ibrams and Gregory* (1981) 74 Cr App Rep 154, CA; *Richens* [1993] 4 All ER 877, CA.
[162] *Richens* [1993] 4 All ER 877, CA.

respect of the new defence, whether 'loss of self-control' refers to a failure to exercise self-control or an inability to exercise self-control. As the Law Commission noted:

> 'To ask whether a person could have exercised self-control is to pose an impossible moral question. It is not a question which a psychiatrist could address as a matter of medical science...'[163]

Qualifying trigger

8.84 Section 54(1)(b) requires that D's loss of self-control must have had a qualifying trigger. By s 55(2), a loss of self-control had a qualifying trigger if s 55 (3), (4) or (5) applies, ie:

- if D's loss of self-control was attributable to D's fear of serious violence from V against D or another identified person (s 55(3)); or
- if D's loss of self-control was attributable to a thing or things done or said (or both) which –
  (a) constituted circumstances of an extremely grave character, and
  (b) caused D to have a justifiable sense of being seriously wronged (s 55(4)); or
- if D's loss of self-control was attributable to a combination of the matters mentioned in s 55(3) and (4) (s 55(5)).

The first trigger: fear of serious violence from V against D or another identified person

8.85 Whereas the second trigger has an ancestry in the old defence of provocation, this trigger is novel. It is intended, inter alia, to rectify the defect with the defence of provocation, referred to in para 8.74, that it discriminated against women in its application. As already indicated, however, the requirement of loss of self-control may rule out many defendants who would otherwise satisfy this trigger and the other requirements of the defence. This is especially true in the second type of case below. *Assuming that there was a loss of self-control*, the present trigger would be satisfied in the following two cases:[164]

- V has frequently hit his partner, D, when he comes home drunk. One night D comes home drunk and D fears that V would hit her yet again. D goes to the kitchen, fetches a knife and intentionally and fatally stabs V in the chest. D was not suffering from an abnormality of mental functioning arising from a medically recognised condition and therefore cannot rely on the partial defence of diminished responsibility. Nor is the complete defence of self-defence available because the force used by D is not reasonable force (as required by that defence) in the light of the facts that the serious

---

[163] *Partial Defences to Murder* (2004) Law Com No 290, para 3.28.
[164] These examples are based on ones given by the Law Commission in *Murder, Manslaughter and Infanticide* Law Com No 304, para 5.50.

violence is anticipated and not imminent and that D's response is disproportionate to the threatened violence.

- D, an armed police officer, is sent to a house where a neighbour has reported that V has what looks like a gun. When D enters the house he sees V with something in his hand. V does not respond to D's request to show what it is. D intentionally shoots V in the chest. V dies. It transpires that V, who was stone deaf, had something harmless in his hand. D could plead self-defence but, although that defence is based on the facts as D believed them to be, that defence will fail if the jury find that the force used was unreasonable on those facts.

The present trigger is intended to avoid the unfairness which would be engendered if, in the event that self-defence failed, the defendant had to be convicted of murder (and given the mandatory life sentence). If the present trigger (and the other requirements of s 54(1)(a) and (c)) are satisfied, the proper verdict will be a manslaughter verdict. It is for D to decide how to run D's defence, but if D is not confident that a self-defence plea will succeed D can plead the defence of loss of self-control via fear of serious violence instead of, or in addition to, the defence of self-defence.

8.86 There are two limits to this trigger:

- the fear of serious violence must be of violence from V, the person killed, and
- the fear must be of such violence to D or some other identified person.

Presumably, the fear of violence must have been induced by V or a third party, and a self-induced fear will not suffice. If D kills V, a wholly innocent person, because X has threatened D that he will do D's son serious violence if he does not, the trigger is not satisfied and D has no defence.[165] Nor is the trigger satisfied if D kills V after a threat that V will 'cripple someone'.

8.87 Section 55(6)(a) provides that, in determining whether a loss of self-control had a qualifying trigger, D's fear of serious violence must be disregarded to the extent that it was caused by a thing which D incited to be done or said for the purpose of providing an excuse to use violence. The good sense of this is obvious.

8.88 It is not a bar that D is partly responsible for the situation in which he found himself, as where D had voluntarily put himself in a position where he might be threatened with serious violence, as where he joins a criminal gang, knowing that members of that gang or another gang may threaten him with serious violence. If such a threat is made and D loses self-control and kills by way of pre-emptive strike he is not debarred from relying on the defence of loss of control. It is noteworthy that such a bar does not operate in this type of case in respect of the defence of self-defence[166] but it does in respect of the defence of duress by threats.[167] The Law Commission thought that in many cases

---

[165] D will not have the defence of duress by threats: see paras 16.53 and 16.54.
[166] Para 16.32.   [167] Para 16.49.

of this type, however, the defence of loss of control would fail under the third, objective requirement.[168]

The second trigger: gross provocation

8.89 The second trigger is that D's loss of self-control was attributable to a thing or things done or said (or both) which –

- constituted circumstances of an *extremely grave character*, and
- caused D to have a *justifiable sense of being seriously wronged*.

This trigger deals with cases of gross provocation. Its two requirements, not made by the old defence of provocation, mean that many cases where a defence of provocation under the old law would have succeeded will not succeed under the new law.[169] The terms of this trigger are strict; it will only be satisfied in a small number of cases. Examples might be where a rape-victim loses self-control and kills the rapist who has taunted her or where a father loses self-control and kills a man who he finds trying to rape his daughter. Many defendants who snap under extreme pressure and whose culpability is far removed from the stereotype cold, calculating murderer will receive a murder conviction and concomitant mandatory life sentence.

8.90 Section 55(6)(b) and (c)) provide that, in determining whether a loss of self-control had a qualifying trigger:

- **a sense of being seriously wronged by a thing done or said is not justifiable if D incited the thing to be done or said for the purpose of providing an excuse to use violence (s 55(6)(b));**
- **the fact that a thing done or said constituted sexual infidelity must be disregarded (s 55(6)(c)).**

The second of these bars is oddly drafted: how can a 'thing said' constitute sexual infidelity? The bar was highly controversial in Parliament. Ultimately the Government's view prevailed and it was restored. The Government's view was that it was quite unacceptable for a defendant who killed an unfaithful partner to seek to blame the victim for what occurred; sexual infidelity could never justify reducing murder to manslaughter. This seems to be an extreme view. The requirements of the trigger and the other provisions relating to the defence would have been enough to limit the defence to exceptional cases of sexual infidelity killings. Why should this one situation be singled out for express exclusion?

---

[168] Law Com No 304, para 5.82.
[169] The duty of the judge to withdraw a loss of control claim from the jury on the ground that it could not reasonably accept it (see para 8.94) is a further protection against such a claim succeeding in cases of provocation which is not gross.

Objective requirement

8.91 Section 54(1)(c) provides that, **assuming the other two requirements are satisfied. D is not guilty of murder if a person of D's sex and age, with a normal degree of tolerance and self-restraint and in the circumstances of D, might have reacted in the same or in a similar way to D.** As can be seen this requirement is not wholly objective. It is not simply concerned with whether someone with a normal degree of tolerance and self-restraint *might* have reacted in the same or a similar way as D did but also whether a person of D's sex and age (the latter in particular may be relevant to tolerance and self-restraint) and in D's circumstances might have reacted as D did.

8.92 Not all of D's circumstances, however, can be taken into account. This is because s 54(3) provides that the reference in s 54(1)(c) to **'the circumstances of D' is a reference to all of D's circumstances other than those whose only relevance to D's conduct is that they bear on D's general capacity for tolerance or self-restraint.** Clearly, D's circumstances to which reference may be made under s 54(1)(c) include not only D's external circumstances, present or past, but also those of his characteristics which affect the gravity of the 'triggering conduct' to D. For example, the fact that D is a dwarf (or exceptionally disfigured, of black skin or a paedophile) and D killed V after being taunted by insults relating to his height (or looks, skin colour or sexual proclivities) can be referred to. This is obviously correct. It is this characteristic which puts the 'sting' into the taunts. The same would be true in the absence of a taunt or other conduct specifically directed at a characteristic. Thus, if D kills V, her partner, who was roaring drunk at the time, reference can be made to the matter that the effect of V's conduct on D was aggravated by the fact that D suffered battered woman syndrome as a result of V's past behaviour to D when drunk.

The closing words of s 54(3) make it clear that characteristics or other circumstances whose only relevance to D's conduct is that they bear on D's general capacity for tolerance or self-restraint cannot be referred to in applying the present requirement. Thus, the fact that D was intoxicated or intolerant or irritable or excessively jealous or had problems in controlling his impulses or otherwise had impaired powers of self-control must be ignored.[170] If it could be taken into account it would subvert the essential function of the objective requirement, viz to mark the distinction between a partially excusable loss of self-control and an inexcusable one by reference to an objective standard of self-control. Taking into account those characteristics of the defendant which affected the gravity of the 'triggering conduct' to him does not affect that essential function. It simply recognises as a matter of common sense that the effect of the conduct on a reasonable person can only be assessed in the light of those characteristics of the defendant which are relevant to the effect of that conduct. It is a different matter to take into account also characteristics which affected the defendant's self-control.

---

[170] If the factor affecting tolerance or self-restraint was due to a recognised medical condition, the defence of diminished responsibility (see para 8.53) may apply.

8.93 It should be noted that what D did by way of reaction need not bear a reasonable relationship (ie be proportionate) to the serious violence feared by D, or the things said or done which caused D to have a justifiable sense of being wronged. This is obviously sensible. How could someone who had lost self-control be required to keep his response proportionate? At most, proportionality is a factor to be taken into account in considering whether a person of D's sex and age, with a normal degree of tolerance and self-restraint and in the circumstances of D (as explained above), might have reacted in the same way or a similar way to D. It will be noted that the question is not whether that person might have reacted and killed, but whether that person might have reacted in the same or a similar way to D (eg inflicting numerous injuries to V's head after knocking him senseless to the ground). This is a further limitation on the second trigger.

Function of judge and jury

8.94 Section 54(5) provides that, if sufficient evidence is adduced to raise an issue with respect to the defence under s 54(1), the jury must assume that the defence is satisfied unless the prosecution proves beyond reasonable doubt that it is not. For these purposes, sufficient evidence is adduced to raise an issue with respect to the defence if evidence is adduced on which, in the opinion of the trial judge, a jury, properly directed, could reasonably conclude that the defence might apply.[171]

What this means is that the judge may only leave the defence of loss of control to the jury if there is evidence (normally, but not necessarily, from the defendant, and whether or not the defendant has pleaded the defence) on which, in the judge's opinion, a properly directed jury could reasonably conclude that the three requirements of the defence might be satisfied. If the judge is not of this opinion, the judge must withdraw the defence of loss of control from the jury. If the judge is of this opinion the judge must leave the defence to the jury with an appropriate direction, and the jury must find that the defence is satisfied unless the prosecution proves beyond reasonable doubt that it (ie one or more of its requirements) is not.

Involuntary manslaughter

Key points 8.6

A person who causes the death of another is guilty of involuntary manslaughter if he does so:

- by an act which is unlawful and dangerous;
- with gross negligence; or
- with recklessness as to the risk of death or serious bodily harm.

---

[171] C&JA 2009, s 54(6).

8.95 Important distinctions between the involuntary manslaughter by an unlawful or dangerous act and the other two types of involuntary manslaughter listed above are that in the last two types it is irrelevant whether or not the defendant's act would have constituted an offence if death had not resulted,[172] and that in the last two types liability can be based on an omission to act[173] (but only if the defendant was under a duty to act recognised by the criminal law).[174] Despite these distinctions the three types of involuntary manslaughter are not mutually exclusive; in some circumstances a defendant may be guilty of involuntary manslaughter by more than one route.[175]

8.96 Following the obscure decision of the House of Lords in 1983 in *Seymour*[176] it appeared that the last two types of involuntary manslaughter listed above no longer survived and had been replaced by a new type of involuntary manslaughter based on the concept of *Caldwell* recklessness[177] as to an obvious and serious risk of injury to the person, despite the fact that manslaughter by gross negligence had been affirmed in 1937 by the House of Lords in *Andrews v DPP*.[178] There was, however, uncertainty about the effect of *Seymour* on the pre-existing law, since the House of Lords did not consider the point.

The matter was resolved in 1994 in relation to manslaughter by gross negligence, by the House of Lords in *Adomako*.[179] The House affirmed the continued existence of such an offence and overruled the decision in *Seymour* and, thus, the type of involuntary manslaughter postulated in it. It has subsequently become clear that 'reckless manslaughter' also survives.

Manslaughter by killing by an unlawful and dangerous act

Key points 8.7

To secure a conviction on the above basis, the prosecution must prove three things:

- the commission of an unlawful act by the defendant;
- that that act was dangerous, in the sense that it was likely to cause harm to another; and
- that the unlawful and dangerous act caused death.

It is irrelevant that the defendant is unaware that his act is unlawful or dangerous.[180]

---

[172] *Larkin* [1943] 1 All ER 217 at 219 (the passage in question does not appear in [1943] KB 174); *Gray v Barr* [1971] 2 QB 554 at 576–577, per Salmon LJ.

[173] The statement in *Khan and Khan* [1998] Crim LR 830, CA, that an omission would only suffice in the case of gross negligence manslaughter was made without advertence to reckless manslaughter.

[174] *Stone and Dobinson* [1977] QB 354, CA.

[175] See *Willoughby* [2004] EWCA Crim 3365, where this was recognised in relation to the first two types in the text.

[176] [1983] 2 AC 493, HL.   [177] Para 3.35.   [178] [1937] AC 576, HL.

[179] [1995] 1 AC 171, HL.   [180] *DPP v Newbury* [1977] AC 500, HL; *Ball* [1989] Crim LR 730, CA.

8.97 This mode of committing manslaughter is commonly known as 'constructive manslaughter' because liability is constructed (ie based) on another offence in the course of which death results.

Commission of an unlawful act

8.98 At one time the unlawful act could consist of a tort[181] but now **only a criminally unlawful act will suffice;**[182] this has been confirmed in recent years by the Court of Appeal in *Dias* and *Andrews* and by the House of Lords in *Kennedy (No 2)*, all of which are referred to in para 8.99. There are two further qualifications on the nature of the unlawful act.

- **An act which has become criminally unlawful simply because it was negligently performed, eg dangerous or careless driving, does not constitute an unlawful act for the purposes of 'constructive manslaughter'.** In other words where negligence is the very essence of the offence[183] the offence cannot be an 'unlawful act' for the purposes of constructive manslaughter. The authority is *Andrews v DPP*[184] where the defendant had killed another while committing the offence of dangerous driving and was convicted of manslaughter. On appeal to the House of Lords, Lord Atkin (with whom the rest of the House of Lords agreed) said that 'There is an obvious difference in the law of manslaughter between doing an unlawful act and doing a lawful act with a degree of carelessness which the legislature makes criminal',[185] and that the latter type of act did not necessarily make the driver guilty of manslaughter if death resulted; the doctrine of 'constructive manslaughter' did not apply to such an act, although there might be liability for manslaughter on the basis of gross negligence.[186]

- As we have seen, there are a number of statutory offences which are constituted by an omission to do something, rather than a positive act. An example is the neglect of a child by its parent or guardian in a manner likely to cause it unnecessary suffering or injury to health, which, if wilful, is an offence under the Children and Young Persons Act 1933, s 1. It was thought that the unintentional causing of death as a

---

[181] *Fenton* (1830) 1 Lew CC 179.

[182] *Franklin* (1883) 15 Cox CC 163; *Lamb* [1967] 2 QB 981, CA.

[183] Para 3.60.

[184] [1937] AC 576, HL.

[185] [1937] AC 576 at 585. An alternative interpretation of these words, viz that only offences which require more than mere negligence will suffice for constructive manslaughter (which would prohibit reliance on an offence of strict liability as well as an offence of negligence as the basis of the unlawful act), see Ormerod [2003] Crim LR 479, would seem to put an interpretation on Lord Atkin's words which they cannot bear. In *Andrews* [2002] EWCA Crim 3021, where D had injected V, who was prone to alcohol abuse, with insulin to give her a 'rush', liability for constructive manslaughter was confirmed on the basis of the commission of the strict liability offence of administering a prescription-only drug otherwise than on medical direction, contrary to the Medicines Act 1968, ss 58 and 67. There was, however, no argument on the relevance of the fact that the offence was one of strict liability.

[186] Paras 8.119–8.130.

result of the commission of such a statutory offence of omission could constitute constructive manslaughter. In *Senior*,[187] for instance, where owing to D's religious belief his child was not provided with medical attendance and died in consequence, it was held that manslaughter had been committed. However, the Court of Appeal in *Lowe*[188] held that *Senior* was no longer good law and that **an omission does not suffice for constructive manslaughter**. D's baby died some 10 weeks after birth and at the time of her death was grossly dehydrated and emaciated. D was convicted of wilfully neglecting the child and of manslaughter after the judge had told the jury that a conviction for manslaughter must follow if wilful neglect had caused the child's death. D's appeal against the latter conviction was allowed by the Court of Appeal, who held that a finding of manslaughter did not inexorably follow from a finding of wilful neglect. There was a clear distinction between an omission likely to cause harm and an act likely to cause harm:

> '...if I strike a child in a manner likely to cause harm it is right that if the child dies I may be charged with manslaughter. If, however, I omit to do something with the result that it suffers injury to health which results in death, we think that a charge of manslaughter should not be an inevitable consequence, even if the omission is deliberate.'[189]

It is difficult to see the distinction between the person who causes the death of his child by deliberate inaction and the one who does so by positive action.

Proof of an unlawful act requires proof of the actus reus of an offence

8.99 It will be remembered that an act is never criminally unlawful in itself. One of the things which is required to render an act criminally unlawful is that it should occur in those circumstances and/or lead to those consequences prescribed by law as constituting the *actus reus* of an offence. For instance, an act of punching is not criminal but it may become so (as a battery) if it results in the consequence that someone is unlawfully hit. Thus, if a boxer unexpectedly dies from a blow delivered by D within the Queensberry rules at a boxing match, there will be no unlawful act by D (and consequently no manslaughter) because the victim will have validly consented to being so hit.[190] On the other hand, if he is hit by D outside the rules (eg 'after the bell' when he was returning to his corner), the force is unlawful and D commits a battery (and, doubtless, other offences); since D's act is unlawful, he will be guilty of constructive manslaughter if death unexpectedly results. (Of course, if D intended grievous bodily harm, he would be guilty of murder.) In

---

[187] [1899] 1 QB 283. Also see *Watson and Watson* (1959) 43 Cr App Rep 111, CCA.

[188] [1973] QB 702, CA. Overruled on the meaning of 'wilful neglect', but not on the present point, by the House of Lords in *Sheppard* [1981] AC 394. For the House of Lords' definition of wilful neglect, see para 6.30. For criticism of *Lowe*, see [1976] Crim LR 529.

[189] [1973] QB 702 at 709.

[190] Paras 7.9 and 7.10.

some cases, the unlawfulness of an act may turn on whether a consent to it given by the victim is a valid consent, a matter dealt with in paras 7.1 to 7.24.

There were indications in the decisions of the Court of Appeal in *Cato*[191] and the later case of *Kennedy (No 1)*[192] that there could be an unlawful act even if the *actus reus* of an offence has not been committed. It is now clear that this does not represent the law. In *Dias*,[193] the Court of Appeal held that 'in [the present] context "unlawful" means that the act has to be a criminal offence'. A differently constituted Court of Appeal in *Andrews*[194] agreed with this. The matter has been put beyond doubt by the House of Lords in *Kennedy (No 2)*, where Lord Bingham, giving the opinion of the House, said that: 'To establish the crime of unlawful act manslaughter it must be shown...: (1) that the defendant committed an unlawful act; (2) that such unlawful act was a crime...'[195]

8.100 Common examples of unlawful acts for the purposes of constructive manslaughter are offences involving a battery, but the fatal commission of the *actus reus* of an assault (in its strict sense)[196] or of some other offence besides an offence of the types referred to in para 8.98 can suffice.[197] In *Cato*, for instance, the Court of Appeal, upholding a conviction for manslaughter, relied on the fact that the defendant, who had administered heroin to the deceased at the latter's request, had committed the *actus reus* of the offence of unlawfully and maliciously administering a noxious thing so as thereby to endanger life or inflict grievous bodily harm, contrary to the Offences Against the Person Act 1861, s 23. Many offences, however, will not satisfy one or both of the other requirements of constructive manslaughter, viz that the unlawful act must be a cause of death and dangerous. For example, although it is an offence under the Misuse of Drugs Act 1971, s 4(3) unlawfully to supply a controlled drug to another, this cannot amount to constructive manslaughter if the person supplied dies as a result of taking it because that act is not itself dangerous; any danger which arises will be due to what the recipient of the drug does with it.[198] In any event, if what the recipient does with the drug is free, deliberate and informed there would be no chain of causation between the offence of supplying and the death.

The importance of proving that the defendant has committed the *actus reus* of an offence was emphasised by the Court of Appeal's decision in *Arobieke*,[199] where D had been convicted of the manslaughter of V who had been electrocuted while trying to cross an electrified railway line. Fearing that D was looking for him, V had gone to a railway station to escape. There was evidence that D had gone to the station and looked in the windows of carriages. Allowing D's appeal, the Court of Appeal held (inter alia) that, although the jury could properly conclude that D had gone to the station to injure or

---

191 [1976] 1 All ER 260, CA.   192 [1999] Crim LR 65, CA.
193 [2001] EWCA Crim 2986 at [9].   194 [2002] EWCA Crim 3021.
195 [2007] UKHL 38 at [7].   196 As, for example, in *Larkin* [1943] KB 174, CCA; para 8.109.
197 The prosecution should specify the unlawful act alleged: *Jennings* [1990] Crim LR 588, CA. This has not always been done in the past: see *Kennedy (No 1)* [1999] Crim LR 65, CA.
198 *Dalby* [1982] 1 WLR 425 at 429; *Kennedy (No 2)* [2007] UKHL 38 at [7].
199 [1988] Crim LR 314, CA.

threaten V, there was no evidence of any criminally unlawful act by D; in particular, there was no assault, since D would not have put V in fear of immediate force.[200] Consequently, there could be no conviction on the basis of constructive manslaughter. It would have been different if D had put V in fear of immediate force, for example by chasing him.

Must defendant have *mens rea* for offence whose *actus reus* he has committed?

8.101 The fact that a person has committed the *actus reus* of an offence does not in itself make his act criminally unlawful; it only does so if the defendant has the *mens rea* required for that offence. To take the example of punching given above, to punch another is only criminally unlawful (a battery) if the puncher intends that his fist should hit another or is reckless as to whether it does. This means that, **as a matter of principle, the defendant's fatal act cannot be an 'unlawful act' for the purposes of constructive manslaughter unless he had the requisite *mens rea* for an offence whose *actus reus* he has committed.**

8.102 Until the House of Lords' decision in 1976 in *DPP v Newbury*,[201] it seemed clear that the law of constructive manslaughter corresponded with this statement of principle. *Lamb*,[202] decided in 1967, was a strong authority to this effect. In that case D pointed a loaded revolver at his friend, V, as a joke. D and V knew that there were two bullets in the revolving cylinder of the revolver. They believed that it was safe to pull the trigger because neither of the chambers containing a bullet was opposite the barrel and they did not know that, when the trigger was pulled, the cylinder would rotate clockwise before the firing pin struck. When the trigger was pulled, and the firing pin struck, the pin detonated a bullet in one of the two loaded chambers and V was killed. The question for the Court of Appeal was whether the trial judge had been correct to direct the jury that there had been an unlawful act for the purposes of constructive manslaughter. The Court of Appeal answered 'no'. There had been no assault or battery, which would have been required for an unlawful act; there was no assault because V was treating the thing as a joke and was therefore not put in fear of immediate force, and there was no assault (on another ground) or battery because D did not foresee that V would be alarmed or shot. (Obiter, the court held that, if properly directed, it might have been open to the jury to convict of involuntary manslaughter on another ground: killing by gross negligence.)

In *Newbury*, two teenage boys pushed part of a paving stone off a railway bridge as a train approached. The stone came through the window of the cab and killed the guard. The House of Lords, upholding the boys' conviction for manslaughter, held that a defendant is guilty of manslaughter if it is proved that he intentionally did an act which was unlawful and dangerous. Lord Salmon, with whose speech the other Law Lords concurred, held that a conviction for constructive manslaughter required proof of *mens rea* but that, as manslaughter was a crime of 'basic' as opposed to 'specific' intention, the

---

[200] The decision on the above ground might be different now in view of the liberal approach taken in recent cases to the requirement for an assault of 'fear of immediate force'; paras 7.39–7.43.

[201] [1977] AC 500, HL.   [202] [1967] 2 QB 981, CA.

necessary *mens rea* was simply 'an intention to do the acts which constitute the crime'. In his speech, Lord Edmund-Davies stated that 'what is required is no more than the *intentional* committing of an unlawful act of the designated type or nature'.

These statements appeared to be inconsistent with the previous case law. That law, however, was not expressly overruled. Lord Salmon referred to *Lamb* with approval, but only to the effect that it showed that a 'guilty mind' was required for constructive manslaughter. He did not indicate what he understood by that term in the present context.

8.103 In subsequent cases the Court of Appeal has not been uniform in its approach. In *Mitchell*,[203] it said that, for constructive manslaughter, 'there must be an act which is unlawful' and 'the act must be intentional' or, as it later expressed it, 'deliberate or intentional'. In two other cases, however, it has proceeded on the basis that the *mens rea* of the unlawful act (offence) must be proved on a charge of constructive manslaughter. For example, in *Scarlett*,[204] the Court of Appeal proceeded on the basis that, where the unlawful act in question was a battery, the full *mens rea* for a battery had to be proved, viz an intention to apply unlawful force to another or recklessness as to such force being applied. On the other hand, the statements of Lord Hope in *A-G's Reference (No 3 of 1994)*,[205] with whose speech the other Law Lords agreed, are in line with those in *Newbury*. Lord Hope said that 'All that need be proved is that he intentionally did what he did' and that 'As Lord Salmon put it in *DPP v Newbury*, manslaughter is one of those crimes in which only what is called a basic intention need be proved – that is an intention to do an act which constitutes the crime'. Lord Hope said that this was 'clear from the authorities' but he made no reference to *Lamb* or *Scarlett*, neither of which were cited to the House of Lords, and relied principally on Lord Salmon's speech in *Newbury*.

8.104 **The statements in *Newbury* and *A-G's Reference (No 3 of 1994)* are open to two interpretations. The first, which seems to be better supported by the actual words used in the speeches, is that the only state of mind that must be proved on the part of the defendant is that he deliberately or consciously did the act, ie that there was a voluntary act on his part, and that it is irrelevant whether or not the defendant had the requisite *mens rea* for an offence whose *actus reus* he has committed.** As such, the use of the word 'intention' is otiose: it merely states what is normally implied as a defence, viz that involuntary conduct is not criminal. It is noteworthy that Lord Salmon's definition of 'basic intent' differs from that adopted in other contexts, where it has been defined as involving foresight of the consequences of the *actus reus* in question. One is prompted to ask whether this difference in definition was a considered one. If the first interpretation is the correct one, the question of the unlawfulness of an act in this context must be assessed on a different basis to that otherwise used in the criminal law. It is also open to the objection that under it a defendant can be convicted of manslaughter without the *mens rea* required

---

[203] [1983] QB 741, CA.

[204] [1993] 4 All ER 629, CA. Note this case must now be read in the light of *Owino* [1996] 2 Cr App Rep 128, CA; para 16.14. See also *O'Driscoll* (1977) 65 Cr App Rep 50, CA, which decision also proceeds on the basis that the *mens rea* of the unlawful act (offence) must be proved on a constructive manslaughter charge.

[205] [1998] AC 245, HL.

for the unlawful act (offence) on which his liability is based. It would certainly be odd that, whereas a person who committed the *actus reus* of (say) a battery could not be convicted of that offence if he lacked the *mens rea* for it, he might nevertheless be convicted of manslaughter if death unexpectedly resulted.

The second interpretation, which is preferable but somewhat strained on the wording of the speeches in *Newbury and A-G's Reference (No 3 of 1994)*, is that, since an act can only be unlawful if accompanied by the relevant *mens rea*, their Lordships must have meant to imply the requirement that the defendant must have the *mens rea* for the unlawful act (offence) and that their reference to intention to do the unlawful act is simply an unnecessary reference to the need for voluntary conduct and does not purport to define exhaustively the state of mind required on the part of the defendant. If this is so, it is a great pity that their Lordships did not make the point clear. The second interpretation gains support from the fact that the case law in support of it, and inconsistent with the first interpretation, was not expressly overruled by the House of Lords in either of its two decisions. There is also some support for it in one passage in Lord Hope's speech in *A-G's Reference (No 3 of 1994)*, where he said that he considered it sufficient for manslaughter that the defendant had the *mens rea* required for an assault (the unlawful act in question). It would have been an even more supportive statement had 'necessary' been used instead of 'sufficient'. This would clearly have countered Lord Hope's other statements referred to above. The statements in *Dias*, *Andrews* and *Kennedy (No 2)* that there must be a 'criminal offence' for an act to be 'unlawful' also lend support to the second interpretation.

No unlawful act if defendant has defence to offence

8.105 An act will not be an 'unlawful act' for the purposes of constructive manslaughter if the defendant has available to him a legally recognised defence to the offence in question.[206]

Unlawful act need not be directed at the victim

8.106 In 1981, in *Dalby*,[207] the Court of Appeal stated that the unlawful act in constructive manslaughter had to be directed at the victim. In *Dalby* D was a drug addict who unlawfully supplied a controlled drug to a friend, V, in whose flat he was staying. D and V both injected themselves with the drug. Later that night someone else helped V to inject two quantities of an unspecified substance. V died the next day. In the Crown Court, D pleaded guilty to supplying a controlled drug, but not guilty to manslaughter. Dealing with constructive manslaughter, the judge directed the jury that D could be convicted if he had intentionally supplied the drug and that unlawful act had been a dangerous one and had caused V's death. The jury convicted D. Allowing D's appeal, the Court of Appeal held that, where a charge of manslaughter is based on an unlawful and dangerous act,

---

[206] See, for example, *Jennings* [1990] Crim LR 588, CA.   [207] [1982] 1 All ER 916, CA.

that act must be directed at the victim, and the unlawful act of supplying drugs had not been. As stated in para 8.100, there were other reasons why D was not guilty.

8.107 Subsequently, the import of what had been held in *Dalby* was thrown into doubt by two decisions of the Court of Appeal, *Mitchell*[208] and *Goodfellow*,[209] where that Court explained that the statement in *Dalby* did not mean what it appeared to mean. In *Mitchell*, the Court stated that 'the court [in *Dalby*] was concerned with the quality of the act rather than the identity of the person at whom it was aimed', whatever that may mean. It added that if the court in *Dalby* was saying that the unlawful act had to be directed at the victim, then that was not part of the ratio decidendi of the case; this is hard to accept. In *Mitchell*, D hit X, causing him to fall against V who died as a result. The Court of Appeal dismissed D's appeal against conviction for manslaughter on the ground that it did not matter that D's act was directed at someone other than the actual victim on whom it unexpectedly took effect. In *Goodfellow,* the Court said that *Dalby* simply meant that there must be 'no fresh intervening cause' between the unlawful act and death.[210] This explanation was not easily reconciled with the actual words of the Court of Appeal in *Dalby* but is a convenient way out. It was confirmed by Lord Hope in *A-G's Reference (No 3 of 1994)* that the unlawful act need not be directed at the victim.[211] This is to be welcomed, although it has to be said that bad decisions force subsequent courts into artificial explanations of them!

A requirement that the defendant's act be directed at the victim would exclude a substantial number of unlawful acts from the ambit of constructive manslaughter. It would also make a number of leading cases difficult to explain. For example, it is by no means obvious that the unlawful act in *DPP v Newbury* was directed at the victim.

8.108 The importance of the rule that the unlawful act need not be directed at the victim is shown by reference to the facts of *A-G's Reference (No 3 of 1994)*, described in paras 8.31 and 8.110, and of *Goodfellow*. In *Goodfellow*, D lived in a council house. He was harassed by two men and wanted to move. He had no chance of exchanging his house, so he conceived the idea of setting the house on fire as if it had been caused by a firebomb. He poured petrol over the furniture and ignited it. His wife, his girlfriend and his young son were killed. Dismissing D's appeal against conviction for manslaughter, the Court of Appeal held that a person could be convicted of constructive manslaughter despite the fact that his unlawful act was not directed at his victim.

Unlawful act must be dangerous

8.109 Not every unlawful act will suffice. At one time it was thought that death occasioned by any unlawful act would amount to manslaughter, although it was not likely to cause physical harm to anyone. It is now clear that an unlawful act causing death must be

---

208 [1983] QB 741, CA.   209 (1986) 83 Cr App Rep 23, CA.
210 As to this, see paras 2.37–2.43 and 2.45–2.55.   211 [1998] AC 245 at 274.

dangerous, in the sense that there is a risk that it will cause some harm to someone, as well as being unlawful.

This requirement was introduced in its initial form by the Court of Criminal Appeal in *Larkin* in 1942. In *Larkin*,[212] D produced a razor at the house of a man with whom his partner had been associating; D did so in order to frighten him. D's partner, who was drunk, blundered against the razor and was killed. The Court of Criminal Appeal, in dismissing an appeal against conviction for manslaughter, held that where the act which a person is engaged in performing is unlawful, then, if at the same time it is an act likely to injure another person, and that person dies, the defendant is guilty of manslaughter.

The present requirement was further explained in *Church* where the Court of Criminal Appeal said:

> 'An unlawful act causing the death of another cannot, simply because it is an unlawful act, render a manslaughter verdict inevitable. For such a verdict inexorably to follow, **the unlawful act must be such as all sober and reasonable people would inevitably recognise must subject the other person to, at least, the risk of some harm resulting therefrom, albeit not serious harm.**'[213]

This objective test, which was approved in *DPP v Newbury*,[214] is not concerned with proving a risk which the defendant must foresee, but with delimiting the type of unlawful act which will suffice for liability for manslaughter. Thus, the test is unaffected by the Criminal Justice Act 1967, s 8, which is not concerned with when foresight has to be proved but with how it is to be proved when it is required.[215] The test is satisfied where the defendant has considered whether there was a risk of harm and wrongly concluded there was none, unless a reasonable person would also have reached that conclusion.

There is a significant difference between the formulation in *Larkin*, where the Court of Criminal Appeal referred to the *likelihood* of injury, and that in *Church*, where the Court of Criminal Appeal referred to a *risk* of some harm, which is a lower level of chance. In *Carey*,[216] the Court of Appeal adopted the *Church* formulation on the ground that it was more recent, was expressly approved in *Newbury* and was more satisfactory. Thus, *Larkin* should not now be regarded as a definitive statement but simply as an important step towards the law as it now is.

The fact that an objective risk of some bodily harm suffices means that this threshold is relatively low. If the law has to have constructive manslaughter it would be better if the objective test under our law was held to relate to the risk of serious bodily harm, as has been required in the Australian case of *Wills*.[217]

---

212 [1943] KB 174, CCA. Also see *Hall* (1961) 45 Cr App Rep 366, CCA.
213 [1966] 1 QB 59 at 70. Emphasis added. Also see *Mackie* (1973) 57 Cr App Rep 453, CA.
214 [1977] AC 500, HL; para 8.102.
215 *Lipman* [1970] 1 QB 152, CA; *DPP v Newbury* [1977] AC 500 at 510, per Lord Edmund-Davies.
216 [2006] EWCA Crim 17.   217 [1983] 2 VR 201, SC of Victoria.

8.110 Although the test in *Church* was framed in terms of an objective risk that the act 'must subject the other person [ie the victim] to the risk of some harm', the House of Lords in *A-G's Reference (No 3 of 1994)*[218] held that **where the objective risk of harm is of harm not to the victim but to another person this will also render the act dangerous, and this is so even if the victim is outside any category of persons whom a reasonable person might consider potentially at risk**. The question was 'was it foreseeable that the act might harm somebody?' No doubt the reason why the formulation was expressed as it was in *Church* was the fact that the objective risk there was to the victim and the Court had that situation in mind when expressing it. As already explained, in *A-G's Reference (No 3 of 1994)*, D stabbed a pregnant woman with the intention of harming her alone. As a result of the attack, the woman went into premature labour and the child, although born alive, subsequently died because of its prematurity. The House of Lords held that, although the defendant in such a case could not be convicted of murder, he could be convicted of constructive manslaughter. On the facts of the case there was a dangerous unlawful act (stabbing the mother) because it was likely to cause harm to somebody (the mother) and the other requirements of constructive manslaughter were satisfied.

8.111 **The objective test is applied on the basis of the facts known to the defendant at the time of his unlawful act**, ie the question is whether – on the facts known to the defendant at that time – a reasonable person would have realised that the act must subject somebody to, at least, the risk of some harm resulting therefrom.[219] It follows that if, unknown to the defendant, the victim had some special susceptibility to death in the circumstances in question, this must not be taken into account in applying the objective test. In *Dawson*,[220] V, a filling station attendant, had suffered a fatal heart attack following an armed robbery by D in the course of which V was threatened with violence. There was no evidence that D knew that V suffered from a serious heart condition from which he was likely to die at any time. The Court of Appeal quashed convictions for manslaughter because the jury might have been given to understand by the judge that they could take into account the heart condition in reaching their verdict.

8.112 For the purpose of the rule that the reasonable person is endowed with such knowledge as the defendant had at the time of his unlawful act, the duration of that act is not the time, possibly very brief, when the 'unlawful act' offence is technically committed but instead is that period in which the act can be said in commonsense terms to continue. In *Watson*,[221] D had entered a house as a trespasser with intent to steal (and thereby committed an unlawful act, a burglary) and, while in the house, had discovered that it was occupied by V, a frail, 87-year-old man, who died from a heart attack an hour and a half later. The Court of Appeal held that the unlawful act comprised the whole of the burglarious intrusion and did not end with D's entry. Consequently, it held, the trial judge had correctly directed the jury that D's knowledge of the V's age and frailty, acquired during that intrusion, could be attributed to the reasonable person.

---

[218] [1998] AC 245, HL.
[220] (1985) 81 Cr App Rep 150, CA.

[219] *Dawson* (1985) 81 Cr App Rep 150, CA.
[221] [1989] 2 All ER 865, CA.

8.113 By way of limitation on *Dawson*, it must be remembered that the reasonable person does not make unreasonable mistakes. Thus, in *Ball*,[222] D's unreasonably mistaken belief that the live cartridge which he loaded into a gun was a blank was not imputed into the reasonable person's appreciation of the risk.

8.114 **The 'harm' referred to in the test in *Church* is physical harm.** This was affirmed by the Court of Appeal in *Dawson*,[223] where it was held that the risk of emotional disturbance produced by terror is not enough; but it assumed that it would be if the risk of physical harm (eg a heart attack) from shock emanating from fright was reasonably foreseeable. In *Carey*,[224] the Court of Appeal noted the difference between emotional disturbance and shock and stated that, had the evidence supported it, the jury could have been allowed to consider whether there was a risk of physical harm emanating from shock. *Dawson* and *Carey* can be contrasted with other decisions to the effect that where actual bodily harm is in issue in other contexts it includes an identifiable psychiatric injury.[225]

8.115 One result of *Dawson* is that, although it is possible to commit constructive manslaughter by frightening a person (an assault) with fatal consequences, such cases will not be very common in practice because in normal circumstances a reasonable person would not realise that frightening a person gave rise to a risk of causing somebody physical harm.

8.116 Very often, a person who commits an unlawful and dangerous act will himself realise the risk of some physical harm to another resulting, but the important thing about the present requirement is that such a person can be convicted of constructive manslaughter even though he does not realise this risk, provided that a reasonable person with the defendant's knowledge of the facts would realise the risk of physical harm.

Unlawful and dangerous act must cause death

8.117 Not only must an unlawful and dangerous act on the defendant's part be proved, but it must also be proved that that unlawful and dangerous act, as opposed to any other act by the defendant, caused the death of the victim.[226] There must be no intervening act or event which would break the chain of causation between the unlawful act and the death.[227] The unlawful and dangerous act need not have been the only cause, but it must have been a substantial cause of the death of another human being, in the sense that it

---

[222] [1989] Crim LR 730, CA.

[223] (1985) 81 Cr App Rep 150, CA. See Stallworthy 'Can Death by Shock be Manslaughter?' (1986) 136 NLJ 51; Busuttil and McCall-Smith 'Fright, Stress and Homicide' (1990) 54 JCL 257.

[224] [2006] EWCA Crim 17 at [37].

[225] *Chan-Fook* [1994] 2 All ER 552, CA; para 7.59.

[226] See, for example, *Mitchell* [1983] QB 741, CA; *Williams* [1992] 2 All ER 183, CA; *Evans* [1992] Crim LR 659, CA; *Carey* [2006] EWCA Crim 17.

[227] See paras 2.28–2.57.

contributed more than negligibly to it. This is, of course, in line with the normal rules of causation. The present requirement was stated as follows by Lord Woolf MR (as he then was) in *Inner South London Coroner, ex p Douglas-Williams*:[228]

> '[I]t is an essential ingredient that the unlawful...act must have caused the death at least in the manner described [ie more than a minute or negligible contribution]. If there is a situation where, on examination of the evidence, it cannot be said that the death in question was caused by an act which was unlawful...as I have described, then a critical link in the chain of causation is not established.'

The point was repeated by the House of Lords in *Kennedy (No 2)*.[229]

The present point was in issue in *Carey*,[230] where the defendants had been convicted of affray (which requires a person to use or threaten another in such a way as to cause a person of reasonable firmness present at the scene to fear for his personal safety) and manslaughter by an unlawful and dangerous act, after they had confronted the deceased (V) and her friends. During the confrontation one of them had punched V who fled. Later V, an apparently healthy 15-year-old, died from a heart attack which was most likely to have been precipitated by her flight. The Court of Appeal quashed the manslaughter convictions because the punch, which certainly was an unlawful and dangerous act, had not caused the death, and the act and threats used in the course of the affray were not in themselves dangerous acts.

8.118 The Court of Appeal's decision in *DJ and* others[231] illustrates the difficulty that can arise in proving a causal link between an unlawful and dangerous act and the deceased's death. In that case a gang of youths, including the five defendants, approached V while he was playing cricket with his son on a tennis court at a leisure centre. An exchange of words took place between members of the gang and V which led to abuse being directed towards V and his son. This escalated into spitting by some of the gang at V and ultimately stones and pieces of wood being thrown at V; at least one of the stones hit V on the head. Very shortly after being hit, V died of a heart attack. There was no real doubt that the defendants had caused V's death but there was doubt as to whether the irregular heart rhythm (arrhythmia) that led to the heart attack was triggered by the unlawful and dangerous acts involved in the throwing of the stones and wood or whether it had already been triggered by the earlier spitting and verbal abuse which, although it may have involved unlawful acts, did not involve dangerous acts. The Court of Appeal quashed the defendants' convictions for manslaughter because the possibility that the earlier spitting and verbal abuse was the sole cause of the arrhythmia and consequent death could not safely be excluded.

---

[228] [1999] 1 All ER 344 at 350.
[230] [2006] EWCA Crim 17, [2006] CA.

[229] [2007] UKHL 38 at [7].
[231] [2007] EWCA Crim 3133.

Manslaughter by killing with gross negligence

Key points 8.8

The requirements for manslaughter by gross negligence are:

- the defendant must have owed a duty of care to the victim; and
- there must have been a gross breach of that duty by the defendant; and
- that breach must have caused the death.

8.119 As stated in para 8.96, the continued existence of this type of involuntary man-slaughter was affirmed by the House of Lords in *Adomako*.[232] In *Adomako*, D was the anaesthetist during an eye operation. A disconnection occurred in a tube which ena-bled the patient (V) to breathe by mechanical means. D failed to notice or remedy this. As a result the supply of oxygen to V ceased and nine minutes later V had a cardiac arrest and died. Four and a half minutes after the disconnection, an alarm sounded on the machine which monitored V's blood pressure. D checked the equipment and administered atropine, but at no stage before the cardiac arrest did he check the tube connection. At D's trial for manslaughter, at which two expert witnesses had described D's conduct as 'abysmal' and 'as a gross dereliction of duty', the judge directed the jury that the test to be applied was whether D was guilty of gross negligence. The jury convicted D, who appealed on the ground that the judge had been wrong so to direct the jury. The Court of Appeal dismissed the appeal, and so did the House of Lords, on the ground that a direction in terms of gross negligence had been the appropriate direction.

Lord Mackay LC, with whom the rest of the House of Lords agreed, having reviewed *Bateman*[233] and *Andrews v DPP*,[234] the previous leading cases on manslaughter by gross negligence, concluded that those two cases provided a satisfactory basis for the offence. According to Lord Mackay's speech:

'...the ordinary principles of the law of negligence apply to ascertain whether or not the defendant has been in breach of a duty of care towards the victim who has died. If such breach of duty is established the next question is whether that breach of duty caused the death of the victim. If so, the jury must go on to consider whether that breach of duty should be characterised as gross negligence and therefore as a crime.'[235]

As a result, gross negligence manslaughter can be proved without the need to inquire into the defendant's state of mind.[236]

---

[232] [1995] 1 AC 171, HL.   [233] (1925) 19 Cr App Rep 8, CCA.
[234] [1937] AC 576, HL.   [235] [1995] 1 AC 171 at 187.
[236] This was confirmed in *A-G's Reference (No 2 of 1999)* [2000] QB 796, CA.

8.120 Lord Mackay's statement in *Adomako* gives rise to the following requirements, which he derived from *Bateman* and *Andrews v DPP* and which have been held to be sufficiently precisely defined to satisfy the ECHR, Article 7.[237]

Duty of care to the victim

8.121 Under the 'ordinary principles of the law of negligence' referred to by Lord Mackay in *Adomako*, the determination of the existence of a duty of care has been summarised as follows by Lord Bridge in *Caparo Industries plc v Dickman:*

> '...in addition to the foreseeability [ie reasonable foreseeability] of damage, necessary ingredients in any situation giving rise to a duty of care are that there should exist between the party owing the duty and the party to whom it is owed a relationship characterised by the law as one of 'proximity' or 'neighbourhood' and that the situation should be one in which the court considers it fair, just and reasonable that the law should impose a duty of a given scope upon the one party for the benefit of the other.'[238]

As has been pointed out,[239] only very rarely can it be said that even though the victim's death was reasonably foreseeable there was no proximity between them, or that it was not fair, just and reasonable to impose a duty of care.

8.122 Despite Lord Mackay's unqualified reference to the 'ordinary principles of the law of negligence', it is clear from the decision of the Court of Appeal in *Wacker*[240] that that reference is not to be understood to mean that the duty of care in manslaughter should automatically correspond with that in tort, whose existence is influenced by considerations of public policy about who should bear the loss.

In *Wacker,* 60 illegal Chinese immigrants were loaded into D's container lorry near Rotterdam. The only way that air could get into the container was through a vent. Shortly before arriving at Zeebrugge D closed the vent. By the time that the container was searched on disembarkation at Dover, 58 of those inside it had died of suffocation. D was charged with 58 offences of manslaughter and convicted of all of them. He appealed unsuccessfully to the Court of Appeal against these convictions. He contended that he did not owe a duty of care to any of the 58 for the purposes of manslaughter because they and D were participants in the criminal activity of seeking to enter the United Kingdom illegally and one of the 'ordinary principles of the law of negligence' was that it did not recognise a duty of care between participants in a criminal activity; this is undoubtedly

---

[237] *Misra and Srivastava* [2004] EWCA Crim 2375. As to Art 7 see para 1.60.

[238] [1990] 2 AC 605 at 617–618.

[239] Herring and Palser 'The Duty of Care in Gross Negligence Manslaughter' [2007] Crim LR 24 at 30. Indeed, as the authors point out there are dicta that where the nature of the harm suffered is direct physical harm, as in manslaughter by gross negligence cases, reasonable foreseeability of the risk is the only test that need be applied to determine whether a duty of care exists: *Alcock v Chief Constable of South Yorkshire Police* [1992] 1 AC 310 at 396, per Lord Keith; *Perrett v Collins* [1998] 2 Lloyd's Rep 255 at 262, per Hobhouse LJ.

[240] [2002] EWCA Crim 1944.

an ordinary principle of the law of tort under the principle *ex turpi causa non oritur actio* (an action cannot be founded on an illegal cause).

The Court of Appeal rejected this argument. It held that the criminal law should not be disapplied simply because the civil law was (as a matter of policy) disapplied. The criminal law had its own public policy aim (the protection of citizens and giving effect to the state's duty to try those who have deprived citizens of life, limb or property) which might require it to be applied where public policy did not require the law of tort to apply. There was no justification for concluding that the criminal law should decline to hold a person criminally liable for the death of another simply because he and the victim were engaged in some joint unlawful activity, or, indeed, because there might have been some element of acceptance of risk by the victim in order to advance the joint unlawful activity. It added that:

> 'In so far as Lord Mackay referred to "ordinary principles of the law of negligence" we do not accept for one moment that he was intending to decide that the rules relating to *ex turpi causa* were part of those ordinary principles. He was doing no more than holding that in an "ordinary" case of negligence, the question whether there was a duty of care was to be judged by the same legal criteria as governed whether there was a duty of care in the law of negligence. That was the only issue relevant to the case...'[241]

In practice it will normally not be difficult to establish whether there was a duty of care, where it is alleged a duty of care existed and manslaughter is in issue. However, where the allegation is that death was caused by a failure to act, it must not be forgotten that it is not enough that it was reasonably foreseeable that the defendant's negligent failure to act would imperil the victim because there can only be liability if the defendant was legally obliged to do the act which he is alleged to have failed to have done.[242]

8.123 The decision of the Court of Appeal in *Evans (Gemma)*[243] provides an example of a situation where a legal duty to act (and therefore a duty of care) can arise for the purposes of manslaughter by gross negligence. The Court held that, for the purposes of gross negligence manslaughter, when a person had created or contributed to the creation of a state of affairs which he knew, or ought reasonably to have known, had become life-threatening to another person, a consequent duty would normally arise on him to act by taking reasonable steps to save the other's life.

In *Evans (Gemma)*, D purchased some heroin which she handed to V, her 16-year-old half-sister. V self-injected the heroin in the house where she lived with D and their mother and she then proceeded to develop and complain of symptoms consistent with an overdose. D appreciated that V's condition was very serious and indicative of an overdose and, together with her mother, she believed that she was responsible for V's care. D and her mother decided not to seek medical assistance because they feared that they, and possibly V, would get into trouble. They put V to bed, hoping that she would recover spontaneously, and remained at the house, checking on V periodically and then sleeping in

---

[241] [2002] EWCA Crim 1944 at [37].   [242] See para 2.11.   [243] [2009] EWCA Crim 650.

the same room as her. The following morning V was dead. The cause of death was heroin poisoning. D was charged with manslaughter.

D could not have been guilty of manslaughter on the basis of her act of supplying the heroin, because V took it freely, voluntarily and informedly and therefore broke the chain of causation between D's act and her death. Thus, the question was whether D was guilty of gross negligence manslaughter on the basis of her subsequent omission to get medical help for V. The jury convicted D of gross negligence manslaughter after the judge had ruled that on the facts D could owe a duty of care to V.

D appealed unsuccessfully to the Court of Appeal. The question for the Court of Appeal was whether, notwithstanding that D and V's relationship lacked the features of familial duty which marked D's mother's relationship with V, D was under a duty to take reasonable steps for V's safety once D appreciated that the heroin she had procured for V was having a potentially fatal effect on V. Relying on *Miller*, discussed in para 2.13, a full (ie five-judge) Court of Appeal held that D was under such a duty. It held that, for the purposes of gross negligence manslaughter, if a person created or contributed to the creation of a state of affairs which he knew, or ought reasonably to have known, had become life-threatening, a consequent duty on him to act by taking reasonable steps to save the other's life would normally arise.[244]

8.124 Before *Evans (Gemma)*, it was a matter of dispute whether the existence of a duty of care in a particular case was *purely* a question of law for the judge,[245] or whether the judge's task was simply to rule whether a duty of care *could* arise on the facts, leaving it to the jury to decide in the light of the judge's direction whether it actually did arise.[246] In principle, the latter is preferable; it is normally the jury's function to determine whether or not an element of an offence is proved (albeit on the basis of a direction on the relevant law from the judge).

The conflict between the cases was resolved by the Court of Appeal in *Evans (Gemma)*, where it was held that the correct view of the law was the latter one. The Court of Appeal held that, although the existence, or otherwise, of a duty of care, or a duty to act, ie whether a duty could arise on the facts, was a stark question of law, the question whether the facts actually established the existence of the duty was for the jury. It added that in some cases, such as those arising from a doctor/patient relationship where the existence of the duty was not in dispute, the judge might well direct the jury that a duty existed. Such a direction would be proper. However, it said, in any cases where the issue was in dispute, and assuming that the judge had found that it would be open to the jury to find that there was a duty of care, or a duty to act, ie a duty could arise on the facts, the jury should be directed that if facts (a) plus (b) and/or (c) or (d) were established, then in law a

---

[244] For critical discussions of the aspect of *Evans (Gemma)* dealt with in this paragraph see Rogers 'Death, Drugs and Duties' [2009] 6 Archbold News 6; Williams 'Gross Negligence Manslaughter and Duty of Care in "Drugs" Cases' [2009] Crim LR 631.

[245] The view taken in *Singh* [1999] Crim LR 582, CA.

[246] The view favoured in *Khan and Khan* [1998] Crim LR 830, CA; *Sinclair* (1998) 148 NLJ 1353, CA; and *Willoughby* [2004] EWCA Crim 3365.

duty would arise, but if facts (x) or (y) or (z) were present, the duty would be negatived. On the facts, the Court of Appeal held, D was under a plain and obvious duty to take reasonable steps to assist or provide assistance for V. The remaining ingredients of the offence were proved. D's appeal was therefore dismissed.

Gross breach of duty of care

8.125 Normally, proof of negligence simply involves proof that, whether or not he realised the risk (of which he should have been aware), the person subject to the duty did something, or failed to do something, in a way which fell below the standard of conduct expected of a reasonable person in all the circumstances (including the defendant's expertise and training, if they are relevant in the context). In the case of gross negligence, however, it is not enough that the defendant's conduct fell, however slightly, below the standard of care to be expected, as it would be in an action in tort or in a prosecution for careless driving. In *Bateman*[247] the Court of Criminal Appeal stated that gross negligence required that:

> 'the negligence of the accused went beyond a mere matter of compensation between subjects and showed such disregard for the life and safety of others, as to amount to a crime against the State and conduct deserving of punishment.'[248]

8.126 For there to be liability for manslaughter by gross negligence:

- **The defendant's conduct must have involved a reasonably foreseeable risk of the death of another.** This point which can be gathered from Lord Mackay's speech in *Adomako* was confirmed by the Court of Appeal in *Singh*,[249] where the Court approved the judge's direction that a risk merely of injury or even of serious injury would not do, and in *Misra and Srivastava*,[250] where the Court held that the relevant risk had to be of death, not merely a risk of bodily injury or injury to health. It is not enough that the reasonably foreseeable risk of death was a remote risk; the circumstances must be such that a reasonably prudent person would have foreseen a serious and obvious risk of death.[251] Indeed, according to the Privy Council in *Brown (Uriah) v R*,[252] the defendant's conduct must be such as to create a very high degree of risk of death.

- As Lord Mackay's speech in *Adomako* indicates, in respect of the reasonably foreseeable risk of death the defendant's conduct in all the circumstances in which he was placed must have fallen so far below the standard to be expected of a reasonable person, ie be so bad, that it should be judged criminal. There is force in

---

[247] (1925) 19 Cr App Rep 8, CCA.   [248] (1925) 19 Cr App Rep 8 at 11.
[249] [1999] Crim LR 582, CA. Also see *R (on the application of Lewin) v CPS* [2002] EWHC 1049 (Admin), DC.
[250] [2004] EWCA Crim 2375. See also *Yaqoob* [2005] EWCA Crim 2169.
[251] *Singh* [1999] Crim LR 582, CA; *Yaqoob* [2005] EWCA Crim 2169.   [252] [2005] UKPC 18.

the argument[253] that, since careless driving is also criminal, the question must be whether the conduct was so bad as to be condemned as the very grave crime of manslaughter. Otherwise, the element of grossness of the negligence is inadequately conveyed.

The requirement of a risk of death can be compared with the lower requirement of a risk of some physical harm in constructive manslaughter. The objective nature of manslaughter by gross negligence would be particularly open to objection if the risk required had only to relate to the risk of non-fatal injury.

8.127 In *Adomako,* Lord Mackay LC said that whether there has been a gross breach of duty of care:

> 'will depend on the seriousness of the breach of duty committed by the defendant in all the circumstances in which the defendant was placed when it occurred. The jury will have to consider whether the extent to which the defendant's conduct departed from the proper standard of care incumbent upon him, involving as it must have done a risk of death…, was such that it should be judged criminal.'[254]

Lord Mackay continued:

> 'It is true that to a certain extent this involves an element of circularity, but in this branch of the law I do not believe that is fatal to its being correct as a test of how far conduct must depart from accepted standards to be characterised as criminal. This is necessarily a question of degree and an attempt to specify that degree more closely is I think likely to achieve only a spurious precision. The essence of the matter, which is supremely a jury question, is whether, having regard to the risk of death involved, the conduct of the defendant was so bad in all the circumstances as to amount in their judgement to a criminal act or omission.'[255]

While the above approach may be a workable one, it does mean that what constitutes gross negligence comes down to a moral judgement by the jury.

8.128 Although evidence of the defendant's state of mind is not a prerequisite to liability for manslaughter by gross negligence, there may be cases where his state of mind is relevant to the issue of the criminality of his conduct.[256] For example, a defendant who is reckless as to a risk to his victim, even if he only foresaw a risk of injury to that person's health and welfare, 'may well be the more readily found to be grossly negligent to a criminal degree'.[257]

---

[253] See commentary to *Litchfield* [1998] Crim LR 507 at 508.   [254] *Adomako* [1995] 1 AC 171 at 187.

[255] *Adomako* [1995] 1 AC 171 at 187.   [256] *A-G's Reference (No 2 of 1999)* [2000] QB 796 at 809.

[257] *A-G's Reference (No 2 of 1999)* [2000] QB 796 at 809; *DPP, ex p Jones* [2000] IRLR 373, DC.

Breach of duty must cause death

8.129 This, the third limb of negligence, according to the 'ordinary principles of negligence', simply involves the application of the rules on causation discussed in paras 2.28 to 2.57. As Lord Woolf MR (as he then was) said in *Inner South London Coroner, ex p Douglas-Williams*:

> '[I]t is an essential ingredient that the...negligent act must have caused the death at least in the manner described [ie more than a minute or negligible contribution]. If there is a situation where, on examination of the evidence, it cannot be said that the death in question was caused by an act which was...negligent as I have described, then a critical link in the chain of causation is not established.'[258]

It must not be forgotten that there will not be a causal link if the death would still have occurred even if there had not been the grossly negligent conduct on the defendant's part.[259]

Abolition of corporate liability for manslaughter by gross negligence

8.130 As noted in para 8.142, the common law offence of manslaughter by gross negligence is abolished in its application to corporations, or any other organisation which can commit corporate manslaughter to which it might have applied, except in relation to an offence committed wholly or partly before 6 April 2008.

Manslaughter by killing with recklessness as to death or serious bodily harm

8.131 It will be recalled that a person is reckless as to a risk if he himself foresees that risk as a consequence of his conduct and he takes that risk, and in all the circumstances it is an unreasonable risk for him to take.[260] Prior to the House of Lords' decision in *Seymour*[261] there was authority that it was manslaughter to kill another with the appropriate degree of recklessness.[262] As with manslaughter by gross negligence, *Seymour* threw doubt on the survival of this species of manslaughter. Just as the overruling of *Seymour* led the House of Lords in *Adomako*[263] to recognise the continued existence of manslaughter by gross negligence, so, it seemed, did it have to be recognised that recklessness of the appropriate degree could still provide the *mens rea* for involuntary manslaughter. Support for this statement could be found in an obiter dictum by Lord Mackay LC in *Adomako*.[264] Doubt seemed to be cast, however, on this submission in two post-*Adomako* decisions where

---

[258] [1999] 1 All ER 344 at 350.   [259] *Dalloway* (1847) 2 Cox CC 273; para 2.30.

[260] Paras 3.32–3.34.   [261] [1983] 2 AC 493, HL.

[262] *Pike* [1961] Crim LR 547, CCA; *Gray v Barr* [1971] 2 QB 554 at 577, per Salmon LJ; *Stone and Dobinson* [1977] QB 354, CA.

[263] [1995] 1 AC 171, HL.   [264] [1995] 1 AC 171 at 187.

the Court of Appeal, without a discussion of the matter, appeared to regard involuntary manslaughter as consisting only of two types: constructive manslaughter and manslaughter by gross negligence.[265] Subsequently, however, in *Lidar*,[266] the Court of Appeal affirmed that there remained a separate species of involuntary manslaughter based on recklessness.

In *Lidar*, D, as a result of a dispute, drove his car away from a pub. V, who was hanging from the window, with his body half in the car, was carried 225 metres before his feet were caught in a wheel and he fell to the ground. V was run over and died from his injuries. D appealed unsuccessfully against his conviction for manslaughter on the ground that the trial judge had been wrong to direct the jury in terms of recklessness and should have directed them in terms of gross negligence. The Court of Appeal held that nothing in *Adomako* suggested that recklessness could no longer be a basis for proving involuntary manslaughter, and that – since a recklessness direction was necessary – a gross negligence direction would have been 'superfluous and unnecessary'.

Lidar clarified the risk which the defendant must actually foresee in order to be guilty of the present type of involuntary manslaughter. According to the case law preceding *Seymour* referred to above, it was not necessary that the defendant should have been reckless as to the risk of death resulting since it sufficed that the defendant foresaw bodily harm as a risk;[267] indeed, in one case the Court of Appeal held that foresight of the risk of an injury to health and welfare sufficed.[268] In *Lidar*, however, the Court of Appeal held that the defendant must have been reckless as to the risk of serious injury. In addition, the Court indicated that recklessness bears a special meaning in the present context. Normally, a person satisfies the definition of recklessness, in terms of foresight of risk, if he foresees the risk in question as a possible consequence of his conduct and takes the unreasonable risk of it occurring. In *Lidar*, it was held that, **for present purposes, the defendant must foresee the risk of serious injury as highly probable and take the unreasonable risk of it. A fortiori, someone who foresees the risk of death as highly probable and unreasonably runs it satisfies this test.**

8.132 The present type of involuntary manslaughter will often overlap with constructive manslaughter and manslaughter by gross negligence, but it will not do so where the fatal act is not otherwise 'unlawful' (as that term is defined for the purposes of constructive manslaughter) and, although the defendant knowingly takes the unreasonable risk of serious bodily harm, there is no risk of death and/or no gross breach of a duty of care (which will be unusual). No doubt the overlap with the other two types of involuntary manslaughter is the reason why this species of involuntary manslaughter is not commonly prosecuted and the reason why Lord Bingham, giving the opinion of the House of Lords in *Kennedy (No 2)*, regarded it as 'well-established and not in any way controversial

---

[265] *Khan and Khan* [1998] Crim LR 830, CA; *Inner South London Coroner, ex p Douglas-Williams* [1999] 1 All ER 344, CA.

[266] [2000] 4 Archbold News 3, CA.   [267] *Pike* [1961] Crim LR 547, CCA.

[268] *Stone and Dobinson* [1977] QB 354, CA.

that a charge of manslaughter may be founded either on the unlawful act of the defendant ("unlawful act manslaughter") or on the gross negligence of the defendant'.[269]

Conclusions on involuntary manslaughter

8.133 Similar problems are raised by each of the first two types of involuntary manslaughter. Why should someone be liable to a maximum punishment of life imprisonment if he inadvertently causes death by a common assault for which he could not receive more than a minimal term of imprisonment if he had not caused death? Why should someone who grossly negligently causes death be liable to be convicted of manslaughter whereas, had he 'merely' caused serious bodily harm, he would not have been guilty of any offence against the person (since there is no general offence of causing non-fatal bodily harm by negligence) and probably of no offence at all, particularly when whether or not the victim dies may depend on pure chance, such as the skill of a surgeon?

Reform

8.134 In its report, *Murder, Manslaughter and Infanticide*, published in 2006,[270] the Law Commission has recommended that there should be two offences of manslaughter which would replace the existing offences of involuntary manslaughter:

'(1) killing another person through gross negligence ("gross negligence manslaughter"); or

(2) killing another person:
 (a) through the commission of a criminal act intended by the defendant to cause injury, or
 (b) through the commission of a criminal act that the defendant was aware involved a serious risk of causing some injury ("criminal act manslaughter").'[271]

Manslaughter would continue to be punishable with a maximum of imprisonment for life.

The definition of causing death by gross negligence would be as follows. It would be manslaughter of this type if:

'(1) a person by his or her conduct causes the death of another;

(2) a risk that his or her conduct will cause death would be obvious to a reasonable person in his or her position;

---

[269] [2007] UKHL 38 at [6].

[270] Law Com No 304, paras 2.159–2.165 and 3.41–3.60, and Appendix A, paras A.3–A.4. For previous recommendations for the reform of involuntary manslaughter see the Law Commission: *Legislating the Criminal Code: Involuntary Manslaughter*, Law Com No 237 (1996).

[271] Law Com No 304, para 2.163.

(3) he or she is capable of appreciating that risk at the material time; and

(4) his or her conduct falls far below what can reasonably be expected of him or her in the circumstances.'[272]

The reference to the defendant's capability to appreciate the risk of death avoids the rigours of the wholly objective approach inherent in the current law of manslaughter by gross negligence. The last part of the definition of the recommended offence avoids the circularity of the existing definition of gross negligence. A satisfactory answer has yet to be given to the question why gross negligence should suffice for liability when it has resulted in death but not when it has resulted in some personal injury, including serious injury.

While the recommendation relating to criminal act manslaughter is slightly less draconian than unlawful and dangerous act manslaughter, because it replaces the objective test of dangerousness with a requirement that the defendant must at least be aware of a serious risk of causing injury, the need for this offence has not satisfactorily been demonstrated. The illegal violence in question can be dealt with by the armoury of non-fatal offences. Why should the defendant be guilty of manslaughter because of an unforeseen, and unforeseeable, occurrence, if he was unaware of the risk of serious injury?

Given that manslaughter is intended to be the third tier of its proposed ladder of general homicide offences,[273] it is puzzling that the Law Commission ultimately recommended against a fixed maximum period of imprisonment and settled instead for a maximum of life imprisonment, the same maximum as would apply to the offence of second-degree murder under its recommendations.

Infanticide

8.135 The Infanticide Act 1938 (IA 1938), s 1, as amended by the Coroners and Justice Act 2009, s 57 (the amendments are italicised), provides:

'(1) Where a woman by any wilful act or omission causes the death of her child being a child under the age of 12 months, but at the time of the act or omission the balance of her mind was disturbed by reason of her not having fully recovered from the effect of giving birth to the child or by reason of the effect of lactation consequent upon the birth of the child, then, *if* the circumstances were such that but for this Act the offence would have amounted to murder *or manslaughter*, she shall be guilty of an offence, to wit of infanticide, and may for such offence be dealt with and punished as if she had been guilty of the offence of manslaughter of the child.

(2) Where upon the trial of a woman for the murder of her child, being a child under the age of 12 months, the jury are of opinion that she by any wilful act or omission caused its death, but that at the time of the act or omission the balance of her mind

---

[272] Law Com No 304, para 3.60.   [273] Para 8.38.

> was disturbed by reason of her not having fully recovered from the effect of giving birth to the child or by reason of the effect of lactation consequent upon the birth of the child, then the jury may, *if* the circumstances were such that but for the provisions of this Act they might have returned a verdict of murder *or manslaughter*, return in lieu thereof a verdict of infanticide.'

Thus, infanticide can either be charged in the first instance as the offence of infanticide (s 1(1)) or serve as a partial defence reducing liability from murder or manslaughter to infanticide (s 1(2)). The offence, and defence, of infanticide were originally created by the Infanticide Act 1922. Their obvious purpose was to mitigate the rigours of the law relating to murder, especially the mandatory death sentence which then applied. They have no application to unborn children, but only to those who attain an existence independent of the mother.

The amendments to s 1 come into force on 4 October 2010. Until then the unamended version of s 1 will appear on the companion website to this book.

8.136 Prior to the amendments, the Court of Appeal in *Gore*[274] had ruled that there was no requirement that the offence of infanticide only applied where the *mens rea* for murder was proved. It held that the *mens rea* of the offence was contained expressly in the first few words of the IA 1938, s 1(1), viz a requirement of proof that the act or omission was wilful. There was no reference to any intention to kill or cause serious bodily harm; and if there was such a requirement, the use of the word 'wilful' would be superfluous. Further, the Court of Appeal held, the section created an offence in s 1(1) and it also provided a partial defence and possible alternative verdict to murder in s 1(2). If s 1(1) had been intended to be used only where the mental element for murder was proved, s 1(2) would be superfluous since the offence created by s 1(1) could always have been left open to the jury as an alternative charge to murder. The view adopted in *Gore* came as a surprise; it had previously been assumed that the offence under s 1(1) required proof of the *mens rea* for murder. *Gore* extended the offence to a much wider range of cases where a child dies. It took the offence far beyond its original mischief.

8.137 An effect of *Gore* was to make it possible for a woman to be charged with infanticide in cases which would not otherwise be an offence of homicide at all. This was because the phrase 'wilful act or omission' in the IA 1938, s 1(1) in its original form was open to the interpretation that it included negligence falling below the level of gross negligence – or, even, that it simply referred to a mere voluntary act or omission without reference to negligence – neither of which would involve liability for involuntary manslaughter. In its consultation paper, *Murder, Manslaughter and Infanticide: Proposals for Reform of the Law*, referred to in para 8.38, the Government, while accepting that the offence of infanticide did not require proof of the *mens rea* for murder, thought that this possibility was an unintended one and that such a widening of the law was inappropriate. The amendments

---

[274] [2007] EWCA Crim 2789.

to s 1(1) are designed to make it clear that infanticide cannot be charged in cases that would not otherwise be murder or manslaughter.[275]

8.138 The defence of infanticide under the IA 1938, s 1(2), as amended, enables a woman to plead as a defence to murder or manslaughter mental disturbance of such a nature as would not amount to insanity under the rule in *M'Naghten's Case*,[276] although it would now often amount on a murder charge to a defence of diminished responsibility. Legally, infanticide is strictly limited to the conditions laid down in the Act, and the fact that the deceased child was less than 12 months old is not sufficient unless there is also evidence that the balance of the mother's mind was disturbed for one of the stated reasons.[277]

Although the mother who raises infanticide as a defence on a murder or manslaughter charge must adduce evidence sufficient to raise the defence, the burden of disproving it rests on the Crown; infanticide as a defence differs from the defences of insanity and diminished responsibility where the burden of proving the defence is on the defendant.[278]

8.139 In *Kai-Whitewind*,[279] the Court of Appeal regarded the law of infanticide as unsatisfactory and outdated because IA 1938, s 1(1) does not include the common case where the balance of the mother's mind is disturbed by environmental or other stress subsequent to the birth and connected with it, but not consequent on birth. It called for urgent reform. It will be noted that no amendment has been made to address this concern of the Court of Appeal, nor to take account of cases where the mother's mind was disturbed by reason of circumstances (other than the effect of lactation) consequent on birth.

Other homicide offences: (1) corporate manslaughter

> **Key points 8.9**
>
> A corporation (or other organisation of a specified type) is guilty of the offence of corporate manslaughter if the way in which its activities are managed or organised causes a person's death and amounts to a gross breach of a relevant duty of care owed by the organisation to the deceased person.

8.140 A corporation, such as an incorporated company, a limited liability partnership under the Limited Liability Partnership Act 2000 or a local authority, is a separate person in law. A limited company, for example, is distinct from its shareholders (otherwise called

---

[275] *Murder, Manslaughter and Infanticide: Proposals for Reform of the Law* Ministry of Justice, Consultation Paper 19/08, para 125.
[276] Paras 15.16–15.47.　[277] *Soanes* [1948] 1 All ER 289, CCA.
[278] Paras 4.7 and 8.61.　[279] [2005] EWCA Crim 1092.

members), its directors and its employees. As is explained in Chapter 18,[280] a corporation is criminally liable for an offence requiring *mens rea* if it can be proved that an individual whose acts and state of mind can be attributable to the corporation committed the *actus reus* for that offence with the appropriate *mens rea* when acting within the scope of his office. In the case of a common law offence and some statutory offences a person must be part of the directing mind and will of the corporation in order to be identified with it.

Until the Corporate Manslaughter and Corporate Homicide Act 2007 came into force it was possible to convict a corporation on this basis of the common law offence of manslaughter by gross negligence. However, it was difficult to secure such a conviction, especially if the corporation was a large- or medium-sized one. Corporations have only been convicted of manslaughter by gross negligence in eight cases (all of which have concerned small companies).[281]

The failure of prosecutions against corporations after the capsizing of the *Herald of Free Enterprise* and the Paddington and Hatfield train crashes, and the failure of manslaughter prosecutions against corporations in 24 other cases between 1992 and 2005, heightened awareness of the difficulty of convicting a corporation of manslaughter, on the basis of gross negligence, because of the need to find the elements of the offence proved on the part of an individual controlling officer. The immediate cause of the death will usually be an operational failure of systems controlling the risk associated with the carelessness of individuals who are junior employees; while this may result from the corporation's failure to have effective management control systems, that failing cannot be 'pinned' on an individual identifiable with the corporation.

It was for this reason that the Corporate Manslaughter and Corporate Homicide[282] Act 2007 (CMCHA 2007) was enacted. The Act can trace its roots back to a Law Commission report, published in 1996,[283] which recommended a new offence of corporate manslaughter. In 2005, the Government published for consultation a draft Corporate Manslaughter Bill,[284] from which the CMCHA 2007 differs in a number of significant respects. The CMCHA 2007, s 1 established the offence of corporate manslaughter whose terms avoid the difficulties experienced under the general principles of corporate liability by abandoning the need to pin the guilt on an individual identifiable with the corporation in favour

---

[280] Paras 18.23–18.43.

[281] See www.corporateaccountability.org/manslaughter/cases/main.htm. Prior to these cases it had been held in judicial review proceedings that a corporation could be held guilty of manslaughter: *HM Coroner for East Kent, ex p Spooner* (1989) 88 Cr App Rep 10, DC, and it had been ruled at a criminal trial that a charge of manslaughter against a corporation was recognised in law, although the judge subsequently directed acquittals on the ground that there was no case to answer on the facts: *P & O European Ferries (Dover) Ltd* (1991) 93 Cr App Rep 71, Crown Ct. There is implicit recognition in the decision of the Court of Appeal in *A-G's Reference (No 2 of 1999)* [2000] QB 796 that a corporation could be convicted of manslaughter.

[282] See n 285.

[283] *Legislating the Criminal Code: Involuntary Manslaughter* Law Com No 237.

[284] Home Office: *Corporate Manslaughter: the Government's Draft Bill for Reform* Cm 6497. For a detailed review of the draft Bill, see Clarkson 'Corporate Manslaughter: Yet More Government Proposals' [2005] Crim LR 677.

of liability based on gross management failure. **The name of the offence**[285] **is misleading because it can also be committed by certain organisations other than corporations.**

8.141 The CMCHA 2007 was generally brought into force on 6 April 2008, with the exception of the provisions relating to death in custody (s 2(1)(d), (2)) and to publicity of conviction (s 10). Section 10 is now in force.

8.142 Under the CMCHA 2007, s 20, the common law offence of manslaughter by gross negligence is abolished, except in relation to an offence committed wholly or partly before 6 April 2008,[286] in its application to corporations, and in any application it had to other organisations to which the offence of corporate manslaughter applies.[287]

The offence

8.143 The CMCHA 2007, s 1(1) provides:

> 'An organisation to which this section applies is guilty of an offence if the way in which its activities are managed or organised –
>
> (a) causes a person's death, and
>
> (b) amounts to a gross breach of a relevant duty of care owed by the organisation to the deceased.'

By s 1(3), an organisation is guilty of an offence under the CMCHA 2007, s 1 only if the way in which its activities are managed or organised by its senior management is a substantial element in the breach referred to in s 1(1). Because the offence requires a gross breach of a duty of care this offence is one requiring proof of gross negligence within its terms.

Section 1 does not apply to anything done or omitted before 6 April 2008.[288]

Organisations to which s 1 applies

8.144 By the CMCHA 2007, s 1(2):

> 'The organisations to which s 1 applies are:
>
> (a) a corporation;
>
> (b) a government department or other body listed in Schedule 1;[289]

---

[285] The name is given by the CMCHA 2007, s 1(5)(a). The name 'corporate homicide' is given to the corresponding offence in Scottish law: CMCHA 2007, s 1(5)(b).

[286] CMCHA 2007, s 27(4). See also n 295.

[287] There is no authority that the common law offence of manslaughter by gross negligence applied to any such organisation other than a corporation.

[288] CMCHA 2007, s 27(3).

[289] The Secretary of State has power to amend Sch 1: CMCHA 2007, s 22.

(c) a police force;

(d) a partnership,[290] or a trade union or employers' association, that is an employer.'[291]

The effect of s 1(2), coupled with s 11,[292] is that the normal presumption that a statute does not apply to the Crown[293] is rebutted in respect of the offence of corporate manslaughter. Among the Government departments and bodies listed in Sch 1 (as amended) are the Ministry of Defence, the Home Office, HM Revenue and Customs and the Ministry of Justice.

Senior management

8.145 The CMCHA 2007, s 1(4)(c) provides that

'"senior management", in relation to an organisation, means the persons who play significant roles in –

(i) the making of decisions about how the whole or a substantial part of its activities are to be managed or organised, or

(ii) the actual managing or organising of the whole or a substantial part of those activities.'

Although the definition of 'senior management' is wider than the definition of those (persons part of the corporation's directing mind and will) who could have involved a corporation in criminal liability for the common law offence of manslaughter by gross negligence, it still restricts the range of people whose misconduct can result in liability for corporate liability. It is arguable that the definition of 'senior management' is too narrow. There is a risk that cynical organisations will delegate their decision-making and management and organisation in areas related to health and to safety to people falling outside the definition.

Relevant duty of care

8.146 The meaning of 'relevant duty of care' for the purposes of the CMCHA 2007, s 1, is provided by the CMCHA 2007, s 2. Section 2(1) and (2) provides that:

'(1) A "relevant duty of care" in relation to an organisation, means any of the following duties owed by it under the law of negligence:[294]

---

[290] Ie a partnership within the Partnership Act 1890 or a limited partnership registered under the Limited Partnerships Act 1907, or a firm or entity of a similar character formed under the law of a country or territory outside the United Kingdom: CMCHA 2007, s 25.

[291] The Secretary of State has power to amend s 1 so as to extend the categories of organisation to which s 1 applies: CMCHA 2007, s 21.

[292] Section 11 expressly removes Crown immunity.

[293] *Tamlin v Hannaford* [1950] 1 KB 18, CA; *Lord Advocate v Dumbarton District Council* [1990] 2 AC 580, HL.

[294] 'The law of negligence' includes the Occupiers' Liability Acts 1957 and 1984 and the Defective Premises Act 1972: CMCHA 2007, s 2(7).

    (a) a duty owed to its employees or to other persons working for the organisation or performing services for it;

    (b) a duty owed as occupier of premises;

    (c) a duty owed in connection with –

        (i) the supply by the organisation of goods or services (whether for consideration or not);

        (ii) the carrying on by the organisation of any construction or maintenance operations;

        (iii) the carrying on by the organisation of any other activity on a commercial basis; or

        (iv) the use or keeping by the organisation of any plant, vehicle or other thing;

    (d) (not yet in force) a duty owed to a person who, by reason of being a person within subsection (2), is someone for whose safety the organisation is responsible.[295]

(2) (not yet in force) A person is within this subsection if –

    (a) he is detained at a custodial institution or in a custody area at a court or police station;

    (b) he is detained at a removal centre or short-term holding facility;

    (c) he is being transported in a vehicle, or being held in any premises, in pursuance of prison escort arrangements or immigration escort arrangements;

    (d) he is living in secure accommodation[296] in which he has been placed;

    (e) he is a detained patient.'[297]

Whether a particular organisation owes a duty of care to a particular individual is a question of law (and therefore is determined by the judge).[298]

Any rule of the common law that has the effect of preventing a duty of care from being owed:

- by one person to another by reason of the fact that they are jointly engaged in unlawful conduct; or

- to a person by reason of his acceptance of a risk of harm,

is to be disregarded.[299] Thus, the rules of *ex turpi causa non oritur actio* (an action cannot be founded on an illegal cause) and *volenti non fit iniuria* (no legal wrong is done to

---

[295] By the CMCHA 2007, s 2(4), a reference in s 1(1) to a duty owed under the law of negligence includes a reference to a duty that would be owed under the law of negligence but for any statutory provision under which liability is imposed in place of liability under that law.

    The CMCHA 2007, s 20 (abolition of common law offence of manslaughter by gross negligence in its application to corporations and other organisations) does not apply in relation to anything done or omitted before s 2(1)(d) comes into force: Corporate Manslaughter and Corporate Homicide Act 2007 (Commencement No 1) Order 2008.

[296] Ie accommodation, outside a custodial institution, provided for the purpose of restricting the liberty of persons under 18: CMCHA 2007, s 2(7).

[297] 'Detained patient' means someone detained under specified mental health legislation or someone deemed to be in legal custody by it: CMCHA 2007, s 2(7).

[298] CMCHA 2007, s 2(5).

[299] CMCHA 2007, s 2(6).

a willing person: voluntary assumption of the risk) which exist in the law of torts do not apply to the offence of corporate manslaughter.

Exclusions from 'relevant duty of care'

8.147 The CMCHA 2007, ss 3 to 7 set out a number of exceptions from the 'relevant duty of care'. Essentially, but not entirely, these relate to bodies in the public sector.

8.148 *Public policy decisions, exclusively public functions and statutory functions* Any duty of care owed:

- by a public authority in respect of a decision as to matters of public policy (including in particular the allocation of public resources or the weighing of competing public interests) is not a 'relevant duty of care';

- in respect of things done in the exercise of an exclusively public function[300] is not a 'relevant duty of care' unless it falls within s 2(1)(a), (b) or (when in force) (d);

- by a public authority in respect of inspections carried out in the exercise of a statutory function[301] is not a 'relevant duty of care' unless it is owed by an employer or occupier under s 2(1)(a) or (b).[302]

8.149 *Military activities* In addition, any duty of care owed by the Ministry of Defence in respect of:

- operations, including peacekeeping operations and operations for dealing with terrorism, civil unrest or serious public disorder, in the course of which members of the armed forces come under attack or face the threat of attack or violent resistance;

- activities carried on in preparation for, or directly in support of, such operations;

- training of a hazardous nature, or training carried out in a hazardous way, which it is considered needs to be carried out, or carried out in that way, in order to improve or maintain the effectiveness of the armed forces with respect to such operations; or

- activities carried out by members of the special forces,[303]

is not a 'relevant duty of care'.[304]

8.150 *Policing and law enforcement* Any duty of care owed by a public authority in respect of:

- operations for dealing with terrorism, civil unrest or serious disorder, which involve policing or law enforcement activities in the course of which officers or employees of the authority come under attack or face the threat of attack or violent resistance;

---

[300] Ie a function falling within the prerogative of the Crown or, by its nature, exercisable only with authority conferred by the exercise of that prerogative, or by or under a statutory provision: CMCHA 2007, s 3(4).
[301] Ie a function conferred by or under a statutory provision: CMCHA 2007, s 3(4).
[302] CMCHA 2007, s 3(1)–(3).
[303] As defined by the CMCHA 2007, s 4(4), eg the SAS.
[304] CMCHA 2007, s 4(1)–(3).

- activities carried on in preparation for, or directly in support of, such operations; or

- training of a hazardous nature, or training carried out in a hazardous way, which it is considered needs to be carried out, or carried out in that way, in order to improve or maintain the effectiveness of officers or employees of the public authority with respect to such operations,

is not a 'relevant duty of care'.[305]

In addition, any duty of care owed by a public authority in respect of other policing or law-enforcement activities is not a 'relevant duty of care' unless it is owed by an employer or occupier under s 2(1)(a) or (b) or, when in force, by a custodian under s 2(1)(d).[306]

It has been suggested that the extent of the exceptions relating to army or police organisations in ss 4 and 5 is unwarranted and may result in individual soldiers or police officers being more at risk of liability than, say, a nurse whose hospital is not protected by an exception from corporate manslaughter when death is caused by serious negligence.[307]

8.151 *Emergencies*   Any duty of care owed by:

- a fire and rescue authority;

- any other organisation providing a service of responding to emergency circumstances either in pursuance of arrangements made with a fire and rescue authority, or (if not in pursuance of such arrangements) otherwise than on a commercial basis;

- a relevant NHS body;

- an organisation providing ambulance services;

- an organisation providing services for the transport of organs, blood, equipment or personnel under arrangements with an ambulance-services organisation;

- an organisation providing a rescue service;

- the armed forces,

in respect of the way in which they respond to emergency circumstances[308] is not a relevant duty of care unless it falls within s 2(1)(a) or (b).[309]

---

[305] CMCHA 2007, s 5(1), (2).

[306] CMCHA 2007, s 5(3).

[307] Horder 'The Criminal Liability of Organisations for Manslaughter' in *Halsbury's Laws of England Centenary Essays* (2007) (Hetherington (ed)) at 116–120.

[308] 'Emergency circumstances' means circumstances that are present or imminent and are causing, or are likely to cause, serious harm or a worsening of such harm, or are likely to cause the death of a person: CMCHA 2007, s 6(7). For these purposes, 'serious harm' means (a) serious injury to or the serious illness (including mental illness) of a person; (b) serious harm to the environment (including the life and health of plants and animals); (c) serious harm to any building or other property: CMCHA 2007, s 6(7). A reference in s 6 to emergency circumstances includes a reference to circumstances that are believed to be emergency circumstances: CMCHA 2007, s 6(8).

[309] CMCHA 2007, s 6(1) and (2). For these purposes, the way in which an organisation responds to emergency circumstances does not include the way in which medical treatment is carried out or decisions within s 6(4) are made: CMCHA 2007, s 6(3). Decisions within s 6(4) are decisions as to the carrying out of medical treatment, other than decisions as to the order in which persons are to be given such treatment.

Any duty of care owed in respect of the carrying out, or attempted carrying out, of a rescue operation at sea in emergency circumstances is not a 'relevant duty of care' unless it falls within s 2(1)(a) or (b).[310]

Any duty of care owed in respect of action taken to comply with a safety direction under the Merchant Shipping Act 1995 or in lieu of such a direction is not a 'relevant duty of care' unless it falls within s 2(1)(a) or (b).[311]

8.152 *Child protection and probation functions* A duty of care that a local authority or other public authority owes in respect of the exercise of its functions under the Children Act 1989 relating to the care and supervision, and protection, of children is not a 'relevant duty of care' unless it falls within a 2(1)(a), (b) or (when in force) (d); and the same is true in respect of the duty of care that a local probation board, a provider of probation services or other public authority owes in respect of its exercise of specified functions and activities.[312] Thus, for example, a local authority which failed to identify that a child was at risk and therefore did not take it into care, with the result that it was killed, would not owe a relevant duty of care because its duty of care in this case would not be owed as an employer or occupier or custodian.

Gross breach of duty

8.153 The CMCHA 2007, s 1(4)(b) provides that:

> 'a breach of a duty of care by an organisation is a "gross" breach if the conduct alleged to amount to a breach of that duty falls far below what can reasonably be expected of the organisation in the circumstances.'

This is a matter to be determined by the jury.

8.154 To help the jury to determine whether this test is satisfied, s 8(1) and (2) provide that, where:

- it is established that an organisation owed a relevant duty of care[313] to a person,[314] and

- it falls to the jury to decide whether there was a gross breach of that duty,

the jury must consider whether the evidence shows that the organisation failed to comply with any health and safety legislation that relates to the alleged breach, and if so how serious that failure was and how much of a risk of death it posed.[315]

Without prejudice to having regard to other matters, the jury may also:

- consider the extent to which the evidence shows that there were attitudes, policies, systems or accepted practices within the organisation that were likely to have encouraged any failure to comply with health and safety legislation, or to have produced

---

[310] CMCHA 2007, s 6(5).   [311] CMCHA 2007, s 6(6).   [312] CMCHA 2007, s 7(1)–(3).
[313] Para 8.146.   [314] See para 8.146.   [315] CMCHA 2007, s 8(1) and (2).

tolerance of it, for example consistently failing to ensure that building workers wore 'hard hats' on site or systems which meant that employees had to take unnecessary risks;

- have regard to any health and safety guidance[316] that relates to the alleged breach.[317]

Causing death

8.155 The death in question must be caused[318] by the way in which the activities are managed or organised, that way amounting to a gross breach of duty.[319]

Prosecution, trial and punishment

8.156 A prosecution for corporate manslaughter may not be instituted without the consent of the Director of Public Prosecutions.[320]

The offence of corporate manslaughter is triable only on indictment and an organisation guilty of it is liable to an unlimited fine.[321]

In addition, under the CMCHA 2007, s 9, the court has power on the application of the prosecution to impose a remedial order against an organisation convicted before it of corporate manslaughter requiring it to take specified steps within a specified period to remedy:

- the breach;
- any matter appearing to have resulted from it and to have been a cause of the death;
- any health and safety deficiency in the organisation's policies, systems or practices appearing to be indicated by the breach.[322]

Under CMCHA 2007, s 10 the court can make a publicity order, which requires the convicted organisation to publish in a specified manner the fact that it has been convicted of corporate manslaughter, specified particulars of the offence, the amount of the fine and the terms of the remedial order made.[323] The resulting damage to the organisation's reputation and the knock-on effects of that mean that the publicity order must not be underestimated as a sanction.

An organisation which fails to comply with a remedial order or a publicity order commits an offence triable only on indictment and punishable with an unlimited fine.[324]

---

[316] Ie any code, guidance, manual or similar publication concerned with health and safety matters and made or issued by an authority responsible for the enforcement of health and safety legislation: CMCHA 2007, s 8(5). Examples of such guidance would be Health and Safety Executive guidance or a code of practice approved by the Health and Safety Commission.

[317] CMCHA 2007, s 8(3) and (4).

[318] Paras 2.28–2.57. The Law Reform (Year and a Day Rule) Act 1996 applies to the offence of corporate manslaughter.

[319] CMCHA 2007, s 1(1).　　[320] CMCHA 2007, s 17(a).

[321] CMCHA 2007, s 1(6).　　[322] CMCHA 2007, s 9(1), (2) and (4).

[323] CMCHA 2007, s 10(1)–(3).　　[324] CMCHA 2007, ss 9(5), 10(4).

No individual liability

8.157 The CMCHA 2007, s 18(1) provides that an individual cannot be guilty of aiding and abetting, counselling or procuring the commission of an offence of corporate manslaughter. Nor can he be liable for corporate manslaughter on any other basis.

On the other hand, an individual whose gross negligence contributed to the organisation's liability for corporate manslaughter, and was a cause of the death, may be convicted of the common law offence of manslaughter by gross negligence. However, it may be impossible to prove this against a member of senior management in the case of a large- or medium-sized organisation. Alternatively, if an individual is a director or similar senior officer of a corporation, it may be possible to prove an offence under the Health and Safety at Work etc Act 1974 against him by virtue of s 37(1) of that Act,[325] whereby if *an offence under the 1974 Act* has been committed with the consent or connivance of such a person, or is attributable to neglect on his part, he is guilty of *that offence* without proof that he was grossly negligent. However, the maximum term of imprisonment for a person convicted under s 37(1) is only two years. A company director convicted of common law manslaughter by gross negligence or of an offence under the 1974 Act can be disqualified from acting as a director for up to 15 years.[326]

There are many who think that the CMCHA 2007 should have incorporated a recommendation by a joint report of two parliamentary committees[327] that individual directors or managers should be liable for an offence of corporate manslaughter punishable with up to 14 years' imprisonment if the offence was committed with their consent or connivance or attributable to their neglect. The exclusion of individual liability for corporate manslaughter has been described as a grave shortcoming.[328]

The CMCHA 2007, s 18(1A)[329] provides that an individual cannot be guilty of an offence of encouraging or assisting crime contrary to the Serious Crime Act 2007, Pt 2 (which offences do not require an offence encouraged or assisted to be committed) by reference to an offence of corporate manslaughter.

Jurisdiction

8.158 The CMCHA 2007, s 1 applies if the harm resulting in death is sustained in the United Kingdom or:

- within the seaward limits of the territorial sea adjacent to the United Kingdom;
- on a British registered ship;

---

[325] Referred to in para 18.44.

[326] For a review of the operation of the 1974 Act, s 37 and the power to make disqualification orders (very few have been made so far in respect of company directors convicted under s 37), see Wright 'Criminal Liability of Directors and Senior Managers for Deaths at Work' [2007] Crim LR 949.

[327] First Joint Report: Home Affairs and Work and Pensions Committee: *Draft Corporate Manslaughter Bill*.

[328] Clarkson 'Corporate Manslaughter: Yet More Government Proposals' [2005] Crim LR 677 at 689.

[329] Inserted by the Serious Crime Act 2007, s 62.

- on a British-controlled aircraft;

- on a British-controlled hovercraft;

- in, on or above, or within 500 metres of, an offshore installation in United Kingdom territorial waters or a designated area of the United Kingdom's continental shelf.[330]

The limited nature of these jurisdictional provisions is unfortunate in the light of the increasing globalisation of corporate activities, particularly in respect of activities in the European Union.

Other homicide offences: (2) causing death by dangerous or careless driving etc

---

Key points 8.10

Four types of offence fall within this heading:

- causing death by dangerous driving;

- causing death by careless, or inconsiderate, driving;

- causing death by careless, or inconsiderate, driving when under the influence of drink or drugs; or

- causing death by driving when unlicensed, disqualified or uninsured.

Common elements

Driving

8.159 The offences below refer to driving a mechanically propelled vehicle or a motor vehicle on a road or other public place. Whether a person is 'driving' is essentially a question of fact; the test of 'driving' is whether the person concerned is in a substantial sense controlling the movement and direction of the vehicle,[331] provided that what occurs can in any ordinary meaning of the word be regarded as 'driving'.[332] Thus, a person who releases the handbrake and 'coasts' downhill in a car is 'driving' it (and this is so even though the steering is locked).[333] On the other hand, a person who is pushing a car and

---

[330] CMCHA 2007, s 28(3).

[331] *MacDonagh* [1974] QB 448, CA; *Burgoyne v Phillips* (1983) 147 JP 375, DC; *McKoen v Ellis* (1986) 151 JP 60, DC; *Gunnell v DPP* [1994] RTR 151, DC. Also see *Tyler v Whatmore* [1976] RTR 83, DC; para 17.4.

[332] *MacDonagh* [1974] QB 448, CA; *Jones v Pratt* [1983] RTR 54, DC; *McKoen v Ellis* (1986) 151 JP 60, DC.

[333] *Burgoyne v Phillips* (1983) 147 JP 375, DC. Also see *Saycell v Bool* [1948] 2 All ER 83, DC.

steering it with his hand through the window is not driving it,[334] nor is someone who, not intending to exercise any control over the vehicle, accidentally causes it to move (eg by accidentally touching the accelerator during a struggle).[335] A person in the driver's seat of a vehicle which is being towed is driving it if he has the ability to control its movements or direction by means of the brakes or steering,[336] and so is a person sitting astride a motor cycle, propelling it with his feet, with his hands on the handlebars but without the engine running.[337]

Mechanically propelled vehicle and motor vehicle

8.160 A 'mechanically propelled vehicle' is not specifically defined by the legislation but it has been held to include a vehicle whose engine has been removed, where there is a possibility that it may soon be replaced,[338] and a vehicle which has broken down because of mechanical failure.[339] Thus, someone who coasts dangerously down a hill in an engineless or broken down vehicle and kills someone can be convicted of causing death by dangerous driving.

'Motor vehicle' has a more limited meaning. It is defined by the Road Traffic Act 1988 (RTA 1988), s 185 as 'a mechanically propelled vehicle intended or adapted for use on roads' (other than a mechanically propelled invalid carriage of a prescribed type) but by the RTA 1988, s 189 certain mechanically propelled vehicles controlled by a pedestrian and certain electrically assisted pedal cycles are deemed not to be motor vehicles. The Divisional Court has held that whether or not the definition in s 185 is satisfied depends on whether a reasonable person looking at the vehicle would say that one of its uses would be use on a road, whether or not it is suitable for such use.[340] On this basis, for example, it has been held[341] that a motorised scooter known as a 'Go-ped' was a motor vehicle within s 185. The Go-ped consisted of a small foot platform attached to a subframe on which the person using it would stand. Its maximum speed was 20mph. Its brakes and steering were inadequate. The Divisional Court said that the capability of a vehicle to be used safely on a road was not conclusive. There was no obvious place in which a Go-ped could be used, other than on a road. It could not travel on rough ground, soft or uneven surfaces. Regardless of the fact that the manufacturers said that it was not to be used on a road, a reasonable person would say that one of its uses would be on the roads. In comparison, by an application of the same test, a go-kart has been held not to be a motor vehicle,[342] although it is undoubtedly a mechanically propelled vehicle.

---

[334] *MacDonagh* [1974] QB 448, CA.   [335] *Blayney v Knight* (1974) 60 Cr App Rep 269, DC.

[336] *McQuaid v Anderton* [1980] 3 All ER 540, DC; *Whitfield v DPP* [1998] Crim LR 349, DC; *R (on the application of Traves) v DPP* [2005] EWHC 1482 (Admin), (Bean J).

[337] *Gunnel v DPP* [1994] RTR 151, DC.   [338] *Newberry v Simmonds* [1961] 2 QB 345, DC.

[339] *Paul* [1952] NI 61, NI CCA.   [340] *Burns v Currell* [1963] 2 QB 433, DC.

[341] *DPP v Saddington* (2001) 165 JP 122, DC.   [342] *Burns v Currell* [1963] 2 QB 433, DC.

Road or other public place

8.161 The RTA 1988, s 192 provides that 'road' means 'any highway[343] and any other road to which the public has access, and includes bridges over which a road passes'. There is an element of circularity in this definition, in that it says that a 'road' means 'any other road to which the public has access'. This leaves open the question of what exactly is meant by a 'road', leaving aside a 'highway'. In *Cutter v Eagle Star Insurance Co Ltd; Clarke v Kato*,[344] Lord Clyde, giving the only reasoned speech in the House of Lords, held that whether a particular area was or was not a 'road' in the context of 'any other road to which the public has access' eventually came to a matter of fact. He stated that one obvious feature of a 'road' as commonly understood was that its physical limits are defined or at least definable as a route or way, and that another feature was its function as a means of access leading from one place to another. Lord Clyde stated that as a matter of ordinary language, a car park did not qualify as a road. In character and more especially in function the two were distinct. The proper function of a road was to enable movement along it to a destination, whereas the proper function of a car park was to enable vehicles to stand and wait.

Whether a 'road' which is not a highway is a road for the purposes of s 192 depends on whether the public has 'access to it'. What is said below about the corresponding phrase in the definition of 'public place' for the purposes of the RTA 1988 is equally applicable in the present respect. Where a road traffic offence can alternatively be committed in a 'public place', it is irrelevant whether or not the place in question is a 'road' if it can be categorised as a 'public place'.

8.162 A 'public place' means a place, such as a sports field or a car park or the 'airside' part of an airport terminal, to which members of the public, whether on payment or otherwise, are admitted or have access at the material time.[345] The absence of a physical obstruction or of a notice forbidding entry does not of itself mean that the public have access.[346] It is irrelevant that the public could have had access; the question is whether they have actually had access to the place in question.[347] If they have, the fact that it has been in defiance of an express prohibition is irrelevant.[348]

Access must be by virtue of being a member of the public. If people only have access to a place because of some special qualification not possessed by members of the public in general, such as membership of a club, the place is not a public place because access

---

[343] Basically, a highway is a way over which all members of the public have the right to pass and repass by foot, on horseback, or accompanied by a beast of burden or with vehicles or cattle. It follows that the term embraces carriageways, bridleways and footpaths.

[344] [1998] 4 All ER 417, HL.

[345] *Collinson* (1931) 23 Cr App Rep 49, CCA; *Elkins v Cartlidge* [1947] 1 All ER 829, DC; *DPP v Vivier* [1991] 4 All ER 18, DC; *DPP v Neville* [1996] NLJR 992, DC.

[346] *Spence* [1999] RTR 353, CA.

[347] *Spence* [1999] RTR 353, CA.

[348] Assumed in *DPP, ex p Taussik* [2000] 9 Archbold News 2, DC.

is not by virtue of their membership of the public.[349] Thus, a caravan park open only to members of the Caravan Club, or a car park at a factory to which only employees and customers are admitted or have access, is not a public place, whereas a caravan park or car park to which any member of the public is admitted, or has access, on payment of a fee is a public place.[350]

Trial and punishment

8.163 The mode of trial and the maximum punishments for the offences described below are provided by the Road Traffic Offenders Act 1988, Sch 2, as amended on a number of occasions. The provisions relating to disqualification from driving referred to are set out in s 34 of, and Sch 2 to, that Act. When s 35A (added by the C&JA 2009, Sch 16) comes into force, where the offender has been sentenced to an immediate term of imprisonment for the offence for which he is to be disqualified, the court must add to the period of disqualification determined under s 34 an extension period (broadly, the custodial period which must be served). This is designed to require that the former period of disqualification takes effect after the offender's release from imprisonment.

Causing death by dangerous driving

8.164 The RTA 1988, s 1, as substituted by the Road Traffic Act 1991 (RTA 1991), s 1, provides that:

> 'A person who causes the death of another person by driving a mechanically propelled vehicle dangerously on a road or other public place is guilty of an offence.'

The offence is punishable with up to 14 years' imprisonment and is triable only on indictment. Unless there are special reasons, disqualification for a minimum of two years is obligatory. In addition, the driver must also be ordered to take an extended driving test and he will remain disqualified after the period of disqualification until he has passed the test. The offence replaced the offence of causing death by reckless driving.

8.165 Off-road authorised motoring events are excluded from the offence of causing death by dangerous driving by the RTA 1988, s 13A. Section 13A provides that a person is not guilty of causing death by dangerous driving if he proves that he was driving in a public place other than a road in accordance with an authorisation for a motoring event given under regulations[351] made under that section.

---

349 *DPP v Vivier* [1991] 4 All ER 18, DC; *DPP v Coulman* [1993] RTR 230, DC.
350 *DPP v Vivier* [1991] 4 All ER 18, DC; *Havell v DPP* (1993) 158 JP 680, DC; *Spence* [1999] RTR 353, CA.
351 Motor Vehicles (Off-Road Events) Regulations 1995.

Dangerous driving

8.166 Dangerous driving is defined by the RTA 1988, s 2A (which was introduced by the RTA 1991). Section 2A(1) provides that a person is to be regarded as driving dangerously if:

> '(a) the way he drives falls far below what would be expected of a competent and careful driver; and
>
> (b) it would be obvious to a competent and careful driver that driving in that way would be dangerous.'

The test in s 2A(1)(a) is a purely objective one; it would be no defence that the defendant was doing his incompetent best, nor that he did not intend to drive dangerously.[352] The reference to the way the vehicle is driven falling far below what would be expected of a competent and careful driver sets a high threshold.[353] It is what distinguishes this offence from that of causing death by driving without due care and attention, where merely falling below the standard of such a driver suffices.

8.167 The test in s 2A(1) is concerned with the manner of the defendant's driving. However, driving may also be rendered dangerous by virtue of the current state of the vehicle, since the RTA 1988, s 2A(2) provides that:

> 'A person is also to be regarded as driving dangerously ... if it would be obvious to a competent and careful driver that driving the vehicle in its current state would be dangerous.'

In determining the state of the vehicle, regard may be had to anything attached to or carried on or in it, and to the manner in which it is attached or carried.[354] Because the danger involved in driving the vehicle in its current state must be obvious, the offence will not be committed if the defect involved is a latent one.[355] 'Current state' in s 2A(2) implies a state different from the original or manufactured state.[356] Thus, where the alleged danger relates solely to something inherent in the original design of the vehicle (eg spikes forming part of a grab unit at the front of an agricultural vehicle) dangerous driving is not committed.[357] It would be different if the original, unaltered state of the vehicle made the manner of the driving dangerous.[358]

---

[352] *A-G's Reference (No 4 of 2000)* [2001] EWCA Crim 780 (bus driver unintentionally pressed accelerator when meant to press brake; as a result bus travelled across pedestrian island and pedestrians were killed. Lack of intention to drive dangerously no defence).

[353] *Conteh* [2003] EWCA Crim 962. A breach of the Highway Code does not necessarily mean that an offence has been committed: *Conteh*. However, the Code's provisions can be considered by a jury provided that it is clearly explained that those provisions do not provide a 'standard': *Taylor* [2004] EWCA Crim 213.

[354] RTA 1988, s 2A(4).

[355] *Marchant* [2003] EWCA Crim 2099.   [356] *Marchant* [2003] EWCA Crim 2099.

[357] *Marchant* [2003] EWCA Crim 2099.   [358] *Marchant* [2003] EWCA Crim 2099.

8.168 For the purposes of both types of dangerous driving, 'dangerous' is defined by the RTA 1988, s 2A(3). It refers to danger either of injury to any person or of serious damage to property.

Section 2A(3) adds that, in determining what would be expected of, or obvious to, a competent and careful driver, regard must be had not only to the circumstances of which he could be expected to be aware (eg the obvious unroadworthiness of the vehicle or the icy condition of the road) but also to any circumstances shown to have been within the defendant's knowledge (eg a dangerous defect in the vehicle of which the defendant was aware, although it would not have been obvious). On the other hand, regard should not be had to any circumstance which the defendant wrongly believed to exist. Consequently, it has been held that, where a police officer pursued a stolen car at speed through traffic lights at red, his mistaken belief that the junction was being controlled by other officers (so that he could cross safely) was irrelevant to the issue of dangerous driving.[359] The defendant's special skill as a driver (eg that the defendant had taken an advanced police driving course) is an irrelevant consideration when considering whether driving was dangerous.[360] This somewhat surprising rule has been justified on the ground that to take into account the driver's special skill would be inconsistent with the objective test of the competent and careful driver.[361]

8.169 The definition of dangerous driving clearly indicates that the offence can only be committed if the manner of the driving or the condition of the vehicle is dangerous within s 2A(1) or s 2A(2) respectively. It follows that, since driving in a dangerously defective state through drink or drugs is not in itself dangerous driving, evidence of intoxication cannot by itself prove dangerous driving.[362]

On the other hand, the Court of Appeal decision in *Woodward*[363] established that evidence that the defendant had consumed alcohol is admissible as evidence under s 2A(3) as to the danger of injury or serious damage if it tends to show that the amount taken was such as would have adversely affected a driver or had adversely affected the particular driver. Surprisingly, it was held by the Court of Appeal in *Pleydell*[364] that evidence of the consumption of cocaine shortly before driving is admissible even if there is no evidence as to the quantity consumed or as to the particular driver having been adversely affected. The reason for this distinction was not explained by the Court of Appeal.

Causing of death

8.170 The prosecution must prove a causal link between the defendant's dangerous driving and the death of the other person.[365] What was said in Chapter 2 and earlier in this chapter about the victim of an offence of homicide and the requirement of causation

---

[359] *Collins* [1997] RTR 439, CA.   [360] *Bannister* [2009] EWCA Crim 1571, CA.
[361] *Bannister* [2009] EWCA Crim 1571 at [16].
[362] *Webster* [2006] EWCA Crim 415, explaining *Woodward* [1995] 3 All ER 79, CA, on this point.
[363] [1995] 3 All ER 79, CA.   [364] [2005] EWCA Crim 1447.   [365] Paras 2.28–2.57.

applies to the present offence.[366] In particular, it should be noted that the defendant's dangerous driving need not be the sole cause of death; it is enough that it is a substantial (ie more than minute or negligible) contribution to the death.[367]

No *mens rea* need be proved as to the risk of death resulting from the dangerous driving; it follows that it is irrelevant that that risk was unforeseen or even unforeseeable.

In *Loukes*,[368] the Court of Appeal held that the offence of causing death by dangerous driving consisted only of an *actus reus* and that *mens rea* played no part in it. The practical effects of this can be seen in paras 15.35 and 17.25.[369]

Relationship with manslaughter by gross negligence

8.171 Some cases of causing death by dangerous driving may also amount to manslaughter by gross negligence, although Lord Mackay LC considered in *Adomako*[370] that charges of gross negligence manslaughter would be rare in such cases. The fact that proof of gross negligence manslaughter requires proof that the defendant's conduct gave rise to a risk of death, whereas the risk need only have been of any injury to a person or of serious damage to property in causing death by dangerous driving, is a disincentive to a prosecution for a manslaughter by gross negligence unless the risk of death is clear-cut. The Crown Prosecution Service's policy is to charge manslaughter by gross negligence only if the evidence shows a very high risk of death, making the case one of utmost gravity.[371]

Causing death by careless, or inconsiderate, driving

8.172 The RTA 1988, s 2B, inserted by the Road Safety Act 2006, s 20(1), provides:

> 'A person who causes the death of another person by driving a mechanically propelled vehicle on a road or other public place without due care and attention, or without reasonable consideration for other persons using the road or place, is guilty of an offence.'

An offence under the RTA 1988, s 2B is triable either way and punishable with up to five years' imprisonment on conviction on indictment. Unless there are special reasons, disqualification for a minimum of 12 months is obligatory.

Section 2B creates two offences – causing death by careless driving and causing death by driving without reasonable consideration.

---

[366] The Law Reform (Year and a Day Rule) Act 1996 applies to the present offence and the other offences of causing death by driving.
[367] *Curphey* (1957) 41 Cr App Rep 78; *Hennigan* [1971] 3 All ER 133, CA; *Skelton* [1995] Crim LR 635, CA.
[368] [1996] 1 Cr App Rep 444, CA.   [369] Also see para 3.60.   [370] [1995] 1 AC 171, HL.
[371] Crown Prosecution Service Policy for Prosecuting Cases of Bad Driving (2007).

Careless, or inconsiderate, driving

8.173 The definitions of careless driving and inconsiderate driving under the RTA 1988, s 3ZA[372] apply to an offence under the RTA 1988, s 2B.[373]

Section 3ZA(2) encapsulates the definition of careless driving established by case law. It provides:

> 'A person is to be regarded as driving without due care and attention if (and only if) the way he drives falls below what would be expected of a competent and careful driver.'

This is a purely objective test. Consequently, a person whose driving simply falls below the standard of a competent and careful driver and who thereby causes the accidental death of another person (see below) is guilty of a serious offence, even though he is doing his incompetent best. Section 3ZA(3) mirrors s 2A(3) by providing that in determining for the purposes of s 3ZA(2) what would be expected of a careful and competent driver in a particular case, regard shall be had not only to the circumstances of which he could be expected to be aware but also to any circumstances shown to have been within the knowledge of the defendant.

The RTA 1988, s 3ZA(4) provides:

> 'A person is to be regarded as driving without reasonable consideration for other persons only if those persons are inconvenienced by his driving.'

The justification for making a driver who would otherwise only be guilty of one or other of the non-imprisonable offences of careless, or inconsiderate, driving guilty of a much more serious offence simply because death has accidentally resulted is not obvious.[374]

Causing of death

8.174 What was said in para 8.170 about the victim and causation is equally applicable, with the substitution of 'careless or inconsiderate driving' for 'dangerous driving' to the present offence.

Analogy with the offence of causing death by dangerous driving indicates that no *mens rea* need be proved as to the risk of death resulting from the careless or inconsiderate driving; it follows that it is irrelevant that that risk was unforeseen or even unforeseeable.

---

[372] Inserted by the Road Safety Act 2006, s 30.

[373] The definitions are applied to the RTA 1988, s 2B by the RTA 1988, s 3ZA(1).

[374] For arguments that the offences under the RTA 1988, s 2B are undesirable and ought not to have been created, see Cunningham 'Punishing Drivers Who Kill: Putting Road Safety First?' [2007] 27 LS 288.

Causing death by careless, or inconsiderate, driving when under the influence of drink or drugs

8.175 The relevant provision is the RTA 1988, s 3A, which was inserted by the RTA 1991, s 3 and amended by the Road Safety Act 2006, s 31. Section 3A(1) provides that:

> 'If a person causes the death of another person by driving a mechanically propelled vehicle on a road or other public place without due care and attention, or without reasonable consideration for other persons using the road or place, and:
>
> (a) he is, at the time when he is driving, unfit to drive through drink or drugs; or
>
> (b) he has consumed so much alcohol that the proportion of it in his breath, blood or urine at that time exceeds the prescribed limit; or
>
> (c) he is, within 18 hours after that time, required to provide a specimen for analysis in pursuance of s 7 of this Act, but without reasonable excuse fails to provide it, or
>
> (d) he is required by a constable to give his permission for a laboratory test of a specimen of blood taken from him under s 7A of this Act, but without reasonable excuse fails to do so,
>
> he is guilty of an offence.'

An offence under s 3A is triable only on indictment and is punishable with a maximum of 14 years' imprisonment. Unless there are special reasons, disqualification for a minimum of two years is obligatory.

8.176 The elements of an offence under s 3A have largely been explained already. As with the offence under s 2B, the prosecution must prove that the defendant drove a mechanically propelled vehicle on a road or other public place and that he did so without due care and attention (as defined by the RTA 1988, s 3ZA),[375] or without reasonable consideration for other users of the road or other public place, depending on which type of offence is charged. The prosecution must also prove that the careless driving caused the death of another and that the defendant falls within one of four categories of case.

The first is that, at the time that he was driving, he was unfit to drive through drink or drugs. 'Drink' means alcoholic drink and 'drug' means any intoxicant other than alcohol,[376] and includes medicines[377] and glue.[378] 'Unfitness to drive' means impairment of the ability to drive properly.[379]

The second, third and fourth categories only operate in relation to a person driving a motor vehicle,[380] as opposed to any other type of mechanically propelled vehicle. The

---

[375] Applied to the RTA 1988, s 3A, by the RTA 1988, s 3ZA(1).   [376] RTA 1988, s 11(2).
[377] *Armstrong v Clark* [1957] 2 QB 391, DC.   [378] *Bradford v Wilson* (1983) 147 JP 573, DC.
[379] RTA 1988, s 3A(2).   [380] RTA 1988, 3A(3).

second category of case is where the driver had consumed so much alcohol that the proportion of it in his blood, breath or urine, at the time when he was driving, exceeded the prescribed limit. The provisions relating to that limit, to the taking of specimens for analysis are contained in the RTA 1988, ss 6 to 9.

The third category of case is where the driver of the motor vehicle, within 18 hours of the time of his careless driving, was required to provide a specimen for analysis in pursuance of s 7 of the Act but without reasonable excuse failed to do so.

The fourth category of case is where it appeared to a constable that the driver had been involved in an accident and that he might be incapable for medical reasons of giving a valid consent to the taking of a specimen of blood for analysis under the Act, and a medical practitioner was requested to take a blood specimen which the driver subsequently refused without reasonable excuse to permit to be subjected to a laboratory test.

In the third and fourth categories it is irrelevant that the driver had not taken any drink (or drugs) or was not 'over the limit' (or did not have impaired driving ability).[381]

Causing death by driving: unlicensed, disqualified or uninsured drivers

8.177 The RTA 1988, s 3ZB, inserted by the Road Safety Act 2006, s 21(1), provides that a person will be guilty of an offence if he causes the death of another person by driving a motor vehicle on a road and, at the time when he is driving, the circumstances are such that he is committing an offence of:

- driving otherwise than in accordance with a licence;[382]
- driving while disqualified;[383]
- using a motor vehicle while uninsured or unsecured against third party risks.[384]

Such an offence is triable either way and punishable with a maximum of two years' imprisonment on conviction on indictment. Unless there are special reasons, disqualification from driving for not less than 12 months is obligatory.

There is no need for the driving to be dangerous or careless, but it must have caused the death. Further discussion of this offence is outside the scope of this book.

---

[381] This rather obvious point was confirmed in *Coe* [2009] EWCA Crim 1452.
[382] Contrary to the RTA 1988, s 87(1).
[383] Contrary to the RTA 1988, s 103(1)(b).
[384] Contrary to the RTA 1988, s 143.

Offences related to homicide

> **Key points 8.11**
>
> The last part of this chapter deals with the following offences related to homicide:
>
> - causing or allowing the death of a child or vulnerable person;
> - solicitation of murder;
> - threats to kill;
> - abortion; and
> - child destruction.

Causing or allowing death of a child or vulnerable adult

8.178 Where a child or vulnerable adult has died and it is clear that this was non-accidental and caused by a parent or someone else with the care of him, it may be difficult or impossible to prove which of the persons with care caused the death, or impossible to prove that one carer was an accomplice to the fatal conduct of another carer. Only if it can be proved in such a case that carer A must have been an accomplice to carer B causing the death or that carer B must have been an accomplice to carer A causing the death, can A and B be convicted of murder or manslaughter.

8.179 These problems have been resolved by the Domestic Violence, Crime and Victims Act 2004 (DVCVA 2004), s 5, which implemented, with significant differences, recommendations made by the Law Commission.[385]
Section 5(1) provides:

> 'A person (D) is guilty of an offence if –
>
> (a) a child or vulnerable adult (V) dies[386] as a result of the unlawful act of a person who –
>   (i)   was a member of the same household as V, and
>   (ii) had frequent contact with him;
> (b) D was such a person at the time of that act,

---

[385] Law Commission: *Children: Their Non-Accidental Death or Serious Injury (Criminal Trials)* (2003) Law Com No 282.

[386] The Law Reform (Year and a Day Rule) Act 1996 applies to an offence under s 5: see para 8.15, n 33.

(c) at that time there was a significant risk of serious physical harm[387] being caused to V by the unlawful act of such a person, and

(d) either D was the person whose act caused V's death or –
  (i) D was, or ought to have been, aware of the risk mentioned in paragraph (c),
  (ii) D failed to take such steps as he could reasonably have been expected to take to protect V from the risk, and
  (iii) the act occurred in circumstances of the kind that D foresaw or ought to have foreseen.'

The offence is triable only on indictment; the maximum term of imprisonment is 14 years.[388]

The victim

8.180 The victim (V) must be a child or vulnerable adult and must have died as a result of an unlawful act.[389] For these purposes:

- 'child' means a person under 16;[390]

- 'vulnerable adult' means a person aged 16 or over whose ability to protect himself from violence, abuse or neglect is significantly impaired through physical or mental disability or illness, through old age or otherwise.[391] The state of vulnerability need not be long-standing. It may be short, or temporary.[392] A fit adult may become vulnerable as a result of accident, or injury, or illness;[393]

- an 'unlawful act' is an act that (a) constitutes an offence, or (b) except in relation to an act of D, would constitute an offence but for being the act of a person who is under 10 or who has the defence of insanity.[394] 'Act' includes a course of conduct and also includes an omission.[395] Typical examples of an unlawful omission in the context of the present offence would be a failure to feed, or to clothe, or to seek medical attention for, a child contrary to the Children and Young Persons Act 1933, s 1. It is noteworthy that, in terms of omissions to act, s 5 imposes criminal liability on a wider range of people than would, at common law or otherwise under statute, be under a legal duty to take steps to care for the victim.[396]

---

[387] By the DVCVA 2004, s 5(6), 'serious' harm means harm that amounts to grievous bodily harm for the purposes of the Offences Against the Person Act 1861; para 7.78.

[388] DVCVA 2004, s 5(7).   [389] DVCVA 2004, s 5(1)(a).

[390] DVCVA 2004, s 5(6).   [391] DVCVA 2004, s 5(6).

[392] *Khan* [2009] EWCA Crim 2 at [27].

[393] *Khan* [2009] EWCA Crim 2 at [27]. The Court of Appeal at [26] did not rule out the possibility that an adult who is utterly dependent on others, even if physically young and apparently fit, may fall within the protective ambit of s 5(1).

[394] DVCVA 2004, s 5(5).   [395] DVCVA 2004, s 5(6).

[396] See paras 2.8, n 14 and 2.11.

The killer and the defendant

8.181 The person whose unlawful act, course of conduct or omission results in the victim's death must be a person who:

- was a member of the same household as V, and
- had frequent contact with V.[397]

The defendant must have been such a person at the time of the unlawful act.[398]

Every person living in a household is clearly a member of it. In addition, by s 5(4)(a), a person is to be regarded as a 'member' of a particular household, even if he does not live in that household, if he visits it so often and for such periods of time that it is reasonable to regard him as a member of it. The fact that a person has a caring responsibility for V, as in the case of a social worker or babysitter, is not in itself enough to satisfy s 5(4)(a). Section 5(4)(b) provides that where V lived in different households at different times, 'the same household as V' refers to the household in which V was living at the time of the act that caused V's death.

'Frequent contact' is not defined. In *Khan*,[399] the Court of Appeal rejected the argument that the frequency of contact must be examined in the context of the risk against which V required protection, and the defendant's awareness of that risk.[400] It held that the question whether contact between D and V was frequent was free-standing; these matters were irrelevant to its determination.

Significant risk of serious physical harm

8.182 Section 5(1)(c) requires that at the time of the unlawful act there was a significant risk of serious physical harm being caused to V by the unlawful act of a person who was a member of the same household as V and had frequent contact with V.

The DVCVA 2004, s 5(1)(c) indicates that the offence is essentially one of negligence as to the risk of serious harm. In *Stephens*,[401] the Court of Appeal held that 'significant risk of serious physical harm' in s 5(1)(c) is intended to bear its ordinary, normal meaning, and that the decision as to whether the risk of serious physical harm was significant is one of fact for the jury applying their collective understanding of the word. To leave the meaning of 'significant' to the jury is fraught with the danger that they may understand 'significant' as involving a relatively low level of risk, whereas it was intended to set 'quite a high threshold'.[402] In *Stephens*, it was held by the Court of Appeal that the trial judge had been wrong to tell the jury that significant meant 'more than minimal' (as it does in causation) but the decision of the Court is, somewhat paradoxically, that the judge should not define it to the jury. The threshold involved in 'significant' is an important one, given

---

[397] DVCVA 2004, s 5(1)(a).   [398] DVCVA 2004, s 5(1)(b).

[399] [2009] EWCA Crim 2.   [400] Ie the factors specified in DVCVA 2004, s 5(1)(d)(i) and (iii).

[401] [2007] EWCA Crim 1249.

[402] This was stated by the Government minister responsible for the legislation during debates in the House of Lords: HL Deb, col 1158.

that the offence is one of negligence, not requiring the defendant actually to be aware of the risk.

Section 5(1)(d)

8.183 Section 5(1)(d) provides the last condition for liability for an offence under s 5(1):

'[E]ither D was the person whose act caused V's death or –
  (i)   D was, or ought to have been, aware of the risk mentioned in [s 5(1)(c)],
  (ii) D failed to take such steps as he could reasonably have been expected to take to protect V from the risk, and
  (iii) the act occurred in circumstances of the kind that D foresaw or ought to have foreseen.'

By s 5(2), the prosecution does not have to prove whether it is the first alternative in s 5(1)(d) or the second (sub-paras (i) to (iii)) that applies. The fact that the prosecution need only prove that D either satisfies the first alternative or the second is of considerable importance.

Section 5(1)(d) was discussed by the Court of Appeal in *Khan*.[403] V, a 19-year-old woman, was brought from Pakistan to England in order to marry X. She spoke no English, had no friends here and did not leave the house. V suffered at least three incidents of serious violence from X, the last of which caused her death. X was convicted of V's murder and four other members of the same household (including D1, D2 and D3) were subsequently charged with allowing the death of a vulnerable adult contrary to the DVCVA 2004, s 5(1). The prosecution's case against the four was that X had been beating V during the three-week period before her death and that V's condition during that period was such that it must have been apparent to the four that she was being subjected to serious violence. The four were convicted of the offence under s 5(1). D1, D2 and D3 appealed unsuccessfully against their convictions.

One of the grounds of appeal in *Khan* arose from the fact that the fatal beating of V occurred at night in a garage outside the house when the appellants were asleep, and involved violence which was markedly different and more extreme than that inflicted during the previous three weeks. The circumstances, it was argued, were utterly different and none of the individual defendants foresaw or ought to have foreseen such an attack. Section 5(1)(d)(iii) states that the fatal unlawful act must have occurred in circumstances of *the kind* that the defendant foresaw or ought to have foreseen. It was argued that the judge's direction was defective because he had simply followed the terms of s 5(1)(d)(iii) whereas he should have provided a more informative direction. The Court of Appeal rejected this. It held:

'The act or conduct resulting in death must occur in circumstances of the kind which were foreseen or ought to have been foreseen by the defendants. They need not be identical. The

---

[403] [2009] EWCA Crim 2.

violence to which [V] was subjected on the night she was killed was of the same kind but it was violence of an even more extreme degree than the violence to which her husband had subjected her on earlier occasions. The place where the fatal attack took place was irrelevant. Although ultimately a jury question, the circumstances would probably have been the same kind, if not identical, if the fatal attack had occurred while the couple were on holiday, away from their home.[404]

8.184 It is important to note that, although s 5 was introduced to deal with the case where it is unclear which of two defendants killed the vulnerable person, its drafting is not limited to this type of case. Consequently, as Khan shows, it can apply to make D guilty under it where it is clear that E killed a child or vulnerable person and that D failed to protect him. As Herring has pointed out,[405] most of the prosecutions so far under s 5 have involved women who have 'stood by' while their male partner has killed a child. Rightly, he argues that this use of s 5 is a matter of grave concern where the woman has been the victim of domestic violence. His grounds are, inter alia, that domestic violence very often has a significant psychological impact on the victim, and this can mean that little or no blame should attach to her for failing to protect the child, and that the use of s 5 in such a case involves the prosecution of women when they and their children have been let down by the State's failure to provide adequate protection and support for battered women. He concludes that the law should focus on protecting mothers and children from violent men, rather than punishing women who are themselves the victims of violence.

In *Khan*, the Court of Appeal noted Herring's concern but pointed out that the defendant cannot be convicted unless he or she failed to take the steps which could reasonably have been expected to protect V (s 5(1)(d)(ii)). This precondition, it said, requires close analysis of the defendant's personal position. By way of example, it added:

'In the present case, if either of the female appellants [D1 and D2] had herself been subjected by [X] to serious violence of the kind which engulfed [V], the jury might have concluded that it would not have been reasonable to expect her to take any protective steps, or that any protective steps she might have taken, even if relatively minor, and although in the end unsuccessful to save the deceased, were reasonable in the circumstances.'[406]

Section 5(3)

8.185 Section 5(3) provides that if D was not the mother or father of V –

- D may not be charged with an offence under s 5 if he was under the age of 16 at the time of the act that caused V's death;

---

[404] [2009] EWCA Crim 2 at [39].
[405] 'Familial Homicide, Failure to Protect and Domestic Violence: Who's the Victim?' [2007] Crim LR 923.
[406] [2009] EWCA Crim 2 at [33].

- for the purposes of s 5(1)(d)(ii), D could not have been expected to take any such step as is referred to there before attaining that age.

Solicitation of murder

8.186 The Offences Against the Person Act 1861, s 4, as amended by the Criminal Law Act 1977, s 5(10), provides:

'Whosoever shall solicit, encourage, persuade or endeavour to persuade, or shall propose to any person, to murder any other person, whether he be a subject of her Majesty or not, and whether he be within the Queen's dominions or not, shall be guilty of [an offence], and being convicted thereof shall be liable to [a maximum of] imprisonment for life.'

The offence is triable only on indictment. It applies not only to inciting another to perpetrate a murder, but also to soliciting someone to be an accomplice to murder. This was held by the Court of Appeal in *Winter*,[407] upholding the conviction of a man who had solicited another to assist him in murdering his wife. As the Court pointed out, and as stated in para 17.8, an accomplice to murder is guilty of murder, but it nevertheless seems strange that he can be said to be 'solicited to murder' a person as s 4 requires.

8.187 The solicitation need not be directed to a particular person; it can, for example, be made by an article in a newspaper.[408]

8.188 There can be an offence under s 4 even if the solicitation to murder relates to the murder of members of a class of people, provided that the class is a sufficiently well-defined one. In *Antonelli and Barberi*,[409] where the indictment for solicitation to murder referred to the proposed murder of 'sovereigns and rulers of Europe', Phillimore J considered 'rulers' a somewhat vague term, but thought that as there were 18 or 20 sovereigns in Europe 'sovereign' referred to a sufficiently well-defined class. There can be a solicitation to murder, contrary to s 4, even though the proposed victim is still in the womb if it relates to the killing of the child after birth, as where D solicits a pregnant woman to kill her child when it is born,[410] but not if the solicitation was to destroy the child in the womb (because that destruction would not be murder).[411]

8.189 The solicitation must come to the notice of the person intended to act on it, though it need not be effective in any way,[412] but, if it is and the person incited agrees to commit the offence, he and the inciter may be guilty of statutory conspiracy. Where the solicitation does not reach the mind of another because, for instance, the letter soliciting the

407 [2007] EWCA Crim 3493.   408 *Most* (1881) 7 QBD 244, CCR.   409 (1905) 70 JP 4.
410 *Shephard* [1919] 2 KB 125, CCA.   411 Para 8.7.   412 *Krause* (1902) 18 TLR 238.

commission of murder never arrives, the person making it may be guilty of an attempt to solicit to murder.

8.190 Not only does s 4 expressly provide that it applies whether or not the person to be murdered is a British subject and wherever the proposed murder is to take place, but it was held in *Abu Hamza*[413] that on its natural meaning it covers the soliciting of a foreign national in England and Wales to commit murder abroad (even though a murder abroad is only indictable in England and Wales if it is committed by a British citizen[414]).

Threats to kill

8.191 The Offences Against the Person Act 1861 (OAPA 1861), s 16, as substituted by the Criminal Law Act 1977, Sch 12, provides:

> 'A person who without lawful excuse makes to another a threat, intending that that other would fear it would be carried out, to kill that other or a third person is guilty of [an offence] and liable on conviction on indictment to imprisonment for a term not exceeding ten years.'

The offence is triable either way.[415]

The threat may be conditional and it may be implied as well as express.[416] It may be made by any means.[417] A threat to kill in England and Wales made from abroad (eg by telephone or e-mail) can suffice.[418] A threat to 'kill' a foetus in the womb is not an offence under s 16, since the foetus is not another person distinct from its mother.[419]

'Without lawful excuse' is not defined, but self-defence, the prevention of crime or related justifications constitute a lawful excuse provided that it was reasonable in the circumstances to make the threat.[420]

---

[413] [2006] EWCA Crim 2918.

[414] Or a British Overseas citizen, citizen of British overseas territories or British National (Overseas): see the British Nationality Act 1948, s 3(1), the British Nationality Act 1981, s 51, and the Hong Kong (British Nationality) Order 1986.

[415] Magistrates' Courts Act 1980, s 17(1) and Sch 1.

[416] *Solanke* [1969] 3 All ER 1383, [1970] 1 WLR 1, CA.

[417] See eg *Williams* (1986) 84 Cr App Rep 299, CA (threatening telephone calls).

[418] *M (Rizwan)* [2003] EWCA Crim 3067.

[419] *Tait* [1990] 1 QB 290, [1989] 3 All ER 682, CA; para 8.8. A threat to kill the child after its birth made at a time when it was still a foetus appears to amount to an offence under s 16: *Tait* at 688–689.

[420] *Cousins* [1982] QB 526, 74 Cr App Rep 363, CA. Lawful excuse does not depend on whether the life of the defendant was in immediate jeopardy when he made the threat: *Cousins*.

Abortion and child destruction

Abortion

8.192 The OAPA 1861, s 58 provides the offence of attempting to procure a miscarriage, which is popularly known as abortion. It states:

> 'Every woman being with child who, with intent to procure her own miscarriage, shall unlawfully administer to herself any poison or other noxious thing, or shall unlawfully use any instrument or other means whatsoever with the like intent, and whosoever, with intent to procure the miscarriage of any woman whether she be or be not with child, shall unlawfully administer to her or cause to be taken by her any poison or other noxious thing, or shall unlawfully use any instrument or other means whatsoever with the like intent, shall be liable to [a maximum of] imprisonment for life.'

The offence is triable only on indictment. As can be seen, it is committed in two cases:

- where a woman 'being with child', with intent to procure her own miscarriage, unlawfully administers to herself any poison or noxious thing or unlawfully uses any instrument or other means; or

- where any other person, with intent to procure the miscarriage of any woman, whether or not she is 'with child', unlawfully administers to her or causes to be taken by her any poison or noxious thing or unlawfully uses any instrument or other means.

In neither case is a miscarriage required to result from the defendant's conduct. However, there are these distinctions between the woman who tries to procure her own miscarriage and any other persons who try to procure another's miscarriage:

- A woman who administers poison etc to herself can only be guilty if she is in fact 'with child'; if she merely believes herself to be pregnant, but is not, she is not guilty under the OAPA 1861, s 58. If another person administers etc, it is irrelevant that the woman concerned was not in fact 'with child' provided that the intent to procure a miscarriage can be proved. The importance of this distinction is diminished by the fact that if the non-pregnant woman conspires with another to administer to herself a noxious thing, or to use something, to procure her miscarriage she may be convicted of conspiracy[421] to commit an offence under s 58.[422]

- A person other than the woman herself can commit the offence by causing to be taken by the woman any poison or noxious thing. This will occur, for example, where

---

[421] *Whitchurch* (1890) 24 QBD 420, CCR.

[422] A non-pregnant woman can also be convicted as an accomplice to an offence under s 58 if she aids, abets, counsels or procures another to perpetrate an offence under s 58 in respect of her: *Sockett* (1908) 72 JP 428, CCR.

the woman is deceived by the defendant into thinking that the substance in question is harmless and takes it on the directions of the defendant.[423]

Means

8.193 The OAPA 1861, s 58 is concerned with the unlawful administration of poison or a noxious thing or the use of an instrument or any other means with intent to procure a miscarriage. 'Poison' has been said to mean a recognised poison, and it has been stated in the same case that if the thing administered is a recognised poison the offence may be committed, even though the quantity given is so small as to be incapable of doing harm.[424] 'Noxious thing' has been defined as something, other than a recognised poison, which is harmful in the dosage in which it was administered, even though it might be harmless in small quantities.[425] 'Any other means' is obviously a wide term, covering digital interference with a foetus and hitting a woman in the lower part of her body[426] among other things. It is irrelevant that, unknown to the defendant, the means used were incapable of procuring a miscarriage.[427] Although in most cases the woman will be a consenting party, the offence also covers non-consensual conduct.[428]

With intent to procure a miscarriage

8.194 What is required for a 'miscarriage'? Must the fertilised ovum have become implanted in the endometrium of the uterus or does the term include failure or prevention of implantation? The issue arose in *R (on the application of Smeaton) v Secretary of State for Health*[429] where a ministerial order enabling pharmacists to dispense the 'morning-after pill', which prevents implantation of a fertilised ovum, was challenged in judicial review proceedings on the ground that the use of such a pill involved an intent to procure a miscarriage. Munby J (as he then was) held that the answer was the former of the two possibilities: in the light of modern medical knowledge, 'miscarriage' had to be construed as presupposing that the fertilised ovum had become implanted in the endometrium of the uterus. The use of a pill to prevent implantation of a fertilised ovum would therefore not be done with intent to procure a miscarriage.[430] Munby J entirely agreed with the only previous decision directly on the point, the unreported decision of Wright J in *Dhingra*.[431] In that case Wright J had held that the use of an intra-uterine device which prevents the implantation of a fertilised ovum did not involve an intent to procure a miscarriage.

---

[423] See para 7.119.

[424] *Cramp* (1880) 5 QBD 307 at 309–310, per Field J; see also Stephen J, at 310. See also *Hennah* (1877) 13 Cox CC 547 at 549, per Lord Cockburn CJ.

[425] *Cramp* (1880) 5 QBD 307, CCR.   [426] *Spicer* (1955) 39 Cr App Rep 189.

[427] *Spicer* (1955) 39 Cr App Rep 189; *Marlow* (1964) 49 Cr App Rep 49.

[428] See Price 'Selective Reduction and Feticide: The Parameters of Abortion' [1988] Crim LR 199 at 206.

[429] [2002] EWHC 886 (Admin), Munby J.

[430] For criticism of this decision see Keown '"Morning-after Pills", "Miscarriage" and Muddle' (2005) 25 LS 296.   [431] (1991), unreported.

In *Dhingra*, Wright J held that a 'miscarriage' required the 'spontaneous expulsion of the contents of the products of pregnancy' and that there could be no pregnancy until implantation of a fertilised ovum. On the basis of this decision, and the agreement with it expressed by Munby J in *Smeaton*, the selective reduction of a multiple pregnancy (where one or more foetuses is destroyed in the womb) in early pregnancy in the interests of the remaining foetuses and the mother is not normally caught by the OAPA 1861, s 58, because it usually results not in the expulsion of the foetus(es) but in its (or their) natural absorption into the womb. However, there appears to be an inconsistency between this view and the latter part of the Abortion Act 1967, s 5(2), referred to in para 8.197, which assumes that selective reduction of a multiple pregnancy does constitute a miscarriage for the purposes of s 58.

Unlawfully

8.195 By the Abortion Act 1967, s 5(2), anything done with intent to procure a woman's miscarriage (or, in the case of a woman carrying more than one foetus, her miscarriage of any foetus) is unlawfully done unless authorised by the Abortion Act 1967, s 1. The effect of this is to prevent the justification of an abortion as lawful under the common law principles relating to necessity. On the other hand, it does not preclude the application of the general defence of duress of circumstances in cases where it is impossible to comply with the procedural requirements of the Act (as where a foreign doctor who is not a registered medical practitioner performs an abortion on a train stuck in deep snow drifts in order to save the mother from immediate death).

8.196 Under the Abortion Act 1967, s 1(1), an offence under the OAPA 1861, s 58 is not committed when:

'a pregnancy is terminated by a registered medical practitioner if two registered medical practitioners are of the opinion, formed in good faith –

  (a) that the pregnancy has not exceeded its twenty-fourth week[432] and that the continuance of the pregnancy would involve risk, greater than if the pregnancy were terminated, of injury to the physical or mental health of the pregnant woman or any existing children of her family; or

  (b) that the termination is necessary to prevent grave permanent injury to the physical or mental health of the pregnant woman;[433] or

  (c) that the continuance of the pregnancy would involve risk to the life of the pregnant woman, greater than if the pregnancy were terminated; or

  (d) that there is a substantial risk that if the child were born it would suffer from such physical or mental abnormalities as to be seriously handicapped.'

---

[432] The Act does not define the point of time at which pregnancy begins.

[433] In the determination of (a) or (b), account may be taken of the mother's actual or reasonably foreseeable environment: Abortion Act 1967, s 1(2).

Whether the necessary opinions were formed in good faith is a question for the jury; the medical evidence, although important, is not conclusive.[434]

8.197 Section 1(1) refers to the termination of a pregnancy. As indicated in para 8.194, the existing case law indicates that the selective reduction of a multiple pregnancy does not usually constitute a miscarriage for the purposes of the OAPA 1861, s 58. Even if it did, the latter part of the Abortion Act 1967, s 5(2), which is not limited to selective reduction, provides that, in the case of a woman carrying more than one foetus, anything done with intent to procure miscarriage of any foetus is authorised by s 1 if the ground for termination of the pregnancy specified in the Abortion Act 1967, s 1(1)(d) applies in relation to any foetus and the thing is done for the purpose of procuring the miscarriage of that foetus, or if any of the other grounds for termination of the pregnancy specified in s 1 applies.

8.198 Any treatment for the termination of pregnancy is lawful only if it is carried out in a National Health Service hospital, a Primary Care Trust, NHS Trust or NHS Foundation Trust hospital or other approved place (or class of place).[435] This limitation and the requirement for the opinion of two registered medical practitioners do not apply in an emergency where a registered medical practitioner performs an abortion, having formed the opinion in good faith that this is immediately necessary to save the mother's life or to prevent grave permanent injury to her physical or mental health.[436]

8.199 The reference in the Abortion Act 1967, s 1(1) to the termination of pregnancy was held by the House of Lords in *Royal College of Nursing of the United Kingdom v Department of Health and Social Security*[437] to mean the whole process of treatment undertaken to terminate a pregnancy. Two results follow from this. First, as their Lordships admitted, provided the various conditions are satisfied, s 1(1) applies where the thing administered or used to abort fails to procure a miscarriage or for some reason the operation is not completed. Second, provided a registered medical practitioner has prescribed the treatment for the termination of a pregnancy, remained in charge and accepted responsibility throughout, and the treatment was carried out in accordance with his directions, the 'termination' will have been by a registered medical practitioner for the purposes of the Abortion Act 1967 and the exemption from liability provided by s 1(1) will extend to any person, such as a nurse, participating in that treatment. This is of particular importance because of a method of termination, known as medical induction, in which a very significant part in the treatment is played by nurses.

---

434 *Smith* [1974] 1 All ER 376, CA.   435 Abortion Act 1967, s 1(3) and (3A).
436 Abortion Act 1967, s 1(4).   437 [1981] AC 800, HL.

8.200 The Abortion Act 1967, s 4(1) provides that no one shall be under a legal duty to participate[438] in any treatment authorised by the Act to which he has a conscientious objection, but s 4(2) provides that nothing shall affect any duty to participate in treatment which is necessary to save the life or to prevent grave permanent injury to the physical or mental health of the pregnant woman.

Child destruction

8.201 The Infant Life (Preservation) Act 1929 (IL(P)A 1929), s 1 provides:

> 'any person who, with intent to destroy the life of a child capable of being born alive, by any wilful act causes a child to die before it has an existence independent of its mother, shall be guilty of an offence, to wit of child destruction, and shall be liable on conviction thereof on indictment to [a maximum of] imprisonment for life...'

Like abortion, the offence is triable only on indictment.

8.202 The offence under the IL(P)A 1929 can be distinguished from that under the OAPA 1861, s 58 since it requires the actual destruction of the child, while the latter offence is constituted by the act which attempts to procure a miscarriage.

8.203 Another distinction is that child destruction can be committed only in respect of a child capable of being born alive. 'Capable of being born alive' means capable of being 'born alive' if delivered at the time when the act was done. A child is 'capable of being born alive' when it has reached such a stage of development in the womb that it is capable, if born then, of living and breathing through its lungs alone[439] without any connection with its mother.[440] Provided that this test is satisfied, it is irrelevant that the child is not viable, in the sense that it has no capacity for sustained survival, but only has the capacity to live for a short time after extrusion from the mother.[441]

---

[438] 'Participate' refers to actually taking part in treatment in a NHS hospital, a Primary Care Trust, NHS Trust or NHS Foundation Trust hospital or other approved place (or class of place) for the purpose of terminating a pregnancy, as opposed to making arrangements preliminary to, and intended to bring about measures aimed at, terminating a pregnancy, such as typing letters of referral: *Janaway v Salford Area Health Authority* [1989] AC 537, HL. The act of referral for abortion by a general practitioner would therefore seem not to be a participation in treatment for the purposes of s 4(1), but see Foster 'When Two Freedoms Collide' (2005) 155 NLJ 1624 for arguments to the contrary.

[439] Either naturally or aided by a ventilator: *C v S* [1988] QB 135, High Ct and CA; *McDonald* [1999] NI 150, NI Crown Ct.

[440] *Rance v Mid-Downs Health Authority* [1991] 1 QB 587. Also see *C v S* [1988] QB 135, High Ct and CA.

[441] *Rance v Mid-Downs Health Authority* [1991] 1 QB 587; *McDonald* [1999] NI 150, NI Crown Ct; Wright 'Capable of Being Born Alive?' (1981) 131 NLJ 188; Wright 'Legality of Abortion by Prostaglandin' [1984] Crim LR 347 and [1985] Crim LR 140. Cf Tunkel 'Late Abortions and the Crime of Child Destruction' [1985] Crim LR 133 and Keown 'The Scope of the Offence of Child Destruction' (1988) 104 LQR 121 who argue that viability of the foetus is an essential requirement of 'being born alive', a view which can only be justified by reading words into the statute. This is only permissible if (a) the words are necessarily implied by words already in the statute (*Federal Steam Navigation Co Ltd v Department of Trade and Industry* [1974] 2 All ER 97, HL) or (b) if it

The IL(P)A 1929, s 1(2) provides that the fact that the pregnancy has lasted for 28 weeks is prima facie evidence that the child was capable of being born alive within the definition of child destruction. However, if it is proved that a foetus of less than 28 weeks was nevertheless so developed as to be capable of being born alive, and this is possible in the case of a foetus of 22 weeks or more, it also is protected by the offence of child destruction.

8.204 Although the woman will normally be a consenting party, it appears that the offence also covers non-consensual conduct.[442] While the act in question will normally be some sort of surgical interference, any act done with the relevant intent and effect will do, eg hitting the woman. The IL(P)A 1929, s 1 contains a proviso that the prosecution must prove 'that the act which caused the death of the child was not done in good faith for the purpose only of preserving the life of the mother', which has been construed as including preserving the mother's physical or mental health.[443] This construction is to be found only in directions by trial judges, and is therefore not binding on any other judge. Arguably, it ignores the word 'only' which appears in the provision.[444] In addition, the Abortion Act 1967, s 5(1) provides that no offence under the IL(P)A 1929 is committed by a registered medical practitioner who terminates a pregnancy in accordance with the provisions of the 1967 Act.

8.205 The offence under the IL(P)A 1929 was not originally intended to prevent late abortions. Instead, it was introduced to fill the gap between abortion and homicide by providing for the conviction of a person who destroys a child in the process of birth in circumstances where it could not be proved that the child had had an existence independent of the mother[445] so as to be in law the object of murder. However, as a result of the language used, the offence covers the termination of a pregnancy by a method which destroys a foetus capable of being born alive.

Interrelation of abortion and child destruction

8.206 In spite of the distinctions between them, there is an obvious overlap between child destruction and abortion. A successful abortion can be charged as child destruction if it can be proved that the child was capable of being born alive and, except when the destruction occurs while the child is being born, all child destruction can be charged as abortion.

is necessary to imply the words to make it compatible with the ECHR (see para 1.65). Neither (a) nor (b) applies here. For a third approach, see Price 'How Viable is the Present Scope of the Offence of Child Destruction?' (1987) 16 Anglo-American LR 220.

[442] See Price 'Selective Reduction and Feticide: The Parameters of Abortion' [1988] Crim LR 199 at 206.

[443] *Bourne* [1939] 1 KB 687; *Newton and Stungo* [1958] Crim LR 469.

[444] See Poole [1985] Crim LR 807 (letter).

[445] Para 8.7.

FURTHER READING

Ashworth 'Principles, Pragmatism and the Law Commission's Recommendations on Homicide Law Reform' [2007] Crim LR 333

Ashworth and Mitchell (eds) *Rethinking English Homicide Law* (2000)

Beaumont 'The Unborn Child and the Limits of Homicide' (1997) 61 JCL 86

Elliott 'What Future for Voluntary Manslaughter?' (2004) 68 JCL 253

S Gardner 'Manslaughter by Gross Negligence' (1995) 111 LQR 22

Goff 'The Mental Element in the Crime of Murder' (1988) 104 LQR 30

Grubb 'The New Law of Abortion: Clarification or Ambiguity?' [1991] Crim LR 659

Herring and Palser 'The Duty of Care in Gross Negligence Manslaughter' [2007] Crim LR 24

Horder 'The Criminal Liability of Organisations for Manslaughter and Other Serious Offences' in *Halsbury's Laws of England Centenary Essays* (2007) (Hetherington (ed)) 103

Keown '"Miscarriage": A Medico-Legal Analysis' [1984] Crim LR 604

Keown 'Selective Reduction of Multiple Pregnancy' (1987) 137 NLJ 1165

Keown 'The Scope of the Offence of Child Destruction' (1988) 104 LQR 121

Maier-Katkin and Ogle 'A Rationale for Infanticide Laws' [1993] Crim LR 903

Mitchell 'More Thoughts about Unlawful and Dangerous Act Manslaughter and the One-Punch Killer' [2009] Crim LR 502

O'Donovan 'The Medicalisation of Infanticide' [1984] Crim LR 259

Ormerod and Taylor 'The Corporate Manslaughter and Corporate Homicide Act 2007' [2008] Crim LR 589

Price 'Selective Reduction and Feticide: The Parameters of Abortion' [1988] Crim LR 199

Price 'How Viable is the Present Scope of the Offence of Child Destruction?' (1987) 16 Anglo-American LR 220

Seaborne Davies 'Child-Killing in English Law' in *Modern Approach to Criminal Law* (1945) (Radzinowicz and Turner (eds)) 301

Seneviratne 'Pre-Natal Injury and Transferred Malice: The Invented Other' (1996) 59 MLR 884

Taylor 'The Nature of "Partial Defences" and the Coherence of (Second Degree) Murder' [2007] Crim LR 345

Tunkel 'Late Abortions and the Crime of Child Destruction' [1985] Crim LR 133

Virgo 'Reconstructing Manslaughter by Defective Foundations' (1995) 54 CLJ 14

Williams 'The Mens Rea for Murder: Leave It Alone' (1989) 105 LQR 387

Williams *The Sanctity of Life and the Criminal Law* (1958) Ch 6

Wilson 'A Plea for Rationality in the Law of Murder' (1990) 10 LS 307

Wilson 'The Structure of Criminal Homicide' [2006] Crim LR 471

Wright 'Capable of Being Born Alive?' (1981) 131 NLJ 188

Wright 'Legality of Abortion by Prostaglandin' [1984] Crim LR 347 and [1985] Crim LR 140

Yale 'A Year and a Day in Homicide' [1989] CLJ 202

9

Sexual offences

OVERVIEW

This chapter deals with most of the sexual offences contained in the Sexual Offences Act 2003:

- rape, sexual assault and other non-consensual sexual offences;
- sexual offences involving children under 16;
- abuse of a position of trust where a child is under 18;
- familial sex offences;
- sex with an adult relative;
- sexual offences against people with a mental disorder;
- preparatory offences; and
- exposure, voyeurism and other minor offences.[1]

The Sexual Offences Act 2003 also contains offences relating to abuse of children through prostitution and pornography, exploitation of prostitution and trafficking.

Introduction

9.1 The modern law of sexual offences is protective in purpose. It does not seek to enforce social morality. Until the law of sexual offences was thoroughly overhauled and modernised by the Sexual Offences Act 2003 (SOA 2003), which governs virtually all offences relating to sexual behaviour, the law relating to sexual offences lacked coherence or structure. Much of it reflected the social attitudes towards sexual behaviour and the roles of men and women of the latter part of the nineteenth century. In particular, many of its offences were gender-specific in terms of the sex of the offender and the victim. Where a sex was specified, it was, with one exception, the masculine sex in the case of the offender and, normally, the feminine sex in the case of the other party. The old law was also discriminatory because it treated male homosexual activity in a different way from other

---

[1] For special rules relating to extra-territorial jurisdiction over many of the offences described in this chapter, see paras 9.133 and 9.134.

types of sexual activity. The SOA 2003 is gender-neutral in terms of offender and victim and treats people equally, regardless of their sexual orientation.

9.2 The old law did not reflect the increased knowledge of the profound and long-lasting effects of sexual abuse, nor did it provide adequate protection against such abuse. There were unacceptable gaps in the law and many maximum penalties were too low. The protection of children and other groups of vulnerable people lies at the heart of the SOA 2003.

Age of consent

9.3 Subject to what is said below, the general age of legal consent to sexual activity (whether heterosexual or homosexual) is 16. The fact that a child is under the age of legal consent does not, of course, mean that he or she is incapable of *actually* consenting for the purposes of offences such as rape which require the absence of consent on the part of the victim; it simply means that a child's consent is irrelevant for those offences, such as sexual activity with a child, where the absence of consent is not an element.

9.4 The SOA 2003 introduced a lower age, 13, beneath which a child cannot in law consent to any sexual activity,[2] ie is legally incapable of *actually* consenting to any sexual activity. It did so in order to provide absolute protection for younger children in respect of non-consensual sexual offences on the ground that there must be an age below which there should be no question whether the child consented or not. The thinking behind the minimum age of actual consent is implemented by having a number of sexual offences with a child under 13 which are parallel to the non-consensual offences of rape, assault by penetration, sexual assault and causing a person to engage in sexual activity without consent and which make no reference to the absence of consent.[3]

9.5 Other than the age of criminal responsibility (10), there is no minimum age for the *perpetrator* of any sexual offence based on the fact that the other party is under 16 (or 13). The *blanket* criminalisation of *all* consensual sexual activity, or related conduct, involving a child under 16 is controversial. It is particularly controversial when both participants are under 16, especially when that activity can simply consist of kissing or cuddling, or of A causing B to look at a pornographic video for A's sexual gratification. Speaking of the age of consent in 2001, Lord Millett said in *K*:[4]

> '... the age of consent has long ceased to reflect ordinary life, and in this respect Parliament has signally failed to discharge its responsibility for keeping the criminal law in touch with the needs of society.'

---

[2] This was confirmed in *A-G's Reference (Nos 74 and 83 of 2007)* [2007] EWCA Crim 2550.
[3] Paras 9.35, 9.44, 9.49 and 9.55.   [4] [2001] UKHL 41 at [44].

Is it sensible to make non-exploitative sexual experimentation between two youngsters an offence – especially when the offence is a serious one? The case for saying 'no' is particularly strong where the activity does not involve penetration. The fact that, if the conduct is truly consensual, the Crown Prosecution Service is most unlikely to prosecute may make the youngsters think that the law is an ass and can generally be ignored with impunity. On the other hand, the fact that engaging in experimentation in what comes naturally is technically criminal may deter children from seeking advice and assistance about their sexual development or about contraception, pregnancy and sexually-transmitted diseases.

Arguments in favour of criminalisation where both parties are under 16 centre round the need to protect under-16-year-olds against coercion, exploitation, abuse or sexual harassment, but, depending on the circumstances, this could be dealt with by a prosecution for an offence under the general law, such as an offence contrary to the Protection from Harassment Act 1997.[5]

By way of some recognition of the above arguments, the SOA 2003 provides that where the defendant to a charge involving sexual activity with someone under 16 is himself under 18 a lesser offence is committed than in the case of a defendant aged 18 or over.[6]

Sexual

9.6 'Sexual' is a recurring adjective in the SOA 2003. The SOA 2003, s 78 provides that for the purposes of the various sexual offences in the SOA 2003, Pt 1 (ss 1 to 79), except sexual activity in a public lavatory:

> 'penetration, touching or any other activity is sexual if a reasonable person would consider that –
>
> (a) whatever its circumstances or any person's purpose in relation to it, it is because of its nature sexual, or
>
> (b) because of its nature it may be sexual and because of its circumstances or the purpose of any person in relation to it (or both) it is sexual.'

Section 78 requires penetration, touching or any other activity to pass one or other of two tests in order to be sexual.

9.7 **The first test (s 78(a)) concentrates on the nature of the act. Would a reasonable person consider that because of its *nature* the act is sexual? If so, the act *is* sexual.** The jury or magistrates must look at the act itself, and not at its surrounding circumstances or the purpose with which it is done. The first test is not satisfied if objectively the nature of the act is simply capable of being (ie may or may not be) sexual; it is only satisfied if objectively the act is such that it is because of its nature sexual. Examples of conduct which because of their *nature* would always satisfy the present test would be anal or

---

[5] Paras 7.137–7.145. [6] Para 9.70.

vaginal sexual intercourse, oral sex, and inserting a vibrator into a woman's vagina or a person's anus.

9.8 The second test (s 78(b)) deals with the case where, although a reasonable person would not consider that an activity is because of its nature sexual, the reasonable person would nevertheless consider that because of its nature it *may be* sexual. Examples of such a case would be inserting a finger into a woman's vagina or someone's anus or where someone removes another person's clothes, or where someone touches the genital organs of himself, of another person or of an animal, or kisses another person, or strokes another person's knee (whether clad or not).

The second test contains two requirements.[7] **The first is whether a reasonable person would consider that because of its nature the actual act *may* be sexual.** In relation to this requirement, the circumstances before or after the act took place, or any evidence as to the purpose of any person in relation to it, are irrelevant. **If the answer to the question posed by this requirement is 'No', the act is not sexual. If the answer to the question is 'Yes', the second requirement comes into play, and requires the jury or magistrates to ask themselves whether because of the circumstances of the activity or the purpose of *any* person in relation to it (not just the person who does the act, but (for example) someone who encourages the act to be done), or both, the activity *is* sexual.**[8]

By way of example of the operation of the second test, a reasonable person might consider that the removal of a shoe *may* be sexual by nature[9] and that because of the shoe remover's fetishistic purpose it is sexual, whereas he would consider that the removal of the shoe for legitimate purposes by an assistant in a shoe shop is not sexual in the light of the assistant's purpose and the circumstances. Likewise, a reasonable person would consider that any touching of a woman's breast *may* because of its nature be sexual, and would consider that 'groping' a woman's breast for sexual gratification was sexual in the light of the purpose with which the touching is done. On the other hand, a reasonable person would not consider that touching a woman's breasts was sexual if it was done as part of acts of self-defence against an attack by the woman or by a doctor who was making a bona fide medical examination and touched the breasts for medical reasons.

Another example is where a mother tells her young child to strip in her presence before the child takes a bath; a reasonable person would consider that the child's act of stripping by its nature *may* be sexual, but no reasonable person would conclude from its circumstances or the purpose of anyone (including the mother) that it is sexual. Suppose, on the other hand, that a man bribed a young child into stripping in front of him in his bed-sit for purposes of sexual gratification. A reasonable person would consider that the act because of its nature *may* be sexual, and would consider (by reference to its circumstances and the man's purpose) that it is sexual.

---

[7] *H (Karl Anthony)* [2005] EWCA Crim 732.

[8] See *H (Karl Anthony)* [2005] EWCA Crim 732 at [12] and [13].

[9] In *H (Karl Anthony)* [2005] EWCA Crim 732 at [11] the Court of Appeal expressed reservations as to whether or not the removal of shoes was capable, by the nature of the act, of being sexual. It is submitted that the Court of Appeal was unduly cautious.

By way of two further examples, reference may be made to the facts of two cases decided under the law before the SOA 2003. If, to adopt the facts of *Beal v Kelly*,[10] a man exposes himself to a 14-year-old boy and invites the boy to handle him, but the boy refuses, whereupon the man reaches out and grabs the boy, a jury might find that a reasonable person would consider that by its nature the grabbing *may* be sexual. If so, it would undoubtedly find it sexual in the light of its circumstances and the man's purpose. If, to adopt the facts of *Court*,[11] a man spanks a clothed 11-year-old child, a reasonable person would consider that by its nature that act *may* be sexual. If the man's purpose is sexual gratification (as it was in *Court* where the man was a buttock-fetishist), a reasonable person would clearly think that the act was sexual. On the other hand, if the man's purpose was simply to chastise the girl whom he has found shoplifting in his store, a reasonable person would not find the act sexual in the light of its purpose. The man would, of course, be guilty of a battery or of assault occasioning actual bodily harm, depending on whether such harm was caused.[12]

Where an act is done for a sexual purpose but does not satisfy the first requirement of the second test, it may result in liability for committing an offence with the intention of committing a relevant sexual offence, contrary to the Sexual Offences Act 2003, s 62.[13]

'Not reasonably believe'

9.9 In many offences under the SOA 2003 a defendant will only be guilty if he did not reasonably believe a specified fact, such as that the victim is consenting or is over 16. A defendant will not reasonably believe that 'the victim' consents or is 16 or over and so on, if he:

- knows,
- believes,
- is aware of the risk (but runs it),
- has thought about the risk but wrongly and unreasonably concluded that there is no risk, or
- has not thought about whether there is a risk,

that the victim is not consenting or under 16, and so on.

'Not reasonably believe' postulates an objective test, just like 'reasonable cause to believe', 'reason to believe', 'reason to suspect' or 'no reason to suspect'.[14]

9.10 Whether an alleged belief in consent or age, and so on, was reasonable must be answered by reference to the surrounding circumstances and the antecedent history of

---

[10] [1951] 2 All ER 763, DC.   [11] [1989] AC 28, HL.
[12] The defendants in *Beal v Kelly* and *Court* were held guilty of offences of indecent assault abolished by SOA 2003.   [13] Para 9.123.
[14] See, for example, *Young* [1984] 2 All ER 164, C-MAC. As to this court, see para 2.32, n 91.

the case. What about the defendant's characteristics in so far as they affect his perception of the relevant facts? Can they also be taken into consideration in assessing the reasonableness of that belief. We saw in para 3.59 that the answer is normally 'no', although it is possible for Parliament to provide that 'not reasonably believe' should be assessed by taking into account the defendant's characteristics. Such provision appears to have been made in relation to 'not reasonably believe that B [the victim] consents' in the definitions of rape and the other non-consensual offences under ss 1–4 of the SOA 2003 dealt with below by a provision that: 'Whether a belief is reasonable is to be determined having regard to *all* the circumstances.'[15] These words appear to include relevant characteristics of the defendant.[16] On the other hand, the appearance of these words in these sections of the Act and their non-appearance in other sections would seem to exclude any argument that 'not reasonably believe' elsewhere in the Act should be assessed by reference to the defendant's characteristics.

9.11 The objectivity of 'not reasonably believe' (even when subjectivised in the cases of the above non-consensual sexual offences) means that the fault element of the offences in which the words appear is negligence. It is easier to accept negligence as a basis of liability if the defendant is only liable where he could, given his mental ability and other relevant characteristics, have avoided being negligent.

Non-consensual sexual offences

Key points 9.1

The SOA 2003, ss 1 to 8 provides the following non-consensual offences:

- rape (s 1);
- rape of a child under 13 (s 5);
- assault by penetration (s 2);
- assault of a child under 13 by penetration (s 6);
- sexual assault (s 3);
- sexual assault of a child under 13 (s 7);
- causing a person to engage in sexual activity without consent (s 4); and
- causing or inciting a child under 13 to engage in sexual activity (s 8).

The offences against a child under 13 are non-consensual because the child is deemed in law to be incapable of actually consenting. The other offences require proof that the complainant did not consent. For this purpose, a person consents if he agrees by choice, and has the freedom and capacity to make that choice.

---

[15] Italics supplied.   [16] See further para 9.29.

Consent

9.12 Until the SOA 2003 there was no statutory definition of 'consent' for the purposes of non-sexual offences. The jury were left to wrestle with the concept by giving it its 'ordinary meaning', although they had to be told that 'real consent' was a different state of mind from 'mere submission'; 'mere submission' was not consent but 'reluctant acquiescence' was,[17] a highly controversial[18] distinction and a difficult one to make. The absence of a statutory definition of consent was a major defect of the old law.

9.13 The SOA 2003, s 74 defines 'consent' for the purposes of the offences under ss 1 to 4 and other offences under the Act involving the absence of consent in a way which avoids the need for the jury to grapple with the distinction between 'reluctant acquiescence' and 'mere submission'. The definition is as follows:

> '...a person consents if he agrees by choice, and has the freedom and capacity to make that choice.'

It would be wrong for a jury to assume that this definition is satisfied because the alleged victim did not protest or resist or do anything.[19]

Although s 74 provides more guidance than under the previous law, juries can face a difficult task in applying it in some cases.

The agreement referred to in s 74 can be express or implied, and may be evidenced by words or conduct, past or present.

The SOA 2003, ss 75 and 76 lay down some evidential and conclusive presumptions as to the absence of consent in respect of the offences under the SOA 2003, ss 1–4. They are dealt with in paras 9.31–9.33.

9.14 The application of s 74 indicates that there will not be a consent under it in the same types of case as in non-fatal offences against the person generally.

A person who is asleep or otherwise unconscious at the time of the relevant act will not consent because he will not agree to what is done. The SOA 2003, s 75(1), referred to in para 9.31, assumes, however, that there may be exceptions. One would be where, although the complainant was asleep at the material time, it could be implied from previous practice that there was a consent to sex in such a circumstance, as where a couple have routinely engaged in 'sleepy sex' in which the other slowly wakes the other by making love to him or her.

9.15 If there appears to be an agreement, it may be vitiated by incapacity, lack of freedom of choice or by mistake.

---

[17] *Olugboja* [1982] QB 320, CA.
[18] See the commentary by JC Smith in [1981] Crim LR at 718.
[19] See para 9.26.

Capacity to choose

9.16 The SOA 2003, s 74 speaks of a person agreeing by choice and having the capacity to make that choice. A person's agreement to sexual activity is invalid if he lacks the mental capacity to choose to engage in it. 'Capacity to make a choice' implies that the person must be aware of the proposed sexual activity; one cannot choose something of which one is unaware. A person may lack the capacity to choose if he lacks the mental capacity to consent because, for example, he is mentally impaired,[20] drugged, seriously intoxicated, hypnotised or semi-comatose.

9.17 Neither the SOA 2003, s 74 nor any other section in the SOA 2003 lays down a specific test of capacity. In *X City Council v MB*,[21] however, Munby J (as he then was) regarded the common law test of capacity to consent as being preserved by s 74. **A person will thus lack capacity to consent if he or she has no real understanding of what is involved, or has such limited knowledge, awareness or understanding as to be in no position to decide whether to agree.**[22] In *Morgan* the Supreme Court of Victoria held that for a woman to be found to lack capacity to consent to intercourse:

> '…it must be proved that she has not sufficient knowledge or understanding to comprehend (a) that what is proposed to be done is the physical fact of penetration of her body by the male organ or, if that is not proved, (b) that the act of penetration proposed is one of sexual connection as distinct from an act of a totally different character.'[23]

The court went on to say:

> 'That knowledge or understanding need not, of course, be a complete or sophisticated one. It is enough that she has sufficient "rudimentary knowledge" of what the act comprises and of its character to enable her to decide whether to give or withhold consent.'[24]

In *X City Council v MB*, Munby J held that *Morgan* was 'an essentially correct summary and statement of the common law rule'. He continued:

> 'The…question is whether she (or he) lacks the capacity to understand the sexual nature of the act. Her knowledge and understanding need not be complete or sophisticated. It is enough that she has sufficient rudimentary knowledge of what the act comprises and of its sexual character to enable her to decide whether to give or withhold consent.'[25]

Munby J also pointed out that **not only is capacity to consent 'issue-specific' in relation to different types of transaction (so that someone may have capacity for one purpose but not for another), but it is also issue-specific in relation to different transactions of**

---

[20] Special provision is made for persons with a mental disorder impeding choice by the offences described in paras 9.106–9.112.

[21] [2006] EWHC 168 (Fam) at [82].   [22] *Howard* [1966] 1 WLR 13, CCA.   [23] [1970] VR 337 at 341.

[24] [1970] VR 337 at 342.   [25] [2006] EWHC (Fam) 168 at [74].

the same type (so that a vulnerable adult (B) may have the capacity to consent to one type of sexual activity whilst lacking the capacity to consent to some other (and to B unfamiliar) type of sexual activity).

9.18 In *X City Council v MB*, Munby J went on to say that capacity to consent is not 'person-specific'. The Court of Appeal in *C*[26] agreed, and added that capacity to choose is also not 'situation-specific', and that an irrational fear which prevents the exercise of choice cannot be equated with lack of capacity to choose. However, when *C* went on appeal to it, the House of Lords disagreed with these statements.[27] The House of Lords held that **capacity to choose can be 'person-specific' or 'situation-specific' as well as 'issue-specific'**. It was difficult to think of an activity which was more person- and situation-specific than sexual relations. One did not consent to sex in general; one consented to 'this act of sex with this person at this time and in this place'. Autonomy entailed the freedom and capacity to make a choice of whether or not to do so. That was entirely consistent with the respect for autonomy in matters of private life as guaranteed in the ECHR, Article 8. The Court of Appeal had therefore been wrong in holding that a lack of capacity to choose could not be person- or situation-specific.

9.19 In *Bree*,[28] the Court of Appeal dealt with the case where the complainant is drunk at the time of sexual intercourse. It held that if through drink (or for any other reason) the complainant (B) has temporarily lost capacity to choose whether to have intercourse on the relevant occasion, B is not consenting, and, subject to questions about whether the defendant had *mens rea*, if intercourse takes place, this will be rape. However, it said, where B has voluntarily consumed even substantial quantities of alcohol, but nevertheless remains capable of choosing whether or not to have intercourse, and in drink agrees to do so, this will not be rape. The Court stated that as a matter of practical reality, capacity to consent may evaporate well before B becomes unconscious. It said that whether this is so or not, however, is fact specific, or, more accurately, depends on the actual state of mind of the individuals involved on the particular occasion. This is equally applicable in the context of offences involving other types of non-consensual conduct under the SOA 2003.

Freedom to choose

9.20 A person may not have a freedom to make a choice whether or not to agree if violence is being used against him, or he is caused to fear that it is being used against another, at the time of the relevant conduct or immediately beforehand. The same is the case if he is caused to fear at the time of the relevant act or beforehand that violence would be used against him or another person.

A person may lack freedom of choice for reasons other than violence or a fear of violence. An example would be where someone agrees because he or she has been abducted

---

[26] [2008] EWCA Crim 1155.

[27] [2009] UKHL 42 (reported elsewhere as *Cooper*). See further para 9.110 as to irrational fear.

[28] [2007] EWCA Crim 804. See also *H* [2007] EWCA Crim 2056.

or is unlawfully detained. Another example might be the use of violence, or threat of violence, to destroy property which was of special value, financially or emotionally. Other examples would be a threat of dismissal by an employer to an employee, a threat to remove children or deny access, a threat to report a serious offence to the police or a threat to withdraw economic support from an illegal immigrant who was being sheltered by the defendant. It would all depend on the nature of the threat and the other circumstances (including the complainant's age and mental capacity, whether there was a realistic expectation that it would or could be carried out and whether the complainant could have taken steps to neutralise the threat), and the perception of the complainant, and whether in the light of these factors the complainant was not in reality free to agree or disagree.

9.21 It would seem that there must be some sort of external coercion; some actual or threatened harm. Provided that it is rational (and therefore there is capacity to choose), self-induced fear cannot suffice. On the other hand, there is no reason why a fear induced by an implied threat by another should not suffice, nor why the threatening or other conduct should not come from a third party or external circumstances. In *K (Peter) and K (Terence)*,[29] B, aged 14, who had been sexually abused by A's brother, and to a lesser extent by A, from the age of eight, agreed to have sex with A in exchange for £3.25 for food at a time when she was homeless, tired, dirty and hungry, having run away from home and lived on the streets for some time. At A's trial for rape, contrary to the Sexual Offences Act 1956, s 1 (repealed), the prosecution's case was that A had taken advantage of a hungry and vulnerable child whom he knew had been abused by his brother and himself, and that B had submitted because her will had been overcome by hunger and desperation and therefore did not consent. The judge directed the jury that there would be no consent if B had submitted to sex because her will had been overborne. A was convicted and appealed unsuccessfully to the Court of Appeal. Although the appeal was concerned with the precise wording of the judge's direction, the Court's decision is based on acceptance that there can be lack of consent in such a case. It should not be thought anyone who agrees to sex out of desperation does not consent. The question is whether the complainant was free to choose. The background of sexual abuse by A and A's brother (of which A was aware), and B's consequent vulnerability and desperation, were clearly important factors.

It remains to be decided whether it is enough simply that the complainant has placed his trust in another who has then taken unfair advantage of him. It is submitted that, while such conduct has relevance in the law of contract, it has no relevance to the law of sexual offences where the complainant is a mentally sound adult, deserving as it is of moral censure. The special need for protection against abuse of positions of trust in relation to children and the mentally infirm is recognised by offences dealt with later in this chapter[30] which do not require proof of the absence of consent.

---

[29] [2008] EWCA Crim 434.   [30] See paras 9.76–9.89 and 9.106–9.122.

Mistake

9.22 Some mistakes may vitiate an apparent agreement, whether they are induced by the defendant's fraud or self-induced. This will certainly be the effect of a mistaken belief as to the nature of the act or that the defendant is someone known personally to the complainant. In neither case does the complainant agree to what is done. The same is true where there is a mistake as to the purpose of the act, as is confirmed by the SOA 2003, s 76 discussed later. There is a clear difference between agreeing to be touched in an intimate part of the body, for example, digital penetration, when it is done by a doctor for clinical reasons and when the touching – even by a doctor – is done purely for reasons of sexual gratification.

9.23 Does SOA 2003, s 74 mean that a mistake as to a collateral matter, such as the attributes of the defendant or the quality of an act,[31] can prevent *'agreement* by choice', or indeed that there is in law no such agreement whenever a person (V) consents to a sexual activity under a mistake as to any fact which is such that V would not have consented if V had known the truth?[32] The decision in B[33] seems to indicate that the answer to both questions is 'no', although there may be an exception in the case of a mistake as to the quality of an act (as there currently is in respect of non-fatal offences against the person).[34]

In *B*, the Court of Appeal held that, where one party to sexual activity has a sexually transmissible disease which is not disclosed to the other party, any consent that may have been given to that activity by the other party is not thereby vitiated. The act remains a consensual act. Therefore, the Court held, the fact that D might not have disclosed his HIV status is not a matter which could in any way be relevant to the issue of consent under the SOA 2003, s 74 in relation to the sexual activity between D and the complainant. The Court noted that the party suffering from the sexually transmissible disease will not have any defence to a charge (eg under the Offences Against the Person Act 1861, s 20) which may result from harm created by that sexual activity, merely by virtue of that consent, because such consent does not include consent to the risk of infection by the disease.[35]

Under the law as it was before the SOA 2003, if a person consented to sexual intercourse having been deceived by a promise which the promisor did not intend to fulfil, the fraudulent promise did not vitiate that consent. In *Linekar*,[36] for example, a prostitute consented to sexual intercourse with a man after he had falsely led her to believe that he intended to pay her for her services. After they had had intercourse he failed to pay. The Court of Appeal held that he was not guilty of rape because his fraudulent promise had

---

[31] Such a mistake was held capable of invalidating consent for the purposes of a battery in the offence of indecent assault under the Sexual Offences Act 1956 (since repealed): *Tabassum* [2000] 2 Cr App Rep 328, CA.

[32] For an argument that s 74 enables the court to develop the latter approach, see Herring 'Mistaken Sex' [2005] Crim LR 511.

[33] [2006] EWCA Crim 2945. Also see *Dica* [2004] EWCA Crim 1103; para 7.32. According to *Tabassum*, n 31, the mistake in *B* was not one as to the 'quality' of the act.

[34] Para 7.30. What constitutes a 'quality' of an act is not yet clear: para 7.31.   [35] Para 7.32.

[36] [1995] QB 250, CA.

not vitiated the woman's consent. The position would seem to be the same under the SOA 2003. A person who agrees to sexual intercourse because of a fraudulent promise of marriage or the fraudulent promise of a job agrees by choice and has the freedom and capacity to make that choice.

Rape

9.24 The SOA 2003, s 1(1) provides:

> 'A person (A) commits an offence if –
>
> (a) he intentionally penetrates the vagina, anus or mouth of another person (B) with his penis,
>
> (b) B does not consent to the penetration, and
>
> (c) A does not reasonably believe that B consents.'

An offence under s 1 is triable only on indictment. The maximum punishment is life imprisonment.[37]

Actus reus

9.25 There must be 'penetration' of the vagina, anus or mouth by the defendant's penis. For the purposes of the SOA 2003, 'penetration' is a continuing act from entry to withdrawal.[38] It follows that, if someone consents to penetration at the time of entry, but withdraws consent and the penetration continues, the continuing penetration will be without consent.[39] It also follows that if the penetrator only acquires *mens rea* as to the fact that a victim is not consenting after he has penetrated him or her but intentionally continues the intercourse, he can be convicted of rape.[40] The slightest degree of penetration is enough.[41]

References in the SOA 2003 to 'penis', 'vagina' and other parts of the body include references to a part surgically constructed (in particular through gender reassignment surgery).[42] It is for this reason that vaginal rape can be committed by a female to male transsexual or in respect of a male to female transsexual.

9.26 The penetration must occur without the consent of the complainant. As already indicated, the absence of consent does not have to be demonstrated by offering resistance or by communicating it to the defendant,[43] but if it is not communicated the *mens rea* as

---

[37] SOA 2003, s 1(4).

[38] SOA 2003, s 79(2).

[39] *Cooper and Schaub* [1994] Crim LR 531, CA.

[40] *Kaitamaki v R* [1985] AC 147, PC.

[41] *Hughes* (1841) 9 C & P 752; *Lines* (1844) 1 Car & Kir 393.

[42] SOA 2003, s 79(3).

[43] This was held by the Court of Appeal in *Malone* [1998] 2 Cr App Rep 447 in relation to the offence of rape under the now repealed Sexual Offences Act 1956; it was confirmed by the Court of Appeal in *H* [2007] EWCA Crim 2056 in respect of all the non-consensual offences under SOA 2003.

to the absence of consent may be more difficult to prove. Consent to penetration of one of the bodily orifices referred to is not consent to penetration of another of them.

9.27 The presumptions in the SOA 2003, ss 75 and 76 referred to in paras 9.31–9.33 will often be of great importance in respect of proof of the absence of consent.

Mens rea

9.28 The defendant must intentionally (ie deliberately)[44] penetrate the vagina, anus or mouth of another person with his penis. It will be a most exceptional case where, once penetration has been proved, it will not be inferred that the perpetrator intended it.

9.29 In addition, the defendant must not reasonably believe that the other person consents to the penetration. We saw in para 9.9 that 'not reasonably believe' is an objective test; negligence is the *mens rea* as to lack of consent.

The present requirement is harsher than the one which applied to the offence of rape under the Sexual Offences Act 1956. That Act simply required the defendant to know or be reckless as to the absence of consent, so that a defendant who unreasonably believed that the other party was consenting was not guilty of rape.

The SOA 2003, s 1(2) provides that:

> 'Whether a belief [in consent] is reasonable is to be determined having regard to all the circumstances, including any steps A [the defendant] has taken to ascertain whether B [the complainant] consents.'

The words '*all* the circumstances' must refer to those which might be relevant to the issue, including any characteristic of the defendant, permanent or transient, which might affect his ability to perceive or understand whether or not the victim is consenting. Examples would be a learning disability, mental illness, deafness, blindness, immaturity, extreme youth and sexual inexperience.

Despite the reference to *all* the circumstances, characteristics should obviously only be taken into account to the extent that they could reasonably affect the defendant's perception or understanding of whether or not the complainant is consenting. Other characteristics would not be factually relevant to the reasonableness of the defendant's belief. The fact, for example, that the defendant finds women in tight trousers irresistible should not be taken into account.

The same point could be made about circumstances other than the characteristics of the defendant. For example, it is submitted that the circumstance that the complainant was provocatively dressed or where the incident occurred should not be taken into account by a jury because it could not reasonably affect the defendant's perception or understanding of whether or not the complainant is consenting. On the other hand, the

---

[44] Para 9.47. Thus, in the unlikely event that a defendant accidentally or recklessly penetrated the other person the defendant would not be guilty of rape.

complainant's behaviour, at least at the time, or the complainant's relationship with the defendant, even if it had ceased, would seem to be circumstances which could reasonably affect the defendant's perception or understanding of whether or not the complainant is consenting.

Proof of lack of consent and of the mens rea relating to it

> **Key points 9.2**
>
> Where the circumstances fall within the terms of SOA 2003, s 75 or s 76, proof of lack of consent and of the *mens rea* relating to it is assisted by the SOA 2003, ss 75 and 76, which provide evidential and conclusive presumptions as to the lack of consent and the lack of a reasonable belief in consent. Sections 75 and 76, which are applied to the SOA 2003, s 1 by s 1(3), also apply to the offences of assault by penetration, sexual assault and causing a person to engage in sexual activity without consent, contrary to the SOA 2003, ss 2, 3 and 4 respectively.[45] They do not apply to any other offence under the Act where consent is relevant.

9.30 Sections 75 and 76 refer to the defendant having done 'the relevant act'.[46] For the purposes of rape, 'the relevant act' is that the defendant intentionally penetrated, with his penis, the vagina, anus or mouth of another person ('the complainant').[47]

Evidential presumptions

9.31 The SOA 2003, s 75(1) provides:

'If in proceedings for an offence to which this section applies it is proved –

(a) that the defendant did the relevant act,

(b) that any of the circumstances specified in subs (2) existed, and

(c) that the defendant knew[48] that those circumstances existed,

the complainant is to be taken not to have consented to the relevant act unless sufficient evidence is adduced to raise an issue as to whether he consented, and the defendant is to be taken not to have reasonably believed that the complainant consented unless sufficient evidence is adduced to raise an issue as to whether he reasonably believed it.'

Thus, if the prosecution proves (a), (b) and (c) a rebuttable presumption arises that the complainant did not consent to the relevant act and that the defendant did not

---

[45] SOA 2003, ss 2(3), 3(3) and 4(3).

[46] Because the provisions require proof that the defendant 'did' the relevant act, they have no application to an attempt to do the relevant act and therefore are inapplicable on a charge of attempt to commit one of the offences to which they apply: see Rodwell 'Problems with the Sexual Offences Act 2003' [2005] Crim LR 290.

[47] SOA 2003, s 77.   [48] Para 3.43.

reasonably believe that the complainant consented. Rebuttal of either presumption does not require the defendant to prove the opposite; the defendant does not have a persuasive burden. Instead, the presumptions will be rebutted if sufficient evidence is adduced to raise an issue as to whether the presumed fact existed. Such evidence will normally be adduced by the defendant, but it does not have to be; it can be adduced by any other witness.

It is for the judge to decide whether sufficient evidence has been adduced. There will be sufficient evidence if there is evidence which (if believed) might leave a jury in reasonable doubt as to whether the presumed fact existed.[49]

Where the judge is satisfied that an issue has been raised on the evidence, the judge must leave it to the jury (whether it has been mentioned by the defendant or not) and in the normal way it will be for the prosecution to prove beyond reasonable doubt the matter which had been (but is no longer) rebuttably presumed, ie the prosecution will have a persuasive burden in such a case. The jury will have to be directed to this effect. They will also, of course, have to be directed about the need for the other elements of the offence to be proved.

On the other hand, if the judge does not think that the evidence adduced is sufficient to raise an issue (or if no evidence is adduced in this respect), the judge will direct the jury to convict the defendant if they are sure that the defendant intentionally did the relevant act, that one of the six circumstances in s 75(2) is proved and that the defendant knew that.

9.32 The circumstances specified in the SOA 2003, s 75(2), one of which the prosecution must prove as one of the preconditions of the rebuttable presumptions arising, are that:

- **any person was, at the time of the relevant act or immediately before it began, using violence against the complainant or causing the complainant to fear that immediate violence would be used against him.** The person using or threatening the violence need not be the person doing the relevant act. It remains to be seen how the courts interpret 'immediately'. It will be noted a threat of something other than violence, eg to damage property or to reveal something discreditable, is not covered;

- **any person was, at the time of the relevant act or immediately before it began, causing the complainant to fear that violence was being used, or that immediate violence would be used, against another person.** An example would be where violence is threatened against the complainant's child unless the complainant agrees to have sexual intercourse. The other person need not be related in any way to the complainant. The comments made in respect of the first circumstance are equally applicable here;

---

[49] Para 4.10.

- the complainant was, and the defendant was not, unlawfully detained at the time of the relevant act. The defendant need not be the person detaining the complainant but he must not be another unlawfully detained person;

- the complainant was asleep or otherwise unconscious at the time of the relevant act. 'Otherwise unconscious' covers people who are, for example, unconscious through drink or drugs;

- because of the complainant's physical disability, the complainant would not have been able at the time of the relevant act to communicate to the defendant whether the complainant consented. It will be noted that this circumstance is limited to physical disability; it does not apply to mental disability.[50] In the present circumstance, s 75 rebuttably presumes that a person who is unable to communicate because of a physical disability has not consented; it is up to the defendant to adduce evidence to the contrary;

- any person had administered to or caused to be taken[51] by the complainant, without the complainant's consent, a substance which, having regard to when it was administered or taken, was capable of causing or enabling the complainant to be stupefied or overpowered at the time of the relevant act.[52] This provision is obviously designed to deal with date rape drugs. It does not cover the case where B is induced voluntarily to consume alcohol in a quantity capable of stupefying or overpowering B. The defendant need not be the person who administers or causes the substance to be taken.

An example of rebuttal of the presumptions in s 75 would be where A, who is proved to have penetrated B vaginally immediately after deliberately using violence on her, adduces sufficient evidence that he and B had in accordance with their customary practice been engaging in sado-masochistic conduct and thereby raises the issue as to whether B consented and whether A reasonably believed that B consented. Another example (which relates to sexual assault) would be where A, who is proved to have had oral sex with B when B was asleep, adduces sufficient evidence that B had asked her (A) to wake him (B) on his birthday by performing this act on him and thereby raises the issue just referred to. Once the issue is raised, the presumptions will be rebutted (and A will not be guilty) unless the prosecution proves beyond reasonable doubt that B did not consent and that A did not reasonably believe that B had consented.

---

[50] The SOA 2003, ss 30–33 provide special offences to deal with those who engage in sexual activity with a person who because of, or for a reason related to, mental disorder are incapable of communicating a choice whether to agree to it: see paras 9.106–9.112.

[51] Presumably these terms bear the same meaning as under the Offences Against the Person Act 1861, ss 23 and 24: paras 7.115–7.119.

[52] For a detailed analysis of the circumstance in the last bullet point, indicating the need for interpretation and clarification, see Finch and Munro 'The Sexual Offences Act 2003: Intoxicated Consent and Drug Assisted Rape Revisited' [2004] Crim LR 789.

Conclusive presumptions

9.33 The SOA 2003, s 76(1) provides:

> 'If in proceedings for an offence to which this section applies it is proved that the defendant did the relevant act and that any of the circumstances specified in subs (2) existed, it is to be conclusively presumed –
>
> (a) that the complainant did not consent to the relevant act, and
> (b) that the defendant did not believe that the complainant consented to the relevant act.'

The circumstances specified in s 76(2) are that:

> '(a) the defendant intentionally deceived the complainant as to the nature or purpose of the relevant act;
> (b) the defendant intentionally induced the complainant to consent to the relevant act by impersonating a person known personally to the complainant.'

In *Jheeta*,[53] the Court of Appeal emphasised that the conclusive presumption only arises in these two very limited types of circumstance. No conclusive presumption arises because the complainant was deceived in some other way. It considered that deception as to the nature and purpose of the relevant act of penetration by a penis would be comparatively rare; no doubt the same is true, perhaps even more true, in the case of impersonation of someone personally known to the complainant.

The conclusive (ie irrebuttable) presumptions under s 76 might at first glance be thought to raise questions about their compatibility with the presumption of innocence under ECHR, Article 6(2); but they do not. They merely help to define the concept of consent.

Other circumstances

9.34 The list of circumstances which give rise to evidential or conclusive presumptions are not, of course, the only ones where an apparent consent may not be a true consent. In the case of other circumstances, it will be for the prosecution from the start to prove the absence of consent (as defined above) and of a reasonable belief in consent.

Rape of a child under 13

9.35 The principle in the SOA 2003 that a child under 13 cannot consent in law to any sexual activity, ie is legally incapable of actually consenting,[54] is implemented in respect of penile penetration by s 5.

---

[53] [2007] EWCA Crim 1699.   [54] Para 9.4.

The SOA 2003, s 5(1) provides:

'A person commits an offence if –

    (a) he intentionally[55] penetrates the vagina, anus or mouth of another person with his penis,[56] and

    (b) the other person is under 13.'

An offence under s 5 is triable only on indictment. The maximum punishment is life imprisonment.[57]

9.36 Other offences dealing with sexual activity in respect of children under 16 or children under 18 have detailed provisions as to their *mens rea* in respect of the child's age but s 5 contains nothing about *mens rea* in this respect. In *G*[58] where D, aged 15, had pleaded guilty to the offence under the SOA 2003, s 5 in respect of a girl of 12 but only on the basis that she had been willing and that on the basis of what she had told him he had reasonably believed that she was 15, the Court of Appeal upheld his conviction. It held that the offence under s 5 is an offence of strict liability as to age; a defendant can be convicted of it even if he reasonably believed that the child was 13 or over.[59] It also rejected the argument that the imposition of strict liability infringed ECHR, Article 6(1) (right to fair trial) or (2) (presumption of innocence),[60] a conclusion with which the House of Lords agreed when this point was appealed to it.[61]

Exceptions to aiding, abetting and counselling

9.37 An offence under s 5 is one of the offences in respect of which there are under the SOA 2003, s 73 exceptions from criminal liability on the basis of aiding, abetting or counselling the commission of the offence if a person acts for the purpose of:

- protecting the child from sexually transmitted infection;
- protecting the physical safety of the child;
- preventing the child from becoming pregnant; or
- promoting the child's emotional well-being by the giving of advice,

and not for the purpose of obtaining sexual gratification or for the purpose of causing or encouraging the activity constituting the offence or the child's participation in it.

The rationale for these exceptions is that one of the aims of the SOA 2003 is to protect from sexual abuse those who are vulnerable. This aim might be defeated if people were prevented from giving sex education or counselling or contraceptives to a child because of fear that they might be convicted of being a secondary party to a sexual

---

[55] See para 9.28.   [56] See para 9.25.   [57] SOA 2003, s 5(2).
[58] [2006] EWCA Crim 821.   [59] See para 6.33.
[60] See para 6.8.   [61] [2008] UKHL 37 at [55].

offence subsequently committed with that child on the ground that they had assisted or encouraged that offence.

Child offenders

9.38 Like any other sexual offence, the minimum age at which this offence can be committed is the age of criminal responsibility, which is the tenth birthday. If A and B, aged between 10 and 13, consensually experiment together and A intentionally penetrates B with his penis, it follows that he is guilty of raping a child, even if he is younger and less experienced or knowledgeable than B, and acts in accordance with B's instructions. Many of the more absurd consequences of this can, however, be avoided by the proper exercise of prosecutorial discretion. It is recognised that the prosecution of a young offender may not always be appropriate, and an inappropriate decision to prosecute may be open to judicial review. Even if some form of prosecution is appropriate, a charge under s 5 may be considered unduly heavy-handed if it is clear that the complainant fully understood and consented to what took place. The Court of Appeal acknowledged this in G[62] and the House of Lords does not appear to have dissented from that. The initial complaint in G had been one of forcible rape, which would fully have justified the initial charge under s 5, but (as already noted) D pleaded guilty on the basis of the girl's willingness and his belief that she was 15. A majority of the House of Lords (3–2) held that neither s 5, nor the prosecution and conviction of D in such circumstances for an offence under s 5 (rather than the less serious offence under s 13[63]), nor the sentence imposed (a conditional discharge), breached D's rights under ECHR, Article 8(1) (right to respect for private life). It was appropriate for the girl's willingness and D's mistaken belief to be reflected merely in the sentence imposed, rather than by the substitution of a charge of a less serious offence under s 13. Baroness Hale concluded:

'The word "rape" does indeed connote a lack of consent. But the law has disabled children under 13 from giving their consent. So there was no consent. In view of all the dangers resulting from under age sexual activity, it cannot be wrong for the law to apply that label even if it cannot be proved that the child was in fact unwilling. The fact that the appellant was under 16 is obviously relevant to his relative blameworthiness and has been reflected in the second most lenient disposal available to a criminal court. But it does not alter the fact of what he did or the fact that he should not have done it. In my view the prosecution, conviction and sentence were both rational and proportionate in the pursuit of the legitimate aims of the protection of health and morals and of the rights and freedoms of others.'[64]

Assault

9.39 The SOA 2003, ss 2, 3, 6 and 7 provide four offences which their headings describe as:

- assault by penetration (s 2);
- assault of a child under 13 by penetration (s 6);

---

[62] [2006] EWCA Crim 821.   [63] See para 9.70.   [64] [2008] UKHL 37 at [55].

- sexual assault (s 3); and

- sexual assault of a child under 13 (s 7).

The headings to each of the four sections are misleading. The sections require bodily contact, either through penetration or some other form of touching. Such conduct constitutes a battery if it is done with the requisite mental element. It does not necessarily involve an assault. If A causes B to apprehend that he is about to touch her breast, for example, but stops him before he can do so, A will be guilty of an assault but not of sexual assault, although he may be guilty of an attempt to commit that offence.

Pursuant to the general principle in the SOA 2003 that a child under 13 cannot consent in law to any sexual activity, ss 6 and 7 provide offences of sexual assault by non-penile penetration of a child under 13 and by touching a child under 13, where the absence of consent is not an element.

Assault by penetration

9.40 The SOA 2003, s 2(1) provides:

'A person (A) commits an offence if –

(a) he intentionally penetrates the vagina or anus of another person[65] (B) with a part of his body or anything else,

(b) the penetration is sexual,[66]

(c) B does not consent to the penetration, and

(d) A does not reasonably believe that B consents.'

The offence is triable only on indictment. The maximum punishment is life imprisonment,[67] the same as for rape.

9.41 The penetration of the vagina or anus may be by any part of the defendant's body, eg a finger or a fist. Alternatively, the penetration of the vagina or anus may be achieved by the defendant by anything else, eg by his use of part of the body of an unwilling third party or of an animal or by his use of a bottle or other article.

There is no need for a hostile intent to be proved on the defendant's part, but the penetration must be done without the victim's consent.

9.42 The *mens rea* is similar to that for rape contrary to s 1.

The prosecution must prove that the defendant intentionally (ie deliberately)[68] penetrated the complainant's vagina or anus. In addition, the prosecution must prove that A, the defendant, did not reasonably believe[69] that B, the complainant, consented to the penetration. As in the case of rape contrary to s 1, whether a belief is reasonable is to be

---

[65] As to 'penetrates the vagina or anus of another person' see para 9.25.   [66] Para 9.6.
[67] SOA 2003, s 2(4).   [68] Para 9.28.   [69] Para 9.9.

determined having regard to all the circumstances, including any steps the defendant has taken to ascertain whether B consents.[70]

9.43 If it is proved that the defendant intentionally penetrated, with a part of his body or anything else, the vagina or anus of B ('the complainant') in circumstances where the penetration was sexual, and that (as the defendant knew) one of the circumstances in s 75(2) existed, the evidential presumptions about the absence of consent and of a reasonable belief in consent in s 75 also apply to the present offence.[71]

If it is proved that the defendant (A) intentionally penetrated, with a part of his body or anything else, the vagina or anus of another person (B, 'the complainant') in circumstances where the penetration was sexual, and that A intentionally deceived B as to the nature or purpose of that act, or that A intentionally induced B to consent to that act by impersonating someone known to B, it is to be conclusively presumed that B did not consent to that act and that A did not believe that B consented to the relevant act.[72]

Assault of a child under 13 by penetration

9.44 The SOA 2003, s 6(1) provides:

> 'A person commits an offence if –
>
> (a) he intentionally penetrates the vagina or anus of another person[73] with a part of his body or anything else,
>
> (b) the penetration is sexual, and
>
> (c) the other person is under 13.'

The offence, like that under s 5 (rape of a child under 13), is one of strict liability as to age.

An offence under s 6 is triable only on indictment. The maximum punishment is life imprisonment.[74] Under the SOA 2003, s 73, the exceptions from liability for aiding, abetting or counselling (para 9.37) apply to an offence under s 6.

Sexual assault

9.45 The SOA 2003, s 3(1) provides:

> 'A person (A) commits an offence if –
>
> (a) he intentionally touches another person (B),
>
> (b) the touching is sexual,[75]

---

[70] SOA 2003, s 2(2).　　[71] SOA 2003, ss 2(3) and 77; see paras 9.31–9.32.
[72] SOA 2003, ss 2(3), 76 and 77; see para 9.33.
[73] As to 'intentionally penetrates the vagina or anus of another person' see paras 9.25 and 9.28.
[74] SOA 2003, s 6(2).　　[75] Para 9.6.

> (c) B does not consent to the touching, and
>
> (d) A does not reasonably believe that B consents.'

An offence under s 3 is triable either way and punishable with a maximum of 10 years' imprisonment on conviction on indictment.[76]

9.46 The use of 'touch' in s 3(1)(a) means that the most minimal contact with B suffices under s 3. As elsewhere in the SOA 2003 whenever the term appears, 'touching' includes:

> 'touching –
>
> (a) with any part of the body,
>
> (b) with anything else,
>
> (c) through anything,
>
> and in particular includes touching amounting to penetration.'[77]

An example of a touching by something other than a part of anyone's body would be holding a sex toy against a private part of the victim's body. The Court of Appeal in *H (Karl Anthony)*,[78] where D had approached a woman and said 'Do you fancy a shag?' before grabbing her tracksuit bottom and pulling her towards him, held that 'touching' includes touching a person's clothing without applying any form of pressure to his body.

The touching must be without the victim's consent. Because no hostile intent is required, a man who tries (somewhat misguidedly) to 'win over' his partner after a quarrel by touching her sexually without her consent will commit the present offence, subject to the *mens rea* as to lack of consent being proved.

9.47 The defendant must intentionally touch the complainant. In *Heard*,[79] the Court of Appeal held that 'intentional touching' in s 3 simply means a deliberate touching which is in fact sexual; it was not necessary to prove that the defendant intended to touch sexually.[80] There can be no doubt that what was held in *Heard* is true in respect of other offences in the SOA 2003 which require that the defendant 'intentionally' touches or penetrates another. Because there must be a deliberate touching, not only will an accidental touching not suffice but nor will a reckless touching (as where a defendant intends to avoid actual physical contact by a very slight margin, but realises that he may not do so).[81] As can be seen, intention in the present context bears a much more limited meaning then it normally does.[82]

---

[76] SOA 2003, s 3(4).   [77] SOA 2003, s 79(8).

[78] [2005] EWCA Crim 732.   [79] [2007] EWCA Crim 125. See, further, para 15.79.

[80] The defendant's purpose may, of course, be relevant in respect of whether the touching was sexual: para 9.8.

[81] This rather obvious point was confirmed in *Heard* [2007] EWCA Crim 125.   [82] Paras 3.5–3.19.

In addition, the defendant must not reasonably believe[83] that the complainant consents to the sexual touching. As in the case of rape contrary to s 1, whether a belief is reasonable must be determined with regard to all the circumstances, including any steps the defendant has taken to ascertain whether the complainant consents.[84]

9.48 In terms of the requirement of the absence of consent by the complainant and 'no reasonable belief' in consent on the defendant's part, the prosecution is assisted by the evidential and conclusive presumptions in ss 75 and 76 referred to in paras 9.31–9.33 which also apply to the present offence.[85] As noted in para 9.30, both s 75 and s 76 refer to the defendant having done the 'relevant act'. For the purposes of the present offence, the 'relevant act' is: 'the defendant intentionally touching another person ("the complainant"), where the touching is sexual'.[86]

Sexual assault of a child under 13

9.49 As with the offences of rape and assault by penetration, a separate offence of sexual assault of a child under 13 is provided, in which absence of consent is not an element.

The SOA 2003, s 7(1) provides:

> 'A person commits an offence if –
>
> (a) he intentionally touches another person,[87]
>
> (b) the touching is sexual,[88] and
>
> (c) the other person is under 13.'

The offence under s 7 is triable either way and is punishable with a maximum of 14 years' imprisonment on conviction on indictment.[89] The exceptions under the SOA 2003, s 73 from liability for aiding, abetting or counselling (para 9.37) apply to an offence under s 7.

As in the case of the offences under ss 5 and 6, there is no exemption for the case of consensual sexual touchings, including kissing or fondling over clothes, where the toucher is also a youngster, perhaps under 13 as well, and no exploitation or abuse is involved.

The offence, like that under s 5 (rape of a child under 13), is one of strict liability as to age.

Causing a person to engage in sexual activity without consent

9.50 Compelling or otherwise causing someone to engage in a sexual activity without consent is potentially a very serious infringement of that person's sexual autonomy, and is clearly deserving the label of 'criminal'.

---

[83] Para 9.9. [84] SOA 2003, s 3(2). [85] SOA 2003, s 3(3).
[86] SOA 2003, s 77. [87] See paras 9.46 and 9.47. [88] Para 9.6. [89] SOA 2003, s 7(2).

It was noted in para 9.25 that rape can only be physically committed by non-consensual penile penetration. The result is that where a woman compels a man to penetrate her without his consent, the woman cannot be convicted of rape. Such conduct is covered by the offences of causing a person to engage in sexual activity without consent, contrary to the SOA 2003, s 4.

Section 4 also covers the case where A causes B to perform the sexual activity on himself or herself without consent, eg self-penetration with a vibrator, self-masturbation without consent or stripping for A's sexual gratification. In addition, it covers the case where A causes B to engage in sexual activity, to which B does not consent, with a third party or an animal or corpse, eg to masturbate X or be penetrated by an animal.

9.51 The SOA 2003, s 4(1) provides:

'A person (A) commits an offence if –

(a) he intentionally causes another person (B) to engage in an activity,

(b) the activity is sexual,[90]

(c) B does not consent to engaging in the activity, and

(d) A does not reasonably believe that B consents.'

Where the activity caused involved:

(a) penetration of B's anus or vagina (whether by a penis, other part of the body or anything else);

(b) penetration of B's mouth with a person's penis;

(c) penetration of a person's anus or vagina with a part of B's body or by B with anything else; or

(d) penetration of a person's mouth with B's penis,

the offence is triable only on indictment and punishable with a maximum of life imprisonment.[91] It will be noted that penetration of an animal by B's penis is not included in this list, nor is penetration of B's mouth by an animal's penis, whereas penetration of B's anus or vagina by an animal's penis is.

In any other case, an offence under s 4(1) is triable either way and punishable with a maximum of 10 years' imprisonment on conviction.[92]

Because there are two separate maxima dependent on a difference in the facts established, there are two separate offences under s 4: causing another to engage in penetrative sexual activity in one of the above ways, and causing another to engage in 'non-penetrative' sexual activity. This is the effect of the rule in *Courtie*.[93]

9.52 A person (A) causes another (B) to engage in sexual activity without consent if B engages in the activity in consequence[94] of A exerting a capacity which he possesses to

---

[90] Para 9.6. [91] SOA 2003, s 4(4). [92] SOA 2003, s 4(5).
[93] [1984] AC 463, HL; para 3.50, n 111. [94] As to causation see paras 2.28–2.57.

control or influence B's acts. It is not enough simply to prove that some antecedent event or condition produced by A contributed to the determination of the will of B to engage in the sexual activity, or that in producing that antecedent event or condition A was actuated by desire that B should engage in it. Cause requires proof of an act.[95] It would not be enough if A simply allowed (ie failed to stop) someone (X) engaging in sexual activity with B without B's consent, even if A owed a legal duty of care in respect of B or had a right of control over X[96] (although in these cases A could be convicted as a secondary party to the offence committed by X if he failed to take reasonable steps to prevent that offence being committed).[97]

9.53 In addition to an intent to cause the complainant to engage in the sexual activity, the defendant must also not reasonably believe[98] that the complainant consents to engaging in the activity.[99] As in the case of rape contrary to s 1, whether a belief is reasonable must be determined with regard to all the circumstances, including any steps the defendant has taken to ascertain whether the complainant consents.[100]

9.54 In terms of the requirements of the absence of consent by the complainant and 'no reasonable belief' in consent on the defendant's part, the prosecution is assisted by the evidential and conclusive presumptions in ss 75 and 76 referred to in paras 9.31–9.33 which also apply to the present offence.[101] As noted in para 9.30, both s 75 and s 76 refer to the defendant having done the 'relevant act'. Section 77 provides that, for the purposes of the present offences, the 'relevant act' is the defendant intentionally causing the complainant to engage in an activity, where the activity is sexual.

Devonald[102] is an interesting example in the context of an offence under the SOA 2003, s 4 of the application of the SOA 2003, s 76(2)(a) which provides that the conclusive presumptions under s 76(1) arise where the defendant intentionally deceived the complainant as to the nature or purpose of the *relevant act*. In relation to offences under s 4, it might initially be supposed that 'the relevant act' must be the sexual activity that the complainant engages in, but, as stated above, the SOA 2003, s 77 provides that the 'relevant act' in the context of s 4 is the defendant (A) intentionally causing the complainant (B) to engage in an activity, where the activity is sexual. B need not be deceived as to the nature of his own act, and cannot be deceived as to his own purpose in so acting. It is the defendant's purpose that matters. In *Devonald*, A sought to exact revenge on his daughter's former boyfriend, B, by contacting him online and pretending to be a young woman who wanted to see him expose himself on a webcam and masturbate for her. His real purpose was to humiliate B. B fell for the deception. A was convicted of an offence under s 4. Upholding this conviction, the Court of Appeal said:

> '[I]t is difficult to see how the jury could have concluded otherwise than that the complainant was deceived into believing that he was indulging in sexual acts with, and for the sexual gratification of, a 20-year-old girl with whom he was having an on-line

---

[95] *Price v Cromack* [1975] 2 All ER 113, DC.   [96] *Price v Cromack* [1975] 2 All ER 113, DC.
[97] Para 17.13.   [98] Para 9.9.   [99] SOA 2003, s 4(1)(d).
[100] SOA 2003, s 4(2).   [101] SOA 2003, s 4(3).   [102] [2008] EWCA Crim 527.

relationship. That is why he agreed to masturbate over the sex cam. In fact, he was doing so for the father of his ex girlfriend who was anxious to teach him a lesson, doubtless by later embarrassing him or exposing what he had done.'[103]

Causing or inciting a child under 13 to engage in sexual activity

9.55 The SOA 2003, s 8(1) provides:

'A person commits an offence if –

    (a) he intentionally causes or incites another person (B) to engage in an activity,

    (b) the activity is sexual,[104] and

    (c) B is under 13.'

Absence of consent is not an element of such an offence.

Under s 8(2), an offence under s 8 is triable only on indictment if the activity caused or incited involved 'penetration' (in one of the same ways as in s 4). In such a case, the maximum punishment is life imprisonment. Otherwise, an offence under s 8 is triable either way and punishable with a maximum of 14 years' imprisonment on conviction on indictment.[105]

In the light of the *Courtie* principle[106] and of the fact that it has been confirmed[107] that 'causing' and 'inciting' involve separate offences, there are four offences under s 8:

- causing a child under 13 to engage in penetrative sexual activity (in one of the ways defined in s 8(2));
- inciting a child under 13 to engage in such activity;
- causing a child under 13 to engage in 'non-penetrative' sexual activity; and
- inciting a child to engage in such activity.

9.56 The sexual activity may be with A himself (as where A incites B to masturbate him), with a third party (as where A incites B to have sexual intercourse with A's friend, C) or by B on himself (as where A incites B to masturbate himself or to strip for A's sexual gratification).

As to the 'causing offences' see para 9.52. The 'inciting offences' under s 8 are important where an incitement of a child to engage in sexual activity does not achieve that result (either because the child is not persuaded to so engage or because things do not progress

---

[103] [2008] EWCA Crim 527 at [7].   [104] Para 9.6.
[105] SOA 2003, s 8(2) and (3).   [106] Para 3.50, n 111.   [107] *Walker* [2006] EWCA Crim 1907.

sufficiently far) and where although the child does engage in sexual activity it cannot be proved that this was caused by the person who incited it.

Incitement requires an element of persuasion or encouragement[108] (eg offering a bribe) or of threats or other pressure to commit an offence,[109] which may be implied as well as expressed. The mere expression of a desire that someone should do the prohibited activity, for instance, does not suffice because it does not amount to encouragement or persuasion. The persuasion, encouragement, threats or other pressure must come to the notice of the child incited,[110] though it need not be effective in any way.[111] If the persuasion etc does not come to the child's notice there can be a conviction of an attempt to commit an offence under SOA 2003, s 8 on appropriate facts.

Provided that the defendant does something which in specific terms directly incites a child or children under 13 to engage in sexual activity, it does not matter if it is not possible to identify any specific or identifiable child to whom the incitement was addressed. This was held by the Court of Appeal in *Jones (Ian Anthony)*,[112] where the Court stated the criminality at which the offence was directed was the incitement. It mattered not that that was directed at a particular child, a very large group of children or whether they could be identified or not. This decision would appear equally applicable (save for the reference to a child or children under 13) to other offences of incitement to sexual activity in SOA 2003.

9.57 Where an offence of causing is in issue, it must be proved that the defendant intended to cause the child to engage in sexual activity. It might have been thought that where incitement is in issue it would have to be proved that the defendant intended that the sexual activity incited should take place, but in *Walker*[113] the Court of Appeal rejected this proposition. It held that the requirement that the incitement to engage in sexual activity must be intentional simply meant that the incitement must be deliberate, or done on purpose, and the defendant must know what he is saying or doing. This is a surprising conclusion. It means, for example, that a mere joke or put-down can constitute an incitement for the purposes of s 8. There can be no doubt that the conclusion is equally applicable to the other incitement offences under SOA 2003.

The offence under SOA 2003, s 8, like that under s 5 (rape of a child under 13), is one of strict liability as to age.

---

[108] *Hendrickson and Tichner* [1977] Crim LR 356, CA; *Marlow* [1997] Crim LR 897, CA.

[109] *Race Relations Board v Applin* [1973] QB 815 at 825, per Lord Denning MR; *Invicta Plastics Ltd v Clare* [1976] RTR 251, DC.

[110] *Banks* (1873) 12 Cox CC 393. See also *Walker* [2006] EWCA Crim 1907 at [37].

[111] *De Kromme* (1892) 66 LT 301, CCR.

[112] [2007] EWCA Crim 1118.

[113] [2006] EWCA Crim 1907.

Child sex offences

Key points 9.3

The SOA 2003, ss 9 to 15 provide the following sex offences which are committed against children under 16:

- sexual activity with a child (s 9);
- causing or inciting a child to engage in sexual activity (s 10);
- engaging in sexual activity in the presence of a child (s 11);
- causing a child to watch a sexual act (s 12);
- child sex offences committed by a child or young person (s 13);
- arranging or facilitating the commission of a child sex offence of the above types (s 14);
- meeting a child following sexual grooming etc (s 15).

The child's consent is irrelevant because the absence of consent is not an element of these offences.

Sexual activity with a child

9.58 The SOA 2003, s 9(1) provides:

> 'A person aged 18 or over (A) commits an offence if –
>
> (a) he intentionally touches another person (B),
>
> (b) the touching is sexual,[114] and
>
> (c) either –
>   (i) B is under 16 and A does not reasonably believe that B is 16 or over, or
>   (ii) B is under 13.'

The exceptions from liability for aiding, abetting or counselling under the SOA 2003, s 73 (para 9.37) apply to an offence under s 9. An offence under s 9(1) where B is under 13 is also an offence under s 5, s 6 or s 7 depending on the nature of the touching.

An offence under s 9(1) is triable only on indictment, with a maximum punishment of 14 years' imprisonment, if the touching involved:

(a) penetration of B's anus or vagina with a part of A's body or anything else;

(b) penetration of B's mouth with A's penis;

---

[114] Para 9.6.

(c) penetration of A's anus or vagina with a part of B's body; or

(d) penetration of A's mouth with B's penis.[115]

In other cases, an offence under s 9 is triable either way, the maximum punishment on conviction on indictment also being 14 years' imprisonment.[116]

9.59 'Touching' covers all forms of physical contact, including penetration.[117] Because of the requirement of 'touching', if an under-16-year-old (B) takes the only active part in sexual activity (so that he is not touched by A, an adult), as where B masturbates a supine A, A does not commit an offence under s 9(1), although he would commit an offence under s 10 if he caused or incited B to engage in the activity.

9.60 A must intentionally touch B. By analogy with SOA 2003, s 3, all that is required is a deliberate touching which is in fact sexual, and it is not necessary to prove that the touching was done for any sexual purpose.[118]

As to the requirement that A must not reasonably believe that B was 16 or over, see para 9.9. Unlike corresponding requirements in respect of the offences of abuse of trust and familial child sex offences mentioned later,[119] A does not have an evidential burden in respect of this requirement. Where B is under 13 at the time of the touching an offence under s 9(1) is one of strict liability as to age, like the offences under the SOA 2003, ss 5 to 8, so that not even a reasonable belief that B is aged 16 or over will excuse. The structure of s 9(1)(c) makes it clear beyond doubt that the presumption that *mens rea* (as to age) is required is rebutted in this type of case. This is also the case in respect of the offences under ss 10–12 described in paras 9.61–9.69.

Causing or inciting a child to engage in sexual activity

9.61 The SOA 2003, s 10(1) provides:

> 'A person aged 18 or over (A) commits an offence if –
>
> (a) he intentionally causes or incites another person (B) to engage in an activity,
>
> (b) the activity is sexual,[120] and
>
> (c) either –
>   (i) B is under 16 and A does not reasonably believe[121] that B is 16 or over, or
>   (ii) B is under 13.'

Any offence under s 10(1) involving a child under 13 is also an offence under s 8(1).

Like an offence under s 9, an offence under s 10 is triable only on indictment if the activity caused or incited involved:

(a) penetration of B's anus or vagina (with a part of the body or anything else);

---

[115] SOA 2003, s 9(2).   [116] SOA 2003, s 9(3).   [117] Para 9.46.   [118] See para 9.47.
[119] See paras 9.85 and 9.94.   [120] Para 9.6.   [121] Para 9.9.

(b) penetration of B's mouth with a person's penis;

(c) penetration of a person's anus or vagina with a part of B's body or by B with anything else; or

(d) penetration of a person's mouth with B's penis.[122]

In such a case, the maximum punishment is 14 years' imprisonment.[123] In other cases, a s 10 offence is triable either way, the maximum punishment on conviction on indictment also being 14 years' imprisonment.[124]

There are separate offences under s 10 of 'causing' and of 'inciting'. 'Intentionally causing' and 'intentionally inciting' were discussed in paras 9.52 and 9.56. Whether or not the child consented to the activity is irrelevant.

9.62 Examples of an offence of causing under s 10(1) are where A, aged 18, not reasonably believing that B is 16 or over:

- causes B, aged 14, to masturbate *him* (A). In such a case, there is an overlap with an offence under s 9(1), if A touches B during the activity;
- causes B, aged 14, to masturbate *himself* (B); or
- causes B, aged 14, to masturbate A's friend, C.

For 'masturbate' in the above list one could of course substitute any other form of sexual activity, eg 'have sexual intercourse with' or 'strip'.

Engaging in sexual activity in the presence of a child

9.63 This offence covers the case where, instead of engaging in sexual activity with the child, or causing (or inciting) a child to engage in sexual activity, A engages in a sexual activity (eg masturbation) with himself or with a third party in the presence of a child, B, or when he can be observed by B, provided A engages in it in B's presence etc for the purpose of obtaining sexual gratification.

9.64 The SOA 2003, s 11(1) provides:

'A person aged 18 or over (A) commits an offence if –

(a) he intentionally engages in an activity,

(b) the activity is sexual,[125]

(c) for the purpose of obtaining sexual gratification, he engages in it –
  (i) when another person (B) is present or is in a place from which A can be observed, and
  (ii) knowing or believing that B is aware, or intending that B should be aware, that he is engaging in it, and

---

[122] SOA 2003, s 10(2).   [123] SOA 2003, s 10(2).
[124] SOA 2003, s 10(3).   [125] Para 9.6.

(d) either –
  (i) B is under 16 and A does not reasonably believe[126] that B is 16 or over, or
  (ii) B is under 13.'

Unlike an offence under the SOA 2003, s 9 or s 10, the present offence is always triable either way and punishable with a maximum of 10 years' imprisonment on conviction on indictment.[127]

9.65 The defendant (A) must engage in the sexual activity for the purpose of deriving sexual gratification from the facts that the other person (B) is present *or in a place from which A can be observed* and must know or believe that B is aware, or intend that B should be aware, that A is engaging in it. The words italicised will remove the necessity in many cases to engage in argument about the meaning of being 'present'. 'Observed' is defined by the SOA 2003, s 79(7) to mean 'observation whether direct or by looking at an image' produced by any means. The italicised words cover the case where B is at a distance but can observe A through a telescope or where B is miles away but can see A masturbating by watching an image created by a webcam or other remote viewing system. B must be present or able to observe at the time that A is engaging in sexual activity.

A's purpose (or presumably one of his purposes) in engaging in the sexual activity in B's presence must be the purpose of obtaining sexual gratification from doing so in B's presence.[128] If A, aged 21, has sexual intercourse with his 18-year-old partner in the presence of B, his one-year-old daughter, who is lying awake in her cot alongside them, he may know that the child is aware that he is engaging in the activity (presumably B is not required to understand that the activity is sexual, otherwise the offence could not be committed where B is young), but he would be most unlikely to be engaging in intercourse in B's presence for the purpose of obtaining sexual gratification from being watched.

Causing a child to watch a sexual act

9.66 The SOA 2003, s 11 deals with an adult who, for sexual gratification, engages in a sexual activity in the presence of, or which is observable by, a child under 16. The SOA 2003, s 12 deals with an adult (A) who, for the purpose of sexual gratification:

- causes a child under 16 to watch sexual activity not by him (A) but by a third party (eg forcing B, a child under 16, to watch C masturbate himself) or by third parties (eg persuading B to watch C and D have sexual intercourse); or

- causes a child to look at a photograph or pseudo-photograph or other image of a person (who may be A) engaging in a sexual activity, as where A persuades B to watch a pornographic video or pornographic images as he downloads them from the Internet.

---

[126] Para 9.9.   [127] SOA 2003, s 11(2).   [128] See para 9.69.

9.67 Section 12(1) provides:

'A person aged 18 or over (A) commits an offence if –

(a) for the purpose of obtaining sexual gratification, he intentionally causes[129] another person (B) to watch a third person engaging in an activity, or to look at an image[130] of any person engaging in an activity,

(b) the activity is sexual,[131] and

(c) either –
  (i)   B is under 16 and A does not reasonably believe[132] that B is 16 or over, or
  (ii) B is under 13.'

Like an offence under s 11, the present offence is triable either way. On conviction on indictment, the maximum punishment is ten years' imprisonment,[133] the same maximum as a s 11 offence.

9.68 'Watch' includes watching a person engaging in sexual activity in front of a webcam. Section 12(1) does not require the sexual activity seen by B to be contemporaneous; A will commit the offence if he causes B to look at an image of any person (real or imaginary) engaging in sexual activity. That image could be in a pornographic video or a photograph, or a cartoon, for example, or a three-dimensional figure.

9.69 It is an important requirement that the defendant must not only intentionally cause the watching or looking; he must also do so for the purpose of obtaining sexual gratification. The Court of Appeal held in *Abdullahi*[134] that that gratification does not have to be taken immediately, ie it is not required that the purposed sexual gratification and the viewed sexual act, or display of images, are simultaneous, or contemporaneous or synchronised. The Court held that the offence can be committed where the defendant's purpose involves immediate or deferred or immediate and deferred gratification. Thus, the offence can be committed, for example, where the defendant causes a child to watch a sexual act to put the child in the mood for future sexual abuse, as well as where he does so because he derives enjoyment from seeing him watch the sexual act. This means that there is a degree of overlap between the offence under the SOA 2003, s 12 and the offence of arranging or facilitating the commission of a child sex offence, contrary to the SOA 2003, s 14 (referred to in para 9.71).

---

[129] See para 9.52.

[130] By the SOA 2003, s 79(4), 'image' means a moving or still image, however produced, and, where – as here – the context permits, a three-dimensional image. It does not include written material. By s 79(5), references to an image of a person include references to an image of an imaginary person.

[131] Para 9.6. [132] Para 9.9. [133] SOA 2003, s 12(2).

[134] [2006] EWCA Crim 2060.

Child sex offences committed by children or young persons

9.70 The SOA 2003, s 13(1) provides:

> 'A person under 18 commits an offence if he does anything which would be an offence under any of sections 9 to 12 [paras 9.58–9.69] if he were aged 18.'

An offence under s 13 is less serious than an offence under ss 9 to 12. It is triable either way and punishable with a maximum of five years' imprisonment on conviction on indictment.[135] The exceptions from liability for aiding, abetting or counselling under the SOA 2003, s 73 (para 9.37) apply to an offence under s 13 if what is done would be an offence under s 9 if the offender were aged 18 or over.

Arranging or facilitating the commission of a child sex offence

9.71 The SOA 2003, s 14(1) provides:

> 'A person commits an offence if –
>
> (a) he intentionally arranges or facilitates something that he intends to do, intends another person to do, or believes that another person will do, in any part of the world, and
>
> (b) doing it will involve the commission of an offence under any of ss 9 to 13.'

An offence under s 14(1) is triable either way and punishable with a maximum of 14 years' imprisonment on conviction on indictment.[136] It is a species of preparatory offence, as confirmed by the Court of Appeal in *R*.[137] In *R*, the Court stated that s 14 covered taking preparatory steps (with the necessary intent) to commit an offence under ss 9 to 13 even if the defendant's conduct had not got as far as amounting to an attempt to commit such an offence. It noted that the section did not further define or limit those steps other than by requiring their object to involve the commission of a relevant child sex offence. It stated that:

> 'An arrangement may be made without the agreement or acquiescence of anyone else. A defendant may take steps by way of a plan with the criminal objective identified in [s 14] without involving anyone else and the mere fact that no-one else is involved would not necessarily mean that no arrangement was made.'[138]

---

[135] SOA 2003, s 13(2).
[137] [2008] EWCA Crim 619 (reported elsewhere as *Robson*).
[136] SOA 2003, s 14(4).
[138] [2008] EWCA Crim 619 at [8].

The Court of Appeal in *R* also held that, although the offence under s 14 covers preparatory conduct, it remains a substantive offence and there is nothing in the Criminal Attempts Act 1981 that precludes the application to s 14 of the offence of attempt. In *R*, A was alleged to have asked a prostitute to find a girl of 12 or 13 for sex. On the evidence the prostitute did not say that she would do so, nor did she give A any reason to believe that she would do so. Allowing the prosecution's appeal against a ruling given by the trial judge that those facts did not constitute an offence under s 14 or an attempt to commit it, the Court of Appeal held that a mere request was capable of amounting to an attempt to commit an offence under s 14, although whether there actually had been a more than merely preparatory act to the commission of such an offence would have to be left to the jury. It did not need to decide whether the acts constituted the substantive offence under s 14, but it stated that nothing it had said was meant to indicate that what was alleged might not constitute the substantive offence of arranging contrary to s 14.

If a person agrees to the defendant's request to find a child with whom the defendant can engage in sexual activity, the defendant will have made an arrangement for the purposes of s 14; it is not necessary for the child to agree.[139]

9.72 Section 14(2) and (3) provides exceptions for people who seek to protect a child from pregnancy or sexually transmitted disease or to protect a child's physical safety or to give it advice, where they do not intend that the child will commit an offence under the SOA 2003, ss 9 to 13 but believe that it will.

Section 14(2) provides that:

'a person does not commit an offence under s 14 if:

(a) he arranges or facilitates something that he believes another person will do, but that he does not intend to do or intend another person to do; and

(b) any offence [within ss 9 to 13] which the doing of that thing would involve would be an offence against a child for whose protection he acts.'

Section 14(3) provides that, in this context:

'a person acts for the protection of a child if he acts for the purpose of –

(a) protecting the child from sexually transmitted infection,

(b) protecting the physical safety of the child,

(c) preventing the child from becoming pregnant, or

(d) promoting the child's emotional well-being by the giving of advice,

and not for the purpose of obtaining sexual gratification or for the purpose of causing or encouraging the activity constituting [an offence within ss 9 to 13] or the child's participation in it.'

---

[139] *Robson (John Paul)* [2009] EWCA Crim 1472.

Examples would be giving an under-age boy a condom (if done for the purpose of protecting the boy against a sexually transmitted infection, but not if done to protect the boy against the risk of his 16-year-old girlfriend becoming pregnant); giving an under-age girl a condom (if done for the purpose of protecting her against a sexually-transmitted infection or pregnancy); giving advice (eg by an 'agony aunt' or counsellor) to an under-age child or children about protected sex (if done for the purpose of protection against sexually-transmitted infection, or, where the advice is given to a girl, pregnancy, or to promote the child's emotional well-being).

Meeting a child following sexual grooming etc

9.73 'Grooming' occurs where paedophiles gain the trust and confidence of children and thereby befriend them for their own purposes. Typically, the paedophiles have deceived children in chatrooms into believing that they are also children or teenagers sharing the same interests and have then arranged meetings with them with a view to engaging or involving the child in sexual activity.

The SOA 2003, s 15(1), as amended,[140] provides:

'A person aged 18 or over (A) commits an offence if –

  (a) A has met or communicated with another person (B) on at least two occasions and subsequently –
    (i)   A intentionally meets B,
    (ii) A travels with the intention of meeting B in any part of the world or arranges to meet B in any part of the world, or
    (iii) B travels with the intention of meeting A in any part of the world,

  (b) A intends to do anything to or in respect of B, during or after the meeting mentioned in paragraph (a)(i) to (iii) and in any part of the world, which if done will involve the commission by A of a relevant offence,

  (c) B is under 16, and

  (d) A does not reasonably believe that B is 16 or over.'

An offence under s 15 is triable either way and punishable with a maximum of 10 years' imprisonment on conviction on indictment.[141] It is a species of preparatory offence. Although its mischief is grooming via the Internet, it is not limited to those who groom in that way.

9.74 The requirements of s 15(1)(a) can be expressed as follows. Having met or communicated (eg by chatroom conversation or by telephone or text communication) with B (aged under 16) on at least two earlier occasions, A (aged 18 or over) must have intentionally *met B*, or *arranged to meet* B or *travelled* with the intention of meeting B.

---

[140] By the Criminal Justice and Immigration Act 2008, Sch 15.   [141] SOA 2003, s 15(4).

Alternatively, after A has met or communicated with B (aged under 16) on at least two occasions, *B must have travelled with the intention of meeting A*. The effect of s 15(1)(c) is that, if B was under 16 at the time of the previous meetings or communications, but has had his sixteenth birthday at the time of the meeting, arranging to meet or travelling to meet, an offence under s 15 is not committed.

The reference to A *having met or communicated* with B is a reference to A having met B in any part of the world or having communicated with B by any means from, to or in any part of the world.[142] Thus, if A meets B in England and Wales[143] after communicating with her on a number of occasions from Berlin via the Internet or by telephone or after meeting her on two occasions during a holiday in Turkey the offence can be committed.

The past meetings or communications need only amount to two; one meeting and one communication, for example, will do. This is a minimal requirement for an offence aimed at grooming. The meetings or communications need not have an explicitly sexual content. They could consist, for example, simply of A meeting B to swap CDs or chance meetings through a friend or chatroom conversations about 'pop' music.

Although it is not necessary that A should actually have met (or arranged to meet) B, A or B must at least have travelled with intent to meet the other; s 15 does not require the journey to be completed or that a meeting (actual or intended) be pre-arranged. Thus, for example, travelling by A with the intention of meeting B on B's way home from school, unknown to B, will suffice.

9.75 At the time of the meeting, or travelling, A must intend to do anything to or in respect of B, during or after the meeting and in any part of the world, which if done will involve the commission by A of a relevant offence. It is this requirement which excludes those whose conduct is innocent. A 'relevant offence' means an offence under the SOA 2003, Pt 1 (which includes all the sexual offences referred to in this chapter) and also anything done outside England and Wales which is not an offence under Pt 1 but would be if done in England and Wales.[144] Thus, an offence will be committed if A meets B in Newcastle intending to take B to Scotland (or travels from London to Dover to meet B and to take B to France) and there to engage in sexual activity with B which would be a Pt 1 offence if done in England.

A does not commit an offence if he reasonably believes B is 16 or over (even if B is under 13); the prosecution must prove that A does not so believe.[145]

---

[142] SOA 2003, s 15(2)(a).

[143] Or outside the United Kingdom if the extra-territorial jurisdiction rules described in paras 9.133 and 9.134 are satisfied.

[144] SOA 2003, s 15(2)(b) (as amended by the Sexual Offences (Northern Ireland) Consequential Amendments Order 2008).

[145] SOA 2003, s 15(1)(d).

Abuse of position of trust

Key points 9.4

The SOA 2003, ss 16 to 19 provide the following offences to deal with abuse of a position of trust involving sexual activity with a child:

- sexual activity with a child (s 16);
- causing or inciting a child to engage in sexual activity (s 17);
- sexual activity in the presence of a child (s 18); and
- causing a child to watch a sexual act (s 19).

The prohibited behaviour in each offence is identical to that prohibited by the child sex offences in the SOA 2003, ss 9 to 12, except that for the abuse of position of trust offences the child may be 16 or 17 and, of course, the defendant must be in a position of trust in relation to the child.

There are exceptions from these offences where the two parties are spouses or civil partners and in the case of relationships which preceded the position of trust.

9.76 Sexual activity with a child is inappropriate within relationships of trust. This is not simply because the power differentials make consent problematic, but also because sexual activity within such a relationship is incompatible with the ethical and moral responsibilities of those in a position of trust. The SOA 2003, ss 16 to 19 are designed to punish such activity.

The offences under ss 16 to 19 are triable either way and punishable with a maximum of five years' imprisonment on conviction on indictment.[146] No distinction is drawn in any of the offences between penetrative and non-penetrative activity.

9.77 *Abuse of position of trust: sexual activity with a child* This offence is provided by s 16. The SOA 2003, s 16(1) provides:

'A person aged 18 or over (A) commits an offence if –

    (a) he intentionally touches[147] another person (B),

    (b) the touching is sexual,[148]

    (c) A is in a position of trust[149] in relation to B,

    (d) ..., and

    (e) ...B is under 18...'

B's consent is, of course, irrelevant.

---

[146] SOA 2003, ss 16(5), 17(5), 18(5) and 19(5).   [147] Paras 9.46 and 9.47.

[148] Para 9.6.   [149] Paras 9.81–9.83.

The exceptions from liability for aiding, abetting or counselling this offence under s 73 apply to this offence if B is under 16.[150]

9.78 *Abuse of position of trust: causing or inciting a child to engage in sexual activity* Section 17 deals with a person in a position of trust who causes or incites a child under 18 to engage in sexual activity with himself (ie the child), such as masturbation, or with a third party (who need not be in a position of trust with the child), or with the person in a position of trust.

The SOA 2003, s 17 (1) provides:

> 'A person aged 18 or over (A) commits an offence if –
>
> (a) he intentionally causes[151] or incites[152] another person (B) to engage in an activity,
> (b) the activity is sexual,[153]
> (c) A is in a position of trust[154] in relation to B,
> (d) ..., and
> (e) ...B is under 18.'

As in the case of other offences under the SOA 2003 of causing or inciting under-age sexual activity, there are separate offences under s 17, one of causing and the other of inciting.

9.79 *Abuse of position of trust: sexual activity in the presence of a child*   Section 18 deals with this. The typical example would be the person who masturbates in front of a child in respect of whom he is in a position of trust. The SOA 2003, s 18 (1) provides:

> 'A person aged 18 or over (A) commits an offence if –
>
> (a) he intentionally engages in an activity,
> (b) the activity is sexual,[155]
> (c) for the purpose of obtaining sexual gratification,[156] he engages in it –
>   (i) when another person (B) is present or is in a place from which A can be observed, and
>   (ii) knowing or believing that B is aware, or intending that B should be aware, that he is engaging in it,
> (d) A is in a position of trust[157] in relation to B,
> (e) ..., and
> (f) ...B is under 18...'

9.80 *Abuse of position of trust: causing a child to watch a sexual act*   This offence catches the person (A) who causes the child to watch a sexual activity which is being engaged in

---

[150] Para 9.37.   [151] Para 9.52.   [152] Para 9.56.   [153] Para 9.6.
[154] Paras 9.81–9.83.   [155] Para 9.6.   [156] Para 9.69.   [157] Paras 9.81–9.83.

by a third party and not by A, or to look at an image (eg a photograph) of anyone (including A) engaging in a sexual activity. The SOA 2003, s 19(1) provides:

> 'A person aged 18 or over (A) commits an offence if –
>
> (a) for the purpose of obtaining sexual gratification,[158] he intentionally causes another person (B) to watch a third person engaging in an activity, or to look at an image of any person engaging in an activity,
>
> (b) the activity is sexual,[159]
>
> (c) A is in a position of trust[160] in relation to B,
>
> (d) …, and
>
> (e) …B is under 18…'

Position of trust

9.81 The SOA 2003, s 21(1) provides that, for the purposes of the above offences, a person (A) is in a position of trust in relation to another person (B) if:

- any of sub-ss (2) to (13) of s 21 applies; or
- any condition specified in an order made by the Secretary of State is met. No order has yet been made.

9.82 Section 21(2) to (13) provides that A is in a position of trust in respect of B if, inter alia:

(a) A looks after persons under 18 who are detained in an institution, such as a secure training centre or a young offenders institution, by virtue of a court order or under an enactment and B is so detained in that institution;

(b) A looks after persons under 18 who are resident in a home for children in residential care, and B is in residential care there;

(c) A looks after persons under 18 who are accommodated and cared for in a hospital, a care home, a community home, or the like, and B is accommodated and cared for in that institution;

(d) A looks after persons under 18 who are receiving full- or part-time education at an educational institution and B is receiving, and A is not receiving, education at that institution;

(e) A is engaged in the provision of a careers service or similar service and, in that capacity, looks after B on an individual basis;

---

[158] Para 9.69.   [159] Para 9.6.   [160] Paras 9.81–9.83.

(f) A regularly has unsupervised contact with B (whether face to face or by any other means) in the provision of accommodation for children in need thereof or in police protection or detention or on remand; or

(g) B is subject to a care order, a supervision order or an education supervision order and A looks after B on an individual basis.

'Looking after'

9.83 For the purposes of (a), (b), (c) and (d) above, a person looks after persons under 18 at an institution or the like if he is *regularly* involved in caring for, training, supervising or being in sole charge of *such persons* there,[161] not necessarily the child abused.

Points (e) and (g) refer to a person looking after another *on an individual basis.* A person (A) looks after another (B) on such a basis if:

(a) A is *regularly* involved in caring for, training or supervising B; and

(b) in the course of his involvement, A regularly has unsupervised contact with B (whether face to face or by any other means).[162]

A number of other people who have (or may have) a relationship of trust with a youngster fall outside the categories in s 21. Examples are doctors; clergymen; sports coaches; youth and community workers; voluntary group leaders and scout masters.

Mens rea

9.84 In addition to requiring the defendant intentionally to do the thing specified by sub-s (1)(a) of each individual section, the SOA 2003, ss 16 to 19 make further provision in a somewhat involved way as to the *mens rea* required in respect of the child's age and the existence of a position of trust.

As to age

9.85 In terms of the *mens rea* as to the age of the child (B), the SOA 2003, ss 16(1)(e), 17(1)(e), 18(1)(f) and 19(1)(e) provide that the defendant (A) must not reasonably believe that B is 18 or over. However, this provision does not apply if B is under 13 at the material time; in such a case the offences are undoubtedly ones of strict liability as to age. Although the prosecution ultimately has the persuasive burden of proof of the requisite *mens rea* as to the age of B where B is aged 13 to 17, the prosecution is assisted by ss 16(3), 17(3), 18(3) and 19(3) which all provide:

'Where in proceedings for an offence under this section it is proved that the other person was under 18, the defendant is to be taken not to have reasonably believed that that person was 18 or over unless sufficient evidence is adduced to raise an issue as to whether he reasonably believed it.'

---

[161] SOA 2003, s 22(2).   [162] SOA 2003, s 22(3).

If such evidence is adduced, the prosecution must prove the *mens rea* as to age.

As to position of trust

9.86 The SOA 2003, ss 16(1)(d), 17(1)(d), 18(1)(e) and 19(1)(d) deal with the *mens rea* required in relation to the existence of a position of trust in cases to which sub-s (2) of each section applies. Sections 16(2), 17(2), 18(2) and 19(2) apply where A is in a position of trust in relation to B by virtue of circumstances within points (a) to (d) in para 9.82, ie:

(a) B detained in an institution by virtue of a court order or under an enactment;

(b) B in residential care;

(c) B accommodated and cared for in a hospital, care home, community home or the like; or

(d) B receiving education at an educational institution,

and, in each case, A is not also in a position of trust by virtue of other circumstances.

These four circumstances are ones where A looks after persons under 18 at an institution and B is at that institution (but not necessarily looked after by A).

Sections 16(1)(d), 17(1)(d), 18(1)(e) and 19(1)(d) provide that in these cases, it must be proved that A knew or could reasonably be expected to know of the circumstances by virtue of which he is in a position of trust in relation to B. Proof of this *mens rea* is aided by ss 16(4), 17(4), 18(4) and 19(4), which provide that, where it is proved that A was in a position of trust in relation to the other person by virtue of the four circumstances just referred to, and it is not proved that he was in such a position of trust by virtue of other circumstances, it is to be presumed that A knew or could reasonably have been expected to know of the circumstances by virtue of which he was in such a position of trust unless sufficient evidence is adduced to raise an issue as to whether he knew or could reasonably have been expected to know of those circumstances. If such evidence is adduced the prosecution will have to prove the *mens rea* as to a position of trust.

9.87 Where a position of trust arises wholly or partly by virtue of the other categories of circumstance referred to in the SOA 2003, s 21, it does so on the basis of an individual's personal relationship of trust between A and B. Not surprisingly, the Act does not require proof of any *mens rea* as to the position of trust where such a position of trust is involved.

Exceptions for spouses and civil partners and for pre-existing relationships

9.88 The SOA 2003, ss 23 and 24 set out exceptions from liability for the above offences.

They provide that conduct by a person (A) which would otherwise be one of the offences against another person (B) is not such an offence if, respectively:

(a) **B was 16 or over, and the defendant proves that at the time of the conduct A and B were lawfully married or civil partners**[163] **of each other.**[164] The defendant's mistaken belief that a marriage or civil partnership had been validly concluded appears to be no defence, however reasonable it may be; or

(b) **the defendant proves that immediately before the position of trust arose, a sexual relationship existed between A and B,**[165] as where A and B were in a sexual relationship immediately before B became a hospital patient or pupil of A. This exception does not apply if at *that* time sexual intercourse between A and B would have been unlawful, eg because B was under 16.[166]

9.89 Placing a persuasive burden on the defendant to prove one of the present exceptions would appear not to be incompatible with the presumption of innocence under ECHR, Article 6(2).[167] If it was, it would be possible to read down the provisions under the Human Rights Act 1998, s 3, so as to impose an evidential burden.

Familial child sex offences

Key points 9.5

The SOA 2003, ss 25 and 26 provide offences dealing with sexual activity involving two members of a family, one of whom is under 18:

- sexual activity with a child family member aged under 18 (s 25); and

- inciting a child family member aged under 18 to engage in sexual activity (s 26).

The family relationships covered are widely defined.

  There are exceptions from these offences where the two persons are spouses or civil partners and in the case of relationships which preceded the family relationship.

Sexual activity with a child family member

9.90 The SOA 2003, s 25(1) provides:

'A person (A) commits an offence if –

  (a) he intentionally touches[168] another person (B),

---

[163] As to civil partnership (ie registered same-sex partnership) see the Civil Partnership Act 2004, s 1.
[164] SOA 2003, s 23(1) and (2) (as amended by the Civil Partnership Act 2004, Sch 27).
[165] SOA 2003, s 24(1), (3).   [166] SOA 2003, s 24(2).
[167] See Card, Gillespie and Hirst *Sexual Offences* (2008) 5.41–5.43.
[168] Paras 9.46 and 9.47.

> (b) the touching is sexual,[169]
>
> (c) the relation of A to B is within s 27,
>
> (d) A knows or could reasonably be expected to know that his relation to B is of a description falling within that section, and
>
> (e) either –
>
> > (i)   B is under 18 and A does not reasonably believe that B is 18 or over, or
> >
> > (ii) B is under 13.'

The exceptions from liability for aiding, abetting or counselling an offence, provided by the SOA 2003, s 73 (para 9.37), apply to an offence under s 25 if B is under 16.

Where A is 18 or over at the time of the offence and the touching involved:

(a) penetration of B's anus or vagina with a part of A's body or anything else;

(b) penetration of B's mouth with A's penis;

(c) penetration of A's anus or vagina with part of B's body (but not with anything else); or

(d) penetration of A's mouth by B's penis,[170]

an offence under s 25 is triable only on indictment and punishable with a maximum of 14 years' imprisonment.[171] In any other case where A was 18 or over at the material time, the offence is triable either way. The maximum punishment on conviction on indictment is, however, the same as in a case of penetration.[172]

Where A was not 18 or over at the material time, an offence under s 25 is triable either way and punishable with a maximum of five years' imprisonment on conviction on indictment.[173]

Because there are different maximum punishments depending on the facts established, the application of the principle in *Courtie*[174] means that there are two separate offences under s 25:

- sexual touching of someone under 18 in a familial relationship by someone aged 18 or over; and

- sexual touching of someone under 18 in a familial relationship by someone under 18.

9.91 Where it is proved that the relation of the defendant to the other person was of a description falling within the SOA 2003, s 27, it is to be taken that the defendant knew or could reasonably have been expected to know that his relation to the other person was of that description unless sufficient evidence is adduced to raise an issue as to whether he knew or could reasonably have been expected to know that it was.[175] If sufficient evidence

---

[169] Para 9.6.   [170] SOA 2003, s 25(6). As to 'penetration', 'vagina' and 'anus' see para 9.25.

[171] SOA 2003, s 25(4).   [172] SOA 2003, s 25(4).   [173] SOA 2003, s 25(5).

[174] [1984] AC 463, HL; para 3.50, n 111. There is nothing to rebut the presumption to this effect.

[175] SOA 2003, s 25(3).

to raise the issue is adduced, it will be for the prosecution to prove beyond reasonable doubt that the defendant knew or could reasonably have expected that his relation to the other person was of a description falling within s 27. Thus, if A, adopted soon after birth, meets B, his natural younger sister, aged 17, when he is 22 and has sexual intercourse with her without realising that she is his natural sister, he will not be guilty under s 25 if he did not know and could not reasonably be expected to know that his relation to B was that of brother-sister or any other prescribed relationship, but he will be taken to have had the requisite *mens rea* as to familial relationship unless sufficient evidence is adduced to raise an issue as to whether he knew or could reasonably have been expected to know that his relation to B was of a description within s 27. If such evidence is adduced, it will be for the prosecution to prove the requisite *mens rea* as to familial relationship.

9.92 The prosecution must also prove that either:

(a) B is under 18 and A did not reasonably believe that B was 18 or over, or

(b) B is under 13.[176]

There can be no doubt from this formulation that where B is under 13 an offence under s 25 (like that under s 5) is one of strict liability as to age. Otherwise, where it is proved that the other person (ie B) was under 18, the defendant (A) is to be taken not to have reasonably believed that that person was 18 or over, unless sufficient evidence is adduced to raise an issue as to whether he reasonably believed it.[177]

Inciting a child family member to engage in sexual activity

9.93 The SOA 2003, s 26(1) provides:

'A person (A) commits an offence if –

(a) he intentionally incites another person (B) to touch,[178] or allow himself to be touched by, A,

(b) the touching is sexual,[179]

(c) the relation of A to B is within s 27,

(d) A knows or could reasonably be expected to know that his relation to B is of a description falling within that section, and

(e) either –
(i)   B is under 18 and A does not reasonably believe that B is 18 or over, or
(ii) B is under 13.'

---

[176] SOA 2003, s 25(1)(e).　　　　　　　　　　　　　　　[177] SOA 2003, s 25(2).
[178] As to these terms, see paras 9.46, 9.56 and 9.57.　　[179] Para 9.6.

An offence under s 26 is triable and punishable in the same way as an offence under s 25.[180] For the same reasons as in s 25, there are two offences under s 26 of inciting a child family member to engage in sexual activity (one committed by someone aged 18 or over and the other committed by someone aged 18).

9.94 The *mens rea* in respect of the fact that the relation of A to B is within s 27 is the same as that in s 25. Where it is proved that the relation of A to B was of a description falling within s 27, it is to be taken that A knew or could reasonably have been expected to know that his relation to B was of that description unless sufficient evidence is adduced to raise an issue as to whether he knew or could reasonably have been expected to know that it was.[181]

Likewise, in respect of the *mens rea* in s 26(1)(e)(i) (no reasonable belief (where B is not under 13) that B is 18 or over), where it is proved that B was under 18, A is to be taken not to have reasonably believed that that person B was 18 or over unless sufficient evidence is adduced to raise an issue as to whether he reasonably believed it.[182]

As in the case of an offence under s 25, an offence under s 26 is one of strict liability as to age if B is under 13.

Family relationships

9.95 Under the SOA 2003, ss 25 and 26 the relation of the defendant and the 'victim' must be within s 27. The relation of one person (A) to another (B) is within the SOA 2003, s 27 if:

(a) it is within s 27(2) to (4), including an adoptive relationship; or

(b) it would be but for the fact that one (or both) of them is adopted.[183]

The effect of (b) is that the categories of relationship set out in s 27(2) to (4) continue to apply to an adopted child's biological family relationships if the child is adopted. Thus, contrary to the normal legal rule that an adopted child is the child of the adoptive parent(s), and not the biological parents, a child is treated as the child of both sets of parents and as the sibling of both biological and adoptive siblings.

9.96 The relation of A and B is within s 27(2) if:

'(a) one of them is the other's parent, grandparent, brother, sister, half-brother, half-sister,[184] aunt or uncle, or

(b) A is or has been B's foster parent.'

'Aunt' means the sister or half-sister, and 'uncle' the brother or half-brother, of a person's parent.[185]

---

[180] SOA 2003, s 26(4), (5) and (6).   [181] SOA 2003, s 26(3).   [182] SOA 2003, s 26(2).
[183] SOA 2003, s 27(1) (as amended by the Criminal Justice and Immigration Act 2008, Sch 15).
[184] Ie a son or daughter of either of one's parents by another partner.
[185] SOA 2003, s 27(5)(a).

9.97 The relation of A to B is within s 27(3):

> 'if A and B live or have lived in the same household, or A is or has been regularly involved in caring for, training, supervising or being in sole charge of B, and –
>
> (a) one of them is or has been the other's step-parent,[186]
>
> (b) A and B are cousins,
>
> (c) one of them is or has been the other's stepbrother or stepsister,[187] or
>
> (d) the parent or present or former foster parent of one of them is or has been the other's foster parent.'

A 'step-parent' includes someone who is neither married to, nor the civil partner of, a parent, if that person is a parent's 'partner'.[188] This is not as wide as may at first seem because a person is another's 'partner' (whether they are of different sexes or the same sex) only if they live together as partners in an enduring family relationship.[189] In s 27(3)(b), 'cousin' means the child of an 'aunt' or 'uncle', as defined above.[190] In s 27(3)(c), 'stepbrother' and 'stepsister' are not limited to the case where one child's parent is married to, nor the civil partner of, the parent of the other child; the terms include the child of a parent's 'partner',[191] as defined above. Section 27(3)(d) refers to foster siblings. Like stepsiblings they are particularly vulnerable to peer sexual abuse when they live, or have lived, in the same household.

For a case to fall within s 27(3) something more is required than the simple relationship referred to in s 27(3)(a) to (d); A and B must live or have lived in the same household, or A must be or have been regularly involved in caring for, training or supervising or being in sole charge of B. It is not enough, for example, simply for A to be the partner of B's parent or a cousin of B.

9.98 The relation of A and B is within s 27(4) if:

> '(a) A and B live in the same household, *and*
>
> (b) A *is* regularly involved in caring for, training, supervising or being in sole charge of B.'

The definition in s 27(4)(a) can be satisfied by someone who would not normally be regarded as being in a family relationship with other members of the household, eg a lodger or au pair.

---

[186] In (a) and (c) references to a step-parent or stepbrother/stepsister are to be read as follows: the step-parent of a person (X) includes someone who is the civil partner of X's parent (but is not X's parent), and X's stepbrother/stepsister includes someone who is the son/daughter of the civil partner of X's parent (but is not the son/daughter of either of X's parents): Civil Partnership Act 2004, ss 246, 247, Sch 21 (amended by the Civil Partnership Act 2004 (Relationships Arising Through Civil Partnership) Order 2005).

[187] See n 186.   [188] SOA 2003, s 27(5)(e).   [189] SOA 2003, s 27(5)(d).

[190] SOA 2003, s 27(5)(b).   [191] SOA 2003, s 27(5)(e).

Exceptions for spouses and civil partners and for pre-existing relationships

9.99 Conduct by a person (A) which would otherwise be an offence under the SOA 2003, ss 25 or 26 against another person (B) is not an offence if one of the two following exemptions apply. The exceptions correspond (the second broadly) with those which apply to offences of abuse of trust.[192]

9.100 The first exception is that B is 16 or over at the time of the conduct and A and B are lawfully married or civil partners of each other at that time.[193] It is for the defendant to prove that A and B were lawfully married or civil partners at the time.[194] A's mistaken belief that a marriage or civil partnership has been validly concluded is apparently no defence, however reasonable the mistake.

9.101 The second exception is where the defendant proves that:

- **the relation of A to B is not within s 27(2);**
- **where A or B (or both) is adopted, the relationship would not be within s 27(2) if there had not been the adoption; and**
- **immediately before the relation of A to B first became such as to fall within s 27, a sexual relationship existed between A and B.**[195]

This does not apply if immediately before the relation of A to B first became such as to fall within s 27 sexual intercourse between A and B would have been unlawful,[196] as where B was under 16.

Sex with an adult relative

> ### Key points 9.6
>
> The SOA 2003, ss 64 and 65 provide offences to deal with those who engage in consensual penetrative sex with an adult relative.

9.102 By s 64(1):

> 'A person aged 16 or over (A) commits an offence if –
>
> (a) he intentionally penetrates another person's vagina or anus with a part of his body or anything else, or penetrates another person's mouth with his penis,[197]

---

[192] Para 9.88.   [193] SOA 2003, s 28(1) (as amended by the Civil Partnership Act 2004, Sch 27).
[194] SOA 2003, s 28(2) (as amended by the Civil Partnership Act 2004, Sch 27).
[195] SOA 2003, s 29(1), (3).   [196] SOA 2003, s 29(2).   [197] See paras 9.25 and 9.28.

> (b) the penetration is sexual,
>
> (c) the other person (B) is aged 18 or over,
>
> (d) A is related to B in a way mentioned in subs (2), and
>
> (e) A knows or could reasonably be expected to know that he is related to B in that way.'

Section 65(1) provides:

> 'A person aged 16 or over (A) commits an offence if –
>
> (a) another person (B) penetrates A's vagina or anus with a part of B's body or anything else, or penetrates A's mouth with B's penis,
>
> (b) A consents[198] to the penetration,
>
> (c) the penetration is sexual,[199]
>
> (d) B is aged 18 or over,
>
> (e) A is related to B in a way mentioned in subs (2), and
>
> (f) A knows or could reasonably be expected to know that he is related to B in that way.'

Both offences are triable either way and punishable with a maximum of two years' imprisonment on conviction on indictment.[200]

9.103 Sections 64(2) and 65(2) define the ways that A may be related to B. The list of relationships is much narrower than the list which applies to offences under ss 25 and 26. The ways that A and B may be related to each other for the purposes of ss 64 and 65 are: as a parent, grandparent, child, grandchild, brother, sister, half-brother, half-sister, uncle, aunt, nephew or niece. 'Uncle' means the brother of a person's parent, and 'aunt' has a corresponding meaning. Consequent on the definition of 'uncle' and 'aunt', 'nephew' and 'niece' mean the child of a person's brother or sister.[201]

Subject to what is said below, where a person is adopted adoptive relationships are excluded from the application of s 64 or s 65 but biological ones are not. Thus, an offence is not committed where, for example, A and B are adoptive brother and sister, adoptive grandparent and grandchild or adoptive uncle and niece. There is an exception in respect of penetration involving an adoptive parent and his or her adopted child. This is because ss 64(3) and 65(3) each provide that 'parent' includes an adoptive parent and that 'child' includes an adopted person.[202] However, s 64(3A) and s 65(3A)[203] each go on to provide that, where s 64(1) or s 65(1) applies in a case where A is related to B as B's child by virtue

---

[198] Paras 9.12–9.23.   [199] Para 9.6

[200] SOA 2003, ss 64(5) and 65(5).   [201] SOA 2003, ss 64(3) and 65(3).

[202] SOA 2003, ss 64(3)(za), (zb), 65(3)(za), (zb) (inserted by the Criminal Justice and Immigration Act 2008, Sch 15).

[203] Inserted by the Criminal Justice and Immigration Act 2008, Sch 15.

of being B's adopted child, A does not commit an offence under s 64(1) or s 65(1), as the case may be, unless A is 18 or over.

Unlike the corresponding provisions in s 25, ss 64 and 65 are limited to penetrative sexual activity. The requirement that a penetration be sexual is clearly going to be satisfied with ease where the penetration is by a penis. In the case of other penetration, it will depend on the circumstances. An example of a case where the requirement would serve to exclude conduct from the offence would be where one sibling helps another to insert a pessary for medical reasons.

9.104 In terms of the requirement that the prosecution must prove that the defendant (A) knew or could reasonably be expected to know that he is related to B in a way mentioned in s 64(2) or s 65(2), as the case may be, s 64(4) and s 65(4) provide an evidential presumption in identical terms. They provide:

> 'Where in proceedings for an offence under this section it is proved that the defendant was related to the other person in any of [the ways prescribed by s 64(2) or s 65(2), as the case may be], it is to be taken that the defendant knew or could reasonably be expected to know that he was related in that way unless sufficient evidence is adduced to raise an issue as to whether he knew or could reasonably be expected to know that he was.'[204]

Offences against people with a mental disorder

Key points 9.7

The SOA 2003, ss 30 to 41 provide a range of offences specifically aimed at protecting people with a mental disorder (whether permanent or temporary) of whatever degree. The offences are grouped as follows under three headings:

- offences against persons with a mental disorder impeding choice (ss 30 to 33);
- inducements etc to persons with a mental disorder (ss 34 to 37); and
- offences by care workers against persons with a mental disorder (ss 38 to 41).

Conduct may well fall within more than one of these groups of offences.

9.105 For the purposes of these offences, 'mental disorder' has the meaning given by the Mental Health Act 1983, s 1, viz 'any disorder or disability of the mind'.[205]

---

[204] What is said in para 9.31 about the operation of the evidential presumption is equally applicable to the present evidential presumption.

[205] SOA 2003, s 79(6).

Offences against persons with a mental disorder impeding choice

9.106 The offences in the SOA 2003, ss 30 to 33 deal with cases where:

- A intentionally engages in sexual activity with B, a person with a mental disorder (s 30);[206]
- A intentionally causes or incites B, a person with a mental disorder, to engage in sexual activity (s 31);
- A intentionally, and for the purpose of sexual gratification, engages in sexual activity in the presence of B, a person with a mental disorder (s 32);
- A intentionally, and for the purpose of sexual gratification, causes B, a person with a person with a mental disorder, to watch a sexual act (s 33),

and, because B has a mental disorder or for a reason related to it, B is unable to refuse. Each offence requires that A knows or could reasonably be expected to know that B has a mental disorder and that because of it or for a reason related to it B is *likely* to be unable to refuse.

The offence under s 30 or an offence under s 31 of 'intentionally causing' might be thought to be redundant because of its apparent overlap with the non-consensual sexual offences under the SOA 2003, ss 1 to 4, because if B is unable to refuse under ss 30 or 31, B will also lack capacity to consent under ss 1 to 4. However, this is not so because the definition of inability to refuse covers some people who have capacity to consent (see para 9.111), and because the *mens rea* as to the 'consent issue' may be easier to prove.

9.107 Where a person is unable to refuse *because of* a mental disorder there is a direct causal link between the disorder and the inability to refuse. The alternative, that a person is unable to refuse consent *for a reason related to* a mental disorder, widens the test to cover other people who are equally vulnerable. This is because the alternative covers people who are unable to refuse partly for a reason other than the fact of their mental disorder as such but related to their mental disorder. One example would be where someone taking medication for a mental disorder was rendered unable to refuse. Another would be where someone has spent all his life in an institutional environment, and has become very compliant with requests that staff make of him, or has had no opportunity to become aware of what sexual activity entails, or does not know that there is a choice to be made when it comes to engaging in sexual activity.

9.108 An offence under s 30 or s 31 is triable only on indictment and punishable with a maximum of life imprisonment if penetration[207] is involved.[208] Otherwise the above

---

[206] The exceptions from liability for aiding, abetting or counselling an offence, provided by the SOA 2003, s 73 (para 9.37), apply to an offence under s 30 if B is under 16.

[207] Ie in the same way as in SOA 2003, s 25(6): see para 9.90, n 170. [208] SOA 2003, ss 30(3), 31(3).

offences are triable either way and punishable with a maximum of 14 years' imprisonment (ss 30 and 31) or 10 years' (ss 32 and 33).[209]

9.109 Subsection (2) of each section defines what is meant by the requirement of inability to refuse in the context of the particular section in terms of:

(a) **the absence of the capacity to choose whether to agree to the material conduct; or**

(b) **inability to communicate such a choice to the defendant.**

9.110 *Absence of the capacity to choose whether to agree to the material conduct* Under this heading, ss 30(2)(a) and 31(2)(a) provide that B is unable to refuse if:

> 'he lacks the capacity to choose whether to agree to the [material conduct][210] (whether because he lacks sufficient understanding of the nature or foreseeable consequences of what is being done, or for any other reason).'

Sections 32(2)(a) and 33(2)(a) make the same provision in respect to the material conduct,[211] except that (for obvious reasons) they do not contain the words 'or foreseeable consequences of what is being done'.

Further explanation of 'inability to refuse' was given in *C*,[212] where the House of Lords was concerned with s 30(2). B was a 28-year-old woman with schizo-affective disorder and an emotionally unstable personality disorder. The effects and manifestations of the disorders were intermittent. B had met A while she was suffering from a relapse. She was in a distressed, agitated state, and told A that she wanted to leave the area in which she was living for her own safety. B alleged that A offered to help her and took her to his friend's house, where she was given crack cocaine and asked by A to engage in a sexual activity. B stated that she had been 'really panicky and afraid' and had wanted to leave the premises, but that, through fear of death, she had stayed and complied with A's request. In his summing up, the trial judge stated that B would have been unable to refuse to consent under s 30(2)(a) if she lacked the capacity to choose whether to agree to the sexual touching 'for any reason', which included an irrational fear or such confusion of mind arising from her mental disorder that she felt unable to refuse any request by A for sex. The Court of Appeal allowed A's appeal against conviction. It held that an irrational fear resulting from a mental disorder could not be equated with a lack of capacity to choose, and that there was no evidence that B was physically unable to communicate any choice that she had made. It further ruled in respect of s 30(2)(a) that a lack of capacity to choose to agree to sexual activity could not be person-specific or situation-specific. The House of Lords allowed the prosecution's appeal against the Court of Appeal's decision.

---

[209] SOA 2003, ss 30(4), 31(4), 32(3), 33(3).

[210] Ie the touching (s 30) or engaging in the activity caused or incited (s 31).

[211] Ie being present (s 32) or watching or looking (s 33).

[212] [2009] UKHL 42 (reported elsewhere as *Cooper*).

The House held that the words 'for any other reason' in s 30(2)(a) were clearly capable of encompassing a wide range of circumstances in which a person's mental disorder might rob him or her of the ability to make an autonomous choice, even though he or she might have sufficient understanding of the information relevant to making it. Those circumstances could include the kind of compulsion which drove a person with anorexia to refuse food, the delusions which drove a person with schizophrenia to believe that she had to do something, or the phobia or irrational fear which drove a person to refuse a life-saving injection. Irrational fear plainly was capable of depriving a person of capacity; the question was whether it did in a particular case. The Court of Appeal had therefore been wrong in holding that an irrational fear that prevented the exercise of choice could not be equated with a lack of capacity to choose.

As noted in para 9.18, the House of Lords held in C that capacity to choose in s 30(2)(a) can be 'person-specific' or 'situation-specific' as well as 'act-specific'. It stated that, once it was accepted that choice was an exercise of free will, and that a mental disorder might rob a person of free will in a number of different ways, and in a number of different situations, then a mentally disordered person might be quite capable of exercising choice in one situation but not in another.

As can be seen, this first type of inability to refuse amounts to the same thing as inability to consent.

9.111 *Inability to communicate choice* Sections 30(2)(b), 31(2)(b), 32(2)(b) and 33(2)(b) each provide, as an alternative, that B is unable to refuse if he is unable to communicate a choice to agree to the material conduct. This second type of inability to refuse covers people who may be able to make a choice but are unable because of mental disorder or a reason related to it to communicate it. In C, the trial judge had also directed the jury that she would have been unable to refuse under s 30(2)(b) if, through her mental disorder, she was unable to communicate that choice to D, even if she was physically able to communicate with him. The Court of Appeal held that this was wrong; s 30(2)(b) required that the complainant was physically unable to communicate because of or by reason of his or her mental disorder. The House of Lords disagreed; it was quite clear that in the SOA 2003, Parliament had had in mind an inability to communicate which was the result of or associated with a disorder of the mind. There was no warrant at all for limiting it to a physical inability to communicate. It had to include a person with such a degree of learning difficulty that he or she had never acquired the gift of speech, so that it was impossible to discover whether or not he or she could understand or make a choice. In a case of physical inability to communicate, a rebuttable presumption of the absence of consent arises under s 75(2) and there can alternatively be a conviction of the appropriate offence under ss 1 to 4 where the defendant's conduct falls within s 30 or (in a case of 'intentionally causing') s 31.

Hulme v DPP[213] provides an example of a case falling within head (b) which did not involve physical inability to communicate. B, a woman aged 27, suffered from cerebral

---

[213] [2006] EWHC 1347 (Admin), DC.

palsy and had a mental age well below 27. A touched B on her private parts and caused her to touch his penis. A was convicted of sexual activity with a person with a mental disorder impeding choice, contrary to s 30. On appeal to the Divisional Court by case stated, the question was whether there was evidence on which the magistrates could conclude that B was unable to refuse to be touched sexually. The Divisional Court answered 'yes'. Although the magistrates' findings indicated that B did not want A to act in the way that he did (ie she was capable of choosing whether to agree to his conduct), their findings also indicated a finding that B was unable effectively to communicate her choice to A because of her mental condition. There was evidence to support that finding because:

- in her evidence, B had said that on A touching her private parts and pressing hard, she did not know what to do or say, and that, said the Divisional Court, could only reasonably be because of her mental condition; and

- in her evidence, B had said that when she touched A's penis she did so because A made her and because he wanted her to, although she did not want to, and that, said the Divisional Court, was explicable on the basis that, because of her mental condition, B was unable effectively to communicate her wishes in the way that a woman of 27, not suffering from her disabilities, would have done in similar circumstances.

Because there was evidence to support the finding A's conviction was proper.

9.112 As can be seen from the list of offences, each of the offences in the SOA 2003, ss 30 to 33 is concerned with a different type of sexually related conduct, each type of which replicates the type of conduct dealt with by each of the sections dealing with child sex offences (SOA 2003, ss 9 to 12) and abuse of trust offences (SOA 2003, ss 16 to 19).

Inducement, threat or deception to a person with a mental disorder

9.113 The SOA 2003, ss 34 to 37 provide the following offences under this heading:

- intentionally touching sexually a person with a mental disorder with that person's agreement, where that agreement is obtained by inducement, threat or deception (s 34);[214]

- intentionally causing a person with a mental disorder to engage in or agree to engage in sexual activity by inducement, threat or deception (s 35);

- intentionally, and for the purpose of sexual gratification, engaging in sexual activity in the presence, procured by inducement, threat or deception, of a person with a mental disorder (s 36); and

- intentionally, and for the purpose of sexual gratification, causing a person with a mental disorder to watch a sexual act by inducement, threat or deception (s 37).

---

[214] The exceptions from liability for aiding, abetting or counselling an offence, provided by the SOA 2003, s 73 (para 9.37), apply to an offence under s 34 if the mentally disordered person is under 16.

These offences require that the defendant knows or could reasonably be expected to know of the person's mental disorder.

9.114 The key difference between these offences and those in ss 30 to 33 is that **in these offences it is not necessary to prove that the mentally disordered person was unable to refuse.** Indeed it is an element of each offence that the 'victim' agrees. **Instead, it is necessary to prove that the 'victim's' agreement was procured by inducement, threat or deception on the part of the defendant in respect of the mentally disordered person.** It is this element which puts the 'sting' in what has occurred in respect of a person whose mental disorder may not be of the same depth as required for an offence under ss 30 to 33.

9.115 An offence under s 34 or s 35 is triable only on indictment and punishable with a maximum of life imprisonment if penetration[215] is involved.[216] Otherwise the above offences are triable either way and punishable with a maximum of 14 years' imprisonment (ss 34 and 35) or 10 years' (ss 36 and 37).[217]

Offences by care workers with persons with a mental disorder

9.116 A person with a mental disorder but who nevertheless has the capacity to consent to sexual activity may not be able to make rational decisions about sexual relationships and, because of familiarity with, and dependency on, a carer may be likely to be strongly influenced by such a person. Mentally disordered people are, therefore, vulnerable to sexual exploitation by their carers because their sexual autonomy – the right to choose whether or not to engage in sexual activity – is constrained in such a situation.

9.117 The SOA 2003, ss 38 to 41 create a set of offences to deal with care workers who involve persons with a mental disorder in sexual activity in a range of ways. The offences in ss 38 to 41 are particularly important where the mentally disordered person is over the age of legal consent (or, if aged 16 or 17, there is no relationship of trust, as defined by the SOA 2003, s 21), so that there may not be any other criminal liability for involving the victim in sexual activity.

The offences mirror those offences under ss 16 to 19 relating to an abuse of trust in respect of a child. The offences are:

- care worker intentionally touching sexually a person with a mental disorder (s 38);[218]
- care worker intentionally causing or inciting sexual activity with a person with a mental disorder (s 39);

---

[215] Ie in the same way as in the SOA 2003, s 25(6): see para 9.90, n 170.

[216] SOA 2003, ss 34(2), 35(2).

[217] SOA 2003, ss 34(3), 35(3), 36(2), 37(2).

[218] The exceptions from liability for aiding, abetting or counselling an offence, provided by the SOA 2003, s 73 (para 9.37), apply to an offence under s 38 if the mentally disordered person is under 16.

- care worker intentionally, and for the purpose of sexual gratification, engaging in sexual activity in the presence of a person with a mental disorder (s 40); and
- care worker intentionally, and for the purpose of sexual gratification, causing a person with a person with a mental disorder to watch a sexual act (s 41).

The offences require that the care worker knows or could reasonably be expected to know of the person's mental disorder.

There is no need to prove that the care worker exercised any form of undue influence.

An offence under s 38 or s 39 is triable only on indictment and punishable with a maximum of 14 years' imprisonment if penetration[219] is involved.[220] Otherwise the above offences are triable either way and punishable with a maximum of 10 years' imprisonment (ss 38 and 39) or seven years' (ss 40 and 41).[221]

Care worker

9.118 The offences under ss 38 to 41 are concerned with the situation where a person (A) is involved in the care of another person (B), a person with a mental disorder, in a way which falls within the SOA 2003, s 42. For this purpose, a person (A) is involved in the care of another (B) ('care worker' for short) if s 42(2), (3) or (4) applies.[222] The definition of a care worker is a wide one.

9.119 Section 42(2) applies if:

'(a) B is accommodated and cared for in a care home, community home, voluntary home or children's home, and

(b) A has functions to perform in the home in the course of employment which have brought him or are likely to bring him into regular face to face contact with B.'

An example would be where A is a member of staff at a care home and B is a resident there. The requirement of 'regular face to face contact' will have the effect of excluding people whose functions in the home do not bring them into regular face to face contact with B, for example, a finance officer.

9.120 Section 42(3) applies:

'if B is a patient for whom services are provided –

(a) by a National Health Service body or an independent medical agency, or

(b) in an independent clinic or an independent hospital,

and A has functions to perform for the body or agency or in the clinic or hospital in the course of employment which have brought him or are likely to bring him into regular face to face contact with B.'

---

[219] Ie in the same way as in SOA 2003, s 25(6): see para 9.90, n 170.   [220] SOA 2003, ss 38(3), 39(3).
[221] SOA 2003, ss 38(4), 39(4), 40(3), 41(3).   [222] SOA 2003, s 42(1).

This definition deals with cases where B is not a resident in a care home or children's home but is an in- or out-patient at a hospital etc. An example would be where B attends a clinic every week and A is a receptionist there whom B sees every week.

9.121 Section 42(4) applies if A:

> '(a) is, whether or not in the course of employment, a provider of care, assistance or services to B in connection with B's mental disorder, and
>
> (b) as such, has had or is likely to have regular face to face contact with B.'

'Care, assistance or services' is a wide description. It would, for example, include someone providing training, a complementary therapist, a psychotherapist or a volunteer counsellor. This definition is of particular importance where B is not being cared for in any form of institution but lives at home.

Exceptions for spouses and civil partners and for pre-existing relationships

9.122 Like the abuse of trust offences, two exceptions are provided from the offences under the SOA 2003, ss 38 to 41. The exceptions are set out in the SOA 2003, ss 43 and 44, which provide that conduct by a person (A) which would otherwise be an offence under ss 38 to 41 against another person (B) is not such an offence if respectively:

(a) **B was 16 or over at the time of the conduct and the defendant proves that A and B were lawfully married or civil partners at that time.**[223] This exemption applies even if the marriage or registration of the civil partnership only took place after the care relationship began;[224] or

(b) **the defendant proves that immediately before A became involved in B's care in a way falling within s 42, a sexual relationship existed between A and B,**[225] as where A and B were in a sexual relationship before B became a patient at the care home where A works. This exception does not apply if at *that* time – ie the 'immediately before' time – sexual intercourse between A and B would have been unlawful (ie criminal),[226] eg because B was under 16 or was A's learning disabled granddaughter.

It follows from (b) that, although a care worker who starts an affair with a mentally disordered patient a day after he starts a job at a care home can be convicted of an offence under s 38, a care worker who was involved in a sexual relationship with such a person when he became her care worker cannot, even if he became a care worker in order to have better access to, and influence over, her.

---

[223] SOA 2003, s 43(1) and (2) (as amended by the Civil Partnership Act 2004, Sch 27).

[224] A's mistaken belief that he is lawfully married to B, or that a civil partnership with B has been legally registered, is apparently no defence, however reasonable the mistake.

[225] SOA 2003, s 44(1) and (3).   [226] SOA 2003, s 44(2).

Preparatory offences

9.123 The SOA 2003, ss 61 to 63 provide preparatory offences of:

(a) intentionally administering a substance to, or causing a substance to be taken by,[227] another person (B), knowing that B does not consent, and with the intention of stupefying or overpowering B so as to enable any person to engage in sexual[228] activity involving B (s 61), eg putting a date rape drug in a woman's drink with the necessary intent;

(b) committing an offence with intent to commit a relevant sexual offence (s 62); and

(c) knowingly or recklessly trespassing[229] on any premises[230] with intent to commit a relevant sexual offence (s 63).

In respect of s 62, obvious examples of an offence which may be committed with intent to commit a relevant sexual offence are kidnapping and false imprisonment but it is possible to think of a wide range of other offences which could be committed with that intent. The principal reason for the offence under s 62 is to make notification requirements which apply to sex offenders ('signing on the sex offenders' register') applicable to people who are convicted of the offence.

For the purposes of ss 62 and 63, a 'relevant sexual offence' is any offence under the SOA 2003, Pt 1 (ss 1–79), ie any of the offences under the SOA 2003 referred to in the overview to this chapter, including aiding, abetting, counselling or procuring such an offence.[231]

Of course, the intended sexual activity or sexual offence referred to in ss 61 to 63 need not occur or be committed, as the case may be, or be attempted. However, proof of the necessary intent may be difficult if the defendant has not got near to attempting the sexual activity or offence.

Other examples of preparatory offences in the Act are the offences of arranging or facilitating the commission of a child sexual offence, contrary to s 14 (in some of its applications) and meeting a child etc following sexual grooming etc, contrary to s 15. Another preparatory offence under the Act is referred to in para 9.128. These preparatory offences bite at an earlier point of time than the law of attempt in relation to the intended sexual offence (and therefore catch people who are thwarted or give up before getting as far as an attempt).

---

[227] As to 'administering' and 'causing to be taken', see paras 7.116–7.119.

[228] See para 9.6.

[229] As to 'trespassing', see para 11.6. Unlike burglary the entry to the premises need not be as a trespasser, so that the offence can be committed by someone who enters lawfully but becomes a trespasser when his permission to be there terminates.

[230] 'Premises' is not limited to a building. It can include land in the open air, so that a playing field or school playground is included. In addition, 'premises' includes a structure or part of a structure, and 'structure' includes a tent, vehicle or vessel or other temporary or movable structure: s 63(2).

[231] SOA 2003, ss 62(2), 63(2).

The offences under ss 61–63 are, with one exception, triable either way and punishable with a maximum of 10 years' imprisonment. The exception is that if an offence under s 62 involves false imprisonment or kidnapping with intent to commit a sexual offence it is triable only on indictment and punishable with life imprisonment.

Other offences

Key points 9.8

The SOA 2003, ss 66 to 71 provide a number of other less serious offences relating to:

- exposure (s 66);
- voyeurism (s 67);
- intercourse with an animal (s 69);
- sexual penetration of a corpse (s 70); and
- sexual activity in a public lavatory (s 71).

9.124 Besides the last offence, all these offences are triable either way and punishable with a maximum of two years' imprisonment.[232]

Exposure

9.125 The SOA 2003, s 66(1) provides a gender-neutral offence of exposure. It states:

'A person commits an offence if –

(a) he[233] intentionally exposes his genitals, and

(b) he intends that someone will see them and be caused alarm or distress.'

9.126 The indecent exposure of any part of the body in a place to which the public has access, or where it is capable of public view, can constitute the common law offence of outraging public decency, referred to in para 14.98, if it is capable of being seen by two or more people who are actually present and the exposure outrages the minimum contemporary standards of decency. This offence is rarely invoked to deal with indecent exposure. It should not be invoked in a case covered by the terms of s 66 unless there is good reason for doing so.[234]

---

[232] SOA 2003, ss 66(2), 67(5), 69(3) and 70(2).

[233] As elsewhere in statute law, in the absence of a contrary intention, 'he'/ 'his' includes 'she'/ 'her': Interpretation Act 1978, s 6.

[234] *Rimmington; Goldstein* [2005] UKHL 63 at [30], [52]–[54], per Lords Bingham and Rodger.

Voyeurism

9.127 The SOA 2003, s 67(1) provides that:

'A person commits an offence if –

  (a) for the purpose of obtaining sexual gratification,[235] he observes another person doing a private act, and

  (b) he knows that the other person does not consent to being observed for his sexual gratification.'

For the purposes of s 67, a person is doing a private act if the person is in a place which, in the circumstances, would reasonably be expected to provide privacy, and –

- the person's genitals, buttocks or breasts[236] are exposed or covered only with underwear,
- the person is using a lavatory, or
- the person is doing a sexual act that is not of a kind ordinarily done in public.[237]

In *Bassett*[238] the Court of Appeal held that in the context of communal showers or changing rooms there is no reasonable expectation of privacy from casual observation by other users of the communal showers or changing rooms, whereas there is a reasonable expectation of privacy from being spied on in such places by someone who has drilled a hole in the wall for this purpose. Thus, casual observation of other users of communal showers or changing rooms does not amount to the offence of voyeurism, even if the observer gains sexual gratification from what he sees. The Court of Appeal added that:

'[T]he question of whether the person observed had a reasonable expectation of privacy from the kind of observation which ensued is one for the jury in each case. We accept that that may well mean that in many cases the question of whether there is or is not a reasonable expectation of privacy will be closely related to the nature of the observing which is under consideration. That in turn may mean that the question of expectation of privacy may have an indirect link to the purpose of the observer. It is however plain that it is the nature of the observation rather than the purpose of the observation which *may* be relevant to the expectation of privacy. As we have already said, the presence of sexual gratification in the observer does not *ipso facto* mean that the observation is one from which there is a reasonable expectation of privacy.'[239]

9.128 Sections 67(2)–(4) provide additional offences relating to:

- operating equipment (eg a hidden webcam) with intent to enable someone else to engage in voyeurism;

---

[235] See para 9.69.
[236] This reference to breasts is limited to female breasts: *Bassett* [2008] EWCA Crim 1174.
[237] SOA 2003, s 68(1).   [238] [2008] EWCA Crim 1174.   [239] [2008] EWCA Crim 1174 at [11].

- recording (eg photographing or videoing) another doing a private act with intent to enable oneself or another to engage in voyeurism, and
- installing equipment, or constructing or adapting a structure,[240] with the intention of enabling oneself or another to commit an offence under s 67(1) (eg rigging up a secret camera in a women's lavatory or changing room or making a peephole in a partition between two lavatory cubicles).

Intercourse with an animal

9.129 The SOA 2003, s 69 introduces two offences, which have similar elements, to deal with what may be called active and passive sexual intercourse with a living animal respectively.

Section 69(1) provides:

'A person commits an offence if –

(a) he intentionally performs an act of penetration with his penis,[241]

(b) what is penetrated is the vagina or anus of a living animal,[242] and

(c) he knows that, or is reckless as to whether, that is what is penetrated.'

Section 69(2) provides:

'A person (A) commits an offence if –

(a) A intentionally causes, or allows, A's vagina or anus to be penetrated,

(b) the penetration is by the penis of a living animal, and

(c) A knows that, or is reckless as to whether, that is what A is being penetrated by.'

Sexual penetration of a corpse

9.130 By SOA 2003, s 70(1):

'A person commits an offence if –

(a) he intentionally performs an act of penetration with a part of his body or anything else,

(b) what is penetrated is a part of the body of a dead person,

(c) he knows that, or is reckless as to whether, that is what is penetrated, and

(d) the penetration is sexual.'[243]

---

[240] In s 67, 'structure' includes a tent, vehicle or vessel or other temporary or movable structure: s 68(2).

[241] Para 9.25.

[242] In relation to an animal, references to the vagina or anus include references to any similar part: SOA 2003, s 79(10).

[243] Para 9.6.

Sexual activity in a public lavatory

9.131 The SOA 2003, s 71(1) provides:

'A person commits an offence if –

(a) he is in a lavatory to which the public or a section of the public has or is permitted to have access, whether on payment or otherwise,

(b) he intentionally engages in an activity, and

(c) the activity is sexual.'

An offence under s 71 is only a summary offence.[244] A person guilty of it is liable to a maximum of six months' imprisonment[245] or a fine not exceeding level 5 on the standard scale or both.[246] The definition of 'sexual' provided by the SOA 2003, s 78, referred to in para 9.6, does not apply to s 71. Instead, s 71(2) provides that, for the purposes of s 71, an activity is sexual if a reasonable person would, in all the circumstances but regardless of any person's purpose, consider it to be sexual.

Because the offence under s 71 is summary only, it is not an offence to attempt to commit it.

Jurisdiction over paedophile offences outside the United Kingdom

Key points 9.9

The normal rule that our courts only have jurisdiction over offences committed in England and Wales[247] would result in an unacceptable gap in the law in respect of those who organise or engage in 'sex tourism', ie a practice whereby adults, usually male, visit underdeveloped countries for sexual pleasure on a commercial basis with young children. Statute has intervened to correct this defect in respect of sexual offences outside the United Kingdom. The principal provision is SOA 2003, s 72.

---

[244] SOA 2003, s 71(3). A prosecution for the common law offence of outraging public decency is possible but, as in the case of indecent exposure, should not be invoked in a case covered by s 71 unless there is good reason for doing so: *Rimmington; Goldstein* [2005] UKHL 63 at [30], [52]–[54], per Lords Bingham and Rodger.

[245] This will be increased to 51 weeks when the Criminal Justice Act 2003, s 281(4) and (5) comes into force.

[246] SOA 2003, s 71(3).

[247] Key Points 1.3.

Sexual Offences (Conspiracy and Incitement) Act 1996

9.132 A modest approach to deal with the problem of jurisdiction was made by the Sexual Offences (Conspiracy and Incitement) Act 1996, which extended the jurisdiction of the courts of England and Wales to conspiracy or incitement in England and Wales to commit outside the United Kingdom one of a number of specified sexual offences[248] against a person under 16. The provisions of the Act relating to conspiracy were repealed[249] in 1998 and subsumed within the Criminal Law Act 1977, s 1A, dealt with in para 14.77. The provisions about incitement (which offence was abolished by the Serious Crime Act 2007, s 59) now apply in respect of an offence of encouragement or assistance of crime.[250] However, they were rendered largely otiose by a much more extensive provision now contained in the SOA 2003, s 72 and Sch 2. The Sexual Offences (Conspiracy and Incitement) Act 1996 continues to be the only available provision to deal with the case of D's encouragement or assistance in this country of the commission abroad of a specified sexual offence by a foreign national who is not resident in the United Kingdom[251] and who would not himself be subject to English criminal law were he to act as D encourages or assists him to do.

Sexual Offences Act 2003, s 72

9.133 The SOA 2003, s 72, as substituted and amended in 2008,[252] provides:

'(1) If –
  (a) a United Kingdom national does an act in a country outside the United Kingdom, and
  (b) the act, if done in England and Wales, would constitute a sexual offence to which this section applies,

  the United Kingdom national is guilty in England and Wales of that sexual offence.

(2) If –
  (a) a United Kingdom resident does an act in a country outside the United Kingdom,
  (b) the act constitutes an offence under the law in force in that country, and
  (c) the act, if done in England and Wales, would constitute a sexual offence to which this section applies,

---

[248] As a result of an amendment by the SOA 2003, the specified offences are those under the SOA 2003, ss 1–12, 14–26.

[249] By the Criminal Justice (Terrorism and Conspiracy) Act 1998, Sch 2.

[250] References to incitement in the 1996 Act have effect instead as references to the offence of encouraging or assisting crime contrary to the Serious Crime Act 2007, Pt 2: Serious Crime Act 2007, s 63(1), Sch 6, Pt 1.

[251] And who has not become a United Kingdom national or resident by (and at) the time proceedings are brought.

[252] As substituted by the Criminal Justice and Immigration Act 2008, s 72(1), and amended by the Sexual Offences (Northern Ireland Consequential Amendments) Order 2008.

the United Kingdom resident is guilty in England and Wales of that sexual offence.

(3) If –

  (a) a person does an act in a country outside the United Kingdom at a time when the person was not a United Kingdom national or a United Kingdom resident,

  (b) the act constituted an offence under the law in force in that country,

  (c) the act, if done in England and Wales, would have constituted a sexual offence to which this section applies, and

  (d) the person meets the residence or nationality condition at the relevant time,

  proceedings may be brought against the person in England and Wales for that sexual offence as if the person had done the act there.

(4) The person meets the residence or nationality condition at the relevant time if the person is a United Kingdom national or a United Kingdom resident at the time when the proceedings are brought.'

For the above purposes, a 'United Kingdom national' is defined by the SOA 2003, s 72(9) as an individual who is –

(a) a British citizen, a British Overseas Territories citizen, a British National (Overseas) or a British Overseas citizen;

(b) a person who under the British Nationality Act 1981 is a British subject; or

(c) a British protected person within the meaning of that Act.

In respect of the condition in s 72(2)(b) or s 72(3)(b) there is a presumption that it is satisfied unless the defence serves on the prosecution a notice stating that in their opinion it is not satisfied, and giving the grounds for that opinion. If this is done, the prosecution must prove that the condition is satisfied.[253] In the Crown Court, whether the condition is satisfied is to be decided by the judge alone.[254]

9.134 The list of offences to which the SOA 2003, s 72 applies is contained in Sch 2 to the SOA 2003.[255] The offences are not limited to sex-tourism offences (at least, as far as such offences are commonly understood) but they are restricted (either by their own requirements or by Sch 2) to offences involving a person under 18, except where 16 (or 13) is the upper limit in respect of the offence itself. Schedule 2 provides that the following are sexual offences to which s 72 applies:

• an offence under any of the following sections of the SOA 2003:
  – s 5 (rape of a child under 13);
  – s 6 (assault of a child under 13 by penetration);
  – s 7 (sexual assault of a child under 13);
  – s 8 (causing or inciting a child under 13 to engage in sexual activity);

[253] SOA 2003, s 72(6).   [254] SOA 2003, s 72(8).
[255] As amended by the Criminal Justice and Immigration Act 2008, s 72(2), (3), and the Order referred to in n 252.

- s 9 (sexual activity with a child);
- s 10 (causing or inciting a child to engage in sexual activity);
- s 11 (engaging in sexual activity in the presence of a child);
- s 12 (causing a child to watch a sexual act);
- s 13 (child sex offences committed by children or young persons);
- s 14 (arranging or facilitating commission of a child sex offence);
- s 15 (meeting a child following sexual grooming etc);
- ss 16–19 (offences of abuse of position of trust);
- ss 25 and 26 (familial child sex offences);
- ss 47–50 (abuse of children through prostitution or child pornography);

- an offence under any of the following sections of the SOA 2003:
  - s 1 (rape);
  - s 2 (assault by penetration);
  - s 3 (sexual assault);
  - s 4 (causing a person to engage in sexual activity without consent);
  - ss 30–41 (offences against persons with a mental disorder impeding choice, offences relating to inducements etc to persons with a mental disorder, and offences committed by careworkers with such persons);
  - s 61 (administering a substance with intent),

  where the victim of the offence was under 18 at the time of the offence;

- an offence under the SOA 2003, s 62 or s 63 (committing offence with intent to commit a sexual offence or trespass with intent to commit a sexual offence, respectively), *where the intended offence was an offence against a person under 18;* and

- an offence under the Protection of Children Act 1978, s 1 (taking, making, distribution etc of indecent photographs of children), or the Criminal Justice Act 1988, s 160 (possession of indecent photograph of child).

References to one of these offences also include a reference to an attempt, a conspiracy, or an encouragement or assistance,[256] to commit that offence and to secondary participation in it, so that extra-territorial jurisdiction also exists under s 72 in respect of such activities.

FURTHER READING

Card, Gillespie and Hirst *Sexual Offences* (2008)

Elvin 'The Concept of Consent under the Sexual Offences Act 2003' (2008) 72 JCL 519

Power 'Towards a Redefinition of the *Mens Rea* of Rape' (2003) 23 OJLS 379

Rook and Ward *Sexual Offences: Law and Practice* (3rd edn, 2004)

---

[256] SOA 2003, Sch 2 refers to 'incitement' but this now has effect as a reference to an offence of encouraging or assisting crime contrary to the Serious Crime Act 2007, Pt 2: Serious Crime Act 2007, s 63(1), Sch 6, Pt 1.

JR Spencer 'The Sexual Offences Act 2003: Child and Family Offences' [2004] Crim LR 347

Temkin *Rape and the Legal Process* (2002)

Temkin and Ashworth 'The Sexual Offences Act 2003: Rape, Sexual Assault and the Problems of Consent' [2004] Crim LR 328

Wallerstein 'A Drunken Consent is Still Consent – Or is It?' (2009) 73 JCL 318

10

Theft and related offences

OVERVIEW

The Theft Act 1968 and what remains of the Theft Act 1978 are dealt with in this and the next chapter. This chapter deals with theft and the following related offences:

- robbery;
- removal of an article from a place open to the public;
- taking a conveyance;
- aggravated vehicle-taking; and
- making off without payment.

10.1 Before the Theft Act 1968 came into force, the law concerning theft and related offences (almost wholly contained in the Larceny Act 1916) was quite different. It is fortunately unnecessary to say anything about it because the Theft Act 1968, which is based on the Eighth Report of the Criminal Law Revision Committee,[1] and what remains of the Theft Act 1978 are an entirely new code. Together with the Theft Act 1978, the Theft Act 1968 also made provision for a number of offences involving deception. These have been repealed by the Fraud Act 2006 and replaced by an offence of fraud and an offence of obtaining services dishonestly, which are dealt with in Chapter 12. The offence of making off without payment is the only offence under the Theft Act 1978 which survives.

Theft

Key points 10.1

Theft is governed by the Theft Act 1968 (TA 1968), ss 1 to 7.[2] The TA 1968, s 1(1) provides that:

'A person is guilty of theft if he dishonestly appropriates property belonging to another with the intention of permanently depriving the other of it…'

---

[1] *Theft and Related Offences* (Cmnd 2977) (1966).
[2] For special rules relating to jurisdiction over theft, see paras 12.69–12.71.

10.2 Theft is triable either way.[3] By the TA 1968, s 7, it is punishable with a maximum of seven years' imprisonment on conviction on indictment.

The *actus reus* of theft is the appropriation of property belonging to another. The *mens rea* is dishonesty coupled with the intention of permanently depriving the other of the property appropriated.

Actus reus of theft

Appropriation

Key points 10.2

An appropriation of property:

- involves an assumption of any of the rights of the owner;
- need not have any effect on the property or the owner's enjoyment of it;
- may occur even though the owner consents to or authorises what the defendant does;
- may occur:
  - simply by taking possession of the property; or
  - even though the defendant is already in possession of the property; or
  - even though the defendant never possesses the property; or
  - even though what the defendant does with the property is not unlawful in civil law; or
  - even though the defendant acquires a right to the property which cannot be annulled in civil law;
- cannot occur simply by deceiving the victim into doing something with the property.

10.3 The TA 1968, s 3(1) provides that:

'Any assumption by a person of the rights of an owner amounts to an appropriation, and this includes, where he has come by the property (innocently or not) without stealing it, any later assumption of a right to it by keeping or dealing with it as owner.'

As will be seen, this provision has been interpreted by the House of Lords in ways which give 'appropriation' a very wide meaning and which seem inconsistent with the clear meaning of s 3(1) but which must be accepted as binding.

---

[3] Magistrates' Courts Act 1980, s 17(1) and Sch 1.

Assumption of any of the rights of the owner

10.4 The essence of the TA 1968, s 3(1) is an 'assumption...of the rights of an owner'. An owner of property has many rights in relation to it; they include the rights to use the property in question, to destroy it, to give it away, to sell it and so on.

In the consolidated appeals, *Morris; Anderton v Burnside*[4] (hereafter simply referred to as *Morris*), where the rest of their Lordships simply agreed with the speech of Lord Roskill, the House of Lords held that, despite the use of the words 'the rights' in the above phrase, s 3 as a whole indicated that an appropriation does not require an assumption of all the rights of an owner and that **it is enough that there has been an assumption of *any* of the rights of *the* owner**. Thus, it held that the defendant's conduct in switching price labels in a shop was an appropriation because the right to fix the price of goods on sale was one of the owner's rights. This interpretation is difficult to reconcile with the clear words of the section, but it must now be regarded as representing the interpretation of the words in question,[5] particularly in the light of the acceptance of this aspect of *Morris* by the House of Lords in *Gomez*.[6] Although it seems odd that the phrase 'assumption of the rights of an owner' should mean 'assumption of any of the rights of the owner', it must be admitted that the offence of theft would be unworkable if *all* the rights of an owner had to be assumed. We shall see later on that it is possible for an owner of property to steal it from someone (like a hirer) who is not the owner but to whom the property 'belongs' for the purposes of theft. Presumably, 'the owner' in the House of Lords' formulation must be read as including 'another person to whom the property belongs' where the alleged theft is not from the owner.

10.5 The importance of the interpretation given to s 3(1) in *Morris* is shown by *Governor of Pentonville Prison, ex p Osman*.[7] In *ex p Osman* the Divisional Court was concerned with the situation where P's bank account is in credit, and D dishonestly presents a cheque or sends instructions to P's bank to draw on that account. It held that such conduct would constitute an appropriation of the bank credit. The reason was that presenting the cheque[8] or sending the instruction is the exercise of one of the rights of the owner of the bank credit, the right to have his cheques or instructions relating to the account met[9] (which is more appropriately expressed as assuming the right of the owner of the bank credit to destroy or diminish it). It would not matter, it held, that the account was never in fact debited. In so holding, it did not follow an obiter dictum by the Court of Appeal in *Kohn*,[10] to the effect that 'the completion of the theft does not take place until the transaction has gone through to completion'.

---

[4] [1984] AC 320, HL.

[5] This was accepted by the Privy Council in *Chan Man-sin v A-G of Hong Kong* [1988] 1 All ER 1.

[6] [1993] AC 442, HL.   [7] [1989] 3 All ER 701, DC.

[8] Merely signing the cheque is only a preparatory act and insufficient: *Ngan* [1998] 1 Cr App Rep 331, CA.

[9] Cf *Tomsett* [1985] Crim LR 369, CA, where the contrary view was taken by the Court of Appeal after prosecuting counsel had declined to argue the point. In *Governor of Pentonville Prison, ex p Osman* the Divisional Court held that consequently the decision in *Tomsett* was not a binding authority on the point.

[10] (1979) 69 Cr App Rep 395, CA.

Appropriation need not have any effect

10.6 It follows from *ex p Osman* that it is irrelevant that the assumption of a right of the owner has no effect on the owner's property or his enjoyment of it. This being so, the view of the Court of Appeal in *Hilton*,[11] where the Court upheld the conviction for theft of the chairman of a charity who, in order to settle his personal debts, had caused its bank to transfer sums from the charity's account to another account on a number of occasions, twice by faxing instructions to the bank and once by the presentation of a cheque, is surprising in the following respect. The Court stated that the chairman had appropriated the credit balance by assuming the rights of the owner by causing the transfer to be made. His instructions by fax or cheque were the key which set the relevant inter-account machinery in motion. It then added, unnecessarily and oddly, and without appearing to realise the inconsistency with previous authority, that 'the fact that the transfer was made was enough to complete the offence'. Subsequently, the Court of Appeal in *Ngan*[12] approved and applied what was said in *ex p Osman* without reference to *Hilton* or any need for a resulting transfer to complete the theft. It held that the act of presenting the cheque was 'the act of theft'. More recently, it has been confirmed that it is not necessary that any person to whom the property belongs should be the poorer because of the appropriation; 'deprivation' is not required.[13]

Owner's consent or authorisation irrelevant

10.7 There may be an assumption of a right of the owner, and therefore an appropriation of property belonging to another, even though the owner consents to or authorises the act in question. This was held by the House of Lords by a majority of four to one in *Gomez*,[14] where an irreconcilable conflict on this point between two earlier House of Lords' decisions, *Lawrence v Metropolitan Police Comr*[15] and *Morris*,[16] was resolved. In *Lawrence v Metropolitan Police Comr* Viscount Dilhorne, giving the judgment of the House of Lords, stated that the words 'without the consent of the owner' are not to be implied into the definition of the offence. However, in *Morris* Lord Roskill, giving the judgment of the majority of the House of Lords and having referred to the decision in *Lawrence*, stated that, for there to be an assumption of the rights (or any right) of the owner, there must be an act by way of adverse interference with or usurpation of those rights (or any of them), and there would not be such an interference or usurpation if what was done with the property was expressly or impliedly authorised by the owner of it.

Despite the fact that *Morris* had generally been followed on the present point, the majority of the House of Lords in *Gomez* held that *Lawrence* represented the correct

---

[11] [1997] 2 Cr App Rep 445, CA. [12] [1998] 1 Cr App Rep 331, CA.

[13] See *R (on the application of A) v Crown Court at Snaresbrook* [2001] EWHC 456 (Admin) at [25]; *Wheatley v Commissioner of Police of the British Virgin Islands* [2006] UKPC 24 at [10]–[11].

[14] [1993] AC 442, HL. See Cooper and Allen 'Appropriation after *Gomez*' (1993) 57 JCL 186; Shute and Horder 'Thieving and Deceiving: What is the Difference?' (1993) 56 MLR 548; Clarkson 'Theft and Fair Labelling' (1993) 56 MLR 554.

[15] [1972] AC 626, HL. [16] [1984] AC 320, HL.

view, and not (on this point) *Morris*. The majority did not discuss in detail the merits of the two views, but relied on the fact that Viscount Dilhorne's statement in *Lawrence* was part of the ratio decidendi,[17] while Lord Roskill's was only an obiter dictum. In *Gomez* the certified question related to the situation where consent had been obtained by fraud. However, as was recognised by Lord Steyn, giving the judgment of the majority of the House of Lords in *Hinks*,[18] the majority in *Gomez* did not differentiate between cases of consent induced by fraud and consent given in other circumstances.

The interpretation in *Gomez* seems to strain the meaning of 'appropriation' and 'assumption' as those terms are normally understood. If the owner has consented to, or authorised, the exercise of one of his rights to property, one would not ordinarily describe that exercise as an appropriation or as an assumption of that right. The interpretation in *Gomez* is also open to the objection that the Criminal Law Revision Committee intended 'appropriation' and 'assumption' to have the meaning given in *Morris*, as Lord Lowry demonstrated in his dissenting speech in *Gomez*.[19] Indeed, the TA 1968 itself assumes this because in s 2(1)(b) it states that a person is not dishonest if he believes that the victim would have consented to the appropriation. Parliament would not have provided this if it did not think that actual consent would prevent an appropriation. The consequences of *Gomez* are returned to below, especially para 10.18.

10.8 The facts of *Gomez* were that D1, an assistant manager of an electrical goods shop, induced his manager to authorise the supply of goods to D2 in exchange for two building society cheques which were worthless because they were stolen. D1 and D2 knew that the cheques were stolen but D1 concealed this from the manager, telling him that the cheques were 'as good as cash'. D1 and D2 were convicted of the theft of the goods.

The Court of Appeal held that the judge had been wrong to hold that, on these facts, there had been an appropriation of the goods by D2 when he took possession of them. Its reason, following the dictum in *Morris* that appropriation required an unauthorised exercise of one of the owner's rights, was that D2 was entitled (ie authorised) to take possession of the goods under the voidable contract of sale. It declined to follow *Dobson v General Accident Fire and Life Assurance Corpn plc*,[20] where a rogue induced the sale to him of a watch and a ring in a telephone conversation with their owner. A day later he paid with a stolen and worthless cheque and took the articles away with him. On the question of whether the rogue had stolen the articles (which was material because the owner's insurance policy covered loss by theft), the Court of Appeal (Civil Division) held that the articles had been stolen. One of the arguments put against this conclusion had

---

[17] It is doubtful that the statement was part of the ratio decidendi since, in Viscount Dilhorne's opinion, the facts of the case fell far short of establishing consent on the part of the owner.

[18] [2001] 2 AC 241 at 251.

[19] For contrasting views on whether or not *Gomez* is a good decision, see JC Smith [1993] Crim LR 304 and S Gardner 'Appropriation in Theft: The Last Word?' (1993) 109 LQR 194.

[20] [1990] 1 QB 274, CA. This decision is discussed in an article by Heaton 'Deceiving without Thieving' [2001] Crim LR 712.

been that the contract of sale had been made over the telephone, ie before delivery, and that accordingly the rogue would have taken delivery of his own property because ownership would have passed to him at the time of the contract. Parker LJ doubted that the property was intended to pass on contract, but held that if ownership had passed by that time,[21] he would hold that, by making the contract, the rogue had assumed the rights of the owner over the articles and at that time they did belong to another (the owner).[22] The other judge did not deal with this point.

The prosecution in *Gomez* appealed successfully to the House of Lords, the majority of whom, as indicated above, held that a person could appropriate property even though he had the owner's consent or authority to exercise the right in question. In doing so, the House placed considerable reliance on what Parker LJ had said in *Dobson v Accident Fire and Life Assurance Corpn plc*.

Appropriation by controllers of corporations

10.9 A corporation, such as a limited company, a local authority or a limited liability partnership under the Limited Liability Partnerships Act 2000 is a separate person in law and can own property. A limited company, for example, is distinct from its shareholders (otherwise called members), so that a shareholder can steal the company's property from it, just as an employee can. A corporation can only act through certain people whose acts and state of mind are the company's acts and state of mind.[23]

One of the points clarified by *Gomez* is that **those who control a company can appropriate the company's property**, and thereby commit theft in relation to it. Previously, the authorities had been in conflict.[24] In *Gomez* Lord Browne-Wilkinson stated that the approach taken to 'appropriation' by the majority in that case meant that, even if those who control a company consent or purport to consent to a dealing with its property by them (or one of them), that dealing will be an appropriation of property belonging to another (the company)[25] and, provided the appropriation is made dishonestly and with intent permanently to deprive the company, theft will be committed. Proof of dishonesty may not be easy. As was said in the later case of *R (on the application of A) v Snaresbrook Crown Court*,[26] the reason why directors who dispose of a company's property are not in the normal way guilty of theft is because their appropriation is not dishonest.

---

[21] Under a sale of goods contract of the type in question, ownership can pass under such a contract as soon as it is made and before the price has been paid, depending on the parties' intention: Sale of Goods Act 1979, s 18, r 1.

[22] [1990] 1 QB 274 at 280.

[23] Key points 18.3.

[24] *McHugh and Tringham* (1988) 88 Cr App Rep 385, CA (cannot be appropriation); cf *A-G's Reference (No 2 of 1982)* [1984] QB 624, CA; *Philippou* (1989) 89 Cr App Rep 290, CA (can be appropriation).

[25] [1993] AC 442 at 496.

[26] [2001] EWHC Admin 456, DC.

Relevance to appropriation of defendant's state of mind

10.10 In *Gomez* Lord Browne-Wilkinson stated that 'appropriation' is an 'objective description of the act done irrespective of the mental state' of the defendant.[27] It is, however, difficult to accept that the state of mind with which the defendant acted in relation to property can never be relevant to the question of whether he appropriated it. In some cases, it may be crucial; an example appears in para 10.21.

Aside from the issue of appropriation, the defendant's state of mind is of crucial importance in other ways. The effect of the House of Lords' decisions in *Lawrence*, *Gomez* and *Hinks*[28] is to make 'appropriation' an extremely wide concept; almost any dealing with property amounts to an 'appropriation'.[29] It is the requirements that the defendant should act dishonestly and with the intention of permanently depriving the victim which control the potential width of the offence of theft. In *Hinks*,[30] Lord Steyn expressed the opinion that they provided adequate protection against injustice. However, the uncertainty of what constitutes 'dishonestly'[31] means that his opinion is questionable.

Examples of appropriation

10.11 The most common type of appropriation is that of taking possession of property; taking possession is clearly one of the rights of the owner. A pickpocket who takes someone's wallet clearly appropriates it. A shopper who removes goods from a shelf in a supermarket thereby appropriates them,[32] since the moving of the goods is one of the rights of the owner, and if he does so dishonestly and with the intention of permanently depriving the other of them he commits theft. Of course, if he intends to pay at the checkout, he would not be found to be dishonest.[33] In *Gallasso*,[34] which was decided by the Court of Appeal a fortnight after *Gomez*, the Court of Appeal held that there could not be an appropriation without a 'taking', but there is nothing in *Gomez* to warrant this, and it is inconsistent with other decisions referred to in this chapter, which are still good law in the light of *Gomez*. Since it cannot be squared with *Gomez*, in particular, the point must be regarded as wrongly decided.

A person can appropriate property even though he does not take possession of it in a technical sense but merely assumes control of it, however momentarily. This is shown by the decision in *Corcoran v Anderton*,[35] where it was held that a robbery (which requires a theft, and therefore an appropriation) was committed where a woman's handbag was wrested from her grasp, even though it then fell to the ground and was not made off with. Indeed, it would seem that the robber appropriated the handbag merely by taking hold of it because thereby he assumed a right of the owner.

The right to price goods is a right of the owner. Thus, in *Pilgram v Rice-Smith*[36] it was held that a supermarket assistant, who, in league with a customer, wrapped goods and

---

[27] [1993] AC 442 at 495. See also *Gallasso* (1992) 98 Cr App Rep 284, CA.   [28] See para 10.18.

[29] For two situations where there is not an appropriation, see paras 10.15 and 10.20.

[30] [2001] 2 AC 241 at 253.

[31] Paras 10.69–10.75.   [32] *McPherson* (1972) 117 Sol Jo 13, CA.   [33] Para 10.74.

[34] (1992) 98 Cr App Rep 284, CA.   [35] (1980) 71 Cr App Rep 104, DC.

[36] [1977] 2 All ER 658, DC.

understated their price on the wrapper so that the customer would be charged less than the true price at the checkout, had thereby appropriated the goods.

Appropriation by a person in possession

10.12 As already indicated, a person can appropriate property even though he is already in possession or control of it. This is made clear by the latter part of the TA 1968, s 3(1), which provides that 'appropriation':

> 'includes, where he [the defendant] has come by property (innocently or not) without stealing it,[37] any later assumption of a right to it by keeping or dealing with it as owner.'

Suppose that D helps himself to V's umbrella in order to go out during a shower but intending to return it when he comes back. He does not steal it at that stage because, although there is an appropriation of the umbrella, it is not accompanied by an intention permanently to deprive V. However, if D subsequently decides to keep the umbrella or to sell it, and does so, he may be convicted of theft because his later assumption of a right to it, by keeping or dealing with it as owner, constitutes an appropriation which is accompanied by an intention permanently to deprive V. Likewise, a person who finds V's lost property and picks it up, intending to return it to V, but later dishonestly decides to keep it, commits theft by keeping it because he thereby dishonestly appropriates it with an intention of permanently depriving V of it.

A common type of theft is theft by a bailee of property; a bailee is someone such as a borrower of goods or a person to whom goods have been hired.[38] If, for example, D hires a car from V and later purports to sell it as his own to X, he thereby appropriates it because V will have retained some of the rights of the owner and D will have assumed one of those retained rights, the right to sell. The same would be true if D simply offered to sell the car because he would have assumed a right retained by V.

Appropriation by a person not in possession

10.13 There can be an appropriation by a person even though he never possesses the property concerned, as where:

- D enters V's house in V's absence and offers to sell V's furniture to X, since the right to sell is one of the rights of ownership;[39] or

---

[37] See, further, para 10.22. 'Stealing' here refers to theft in terms of English law whether the conduct in question occurred in this country or abroad: *Atakpu* [1994] QB 69, CA. This is surprising in relation to conduct abroad since, on a correct application of the law of jurisdiction, conduct abroad cannot constitute the offence of theft under English law and English courts would lack jurisdiction to try someone on a charge of such a theft abroad. In *Atakpu* the Court of Appeal considered that such conduct did constitute theft under English law but that an English court would lack jurisdiction to try it. For a critical analysis of this decision, see Sullivan and Warbrick 'Territoriality, Theft and *Atakpu*' [1994] Crim LR 650.

[38] See para 10.41.

[39] *Pitham and Hehl* (1976) 65 Cr App Rep 45, CA. The actual decision in this case is open to criticism on its facts because, as the offeror knew, the offeree knew that the offeror was not the owner of the furniture and did not have the owner's authority to sell the property, so that in reality D was not offering to sell the furniture but

- D destroys V's property without touching it, eg by throwing stones at a window or shooting domestic animals, since the right of destruction is one of the rights of the owner. However, such conduct would also constitute an offence under the Criminal Damage Act 1971 and would be more appropriately charged under that Act.

Other examples are provided by reference to *Governor of Pentonville Prison, ex p Osman* and *Dobson v Accident Fire and Life Assurance* which were dealt with in paras 10.5 and 10.8 respectively.

Obtaining ownership by deception or duress: an appropriation?

10.14 It seems to have been accepted by the House of Lords in *Gomez*[40] that, **where a person receives property simultaneously with the transfer of ownership of it to him as a result of a deception, he appropriates it by taking physical possession of it**. An example would be where D has deceived V into making a gift to him. The ownership of the gift would pass on delivery to D, the time that D receives it. At the split second of time that D receives the property from V it will belong to V, although a split second later it will not. The same would be true if the obtaining of ownership had been by duress. Indeed, a person who has acquired another's full proprietary interest with consent appropriates it if he simultaneously receives it, even if no deception or duress is involved. Lord Steyn, giving the majority judgment in *Hinks*,[41] and relying on *Lawrence* and *Gomez*, rejected a submission that a person does not appropriate property unless the other (the owner) retains, beyond the instant of the alleged theft, some proprietary interest or the right to recover some proprietary interest.

Deceiving the victim into doing something with the property

10.15 The definition of appropriation requires D's conduct in relation to property to manifest an assumption of any of the rights of the owner. This being so, does D thereby appropriate property if he induces V to do something in respect of V's property in relation to which D does not then have possession, control or physical contact? In *Briggs*[42] the Court of Appeal answered 'no'. In that case, D deceived her elderly relatives, who were selling their house, to give her a letter of authority which she presented to the licensed conveyancers handling the sale. The letter authorised the conveyancers to transfer some of the proceeds (£49,500) of the sale of the house to D's solicitors' bank account. This was done after completion of the sale of the house and was used to purchase a house in the name of D and her father. D was convicted of the theft of the credit balance representing the £49,500 transferred by the licensed conveyancers to D's solicitors' bank account. The Court of Appeal allowed D's appeal against conviction. The prosecution had alleged that she had appropriated the credit balance when she caused the licensed conveyancers

---

making a proposal for the joint theft of it: see *Smith's Law of Theft* (9th edn, 2007) (Ormerod and Williams (eds)) para 2.79.

[40] [1993] AC 442, HL.   [41] [2001] 2 AC 241 at 253.   [42] [2003] EWCA Crim 3662.

to transfer the £49,500 to her solicitors for her own purposes. The Court of Appeal disagreed. **It held that, where a victim causes a payment to be made in reliance on deceptive conduct by the defendant, there is no 'appropriation' by the defendant.**

The Court distinguished its decision that there had been an appropriation in *Hilton*,[43] where it had held that the chairman of a charity who had caused a bank transfer from the charity's account to another account on a number of occasions by issuing instructions to the bank had appropriated the charity's bank balance by assuming the charity's right to the balance, on the ground that the defendant had direct control of the charity's bank balance and had caused payments from it to be made by his bank (which was, of course, an innocent agent) to settle his personal debts.

The Court of Appeal was 'fortified' in coming to its decision by a number of factors including the following:[44]

- 'no case has been cited to us where it has been held that an "appropriation" occurs where the relevant act is committed by the victim albeit as a result of deception.' It is unfortunate that *Gomez* was not cited to the Court of Appeal because, while it is not absolutely inconsistent with *Briggs*, it results in a distinction which is hard to explain between the case where D does an act in relation to property which he possesses or controls with the victim's consent which has been obtained by deception (appropriation: *Gomez*), and the case where D by deception causes the victim to transfer his property or to do some other act with it which would be an appropriation if done by D personally (not an appropriation: *Briggs*).[45]

- 'the word "appropriation" in s 3(1) of the Theft Act 1968…is a word which connotes a physical act rather than a more remote action triggering the payment which gives rise to the charge. The Oxford English Dictionary defines "appropriation" as "to take possession for one's own, to take to oneself". It is not easy to see why an act of deceiving an owner to do something would fall within the meaning of "appropriation".' This statement must be treated with caution. While, as a general rule, an act is required for an appropriation, the case law referred to in this chapter shows that that act need not be a physical one.

Innocent obtaining of ownership

10.16 Where an owner transfers his full proprietary interest to D simultaneously with D's receiving the property, and D acts innocently (ie without the *mens rea* for theft), D cannot be convicted of theft because of his lack of *mens rea* at that point in time. In addition, any subsequent dealing with the property done with the *mens rea* for theft will not amount to theft. The reason is that the owner's consent to the transfer of his full proprietary interest will mean that, at the time of the later appropriation, the property will not belong to another. Thus, if D fills his tank at a self-service station, intending to pay, but

---

[43] [1997] 2 Cr App Rep 445, CA.   [44] [2003] EWCA Crim 3662 at [13].
[45] See, further, the commentary to *Briggs* in [2004] Crim LR 495, CA, and Heaton 'Cheques and Balances' [2005] Crim LR 747.

changes his mind en route to the cashier and drives off, he cannot be convicted of theft of the petrol because at the time of any appropriation with the *mens rea* for theft the petrol does not belong to another.[46] D could, however, be convicted of making off without payment, contrary to the Theft Act 1978, s 3.[47]

A lawful act can be an appropriation

10.17 Despite the arguments of an eminent academic lawyer,[48] an act which is lawful in civil law may nevertheless constitute an appropriation and, if done dishonestly and with intent permanently to deprive, theft. The TA 1968, s 1(1) requires an appropriation, not an unlawful appropriation. The whole tenor of the decisions in *Lawrence* and *Gomez* is against implying 'unlawful' before 'appropriation' in s 1(1), although the point was not specifically addressed in them. In *Hinks*,[49] the majority of the House of Lords (Lord Hobhouse dissenting) held that such an implication should not be made; to do so would run counter to the decisions in those two cases. Nevertheless, it must be admitted that it will be unusual for an appropriation not to involve a dealing with property which is unlawful in civil law.

Where a person acquires an indefeasible right to property: can there be an appropriation?

10.18 As indicated above, a person who obtains ownership of property by deception or duress thereby appropriates it. Such a person does not acquire an indefeasible right (ie a right not liable to be annulled) to the property. Nor, for example, does someone who receives property, by gift, from a person who is mentally incapable of making the gift, or someone who has exercised undue influence over the donor.

On the other hand, someone who obtains ownership of property under a mistake on the part of its owner, which was not induced by misrepresentation, normally acquires an indefeasible right to it. So does someone who receives a gift from a donor whose mental capacity is impaired, but not to the extent of rendering the donor mentally incapable of making a valid gift. The case where the recipient of property acquires an indefeasible right to it was not specifically addressed in *Lawrence* or *Gomez*. However, in *Hinks*,[50] where a conflict in the previous authority[51] was resolved, the majority of the House of Lords (Lord Hobhouse dissenting) held that such a recipient does appropriate the property because, following *Lawrence* and *Gomez*, it is irrelevant that the receipt was made with the consent of the owner. Thus, **provided that such a recipient was dishonest and intended permanently to deprive the transferor at the time of the acquisition, the recipient is guilty of**

---

[46] *Edwards v Ddin* [1976] 3 All ER 705, DC.   [47] See para 10.125.

[48] Williams 'Theft, Consent and Illegality' [1977] Crim LR 127.

[49] [2001] 2 AC 241, HL.   [50] [2001] 2 AC 241, HL.

[51] *Mazo* [1997] 2 Cr App Rep 518, CA (Court of Appeal accepted that a person who acquires indefeasible right to property did not steal it apparently because he did not appropriate it); *Kendrick and Hopkins* [1997] 2 Cr App Rep 524, CA (Court of Appeal implicitly disapproved the proposition accepted in *Mazo*). See S Gardner 'Property and Theft' [1998] Crim LR 35 at 36, and the reply by JC Smith, ibid, 80.

theft, even though in civil law he has an indefeasible right to receive the property and thereafter to retain it (or to recover it if taken from him).

In *Hinks*, D was convicted of four counts of theft of money. The prosecution alleged that she had encouraged V, a naive, gullible man of limited intelligence, to withdraw sums amounting to £60,000 from his building society, which were then deposited to her account. D was also convicted on another count of theft, which alleged that D had taken a television set by similar means. D's defence was that the money and the television had been handed over as valid gifts, that the title in them had passed to her and that therefore there could be no theft. Having appealed unsuccessfully to the Court of Appeal against these convictions, D appealed to the House of Lords, the certified question being 'whether the acquisition of an indefeasible title to property is capable of amounting to an appropriation of property belonging to another for the purposes of s 1(1) of the Theft Act 1968'.

By a majority of three to two, the House of Lords dismissed D's appeal. The three Law Lords in the majority plus Lord Hutton [52] answered the certified question in the affirmative. Lord Steyn, with whose speech Lords Slynn, Jauncey and (on *this* point) Hutton agreed, held that it was clear from *Lawrence* and *Gomez* that the consent or authorisation of the owner was irrelevant to the issue of whether or not there had been an appropriation. He refused to restrict those decisions by interpolating 'unlawfully' before 'appropriates' or by accepting an argument that a person does not appropriate property unless the owner retains, beyond the instant of the alleged appropriation, some proprietary interest or the right to resume or recover some proprietary interest. His Lordship was not persuaded that there were convincing reasons for such a restriction. He was content that the mental elements of the offence provided adequate protection from injustice, and that the wider definition of appropriation eliminated the need for judges to give directions about the civil law 'in an overly complex corner of the law'.

10.19 While the decision in *Hinks* may be a logical conclusion from the decision of the majority in *Gomez*, and while one may view D's conduct with distaste, it seems bizarre that a person who lawfully receives a gift may be convicted of the theft of it (if he is dishonest and intends permanently to deprive the transferor of it).[53] The same comment applies to those who obtain an indefeasible right to property by way of contract, to whom the reasoning in *Hinks* is equally applicable. Thus, the receipt of property accompanied by the acquisition of an indefeasible right to it, in accordance with the transferor's intentions, amounts to an appropriation of property which, apparently, at that split second of time, belonged to the transferor. Indeed, the culmination of the reasoning in *Lawrence* and *Gomez* in *Hinks* leads to the conclusion that, with the notable exception of conduct

---

[52] Lord Hutton dissented from the dismissal of D's appeal on the ground that the trial judge had misdirected the jury on dishonesty. The majority did not consider it appropriate to review the judge's summing-up on dishonesty for a number of reasons, in particular because it did not have adequate information as to how the defence case had been deployed in the Crown Court. A summing-up 'must always be tailored to the particular facts of each case': per Lord Steyn [2001] 2 AC 241 at 253.

[53] For a refutation of the criticisms of the decision in *Hinks*, see Shute 'Appropriation and the Law of Theft' [2002] Crim LR 445. Also see Bogg and Stanton-Ife 'Protecting the Vulnerable: Legality, Harm and Theft' [2003] 23 LS 402.

of the type to which the decision in *Briggs*[54] refers, there are almost no limits to what can constitute an 'appropriation' of property belonging to another,[55] and that a person who in civil law acquires an indefeasible right to property and thereafter to retain it (or to recover it if taken from him) is guilty of theft if he does so dishonestly and with intent permanently to deprive the transferor of it. Although it can be accepted that an act need not be unlawful in civil law in order to be an appropriation, there is a material difference between this and agreeing that a person can be said to appropriate property (and to be liable to be convicted of theft if he has the *mens rea*) when he has acquired an indefeasible right to it.

There is much to be said for the view expressed by Lord Hobhouse in his dissenting judgment in *Hinks*. Lord Hobhouse considered that the words and phrases in ss 1 to 6 of the TA 1968 had an interrelationship with each other and should be read as a whole, rather than being interpreted in isolation. He also thought that the application of the law of theft in the present context should involve a consideration of the law of gift. In the light of these matters, he concluded that if there is a valid gift there can be no theft.

It must be emphasised that the majority decision in *Hinks* related to the question posed in the certified question. It does not mean that all recipients of gifts in like circumstances commit theft. As already implied, and as recognised by Lord Steyn, a jury could find that the transferee of the gift was not dishonest.

An exception for the bona fide purchaser[56]

10.20 The TA 1968, s 3(2) excludes a particular type of case which falls within the definition of appropriation in s 3(1) from being an appropriation. Section 3(2) provides that:

> 'where property or a right or interest in property is or purports to be transferred for value to a person acting in good faith, no later assumption by him of rights which he believed[57] himself to be acquiring shall, by reason of any defect in the transferor's title, amount to theft of the property.'

The effect of the subsection is that, if A steals goods from B and sells them to D who acts in good faith (ie D neither knows nor suspects that they are stolen), a refusal by D to restore the goods (or his disposal of them) after his discovery of the theft by A is not theft by him from B. Although the refusal or disposal in itself would be no offence, if D, having discovered the truth, sold the goods this would amount to the offence of fraud, contrary to the Fraud Act 2006, s 1.[58] In addition, if he sold them with a view to giving the purchase price to someone else, he could also be convicted of handling stolen goods.[59]

---

[54] See para 10.15.

[55] See Parsons 'Dishonest Appropriation after *Gomez* and *Hinks*' (2004) 68 JCL 520.

[56] See the articles cited in para 11.50, n 113.

[57] Ie at the time of the initial acquisition: *Adams* (1993) 15 Cr App Rep (S) 466, CA.

[58] Para 12.3.   [59] Paras 11.33–11.55.

It must be emphasised that the exception in s 3(2) is limited to cases where the goods were transferred for value to the defendant who acted in good faith. If D receives goods as a gift and later, on discovering that they are stolen, decides to keep them, he may be convicted of theft; so may D if he buys stolen goods, aware that they are or may be stolen.

Although the above examples have referred to the case where the defect in the transferor's title is due to the fact that the goods are stolen, it must not be forgotten that the exception in s 3(2) is not limited to such a case; it applies to defects in the transferor's title in general.

Section 3(2) is not limited to the buyers of property. A pawnbroker, for example, with whom goods are pledged (ie possession is transferred in exchange for a loan) will satisfy the terms of s 3(2) if he receives the goods without realising a defect in the pledgor's title and, on learning the truth, retains them or sells them when the pledgor fails to redeem the pledge on the due date. On the other hand, it would seem that the pawnbroker would appropriate them if he sells them before that time because this would not be a right which he believed himself to be acquiring.

Appropriation by omission

10.21 As a general rule, the 'assumption of the rights of an owner' required for an appropriation requires that the defendant does an act manifesting such an assumption; the natural meaning of 'assumption' in the present context is an active one, viz the act of taking for or upon oneself any of the rights of an owner, as illustrated by the examples already given.

By way of exception to the general rule, an appropriation can be made by a mere omission to restore property to its owner or other person entitled to its possession. This is implicit in the TA 1968, s 3(1) which speaks of a person appropriating by 'keeping as owner' property which he has come by innocently, since 'keeping' does not necessarily involve doing any act but may be effected by a person failing to return property. Whether or not a particular omission in relation to property can constitute 'keeping it as owner' depends on the circumstances and state of mind of the defendant. Merely 'keeping' the thing is insufficient. There must be a 'keeping as owner'. There can be no 'keeping as owner' by D during a period while he remains undecided about what to do with the property.[60]

Other points

10.22 Once a person has appropriated property belonging to another with the appropriate *mens rea* he is guilty of theft. **Such an appropriation, even though it may continue for a short period of time, is a once and for all happening and subsequent appropriations of the property by the thief do not constitute fresh commissions of theft.** As has been said: 'Otherwise it would be possible, in theory, to convict a thief of theft of a silver teapot

---

[60] *Broom v Crowther* (1984) 148 JP 592, DC.

every time he uses it to make the tea'.[61] This view is supported by the statement in the TA 1968, s 3(1) that a later assumption of a right to the property may amount to an appropriation where the defendant has come by the property 'without stealing' it, which implies that where someone has come by property by stealing it, any later assumption by him of a right to it by keeping or dealing with it as owner does not amount to a fresh appropriation. It was affirmed by the Court of Appeal in *Atakpu*[62] that 'if goods have once been stolen, they cannot be stolen again by the same thief'.

10.23 As indicated above, **an appropriation need not be instantaneous: it may continue for a short period of time**. This is important, for example, in relation to the offence of robbery.[63] Case law[64] before *Gomez* supported the view that an appropriation could be a continuing act, but those cases were not referred to by the House of Lords in that case and, on a strict reading of *Gomez*, since any dishonest assumption of a right of the owner with the necessary intent constitutes theft, little room seems to be left for an appropriation by a continuous course of action. However, in *Atakpu*[65] the Court of Appeal, having reviewed *Gomez* and the other case law on the point, held, obiter, that it remained the law that an appropriation could be a continuous course of action; it considered that it should be left to the common sense of the jury to decide that the appropriation could continue for so long as the thief can sensibly be regarded as in the act of stealing, ie so long as he is 'on the job'. Subsequently, in *Lockley*,[66] the Court of Appeal confirmed that the view that an appropriation could be a continuing act had not been overruled by *Gomez*.

10.24 A person cannot be convicted of theft unless it is proved that he appropriated a **specific piece of property** belonging to another with the appropriate *mens rea*. It is not in itself enough that D's conduct leads (as D realises) to someone else becoming indebted to another. This is shown by *Navvabi*,[67] where D, by unauthorisedly issued cheques for £50 or £100 backed by a cheque card, obtained gaming chips in a casino. Because the cheques were backed by the cheque card, the bank was bound to honour them, ie it became indebted to the casino. The Court of Appeal quashed D's convictions on counts of the theft of £50 or £100 from the bank, since there was no appropriation by him of that part of the bank's funds to which the sums specified in the cheques corresponded. Clearly, it was impossible to point to any specific property of the bank which had been appropriated.[68] On the other hand, if D takes V's cheque made out in V's favour by X, and presents it for payment, D commits the *actus reus* of theft of V's credit balance (V's right to sue the bank, a debtor, for that amount is a piece of property) or of V's right to overdraw (V's right to

---

[61] Williams 'Appropriation: A Single or Continuous Act?' [1978] Crim LR 69. See also [1978] Crim LR 313.

[62] [1994] QB 69, CA. Contrast *Ascroft* [2004] EWCA Crim 2365, where the Court of Appeal, in upholding a confiscation order imposed after a conviction to steal, reached a different conclusion.

[63] Para 10.103.

[64] *Hale* (1978) 68 Cr App Rep 415, CA; *Gregory* (1982) 77 Cr App Rep 41, CA.

[65] [1994] QB 69 at 80.

[66] [1995] Crim LR 656, CA.

[67] [1986] 3 All ER 102, CA. Contrast *Monaghan* [1979] Crim LR 673, CA, and commentary.

[68] On the other hand, such a person could be convicted of the offence of fraud, contrary to the Fraud Act 2006, s 1.

the overdraft is a piece of property).[69] The reason is that D has assumed the rights of the owner over the intangible piece of property (the right) in question. If, as appears to be the case, he has the *mens rea* of theft he can be convicted of that offence.[70]

10.25 A person charged with stealing a part of specific property can be convicted on that charge even though it emerges at the trial that he is guilty of stealing all of it,[71] and it seems that the converse is also true.[72]

Property

> **Key points 10.3**
>
> 'Property' means anything which is capable of being owned, but electricity is not property for the purposes of theft, and there are restrictions on when land and things forming part of it, and wild creatures and their carcasses, can be stolen.

10.26 By the TA 1968, s 4(1),

> '"property" includes money and all other property, real or personal, including things in action and other intangible property.'

There is an element of circularity in this definition, in that 'property' is defined as including 'all other property'. In this respect it may be helpful to remember that the appropriate definition of property is that it means something which may be the subject of ownership.

10.27 'Money' refers to current coins and bank notes (including foreign ones), and 'personal property' refers in a tangible sense to movable property, ie goods. The reference to 'real property' means that land, things forming part of it, and rights in it, are included in the definition of 'property'. However, there are special provisions restricting the theft of land and things forming part of it, which are dealt with later.[73] Likewise there are special provisions restricting the theft of wild creatures and their carcasses.[74]

10.28 A 'thing in action' (normally described by its traditional title 'chose in action') is a personal right of property which can only be claimed or enforced by a legal action and not by taking physical possession,[75] and its inclusion in the definition of property means that one who dishonestly assumes a right of ownership over a thing in action, such as a

---

[69] Para 10.28.   [70] *Hallam and Blackburn* [1995] Crim LR 323, CA.

[71] *Pilgram v Rice-Smith* [1977] 2 All ER 658, DC.

[72] Certainly on a charge of stealing several specific items there can be a conviction of stealing some of them if theft of all of them is not proved: *Machent v Quinn* [1970] 2 All ER 255, DC.

[73] Paras 10.34 and 10.35.   [74] Para 10.36.

[75] *Torkington v Magee* [1902] 2 KB 427 at 430, per Channell J.

debt, a copyright or a registered trade mark, with the intention of permanently depriving the person entitled to it, is guilty of theft. Thus, if D dishonestly purports to assign to X a debt owed to D and his partner, V, in order to defeat V's rights, D is guilty of the theft of a thing in action belonging to V. Likewise, if D dishonestly purports to sell to X the copyright owned by V in a book, this is theft by D of a thing in action belonging to V.

A bank account in credit is a thing in action because it constitutes a debt owed by the bank to the customer.[76] Thus, for example, if a company accountant dishonestly draws a cheque on his employer's bank account for an unauthorised purpose and presents it for payment, he is guilty of the theft of the thing in action (the amount of the bank balance) belonging to his employer.[77] The exercise of the right to destroy or diminish the thing in action (bank credit) is the equivalent of an appropriation of tangible property by destroying it.[78] There would also have been a theft in the above example, even if the bank account is not in credit, provided that, or to the extent that, the amount drawn is within the limit of an agreed overdraft facility, because the account holder's right to draw within that limit under such a facility is a thing in action.[79] Likewise, it has been held that, if D, who has control of another's bank account, gives instructions for the transfer of funds from that account to another bank account by CHAPS (the electronic clearing house automated payment system) or by telegraphic means, he appropriates the bank balance represented by the amount transferred.[80] Similarly, someone who dishonestly obtains a cheque from V and presents it for payment appropriates the amount of V's bank credit represented by the cheque,[81] or V's right to overdraw, as the case may be.

'Other intangible property' covers such things as gas stored in pipes, which is undoubtedly capable of being owned. It also covers patents.[82] In *A-G of Hong Kong v Chan Nai-Keung*,[83] the Privy Council held that export quotas, which could be freely bought and sold and which gave an expectation of an export licence to the amount of the quotas (although no enforceable right to it), were 'intangible property'.

Things which are not property

10.29 In spite of the broad definition of property in the TA 1968, s 4(1), there are some things which do not, or may not, come within the definition of property and hence cannot be stolen.

---

[76] *Davenport* [1954] 1 All ER 602 at 603. The money represented by the account is the money of the banker and not of the customer.

[77] *Kohn* (1979) 69 Cr App Rep 395, CA; *Graham* [1997] 1 Cr App Rep 302 at 325. As to the time of the appropriation, see para 10.5.

[78] *Kohn* (1979) 69 Cr App Rep 395, CA; *Graham* [1997] 1 Cr App Rep 302, CA (addendum).

[79] *Kohn* (1979) 69 Cr App Rep 395 at 410.

[80] At least, when the transfer is made: *Hilton* [1997] 2 Cr App Rep 445, CA, see para 10.6. There would not, however, be an appropriation where D simply procured a bank account holder (X) by deception to initiate the transfer from his (X's) bank account to another: *Naviede* [1997] Crim LR 662, CA; *Briggs* [2003] EWCA Crim 3662; para 10.15.

[81] *Williams (Roy)* [2001] 1 Cr App Rep 362, CA; see Heaton 'Cheques and Balances' [2005] Crim LR 747. As to the time of the appropriation, see para 10.5.

[82] These are declared not to be things in action: Patents Act 1977, s 30.   [83] [1987] 1 WLR 1339, PC.

10.30 A human corpse, or a part of a corpse, is not property,[84] since it cannot be owned. On the other hand, the shroud in which a dead body is wrapped remains the property of the person to whom it previously belonged, and continues to belong. Consequently, grave robbers who take a body wrapped in a shroud can be convicted of theft of the shroud, although not of the body.[85]

A qualification of the above rule is that **a corpse or part of a corpse becomes property if it has acquired different attributes by the application of human skill, such as embalming or dissection for exhibition or teaching purposes.**[86] Thus, an anatomical or pathological specimen (eg a skeleton or cadaver) which has been embalmed or dissected for teaching purposes or exhibition is property. On the other hand, a body or part of a body which has been preserved at a post mortem, eg by fixing a brain in paraffin, is not property because such preservation is not on a par with embalming or dissecting a corpse for teaching purposes or exhibition.[87] It follows from this that a corpse stored for research or teaching purposes in a medical school, or a part of a body intended for transplantation, is not regarded as property.

While it is clear that a live human body is not property, people have been convicted of the theft of products of the human body, such as hair or urine.[88] Although these convictions have never been tested in an appellate court, the Court of Appeal (Civil Division) has held that a sperm sample from a person undergoing chemotherapy, which a hospital stored in case he became infertile after the treatment, was owned by that person and was therefore property.[89]

10.31 It has been held that **confidential information, such as an official secret, a trade secret or the contents of a future examination paper, is not property** for the purposes of theft,[90] so that the mere abstraction of it (eg by photocopying it) is not theft. However, the 'borrowing'[91] or outright taking of a piece of paper on which the secret information is recorded may well amount to the theft of the piece of paper. In addition, if the information is stored in a computer its dishonest abstraction will involve an offence under the TA 1968, s 13 of abstracting electricity (which is described in para 10.33) or, more appropriately, under the Computer Misuse Act 1990, s 1. Official secrets are protected by the Official Secrets Acts 1911 and 1989.

---

[84] *Haynes' Case* (1613) 12 Co Rep 113; *Handyside's Case* (1749) 2 East PC 652; *Sharpe* (1857) 26 LJMC 47 at 48, per Erle CJ; *Kelly and Lindsay* [1999] QB 621 at 630. See Smith 'Stealing the Body and its Parts' [1976] Crim LR 622; Harris 'Who Owns My Body?' (1996) 16 OJLS 55. It is a common law offence to remove a corpse from a grave without lawful authority: *Lynn* (1788) 2 Term Rep 733.

[85] *Haynes' Case* (1613) 12 Co Rep 113.

[86] *Kelly and Lindsay* [1999] QB 621, CA, applying *Doodeward v Spence* (1908) 6 CLR 406, High Ct of Australia, and *Dobson v North Tyneside Health Authority* [1996] 4 All ER 474 at 479, per Peter Gibson LJ. The matter is discussed by Pavlowski 'Dead Bodies as Property' (1996) 146 NLJ 1828.

[87] *Dobson v North Tyneside Health Authority* [1996] 4 All ER 474, CA.

[88] *Herbert* (1960) 25 JCL 163; *Welsh* [1974] RTR 478, CA (sentencing appeal).

[89] *Yearworth v North Bristol NHS Trust* [2009] EWCA Civ 37.

[90] *Oxford v Moss* (1978) 68 Cr App Rep 183, DC. See Tettenborn 'Stealing Information' (1979) 129 NLJ 967; Hammond 'Theft of Information' (1984) 100 LQR 252; Coleman 'Trade Secrets and the Criminal Law: The Need for Reform' (1985) Comp L & P 111.

[91] Para 10.89.

The use or disclosure of trade secrets can have more serious consequences for a business than the theft of its property. The law of theft offers adequate protection against the appropriation of a patent or registered trade mark, but it does not offer any against the misuse of a trade secret, although the sanctions available in the civil law for breach of confidence may often provide a sufficient deterrent for the type of people involved in the 'theft' of trade secrets.[92] If the person who misuses a trade secret occupies a position in which he is expected to safeguard, or not to act against, the financial interests of the owner of a trade secret he can be convicted of fraud contrary to the Fraud Act 2006, s 1, if the terms of s 4[93] thereof are satisfied.

10.32 Rides in cars, coaches or trains are not property, nor are lodgings for the night and other services, but those who obtain them dishonestly may be guilty of an offence of obtaining services dishonestly, contrary to the Fraud Act 2006, s 11.[94]

10.33 Electricity is not property within the TA 1968, s 4, and cannot be stolen,[95] but under the TA 1968, s 13, it is an offence for a person dishonestly[96] to use without due authority, or dishonestly to cause to be wasted or diverted, any electricity. This offence is triable either way, and punishable with a maximum of five years' imprisonment on conviction on indictment. The 'use' of any electricity means the consumption of electricity which would not occur but for the defendant's act.[97] The use, diversion or wastage of electricity can constitute a serious offence, as where a person reconnects his electricity supply after it has been cut off for non-payment, or where a malicious prankster enters someone's empty house, switches on all the electrical gadgets and leaves them running, or where a person runs electrical equipment after interfering with the electricity meter so that it does not record. However, it is possible to think of many trivial examples. If D turns on V's radio without V's authority, he may be convicted of an offence under s 13, as may someone who inserts a false disc in an electrical weighing machine and weighs himself.

Someone who dishonestly uses a telephone system without authority is guilty of an offence under s 13, but it is more likely that the prosecution would be brought under the Communications Act 2003, s 125, by which a person who dishonestly obtains 'an electronic telecommunication service' (a term which can include simply making a telephone call) with intent to avoid payment is guilty of an offence triable either way. On conviction on indictment the maximum punishment is five years' imprisonment.

---

[92] In 1997 the Law Commission provisionally proposed that there should be a new offence to punish the misuse of trade secrets. It would have been committed by any person who used or disclosed a trade secret belonging to another (ie the person entitled to the secret) without that other's consent. See *Legislating the Criminal Code: Misuse of Trade Secrets* (1997) Law Com Consultation Paper No 150. The proposal attracted majority support but strong opposition from a minority. See Hull 'Stealing Secrets: A Review of the Law Commission's Consultation Paper on the Misuse of Trade Secrets' [1998] Crim LR 246 for a valuable critique of the proposals. The Law Commission concluded that it would not be right to continue with the project for a number of reasons: see Law Commission *Annual Report 2004/05*, para 5.12.

[93] Paras 12.24–12.28.   [94] Para 12.35.   [95] *Low v Blease* (1975) 119 Sol Jo 695, DC.

[96] See paras 10.73–10.75. The TA 1968, s 2 (paras 10.69 and 10.79) does not apply to an offence under s 13.

[97] *McCreadie and Tume* (1992) 96 Cr App Rep 143, CA.

Land and things forming part of it

10.34 Severe restrictions on the theft of land and things forming part of land are imposed by the TA 1968, s 4(2) and (3). These restrictions do not apply to incorporeal hereditaments,[98] another form of real property, examples of which are easements and profits à prendre. Thus incorporeal hereditaments are stealable by anyone.

The soil and plants and other growing things are clearly things forming part of land, as are houses, walls and other similar permanent structures (or parts of them, such as bricks or fixtures) built into the land. At the other extreme, a workman's hut temporarily resting on the land while the workmen are there does not form part of the land, nor does a pile of gravel or other material on the land. In borderline cases, the issue is decided by looking at the degree of annexation (ie attachment or integration) and the object of that annexation, and deciding whether these are sufficient for it to be said that the thing forms part of the land.[99] A mobile home which can fairly easily be removed, albeit connected to mains services such as water and electricity, does not form part of the land, whereas (for example) a timber-framed bungalow resting on concrete foundation blocks in the ground which can only be moved by destroying it does.[100] A houseboat attached to the river bed, a pontoon and the river wall by mooring lines has been held not to form part of the land.[101] Quite apart from the question of 'which land?', all the attachments could simply be undone and the houseboat moved, and the object of the attachment was to prevent the vessel moving rather than to enable it to be used as a home. Consequently, neither the degree nor the object of the annexation was sufficient for it to form part of the land.

10.35 The TA 1968, s 4(2) and (3) provide:

'(2) A person cannot steal land, or things forming part of land and severed from it by him or by his directions, except in the following cases, that is to say:

(a) when he is a trustee or personal representative, or is authorised by power of attorney, or as liquidator of a company, or otherwise, to sell or dispose of land belonging to another, and he appropriates the land or anything forming part of it by dealing with it in breach of the confidence reposed in him; or

(b) when he is not in possession of the land and appropriates anything forming part of the land by severing it or causing it to be severed, or after it has been severed; or

(c) when, being in possession of the land under a tenancy, he appropriates the whole or part of any fixture or structure let to be used with the land.

(3) A person who picks mushrooms growing wild on any land, or who picks flowers, fruit or foliage from a plant growing wild on any land, does not (although not in possession of the land) steal what he picks, unless he does it for reward or for sale or other commercial purpose…'

---

[98] TA 1968, s 4(2) provides that 'land' in s 4(2) does not include incorporeal hereditaments.

[99] *Elitestone Ltd v Morris* [1997] 2 All ER 513, HL. Also see *Holland v Hodgson* (1872) LR 7 CP 328 at 334, per Blackburn J.

[100] *Elitestone Ltd v Morris* [1997] 2 All ER 513, HL.

[101] *Chelsea Yacht and Boat Club Ltd v Pope* [2001] 2 All ER 409, CA.

The effect of these provisions is as follows

- *Land as a whole* cannot be stolen except where the appropriator is of a defined class and acts in a defined way (TA 1968, s 4(2)(a)). The class of appropriators comprises a trustee or personal representative, or a person authorised by power of attorney, or as a liquidator of a company, or otherwise, to sell or dispose of land belonging to another. The defined mode of appropriation is dealing with the land in breach of the confidence reposed in him. The result is that a person cannot steal land as a whole by moving a boundary fence or by occupying it as a squatter; if, in moving the boundary fence, he resorts to any false representation in order to obtain the land or damages his neighbour's property, he may be guilty of fraud or criminal damage respectively, but as the law is at present he commits no offence merely by squatting.

- *Things forming part of land* can only be stolen in the following cases:
  - As for land as a whole, by the defined persons in the defined way (TA 1968, s 4(2)(a));
  - *Where a person not in possession of the land appropriates the thing by severing it or causing it to be severed* (TA 1968, s 4(2)(b)). If a trespasser or other person not in possession of the land digs gravel, removes tiles and bricks from a building or part of a wall, cuts turf, digs up flowers or other growing things, picks a flower from a cultivated plant or cuts down a tree or saws off one of its branches, or causes such severance to be done (eg letting loose a pig on the land where it uproots vegetables), he may be convicted of theft.

  This provision does not apply to the picking of wild mushrooms or fungi nor to picking from wild plants and the like. Such conduct is governed instead by the special provisions of the TA 1968, s 4(3), as follows. First, the picking of wild mushrooms or other fungi [102] by a person not in possession of the land is not theft (although clearly there has been a severance) unless it is done for reward or for sale or other commercial purpose. Second, where a person not in possession of the land picks flowers, fruit or foliage *from* a plant, shrub or tree,[103] growing wild, he cannot commit theft (although, again, there has clearly been a severance) unless the picking is done for reward or for sale or other commercial purpose. 'Picking from' is a narrow term. It does not include uprooting a wild plant or lopping off a branch from a wild shrub; these are covered by s 4(2)(b) and are unaffected by s 4(3).

  The operation of these provisions is as follows: shortly before Christmas a florist and an electrician go out in their cars; both pick holly from a tree which is cultivated in a garden and both may be convicted of theft because the tree is not wild. They continue and both pick holly from a tree which is wild; the florist is intending to sell it in his shop and may be convicted of theft, whereas the electrician is intending to decorate his home and cannot be so convicted. Both dig up small fir

---

[102] By the TA 1968, s 4(3), 'mushroom' includes a fungus.
[103] By the TA 1968, s 4(3), 'plant' includes any tree or shrub.

trees growing wild and both may be convicted of theft, whatever their purpose, because the severance by them has gone beyond 'picking from'.

- *Where a tenant appropriates a fixture or structure let to be used with the land* (TA 1968, s 4(2)(c)). Generally, a person in possession of land under a tenancy[104] cannot steal things forming part of it; consequently, if he extracts gravel from the land and sells it, or digs up a plant on the land and gives it to a friend, or picks blackberries from a wild bush on the land and sells them, he cannot be convicted of theft. The only exception is provided by s 4(2)(c). It relates to the whole or part of any structure or fixture let to be used with the land; such is stealable by a tenant and is stealable by any means (ie a severance is not necessary). The obvious example of a 'structure' is a building, but the term also includes things such as a wall or a bridge. Basically, a 'fixture' is an object, such as a washbasin or fireplace, which is attached to land or to a building for the purpose of making a permanent improvement to the land or building; by the ordinary law of land it becomes part of the land. It follows from all this that if a tenant demolishes a coalshed on the land of which he is a tenant, or removes an antique fireplace there in order to sell it, or sells the fireplace *in situ* with a promise to remove it later, he may be convicted of theft.

Of course, once a thing has been severed from land it ceases to form part of it and is no longer subject to any restriction on its being stolen.

Wild creatures

10.36 The TA 1968, s 4(4) provides:

> 'Wild creatures tamed or untamed shall be regarded as property; but a person cannot steal a wild creature not tamed nor ordinarily kept in captivity, or the carcase of any such creature, unless either it has been reduced into possession by or on behalf of another person and possession of it has not since been lost or abandoned, or another person is in course of reducing it into possession.'

While they are alive, wild creatures which are neither tamed nor ordinarily kept in captivity are not owned by anyone, but on being killed or taken they become the property of the owner of the land on which they are killed or taken, or, if he has granted the sporting rights to someone else, the grantee of those rights.[105] Section 4(4) distinguishes two groups of wild creatures:

Wild creatures which have been tamed or are ordinarily kept in captivity **Such a creature can be stolen in the same ways as any other property.** Thus a person may be guilty of theft by dishonestly appropriating a tamed fox or a bear from a zoo.

[104] By the TA 1968, s 4(2), 'tenancy' means a tenancy for years or any less period and includes an agreement for such a tenancy. In addition, someone who after the end of the tenancy remains in possession is to be treated as having possession under the tenancy: TA 1968, s 4(2). 'Let' is construed accordingly: TA 1968, s 4(2).

[105] *Blades v Higgs* (1865) 11 HL Cas 621, HL.

Wild creatures neither tamed nor ordinarily kept in captivity Such a creature or its carcase cannot normally be stolen but becomes 'stealable':

- if reduced into possession by or on behalf of another (in which case it remains 'stealable' so long as possession has not subsequently been lost or abandoned);[106] or

- if another person is in course of reducing it into possession.

Thus, it is not theft to poach game on another's land, unless for instance the game is taken from a sack into which another, even another poacher, has put the product of his own shooting (because there has been a reduction into possession by another) or the game is picked up from the ground where it is lying after it has been shot by another but not yet picked up by him (because another is in the course of reducing it into his possession).[107] Poaching is subject to its own legislation.

The term 'reduced into possession by or on behalf of another' covers (inter alia) the shooting and taking of game by a gamekeeper on his employer's behalf, since by doing so the gamekeeper reduces the game into possession on behalf of his employer ('another'), and the gamekeeper can be convicted of theft if he subsequently appropriates it.

Deciding whether or not a wild creature has been reduced into possession may involve the drawing of fine distinctions. There can be no doubt that, if a person stocks tanks on his fish farm with trout, the trout are reduced into his possession. On the other hand, unless it is a very small pond, a person who stocks open water with trout for the purpose of fly fishing would not seem to have sufficient control over them for the trout to be in his possession.[108]

Other offences relating to wild creatures

10.37 The Eighth Report of the Criminal Law Revision Committee recommended that the whole law with regard to poaching should be considered by an appropriate committee.[109] This has not occurred. As a result, certain provisions of the Larceny Act 1861

---

[106] Possession of a live wild creature is abandoned if the possessor allows it to escape from his possession; it is lost if a wild creature not ordinarily kept in captivity escapes of its own volition. Possession of the carcass of a wild creature is not lost by a person who mislays it: see para 10.40 and *Smith's Law of Theft* (9th edn, 2007) (Ormerod and Williams (eds)) para 2.155.

[107] In *Cresswell v DPP; Currie v DPP* [2006] EWHC 3379 (Admin), DC, which was concerned with 'in the course of reducing into possession' in the similarly worded provision in the Criminal Damage Act 1971, s 10(1)(a), Keene LJ held that merely to entice a wild animal to a particular spot from time to time by providing food there, even with the ultimate object of killing it in due course, does not form part of a course normally of reducing it into possession and that where a trap has been set one cannot identify a wild creature as being in the course of being reduced into possession until the stage at least when it is in the process of entering the set trap. Walker J did not reach a conclusion on this point.

[108] Arguably, the trout in the first example are kept in captivity, but those in the second example retain far too much freedom for there to be any possibility of this.

[109] Cmnd 2977, para 53.

punishing summarily the unlawful taking or destroying of fish in private waters or in waters in which there is a private right of fishery, which were inserted on a temporary basis in a modified form in the TA 1968, Sch 1 remain in force. Various Victorian statutes provide summary offences relating to the poaching of game (including rabbits), whose gist is trespassing in pursuit of game and which do not require any actual taking or destroying of game. The Deer Act 1991, s 1 provides summary offences relating to the intentional taking, killing or injuring of deer without the consent of the owner or occupier of the land or other lawful authority.

These offences relating to fish, game and deer are separate offences and are quite distinct from the offence of theft.

Under the Wildlife and Countryside Act 1981, s 1(1) it is a summary offence intentionally to kill, injure or take away any wild bird, and under s 9(1) it is a summary offence intentionally to kill, injure or take away certain wild animals. These offences are also quite distinct from that of theft.

Belonging to another

> **Key points 10.4**
>
> Property belongs to another if anyone other than the defendant has possession or control of it, or owns it or has any proprietary right or interest in it less than complete ownership.

10.38 The property appropriated must belong to another at the time of its appropriation. In ordinary language property is frequently said to belong to someone only when he owns it, but under the TA 1968, s 5(1) property is also regarded as belonging to any person who has possession or control of it, or any proprietary right or interest in it falling short of complete ownership. This raises questions of civil law.

Ownership and possession

10.39 Before discussing s 5(1), it is necessary to say something about ownership and possession. **Ownership of goods or money or other property is the ultimate right to control. It lasts longer than any other right to control, but ownership does not necessarily entail physical control.** For example, A may have hired his car to B for a day and C's £10 note may have been taken by E, a pickpocket, who placed it in his wallet; A and C are still the owners of their car and £10 note respectively, although B and E have possession. Even if C's £10 note were mixed with E's other money, C would remain its owner (although he would probably not be able to identify it) but E could make someone who gave value and received the £10 note in good faith its owner. This is because money is negotiable; a thief can give a better title to it than he has got. Goods are not negotiable: hence, if G steals H's watch and sells it to J who acts in good faith, H remains the owner of the watch (and can sue J for its return).

Mention may also be made of the rules which determine when ownership passes on the sale of goods. The principal rule is that ownership passes when the parties intend it to pass. If their intention is not clear, special rules apply. For example, in the case of an unconditional sale of specific goods (ie goods identified and agreed on at the time of the contract of sale, eg Ford Focus registration number XY 59 ABC) in a deliverable state, ownership passes when the contract is made, even if payment or delivery is made afterwards. Whereas, in the case of a sale of non-specific goods (eg a retail sale of petrol), ownership cannot pass until the goods are irrevocably earmarked as the goods to be used to perform the contract, as where the petrol is put in the tank, but it will pass then even though payment is only made later.[110]

Generally speaking, if a person intends to transfer ownership to another, the ownership passes even though the transferor acts under a mistake. The only exceptions are where the transferor acts under a mistake, known to the transferee, as to the identity of the transferee or of the property transferred, or as to the quantity of money paid.

Since the owner of a vending (or gaming) machine only intends to pass ownership to someone who inserts appropriate coins, the ownership of property (or money) issued by such a machine does not pass if it is obtained by a jemmy, a false token or foreign coins.[111]

An example of the fine detail which questions of ownership can raise can be illustrated by reference to the apparently simple example of a train ticket or a car park ticket. If someone sells or, even, gives a used but still-valid ticket for use by another, he may, to his surprise, be guilty of theft.[112] He will thereby have appropriated the ticket, he will have intended permanently to deprive the original seller[113] and he may be found to have appropriated the ticket dishonestly. The case will turn on whether the original seller retained ownership of the ticket. This will depend on whether under the terms of the contract the original seller has retained ownership. If the original seller has purported to retain ownership, eg by a statement on the ticket or in a notice, the statement will only be a term of the contract if reasonable notice of it was given.[114] If it was, it is irrelevant that the original buyer had not read the words giving the notice.

10.40 Possession is essentially physical control, but:

- Possession may mean something more than mere physical control; for example, a guest has not got possession of the cutlery with which he eats a meal in his host's house; nor has a customer who examines goods in a shop, nor an employee in a shop in control of the employer's goods. In each of these cases, the host, shopkeeper or

---

[110] For the basic provisions, see the Sale of Goods Act 1979, s 16, 17 and 18.

[111] *Goodwin* [1996] Crim LR 262, CA.

[112] See Smith 'Stealing Tickets' [1998] Crim LR 723.

[113] See para 10.87.

[114] *Parker v South Eastern Rly Co* (1877) 2 CPD 416, CA. The issue of whether London Underground had retained ownership of the tickets in *Marshall* [1998] 2 Cr App Rep 282, CA, para 10.87, was not the subject of the subsequent appeal in that case.

employer, as the case may be, retains possession (as well as ownership, if he is the owner).

- Possession may also mean less than physical control; for example, a householder possesses that which is in his house when he is at his office.

Possession cannot begin until the person with control is aware that the thing is under his control, although this can include the case where property is left for him in a place (eg his home) under his control by prior arrangement with him. Once begun, possession can continue despite the fact that the possessor forgets about the thing.

A person does not lose possession (or ownership, if he has it) of a thing simply by mislaying it, but he will lose possession (but not ownership, if he has it) if (and when) someone else assumes physical control of it. Thus, if a purse falls out of a woman's bag in the street, she continues to possess it until someone else assumes control. On the other hand, **if property is abandoned by someone, and this requires that he should be completely indifferent as to what is done to or with the property by anyone else, he loses any rights to possession of the property, including ownership if he is the owner.** The result is that, unless the property also belongs to another person (V) or unless and until the abandoned property falls into the control or possession of another (V),[115] it cannot be stolen by D.[116] The test of abandonment is a strict one; a person does not, for example, abandon goods which he puts in his dustbin because he has put the goods there for collection by the council's refuse collectors and is therefore not indifferent to what happens to the goods.[117]

10.41 As already indicated, ownership and possession may be vested in different people. An example is provided by reference to a bailment. Bailment embraces all situations in which possession of goods is given by one person (A) to another (B) upon the condition that they shall be restored to A by B (as where goods are hired or lent or left for repair), or dealt with as he directs, upon expiry of the agreed period of possession.[118] B (the bailee) obtains possession but A (the bailor) retains ownership. (A loan of money, however, involves the transfer of ownership, as well as of possession, by the lender since by the nature of the thing he does not expect the very notes or coins transferred to be returned, although, of course, he expects to be repaid. The same is true about the 'loan' of a bag of sugar or a pint of milk or the like.)

10.42 In law, the ownership of goods is often spoken of as 'the property in the goods'. This use of the word 'property' is confusing and it is simpler to use that word only in its other sense, which is the one used earlier in this chapter, namely to cover those things which may be the subject of ownership. It is in the latter sense that the word 'property' is used in the TA 1968.

---

[115] For a review of the criminal and civil authorities on the issue of abandoned goods and a proposal for a new approach, see Hickey 'Stealing Abandoned Goods: Possessing Title in Proceedings for Theft' (2006) 26 LS 584.

[116] See para 10.44 in respect of the abandonment of property on occupied land.

[117] *Williams v Phillips* (1957) 41 Cr App Rep 5, DC.

[118] *TRM Copy Centres (UK) Ltd v Lanwall Services Ltd* [2009] UKHL 35 at [10] per Lord Hope.

Section 5(1)

10.43 The TA 1968, s 5(1) provides that:

> 'Property shall be regarded as belonging to any person having possession or control of it, or having in it any proprietary right or interest (not being an equitable interest arising only from an agreement to transfer or grant an interest).'

Possession or control

10.44 Possession or control is not required to be lawful.[119] It follows that property can be stolen from someone who is not in lawful possession or control of it. **'Control' covers cases where a person in physical control of property is nevertheless not in possession of it,** such as the guest using his host's cutlery or the customer examining goods in a shop. It also covers cases where it is doubtful whether a person in control of property can be said to be in possession of it.

In *Woodman*,[120] it was held that the knowledge that the thing is under one's control it not necessary for one to come into control of it; as already stated, such knowledge is necessary for possession. The defendant in *Woodman* took some scrap metal from a dis-used factory belonging to English China Clays. Originally there had been a substantial amount of scrap metal on the site. This had been sold to a company which removed the bulk of it but some was too inaccessible to be removed in such a way as to be attractive to the company: it was left on the site for perhaps a couple of years until the defendant took it away. After the company had removed the bulk of the scrap, English China Clays erected a barbed wire fence and put up notices such as 'Private Property, Keep Out' and 'Trespassers will be prosecuted'. Dismissing an appeal against a conviction for theft of scrap from the site, the Court of Appeal held that there was ample evidence that English China Clays were in control of the site and therefore in control of articles which were on the site, in spite of the fact that they were not aware of the existence of the scrap: control of a site by excluding others was prima facie control of the articles on the site as well.

The fact that an occupier can be in control of items of property on the land even though unaware of their existence is of significance where the owner of the items has abandoned them on occupied land (and thereby lost ownership and possession of them). In such a case the fact that the items can nevertheless belong to another, the occupier in control of them, means that someone else who dishonestly appropriates them can be convicted of their theft. In *Rostron and Collinson*[121] the Court of Appeal dismissed appeals against conviction for theft of golf balls which had been hit into a lake by golfers and abandoned by them. The Court of Appeal held that there was evidence to justify the finding that the balls belonged to another, the club.

---

[119] *Lloyd* [1998] 3 All ER 741, CA. See also *Turner (No 2)* [1971] 2 All ER 441 at 443.
[120] [1974] QB 754, CA.   [121] [2003] EWCA Crim 2206.

Proprietary right or interest

10.45 The best example of a 'proprietary right or interest' is complete ownership of property, but the phrase **also covers proprietary rights or interests falling below that of complete ownership.**

Whether a person other than the defendant had a proprietary right or interest in the property at the time of the appropriation is not determined by the Act but depends on the complexities and niceties of the civil law. A full examination of these is outside the scope of this book, but **an example of a proprietary interest less than complete ownership is the interest (called a beneficial interest) which a beneficiary of a trust has in the trust fund or a legatee has under the will of a deceased person.** Whether or not there is a trust on given facts is for the judge to decide as a matter of law.[122] Where the transaction is in writing, it is for the judge to decide whether it creates a trust and to direct the jury whether or not it does.[123] If the transaction is not in writing (or not wholly in writing), the judge should direct the jury that, if they find that the relevant facts are proved, they should conclude that there is a trust.[124]

10.46 One type of trust is a constructive trust. This is a trust imposed by the law of equity without reference to any presumed intention of the parties in order to do justice in cases of breach of a fiduciary duty or some other unconscionable dealing. The principal category of constructive trust is that referred to by Lord Browne-Wilkinson in *Westdeutsche Landesbank Girozentrale v Islington London Borough Council*,[125] viz: 'Although it is difficult to find clear authority for the proposition, when property is obtained by fraud equity imposes a constructive trust on the fraudulent recipient: the property is recoverable and traceable in equity.' In *A-G's Reference (No 1 of 1985)*,[126] the Court of Appeal was of the view that an interest under a constructive trust was not a proprietary interest for the purposes of the TA 1968, s 5(1). Dealing with a case where a pub manager had made secret profits by selling his own beer in his employer's pub, the Court held that, even if an employee did hold a secret profit on constructive trust for his employer (see below), that constructive trust did not give the employer a proprietary interest for the purposes of s 5(1). Such an interpretation involves adding words to s 5(1) and it can be contrasted with the decision of another Court of Appeal in *Shadrokh-Cigari*,[127] where it was held an interest which could only have arisen under a constructive trust was a proprietary interest for the purposes of s 5(1). This decision renders doubtful that in *A-G's Reference* on the present point. In *Holmes v Governor of Brixton Prison*,[128] the Divisional Court, obiter, took the provisional view that property subject to a constructive trust is regarded as belonging to the person entitled to the beneficial interest for the purposes of s 5(1). It distinguished

---

[122] *Clowes (No 2)* [1994] 2 All ER 316, CA.   [123] *Clowes (No 2)* [1994] 2 All ER 316, CA.

[124] Such an approach has been taken in respect of the TA 1968 s 5(3): see para 10.55.

[125] [1996] AC 669 at 716.

[126] [1986] QB 491, CA; see also para 10.56. The Court of Appeal did not consider the applicability of the TA 1968, s 5(2): para 10.51.

[127] [1988] Crim LR 465; see also para 10.61.   [128] [2004] EWHC 2020 (Admin), DC.

A-G's Reference (No 1 of 1985) on the ground that it concerned a secret profit whereas *Holmes v Governor of Brixton Prison* concerned a fraudulent taking of property.

If property subject to a constructive trust can belong to another under s 5(1) in all or some cases, the question of whether or not there is a constructive trust can raise complicated questions of civil law. For example, is an employee who receives a bribe, or who makes a secret profit by the misuse of his employer's time and/or property, a constructive trustee of that money for his employer? According to *Lister & Co v Stubbs*,[129] a decision binding on the Court of Appeal (and relied on in *A-G's Reference (No 1 of 1985)*), the answer is 'no'; the employee merely has to account to the employer as a debtor for the bribe or secret profit. However, according to the more recent decision of the Privy Council in *A-G of Hong Kong v Reid*,[130] *Lister & Co v Stubbs* was wrongly decided and the answer is 'yes'. Although decisions of the Privy Council are only persuasive, it would be open to a future Court of Appeal or a High Court judge in a civil case to depart from *Lister v Stubbs* and apply *A-G for Hong Kong v Reid*.[131] If it does, and if the view adopted in *Shadrokh-Cigari* and *Holmes v Governor of Brixton Prison* is extended to this type of case, a bribe or secret profit would belong to another under s 5(1) because the employer would have a proprietary interest in it. It would follow that the employee could be convicted of the theft of the bribe or secret profit if he appropriated it.[132] The matter is now less important than hitherto because an employee who receives a bribe or makes a secret profit can be convicted of the offence of fraud under the Fraud Act 2006, s 1 by virtue of s 4 of this Act.

10.47 Section 5(1) says that 'proprietary right or interest' in the present context does not include 'an equitable interest arising only from an agreement to transfer or grant an interest'. This needs to be explained to those who have not yet encountered the rules of equity. When a person makes a specifically enforceable contract to buy, for example, a unique chattel, he thereby receives what is called an equitable interest in it although legally the person contracting to sell retains the legal ownership until that is transferred. The above words are designed to ensure that an owner who contracts to sell his property to A, and then contracts to sell it to B, does not steal it from A.

---

[129] (1890) 45 Ch D 1, CA.

[130] [1994] 1 AC 324, PC; Smith 'Lister v Stubbs and the Criminal Law' (1994) 110 LQR 180.

[131] *Smith v Leech Brain & Co Ltd* [1962] 2 QB 405 at 415; *Doughty v Turner Manufacturing Co Ltd* [1964] 1 QB 518, CA. So far *A-G of Hong-Kong v Reid* has been judicially preferred, but not applied, in three High Court cases; two of them (the third is below) are *Ocular Sciences Ltd v Aspect Vision Care Ltd* [1997] RPC 289; *Fyffes Group Ltd v Templeman* [2000] 2 Lloyd's Rep 643. However, in another High Court case, *A-G v Blake* [1997] Ch 84 (point not dealt with on appeal: [1998] Ch 439, CA; [2001] 1 AC 268, HL), and in a Court of Appeal case, *Halifax Building Society v Thomas* [1996] Ch 217, the judges treated *Lister & Co v Stubbs* as still binding. In the third High Court case mentioned above, *Daraydan Holdings Ltd v Solland International Ltd* [2004] EWHC 622 (Ch), the judge stated that, if he had not been able to distinguish *Lister & Co v Stubbs*, he would have applied *A-G of Hong Kong v Reid*.

[132] *Powell v MacRae* [1977] Crim LR 571, DC, where it was held that an employee could not be convicted of theft of a bribe because the bribe did not belong to another, was, of course, decided before *A-G of Hong Kong v Reid*.

Property may belong to more than one person

10.48 The result of the definition of 'belonging to another' in the TA 1968, s 5(1) is that property may 'belong' to more than one person. If A delivers goods to B with instructions to keep them safely for him, and D appropriates them dishonestly and with intent permanently to deprive A and B of them, he will commit theft from both A and B.

10.49 Another result is that a person to whom property 'belongs' under s 5(1) may steal the goods from someone else to whom they 'belong'. For instance, in the above example, if it is B who dishonestly appropriates the goods, he can be convicted of theft from A. Indeed, an owner may be convicted of stealing his own property. If D lets a car to V for a month and the next week surreptitiously takes it away, he can be convicted of theft – even though he is still the owner of the car – because the car is in V's possession; the same would be true if D removed his goods, without redeeming them, from G's pawnbroker's shop, or if D removed his shoes from J's shoe repair shop without paying for the repairs. Another example that an owner can steal his own property is provided by *Turner (No 2)*,[133] where D, whose car had been repaired, took the car from outside the repairer's garage with the object of evading payment of the repairer's charges. The Court of Appeal dismissed D's appeal against conviction for theft of the car because he had appropriated property belonging to another; it held that the car had clearly been in the 'possession or control' of the repairer when D had appropriated it by taking it. This decision shows the width of the TA 1968, s 5(1) because although the repairer presumably had a lien (a right to retain until payment) over the car, the trial judge had told the jury to ignore questions of lien and the Court of Appeal had to decide the appeal on the basis that there was no lien. If there was no lien, the repairer would only have been in possession of the car as a bailee at will (ie under a bailment immediately terminable at any time by the bailer). The Court of Appeal rejected an argument that possession as a bailee at will was insufficient. It said:

> 'There is no ground for qualifying the words "possession or control" in any way. It is sufficient if it is found that the person from whom the property is taken, or to use the words of the Act, appropriated, was at the time in fact in possession or control'.[134]

The somewhat surprising result of *Turner (No 2)* is that someone with a better right to possession than the possessor can be convicted of theft if he dishonestly appropriates the property with the intent permanently to deprive the possessor of it.[135]

A partner may likewise be held guilty of stealing partnership property, for partners are co-owners of their property and each of them has a proprietary right in it.[136] A thief may

---

[133] [1971] 2 All ER 441, CA.   [134] [1971] 2 All ER 441 at 443.

[135] Cf *Meredith* [1973] Crim LR 253, Crown Ct, where a Circuit judge ruled that it was not theft, where a car owner recovered the car from a police yard where it had been impounded, because the police had no right to retain possession of it; their power to remove a vehicle which was obstructing the highway did not extend to keeping it from the owner. This seems inconsistent with *Turner (No 2)* but lacks the authoritative force of that decision.

[136] *Bonner* [1970] 2 All ER 97n, CA.

steal from another thief, as where he appropriates goods whose ownership and possession the latter has obtained by deception.[137]

As was said in paras 10.45 and 10.46, a beneficiary under a trust (with the possible exception of certain types of a constructive trust) has a proprietary right or interest under s 5(1), and therefore the trust property is regarded for the purposes of the Act as belonging to the beneficiary as well as to the trustees who are the legal owners. If D holds goods, money or shares in trust for V, D as trustee has the legal ownership of the goods, money or shares, but V has a proprietary interest in them. Thus, D will be guilty of theft if he dishonestly appropriates them with the intention of defeating the trust by permanently depriving V of them.[138]

Property of defendant's spouse or civil partner

10.50 Spouses and civil partners[139] may be guilty of stealing each other's property, although in many instances their possession, and in some instances their ownership, is joint. However, a prosecution may not be instituted against a person for the theft of property which belonged to his or her spouse or civil partner at the time of the offence except by or with the consent of the Director of Public Prosecutions. The only exceptions are:

- where the property also belonged to a third party and both spouses or both civil partners are charged with its theft;

- in the cases of spouses, where the spouses were, by virtue of a judicial decree or order, not obliged to cohabit at the time of the offence;[140]

- in the case of civil partners, where an order is in force providing for their separation.[141]

Special cases

Key points 10.5

The TA 1968, s 5 contains four subsections other than s 5(1). These deal with specific situations where either the property does not belong to another under s 5(1) or where, although it does so belong by virtue of complicated rules of civil law, the matter is simplified by a special rule. By virtue of the rules laid down by these four subsections, property is deemed to belong to another in the specified situations for the purposes of the definition of theft in s 1.

---

[137] *Meech* [1974] QB 549, CA; para 10.55.   [138] See *Clowes (No 2)* [1994] 2 All ER 316, CA.

[139] As to civil partnerships (ie registered same-sex partnerships), see the Civil Partnership Act 2004, s 1.

[140] 'Judicial decree or order' includes a non-molestation order: *Woodley v Woodley* [1978] Crim LR 629, DC.

[141] TA 1968, s 30(4) (amended by the Civil Partnership Act 2004, Sch 27). The provisions of s 30(4) also apply to a charge of attempting or conspiring to commit theft of property belonging to the defendant's spouse or civil partner and to a charge of encouraging or assisting such a theft contrary to the Serious Crime Act 2007, Pt 2: Serious Crime Act 2007, s 63(1), Sch 6, Pt 1.

Trusts

10.51 As we have seen, property subject to a trust is regarded under s 5(1) as belonging to the beneficiaries as well as to the trustees. However, there are some trusts where there are no individual beneficiaries (in the legal sense of persons owning a beneficial interest in the trust property). Charitable trusts are an example.[142] Without special provision, a dishonest appropriation of property subject to a charitable trust by a sole trustee or all the trustees would not be theft because the property would not belong to another. For this reason, special provision is made by the TA 1968, s 5(2), which provides that:

> 'Where property is subject to a trust, the persons to whom it belongs shall be regarded as including any person having a right to enforce the trust, and an intention to defeat the trust shall be regarded accordingly as an intention to deprive of the property any person having that right.'

Therefore, if trustees hold property on trust for charitable purposes, the Attorney-General, as a person who, though not a beneficiary, has the right to enforce such a trust, is someone to whom the property 'belongs', and the trustees may be convicted of theft if they dishonestly appropriate it.

Property received under an obligation to retain and deal with it in a particular way

10.52 The TA 1968, s 5(3), which is in terms which include property received from another under an obligation short of actual trusteeship,[143] provides that:

> 'Where a person receives property from or on account of another, and is under an obligation to the other to retain and deal with that property or its proceeds in a particular way, the property or proceeds shall be regarded (as against him) as belonging to the other.'

Slightly more fully, s 5(3) can be expressed as follows. If:

- the defendant has received property (usually money) from or on account of another (V, the person from whom the property is alleged to have been stolen), and

- the defendant is under an obligation in civil law [144] (as opposed to a moral obligation) to V to retain and deal with the property or its proceeds in a particular way,

that property or its proceeds is regarded (as against the defendant) as belonging to another (ie V).

---

[142] Another example is a discretionary trust for a very large class: *Vestey v IRC* [1980] AC 1148, HL.

[143] *Arnold* [1997] 4 All ER 1 at 9.

[144] *Meech* [1974] QB 549, CA; *Mainwaring* (1981) 74 Cr App Rep 99, CA; *Wakeman v Farrar* [1974] Crim LR 136, DC; *DPP v Huskinson* (1988) 20 HLR 562, DC; *Breaks and Huggan* [1998] Crim LR 349, CA.

'Proceeds' refers to money or other property (including a bank credit) representing what was originally received.

The existence of a legal obligation to retain and deal with the property or its proceeds in a particular way is not enough for s 5(3) to apply. In addition, **the defendant must have personal knowledge of the obligation and its extent.**[145] The knowledge of an agent cannot be imputed to him for this purpose.[146] Thus, if an assistant of D receives a cheque payable to D's company from a client, the money to be used in a specified way, and D, not knowing of the client's instructions, uses the cheque for the ordinary purposes of the business, D is not guilty of theft because, as against D, the money does not belong to another under s 5(3) in view of D's ignorance of the obligation.

Receipt of property from or on account of another

10.53 The TA 1968, s 5(3) requires that the defendant should have 'received' the property 'from or on account of' another to whom he is under a legal obligation to retain and deal with it in a particular way. This requirement is clearly satisfied where D receives money *from* V which he is legally obliged to V to use in a particular way. It is also satisfied where D (a shop assistant) receives money from a customer for some of his employer's goods since he has received the money *on account of* another (the employer) and is legally obliged to the employer to retain and deal with it in a particular way (eg to put it in the till). It will be noted that an 'obligation to retain and deal with' property in a particular way may be owed to the person from whom it was received (in which case it will belong to him under s 5(3)) or to the person on whose account it was received (in which case it will belong to that person under s 5(3)). Which, if any, is the case depends on the facts and the applicable civil law.

10.54 The requirement that D must have 'received' the property from or on account of another would seem not to be satisfied where a sum of money is credited to V's account by a bank transfer (as opposed to being credited by the paying in of a cheque received by D). The credit is new property, a thing in action belonging to D which has never belonged to anyone else.[147] Consequently, D has not 'received' it and the property cannot, under s 5(3), belong to another from or on whose account it was received.[148] The Court of Appeal in *Klineberg and Marsden*[149] did not advert to this point when it failed to distinguish between separate sums provided by cash or cheque received from another and those provided by bank transfer.[150]

---

[145] *Wills* (1990) 92 Cr App Rep 297, CA. Presumably, he need not know that it is a legal obligation.

[146] *Wills* (1990) 92 Cr App Rep 297, CA.

[147] *Preddy* [1996] AC 815, HL.

[148] The credit would belong to another under s 5(1) if the person whose bank account has been debited as a result of the transfer has an equitable interest in the credit: see JC Smith [1999] Crim LR 419.

[149] [1999] 1 Cr App Rep 427, CA.

[150] See also *Re Kumar* [2000] Crim LR 504, DC, where the court was likewise inadvertent to the present point.

Obligation to the other to retain and deal with the money or its proceeds in a particular way

10.55 Where the transaction is in writing, it is for the judge to decide whether it creates a legal obligation of the above type and to direct the jury whether or not it does.[151] Where the transaction is not in writing (or not wholly in writing), it cannot be known whether or not the relevant circumstances existed until the facts have been established. It is for the jury to establish these circumstances if the facts are in dispute and, where they are, the judge must direct the jury to make their findings on the facts and then say to them: 'If you find the facts to be such-and-such, then I direct you as a matter of law that a legal obligation arose to which s 5(3) applies.'[152]

The judges (including appellate judges) have on occasions reached surprising conclusions on whether or not a legal obligation of the type referred to in s 5(3) would arise in given circumstances. *Meech*[153] provides an example. V fraudulently obtained a cheque for £1,450 from a finance company. He asked D to cash the cheque for him. D agreed and paid it into his own bank account. Two days later, having discovered V's fraud, D withdrew £1,410 from his account. This represented the £1,450 less a debt of £40 which V owed him. D had arranged with E and F to stage a fake robbery with him as victim, so that he could give an excuse for not returning the money to V, and this was carried out. D, E and F were convicted of the theft of the £1,410 and appealed unsuccessfully to the Court of Appeal. The Court held that at the time of the appropriation, which (it held) was when the money was divided up after the fake robbery,[154] the money (the proceeds of the cheque) belonged to another, V, under s 5(3) because D had initially received the cheque from V under an obligation to retain and deal with it or its proceeds in a particular way. This obligation was not affected by the fact that V, having acquired the cheque illegally, could not have enforced it in a court.

It is difficult to see how there was a legal obligation of the type specified in s 5(3). The Court of Appeal held that there was an initial obligation owed to V by D to retain and deal with the cheque and its proceeds in a particular way and that this sufficed for the purposes of s 5(3), even if the obligation ceased on D's discovery of V's fraud. The Court based this initial obligation on the fact that on D's knowledge of the facts there was an obligation to V, but s 5(3) does not talk in terms of an obligation believed by the defendant to exist, but of an actual obligation. Moreover, it appears to require the existence of such an obligation at the time of the appropriation. It is certainly odd that, on the view taken by the Court of Appeal, an obligation which may never have existed and which did not exist at the time of the appropriation could be held to suffice for the purposes of s 5(3). It

---

[151] *Clowes (No 2)* [1994] 2 All ER 316, CA.

[152] *Mainwaring* (1981) 74 Cr App Rep 99, CA. Also see *Dubar* [1995] 1 All ER 781, C-MAC (as for this court, see para 2.32, n 91); *Breaks and Huggan* [1998] Crim LR 349, CA. Where the relevant facts are not in dispute, the judge should normally rule on them before, or at the commencement of, the trial: *Breaks and Huggan* [1998] Crim LR 349, CA.

[153] [1974] QB 549, CA.

[154] Following *Gomez*, D would now have appropriated the money when he withdrew it from the bank; see para 10.7.

is submitted that the view taken in *Meech* is wrong and would not now be followed by the Court of Appeal.

10.56 It cannot be over-emphasised that, for property to belong to another under the TA 1968, s 5(3), **the defendant must be under a specific legal obligation to the person from or on whose account he received the property to retain and deal with that property or its proceeds in a particular way;** the fact that he is under some contractual obligation to that person to do something will not normally mean that he is obliged to retain and deal with the property received in a particular way. For example, where an employee receives money from a customer for goods which (contrary to his terms of employment) he is selling on his own account on the employer's premises (as where the manager of a pub is selling his own beer),[155] or where an employee receives money as a result of misusing his employer's property (such as out of hours use of a taxi by an employed taxi driver),[156] the money will not belong to another under s 5(3). The reason is that in neither of these cases is the money received from or on account of another to whom the employee is legally obliged to retain and deal with it in a particular way. (As to whether there could be a constructive trust in such a case, see para 10.46). Likewise, a person who receives and cashes a cheque for housing benefit to which he is entitled and who dishonestly uses the money for his own purposes instead of paying rent arrears does not satisfy the requirement of s 5(3) because there is no obligation on him, statutory or contractual, to retain and deal in a particular way with the money received.[157]

By way of further example, if V makes a contract with D, a decorator, to have his house painted and pays to D a down payment of £500, the £500 will belong only to D. It will not belong to V under s 5(3) because, although D is under a legal (contractual) obligation to paint the house, he is not under a legal obligation to retain and deal with the £500 (or its proceeds) in a particular way; he can do what he likes with it. It would be different if the £500 is handed over specifically to enable D to buy the necessary materials to paint the house; here D is under a legal obligation to retain and deal with the money or its proceeds (eg the paint) in a particular way; therefore it belongs to V under s 5(3) and D can be convicted of theft if he dishonestly appropriates it. This distinction can be illustrated by reference to *Hall*.[158]

D, a travel agent, received money from clients as deposits and payments for air trips to America: in some instances a lump sum was paid by schoolteachers in respect of charter flights for their pupils; in other instances individuals made payments in respect of their own projected flights. In none of the seven cases covered by the charges did the flights materialise and in none was there any refund. D claimed to have paid into his

---

[155] *A-G's Reference (No 1 of 1985)* [1986] QB 491, CA; *Cooke* [1986] AC 909, HL. If two or more agree to do this, they can be convicted of conspiracy to defraud: *Cooke.*

[156] *Cullen* (1873) LR 2 CCR 28, CCR.

[157] *DPP v Huskinson* (1988) 20 HLR 562, DC.

[158] [1973] QB 126, CA. Also see *Hayes* (1976) 64 Cr App Rep 82, CA. Note: the statements in these cases that it is for the jury to determine not only the facts but also whether, on those facts, an obligation arose have been disapproved and are not to be followed: *Dubar* [1995] 1 All ER 781, C-MAC (as to this court see para 2.32 note 91). The correct approach is that given in para 1 of para 10.55: ibid.

firm's general trading account all sums received by him and asserted that those sums had become his own property and had been applied by him in the conduct of the firm's business; he submitted that he could not be convicted of theft just because the firm had not prospered and there was no money. D was convicted but appealed successfully to the Court of Appeal who held that, although D was under a legal obligation to fulfil the customers' expectations under the contracts, it was not established, in the absence of some further arrangement, that D had been under an obligation to the clients concerned to retain and deal with the money in a particular way; therefore the money did not belong to another under s 5(3) at the material time.

It would have been different if D had been required by the terms of the contracts to pay the money into a separate account and use it to purchase the tickets. In that case he would have been under a legal obligation to retain and deal with the money or its proceeds in a particular way and it would have belonged to another under s 5(3). It would also have been different if D had been obliged to the customers or the airline to retain in the firm's general trading account funds (less any commission) representing the amount received from the customers and paid in by him, and to pay it to the airline. In such a case, a failure by D to maintain the level of the account at or above the amount payable would amount to the appropriation of the bank balance (a thing in action) which was the proceeds of the money received from the customers (or on account of the airline, as the case might be) which he was under an obligation to the customers (or the airline, as the case might be) to retain and deal with in a particular way.[159]

Care must be taken in framing the terms of an indictment, information or charge. In *Dyke and Munro*,[160] two trustees of a charitable trust were convicted of stealing money which had been collected in collecting tins by street collectors but had not been paid into the charity's bank account by the two trustees; instead the money had been taken by them. The indictment alleged that they had stolen 'monies belonging to a person or persons unknown' (viz those who had contributed). Allowing their appeal against conviction, the Court of Appeal held that they could not be convicted of theft as charged. The ownership of the money had passed to the charitable trust when the money was put in the tins and, although the trustees had been legally obliged to retain and deal with the money in a particular way, that obligation had not been owed to the individual contributors. The money therefore did not belong to the individual contributors under s 5(3). On the other hand, the trustees could have properly been convicted if the indictment had alleged that the money had belonged to the Attorney-General to whom the trustees were obliged to retain and deal with the money in accordance with the terms of the charitable trust.[161]

10.57 Another example of the limits and operation of the TA 1968, s 5(3) is as follows. If D is engaged by V to collect rent from V's tenants, or football pool money, and to account to V for the money he receives (less any commission or other reward), the money collected will belong to another (V) under s 5(3) if under their arrangement the circumstances are such that D is legally obliged to hand over the actual money received or to

---

[159] See *Re Kumar* [2000] Crim LR 504, DC.   [160] [2001] EWCA Crim 2184.   [161] Para 10.51.

maintain a distinct fund containing the money received or other money or a bank credit representing it (its proceeds) or to retain in his general account a sum representing it. In such a case a dishonest appropriation by D of any of the money or its proceeds to which he is not entitled can be theft. However, the money or its proceeds will not belong to V under s 5(3) if the relationship between D and V is simply one of debtor and creditor (ie D is not obliged to V to hand over the actual money received or to keep the money or its proceeds in a particular fund or to retain in his general bank account a sum representing the money received, and merely has to account in due course to V for an equivalent sum). In such a case, D will not commit theft by dishonestly appropriating the money, unless in some way an obligation to the tenants or punters has arisen to keep the money or its proceeds in a particular fund (in which event the money or its proceeds will belong to them under s 5(3)).

Where a person receives money or other property for onward transmission to another there is clearly an obligation, to the person entrusting it for transmission, to retain and deal with it or its proceeds in a particular way (to keep it or its equivalent separate and to hand it over). An example is provided by *Wain*.[162] D, by organising events, raised money for a company which distributed money among charities. D paid what he had raised into a special bank account which he had opened and thereafter, with the consent of a representative of the company, into his own account. D then dishonestly dissipated the credit in his account. The Court of Appeal held that D thereby appropriated property belonging to another because he was under an obligation to retain the proceeds of the money collected (the money credited in the successive bank accounts) and deal with them in a particular way (to hand them over to the company).

Utility of s 5(3)

10.58 Where the defendant has received the property as a bailee or trustee, it belongs to another under s 5(1) (or under s 5(2) in the case of some trusts) for reasons already explained. Consequently, although property which has been bailed or handed over subject to a trust clearly belongs to another under the TA 1968, s 5(3), recourse to that subsection is unnecessary.

In fact, it may be that s 5(3) is virtually otiose since, in nearly every other case covered by it, it can be established that, under the civil law, someone other than the recipient (ie the defendant) had a 'proprietary interest' in the property or proceeds in question, so that it belonged to another under s 5(1). In *Klineberg and Marsden*[163] the Court of Appeal described s 5(3) as 'essentially a deeming provision by which property or its proceeds "shall be regarded" as belonging to another, even though, on a strict civil law analysis, it does not'. One case which may be covered by s 5(3), but not by s 5(1), is where V sells D a non-transferable ticket on terms that D will return it at the end of a journey. In such a case, the entire proprietary interest in the ticket may pass to D[164] but D's retention of the

---

162 [1995] 2 Cr App Rep 660, CA, disapproving *Lewis v Lethbridge* [1987] Crim LR 59, DC.
163 [1999] 1 Cr App Rep 427 at 432. Also see *Floyd v DPP* [2000] Crim LR 411, DC.
164 See para 10.39.

ticket after the journey, with intent permanently to deprive V of it, could be theft of the ticket by virtue of s 5(3) on the basis that D was under an obligation to 'retain and deal with it in a particular way'.

Even if s 5(3) is virtually otiose, the civil law in this area is complex and s 5(3) plays a useful role in making it quite clear that, in the circumstances fairly simply specified by it, the property or its proceeds shall be regarded as 'belonging to another' for the purposes of theft.

Property transferred under a mistake

10.59 As already explained, a person (D) who, despite a mistake on the transferor's part, obtains ownership of property at the time he takes property thereby appropriates that property. At that point of time the property will still belong to another (the transferor) under the TA 1968, s 5(1), although a split second later the transferor will lose ownership and possession of it. If D has the necessary *mens rea* he can be convicted of theft.

10.60 We are concerned here with the situation where an appropriation with *mens rea* only occurs after the defendant has obtained ownership and possession of the property, as where property is transferred under a mistake which the defendant only discovers subsequently. In such a case the defendant will only commit theft if he then appropriates the property by keeping or dealing with it as owner with the necessary *mens rea and* the property belongs to another at that point of time.

Section 5 (1)

10.61 Although s 5(1) does not make express provision for mistake, property will still belong to the transferor in such a case under s 5(1) if the facts fall within a rule of civil law of restitution which was applied to the law of theft in *Shadrokh-Cigari*.[165] The rule is that, **where an action will lie under the law of restitution to recover money or other property which is transferred under a mistake, the person paying or transferring it under the mistake has a proprietary interest in it, at least once the recipient knows of the mistake.**[166] In *Shadrokh-Cigari*, $286,000 was transferred from an American bank to the English bank account of X, a boy, instead of the $286 actually due. X's guardian, D, procured X to authorise the English bank to issue banker's drafts drawn in favour of D for most of the sum of $286,000. D then used the drafts for his own purposes. The Court of Appeal upheld D's conviction for theft of the drafts from the English bank; D had appropriated the drafts and they belonged to another (the English bank) for the purposes of s 5(1) because, having transferred them to D under a mistaken belief that D could properly deal with the funds in the account, the bank, although it transferred ownership, retained a proprietary interest in them.

---

[165] [1988] Crim LR 465, CA. See also *Gresham* [2003] EWCA Crim 2070.

[166] *Chase Manhattan Bank NA v Israel-British Bank (London) Ltd* [1981] Ch 105; *Westdeutsche Landesbank Girozentrale v Islington London Borough Council* [1996] AC 669 at 715, per Lord Browne-Wilkinson.

Under the rules of equity, where the transferor (T) of money or other property transferred under a mistake retains a proprietary interest in it, and that money or other property is used to acquire property or is combined with other money to do so, T can 'trace'[167] his interest in that property or fund with the result that he will have a proprietary interest in those proceeds to the extent that they represent the original money or other property, and they will also belong to T for the purposes of s 5(1).

Too much must not be made of the decision in *Shadrokh-Cigari*, since the situations in which an action will lie to recover money or other property transferred under a mistake, or, in other words, situations where the transferee is under a legal obligation to make restoration of such money or property, are limited. This is a point dealt with in slightly more detail in para 10.63. What is said there about an obligation to restore is equally applicable in the present context.

Section 5(4)

10.62 Section 5(1) does not make express provision for mistake. The TA 1968, s 5(4), on the other hand, does.

Section 5(4) provides that:

> 'Where a person gets property by another's mistake, and is under an obligation to make restoration (in whole or in part) of the property or its proceeds or of the value thereof, then to the extent of that obligation the property or proceeds shall be regarded (as against him) as belonging to the person entitled to restoration, and an intention not to make restoration shall be regarded accordingly as an intention to deprive that person of the property or proceeds.'

To bring s 5(4) into play it is not enough simply that V has acted under a mistake; in addition, the transferee, D, must be under a legal[168] obligation under the law of restitution[169] to make restoration (in whole or in part) of the property received from V or its proceeds or its value. Only then, and to the extent of that obligation, is the property or proceeds regarded under s 5(4) as belonging to the person entitled to restoration. It is a matter of law for the judge whether or not an obligation to restore existed in particular circumstances. It is for the jury to establish whether or not these circumstances existed if the transaction was not wholly in writing and the facts are in dispute, and the judge should direct them in a similar way to that described in para 10.55 in relation to s 5(3).

10.63 When does a legal obligation to make restoration arise for the purposes of the TA 1968, s 5(4)? The answer to this could only be exhaustively attempted by a lengthy discussion of the civil law of restitution, which would not be appropriate for a book such as this.

---

[167] Subject to the normal restrictions on tracing; see Pearce and Stevens *The Law of Trusts and Equitable Obligations* (4th edn, 2006) Ch 31.

[168] *Gilks* [1972] 3 All ER 280, CA.

[169] In *A-G's Reference (No 1 of 1983)* [1985] QB 182, CA, the Court held that 'make restoration' in s 5(4) meant make restitution.

Suffice it to say that the most obvious case where an obligation to make restoration arises in a case where the mistake has not prevented ownership passing is where V transfers money under a mistake (whether of fact or of law)[170] which leads him to believe that D is legally entitled to the money.[171] It is this type of case which s 5(4) was principally intended to cover. For example, if V, an employer, pays D, an employee, a week's wages of £380, forgetting that he has already paid D £160 as an advance against wages, this mistake does not prevent ownership of the £380, which V intended to pay, passing to D, but D is under an obligation in civil law to make restoration to V of the £160 excess and, to the extent of that obligation, the money is regarded as belonging to V. If D spends the excess on becoming aware of the mistake, he can be convicted of the theft of £160, since it belongs to another (to V) under s 5(4).

10.64 The application of the TA 1968, s 5(4) is illustrated by *Davis*.[172] D was entitled to housing benefit from the local authority. Because of an administrative mistake, D was sent two housing benefit cheques (which we shall call 'duplicate cheques') every month for eight months; each cheque was for the full amount due. D then ceased to be entitled to housing benefit but he still received a single housing benefit cheque each month. Instead of returning the cheques, D dishonestly endorsed them. Some of the duplicate cheques were endorsed to his landlord for rent. The Court of Appeal quashed his conviction of theft of *money* in relation to this conduct because D had not thereby received, and therefore could not appropriate, money.

In relation to one set of duplicate cheques and some of the single cheques, D had endorsed these to shopkeepers for cash. The Court of Appeal upheld his conviction of theft of money in relation to these.

Dealing with the single cheques, it held that, since the cheques (ie the cheque forms as opposed to the thing in action which they represented) had been got by mistake in circumstances where D was under a legal obligation to make restoration of them, and since the cash into which D converted the cheques was the 'proceeds' of that property (the cheques) which D had received under a mistake, D was under a legal obligation to make restoration of those proceeds and therefore they belonged to another (the local authority) under s 5(4).

In the case of the set of duplicate cheques which had been cashed, it could not be proved which was the one to which D was entitled and which one had been sent under a mistake. The Court of Appeal dealt with this by holding that they were to be treated together as 'got' by another's mistake in the same way as if the excessive payment had been made in

---

[170] *Kleinwort Benson Ltd v Lincoln City Council* [1999] 2 AC 349, HL.

[171] *Kelly v Solari* (1841) 9 M & W 54. Other examples would be where money is paid under a void contract under the mistaken belief (whether the mistake was one of fact or of law) that it was valid: *Kleinwort Benson Ltd v Lincoln City Council* [1999] 2 AC 349, HL, or where an overpayment is made under a mistake (of fact or of law) but for which no overpayment would have been made (although this may only apply where the mistake was directly related to the overpayment and/or was connected to the payer/payee relationship): *Nurdin & Peacock plc v D B Ramsden & Co Ltd* [1999] 1 All ER 941. There are various bars to restitution for mistake: see *Barclays Bank Ltd v W J Simms Son & Cooke (Southern) Ltd* [1980] QB 677 at 695–696.

[172] (1988) 88 Cr App Rep 347, CA.

a single cheque, and that D was under a legal obligation to make restoration to the local authority in part of them or their proceeds to the extent of that obligation, and that therefore the proceeds to that extent belonged to another (the local authority) under s 5(4).

10.65 Another example is provided by *A-G's Reference (No 1 of 1983)*.[173] The defendant was a woman police officer. She was paid by her employer by direct debit. Once she was overpaid by £74. When she realised this, she decided to do nothing about it, although she did not withdraw any of this money. At the defendant's trial for theft, the judge directed an acquittal. On a reference by the Attorney-General, the Court of Appeal held that, to the extent of the overpayment, the debt due to the defendant from her bank (a thing in action) was property which belonged to another under the TA 1968, s 5(4). This was because the defendant had got that property under another's (the employer's) mistake as to her legal entitlement and was under an obligation in civil law to make restoration. This obligation to make restoration did not relate to the property (the debt), since it was not something which could be restored, nor did it relate to the proceeds of that property, since there were no proceeds to restore. Instead, it related to the value of the property – £74; under the civil law of restitution the defendant was obliged to restore or pay for the value of the benefit which she had received. Therefore, as against the defendant, the property (the debt) was regarded as belonging to another, the person (the employer) entitled to restoration, under s 5(4).

10.66 As seen,[174] in *Shadrokh-Cigari*[175] the Court of Appeal applied to the law of theft the rule of civil law that, where an action will lie to recover money or other property transferred under a mistake of fact, the transferor has a proprietary interest in it, at least once the recipient knows of the mistake, which can be 'traced' into things into which it is converted.[176] Consequently, the original money or other property or its proceeds will belong to another (the transferor) for the purposes of the TA 1968, s 5(1). In the light of the application of this principle, situations covered by s 5(4) will, for practical purposes, also be covered by s 5(1). A similar point was made in para 10.58 about s 5(3) and a similar comment can be made here as there. This is that the TA 1968, s 5(4) makes clear in fairly simple terms that, in the circumstances specified by it, property is regarded as belonging to another and avoids the need for the criminal courts to get involved in esoteric points of law relating to proprietary interests. Since, as the Court of Appeal admitted in *Shadrokh-Cigari*, s 5(4) was an alternative route to a finding in that case that the property in question belonged to another, it seems an unnecessary complication for it to have based its decision primarily on s 5(1) by an application of such points of law.

Corporation sole

10.67 The TA 1968, s 5(5) deals with a different kind of special case from those covered by s 5(2)–(4). It provides that the property of a corporation sole, examples of which are a

---

[173] [1985] QB 182, CA. See also *Stalham* [1993] Crim LR 310, CA.
[174] Para 10.61.   [175] [1988] Crim LR 465, CA.
[176] See Pearce and Stevens *The Law of Trusts and Equitable Obligations* (4th edn, 2006) Ch 31.

bishop and the Treasury Solicitor, shall be regarded as belonging to the corporation not-withstanding a vacancy in the corporation. This is simply to guard against the possibility that, for example, the property of a bishopric might be regarded as belonging to no one, and therefore incapable of being stolen, during a vacancy in the see.

Mens rea of theft

10.68 The TA 1968, s 1(2) states that it is immaterial that the appropriation is not made with a view to gain or is not made for the thief's own benefit (so that D can be convicted of theft if he throws V's ring into a river or tears to pieces V's clothing, although a charge of criminal damage would be more appropriate in the latter case).

The *mens rea* required for theft by the TA 1968, s 1(1) is that the appropriation must have been made dishonestly and with the intention of permanently depriving another person to whom the property belongs.[177]

The extreme width of the requirement of 'appropriation' means that these require-ments of *mens rea*, particularly that of dishonesty, play a crucial role in the offence in limiting the offence of theft within reasonable bounds.

'Dishonestly'

Key points 10.6

By the TA 1968, s 2(1) a person does not appropriate property dishonestly if he acts with one of three beliefs. If one of these beliefs is alleged, the judge will tell the jury that, as a matter of law, the defendant's appropriation of property is not to be regarded as dishon-est, unless the alleged belief is disproved. In any other case, the question of dishonesty is one of fact for the jury and not of law for the judge. In answering the question of fact the jury will apply the tests laid down by the Court of Appeal in *Ghosh*.

Section 2(1)

10.69 The TA 1968, s 2(1) provides:

'A person's appropriation of property belonging to another is not to be regarded as dishonest:

   (a) if he appropriates the property in the belief that he has in law the right to deprive the other of it, on behalf of himself or of a third person; or

---

[177] The defendant must, of course, have this *mens rea* at the time of the appropriation alleged; see *Hayes* (1976) 64 Cr App Rep 82, CA.

(b) if he appropriates the property in the belief that he would have the other's consent if the other knew of the appropriation and the circumstances of it; or

(c) (except where the property came to him as trustee or personal representative) if he appropriates the property in the belief that the person to whom the property belongs cannot be discovered by taking reasonable steps.'

Where one of these beliefs is alleged, it is irrelevant that it was unreasonable,[178] although, of course, the reasonableness of an alleged belief is of evidential importance when the issue of its genuineness is being considered.[179]

10.70 The Theft Act 1968, s 2(1)(a) means that the defendant's appropriation is not dishonest if he acts under a claim of right (ie a *belief* in a legal right to deprive) which means that a mistake of civil law may excuse, as where a creditor seizes property belonging to his debtor, intending to recoup himself thereby, under the erroneous belief that the law permits debts to be recovered in this way. The concluding words of s 2(1)(a) make it plain that someone who appropriates property in the belief that he is entitled to do so on behalf of, for example, the company by which he is employed is not guilty of theft. If the defendant genuinely believes that he has the right in law to deprive another of the property, he cannot be convicted of theft even though he knows that he has no legal right to appropriate it in the way which he does, eg by the use of force.[180]

Section 2(1)(a) is limited to beliefs in a legal right to deprive another of property, as opposed to beliefs in a moral right to do so (such as Robin Hood had when he stole from the rich to feed the poor). Where the defendant believes that he has a moral right to deprive, the question of his dishonesty depends on the tests outlined in para 10.74.

10.71 The TA 1968, s 2(1)(b) (*belief* that the person to whom the property belongs would have consented if he had known of the appropriation and its circumstances) would clearly cover the case of a student who takes a bottle of lager from a friend's room, leaving the price behind him and believing that his friend would have consented had he known of all the circumstances. A defendant's belief that he would have had the other's consent must be a belief that he would have had a 'true consent, honestly obtained'.[181]

10.72 The TA 1968, s 2(1)(c) (*belief* that the person to whom the property belongs cannot be discovered by taking reasonable steps) does not apply where the property came to the defendant as trustee or personal representative. It aims principally at protecting the honest finder as long as he remains honest. There is no dishonesty, and therefore no theft, if, believing that the owner of goods or money found by him cannot be discovered by taking reasonable steps, the finder appropriates the goods or money during the currency of that belief.

It is important to appreciate the extremely limited nature of the immunity conferred on the honest finder. In the first place property may, as we have seen, belong to more than

---

[178] *Holden* [1991] Crim LR 478, CA.

[179] Para 5.9.   [180] *Robinson* [1977] Crim LR 173, CA; para 10.98.

[181] *A-G's Reference (No 2 of 1982)* [1984] QB 624 at 641.

one person for the purpose of the Act. Although someone who finds goods on or embedded in another's land may well believe that their owner, the loser, cannot be discovered by taking reasonable steps, the goods would probably be held to belong also to the occupier of the land on the ground that he has possession or control of them.[182] Appropriation with knowledge of the occupier's rights would be theft. Secondly, if, while he is in possession of the goods, the finder becomes aware of the person to whom they belong, he may be guilty of theft in consequence of any subsequent appropriation by keeping or disposing of the goods with the intention of permanently depriving that person. There is no equivalent to the protection of honest purchasers from thieves conferred by the TA 1968, s 3(2).[183]

Section 2(1)(c) is not limited to honest finders. For example, it also protects a shoe repairer who, believing that he cannot find the owner of some uncollected shoes, appropriates them.

Cases not covered by section 2(1)

10.73 The negative definition of dishonesty in the TA 1968, s 2(1) is only a partial definition. Consequently, a defendant's appropriation may not have been made dishonestly even though the case falls outside s 2(1). This was held by the Court of Appeal in 1973 in *Feely*.[184] Moreover, as the court made clear in that case, in situations other than those referred to in s 2(1) the meaning of dishonesty is not a matter of law for the judge to decide but a matter of fact for the jury. This means that in such situations it is not for the judge to tell the jury whether or not the defendant's appropriation, assuming his version of the facts is not disproved, was made dishonestly but for the jury to decide this.

In *Feely*, D was employed by a firm of bookmakers as a manager of one of their branches. D's employers sent a circular to all their managers stating that the practice of borrowing from tills was to stop and after receiving that circular D knew that he had no right of any kind to take money from a till or safe for his own purposes. Subsequently, D took about £30 from a safe at his branch in order to give it to his father. When the deficiency was discovered, D gave an IOU to his successor as branch manager and said that he intended to repay the sum, taking it out of money due to him by his employers, who owed him about twice that amount. The judge in his summing up told the jury '...as a matter of law...I am bound to direct you, even if he were prepared to pay back the following day and even if he were a millionaire, it makes no defence in law to this offence'. The Court of Appeal held that this was wrong: it may happen that an employee is acting dishonestly when he removes money from a till but it is for the jury to decide. 'We do not agree', said Lawton LJ, 'that judges should define what "dishonestly" means'. Instead, the question of whether the defendant's appropriation was dishonest should be left to the jury to decide and the jury should apply to that question the current standards of ordinary decent people.

---

[182] Paras 10.39–10.44.   [183] Para 10.20.
[184] [1973] QB 530, CA. For a criticism of this decision, see Elliott 'Law and Fact in Theft Act Cases' [1976] Crim LR 707.

'Dishonestly' is not intended to characterise a course of conduct but to describe a state of mind.[185] What this means, for the purpose of the above test, is that the jury (or magistrates), having determined the defendant's state of mind at the time of the appropriation, must ask themselves whether, given that state of mind (eg an intention to repay coupled with a belief, whether reasonable or not,[186] that he will be able to do so), the defendant was acting dishonestly according to the current standards of ordinary decent people.

10.74 In *Ghosh*,[187] a case concerned with other (subsequently repealed) offences of dishonesty under the Act but the decision in which is expressly applicable to theft, the Court of Appeal added a second, subjective, test to the objective test laid down in *Feely*. It held that:

> 'In determining whether the prosecution has proved that the defendant was acting dishonestly, a jury [or magistrates] must first of all decide whether according to the ordinary standards of reasonable and honest people what was done was dishonest. If it was not dishonest by those standards, that is the end of the matter and the prosecution fails. If it was dishonest by those standards, then the jury [or magistrates] must consider whether the defendant himself must have realised that what he was doing was by those standards dishonest.'[188]

This two-fold test can be summarised as follows: Was what the defendant did dishonest according to the ordinary standard of reasonable and honest people? If so did the defendant realise that what he was doing was dishonest by those standards? If the answer to both questions is 'yes', the defendant's appropriation is dishonest.

If the defendant did not realise that what he was doing was dishonest by the ordinary standards of reasonable and honest people, then, however irrational or bigoted his state of mind may be,[189] his appropriation will not have been dishonest. In most cases where, given his state of mind, the defendant's actions are obviously dishonest by ordinary standards, there will be no doubt that he himself knew he was acting dishonestly by the ordinary standards of reasonable and honest people.

It must be emphasised that the second test is not whether the defendant believed that his behaviour was not dishonest by his standards. It is no defence for him to say: 'I knew that what I was doing is generally regarded as dishonest, but I did not regard it as dishonest myself.'[190] On the other hand, it is a defence to say – unless disproved: 'I did not know that ordinary people would regard what I was doing as dishonest.' In other words, under this test 'dishonestly' is not governed by the defendant's own moral standards but by his understanding of the moral standards of ordinary, decent people. Of course, the more outrageous his alleged understanding of them is the less likely he is to be believed.

[185] *Ghosh* [1982] QB 1053 at 1063. [186] *Lewis* (1975) 62 Cr App Rep 206, CA.
[187] [1982] QB 1053, CA. The approach to 'dishonesty' in this case has been held to be of general application, even outside the Theft Acts: *Lockwood* [1986] Crim LR 244, CA.
[188] These tests are discussed by Campbell 'The Test of Dishonesty in *R v Ghosh*' (1984) 43 CLJ 349 and Halpin 'The Test for Dishonesty' [1996] Crim LR 283.
[189] *Mitchell* (1990) unreported, CA. [190] *Ghosh* [1982] QB 1053 at 1064.

In *Ghosh,* the Court of Appeal stated that Robin Hood would act dishonestly because he would know that ordinary people would consider his actions to be dishonest. However, assuming that the jury did consider that Robin Hood's actions were dishonest by the current standards of ordinary decent people, it is by no means certain that a claim by Robin Hood that he thought an ordinary person would not regard his actions as dishonest would easily be disproved.[191]

10.75 The approach laid down in *Ghosh* is liable to create an additional ground for contested trials, to complicate the judge's direction, and to lead to arbitrary and inconsistent verdicts by different juries or benches of magistrates as to what is dishonest.[192] It would be much better if statute laid down as a matter of law a full definition of what is (or what is not) dishonesty. Because the element of 'dishonestly' has a crucial function in determining whether conduct with property is or is not theft, the law should state in advance what is and what is not forbidden. That task should not be left to the moral standards of the jury or magistrates in a particular case.

It may be that the *Ghosh* approach contravenes the ECHR, Article 7 (no punishment without law). Article 7 is infringed if a defendant is punished in a case where the 'quality of law' requirement referred to in para 1.58 is not satisfied, ie if the defendant was unable – even with appropriate advice if necessary – to foresee to a *reasonable degree* whether or not his conduct was criminal. This was applied, for example, by the European Court of Human Rights in *Hashman and Harrup v United Kingdom,*[193] where the applicants (anti-hunt protesters) had been bound over to keep the peace and be of good behaviour after a finding that they had acted *contra bonos mores. Contra bonos mores* meant 'wrong rather than right in the judgement of the majority of citizens'. The European Court held that this definition failed to meet the quality of law requirement because it failed to describe the behaviour covered by it, even by reference to its effects.[194] The same could clearly be said of the *Ghosh* approach. However, the European Court in *Hashman and Harrup v United Kingdom* said that the offences of 'dishonesty' under the Theft Acts were different from binding over for behaviour *contra bonos mores* because dishonesty (ie the *Ghosh* approach) was 'but one element of a more comprehensive definition of the proscribed behaviour'. In the light of the width of 'appropriation' in theft, this would appear to underestimate the importance of the element of dishonesty in the case of the offence of theft. Despite what was said in *Hashman and Harrup* about 'dishonesty', a quality of law challenge to the *Ghosh* approach would not necessarily be doomed.

---

[191] For a critical evaluation of the position after *Ghosh,* see Elliott 'Dishonesty in Theft: A Disposable Concept' [1982] Crim LR 395. Also see Williams 'The Standard of Honesty' (1983) 133 NLJ 636. For suggestions for reform, see Elliott, loc cit; *Smith's Law of Theft* (9th edn, 2007) (Ormerod and Williams (eds)), paras 2.310–2.314; Williams 'Innocuously Dipping into Trust Funds' (1985) 5 LS 183; Halpin 'The Test for Dishonesty' [1996] Crim LR 283.

[192] These and other objections are neatly summarised by Griew 'Dishonesty: Objections to *Feely* and *Ghosh*' [1985] Crim LR 341.

[193] (2000) 30 EHRR 241, ECtHR.

[194] Provisions which describe behaviour by reference to its effects are acceptable: *Steel v United Kingdom* (1999) 28 EHRR 603, ECtHR.

General

10.76 The judge is not required to direct the jury about the TA 1968, s 2(1), unless there is evidence that the defendant appropriated the property with one of the beliefs specified in that provision. In such a case the jury should be directed about the effect of that belief. The judge must tell the jury that as a matter of law they must acquit the defendant unless the prosecution disproves his alleged belief beyond reasonable doubt.[195]

10.77 Where the evidence is otherwise, a *Ghosh* direction is not always necessary; the Court of Appeal has emphasised on a number of occasions that it is not necessary to give a *Ghosh* direction in every case.[196] Essentially, a *Ghosh* direction is necessary where ordinary people might take a different view from the defendant about whether his appropriation was dishonest. On the other hand, if this is not the issue but the issue simply relates to something which, if true, would undoubtedly negative dishonesty, as where the defendant alleges that he believed the property was abandoned, a *Ghosh* direction is unnecessary.[197] Nor is a *Ghosh* direction necessary if the defendant simply denies the alleged conduct and there is nothing to suggest that the defendant was not dishonest.[198]

10.78 Where a *Ghosh* direction is necessary, the judge must tell the jury to determine what the defendant's state of mind actually was (ie what his beliefs and intentions were); unless the defendant's alleged state of mind is disproved by the prosecution the jury will, of course, have to find that it existed. In giving a *Ghosh* direction the judge should use the precise form of words in that case.[199] The judge must tell the jury that they must acquit the defendant unless the prosecution satisfy them that the defendant's appropriation was dishonest.

Section 2(2)

10.79 For the sake of completeness it should be noted that the TA 1968, s 2(2) expressly says what has already been implied:

> 'A person's appropriation of property belonging to another may be dishonest notwithstanding that he is willing to pay for the property.'

Someone who knows that the owner of a picture does not wish to sell it might well be held to have acted dishonestly and to be guilty of theft if he took the picture, intending to deprive the owner permanently of it but leaving the price behind. On the other hand, a student who takes a bottle of lager from a friend's room, leaving the price, might not be held to have acted dishonestly under *Ghosh*, even if he did not believe that the owner

---

[195] See *Wootton and Peake* [1990] Crim LR 201, CA, where this point is made, albeit rather weakly.

[196] See, for example, *Roberts* (1987) 84 Cr App Rep 117, CA; *Price* (1989) 90 Cr App Rep 409, CA; *Buzaleck and Schiffer* [1991] Crim LR 130, CA; *O'Connell* (1991) 94 Cr App Rep 39, CA.

[197] *Wood* [2002] EWCA Crim 832.   [198] *Cobb* [2005] EWCA Crim 1549.

[199] *Hyam* [1997] Crim LR 439, CA.

would have consented to the appropriation (so that the case would not be covered by the provisions of s 2(1)).

In *Wheatley v Commissioner of Police of the British Virgin Islands*,[200] the Privy Council held that, for the purposes of the offence of theft within the meaning of the Criminal Code of the British Virgin Islands, ss 203–208, which were closely modelled on the Theft Act 1968, ss 1–6, the prospect of loss was not determinative of dishonesty. The Privy Council held that, although, in most cases of theft there would be an original owner of money or goods who would be poorer because of the defendant's appropriation, the provision in s 204(2) of the Code (the equivalent of the TA 1968, s 2(2)) that an appropriation might be dishonest despite a willingness to pay showed that the prospect of loss was not determinative of dishonesty.

Intention of permanently depriving

> ### Key points 10.7
>
> The TA 1968, s 1(1) requires that the defendant 'dishonestly appropriates property belonging to another with the intention of permanently depriving the other of it'. In some cases, a person is deemed by the TA 1968, s 6 to intend permanently to deprive the other person of the property even though he does not mean him permanently to lose the thing.

10.80 Actual permanent deprivation is not required for theft, but the defendant must be proved to have intended at the time he appropriated property belonging to another (V) to deprive V permanently of it (the thing appropriated). If D dishonestly takes V's watch, intending to deprive V permanently of it, D is guilty of theft, even though he is arrested almost immediately afterwards and the watch is returned to V.

10.81 Because the defendant must intend permanently to deprive the other **'of it', ie the actual thing appropriated,** an appropriator of money who intends to spend it but to repay it with other notes nevertheless has an intention permanently to deprive (although he may be found not to have acted dishonestly).[201] The same is, of course, true where other property, such as some milk, is appropriated with the intention of consuming it and of replacing it with its equivalent.

10.82 Normally, D will intend permanently to deprive V by the act of appropriating V's property itself, but this is not necessary. Provided that it exists at the time of the appropriation, an intent to deprive V in the future by some subsequent act will do.[202]

---

[200] [2006] UKPC 24.   [201] *Velumyl* [1989] Crim LR 299, CA.

[202] This follows from the decision in *Morris; Anderton v Burnside* [1984] AC 320, HL, where the appropriation consisted of label-swapping but the intended deprivation would only have occurred through an act of buying at the checkout.

10.83 The question of whether or not there was an intention permanently to deprive the person to whom the property belongs gives rise to no difficulty in the ordinary case because the defendant's conduct with the property will often provide a clear inference as to his intention. For example, if D takes V's bricks and builds them into a wall on his property, or if D takes V's money and spends it in a pub, the inference of an intention permanently to deprive is very strong indeed (although it would be a misdirection for a judge to tell a jury that they must draw it). On the other hand, if D picks up V's copy of this book in the student work room and takes it over to his desk and reads it, or if D takes V's squash racquet and, after using it, leaves it elsewhere at the squash club, it is unimaginable that an inference could be drawn on these facts that D appropriated the property with an intention permanently to deprive.

10.84 In one case a person can intend permanently to deprive even though at first sight it may appear that he only intends a purely temporary borrowing. This is where a victim of an appropriation has a limited interest in the property. For example, if V hires a power tool for a week from X and during that week D, knowing these facts, takes the tool, intending to return it to X ten days later, D can be convicted of the theft of the tool from V (since he intended permanently to deprive V of the whole of his interest in the property) but not of the theft of it from X (because he did not so intend in relation to X).

Section 6

10.85 In certain exceptional cases a person can be convicted of theft even though he did not mean permanently to deprive anyone to whom the property belonged, and even though he positively intended to return the actual property at some future date (or did actually return it). A conviction in such a case is possible if the case falls within the TA 1968, s 6, which extends the meaning of 'intention of permanently depriving'.

It cannot be emphasised too much that s 6 does not provide a complete definition of 'intention of permanently depriving'; instead it simply extends or clarifies that phrase. In the vast majority of cases it need not be referred to at all, and it certainly should not be referred to if the issue of whether or not the defendant had the intention of permanently depriving can be determined without reference to it.[203] The Court of Appeal in *Lloyd*[204] said that reference to s 6 should be made in exceptional cases only, and these are cases where D does not mean V permanently to lose the thing itself but has acted in a way which may fall within s 6. Despite such statements, s 6 continues to be invoked in inappropriate cases by students in their answers. The message that s 6 should only be referred to in the type of case outlined in *Lloyd* is clearly one which is not easy to get across.

10.86 Despite a statement by the Court in *Lloyd* that s 6 should be interpreted in such a way as to ensure that nothing is construed as an intention permanently to deprive which would not have been so construed before the TA 1968, it is now clear that the

---

[203] *Lloyd* [1985] QB 829 at 835–836. Also see *Warner* (1970) 55 Cr App Rep 93, CA; *Cocks* (1976) 63 Cr App Rep 79, CA; *Coffey* [1987] Crim LR 498, CA. [204] [1985] QB 829, CA.

courts interpret the words of s 6 without reference to the law before the Act. Indeed, in *Bagshaw*,[205] the Court of Appeal stated that what was said in *Lloyd* on the present point was obiter and that there might be other occasions on which s 6 applies. The reported cases, referred to in para 10.87, are examples of such other occasions on which s 6 has been applied.

Section 6(1): Part 1

10.87 The first part of the TA 1968, s 6(1) provides that:

'A person appropriating property belonging to another without meaning the other permanently to lose the thing itself is nevertheless to be regarded as having the intention of permanently depriving the other of it if his intention is to treat the thing as his own to dispose of regardless of the other's rights,...'

These words are the key part of s 6. They deem an appropriator of another's property to have intended permanently to deprive the other of it if he intends to treat the thing as his own to dispose of regardless of the other's rights, even though he does not mean (ie intend) the other permanently to lose the thing itself. The following are examples of cases which are caught by the above words of s 6(1).

D takes V's Ming vase, intending to sell it back to V (or to hold it to ransom) and to return it to V only if V pays the asking price (or ransom). D clearly intends to treat the thing as his own to dispose of regardless of the rights of the other (V), since he intends that V should only get back what he is already entitled to [206] by paying for it, even though he does not mean V to be permanently deprived because he hopes that V will pay the asking price (or ransom).[207] This was recognised by the Court of Appeal in *Raphael*,[208] where the defendants had taken the victim's car by force and demanded payment for its return. Rejecting appeals against convictions for conspiracy to rob (robbery requires the commission of theft), the Court of Appeal stated that an intention on the part of a taker of property 'to treat the thing as his own to dispose of regardless of the other's rights' includes the situation where the defendant makes an offer to sell the other's own property back to him subject to a condition or conditions (eg payment of the price demanded) for its return inconsistent with his right to possession of his own property.

In *Downes*,[209] D was in possession of vouchers in his name. The vouchers belonged to the Inland Revenue. They could be used to obtain tax advantages. D sold the vouchers to others who, as he knew, would submit them for this purpose. The Court of Appeal held that, by doing so, D had committed theft. Although he knew that the vouchers would

---

[205] [1988] Crim LR 321, CA.
[206] Section 6(1) would not apply if V was not entitled to the property without paying for it: *Johnstone* [1982] Crim LR 454 and 607, Crown Ct.
[207] Such an example was given in *Lloyd* [1985] QB 829, CA.   [208] [2008] EWCA Crim 1014.
[209] (1983) 77 Cr App Rep 260, CA.

return to the Inland Revenue when submitted by the buyers, he had treated them as his own to dispose of regardless of the other's (Inland Revenue's) rights by selling them.

Marshall[210] provides another example of the operation of the first part of s 6(1). There, the defendants had collected from people exiting London Underground stations tickets which had been used but were still valid, and resold them to others. The issue addressed by the Court of Appeal[211] was whether, in respect of charges of theft of the tickets, the trial judge had been correct to take the view that there was evidence of an intention permanently to deprive London Underground by virtue of s 6(1). The Court of Appeal answered 'yes': by acquiring and reselling the tickets the defendants had intended to treat the tickets as their own to dispose of regardless of the rights of London Underground (who had the exclusive right to sell its tickets). It was irrelevant that the tickets might find their way back into the possession of London Underground, albeit with their usefulness or 'virtue' exhausted.

In *DPP v Lavender*,[212] where D had surreptitiously removed two doors from a nearby council house to replace doors in his council house, the Divisional Court held that he had acted with an intent permanently to deprive the council of the doors, by virtue of s 6(1). This is not easy to accept. D had certainly acted with intent to treat the doors as his own regardless of the rights of the council, but it is far from obvious that he acted with intent to treat the doors as his own *to dispose of* regardless of the rights of the council. The only way in which this decision can be justified is if 'treat as one's own to dispose of' means 'to have the disposal of', ie to *deal with* regardless of the rights of the other. This may be what the Divisional Court meant when it said that 'to dispose of' should not be given a narrow dictionary definition. However, such a narrow definition was cited with apparent approval in *Cahill*,[213] which was not referred to by the Court in *DPP v Lavender*. Moreover, if 'to dispose of' is to be understood in the wider sense referred to, the requirement that the defendant must 'intend to treat the thing as his own to dispose of *regardless of the rights of the other*' is redundant.

Another type of case which can fall within the above words of s 6(1) is where the defendant abandons the property and he is indifferent as to whether it is recovered by the person to whom it belongs (or he may even hope that it is). If, by the circumstances of the abandonment and/or the nature of the property, it is (to the defendant's knowledge) unlikely that the property will be recovered, he can be said to intend to treat the thing as his own to dispose of regardless of the rights of the other.[214] An obvious example of a case which would be caught by s 6(1) would be where D takes V's watch in Leicester and abandons it in Newcastle. At the other extreme D, who took and used V's squash racquet and then left it elsewhere at the squash club, would not be caught by s 6(1), and neither, generally

---

[210] [1998] 2 Cr App Rep 282, CA. See JC Smith 'Stealing Tickets' [1998] Crim LR 723.

[211] For another issue raised by the case but not discussed by the Court of Appeal, see para 10.39.

[212] [1994] Crim LR 297, DC.

[213] [1993] Crim LR 141, CA.

[214] In *Fernandes* [1996] 1 Cr App Rep 175, the Court of Appeal stated that s 6(1) may apply to a person in possession or control of another's property who dishonestly and for his own purpose deals with property in such a manner that he knows he is risking its loss.

speaking, would a person who takes another's car and then abandons it, because it is a well-known fact that cars which are abandoned are almost invariably returned to their owners. See also para 10.90.

If D appropriates V's piano by pretending to be its owner and purporting to sell it to X, knowing that V's imminent return will prevent the removal of the piano, he can be convicted of its theft since he intends to treat it as his own to dispose of regardless of V's rights and is therefore deemed by s 6(1) to intend permanently to deprive V of it. (However, it would be more appropriate to charge D with fraud, contrary to the Fraud Act 2006, s 1.) The decision of the Privy Council in *Chan Man-sin v A-G of Hong Kong*[215] provides an interesting example of the fact that the requirements of s 6(1) can be satisfied even where D knows that the person to whom the property belongs will not lose anything. A company accountant drew and presented forged cheques in his favour on the company's account. The Privy Council held that there was evidence from which it could be inferred that his appropriations of a thing in action (the credit in the company's bank account) had been accompanied by an intention permanently to deprive the company of that thing because he intended to treat the bank credit as his own to dispose of regardless of the company's rights, and it would not matter if he had realised that the fraud would be discovered and that the company's credit balance would be unaffected.

10.88 The first part of s 6(1) expresses the critical notion of s 6. The second part of s 6(1) and also s 6(2) provide specific illustrations of the application of that notion.[216]

Section 6(1): Part 2

10.89 Section 6(1) of the TA 1968 goes on to provide that:

> 'a borrowing or lending of it [the property appropriated] may amount to so treating it [ie treating it as the defendant's own to dispose of regardless of the rights of the other] if, but only if, the borrowing or lending is for a period and in circumstances making it equivalent to an outright taking or disposal.'

In *Lloyd*,[217] the Court of Appeal held that **this part of s 6(1) 'is intended to make clear that a mere borrowing is never enough to constitute the necessary [*mens rea*] unless the intention is to return the "thing" in such a changed state that it can truly be said that all its goodness or virtue has gone'.** It is clear from the example given in *Lloyd* and set out below that 'changed state' does not mean that the thing's physical state must have changed.

An example of a case covered by the second part of s 6(1), which was given by the Court of Appeal in *Lloyd*, is where someone takes railway tickets intending that they should be returned to the railway company only after the journeys have been completed. Clearly, the

---

[215] [1988] 1 All ER 1, PC. Also see *Hilton* [1997] 2 Cr App Rep 445, CA.
[216] *Fernandes* [1996] 1 Cr App Rep 175 at 188.
[217] [1985] QB 829 at 836, CA.

borrowing here is for a period and in circumstances equivalent to an outright taking or disposal because, if the tickets are returned as intended, all their goodness or virtue will have gone. The same can be said if D takes V's football season ticket, intending to return it at the end of the season. D's borrowing is clearly for a period and in circumstances making it equivalent to an outright taking since, when it is returned as he intends, the season ticket will be a virtually worthless piece of paper. His intention to borrow the season ticket in this way amounts to the intention to treat the thing as his own to dispose of regardless of V's rights and is thereby deemed by s 6(1) to be an intention permanently to deprive V of it. Likewise, in *DPP v SJ*,[218] Silber J, sitting in the Administrative Court, held that the magistrates' court had been wrong to accept a submission of no case to answer where D had snatched V's stereo headphones and snapped them before returning them to V. The judge noted that the headphones had no conceivable use after being broken.

If D took a battery from V's shop for his torch, intending to return it when the battery was exhausted, he would be deemed to intend permanently to deprive V of the battery. (He could, of course, also be convicted of the offence of abstracting electricity, which might be a more appropriate charge.) By way of further example, although confidential information in an examination paper is not property and cannot be stolen, if a student surreptitiously borrows a college examination paper a week before the examination, intending to copy it and then to return it, his appropriation of the piece of paper will be regarded under s 6(1) as done with the intention of permanently depriving the college authorities of it (the paper). The borrowing is clearly for a period and in circumstances making it equivalent to an outright taking or disposal because, if the paper is returned as intended, all its goodness or virtue will have gone.

10.90 In these cases the property would have lost *all* its virtue at the time of the intended return. According to the test in *Lloyd*, s 6 would not catch the case where the property at the time of its intended return would have some goodness or virtue, albeit that it would have substantially or essentially lost its virtue (as where the season ticket had one match's unexpired use). In *Lloyd*, the defendant removed films from a cinema, for a few hours on each occasion, in order to make 'pirate' copies of them. The Court of Appeal held that this did not constitute theft of the films because, although great financial harm would be caused to the copyright owner and others, the goodness and virtue of the films would not have gone out of them on their return; they could still be projected to cinema audiences. Therefore, the borrowing was not for a period, or in circumstances, making it equivalent to an outright taking or disposal.

Clinton (Chief Inspector of RUC) v Cahill is to like effect.[219] D was a tenant of a property heated by a district heating system under which hot water from a heating station passed through radiators in properties and returned to the station. Seals on D's meter were broken and she received hot water for which she had not paid. The Court of Appeal of Northern Ireland held that, although D had dishonestly appropriated water belonging to another, the appropriation consisting in the abstraction of heat from the water, she had not intended

---

[218] [2002] EWHC 291 (Admin).   [219] [1998] NI 200, NICA.

permanently to deprive the other of it. Clearly, she had not meant the other permanently to lose the water itself, and she was not caught by s 6(1) because, on the facts found, the virtue in the water had not wholly (or even substantially or essentially) disappeared when the water returned from her radiators to the system. Some heat was still retained in it. Therefore D's use of it was not the equivalent of an outright taking or disposal.

The decision of the Court of Appeal in *Mitchell*[220] confirms that a person who takes another's motor vehicle and then abandons it does not, generally speaking, intend by virtue of s 6(1) permanently to deprive the owner of it. Referring to the second part of s 6(1), it held that, because a 'borrowing or lending' could only be deemed by s 6(1) to amount to an 'intention of permanently depriving' the owner of the article if the intention of the borrower or lender was that the article be returned to the owner in such a changed state that it had lost all its practical value, the offence of theft was not made out in the above circumstances.

10.91 In principle, it would appear that, where D appropriates a cheque intending to pay it into his bank account, the case would be covered by the second part of s 6(1). However, in *Preddy*[221] Lord Goff, with whose speech the rest of the House of Lords agreed, held that if by deception D obtains a cheque form belonging to the drawer of the cheque there would be 'no intention on the part of [D] permanently to deprive the drawer of the cheque form, which would on presentation of the cheque for payment be returned to the drawer via his bank'.[222] Lord Goff seems to have assumed that D was aware of what ultimately happens to a cheque after presentation; if D was not, there should be no problem in establishing the necessary intent. The case for finding an intent permanently to deprive where D is aware that the cheque will return to the drawer's bank is arguably stronger than in respect of the tickets which were resold in *Marshall*.[223] When the cheque is returned to the drawer's bank after payment and is available to him, it will have changed its nature. Before it is paid it is a valuable security,[224] a 'key' to payment of the amount specified in it; after payment it is a worthless piece of paper. Although D may not mean the drawer of the cheque permanently to lose that thing itself, it would seem in principle that D is to be regarded as intending permanently to deprive the drawer of the cheque by reference to both parts of s 6(1). This argument finds support in the decision of the Court of Appeal in *Arnold*.[225] Dealing with a case where D had appropriated a bill of exchange (another form of valuable security) handed over on the basis that he would retain and deal with it in a particular way, the Court stated:

> 'there is good reason for the application of s 6(1) if the intention of the transferee at the time of the appropriation is that the document should find its way back to the

---

[220] [2008] All ER (D) 109 (Apr), CA.   [221] [1996] AC 815 at 836–837.

[222] It does not appear to be the modern practice for cheques to be returned to the drawer, although – once cleared – they are available to the drawer via his bank.   [223] Para 10.87.

[224] A 'valuable security' means any document creating, transferring, surrendering or releasing any right to, in or over property, or authorising the payment of money or delivery of any property, or evidencing such creation etc, or such payment etc, or the satisfaction of any obligation.   [225] [1997] 4 All ER 1, CA.

transferor only after all the benefit to the transferor has been lost or removed as a result of its use.'[226]

However, in *Clark*,[227] where *Arnold* was not referred to, the Court of Appeal held that 'the decision' in *Preddy* (ie Lord Goff's statement about cheques) was not merely obiter, particularly as it had been followed by the Court of Appeal in *Graham*.[228] Consequently, with some apparent reluctance, it declined to hold that there is an intent permanently to deprive where the property in question is a cheque. *Clark* is an unfortunate decision. It is by no means obvious that what was said about cheques by Lord Goff was part of the ratio in *Preddy* and the fact that a case is subsequently followed is not in itself relevant to whether a statement is part of its ratio. Moreover, *Graham* is not a strong authority in support because the Court of Appeal simply relied on Lord Goff's statement without discussion. As explained above, the case of cheques seems to fall four-square within s 6(1).[229] In *Mitchell*,[230] where *Preddy*, *Graham* and *Clark* do not appear to have been considered, the Court of Appeal took the contrary view obiter to that taken in those cases.

10.92 So far, we have been concerned with 'borrowings'; an example of a lending falling within s 6(1) would be where D, assistant to a florist (V), lends some cut flowers to X, telling X that he can have them for a week. If the short life of the cut flowers means that when they are returned as intended they will have lost all their goodness and virtue, the lending is for a period and in circumstances equivalent to an outright disposal and D is deemed by s 6(1) to intend permanently to deprive V of the flowers, even though he does not mean V to be so deprived.

Section 6(2)

10.93 The TA 1968, s 6(2) provides a further explanation of 'treating as one's own to dispose of regardless of the other's rights'. It provides that:

'Without prejudice to the generality of [s 6(1)], where a person, having possession or control (whether lawfully or not) of property belonging to another, parts with the property under a condition as to its return which he may not be able to perform, this (if done for purposes of his own and without the other's authority) amounts to treating the property as his own to dispose of regardless of the other's rights.'

Thus, where D, who is in possession or control of V's property, pawns it, intending to redeem it and return it if he wins a bet, this amounts to 'treating as his own to dispose of regardless of the rights of the other [V]' and his intention to do so is deemed by s 6(1) to be an intention permanently to deprive V of it. The wording of s 6(2) seems clearly to indicate that it applies even though D is convinced that he will be able to perform the condition for return (ie to

---

[226] [1997] 4 All ER 1 at 15.
[227] [2002] 1 Cr App Rep 141, CA. See JC Smith's commentary in [2001] Crim LR 573.
[228] [1997] 1 Cr App Rep 302, CA.
[229] For an analysis of the problems posed by the law in relation to the theft of cheques, see Heaton 'Cheques and Balances' [2005] Crim LR 747.   [230] [2008] All ER (D) 109 (Apr), CA.

redeem the property) if, in fact, he may not be able to do so.[231] In such a case, however, the circumstances may be such that he would be found not to have been dishonest.

Conditional intention

10.94 This rather misleading term is commonly used to describe the defendant's state of mind in the type of case where he looks for something to steal, as where he rifles through V's handbag, intending to keep anything worth keeping but finds nothing worthwhile. In such a case the defendant cannot be convicted of the theft of the handbag or any of its actual contents,[232] although he may be convicted of attempted theft of some or all of the contents of the handbag.[233] The true reason why D cannot be convicted of theft in such a case, and the reason why 'conditional intention' is a misleading description of the defendant's state of mind in relation to the handbag and its actual contents, is that the defendant has no intention permanently to deprive V of the handbag or its actual contents. On the other hand, if D finds something which may, on further examination be worth keeping and he retains it for further examination, it is arguable, at least where he expects that the thing will be worth keeping, that he does commit theft of it because his appropriation at that stage is accompanied by an intention permanently to deprive V of the thing.[234]

Comment

10.95 Except to the extent that s 6 applies, the requirement of an intention of permanent deprival excludes from the law of theft dishonest borrowing, which many think should be included, but this is a question of the proper sphere of the criminal law. Are people to be punished for simply being a nuisance to others? Is it wise to have prohibitory laws (and there are plenty of them as it is) which work only provided that there are no prosecutions in venial cases?[235] Such offences of unauthorised borrowing as exist are covered in paras 10.108–10.124.

Robbery

Key points 10.8

Robbery is stealing aggravated by the use of force or the threat of force immediately before or at the time of doing so, and in order to do so.

---

[231] For a contrary view see *Smith's Law of Theft* (9th edn, 2007) (Ormerod and Williams (eds)) paras 2.339–2.343.

[232] *Easom* [1971] 2 QB 315, CA.

[233] Para 14.119.

[234] See Griew *Theft Acts 1968 and 1978* (7th edn, 1995), paras 2.114–2.187.

[235] For argument in favour of abolishing the requirement of intention permanently to deprive, see Williams 'Temporary Appropriation Should be Theft' [1981] Crim LR 129.

10.96 The TA 1968, s 8(1) provides that:

> 'A person is guilty of robbery if he steals, and immediately before or at the time of doing so, and in order to do so, he uses force on any person or puts or seeks to put any person in fear of being then and there subjected to force.'

Robbery is triable only on indictment. The maximum punishment is life imprisonment.[236]

Need for a theft

10.97 Although the Court of Appeal in *Forrester*[237] regarded it as an open question whether the reference in the TA 1968, s 8 to 'steals' is to be regarded as subject to the definition of theft in the TA 1968, ss 1 to 6, there can be no real doubt that it is to be so regarded.[238] It would be most surprising if the TA 1968, having established in ss 1 to 6 a detailed definition for the purposes of the offence of theft, had then gone on to provide that 'steals' in s 8 was subject to some other undefined meaning. That there can be no real doubt that 'steals' in s 8 is subject to the definition of theft in ss 1 to 6 gains support from *Raphael*[239] and *Mitchell*[240] where the Court of Appeal clearly considered that ss 1 and 6 (and no doubt ss 2 to 5, the other sections subsidiary to s 1) applied to s 8. *Forrester* was not cited to the Court. Presumably it was for that reason that the Court did not consider the correctness of the above statement in that case. Although *Forrester* was not considered in *Raphael* or *Mitchell* it may now safely be considered to be wrong on the present point.

10.98 On the basis that 'steals' means 'commits theft contrary to the TA 1968, s 1', it follows that the necessary ingredients of that offence must be proved on a robbery charge. Thus, for example, a person who forces another to hand over money, believing that he has a legal right to it, is not guilty of robbery since, not being dishonest,[241] he is not guilty of theft, and this is so even though he does not believe he was entitled to use force to get the money.[242] In *Robinson*,[243] for example, it was alleged that D, who was owed £7 by V's wife, approached V, brandishing a knife. A fight followed, during which V dropped a £5 note. D picked it up and demanded the remaining £2 owed to him. Allowing D's appeal against conviction for robbery, the Court of Appeal held that the prosecution had to prove that D was guilty of theft, and that he would not be (under the TA 1968, s 2(1)(a)) if he believed that he had a right in law to deprive V of the money, even though he knew he was not enti-

---

[236] Magistrates' Courts Act 1980, s 17(1) and Sch 1; TA 1968, s 8(2).

[237] [1992] Crim LR 793, CA.

[238] It may be noted that the concluding words of the TA 1968, s 1(1) state that 'steal' is to be construed in accordance with the definition of theft in s 1(1), set out in Key Points 10.1, and that, by s 1(3), ss 2–5 have effect as regards the interpretation and operation of s 1.

[239] [2008] EWCA Crim 1014. See also *Robinson* [1977] Crim LR 173, CA; para 10.98.

[240] [2008] All ER (D) 109 (Apr), CA.   [241] Para 10.70.

[242] *Skivington* [1968] 1 QB 166, CA; *Robinson* [1977] Crim LR 173, CA.

[243] [1977] Crim LR 173, CA.

tled to use the knife to get it. Therefore the trial judge had been wrong to tell the jury that D must have believed he had the legal right to take the money in the way he did.

10.99 Where the defendant has used force on another (or put another person in fear of force) in order to steal but has not achieved the appropriation of any property, and is therefore not guilty of robbery, he can be convicted of assault with intent to rob, which is triable only on indictment and punishable with a maximum of life imprisonment.[244]

Additional elements

10.100 To constitute robbery, a thief must immediately before or at the time of stealing, and in order to do so, use force on any person or put or seek to put any person in fear of force being there and then applied.

10.101 The words 'puts or seeks to put any person in fear' in the TA 1968, s 8(1), make it clear that it is **irrelevant whether or not the person threatened is actually put in fear of being subjected to force**. This was confirmed by the Divisional Court in *B v DPP; R v DPP*,[245] where a submission of no case to answer at a robbery trial in a youth court on the ground that the victim had given evidence that he had not felt threatened or been put in fear had been rejected. The Divisional Court held that this rejection had been correct. It was the intention of the perpetrator rather than the fortitude of the victim which was the touchstone of whether there had been a robbery. The fact that the victim was not put in fear had no bearing on the question of whether the defendant sought to put any person in fear of force being then and there subjected to force.

10.102 The force used or threatened need not be used or threatened against the owner or possessor of the property stolen.[246] Consequently, if a gang uses force against a signalman only in order to stop and steal from a train, its members are guilty of robbery. Difficult questions of degree can arise. If the signalman were bound and gagged by force an hour before the stealing from the train, the gang having operated the signals in the meantime, it could be argued that the force was used immediately before the theft, but there must be some limit unless the word 'immediately' becomes meaningless. Questions of degree are, however, difficult to avoid if the definition of robbery is not to be unduly wide.

10.103 It is clear that there is **no robbery if the force is used or threatened after 'the time' of the stealing** (ie the theft). The thief who uses force to defend his possession after he has taken the goods is guilty of robbery only if it can be established that he is doing so at 'the time' of the theft. This is not limited to the period (possibly a split second of time) during which the appropriation with the *mens rea* for theft initially occurs, since an act of appropriation may be a continuing one.[247] 'The time' of the theft lasts as long as the theft

[244] TA 1968, s 8(2).   [245] [2007] EWHC 739 (Admin), DC.
[246] *Taylor* [1996] 10 Archbold News 2, CA.
[247] *Hale* (1978) 68 Cr App Rep 415, CA; *Gregory* (1982) 77 Cr App Rep 41, CA; para 10.23.

can be said to be still in progress in commonsense terms, ie so long as the defendant is 'on the job'.[248]

10.104 Where force is used, it must be used 'on' a person. In *Clouden*,[249] the Court of Appeal held that this does not require that force be used on the actual person to overpower his resistance, and that force used only to get possession of property can be used 'on' a person. In this case a man who had wrenched a shopping basket from the hands of a woman was held to have been rightly convicted of robbery. The Court of Appeal's view was consciously different from that of the Criminal Law Revision Committee, who did not regard the mere snatching of property, such as a handbag, from an unresisting woman as using force for the purpose of the definition of robbery, though they thought that it might be so if the owner resisted.[250]

10.105 In the case of a threat of force, a threat of future force is insufficient: the threat must be 'then and there' to subject another to force. Whether what the defendant has done or threatened is 'force' is a question of fact for the jury.[251]

10.106 The force must be used or threatened in order to steal; a man who knocks a woman to the ground to rape her and comes close to doing so, but then changes his mind and instead takes her handbag which she has dropped, is not guilty of robbery or assault with intent to rob, although he may be convicted of theft and of attempted rape.

It follows from the requirement that force must be used or threatened in order to steal that an unintentional use or threat of force cannot suffice. Where a threat of force is involved the intention must be to put another in fear for himself; an intent to put someone in fear for another is not enough.[252]

10.107 Robbery is an extremely broad offence. The use of slight force (eg a push) or the threat of slight force in order to steal property suffices to convert a theft into robbery, and constitutes the same single offence as the use of extreme violence or the threat of it. Professor Ashworth has argued that, just as the law of non-fatal offences against the person differentiates between degrees of harm and culpability by a ladder of offences, so as to mark out particularly serious cases from less serious ones, so should robbery. Alternatively, and more radically, robbery could be abolished as an offence, leaving its theft and offence against the person ingredients to be charged separately.[253]

---

[248] *Hale* (1978) 68 Cr App Rep 415, CA; *Atakpu* [1994] QB 69 at 80; *Lockley* [1995] Crim LR 656, CA.

[249] [1987] Crim LR 56, CA.

[250] *Eighth Report of the Criminal Law Revision Committee: Theft and Related Offences* (Cmnd 2977) (1966), para 65.

[251] *Dawson and James* (1976) 64 Cr App Rep 170, CA; *Clouden* [1987] Crim LR 56, CA.

[252] *Taylor* [1996] 10 Archbold News 2, CA.

[253] Ashworth 'Robbery Re-Assessed' [2002] Crim LR 851.

Unauthorised borrowing

Key points 10.9

Whereas theft and robbery require an appropriator of property belonging to another to intend permanently to deprive the other of it, in the following offences under the TA 1968, ss 11, 12 or 12A an intention temporarily to deprive is enough.

Removal of an article from a place open to public

10.108 The TA 1968, s 11(1) provides that:

> 'where the public have access to a building in order to view the building or part of it, or a collection or part of a collection housed in it, any person who without lawful authority removes from the building or its grounds the whole or part of any article displayed or kept for display to the public in the building or that part of it or in its grounds shall be guilty of an offence.'

Such an offence is triable either way[254] and punishable on conviction on indictment with a maximum of five years' imprisonment.[255]

10.109 The offence under s 11(1) covers removals only from non-commercial collections, but if the thing removed is there otherwise than as forming part of, or being on loan for exhibition with, a collection intended for permanent exhibition,[256] it must be removed on a day when the public has access to the building or grounds.[257] Thus, the offence is not committed if a painting is removed from a wholly temporary art exhibition in a church hall on a day when the hall is closed.

10.110 The defendant's belief that he had lawful authority for the removal of the thing in question or that he would have it if the person entitled to give it knew of the removal and its circumstances is a defence.[258] The belief does not have to have been a reasonable one, and the burden of proving it is not borne by the defendant (although he does have an evidential burden in respect of it).[259]

Taking conveyances without authority

10.111 The TA 1968, s 12(1) provides that:

> 'a person shall be guilty of an offence if, without having the consent of the owner or other lawful authority, he takes any conveyance for his own or another's use...'

---

[254] Magistrates' Courts Act 1980, s 17(1) and Sch 1.   [255] TA 1968, s 11(4).
[256] See *Durkin* [1973] QB 786, CA.   [257] TA 1968, s 11(2).
[258] TA 1968, s 11(3).   [259] Ch 4.

The offence is triable only summarily and punishable with imprisonment for up to six months[260] or a fine not exceeding level 5 on the standard scale or both.[261]

Although an offence under s 12(1) is a summary one, the Criminal Justice Act 1988, s 40(1) provides that a count charging a person with it may be included in an indictment if the charge:

- is founded on the same facts or evidence as a count charging an indictable offence; or
- is part of a series of offences of the same or similar character as an indictable offence which is also charged,

but only if (in either case) the facts or evidence relating to the offence were disclosed in material served on a person sent for trial for the indictable offence. If convicted on indictment for an offence under s 12(1) an offender is punishable in the same way as he could have been on summary conviction.[262]

Where a conveyance has been taken and driven away there can be a charge of stealing the fuel consumed, but usually the prosecution rely simply on a charge under s 12(1).

As an offence under s 12(1) is a summary one, an attempt to commit it is not an offence.[263] However, the Criminal Attempts Act 1981, s 9 provides a separate preparatory offence of interference with a motor vehicle with the intention that an offence under the TA 1968, s 12 shall be committed. There is no corresponding offence in relation to other types of conveyance, such as boats and aircraft.

Conveyance

10.112 Although a dictionary definition of a conveyance confines it to a vehicle or carriage, there is no such limitation for the purposes of the TA 1968, s 12, which defines it as '**any conveyance constructed or adapted for the carriage of a person or persons whether by land, water or air, except that it does not include a conveyance constructed or adapted for use only under the control of a person not carried in or on it**'.[264] Thus, an aeroplane or boat is a conveyance, as well as something (like a motor car or motor cycle) which is purely land-based. As the definition implies a thing can be a 'conveyance' even though it lacks either wheels or engine, but it has been held that a horse is not a conveyance for the purpose of s 12 and that s 12 is directed towards artefacts rather than towards animals.[265] It is clear that a conveyance cannot include either a handcart or a trailer because, although passengers can be carried in them, they are not constructed or adapted for this purpose and anyway, even if they are, they are constructed for use only under the control of a person not carried in or on them. For this latter reason, perambulators, pedestrian-controlled trollies and most lawnmowers are not conveyances. However, a conveyance would undoubtedly include a lawnmower constructed or adapted for use

---

[260] This will be increased to 51 weeks when the Criminal Justice Act 2003, s 281(4) and (5) comes into force.
[261] TA 1968, s 12(2).   [262] Criminal Justice Act 1988, s 40(2).   [263] Para 14.105.
[264] TA 1968, s 12(7)(a).   [265] *Neal v Gribble* [1978] RTR 409, DC.

under the control of a person carried on it; it would also include an invalid carriage, whether powered or not, constructed or adapted for use under the control of the occupant. Read literally, the definition includes roller-skates, ice-skates or skis. Such an interpretation would doubtless be avoided if the issue arose, although powered roller-skates (which are powered by a small, integral petrol engine controlled by the skater)[266] would seem to be a different proposition.

Taking

10.113 **The mere unauthorised assumption of possession of a conveyance is not enough to constitute a taking; some movement, however small, must also take place,**[267] **and the movement must not be accidental.**[268] If someone assumes possession of, and moves, a conveyance which has been taken without consent or other authority and then been abandoned, he can be convicted of taking it contrary to the TA 1968, s 12 because there will be a fresh assumption of possession and therefore a 'taking'.[269] It remains to be seen whether there would also be a 'taking' contrary to s 12 if the previous 'taker' had not abandoned the conveyance. As explained in para 10.119, there is a separate offence of driving a conveyance, knowing that it has been taken without authority. It may be that it will be held to exclude the application of the offence of 'taking' where the taker had the requisite knowledge. On the other hand, it would be surprising if a person who assumes possession of, and moves, a conveyance which (unknown to him) has already been 'taken' by another, and not been abandoned, did not commit any offence under s 12.

10.114 **Unauthorised use of a conveyance by a person already in lawful possession or control of a conveyance may amount to a taking.**

An employee who uses his employer's lorry for his own purposes after the expiry of the period for which he is authorised to use it, usually the working day, thereby takes it.[270] So does an employee who, during the period for which he is authorised to use it, appropriates the employer's lorry to his own use in a manner which is inconsistent with the rights of the employer and shows that he has assumed control of it for his own purposes. Consequently, a serious deviation from the employee's proper route may be a taking. In *McKnight v Davies*,[271] D crashed his employer's lorry while driving back to the depot after making some deliveries. Scared by this, he drove to a public house for a drink, then took three men to their houses, then drove to another public house for another drink, parked the lorry near his house and only on the following day returned it to the depot. The Divisional Court, upholding D's conviction under s 12, said that not every brief unauthorised diversion from his proper route by an employed driver during the working day would necessarily involve taking; however, it would if he appropriated the vehicle to his own use in a manner which repudiated the rights of the true owner and showed that

---

[266] It was reported in *The Guardian* on 1 August 2007 that such skates are on sale in the United Kingdom.
[267] *Bogacki* [1973] QB 832, CA.   [268] *Blayney v Knight* (1974) 60 Cr App Rep, 269, DC.
[269] *DPP v Spriggs* [1994] RTR 1, DC.   [270] See, for instance, *Wibberley* [1966] 2 QB 214, CA.
[271] [1974] RTR 4, DC.

he had assumed control of the vehicle for his own purposes, which D had done on leaving the first public house.

A similar principle applies to a bailee. A bailee of a conveyance takes it if he uses it for a purpose other than that for which he has been given permission or after the end of the bailment. In *Phipps and McGill*,[272] D asked the owner of a car if he could borrow it to take his (D's) wife to a London station. The owner agreed on the express condition that D returned the car immediately after dropping his wife, but apparently D brought his wife back because she had missed the train. Instead of returning the car, D drove it to Hastings and did not return it until two days later; the Court of Appeal held that D had taken the car as soon as he drove it outside the purpose or condition of the bailment.

For the defendant or another's use

10.115 The taking must be for the defendant's use or that of another. In *Bow*,[273] the Court of Appeal held that this required that the conveyance should actually be used as a conveyance, as it will be if the defendant drives a car, or coasts downhill in it, or is carried away in a boat as it drifts with the tide. It is clear from the Court of Appeal's decision in *Marchant*[274] that, despite what was said in *Bow*, a conveyance is also taken for the defendant's use or that of another where, even though it is not used as a conveyance, it is taken for later use as a conveyance. Consequently, as in *Pearce*,[275] a person who puts another's dinghy on a trailer and tows it away for later use as a conveyance thereby takes it for his own use, as does someone who pushes a car a few feet, intending to use it later as a conveyance.[276] Provided someone acts in one of the two ways referred to in this paragraph, his motive is irrelevant; thus, a person who drives another's vehicle a few yards to remove it as an obstruction may be convicted of the present offence.[277]

Examples of cases where there is no taking for the use of the defendant or another are where the defendant releases the handbrake of a car so that it runs downhill empty or where he pushes an obstructing vehicle out of the way. Of course, if an intent permanently to deprive can be proved, as where D casts adrift a boat on tidal waters in stormy conditions, there can be a conviction for theft.

Without consent or other lawful authority

10.116 The taking must be without the consent of the owner or other lawful authority. The offence will not be committed if the owner has actually consented to the taking; if there is no actual consent at the time of the taking, the fact that the owner would have consented if he had been asked does not prevent the taking being without consent.[278]

---

[272] (1970) 54 Cr App Rep 300, CA. Also see *Singh v Rathour* [1988] 2 All ER 16, CA.
[273] [1977] RTR 6, CA. Also see *Stokes* [1983] RTR 59, CA.   [274] (1985) 80 Cr App Rep 361, CA.
[275] [1973] Crim LR 321, CA; applied in *Marchant* (1985) 80 Cr App Rep 361, CA, where it was assumed that the defendant in *Pearce* intended to make later use of the dinghy.
[276] See *Marchant* (1985) 80 Cr App Rep 361, CA.
[277] *Bow* (1976) 64 Cr App Rep 54, CA; *Stokes* [1983] RTR 59, CA.   [278] *Ambler* [1979] RTR 217, CA.

A consent obtained by means of a deception is nevertheless valid and cannot prevent the offence being committed. Unlike the situation elsewhere in the criminal law,[279] this is so even if the mistake induced is as to the identity of the deceiver.[280] There is no obvious reason why the law is different here. In *Whittaker v Campbell*[281] D found a driving licence belonging to X, and used it to hire from V a motor vehicle, representing that he was X. The Divisional Court held that, even if V had made a mistake of identity which would have rendered void the contract of hire between him and D, this did not render invalid his consent to D's taking of the conveyance for the purposes of the TA 1968, s 12. *Peart*[282] provides another example. D in Newcastle obtained the owner's consent to the loan of a van by falsely saying that if he were not in Alnwick by 2.30pm he would lose an important contract, whereas his actual intention was to drive to Burnley which is much further away. It was held that the initial taking was with the consent of the owner. Of course, as *Phipps and McGill*[283] shows, once the defendant used the vehicle outside the terms of the bailment the taking became without consent. In addition, those who obtain consent to their taking a conveyance by a false representation may be convicted of fraud contrary to the Fraud Act 2006, s 1.[284]

It remains to be decided whether a consent obtained by force or the threat of force is nevertheless valid so as to prevent an offence under s 12 being committed, but the better view is that it would not be valid.[285]

The TA 1968, 12(7)(b) provides that, in relation to a conveyance which is subject to a hiring agreement or a hire-purchase agreement, 'owner' means the person in possession of it under that agreement. It follows that during the currency of the agreement such a person cannot commit the present offence since he can hardly be said to act without the consent of the owner.

10.117 A taking is not without lawful authority where it is by police or local authority officers in the exercise of statutory powers to remove vehicles which constitute obstructions or are dangerous, or where bailors of conveyances recover them under a term in the bailment.

Belief in lawful authority or that owner would have consented

10.118 Under the TA 1968, s 12(6):

'a person does not commit an offence under [s 12] by anything done in the belief that he has lawful authority or that he would have the owner's consent if the owner knew of his doing it and of the circumstances of it'.

---

[279] Para 7.28.

[280] *Peart* [1970] 2 QB 672, CA; *Whittaker v Campbell* [1984] QB 318, DC.

[281] [1984] QB 318, DC.

[282] [1970] 2 QB 672, CA.

[283] (1970) 54 Cr App Rep 300, CA; para 10.114.

[284] Para 12.3.

[285] *Smith's Law of Theft* (9th edn, 2007) (Ormerod and Williams (eds)), para 10.43; *Hogdon* [1962] Crim LR 563, CCA.

Such a belief does not have to be reasonable; the burden of proving it is not borne by the defendant, but he does have an evidential burden in relation to it.[286] One case where a defendant will believe that he has lawful authority is where he believes the conveyance is his.[287]

Other offences under section 12

Driving or allowing oneself to be carried on conveyance taken contrary to the TA 1968, s 12

10.119 The TA 1968, s 12(1) contains an ancillary offence which is committed where the defendant,

> 'knowing that any conveyance has been taken without [the owner's consent or other lawful authority], drives[288] it or allows himself to be carried in or on it'.

This offence covers cases where the driving is done with the consent of the 'taker' as well as those where it is not. It is triable and punishable in the same way as the 'taking' offence.

In order to be 'carried in or on' a conveyance there must be some movement of it; it is not enough merely to be in or on it.[289]

No doubt the requisite knowledge includes wilful blindness,[290] as it normally does in other statutes.

A person may be guilty of the present offence if the conveyance has, to his knowledge, been stolen and not merely taken temporarily.[291]

Corresponding offences relating to pedal cycles

10.120 Although a pedal cycle falls within the definition of 'conveyance', referred to in para 10.112, the above offences under the TA 1968, s 12(1) do not apply to them.[292] Instead, two similar offences, triable only summarily and punishable with a fine not exceeding level 3 on the standard scale, apply to pedal cycles.[293] A bicycle, tricycle or other vehicle propelled (by pedals) solely by human energy is clearly a pedal cycle. It is a moot point whether 'pedal cycle' also includes an electrically assisted pedal cycle (if it does not, s 12(1) will apply to such a cycle).

---

[286] *MacPherson* [1973] RTR 157, CA; *Briggs* [1987] Crim LR 708, CA; *Gannon* [1988] RTR 49, CA.
[287] *Gannon* [1988] RTR 49, CA.   [288] Para 8.159.
[289] *Miller* [1976] Crim LR 147, CA; *Diggin* (1980) 72 Cr App Rep 204, CA.   [290] See para 3.43.
[291] *Tolley v Giddings* [1964] 2 QB 354, DC.   [292] TA 1968, s 12(5).   [293] TA 1968, s 12(5).

Aggravated vehicle-taking

10.121 The TA 1968, s 12A, which was added by the Aggravated Vehicle-Taking Act 1992, s 1, is aimed at joy-riders who pose a particular danger to society in terms of the risk of death, injury or damage to property. It is limited to mechanically propelled vehicles,[294] and does not cover other types of conveyance such as boats, aeroplanes or horse-drawn coaches. The TA 1968, s 12A provides that:

> '(1) Subject to subsection (3) below, a person is guilty of aggravated vehicle-taking of a vehicle if –
>
> (a) he commits an offence under s 12(1) (in this section referred to as "the basic offence") in relation to a mechanically propelled vehicle; and
>
> (b) it is proved that, at any time after the vehicle was unlawfully taken (whether by him or another) and before it was recovered, the vehicle was driven, or injury or damage was caused, in one or more of the circumstances set out in paragraphs (a) to (d) of subsection (2) below.
>
> (2) The circumstances referred to in subsection (1)(b) are –
>
> (a) that the vehicle was driven dangerously[295] on a road or other public place;[296]
>
> (b) that, owing to the driving of the vehicle, an accident[297] occurred by which injury was caused to any person;
>
> (c) that, owing to the driving of the vehicle, an accident occurred by which damage was caused to any property, other than the vehicle;
>
> (d) that damage was caused to the vehicle.'

10.122 Under s 12A(1)(b) and (2), the prosecution does not have to prove that the dangerous driving, injury or damage was caused by the defendant's driving or by the defendant at all. Nor, under s 12A(2)(b) or (c), need it be proved that there was any fault in the driving of the vehicle.[298] Thus, in *Marsh*,[299] where D, who had taken a pub landlord's car without consent in order to give a barmaid a lift home, hit a woman through no fault of his own when she ran into the road, the Court of Appeal dismissed his appeal against conviction of a s 12A offence. The terms of s 12A(2)(b) had been satisfied, since there was a causal connection between the moving of the car and the accident, and no fault in the driving of the car was required.

---

[294] Para 8.160.

[295] This has the same meaning as 'dangerous driving' under the Road Traffic Act 1988, s 2A(1) (see para 8.166): TA 1968, s 12A(7).

[296] Paras 8.161 and 8.162.

[297] 'Accident' in this context includes a situation where a person has deliberately caused injury: *Branchflower* [2004] EWCA Crim 2042.

[298] *Marsh* [1997] 1 Cr App Rep 67, CA.

[299] [1997] 1 Cr App Rep 67, CA.

10.123 Once it is proved that that driving, injury or damage was caused during the period between the taking of the vehicle contrary to s 12(1) and its recovery,[300] the defendant is fixed with liability for an offence contrary to s 12A, unless he can prove one of the defences under the TA 1968, s 12A(3) in relation to any driving, injury or damage proved by the prosecution. Section 12A(3) provides:

> 'A person is not guilty of an offence under this section if he proves that, as regards any such proven driving, injury or damage as is referred to in subsection (1)(b) above, either –
>
> (a) the driving, accident or damage referred to in subsection (2) occurred before he committed the basic offence; or
>
> (b) he was neither in nor on nor in the immediate vicinity of the vehicle when that driving, accident or damage occurred.'

10.124 An offence under s 12A(1) is triable either way. It is punishable on conviction on indictment with a maximum of two years' imprisonment, or 14 years' if the death of a person is caused by an accident falling within s 12A(2)(b).[301] However, if the only aggravating feature is damage to the vehicle or to other property, which is under £5,000 in value, the offence must be treated as if it was only triable summarily,[302] the maximum punishment being six months' imprisonment[303] or a fine not exceeding the statutory maximum, or both. Unless there are special reasons, a person convicted of an offence under s 12A must be disqualified from driving for not less than 12 months.[304]

Because of the different maxima, s 12A creates two offences, one with a maximum of two years, and one (where death is caused in the specified way) with a maximum of 14.[305]

Making off without payment

> **Key points 10.10**
>
> The offence of making off without payment differs from those dealt with so far in this chapter because it does not require anything to be done with property. Instead, it punishes those who dishonestly make off without payment for goods supplied or services done knowing that payment on the spot is required or expected and intending never to pay. In everyday speech they are often referred to as 'bilkers'.

[300] A vehicle is recovered when it is returned to its owner or other lawful possession or custody, and for this purpose 'owner' means the same as in s 12 (see para 10.116): TA 1968, s 12A(8).
[301] TA 1968, s 12A(4).
[302] Magistrates' Courts Act 1980, s 22 and Sch 2.
[303] This will be increased to 12 months' imprisonment when the Criminal Justice Act 2003, s 282 is in force.
[304] Road Traffic Offenders Act 1988, s 34 and Sch 2. See also s 35A; para 8.163.
[305] *Sherwood; Button* [1995] RTR 60, CA.

10.125 The definition of the offence is set out in the TA 1978, s 3(1), which provides that:

> '…a person who, knowing that payment on the spot for any goods supplied or service done is required or expected from him, dishonestly makes off without having paid as required or expected and with intent to avoid payment of the amount due shall be guilty of an offence.'

An offence under s 3(1) is triable either way and punishable on conviction or indictment with a maximum of two years' imprisonment.[306]

Actus reus

10.126 The defendant must make off without paying as required or expected, in circumstances where payment on the spot for any goods supplied or service done is required or expected.

Making off

10.127 'Makes off' refers to making off from the spot where payment is required or expected; what is the 'spot' depends on the circumstances of each case. It is clear that the following are examples of this offence: walking out of a restaurant without paying the bill and jumping out of a taxi and running off without paying the fare.[307] On the other hand, walking towards the exit of the restaurant or moving towards the door of the taxi, with intent to leave and avoid payment, will not suffice for an offence under the TA 1978, s 3, since there has not yet been a 'making off' from the spot where payment is required or expected (although it may constitute an attempt to commit that offence).[308]

10.128 A moot point is whether a person 'makes off' if he leaves without payment with the consent of the creditor (albeit that it is procured by a false representation). We are not concerned here with the type of case where a taxi driver allows a passenger to leave his taxi in order to go into a house to collect the fare and the passenger never returns, because the driver has not consented to the passenger leaving without paying him and there is no difficulty in saying he makes off without payment. The difficulty is where someone leaves without payment, having deceived the creditor into believing that payment has been made, as where X walks out of a hotel with his suitcases, having told the proprietor that he has paid the receptionist. A Circuit judge appears to have held that one cannot make off if the creditor consents to one's leaving without paying him,[309] but this interpretation is not warranted by the wording of the section and, it is submitted, is not

---

[306] TA 1978, s 4.   [307] *Moberly v Allsop* (1992) 156 JP 514, DC.

[308] *McDavitt* [1981] Crim LR 843, Crown Ct; *Brooks and Brooks* (1982) 76 Cr App Rep 66, CA.

[309] *Hammond* [1982] Crim LR 611, Crown Ct. See also [1983] Crim LR 205 and 573.

the correct view. However, a charge of fraud contrary to the Fraud Act 2006, s 1 would be more appropriate in such a case.

Without payment

10.129 Making off without payment is only an offence if payment on the spot (ie there and then)[310] is required or expected of the defendant for any goods supplied or service done, as in the above examples. 'Goods' has the same meaning[311] as in the TA 1968.[312]

'Payment on the spot' includes cases where payment is required or expected at the time of collecting goods on which work has been done or in respect of which service has been provided.[313] It is not necessary that payment by cash is required or expected; cases where the common understanding is that payment on the spot will be by cheque or credit card or debit card are therefore covered. Normally, the spot on which payment is initially required or expected is the spot from which the defendant makes off without payment but s 3 does not require this. If payment there and then continues to be required, the 'spot' can move from one place to another. This is shown by *Aziz*[314] where D1 and D2, passengers in a taxi, refused to pay the fare on arrival at their destination. The driver said that he would drive them back to their hotel but he then headed for the police station. En route, D1 and D2 made off without payment. The Court of Appeal dismissed D1 and D2's appeals against conviction for making off without payment since, when they made off from the taxi, payment 'on the spot' (ie there and then) was required, as they knew.

10.130 The Court of Appeal has held that the requirement that the defendant must make off 'without having paid as required or expected' is not satisfied if the creditor (or his agent) has agreed that payment would be postponed, because there will be no expectation of payment on the spot, even if that agreement has been procured by a dishonest deception.[315] A moot point is whether a person who purports to pay but does so with a cheque which 'bounces' or with a forged cheque makes off without payment when he leaves the spot where payment is required. Assuming that a person who leaves with the creditor's consent can nevertheless be said to 'make off', the better view is that in the case of a bouncing cheque the person will not make off without payment (because by giving the cheque he discharges, conditionally at least,[316] his liability to pay), whereas in the case of a forged cheque he will make off without having paid as required or expected (because

---

[310] This paraphrase was referred to by the Court of Appeal in *Aziz* [1993] Crim LR 708, CA.

[311] Ie the meaning given by the TA 1968, s 34(2)(b): see para 11.43.   [312] TA 1978, s 5(2).

[313] TA 1978, s 3(2).   [314] [1993] Crim LR 708, CA.   [315] *Vincent* [2001] EWCA Crim 295.

[316] Where a cheque is accepted in payment of a debt it is rebuttably presumed that the parties intend it to be only a conditional discharge of the debt: *Re Romer and Haslam* [1893] 2 QB 286, CA. So far the debt has been satisfied (ie payment has been made) but if the cheque is dishonoured (ie bounces) the right to sue on the original debt revives: *Sayer v Wagstaff* (1844) 5 Beav 415; *Re Romer and Haslam* [1893] 2 QB 286, CA. If the creditor expressly or impliedly promises, in accepting the cheque, to discharge the debtor from his liability to pay the debt regardless of whether the cheque is honoured, the debt is not only satisfied but it does not revive if the cheque is dishonoured, with the result that the creditor's right to sue on it does not revive (although he can sue on the cheque): *Sard v Rhodes* (1836) 1 M & W 153. The case is even stronger where a credit card or debit card is used, but for some reason payment to the creditor is not made by the card company, because there is a

a forged cheque is void and, just like payment with counterfeit money or forged notes, does not operate even as a conditional discharge of the obligation to pay).[317] These points, however, are somewhat academic since the appropriate offence to charge in such a case is generally that of fraud, contrary to the Fraud Act 2006, s 1.

10.131 **An offence is not committed under the TA 1978, s 3 if the payment avoided relates to the supply of goods or the doing of services which is contrary to law, or where the service done is such that payment is not legally enforceable.**[318] For example, a contract with a prostitute for her services is illegal and unenforceable in civil law; in consequence a man who has intercourse with a prostitute and then leaves, having refused to pay her the agreed fee, does not commit an offence under s 3. However, if, unknown to the prostitute, he did not intend to pay before he received the prostitute's services, he could be convicted of obtaining services dishonestly, contrary to the Fraud Act 2006, s 11,[319] but not (it would seem) of rape or other non-consensual sexual offence.[320]

10.132 **An offence is not committed under s 3 if the payment required or expected is not legally due;** for example, the offence is not committed by a passenger who refuses to pay anything to a taxi driver, and makes off, after the driver has in breach of contract abandoned the journey before reaching its destination.[321]

Mens rea

10.133 The *mens rea* required of a person charged with making off without payment is that, **knowing**[322] **that payment on the spot was required or expected, he made off dishonestly and with intent to avoid payment of the amount due.**

10.134 In *Allen*,[323] the House of Lords held that an intent permanently to avoid payment is required; an intent to defer or delay payment is not sufficient. In this case, the defendant left a hotel without paying. At his trial for making off without payment, he put forward the defence that he had been prevented from paying the bill by temporary financial difficulties but had expected to be able to do so subsequently. The House of Lords held that the trial judge had been wrong to tell the jury that an intent not to pay on the spot would suffice, since the defendant could only be convicted if he was proved to have intended never to pay.

---

presumption that the use of the card is accepted by the creditor as an absolute discharge: *Re Charge Card Services Ltd* [1989] Ch 497, CA.

[317] Syrota 'Are Cheque Frauds Covered by Section 3 of the Theft Act 1978?' [1981] Crim LR 412. Also see *Hammond* [1982] Crim LR 611, Crown Ct.

[318] TA 1978, s 3(3).

[319] See paras 12.35–12.42.

[320] Para 9.23.

[321] *Troughton v Metropolitan Police* [1987] Crim LR 138, DC.

[322] No doubt 'knowing' includes being wilfully blind; para 3.43.

[323] [1985] AC 1029, HL.

10.135 Where there is evidence which may cause a jury to find that the defendant was not dishonest, dishonesty is a question of fact, to be determined by answering the questions set out by the Court of Appeal in *Ghosh*.[324] The provisions of the TA 1968, s 2(1) do not apply to 'dishonestly' in the offence of making off without payment because they only apply to the offence of theft.[325]

FURTHER READING

Arlidge and Parry on Fraud (3rd edn, 2007), Ch 9

Griew *The Theft Acts 1968 and 1978* (7th edn, 1995) Chs 1, 2, 3, 5, 6 and 13

Ormerod and Williams (eds) *Smith's Law of Theft* (9th edn, 2007) Chs 1, 2, 6, 7, 10 and 11

Simester and Sullivan 'The Nature and Rationale of Property Offences' in *Defining Crimes* (2005) (Duff and Green (eds))

ATH Smith *Property Offences* (1994) Chs 1–9, 12–14 and paras 20.69–20.105

JN Spencer 'The Aggravated Vehicle-Taking Act 1992' [1992] Crim LR 699

[324] See paras 10.73–10.75.   [325] See TA 1968, s 1 (3).

11

Other offences under the
Theft Act 1968

OVERVIEW

This chapter deals with burglary, aggravated burglary, blackmail, handling stolen goods, dishonestly retaining a wrongful credit and going equipped for stealing or burglary.

11.1 Unless otherwise indicated the offences discussed in this chapter are triable either way,[1] the maximum punishments stated relating to convictions on indictment.[2]

Burglary and aggravated burglary

Key points 11.1

There are two types of burglary:

- entering a building or part of a building as a trespasser with intent to steal in the building or part trespassed in or to inflict grievous bodily harm on any person therein or to do unlawful damage to the building or anything therein;

- having entered a building or part of a building as a trespasser, stealing anything in the building or part trespassed in or inflicting grievous bodily harm on any person therein or attempting to do so.

It is aggravated burglary to commit burglary of either type when the defendant has with him a firearm, imitation firearm, explosive or weapon of offence.

---

[1] Magistrates' Courts Act 1980, s 17(1) and Sch 1.
[2] For special rules relating to jurisdiction over blackmail, handling stolen goods and retaining a wrongful credit, see paras 12.69–12.71.

Burglary

11.2 The TA 1968, s 9, as amended by the Sexual Offences Act 2003, provides:

> '(1) A person is guilty of burglary if –
>   (a) he enters any building or part of a building as a trespasser and with intent to commit any such offence as is mentioned in sub-s (2) below; or
>   (b) having entered any building or part of a building as a trespasser he steals or attempts to steal anything in the building or that part of it or inflicts or attempts to inflict on any person therein any grievous bodily harm.
> (2) The offences referred to in sub-s (1)(a) above are offences of stealing anything in the building or part of a building in question, of inflicting on any person therein any grievous bodily harm therein, and of doing unlawful damage to the building or anything therein.'

There are two separate types of burglary, under s 9(1)(a) and (b) respectively.[3] Both are punishable with a maximum of 14 years' imprisonment if committed in respect of a building or part of a building which is a dwelling but otherwise with a maximum of 10 years.[4] Because the maximum punishment for each type of burglary depends on whether or not a dwelling is alleged and proved to have been involved, each type consists of two distinct offences: burglary in a dwelling and burglary in any other type of building.[5]

Burglary comprising the commission of, or an intention to commit, an offence triable only on indictment is itself triable only on indictment. So is burglary in a dwelling if a person there was subjected to violence or the threat of violence[6] or if the defendant was over 18 and had two previous convictions for burglary in a dwelling at the time of the burglary.[7]

The first type of burglary

11.3 This is defined by the TA 1968, s 9(1)(a), whose effect is that a person is guilty of burglary if he enters any building or part of a building as a trespasser and with intent to commit one of the offences specified in s 9(2).

Actus reus

Entry

11.4 The TA 1968 does not define what constitutes an 'entry' into a building (or part) for the purposes of s 9. In *Collins*,[8] it was said by the Court of Appeal that there had to be an 'effective and substantial' entry, which seemed narrower than the rule which had applied

---

[3] *Downer* [2009] EWCA Crim 1361.   [4] TA 1968, s 9(3).
[5] This is the effect of *Courtie* [1984] AC 463, HL; para 3.50, n 111.
[6] Magistrates' Courts Act 1980, s 17(1) and Sch 1.
[7] Powers of Criminal Courts (Sentencing) Act 2000, s 111(4).   [8] [1973] QB 100 at 106.

to 'entry' under earlier legislation, viz that the insertion, however minimal, of any part of the body, whether to commit the further offence or to effect entry, sufficed.[9] However, in *Brown*,[10] the Court of Appeal rejected the 'substantial' requirement, saying that an **entry need only be 'effective' and that this was a question for the jury**. It held that there could be an entry, for the purpose of s 9, by a person whose whole body had not been inside the building (or part) and that consequently there had been an entry by a defendant who had been seen half inside a shop window, rummaging inside it. In fact, the Court of Appeal held that it would be astounding if it was held that there was not an entry by a smash-and-grab raider who inserted a hand through a shop window to grab goods. *Brown* was followed in *Ryan*,[11] which shows that 'effectiveness' does not require that the insertion of the defendant's body should be effective for the purpose of committing the relevant further offence. In *Ryan* the Court of Appeal held that it was clear from *Brown*[12] that, for the purpose of s 9, a person could enter a building even if only part of his body was within the building and that it was totally irrelevant that he was incapable of committing his intended crime (stealing) because he had become trapped. The Court dismissed the appeal against conviction, based on the absence of an entry, of the defendant who had become trapped in a window after only his head and right arm had been inserted, the rest of his body remaining outside the building.

While the meaning of the word 'effective' in this context is unclear, minimal intrusions, as where the defendant's fingers are inserted through a gap between a window and its frame in order to open the window, would be very unlikely to be held to be effective entries by a jury.

11.5 Under the pre-Theft Act law on burglary, an entry could be effected merely by the insertion of an instrument without the intrusion of any part of the body provided it was inserted to commit a relevant further offence (eg a hook to extract (steal) a ring), but not if it was inserted merely to facilitate access by a person's body.[13] It remains to be decided to what extent, if any, such an insertion, even if effective, can be an entry, but it would seem that, at least, an insertion to facilitate entry cannot be (although it could amount to an attempt to enter).

As a trespasser

11.6 Trespass is a concept of the civil law. In *civil* law a person enters a building or part of a building as a trespasser if he intentionally, recklessly or negligently **enters a building or part of a building in the possession of another and he enters without a right by law or permission to do so**.[14] However, a negligent entry does not suffice for burglary,[15] subjective *mens rea* is required. A person who involuntarily enters a building, as where he is dragged in, cannot be a trespasser.

---

[9] *Bailey* (1818) R & R 341.

[10] [1985] Crim LR 212, CA. This report does not contain all the points contained in the transcript of the Court of Appeal's judgment.

[11] (1996) 160 JP 610, CA.   [12] [1985] Crim LR 212, CA.   [13] *Anon* (1584) 1 And 117.

[14] See Murphy *Street on Torts* (12th edn, 2007) 286–287.   [15] See para 11.12.

11.7 Rights of entry are granted by statute to certain people for certain purposes. For instance, a police officer entering a building with a search warrant authorised under some statute is not a trespasser if he enters with the intention of searching pursuant to such a warrant, but he is if he enters with the intention of stealing something inside the building or for some other purpose.

11.8 Likewise, a permission to enter will be granted for a particular purpose or purposes. If someone, who has permission to enter for a particular purpose or purposes, enters for some purpose for which he does not have permission, he enters in excess of permission and, therefore, as a trespasser. For example, in *Jones and Smith*,[16] it was held that a man who had a general permission to enter his father's home entered it as a trespasser when he entered it to steal his father's television set because he entered in excess of his permission. Clearly, his permission did not extend to entering the house to steal.

It appears that permission to enter for a particular purpose may be given by someone (X) other than the person (Y) in possession of the premises if that person (X) has Y's authority (express or implied) to do so. In the famous case of *Collins*,[17] the Court of Appeal said that it was unthinkable that an 18-year-old woman was unable to give such permission in the circumstances, whatever the position in the law of tort. The issue is of some importance because members of a family, lodgers and employees, for example, are impliedly (and often expressly) authorised to invite other people generally, or particular classes of persons or particular persons to enter (eg the family home, lodging house or business premises). Thus, if a lodger is authorised by her landlord to invite women, but not men, to her room and Jill and Jack come to her room at her invitation, Jill is not a trespasser but Jack is. Such an authority can, of course, be withdrawn or altered in terms of who may be invited. In addition, it would be most unlikely to be found that a very young child had any implied authority. If a family member, lodger, employee, and so on, does not have authority or acts in excess of a limited authority, and the entrant knows or is reckless that that person does not have authority to invite him in, the entrant can be convicted of burglary under the TA 1968, s 9(1)(a) if he has the necessary intent.

11.9 Permission to enter may be express or implied. For instance, in the case of shops there is an implied permission during opening hours for members of the public to enter for the purposes of inspecting goods on display or making purchases. A person who enters a building with permission, intending to commit a relevant offence, enters in excess of his permission and enters as a trespasser.

A permission to enter may not necessarily extend to every part of the building. Thus, a person may lawfully enter a building, such as an hotel or shop, but enter the manager's office or stockroom as a trespasser; equally he may be a lawful guest at a meal in a private house but enter a bedroom as a trespasser. In both of these cases the entry as a trespasser will be into a 'part of a building'.[18] On the other hand, if a person lawfully enters a building (or part of a building) and then stays on after the expiry of his entitlement (as where

---

[16] [1976] 3 All ER 54, CA. See, further, Pace 'Burglarious Trespass' [1985] Crim LR 716.
[17] [1973] QB 100, CA.
[18] *Hillen and Pettigrew v ICI (Alkali) Ltd* [1936] AC 65 at 69–70, per Lord Atkin.

someone, who has entered a shop for a lawful purpose, decides to hide and stay on after the shop closes, and does so, in order to steal) he cannot be convicted of burglary because, although he becomes a trespasser by staying 'after hours', he has not entered the building (or part) as a trespasser.[19] If, however, he then moves into another part of the building to carry out the theft, he will then commit burglary because he will have entered that part as a trespasser with the requisite intent.

Building or part of a building

11.10 The TA 1968, s 9(4) states that **references to a building also apply to an inhabited vehicle or vessel (whether or not the person having a habitation in it is there at the time).** Clearly, a caravan or houseboat which is someone's permanent home is an 'inhabited vehicle or vessel', even though he is not there at the time; so is a caravan or houseboat which is used as a holiday home during the summer during those weeks or weekends in which it is being so used, but whether it is inhabited during the rest of the summer is open to doubt. Certainly, a 'holiday home' caravan or boat is not inhabited when it is closed up for the winter.

Apart from s 9(4), the Act is silent. **However, it seems that a substantial portable structure with most of the attributes normally found in buildings can be a 'building' for the purpose of burglary, provided there is an element of permanence in the site which it occupies.** In *B and S v Leathley*,[20] a decision by the Crown Court in its appellate capacity, it was held that a freezer container measuring 25ft by 7ft by 7ft and weighing three tons, which had occupied the same position for three years and was likely to remain there for the foreseeable future, had doors and was connected to mains electricity, was a 'building' for the purposes of burglary. This decision can usefully be contrasted with *Norfolk Constabulary v Seekings*,[21] where articulated trailers which had been used as temporary stores for about a year, and which had electric power, steps and lockable shutters, were held by the Crown Court in its appellate capacity not to be 'buildings' for the purposes of burglary. Clearly, a tent is not a building.

It has not yet been decided when a partially erected house or similar structure becomes a building.

11.11 A 'part of a building' does not necessarily mean a separate room; it also includes a physically marked-out area in a room, such as the area behind a counter in a shop, from which the defendant is plainly excluded, whether expressly or impliedly.[22]

Mens rea

As to entry as a trespasser

11.12 Part of the *mens rea* required for an offence of burglary under the TA 1968, s 9(1) (a) is that **the defendant must know that he is entering as a trespasser (ie he must know**

---

[19] *Laing* [1995] Crim LR 395, CA.
[21] [1986] Crim LR 167, Crown Ct.
[20] [1979] Crim LR 314, Crown Ct.
[22] *Walkington* [1979] 2 All ER 716, CA.

he is entering without a right by law or permission to do so) or be reckless as to this fact. Negligence as to the trespass is insufficient. This was established by the Court of Appeal in *Collins*,[23] decided at a time (before the Sexual Offences Act 2003 amended s 9) when entry as a trespasser with intent to rape was burglary. About two o'clock early one morning in June an 18-year-old woman went to bed. She (V) wore no night apparel and the bed was very near the open lattice-type window of her room. V awoke about two hours later and saw in the moonlight a vague form crouched in the open window. V leapt to the conclusion that her boyfriend was paying her an ardent nocturnal visit; she sat up in bed, and (according to D, who had arrived to have intercourse with her, by force if necessary) helped him to enter the room, after which they had full intercourse; then V realised that he was not her boyfriend but D, who was later convicted of burglary. The Court of Appeal, allowing D's appeal, held that the prosecution had to prove that D entered as a trespasser and knew it or was reckless as to this, and that, on the basis that D had not entered the room before he was helped in by V, the trial judge had not directed the jury adequately on the need for D's entry to have been accompanied by knowledge on his part that he was entering as a trespasser, or recklessness as to this. In a case such as *Jones and Smith*,[24] the defendant must know that he is entering in excess of the permission given to him or be reckless as to this.

Ulterior intent

11.13 The defendant's entry must be accompanied by the ulterior intent to commit one of the offences specified in the TA 1968, s 9(2), viz:

- to steal anything in the building or, as the case may be, the part of the building trespassed in; or
- to inflict grievous bodily harm on any person in the building or, as the case may be, the part of the building trespassed in; or
- to do unlawful (ie criminal) damage to the building or anything therein (whether or not the defendant has trespassed in the part in which the damage is intended to occur).

Although the wording of the provision is not entirely free from doubt, it would seem that the defendant's intention at the time of entry must relate to property or a person then in the building (or part) entered as a trespasser;[25] for example, to steal property then in the building trespassed in. Consequently, it is not burglary to enter a bank as a trespasser, intending to steal some bullion when it is delivered to the bank; nor is it burglary to enter

---

[23] [1973] QB 100, CA.

[24] [1976] 3 All ER 54, CA; para 11.8. In *Collins* [1973] QB 100, CA, the Court of Appeal did not discuss whether Collins knew or was reckless as to whether he was entering in excess of the supposed permission. The case is not easy to reconcile with *Jones and Smith*.

[25] For a discussion of this point, see White 'Lurkers, Draggers and Kidnappers: The Further Offence in Burglary' (1986) 150 JPN 37 and 56.

a building as a trespasser, intending to inflict grievous bodily harm on someone who is being dragged in behind.

The requisite intent will exist only if the defendant's intended conduct would, if carried out in accordance with his intentions, amount to the offence allegedly intended. Thus, a person who trespasses in a building to take something to which he believes he has a legal right lacks an intent to steal and does not commit burglary.

11.14 Where a person is charged with entry into a building or part of a building with intent to steal, and the indictment does not assert an intention to steal a specific or identified object, the defendant can be convicted if at the time of entry he had the necessary intent to steal something therein, even though he did not intend to steal a specific thing but merely intended to steal anything that he might find worth stealing, or even though there was in fact nothing there worth his while to steal.[26] Thus, a person who enters part of a department store, intending to steal from the till, can be convicted of burglary even though the till is empty. This is an example of the fact that it is irrelevant that it is impossible for the defendant to carry out his ulterior intention.[27]

11.15 The punishment for burglary by entry with intent is a branch of preventive justice, like the punishment of attempts to commit crime. It goes further than an offence of attempt, however, because it punishes mere preparation for crime, whereas an attempt requires conduct which is more than merely preparatory.[28]

The second type of burglary

11.16 A person is guilty of the second type of offence of burglary, defined by the TA 1968, s 9(1)(b), if, having entered any building or part of a building as a trespasser, he steals or attempts to steal anything in the building or that part of it or inflicts or attempts to inflict on any person therein any grievous bodily harm.

'Trespasser' and 'building' have the same meanings as in the other type of burglary. The important distinction is that this type of offence requires the defendant, having entered the building or part as a trespasser, actually to have committed or attempted the offence of theft or the offence of inflicting grievous bodily harm, contrary to the Offences Against the Person Act 1861, s 20,[29] in terms both of the *actus reus* and *mens rea* of the relevant offence;[30] on the other hand he is not required to have had the intent to commit such an offence when he entered. The defendant must know or be reckless

---

[26] *Walkington* [1979] 2 All ER 716, CA; *A-G's References (Nos 1 and 2 of 1979)* [1980] QB 180, CA.

[27] For another example, see *Ryan* (1996) 160 JP 610, CA; para 11.4.   [28] See para 14.104.

[29] Or an offence of administering etc poison etc so as thereby to endanger life or inflict grievous bodily harm, contrary to the Offences Against the Person Act 1861, s 23; para 7.114.

[30] The suggestion in an unanswered question by the Court of Appeal in *Jenkins* [1983] 1 All ER 1000, that the infliction of grievous bodily harm need not amount to an offence (so that a trespasser could be guilty of burglary if his entry caused unforeseen harm to an occupant, such as a heart attack through shock) was not commented on by the House of Lords on appeal ([1984] AC 242). It would be unfortunate if it ever became the law, since it would extend a serious offence to cover something which is not in itself an offence.

that he has entered as a trespasser when he commits or attempts one of these offences. It is irrelevant whether or not he realised at the time of entry that he was entering as a trespasser. Thus, if a person enters a building, thinking that he has permission, and later realises that he has not and then steals something inside or inflicts grievous bodily harm on someone inside (eg the occupier who is trying to eject him), he is guilty of burglary of the present type. Of course, if the trespasser's conduct does not constitute theft (eg because he thought he had a right in law to the property) or an offence of infliction of grievous bodily harm (eg because he was acting in reasonable self-defence against a lethal attack by another trespasser), or an attempt to commit such an offence, he is not guilty of burglary of the present type.

11.17 There is no obvious reason why s 9(1)(b) does not cover such entrants who proceed to commit criminal damage in the building; depending on the circumstances criminal damage may be subject to a lower maximum than burglary, sometimes significantly.[31]

General

11.18 Both types of offence require a trespassory entry into a building or part of a building. To be guilty of the first (s 9(1)(a)) type of offence, it must be proved that, at the time of his trespassory entry, the defendant intended to commit one of the specified offences. Someone who enters a building as a trespasser with the intention of going to sleep inside is not guilty of burglary of the first type if he subsequently forms the intention of stealing something from the premises, but if he actually steals or attempts to steal the thing in question, he is then guilty of burglary of the second (s 9(1)(b)) type by virtue of the commission or attempted commission of theft. Where a person enters a building, or part, as a trespasser with intent to steal or inflict grievous bodily harm, and commits the intended offence or attempts to do so, he can be charged with either type of offence, since the two types are not mutually exclusive;[32] in practice he will normally be charged with the second type of offence in such a case.

Aggravated burglary

11.19 By the TA 1968, s 10(1):

> 'A person is guilty of aggravated burglary if he commits any burglary and at the time has with him any firearm or imitation firearm, any weapon of offence, or any explosive.'

Aggravated burglary is punishable with a maximum of imprisonment for life,[33] and is triable only on indictment.

---

[31] Para 13.2.   [32] *Taylor* [1979] Crim LR 649, CA.   [33] TA 1968, s 10(2).

To commit aggravated burglary, a person must have with him a firearm or imitation firearm, a weapon of offence or an explosive at the time he commits burglary. Where the burglary alleged is entry as a trespasser with intent to steal etc, this means the time of the entry into a building, or part, as a trespasser with an appropriate ulterior intent. Where the burglary alleged is that, having entered as a trespasser, the defendant stole etc, it means the time when, having entered a building or part as a trespasser, a person actually steals or inflicts grievous bodily harm, or attempts such, whether or not he had with him the article when he entered.[34] Thus, a trespasser who uses a weapon of offence, which he has found after entry, to inflict grievous bodily harm can be convicted of aggravated burglary of the second type.

Definitions of articles specified in s 10(1)

11.20 'Firearm' includes an airgun or air pistol, and 'imitation firearm' means anything which has the appearance of being a firearm, whether capable of being discharged or not.[35]

11.21 'Explosive' means any article manufactured for the purpose of producing a practical effect by explosion, or intended by the person having it with him for that purpose.[36]

11.22 A 'weapon of offence' means any article made or adapted for use for causing injury to or incapacitating a person, or intended by the person having it with him for such use.[37] A rubber hose filled with metal would be an article adapted for use for causing injury and a screwdriver would be a 'weapon of offence' if intended for use for causing injury. Handcuffs are an example of an article made for incapacitation, and rope is an example of one intended for such use if it is intended to use it to tie up someone in the building. Where there is an issue as to whether the article was made or adapted for one of the specified purposes, it is for the jury to decide.[38] In the case of flick-knives, butterfly knives and certain similar articles, judicial notice has been taken of the fact that they are made for the purpose of causing injury, and the judge can direct the jury to find them to be made for use for causing injury.[39] In the case of an article made or adapted for one of the specified purposes, it is irrelevant that the defendant did not intend to use it for such a purpose.

There is authority that an article not made or adapted for an offensive purpose which the defendant did not have with him for the purpose of injury or incapacitation will become an article 'intended for such use' if, having formed the intention so to use it, he instantly uses it for such a purpose.[40] On this basis, if D uses a screwdriver in order to gain entry to a house and then, when confronted by its occupier as he steals something,

---

[34] *Francis* [1982] Crim LR 363, CA; *O'Leary* (1986) 82 Cr App Rep 341, CA; *Kelly* (1992) 97 Cr App Rep 245, CA.

[35] TA 1968, s 10(1)(a).   [36] TA 1968, s 10(1)(c).   [37] TA 1968, s 10(1)(b).

[38] *Williamson* (1977) 67 Cr App Rep 35, CA.

[39] *Simpson* [1983] 3 All ER 789, CA; *DPP v Hynde* [1998] 1 All ER 649, DC.

[40] *Kelly* (1992) 97 Cr App Rep 245, CA.

he decides to use it (and he does use it) to injure the occupier, D can be convicted of aggravated burglary. This can be contrasted with the situation in respect of the corresponding definition of 'offensive weapon' under the Prevention of Crime Act 1953, s 1, under which a person commits an offence if he has with him an offensive weapon in a public place. There, an article not made or adapted to cause injury and which was not previously intended to cause injury does not become an offensive weapon if the person who has it with him suddenly forms the intent to use it to injure and then and there does so.[41]

For the purposes of being an article intended for use for causing injury to or incapacitating someone, it is not necessary that the defendant intended to use the article to injure or incapacitate someone in the course of the burglary itself. It suffices that he had it with him for such use on another occasion.[42]

Has with him

11.23 The nub of s 10 is to punish those who are armed with a relevant article while committing burglaries. If a weapon is carried not by a burglar but by an accomplice waiting outside the building, aggravated burglary is not committed.[43] Reference to the case law on other similarly worded offences relating to firearms and offensive weapons[44] suggests that, in order for a burglar to have with him a firearm etc, the article need merely be near to him and be readily accessible to him, but in *Klass*[45] the Court of Appeal took a stricter approach in respect of aggravated burglary, which requires the burglar to be carrying (ie armed with) the relevant article at the time of the burglary.

11.24 The case law on other offences also suggests that 'has with him' means 'knowingly has with him' the thing which is a firearm, imitation firearm, weapon of offence or explosive[46] (so that, for example, a burglar whose swagbag contains a revolver is not guilty of aggravated burglary if he thought the bag was empty). However, it would appear from such cases that a defendant does have sufficient knowledge if he knows that he has something with him although he does not know that it is a firearm, imitation firearm etc.[47] If the courts follow this case law, an offence carrying a maximum of life imprisonment will be one of strict liability as to the nature of the thing which the defendant has with him.

---

[41] *Ohlson v Hylton* [1975] 2 All ER 490, DC.

[42] *Stones* [1989] 1 WLR 156, CA. For a criticism of this decision, see Reville 'The Mischief of Aggravated Burglary' (1989) 139 NLJ 835.

[43] *Klass* [1998] 1 Cr App Rep 453, CA.   [44] *Pawlicki* [1992] 3 All ER 902, CA.

[45] [1998] 1 Cr App Rep 453, CA.   [46] *Cugullere* [1961] 2 All ER 343, CCA.

[47] See, for example, *Vann and Davis* [1996] Crim LR 52, CA (having with one a firearm in a public place, contrary to the Firearms Act 1968, s 19); *Hussain* [1981] 2 All ER 287, CA (possession of firearm without a certificate); *Bradish* [1990] 1 QB 981, CA (possession of a prohibited weapon).

Blackmail

Key points 11.2

Blackmail consists of making an unwarranted demand with menaces with a view to gain for oneself or another or an intent to cause loss to another.

11.25 By the TA 1968, s 21(1):

'A person is guilty of blackmail if, with a view to gain for himself or another or with intent to cause loss to another, he makes any unwarranted demand with menaces; and for this purpose a demand with menaces is unwarranted unless the person making it does so in the belief –

(a) that he has reasonable grounds for making the demand; and

(b) that the use of the menaces is a proper means of reinforcing the demand.'

Blackmail is an offence triable only on indictment and punishable with imprisonment for a maximum of 14 years.[48]

Actus reus

Demand

11.26 The essence of the offence is a demand, so that if the other ingredients of blackmail are present a person whose demand is unsuccessful is guilty of blackmail and not merely of an attempt. **The demand need not be express**, since (taken together with the menaces) it may be implied by a request or suggestion[49] or other conduct. **The nature of the act or omission demanded is immaterial;**[50] the offence is not limited to a demand for the transfer of property, although this represents the usual type of blackmail.

In *Treacy v DPP*,[51] the House of Lords held by a majority that a demand by letter is made when the letter is posted; it is therefore irrelevant that the letter is never delivered (or that its recipient is illiterate). A similar rule probably applies to an oral demand, so that it is irrelevant that the addressee is, for instance, deaf or cannot understand what is said (at least, if an ordinary person would have understood).

---

[48] TA 1968, s 21(3).

[49] As in the pre-Act cases of *Studer* (1915) 11 Cr App Rep 307, CCA, and *Collister and Warhurst* (1955) 39 Cr App Rep 100, CCA.

[50] TA 1968, s 21(2).   [51] [1971] AC 537, HL.

Menaces

11.27 When the word was first used in this branch of the law, 'menaces' was limited to threats of violence, but it has long since come to include **'threats of action detrimental to or unpleasant to the person addressed'**.[52] It is immaterial whether the menaces do or do not relate to action to be taken by the person making the demand.[53] The thug who says 'Give me money or the boys will beat you up', and the man who says 'Give up your claim to my Picasso or my daughter will tell the world that you seduced her', are both as guilty of blackmail as the man who reinforces his demands with threats of action by himself.

It was held by the Court of Appeal in *Lawrence and Pomroy*[54] that the word 'menaces' is an ordinary word which a jury can be expected to understand and that consequently it is only rarely that a judge will need to enter on a definition of that word. However, there are two occasions[55] when a direction may be required:

- If, on the facts known to the defendant, his threats might have affected the mind of an ordinary person of normal stability, although they did not affect the addressee, the jury should be told that they would amount to menaces.[56]
- If, although they would not have affected the mind of a person of normal stability, the threats affected the mind of the victim, the jury should be told that the menaces would be proved if the defendant was aware of the likely effect of his actions on the victim, eg because he knew of some unusual susceptibility on the victim's part.[57]

Mens rea

11.28 The demand with menaces must be made by the defendant with a view to gain for himself or another, or with intent to cause loss to another. Under the TA 1968, s 34(2)(a) 'gain' and 'loss' are confined to money or other property.[58] Consequently, it is not blackmail to demand with menaces that a person should cease committing adultery or should commit adultery or should surrender the custody of a child. On the other hand, it is not necessary that the defendant should be motivated by the desire to achieve economic gain or to cause economic loss. In *Bevans*,[59] for example, a man in severe pain, who threatened to shoot a doctor if he did not give him an injection of morphine, was held guilty of blackmail. The drug was property, the man had demanded it with menaces (and thereby acted with a view to gaining it for himself); it was irrelevant that his motive had been to gain relief from pain rather than economic gain.

---

[52] *Thorne v Motor Trade Association* [1937] AC 797 at 817, per Lord Wright.   [53] TA 1968, s 21(2).

[54] (1971) 57 Cr App Rep 64, CA. See also *Garwood* [1987] 1 All ER 1032, CA; *Venn* [2009] All ER (D) 153 (Nov), CA.

[55] *Garwood* [1987] 1 All ER 1032, CA.   [56] Also see *Clear* [1968] 1 QB 670, CA.

[57] *Garwood* [1987] 1 All ER 1032, CA.

[58] 'Property' bears the meaning given by the TA 1968, s 4(1) (see para 10.26): TA 1968, s 34(1).

[59] (1988) 87 Cr App Rep 64, CA.

11.29 The gain in view or loss intended need not be permanent,[60] which differentiates blackmail from theft and robbery. Hence, woman D, who tells woman V that D will reveal details of V's sexual aberrations to her fiancé unless V lends her a dress for a ball, is guilty of blackmail.

11.30 Under the TA 1968, s 34(2)(a), **'gain' includes a gain by keeping what one has, as well as getting what one has not; 'loss' includes a loss by not getting what one might get, as well as losing what one has.** The width of these terms means that blackmail extends to a wide variety of demands with menaces which do not involve a demand for the transfer of property. For example, a demand that the victim should abandon a claim against the defendant to specific and identifiable property can constitute blackmail if it is accompanied by menaces, because the defendant has a view to gain by keeping what he has; of course, he also has an intent to cause loss to the victim by the victim not getting what he might get. A person who demands with menaces that compromising letters be destroyed acts with an intent to cause loss to another (by the latter losing what he has) and therefore he can be convicted of blackmail. However, it has been held that, where the abandonment of a claim to property is demanded, the particular property must be specific and identifiable; consequently, where the demand is that the victim should forebear to sue to enforce a debt it is not made with a view to gain or with intent to cause loss.[61] This is not a necessary, or even obvious, interpretation of the words of s 34(2).

A person who demands with menaces a job can be convicted of blackmail since he acts with a view to gain for himself. A person acts with a view to gain if he seeks to recover a debt, for he is endeavouring to get money which he has not got although it is legally due to him,[62] but so long as the menaces go no further than the threat of legal proceedings no offence is committed since it is inconceivable that the demand with menaces would be found to be unwarranted.

Unwarranted demand with menaces

11.31 As was stated above, the demand with menaces must be unwarranted. For this purpose the TA 1968, s 21(1) provides that **a demand with menaces is unwarranted unless the person making it does so in the belief that he has reasonable grounds for making the demand and that the use of the menaces is a proper means of reinforcing the demand.** Legally, it is irrelevant whether or not the defendant's beliefs are reasonable; the question is whether he had such beliefs, but, of course, the reasonableness of his alleged belief is evidentially important in relation to his credibility. The defendant does not have to prove these beliefs, but this does not mean that the prosecution must negative the existence of a belief for which there is no evidence. Instead, the defendant has an evidential burden and, unless he adduces evidence (or there is evidence from another

---

[60] TA 1968, s 34(2)(a).   [61] *Golechha and Choraria* [1989] 3 All ER 908, CA.
[62] *Parkes* [1973] Crim LR 358, Crown Ct; approved in *A-G's Reference (No 1 of 2001)* [2002] 3 All ER 840, CA.

source) which raises the issue that he had the beliefs required, the jury will be obliged to find that the demand with menaces was unwarranted.[63]

Assuming that the issue is raised, the prosecution must negative either the defendant's alleged belief that he had reasonable grounds for making the demand, or his alleged belief that the use of the menaces was a proper means of reinforcing it; otherwise the jury must find that the demand with menaces was not unwarranted and must acquit the defendant. Normally, it will be easier to negative the second of these alleged beliefs, since a person who makes a demand with menaces may well believe he has reasonable grounds for making the demand but realise that the use of the menaces in question was not a proper means of reinforcing the demand. For example, a prostitute may well believe that she has reasonable grounds for demanding payment of a debt by a customer (although she knows the debt is not legally enforceable), but realise that her threat to have the customer beaten up otherwise is not a proper means of reinforcing the demand.

11.32 It seems clear that, subject to what was said in *Harvey*, below, and unlike the tests of dishonesty under *Ghosh*,[64] the defendant is to be judged solely according to his own understanding of general moral standards. It follows that the person whose understanding of general moral standards is of standards which are low may succeed in a defence in a case where another person who understands standards to be higher may not, even though the jury thinks that he acted reasonably.

It was held by the Court of Appeal in *Harvey*[65] that no threat of an act known or suspected by the defendant to be unlawful could be believed by him to be proper, even though he might regard it as justified. This seems incontrovertible where the act is a serious crime since D cannot credibly say that he believed that a threat of murder or rape, as in *Harvey*, was proper according to general moral standards. On the other hand, it is less acceptable where the threatened act involves a minor illegality since D may well believe that to threaten a minor offence is proper according to his understanding of general moral standards.

Handling

> ### Key points 11.3
>
> The offence of handling stolen goods can be committed in 18 different ways. 'Stolen goods' are not limited to goods obtained by theft. In particular, they also include goods obtained by blackmail or fraud, and the proceeds of goods obtained by theft, blackmail or fraud. The goods must remain stolen at the time of handling. The handling must occur after the end of the course of 'stealing' and must be done dishonestly and with knowledge or belief that the goods are 'stolen'.

---

[63] *Lawrence and Pomroy* (1971) 57 Cr App Rep 64, CA. [64] Para 10.74.
[65] (1981) 72 Cr App Rep 139, CA.

11.33 By the TA 1968, s 22:

> 'A person handles stolen goods if (otherwise than in the course of the stealing) knowing or believing them to be stolen goods he dishonestly receives the goods, or dishonestly undertakes or assists in their retention, removal, disposal or realisation by or for the benefit of another person, or if he arranges to do so.'

Handling stolen goods is punishable with imprisonment for a maximum of 14 years.

11.34 There is a considerable overlap between handling and theft. In many instances, a person who 'handles' stolen goods is thereby appropriating property belonging to another and is also guilty of theft if he has the necessary *mens rea*.[66] Nevertheless, there are two reasons for having the separate offence of handling. One is that sometimes handling stolen goods does not involve the dishonest appropriation of property belonging to another with the intention of permanently depriving that person; for example, because the dealing with them does not constitute an appropriation (as in the case of handling by 'arranging' to do something with them, which is discussed below). The other reason is that professional receivers or disposers of stolen property (otherwise known as 'fences' and 'placers', respectively) are a serious nuisance and it is widely believed that without them there would be fewer thieves[67] since many 'professional' thieves would be deterred from their activities if they could not pass on to others the task of disposing of stolen goods at a profit or the task of laundering them. The existence of the separate offence of handling, which is more severely punishable than theft, ensures that large-scale fences and placers can be punished more severely than the thieves for whom they act.

Actus reus

Forms of handling

11.35 The TA 1968, s 22(1) states that handling consists of receiving stolen goods, or undertaking or assisting in their retention, removal, disposal or realisation by or for the benefit of another, or arranging to do one of these things. As will be shown later, this definition comprises 18 different forms of handling.[68] However, although Lord Bridge stated, obiter, in *Bloxham*[69] that s 22(1) creates two distinct offences (one of receiving, and the other capable of being committed in the other ways specified in s 22(1)), the weight of authority[70] is in favour of the view that the provision creates only one offence, which can be committed by receiving or by any of the other ways specified.

---

[66] *Dolan* (1975) 62 Cr App Rep 36, CA; *Sainthouse* [1980] Crim LR 506, CA.
[67] A point made by the Court of Appeal in *Shelton* (1986) 83 Cr App Rep 379, CA.
[68] *Nicklin* [1977] 2 All ER 444, CA.   [69] [1983] 1 AC 109 at 113.
[70] *Nicklin* [1977] 2 All ER 444, CA; *Griffiths v Freeman* [1970] 1 All ER 1117, DC.

If Lord Bridge's view was correct, an indictment alleging an unparticularised offence of handling would be bad for duplicity, but it has been held by the Court of Appeal[71] and by the Divisional Court[72] that such an indictment is not defective, although the better practice is to particularise the form of handling relied on, and, if there is any uncertainty about the form of handling in question, it will be advisable to have more than one count in the indictment. In the case of uncertainty, only two counts should generally be inserted since they will normally cover every form: one count for receiving, and the other either for the other forms of handling or for one or two of those forms (eg assisting in the removal or disposal of stolen goods by another).[73] Similar principles apply to charges before a magistrates' court.[74] If the defendant is charged solely with receiving, he may not be convicted on that count of some other form of handling.[75]

The various forms of handling are set out below.

Receiving

11.36 **Receiving consists of a 'single finite act' whereby 'the defendant came into possession' of the goods.**[76] 'Possession' here means exclusive control. **'Receiving' also involves a receipt from someone else,** so that a person who finds stolen goods and helps himself to them does not receive them.[77] It is possible for a receiver to be in joint possession with the thief or another receiver if he shares exclusive control with such a person.

It follows from the requirement of possession that a person who holds goods while he inspects them during negotiations with the thief does not receive them, nor does someone who helps the thief to unload the goods from a lorry.[78] In order to be in possession (and therefore to be a receiver), a person need not have physical contact with the goods so long as he takes them under his exclusive control or an agent or employee does so acting under his orders, in which case the agent or employee is also a receiver if he has the necessary *mens rea*.[79] Of course, the defendant can only be convicted of handling if at the relevant time, here the time of the receiving, he had the requisite *mens rea*. If he did not, but later discovers that the goods are stolen, any subsequent dealing with them by him may constitute a handling of the types outlined in paras 11.39 to 11.41.

Arranging to receive

11.37 **This requires preparation by the defendant, or a concluded agreement between the defendant and another (eg the thief), for the receiving of stolen goods by the defendant.** A mere offer to receive stolen goods, or the participation in negotiations for their receipt by him (as where the defendant negotiates to purchase stolen goods), will not

---

[71] *Nicklin* [1977] 2 All ER 444, CA.   [72] *Griffiths v Freeman* [1970] 1 All ER 1117, DC.
[73] *Nicklin* [1977] 2 All ER 444, CA; *Willis* [1972] 3 All ER 797, CA.
[74] *Griffiths v Freeman* [1970] 1 All ER 1117, DC.   [75] *Nicklin* [1977] 2 All ER 444, CA.
[76] *Smythe* (1980) 72 Cr App Rep 8 at 13.   [77] *Haider* (1985) unreported, CA.
[78] *Hobson v Impett* (1957) 41 Cr App Rep 138, DC.   [79] *Smith* (1855) Dears CC 559.

suffice. However, certainly in the case of an offer, it may amount to an attempt to handle (in that it is an attempt to arrange to receive).

11.38 The other forms of handling set out below differ in one vital respect from receiving or arranging to receive in that they must all be done 'by another' or 'for the benefit of another'. If D1 and D2 are jointly charged in one count of an indictment with an act of handling 'by or for the benefit of another', the other person must be someone other than D1 and D2.[80]

Undertaking the retention, removal, disposal or realisation of stolen goods for the benefit of another

11.39 These four forms of handling are appropriate to cover the case where it is the defendant, either alone or with another, who retains, removes, disposes of or realises the stolen goods for the benefit of another. A person who undertakes one of the four activities solely for his own benefit cannot be convicted of handling, unless he has received the goods with the relevant *mens rea*. Thus, if C who has innocently received the goods simply retains them for his own benefit, he cannot be convicted of handling, although (unless he paid for them) he may be guilty of theft.

The four activities can be explained as follows.

- 'Retention' means 'keeping possession of, not losing, continuing to have'.[81]
- 'Removal' clearly refers to the movement of stolen goods from one place to another. Thus, a person undertakes the removal of stolen goods for the benefit of another if he transports the goods to a hideout for the benefit of the thief or some other person. However, a very slight movement of goods probably does not suffice.
- 'Disposal' covers not only the dumping or giving away of stolen goods but also their destruction or transformation, as where the defendant melts down stolen candlesticks for the benefit of the thief or another.[82]
- 'Realisation' means the exchange of stolen goods for money or some other property; the realisation is by the seller, not the buyer.[83] A person who sells stolen goods as agent for a third party (eg the thief) undertakes their realisation for the benefit of another. However, as was held by the House of Lords in *Bloxham*,[84] a person who sells stolen goods on his own behalf does not undertake their realisation for the benefit of another because the buyer benefits from the purchase and not from the realisation

---

[80] *Roberts* [1993] 9 Archbold News 2, CA; *Gingell* [2000] 1 Cr App Rep 88, CA. This restriction does not apply to a conspiracy to handle where one co-defendant has agreed to commit one of these forms of handling by or for the benefit of another co-defendant: *Slater and Suddens* [1996] Crim LR 494, CA.

[81] *Pitchley* (1972) 57 Cr App Rep 30, CA.

[82] Griew *The Theft Acts 1968 and 1978* (7th edn, 1995) paras 15–26; contrast Williams *Textbook of Criminal Law* (2nd edn, 1983) 687 ('disposal' limited to alienation).

[83] *Bloxham* [1983] 1 AC 109, HL.   [84] [1983] 1 AC 109, HL.

(which benefits the seller only). In such a case, the seller can only be convicted of handling if he received the stolen goods with the relevant *mens rea*.

Assisting in the retention, removal, disposal or realisation of stolen goods by another

11.40 These four forms of handling are appropriate to cover cases where the defendant provides assistance to another person who is undertaking or going to undertake the retention, removal, disposal or realisation of stolen goods.

'Assist' was construed in a wide way by the Court of Appeal in *Kanwar*.[85] Here, D was charged with assisting in the retention of stolen goods but the Court's statement would seem to apply to the other three forms of assistance. **'Assistance', the Court held, requires that something be done by the defendant for the purpose of enabling the goods to be retained etc**; it is not limited to physical acts since verbal representations, whether oral or written, for the purpose of enabling stolen goods to be retained etc can suffice. The requisite assistance, the Court stated, need not be successful in its object. Further elucidation of 'assist' was provided by the Court of Appeal in *Coleman*,[86] where it was held that the term includes helping or encouraging.

Although the decision in *Kanwar* does not refer to the possibility of assisting by failing to do something, there is authority (as will be seen shortly) that in one case a person can assist in the retention of stolen goods by another by an omission to act.

There is some overlap with cases of 'undertaking'. For example, a person who joins with another in removing stolen goods for the latter's benefit not only undertakes their removal for the benefit of another, but also assists in that removal by another.

'Retention', 'removal', 'disposal' and 'realisation' have already been defined, but the following are examples of these terms in the context of assistance.

11.41 A person assists in the retention of stolen goods by another if he puts the thief in touch with a warehouse keeper, or covers stolen goods in the possession of a handler in order to conceal them, or tells lies so as to make it more difficult for the police to find stolen goods retained by the thief. On the other hand, a refusal to answer questions put by the police as to the whereabouts of stolen goods does not amount to handling,[87] even though it may well assist in their retention by another. However, if the goods have been left on his premises by the thief or a handler such a refusal may be evidence that the defendant has permitted them to remain there, which does constitute assisting in their retention.[88] Where the permission has not been communicated to the other but the defendant passively allows the goods to remain under his control, there is only an omission to get rid of the goods on his part. Nevertheless, it has been held that this constitutes assistance in their retention.[89] This is the exceptional case where an omission can

---

[85] [1982] 2 All ER 528, CA.   [86] (1985) 150 JP 175, CA.   [87] *Brown* [1970] 1 QB 105, CA.
[88] *Brown* [1970] 1 QB 105, CA.
[89] *Brown* [1970] 1 QB 105, CA; *Pitchley* (1972) 57 Cr App Rep 30, CA.

constitute 'assistance'. Merely to use stolen goods does not suffice, since it does not in itself amount to assistance in their retention.[90]

There will be assistance in the removal of stolen goods by another if the defendant lends a lorry for their removal. An example of assistance in the disposal of stolen goods by another occurs where the defendant advises the thief as to how to get rid of stolen goods. On the other hand, merely to accept the benefit of a disposal by another does not in itself suffice, since it does not amount to assistance in the disposal,[91] although if the benefit consists of the proceeds[92] of the original stolen goods and they are received by the defendant he may be convicted of handling by receiving.

A person assists in the realisation of stolen goods by another if he puts a thief in touch with a fence.

Arranging to undertake or assist in the retention, removal, disposal or realisation of stolen goods by or for the benefit of another

11.42 These eight forms of handling require no explanation in the light of what has been said in paras 11.39 to 11.41. An example covered by these forms is agreeing to send a van to collect the thief and the stolen goods, which constitutes arranging to assist in the removal of stolen goods by another.

Because the offence of handling can only be committed if the goods are already stolen at the time of the alleged act of handling, any arrangement, including an arrangement to receive, made before goods are stolen will not constitute handling stolen goods.[93] It may, however, constitute the separate offence of conspiracy to handle.[94]

Stolen goods

11.43 The TA 1968, s 34(2)(b) states that 'goods':

'includes money and every other description of property,[95] except land, and includes things severed from the land by stealing.'

It will be noted that, although it would not normally be so described, a thing in action is 'goods' for the present purpose because it falls within 'every other description of property'.

11.44 By the TA 1968, s 24, as amended by the Fraud Act 2006 (FA 2006), Sch 1, '**stolen goods' is not limited to goods which have been stolen (contrary to the TA 1968, s 1); the term also includes goods obtained by blackmail (contrary to the TA 1968, s 21)**[96] **or by fraud (within the meaning**[97] **of the FA 2006).**[98] References hereafter to 'steal', 'stolen',

---

[90] *Sanders* (1982) 75 Cr App Rep 84, CA.   [91] *Coleman* (1985) 150 JP 175, CA.
[92] Para 11.46.   [93] *Park* (1987) 87 Cr App Rep 164, CA.
[94] *Park* (1987) 87 Cr App Rep 164 at 173. For conspiracy, see Ch 14.
[95] 'Property' has the meaning given by the TA 1968, s 4(1) (see para 10.26): TA 1968, s 34(1).
[96] Paras 11.25–11.32.   [97] Paras 12.3–12.28.   [98] TA 1968, s 24(4).

'theft' and 'thief' must be understood in this extended sense.[99] Because a child under the age of criminal responsibility (10) cannot be guilty of an offence, someone of the age of criminal responsibility cannot handle goods 'stolen' by such a child.[100] The same would be true when the goods were 'stolen' by someone who lacked the necessary *mens rea* or who had the defence (incapacity) of insanity. The person handling the goods in such a case would normally, however, be guilty of the theft of them. On the other hand, where the goods were stolen by someone who committed the relevant *actus reus* with the necessary *mens rea* but who had an excuse such as duress by threats, they would be stolen goods. This is because the fact that a person has an excuse does not mean that an offence has not been committed, but simply that that person is excused from liability for it.[101]

In addition, goods which have not been stolen in England or Wales are stolen goods if they have been the subject of an act elsewhere (including Scotland and Northern Ireland) and that act:

(a) **was criminal when and where it occurred, and**

(b) **if it had occurred in England and Wales would have satisfied the requirements of the TA 1968, s 1 or 21 or of fraud within the meaning of the FA 2006.**[102]

Lastly, references to stolen goods also include money which is dishonestly withdrawn from an account to which a 'wrongful credit' has been made, but only to the extent that the money derives from the credit.[103] 'Wrongful credit' is defined by s 24A(2A); see para 11.59.

The fact that the goods were stolen may be proved by evidence of the conviction of the thief; in such a case he must be taken to have stolen the goods unless the contrary is proved.[104]

If the alleged thief has not been tried, or has been tried but has been acquitted, in respect of the alleged theft, this does not prevent the goods being found to be stolen on a handling charge if the evidence persuades the jury at the trial for handling that the goods were stolen. That evidence may consist of admissions by the defendant of facts within his knowledge (such as how he acquired the goods) from which the jury may legitimately infer that the goods were stolen.[105] On the other hand, the defendant's belief that the goods were stolen is not enough on its own to permit an inference by the jury that the goods were stolen.[106]

11.45 For the offence of handling to be committed **the goods must not only have been stolen, but remain stolen at the time of their handling.** In this context the TA 1968,

---

[99] TA 1968, s 24(4).   [100] *Walters v Lunt* [1951] 2 All ER 645, DC.

[101] See paras 2.20, 2.25.   [102] TA 1968, s 24(1).

[103] TA 1968, s 24A(8), inserted by the Theft (Amendment) Act 1996, s 2(1), provides this. Section 24A(7) applies this to all references to 'stolen goods' in the TA 1968.

[104] Police and Criminal Evidence Act 1984, s 74(1), (2).

[105] *McDonald* (1980) 20 Cr App Rep 288, CA.

[106] *A-G's Reference (No 4 of 1979)* (1980) 71 Cr App Rep 341, CA.

s 24(3) is important. It provides that no goods which have been stolen are to be regarded as having continued to be stolen after one of the following events has occurred:

- *After they have been restored to the person from whom they were stolen or to other lawful possession or custody* These words were not satisfied in *Greater London Metropolitan Police Commissioner v Streeter*,[107] for example, where cartons of cigarettes stolen from V were seen on the thief's lorry by V's security officer. The security officer marked the cartons for future identification and informed the police. The police then followed the lorry to D's shop where he took delivery of the cartons. The Divisional Court held that neither the security officer nor the police had purported to exercise possession or control over the cartons, but had merely waited to see what happened. The cartons had therefore not ceased to be stolen when they were handled by D. It is often difficult to decide whether goods have been restored to lawful possession or custody, particularly when the police have traced the goods. **The crucial question here is whether the police officer has reduced the stolen goods into his possession, and this depends upon the intention with which he has acted.** In *A-G's Reference (No 1 of 1974)*[108] it was held that a police officer, who had removed the rotor arm of a car containing goods about which the officer wished to question the driver, would have reduced them into his possession if he had acted with intent to take charge of them so that they could not be removed and so that he could have the disposal of them; but, if he had retained an open mind as to whether he should take possession and merely removed the rotor arm in order that the driver should not get away without interrogation, he would not have reduced them into his possession.

- *After the person from whom they were stolen and any other person claiming through him have otherwise ceased as regards those goods to have any right to restitution in respect of the theft* An illustration of this provision is where A, the thief, obtains the goods from B under a contract which is voidable because of A's misrepresentation. If B, on realising the misrepresentation, affirms the contract, he thereby ceases to have any right to restitution of the goods and they therefore cease to be stolen goods at that point of time.

11.46 For the purpose of the offence of handling stolen goods, **references to 'stolen goods' include the proceeds of such goods within the terms of the TA 1968, s 24(2)(a) and (b).** Section 24 states that:

> 'references to stolen goods include, in addition to the goods originally stolen and parts of them (whether in their original state or not), –
>
> (a) any other goods which directly or indirectly represent or have at any time represented the stolen goods in the hands of the thief as being the proceeds of any disposal or realisation of the whole or part of the goods stolen or of goods so representing the stolen goods; and

---

[107] (1980) 71 Cr App Rep 113, DC.   [108] [1974] QB 744, CA.

> (b) any other goods which directly or indirectly represent or have at any time represented the stolen goods in the hands of a handler of the stolen goods or any part of them as being the proceeds of any disposal or realisation of the whole or part of the stolen goods handled by him or of goods so representing them.'

'The thief' means the person by whose conduct, with the appropriate *mens rea*, the goods were originally stolen or obtained by fraud or blackmail. 'A handler' means any person who has committed the *actus reus* of handling with the appropriate *mens rea*. The requirement that the goods must directly or indirectly represent or have at any time represented the stolen goods 'in the hands' of the thief or a handler is wider than it may seem because 'in the hands of' means 'in the possession or under the control of'.[109]

11.47 The operation of s 24(2) can be illustrated as follows. A steals a car (or obtains it by fraud or blackmail). He sells it to B for £1,000 and receives that sum in cash. The car and cash are now both stolen goods, the latter because it directly represents the original stolen goods (the car) in the hands of the thief (A) as the proceeds of the car's realisation or disposal. Therefore, if A then gives £500 of the £1,000 to C, who receives the money knowing that it has represented part of the original stolen goods, C can be convicted of handling. If C buys a camera with the £500, the camera becomes stolen goods once it is in his hands because it indirectly represents the original stolen goods in the hands of a handler as the proceeds of the realisation or disposal of goods representing the original stolen goods. Consequently, if E receives the camera from C, knowing that it has represented part of the stolen goods in the hands of C, E can be convicted of handling stolen goods. However, if F receives the camera from E, unaware that it represents the original stolen goods, and then sells it for cash, the cash which F receives will not become stolen goods because, lacking *mens rea*, F is not a handler and therefore that cash does not represent the original stolen goods in the hands of a handler as proceeds of their realisation or disposal. Thus, if G receives that cash from F, G cannot be convicted of receiving stolen goods, even though he knows all the material facts.

Limitation

11.48 The requirement that the handling must have been 'otherwise than in the course of the stealing' (ie the stealing by which the goods originally became stolen goods) means that the original thief cannot commit handling so long as the stealing continues, nor can an accomplice to the theft (ie someone who had aided, abetted, counselled or procured it). The purpose of the limitation seems to be to protect a perpetrator of, or an accomplice to, a stealing from being liable for handling on the basis of acts done as part of their enterprise of stealing. Suppose that D1 steals a leather coat at D2's request. He walks 20 yards to D2's car and hands the coat to D2. D1 and D2 are arrested a few seconds later. D1 has undertaken the removal of the stolen goods for the benefit of another (D2) and D2 has received those goods. However, if both these forms of conduct were in the course of D1's stealing neither can be convicted of handling the stolen coat.

---

[109] *Forsyth* [1997] 2 Cr App Rep 299, CA.

It is difficult to define exactly when the course of the stealing finishes, but clearly, as in the case of the 'time' of stealing in robbery,[110] it is not limited to the period (possibly a slight second of time) during which the act of appropriation with *mens rea* whereby the goods were stolen initially occurs. It would seem that, by analogy with robbery, 'the course of the stealing' lasts as long as the stealing can be said to be still in progress in commonsense terms.[111] If so, any handling of goods which have been stolen by a person will be done in the course of the stealing if it is done at the scene of the crime or while he is leaving the immediate vicinity of the theft with the goods; on the other hand, handling of the goods four hours later after they have been driven 200 miles from the scene of the crime is clearly not done in the course of the stealing. The difficulty, of course, comes in drawing the line in between; this may be more difficult, however, in the abstract than in a concrete case.

It must be emphasised that, once the course of the stealing has ended, even the original thief of the goods can be convicted of handling them. An example would be if, after the course of the stealing, he helps a fence to whom he has sold them to move the stolen goods from one hiding place to another, since he would be assisting in their removal by another.

11.49 Unless there is an issue on the evidence that the defendant was the thief or that the handling was in the course of the stealing, the prosecution does not have to prove that the handling was 'otherwise than in the course of the stealing'; indeed, the judge should not even tell the jury about these words.[112]

Mens rea

Knowledge or belief[113]

11.50 **None of the actions described above is enough to amount to handling unless the defendant either knows or believes that the goods are stolen at the time of the act of**

---

[110] Para 10.103.

[111] See further the comments in para 10.103, which would seem to be equally applicable here. Depending on the facts, the 'course of the stealing' may be very brief, as in *Pitham and Hehl* (1976) 65 Cr App Rep 45, CA. In that case, X offered to sell V's furniture to D1 and D2. D1 and D2 inspected the furniture and agreed to buy it. They paid X and then removed the furniture. They were convicted of handling stolen goods and appealed unsuccessfully against conviction, contending that their acts did not take place 'otherwise than in the course of stealing'. The Court of Appeal dismissed their appeals on the ground that X's offer to sell amounted to appropriation (see para 10.13) and the offence of theft was complete at that stage. What D1 and D2 had done thereafter had been done after the course of the stealing had concluded. Although this decision has been criticised (see *Smith's Law of Theft* (9th edn, 2007) (Ormerod and Williams (eds)) para 13.77), it can be supported on the ground that X's part in the stealing (theft) was complete and there was no evidence that D1 and D2 had aided, abetted, counselled or procured X to commit that stealing. Therefore, the involvement of the only party to the enterprise of stealing the furniture was complete. See Allen *Criminal Law* (10th edn, 2009) 540–541 for a similar argument.

[112] *Cash* [1985] QB 801, CA.

[113] JR Spencer 'Handling, Theft and the Mala Fide Purchaser' [1985] Crim LR 92; Williams 'Handling, Theft and the Purchaser who Takes a Chance' [1985] Crim LR 432; JR Spencer 'Handling and Taking Risks – A Reply to Professor Williams' [1985] Crim LR 440.

handling alleged.[114] It follows that, goods being received at the moment when they come into the possession of a person, the subsequent acquisition of knowledge by that person that they are stolen does not of itself make him a handler,[115] although if he then goes on to commit some other act of handling, such as undertaking their disposal for the benefit of another, he can be convicted of handling on that ground. 'Undertaking' and 'assisting' can be continuing forms of conduct, and where this occurs it is enough that the defendant only discovers that the goods are stolen after he began to handle them in one of these ways, provided he has not yet ceased to do so.

It must be remembered that if a person, who has innocently received as a gift stolen goods, subsequently decides to keep them when he discovers that they are stolen, he commits theft, since his keeping them as owner amounts to an appropriation under the TA 1968, s 3(1). It would be different if the goods were transferred to him for value in good faith because the TA 1968, s 3(2) would prevent him being guilty of theft (see para 10.20).

11.51 A person 'knows' that goods are stolen if he is certain of this, as where he is told by the thief or someone else with first-hand knowledge that they are stolen.[116] The Court of Appeal stated in *Hall*[117] that 'belief' was something short of 'knowledge', and might be said to be the state of mind of a person who said to himself: 'I cannot say I know for certain that those goods are stolen, but there can be no other reasonable conclusion in the light of all the circumstances, in the light of all that I have heard and seen'.[118] In other words, **for 'belief' the defendant must be virtually certain. It is clear that suspicion – even a very strong one – that goods are stolen is not enough,[119] nor is wilful blindness.**[120] However, it has been held that knowledge or belief may be inferred from wilful blindness,[121] which is somewhat difficult to understand if the suspicion involved in wilful blindness is not enough for 'belief'. What is it which is inferable from wilful blindness which constitutes 'belief'? The courts have not supplied an answer.

---

[114] *Brook* [1993] Crim LR 455, CA. For an analysis of the position of the innocent receiver with subsequent *mens rea*, see Tunkel (1983) 133 NLJ 844.

[115] *Brook* [1993] Crim LR 455, CA.

[116] *Hall* (1985) 81 Cr App Rep 260, CA. The test of 'knowledge or belief' being subjective, it is not enough that a person ought to have known the goods were stolen: *Atwal v Massey* [1971] 3 All ER 881, DC.

[117] (1985) 81 Cr App Rep 260, CA.

[118] The Court of Appeal in *Hall* continued that this was enough for belief even if the defendant said to himself: 'Despite all that I have seen and all that I have heard, I refuse to believe what my brain tells me is obvious'. The Court of Appeal in *Forsyth* ([1997] 2 Cr App Rep 299, CA) held that this was potentially confusing because a jury might conclude that a defendant was guilty if there were circumstances of great suspicion from which the only reasonable conclusion was that the goods were stolen but which the defendant could not bring himself to believe.

[119] *Grainge* [1974] 1 All ER 928, CA; *Moys* (1984) 79 Cr App Rep 72, CA.

[120] *Griffiths* (1974) 60 Cr App Rep 14, CA; *Moys* (1984) 79 Cr App Rep 72, CA. As to 'suspicion' and 'wilful blindness' see further paras 3.45 and 3.48.

[121] *Griffiths* (1974) 60 Cr App Rep 14, CA; *Moys* (1984) 79 Cr App Rep 72, CA; *Forsyth* [1997] 2 Cr App Rep 299, CA.

Clearly, there is little difference between 'knowing' and 'believing' in this context (as in others). It has been held that 'knowledge or belief' are words in ordinary usage in English and that it is not necessary in every case for the jury to be given any definition of them,[122] which is rather surprising in the light of what has just been said about these terms. It has also been held, however, that in cases 'where much reference is made to suspicion, it will be prudent to give [a direction]'.[123]

11.52 The answer to the question, 'How much must the defendant know or believe?' is this. The defendant need not know the nature of the goods,[124] an important point if they are in a locked trunk, for example, but he must know or believe enough facts about the way in which the goods have been acquired or dealt with as to indicate that, in law (whether or not he realises this),[125] they have been 'stolen'. Where the charge relates to the proceeds of the original stolen goods the defendant must know the relevant history of those proceeds.

Proof of knowledge or belief

11.53 This may be assisted by the so-called 'doctrine of recent possession'. This common law 'doctrine' applies where the defendant received or otherwise handled[126] recently stolen goods. Under the 'doctrine', the judge may direct the jury that they may, if they think fit, in the absence of an explanation by the defendant or if they are satisfied beyond reasonable doubt that any explanation given is untrue, infer that he knew or believed that they were stolen.[127] Of course, the jury are not obliged to draw the inference, and the onus of proving knowledge or belief remains on the prosecution throughout.[128]

The 'doctrine of recent possession' is misnamed,[129] since it has nothing to do with goods recently possessed but concerns the possession or handling of recently stolen goods. Moreover, it is not even a doctrine since it is merely an application of the ordinary rules of circumstantial evidence.

11.54 Quite apart from the common law 'doctrine', the TA 1968, s 27(3)[130] lays down a special rule to assist in the proof of knowledge or belief. The rule supplements the general rules about the admissibility of 'bad character evidence'. It applies where the defendant is being prosecuted at the trial in question[131] only for handling stolen goods and evidence

---

[122] *Smith* (1976) 64 Cr App Rep 217, CA; *Harris* (1986) 84 Cr App Rep 75, CA; *Reader* (1977) 66 Cr App Rep 33, CA.

[123] *Toor* (1986) 85 Cr App Rep 116, CA.   [124] *McCullum* (1973) 57 Cr App Rep 645, CA.

[125] Ignorance of the criminal law is no defence: para 3.73.   [126] *Ball* [1983] 2 All ER 1089, CA.

[127] *Schama and Abramovitch* (1914) 11 Cr App Rep 45, CCA; *Aves* [1950] 2 All ER 330, CCA.

[128] *Schama and Abramovitch* (1914) 11 Cr App Rep 45, CCA; *Aves* [1950] 2 All ER 330, CCA.

[129] *Ball* [1983] 2 All ER 1089 at 1092.

[130] For a discussion of this provision, see Munday 'Handling the Evidential Exception' [1988] Crim LR 345.

[131] *Bradley* (1979) 70 Cr App Rep 200, CA.

has been given of his having or arranging to have in his possession the goods in question, or of his undertaking or assisting in, or arranging to undertake or assist in, their retention, removal, disposal or realisation. In such a case s 27(3) provides that the following evidence is admissible:[132]

> 'for the purpose of proving that [the defendant] knew or believed the goods to be stolen goods:
>
> (a) evidence that he has had in his possession, or has undertaken or assisted in the retention, removal, disposal or realisation of, stolen goods from any theft taking place not earlier than 12 months before the offence charged; and
>
> (b) (provided that seven days' notice in writing has been given to him of the intention to prove the conviction) evidence that he has within the five years preceding the date of the offence been convicted of theft or of handling stolen goods.'

Section 27(3) does not authorise the introduction of evidence which goes beyond what it specifically describes.[133] Thus, evidence given under para (a) is limited to the fact that the defendant has had in his possession, or has undertaken or assisted in the retention etc of, stolen goods from any theft taking place not earlier than 12 months before the offence of handling charged and to the description of those goods. The result is that evidence may not be given under s 27(3) that the defendant knew or believed those goods to be stolen or as to the circumstances whereby he came by them.[134] Likewise, evidence given under para (b) is limited to a recital of the conviction, when and where it occurred, and a description of the goods[135] (with the result that evidence of other details may not be given under that paragraph).

Dishonesty

11.55 Knowledge or belief that the goods were stolen is not enough. The prosecution must also prove that, when he handled the goods, the defendant did so dishonestly. **Dishonesty is a question of fact, to be determined by answering the questions set out in *Ghosh* by the Court of Appeal.**[136] The provisions of the TA 1968, s 2(1) do not apply to 'dishonestly' in the offence of handling stolen goods because they only apply to the offence of theft.[137] No doubt, on the ground that he was not dishonest a person would not be found to have dishonestly handled stolen goods, even if he knew them to be stolen, if he acquired them in order to return them to the owner, or to hand them over to the police.

---

[132] Subject to the judge's discretion to exclude it if the prejudicial effect of the evidence outweighs its probative value: *Knott* [1973] Crim LR 36, CA; *Hacker* [1995] 1 All ER 45, HL.

[133] The evidence described in (a) and (b) cannot be used for any other purpose, eg to prove dishonesty (*Duffus* (1994) 158 JP 224, CA) or an act of handling. Thus, if the defendant admits knowledge or belief that the goods were stolen, evidence of type (a) or (b) is inadmissible: *Duffus* (1994) 158 JP 224, CA.

[134] *Bradley* (1979) 70 Cr App Rep 200, CA; *Wood* [1987] 1 WLR 779, CA.

[135] *Hacker* [1995] 1 All ER 45, HL.

[136] Paras 10.73–10.75.   [137] See the TA 1968, s 1(3).

Likewise, it would be most unlikely for a person to be found to have dishonestly handled stolen goods if he induced a thief to hand a stolen gun over to him in order to prevent the thief committing suicide by shooting himself.

Overlap with money laundering offences

11.56 The offence of handling stolen goods is, strictly, no longer necessary in virtually every case covered by it because of the wider money laundering provisions of the Proceeds of Crime Act 2002 (PCA 2002), Pt 7 (ss 327–340). Stolen goods in all their forms fall within the definition of 'criminal property' within the PCA 2002, s 340(3) which provides that:

'Property is criminal property if –

(a) it constitutes a person's benefit from criminal conduct or it represents such a benefit (in whole or part and whether directly or indirectly), and

(b) the alleged offender knows or suspects that it constitutes or represents such a benefit.'

The PCA 2002, s 327 makes it an offence to conceal, disguise, convert or transfer criminal property, or to remove it from England and Wales. The PCA 2002, s 328 provides that it is an offence for a person to enter into or become concerned in an arrangement which he knows or suspects facilitates (by whatever means) the acquisition, retention, use or control of criminal property by or on behalf of another person. By the PCA 2002, s 329, it is an offence for a person to acquire, use or possess criminal property, unless he did so for adequate consideration. Although many instances of handling fall outside the popular conception of money laundering, the offences in ss 327–329 are, between them, capable of covering virtually anything[138] which constitutes handling stolen goods. In addition, although the maximum sentences for these offences are the same as for handling (14 years' imprisonment), their *mens rea* requirement is less demanding since the defendant is not required to know or believe that the property constitutes or represents the benefit from criminal conduct, but is simply required to know or suspect this. In addition, there is no requirement of 'dishonesty'.[139] The offences clearly have the potential to be more attractive to a prosecutor than that of handling stolen goods.

---

[138] One exception would be where the offence of handling consisted of 'acquisition, use or possession' of the stolen goods for adequate consideration. Because of the adequate consideration there would not be an offence under the PCA 2002, s 329.

[139] The offences under the PCA 2002, ss 327–329 are, however, subject to a limitation whereby an offence is not committed in the case of making an authorised disclosure to a police officer or other specified authority before the conduct in question (or intending to do so but failing with reasonable excuse to do so).

In *R (on the application of Wilkinson) v DPP*,[140] the Divisional Court considered the increasingly common practice of the Crown Prosecution Service to charge offences under the PCA 2002, s 329 as opposed to charging the offence of handling stolen goods. Recognising that the offence under s 329 is easier to prove in terms of *mens rea*, it held that:

- when the offence under the PCA 2002, s 329 was created it was in the context of legislation directed primarily at money laundering and matters of serious criminality;
- the PCA 2002, s 329 should be resorted to only in serious cases, as is clear from the Crown Prosecution Service's guidance;
- if an offence was inappropriately charged, the judge could encourage the prosecution to charge handling stolen goods, but could do no more than that.

This clearly offers little protection against inappropriate charges of money laundering.

Section 23

11.57 The TA 1968, s 23 punishes as a summary offence, with a fine not exceeding level 3 on the standard scale, public advertisements of a reward for the return of stolen or lost goods with statements to the effect that no questions will be asked, or that the person returning them will be safe from apprehension or inquiry, or that money paid or loaned for the goods will be returned. It is not obvious why it should be an offence for an advertisement simply to state that no questions will be asked. What is being proposed would not be an offence under the Criminal Law Act 1967, s 5(1) (concealing an offence for reward)[141] or otherwise. Indeed, the need for the offence as a whole is doubtful. It was inserted because it was thought that the advertisements covered by it might encourage dishonesty.[142] This may provide a justification where advertisements are addressed to the thief (because they would offer a safe route for the realisation of the goods), but it hardly justifies criminalising advertisements directed to innocent members of the public or bona fide purchasers of the stolen goods.

It was held by the Divisional Court in *Denham v Scott*[143] that the offence is one of strict liability in relation to the publication of such an advertisement, so that someone who

---

140 [2006] EWHC 3012 (Admin), DC.
141 Para 17.87.
142 *Eighth Report of the Criminal Law Revision Committee: Theft and Related Offences* (Cmnd 2977) (1966), para 144.
143 (1983) 77 Cr App Rep 210, DC.

publishes such an advertisement without knowledge of its inclusion can be convicted of the offence.

Dishonestly retaining a wrongful credit

> **Key points 11.4**
>
> The offence of handling is not committed by someone to whose bank account a 'wrongful credit', as defined below, has been made because that credit itself is not stolen goods; but this gap has been filled by the offence of dishonestly retaining a wrongful credit, contrary to the TA 1968, s 24A.

11.58 The TA 1968, s 24A was inserted by the Theft (Amendment) Act 1996, s 2. Section 24A(1) provides that:

> 'A person is guilty of an offence if –
>
> (a) a wrongful credit has been made to an account kept by him or in respect of which he has any right or interest;
>
> (b) he knows or believes that the credit is wrongful; and
>
> (c) he dishonestly fails to take such steps as are reasonable in the circumstances to secure that the credit is cancelled.'

The maximum punishment is 10 years' imprisonment.[144] This can be compared with the maximum of 14 years' for the offence of handling.

Actus reus

11.59 **What is required is the failure to take such steps as are reasonable in the circumstances to secure the cancellation of a wrongful credit made to an account kept by the defendant or in respect of which he has any right or interest.** Nothing need be done by the defendant. The mere omission to take reasonable steps to secure the cancellation of a wrongful credit suffices. For this purpose, 'cancellation' means cancelling the original credit so as to achieve the same effect as if it had not been made in the first place; it does not occur where the defendant withdraws money to spend for his own benefit.[145]

---

[144] TA 1968, s 24A(6).   [145] *Lee* [2006] EWCA Crim 156.

A 'credit' refers to a credit of an amount of money in an account.[146] By the TA 1968, s 24A(2A), **a credit to an account is wrongful to the extent that it derives from:**

- **theft;**
- **blackmail;**
- **fraud (contrary to the Fraud Act 2006, s 1); or**
- **stolen goods.**[147]

Although a bank credit can be 'goods' for the purposes of handling, a wrongful credit of the above type is not stolen goods because it has not represented the original stolen goods, directly or indirectly, 'in the hands of the thief or a handler' as the proceeds of their disposal or realisation but is a new thing in action which has never been in those hands. In determining whether a credit to an account is wrongful, it is immaterial whether the account is overdrawn before or after the credit is made.[148]

Mens rea

11.60 **The defendant must know or believe**[149] **that the credit is wrongful;** he must know or believe the facts which make the credit 'wrongful' in law, although he need not know that they have this effect.[150]

Because failing to take steps is an omission which can continue over a period of time, it suffices that *mens rea* exists at some point during it; it need not exist from the outset.[151] It follows that those who only become aware of a wrongful credit after it has been made can commit an offence under the TA 1968, s 24A.

---

[146] TA 1968, s 24A(2). 'Account' means an account kept with: (a) a bank; (b) a person carrying on a business which falls within s 24A(10) below; or (c) an issuer of electronic money (as defined for the purposes of the Financial Services and Markets Act 2000 (FSMA 2000), Pt 2): TA 1968, s 24A(9), inserted by the Fraud Act 2006 (FA 2006), Sch 1. A business falls within the TA 1968, s 24A(10) if: (a) in the course of the business money received by way of deposit is lent to others; or (b) any other activity of the business is financed, wholly or to any material extent, out of the capital of or the interest on money received by way of deposit: TA 1968, s 24A(10), inserted by FA 2006, Sch 1. References in the TA 1968, s 24A(10) above to a deposit must be read with: (a) the FSMA 2000, s 22; (b) any relevant order under that section; and (c) the FSMA 2000, Sch 2; but any restriction on the meaning of deposit which arises from the identity of the person making it is to be disregarded: TA 1968, s 24A(11), inserted by the FA 2006, Sch 1. For the purposes of the TA 1968, s 24A(10): (a) all the activities which a person carries on by way of business are to be regarded as a single business carried on by him; and (b) 'money' includes money expressed in a currency other than sterling: TA 1968, s 24A(12), inserted by the FA 2006, Sch 1.

[147] TA 1968, s 24A(2A) was inserted by the FA 2006, Sch 1. 'Stolen goods' has been amended for the purposes of the TA 1968 in general by the TA 1968, s 24A(7) (as amended by the FA 2006, Sch 1) and (8); see para 11.44.

[148] TA 1968, s 24A(5).

[149] As to the meaning of these terms, see para 11.51. There is no equivalent, in respect of proof of knowledge or belief, of the TA 1968, s 27(3); para 11.54.

[150] Ignorance of the criminal law is no defence: para 3.73.

[151] Para 3.65.

11.61 The defendant must dishonestly fail to take such steps which are reasonable in the circumstances to secure that the wrongful credit is cancelled. The approach to this question is the same as in the offence of handling.[152]

Width

11.62 The TA 1968, s 24A covers a range of situations. It catches the thief, blackmailer, fraudster or handler who pays into his own account the proceeds of his offence, if he dishonestly fails to take reasonable steps to secure its cancellation, because the credit which he has failed to cancel is wrongful under s 24A(2A).

Section 24A is not, however, aimed at this type of case but at the following. Suppose that Y pays money which he has stolen (or obtained by blackmail or by selling stolen goods) into his bank account, and that Y then transfers the credit thereby created to D's bank account. If D dishonestly fails to take reasonable steps to cancel that credit he can be convicted of an offence under s 24A, because the credit will be wrongful under s 24A(2A). It would be likewise if the credit transferred to D's account had derived from a fraud committed by Y, contrary to the FA 2006, s 1.

Going equipped for stealing or burglary

11.63 The TA 1968, s 25(1), as amended by the FA 2006, Sch 1, provides that:

> 'A person shall be guilty of an offence if, when not at his place of abode, he has with him any article for use in the course of or in connection with any burglary or theft.'

For this purpose, 'theft' includes an offence under the TA 1968, s 12(1) (ie taking a conveyance other than a pedal cycle).[153] The offence under s 25(1) is a species of preparatory offence. Generally, the law does not penalise mere preparation for crime[154] but the offence under s 25(1) is an exception. It is punishable with a maximum of three years' imprisonment.[155]

11.64 The sidenote to the TA 1968, s 25 describes the offence as 'going equipped for stealing etc'. However, a sidenote cannot restrict the clear meaning of the section to which it relates.[156] Consequently, although the decision of the Divisional Court in *In the matter of McAngus*,[157] that a person who had with him counterfeit shirts in a warehouse for use in connection with a cheat had properly been convicted of an offence under s 25 is surprising, it undoubtedly falls within the words of s 25. The phrase 'has with him' has not been judicially considered in a reported case, but it would seem to bear the same meaning as in offences relating to firearms and offensive weapons, ie that the article is near to the

---

[152] Paras 10.73–10.75 and 11.55. [153] TA 1968, s 25(5). [154] See para 14.104.
[155] TA 1968, s 25(2). [156] *Chandler v DPP* [1964] AC 763, HL. [157] [1994] Crim LR 602, DC.

defendant and readily accessible, rather than the narrower meaning it has in aggravated burglary.[158]

11.65 It is not an offence for a person to have at his place of abode articles which are for use in the course of any burglary or theft, but if he is away from his place of abode he commits an offence if he has with him any such article. Where a person lives, and drives around, in a car in which he keeps his tools for burglary, the car is his place of abode for the present purpose only when it is on a site where he intends to abide.[159]

11.66 Some articles are specifically and clearly made or adapted for use in committing a burglary or theft, and possession of these is evidence that they were intended for such use,[160] but there must be very few of them, since most articles have both innocent and criminal uses. In all cases, the jury must be satisfied that the article in question was intended for one of the specified uses.

11.67 The defendant must intend that the article is used in the course or in connection with a burglary or theft.[161] It is not necessary, however, to prove that the defendant intended the article to be used in the course of or in connection with any particular burglary or theft; it is enough to prove a general intention that it should be used for some burglary or theft if the opportunity arises.[162] On the other hand, the offence is not committed if the defendant does not have a firm intention to use the thing for a burglary or theft, given the opportunity.[163]

11.68 It is not necessary to prove that the defendant intended to use the article himself; it is sufficient that he has the article with him for future use by another in the course of or in connection with burglary or theft.[164] However, it is not enough to prove that the article had been used before the defendant came into possession of it.[165] Nor is it enough to prove that the articles were used to get a job which would give the opportunity to steal.[166]

11.69 The phrase 'for use...in connection with' extends the scope of the offence, since it covers the case where the article is intended for use while making preparations for a burglary or theft, or while making an escape after it has been committed.[167]

11.70 The Divisional Court has held that a person who has embarked on the commission of a burglary or theft and, for the first time, comes into possession of, and decides to make immediate use of, some implement to help him do so (eg something which he has just found) can be convicted of the present offence.[168] This is odd; it cannot be said in commonsense terms that he has the thing with him for use in the course of or in connection with a burglary or theft.

---

[158] See para 11.23.   [159] *Bundy* [1977] 2 All ER 382, CA.
[160] TA 1968, s 25(3).   [161] *Ellames* [1974] 3 All ER 130, CA.
[162] *Ellames* [1974] 3 All ER 130, CA.   [163] *Hargreaves* [1985] Crim LR 243, CA.
[164] *Ellames* [1974] 3 All ER 130, CA; *In the matter of McAngus* [1994] Crim LR 602, DC.
[165] *Ellames* [1974] 3 All ER 130, CA.   [166] *Mansfield* [1975] Crim LR 101, CA.
[167] *Ellames* [1974] 3 All ER 130, CA.   [168] *Minor v DPP* (1987) 86 Cr App Rep 378, DC.

FURTHER READING

Alldridge 'Attempted Murder of the Soul: Blackmail, Piracy and Secrets' (1993) 13 OJLS 368

Griew *The Theft Acts 1968 and 1978* (7th edn, 1995) Chs 4, 14, 15 and 16

Lamond 'Coercion, Threats and the Puzzle of Blackmail' in *Harm and Culpability* (1996) (Simester and ATH Smith (eds)) 215

Ormerod and Williams (eds) *Smith's Law of Theft* (9th edn, 2007) Chs 8, 9 (paras 9.01–9.26), 12 and 13

ATH Smith *Property Offences* (1994) Chs 15, 28, 30 and 31

Spencer 'The Mishandling of Handling' [1981] Crim LR 682

12

Fraud and related offences

OVERVIEW

This chapter deals principally with the offence of fraud and related offences contrary to the Fraud Act 2006 and with the offence of forgery and related offences under the Forgery and Counterfeiting Act 1981. It also deals briefly, between the discussion of these two Acts, with a number of offences under the Theft Act 1968 which are fraudulent in nature.[1]

The chapter concludes with an account of the special jurisdictional provisions relating to these offences and to theft and certain other offences under the Theft Act 1968.

Fraud Act 2006

Key points 12.1

The following offences under the Fraud Act 2006 are dealt with below:

- fraud;
- possession or control of an article for use in the course of, or in connection with, any fraud;
- making, adapting or supplying such an article; and
- obtaining services dishonestly.[2]

12.1 The Fraud Act 2006 (FA 2006) is the culmination of law reform proposals stretching back over more than 30 years. The group of offences provided by the FA 2006 enable the criminal law to address problems hitherto posed by developments in technology, commercial transactions and property transfer. In doing so, the Act has simplified the

---

[1] For special rules relating to jurisdiction over all the offences dealt with in this chapter besides that in para 12.46, see paras 12.69–12.71.

[2] The FA 2006 also provides an offence of participating in a fraudulent business carried on by a sole trader etc (s 9), which corresponds to the offence of fraudulent trading by a company contrary to the Companies Act 2006, s 993. Both offences are outside the scope of this book.

law and provided offences which are flexible enough to meet future developments of the above type. The offences of fraud and of obtaining services dishonestly are based, with some amendments, on offences recommended by the Law Commission in its report, Fraud,[3] published in 2002.

Fraud

Key points 12.2

There is one offence of fraud. It can be committed in three different ways:

- by false representation;
- by failing to disclose information;
- by abuse of position,

in each of which the defendant's conduct must occur dishonestly and with intent to gain for himself or another or to cause loss to another or to expose another to a risk of loss.

12.2 The FA 2006, s 1 creates the offence of fraud which has replaced a total of eight deception offences under the Theft Acts 1968 and 1978: obtaining property by deception, obtaining a money transfer by deception, obtaining a pecuniary advantage by deception, procuring the execution of a valuable security by deception, obtaining services by deception, obtaining the remission of an existing liability to make a payment by deception, inducing a creditor to forgo or wait for payment of an existing liability to pay by deception, and obtaining the exemption from, or abatement of, a liability to make a payment by deception. The replacement of these offences was welcomed by lawyers, since they posed difficult problems in practice. These problems resulted in part from the need to prove a deception (a computer or other machine cannot be deceived).[4] They also resulted from the need to prove that the deception was an operative cause of the property, money transfer, pecuniary advantage etc, as the case might be, being obtained or induced (which could only be proved by an artificiality in most cases where the use of a credit, debit or cheque card involved a false representation). In addition, the law about deception was criticised on the grounds that there were too many offences and too much overlap, and on the ground that they were over-particularised (with the result that some conduct deserving of punishment fell into gaps between offences). Where two or more people agreed to pursue a course of conduct which fell into a gap, the problem could be resolved by a prosecution and conviction for the much-criticised offence of conspiracy to defraud, dealt with in Chapter 14, but if only one person was involved the law was powerless.[5] The offence of fraud should reduce the need to rely on conspiracy to defraud.

[3] Law Com No 276.   [4] *Holmes v Governor of Brixton Prison* [2004] EWHC 2020 (Admin), DC.
[5] Unless, as could happen, the conduct constituted an offence under other legislation.

Offence of fraud

12.3 The FA 2006, s 1(1) and (2) provides:

> '(1) A person is guilty of fraud[6] if he is in breach of any of the sections listed in subs (2) (which provide for different ways of committing the offence).
>
> (2) The sections are:
> (a) section 2 (fraud by false representation);
> (b) section 3 (fraud by failing to disclose information), and
> (c) section 4 (fraud by abuse of position).'

Thus, there is one offence of fraud which can be committed in the three different ways specified by the FA 2006, ss 2 to 4. As will be seen, the offence is a 'conduct crime';[7] unlike the repealed deception offences under the Theft Acts 1968 and 1978, no consequence is required by ss 2 to 4 to result from the defendant's fraudulent conduct.

The offence of fraud is triable either way, and punishable with a maximum of 10 years' imprisonment on conviction on indictment.[8]

The three ways of committing fraud

Fraud by false representation

12.4 By the FA 2006, s 2(1), a person is in breach of the FA 2006, s 2 if he:

> '(a) dishonestly makes a false representation, and
> (b) intends, by making the representation –
> (i) to make a gain for himself or another, or
> (ii) to cause loss to another or to expose another to a risk of loss.'

This is the widest of the three ways of committing fraud. It covers virtually all the conduct that previously fell within the eight deception offences under the Theft Acts 1968 and 1978. It is the most common way by which fraud is committed.

Actus reus

12.5 The *actus reus* is a simple one: **making a false representation (ie making a representation in the circumstance that it is false)**. No one is required to be deceived by it or to have acted on it. Indeed, it is irrelevant that the intended recipient is never aware of the representation because, for example, the defendant's false begging letter never arrives. Nothing (in particular, no gain or loss or risk of loss) is required to result from the representation, although doubtless in most cases it will have. The offence is complete

---

[6] For a special provision relating to the liability of its controlling officers when this offence is committed by a corporation, see para 12.47.

[7] Para 2.17.   [8] FA 2006, s 1(3).

as soon as the false representation is made with the requisite *mens rea*. There is merit in the claim[9] that s 2 appears to criminalise lying.

12.6 *'Representation'*   The FA 2006, s 2(3) provides:

> '"Representation" means any representation as to fact or law, including a representation as to the state of mind of –
>
> (a) the person making the representation, or
>
> (b) any other person.'

It will be noted that s 2(3) does not actually define what amounts to a 'representation' but defines what a 'representation' must be about.

The FA 2006, s 2(4) provides that **a representation may be express or implied**.

12.7   An obvious example of a representation of fact (ie a past or present verifiable thing) would be a statement that a worthless ring was a diamond ring. A statement as to the meaning of a statute is clearly a representation of law, for example. Representations of facts are common; representations of law are not.

12.8   Because 'representation' includes a representation as to the state of mind of the representor or another, the making of a false statement of the present intentions of the person making the statement or another person (eg a false promise) can amount to a false representation. The intention may, of course, be implied from the nature of the transaction in which the defendant engages. A request for a loan of money implies an intention to repay, and the ordering of a meal in a restaurant implies a representation that the representor (or, possibly, another) intends to pay for it.

12.9   The requirement that the representation must be as to fact (ie a past or present verifiable thing) or law, or as to a state of mind, means that a statement which merely expresses an opinion does not in itself constitute a false representation if the opinion turns out to be unjustified. By way of example, if a statement that a picture is worth £1,000, or that a car is reliable, or that the profits of a business in the next financial year will be £1m turns out to be unjustified there is no false representation. However, if the person making the statement is aware that the opinion is unjustified he will at the same time by his conduct make a false representation as to his state of mind, because he will impliedly represent that he believes the opinion is justified when in fact he does not so believe.

12.10   There is no limit on how an express representation may be made. Thus, it can be stated by words, whether oral or written (eg on an application form for a loan or job, or in a 'phishing' e-mail,[10] or posted on a website), or communicated by conduct (as where a rogue dresses up in a security guard's uniform in order to convey the impression that he is a security guard).

---

[9] Ormerod 'The Fraud Act 2006 – Criminalising Lying?' [2007] Crim LR 193 at 196.

[10] Explanatory notes to the FA 2006. 'Phishing' occurs where a person disseminates an e-mail to large groups of people falsely representing that it has been sent by a legitimate financial institution and seeking to prompt

12.11 An implied representation may be made by words or by conduct, such as the implied representation by conduct, referred to above, made by someone who orders a meal in a restaurant that he (or, possibly, another) intends to pay for it, or such as that made by someone who sells property that he has a right to do so. Similarly a person who proffers an obsolete foreign banknote for exchange at a bureau de change impliedly represents the fact that it is valid as currency in its country of origin.[11]

A common example of an implied false representation by conduct concerns 'bouncing cheques'. The giver of a cheque impliedly represents that the state of facts existing at the date of the delivery of the cheque is such that the cheque will be honoured in the ordinary course of events on presentation for payment on or after the date specified on the cheque.[12] If the facts are not as represented, a false representation is made.

If a credit card or debit card is used, or a cheque is supported by a cheque card, then, provided any conditions referred to by the card are complied with, the card company or bank is legally obliged to honour the transaction or cheque, because a contract to this effect is brought into being between the payee and the card company or bank. It is irrelevant that the user's authority to use the card has been withdrawn or that he is exceeding it, or that the drawer was a thief (and not the authorised signatory) and forged a signature resembling that of the authorised signatory.[13] In such a case, there will not be a false representation about payment. However, a person who uses a credit card or debit card or who draws a cheque backed by a cheque card, impliedly represents by his conduct that he has actual authority from the card company or bank to use the card to make a contract with the payee on behalf of the bank that it will honour the transaction or the cheque on presentation. If he has no such authority the representation as to it is false.[14]

12.12 By the FA 2006, s 2(5), a representation may be regarded for the purposes of s 2 as made if it (or anything implying it) is submitted in any form to any system or device designed to receive, convey or respond to communications (with or without human intervention). **As a result of the wording of the FA 2006, s 2(1) (absence of a requirement that someone be deceived) and s 2(5), s 2 can be breached where the false representation is submitted to a computer or other machine, rather than being addressed to a human being, as where a person unauthorisedly enters someone else's number into a 'CHIP and PIN' machine or where a person feeds an imitation coin into a car park machine.**

12.13 *False representation*   By the FA 2006, s 2(2):

> 'A representation is false if –
>
> (a) it is untrue or misleading, and
>
> (b) the person making it knows that it is, or might be, untrue or misleading.'

---

readers of the e-mail to provide information, such as credit or bank account numbers, so that he can make use of the information obtained for personal gain.

[11] *Williams* [1980] Crim LR 589, CA. Also see *Hamilton* (1991) 92 Cr App Rep 54, CA.

[12] *Gilmartin* [1983] QB 953, CA.   [13] *First Sport Ltd v Barclays Bank plc* [1993] 3 All ER 789, CA.

[14] *Comr of Police of the Metropolis v Charles* [1977] AC 177, HL; *Lambie* [1982] AC 449, HL.

According to the explanatory notes to the FA 2006, 'misleading' refers to something 'less than wholly true and capable of an interpretation to the detriment of the victim'.[15]

It has been suggested[16] that 'trade puffs', such as may be used by second-hand car salesmen and street traders, for example false statements that a car has 'always been well maintained' or that a mobile phone is 'as good as a Nokia', can be false representations under the FA 2006, s 2. There is merit in the suggestion. The statements could be regarded as ones of fact and, if not completely untrue, they would seem to be misleading. Their maker would probably know that they were, or might be, untrue or misleading. This does not, however, mean that such persons will necessarily be guilty of fraud by way of s 2. It might be difficult to prove the *mens rea* required,[17] as will be seen.

12.14 The definition of 'false representation' does not deal with **whether a failure to state the truth can constitute a false representation.** Three types of case, at least, can be identified for examination:

- A representation may be a half-truth because, although it is literally true, it omits a material matter, as where an applicant for a job correctly states that he does not have a criminal record but fails to state that he has been charged with theft to which he intends to plead guilty. Such a statement constitutes a misrepresentation (ie a false representation) in civil law[18] and there seems **no reason why a half-truth should not also be so for the purposes of the FA 2006, s 2, particularly as it makes the representation misleading.**

- A representation may be true when made, but, to the representor's knowledge, become untrue while it is still operative, as where a person orders a meal in a restaurant, intending to pay but changes his mind before being served. His representation that he intends to pay is true when made but it is a continuing representation which becomes false. It is **submitted that, as was the law in respect of the repealed offences of deception,**[19] **there is a false representation if the representor knowing of the change does not inform the representee** (the waiter, in the example). The initially true representation made by the representor is continuing in effect and has become a false one in such circumstances. If this is not accepted, reliance will have to be placed on the second way of committing fraud, ie under the FA 2006, s 3 (fraud by failure to disclose information one is legally obliged to disclose), because once a person becomes aware of the change from truth to falsehood he becomes under a duty in civil law to disclose the truth.[20]

- In the above instances there is a representation, by words or by conduct, by the defendant which is or becomes false. Under the old offences of deception, someone who **simply refrained from stating something which it was his legal duty to disclose** committed a deception if it led the person to whom the duty was owed being

---

[15] Home Office Explanatory Notes, para 19.
[16] Ormerod 'The Fraud Act 2006 – Criminalising Lying?' [2007] Crim LR 193 at 198.
[17] Paras 12.15–12.19. [18] *Dimmock v Hallett* (1866) 2 Ch App 21.
[19] *DPP v Ray* [1974] AC 370, HL. [20] *With v O'Flanagan* (1936) Ch 575, CA.

deceived.[21] This seemed to stretch the concept of deception. Section 2 speaks not of 'deception' (which requires that someone was deceived by the defendant) but simply of '*making a false representation*'. In the present type of case the person who simply fails to disclose has not done anything; **how can he have** *made* **a false** *representation?* Cases of the present type clearly fall within s 3 (fraud by failing to disclose information) and it is submitted that the courts should avoid the temptation to give an artificial interpretation to s 2 so as to bring within that section as well a failure to discharge a legal duty to disclose which conveyed a false impression.

Mens rea

12.15 The *mens rea* required for a breach of s 2 consists of three elements.

12.16 **The defendant must know that his representation is, or might be, untrue or mis-leading.**[22] It will be noted that the defendant need not know that his misrepresentation is untrue or misleading; it is enough that he knows that it *might be* (ie that there is a risk that it is). This extends the ambit of the offence. It is similar to the concept of recklessness but differs from that concept because it does not require that the risk is an unreasonable one to take.

12.17 **The defendant must make the false representation dishonestly.**[23] Whenever it is in issue under the FA 2006, ss 2 to 4, the question of dishonesty will have to be determined by answering the questions set out in *Ghosh*,[24] in the same way as in a trial for theft. It might be difficult to prove dishonesty against those who make false trade puffs. Since the *actus reus* of the form of fraud under the FA 2006, s 2 consists simply of telling a lie, 'dishonesty' is liable to play a crucial role in the determination of whether telling a lie in a particular case is or is not an offence. 'Dishonesty' plays a similar crucial role in the two other ways in which fraud can be committed. On this ground, it might be thought that the offence of fraud would fail to satisfy the quality of law requirement, under the ECHR, Article 7, of foreseeability (or legal certainty) as to whether a particular piece of conduct is criminal. Perhaps surprisingly, the Joint Parliamentary Committee on Human Rights concluded that the offence had a sufficient conduct element to be compatible with Article 7.[25]

12.18 **The defendant must intend, by making the representation,**

- **to make a gain for himself or another, or**
- **to cause loss to another or to expose another to a risk of loss.**[26]

Presumably the necessary intent can be proved by proving that the defendant's aim or purpose in making the false representation was thereby to make a gain or cause a loss or expose to loss or by proving that a gain or loss or exposure to the risk of loss was vir-tually certain to result from his making of the false representation and that he foresaw this virtual certainty.[27] If so, a person who tells a lie for the purpose of admission to an

---

[21] *Firth* (1990) 91 Cr App Rep 217, CA. [22] FA 2006, s 2(2)(b).   [23] FA 2006, s 2(1)(a).
[24] [1982] QB 1053, CA; paras 10.73–10.75. [25] *Fourteenth Report of the Joint Committee*, para 2.14.
[26] FA 2006, s 2(1)(b).   [27] Paras 3.5–3.19.

association can be convicted of fraud if he knows that all members automatically receive a gift on admission, because, as he foresees, he is virtually certain to make that gain by making the representation. Likewise a person can be convicted of fraud if he makes a false representation on an insurance application form because, although his purpose is to secure insurance, he will realise that by making the representation he is exposing the insurance company to the risk of loss, even though he hopes that it never has to 'pay up'.

It will be noted that the defendant must intend, **by making the representation,** to make a gain or cause a loss or expose to loss. This might be difficult to prove against someone who makes false trade puffs because customers do not normally take notice of trade puffs and are therefore unconcerned about their veracity. It follows that, unless he is aware that this will not be so in the instant case (as where the customer has shown that the content of the puff is important), the maker of the puff will not make his false statement to bring about his intended gain.[28]

This type of case can be distinguished from that where the defendant makes use of a credit card or other 'piece of plastic' which is unauthorised, eg because it has been stolen by him. This – as seen – constitutes an implied false representation of his authority to use it. The other party, knowing that he will be paid by the card company, may act without a positive belief that that representation is true but unless he is a highly unusual person he would not accept payment by the card if he knew the truth. If the defendant realises this he will intend, by making the false representation, to make a gain.

12.19 By the FA 2006, s 5(1), the reference to gain and loss in s 2 is to be read in accordance with s 5 which defines 'gain' and 'loss' in the same way as in the Theft Act 1968, s 34(2)(a). By s 5(2), **'gain' and 'loss' are confined to gain or loss (whether temporary or permanent) in money or other property.**[29] Because an intended gain or loss need only be temporary D, who tells a lie in order to induce someone to let him borrow his car, can be convicted of fraud even though he intended to return the car as promised.

Under s 5(3) **'gain includes a gain by keeping what one has, as well as a gain by getting what one does not have', and under s 5(4) 'loss includes a loss by not getting what one might get, as well as a loss by parting with what one has'.** The width of these terms means that fraud extends to cases where the intended outcome of the false representation is not the transfer of property. For example, a false representation made with intent to induce the representee to abandon a claim against the defendant's (or X's) specific and identifiable property can constitute fraud because the representor (defendant) has an intention that he (or X) should keep what he has and therefore has an intent to make a gain for himself (or another, X, as the case may be); of course, he also has an intent to cause loss to the representee by that person not getting what he might get. A person who tells a lie in order to get a job can be convicted of fraud because he intends by the lie to make a gain for himself. Likewise, so can someone who tells a lie in order to get a debtor of his to pay

---

[28] See S Gardner [2007] Crim LR 661 (letter).

[29] 'Property' means any property whether real or personal (including things in action and other intangible property): FA 2006, s 5(2).

up, for he intends by the lie to get money which he has not got (although he may well be acquitted of fraud on the ground that he is not dishonest). In both cases, of course, he also has an intent by the representation to cause loss to another.[30]

Normally, if a person has one of the above two intentions he will also have the other, but there can be cases where this is not so. Suppose D knows that V is looking after some compromising letters for X. If D imitates X over the telephone and tells V that he (supposedly X) wants the letters destroyed, D will act with intent to cause loss to another but not with intent to make a gain for himself or another.

These definitions of 'gain' and 'loss' have the effect of ensuring that, as in the case of blackmail, fraud is an economic crime; it does not cover the case where someone intends to obtain a non-economic benefit, such as sexual intercourse, by a false representation.

Fraud by failing to disclose information

12.20 A person is in breach of the FA 2006, s 3 if he:

'(a) dishonestly fails to disclose to another person information which he is under a legal duty to disclose, and

(b) intends, by failing to disclose the information –
(i) to make a gain for himself or another, or
(ii) to cause loss to another or to expose another to a risk of loss.'[31]

Actus reus

12.21 The *actus reus* consists simply in a failure by the defendant to disclose to another person information which the defendant is under a legal duty to disclose. Nothing (in particular, no gain or loss) is required to result from the failure to disclose.

'Legal duty to disclose' is not defined by the FA 2006. 'Legal duty' refers to a duty in civil law. Such a duty of disclosure may derive from statute (eg the provisions governing company prospectuses); from the fact that the transaction in question is one of the utmost good faith (eg an insurance contract);[32] from the express or implied terms of a contract; from the custom of a particular trade or market; from the existence of a fiduciary relationship between the parties (eg in certain well-established relationships such as solicitor (or other professional person) and client, trustee and beneficiary, director and company, partner and partner, employee and employer and agent and principal, or where one person has placed himself in such a position that he becomes obliged to act fairly and with due regard to the interests of the other party);[33] or from a change in circumstances

[30] Support for the statements in this paragraph can be derived from the case law on the corresponding provisions relating to blackmail: para 11.30.

[31] FA 2006, s 3.

[32] See *Cheshire, Fifoot and Furmston's Law of Contract* (15th edn, 2007) (Furmston (ed)) 372–379.

[33] See *Cheshire, Fifoot and Furmston's Law of Contract* (15th edn, 2007) (Furmston (ed)) 379–380. Most of these instances were given by the Law Commission (*Fraud* (2002), Law Com No 276, para 7.28) and are reproduced in the explanatory notes to the FA 2006, para 18.

whereby an initially true (positive) representation has become untrue to the representor's knowledge while it is still operative.

Originally, the Law Commission had proposed that the present form of fraud should also apply to non-disclosure in breach of a moral duty to disclose, as where an art dealer knows that a prospective purchaser (X) of a painting thinks that it is by Picasso, whereas in fact it is a painting of little value by an artist called Piccolo, and the dealer does not disabuse X of his mistake. This was rejected by the Government, as a result of its consultation process, as too uncertain and as productive of an undesirably wide offence which would render a person criminally liable for the non-disclosure of information which he was not obliged by the civil law to disclose.

12.22 If a false representation could be made under s 2 in the absence of any positive representation by the defendant but simply on the ground of a failure to fulfil a legal duty of disclosure which created a false impression, there would be few, if any, cases under s 3 which would not also fall within s 2. Quite apart from the linguistic argument made in para 12.14, this strongly indicates that s 2 is not meant to cover cases dealt with by s 3 where no positive representation is made. On this basis, the only area of overlap would be where the defendant has made a positive representation which to his knowledge becomes false while it is still operative and which he does not disclose in breach of his legal duty to do so. One can be confident that the courts will hold that this constitutes the making of a false representation (on the ground that what was true has become false) under s 2. To this extent there is clearly an overlap between the two sections.

Mens rea

12.23 The *mens rea* expressly required by the FA 2006, s 3 is that the defendant must:

- **fail to disclose the information dishonestly;**[34]
- **intend, by failing to disclose the information**
  - **to make a gain for himself or another, or**
  - **to cause loss to another or to expose another to a risk of loss.**[35]

Section 3 does not expressly require the defendant to know that he is under a legal duty to disclose the information to the other person or be aware that he might be, but it is submitted that such a requirement should be read into s 3 on the basis that the presumption that *mens rea* is required as to this element of the *actus reus*[36] is not rebutted clearly or by necessary implication. In any event, dishonesty could be difficult to prove against a defendant who neither knew of the circumstances giving rise to the duty to disclose the information nor was aware that they might exist.

---

[34] FA 2006, s 3(a). As to 'dishonestly', see para 12.17.

[35] FA 2006, s 3(b). As to this, see paras 12.18 and 12.19.

[36] Ch 6. It must be admitted, however, that the presence of a 'knowledge-requirement' in the FA 2006, s 2, and its absence in s 3 (and in s 4) may tell against this submission.

Fraud by abuse of position

12.24 By the FA 2006, s 4(1), a person is in breach of the FA 2006, s 4 if he:

> '(a) occupies a position in which he is expected to safeguard, or not to act against, the
>   financial interests of another person,
>
> (b) dishonestly abuses that position, and
>
> (c) intends, by means of the abuse of that position –
>   (i)   to make a gain for himself or another, or
>   (ii) to cause loss to another or to expose another to a risk of loss.'

Actus reus

12.25 The *actus reus* consists of an abuse by the defendant of a position in which he is
expected to safeguard, or not to act against, the financial interests of another person.
The abuse need not be secret[37] but doubtless it will normally be so. In its report on fraud
the Law Commission stated that the difference between a case under s 4 and the case of
non-disclosure under s 3 was that in a case under s 4:

> 'the defendant does not need to enlist the victim's co-operation in order to secure the
> desired result. An example would be the employee who, without the knowledge of
> his employer, misuses his or her position to make a personal profit at the employer's
> expense [eg the barman who sells his own drink, and not his employer's, and pockets the
> proceeds]'.[38]

It also covers the rather more serious case where an employee of a software company uses
his position to clone software products with the intention of selling the products on, and
the case where a person employed to care for an elderly person has access to that person's
bank account and abuses his position by transferring funds to invest in shares in a high-
risk business venture of his own.[39] Also covered is the case of a company director who
diverts a contract that he is legally obliged to obtain for the company for his own personal
gain.[40]

12.26 By the FA 2006, s 4(2), a person may be regarded as having abused his position
even though his conduct consisted of an omission rather than an act, as, for example,
where an employee fails to take up the chance of a crucial contract in order that a rival
company can take it up instead at the expense of his employer.[41]

---

[37] Law Commission: *Fraud* (2002), Law Com No 276, para 7.40, had recommended a requirement of secrecy
but this was not included in the Bill presented to Parliament by the Government.

[38] Law Commission: *Fraud* (2002), Law Com No 276, para 7.36.

[39] Explanatory notes to the FA 2006, paras 22 and 23.

[40] This example is given by Sullivan in 'Fraud – The Latest Law Commission Proposals' (2003) 67 JCL 139
at 145.

[41] This example is given in the explanatory notes to the FA 2006, para 21.

Apart from this, the Act leaves 'abuse of position' undefined because it is intended to cover a wide range of conduct.[42]

12.27 The Act also provides no guidance as to when a person occupies a position in which he is expected to safeguard, or not to act against, the financial interests of another person. The Law Commission stated:

> 'The essence of the kind of relationship [to which s 4 refers] is that the victim has voluntarily put the defendant in a privileged position, by virtue of which the defendant is expected to safeguard the victim's financial interests or given power to damage those interests. Such an expectation to safeguard or power to damage may arise, for example, because the defendant is given authority to exercise a discretion on the victim's behalf, or is given access to the victim's assets, premises, equipment or customers. In these cases the defendant does not need to enlist the victim's *further* co-operation in order to secure the desired result, because the necessary co-operation has been given in advance.
>
> The necessary relationship will be present between trustee and beneficiary, director and company, professional person and client, agent and principal, employee and employer, or between partners. It may arise otherwise, for example, within a family, or in the context of voluntary work, or in any context where the parties are not at arm's length. In nearly all case where it arises, it will be recognised by the civil law as importing fiduciary duties, and any relationship that is so recognised will suffice. We see no reason, however, why the existence of such duties should be essential. This does not of course mean that it would be entirely a matter for the fact-finders whether the necessary relationship exists. The question whether the particular facts alleged can properly be described as giving rise to that relationship will be an issue capable of being ruled upon by the judge and, if the case goes to the jury, of being the subject of directions.'[43]

Unless the appellate courts give the present requirements a narrow interpretation, this form of the offence is potentially a wider one than one might expect to find in an offence of fraud, particularly in the light of the non-definition of 'abuse'.

Nothing (in particular, no gain or loss) is required to result from the abuse of position.

Mens rea

12.28 The *mens rea* required is that the defendant must:

- dishonestly abuse the position which he occupies in which he is expected to safeguard, or not to act against, the financial interests of another;[44]
- intend, by means of the abuse of that position –
  - to make a gain for himself or another, or
  - to cause loss to another or to expose another to a risk of loss.[45]

---

[42] Explanatory notes, para 21.

[43] Law Commission: *Fraud* (2002), Law Com No 276, para 7.37–7.38.

[44] FA 2006, s 4(1)(b); given the potential width of this form of fraud 'dishonestly' has a particularly crucial function. As to 'dishonesty', see para 12.17.

[45] FA 2006, s 4(1)(c). As to this see paras 12.18 and 12.19.

Section 4 does not expressly require the defendant to know that he is in a position where he is expected to safeguard, or not to act against, the financial interests of another or be aware that he might be, but it is submitted that such a requirement should be read into s 4.[46] In any event, dishonesty would be difficult to prove against a defendant who neither knew nor was aware of this.

Possession etc of articles for use in frauds

12.29 The FA 2006, s 6(1) provides that:

> 'A person is guilty of an offence[47] if he has in his possession or under his control any article for use in the course of or in connection with any fraud.'

This offence is a species of preparatory offence. It is triable either way and punishable with a maximum of five years' imprisonment on conviction on indictment.[48] It is, therefore, a more serious offence than that of going equipped for stealing or burglary, contrary to the Theft Act 1968, s 25, referred to in para 11.63, whose maximum punishment is three years' imprisonment.

12.30 'Possession' and 'control' are not defined by the Act but 'possession' when used in the alternative to 'control' seems to bear the meaning set out in para 10.40, and 'control' seems to cover the case where a person in physical control of the article is nevertheless not in possession of it or where it is doubtful whether he can be said to be. A person would be in possession or control of data held on a computer in his possession or control, but would not be in possession or control of an article stored, with his knowledge and permission, in the matrimonial home by his spouse.[49] It remains to be seen what element, if any, of *mens rea* the courts read in regarding 'possession or control'.

As has been pointed out,[50] virtually any 'article' might be used in the course of or in connection with a fraud. Obvious examples would be credit card cloning devices, equipment to be inserted at ATM machines to skim bank details and devices to cause a gas or electricity meter to under-record consumption. Paper, pens, PCs, printers and identity badges are other obvious examples. For these purposes, 'article' includes any programme or data held in electronic form.[51] Thus, programmes for generating credit card numbers or e-mails for use in phishing attacks are 'articles'.[52]

---

[46] For the same reason as given in respect of the FA 2006, s 3 (para 12.23, but note n 36).

[47] For a special provision relating to the liability of its controlling officers when this offence is committed by a corporation, see para 12.47. [48] FA 2006, s 6(2).

[49] See, for example, *Kousar* [2009] EWCA Crim 139 (which concerned an offence under the Trade Marks Act 1994, s 92). However, if it could be proved that spouse A has assisted or encouraged spouse B's possession of the article, spouse A could be convicted as an accomplice to the offence committed by spouse B.

[50] *Smith's Law of Theft* (9th edn, 2007) (Ormerod and Williams (eds)) para 9.69.

[51] FA 2006, s 8(1). [52] Yeo 'Bull's-eye (2)' (2007) 157 NLJ 418.

Presumably, 'fraud' refers to the offence contrary to the FA 2006, s 1, described in para 12.3.

12.31 Unlike the offence under the Theft Act 1968, s 25, there is no requirement that the thing possessed or controlled by the defendant should be outside his place of abode. Thus, a person who has a computer programme stored on his PC at home for use in connection with the perpetration of a fraud is caught by the FA 2006, s 6. The defendant need not have begun to commit any fraud. For these reasons, the offence is a particularly wide one.

12.32 It is to be hoped that, by analogy with the interpretation given to the corresponding offence under the Theft Act 1968, s 25, the defendant must possess or control the article with the intention that it is used in the course of, or in connection with, a fraud, although he need not intend this in relation to a particular fraud; if so a general intention that the article be used for a fraud if the opportunity arises suffices.[53] The Government's intention was that this approach should apply to the present offence. It is unfortunate that they refused to insert a provision to this effect when the Act was before Parliament.[54] If the courts are not prepared to read in such a requirement the offence would be a wide one, and would be intolerably so if they also refused to read in a full *mens rea* requirement in respect of what is possessed or controlled.

Making or supplying articles for use in frauds

12.33 The FA 2006, s 7(1) provides that:

'A person is guilty of an offence[55] if he makes, adapts, supplies or offers to supply any article –

(a) knowing that it is designed or adapted for use in the course of or in connection with fraud, or

(b) intending it to be used to commit, or assist in the commission of, fraud.'

The offence is triable either way and punishable with a maximum of 10 years' imprisonment on conviction on indictment.[56]

12.34 Authorities on the offence of supplying a controlled drug suggest that 'supply' connotes more than the mere transfer of physical control from one person to another; it means to furnish to another the article for the purpose of enabling the other to use it for his own purposes.[57]

---

[53] See *Ellames* [1974] 3 All ER 130, CA; para 11.67.
[54] See Ormerod 'The Fraud Act 2006 – Criminalising Lying?' [2007] Crim LR 193 at 211.
[55] For a special provision relating to the liability of its controlling officers when this offence is committed by a corporation, see para 12.47.
[56] FA 2006, s 7(2).   [57] *Maginnis* [1987] AC 303, HL.

Presumably, 'fraud' refers to the offence contrary to the FA 2006, s 1. 'Article' includes any programme or data held in electronic form.[58] Examples of types of article covered by the FA 2006, s 7 appear in para 12.30.

In some cases, the offence of making under s 7(1) overlaps with the offence of forgery, dealt with later.[59] Like forgery, it is a preparatory offence.

Obtaining services dishonestly

Key points 12.3

The offence of dishonestly obtaining services deals with the person who, by a dishonest act, obtains for himself or another a service, other than a free service, without paying the price for it and intending not to do so.

12.35 The FA 2006, s 11(1) and (2) provides:

'(1) A person is guilty of an offence[60] under this section if he obtains services for himself or another –
   (a) by a dishonest act, and
   (b) in breach of subsection (2).
(2) A person obtains services in breach of this subsection if –
   (a) they are made available on the basis that payment has been, is being or will be made for or in respect of them,
   (b) he obtains them without any payment having been made for or in respect of them or without payment having been made in full, and
   (c) when he obtains them, he knows –
     (i) that they are being made available on the basis described in paragraph (a), or
     (ii) that they might be,
  but intends that payment will not be made, or will not be made in full.'

The offence of obtaining services dishonestly is triable either way and punishable with a maximum of five years' imprisonment on conviction on indictment.[61] Unlike the offence of fraud, contrary to the FA 2006, s 1, the offence is a 'result crime'; services must be obtained as a result of the defendant's act.

---

[58] FA 2006, s 8(1).   [59] Paras 12.49–12.59.

[60] For a special provision relating to the liability of its controlling officers when this offence is committed by a corporation, see para 12.47.   [61] FA 2006, s 11(3).

Actus reus

12.36 A person commits the *actus reus* of the offence if he does an act and thereby obtains services for himself or another by an act and in breach of s 11(2)(a) and (b), ie where

- the services are made available on the basis that payment has been, or is being or will be, made for or in respect of them,[62] and
- he obtains them without any payment having been made for or in respect of them or without payment having been made in full.[63]

12.37 Unlike the repealed offence of obtaining services by deception, contrary to the Theft Act 1978 (TA 1978), s 1, the s 11 offence does not require the services to be obtained by deception. It simply requires them to be obtained by an act. Thus, someone who sneaks into a cinema and watches a film without paying can be convicted of the offence, although he would not have committed the offence under the TA 1978, s 1. If a person obtained such admission without payment by a false representation, he would not only be committing an offence under the FA 2006, s 11, but also the offence of fraud contrary to the FA 2006, s 1 (by virtue of the FA 2006, s 2).

Because no deception is required, the s 11 offence can be committed where the defendant obtains services through a machine. Examples are where the defendant downloads, via the Internet, software or data for which a charge is made, or which is only available to those who have paid a subscription for the service, by giving false identification details, or where the defendant receives satellite television transmissions by using a cloned decoder. The offence also catches people who obtain a free train ride by feeding imitation coins into an electronic ticket machine. In this case, however, there could also be a conviction for fraud, contrary to the FA 2006, s 1 (by virtue of s 2).

Act

12.38 The requirement of an act would seem to exclude the possibility of an offence under the FA 2006, s 11 being committed by a failure to do something which one is legally obliged to do. A person who obtains services by failing to disclose a material fact would, therefore, not fall within the FA 2006, s 11. Nor would a person who, having innocently gone to a lecture, thinking it was free, stayed on to hear the lecture without paying after hearing a request that those who had not paid the fee should do so immediately. He would lack the necessary *mens rea* for the offence at the time of his act of entering the lecture room, and his subsequent failure to leave when he knew the truth and had the *mens rea* for the offence cannot suffice.

---

[62] FA 2006, s 11(2)(a).   [63] FA 2006, s 11(2)(b).

Obtaining services

12.39 The FA 2006 does not provide a definition of 'services', but the concept of a 'service' is unlikely to cause many problems to the courts. **The services must be obtained for the defendant or another by the defendant's act.** There is, therefore, a requirement of causation. It follows that, if someone obtains services not because of what he has done but because of a mistake by the service-provider, he does not commit the present offence. As noted in para 10.32, 'services' are not property within the TA 1968, s 4(1) and therefore cannot be the subject of theft, contrary to the TA 1968, s 1, but the new offence is a 'theft- like' one.

12.40 **The requirement that the services must be made available on the basis that payment has been, is being or will be made for or in respect of them means that obtaining free services by a dishonest act, as where a young person by such an act sneaks into a free film show open only to old age pensioners at a cinema and watches the film, is not caught by the FA 2006, s 11.**

'On the basis' seems to relate to the basis on which the service-provider provides them, and does not require any form of agreement on the part of the defendant. The reference to 'payment' seems to be to an identifiable payment or payments made by or on behalf of the person obtaining the benefit to the person providing the benefit, as opposed to some indirect commercial advantage to the service-provider.

It remains to be seen whether the references to 'payment' are limited to payment in a monetary sense (by cash or otherwise), or whether they also include payment in kind or by the performance of services in return for the services. There is no intrinsic reason why they should not.

If a service-provider is deceived into agreeing to waive the charge which would normally be required for a service, the service will not be provided on the requisite 'basis of payment'. Nor will it be provided if a free service is obtained with a view to a future gain, as where a bank account is opened (a service) free of charge (banks do not charge to open an account) by a dishonest act (eg presenting a bad cheque) with a view to running up an unauthorised overdraft. (However, if the account holder then proceeds to run up the unauthorised overdraft or dishonestly makes use of some other facility of the bank for which a bank charge is made or a fee is paid he may thereby become liable under s 11 if he does not pay the charge or fee in full.) In both of the examples just given of the obtaining of a free service, a false representation will have been involved, with the result that an offence of fraud, contrary to the FA 2006, s 1 may be committed.

12.41 The effect of the requirement that the defendant must obtain the services without any payment having been made for or in respect of them or without payment having been made in full is to exclude from s 11 cases where payment has been made in full. This means that the obtaining of 'to-be-paid-for' services is not caught if the defendant pays for them by cash, 'plastic' or cheque at the relevant time, however dishonest the act by which he obtains them.

Two other types of case are excluded by the present requirement. The first is where the defendant gains admission to a keep-fit class which is open only to residents of a particular locality by pretending to be such a resident and paying the fee. The second is where a parent 'lies about a child's religious upbringing in order to obtain a place at a fee-paying school, with every intention of paying the fee'.[64] Nor could there be a conviction for fraud contrary to the FA 2006, s 1 in either case because although there is a false representation in each case there is no intent to make a gain or to cause loss in the sense required for that offence.

Mens rea

12.42 The *mens rea* requirement is threefold:

- **the defendant's act must be done dishonestly.** Although s 11(1) uses the phrase 'dishonest act', 'dishonest' must refer to the defendant's state of mind just as 'dishonestly' does in TA 1968 and TA 1978 (see the first sentence of the last paragraph of para 10.73) and the approach laid down in *Ghosh*[65] applies to it;

- **when the defendant obtains them, the defendant must know**[66] **that the services are being made available on the basis that payment has been, is being or will be made for or in respect of them, or must know that they *might* be;**

- **when he obtains the services, the defendant must intend that payment will not be made, or will not be made in full.** These words seem to require an intent to make permanent default (in whole or in part) of the expected payment. This is another reason why the offence under the FA 2006, s 11 is 'theft-like'.

Although the second and third elements of *mens rea* must exist at the time of the obtaining of the services, and are not required to exist at the time of the act by which they are obtained, it will often be difficult to prove that the defendant's act was dishonest if he lacks those two elements at the time of that act. Thus, a man who engages the services of a prostitute by promising to pay her but who has changed his mind by the time that he receives her sexual services might well not be convicted of an offence under the FA 2006, s 11 on the ground that his act of promising payment was not dishonest. On the other hand, if he had also induced the prostitute to give her services by falsely reassuring her that he was not HIV positive that act would doubtless be found dishonest and he would be convicted under s 11.

Fraudulent offences under Theft Act 1968

Key points 12.4

The Theft Act 1968, ss 17, 19 and 20 deal with offences of false accounting, false statements by officers of corporations or unincorporated associations, and the destruction, defacement or concealment of a valuable security, will or court or government document.

---

[64] This example was given by the Law Commission: *Fraud* (2002), Law Com No 276, para 8.12.
[65] [1982] QB 1053, CA; paras 10.73–10.75.   [66] Para 3.43.

12.43 All the above offences are triable either way, punishable with a maximum of seven years' imprisonment on conviction on indictment. They do not call for detailed discussion.

False accounting

12.44 The TA 1968, s 17 punishes the dishonest destruction, defacement, conceal-ment or falsification of any account 'or any record or document made or required for any accounting purpose' with a view to gain for oneself or another or with intent to cause loss to another. Section 17 also punishes a person who, with such a view or intent, dishonestly in furnishing information for any purpose produces or makes use of any account, or any such 'record or document', which to his knowledge is or may be mis-leading, false or deceptive in a material particular. This is a very convenient section to use where there has been an elaborate and complicated system of fraud in which it is not easy to identify the particular sums of money and other property of which the owner has been deprived, although it is certainly not limited to this. Like s 20, below, this is one of those sections in which the definitions of gain and loss in s 34, which are discussed in para 11.30, are incorporated, so that it suffices that merely a temporary gain or loss is intended.

False statements by company directors etc

12.45 The TA 1968, s 19 punishes the publishing of a written statement known to be (or possibly to be) misleading, false or deceptive in a material particular by an officer of a body corporate or unincorporated association (or person purporting to act as such), with intent to deceive its members or creditors about its affairs.

Suppression of documents etc

12.46 The TA 1968, s 20, as amended by the Fraud Act 2006, makes it an offence for a person to destroy, deface or conceal any valuable security, any will or any original docu-ment of or belonging to, or filed or deposited in, any court or any government depart-ment, provided that the defendant acted dishonestly and with a view to gain for himself or another or with intent to cause loss to another.

A 'valuable security' means any document creating, transferring, surrendering or releasing any right to, in or over property, or authorising the payment of money or deliv-ery of any property, or evidencing such creation etc, or such payment etc, or the satisfac-tion of any obligation.[67]

---

[67] TA 1968, s 20(3).

Liability of controlling officer for fraud or falsification offence by corporation

12.47 Under the TA 1968, s 18,[68] a director, manager or other similar officer of a corporation (eg a limited company) is liable for offences under the TA 1968, s 17 which have been committed by the body corporate with his connivance or consent.[69]

The Fraud Act 2006, s 12 makes the same provision in respect of an offence under that Act.[70]

If the affairs of a corporation are managed by its members, the above provisions apply in relation to the acts and defaults of a member in connection with his functions of management as if he were a director of the corporation.[71]

Forgery and related offences

Key points 12.5

The following offences under the Forgery and Counterfeiting Act 1981 are dealt with below:

- forgery;
- copying a false instrument;
- using a false instrument;
- using a copy of a false instrument,

all of which require the defendant to intend to induce somebody to accept the false instrument (or copy) as genuine (or as a copy of a genuine instrument) and by reason of so accepting it to do or not to do some act to his own or another's prejudice.

The treatment of these offences is followed by a description of offences relating to the custody or control of money orders, share certificates, cheques and various other instruments, or to the making, custody or control of a machine, implement or material designed or adapted to make such an instrument. The more serious version of each of these offences requires proof of the above intentions; the less serious version does not.

12.48 Forgery and its related offences are complementary to the offence of fraud and a number of other offences dealt with in this and the two previous chapters, in that they penalise overt preparation involving false documents or other instruments. Forgery and

---

[68] As amended by the FA 2006.

[69] TA 1968, s 18(1). See, further, paras 18.44–18.46. Corporate criminal liability is dealt with in Ch 18.

[70] FA 2006, s 12(1) and (2).   [71] TA 1968, s 18(2); FA 2006, s 12(3).

related offences are another exception to the general rule that the law does not penalise mere preparation for crime. The reason seems to be the social and commercial necessity that documents and other instruments which are relied on are authentic.

The law relating to forgery and related offences is governed by the Forgery and Counterfeiting Act 1981 (FCA 1981). This is a codifying Act based largely on the Law Commission's report, *Forgery and Counterfeit Currency*.[72] The Act repealed the whole of the Forgery Act 1913, the whole of the Coinage Offences Act 1936, and a number of other statutory provisions, and abolished the common law offence of forgery. The FCA 1981, Pt I deals with forgery and related offences, and Pt II with counterfeiting. Like the Theft Acts 1968 and 1978, the Criminal Damage Act 1971 and the Fraud Act 2006, the FCA 1981 is a completely new code.

All the offences under the FCA 1981 mentioned hereafter are triable either way, the maximum punishment on conviction on indictment being 10 years' imprisonment (unless otherwise stated).

Forgery

12.49 This offence is defined by the FCA 1981, s 1 which states that:

> 'A person is guilty of forgery if he makes a false instrument, with the intention that he or another shall use it to induce somebody to accept it as genuine, and by reason of so accepting it to do or not to do some act to his own or any other person's prejudice.'

Actus reus

12.50 The *actus reus* of this offence is **making a false instrument**. By the FCA 1981, s 9(2) this includes altering an instrument so as to make it false in any respect.

Instrument

12.51 For the purposes of s 1 and other sections in the FCA 1981, an 'instrument' is defined by the FCA 1981, s 8(1) as:

(a) **any document, whether of a formal or informal character (other than a currency note)**;[73]

(b) **any stamp issued or sold by a postal operator (or a metered postage mark)**;[74]

(c) **any Inland Revenue stamp;**[75] **or**

---

[72] Law Com No 55 (1973).   [73] FCA 1981, s 8(2).   [74] FCA 1981, s 8(3).
[75] As defined by the Stamp Duties Management Act 1891, s 27: FCA 1981, s 8(4).

(d) **any disc, tape, soundtrack or other device on or in which information is recorded or stored by mechanical, electronic or other means.** To be 'recorded' or 'stored' the information must be preserved for an appreciable time with the object of subsequent retrieval or recovery.[76] Examples of items covered are microfilm records, information on computer discs and tachograph record sheets (discs on which a tachograph records information about driving periods, rest breaks etc),[77] but not electronic impulses in a computer or its 'user segment' (which retains or stores information momentarily while the computer searches its memory, eg to check a password).[78] Unauthorised manipulation of such electronic impulses (by computer hacking or otherwise) is covered by the offence of unauthorised access to computer material, contrary to the Computer Misuse Act 1990, s 1.

Until 1987, a difficulty with this definition related to the word 'document' in (a). The Forgery Act 1913 and its predecessor dealt with the forgery of documents but did not define what constituted a 'document' for its purposes. However, judicial decisions suggested that if a thing was intended to have utility apart from the fact that it conveyed information or recorded a promise it was not a document;[79] a document for the purpose of the law of forgery was, it was thought, a writing which was only intended to convey information or record a promise. This view was based on a rationalisation of the difficult decisions in *Closs*[80] (where a picture falsely bearing the signature of a well-known artist was held not to be a document) and *Smith*[81] (where two of the judges held that wrappers made in the same distinctive form as those in which Borwick's baking powder was sold were not documents).

In their report, the Law Commission concluded that only things which conveyed two messages: a message about the thing itself (eg that it is a cheque) and a message to be found in its words or other symbols that is to be accepted and acted on (eg the message in a cheque to the banker to pay a specified sum), needed to be protected by the law of forgery. Thus, they sought to make clear that things like those in *Closs* and *Smith* were excluded from forgery by limiting the forgery of documents to 'instruments', which were defined as 'any instrument in writing whether of a formal or informal character'. In the view of the Commission, 'instrument' was the appropriate term to convey this meaning. However, although the new offence of forgery is concerned with making a false instrument, Parliament, in its wisdom, chose to change the proposed definition of 'instrument' and that is why the Act defines an instrument as including 'any document, whether formal or informal'. This left open the question of the extent of the offence of forgery and left unanswered the difficulties attached to *Closs* and *Smith*.

---

[76] *Gold and Schifreen* [1988] AC 1063, HL.
[77] *A-G's Reference (No 1 of 2000)* [2001] 1 WLR 331, CA.
[78] *Gold and Schifreen* [1988] AC 1063, HL.
[79] Williams 'What is a Document?' (1948) 11 MLR 150 at 160.   [80] (1857) Dears & B 460.
[81] (1858) Dears & B 566.

In 1987, in *Gold and Schifreen*,[82] the Court of Appeal adopted the Law Commission's view that only instruments containing both types of message needed to be protected by the law of forgery, a view which Lord Brandon, delivering the opinion of the House of Lords on appeal, referred to, obiter, with apparent approval.[83]

Applying the two-messages concept, paintings (even if purporting to bear the signature of an artist), a false autograph, and any writing on manufactured articles indicating the name of the manufacturer or country of origin, are not documents and therefore not 'instruments', whereas, for example, letters, wills, title deeds and cheques are. Of course, paintings and other things which are not 'instruments' are not necessarily beyond the reach of the criminal law if they are falsified, since their use (or attempted use) to deceive will usually involve an offence of fraud under the Fraud Act 2006, s 1 (or an attempt to commit such an offence).

False instrument

12.52 The FCA 1981, s 9(1) provides an exhaustive definition of the word 'false' for the purpose of forgery and related offences. An instrument is false for this purpose:

> '(a) if it purports to have been made in the form in which it is made by a person who did not in fact make it in that form; or
>
> (b) if it purports to have been made in the form in which it is made on the authority of a person who did not in fact authorise its making in that form; or
>
> (c) if it purports to have been made in the terms in which it is made by a person who did not in fact make it in those terms; or
>
> (d) if it purports to have been made in the terms in which it is made on the authority of a person who did not in fact authorise its making in those terms; or
>
> (e) if it purports to have been altered in any respect by a person who did not in fact alter it in that respect; or
>
> (f) if it purports to have been altered in any respect on the authority of a person who did not in fact authorise the alteration in that respect; or
>
> (g) if it purports to have been made or altered on a date on which, or at a place at which, or otherwise in circumstances in which, it was not in fact made or altered; or
>
> (h) if it purports to have been made or altered by an existing person but he did not in fact exist.'

Although it is irrelevant, for the purposes of the above definition, whether the falsity in question is or is not material, the nature of the requisite ulterior intent to prejudice is such that an immaterial falsity will not normally suffice.

12.53 A crucial element in this definition is that, **to be false, an instrument must** *purport* **to have been made or altered in a way (specified in s 9(1)(a) to (h) above) in which**

---

[82] [1987] QB 1116, CA.   [83] [1988] AC 1063 at 1071.

it was not made or altered. **An instrument is not false merely because it tells a lie (ie contains a false statement); it must tell a lie about itself** *and* **it must tell a lie about itself by purporting to have been made or altered in a way specified by the FCA 1981, s 9(1),** ie to have been made or altered by (or on the authority of) a person who did not make or alter it (or authorise its making or alteration), or by otherwise purporting to be made or altered in circumstances in which it was not made or altered. This requirement, sometimes described as the requirement of automendacity, was made by the old law relating to forgery.[84] The wording of the FCA 1981, s 9(1) indicates that this continues to be a requirement of the law, and it was affirmed by the House of Lords in 1987 in *More*[85] that it does.

In *More*, D intercepted a cheque for X. He opened a building society account in a false name and paid in the cheque. Later, he presented a withdrawal form for most of the amount paid in and was paid by the building society. The withdrawal form was, of course, completed in the assumed name of X. D was convicted of the forgery of the withdrawal form. He appealed unsuccessfully to the Court of Appeal, which held that the form was a false instrument within s 9(1)(h), since it purported to have been made by an existing person who did not exist, notwithstanding that it did not tell a lie about itself because it was completed by the account holder (albeit he had chosen to be known by a false name). Allowing D's appeal, the House of Lords held that the form was not a false instrument because D was a real person. It was he who was the holder of the account and in that capacity he had signed the withdrawal form. That form clearly purported to be signed by the person who originally opened the account and in this respect it was wholly accurate. Consequently, the House of Lords held, the withdrawal form did not tell a lie about itself and was therefore not a false instrument.

12.54 Despite the affirmation in *More* of the requirement of automendacity, the decision of the Court of Appeal in *Donnelly*[86] in 1984 (which was not referred to by the House of Lords in *More*) appeared to remove its force. This is because that decision suggests that any instrument which tells a lie about a past fact tells a lie about itself and is false within the above definition.

In *Donnelly*, D was the manager of a jeweller's shop. He completed and signed what purported to be a written valuation of jewellery for insurance purposes. The certificate stated that D had examined the items in question. In fact, the items of jewellery did not exist and the valuation was intended to be used to defraud the insurance company. D was convicted of forgery and appealed to the Court of Appeal, which dismissed his appeal. The Court of Appeal's reasoning was that the valuation certificate, the instrument in question, did tell a lie about itself because (within s 9(1)(g), above) it 'purported to be made in circumstances in which it was not made'. However, that phrase must be read in the context of the rest of s 9(1)(g)[87] (which refers to the date on which, or the place at

---

[84] *Re Windsor* (1865) 10 Cox CC 118 at 123, per Blackburn J; *Dodge* [1972] 1 QB 416, CA.

[85] [1987] 3 All ER 825, HL.

[86] [1984] 1 WLR 1017, CA. This decision was criticised by JC Smith [1984] Crim LR 491–492, but supported by Leng 'Falsity in Forgery' [1989] Crim LR 687 at 697–699.

[87] See, for example, *Pengelley v Bell Punch Co Ltd* [1964] 2 All ER 945, CA.

which, the instrument was made); consequently, it must refer to other circumstances directly related to the making of the instrument, eg the presence of witnesses. To give the phrase an unlimited meaning would render redundant all the other provisions set out in s 9(1)(a) to (h), since instruments covered by them and many other instruments telling lies would also be covered by it. In particular, any instrument telling a lie about a past fact would be a forgery because it would purport to be made after the fact occurred.

12.55 The status of *Donnelly* in the light of *More* was uncertain, given that the House did not refer to it in *More*. That uncertainty was increased by two decisions of the Court of Appeal in 1994, *Jeraj*[88] and *Warneford and Gibbs*.[89]

In the first of the two cases, *Jeraj*, D, a bank manager, signed a document on bank notepaper to the effect that he had received a certain letter of credit and that, on behalf of his bank, he had fully endorsed it. He could not have received the letter of credit or endorsed it, because it did not exist. Dismissing D's appeal against conviction for forgery, the Court of Appeal held that the trial judge had been correct in considering that he was bound by *Donnelly*, which (it said) had not been undermined by *More*. The Court of Appeal seems to have regarded the reasoning in *Donnelly* as applying in *Jeraj* (ie that the document was false within s 9(1)(g), above) because, since the letter of credit had never existed, the document had not been made after the letter had been received and endorsed, and therefore 'purported to be made in circumstances in which it was not made'. The Court went on to find a further point which, it said, did not turn on s 9(1)(g), viz that D's document was such as to represent that it, together with the letter of credit, amounted to some kind of articulated document, the letter of credit being subject to an endorsement by reason of D's document which was to be read with it. D's document thus told a lie about itself because it could not be an endorsement of a non-existent letter of credit. If this point did not turn on s 9(1)(g), and since there is no other paragraph in the FCA 1981, s 9(1) which is relevant, this explanation would seem not to involve the document telling a lie about itself in one of the specified ways. *Jeraj*, then, is noteworthy, not only for its affirmation of the standing of *Donnelly*, but also because of its statement to the effect that an instrument can be false if it tells a lie about itself in a way other than that specified in s 9(1). That statement's validity is dubious, to say the least.

In *Warneford and Gibbs*, where *Jeraj* was not cited, a differently constituted Court of Appeal held that *Donnelly* was wrongly decided and incapable of standing alongside *More*. D and E were charged with using a false instrument contrary to the FCA 1981, s 3. The alleged false instrument was 'a purported employer's reference', given to a building society in support of a mortgage application, relating to a person who had never been employed by the establishment in question. It was alleged by the prosecution that the reference was a false instrument within s 9(1)(g) because the fact that the person had never been employed by the establishment was a 'circumstance' in which the document on its face purported to have been made but was not in truth so made. The Court of Appeal allowed D and E's appeals against conviction. It held that s 9(1)(g) was not to be

---

[88] [1994] Crim LR 595, CA.   [89] [1994] Crim LR 753, CA.

construed so as to bring within its compass every document which contains a falsehood. The expression 'otherwise in circumstances in which it was not in fact made' in s 9(1)(g) referred to the circumstances of the making of the document, just as the references to date and places in s 9(1)(g) concerned the date and place of the making of the document. If, for example, it said, the document on its face purported to have been made in the presence of named individuals who were not in fact present, it would fall within s 9(1)(g). The lie had to relate to the actual circumstances of the document's making. A lie about other facts extraneous to the document did not suffice.

There was no way that *Jeraj* (approving *Donnelly*, and indeed going further) and *Warneford and Gibbs* (disapproving *Donnelly*) could be reconciled.

12.56 In 2000, the conflict was resolved by the Court of Appeal in *A-G's Reference (No 1 of 2000)*[90] where the Court held that, in view of *Jeraj*, *Donnelly* was binding on it and that *Warneford and Gibbs, Jeraj* not having been cited, had to be regarded as per incuriam and therefore wrong. The Court of Appeal, however, sought to limit its effects. **It held that an instrument can be false within s 9(1)(g), on the basis that 'it purports to have been made or altered ... in circumstances in which it was not in fact made or altered', if the past fact to which it falsely refers is one which was required to exist (or to have existed) before the instrument could properly (or honestly) be made or altered.** In this case, a coach driver, who was not taking a break, operated his tachograph machine in a way which indicated that he was taking a break and therefore that the coach was being driven by a second driver. As a result the tachograph sheet indicated that he was taking a break required by law when he was not. Truly to make that part of the instrument which was false it was essential for there to be a second driver during the period when the tachograph was operated in the second driver's position. At his trial for forgery, the trial judge ruled that the tachograph sheet did not amount to a false instrument and the driver was acquitted. The Court of Appeal held that the tachograph sheet did amount to a false instrument within s 9(1)(g). Applying *Donnelly* and *Jeraj*, it held that *Donnelly* could be adopted without going so far as to make any instrument which told a lie about some alleged past fact a forgery. In *Donnelly*, it said, the falsity related to an event (an examination) which must have occurred before a genuine valuation could be made. A similar comment could be made about *Jeraj*; there had to be a letter of credit which could be endorsed before the note could honestly be written. The Court admitted that the same was true of the facts in *Warneford and Gibbs* (there had to be an employer/employee situation before an employer's reference could be written) but it took the view that the Court of Appeal in that case would not have formed its view as to the correctness of *Donnelly* if it had been aware of *Jeraj*. The Court of Appeal concluded that *Donnelly* could be justified on the basis that it decided that if the falsity related to some past fact required to exist before an instrument could be 'properly made or altered', and those circumstances did not exist, the instrument would tell 'a lie' about itself because it was saying that it was made in circumstances which did not exist.

---

[90] [2001] 1 WLR 331, CA.

In terms of the facts of the case, the Court of Appeal accepted that there would not have been a false instrument within s 9(1)(g) if the record had been produced by the driver writing it out, as opposed to being produced by the tachograph being operated. In the former case, the falsity would not have related to the making of the instrument, but simply as to its contents, whereas the tachograph record made continuously over the period indicated by the record was capable of being a false instrument during the period when it showed that the driver in question was not driving and that a second driver must therefore have been driving. To make that part of the instrument properly, it was essential for there to be a second driver during the period the tachograph was operated in the second driver position. There was no second driver and therefore the instrument was false. The circumstance which was false was that the record was made during a period when there purported to be a second driver who was driving.

Although *A-G's Reference (No 1 of 2000)* restricts *Donnelly* to some extent, that restriction still leaves *Donnelly* (as explained) with a wide ambit; there are many cases where it will be satisfied. Moreover, the Court of Appeal's explanation of *Donnelly* involves a highly artificial way of squaring that case with *More*, and one which gives rise to fine distinctions. To state in writing, 'My examination of the painting has revealed that it is by Constable', when no examination has taken place, can render the document a forgery because of the lie about the antecedent circumstance which must have existed before the statement could properly be made, but a written statement, 'The painting is by Constable', cannot.

One thing which is surprising about *A-G's Reference (No 1 of 2000)* is that forgery (with all its complexity) was ever charged. It was, and still is, an either-way offence under the Transport Act 1968, s 99(5) knowingly to make a false entry on a tachograph record sheet.

Mens rea

12.57 The FCA 1981, s 1 states that **the defendant must have the ulterior intent 'that he or another shall use [the false instrument] to induce somebody**[91] **to accept it as genuine', and the ulterior intent to induce that person 'by reason of so accepting it to do or not to do some act to his own or any other person's prejudice'**[92] (besides that of the defendant);[93] these intents must exist when the defendant makes the false instrument.[94] It follows that it is not enough simply to intend to induce a person to believe that an instrument is genuine. Thus, making a false birth certificate solely to induce the belief that one comes from a noble family is not forgery.

---

[91] It is not necessary that the person should be identifiable: *Johnson* [1997] 8 Archbold News 1, CA.

[92] It was accepted by the Court of Appeal in *Campbell* (1985) 80 Cr App Rep 47 that intention is required as to both elements. This has been affirmed in a number of subsequent cases, eg *Garcia* (1987) 87 Cr App Rep 175, CA, where it was stated in relation to the intent as to the second element that the question was whether the defendant was aware of the prejudice alleged, and whether he intended it.

[93] *Utting* [1987] 1 WLR 1375, CA.   [94] *Ondhia* [1998] 2 Cr App Rep 150, CA.

The defendant need not intend to induce another human being; it suffices that he intends to induce a machine to respond to the instrument as if it were genuine.[95]

If the defendant makes a false instrument with the necessary intent, it is irrelevant whether or not it is communicated to anyone, and it is irrelevant whether anyone is induced to accept the instrument as genuine or whether prejudice (within the meaning set out below) is caused, except perhaps in an evidential sense.[96]

Provided that the maker of the false instrument has the necessary intents at the time of making it, it is irrelevant that he has not at that time made up his mind about the method of communicating the false instrument to the victim.[97] It must be proved, however, as s 1 requires, that he intends *it* (the false instrument made by him)[98] to be used to induce somebody to accept *it* as genuine and intends to induce that person by reason of so accepting *it* to do something to his own or another's prejudice. This being so, the actual decision of the Court of Appeal in *Ondhia*,[99] where the point just made was stated, is difficult to accept. In that case D had on three occasions made false instruments with intent that his agent would receive a facsimile of each of them from him by fax and transmit it to P, anticipating that P would accept it and treat it as a duplicate of the false original. The Court of Appeal rejected D's appeal against conviction for forgery in respect of the three original false instruments. This is odd because, when he made each of the three original false instruments, D did not intend to use *it* to induce anyone to do anything. He simply intended to use it to make a facsimile which could be used to induce someone to do something.

12.58 The act or omission intended to be induced must be to the prejudice of the person induced or anyone else besides the defendant.[100] 'Prejudice' is exhaustively defined by the FCA 1981, s 10. Section 10(1) states that, for the purposes of the offences under the 1981 Act described in this chapter, **an act or omission intended to be induced is only to a *person's prejudice* if it is one which, if it occurs:**

- **will**[101] **result:**
  - **in *his* temporary or permanent loss of property (including a loss by not getting what one might get as well as a loss by parting with what one has),**[102] as where a false cheque or will is made to cause another either to part with property or not to get property he might have got; or
  - **in *his* being deprived of the opportunity to earn remuneration or greater remuneration,** as where a letter falsely purporting to come from someone asked to give a character reference for an applicant for a job states that he is dishonest; or

---

[95] FCA 1981, s 10(3).
[96] *Ondhia* [1998] 2 Cr App Rep 150, CA.
[97] *Ondhia* [1998] 2 Cr App Rep 150 at 156.
[98] *Ondhia* [1998] 2 Cr App Rep 150 at 156.
[99] [1998] 2 Cr App Rep 150, CA.
[100] *Utting* [1987] 1 WLR 1375, CA.
[101] Ie 'must' and not merely 'may potentially': *Garcia* (1987) 87 Cr App Rep 175, CA.
[102] FCA 1981, s 10(5).

– in *his* being deprived of an opportunity to gain a financial advantage otherwise than by way of remuneration, as where a false testimonial is made to obtain a contract for which a number of different tenders have been made and a genuine tenderer is deprived of what would have been his contract if it had not been for the false statement; or

- will[103] result in somebody being given an opportunity:
  – to earn remuneration or greater remuneration from *him*, as where a false testimonial or degree certificate is made in order to obtain a job or better pay in a job; or
  – to gain a financial advantage from *him* otherwise than by way of remuneration, as where a false aeroplane or theatre ticket is made in order to gain from him a flight or admission; or

- will[104] be the result of *his* having accepted a false instrument as genuine, or a copy of a false instrument as a copy of a genuine one, in connection with his performance of any duty. An example would be where a cheque is falsely endorsed to induce a bank to accept it as genuine in connection with its performance of its duty to pay out only on a valid cheque.[105] Another example would be where a false tachograph record sheet is made to induce a relevant law enforcement officer to be satisfied with the compliance of the record with legal requirements. This last definition shows that the prejudice intended need not have any financial connotation at all.

An act which a person has an enforceable duty to do and an omission to do an act which a person is not entitled to do are to be disregarded.[106] Consequently, it is not forgery to make a false instrument to induce another to do what he is obliged to do, eg to pay a debt, or to refrain from doing what he is not entitled to do.

Where the intended inducement to respond to the instrument as if it were genuine is of a machine (eg a cash dispenser at a bank), the act or omission intended to be induced by the machine is treated as an act or omission to a person's prejudice.[107]

12.59 The above definition of the *mens rea* for forgery is an exclusive one. **Dishonesty is not an element of the offence.**[108] It follows, for example, that it is irrelevant that the defendant believed that he was legally entitled to a gain which he intended to make as a result of falsifying the instrument. Thus, a person commits forgery if, believing that he is legally entitled to property in the possession of another, he makes a false document of title to it in order to obtain the property. Indeed, it is not a defence in itself that the defendant might have actually been entitled to have the property transferred to him if he had made a true claim (but not if he made a false statement). If, as would normally be the case, the

---

103 Ie 'must' and not merely 'may potentially': *Garcia* (1987) 87 Cr App Rep 175, CA.
104 Ie 'must' and not merely 'may potentially': *Garcia* (1987) 87 Cr App Rep 175, CA.
105 *Campbell* (1985) 80 Cr App Rep 47, CA.
106 FCA 1981, s 10(2).   107 FCA 1981, s 10(4).
108 *Campbell* (1985) 80 Cr App Rep 47, CA; *Horsey v Hutchings* (1984) Times, 8 November, DC.

maker of a false instrument is proved to have had the two intentions he can be convicted of forgery.[109]

Copying a false instrument

12.60 By the FCA 1981, s 2:

> 'It is an offence for a person to make a copy of an instrument which is, and which he knows or believes to be, a false instrument, with the intention that he or another shall use it to induce somebody to accept it as a copy of a genuine instrument, and by reason of so accepting it to do or not to do some act to his own or any other person's prejudice.'

Actus reus

12.61 The *actus reus* of this offence is making a copy of a 'false instrument'; the definition of these two words is the same as for the offence of forgery.[110] The fact that the instrument must be false but need not be forged means that a person who, with the necessary intent, copies a false instrument will be liable, even though the instrument may have been made innocently.

There are no limits on the method of making the copy. Photocopying a false instrument is an obvious and easy method.

Mens rea

12.62 The *mens rea* required is that:

- The defendant must know or believe[111] that the instrument copied is false.
- The defendant must have the ulterior intent that he or another shall use the copy of the false instrument to induce somebody[112] to accept it as a copy of a genuine instrument, *and* the ulterior intent to induce that person by reason of so accepting it to do or not to do some act to his own or any other person's prejudice.[113] The elements of these ulterior intents have already been discussed in relation to forgery,[114] and what is said there applies equally here, except that references to 'false instrument' and 'genuine instrument' should be read as 'copy of a false instrument' and 'copy of a genuine instrument'. It follows from the present requirement that

---

[109] *A-G's Reference (No 1 of 2001)* [2002] EWCA Crim 1768. [110] Paras 12.51–12.56.
[111] For guidance as to these terms, see paras 3.43 and 3.44. [112] See para 12.57, n 91.
[113] By analogy with the FCA 1981, ss 1 and 3 (see paras 12.57 and 12.63), it is clear that an ulterior intention is required in both respects. [114] Paras 12.57 and 12.58.

the present offence is not committed by making a copy of a false instrument if the copy-maker intends to represent it as a copy of a false statement.

Using a false instrument or a copy of a false instrument

12.63 By the FCA 1981, s 3:

> 'It is an offence for a person to use an instrument which is, and which he knows or believes to be, false, with the intention of inducing somebody to accept it as genuine, and by reason of so accepting it to do or not to do some act to his own or any other person's prejudice.'

The defendant must be proved not only to have intended to induce somebody[115] to accept the false instrument as genuine, but also to have intended to induce the victim by reason of so accepting it to do or not to do something to his or another's prejudice.[116]

The FCA 1981, s 4 provides a similarly worded offence of using a copy of an instrument which is, and which he knows or believes to be, a false instrument, with the intention of inducing somebody to accept it as a copy of a genuine instrument, and by reason of so accepting it to do or not to do some act to his own or any other person's prejudice.

In the light of the explanations already given, no more need be said about these offences except to point out that 'use' is a wide term and covers (inter alia) a person who offers, delivers, tenders in payment or exchange, or exposes for sale or exchange, an instrument.

Offences relating to money orders, share certificates, cheques etc

12.64 The FCA 1981, s 5[117] provides a number of offences relating to the following instruments:

- money orders or postal orders;
- United Kingdom postage stamps;
- Inland Revenue stamps;
- share certificates;
- cheques and other bills of exchange;
- travellers' cheques;
- bankers' drafts;

---

[115] See para 12.57, n 91.   [116] *Tobierre* [1986] 1 All ER 346, CA.
[117] As amended by the Identity Cards Act 2006, s 44(2).

- promissory notes;
- cheque cards;
- debit cards;
- credit cards; and
- birth, adoption, marriage, civil partnership or death certificates or officially certified copies thereof.

Any such instrument is hereafter referred to as a 'specified instrument'.

12.65 By the FCA 1981, s 5(1) –

> 'It is an offence for a person to have in his custody or under his control a [specified instrument] which is, and which he knows or believes to be, false, with the intention that he or another shall use it to induce somebody to accept it as genuine, and by reason of so accepting it to do or not to do some act to his own or any other person's prejudice.'

'Custody' and 'control' are not explained by the Act, but it appears that 'custody' is intended to mean 'physical custody' and 'control' to import the notion of the power to direct what shall be done with the thing in question. The other elements of the offence have the same meaning as they have where they appear in FCA 1981, ss 1–4.

The relationship between this offence and some of those just described can be illustrated as follows. If someone makes out a false cheque with intent to induce someone to accept it as genuine, and with intent to induce that person by reason of so accepting it to do something to his prejudice, he commits forgery contrary to s 1. If he walks through the streets to a bank, with the false cheque, in order to cash it, he commits the present offence under s 5(1). If he then passes the cheque to a bank official in order to induce him to part with money, he commits the offence of 'using' contrary to s 3. Of course, it may be that different people will commit different offences in the cycle, as where the person who makes the false instrument gets other people to engage in the use of such false instruments.

12.66 If the intents required for an offence under the FCA 1981, s 5(1) cannot both be proved, but custody or control of one of the specified instruments is, the defendant can be convicted of an offence under the FCA 1981, s 5(2). **By s 5(2), it is an offence for a person merely to have in his custody or control, without lawful authority or excuse, a specified instrument which is, and which he knows or believes to be, false.** The maximum punishment on conviction on indictment is two years' imprisonment.[118]

The only part of this offence which requires further elaboration is 'without lawful authority or excuse', which does not appear in s 5(1). The defendant does not have the burden of proving this but merely has an evidential burden. A person who has a settled intention to take a false instrument to the police has a lawful excuse, even if he does not hand the

---

[118] FCA 1981, s 6(4).

instrument over at the earliest opportunity.[119] On the other hand, a solicitor in possession of a false instrument on behalf of a client in order to prepare his client's defence to a criminal charge does not have a lawful authority or excuse;[120] nor does a person who is in a state of indecision as to what to do with an instrument recently discovered to be false.[121]

12.67 The FCA 1981, s 5(3) provides:

> 'It is an offence for a person to make or have in his custody or under his control a machine or implement, or paper or any other material, which to his knowledge is or has been specially designed or adapted for the making of [a specified instrument], with the intention that he or another shall make [a specified instrument] which is false and that he or another shall use the instrument to induce somebody to accept it as genuine, and by reason of so accepting it to do or not to do some act to his own or any other person's prejudice.'

This offence strikes at the would-be forger even before he starts to make a false instrument, and before he has got as far as committing attempted forgery.[122] Like an offence under FCA 1981, s 5(1), an offence under s 5(3) is a species of preparatory offence.

12.68 The FCA 1981, s 5(4) is important where the intents required under s 5(3) cannot be proved, since it makes it an **offence for a person merely to make or have in his custody or under his control any such machine, implement, paper or material, without lawful authority or excuse**. This offence is punishable with a maximum of two years' imprisonment on conviction on indictment.[123]

Jurisdiction

12.69 The traditional approach[124] to jurisdiction over offences where the final constituent element occurred abroad caused serious difficulties in relation to offences of a fraudulent or similar type which increasingly tend to be transnational in nature. These difficulties led to the enactment of the Criminal Justice Act 1993, Pt I of which amended the rules relating to territorial jurisdiction in respect of the offences governed by it, but not other offences, so as to enable the courts of England and Wales to try transnational offences of a fraudulent or similar type.

12.70 Part I applies to what it calls Group A and Group B offences.
Group A offences are:

- theft, false accounting, false statements by an officer of a body corporate or unincorporated association, blackmail, handling stolen goods and retaining a wrongful credit, all of which are offences under the Theft Act 1968;

---

[119] *Wuyts* [1969] 2 QB 474, CA; *Sunman* [1995] Crim LR 569, CA (this case was concerned with a corresponding offence in relation to counterfeits).
[120] *Peterborough Justices, ex p Hicks* [1978] 1 All ER 225, DC.   [121] *Sunman* [1995] Crim LR 569, CA.
[122] Paras 14.120–14.130.   [123] FCA 1981, s 6(4).   [124] Para 1.22.

- fraud, possession etc of articles for use in frauds, making or supplying articles for use in frauds, participating in a fraudulent business carried on by sole trader etc and obtaining services dishonestly, all of which are offences under the Fraud Act 2006;
- forgery, copying a false instrument, using a false instrument or a copy of a false instrument, offences relating to money orders, share certificates, passports etc, and various counterfeiting offences, contrary to the Forgery and Counterfeiting Act 1981;
- possession of a false identity document etc; and
- the common law offence of cheating the public revenue.[125]

Group B offences are:

- encouraging or assisting the commission of a Group A offence;
- conspiracy to commit a Group A offence;
- attempt to commit a Group A offence; and
- common law conspiracy to defraud.[126]

12.71 The Criminal Justice Act 1993, s 2(3) provides that a person may be guilty of a Group A offence if any of the events which are 'relevant events' in relation to the offence occurred in England and Wales. For this purpose, a 'relevant event' is defined by s 2(1) as meaning any act, omission or other event (including any result of one or more acts or omissions) proof of which is required for conviction of the offence. In addition, in relation to an offence of fraud under the Fraud Act 2006, s 1, 'relevant event' includes:

- if the fraud involved an intention to make a gain and the gain occurred, that occurrence;
- if the fraud involved an intention to cause a loss or to expose another to a risk of loss and the loss occurred, that occurrence.[127]

Consequently an offence is regarded as committed in England and Wales if any one such element is committed or results there.

Section 3(1) provides that it is immaterial whether or not the defendant was a British citizen at any material time or was in England and Wales at any such time,[128] or whether the offence is an offence under the law of the foreign country in which part of it occurs.

12.72 The rules relating to jurisdiction over Group B offences are dealt with at the appropriate points in Chapter 14.

---

[125] Criminal Justice Act 1993, s 1(2), as amended by the Theft (Amendment) Act 1996, s 3, the Criminal Justice Act 1993 (Extension of Group A Offences) Order 2000, the Identity Cards Act 2006, s 30(1) and the Fraud Act 2006, Sch 1.

[126] Criminal Justice Act 1993, s 1(3).

[127] Criminal Justice Act 1993, s 2(1A), inserted by the Fraud Act 2006, Sch 1.

[128] Criminal Justice Act 1993, s 3(1).

FURTHER READING

Arlidge and Parry on Fraud (3rd edn, 2007) Chs 2–6, 10–12

Arnheim 'Forgery and Negligence' (1988) 132 SJ 350

Ormerod and Williams (eds) *Smith's Law of Theft* (9th edn, 2007) Chs 3, 4 and 9 (paras 9.27–9.113)

Leng 'Falsity in Forgery' [1989] Crim LR 679

ATH Smith *Property Offences* (1994) Ch 23

Sullivan 'Fraud – The Latest Law Commission Proposals' (2003) 69 JCL 139

13

Offences of damage
to property

OVERVIEW

This chapter deals with the following offences relating to the destruction or damaging of property:

- destroying or damaging property belonging to another;
- destroying or damaging property, intending to endanger life thereby, or being reckless as to life being endangered thereby;
- arson;
- racially or religiously aggravated criminal damage;
- threats to destroy or damage property; and
- possessing anything with intent to destroy or damage property.

All but the racially or religiously aggravated offence are governed by the Criminal Damage Act 1971.

13.1 The law of criminal damage was reformed by the Criminal Damage Act 1971 (CDA 1971) which implemented in the main the Law Commission's report, *Offences of Damage to Property*.[1] The CDA 1971 replaced the complex provisions of the Malicious Damage Act 1861, only a few of whose provisions (which are outside the scope of this book) remain in force. Like the Theft Acts 1968 and 1978, the Forgery and Counterfeiting Act 1981 and the Fraud Act 2006, the CDA 1971 is a completely new code, and no further reference needs to be made here to the repealed legislation.

[1] Law Com No 29 (1970).

Destroying or damaging property belonging to another

> **Key points 13.1**
>
> The CDA 1971, s 1(1) provides that:
> 'A person who without lawful excuse destroys or damages any property belonging to another intending to destroy or damage any such property or being reckless as to whether any such property would be destroyed or damaged shall be guilty of an offence.'

Trial and punishment

13.2 The offence under the CDA 1971, s 1(1) is punishable on conviction on indictment with imprisonment for a maximum of 10 years.[2]

Offences under the CDA 1971, s 1(1) are triable either way.[3] This is subject to the following important qualification. The qualification is that, where the value of the property destroyed or of the alleged damage does not exceed £5,000, a magistrates' court must proceed as if the offence was triable only summarily,[4] in which case the maximum punishment is currently three months'[5] imprisonment or a fine not exceeding level 4 on the standard scale or both.[6] The same applies[7] where the charge is that a person is an accomplice to such an offence or has encouraged or assisted its commission contrary to the Serious Crime Act 2007, Pt 2 or has attempted its commission.[8]

Where:

(a) a defendant is charged on the same occasion with two or more offences of criminal damage[9] under £5,000 which form part of a series of two or more offences of the same or a similar character; or

---

[2] CDA 1971, s 4.

[3] Magistrates' Courts Act 1980, s 17(1) and Sch 1.

[4] Magistrates' Courts Act 1980, s 22 and Sch 2, as amended by the Criminal Justice and Public Order Act 1994, s 46; Serious Crime Act 2007, s 63(1) and Sch 6, Pt 1. If it is not clear whether or not the value of the property destroyed or of the damage allegedly done exceeds £5,000, the magistrates' court must permit the defendant to choose summary trial or trial on indictment: *R (on the application of DPP) v Prestatyn Magistrates' Court* [2002] EWHC 1177 (Admin), DC.

[5] This will be increased to 51 weeks when the Criminal Justice Act 2003, Sch 32, para 27, comes into force.

[6] Magistrates' Courts Act 1980, s 33.

[7] Magistrates' Courts Act 1980, s 22 and Sch 2, as amended by the Criminal Justice and Public Order Act 1994, s 46; Serious Crime Act 2007, s 63(1) and Sch 6, Pt 1.

[8] The qualification referred to in the text does not apply to conspiracy to commit such an offence: paras 14.79 and 14.80.

[9] Or aggravated vehicle-taking only involving damage (whether to the vehicle or to other property) (para 10.121).

(b) the offence charged consists in encouraging or assisting the commission of two or more such offences contrary to the Serious Crime Act 2007, Pt 2,

the above qualification has effect as if any reference in it to the values involved were a reference to the aggregate values involved.[10]

The fact that 'low value' criminal damage has to be proceeded with 'as if' it was triable summarily does not mean that it is a summary offence. On the contrary, like any other offence under the CDA 1971, s 1(1) it is an 'either-way' offence (and therefore an 'indictable offence') for purposes other than trial, such as the offence of attempt.[11]

Although the effect of the qualification under the Magistrates' Courts Act 1980, s 22(1) and (2) is to prevent a magistrates' court sending a defendant for trial in the Crown Court for the offence of criminal damage contrary to the CDA 1971, s 1(1), where the value is below £5,000, the offence may, nevertheless, be tried on indictment if the requirements of the Criminal Justice Act 1988, s 40(1) are satisfied. The Criminal Justice Act 1988, s 40(1) provides that a count charging a person with such an offence (or with being a party to such an offence or with attempting or inciting it) may be included in an indictment if the charge:

(i) is founded on the same facts or evidence as a count charging an indictable offence; or

(ii) is part of a series of offences of the same or similar character as an indictable offence which is also charged;

but only if (in either case) the facts or evidence relating to the offence were disclosed in material served on a defendant sent for trial for the indictable offence.

By the CJA 1988, s 40(2), if a count is included in an indictment under s 40(1) the maximum punishment available on conviction is limited to the maximum for the offence available in a magistrates' court.

A limit on prosecutions

13.3 A prosecution may not be instituted against someone for any offence of 'doing unlawful damage to property' which belonged to his or her spouse (or civil partner) at the time of the offence except by or with the consent of the Director of Public Prosecutions. The only exceptions are:

- where the property also belonged to a third party and both spouses (or civil partners) are charged with damaging it;

---

[10] Magistrates' Courts Act 1980, s 22(11), inserted by the Criminal Justice Act 1988, s 38; Serious Crime Act 2007, s 63(1), Sch 6, Pt 1.

[11] Interpretation Act 1978, Sch 1; *Bristol Magistrates' Court, ex p E* [1998] 3 All ER 798, DC; *Fennell* (2000) 164 JP 386, CA.

- in the case of spouses, where, by virtue of a judicial decree or order,[12] the spouses were not obliged to cohabit at the material time;
- in the case of civil partners, where an order is in force providing for their separation.[13]

Actus reus

13.4 The *actus reus* required to be proved is that the defendant must destroy or damage property belonging to another. The definitions which follow are equally applicable to the other provisions of the Act.

Damage and destruction

13.5 Property may be damaged if it suffers permanent or temporary physical harm or permanent or temporary impairment of its usefulness or value.[14] If part of a machine is removed, without which it cannot work, the machine (but not the part) may be damaged[15] because its usefulness is impaired; likewise if the horizontal bars of scaffolding are removed from the vertical parts, the scaffolding (but not the parts removed) may be damaged.[16] On the other hand, simply to deprive someone of the use of property, for example, by wheel-clamping his car, does not amount to damage,[17] apparently because there is no intrusion into the integrity of the property.[18] A wall may be damaged if slogans are painted on it, as may beer if water is poured into it,[19] because its value is impaired. Grass may be damaged by trampling on it[20] and land may be damaged by tipping loads of rubbish on it; such conduct impairs the usefulness and value of the grass or land (in the latter case the cost of removing the rubbish reduces its present value).[21] Although the property damaged must be tangible, the damage itself need not be tangible.[22] Thus, the

---

[12] 'Judicial decree or order' includes a non-molestation order: *Woodley v Woodley* [1978] Crim LR 629, DC.

[13] Theft Act 1968, s 30(4) (amended by the Civil Partnership Act 2004, Sch 27), whose provisions apply to a charge under the CDA 1971, s 1(1) or s 1(1) and (3) (para 13.23), to a charge of attempting or conspiring to commit such an offence. They also apply to a charge of encouraging or assisting the commission of such an offence contrary to the Serious Crime Act 2007, Pt 2: Serious Crime Act 2007, s 63(1), Sch 6, Pt 1.

The provisions of the Theft Act 1968, s 30(4) would not seem to apply to the offences under the CDA 1971, s 1(2) or s 1(2) and (3) referred to in paras 13.19 and 13.23. Those offences involve more than unlawful damage and the defendant can be convicted of them even if the damaged property only belongs to him. It would be odd if there was a limit on prosecution when the property belonged to the defendant's spouse or civil partner.

[14] *Morphitis v Salmon* [1990] Crim LR 48, DC; *Whiteley* (1991) 93 Cr App Rep 25, CA; *Fiak* [2005] EWCA Crim 2381.

[15] *Fisher* (1865) LR 1 CCR 7, CCR; *Getty v Antrim County Council* [1950] NI 114.

[16] *Morphitis v Salmon* [1990] Crim LR 48, DC.

[17] *Stear v Scott* [1992] RTR 226 (note), DC; *Lloyd v DPP* [1992] 1 All ER 982, DC; *Drake v DPP* [1994] RTR 411, DC.

[18] *Drake v DPP* [1994] RTR 411, DC.   [19] *Roper v Knott* [1898] 1 QB 868, DC.

[20] *Gayford v Chouler* [1898] 1 QB 316, DC.   [21] *Henderson and Battley* (1984) unreported, CA.

[22] *Whiteley* (1991) Times, 6 February, CA.

erasure or alteration of the magnetic particles on an audio or video tape or disc may constitute damage to the tape or disc if it impairs the value or usefulness of the tape or disc, even though there is no physical harm to the tape or disc itself.[23]

The test of physical harm or impairment of the property's usefulness or value does not conclude the matter because, if the harm or impairment is minimal, it is likely to be found that there is no 'damage' for the purposes of the Act. Since it is not necessary that the effect of what has been done should be permanent, the fact that it is rectifiable does not prevent the property being damaged. However, where it is rectifiable the amount (and any cost) of rectification are relevant factors in determining whether there is damage;[24] if these are minimal it may be found that what has occurred is not 'damage'. In *Roe v Kingerlee*,[25] the Divisional Court held that graffiti smeared in mud on the wall of a police cell could be damage, even though it could be washed off. A case where it might be found as a matter of fact and degree that there was no damage might be spitting on someone's raincoat.[26]

Whether what is done to property amounts to 'damage' under the above principles is a question of fact for the jury or magistrates.[27]

A modification of the contents of a computer is not regarded as damaging any computer or computer storage medium unless its effect on that computer or computer storage medium impairs its physical condition.[28] It may, however, constitute an offence under the Computer Misuse Act 1990, s 3 (unauthorised act with intent to impair, or with recklessness as to impairing, operation of computers, etc).

The destruction of property requires something more than damage. Examples of destruction are the demolition of a machine, the pulling down of a wall or other structure, reducing a dinghy to ashes by setting fire to it or the killing of an animal. It would be most unusual for the process of destruction not to involve damage to the property.

Property

13.6 For the purposes of the CDA 1971, 'property' is defined by s 10(1) as:

> 'property of a tangible nature, whether real or personal, including money and –
>
> (a) including wild creatures which have been tamed or are ordinarily kept in captivity, and any other wild creatures or their carcasses if, but only if, they have been

---

[23] *Cox v Riley* (1986) 83 Cr App Rep 54, DC; *Whiteley* (1991) Times, 6 February, CA. Note the actual decisions in these cases in so far as they related to computers would now be different because of the Criminal Damage Act 1971, s 10(5).

[24] See *Cox v Riley* (1986) 83 Cr App Rep 54, DC, for an example of this.

[25] [1986] Crim LR 735, DC. See also *Hardman v Chief Constable of Avon and Somerset Constabulary* [1986] Crim LR 330, Crown Ct; *Fiak* [2005] EWCA Crim 2381.

[26] *A (a juvenile) v R* [1978] Crim LR 689, Crown. Ct. (Crown Court held on appeal, acquitting the defendant, that such spitting did not damage the raincoat where the spittle could be removed by a wipe with a damp cloth.)

[27] *Roe v Kingerlee* [1986] Crim LR 735, DC; *Henderson and Battley* (1984) unreported, CA; *Cox v Riley* (1986) 83 Cr App Rep 54, DC.

[28] Criminal Damage Act 1971, s 10(5), inserted by the Police and Justice Act 2006, s 52, Sch 14, para 2.

> reduced into possession which has not been lost or abandoned or are in the course of being reduced into possession;[29] but
>
> (b) not including mushrooms growing wild on any land or flowers, fruit or foliage of a plant growing wild on any land.'[30]

This definition is very similar to the definition in the Theft Act 1968, s 4 of property which can be stolen; but there are four differences. First, land itself cannot generally be stolen, but there are **no limits on when land can be the subject of criminal damage**. If someone moves his fence to capture a little of his neighbour's lawn, he cannot be convicted of theft of the lawn,[31] but he can be convicted of criminal damage if he damages the lawn in replacing the fence. Second, although intangible property can be stolen, **intangible property is not property for the purposes of criminal damage**. Third, unlike theft (where they can be stolen if picked for sale, reward or other commercial purpose) **wild mushrooms and the flowers, fruit or foliage of any wild plant cannot be the subject of criminal damage**. Fourth, in theft, to be stealable a wild creature not tamed or ordinarily kept in captivity must have been reduced into possession by or on behalf of another person, or another person must be in the course of reducing it into possession; however, there is **no requirement in the corresponding part of the present definition that the reduction into possession be by or on behalf of another person or that another person be in the course of reduction into possession.**

Belonging to another

13.7 The property destroyed or damaged must 'belong to another'. This phrase is defined by the CDA 1971, s 10(2)–(4). Section 10(2) provides:

> 'Property shall be treated for the purposes of this Act as belonging to any person –
>
> (a) having the custody or control of it;
>
> (b) having in it any proprietary right or interest (not being an equitable interest arising only from an agreement to transfer or grant an interest); or
>
> (c) having a charge on it.'

This definition is similar to that of 'belonging to another' in the Theft Act 1968, s 5(1), dealt with in paras 10.38 to 10.49.

There are only two divergences from the Theft Act provision. First, the CDA 1971, s 10(2)(a) speaks of **'custody or control'**, as opposed to 'possession or control'. These terms are not defined by the CDA 1971, but it seems that 'custody' is intended to mean 'physical custody' and 'control' to import the notion of the power to direct what shall be done with the thing in question. These terms consequently avoid the technicalities connected with

---

[29] See para 10.36.

[30] 'Mushroom' includes any fungus and 'plant' includes any shrub or tree: CDA 1971, s 10(2). In relation to various terms in s 10(1), see paras 10.26–10.36. [31] Para 10.35.

the concept of possession. Second, s 10(2)(c) states that **property belongs to a person who has a charge on it** (as where someone mortgages land by way of charge to a building society); such a person will have a proprietary right or interest in the property and it is not obvious why special provision was made for charges by the Act.

The CDA 1971, s 10(3) and (4) provides that, as in the case of theft, where property is subject to a trust, the person to whom it belongs shall include any person having the right to enforce the trust; and that property belonging to a corporation sole is to be treated as belonging to the corporation notwithstanding a vacancy in the corporation.[32]

The requirement that the property destroyed or damaged must belong to another means that a person to whom alone the property belongs cannot be convicted under the CDA 1971, s 1(1), if he destroys or damages it, however dishonest his motive (eg to defraud an insurance company). On the other hand, as in the case of theft, an owner (or someone else to whom the property belongs) can be convicted under s 1(1), if the property also belongs to another.

Mens rea

13.8 **The CDA 1971, s 1(1) requires that the defendant should intend, or be reckless as to, the destruction or damage of property belonging to another.** As was confirmed by the Court of Appeal in *Smith (David)*,[33] it is not enough for the defendant to intend, or be reckless as to, the destruction or damaging of property; he must intend, or be reckless as to, the destruction or damaging of property *belonging to another*, which he will not be if he believes that the property is his.

'Intention' and 'recklessness' are discussed in paras 3.5 to 3.36.

'Without lawful excuse'

13.9 A defendant who has committed the *actus reus* of an offence under the CDA 1971, s 1(1) with the requisite *mens rea* is not guilty of that offence if he has a 'lawful excuse'.

The CDA 1971, s 5(2) provides that:

'A person [charged with an offence under s 1(1), or s 1(1) and (3), or with an offence under s 2 or s 3 other than one of a specified type] shall, whether or not he would be treated for the purposes of this Act as having a lawful excuse apart from this subsection, be treated as having a lawful excuse –

   (a) if at the time of the act or acts alleged to constitute the offence he believed that the person or persons whom he believed to be entitled to consent to the destruction of or damage to the property in question had so consented, or would have consented

---

[32] See the explanation of the corresponding provisions in paras 10.51 and 10.67.

[33] [1974] QB 354, CA; see para 3.81.

> to it if he or they had known of the destruction or damage and its circumstances; or
>
> (b) if he destroyed or damaged or threatened to destroy or damage the property in question or, in the case of a charge of an offence under s 3 above, intended to use or cause or permit the use of something to destroy or damage it, in order to protect property[34] belonging to himself or another[35] or a right or interest in property which was or which he believed to be vested in himself or another, and at the time of the act or acts alleged to constitute the offence he believed –
>   (i) that the property, right or interest was in immediate need of protection; and
>   (ii) that the means of protection adopted or proposed to be adopted were or would be reasonable having regard to all the circumstances.'

Section 5(2) lays down **two statutory grounds of lawful excuse:**

- **belief in consent; and**
- **belief in defence of property.**

For these purposes, **it is immaterial whether the belief is reasonable or not,** provided it is genuinely held.[36] In relation to both grounds, the defendant has the burden of adducing evidence to raise the issue;[37] if there is some evidence, however tenuous or nebulous, it must be left to the jury with a direction about it and the prosecution must prove beyond reasonable doubt that the requirements of the ground in question are not satisfied. On no account should the judge direct the jury to convict.[38]

Belief in consent

13.10 The operation of the CDA 1971, s 5(2)(a) can be exemplified as follows. In *Denton*,[39] D set fire to some machinery on his employer's premises and thereby damaged the premises and their contents. D gave evidence that he had acted at his employer's request, so that the latter could make a fraudulent insurance claim. The Court of Appeal held that D's belief (which was conceded), that the person (his employer) whom he honestly believed to

---

[34] Damage or destruction in order to protect oneself or another person is obviously not covered by this provision: *Baker and Wilkins* [1997] Crim LR 497, CA.

[35] In *Cresswell v DPP; Currie v DPP* [2006] EWHC 3379, (2007) 171 JP 233, DC, Keene LJ held that s 5(2)(b) cannot apply where both the destroyed property and the thing sought to be protected are in the ownership of the same person; the other judge (Walker J) left the point open.

[36] CDA 1971, s 5(3). Even a drunken belief will suffice: *Jaggard v Dickinson* [1981] QB 527, DC; para 15.93.

[37] *Hill and Hall* (1988) 89 Cr App Rep 74, CA. This requirement was interpreted strictly in *Jones (Iorwerth)* [2003] EWCA Crim 894 at [14] where the Court of Appeal, in rejecting a claim that the judge should have left the defence under s 5(2)(b) to the jury, said: 'Before the defence can leave the ground, it is necessary...for the defendant to assert in his evidence, and not merely through the mouth of his counsel and not merely through a defence statement, that he had the necessary belief.'

[38] *Wang* [2005] UKHL 9, disapproving *Hill and Hall* (1988) 89 Cr App Rep 74, CA on this point.

[39] [1982] 1 All ER 65, CA. Other aspects of this decision were criticised in *Appleyard* (1985) 81 Cr App Rep 319, CA.

be entitled to consent to the damage had so consented, provided him with a lawful excuse under s 5(2)(a), despite the employer's dishonest motive.

13.11 *Blake v DPP*[40] shows the limits of s 5(2)(a). D, a vicar, took part in a demonstration against the Gulf War of 1991. He wrote a Biblical quotation with a marker pen on a pillar outside the Houses of Parliament. He claimed that he was carrying out the instructions of God and (inter alia) that he had a lawful excuse under s 5(2)(a) because he believed that God was the person entitled to consent to the damage of the property. Dismissing D's appeal against conviction, the Divisional Court held that a belief that God had consented to the pillar being damaged and that God was entitled to consent could not amount to a lawful excuse under English law.

Belief in defence of property

13.12 In relation to the CDA 1971, s 5(2)(b), the property intended to be protected, unlike that damaged, need not always be tangible; it can also consist of a right or privilege in or over land, whether created by grant, licence or otherwise.[41] Just as a person is entitled in appropriate circumstances to shoot a dog attacking his sheep, so is he entitled to demolish a wall barring a right of way which he has (or believes he has).[42]

13.13 The defendant has a lawful excuse within s 5(2)(b) if:

- he destroyed or damaged the property in *question in order to protect property or a right or interest in it*;
- the property belonged to the defendant or another or, as the case may be, the right or interest was or was believed by the defendant to be vested in himself or another;
- he *believed* the property to be in immediate need of protection; and
- he *believed* that the means adopted to protect it were reasonable, having regard to all the circumstances.

Sometimes, the defence under s 5(2)(b) will overlap with the defence of prevention of crime under the Criminal Law Act 1967 or the common law defence of defence of property but it is available even if the threatened harm is not itself criminal or unlawful,[43] whereas the other defences are not.[44] Thus, for example, a person who damages the equipment of a council (which is being used in pursuance of the council's power to abate a public nuisance), in order to protect his property but knowing that the threatened harm is lawful, can invoke the defence under s 5(2)(b).

13.14 *In order to protect property* Although this requirement would seem to refer solely to the defendant's purpose, ie what *he* was aiming to achieve, and nothing else, it has been

---

[40] [1993] Crim LR 586, DC.   [41] CDA 1971, s 5(4).

[42] *Chamberlain v Lindon* [1998] 2 All ER 538, DC.

[43] *Jones (Margaret)* [2004] EWCA Crim 1981. This point was not dealt with on appeal: [2006] UKHL 16.

[44] Para 16.1.

held that it has an objective aspect to be determined on the facts as the defendant believed them to be. In *Hunt*,[45] D, who assisted his wife in her job as deputy warden of a block of old people's flats, set fire to some bedding in a relatively isolated part of the block. He said that he did so in order to demonstrate that the fire alarm was not working (despite requests that it be repaired) and thereby to protect the flats from the risks posed to them. Affirming D's conviction for arson, contrary to the CDA 1971, as 1(1) and (3), the Court of Appeal held that, while D had acted in order to draw attention to the defective alarm, he had not done so in order to protect property. It said:

> 'The question whether or not a particular act of destruction or damage or threat of destruction or damage was done or made in order to protect property belonging to another must be, on the true construction of the statute, an objective test. Therefore we have to ask ourselves whether, whatever the state of this man's mind and assuming an honest belief, that which he admittedly did was done in order to protect this particular property, namely the old people's home in Hertfordshire?
>
> If one formulates the question in that way, ... it admits of only one answer: this was not done in order to protect property; it was done in order to draw attention to the defective state of the fire alarm. It was not an act which in itself did protect or was capable of protecting property.'[46]

This is tantamount to rewriting the present requirement.

Hunt was followed by the Court of Appeal in two cases where the facts were essentially the same, *Ashford and Smith*[47] and *Hill and Hall*.[48] In *Hill and Hall* D1 and D2 had been convicted of possessing articles with intent to damage the perimeter fence of a naval base without lawful excuse, contrary to the CDA 1971, s 3.[49] They claimed that they had a lawful excuse because the base was an obvious target for a nuclear strike and consequential damage to surrounding property and that they acted to have the base abandoned and thus the danger removed. The Court of Appeal held that the question was whether, on the facts as believed by D1 and D2, their intended act could amount to something done to protect people's homes adjacent to the base.

Further authority for the present point is provided by *Johnson v DPP, Blake v DPP* and *Chamberlain v Lindon*, referred to in para 13.16.

In *Johnson v DPP*,[50] D, a squatter, chiselled off locks from the door of the house. His defence was that he had done so to replace them with a lock of his own, in order to protect his property in the house which he believed to be in immediate need of protection, and that therefore he had a lawful excuse under s 5(2)(b). Dismissing his appeal against conviction for criminal damage, the Divisional Court held that, judged objectively, the damage caused in changing the locks could not have the effect of protecting property, and that, applying the subjective test, D had no belief that his property was in immediate need of protection and that the means of protection were reasonable.

---

[45] (1977) 66 Cr App Rep 105, CA.   [46] (1977) 66 Cr App Rep 105 at 108.
[47] [1988] Crim LR 682, CA.   [48] (1988) 89 Cr App Rep 74, CA.
[49] See para 13.30.   [50] [1994] Crim LR 673, DC.

In *Blake v DPP*, referred to in para 13.11, D also claimed that he had a lawful excuse under s 5(2)(b) because he damaged the pillar to protect property in the Gulf States. Dismissing D's appeal against conviction for criminal damage, the Divisional Court held that, judged objectively, D's conduct could not be said to be done to protect property in the Gulf States, as such protection was too remote from his conduct.

13.15 *Property belonging to the defendant or another* The defendant cannot rely successfully on s 5(2)(b) if what he seeks to protect is neither property belonging to himself or another nor a right or interest in property which is (or which he believes is) vested in himself or another. This was the crucial point in *Cresswell v DPP; Currie v DPP*.[51] D1 and D2 went onto farmland and destroyed badger traps in order to protect wild badgers. On appeal to the Divisional Court against conviction under the CDA 1971, s 1(1), Keene LJ held that, because badgers had not yet entered a set trap (and thereby been reduced into possession) they were not 'property' as defined by s 10(1)(a).[52] Walker J did not come to a concluded view on this point. However, both judges were agreed that the badgers did not belong to anyone within the terms of s 10(2) because no one had possession or control of them, or any proprietary right or interest in them. Thus, D1 and D2 could not rely on s 5(2)(b).

It is odd that, according to the wording of s 5(2)(b), where the defendant acts in order to protect a right or interest in property it is irrelevant that the right or interest is not vested in him or another if he believes that it is, whereas if he acts in order to protect property itself it must actually belong to the defendant or another. The emphasis on the defendant's beliefs in much of s 5(2)(b) might encourage a court, when the occasion arises, to imply that a mistaken belief that the property for whose protection the defendant acts belongs to him or another (as where the defendant acts to protect property which has been abandoned and is ownerless, believing that it belongs to another) can satisfy the present requirement under s 5(2)(b).

13.16 *Belief that the property or right or interest is in need of immediate protection* Whether the defendant believes that the property etc is in need of protection is a subjective question. On the other hand, it has been held that whether the property etc is in need of 'immediate' protection is an objective question, to be determined by the court or jury in the light of all the circumstances as the defendant believed them to be. One such authority is *Hill and Hall*, referred to in para 13.14, where the Court of Appeal went on to hold that there was no evidence on which it could be said that, on the facts as they believed them to be, D1 and D2 believed that the houses near the base were in need of immediate protection. Whether there is a need of immediate protection will depend partially, at least, on whether the perceived threat has taken shape or is merely speculative. Recognition of this may be derived from the decision of the Divisional Court in *Chamberlain v Lindon*,[53] where D had destroyed a wall built on V's land nine months previously, believing that doing so was necessary to protect his own right of vehicular access across that land and

---

[51] [2006] EWHC 3379 (Admin), DC.
[52] Paras 10.36 and 13.6.   [53] [1998] 2 All ER 538, DC.

that the means adopted were reasonable in the circumstances. The Divisional Court held that the magistrates had been entitled to find that D had a lawful excuse for the purposes of s 5(2)(b). On the facts believed by D, his demolition of the wall could, it held, amount objectively to something done to protect his right of way; the fact that he had chosen to demolish the wall to protect his right of way because he hoped to avoid litigation did not mean that the act of destroying the wall was not done by D to protect his right of way on the facts as he believed them. Moreover, it held, the fact that the wall had stood for nine months did not prevent there being, on the facts as D believed them, an immediate need for its removal; there was a present need to remove the wall, and the longer it remained the more urgent the need to remove it so as to avoid any suggestion of acquiescence in the obstruction. Referring to *Hill and Hall*, Sullivan J (with whose conclusions and reasoning Rose LJ agreed) said:

> 'The appellants in [*Hill and Hall*] had professed to be concerned as to the potential con-sequences of a possible nuclear attack in the future. Here, on the facts, as believed by the respondent, his right of way was actually being obstructed... [I]t was not a case of a risk of there being an obstruction at some future speculative date, there was a present need to remove the obstruction. The respondent was not destroying or damaging property as some sort of pre-emptive strike to prevent some future obstruction.'[54]

13.17 *Belief that the means adopted were reasonable*   This is a purely subjective require-ment. In *Chamberlain v Lindon* Sullivan J said:

> '[T]he question is not whether the means adopted by the defendant were objectively rea-sonable having regard to all the circumstances, but whether the defendant believed them to be so.'[55]

This is more liberal than the approach taken in respect of the private and public defences, eg prevention of crime and self-defence, referred to in Chapter 16, which requires the defend-ant's force to be objectively reasonable on the facts as he believed them to be, regardless of whether he believes the force was reasonable.[56] The Law Commission considers that it is anomalous that a more stringent rule should apply when a person injures another in defending himself than when he damages property to protect other property. It has rec-ommended that s 5 should be brought into line with self-defence in this respect.[57]

Other types of defence

13.18 The CDA 1971, s 5(5) provides that the provisions in s 5 are not to be construed as casting doubt on any defence recognised by law as a defence to a criminal charge, eg the

---

[54] [1998] 2 All ER 538 at 544.

[55] [1998] 2 All ER 538 at 546. See also *Jones (Iorwerth)* [2003] EWCA Crim 894.   [56] Para 16.21.

[57] *Legislating the Criminal Code: Offences against the Person and General Principles* (1993), Law Com No 218, para 37.6.

excuses of duress by threats or of circumstances and justifications of prevention of crime and of defence of property.[58] It will be noted that s 5(5) refers to a defence recognised by law. Thus, a person who damages property in the belief that he has the consent of God to do so does not have a lawful excuse because such a belief does not constitute a defence recognised by English law. This was decided by the Divisional Court in *Blake v DPP*.[59] Nor does a motorist have a lawful excuse if he damages a wheel clamp to free his car, having parked on property with knowledge of the risk of being clamped,[60] since his conduct does not fall within any recognised defence.

Destroying or damaging property intending thereby to endanger life or being reckless as to life being endangered thereby

---

Key points 13.2

By the CDA 1971, s 1(2):
'A person who without lawful excuse destroys or damages any property, whether belonging to himself or another –

(a) intending to destroy or damage any property or being reckless as to whether any property would be destroyed or damaged; and

(b) intending by the destruction or damage to endanger the life of another or being reckless whether the life of another would be thereby endangered,

shall be guilty of an offence.'[61]

An offence under the CDA 1971, s 1(2) is triable only on indictment[62] and punishable with a maximum of imprisonment for life.[63]

13.19 There are two separate offences under s 1(2)

- criminal damage with intent to endanger life; and
- criminal damage reckless as to whether life would be endangered.[64]

As a result the jury's verdict of guilty of one of the above offences provides a more specific basis of the facts on which their verdict has been based and thereby assists the judge in sentencing; the two types of *mens rea* involved in the present offences involve very

---

[58] Ch 16.   [59] [1993] Crim LR 586, DC. Also see *Hipperson v DPP* [1996] CLY 1445, DC.
[60] *Lloyd v DPP* [1992] 1 All ER 982, DC.
[61] For the definition of various terms in s 1(2), see paras 13.5 and 13.6.
[62] But see the correspondence in [1979] Crim LR 266 and 607 and [1980] Crim LR 69.
[63] CDA 1971, s 4.   [64] *Roberts* [1998] 1 Cr App Rep 441, CA.

different degrees of *mens rea*. The prosecution should charge two counts, one alleging an offence committed with intent to endanger life and one an offence committed recklessly as to such endangerment, where there is reliance in the alternative on intention and recklessness.[65]

Actus reus

13.20 The *actus reus* of an offence under s 1(2) consists in destroying or damaging any property, whether belonging to the defendant or another. It is not necessary that anyone's life is actually endangered by the destruction or damage caused.[66] Such endangerment is not a requirement of the *actus reus*.

Mens rea

13.21 The defendant must intend to destroy or damage property or be reckless as to this. In addition, he must intend *by that destruction or damage* to endanger the life of another or be reckless as to whether *that destruction or damage* endangers the life of another.

It is not enough merely that the defendant intends to endanger life, or is reckless as to whether life would be endangered, *by the act* which causes the destruction or damage. Accordingly, as was held by the House of Lords in *Steer*,[67] a person who fires a gun from outside a house at a person standing behind a window in it cannot be convicted under s 1(2), even though he may have intended to endanger the life of that person, if he did not intend his intended damaging of the window to endanger life (and was not reckless as to that damage endangering life).

An example of the points made in this paragraph and para 13.20 is *Dudley*.[68] D set fire to V's house with a fire bomb but V was able to extinguish the fire. Only trivial damage was caused and life was not endangered. Nevertheless, the Court of Appeal upheld D's conviction for arson being reckless as to endangering life, contrary to s 1(2) and (3) (below). When D threw the firebomb he had clearly been reckless as to life being endangered by the damage which the bomb might cause, and it was irrelevant that life had not in fact been endangered by the damage caused.

Lawful excuse

13.22 The question whether the defendant had a lawful excuse for the purposes of the CDA 1971, s 1(2), for acting as he did is dependent on the general law, whereas, as we have seen, there are by virtue of s 5 of the CDA 1971 additional statutory defences of lawful excuse in respect of offences of criminal damage contrary to s 1(1).

---

[65] *Hoof* (1980) 72 Cr App Rep 126, CA. Also see *Hardie* [1984] 3 All ER 848 at 853–854.
[66] *Dudley* [1989] Crim LR 57, CA; *Parker* [1993] Crim LR 856, CA.
[67] [1988] AC 111, HL.   [68] [1989] Crim LR 57, CA.

Arson

Key points 13.3

By the CDA 1971, s 1(3), if the destruction or damage contrary to s 1 (ie contrary to s 1(1) or s 1(2)) is by fire, the offence 'shall be charged as arson'.[69]

13.23 Arson contrary to the CDA 1971, s 1(1) and (3) is triable either way;[70] the qualification relating to 'small value' destruction or damage[71] does not apply to it. Arson contrary to s 1(2) and (3) is triable only on indictment. Arson whether contrary to s 1(1) and (3) or s 1(2) and (3) is punishable with a maximum of imprisonment for life. The higher maximum penalty for arson contrary to s 1(1) and (3) than is available for an offence under s 1(1) may be justified by the exceptional danger to life and property involved in the use of fire for the destruction or damaging of property.

13.24 The requirements for arson contrary to s 1(1) and (3) and s 1(2) and (3) respectively are the same as for s 1(1) and s 1(2) respectively, except that it must be proved that the destruction or damage was caused by fire. The provisions of s 5 apply to the defence of lawful excuse in respect of the offence of arson contrary to s 1(1) and (3), but not to arson contrary to s 1(2) and (3).

13.25 There are two offences contrary to s 1(2) and (3):

- arson with intent to endanger life; and
- arson reckless as to whether life would be endangered.[72]

There are therefore three separate offences of arson. As in the case of an offence contrary to s 1(2), an allegation of an offence contrary to s 1(2) and (3) should contain two separate counts: arson with intent to endanger life and arson being reckless as to life being endangered, where there is reliance in the alternative on intention and recklessness.[73]

A typical example of an offence under the CDA 1971, s 1(2) and (3) is where the defendant sets fire to his own house, in order to make an insurance claim, despite being aware that someone is asleep inside it.

---

[69] It is uncertain whether this means that, in the Crown Court, it is mandatory to use the word 'arson', or whether it suffices to allege that the destruction or damage was by fire: see *Drayton* [2005] EWCA Crim 2013, where the point was left open, despite the view taken in *Booth* [1999] Crim LR 144, CA, that the use of 'arson' is mandatory. In a magistrates' court, the use of 'arson' is not mandatory, although it may be helpful if that word is used: *Drayton*.

[70] Magistrates' Court Act 1980, s 17(1) and Sch 1.   [71] Para 13.2.

[72] *Roberts* [1998] 1 Cr App Rep 441, CA.

[73] *Hoof* (1980) 72 Cr App Rep 126, CA. See also *Hardie* [1984] 3 All ER 848 at 853–854.

Racially or religiously aggravated criminal damage

13.26 The Crime and Disorder Act 1998, s 30(1), as amended by the Anti-terrorism, Crime and Security Act 2001, s 39, makes it **an offence to commit an offence under the CDA 1971, s 1(1) which is racially or religiously aggravated.** The 'racially or religiously aggravated element' is similar to that which applies to the offences of racially or religiously aggravated assault, referred to in paras 7.98 to 7.113. However, because of the nature of the offence of simple criminal damage, the definition of racial or religious aggravation in the Crime and Disorder Act 1998, s 28(1) has needed some modification, and this is achieved by the Crime and Disorder Act 1998, s 30(3). As modified – the modification is in italics – s 28(1) provides that an offence is racially or religiously aggravated for the purposes of s 30 if:

- at the time of committing the offence, or immediately before or after doing so, the offender demonstrates towards the *person to whom the property belongs or is treated as belonging for the purposes of the CDA 1971*[74] hostility based on *that person's* actual or presumed membership of, or association with members of, a racial or religious group; or
- the offence is motivated (wholly or partly) by hostility towards members of a racial or religious group based on their membership of that group.

In addition to the requirement of racial or religious aggravation, the prosecution must prove the elements of the offence of criminal damage contrary to the CDA 1971, s 1(1), viz that the defendant has intentionally or recklessly, and without lawful excuse, destroyed or damaged property belonging to another. **Because criminal damage by fire must be charged as arson, punishable with a maximum of life imprisonment, contrary to the CDA 1971, s 1(1) and (3), and is therefore not merely an offence under s 1(1), the offence of racially or religiously aggravated criminal damage cannot be committed by fire.**

13.27 An offence under the Crime and Disorder Act 1998, s 30 is triable either way. The maximum punishment on conviction on indictment is imprisonment for 14 years[75] (as opposed to 10 for an offence under the CDA 1971, s 1(1)).

It is noteworthy that the qualification (referred to in para 13.2) relating to the trial of cases of damage or destruction not exceeding £5,000 in value in the case of an offence under the CDA 1971, s 1(1) does not apply to racially or religiously aggravated criminal damage. While the qualification is appropriate for the 'ordinary' case of criminal damage it is not for the more serious conduct inherent in racially or religiously aggravated criminal damage.

---

[74] See para 13.7.   [75] CDA, s 30(2).

Threats to destroy or damage property

13.28 The CDA 1971, s 2 provides that:

> 'A person who without lawful excuse makes to another a threat, intending that that other would fear it would be carried out,
>
> (a) to destroy or damage any property belonging to that other or a third person; or
>
> (b) to destroy or damage his [ie the defendant's] own property in a way which he knows is likely to endanger the life of that other or a third person;
>
> shall be guilty of an offence.'

The threat must be to do something which would be an offence against the CDA 1971, s 1. It must be made with the intention of inducing a fear in the mind of the recipient that it would be carried out.

In relation to the requirement in a case involving s 2(a) of a threat to destroy or damage the property belonging to a recipient or a third party, the threat must be considered objectively. The first issue is whether a threat was made. The second is in two parts:

- whether the threat, objectively considered, was capable of amounting to a threat to destroy the property of another (a question of law, for the judge in the Crown Court); and
- whether it was, in fact, such a threat (a question of fact, for the jury in the Crown Court).[76]

A similar approach applies to the requirement of a threat in a case involving s 2(b).[77]

It does not matter how the threat is conveyed; a letter, a telephone call or any other method of communication will do. Nor does it matter that the person making the threat does not intend to carry it out, provided that he intends that the addressee should fear that he would. It is irrelevant whether or not the addressee is actually put in such fear.

Where the threat is of the type described in s 2(a) 'without lawful excuse' is subject to s 5 in the same way as the offence under s 1(1), but in the case of a threat falling within s 2(b) 'without lawful excuse' is not.[78]

13.29 An offence under the CDA 1971, s 2 is triable either way;[79] the maximum punishment on conviction on indictment is 10 years' imprisonment.[80]

---

[76] *Cakmak* [2002] EWCA Crim 500.   [77] *Cakmak* [2002] EWCA Crim 500.
[78] CDA 1971, s 5(1).   [79] Magistrates' Courts Act 1980, s 17(1) and Sch 1.
[80] CDA 1971, s 4.

Possessing anything with intent to destroy or damage property

13.30 The CDA 1971, s 3 provides that:

> 'A person who has anything in his custody or under his control intending without lawful excuse to use it or cause or permit another to use it –
>
> (a) to destroy or damage any property belonging to some other person; or
>
> (b) to destroy or damage his own or the user's property in a way which he knows is likely to endanger the life of some other person;
>
> shall be guilty of an offence.'

The offence as described is a species of preparatory offence. Examples of it are possession of a terrorist arsenal, the possession of pickaxe handles by protection racketeers, and even the possession of paint or sprays by those who intend to write graffiti on the walls of buildings.

Although the word 'possession' does not appear in the definition in s 3, the terms 'in his custody or under his control' cover the same situations as possession, but their use avoids the technicalities of the concept of 'possession'. The explosives contained in a warehouse may be in the custody of the keeper of that warehouse but they may also be under the control of the leaders of the terrorist group, who can order their removal and use at any time.

Provided that the requisite intention exists, it is immaterial that there is no immediate intention to use the thing; a so-called conditional intent, ie an intention to use the thing to cause damage should it prove necessary, will suffice.[81]

It would appear that the offence is committed if the thing, eg a stone, is picked up on the spur of the moment with the intention of using it immediately to cause damage.

Where the offence involves an intent falling within the CDA 1971, s 3(a) 'without lawful excuse' is subject to s 5,[82] but in the case of an intent falling within s 3(b) 'without lawful excuse' is not.[83]

13.31 An offence under the CDA 1971, s 3 is triable either way;[84] the maximum punishment on conviction on indictment is 10 years' imprisonment.[85]

FURTHER READING

Elliott 'Endangering Life by Destroying or Damaging Property' [1997] Crim LR 69

ATH Smith *Property Offences* (1994) Ch 27

---

[81] *Buckingham* (1976) 63 Cr App Rep 159, CA.

[82] In para (b) of the definition in s 5(2) set out in para 13.9, the question in s 3 is whether the defendant intended to use or cause or permit the use of something to destroy or damage property in order to protect property etc.

[83] CDA 1971, s 5(1).

[84] Magistrates' Courts Act 1980, s 17(1) and Sch 1.

[85] CDA 1971, s 4.

14

Inchoate offences

OVERVIEW

Criminal liability is not limited to those who actually commit or participate in substantive offences. The criminal law also deals with a person who encourages or assists the commission of an offence, or conspires with others to commit an offence or attempts to commit an offence. If D does an act capable of encouraging or assisting the commission by E of a burglary at V's house, this constitutes encouraging or assisting burglary. If E agrees with D to commit the burglary, this amounts to a conspiracy to commit burglary. If E then goes as far as attempting to enter V's house, but fails because he is discovered as he turns a picklock in the front door, E can be convicted of attempted burglary. As these examples show, a defendant may well be guilty of more than one of these offences. They play an important role in modern crime control where there is an increasing emphasis on the detection and apprehension of those engaged in serious crime at an early stage before harm is caused.

The statutory offences of encouraging or assisting crime, conspiracy and attempt are known as inchoate (ie incomplete or undeveloped) offences since they may be committed notwithstanding that the substantive offence to which they relate is not committed. Indeed, if the substantive offence is committed, no question of attempt normally arises, and where there has been encouragement or assistance the person encouraging or assisting becomes a party (as an accomplice) to the substantive offence and will normally be proceeded against for *that* offence and not for an offence of encouraging or assisting crime. Where conspirators have committed the substantive offence a charge of conspiracy is generally undesirable because it tends to complicate the trial.

For convenience, common law conspiracy is also discussed in this chapter although it is not strictly an inchoate offence since it includes agreements for objects which are not in themselves criminal.

Encouraging or assisting crime

Key points 14.1

Under the Serious Crime Act 2007, Pt 2 the common law offence of incitement (which was limited to the intentional encouragement of crime) was abolished[1] and replaced by three offences of encouraging or assisting crime:

- intentionally encouraging or assisting an offence;
- encouraging or assisting an offence believing it will be committed; and
- encouraging or assisting offences believing one or more will be committed.

14.1 The Serious Crime Act 2007 (SCA 2007), Pt 2 is based on Law Commission report *Inchoate Liability for Assisting and Encouraging Crime*,[2] although it differs from it in a number of respects. The Law Commission considered that the main defect of the previous law was that D1 who encouraged a crime was instantly guilty of inciting it whether or not it took place, while D2 who actively sought to assist a crime could only become guilty of an offence if the offence assisted was subsequently committed or attempted by someone who was actually assisted by D2's conduct.[3]

The abolished common law offence of incitement was relatively simple and straightforward. The three offences which have replaced it are governed by 24 sections and two Schedules of the SCA 2007, a set of provisions which are unnecessarily technical and complex and which significantly extend the scope of liability.

14.2 The three offences of encouraging or assisting crime provided by the SCA 2007, Pt 2 apply to encouraging or assisting any offence with the exception of a number of offences, mainly of an inchoate nature, referred to later. In addition, an *individual* cannot be guilty of an offence under the SCA 2007, Pt 2 by reference to an offence of corporate manslaughter.[4]

Many of the provisions of the SCA 2007, Pt 2 apply to all three offences under it. Most of those provisions are dealt with below after the terms of the offences have been set out.

The offences

Intentionally encouraging or assisting an offence

14.3 The SCA 2007, s 44 provides:

---

[1] Serious Crime Act 2007, s 59.   [2] (2006), Law Com No 300.

[3] Law Com No 300, paras 3.1–3.8. The need to plug this gap had been convincingly argued by Spencer 'Trying to Help Another Person to Commit a Crime' in *Essays in Honour of JC Smith* (1987) (Smith (ed)) 148.

[4] Corporate Manslaughter and Corporate Homicide Act 2007, s 18(1A) (inserted by the SCA 2007, s 62).

'(1) A person commits an offence if –

(a) he does an act capable of encouraging or assisting the commission of an offence; and

(b) he intends to encourage or assist its commission.

(2) But he is not to be taken to have intended to encourage or assist the commission of an offence merely because such encouragement or assistance was a foreseeable consequence of his act.'

An example of an offence under s 44 would be where D sends E a lethal poison pill, knowing that E wants it to murder V and intending to assist the commission of murder. Another example would be where D exhorts E to burgle V's home, intending to encourage E to do so.

Actus reus

14.4 The defendant must do an act capable of encouraging or assisting in the commission of an offence, other than an offence of encouraging or assisting suicide, contrary to the Suicide Act 1961, s 2(1).[5]

Act capable of encouraging or assisting

14.5 The SCA 2007 does not offer a definition of the words 'an act capable of encouraging or assisting the commission of an offence', but s 65 clarifies their meaning:

'(1) A reference in this Part [ie Part 2] to a person's doing an act that is capable of encouraging the commission of an offence includes a reference to his doing so by threatening another person or otherwise putting pressure on another person to commit the offence.

(2) A reference in this Part to a person's doing an act that is capable of encouraging or assisting the commission of an offence includes a reference to his doing so by –

(a) taking steps to reduce the possibility of criminal proceedings being brought in respect of that offence;

(b) failing to take reasonable steps to discharge a duty.

(3) But a person is not to be regarded as doing an act that is capable of encouraging or assisting the commission of an offence merely because he fails to respond to a constable's request for assistance in preventing a breach of the peace.'

14.6 Section 67 provides that any reference in Part 2 to an act includes a reference to a course of conduct, and that doing an act is to read accordingly.

---

[5] SCA 2007, s 51A (inserted by the Coroners and Justice Act 2009, Sch 21).

Indirectly encouraging or assisting

14.7 The SCA 2007, s 66 provides:

> 'If a person (D1) arranges for a person (D2) to do an act that is capable of encouraging or assisting the commission of an offence, and D2 does the act, D1 is also to be treated for the purposes of this Part [ie Part 2] as having done it.'

This covers the type of case where D1 tells D2 to assist in the commission of an offence, and D2 does so; D1 is to be treated as having done the act of assistance done by D2. Both of them can be convicted of an offence of assisting or encouraging crime. If D2 does not do as he was told by D1, neither of them can be.

The reason for this provision is not obvious because D1 can be convicted of the 'encouraging or assisting offence' under the rules relating to secondary liability if D2 carries out the arranged act.

Mens rea

14.8 The *mens rea*, required by s 44(1)(b), is that the defendant must intend to encourage or assist the commission of the offence which his act is capable of encouraging or assisting.

14.9 According to the explanatory notes to the Act,[6] the statement in s 44(2) (that a person is not to be taken to have intended to encourage or assist the commission merely because such encouragement or assistance was a foreseeable consequence of his act) is intended to make clear that foresight of consequences is not sufficient to establish intention, ie that intention in s 44 is limited to direct intention. While the wording of s 44, when contrasted with s 45, supports the view that intention is so limited, it is unfortunate that 'foreseeable', and not 'foreseen', was used in s 44(2), because 'foreseeable' seems to refer to an objective concept. On that basis, s 44(2) simply restates the Criminal Justice Act 1967, s 8.

14.10 Section 47(2) provides that if it is alleged under s 44(1)(b) that a person (D) intended to encourage or assist the commission of an offence, it is sufficient to prove that he intended to encourage or assist the doing of an act which would amount to the commission of that offence.[7] By s 47(8), reference in s 47 to the doing of such an act

> 'includes reference to:
>
> (a) a failure to act,
> (b) the continuation of an act already begun, and
> (c) an attempt to do an act (except an act amounting to the commission of the offence of attempting to commit *another* offence).'[8]

---

[6] Para 146.   [7] See para 14.24.   [8] Italics supplied.

The effect of s 47(8)(c) (taken together with s 47(2)) is that it is an offence under s 44 intentionally to encourage or assist a substantive offence which is expressed as an attempt, such as the offence of attempt to choke with intent to commit an indictable offence, contrary to the Offences Against the Person Act 1861, s 21, or intentionally to encourage or assist an attempt to commit a substantive offence (since such an attempt is itself an offence), but not intentionally to encourage or assist an attempt to attempt to commit a substantive offence (because this is excluded by the bracketed words in s 47(8)(c)).

Further provision about the *mens rea* for an offence under s 44 is made by s 47(5), set out in para 14.24.

Supplemental provision

14.11 If a person's act is capable of encouraging or assisting the commission of a number of offences, s 44 applies separately in relation to each offence that he intends to encourage or assist to be committed.[9] Thus, if D lends E a jemmy, *intending* E to use it to enter two houses (burglary) and to smash shop windows (criminal damage), D can be convicted of three offences of encouraging or assisting under s 44. If D only *believed* that E would use the jemmy in this way he would be guilty of encouraging or assisting these offences under s 45.

Encouraging or assisting an offence believing it will be committed

14.12 The SCA 2007, s 45 provides:

'A person commits an offence if –

    (a) he does an act capable of encouraging or assisting the commission of an offence; and

    (b) he believes –
       (i) that the offence will be committed; and
       (ii) that his act will encourage or assist its commission.'

Actus reus

14.13 The *actus reus* requirement is identical to that under s 44. The provisions of the SCA 2007, ss 65–67 referred to in paras 14.5 to 14.7 apply likewise to s 45.

14.14 Section 49(4)(a) provides that, in reckoning whether (for the purposes of s 45 or s 46, below) an act is capable of encouraging or assisting the commission of an offence:

- offences under ss 44, 45 or 46; and
- 'listed offences'

[9] SCA 2007, s 49(2)(a).

are to be disregarded. As a result, a person cannot be guilty under s 45 of encouraging or assisting an offence under ss 44, 45 or 46 or a listed offence. 'Listed offences' are the offences listed in the SCA 2007, Sch 3, Pts 1, 2 or 3.[10] They are mainly statutory offences of incitement and include the following offences referred to elsewhere in this book:

- solicitation of murder (Offences Against the Person Act 1861, s 4);
- encouraging or assisting suicide (Suicide Act 1961, s 2(1));
- assisting an offender (Criminal Law Act 1967, s 4(1));
- concealing an offence for reward (Criminal Law Act 1967, s 5(1));
- statutory conspiracy (Criminal Law Act 1977, s 1(1));
- common law conspiracy, eg to defraud (Criminal Law Act 1977, s 5(2) and (3));
- attempt (Criminal Attempts Act 1981, s 1(1));
- attempt under a special statutory provision,[11] (ie a statutory offence expressed as an attempt to commit another offence).

It will be noted that there is no corresponding exclusion of offences in respect of s 44. The various offences of incitement under the Sexual Offences Act 2003 are not included in the list in Sch 3 and are therefore capable of being the subject of an offence under s 45 (or s 46 below).

Mens rea

14.15 The crucial distinction between an offence under s 45 and that under s 44 is the *mens rea* required by s 45(b). **Section 45 deals with the case where the defendant does not intend the substantive offence to be committed but believes that the substantive offence will be committed and that his act will encourage or assist its commission.**

Section 49(7) provides that, in relation to the former of these two beliefs, it is sufficient if the defendant believes that the offence will be committed if certain conditions are met. Thus, if D encourages E to beg some money from V and tells him that, if V refuses, E should take some money from V by force, the case is covered by s 49(7) and D can be convicted under s 45 of encouraging or assisting robbery because D believes that the offence (of robbery) will be committed if certain conditions are met (ie if V refuses to hand over money).

14.16 Section 47(3) provides that if it is alleged under s 45(b) that a person (D) believed that an offence would be committed and that his act would encourage or assist its commission, it is sufficient to prove that he believed:

- that an act would be done which would amount to the commission of that offence; and
- that his act would encourage or assist the doing of that act.

---

[10] SCA 2007, s 49(5)(a). Sch 3 has been amended by the Coroners and Justice Act 2009, Sch 21.

[11] The reference to 'attempt under a special statutory provision' has the same meaning as it has for the purposes of the Criminal Attempts Act 1981 (see para 14.142): SCA 2007, Sch 3, Pt 3. It therefore refers to a statutory offence 'expressed as an offence of attempting to commit another offence'.

Reference in s 47 to the doing of such an act includes a reference to a failure to act, the continuation of an act already begun, and an attempt to do an act (except an act amounting to the commission of the offence of attempting to commit another offence).[12] The reference to 'an attempt to do an act' does not mean that a person can be guilty under s 45 if he encourages or assists an attempt merely believing that it will be committed. As stated in para 14.14, a person cannot be guilty *under s 45 or s 46, below,* of encouraging or assisting an attempt to commit an offence. As stated in para 14.10, the phrase refers to situations where an attempt to do an act suffices for the commission of the *actus reus* of a substantive offence which is expressed as an attempt (as opposed to an attempt to commit another offence).

Further provision about the *mens rea* for an offence under s 45 is made by s 47(5), set out in para 14.24.

Supplemental provision

14.17 If a person's act is capable of encouraging or assisting the commission of a number of offences, s 45 applies separately in relation to each offence that he believes will be encouraged or assisted to be committed.[13]

Encouraging or assisting offences believing one or more will be committed

14.18 By the SCA 2007, s 46:

'(1) A person commits an offence if –
  (a) he does an act capable of encouraging or assisting the commission of one or more of a number of offences; and
  (b) he believes –
    (i) that one or more of those offences will be committed (but has no belief as to which); and
    (ii) that his act will encourage or assist the commission of one or more of them.
(2) It is immaterial for the purposes of subsection (1)(b)(ii) whether the person has any belief as to which offence will be encouraged or assisted.'

Section 46(3)(a) requires an indictment for an offence under s 46 to specify the offences alleged to be the 'number of offences' mentioned in s 46(1)(a) that the defendant believed might be committed. For example, if the prosecution allege that D lent his van to E believing that E will use it to commit trafficking for sexual exploitation or handling stolen goods by undertaking their disposal for the benefit of another, the indictment must specify both

---

[12] SCA 2007, s 47(8).　　[13] SCA 2007, s 49(2)(b).

offences. However, by s 46(3)(b) this does not mean that every offence that the defendant could have encouraged or assisted must be specified.

Actus reus

14.19 **The defendant must do an act capable of encouraging or assisting the commission of *one or more of a number of offences*.** The provisions of the SCA 2007, ss 65–67 referred to in paras 14.5 to 14.7 apply likewise to s 46.

14.20 Section 49(4)(b) provides that an offence under ss 44, 45 or 46, or a 'listed offence', is to be disregarded in reckoning whether an act is capable of encouraging or assisting the commission of one or more of a number of offences. See further para 14.14.

Mens rea

14.21 Section 46(1)(b) requires that the defendant must believe:

(a) **that one or more of the offences which his act is capable of encouraging or assisting will be committed (but has no belief as to which); and**

(b) **that his act will encourage or assist the commission of one or more of them.**

By s 46(2), it is immaterial whether the person has any belief as to which offence will be encouraged or assisted.

14.22 For the purposes of (a), it is sufficient for the defendant to believe that one or more of the offences will be committed if certain conditions are satisfied.[14]

14.23 Section 47(4) provides that if it is alleged under s 46(1)(b) that a person believed that one or more of a number of offences would be committed and that his act would encourage or assist the commission of one or more of them, it is sufficient to prove that he believed:

- that one or more of a number of acts would be done which would amount to the commission of one or more of those offences; and

- that his act would encourage or assist the doing of one or more of those acts.

Reference to the doing of such an act includes a reference to a failure to act, the continuation of an act already begun, and an attempt to do an act (except an act amounting to the commission of the offence of attempt).[15] As to the meaning of 'attempt to do an act', see para 14.16.

Further provision about the *mens rea* for an offence under s 46 is made by s 47(5), below.

---

[14] SCA 2007, s 49(7).   [15] SCA 2007, s 47(8).

Common provisions

Further provisions about *mens rea*

14.24 The SCA 2007, s 47(5) sets out the *mens rea* that must be proved under ss 44, 45 or 46 if an offence that it is alleged a person intended or believed would be committed requires proof of fault (ie *mens rea*), circumstances or consequences.

Section 47(5) provides:

> 'In proving for the purposes of this section whether an act is one which, if done, would amount to the commission of an offence –
>
> (a) if the offence is one requiring proof of fault, it must be proved that –
> (i) D believed that, were the act to be done, it would be done with that fault;
> (ii) D was reckless as to whether or not it would be done with that fault; or
> (iii) D's state of mind was such that, were he to do it, it would be done with that fault; and
> (b) if the offence is one requiring proof of particular circumstances or consequences (or both), it must be proved that –
> (i) D believed that, were the act to be done, it would be done in those circumstances or with those consequences; or
> (ii) D was reckless as to whether or not it would be done in those circumstances or with those consequences.'

In the case of an offence under s 44, s 47(5)(b)(i) is to be read as if the reference to 'D believed' were a reference to 'D intended or believed', but D is not to be taken to have intended that an act would be done in particular circumstances or with particular consequences merely because its being done in those circumstances or with those consequences was a foreseeable consequence of his act of encouragement or assistance.[16]

It follows from s 47(5)(a) that, if an offence that D is alleged to have intended or believed would be encouraged or assisted requires *mens rea*, D must believe or be reckless that, if the act encouraged or assisted is done, it would be done with the necessary *mens rea* for it by the person encouraged or assisted, or (by s 47(5)(a)(iii)) D must have the necessary *mens rea* for that offence. The latter point is important where D thinks that the other person will lack the *mens rea*. Thus, the offences under ss 44, 45 or 46 apply to the encouragement or assistance of an innocent agent. Section 47(6) provides that, for the purposes of s 47(5) (a)(iii), D is assumed to be able to do the act in question. Thus, D cannot escape liability in respect of s 47(5)(a)(iii) simply because it is impossible for him to commit the offence encouraged or assisted. Suppose that D (a woman) encourages E to penetrate V with his penis, believing that if E were to do so it would be without V's consent. D knows that E

---

[16] SCA 2007, s 47(7).

will reasonably believe that V is consenting if E acts on D's encouragement. Although a woman cannot perpetrate rape, D can be convicted of encouraging or assisting rape.

It follows from s 47(5)(b) that a requirement to prove *mens rea* applies in respect of any circumstances or consequences of the *actus reus* of the offence that D is alleged to have intended or believed would be encouraged or assisted, and that this is so even though that offence is one of strict liability as to that particular element. For example, the offence of driving a motor vehicle on a road or other public place with excess alcohol, contrary to the Road Traffic Act 1988, s 5, is one of strict liability, for which no *mens rea* is required.[17] If D asks E to drive him to the station, in ignorance that E has been drinking and is 'over the limit', D cannot be convicted of an offence of encouraging or assisting crime (the only relevant one would be that under s 44) because he neither believes nor is he reckless that if E complies with his request the driving would be in the circumstance that E is over the limit, despite the fact that if E did drive D as requested E would commit the substantive offence.

Sometimes, as in the example just given, the *mens rea* requirement is higher for an offence under ss 44 to 46 than for the substantive offence, but in other cases it will be lower. In the offence of handling stolen goods, for example, a defendant must know or believe that the circumstance that the goods are stolen exists,[18] but on a charge under ss 44, 45 or 46 it is enough, by virtue of s 47(5), that he believes or is reckless that they are. Suppose that E asks D to drive him to X's house so that he can pick up some laptops. D knows that X is a 'shady character'. He does not believe that the laptops are stolen but, if he is aware that there is a possibility that they are, D can be convicted of the offence under s 45. It is open to question why a person who is simply reckless as to a circumstance or consequence of the substantive offence should be liable for encouraging or assisting that offence when it may never be committed.

The operation of s 47(5) can also be illustrated as follows. Suppose that D encourages E to beat V up. D clearly believes that E will act with the *mens rea* for assault occasioning actual bodily harm and intends or believes that if the beating up is done the consequence of actual bodily harm would result. He has therefore encouraged or assisted assault occasioning actual bodily harm and can be convicted under s 44. If, however, E actually gives V a particularly severe beating up, intending to cause him serious harm, and kills V, and is thereby guilty of murder, D would not be guilty of encouraging or assisting murder because he would lack the necessary *mens rea* under s 47(5)(a) and (b).

In the case of an offence under s 46:

- it is sufficient to prove the matters referred to in s 47(5) by reference to one offence only,[19] in which case there can be a conviction under s 46 by reference to that one offence;

- the offence or offences by reference to which those matters are proved must be one of the offences specified[20] in the indictment,[21] but this does not affect any enactment or rule of law under which a person charged with one offence may be convicted of another.[22]

---

[17] See para 15.35.   [18] Para 11.50.   [19] SCA 2007, s 48(2).
[20] Ie specified in the indictment by virtue of the SCA 2007, s 46(3)(a) (para 14.18): SCA 2007, s 46(4).
[21] SCA 2007, s 48(3).   [22] SCA 2007, s 48(4).

Commission of offence encouraged or assisted not required

14.25 The SCA 2007, s 49(1) provides that:

> 'A person may commit an offence under [the SCA 2007, ss 44, 45 or 46] whether or not any offence capable of being encouraged or assisted by his act is committed.'

Like the other inchoate offences, the offences under ss 44, 45 and 46 are conduct crimes. An offence under ss 44 to 46 is complete on the doing of an act capable of encouraging or assisting an offence (whether or not anyone is actually encouraged or assisted, or is even aware that he is being encouraged or assisted). It follows that subsequent withdrawal by the person who gave the encouragement or assistance is no defence.

14.26 Where an offence encouraged or assisted has been committed, the offences under ss 44, 45 and 46 exist alongside the rules about secondary liability for the offence encouraged or assisted under the common law rules about aiding, abetting, counselling or procuring crime. The Law Commission[23] considered that there were compelling reasons for retaining secondary liability and not confining liability to that of encouraging or assisting the offence if it was committed. To do otherwise, as it had earlier provisionally proposed,[24] would not accurately label and condemn the encourager or assister for his conduct. It would appear that in practice a person is normally charged as a secondary party to the offence encouraged or assisted if it is committed, and not with an offence under s 44, 45 or 46 in such a case.

Overlap between offences

14.27 The potential overlap between the offences under s 44, 45 or 46 in a given case is obvious. Section 49(3) provides that a person may, in relation to the same act, commit an offence under more than one of s 44, 45 or 46. The following is an example: D lends E a knife and believes that he will enter a building and commit burglary. He also believes that E will use it to commit another offence which will either be to enter another building and commit another burglary or to attack V in the street and wound him. D could be convicted under s 45 of encouraging and assisting burglary. He could also be prosecuted and convicted under s 46 of encouraging and assisting burglary or unlawful wounding.

---

[23] Law Com No 300, paras 2.1–2.26.
[24] *Assisting and Encouraging Crime* Law Commission Consultation Paper No 131 (1993).

Defence of acting reasonably

14.28 The SCA 2007, s 50 provides two defences:

> '(1) A person is not guilty of an offence under [ss 44, 45 or 46] if he proves –
> (a) that he knew certain circumstances existed; and
> (b) that it was reasonable for him to act as he did in those circumstances.
>
> (2) A person is not guilty of an offence under [ss 44, 45 or 46] if he proves –
> (a) that he believed certain circumstances to exist;
> (b) that his belief was reasonable; and
> (c) that it was reasonable for him to act as he did in the circumstances as he believed them to be.'

Section 50(1) applies where the circumstances referred to actually exist and the defendant knows this. Section 50(2) applies where the circumstances referred to may or may not exist but the defendant believes that they do; in such a case his belief must be reasonable.

Section 50(3) sets out a non-exhaustive list of factors to be considered in determining whether it was reasonable for the defendant to act as he did:

> 'Factors to be considered in determining whether it was reasonable for a person to act as he did include –
>
> (a) the seriousness of the anticipated offence (or, in the case of an offence under section 46, the offences specified in the indictment);
>
> (b) any purpose for which he claims to have been acting;
>
> (c) any authority by which he claims to have been acting.'

The defence of acting reasonably is wide enough to cover cases where the defendant acts in order to prevent the commission of crime and can operate to avoid the defendant being liable for an offence under s 44, 45 or 46 in respect of conduct consisting of normal and commonplace activities or, more broadly, activities that might be thought to be within the defendant's rights to engage in. An example given by the Law Commission[25] of the type of case which s 50 is designed to cover is where D is driving at 70 miles per hour in the outside lane of a motorway. E, driving faster, comes up behind D. D, not intending that E should continue speeding, but knowing that pulling over will assist E to continue speeding, pulls over to let E overtake.

Whether it was reasonable for the defendant to act as he did may be a matter on which different juries or magistrates' courts have different views in a particular type of case and therefore the operation of s 50 may be unpredictable.

It appears that s 50(1) and (2) imposes the persuasive burden of proof, but it would be open to a court to read down the provision so as only to impose an evidential burden

---

[25] Law Com No 300, para 6.18.

if this is necessary to render it compatible with ECHR, Article 6(2) (presumption of innocence).

Protective offences: victims not liable

14.29 Section 51 provides that:

> '(1) In the case of protective offences, a person does not commit an offence under [s 44, 45 or 46] by reference to such an offence if –
>   (a) he falls within the protected category; and
>   (b) he is the person in respect of whom the protective offence was committed or would have been if it had been committed.
> (2) "Protective offence" means an offence that exists (wholly or in part) for the protection of a particular category of persons ("the protected category").'

As a result of s 51, for example, a 15-year-old girl who encourages a man to have sexual intercourse with her cannot be convicted of an offence of encouraging or assisting the offence of sexual activity with a child because that offence is a 'protective offence'; she falls within the protected category of persons and she is the person in respect of whom the offence was or would have been committed.

The exemption under s 51 mirrors that for victims under the law relating to secondary liability (aiding and abetting etc), although unlike that law it is clear that it is not limited to protective offences of a sexual nature.

Impossibility

14.30 The SCA 2007, Pt 2 does not provide that the impossibility of committing the offence encouraged or assisted is a defence. The apparent unavailability of a defence of impossibility is consistent with the situation in respect of statutory conspiracy and of attempt, although in those cases the statute makes express provision about impossibility. The fact that express provision is not made by the SCA 2007, Pt 2 about the issue is unfortunate since it leaves it open for defendants to argue that impossibility is a defence to an offence under Pt 2 (just as it was to the common law offence of incitement).[26]

Uncertainty

14.31 The SCA 2007, s 56 deals with the case where it is proved that the defendant must have committed an offence under s 44, 45 or 46 or have committed the 'anticipated offence' as a perpetrator but it is not proved which of those offences he has committed.

---

[26] See *Whitehouse* [1977] QB 868, CA; *Fitzmaurice* [1983] QB 1083, CA.

Section 56 provides that in proceedings for an offence under s 44, 45, or 46 ('the inchoate offence') the defendant may be convicted of the inchoate offence if:

- it is proved that he must have committed the inchoate offence or perpetrated the anticipated offence; but
- it is not proved which of those offences he committed.

The 'anticipated offence' is the offence mentioned in s 47(2),[27] in relation to an offence under s 44, or s 47(3),[28] in relation to an offence under s 45, or an offence specified in the indictment, in relation to an offence under s 46.[29]

Jurisdiction

Substantive offence anticipated to take place wholly or partly in England or Wales

14.32 By SCA 2007, s 52(1), if a person (D) knows or believes that what he anticipates might take place wholly or partly in England or Wales, he may be guilty of an offence under s 44, 45 or 46 no matter where he was at any relevant time. Thus, if D in France e-mails E in Wales encouraging him to kill V in Cardiff, D can be tried and convicted of any offence under s 44 in England and Wales, and the same would be true if he encouraged E2 to post in France a parcel bomb to V in Cardiff.

Substantive offence not anticipated to take place wholly or partly in England or Wales

14.33 The SCA 2007, s 52(2) provides that, if it is not proved that D knows or believes that what he anticipates might take place wholly or partly in England or Wales, he is not guilty of an offence under s 44, 45 or 46 unless Sch 4, para 1, 2 or 3 applies.

Relevant behaviour by D within the jurisdiction

14.34 Schedule 4, para 1 provides:

'(1) This paragraph applies if –
   (a) any relevant behaviour of D's takes place wholly or partly in England or Wales;
   (b) D knows or believes that what he anticipates might take place wholly or partly in a place outside England and Wales; and
   (c) either –
      (i) the anticipated offence[30] is one that would be triable under the law of England and Wales if it were committed in that place; or

---

[27] See para 14.10.   [28] See para 14.16.   [29] SCA 2007, ss 47(9), 56(3).

[30] In relation to an offence under s 46, a reference in Sch 4 to the anticipated offence is to be read as a reference to any of the offences specified in the indictment: SCA 2007, Sch 4, para 4.

> (ii) if there are relevant conditions, it would be so triable if it were committed there by a person who satisfies the conditions.
>
> (2) "Relevant condition" means a condition that –
>
> (a) determines (wholly or in part) whether an offence committed outside England and Wales is nonetheless triable under the law of England and Wales; and
>
> (b) relates to the citizenship, nationality or residence of the person who commits it.'

Thus, if D in London e-mails E (a British citizen) in France, encouraging E to kill V in Paris, D can be tried and convicted in England and Wales of an offence under s 44 because the murder would be triable there, but not if the encouragement was simply to disfigure V because the offence of causing grievous bodily harm would not be triable in England and Wales in such a case.

14.35 Schedule 4, para 2(1) provides:

> 'This paragraph applies if –
>
> (a) paragraph 1 does not apply;
>
> (b) any relevant behaviour of D's takes place wholly or partly in England or Wales;
>
> (c) D knows or believes that what he anticipates might take place wholly or partly in a place outside England and Wales; and
>
> (d) what D anticipates would amount to an offence under the law in force in that place.'

For example, if D in Newcastle sends E in New Zealand software to be used in perpetrating a fraud and that fraud would be an offence under the Fraud Act 2006, s 1 and under New Zealand law, D can be convicted of an offence under s 44. The condition in para 2(1)(d) is deemed to be satisfied unless the defence serve on the prosecution a notice denying this, showing the grounds for that opinion and requiring the prosecution to show that it is satisfied.[31] The question whether the condition is satisfied is to be decided by the judge alone in the Crown Court.[32]

Relevant behaviour by D wholly outside the jurisdiction

14.36 Schedule 4, para 3(1) provides:

> 'This paragraph applies if –
>
> (a) any relevant behaviour of D's takes place wholly outside England and Wales;
>
> (b) D knows or believes that what he anticipates might take place wholly or partly in a place outside England and Wales; and

---

[31] SCA 2007, Sch 4, para 2(2).   [32] SCA 2007, Sch 4, para 2(3).

(c) D could be tried under the law of England and Wales if he committed the anticipated offence in that place.'[33]

Thus, if D (a British citizen) in Canada sends a parcel of poison to E in France encouraging E to use it to murder V (also in France), it would be possible to try and convict D
of an offence under s 44 in England because, as he is a British citizen, the anticipated
offence (murder) would be triable in England and Wales if D committed it himself in
France.[34]

General

14.37 By s 52(3), a reference in s 52 and in Sch 4, paras 1 to 3 to what D anticipates is to
be read as follows:

'(a) in relation to an offence under section 44 or 45, it refers to the act which would
amount to the commission of the anticipated offence;[35]

(b) in relation to an offence under section 46, it refers to an act which would count to
the commission of any of the offences specified in the indictment.'

14.38 The rules contained in s 52 and Sch 4 do not restrict the operation of any special
jurisdictional rules under other statutes,[36] such as those under the Sexual Offences Act
2003, s 72, referred to in para 9.133, and those under the Criminal Justice Act 1993 (CJA
1993), Part I.

Under the CJA 1993, s 5(4) a person may be convicted of encouraging or assisting the commission of a Group A offence[37] (viz one of the offences under the Theft
Act 1968, Forgery and Counterfeiting Act 1981, Fraud Act 2006 and related offences
listed in CJA 1993, s 1: see para 12.70) if the encouraging or assisting takes place
in England and Wales and would be triable in England and Wales but for what the
person charged had in view not being an offence triable in England and Wales (as
where D in Cardiff encourages E in Rome to commit theft there). It is irrelevant
whether or not the defendant was a British citizen at any material time or was in
England and Wales at any such time.[38]

---

[33] For the purposes of sub-para (c), D is to be assumed to be able to commit the anticipated offence: SCA 2007,
Sch 4, para 3(2).
[34] This example is given in the explanatory notes to the Act.
[35] For the meaning of 'the anticipated offence' see para 14.31.
[36] SCA 2007, s 52(5).
[37] Section 5(4) refers to the repealed common law offence inciting the commission of a Group A offence
but the references in the Criminal Justice Act 1993, ss 1(3)(d) and 5(4) have effect as a reference to the offences
under the SCA 2007, Pt 2: SCA 2007, s 63(1), Sch 6, Pt 1. Encouraging or assisting the commission of a Group A
offence is a Group B offence under the CJA 1993, Pt 1: CJA 1993, s 1(3)(d) (as amended by the SCA 2007, s 63(1),
Sch 6, Pt 1).
[38] CJA 1993, s 3(1).

Prosecution, trial and punishment

Prosecution

14.39 No proceedings for an offence triable by virtue of any provision of the SCA 2007, Sch 4[39] may be instituted except by, or with the consent of, the Attorney-General.[40]

14.40 Any provision of any other statute providing that proceedings may not be instituted or carried on otherwise than by, or on behalf or with the consent of, any person, eg the Attorney-General or Director of Public Prosecutions, or conferring power to institute proceedings, eg the power of the Revenue and Customs Prosecution Office to prosecute money laundering offences, has effect with respect to an offence under the SCA 2007, ss 44, 45 or 46 as it has effect with respect to the anticipated offence.[41]

Trial

14.41 An offence under ss 44 or 45 is triable in the same way as the anticipated offence.[42] An offence under s 46 is triable only on indictment.[43]

Punishment

14.42 The following provisions apply if:

- a person is convicted of an offence under the SCA 2007, s 44 or s 45; or
- a person is convicted of an offence under s 46 by reference to *only one* offence ('the reference offence').[44]

If the anticipated or reference offence is murder, the maximum punishment is imprisonment for life.[45] In any other case the maximum punishment is the same as for the anticipated or reference offence.[46] Suppose that D gives E an axe and he is charged under s 46, it being alleged that he believed that either criminal damage or murder would be committed with it. D is convicted under s 46 in relation to the criminal damage but acquitted in relation to the murder. The maximum sentence will be that for arson.

14.43 Where a person is convicted under the SCA 2007, s 46 by reference to *more than one* reference offence ('the reference offences'), the situation is as follows:

- if one of the reference offences is murder, the maximum sentence is life imprisonment;

---

[39] Para 14.33. [40] SCA 2007, s 53.

[41] SCA 2007, s 54(1), (2)(a) and (b). In relation to an offence under s 46: (a) this reference to the anticipated offence is to be read as a reference to any offence specified in the indictment; and (b) each of the offences specified in the indictment must be an offence in respect of which the prosecutor has power to institute proceedings: SCA 2007, s 54(3).

[42] SCA 2007, s 55(1). [43] SCA 2007, s 55(2).

[44] SCA 2007, s 58(1). [45] SCA 2007, s 58(2).

[46] SCA 2007, s 58(3). In the case of encouraging or assisting 'small value criminal damage', the maximum is the lower maximum for small value damage: see para 13.2.

- otherwise, if one or more of the reference offences is punishable with imprisonment, the maximum punishment is the maximum term of imprisonment for any of the offences or the longer (or longest) maximum if the terms differ. Alternatively, a fine may be imposed;
- in any other case, a fine may be imposed.[47]

Thus, if D lends E a van believing that E may use it to traffic people for sexual exploitation and that E may also use it for theft, and D is convicted under s 46 of encouraging or assisting both offences, the maximum sentence will be 14 years' imprisonment (the maximum for the trafficking offence), as opposed to seven years' (the maximum for theft).

14.44 The above provisions relating to offences other than murder are subject to any contrary provision made by or under any Act.[48]

Conspiracy: general

Key points 14.2

There are statutory and common law offences of conspiracy:

- It is a statutory conspiracy to agree with any other person or persons for the commission of an offence or offences.
- It is a common law conspiracy to agree with any person or persons to defraud or, possibly, to corrupt public morals or to outrage public decency.

14.45 Until the Criminal Law Act 1977 (CLA 1977), Pt I came into force, the common law offence of conspiracy was the only general offence of conspiracy known to the criminal law. An agreement was a common law conspiracy if it had one of five types of object:

- to commit a criminal offence;
- to pervert the course of justice. Generally, this did not add much to the first type, since normally the perversion of justice was a criminal offence;
- to commit a tort, such as trespass, provided the execution of the agreement had as its object either:
  - the invasion of the 'public domain', eg trespass in an embassy; or
  - the infliction of injury or damage which was more than nominal;
- to defraud; or
- to corrupt public morals or to outrage public decency.

---

[47] SCA 2007, s 58(4)–(7). If a reference offence is 'small value criminal damage', the comment at n 46 is equally applicable here. [48] SCA 2007, s 58(8)(a).

The width of the non-criminal objects of a conspiracy was open to severe criticism, particularly since it was not obvious why, if a particular act was not criminal when done, an agreement to do it should be criminal. Following the recommendations of the Law Commission,[49] the CLA 1977, Pt I introduced the statutory offence of conspiracy contrary to s 1 of that Act, which basically penalises agreements for the commission of a criminal offence and greatly altered the extent of the common law offence of conspiracy since, except for conspiracies to defraud and, possibly, conspiracies to corrupt public morals or to outrage public decency, the offence of conspiracy at common law was abolished by the CLA 1977, s 5(1). The rules for statutory conspiracy under the CLA 1977 do not apply to common law conspiracy.

Before discussing the separate requirements of statutory conspiracy and what remains of common law conspiracy, reference must be made to some matters which are common to both types of conspiracy.

Agreement[50]

14.46 There cannot be a conspiracy unless there is a concluded agreement for a particular purpose; mere negotiations are insufficient,[51] as is an uncommunicated intention to enter into an agreement.[52] There may be any number of parties to the agreement. **The offence is complete as soon as the parties agree**[53] and it is immaterial that they never begin to put it into effect.[54] In *Saik*,[55] Lord Hope said:

> 'A conspiracy is complete when the agreement to enter into it is formed, even if nothing is done to implement it. Implementation gives effect to the conspiracy, but it does not alter its essential elements. … The question whether its requirements are fulfilled is directed to the stage when the agreement is formed, not to the stage when it is implemented.'

The repentance and withdrawal of a party after the agreement has been made cannot affect his liability for conspiracy,[56] although it may mitigate the sentence imposed.

It is not necessary that all the parties to the agreement should all have been in communication with each other, provided they entertained a common purpose, communicated to at least one other party, expressly or tacitly, in relation to the object of the conspiracy.[57] This can occur, for example, in a 'chain' or 'wheel' conspiracy. In a chain conspiracy D1 agrees with D2, D2 agrees with D3, D3 agrees with D4 and so on. In a wheel conspiracy,

---

[49] *Report on Conspiracy and Criminal Law Reform* (1976) Law Com No 76.
[50] Orchard '"Agreement" in Criminal Conspiracy' [1974] Crim LR 297, 335.
[51] *Jones* (1832) 4 B & Ad 345 at 349, per Denman CJ.
[52] *Scott* (1978) 68 Cr App Rep 164, CA.   [53] *Hobbs* [2002] EWCA Crim 387.
[54] *Poulterer's Case* (1610) 9 Co Rep 55b; *Bolton* (1992) 94 Cr App Rep 74, CA.
[55] [2006] UKHL 18 at [75].
[56] *Mogul Steamship Co Ltd v McGregor, Gow & Co* (1888) 21 QBD 544 at 549; affd [1892] AC 25, HL; *Bolton* (1992) 94 Cr App Rep 74, CA.
[57] *Ardalan* [1972] 2 All ER 257, CA; *Scott* (1978) 68 Cr App Rep 164, CA; *Chrastny (No 1)* [1992] 1 All ER 189, CA.

D1 is the 'hub' of the wheel, who recruits D2, D3, D4 and so on into his plan. This could occur, for instance, with members of a society who had each worked for the same end under some common superior but had never communicated with each other.[58] However, for D1 and D4, for example, to be parties to the same agreement (and therefore to be parties to the same conspiracy), they must be aware of each other's involvement (although not of their identities); otherwise there will be separate agreements (conspiracies) involving those who are aware of each other's involvement.[59]

Although conspiracy is committed as soon as the agreement for the 'unlawful' object is made, **conspiracy is a continuing offence and is committed not only when agreement is first reached but also as long as the agreement to effect the unlawful object continues**, ie until the agreement is terminated by completion of its performance or by abandonment or frustration or however it may be.[60] **The most important result of this is that a number of persons may be held parties to the same conspiracy although they joined it at different times.**[61]

14.47 The fact that there must be two or more parties to constitute an agreement means that:

- **A director who is the 'one man' of a 'one man' company cannot be convicted of conspiring with the company** in spite of the fact that a company can be held guilty of conspiracy and is in law a separate entity from its directors.[62] This is because, in order that there should be a conspiracy, there must be an agreement between two minds, and the director's mind is that of the company only in a purely artificial sense. A company can be convicted of conspiring with several of its directors, but presumably the rule with regard to the one man company would prevent two 'one man' companies with the same 'one man' from being convicted of conspiring together.

- **A person is not guilty of conspiracy if the only other person with whom he agrees is his or her spouse,**[63] a rule stemming from the outmoded principle that spouses are regarded as one person in law,[64] which has been held by the Court of Appeal no longer to apply to the tort of conspiracy.[65] It remains undecided whether the rule applies to a husband and wife whose marriage is of a type which is actually or potentially polygamous.[66] **A person is not guilty of statutory conspiracy if the only other person with whom he agrees is his civil partner.**[67]

---

[58] See summing up of Fitzgerald J in *Parnell* (1881) 14 Cox CC 508 at 516. See also *Meyrick and Ribuffi* (1929) 21 Cr App Rep 94, CCA.   [59] *Griffiths* [1965] 2 All ER 448, CCA.

[60] *DPP v Doot* [1973] AC 807, HL; *Reilly* [1982] QB 1208, CA. See also *Khalil* [2003] EWCA Crim 3467 (defendant became involved after a contract killer (an undercover police officer) had apparently committed the murder; held he could not be convicted of conspiracy to murder).

[61] *Murphy and Douglas* (1837) 8 C & P 297 at 311; *Sweetland* (1957) 42 Cr App Rep 62 at 67.

[62] *McDonnell* [1966] 1 QB 233.

[63] *Mawji v R* [1957] AC 126, PC (common law conspiracy); CLA 1977, s 2(2)(a) (amended by the Civil Partnership Act 2004, Sch 27) (which provides that a person is not guilty of statutory conspiracy if the other person with whom he agrees is (both initially and at all times during the currency of the agreement) his spouse or civil partner).

[64] 1 Hawkins c 27, s 8.   [65] *Midland Bank Trust Co Ltd v Green (No 3)* [1982] Ch 529, CA.

[66] This point was left open in *Mawji v R* [1957] AC 126, PC, in relation to the rule at common law.

[67] CLA 1977, s 2(2)(a): see n 63. There is no 'one person in law' rule in relation to civil partners.

These rules serve no useful purpose and should be abolished.

It seems anomalous that if spouses or civil partners agree between themselves to commit an offence they cannot be convicted of conspiracy, whereas if the substantive offence is committed by one of them pursuant to the agreement they can both be convicted of that offence as perpetrator and accomplice respectively.

A husband and wife (or civil partner and civil partner in the case of a statutory conspiracy) can be convicted of conspiring together with a third party,[68] even if one of them does not know the identity of the third party. However, if A, a spouse or (in the case of statutory conspiracy) civil partner agrees with B, his or her spouse or civil partner, for a relevant object in ignorance of an agreement for that object between B and another (C), A cannot be so convicted; not knowing of B's agreement with C, A cannot be said to have agreed with C but only with his or her spouse or civil partner.[69] This makes the above rules even more anomalous.

Acquittal of all save one

14.48 Suppose D1 and D2 (or D1, D2 and D3) are charged with conspiracy and that D2 is (or D2 and D3 are) acquitted, can D1 nevertheless still be convicted?

In answering this question two situations must be distinguished.

The first is where a conspiracy is charged as being between two or more accused persons (eg D1 and D2 or D1, D2 and D3) and a person or persons unknown, dead or simply not charged. Here, it has long been established that the acquittal of D2 (or D2 and D3) does not prevent the conviction of D1.[70]

The second situation is where two or more persons (eg D1 and D2 or D1, D2 and D3) are charged in the same indictment with conspiracy together (but not with others), and all but one of them (eg D1) are acquitted. This can happen, for example, where evidence is admissible against one conspirator but not against another. At common law, D1 could nevertheless be convicted if he was tried separately from D2 (or D2 and D3)[71] but not if he was tried together with them.[72] However, the CLA 1977, s 5(8) now provides that:

> 'The fact that the person or persons who, so far as appears from the indictment on which any person has been convicted of conspiracy, were the only other parties to the agreement on which his conviction was based have been acquitted of conspiracy by reference to that agreement (whether after being tried with the person convicted or separately) shall not be a ground for quashing his conviction unless under all the circumstances of the case his conviction is inconsistent with the acquittal of the other person or persons in question.'

---

[68] *Whitehouse* (1852) 6 Cox CC 38. For a limitation, see the CLA 1977, s 2(2): para 14.74.

[69] *Chrastny (No 1)* [1992] 1 All ER 189 at 192.

[70] For an authority, see *Anthony* [1965] 2 QB 189, CCA. Also see *Nichols* (1745) cited in 13 East 412n; *Cooke* (1826) 5 B & C 538.   [71] *DPP v Shannon* [1975] AC 717, HL.

[72] *Plummer* [1902] 2 KB 339; *Coughlan* (1976) 64 Cr App Rep 11, CA. In *DPP v Shannon* [1975] AC 717, HL obiter dicta on this point differed.

The effect of this provision was explained by the Court of Appeal in *Longman*,[73] as follows. Where, in a case where D1 and D2 are tried together for conspiracy together but with no one else, the evidence against D1 and D2 is of equal weight or nearly equal weight, so that a verdict of guilty against D1 and of not guilty against D2 would be inexplicable and therefore inconsistent, the judge must direct the jury that the only verdicts open to them are to convict both or to acquit both. He must add that, if they are unsure about the guilt of one of them, they must acquit both. On the other hand, where the strength of the evidence against D1 and D2 in such a case is (in the view of the judge)[74] markedly different, the judge must direct the jury to consider each case separately and direct them that they may conclude that the prosecution has proved that D1 conspired with D2 but has not proved any such conspiracy against D2, in which event they should convict D1 but acquit D2.

Statutory conspiracy

> ## Key points 14.3
>
> Although a number of statutes specially provide that a particular type of conspiracy is an offence, the term 'statutory conspiracy' is used here to describe the offence of conspiracy to commit a criminal offence contrary to the CLA 1977, s 1.
>
> A person is guilty of a statutory conspiracy if he agrees with one or more persons that a course of conduct shall be pursued which, if the agreement is carried out in accordance with their intentions, will necessarily amount to or involve the commission of any offence or offences by one or more of them (or would do so but for the existence of facts rendering the commission of the offence or any of the offences impossible).
>
> The CLA 1977, s 2 sets out a number of exemptions from liability.

14.49 The rules laid down for statutory conspiracy by the CLA 1977, ss 1 and 2 also apply for determining whether a person is guilty of an offence of conspiracy under any other enactment, but conduct which is an offence under such an enactment is excluded from being an offence under s 1.[75]

Because a statutory conspiracy to commit an offence is a separate offence from the substantive offence to which it relates, special rules provided in relation to that offence, such as a reverse onus provision or about orders which can be made on conviction, do not apply to a conspiracy for the commission of that offence,[76] unless statute has decreed otherwise.[77]

---

[73] (1980) 72 Cr App Rep 121, CA. See also *Testouri* [2003] EWCA Crim 3735.

[74] *Roberts* (1983) 78 Cr App Rep 41, CA.   [75] CLA 1977, s 5(6).

[76] *Cuthbertson* [1981] AC 470, HL (forfeiture provision in respect of substantive offence inapplicable on conviction of conspiracy to commit it); *McGowan* [1990] Crim LR 399, CA (defence under Misuse of Drugs Act 1971 inapplicable on charge of conspiracy to produce a controlled drug); *A-G, ex p Rockall* [1999] 4 All ER 312, DC (presumption of corruption provided by Prevention of Corruption Act 1916, s 2, in respect of offence under Prevention of Corruption Act 1906, s 1, inapplicable on charge of conspiracy to commit that offence).

[77] For examples where statute has so decreed, see para 14.78 (b) and (c).

14.50 The CLA 1977, s 1(1), as substituted by the Criminal Attempts Act 1981, s 5(1), provides:

> 'Subject to [the other provisions of the CLA 1977, Pt I], if a person agrees with any other person or persons that a course of conduct shall be pursued which, if the agreement is carried out in accordance with their intentions, either –
>
> (a) will necessarily amount to or involve the commission of any offence or offences by one or more of the parties to the agreement, or
>
> (b) would do so but for the existence of facts which render the commission of the offence or any of the offences impossible,
>
> he is guilty of conspiracy to commit the offence or offences in question.'

Unlike the offences of encouragement or assisting crime there is no defence of acting reasonably.

It is particularly difficult to divide the definition of statutory conspiracy into *actus reus* and *mens rea* because even the element of agreement involves a mental state on the part of the defendant. Nevertheless, for the purposes of exposition some division must be made, although it is not pretended that the division made here is the only possible one.

Actus reus

14.51 There must be an agreement (as explained above) between two or more people which satisfies the terms of the CLA 1977, s 1(1).

The key issue, derived from s 1(1)(a), is whether the course of conduct agreed on by the parties will necessarily amount to or involve the commission of any offence or offences by one or more of them if it is 'carried out in accordance with their intentions'. If D1 and D2, visitors to this country, agree to persuade someone they have met to engage in a 'threesome' with them, mistakenly believing that their intended conduct is an offence, they are not guilty of statutory conspiracy, because if their agreement is carried out it will not amount to the commission of an offence. On the other hand, if D1 and D2 agree to have sexual intercourse with a woman without her consent, there is a statutory conspiracy to rape because the course of conduct agreed on – sexual intercourse – will necessarily amount to or involve the commission of rape if it was carried out in accordance with their intentions.

14.52 Because the CLA 1977, s 1 expressly contemplates that a conspiracy may involve the commission of a substantive offence by one or more, but not all, of the conspirators, a defendant can be convicted of conspiracy where he is the intended 'object' of the substantive offence.[78] An example would be where D agrees with another, or others, for the supply to him of a controlled drug or the publication to him of an obscene article (provided that the indictment makes it clear that the intended supply or publication is to D, and not

---

[78] *Drew* [2000] 1 Cr App Rep 91, CA; *Jackson* [2000] 1 Cr App Rep 97n, CA.

simply to another[79]). This rule does not apply if the person who is the intended object could not be convicted of the substantive offence as a perpetrator or accomplice; see para 14.74.

14.53 In *Hollinshead*,[80] the Court of Appeal held that 'the commission of any offence... by one or more of the parties to the agreement' meant commission by one or more of them as a perpetrator and not simply as an accomplice, so that there could not be a statutory conspiracy to aid, abet, counsel or procure the commission of an offence by someone not party to the agreement. On appeal, the House of Lords did not consider it necessary to decide whether or not this view was correct. It was, however, endorsed by the Court of Appeal in *Kenning*.[81] This endorsement was clearly right; in the context of s 1(1)(a) the natural meaning of 'commission of any offence' must be 'commission of an offence by one or more of the parties as perpetrator' with the result that there cannot be a statutory conspiracy to aid and abet.[82] As a result, if D1 and D2 agree to assist X (not a party to the agreement) to rape a woman they are not guilty of a statutory conspiracy to rape because the course of conduct agreed on would not amount to or involve the commission of rape by one or more of the parties (ie D1 or D2) to the agreement if it was carried out in accordance with their intentions. The same would be true if D1 and D2 agree to encourage X to commit the rape. However, in both cases D1 and D2 could be convicted of a statutory conspiracy to commit (ie perpetrate) the offence under the Serious Crime Act 2007, s 44 of intentionally encouraging or assisting the commission of rape.

Parliament has, from time to time, created offences, such as aiding and abetting suicide (abolished by the Coroners and Justice Act 2009), whose *actus reus* consists of procuring or aiding and abetting something, so that the perpetrator of such an offence is the procurer or aider and abettor. People who conspire for one (or more) of them to perpetrate such an offence can therefore be convicted of a statutory conspiracy to commit it because it amounts to a substantive offence.

14.54 'Carried out in accordance with their intentions' refers not only to the physical course of conduct (and its surrounding circumstances) intended but also to any intended consequences of it; otherwise it would be impossible to convict a person of conspiring to commit an offence whose *actus reus* requires a consequence to result from conduct. Suppose that two terrorists, D1 and D2, agree that D2 should destroy an army tank by putting inside it a time bomb to be supplied by D1. There is a statutory conspiracy to commit criminal damage because the course of conduct agreed on (planting the bomb) would necessarily amount to or involve the commission of criminal damage if it was carried out in accordance with their intentions of causing criminal damage.

Impossibility

14.55 The CLA 1977, s 1(1)(b) deals with agreements which are impossible of fulfilment, as where D1 and D2 agree to murder V by poisoning him, not knowing that he is already

---

[79] *Jackson* [2000] 1 Cr App Rep 97n, CA.
[80] [1985] 1 All ER 850, CA; revsd [1985] AC 975, HL.   [81] [2008] EWCA Crim 1534.
[82] It may be noted that, under the Criminal Attempts Act 1981, an attempt to aid and abet an offence is not criminal; see para 14.106(d).

dead, or where D1 and D2 agree to have intercourse with a girl of 16, thinking that she is 15. Section 1(1)(b) provides that an agreement on a course of conduct which, if the agreement is carried out in accordance with the parties' intentions, would necessarily amount to or involve the commission of an offence or any offences by one or more of the parties but for the existence of facts which render the commission of the offence or any of the offences impossible is a statutory conspiracy.

Section 1(1)(b) may not have been strictly necessary to deal with agreements which are impossible of fulfilment. In cases of impossibility, such as the two examples just given, it would seem that there is a conspiracy within s 1(1)(a), because if the course of conduct agreed on is carried out in accordance with the parties' intentions this will necessarily amount to or involve the commission of an offence. Nevertheless, s 1(1)(b) is useful because it puts the matter beyond doubt. Moreover, the use of the word 'would' [necessarily amount to or involve the commission of an offence] seems more appropriate than 'will' where the existence of facts renders it impossible to commit an offence.

Ifs and buts

Agreement whose object is the achievement of an offence subject to a condition precedent

14.56 **Often parties to an agreement for the commission of an offence make the carrying out of their agreed course of conduct subject to a condition precedent** (as where they agree to rob a bank, provided that on arrival there it seems safe to do so, or where they agree to kill a person, if he arrives at a rendezvous with them). **In such a case they can be convicted of statutory conspiracy** to rob and of statutory conspiracy to murder, respectively, since they have agreed on a course of conduct which, if it is carried out in accordance with their intentions, will necessarily amount to or involve the commission of an offence.[83] In *Saik*,[84] Lord Nicholls said:

'An intention to do a prohibited act is within the scope of s 1(1) even if the intention is expressed to be conditional on the happening, or non-happening, of some particular event. The question always is whether the agreed course of action, if carried out in accordance with the parties' intentions, would necessarily amount to or involve an offence. A conspiracy to rob a bank tomorrow if the coast is clear when the conspirators reach the bank is not, by reason of this disqualification, any less a conspiracy to rob.'

It was stated by the Court of Appeal in *Jackson*[85] that

'"Necessarily" [in s 1] is not to be held to mean that there must inevitably be the carrying out of an offence; it means, if the agreement is carried out in accordance with the plan, there must be the commission of the offence referred to in the conspiracy count.'

---

[83] *Reed* [1982] Crim LR 819, CA.   [84] [2006] UKHL 18 at [5].
[85] [1985] Crim LR 442, CA.

In *Jackson*, the defendants had agreed with X, who was on trial for burglary, that if he was convicted they would shoot him in the leg; they believed that he would receive a more lenient sentence if they did so. The Court of Appeal dismissed the defendants' appeal against conviction for conspiracy to pervert the course of justice.

In *Reed*,[86] the Court of Appeal refused leave to appeal where D1 and D2 had been convicted of conspiring to commit the substantive offence of aiding and abetting suicide after they had agreed that D1 would visit people contemplating suicide and either discourage them or assist them, depending on his assessment of the appropriate course of action.

In *O'Hadhmaill*,[87] it was held by the Court of Appeal that D, a member of the IRA, who had agreed with others to cause explosions if the results of the Northern Ireland peace process did not satisfy them, could be convicted of a conspiracy to cause an explosion.

Agreement whose object is not the commission of an offence but in whose achievement an offence may be committed

14.57 In the cases just discussed the actual object of the agreement is an offence. The position is different where the object of the agreement is not criminal, although (as the parties know) the achievement of that object *may* involve the commission of an offence. In such a case the commission of the offence is only incidental to the object of the agreement, which may be achievable without it; it cannot be said that the parties have agreed on a course of conduct which, if carried out in accordance with their intentions, will or would necessarily amount to or involve the commission of an offence, as required by the CLA 1977, s 1(1).

An example of this was given by the Court of Appeal in *Reed*:[88]

> 'A and B agree to drive from London to Edinburgh in a time which can be achieved without exceeding the speed limits, but only if the traffic which they encounter is exceptionally light. Their agreement will not necessarily involve the commission of any offence, even if it is carried out in accordance with their intentions, and they do arrive from London to Edinburgh within the agreed time. Accordingly the agreement does not constitute the offence of statutory conspiracy or indeed of any offence.'

The Court of Appeal distinguished this type of case from two of the cases referred to in para 14.56, viz where there is an agreement to rob a bank, if on arrival there it is safe to do so, and the actual facts of *Reed*, on the ground that in both cases the agreements would necessarily involve the commission of the substantive offences of robbery and aiding and abetting suicide respectively.

Agreement to commit an offence and, if necessary, another offence

14.58 This heading is concerned with the type of case where D1 and D2 agree to commit an armed robbery on V and agree that, if necessary, eg to rob him or to escape, they will

---

[86] [1982] Crim LR 819, CA.

[87] [1996] Crim LR 509, CA. This point does not appear in the brief report, but is referred to in the commentary.   [88] [1982] Crim LR 819, CA.

shoot to kill. Section 1(1) seems to indicate that they can be convicted of conspiracy to rob but not of conspiracy to murder because, as in the type of case just dealt with in para 14.57, if the agreed course of conduct is carried out in accordance with their intentions, it will necessarily amount to or involve robbery but not necessarily murder. The only difference seems to be that, whereas in the type of case in para 14.57, the object of the agreement is not the commission of an offence, the object of the agreement here is itself an offence.

Despite what appears to be the clear meaning of s 1(1), the Court of Appeal in *Suchedina (A-G's Reference (No 4 of 2003))* was sympathetic to the view that: 'if conspirators agree that they will steal a particular item and that they will, if necessary, either commit burglary or commit robbery in order to obtain that item, that will amount to an agreement to commit the offences of theft, burglary and robbery.'[89] To reach such a view is tantamount to re-writing s 1(1) because if the agreement is carried out in accordance with the parties' intentions it will not *necessarily* amount to or involve the commission of an offence of burglary or robbery. The sooner that the Supreme Court can consider this matter, the better.

Conditions subsequent

14.59 What is the answer where the completion of the substantive offence depends on a condition subsequent to the carrying out of the agreed course of conduct? Such a situation is common and occurs where the parties to an agreement agree that a course of conduct be pursued which, if carried out in accordance with their intentions, will necessarily amount to or involve the commission of an offence by one or more of them only if some contingency occurs after the course of conduct has been carried out. An example is where the substantive offence is a 'result crime' since, taking conspiracy to murder as an example, the course of conduct agreed on – eg firing a gun – will necessarily amount to or involve the offence of murder only if the bullet thereafter hits the victim and kills him. In the present type of case, there can be a conviction for conspiracy to commit the substantive offence if the parties intended that the element(s) necessary to complete that offence should occur, despite the fact that they realised that that occurrence depended on some contingency subsequent to their agreed course of conduct.

'Offence'

14.60 The 'offence' which the agreed course of conduct must necessarily amount to or involve if it is carried out in accordance with the parties' intentions may be an offence which is only triable summarily. However, where in pursuance of the agreement the acts are to be done in contemplation or furtherance of a trade dispute (within the meaning of the Trade Union and Labour Relations (Consolidation) Act 1992) that offence is not an 'offence' for the purposes of conspiracy if it is triable only summarily and not punishable with imprisonment.[90]

For further discussion of 'offence' for the purposes of statutory conspiracy see para 14.77.

---

[89] [2004] EWCA Crim 1944 at [14]. See also *Hussain, Bhatti and Bhatti* [2002] EWCA Crim 6 at [27].
[90] Trade Union and Labour Relations (Consolidation) Act 1992, s 242.

Mens rea

Key points 14.4

The *mens rea* requirements for statutory conspiracy are that:

- if the *actus reus* of the substantive offence (ie the agreed offence) requires for its commission the existence of a fact or circumstance a defendant (D) and at least one other party to the agreement must intend or know that it shall or will exist;

- two parties to the agreement must intend that the agreement is carried out and the substantive offence be committed. Technically, provided that this can be proved another party who is a defendant can be convicted even though he lacked that intention, if he knew of the course of conduct agreed on and what it would involve; but in practice the technical position is ignored and the above intent is required to be proved against an individual defendant; and

- a defendant (D) and at least one other party must have any additional *mens rea* required for the substantive offence.

14.61 As will be explained, this offence is unusual in that liability does not depend merely on the state of mind of the defendant but also on the state of mind of other parties to the agreement. There cannot be a conspiracy unless at least two parties satisfy the requirements of *mens rea*. This is not surprising, given the nature of the offence.

Mens rea as to any fact or circumstance necessary for commission of substantive offence

14.62 A person cannot be convicted of statutory conspiracy unless he and at least one other party to the agreement intend or know that any fact or circumstance necessary for the commission of the *actus reus* of the substantive offence shall or will exist when the conduct constituting the offence is to occur.[91]

This general rule is not stated expressly in the Act but is implied by the CLA 1977, s 1(2), which states that such a rule applies even though the substantive offence does not require knowledge as to a particular fact or circumstance necessary for the commission of the offence, ie an offence where recklessness or negligence as to a circumstance suffices or which is of strict liability as to a fact or circumstance.

14.63 In *Saik*[92] the House of Lords confirmed that the requirement of intention or knowledge in the CLA 1977, s 1(2) was not confined to conspiracies to commit substantive offences which may be committed without knowledge of any fact or circumstance necessary for the commission of the substantive offence. Although s 1(2) did not on its face apply where the substantive offence required the defendant to know of a material fact or circumstance, s 1(2) was to be read as applicable whenever an ingredient of the

---

[91] *Saik* [2006] UKHL 18. [92] [2006] UKHL 18. Baroness Hale gave a dissenting speech.

substantive offence was the existence of a particular fact or circumstance. This decision was an important one. It clarified the meaning of 'knowledge' in s 1(2) because some Court of Appeal[93] decisions had held that it was sufficient for conspiracy that the defendant had the *mens rea*, as to a fact or circumstance, required for the substantive offence, even though that requirement could be satisfied by proof that the defendant suspected (recklessness), or had reason to suspect it (negligence). The House of Lords held that this was wrong: both were insufficient in s 1(2).

An example of the present rule can be given by reference to the offence of engaging in sexual activity with a child under 16. As we saw in para 9.60, this offence is one of negligence as to the child's age (if the child is 13 or over). The effect of the CLA 1977, s 1(2) is that if D1 and D2, both aged 30, agree to have sexual intercourse that night with a girl aged 14 they can only be convicted of conspiracy to commit the s 9 offence if they both know that she is under 16.

Another example can be given by reference to the offence of handling stolen goods, which requires knowledge or belief that the goods are stolen. The effect of s 1(2) is that if D1 and D2 agree to handle some goods which are to be acquired by X and they claim that they thought that that acquisition would be a legitimate one, they can only be convicted of conspiracy to handle stolen goods if it is proved that they both 'intend or know' that the goods shall or will be stolen when the handling occurs.

Intention or knowledge as to fact or circumstance

14.64 Often whether or not a fact or circumstance required for the substantive offence exists will be a matter quite independent of the parties to the agreement and outside their control. In such a case, it is difficult to appreciate how a party when agreeing to a course of conduct can intend that a fact or circumstance shall exist at the time that the conduct constituting the substantive offence is to occur.

It is submitted that, for the purposes of the CLA 1977, s 1(2), the reference to 'intention' describes the *mens rea* for conspiracy where a fact or circumstance required for the *actus reus* of the substantive offence does not exist at the time of the agreement but it is *known* that it will have to exist at the time that the conduct constituting the substantive offence occurs, as where D1 and D2 agree to have intercourse with a woman without her consent who is to be delivered to D1's house the next day by a kidnapper.

It is submitted that reference to 'knowledge' describes the case where a fact or circumstance required for the *actus reus* of the substantive offence exists at the time of the agreement, as where the woman has already expressed her dissent to intercourse, as D1 and D2 know.

14.65 Although generally 'knowledge' includes wilful blindness (a species of recklessness),[94] this is not the case here. As noted in para 14.63, the House of Lords held in *Saik*[95] that in the context of the CLA 1977, s 1(2) the requirement of 'knowledge' as to a fact or circumstance of the *actus reus* is not satisfied by proof of suspicion (another species of

---

[93] See *Rizvi and Christi* [2003] EWCA Crim 3575, and *Sakavickas* [2004] EWCA Crim 2686.
[94] Para 3.45. [95] [2006] UKHL 18.

recklessness) as to a relevant fact or circumstance. Lord Nicholls said that there was no doubt that the requirement in s 1(2) 'was designed to eliminate the risk that someone could be guilty of conspiracy just because he was reckless as to the existence or otherwise of the circumstances that would make the conduct criminal'.[96] In *Saik* D, the sole proprietor of a bureau de change which had a turnover of £1,000 a week until 2001, started purchasing large quantities of $100 bills. Between May 2001 and February 2002, D exchanged some $8 million. He was seen by surveillance officers meeting another alleged conspirator near his office on many occasions, and at these times sacks of sterling were observed. D was charged with a conspiracy to launder the proceeds of crime, contrary to the Criminal Justice Act 1988, s 93C(2) (which offence has been replaced by an offence under the Proceeds of Crime Act 2002, s 327). He pleaded guilty on the basis that he suspected that his dealings involved 'dirty' money.[97] The House of Lords (Baroness Hale dissenting) allowed D's appeal against conviction on the ground that D's suspicion about the source of the money was an insufficient basis for a conviction of conspiracy to launder the proceeds of crime, since the CLA 1977, s 1(2) required D to intend or know that the money shall or will be the proceeds of crime and that requirement was not fulfilled. Lord Nicholls stated that the distinction drawn by s 1(2) between knowledge and lesser states of mind such as recklessness or suspicion:

'is not altogether satisfactory in terms of blameworthiness. But this does not entitle the House to erode the distinction clearly drawn in s 1(2)...[T]he desire to avoid an unattractive outcome in the present case cannot justify a distorted interpretation of s 1(2). It is not for the courts to extend the net of conspiracy beyond the reach set by Parliament.'[98]

14.66 In paras 3.43 and 3.44, it was stated that 'knowledge' normally includes 'belief'. In *Saik* Lord Nicholls, with whose reasoning Lord Steyn agreed, stated[99] that 'know' in the CLA 1977, s 1(2) should be interpreted strictly and not watered down, and went on to reject the notion that 'belief' could suffice for 'knowledge' in s 1(2). If this represented the law, so that an untrue belief would not suffice for conspiracy, it would present problems in respect of agreements to commit an offence which was impossible by virtue of the non-existence of a circumstance because one cannot know something which does not exist but one can believe it, and because if the parties believe that that thing already exists they do not intend that it shall exist. The CLA 1977, s 1(1) contemplates that there can be a conviction in such a case.

Lord Brown thought[100] that 'belief' would suffice for the purposes of knowledge in the CLA 1977, s 1(2).

14.67 Because 'suspicion' will not suffice in CLA 1977, s 1(2), if D1 and D2 merely suspect that a necessary fact or circumstance will exist when the agreed course of conduct is executed but are prepared to carry out the agreed course of conduct whether or not the

---

[96] [2006] UKHL 18 at [58]. [97] This account of the facts appears in [2004] EWCA Crim 2936.
[98] [2006] UKHL 18 at [33]. [99] [2006] UKHL 18 at [26]. [100] [2006] UKHL 18 at [119].

fact or circumstance exists at that time, they are not guilty of statutory conspiracy. An example would be where D1 and D2 agree to have intercourse with a woman, suspecting that she will not consent and agreeing to have the intercourse whether or not she does.

However, in the course of her dissenting speech, in *Saik*, Baroness Hale considered that D1 and D2 could be convicted of conspiracy to rape. Her Ladyship considered that what she called a 'conditional intent' should suffice in s 1(2) just as it does in s 1(1), and that D1 and D2 would be guilty of rape because 'when they agree they have thought about the possibility that [the woman] may not consent. They have agreed that they will go ahead *even if at the time when they go ahead they know that she is not consenting*'.[101] This is a different type of conditional intent from that referred to in paras 14.56 and 14.57 in relation to the words of s 1(1) where the defendant has no doubt that any facts or circumstances required for the *actus reus* of the substantive offence 'shall or will' exist if the contingency occurs, or where there is an unconditional intention to commit one offence and a conditional intention to commit another offence. It cannot be regarded as representing the law, in the light of the view taken by the other members of the House of Lords in *Saik*.

Intent that agreement be carried out and substantive offence be committed

14.68 The wording of the CLA 1977, s 1(1) seems unequivocally to indicate that, as a second element of *mens rea*, a defendant and at least one other party to the agreement must intend that the agreement be carried out to completion and that the substantive offence or offences to which their agreed course of conduct will (or would) necessarily amount, or which it will (or would) involve, will be committed. Consequently, it is amazing that the House of Lords in *Anderson*[102] held that such an intention need not be proved against an individual defendant; it sufficed that a defendant knew the course of action agreed on and what it would involve. This decision has been overlooked or ignored in a number of subsequent appellate decisions on statutory conspiracy,[103] where courts have held that an intention that an agreement be carried out is part of the *mens rea* of a conspirator. In *Edwards*,[104] for example, where D had been charged with a conspiracy to supply amphetamine (a controlled drug), D may have intended to supply ephedrine (not a controlled drug) instead. The Court of Appeal, without reference to *Anderson*, held that the trial judge had been correct to direct the jury that they could only convict D if he had intended to supply amphetamine.

In *McPhillips*,[105] the Court of Appeal of Northern Ireland held that s 1(1) required an intention on the part of a defendant that the agreement be carried out. As a result, D, who had joined a conspiracy to plant a bomb timed to go off during a disco, was held not guilty of conspiracy to murder because he intended to give a warning before the bomb

---

[101] [2006] UKHL 18 at [99].
[102] [1986] AC 27, HL. For the facts of this case, see para 14.71.
[103] *Edwards* [1991] Crim LR 45, CA; *Ashton* [1992] Crim LR 667, CA; *Harvey* [1999] Crim LR 70, CA.
[104] [1991] Crim LR 45, CA.   [105] [1989] NI 360, NICA.

went off. *Anderson* was distinguished on the ground that in that case the defendant had not intended to frustrate the plans of the other conspirators. It is not obvious why this was a material distinction.

In *Yip Chiu-cheung v R*,[106] an appeal from Hong Kong concerning the common law offence of conspiracy to commit an offence, the Privy Council took a view which conflicts with that in *Anderson*. In *Yip Chiu-cheung* an undercover enforcement officer entered into an agreement with D to carry out a drug trafficking offence. The trial judge told the jury to convict D of conspiracy to commit the trafficking offence if they found that the undercover officer had intended to carry out the trafficking offence, because he would be a co-conspirator (so that there would be a conspiracy). The Privy Council held that the judge's direction was correct since: 'The crime of conspiracy requires an agreement between two or more persons to commit an unlawful act with the intention of carrying it out.'[107]

Although *Yip Chiu-cheung* was concerned with common law conspiracy, the requirement in it of an intention on the part of a defendant and at least one other party that the agreement be carried out and the substantive offence committed accords with s 1(1) in a way that *Anderson* does not. If such an intent is required for a common law conspiracy to commit an offence, why should it not for a statutory conspiracy, especially in the light of the clear words of s 1(1)? In principle, the approach in *Yip Chiu–cheung* is right and that in *Anderson* is wrong in relation to s 1(1). Support for the view that to be guilty of conspiracy a defendant must intend that the agreement be carried out and the substantive offence committed can also be found in the speech of Lord Nicholls, with whose legal analysis Lord Steyn agreed, in *Saik*.[108] Nevertheless, until it is overruled the approach in *Anderson* is binding, although in practice it seems likely to continue to be overlooked or ignored or to be distinguished. In any event, a party to a conspiracy who does not intend that the substantive offence be committed but plays a part in the agreed course of conduct can be convicted of the appropriate offence of encouraging or assisting crime.

It may be that the House of Lords thought that not even one party must have had an intention that the agreement be carried out and the substantive offence committed. However, since it did not clearly indicate this, and since such an interpretation would do further violence to the wording of the Act and to the intentions of the Law Commission, it can be assumed – especially in the light of the Privy Council's statement in *Yip Chiu-cheung* – that at least two of the parties to the agreement must have had such an intention and that otherwise there cannot be a statutory conspiracy. If this is so, there cannot be a conviction for statutory conspiracy of either D1 and D2 who are the only parties to an agreement for the commission of an offence if only D1 intends that the agreement be carried out and the substantive offence committed.

14.69 On the assumption made in the last paragraph, where the *actus reus* of the substantive offence requires a specific consequence to be caused, the present requirement necessitates proof of an intention on the part of two or more parties to the agreement that

---

[106] [1995] 1 AC 111, PC.   [107] [1995] 1 AC 111 at 118.   [108] [2006] UKHL 18 at [4].

that consequence should result. Three points arise in relation to this. First, the intent may be conditional, as indicated in paras 14.56 and 14.57. Second, although an intention to cause some lesser consequence may suffice for the substantive offence, such an intention will not suffice on a charge of conspiracy.[109] Consequently, on a charge of conspiracy to murder, an intention that someone be unlawfully killed must be proved, although an intention unlawfully to cause grievous bodily harm suffices for murder itself.[110] Third, there can be little doubt that only a direct intent will do.

It follows from the present requirement that if D1 gives D2 a parcel and tells him to deliver it to V's empty house, which D2 agrees to do, and the parcel contains a bomb with which D1 intends to cause criminal damage (an offence where recklessness suffices) to V's house, neither D1 nor D2 can be convicted of conspiracy to commit criminal damage, unless D2 also knows that the parcel contains a bomb and intends that V's property be damaged or destroyed.

Additional mens rea

Additional *mens rea* required for substantive offence

14.70 **In addition to any** *mens rea* **relating to a specified circumstance or consequence of the** *actus reus* **of the substantive offence, the defendant and at least one other party to the agreement must be proved to have had any ulterior intent or other** *mens rea* **required for that offence.** This was recognised in *Saik*[111] by Lord Nicholls, with whose analysis Lord Steyn agreed. For example, on a charge of conspiracy to steal, the intended course of conduct must be dishonest on their part and they must intend permanently to deprive the other person to whom the property belongs.

Likewise, on a charge of conspiracy to commit an offence of criminal damage being reckless as to life being endangered[112] it is necessary that a defendant and at least one other party have agreed to damage property, being reckless as to whether life will be endangered thereby. A decision to the contrary is that of the Court of Appeal in *Mir and Beg*[113] where it was held that, on a charge of conspiracy to commit such an offence, recklessness as to life being endangered was insufficient. The Court's reason was that the endangerment of life is a fact or circumstance required for the *actus reus* of that offence and that therefore only knowledge or intention on the part of the alleged conspirators that their agreed course of conduct would create a risk to life would do. This decision may be regarded as not binding on the Court of Appeal, because Court of Appeal decisions indicating that the actual endangerment of life is not required and is therefore not a fact or circumstance required for the *actus reus* of aggravated criminal damage[114] were not cited to the Court of Appeal. Although *Mir and Beg* has been applied in two unreported Court of Appeal decisions,[115] they are open to the same

---

[109] *Siracusa* (1989) 90 Cr App Rep 340, CA.
[110] *Siracusa* (1989) 90 Cr App Rep 340 at 350.
[111] [2006] UKHL 18 at [4].   [112] See para 13.21.   [113] (1994) unreported, CA.
[114] Para 13.20.   [115] *Browning and Dixon* (1998) unreported, CA; *Ryan* (1999) unreported, CA

objections. It would seem that they and *Mir and Beg* can now be safely ignored. In *Saik* Lord Nicholls said:

> 'Damaging property, being reckless as to whether life is endangered thereby, is a criminal offence: Criminal Damage Act 1971, section 1(2). Conspiracy to commit this offence requires proof of an intention to damage property, and to do so recklessly indifferent as to whether this would endanger life'.[116]

Must defendant intend to play a part in agreed course of conduct?

14.71 In *Anderson*,[117] Lord Bridge, with whose speech the other Law Lords agreed, specified an additional element of *mens rea* which always had to be proved against a person charged with statutory conspiracy. He stated:

> '[T]he necessary *mens rea* of the crime is, in my opinion, established if, and only[118] if, it is shown that the accused, when he entered into the agreement, intended to play some part in the agreed course of conduct in furtherance of the criminal purpose which the agreed course of conduct was intended to achieve. Nothing less will suffice; nothing more is required.'[119]

This implication of this *mens rea* requirement (on the part, presumably, of each party to the agreement if he is to be guilty) was not supported by any authority and is in no way warranted by s 1(1) or any other part of the CLA 1977. It is pure judicial invention. It does further violence to the unequivocal wording of s 1(1) and to the intentions of the Law Commission.

If Lord Bridge's statement represented the law, a person would not be guilty as a perpetrator of criminal conspiracy who for thoroughly bad motives entered into an agreement with others that a course of conduct be pursued which would necessarily amount to the commission of an offence if it was carried out in accordance with their intentions, if he did not himself intend to play some part in the agreed course of conduct. Conversely, if a police officer or the like who joined a conspiracy in order to entrap the conspirators did intend to play a minor part in the furtherance of the agreed conduct in order to maintain his credibility as a conspirator and to obtain sufficient evidence against them, he would (according to Lord Bridge's statement) be guilty of statutory conspiracy, even though (according to the decision in *Anderson* referred to in para 14.68) he did not intend the substantive offence to be committed. The application of that statement would clearly give rise to some unfortunate results.

Reference to the facts and decision in *Anderson* indicates that Lord Bridge's statement in *Anderson* quoted above was not necessary to the decision[120] and was merely an obiter

---

[116] [2006] UKHL 18 at [4].   [117] [1986] AC 27, HL.

[118] The word 'only' must be read subject to the comments in para 14.68.

[119] [1986] AC 27 at 39. Presumably, this meant that nothing more is required against an individual defendant, but not that nothing more is required against two or more other parties to the agreement.

[120] See commentaries by JC Smith in [1986] Crim LR at 54 and 247.

dictum. In *Anderson*, D had agreed with others to participate, in return for a fee, in a scheme to effect X's escape from prison by providing cutting wire, a rope ladder, transport and safe accommodation. According to D, he had never intended the escape plan to be carried into effect and had only intended to supply the cutting wire, whereafter he was going to go abroad with the part of the fee which had been paid on account and another part he expected to have paid on account. The House of Lords held that on these facts D had correctly been convicted of statutory conspiracy to effect the escape of X. Its reason was that D (as already discussed) did not have to be proved to have intended that the substantive offence be committed and that, in agreeing that a course of conduct be pursued that would, if successful, necessarily involve effecting X's escape from prison, D clearly intended, by providing the wire, to play a part in the agreed course of conduct in furtherance of that criminal objective. Neither the fact that D intended to play no further part in attempting to effect the escape, nor that he believed the escape to be impossible, would have afforded him any defence.

In view of the unfortunate consequences of Lord Bridge's obiter statement, it is pleasing to note that it has been explained by the Court of Appeal in *Siracusa*[121] that Lord Bridge did not mean that the prosecution must prove that the defendant intended to play an active part in the agreed course of conduct. The Court held that he can 'play a part' merely by continuing to concur in the criminal activity of another or others. This explanation of what Lord Bridge said is a highly artificial one, driven by a desire to avoid the unfortunate consequences of that statement while paying the necessary lip-service to it. So explained, the point becomes meaningless in the light of the rule[122] that once one is guilty of agreement one cannot escape liability by changing one's mind and withdrawing from it. One can be confident that the interpretation in *Siracusa* will be followed.

It is unfortunate that the other part of the House of Lords' decision, discussed in para 14.68, must be regarded as part of the ratio decidendi and therefore binding.

No need for knowledge that agreed course of conduct criminal

14.72 A person charged with conspiracy need not know that the course of conduct agreed on, and what it would involve, constitute a criminal offence. This was the position in relation to common law conspiracy to commit an offence,[123] and the wording of s 1(1) of the CLA 1977 makes it clear that this continues to be the case for statutory conspiracy. Thus, it is a statutory conspiracy to agree to manufacture a particular drug which, in law, is categorised as a Class A controlled drug, even though the parties are ignorant of the criminal legislation on drugs and therefore not aware that they are conspiring to commit an offence.[124] Ignorance of the criminal law is no defence.[125]

---

[121] (1989) 90 Cr App Rep 340, CA. Also see *Edwards* [1991] Crim LR 45, CA (commentary).
[122] Para 14.46.　　[123] *Churchill v Walton* [1967] 2 AC 224, HL.
[124] *Broad* [1997] Crim LR 666, CA.　　[125] Para 3.73.

Summary: The above *mens rea* requirements are summarised in the table below which shows when D and other parties, R, S, T, U and Z with different *mens rea*, are guilty of statutory conspiracy.

Mens rea	First party D	*If the only other party is*			
		R	S	T	U
Re facts or circumstances of substantive offence	✓	✓	✓	✗	✓
As to agreement being carried out and substantive offence committed	✓	✓	✓	✓	✗
Additional MR required for substantive offence	✓	✓	✗	✓	✗
Who is guilty of statutory conspiracy?		D: ✓ R: ✓	D: ✗ S: ✗	D: ✗ T: ✗	D: ✗ U: ✗

But if there is a third party besides the two with full mens rea

	D	R	Z		
Re facts or circumstances of substantive offence	✓	✓	✓		
As to agreement being carried out and substantive offence committed	✓	✓	✗		
Additional MR required for substantive offence	✓	✓	✓		
Who is guilty of statutory conspiracy?		D: ✓ R: ✓ Z: ✓ Technically according to *Anderson*	D: ✓ R: ✓ Z: ✗ In practice ignoring *Anderson*		

Conspiracy to do what?

14.73 Liability for conspiracy relates only to the offence or offences which would necessarily be committed if the agreement to pursue a course of conduct is carried out in accordance with the parties' intentions. If D1 and D2 agree to attack and kill V they are guilty of conspiracy to murder, even though there is a chance that V may survive the attack, since the offence of murder would necessarily be committed if the course of conduct agreed by them is carried out in accordance with their intentions. If D1 and D2 agree to do serious harm to V they can be convicted of conspiracy to commit the offence of causing grievous bodily harm with intent, but not of conspiracy to murder, even though if they had carried out their plan and V had died of his injuries they could have been convicted of murder, since that offence is not one which would necessarily be committed if the agreement is carried out in accordance with their intentions.

Exemptions from liability for statutory conspiracy

14.74 The CLA 1977, s 2 provides the following exemptions:

- *The intended victim* The CLA 1977, s 2(1) provides that a person cannot be guilty of a conspiracy to commit any offence if he is the intended victim of that offence. Unlike the corresponding exemption under the Serious Crime Act 2007, s 51, in respect of offences of encouraging or assisting crime, there is no definition of who is a 'victim'. It would seem to refer to a person against whom the substantive offence would be committed if the agreement was carried out but who could not be convicted (either as a perpetrator or as an accomplice) of the substantive offence itself, because it is designed for his protection and he is assumed to fall outside its scope. For example, a child under 16 who has sexual intercourse with an adult cannot be convicted as an accomplice to the offence committed by the adult, even though the child is a willing participant. This matter is discussed later.[126]

- *Section 2(2)* This provides that a person is not guilty of a conspiracy to commit any offence if the only other person or persons with whom he agrees are (both initially and at all times during the currency of the agreement):
  - his spouse or civil partner;[127]
  - under the age of criminal responsibility (ie under 10);[128] or
  - an intended victim or victims of the substantive offence.[129]

  Thus, if D1 agrees with a 15-year-old girl to have intercourse with her he cannot be convicted of conspiracy to engage in sexual activity with a child under 16 since the only other party to the agreement is an intended victim. It would, of course, be different if D1 and D2 had agreed with the girl that they should have intercourse with her because the exemption only applies where the only other party or parties to the agreement are under 10 or intended victims or a spouse or a civil partner; in that case D1 and D2 could be convicted of conspiracy, although the girl would be exempt from liability under s 2(1).

  While this rule can be supported where the only other party is under the age of criminal responsibility, for there can be no 'criminal' agreement between two persons if one of them is legally incapable of agreeing for the purposes of criminal liability, the exemption is difficult to defend in the other two cases and (as said earlier) anomalous in the case of the first.

14.75 By way of comparison, it may be noted that, provided that at least one party to the agreement is capable of being convicted of perpetrating the substantive offence, the fact that another party (X) is not capable of perpetrating it does not mean that X or any

---

[126] Para 17.58.

[127] CLA 1977, s 2(2)(a) (amended by the Civil Partnership Act 2004, Sch 27); para 14.47.

[128] CLA 1977, s 2(2)(b) and (3).   [129] CLA 1977, s 2(2)(c).

other party to the agreement cannot be convicted of conspiracy to commit that offence.[130] Thus, a woman, lacking a penis, cannot perpetrate the offence of rape (although she can be convicted of that offence as an accomplice) but, if she agrees with a man that he will rape V, they can both be convicted of conspiracy to rape. Likewise, the mere fact that an individual party to an agreement (Y) is exempt from prosecution for the substantive offence agreed to does not prevent another party to the agreement (Z) being liable for a conspiracy to commit it.[131] It remains to be determined whether Y's exemption also applies to a conspiracy charge.

Jurisdiction

Conspiracy abroad to commit offence in England and Wales

14.76 Under the common law rules of jurisdiction, the courts of England and Wales have jurisdiction over a conspiracy formed abroad provided that it was intended to result in the commission of an offence under English law in England and Wales, even though no overt act, omission or consequence pursuant to the conspiracy takes place in England and Wales.[132]

Special provision to much the same effect is made by the Criminal Justice Act 1993, s 3(2) in relation to conspiracy to commit a Group A offence, ie one of the offences under the Theft Act 1968, Forgery and Counterfeiting Act 1981, Fraud Act 2006 and related offences listed in s 1 of the 1993 Act (see para 12.70).[133] It provides that a defendant may be convicted of such a conspiracy whether or not he became a party to the conspiracy in England and Wales, and whether or not any act, omission or other occurrence in relation to the conspiracy actually occurred in England and Wales. It is immaterial whether or not a person was a British citizen at any material time or was in England and Wales at any such time.[134]

Conspiracy to commit offence outside England and Wales

14.77 Although the CLA 1977, s 1(4) provides that 'offence' in CLA 1977, Pt I means an offence triable in England and Wales, the importance of this has been much reduced by the CLA 1977, s 1A. Section 1A, inserted by the Criminal Justice (Terrorism and Conspiracy) Act 1998, s 5(1) and amended by the Coroners and Justice Act 2009, s 72(1),

---

[130] *Whitchurch* (1890) 24 QBD 420, CCR.

[131] *Duguid* (1906) 70 JP 294, CCR; *B* [1984] Crim LR 352, CA; *Sherry and El-Yamani* [1993] Crim LR 536, CA.

[132] *Liangsiriprasert v Government of the United States of America* [1991] 1 AC 225, PC; *Sansom* [1991] 2 QB 130, CA; *Al Fawwaz* [2001] UKHL 69.

[133] Conspiracy to commit a Grade A offence is a Group B offence under the Criminal Justice Act 1993, Pt I: CJA 1993, s 1(3)(a).

[134] Criminal Justice Act 1993, s 3(1).

deals with a conspiracy to commit an act outside England and Wales that (if committed in accordance with the conspiracy) would amount to an offence under the law of the country or territory concerned and would have constituted an offence under English law if committed in England and Wales.

Section 1A provides that, where four conditions in s 1A(2) to (5) are satisfied in respect of an agreement, the provisions relating to the offence of statutory conspiracy under the CLA 1977, Pt I (ie ss 1–5, described in this chapter) have effect in relation to the agreement in the same way as they have effect in relation to an agreement falling within the CLA 1977, s 1(1) The four conditions are that:

(a) the pursuit of the agreed course of conduct would at some stage involve:
   (i) an act by one or more of the parties, or
   (ii) the happening of some other event,
   intended to take place in a country or territory outside England and Wales;[135]

(b) that act or other event constitutes an offence under the law in force in that country or territory;

(c) the agreement would fall within the CLA 1977, s 1(1) as an agreement relating to the commission of an offence but for the fact that the offence would not be an offence triable in England and Wales if committed in accordance with the parties' intentions; and

(d) (i) a party to the agreement, or a party's agent, did anything in England and Wales in relation to the agreement before its formation, or
   (ii) a party to the agreement became a party in England and Wales (by joining it either in person or through an agent), or
   (iii) a party to the agreement, or a party's agent, did or omitted anything in England and Wales in pursuance of the agreement.[136]

In respect of condition (b) there is a presumption that this condition is satisfied unless the defence serve on the prosecution a notice stating that in their opinion it is not satisfied, and giving the grounds for that opinion, in which case the prosecution must prove that it is satisfied.[137] Whether condition (b) is satisfied is to be decided by the judge alone.[138]

The Court of Appeal has confirmed that the CLA 1977, s 1A does not create a distinct offence of conspiracy; its purpose was to give English and Welsh courts extra-territorial jurisdiction in relation to conspiracies to commit offences outside England and Wales by extending to them the provisions of the CLA 1977, Pt 1 relating to statutory conspiracy contrary to s 1, provided that the four conditions set out above were satisfied.[139]

As a result of the CLA 1977, s 1A, for example, those who agree in England to damage property abroad are caught by the CLA 1977, s 1 if their agreed conduct is both an offence

---

[135] Ie Great Britain and Northern Ireland: Interpretation Act 1978, s 5 and Sch 1.
[136] CLA 1977, s 1A(2)–(5).   [137] CLA 1977, s 1A(8).   [138] CLA 1977, s 1A(10).
[139] *Patel* [2009] EWCA Crim 67.

under the foreign law and would have been an offence under English law if committed in England. It is immaterial whether or not the defendant was a British citizen at the time of any act or other event whose proof is required by s 1A.[140] Likewise, if D1 and D2 agree in France to take indecent photographs of children in a particular Far Eastern State and D1 comes to this country to collect the necessary equipment they are caught by s 1A, provided that that act constitutes an offence under the law of that State.

If the conditions in s 1A are satisfied, a reference to an offence in the CLA 1977, Pt I is to be read as a reference to what would be the offence in question but for the fact that it is not an offence triable in England and Wales.

No proceedings for an offence triable under s 1 by virtue of s 1A may be instituted except by or with the consent of the Attorney-General.[141]

Prosecution, trial and punishment

Prosecution

14.78 The following restrictions on the institution of prosecutions for statutory conspiracy are provided by CLA 1977:

(a) proceedings for conspiracy to commit any offence or offences cannot be instituted except by or with the consent of the Director of Public Prosecutions if the offence or (as the case may be) each of the offences in question is a summary offence;[142]

(b) proceedings for conspiracy to commit an offence (other than a summary offence), for which a prosecution cannot be instituted otherwise than by, or on behalf of or with the consent of, the Director of Public Prosecutions or any other person, may only be instituted by, or on behalf of or with the consent of, the relevant person;[143] and

(c) where an offence has been committed pursuant to any agreement and any time limit applicable to the institution of a prosecution for that offence has expired, the institution of a prosecution for conspiracy to commit that offence is also barred.[144]

Trial

14.79 Statutory conspiracy is triable only on indictment, even if it relates to the commission of a summary offence (since a conspiracy charge is thought to raise too many difficulties of substance and procedure for magistrates to try); the restriction on prosecutions

---

[140] CLA 1977, s 1A(12).

[141] CLA 1977, s 4(5), inserted by the Criminal Justice (Terrorism and Conspiracy Act) 1998, s 5(2).

[142] CLA 1977, s 4(1). Sometimes the Attorney-General's consent is required instead: CLA 1977, s 4(2).

[143] CLA 1977, s 4(3). If consent has already been given for a prosecution for the substantive offence, a separate consent is nevertheless necessary for a prosecution for conspiracy to commit it: *Pearce* (1980) 72 Cr App Rep 295, CA.

[144] CLA 1977, s 4(4).

for conspiracy to commit a summary offence mentioned in para 14.78 is an attempt to ensure that such prosecutions are only brought in appropriate cases.

Punishment

14.80 The penalties for statutory conspiracy are set out in a somewhat involved fashion by the CLA 1977, s 3. Where the substantive offence, or one of them, is:

- murder, or any other offence whose sentence is fixed by law;
- an offence for which life imprisonment may be awarded, eg robbery; or
- an indictable offence punishable with imprisonment but for which no maximum term is provided,

the maximum sentence is life imprisonment.

In any other case, provided the substantive offence, or one of them, is punishable with imprisonment, the maximum sentence on conviction for statutory conspiracy is the maximum for the substantive offence or the longer (or longest) maximum in the case of different substantive offences.

If none of the substantive offences is punishable with imprisonment, a person convicted of statutory conspiracy is not punishable with imprisonment, although he may be fined.

The maximum punishment in respect of 'small value criminal damage', which is lower than for criminal damage in general,[145] does not apply to a charge of conspiracy to commit such criminal damage; the normal maximum for conspiracy applies.[146]

The maximum penalty for a statutory conspiracy to commit an offence outside the United Kingdom, which conspiracy is triable in England and Wales by virtue of the CLA 1977, s 1A,[147] is the maximum for the equivalent substantive offence under English law, and not the maximum for the offence under the law of the foreign country or territory which was the object of the conspiracy.[148]

Where the substantive offence has been committed

14.81 A conspiracy to commit an offence does not merge with the substantive offence when the latter is committed. However, where there is an effective and sufficient charge of a substantive offence or offences, the addition of a charge for conspiracy is generally undesirable because it tends to prolong and complicate the trial.[149] An exception is where the case is complex and the interests of justice can only be served by presenting an overall picture which cannot be achieved by charging a series of substantive offences.[150] Another exception is where a charge of a substantive offence or offences does not represent the overall criminality of the case, ie where the agreement to commit the substantive

---

[145] Para 13.2. [146] *Ward* (1996) 161 JP 297, CA. [147] See para 14.77.
[148] *Patel* [2009] EWCA Crim 67. [149] *Verrier v DPP* [1967] 2 AC 195 at 223–224.
[150] *Hammersley* (1958) 42 Cr App Rep 207, CCA.

offence is more wicked than that offence.[151] Where an indictment contains substantive counts and a related conspiracy count or counts, the court will expect the prosecution to justify the joinder. If the judge is not satisfied that the joinder is justified, the prosecution must elect to proceed either on the substantive counts or on the conspiracy count or counts.[152]

Recommendations for reform

14.82 In 2006, primarily because of the House of Lords' decision in *Saik*,[153] the Government requested the Law Commission to review the offence of statutory conspiracy. In 2009 the Law Commission responded by publishing its report *Conspiracy and Attempts*,[154] in which it makes recommendations for the reform of statutory conspiracy. It also contains recommendations in relation to attempt[155] which it had aimed to review in any event. The recommendations are intended to ensure that the law relating to the various inchoate offences is consistent and coherent. The report does not review any aspect of common law conspiracy.

The report includes the following recommendations for the reform of statutory conspiracy:

(a) a conspiracy must involve an agreement by two or more persons to engage in the conduct element of an offence and (where relevant) to bring about any consequence element;

(b) a conspirator must be shown to have *intended* that the conduct element of the offence, and (where relevant) the consequence element (or other consequences), should respectively be engaged in or brought about. This would reverse the much criticised decision in *Anderson*;[156]

(c) an alleged conspirator must be shown at the time of the agreement to have been reckless whether a circumstance element of a substantive offence (or other relevant circumstance) would be present at the relevant time, when the substantive offence requires no proof of fault, or has a requirement for proof only of negligence (or its equivalent), in relation to that circumstance;

(d) where a substantive offence has fault requirements not involving mere negligence (or its equivalent), in relation to a fact or circumstance element, an alleged conspirator may be found guilty if shown to have possessed those fault requirements at the time of his or her agreement to commit the offence. Recommendations (c) and (d) would widen the *mens rea* as to circumstance in statutory conspiracy;[157]

---

[151] *Ward* [1997] 1 Cr App Rep (S) 442, CA.
[152] *Practice Direction* [2002] 3 All ER 904 at IV. 34.3, as substituted by *Practice Direction* [2008] 1 WLR 154.
[153] Paras 14.63 and 14.65–14.67.   [154] Law Commission Report No 318.
[155] Para 14.144.   [156] [1986] AC 27, HL; para 14.68.
[157] Paras 14.62–14.67.

(e) the defence of 'acting reasonably' provided by the Serious Crime Act 2007 (SCA 2007), s 50 in respect of offences of encouraging or assisting crime should be applied in its entirety to the offence of conspiracy;

(f) the anomalous immunity for spouses and civil partners referred to in paras 14.47 and 14.74 should be abolished;

(g) the present exemption for a non-victim co-conspirator referred to in para 14.74[158] should be abolished but the present exemption for a defendant (D) who is a victim should be retained if:

    (i) the conspiracy is to commit an offence that exists wholly or in part for the protection of a particular category of persons;

    (ii) D falls within the protected category; and

    (iii) D is the person in respect of whom the offence agreed upon would have been committed;

(h) on the other hand, the rule that an agreement involving a person of or over the age of criminal responsibility and a child under the age of criminal responsibility gives rise to no criminal liability for conspiracy should be retained because there is no meeting of two 'criminal minds';

(i) the present requirement for the Director of Public Prosecutions to give consent if proceedings to prosecute a conspiracy to commit a summary offence are to be initiated need not be retained;

(j) it should be possible to convict the defendant of conspiracy to commit a substantive offence regardless of where any of the defendant's relevant conduct (or any other party's relevant conduct) occurred so long as the defendant knew or believed that the conduct or consequence element of the intended substantive offence might occur, whether wholly or in part, in England or Wales. This would be broadly consistent with the SCA 2007, s 52(1);

(k) by analogy with the relevant provisions of the SCA 2007, Sch 4, it should be possible to convict the defendant of conspiracy to commit a substantive offence, regardless of where any other party's conduct occurred, if: the defendant's relevant conduct (ie any communication forming part of the process which led up to the final agreement) occurred in England or Wales; the defendant knew or believed that the conduct or consequence element of the intended substantive offence might be committed wholly or partly in a place outside England and Wales; and the substantive offence, if committed in that place, would also be an offence under the law in force in that place (however described in that law);

(l) by analogy with the relevant provisions of the SCA 2007, Sch 4, it should be possible to convict the defender of conspiracy to commit a substantive offence, regardless of where any other party's relevant conduct occurred, if: the defendant's relevant conduct occurred in England or Wales; the defendant knew or believed that

---

[158] Ie the exemptions provided by CLA 1977, s 2(1) and s 2(2)(c).

the intended substantive offence might occur wholly or partly in a place outside England and Wales; and the substantive offence, if committed in that place, would be an offence triable in England and Wales (or would be so triable if committed by a person satisfying relevant citizenship, nationality or residence conditions);

(m) by analogy with the relevant provisions of the SCA 2007, Sch 4, it should be possible to convict the defendant of conspiracy to commit a substantive offence, where the defendant's relevant conduct occurred outside England and Wales, if: the defendant knew or believed that the intended substantive offence might occur wholly or partly in a place outside England and Wales and the defendant could be tried in England and Wales (as the perpetrator) if he or she committed the substantive offence in that place; and

(n) by analogy with the SCA 2007, and as is the case with the CLA 1977, s 1A, in cases where it cannot be proved that the defendant knew or believed that the intended substantive offence might be committed wholly or partly in England and Wales, no proceedings may be instituted except with the consent of the Attorney-General.

The proposals made in respect of jurisdiction reflect the need to respond to the growth of organised, cross-border crime.

Common law conspiracy

14.83 As was stated in para 14.45, this offence has now been reduced to conspiracy to defraud and, possibly, conspiracies to corrupt public morals or to outrage public decency.

Conspiracy to defraud

> **Key points 14.5**
>
> There are two types of conspiracy to defraud:
>
> - an agreement by dishonesty to deprive a person of something which is his or to which he is, or would be or might be, entitled or an agreement by dishonesty to injure some proprietary right of his; and
>
> - an agreement dishonestly to bring about a situation which would or might deceive a public official performing public duties to act contrary to such a duty.

14.84 This type of common law conspiracy is expressly preserved by the CLA 1977, s 5(2), although its preservation was intended only to be temporary since it was intended to abolish it once certain unacceptable gaps in the law relating to fraud had been closed by legislation which was expected after the Law Commission had completed its review of the matter. In 2002, the Law Commission completed its review. It concluded that conspiracy to defraud is too wide to offer adequate guidance on the difference between fraudulent and lawful conduct and should be abolished. It proposed the introduction of two new general offences, fraud and obtaining services dishonestly, which could form the object of a statutory conspiracy. In May 2004, the Government announced that it was in basic agreement with this proposal and, subject to the views of consultees, proposed to introduce legislation to implement it when parliamentary time permitted. However, although the Fraud Act 2006[159] introduced the two offences proposed by the Law Commission, it does not contain a provision abolishing conspiracy to defraud because the Government thought that it would be premature to do so before there had been an opportunity to consider the operation of the new offences.[160]

Because there can be a conspiracy to defraud even though the fraudulent object would not constitute an offence if achieved[161] (in fact it need not even be tortious), the offence is currently an important weapon against those who agree to achieve a fraudulent, non-criminal object, as where there is an agreement dishonestly to prejudice another's financial interests (eg depriving him of future income) where no specific property belonging to that person has actually been stolen and no offence of fraud is involved. The introduction of the offence of fraud by the Fraud Act 2006 has greatly reduced the number of cases where the object of a conspiracy to defraud will not be an offence. However, the Government still has concerns that the abolition of conspiracy to defraud would impair the ability to prosecute multiple offences and the largest and most complex cases of fraud.

Basic definition of fraud

14.85 In *Scott v Comr of Police of the Metropolis*,[162] the House of Lords held that **there may be a conspiracy to defraud without any element of deception**. D agreed with the employees of cinema owners to borrow films for a short period of time without the permission of the cinema owners and in return for payment to the employees, so that, without the consent of the owners of the copyright and distribution rights in such films, he could make copies and distribute them commercially. D could not have been convicted of theft or of statutory conspiracy to steal the films, because there had been no intention of permanently depriving the cinema owners of the films,[163] nor could he have been convicted of the offence (since repealed) of obtaining the films by deception or of statutory conspiracy to commit that offence, because he had no such intention and because no deception had been practised to obtain them.[164] The economic interests of owners of the copyright and

---

[159] See paras 12.1 and 12.2.

[160] Lord Goldsmith, Attorney-General, HL Deb Vol 673 col 1447. For an account of the views, almost wholly in favour of abolishing conspiracy to defraud, expressed in the parliamentary debates on the Fraud Act 2006, see Ormerod 'The Fraud Act 2006 – Criminalising Lying?' [2007] Crim LR 193 at 216–218.

[161] See for example, *Scott v Comr of Police of the Metropolis* [1975] AC 819, HL, below.

[162] [1975] AC 819, HL.   [163] Para 10.90.

[164] Nor, had it then existed, could D have been convicted of fraud, contrary to the Fraud Act 2006, s 1, because no false representation had been made, and he had not acted in one of the other ways whereby that offence can be committed.

distribution rights, in particular, had, however, been injured because the existence of 'pirate' copies would affect royalty payments. D was charged with, and convicted of, conspiracy to defraud. Upholding the conviction, the House of Lords held that on such a charge it was not necessary for the Crown to prove an agreement to deprive the owners of their property by deception. **It was sufficient to prove an agreement by dishonesty to deprive a person of something which is his or to which he is, or would be or might be, entitled or an agreement by dishonesty to injure some proprietary right of his.**

In relation to an agreement dishonestly to deprive someone of something to which he is or would be or might be entitled, the Privy Council in *Adams v R*[165] upheld the conviction for conspiracy to defraud of a defendant, a company director, who had been party to an agreement which involved the parties making and retaining a secret profit, because the agreement extended to taking positive steps dishonestly to conceal the profits which he was under a duty to disclose to the company. The Privy Council stated that:

'Since a company is entitled to recover from directors secret profits made by them at the company's expense, it would follow that any dishonest agreement by directors to impede a company in the exercise of its rights of recovery would constitute a conspiracy to defraud. In their Lordships' view a person can be guilty of fraud when he dishonestly conceals information from another which he was under a duty to disclose to that other or which that other was entitled to require him to disclose.'[166]

The conduct in *Adams* is now an offence under the Fraud Act 2006, s 3 or s 4.

It is irrelevant that the execution of the agreement may not involve any actual economic loss on the part of the victim, provided his economic interests are put at risk.[167] It is also irrelevant that that situation is to be brought about by some perpetrator other than the parties to the agreement.[168] Thus, people who agree to supply to retailers falsely labelled bottles of whisky or to make and sell devices to by-pass electricity meters can be convicted of conspiracy to defraud, even though the perpetration of the fraud (on the purchaser of the whisky or the electricity supplier) will be done by the retailer of the whisky or the user of the device respectively.[169] This can be contrasted with statutory conspiracy which is committed only if it is intended that at least one of the parties to the agreement shall perpetrate the offence agreed to be committed.

14.86 There has been conflict in the case law on the issue of whether the causing of economic loss or prejudice must be the purpose of the parties to the agreement.[170] For practical purposes, the point has been resolved against such a requirement by the decision of

---

[165] [1995] 2 Cr App Rep 295, PC.   [166] [1995] 2 Cr App Rep 295 at 309.

[167] *Allsop* (1976) 64 Cr App Rep 29, CA; *Wai Yu-tsang v R* [1992] 1 AC 269 at 280; *Adams v R* [1995] 2 Cr App Rep 295 at 308.

[168] *A-G's Reference (No 1 of 1982)* [1983] QB 751, CA; *Hollinshead* [1985] AC 975, HL. In relation to *Hollinshead*, see [1995] Crim LR 217 and 519.

[169] *A-G's Reference (No 1 of 1982)* [1983] QB 751, CA; *Hollinshead* [1985] AC 975, HL.

[170] Contrast *A-G's Reference (No 1 of 1982)* [1983] QB 751, CA (causing of economic loss or prejudice must be defendant's purpose) with *Allsop* (1976) 64 Cr App Rep 29, CA (causing economic loss or prejudice need not be

the Privy Council in *Wai Yu-tsang v R*,[171] where it was held that it was **enough that the alleged conspirators had dishonestly agreed to bring about a state of affairs which they realised would or might deceive the victim into so acting, or failing to act, that he would suffer economic loss or his economic interests would be put at risk. Doubtless, a similar principle applies where a deception is not involved.** The decision in *Wai Yu-tsang v R* is important because, as the Court of Appeal stated in *Allsop*:[172]

> 'Generally the primary object of fraudsmen is to advantage themselves. The detriment that results to their victims is secondary to that purpose and incidental.'

Fraud not involving economic loss or prejudice

14.87 Although in the vast majority of cases the agreement relates to bringing about a situation which would or might cause some sort of economic prejudice, conspiracy to defraud is not limited to this type of case. **An agreement dishonestly to bring about a situation which would or might deceive**[173] **a public official performing public duties (which phrase does not include bank managers and the like)**[174] **to act contrary to such a duty is a conspiracy to defraud, even though there is no risk of causing economic loss to anyone or of prejudicing his economic interests.**[175] An example would be where D1 and D2 agree dishonestly to deceive a public official into granting a licence or into giving secret information. It may be that this type of conspiracy to defraud is not limited to public officials acting in pursuance of their public duties. In *Wai Yu-tsang v R*,[176] the Privy Council advised, obiter, that it was not so restricted (as shown in para 14.88).

As in the case of a conspiracy to defraud involving the risk of economic loss or prejudice, **it need not be the aim or purpose of the parties to cause the victim to act contrary to his public duty. It is enough that they have dishonestly agreed to bring about a situation which they realised would or might deceive the victim into so acting.**

14.88 In *Scott v Comr of Police of the Metropolis*,[177] Lord Diplock took the view, obiter, that the object of inducing a public official to act contrary to his public duty was a separate type of fraudulent object. In comparison, in *Welham v DPP*,[178] which was concerned with intent to defraud in the context of forgery contrary to the now-repealed Forgery Act 1913, Lord Radcliffe[179] had thought such an object was not to be regarded as a special

the defendant's purpose, but he must have foreseen that economic loss or prejudice was likely if the agreement was carried out).

[171] [1992] 1 AC 269, PC.   [172] (1976) 64 Cr App Rep 29 at 31.

[173] 'To deceive is…to induce a man to believe that a thing is true which is false': *Re London and Globe Finance Corpn* [1903] 1 Ch 728 at 732, per Buckley J.

[174] *DPP v Withers* [1975] AC 842 at 877, per Lord Kilbrandon; *Moses and Ansbro* [1991] Crim LR 617, CA.

[175] *Board of Trade v Owen* [1957] AC 602 at 622, per Lord Tucker; *Welham v DPP* [1961] AC 103, HL; *Scott v Comr of Police of the Metropolis* [1975] AC 819, see especially Lord Diplock at 841; *DPP v Withers* [1975] AC 842 at 873 and 877, per Lords Simon and Kilbrandon respectively.

[176] [1992] 1 AC 269, PC.   [177] [1975] AC 819 at 841.

[178] [1961] AC 103, HL.   [179] [1961] AC 103 at 123–124.

type of fraud, but rather as exemplifying a general principle that intention to defraud is not limited to cases where there is an intent to cause the victim economic loss. That general principle was also enunciated by Lord Denning[180] in *Welham*. Both statements in *Welham*, with which the rest of the House of Lords agreed, were obiter.

The matter was referred to by the Privy Council in *Wai Yu-tsang v R*. Their Lordships agreed, obiter, with the approach taken in *Welham*; the object of inducing public officials to act contrary to their public duties was not a separate type of fraudulent object but merely an example that a conspiracy to defraud was not limited to agreements to cause the victim economic loss. Lord Goff, giving the advice of the Privy Council, having referred with approval to the statements of Lords Denning and Radcliffe in *Welham*, said:

> 'This authority establishes that the expression "intent to defraud" is not to be given a narrow meaning, involving an intention to cause economic loss to another. In broad terms, it means simply an intention to practice a fraud on another, or an intention to act to the prejudice of another man's right.'[181]

This provides the worrying potential for widening the scope of an offence whose ambit is already wide and somewhat imprecise in the terms set out in paras 14.85–14.87. The refusal of the House of Lords in *Norris v Government of the United States of America*[182] to extend the scope of conspiracy to defraud to deal with the situation in issue is therefore to be welcomed.

In *Norris v Government of the United States of America*, the House of Lords had to decide whether an agreement to engage in price-fixing of itself amounted to a conspiracy to defraud. At the time the agreements in question were made there were no previous decisions which even suggested that it did. The House held that to extend conspiracy to defraud to such conduct would infringe the principle of legality.[183]

Dishonesty

14.89 The requirement that the agreement must be by dishonesty to bring about a situation which would or might cause economic loss or prejudice (or would or might cause a public official to act contrary to his public duty) refers partly to the proposed means of achieving that object and partly to the state of mind of the parties to the agreement. In *Landy*,[184] statements by the Court of Appeal suggested that the defendants' belief as to whether or not they were acting honestly was the determinant of dishonesty in conspiracy to defraud. However, subsequently in *Ghosh*,[185] it held that **the test of dishonesty was the same as in offences under the Theft Acts**, viz whether the defendants' proposed means were on the facts known to them dishonest according to the current standards of ordinary decent people, and whether, if they were, the defendants realised that they were

---

[180] [1961] AC 103 at 133.   [181] [1992] 1 AC 269 at 276.   [182] [2008] UKHL 16.

[183] See paras 1.34 and 1.35. See also para 1.33. *Norris v Government of the United States of America* was followed in *GG plc* [2008] UKHL 17.

[184] [1981] 1 All ER 1172, CA.   [185] [1982] QB 1053, CA; para 10.74.

contrary to those standards. The extent to which the judge must leave these questions to the jury is the same as in the case of substantive offences against property.[186]

14.90 Because of the breadth and imprecision of conspiracy to defraud, the element of dishonesty plays a crucial role in determining whether an agreement constitutes that offence. This means, for example, that whether an agreement simply involves sharp practice or the serious offence of conspiracy can be uncertain in advance of a determination by a jury. The Joint Parliamentary Committee on Human Rights has doubted the compatibility of conspiracy to defraud with the requirement of legal certainty (ie reasonable foreseeability of the legal consequence of a course of action) inherent in ECHR, Art 7.[187]

14.91 Of course, there cannot be a conspiracy to defraud unless there are at least two parties to an agreement who satisfy the *mens rea* requirements of the offence which have just been explained. Even if there is a conspiracy to defraud, a person who is ostensibly a party to that agreement cannot be convicted if one of the above requirements is not satisfied in relation to him.

Scope of conspiracy to defraud

14.92 Where the agreed fraudulent course of conduct will not, or will not necessarily, amount to or involve the commission of an offence by one or more parties to the agreement if it is carried out in accordance with the parties' intentions, as where there is an agreement temporarily to deprive a person dishonestly of property, or an agreement permanently to deprive him dishonestly of property which cannot be stolen (such as land, generally), the agreement is only punishable as a common law conspiracy to defraud.

On the other hand, where the agreed fraudulent course of conduct will necessarily amount to or involve the commission of an offence by one or more parties to the agreement if it is carried out in accordance with the parties' intentions, the agreement is punishable either as a statutory conspiracy or as a common law conspiracy to defraud. The Criminal Justice Act 1987, s 12(1) provides that:

'If –

    (a) a person agrees with any other person or persons that a course of conduct shall be pursued; and

    (b) that course of conduct will necessarily amount to or involve the commission of any offence or offences by one or more of the parties to the agreement if the agreement is carried out in accordance with their intentions,

the fact that it will do so shall not preclude a charge of conspiracy to defraud being brought against any of them in respect of the agreement.'

---

[186] *Squire* [1990] Crim LR 341, CA; see paras 10.73–10.76.
[187] *Fourteenth Report*: 2005–2006, para 2.25.

As a result, there is a substantial overlap between statutory conspiracy and conspiracy to defraud. For example, any agreement to commit fraud or to steal (or to commit most other offences under the Theft Acts or the Forgery and Counterfeiting Act 1981) or to commit a host of minor statutory offences can be prosecuted either as a statutory conspiracy or as a conspiracy to defraud. The category of offences covered by this overlap is very wide indeed.

14.93 In 2007, the Attorney-General issued *Guidance on the Use of the Common Law Offence of Conspiracy to Defraud*, according to which a prosecution for conspiracy to defraud instead of a substantive offence, contrary to the Fraud Act 2006 or another Act, or a statutory conspiracy, contrary to CLA 1977, s 1 may be appropriate in two categories of case:

- Conduct that can more effectively be prosecuted as conspiracy to defraud. That is to say cases where the interests of justice can only be served by presenting to a court an overall picture which cannot be achieved by charging a series of substantive offences or statutory conspiracies. Typically such cases will involve some, but not necessarily all, of the following:
  - evidence of several significant but different kinds of criminality;
  - several jurisdictions;
  - different types of victim, eg individual banks, website administrators and credit card companies;
  - organised crime networks.

  Prosecuting such cases as statutory conspiracies could lead to indictments with an unwieldy number of separate counts, and possibly separate trials for separate parts of the conspiracy.

- Conduct which can be prosecuted only as conspiracy to defraud, ie conduct that is not covered by any statutory offence.

Although this guidance has no legal force, the Attorney-General intended it to be binding; conspiracy to defraud is not to be used where there is an effective statutory alternative. Each time that conspiracy to defraud is prosecuted, the prosecutor will have to justify this in writing.[188]

Jurisdiction

14.94 The Criminal Justice Act 1993, s 3(2) provides that a defendant may be convicted of a conspiracy to defraud in England and Wales[189] whether or not he became a party to the conspiracy in England and Wales and whether or not any act, omission or other occurrence in relation to the conspiracy occurred in England and Wales. It is immaterial whether or not a person was a British citizen at any material time or was in England and Wales at any such time.[190]

---

[188] What is said in para 14.81 about charging statutory conspiracy when a substantive offence has been committed applies to conspiracy to defraud.

[189] Conspiracy to defraud is a Group B offence under the Criminal Justice Act 1993, Pt I: CJA 1993, s 1(3)(b).

[190] Criminal Justice Act 1993, s 3(1).

14.95 The Criminal Justice Act 1993, s 5(3) deals with the case where the fraud which the parties had in view was intended to take place outside England and Wales. It provides:

'A person may be guilty of conspiracy to defraud if:

(a) a party to the agreement constituting the conspiracy, or a party's agent, did anything in England and Wales in relation to the agreement before its formation; or

(b) a party to it became a party in England and Wales (by joining it either in person or through an agent); or

(c) a party to it, or a party's agent, did or omitted anything in England and Wales in pursuance of it,

and the conspiracy would be triable in England and Wales but for the fraud which the parties to it had in view not being intended to take place in England and Wales.'

Section s 6(1)[191] provides that a person is only guilty of conspiracy to defraud by virtue of s 5(3) if the pursuit of the agreed course of conduct would at some stage involve:

• an act or omission by one or more of the parties; or
• the happening of some other event,

constituting an offence under the law in force where the act, omission or event was intended to take place. This is an odd provision because the common law offence of conspiracy to defraud does not require the intended commission of an offence under English law. The condition in s 6(1) is deemed to be satisfied unless the defence serve a notice on the prosecution stating that in their opinion it is not, giving their grounds for that opinion and requiring the prosecution to show that it is satisfied.[192] The question whether the condition is satisfied is to be decided by the judge alone.[193]

Conspiracy to corrupt public morals and conspiracy to outrage public decency

Key points 14.6

Although the Criminal Law Act 1977, s 5(3) may have the effect of preserving the common law offence of conspiracy to outrage public decency, it would appear that it does not do so. On the other hand, it may preserve the common law offence of conspiracy to corrupt public morals.

14.96 The existence of both of these types of common law conspiracy was recognised by the House of Lords in the latter half of the twentieth century.

---

[191] As amended by the Criminal Justice (Terrorism and Conspiracy) Act 1998, Sch 1.
[192] Criminal Justice Act 1993, s 6(4).   [193] Criminal Justice Act 1993, s 6(7).

- *Conspiracy to corrupt public morals* In *Shaw v DPP*,[194] decided in 1961, the majority of the House of Lords recognised the continued existence of the offence of conspiracy to corrupt public morals. They accordingly dismissed Shaw's appeal against conviction for this offence, arising out of his agreement with others for the publication of a *'Ladies' Directory'*, giving the names, addresses and practices of prostitutes.

  Shaw was followed by the majority of the House of Lords (Lord Diplock dissenting) in 1972 in *Knuller (Publishing, Printing and Promotions) Ltd v DPP*,[195] where further explanation was given of conspiracy to corrupt public morals. The House held that an agreement to publish advertisements soliciting homosexual acts between consenting adults in private was a conspiracy to corrupt public morals, even though such conduct was no longer an offence. Lords Reid and Simon said that 'corrupt' was a strong word and that 'corrupt public morals' meant more than 'lead morally astray'. Lord Reid thought that 'corrupt' was synonymous with 'deprave',[196] while Lord Simon said that what was required was conduct which 'a jury might find to be destructive of the very fabric of society'.[197] Lord Reid thought that conspiracy to corrupt public morals was something of a misnomer: 'It really means to corrupt the morals of such members of the public as may be influenced by the matter published by the accused.'[198]

  Although the judge must initially rule on whether there is evidence on which the jury can find the case proved, it is for the jury to find whether a particular object is corrupting of public morals and they should do this by applying the current standards of ordinary decent people.[199] It is doubtful whether a jury would find that there was a conspiracy to corrupt public morals if a case similar to *Shaw* or *Knuller* came before it today.

  The vagueness of 'corrupting public morals' leads to considerable uncertainty about the conduct penalised by the criminal law, in apparent breach of the requirement of legal certainty (ie foreseeability of the legal consequences of a course of action) inherent in the ECHR, Article 7.[200]

- *Conspiracy to outrage public decency* In *Knuller (Publishing, Printing and Promotions) Ltd v DPP*, the defendant had also been convicted of conspiracy to outrage public decency. The majority of the House of Lords (Lords Reid and Diplock dissenting) recognised the continued existence of this offence, although the defendant's appeals against conviction were allowed because the jury had not been properly directed on the relevant principles.

---

[194] [1962] AC 220, HL.   [195] [1973] AC 435, HL.   [196] [1973] AC 435 at 456.
[197] [1973] AC 435 at 491.   [198] [1973] AC 435 at 456.
[199] *Shaw v DPP* [1962] AC 220, HL; *Knuller (Publishing, Printing and Promotions) Ltd v DPP* [1973] AC 435, HL.
[200] Para 1.60.

14.97 The CLA 1977, s 5(3) preserves the offence of conspiracy at common law:

> 'if and in so far as it may be committed by entering into an agreement to engage in conduct which –
>
> (a) tends to corrupt public morals or outrages public decency; but
>
> (b) would not amount to or involve the commission of an offence if carried out by a single person otherwise than in pursuance of an agreement.'[201]

This somewhat tentative provision raises the questions of whether substantive common law offences of corrupting public morals and of outraging public decency exist, and (if they do) what their extent is.

14.98 It is now clear that there is a substantive common law offence of outraging public decency. Its existence was less certain in 1977 than it is now, despite the fact that in 1972 in *Knuller (Publishing, Printing and Promotions) Ltd v DPP*[202] the majority of the House of Lords held, obiter, that outraging public decency was a common law offence, and that the existence of the substantive offence had previously been recognised by the Court of Criminal Appeal is *Mayling*.[203] Any doubt as to the existence of the substantive offence has been removed since 1977 by a series of Court of Appeal decisions, *May*,[204] *Gibson and Sylveire*,[205] *Lunderbeck*,[206] *Rowley*[207] and *Hamilton*[208] confirming that the offence exists.

The substantive offence of outraging public decency requires an act or exhibit of such a lewd, obscene or disgusting nature as to result in an outrage to public decency.[209] An act is obscene for this purpose if it offends against recognised standards of propriety and is at a higher level of impropriety than indecency,[210] and a disgusting act is conduct capable of filling the onlooker with loathing or extreme distaste or of causing the onlooker extreme annoyance.[211] It is the nature of the act that the jury must consider;[212] the test is thus objective. It is not enough that the act is lewd, obscene or disgusting. It must outrage minimum standards of public decency as judged by the jury in contemporary society.[213] 'Outrage' is a strong word. 'Outraging public decency' goes

---

[201] No person may, however, be proceeded against for an offence at common law of conspiring to corrupt public morals or of outraging public decency in respect of an agreement to present or give a performance of a play, or to cause anything to be said or done in the course of such a performance: Theatres Act 1968, s 2(4). A similar restriction applies in the case of an agreement to give a film exhibition (see the Obscene Publications Act 1959, s 2(4A)) or to cause a programme to be included in a programme service or to cause anything to be said or done in the course of a programme which is included (see the Broadcasting Act 1990, Sch 15).

[202] [1973] AC 435, HL. [203] [1963] 2 QB 717, CCA. [204] (1989) 91 Cr App Rep 157, CA.

[205] [1990] 2 QB 619, CA. [206] [1991] Crim LR 784, CA. [207] [1991] 4 All ER 649, CA.

[208] [2007] EWCA Crim 2062.

[209] *Mayling* [1963] 2 QB 717, CCA; *Hamilton* [2007] EWCA Crim 2062. The offence is one of strict liability as to this result: *Gibson* [1990] 2 QB 619, CA; para 6.9.

[210] *Stanley* [1965] 2 QB 327, CCA; *Hamilton* [2007] EWCA Crim 2062.

[211] *Mayling* [1963] 2 QB 717, CCA. [212] *Hamilton* [2007] EWCA Crim 2062.

[213] *Knuller (Publishing, Printing and Promotions) Ltd v DPP* [1973] AC 435 at 495, per Lord Simon with whom Lord Kilbrandon agreed; *Hamilton* [2007] EWCA Crim 2062.

beyond offending the susceptibilities of, or even shocking, reasonable people.[214] It is not necessary to prove that the defendant's act in fact outraged any member of the public.[215] It is enough that the conduct would be likely to disgust ordinary members of the public if they saw it, whether or not any actual spectators were disgusted.[216]

The conduct in question must be done in a place to which the public has access though not necessarily as of right, or a place where what is done is capable of public view.[217] It must also be 'public' in the sense that it is capable of being seen by at least two people who are actually present, even if they do not actually see it.[218]

14.99 There can be no real doubt that the substantive offence of outraging public decency is coterminous with outraging public decency as the object of a conspiracy, in which case a conspiracy to outrage public decency will always be a statutory conspiracy and the effect of 5(3) is to abolish the common law offence of conspiracy to outrage public decency.

14.100 The position is more uncertain in relation to corrupting public morals, since the only authority in favour of the existence of a substantive common law offence of corrupting public morals is *Shaw v DPP*[219] where the Court of Criminal Appeal held that there was a common law offence of conduct calculated or intended to corrupt public morals. Unfortunately, the House of Lords on appeal did not decide this point. In *Knuller (Publishing, Printing and Promotions) Ltd v DPP*,[220] the House of Lords did not consider whether there was a substantive offence of corrupting public morals.

As a result one cannot be certain that there is a common law substantive offence of corrupting public morals. If there is not it will not be a statutory conspiracy to conspire to corrupt public morals (unless the intended conduct constitutes some other substantive offence), but by the CLA 1977, s 5(3) it will be a common law conspiracy. If, on the other hand, there is a common law offence of corrupting public morals, the effect of s 5(3) is that a conspiracy to corrupt public morals will *either* only be a statutory conspiracy (if that substantive offence is coterminous with corruption of public morals as the object of a conspiracy) *or* (if the substantive offence has a narrower ambit) will be a statutory conspiracy if the conduct agreed on would amount to a substantive offence but will be a common law conspiracy if that conduct falls outside the substantive offence (or any other substantive offence) but within the definition of the corruption of public morals as the object of a common law conspiracy.

Until this issue is resolved, the prudent course where conspiracy to corrupt public morals is charged is to charge alternative counts of statutory conspiracy and common law conspiracy.

14.101 The reader may be amazed that a statute should leave the law so uncertain. In defence of the legislature it should be pointed out that, like the CLA 1977, s 5(2), s 5(3)

---

[214] *Knuller (Publishing, Printing and Promotions) Ltd v DPP* [1973] AC 435 at 495, per Lord Simon with whom Lord Kilbrandon agreed.

[215] *Mayling* [1963] 2 QB 717, CCA; *Choi* [1999] 5 Archbold News 3, CA.

[216] *May* (1990) 91 Cr App Rep 157, CA; *Choi* [1999] 5 Archbold News 3, CA.

[217] *Walker* [1996] 1 Cr App Rep 111, CA; *Hamilton* [2007] EWCA Crim 2062,.

[218] *Hamilton* [2007] EWCA Crim 2062.   [219] [1961] 1 All ER 330, CCA; affd [1962] AC 220, HL.

[220] [1973] AC 435, HL.

was intended to be purely a temporary holding operation. The Law Commission, whose report on conspiracy was implemented with amendments by the CLA 1977, ss 1 to 5, had recommended that the common law conspiracies to corrupt public morals or to outrage public decency should be abolished, along with the substantive offences of corrupting public morals and outraging public decency (which they thought did exist) and certain other common law offences concerned with morals and decency, and that these substantive offences should be replaced by certain new statutory offences to fill the gaps in the law where desirable.[221] However, by and large, this recommendation was not enacted by the Bill which became the CLA 1977. The Government's reason was that the abolition of these common law conspiracies should be delayed until the whole area of obscenity and indecency in publications, entertainments and the like had been reviewed. This review was completed by the Committee on Obscenity and Film Censorship, which reported in 1979,[222] but its proposals have never been implemented.

Impossibility in common law conspiracy

14.102 This is governed by the decision of the House of Lords in *DPP v Nock*; *DPP v Alsford*,[223] where the reasoning of the House in *Haughton v Smith*[224] concerning impossibility in relation to the common law offence of attempt was held to apply to common law conspiracy.

The position is as follows. **Where the object of the agreement is at the time of the agreement capable of being achieved but cannot actually be achieved because of some supervening event or because the proposed means are insufficient, there can be a conviction for common law conspiracy.** Thus, there can be a conviction for conspiracy to defraud in the case of an agreement to 'borrow' P's book from his locker without his consent, even though the book is subsequently destroyed before this can be done or the skeleton key which is to be used does not fit the lock. **However, in any other case of impossibility, eg where the book has already been destroyed at the time of the agreement, there cannot be a conviction for common law conspiracy.**

As seen in para 14.55, the law on impossibility is tougher in the case of statutory conspiracies; although a conspiracy to commit an offence of fraud, which offence is impossible of commission for reasons other than inadequacy of means or a supervening event, cannot be a common law conspiracy to defraud, it can be a statutory conspiracy.

Trial and punishment

14.103 Common law conspiracy is triable only on indictment.

The maximum punishment for a common law conspiracy to defraud is now governed by statute (the Criminal Justice Act 1987, s 12(3)), and is 10 years' imprisonment. Where

---

[221] Law Commission *Report on Conspiracy and Criminal Law Reform* (1976), Law Com No 76, para 3.86–3.143.
[222] Cmnd 7772.   [223] [1978] AC 979, HL.   [224] [1975] AC 476, HL.

a defendant is convicted for conspiracy to defraud on evidence which would have supported a conviction for the statutory conspiracy for which the maximum sentence would have been lower, the court is not obliged to treat itself as bound by that lower maximum rather than the maximum under s 12(3).[225]

In the case of a common law conspiracy to corrupt public morals or to outrage public decency, to the extent that such an offence survives, statute has not intervened, with the result that these types of common law conspiracy remain punishable with imprisonment for a period fixed at the discretion of the judge.[226]

Attempt

Key points 14.7

It is a criminal offence to attempt to commit an offence triable on indictment.
To be guilty of an attempt the defendant:

- must have done an act which is more than merely preparatory to the commission of the substantive offence (the offence whose attempt is charged), which means that he must have embarked on the commission of that offence; and

- must have acted with intent to commit that offence, which means that he must have acted with intent to commit a sufficient act for the substantive offence, with intent to bring about any consequence required for it, with *mens rea* as to any circumstances required for it and with any additional *mens rea* required for it.

A person may be guilty of attempting to commit an offence even though, unknown to him, the commission of that offence is impossible.

14.104 The common law offence of attempt to commit an indictable offence was abolished by the Criminal Attempts Act 1981 (CAA 1981),[227] and replaced by a statutory offence of attempt which was created by the CAA 1981, s 1. The provisions relating to the statutory offence largely implement recommendations made by the Law Commission.[228]

The CAA 1981, s 1(1) provides that:

'If, with intent to commit an offence to which [s 1] applies, a person does an act which is more than merely preparatory to the commission of the offence, he is guilty of attempting to commit the offence.'

---

[225] *Bright* [2008] EWCA Crim 462.   [226] Para 1.31.   [227] CAA 1981, s 6(1).
[228] *Criminal Law: Attempts and Impossibility in relation to Attempts, Conspiracy and Incitement* (1980), Law Com No 102.

Conduct which is *merely preparatory* to the commission of an offence is not generally an offence. However, mere preparation to commit an offence is criminal if it amounts to one of a number of preparatory offences, for example, under the Theft Act 1968, Criminal Damage Act 1971, Forgery and Counterfeiting Act 1981, Sexual Offences Act 2003 and Fraud Act 2006, as indicated in previous chapters.[229]

The scope of the offence

14.105 The CAA 1981, s 1(4) provides that s 1 applies to any substantive offence which, 'if it were completed, would be triable in England and Wales as an indictable offence' (ie one triable only on indictment or one triable either way).[230] This means that, contrary to the Law Commission's recommendation, **it is not an offence under s 1 to attempt to commit a summary offence**. There is no obvious reason. It is anomalous in the light of the fact that the other inchoate offences can be committed in relation to a summary offence. There are, however, a number of specific statutory offences of attempting to commit a particular summary offence (see para 14.142).

The reference in s 1(4) to 'any offence which, if it were completed, would be triable in England and Wales as an indictable offence' means that normally an attempt in England and Wales to commit an indictable offence abroad is not an offence. The reason is that generally, as explained more fully elsewhere, an offence completed abroad (ie outside England and Wales) is not triable in England and Wales, unless a substantial part of it is committed in England and Wales.[231] Thus, generally speaking, if someone has got as far in London as attempting to commit an offence abroad but not as far as committing a substantial part of it, he cannot be convicted of attempting to commit that offence.

As to attempts committed outside England and Wales see para 14.138.

---

[229] Chs 9–13.

[230] An offence of criminal damage where the value of the property destroyed or of the damage done is less than £5,000 is an 'indictable offence', notwithstanding that it has to be proceeded with 'as if' it was a summary offence (para 13.2): *Bristol Magistrates' Court, ex p E* [1998] 3 All ER 798, DC.

[231] CAA 1981, s 1A, inserted by the Criminal Justice Act 1993, s 5(2), provides that if (a) an act is done in England and Wales, and (b) it would fall within the CAA 1981, s 1(1) as more than merely preparatory to the commission of a Group A offence (ie offences under the Theft Act 1968, Forgery and Counterfeiting Act 1981, Fraud Act 2006 and related offences listed in s 1 of the 1993 Act: see para 12.70) but for the fact that that offence, if completed, would not be an offence triable in England and Wales, what the person doing the act had in view is to be treated as an offence to which the CAA 1981, s 1 applies.

The Criminal Justice Act 1993 (CJA 1993), s 6(2) provides that a person is only guilty of an offence triable by virtue of the CAA 1981, s 1A if what he had in view would involve the commission of an offence under the law in force where the whole or any part of it was intended to take place. The CJA 1993, s 6(4) and (7) referred to in para 14.95, nn 192 and 193 also apply to the CAA 1981, s 1A.

The CAA 1981, s 1A is misconceived because it cannot apply where the substantive offence is triable under English law, and any act done in England and Wales by way of an attempt to commit a Group A offence must be a 'relevant event' under the CJA 1993, s 2(1), and any completed Group A offence triable is under s 2(3) in England and Wale if a relevant event occurs there (see para 12.71).

14.106 The CAA 1981, s 1(4) (as amended by the Coroners and Justice Act 2009, Sch 21) goes on to provide that the offence of attempt under s 1 does not apply to the following:

(a) conspiracy (whether statutory or common law);

(b) assisting an offender, or concealing an offence, contrary to the Criminal Law Act 1967, ss 4(1) or 5(1), respectively;

(c) an offence of encouraging or assisting suicide, contrary to the Suicide Act 1961, s 2(1); or

(d) aiding, abetting, counselling, procuring or suborning the commission of an offence; in other words, attempting to be an accomplice to an offence which is actually committed is not an offence. As already noted in para 14.53, however, Parliament has, from time to time, created offences whose *actus reus* consists of procuring or aiding and abetting something, so that the perpetrator of such an offence is the procurer or aider and abettor of the relevant thing. Where such an offence has been enacted a person who attempts to perpetrate it can be convicted of an attempt to commit it.[232] It is, of course, possible for a person to be liable as an accomplice to an attempt.[233]

Section 1(4) does not preclude a conviction of attempting to commit an offence under the Serious Crime Act 2007, Pt 2 of encouraging or assisting the commission of an offence, or of attempting to commit a preparatory offence. In *R*[234] the Court of Appeal confirmed there could be a conviction for attempting to commit the preparatory offence under the Sexual Offences Act 2003, s 14 of arranging or facilitating the commission of a child sex offence. In these circumstances criminal liability is imposed at a stage distant from the commission of a substantive offence.

14.107 There are a number of other offences which, by their nature, cannot be attempted under the definition in the CAA 1981, s 1.

14.108 **The requirement for an act means that offences which can only be committed by an omission to act are excluded from the offence of attempt.** It appears that Parliament intended that it should be possible to charge attempt by omission in appropriate cases.[235] When the Criminal Attempts Bill was before Parliament, a proposed amendment to add 'omissions' to the list of offences which could not be attempted was defeated after it had been opposed by the Government because it was desired to retain the possibility of charging attempt by omission in certain cases, such as attempting to kill an invalid by failing to feed. Nevertheless, the words of s 1(1) are unambiguous: 'doing an act' could only be construed as meaning 'doing an act or failing to do an act' by an impermissible rewriting of the provision. The limitation of the offence of attempt to the doing of an act is unfortunate because there is morally no difference between those who attempt to commit an

---

[232] *McShane* (1977) 66 Cr App Rep 97, CA; *Chief Constable of Hampshire v Mace* (1986) 84 Cr App Rep 40, DC.

[233] *Dunnington* [1984] QB 472, CA.   [234] [2008] EWCA Crim 619 (reported elsewhere as *Robson*).

[235] See Dennis 'The Criminal Attempts Act 1981' [1982] Crim LR 5 at 7.

offence by doing an act and those who attempt to do so by failing to do something which they are legally obliged to do.[236]

14.109 The requirement of an intent to commit the substantive offence whose attempt is charged means that a charge of attempt to commit involuntary manslaughter is inappropriate because the prosecution would have to prove an intent to kill and if they did this would establish attempted murder. In *Creamer*[237] the Court of Criminal Appeal stated obiter that attempted involuntary manslaughter was an offence unknown to the law. On the other hand, there is no reason in principle why a person who intends to kill, but who would have had the partial defence of loss of control[238] or diminished responsibility or killing in pursuance of a suicide pact if he had killed, should not be guilty of attempted voluntary manslaughter, as opposed to attempted murder, if his attempt is unsuccessful. However, the available authorities on the point deny that this is possible.[239] So, it seems, does the wording of the CAA 1981, s 1.[240]

Mens rea

14.110 In order that a person may be convicted of an attempt to commit an offence, he must be proved to have had an intention to commit that offence, and to have done an act which constituted the *actus reus* of an attempt (ie an act which was more than merely preparatory to the commission of the intended offence). Of these two elements, the first is particularly important because whether a particular act amounts to an attempt will often depend on the intent with which it is done. For example, to strike a match near a haystack may or may not be attempted arson of the haystack, depending on whether there is an intent to set fire to the haystack or to light a cigarette; the intent colours the act. The function of the *actus reus* is to regulate the point at which acts in furtherance of the defendant's intention incur criminal liability. The policy of the law is that it is only when some act is done which sufficiently manifests the social danger present in the intent that authority should intervene.

14.111 The *mens rea* specified for the offence of attempt by the CAA 1981, s 1(1) is an 'intent to commit an offence to which this section [ie s 1] applies' and which the defendant is alleged to have attempted.

---

[236] See Palmer 'Attempt by Act or Omission: Causation and the Problem of the Hypothetical Nurse' (1999) 63 J Crim L 158.

[237] [1966] 1 QB 72 at 81.

[238] This defence will replace the partial defence to murder of provocation when the Coroners and Justice Act 2009, ss 54 and 55 are brought into force on 4 October 2010.

[239] *Bruzas* [1972] Crim LR 367, Crown Ct (provocation not available as a defence to attempted murder); *Campbell* [1997] Crim LR 495, Crown Ct (diminished responsibility not available as defence to attempted murder charge). In *Creamer*, n 237, the Court of Criminal Appeal, in saying that it was 'undoubtedly true that attempted manslaughter is [an offence] unknown to the law' did not advert to the distinction between voluntary and involuntary manslaughter; the case was concerned with liability as an accomplice for the offence of involuntary manslaughter.

[240] This point was made by Sedley J (as he then was) in *Campbell* [1997] Crim LR 495, Crown Ct.

The words quoted involve more complexity than might at first sight appear. The reason is that an intent to commit the offence attempted may involve a number of mental elements.

Intent to commit a sufficient act

14.112 The defendant must always be proved to have intended to commit an act (indeed, he may have done it) or to continue with a series of acts which, when completed, will amount to the offence allegedly attempted[241] (assuming any requisite consequence for that offence has resulted from the act or acts and that any requisite circumstance exists). In this context talk of anything other than a direct intent would seem to be meaningless.

Intent as to any consequence of substantive offence

14.113 Where the definition of the offence allegedly attempted requires that some consequence be brought about by the defendant's conduct, it must always be proved that the defendant intended that consequence to result from his intended sufficient act. Intention in this context can be proved by proving that the defendant had a direct intention to bring it about. However, the jury or magistrates are entitled to find that the defendant intended that consequence if it was virtually certain to result from the intended sufficient act and the defendant foresaw that consequence as virtually certain to result therefrom, although it was not his purpose to bring that consequence about.[242]

It is not enough that the defendant intended some lesser consequence to result from his intended sufficient act, nor is it enough that he was merely reckless as to the specified consequence resulting therefrom.[243] The result is that **the requirement of *mens rea* for attempt may be stricter on a charge of attempt than for the substantive offence which has been attempted**. For example, a person may be convicted of murder if he kills someone when intending merely to cause unlawful grievous bodily harm, whereas on a charge of attempted murder the jury must be satisfied that he intended unlawfully to kill if he is to be convicted.[244] By way of further example, a person may be convicted of criminal damage if he was reckless as to destroying or damaging another's property, but on a charge of attempted criminal damage an intent as to this consequence must be proved.[245]

Mens rea *as to any circumstances of the substantive offence*

14.114 The defendant must be proved to have had *mens rea* in relation to any circumstances of the *actus reus* of the offence allegedly attempted. Subject to what is said below, this is so even if that offence is one of strict liability as to a circumstance or circumstances.

---

[241] *Khan* [1990] 2 All ER 783, CA.

[242] *Pearman* (1984) 80 Cr App Rep 259 at 263; *Walker and Hayles* (1989) 90 Cr App Rep 226, CA (note the reference in this case to 'very high degree of probability' is now wrong).

[243] *Millard and Vernon* [1987] Crim LR 393, CA.

[244] *Whybrow* (1951) 35 Cr App Rep 141, CCA; *Walker and Hayles* (1989) 90 Cr App Rep 226, CA.

[245] See *Millard and Vernon* [1987] Crim LR 393, CA; *O'Toole* [1987] Crim LR 759, CA.

It makes no sense in this context to speak of a direct intention as to a circumstance (ie to speak of a defendant deciding to bring about, in so far as it lies within his power, a circumstance) or of foresight of it resulting from an intended act.

14.115 In the relatively rare case **where the offence allegedly attempted requires knowledge (in the sense of being certain) as to a circumstance (otherwise known as intention as to a circumstance) or 'knowledge or belief' as to a circumstance, knowledge or belief as to it is required on a charge of attempting that offence.** This is supported by the CAA 1981, s 1(3), which, as explained later, relates to impossibility of an attempt. Section 1(3) proceeds on the basis that a defendant can be convicted of an attempt where he mistakenly believes in the existence of facts or circumstances which would render his intended act criminal.[246] Thus, in this case 'belief' in the existence of a circumstance suffices where the defendant is not certain about it. It can hardly be the case that a correct belief in facts or circumstances making the intended act criminal is insufficient until verified and turned into actual knowledge.[247]

14.116 **Where recklessness (which term includes 'wilful blindness') suffices for the offence allegedly attempted, recklessness will also suffice on a charge of attempting to commit it.** In *Khan*,[248] the Court of Appeal held that, since recklessness as to the absence of the woman's consent was sufficient *mens rea* on a charge of rape, contrary to the Sexual Offences Act 1956, s 1 (since repealed),[249] a defendant could be convicted of attempted rape, if he knew that the woman was not consenting or was reckless as to the fact that she might not be. Although *Khan* is strictly an authority only in relation to an attempt to commit the offence of rape under s 1 of the 1956 Act, it is inconceivable that the approach taken in it is not equally applicable to an attempt to commit any other offence for which recklessness as to a circumstance or circumstances suffices.

Since recklessness as to a circumstance suffices on an attempt charge if it suffices for the substantive offence, recklessness will suffice on a charge of attempting to commit an offence in which negligence as to a circumstance suffices or which is one of strict liability as to a circumstance. The reason is that, although a person can be convicted of such an offence even though he is not reckless as to that circumstance, it is no defence that the defendant was actually reckless as to it, so that recklessness clearly suffices in such an offence. The result is, for example, that on a charge of attempting to engage in sexual activity with a child under 16, an offence of negligence in relation to age (unless the child is under 13 in which case it is one of strict liability in this respect), the defendant must be proved actually to have been certain or to have believed that the girl was under 16 or to have been reckless as to this. It may be that the law is harsher than as stated here. In *A-G's Reference (No 3 of 1992)*[250] where another issue concerning the *mens rea* for attempt, dealt with in para 14.117, was under consideration, the Court of Appeal stated that the

---

[246] It would be nonsensical to talk of knowledge in such a case.

[247] Dennis [1981] Crim LR 5 at 12. Also see *Brown* [1984] 3 All ER 1013, CA.

[248] [1990] 2 All ER 783, CA. See Duff 'The Circumstances of an Attempt' (1991) 50 CLJ 100, and the response by Williams 'Intents in the Alternative' (1991) 50 CLJ 120.

[249] By the Sexual Offences Act 2003.   [250] [1994] 2 All ER 121 at 126.

defendant 'in order to be guilty of an offence must be in one of the states of mind required for the commission of the full offence, and did his best, as far as he could to supply what was missing from the completion of the offence'. This statement made without reference to authority or any apparent consideration of its implications must be viewed with caution. If it does represent the law, the effect would be that if the substantive offence was one of negligence or strict liability as to a circumstance of its *actus reus* the same would be true in respect of a charge of attempting to commit it.

Additional mens rea

14.117 The requirement that the defendant must be proved to have intended to commit the offence allegedly attempted means that he must have any other mental element, additional to *mens rea* as to the consequence or circumstances of the *actus reus* of the offence allegedly attempted, required for that offence. Thus, a person can only be convicted of attempted theft if he acted dishonestly and with intent permanently to deprive the person to whom it belonged of the property he intended to appropriate. Likewise, a person can only be convicted of attempting to commit the offence of destroying or damaging property intending or being reckless as to endangering life if (in addition to intending to destroy or damage property) he intended or was reckless as to endangering life by the intended destruction or damage. Thus, recklessness suffices in this respect if it suffices as additional *mens rea* for the offence attempted. *A-G's Reference (No 3 of 1992)*[251] provides authority for this. D threw a lighted petrol bomb at a car containing people. The bomb missed the car. At D's trial for attempting to commit the above offence by fire (arson), being reckless as to whether life would be endangered thereby, the judge directed an acquittal. Her reasons were that D had to intend to commit the offence whose attempt was charged, that it was impossible to intend to be reckless as to endangering life, and therefore that it was impossible to convict someone of the attempt charged if all that could be proved was that he intended to damage property being reckless as to whether life would be endangered thereby. The Court of Appeal held that this was wrong; on a charge of the type in question, in addition to proof of an intent to cause damage by fire, it was sufficient to prove that D was reckless as to life being endangered thereby.

General comments

14.118 *Ignorance of law no defence* The requirement of an intent to commit an offence does not mean that the defendant must be aware that what he intends to do is an offence; the CAA 1981 does not derogate from the general rule[252] that ignorance of the law is no defence.

14.119 *Conditional intent* A person charged with attempting to commit an offence may have acted with a so-called 'conditional intent', ie an intent to commit that offence if

---

[251] [1994] 2 All ER 121, CA. Criticised by Elliott 'Endangering Life by Destroying or Damaging Property' [1997] Crim LR 382 at 393–395.　　[252] Para 3.73.

a particular condition is satisfied. Provided in such a case that the defendant has formed a firm intention to commit the offence if the condition in question is satisfied, and that he has gone beyond mere preparation (and therefore committed the *actus reus* of an attempt), he can be convicted of an attempt to commit that offence.

A common example of a case involving a 'conditional intent' is where the defendant intends to steal whatever he might find worth stealing in his target area, as where D is arrested as he opens V's suitcase, intending to look inside it, to examine its contents and, if there is anything worth stealing, to steal that thing. Provided he is not charged with the attempted theft of specific objects but instead is merely charged with the attempted theft of 'some or all of the contents' of the suitcase, D can be convicted of attempted theft.[253] The proviso is an unsatisfactory one because, if the suitcase does not contain anything worth stealing, D's intention is to steal something other than the contents of the suitcase. Similarly, if D is arrested as he is about to trespass in a building with the intention of stealing anything valuable therein, if he finds such a thing, D can be convicted of attempted burglary;[254] in such a case it is unnecessary for the charge to allege more than 'with intent to steal therein' since the type of offence attempted does not require anything to be stolen.

Another example is where D creeps into V's house intending to kill V if V is alone (or if V is there). Assuming that it is proved that D acted with a firm intention to commit murder if the condition was satisfied, and had gone beyond the stage of mere preparation, D can be convicted of attempted murder despite the condition attached to his intention.

Actus reus

14.120 The CAA 1981, s 1(1) provides that the offence of attempt to commit an offence requires 'an act that is more than merely preparatory to the commission of the offence'. 'The offence' means one to which s 1 applies[255] and which the defendant intends to commit.

The application of the formula 'an act that is more than merely preparatory to the commission of the offence' can be illustrated as follows. If D buys a box of matches he cannot be convicted of attempted arson, even though it may clearly be proved that he intends to set fire to a haystack at the time of the purchase. Nor can D be convicted of this offence if he approaches the stack with the matches in his pocket. However, if he bends down near the stack and lights a match which he extinguishes on seeing that he is being watched, he may be guilty of attempted arson. In the first two instances, D's acts have clearly not gone beyond the stage of mere preparation; in the third the jury (or magistrates) may properly find that they have.

---

[253] *Husseyn* (1977) 67 Cr App Rep 131, CA; *A-G's References (Nos 1 and 2 of 1979)* [1980] QB 180, CA; *Scudder v Barrett* [1980] QB 195, DC; *Bayley and Easterbrook* [1980] Crim LR 503, CA; *Smith and Smith* [1986] Crim LR 166, CA. Also see *Toothill* [1998] Crim LR 876, CA.

[254] *A-G's References (Nos 1 and 2 of 1979)* [1980] QB 180, CA.   [255] Paras 14.105 and 14.108.

14.121 The formula 'an act that is more than merely preparatory to the commission of the offence' is rather vague, particularly since the CAA 1981 offers no explanation of it. The formula was intended by the Law Commission to be a rationalisation of various decisions on what constituted a sufficient act for the common law offence of attempt, some of which were unsatisfactory or not easy to reconcile with others. However, the formula must not be construed according to the previous case law. The reason is that, as the long title of the Act states, it is an Act to amend the law of attempt. Consequently, the correct approach is not to refer to the previous case law and seek to fit some previous test to the words of the formula, but instead to apply the words of the formula according to their plain and natural meaning.[256]

Functions of judge and jury

14.122 The CAA 1981, s 4(3) provides that, where there is evidence sufficient in law to support a finding that the defendant did an act which was more than merely preparatory to the commission of the offence allegedly attempted (ie evidence capable of constituting an attempt), the question whether or not it is proved that his act actually fell within s 1(1) is a question of fact. This is of particular importance in terms of the respective functions of judge and jury in relation to the *actus reus* of attempt. In a condensed fashion, s 4(3) codifies the principles laid down in this respect by the House of Lords in *DPP v Stonehouse*.[257] It was held in that case, and s 4(3) assumes this, that **whether there is evidence of an act sufficient in law to constitute an attempt (ie evidence on which a jury could properly conclude that the defendant had gone beyond mere preparation)**[258] **is a question for the judge. If the judge decides that there is no such evidence on which the jury could properly convict of an attempt (or if the judge decides that, although the matter is not as conclusive as that, it would nevertheless be unsafe to leave the evidence to the jury),**[259] **the judge must direct the jury to acquit the defendant of an attempt.** The effect of s 4(3) is that if, **on the other hand, the judge finds that there is evidence on which a jury could properly conclude that there has been a more than merely preparatory act, the judge must leave it to the jury to decide as a question of fact whether or not the defendant did an act which was more than merely preparatory to the commission of the offence allegedly attempted.** This involves the jury in finding not only that the defendant did a particular act but also that it was more than 'merely preparatory to' the commission of the intended offence. Accordingly, the judge must not direct the jury to convict if they find a relevant act proved, even though on the evidence there can only be an affirmative answer to the question 'was it more than merely preparatory?'[260] Leaving the task to the jury of determining whether an act was actually more than merely preparatory may lead to inconsistency as between juries on materially similar facts.

---

[256] *Gullefer* [1990] 3 All ER 882, CA; *Jones* [1990] 3 All ER 886, CA; *Campbell* (1990) 93 Cr App Rep 350, CA.   [257] [1978] AC 55, HL.
[258] *Gullefer* [1990] 3 All ER 882 at 884.   [259] *Campbell* (1990) 93 Cr App Rep 350, CA.
[260] *Wang* [2005] UKHL 9. See also *Griffin* [1993] Crim LR 515, CA.

More than merely preparatory act

14.123 It is obvious that there is sufficient evidence in law that an act is more than merely preparatory to the commission of an offence in a 'last *act*' case, ie one where the defendant has done the last *act* towards the commission of the alleged attempted offence which, to his knowledge, it was necessary for him to do in order to commit that offence, even though something more remains to be done by another, innocent person. Thus, one who puts poison in another's drink, intending him to drink it and be killed in consequence, may be convicted of attempted murder, and so may someone who posts a parcel bomb to another, intending him to be killed when he opens it.

14.124 However, cases where there may be sufficient evidence that an act is more than merely preparatory to the commission of an offence are not restricted to 'last act' cases; otherwise the offence of attempt would hardly ever be committed and some offences, such as rape, could never be attempted. It is established that there can be sufficient evidence in law of a more than merely preparatory act in a case where the defendant still has to take some further step or steps himself before the substantive offence can be committed[261] but, clearly, there will not always be sufficient evidence of such an act in such a case. The dividing line between acts which will or will not suffice under the formula must, of course, be drawn on the basis of the wording of the CAA 1981, s 1(1), and **the key words are 'more than merely preparatory'**. Obviously, every act in furtherance of a criminal objective can be described as preparatory to the commission of the offence but it will not always be describable as merely preparatory. As is indicated by common sense and by the Court of Appeal in *Gullefer*[262] and in *Jones*,[263] **if the defendant can be said to have got as far as having embarked on the commission of the offence (ie 'on the job'),**[264] **as where he tries to force a door of a house in order to commit burglary or points a loaded gun at someone with intent to kill him,**[265] **there is sufficient evidence of an act more than merely preparatory to the commission of the intended offence.** In such a case, it would be a major understatement to say that there is not sufficient evidence that his acts had gone beyond being merely preparatory, even though (since some further act was required of him) his acts were still at the preparatory stage.

---

[261] *Boyle and Boyle* (1986) 84 Cr App Rep 270, CA; *Gullefer* [1990] 3 All ER 882, CA; *Jones* [1990] 3 All ER 886, CA.

[262] [1990] 3 All ER 882, CA.

[263] [1990] 3 All ER 886, CA. For criticism of *Jones* and *Gullefer* see KJM Smith 'Proximity in Attempt: Lord Lane's "Midway Course"' [1991] Crim LR 576.

[264] A phrase used in *Osborn* (1919) 84 JP 63.

[265] Even if the safety catch is still on and he has yet to put his finger to the trigger: *Jones* [1990] 3 All ER 886, CA. See also *A-G's Reference (No 1 of 1992)* [1993] 2 All ER 190, CA (attempted physical penetration by D's penis of the victim not necessary for case of attempted rape to be left to jury); *Patnaik* [2000] 3 Archbold News 2, CA (not a necessary threshold for attempted rape to be left to the jury that D, who was engaged in violently subduing victim with intent to rape her, should have gone as far as starting to undo or remove her (or his) clothing or to do some other unequivocal sexual act).

14.125 In *Gullefer*, D had jumped onto a greyhound track to stop a race, in which the dog he had backed was losing. He did so in order to have the race declared void whereupon he would have been entitled to recover his bet of £18. The Court of Appeal allowed his appeal against conviction for the attempted theft of the amount of the bet because the judge had been wrong to find that there was sufficient evidence to leave to the jury that D had done an act more than merely preparatory to getting the £18. He had not embarked on the commission of the offence. His act was merely preparatory to getting the £18; it still remained for the stewards to declare the race void and for D then to go to the bookmaker and demand the £18.

14.126 *Gullefer* can be contrasted with *Jones*, where D had got into V's car and pointed a loaded firearm at him. V managed to disarm him. D was charged with attempted murder. The trial judge rejected a submission that there was insufficient evidence to leave to the jury the question of whether D had done a more than merely preparatory act. That submission had been based on the argument that at least three more preparatory acts would have had to be carried out by D before the substantive offence was committed, ie remove the safety catch, put his finger on the trigger and pull it. D appealed unsuccessfully against conviction for attempted murder. The Court of Appeal held that, although D's earlier acts prior to entering V's car could only be regarded as preparatory, once D had got into V's car, taken out the loaded firearm and pointed it at V there was sufficient evidence of a more than merely preparatory act.

14.127 The approach referred to above was purportedly adopted by the Court of Appeal in *Geddes*,[266] **although the words used by the Court raised the threshold of embarking on the commission of the offence by requiring that the defendant should actually have tried to commit the substantive offence**, ie have got as far as the last *acts* necessary on his part to commit the offence. Dealing with the approach to be taken by a judge in deciding whether there is evidence sufficient in law to support a finding by the jury that the defendant did an act merely preparatory to the commission of the offence allegedly attempted, Lord Bingham CJ, as he then was, giving the judgment of the Court said:

> 'It is, we think, an accurate paraphrase of the statutory test and not an illegitimate gloss upon it to ask whether the available evidence, if accepted, could show that a defendant has done an act which shows that he has actually tried to commit the offence in question, or whether he has only got ready or put himself in a position or equipped himself to do so.'[267]

In *Geddes*, D had entered school grounds and been found in a boys' toilet. He ran away and a rucksack discarded by him was found to contain lengths of string, sealing tape and a knife. D was convicted of attempted false imprisonment of a person unknown. He

---

[266] (1996) 160 JP 697, CA.

[267] (1996) 160 JP 697 at 705. See also *Qadir* [1997] 9 Archbold News 1, CA ('Attempt begins at the moment when the defendant embarks upon the crime proper, as opposed to taking steps rightly regarded as merely preparatory.').

appealed against conviction on the ground that the trial judge had been wrong to rule that there was sufficient evidence of more than merely preparatory acts by D for the matter to be left to the jury. The Court of Appeal allowed D's appeal. It held that, although there was no doubt as to D's intention, the evidence was clearly capable of showing no more than that he had made preparations, equipped himself, got ready and put himself in a position to commit the offence whose attempt was charged. There was not evidence sufficient in law to support a finding that he had moved beyond the role of intention, preparation and planning into the area of execution or implementation, ie that he had actually tried to commit the offence of false imprisonment. He had entered the school but he had never had any contact or communication with any pupil.[268]

An earlier decision to like effect was that of the Court of Appeal in *Campbell*,[269] where D had been arrested, armed with an imitation firearm, as he approached within a yard of the door of a post office where he intended to commit a robbery. The Court of Appeal, allowing D's appeal against conviction for attempted robbery, held that there had not been sufficient evidence to leave to the jury that D's acts were more than merely preparatory.

14.128 *Geddes* can be contrasted with the decision of the Court of Appeal in *Tosti*,[270] where the Court of Appeal, having referred to Lord Bingham's paraphrase of the test in s 1(1), upheld a conviction for attempted burglary despite the fact that the defendant had not got as far as 'trying to commit the offence in question'. The question for the Court was whether there had been sufficient evidence to leave to the jury the question of whether the defendants had done an act which was more than merely preparatory to committing burglary. The evidence was that the defendants had equipped themselves with oxyacetylene equipment, driven to the scene, concealed the oxyacetylene equipment in a hedge, approached a barn door and bent down to examine a heavy padlock. Dismissing appeals against conviction for attempted burglary, Beldam LJ, giving the Court's judgment, stated that 'there may be actions which are preparatory which are not merely so and which are essentially the first steps in the commission of the offence'.[271] The Court held that the facts proved in evidence were sufficient for the judge to leave to the jury the question whether those acts were or were not more than merely preparatory. In doing so the Court purported to apply the guidance in *Geddes* but in reality they were adopting the pre-*Geddes* approach indicated by the Court of Appeal in *Gullefer* and *Jones*.

14.129 In making a ruling on whether or not an act was capable of being more than merely preparatory the judge must keep in mind the essential nature of the offence attempted, ie the essential act or transaction on which it hinges and any consequence required to complete it.[272] In *Toothill*,[273] where D had knocked at the door of the house of his intended rape-victim, the Court of Appeal upheld a conviction of attempted burglary

---

[268] The defendant in *Geddes* would now be guilty of an offence under the Sexual Offences Act 2003, s 63 (trespassing with intent to commit a relevant sexual offence).
[269] (1990) 93 Cr App Rep 350, CA.   [270] [1997] Crim LR 746, CA.
[271] These words appear in the transcript but not in the brief report cited in n 270.
[272] *Qadir* [1997] 9 Archbold News 1, CA. See also the commentary to *Nash* [1999] Crim LR 308, CA.
[273] [1998] Crim LR 876, CA.

with intent to rape;[274] the judge had been correct in holding that there was evidence on which the jury could find that D's knocking at the door was more than merely preparatory to the commission of burglary, since commission of that offence simply required for its completion an act of entry as a trespasser (with a requisite intent, such as to rape). It would doubtless have been different if the substantive offence had required the commission of rape for its completion.

Although it is not possible to categorise types of offences, because their individual facts can vary, killing or wounding *usually* concentrates on a particular moment, whereas fraud is *more likely* to involve a plan carried on over a period of time. In the former type of case, an act leading up to the completion of the offence but substantially earlier in time is likely to be merely preparatory, whereas in the latter the moment when an act is done which is more than merely preparatory may be quite remote in time from the completion of the offence.[275]

14.130 Of course, as recognised in *Geddes*, the dividing line cannot always be easily drawn. Quite apart from this, the differences inherent in *Geddes* and *Tosti* mean that the dividing line between 'merely preparatory' and 'more than merely preparatory' has become uncertain.

Whichever approach is adopted, a defendant must have gone a long way down the road towards committing the intended offence to fall within the scope of attempt. This is due not only to the wording 'more than merely preparatory' but also due to the fact that it is implicit in the word 'attempt' itself.

Attempts to do the impossible

14.131 The CAA 1981, s 1(2) and (3) deals with attempts to do the impossible and reverses the decision in *Haughton v Smith*,[276] a House of Lords case where the actual decision and other statements of principle were to the effect that in many cases of impossibility there could not be a conviction for the common law offence of attempt.

Section 1(2) provides that:

'A person may be guilty of attempting to commit an offence to which [s 1] applies even though the facts are such that the commission of the offence is impossible.'

Section 1(3) adds that:

'In any case where –

(a) apart from this subsection [s 1(3)] a person's intention would not be regarded as having amounted to an intent to commit an offence; but

---

[274] The offence of burglary with intent to rape was replaced by the offence of trespass with intent to commit a relevant sexual offence by the Sexual Offences Act 2003.

[275] *Qadir* [1997] 9 Archbold News 1, CA.   [276] [1975] AC 476, HL.

(b) if the facts of the case had been as he believed them to be, his intention would be so regarded,

then, for the purposes of [s 1(1)], he shall be regarded as having had an intent to commit that offence.'

14.132 As a result of the CAA 1981, s 1(2) a person is guilty of attempted murder if his physical objective is capable of commission at the time of his attempt but he fails to achieve it because of a supervening event or inadequate means or lack of skill, as where, intending to kill, he sends a time bomb to V who dies of natural causes before the bomb arrives or where he places a small quantity of poison in a glass of lemonade which he expects his intended victim to drink, the quantity being insufficient to be lethal. Likewise, a person is guilty of attempted burglary where, in order to burgle a house, he tries to force a window with a jemmy which is insufficient.

14.133 The effect of the CAA 1981, s 1(2), in combination with s 1(3), is that a person can be convicted of an attempt even though his physical objective could never have been achieved at the time of his attempt, whatever means or however much skill was used. A person is guilty of attempted murder if he fires at a bolster in a bed, mistakenly believing that it is B whom he intends to kill; a person is guilty of attempted theft if he is charged with attempting to steal from a particular wallet which is in fact empty. Unlike the examples in the previous paragraph, these examples would not have constituted the common law offence of attempt as a result of the views expressed by the House of Lords in *Haughton v Smith*. The rationale behind the distinction between the two types of situation drawn in that case was not easily discernible and the abolition of the distinction is therefore to be welcomed.

14.134 The effect of s 1(2), in combination with s 1(3), is also that a person can be convicted of an attempt where he has achieved or could have achieved his object in physical terms, but owing to some mistake on his part his object does not after all amount to an offence. Following the decision in *Haughton v Smith*, there could not have been a conviction for the common law offence of attempt in such a situation. Given that the essence of the offence of attempt is to punish those who go further than mere preparation to put their 'evil intents' into practice, the reversal of that decision for the purposes of the statutory offence of attempt is clearly right. As a result of the above provisions a person who handles goods, mistakenly believing that they are stolen, can be convicted of attempting to handle stolen goods; a man who mistakenly believes that the girl with whom he has sexual intercourse is under 16 can be convicted of attempting to have penetrative sexual activity with a girl under 16; and a person who takes his own umbrella from a hat stand, thinking it is another's, can be convicted of attempted theft.

Strictly, the people referred to in para 14.133 and the last paragraph could be convicted of an attempt by reference only to the CAA 1981, s 1(2), since they all have the necessary *mens rea* for the attempted offence in question. Section 1(3) is, however, included in the Act to prevent a defence succeeding that the defendant's conduct was objectively innocent.

14.135 The above undoubtedly reflects the current effect of the CAA 1981 on attempts to do the impossible, but between May 1985 and May 1986 the interpretation of the Act was different in relation to cases of the type described in para 14.134, as a result of the House of Lords' decision in May 1985 in *Anderton v Ryan*[277] that they did not constitute an attempt under the Act. The case concerned a defendant who had bought a video recorder, believing it to have been stolen. On the facts as they were assumed to be it was not stolen. The House of Lords (Lord Edmund-Davies dissenting) held that the defendant could not be convicted of attempting to handle stolen goods. It held that on their true construction s 1(2) and, particularly, s 1(3) did not compel the conclusion that a person was guilty of attempting to commit an offence where his acts were 'objectively innocent', although he mistakenly believed facts which if true would have made his acts a complete offence.

This decision was particularly objectionable in that it introduced the concept of 'objective innocence' which it was clearly the CAA 1981's intention to exclude. Consequently, there was a general satisfaction when it was overruled in May 1986 by the House of Lords in *Shivpuri*.[278] Here, D, who had been arrested while in possession of a suitcase, had admitted that he believed that the suitcase contained either heroin or cannabis and that he had been concerned in dealing with it. When analysed the contents turned out not to be a controlled drug at all but a harmless substance. The House of Lords, overruling *Anderton v Ryan*, dismissed D's appeal against conviction for attempting to commit the statutory offence of knowingly being concerned in dealing with a drug whose importation was prohibited. Lord Bridge, with whose speech the other Law Lords agreed, made clear that there is no distinction between 'objectively innocent' and 'objectively guilty' acts in the present sphere. Lord Bridge stated:

> 'I am satisfied that the concept of "objective innocence" is incapable of sensible application in relation to the law of criminal attempts. The reason for this is that any attempt to commit an offence which involves "an act which is more than merely preparatory to the commission of the offence" but which for any reason fails, so that in the event no offence is committed, must, ex hypothesi, from the point of view of the criminal law, be "objectively innocent". What turns what would otherwise, from the point of view of the criminal law, be an innocent act into a crime is the intent of the actor to commit an offence.... A puts his hand into B's pocket. Whether or not there is anything in the pocket capable of being stolen, if A intends to steal his act is a criminal attempt; if he does not so intend his act is innocent.... These considerations lead me to the conclusion that the distinction sought to be drawn in *Anderton v Ryan* between innocent and guilty acts considered "objectively" and independently of the state of mind of the actor cannot be sensibly maintained.'[279]

The House held that, by the CAA 1981, s 1, two things, and two things only, had always to be proved for a conviction for attempt. First, that the defendant had an intention to commit the offence in question. Second, that, with that intent, the defendant had done an act which was more than merely preparatory to the commission of the offence intended by him, which meant that the question to ask was whether the act would have been more

---

[277] [1985] AC 560, HL.   [278] [1987] AC 1, HL.   [279] [1987] AC 1 at 21–22.

than preparatory if the facts had been as the defendant believed them to be. Applying these two tests, it was held, D was clearly guilty of the offence in question, since he had intended to deal with drugs which he believed had been illegally imported, and he had done an act which was more than merely preparatory to the commission of that intended offence.

Shivpuri was applied in *Jones (Ian Anthony)*.[280] In March 2005 a journalist reported to the police that she had seen graffiti on the door of a train toilet, seeking girls aged eight to 13 for sex in return for payment and requesting contact via a mobile telephone number. In consequence, the police began an undercover operation using an officer pretending to be 'Amy', aged 12. As a result of an exchange of text messages, in which D, an adult, incited 'Amy' to penetrative sexual activity, D was arrested and charged, inter alia, with attempting to cause or incite a child under 13 to engage in penetrative sexual activity (ie attempting to commit an offence under the Sexual Offences Act 2003, s 8). At trial, D applied to stay the proceedings as an abuse of process. One of his grounds was that the charge disclosed no offence known to law, because the defendant did not intend to incite any *actual* person under the age of 13 and therefore could not have had the requisite intent. The trial judge rejected D's application. D entered a plea of guilty as a result and appealed to the Court of Appeal against the judge's ruling. Applying *Shivpuri*, the Court of Appeal dismissed D's appeal. D clearly intended to incite 'Amy' to engage in penetrative sexual activity and, on the material before the judge, D had done an act more than merely preparatory to the commission of the offence. The fact that the commission of the offence of incitement was on the facts impossible because 'Amy' was not under 13 was irrelevant.

14.136 Some cases of impossible attempts are hardly deserving of punishment. In such cases, assuming (and this is unlikely) that the case ever came to light, the discretion to prosecute is very likely to be exercised against the institution of a prosecution.

14.137 It must be emphasised that the CAA 1981, s 1(3) only operates where, if the facts of the case had been as the defendant believed them to be, his intention would be regarded as having amounted to an intention to commit an offence. Consequently, whether or not the defendant knows the true facts, if what he intends to do (and may actually do) is not an offence, although because of a mistake as to the criminal law he believes that it is, he cannot be convicted of an attempt. For example, a man who has intercourse with a girl of 17, knowing that she is 17 but mistakenly believing that it is an offence to have intercourse with her because she is under 18, cannot be convicted of an attempt contrary to s 1 because he does not intend to commit an offence to which s 1 applies.

Jurisdiction over attempts outside England and Wales

14.138 The courts in England and Wales have jurisdiction under the common law rules of jurisdiction over an attempt committed abroad provided that it was intended to result

---

[280] [2007] EWCA Crim 1118.

in an offence triable in England and Wales on indictment, even though no overt act or consequence takes place in England and Wales.[281]

Statutory provision to this effect is made by the Criminal Justice Act 1993, s 3(3) in relation to attempts abroad to commit a Group A offence, viz one of the offences under the Theft Act 1968, Forgery and Counterfeiting Act 1981, Fraud Act 2006 and related offences listed in the Criminal Justice Act 1993, s 1 (see para 12.70),[282] which would be triable in England and Wales if committed. Section 3(3) provides that it is immaterial that the attempt was not made in England and Wales and had no effect in England and Wales. It is irrelevant whether or not the defendant was a British citizen at any material time or was in England and Wales at any such time.[283]

Prosecution, trial and punishment

Prosecution

14.139 By the CAA 1981, s 2, where the offence attempted is subject to a statutory provision whereby proceedings for it may not be instituted or carried on otherwise than by, or on behalf or with the consent of, any person (such as the Director of Public Prosecutions), that provision extends to an attempt to commit that offence, and so does any statutory time limit on the institution of proceedings for the offence attempted.

Trial

14.140 The offence of attempt under the CAA 1981, s 1 is triable in the same way as the offence attempted. Consequently, if that offence is triable only on indictment (eg murder or rape) an attempt to commit it must be tried on indictment, whereas if the offence attempted is triable either way (eg theft or sexual assault) an attempt to commit it is triable either way.[284] This is one of the effects of the rather obscure wording of the CAA 1981, s 4(1).

Punishment

14.141 The CAA 1981, s 4(1) also specifies the penalties for a person convicted of an attempt under s 1:

- if the offence attempted is murder or any other offence for which the sentence is fixed by law, the maximum punishment is life imprisonment; and
- in the case of any other attempt, the maximum punishment is the same as is available to the court of trial for the offence attempted.[285]

---

[281] *Latif and Shahzad* [1996] 1 All ER 353, HL.

[282] Attempt to commit a Group A offence is a Group B offence under the Criminal Justice Act 1993, Pt I: CJA 1993, s 1(3)(c).

[283] Criminal Justice Act 1993, s 3(1).   [284] For an exception, see para 13.2.

[285] In the case of attempted 'small value criminal damage', the maximum is the lower maximum for small value damage: see para 13.2.

Specific offences of attempt

14.142 Quite apart from the offence of attempt to commit an indictable offence under the CAA 1981, s 1, there are a substantial number of specific statutory offences of attempt to commit another offence. Many of these specific offences consist of attempts to commit purely summary offences, in which cases the general offence of attempt is inapplicable.

Subject to any inconsistent provision in any other enactment, the CAA 1981, s 3 applies to specific statutory offences of attempt which are '*expressed as an offence of attempting to commit another offence*' rules which correspond to those in s 1 for the general statutory offence of attempt. Thus, s 3(3) provides that a person is guilty of an attempt under a special statutory provision if, with intent to commit the relevant full offence, he does an act which is more than merely preparatory to the commission of that offence. In addition, s 3(4) and (5) provide the same rules as in s 1 in relation to 'impossible attempts', while the CAA 1981, s 4(4) provides that the respective functions of a judge and jury are the same as in the case of an offence under s 1.

The crucial question involved in the italicised words is whether the attempt to do something is expressed as an alternative to that 'something' as a mode of committing the *same* offence, or whether it is expressed as a separate offence from the 'something offence'. Obviously, a specific statutory offence of attempt created by a separate section or subsection from the full offence is 'expressed as an offence of attempting to commit another offence'. The fact that the full offence and the attempt are expressed in the very same provision does not necessarily mean that the opposite is the case. It all depends on the exact wording of the offence. For example, in *Mason v DPP*,[286] the Divisional Court held that s 3 applies to an attempt to drive contrary to the Road Traffic Act 1988, s 5(1)(a) (which states that a person commits an offence if he 'drives or attempts to drive' with excess alcohol in his breath, blood or urine).

In practice, the question of whether a statutory offence of attempt is expressed as an offence of attempting to commit another offence is probably not important because a court is likely to adopt the terms of the CAA 1981, s 1 in relation to offences involving an attempt which are neither an offence under s 1 nor within the scope of s 3. In *Qadir*,[287] the Court of Appeal, having held that it was not clear whether offences of knowingly being concerned in any fraudulent evasion *or attempt* at evasion of a prohibition on the import or export of goods, contrary to the Customs and Excise Management Act 1979, s 170(2), were within the scope of s 3, held that nevertheless the judge had been right to adopt the definition of attempt contained in s 1 as the basis for his approach to the question of whether there were acts capable of amounting to an attempt under the Customs and Excise Management Act 1979.

---

[286] [2009] EWHC 2198 (Admin), DC.   [287] [1997] 9 Archbold News 1, CA.

Abandonment of attempt

14.143 Although no argument of deterrence, reformation or prevention seems to require the punishment of one who abandons his attempt before he has done any harm, being truly repentant, it was the position at common law that once the defendant had committed the *actus reus* of an attempt with the necessary *mens rea* he could not escape liability by abandoning the attempt, however genuine and voluntary his repentance.[288] The CAA 1981 does not change this. Of course, voluntary abandonment may mitigate the sentence imposed.

Recommendations for reform

14.144 In its report *Conspiracy and Attempts,*[289] the Law Commission has made a number of recommendations for the amendment of the CAA 1981:

- that the CAA 1981 be amended to provide expressly that, for the purposes of s 1(1), an intent to commit an offence includes a conditional intent to commit it. This recommendation is intended to avoid the problem, inherent in the procedural proviso formulated by the judges to deal with conditional intention in the case of attempted theft;[290]

- that the CAA 1981 be amended so as expressly to provide that for substantive offences which have a circumstance requirement but no corresponding fault requirement, or which have a corresponding fault requirement which is objective (such as negligence) the defendant could be convicted of attempting to commit the substantive offence only if the defendant was subjectively reckless as to the circumstance at the relevant time;

- that the CAA 1981 be amended so as expressly to provide that, where a substantive offence has fault requirements not involving mere negligence (or its equivalent) in relation to a fact or circumstance, it should be possible to convict the defendant of attempting to commit the substantive offence if the defendant possessed those fault requirements at the relevant time;

- that the CAA 1981 be amended so that the defendant may be convicted of attempted *murder* if (with the intent to kill V) the defendant failed to discharge his or her legal duty to V (where that omission, unchecked, could have resulted in V's death). The Commission concluded that it was neither necessary nor desirable to extend the law of attempt in general terms to encompass omissions by failing to discharge a legal duty.

The Law Commission decided not to recommend the extension of the CAA 1981 to summary offences.

---

[288] *Lankford* [1959] Crim LR 209 at 210; *Haughton v Smith* [1975] AC 476 at 493–494, per Lord Hailsham LC. See Wasik 'Abandoning Criminal Intent' [1980] Crim LR 785.

[289] (2009) Law Commission Consultation Paper No 318.   [290] Para 14.119.

FURTHER READING

Arlidge and Parry on Fraud (3rd edn, 2007) Ch 7

Dennis 'The Rationale of Criminal Conspiracy' (1977) 93 LQR 39

Dennis 'The Criminal Attempts Act 1981' [1982] Crim LR 5

Duff *Criminal Attempts* (1996)

Glazebrook 'Should We Have a Law of Attempted Crime?' (1969) 85 LQR 27

Ormerod and Fortson 'Serious Crime Act 2007: the Part 2 Offences' [2009] Crim LR 389

Ormerod and Williams (eds) *Smith's Law of Theft* (9th edn, 2007) Ch 5

ATH Smith *Property Offences* (1994) Ch 19

JC Smith 'Fraud and the Criminal Law' in *Pressing Problems in the Law* (1995) (Birks (ed)) 1.49

KJM Smith 'Proximity in Attempt: Lord Lane's Middle Course' [1991] Crim LR 576

Spencer 'Encouraging and Assisting Crime: Legislate in Haste, Repent at Leisure' [2008] 9 Archbold News 7

Wasik 'Abandoning Criminal Intent' [1980] Crim LR 785

G Williams 'The Lords and Impossible Attempts, or Quis Custodiet Custodes' (1986) 45 CLJ 33

15

Mental condition defences

OVERVIEW

In this chapter the following matters relating to the mental condition of the defendant are considered:

- infancy;
- insanity;
- automatism; and
- intoxication.

For convenience of exposition, the issue of unfitness to be tried is dealt with, although it is not a defence. The section on automatism also covers other forms of involuntary conduct, although these do not relate to the defendant's mental condition.

Infancy

Key points 15.1

It is not unknown for the person suspected of an offence to be a child under the age of 10 years,[1] but such a child cannot be convicted of an offence because he is under the age of criminal responsibility.

It used to be the law that a child aged 10 or over but under 14 had a defence if he was ignorant at the material time that what he was doing was seriously wrong, and that he was rebuttably presumed incapable of committing an offence unless he was proved to have known that what he was doing was seriously wrong. This defence and the associated presumption have been abolished.

---

[1] In 2006, for example, 2,840 crimes, including sexual offences, burglary, harassment and wounding were recorded where a child under 10 was the subject: *Guardian*, 3 September 2007.

Children under 10

15.1 A child cannot be convicted of an offence which occurs when he is under 10 because it is irrebuttably presumed that no child under the age of 10 years can be guilty of an offence.[2] Such a child is said to be *doli incapax* (not capable of crime). At common law, the age of immunity from responsibility was seven. It was raised to eight by statute in 1933 and, again by statute, to 10 in 1963. The age of 10 can be contrasted with seven in Cyprus, Ireland and Switzerland, eight in Scotland,[3] nine in Malta, 13 in France, 14 in Austria, Bulgaria, Germany Italy and Romania, 15 in the Scandinavian states, 16 in Spain, and 18 in Belgium and Luxembourg.[4] A consequence of the *doli incapax* principle is not only that the child under 10 cannot be guilty of an offence but also that he has not committed an offence.[5]

Children 10–13

15.2 The *common law* laid down two related rules concerning children of 10 years or over but under the age of 14, although it was only established authoritatively in 2009 that the first existed independently of the second. Such children were legally incapable of committing an offence unless they had 'mischievous discretion', ie knowledge at the material time that what they were doing was seriously wrong.[6] In addition, they were presumed to be incapable of committing an offence, although that presumption might be rebutted by proof of 'mischievous discretion'.[7] Thus, a child aged 10 to 13 could be convicted only if the prosecution proved beyond reasonable doubt not simply that he committed the *actus reus* with *mens rea* but also that he knew he was doing something seriously wrong, which could be difficult to prove.

This gave rise to the odd result that children from 'good' homes were more likely to be found guilty than children from 'bad' homes, since children from 'good' homes were more likely to have known the serious wrongfulness of their conduct than children from 'bad' homes, although the latter might have been more in need of the corrective treatment which can follow a finding of guilt.[8]

15.3 In *C v DPP*,[9] the House of Lords stated that the rebuttable presumption gave rise to anomalies and absurdities and presented the prosecution with difficulty in rebutting it. It called on Parliament to reform the law. This invitation was accepted by the Crime and Disorder Act 1998, s 34, which provides that: 'The rebuttable presumption of criminal law that a child aged 10 or over is incapable of committing an offence is hereby abolished'.

---

[2] Children and Young Persons Act 1933, s 50, as amended by the Children and Young Persons Act 1963, s 16.

[3] In 2009 the Scottish Government proposed raising the age of criminal responsibility from eight to 12. A provision which would have this effect is contained in the Criminal Justice and Licensing (Scotland) Bill which is before the Scottish Parliament at the time this book states the law.

[4] HL Deb Vol 564, col WA 82.   [5] For the implications of this, see paras 11.44 and 17.6.

[6] *C v DPP* [1996] AC 1, HL.   [7] *JTB* [2009] UKHL 20.

[8] See Williams 'The Criminal Responsibility of Children' [1954] Crim LR 493 at 495–496.

[9] [1996] AC 1, HL.

It was generally thought that the effect of s 34 was to subject children aged 10 to 13 to the same rules of criminal responsibility as adults. However, it was argued by Professor Walker[10] that all that was abolished was a presumption which implied that a child aged 10 to 13 who did not know that his act was seriously wrong was not guilty of an offence, that the only effect of the presumption was to oblige the prosecution to offer enough evidence to prove that the child did know this, and that therefore the abolition of the presumption did not abolish the defence of 'ignorance of serious wrong'. Instead, the argument concluded, the abolition of the presumption merely laid an evidential burden on the defence to adduce evidence raising a reasonable doubt that the child in question did not appreciate the serious wrongness of his conduct, in which case he would have a defence unless the prosecution proved that the child did know his conduct was seriously wrong.

Professor Walker's argument was referred to by the House of Lords in *JTB*,[11] but did not find favour with the House. The issue before the House was:

- whether the defence of ignorance of serious wrong available to a child aged 10 to 13 accused of an offence and the rebuttable presumption that a child aged 10 to 13 was incapable of committing crime were two different things; and

- if so, whether the Crime and Disorder Act 1998, s 34 had merely abolished the presumption, leaving it open to the child to prove that at the time he was ignorant that his conduct was seriously wrong.

The House of Lords held that the defence and the rebuttable presumption were two different things. However, it held, it had become customary to speak of the presumption as embracing both the presumption and the defence. It concluded that the Crime and Disorder Act 1998, s 34, when read in conjunction with legitimate extrinsic aids to interpretation, particularly reference to parliamentary debates under the rule in *Pepper v Hart*,[12] had abolished the defence of ignorance of serious wrong as well as the presumption. Thus, *JTB* confirms that the effect of s 34 was to subject children aged 10 to 13 to the same rules of criminal responsibility as adults.

It is surprising that the age of criminal responsibility was not increased by the Crime and Disorder Act 1998.[13] In the light of what is now known about child development, even if youngsters of 10 or over up to the low teens commit the *actus reus* of an offence with *mens rea*, are they fully responsible in a moral sense? The Government has been urged by various international bodies to reconsider the low age of criminal responsibility.[14]

---

[10] Walker 'The End of an Old Song?' (1999) 149 NLJ 64.

[11] [2009] UKHL 20. For criticism of the House of Lords' decision see Bennion 'Mens Rea and Defendants Below the Age of Discretion' [2009] Crim LR 757.　　　　　　[12] [1993] AC 593, HL.

[13] In a report published in 2007 by the Centre for Crime and Justice Studies at King's College, London, Allen 'A New Approach to Children in Trouble' in *Debating Youth Justice: From Punishment to Problem Solving?* (Davies and McMahon (eds)) argued that the age of criminal responsibility should be raised to 14 and that children under 14 should be dealt with in the family court proceedings referred to in para 15.5. See also the Commission on Families and the Well-being of Children: *Families and the State: An Inquiry into the Relationship between the State and the Family* (2005); Keating 'Reckless Children?' [2007] Crim LR 547.

[14] See Keating 'Reckless Children?' [2007] Crim LR 550–551. In 2008 the UN Committee on the Rights of the Child criticised the low age of criminal responsibility in England and Wales: see Ashworth [2009] Crim LR 582.

Trial and punishment of children and young persons

15.4 Children charged with an offence are usually tried summarily in a youth court, but in the case of an offence of homicide and certain other serious circumstances they must be tried in the Crown Court;[15] they are subject to a different regime from adults in respect of treatment after conviction. The same applies to young persons (ie those aged 14 or over but under 18).

Civil proceedings

15.5 Whether or not they are under the age of criminal responsibility, offenders under 17 may be dealt with by civil family court proceedings under the Children Act 1989, s 31 (as amended by various statutes) which can result in their being put in the care of the local authority or under the supervision of such an authority. However, in such proceedings the child's welfare is the court's paramount consideration and an order may only be made under s 31 if the court is satisfied:

- that the child concerned is suffering, or likely to suffer, harm, and
- that the harm, or likelihood of harm, is attributable to the care given to the child, or likely to be given to him if the order under s 31 were not made, not being what it would be reasonable to expect a parent to give, or the child's being beyond parental control.

It is, therefore, not enough for such an order simply that the child is guilty of an offence.

In addition, a magistrates' court sitting as a civil family court may make a child safety order under the Crime and Disorder Act 1998, s 11 (as amended by the Children Act 2004) in respect of a child *under 10* if satisfied of one or more of a number of grounds. One of these is that the child has committed an act which, if he had been aged 10 or over, would have constituted an offence. If such an order is made the child is placed, for a period not exceeding 12 months, under the supervision of a social worker or member of a youth offending team, and required to comply with conditions specified in the order.

---

[15] Following the finding of the European Court of Human Rights' decision in *V and T v United Kingdom* (1999) 30 EHRR 121 that the Crown Court trial of two 11-year-old boys for murder involved a breach of the right to a fair trial guaranteed by the ECHR, Art 6, a practice note first issued in 2000 and now contained in the *Practice Direction* [2002] 3 All ER 904 (as amended by *Practice Direction* [2007] 1 WLR 1790), III 30.1–30.18 has sought to tackle many of the problems in that case so as to prevent young defendants being avoidably intimidated, humiliated or distressed by the trial process and to assist them to understand and participate in the proceedings.

Mental disability

Key points 15.2

Mental disability on the part of the defendant may affect the outcome of a case in three ways:

- mental disability after the time when the defendant is sent for trial, or when he is brought for trial, may render him unfit to be tried;

- mental disability at the time of the alleged offence by him may give rise to the defence of insanity or (in the case or murder) of diminished responsibility, dealt with in Chapter 8;[16] or

- mental disability at the time of conviction may result in a hospital order under the Mental Health Act 1983, s 37(1) or some other similar order being made, instead of one of the normal types of sentence being imposed.

Unfitness to be tried

15.6 Whether or not the defendant may have the defence of insanity, and therefore even though there may be no doubt that he was sane at the time of his alleged offence,[17] his mental condition may prevent him being tried at all or may result in his trial being suspended, as opposed to being a defence at a trial.

Urgent need for treatment: transfer direction by Secretary of State

15.7 Where there is an urgent need for in-patient psychiatric treatment, the Secretary of State may be able to exercise powers under the Mental Health Act 1983, s 48. Section 48[18] provides that, where a person has been remanded in custody pending trial, the Secretary of State may order his detention in a mental hospital for treatment without trial. The Secretary of State can only make such an order (a 'transfer direction') if satisfied by two medical reports that the defendant is suffering from mental disorder (ie any disorder or disability of the mind) of a nature and degree which makes it appropriate for him to be detained in a hospital for treatment and that he is in urgent need of treatment. When the defendant no longer requires treatment, or effective treatment cannot be given, he can either be returned to prison, or released on bail, to await trial.

---

[16] Paras 8.53–8.72.

[17] The defendant may, for example, have suffered serious brain damage since the offence.

[18] As amended by the Mental Health Act 2007, Sch 1.

The latest available data shows a striking increase in the number of transfer directions: from 77 in 1987 to 494 in 1997.[19]

Unfitness to plead

Key points 15.3

If the issue of fitness to plead is raised at a trial on indictment in the Crown Court, it is for the judge to decide on the evidence whether the defendant is fit to plead.

If the judge finds that the defendant is under a disability (ie unfit to plead) the trial must not proceed or further proceed but it must be determined by a jury whether they are satisfied that the defendant did the act or made the omission charged as the offence.

If the jury are not satisfied that the defendant did the act or made the omission charged in a count in the indictment, they must acquit the defendant in respect of it.

If there have been findings that the defendant is under a disability and that he did the act or made the omission charged, the judge must make one of a number of orders in respect of the defendant.

15.8 When a defendant whose mental condition has not required the making of a transfer direction, or a defendant who has been returned for trial after being subject to such an order, is arraigned in the Crown Court he may be found unfit to plead (or, as it is often put, 'unfit to stand trial').

In recent years the number of findings of unfitness to plead has averaged 66 a year.[20]

Test of fitness to plead

15.9 The issue of fitness to plead may be raised by the defence, the prosecution or the judge.[21] It is for the court without a jury (ie for the judge)[22] to decide on the evidence whether the defendant is capable:

- of understanding the charge, the difference between a plea of guilty and not guilty and the course of the proceedings so as to make a proper defence;
- of challenging a juror to whom he might wish to object;

---

[19] See Mackay and Machin *Transfers from Prison to Hospital – the Operation of s 48 of the Mental Health Act 1983* (Home Office Research, Development and Statistics Directorate: Research Findings No 84). Also see Mackay and Machin 'The Operation of s 48 of the Mental Health Act 1983' (2000) 40 Brit J Criminal 727.

[20] See Mackay, Mitchell and Howe 'A Continued Upturn in Unfitness to Plead – More Disability in Relation to the Trial under the 1991 Act' [2007] Crim LR 530. This shows a continuing increase in the average figure since the late 1980s. It also contains other statistics relating to the operation of the statutory provisions relating to unfitness to plead.

[21] *MacCarthy* [1967] 1 QB 68, CCA.

[22] Criminal Procedure (Insanity) Act 1964, s 4(5) (substituted by the Criminal Procedure (Insanity and Unfitness to Plead) Act 1991, s 2; amended by the Domestic Violence, Crime and Victims Act 2004, s 22).

- of understanding the details of the evidence; and
- of giving evidence.[23]

As can be seen, this test covers not only some people who are mentally disordered but also others, such as deaf mutes, who are incapable of understanding the proceedings or the evidence or of communicating. On the other hand, an attack of hysterical amnesia rendering it impossible for the defendant to remember what happened at the time of the events in respect of which he is charged has been held not to make him unfit to plead.[24] In such a case, there is no difficulty for the defendant in understanding the proceedings or the evidence, or the difference between a plea of guilty and one of not guilty, or in communicating, although his lack of memory may make it difficult for him to decide whether to plead guilty or not guilty. Likewise, if a defendant is capable of understanding the charge, the difference between a plea of guilty and not guilty, and the course of proceedings so as to make a defence, and is capable of challenging a juror, of understanding the details of evidence and of giving evidence, he is fit to plead, even though he:

- is not capable of acting in his best interests (eg by pleading guilty when it seems unlikely that he is);[25] or
- lacks the ability to make choices and decisions about the conduct of his case as the trial proceeds (eg about whether to allow a relevant line of defence to be run); or
- has delusions about the court's powers of sentence, or its objectivity, or as to evil influences thought to be present in the proceedings.[26]

It would be better if English law adopted an 'effective participation' test along the lines of a concept developed by the European Court of Human Rights, principally in the context of young children in the criminal process.[27] That concept refers to the capacity to participate effectively in the criminal process. In this respect, the test laid down in the law of Jersey in 2003 has much to commend it. Under this test, in determining fitness to plead, the judge should have regard to the ability of the defendant:

- to understand the nature of the proceedings so as to instruct his lawyer and to make a proper defence;
- to understand the substance of the evidence;
- to give evidence on his own behalf;
- to make rational decisions in relation to his participation in the proceedings, including whether or not to plead guilty, which reflect true and informed choices on his part.[28]

---

[23] *Pritchard* (1836) 7 C & P 303; *Berry* (1977) 66 Cr App Rep 156, CA; *Robertson* [1968] 3 All ER 557, CA; *M* [2003] EWCA Crim 3452. For criticism of this test by a psychiatrist, see Grubin 'What Constitutes Fitness to Plead?' [1993] Crim LR 748.

[24] *Podola* [1960] 1 QB 325, CCA.   [25] *Robertson* [1968] 3 All ER 557, CA.

[26] *Moyle* [2008] EWCA Crim 3059.

[27] See, in particular, *V and T v United Kingdom* (1999) 30 EHRR 121, ECtHR; para 15.4, n 15.

[28] See Mackay 'On Being Insane in Jersey Part Three – The Case of *Attorney-General v O'Driscoll*' [2004] Crim LR 291. See also the recommendations of the Scottish Law Commission *Report on Insanity and Diminished Responsibility* (Scot Law Com No 195), Ch 4 and draft Bill, Ch 4.

Where the defendant or the judge has raised the issue of unfitness to plead the defendant has the persuasive burden of proving his unfitness, although he only has to prove his unfitness on the balance of probabilities.[29] However, if the issue is raised by the prosecution it must be established by the prosecution beyond reasonable doubt.[30]

Procedural rules relating to determination of fitness to plead

15.10 Where the issue of fitness to plead is raised, the procedure is governed by the Criminal Procedure (Insanity) Act 1964, s 4.[31] The issue does not have to be determined as soon as it is raised. This is because, to prevent the defendant being found unfit and deprived of his right to trial where he may be entitled to acquittal of the offence charged, the Criminal Procedure (Insanity) Act 1964, s 4(2) provides that the judge has a discretion to postpone the question of fitness to be tried until any time up to the opening of the case for the defence, where he considers it expedient to do so and in the interests of the defendant. The prosecution case may be so strong, and the defendant's condition so disabling, that postponement of the trial would be wholly inexpedient. Conversely, the prosecution case may be so thin that, whatever the degree of disability, it clearly would be expedient to postpone.[32] If there is a reasonable chance that the prosecution case will be successfully challenged, postponement will usually be in the defendant's interests.[33]

Where the issue of fitness to plead is postponed the trial will proceed in the normal way. If at the end of the prosecution evidence there is no case to answer, the jury will be directed to acquit the defendant and the issue of fitness will not be determined. If there is a case to answer, the postponed issue of fitness will be determined by the judge before the defence case is opened.

The judge must not make a determination that the defendant is unfit to plead except on the evidence of two or more registered medical practitioners, at least one of whom is a specialist approved by the Secretary of State.[34]

Determination of whether person found unfit to plead did act or made omission charged

15.11 The Criminal Procedure (Insanity) Act 1964, s 4A[35] lays down the procedure which applies where it is determined by the judge that the defendant is unfit to plead (a finding of disability). It provides that the trial must not proceed or further proceed but it must be determined by a jury (the jury by whom the defendant was being tried, if the

---

[29] *Podola* [1960] 1 QB 325, CCA.   [30] *Robertson* [1968] 3 All ER 557, CA.

[31] As substituted by the Criminal Procedure (Insanity and Unfitness to Plead) Act 1991.

[32] *Burles* [1970] 2 QB 191, CA.   [33] *Webb* [1969] 2 QB 278, CA.

[34] Criminal Procedure (Insanity) Act 1964, s 4(6) (as amended by the Domestic Violence, Crime and Victims Act 2004, s 22), as interpreted in *Ghulam* [2009] EWCA Crim 2285. Section 4(6) does not, therefore, prevent the judge determining that the defendant is fit to plead in the absence of the medical evidence referred to in s 4(6): *Ghulam*.

[35] As substituted by the Criminal Procedure (Insanity and Unfitness to Plead) Act 1991, s 2 and amended by the Domestic Violence, Crime and Victims Act 2004, s 22.

issue of fitness to plead was postponed)[36] whether they are satisfied, as respects the count or each of the counts against the defendant, 'that he did the act or made the omission charged as the offence'.[37] It was held by the House of Lords in *Antoine*,[38] that this means that the jury need only be satisfied that the defendant committed the *actus reus* of the offence, and not whether he did so with the *mens rea* for it; they do not have to consider that issue.[39] On the other hand, surprisingly, the House held that, if 'objective' evidence raises the issue of mistake, accident, self-defence or involuntariness, the jury should not find that the defendant has done the act or made the omission charged unless they are satisfied that the prosecution has disproved that 'defence'. Evidence of mistake or accident seems to be relevant only to the question of whether a defendant had the *mens rea* required for an offence.

Defences which arise only on proof of *actus reus* and *mens rea*, such as diminished responsibility and loss of control on murder charges,[40] are not available when the jury considers whether the defendant did the act or made the omission charged.[41]

The normal rules of criminal evidence and procedure apply to the question of whether the defendant did the act or made the omission charged.[42] So does the normal criminal standard of proof (beyond reasonable doubt).[43] If it is proved that the defendant did the act or made the omission charged, the jury must make a finding to this effect.[44]

Such a finding is not a conviction; the purpose of the availability of the finding is to strike a fair balance between the need to protect a defendant who has not committed the *actus reus* of the offence charged and is unfit to plead and the need to protect the

---

[36] Criminal Procedure (Insanity) Act 1964, s 4A(5) (substituted by the Domestic Violence, Crime and Victims Act 2004, s 22).

[37] Criminal Procedure (Insanity) Act 1964, s 4A(2). This determination must be made on the evidence (if any) already given at the trial, and on any evidence or further evidence adduced by the prosecution or adduced by a person appointed by the judge to put the defendant's case: ibid.

[38] [2001] 1 AC 340, HL.

[39] [2001] 1 AC 340, HL. As recognised in *R (on the application of Young) v Central Criminal Court* [2002] EWHC 548 (Admin), DC, the *actus reus* itself may contain an element in which the defendant's intention is an essential ingredient (see Key Points 2.1, n 10). In such a case, the jury will have to consider the defendant's intentions in the relevant respect in order to decide whether or not he committed the *actus reus*. In *M* [2003] EWCA Crim 357, the Court of Appeal held obiter that, where the 'act' in respect of which the jury is asked to make its finding is the act of participation in a joint criminal venture, it would have to be determined whether there was a common purpose and what it was, and whether the act of the perpetrator went outside its scope; and that in such a case, as with issues such as mistake, the determination will fall to be made as a matter of inference from the independent evidence of witnesses and not from the evidence of the defendant or the suggestions of counsel.

[40] Paras 8.53 and 8.77, respectively.

[41] *Antoine* above (diminished responsibility); *Grant* [2001] EWCA Crim 2611 (provocation: this defence will be abolished and replaced by the defence of loss of control when the relevant provisions of the Coroners and Justice Act 2009 are brought into force on 4 October 2010).

[42] *Chal* [2007] EWCA Crim 2647.

[43] *Antoine* [2001] 1 AC 340 at 375–376, per Lord Hutton; *R (on the application of Young) v Central Criminal Court* [2002] EWHC 548 (Admin) at [38]; *Chal* [2007] EWCA Crim 2647 at [25].

[44] Criminal Procedure (Insanity) Act 1964, s 4A(3).

public from a defendant who has committed an act or made an omission which would have constituted an offence if done with the requisite *mens rea*.[45]

If the jury are not satisfied that the defendant did the act or made the omission charged in a count in the indictment, they must acquit the defendant in respect of it.[46]

15.12 Because it cannot result in a conviction and because any order made following a finding adverse to the defendant is not punitive but is made only for the purpose of protecting the public, the procedure under s 4A for determining whether the defendant did the act or made the omission charged does not involve the determination of a criminal charge. Therefore, the procedure is not incompatible with the ECHR, Article 6 (right to a fair trial).[47]

Orders available if defendant found unfit to plead and to have done act or omission charged

15.13 The Criminal Procedure (Insanity) Act 1964, s 5, as substituted by the Domestic Violence, Crime and Victims Act 2004, s 24, provides that, where there have been findings that the defendant is under a disability (ie unfit to plead) and that he did the act or made the omission charged, the judge must make in respect of the defendant:

- a hospital order (with or without a restriction order);
- a supervision order; or
- an order for his absolute discharge.

Where the finding relates to a murder charge and the judge has power to make a hospital order, the judge has no choice; the judge must make a hospital order. A hospital order may be made with or without an additional direction restricting discharge from hospital, except where the finding relates to murder and a hospital order is made (in which case an order restricting discharge without limit of time, ie indefinite hospitalisation, must be made).[48] For further detail, see para 15.38. Because the judge only has power to make a hospital order if satisfied that the defendant is suffering from mental disorder such that detention in a hospital is appropriate and the most suitable method of disposing of the case, the effect of the provision relating to murder is that the judge is not obliged to make a hospital order in a murder case where the defendant's unfitness to plead is due to something other than mental disorder, as in the case of a deaf mute. Under the law which applied before the substitution of s 5 the judge had to make a hospital order (with a restriction order) in any murder case where the defendant was found to be unfit to plead

---

[45] *Antoine* [2001] 1 AC 340 at 375, per Lord Hutton.
[46] Criminal Procedure (Insanity) Act 1964, s 4A(4).   [47] *H* [2003] UKHL 1.
[48] The number of cases where unfitness to plead has been found remains relatively small, although it is gradually increasing (see n 20), despite the fact that the judges have shown a willingness to make use of their powers to make orders which do not involve hospitalisation for an indefinite period. In the period 1997–2001, there were 329 findings of unfitness to plead; in only 120 of those cases was a restriction order made without limitation of time: see the article by Mackay, Mitchell and Howe cited in n 20 for the full statistics.

and to have done the act or omission charged, even if the defendant was not suffering from a mental disorder warranting compulsory confinement. In *Grant*,[49] the Court of Appeal expressed concern that this might be a breach of the ECHR, Article 5(1)(e);[50] the change to s 5 means that it is compatible with Article 5(1)(e) in the present respect.

Appeal

15.14 The defendant has a right of appeal under the Criminal Appeal Act 1968 to the Court of Appeal against findings that he is under a disability (ie unfit to plead) and that he did the act or made the omission charged.[51] This right is subject to the same conditions as apply to other criminal appeals from the Crown Court generally. Where the Court allows an appeal against a finding that the defendant did the act or made the omission charged it must quash the finding and direct that a verdict of acquittal be recorded.[52] There is no power under the Criminal Appeal Act 1968 to order a retrial.[53] This has been criticised by the Court of Appeal on the ground that there could well be cases where the public interest would not be protected if it considered that such a finding was unsafe and was compelled to direct an acquittal, but nothing further could be done.[54]

Magistrates' courts[55]

15.15 The Criminal Procedure (Insanity) Act 1964, ss 4, 4A and 5 only apply to trials on indictment.[56] There is no procedure expressly devised for the question of fitness to plead in relation to magistrates' courts; in particular, magistrates dealing with a summary-only offence have no power to send a defendant to the Crown Court for a judge to decide his fitness to plead under the procedure in s 4. However, where the offence is punishable with imprisonment and the defendant is suffering from mental disorder (ie any disorder or disability of the mind) and appears unfit to plead, and provided that the offence charged is not triable only on indictment,[57] the magistrates may make use of their power under the Mental Health Act 1983, s 37(3)[58] to make a hospital order or a guardianship order without proceeding to a trial or conviction, if they are satisfied that he 'did the act or made the omission charged'.[59] This phrase doubtless has the same meaning as under the

---

[49] [2001] EWCA Crim 2611.   [50] Para 15.47.

[51] Criminal Appeal Act 1968, s 15. Section 16 deals with the Court of Appeal's powers of disposal of an appeal.   [52] Criminal Appeal Act 1968, s 16(4).

[53] *Norman* [2008] EWCA Crim 1810 at [31].   [54] *Norman* [2008] EWCA Crim 1810 at [34].

[55] Including youth courts. See *R (on the application of P (a juvenile)) v Barking Youth Court* [2002] EWHC 734 (Admin), DC.

[56] *Metropolitan Stipendiary Magistrate, ex p Aniifowosi* (1985) 149 JP 748, DC.

[57] The power under the Mental Health Act 1983, s 37(3) applies whether the offence charged is purely summary or triable either way, but the wording of the provision precludes it applying where the offence is triable only on indictment: *Chippenham Magistrates' Court, ex p Thompson* (1995) 160 JP 207, DC.

[58] As amended by the Mental Health Act 2007, Sch 1.

[59] *Lincolnshire (Kesteven) Justices, ex p O'Connor* [1983] 1 All ER 901, DC.

Criminal Procedure (Insanity) Act 1964, s 4A,[60] viz the magistrates must be satisfied simply that the defendant committed the *actus reus* of the offence charged. Where there is an apparent case that the defendant is unfit to plead, the magistrates should first determine whether the defendant did the act or made the omission charged, and then consider whether a s 37(3) order is appropriate.[61] An order under s 37(3) will only be made after medical evidence has been considered. Where the offence is punishable by imprisonment, the case can be adjourned so that the necessary medical reports can be prepared.[62] Before exercising the power under s 37(3) the court should invite submissions on the course to be adopted.[63]

Defence of insanity

> **Key points 15.4**
>
> Everyone is presumed sane until the contrary is proved.
>
> It is a defence to a criminal prosecution for the defendant to show that he was labouring under such a defect of reason, due to disease of the mind, as either not to know the nature and quality of his act or, if he did know this, not to know that he was doing wrong.
>
> Where the defence is raised by the defendant or the judge, the defendant has the burden of proving these requirements. Sometimes the prosecution can raise the issue of the defendant's insanity, in which case it has the burden of proving the requirements.
>
> If the defence of insanity is made out at a trial in the Crown Court, a special verdict of not guilty by reason of insanity must be returned by the jury and the judge must make one of a number of orders in respect of the defendant. Where the special verdict relates to murder there are special provisions about the type of order.

15.16 The defence of insanity is concerned with the defendant's mental condition at the time of the alleged offence. At that point of time he may have been suffering a permanent or occasional mental malfunction. It would be irrelevant that his mental condition is perfectly normal at the time of the trial.

The defence of insanity is contained in the *M'Naghten Rules*. **The defence is concerned with the defendant's legal responsibility at the time of his alleged offence, and not simply with whether he was medically insane at that time.** In other words, it is concerned with insanity in a legal sense, and not in a medical sense. What the law regards as insanity may be far removed from what would be regarded as insanity by a doctor. The issue of

---

[60] Para 15.11.   [61] *R (on the application of P) v Barking Youth Court* [2002] EWHC 734 (Admin), DC.

[62] Powers of Criminal Courts (Sentencing) Act 2000, s 11.

[63] *R (on the application of Singh) v Stratford Magistrates' Court* [2007] EWHC 1582 (Admin), DC; *Lincolnshire (Kesteven) Justices, ex p O'Connor* [1983] 1 All ER 901, DC.

whether the defendant has the defence of insanity is a matter for the jury (in the Crown Court) to decide in the light of the medical and other evidence.[64]

15.17 Mental illness short of insanity under the *M'Naghten Rules* cannot in itself affect the liability of the defendant; the only exception is the offence of murder where it may give rise to the partial defence of diminished responsibility.[65] Mental illness short of insanity under the *M'Naghten Rules* may, however, provide evidence in support of a plea of lack of *mens rea*, and it may be relevant in respect of the defence of loss of control and some of the general defences to criminal liability.

15.18 The *M'Naghten Rules* were laid down by the judges in their advice to the House of Lords in *M'Naghten's Case*.[66] Their advice was sought in consequence of the acquittal of M'Naghten, who was found to be insane on a charge of murdering Sir Robert Peel's private secretary. Although the rules were not laid down in a case decided by the House of Lords, they have been recognised again and again as representing the present law.

The *M'Naghten Rules* can be summarised thus:

> - Everyone is presumed sane until the contrary is proved.
> - It is a defence to a criminal prosecution for the defendant to show that he was labouring under such a defect of reason, due to disease of the mind, as either not to know the nature and quality of his act or, if he did know this, not to know that he was doing wrong. The defence involves an 'all-or-nothing' test, unlike the defence of diminished responsibility which involves a question of degree as to whether there has been *substantial* impairment in the requisite respect arising from mental abnormality.

As noted in Chapter 4, **when the defence of insanity is pleaded by the defendant the persuasive burden of proof is exceptionally on him,**[67] but he may rebut the presumption of sanity by adducing evidence which satisfies the jury on the balance of probabilities that he was insane within the terms of the *M'Naghten Rules* when he committed the alleged offence.[68] **The same is true if the judge rules that the defendant is raising the defence of insanity.** The effect of the defence being left to the jury in these two cases is to remove from the prosecution the normal need to prove that the defendant voluntarily committed the *actus reus* of the offence with the required *mens rea*. Placing the persuasive burden of proof on the defendant means that, even though there is credible evidence in support of the insanity defence, a defendant will fail to prove it if the jury consider that it is slightly less probable than not (or, even, as probable as not) that he was legally insane. This is anomalous[69] and is arguably incompatible with the presumption of innocence under the

---

[64] See, for example, *Roach* [2001] EWCA Crim 2698.
[65] Para 8.53.   [66] (1843) 10 Cl & Fin 200.
[67] *M'Naghten* (1843) 10 Cl & Fin 200; *Woolmington v DPP* [1935] AC 462, HL; *Sodeman v R* [1936] 2 All ER 1138, PC; para 4.7.
[68] *Sodeman v R* [1936] 2 All ER 1138, PC; para 4.5.
[69] See Jones 'Insanity, Automatism and the Burden of Proof' (1995) 111 LQR 475.

ECHR, Article 6(2).[70] In the case of other general defences, the defendant merely bears the burden of adducing evidence sufficient to raise a particular defence, and there is no reason why someone who pleads insanity should be any worse off.

15.19 Where the medical evidence is clear, unanimous and unchallenged to the effect that the defendant was legally insane and there is no other evidence justifying the jury in rejecting it, a verdict of guilty will be set aside on appeal on the ground that no reasonable jury could have reached such a verdict.[71] On the other hand, a conviction will not be quashed merely because the jury chose to disagree with expert medical opinion[72] or because the medical evidence tends to support the defence, if there is other evidence to the contrary.[73]

Role of the judge

15.20 If the defendant puts his state of mind in issue and there is medical evidence relating to it, it is irrelevant whether or not he expressly pleads the defence of insanity. The reason is that whether or not he has raised that defence is a question of law for the judge in the light of the medical evidence.[74] The medical evidence may indicate the factual nature of the defendant's mental condition but it is for the judge to say whether that is evidence of a defect of reason from disease of the mind. If the judge concludes that there is medical evidence in support of *all* the elements of the *M'Naghten Rules*, he may rule that the defendant is raising the defence of insanity and leave it to the jury to decide whether or not those elements are actually satisfied, despite objections by the defence.[75] In *Dickie*,[76] the Court of Appeal held that the 'circumstances in which a judge will do that will be exceptional and very rare'. If the judge decides to leave the defence of insanity to the jury, he must give counsel on both sides the chance to call evidence on the point before so leaving it.[77] The judge's power to rule that evidence which is not expressly introduced

---

[70] Para 4.8. However, placing the persuasive burden on the defendant may be justified as a proportionate interference with the presumption of innocence because of the practical difficulties of disproof if the persuasive burden was on the prosecution and the need to deal with the problem of false claims of mental disorder. It has been held that placing the persuasive burden on the defendant in respect of diminished responsibility is not incompatible with Art 6(2): see para 8.61. This suggests that a challenge to the present rule would probably fail. In *Chaulk* (1990) 2 CR (4th) 1, SC of Canada, it was held that the reverse burden imposed by the insanity defence was a justified interference with the presumption of innocence under the Canadian Charter of Rights and Freedoms.

[71] This statement is made by analogy with the rule applying to the defence of diminished responsibility: see para 8.70.

[72] *Rivett* (1950) 34 Cr App Rep 87, CCA.   [73] *Latham* [1965] Crim LR 434, CCA.

[74] *Kemp* [1957] 1 QB 399; *Bratty v A-G for Northern Ireland* [1963] AC 386 at 411, per Lord Denning; *Dickie* [1984] 3 All ER 173, CA; *Hennessy* [1989] 2 All ER 9 at 12–13; *Thomas* (1996) 29 BMLR 120, CA. *Charlson* [1955] 1 All ER 859 which is to the contrary (see para 15.58), must now be taken to be wrongly decided, although it has not been expressly overruled. See further, para 15.58.

[75] *Dickie* [1984] 3 All ER 173 at 178; *Thomas* (1996) 29 BMLR 120, CA.

[76] [1984] 3 All ER 173 at 178.   [77] [1984] 3 All ER 173 at 178.

in support of a defence of insanity does in fact raise that defence is of great practical importance, as explained in para 15.41.

The above power does not mean that the judge can seek out further evidence. On the other hand, if he has doubts on the evidence before him, he can seek clarification from the witnesses to enable him to reach a conclusion on that evidence.

Requirements of the defence

Defect of reason

15.21 The defendant must prove that he was suffering from a 'defect of reason' due to disease of the mind when he did the prohibited act. **A 'defect of reason' is more than a momentary confusion or absent-mindedness; a deprivation of reasoning power is required.**[78] In *Clarke*,[79] D was charged with theft by shoplifting. Her defence was that she had no intention to steal but had acted in a moment of absent-mindedness caused by a diabetic depression induced by sugar deficiency. The trial judge ruled that D's defence was one of insanity because she was pleading a defect of reason due to disease of the mind. D did not wish to be found insane and changed her plea to one of guilty. The Court of Appeal, allowing her appeal against conviction, held that D's defence was simply one of lack of *mens rea* and not a defence of insanity, since temporary absent-mindedness due to disease was not a defect of reason due to disease. 'Defect of reason', it held, meant the deprivation of reasoning power; it did not cover people who retain their reasoning power but in moments of confusion or absent-mindedness fail to use it fully. Nor does the term cover those who act under an irresistible impulse or some other defective emotional or volitional state. A defect of reason does not have to be a continuing aspect of the defendant's mental make-up; it may simply be short-lived, as in the case of a blackout.

Disease of the mind

15.22 The defendant must prove that he was suffering from a defect of reason due to a 'disease of the mind' (in the legal sense[80] of that term)[81] at the material time. **The disease must be of the mind; it need not be of the brain.**[82] The meaning of 'disease of the mind' was explained by the House of Lords in *Sullivan*,[83] where the view taken in previous cases[84] was endorsed. Lord Diplock, with whose speech the rest of their Lordships agreed, stated the law as follows:

> 'The nomenclature adopted by the medical profession may change from time to time... But the meaning of the expression "disease of the mind"... remains unchanged for the

---

[78] *Clarke* [1972] 1 All ER 219, CA.   [79] [1972] 1 All ER 219, CA.
[80] 'Disease of the mind' has no agreed psychiatric meaning.
[81] See, for instance, *Sullivan* [1984] AC 156 at 172, per Lord Diplock.
[82] *Kemp* [1957] 1 QB 399; *Burgess* [1991] 2 QB 92, CA.
[83] [1984] AC 156, HL.   [84] Eg *Kemp* [1957] 1 QB 399; *Quick* [1973] QB 910, CA.

purposes of the application of the *M'Naghten Rules*…"Mind" in the *M'Naghten Rules* is used in the ordinary sense of the mental faculties of reason, memory and understanding. If the effect of a disease is to impair these faculties…it matters not whether the aetiology [ie assignment of the cause] of the impairment is organic, as in epilepsy [or arteriosclerosis or brain tumours], or functional [as in the case of schizophrenia, paranoia or manic depression], or whether the impairment itself is permanent or is transient and intermittent, provided it subsisted at the time of the commission of the act.'[85]

To this one may add that it is irrelevant whether the condition of the mind is curable or incurable.[86]

15.23 **The requirement that there must be an impairment of the mental faculties of reason, memory and understanding and that that mental impairment should be caused by disease must be stressed.** The distinction between mental impairment due to disease and mental impairment not due to disease is now established as being between internal and external causes. **For the mental impairment to be due to disease, the immediate cause of the impairment must be internal to the defendant.**[87] 'A malfunctioning of the mind of transitory effect caused by the application to the body of some external factor such as violence, drugs, including anaesthetics, alcohol and hypnotic influences cannot fairly be said to be due to disease' and does not constitute a disease of the mind.[88] The same is true where a woman suffers a state of dissociation resulting (as post-traumatic stress disorder) from being raped[89] or where a diabetic gets into a hypoglycaemic coma as a result of failing to take food after taking insulin (since the consequent effect of the insulin is due to an external factor).[90] It would be different if a diabetic failed to take his insulin and got into a hyperglycaemic coma as a result, because it would be the diabetes itself (an internal factor) which would have caused the coma.[91] The distinction which the law draws between hypoglycaemia (not a disease of the mind) and hyperglycaemia (disease of the mind) is not easy to defend. Why should a distinction be drawn between a diabetic who gets into a hypoglycaemic coma as a result of taking too much insulin or failing to eat adequately after taking the correct dose and a diabetic who gets into a hyperglycaemic coma as a result of not taking his insulin?

---

[85] [1984] AC 156 at 172.   [86] *Kemp* [1957] 1 QB 399 at 407.

[87] *Quick* [1973] QB 910, CA; *Sullivan* [1984] AC 156, HL; *Burgess* [1991] 2 QB 92, CA; *Roach* [2001] EWCA Crim 2698. Where an underlying mental condition which would not otherwise produce a disease of the mind sufficient to satisfy the other parts of the *M'Naghten Rules* is aggravated by external factors so that the defendant has a defect of reason such that he does not know the nature and quality of his act (or that it is wrong), this does not bring the Rules into play: see *A-G for Northern Ireland v Gallagher* [1963] AC 349, HL (para 15.98); *Roach* [2001] EWCA Crim 2698 (para 15.61).

[88] *Quick* [1973] QB 910, CA; *Sullivan* [1984] AC 156 at 172, per Lord Diplock.

[89] *T* [1990] Crim LR 256, Crown Ct.

[90] *Quick* [1973] QB 910, CA. See also *Bingham* [1991] Crim LR 433, CA.

[91] *Hennessy* [1989] 2 All ER 9, CA; para 15.59. Diabetes is a deficiency in the system of the production of the hormone insulin which balances the sugar metabolism. In the absence of that hormone the blood sugar rises and that results in hyperglycaemia and ultimately a hyperglycaemic coma. If a diabetic takes too much insulin to treat his hormonal deficiency, or fails to eat adequately after taking the correct dose in order to counterbalance it, the blood sugar may fall too far and hypoglycaemia and ultimately a hypoglycaemic coma may result.

15.24 In *Bratty v A-G for Northern Ireland*,[92] Lord Denning said: 'It seems to me that any mental disorder which has manifested itself in violence and is prone to recur is a disease of the mind'. However, a significant rider was placed on Lord Denning's statement by the Court of Appeal in *Burgess*,[93] where it was stated that, while the fact that there is a danger of recurrence may be an added reason for categorising a condition as a disease of the mind, the absence of the danger of recurrence is not a reason for saying that it cannot be a disease of the mind.

The rider in *Burgess* is one reason why Lord Denning's statement in *Bratty* should be regarded as misleading. A second reason is that, as pointed out in *Quick*,[94] the statement wrongly suggests that it would be irrelevant that the immediate cause of the mental disorder was an external one. A third reason is that the reference to 'violence' in the statement must not be read as an indication that the defence of insanity is limited to offences of violence. There is no suggestion that it is so limited in the other cases on the defence and it has long been accepted that insanity is generally a defence to a criminal charge. In the light of these comments, Lord Denning's statement seems of little value.

15.25 The distinction between mental impairment due to disease (ie due to an internal cause) and mental impairment not due to disease (ie due to an external cause) is not always easy to draw, as was pointed out by the Court of Appeal in *Burgess*,[95] where D had claimed that he had been sleepwalking when he wounded a woman. There was medical evidence indicating that D's actions had occurred during the course of a sleep disorder due to an internal factor. The Court of Appeal held that the judge had been correct to rule that, on any view of the medical evidence, it amounted to evidence of insanity within the *M'Naghten Rules* because that evidence indicated that the sleepwalking was due to an internal factor. This decision does not deny that sleepwalking due to an external factor (such as excess alcohol) would be non-insane automatism,[96] but it is probably rare for sleepwalking to have as its immediate cause an external factor.[97] It is noteworthy that the Supreme Court of Canada in *Parks*[98] concluded that somnambulism is not suitable to the internal/external factor approach alone and held that the sleepwalking in question in that case was not due to a disease of the mind, although it did not rule out the possibility of a finding of insanity in a sleepwalking case where the facts were different.

15.26 The difficulty in distinguishing between mental impairment due to disease (internal cause) and mental impairment not due to disease (external cause) is shown by reference to cases concerned with whether a dissociative state resulting from a psychological

---

[92] [1963] AC 386 at 412.   [93] [1991] 2 QB 92, CA.   [94] [1973] QB 910, CA.

[95] [1991] 2 QB 92, CA. See Mackay 'The Sleepwalker is Not Insane' (1992) 55 MLR 714.

[96] As in the Scottish case of *Finegan v Heywood* [2000] SCCR 648, HCJ Appeal. As to non-insane automatism induced by intoxication, see para 15.64.

[97] In *Pooley* (2007) unreported, referred to by Mackay 'Epilepsy and the Defence of Insanity – A Time for Change?' [2007] Crim LR 782 at 791, a Crown Court case involving the issue of sleepwalking precipitated by alcohol consumption and environmental change, the Circuit judge dealt with the matter as one of non-insane automatism, stating that: 'Concurrent causes can allow for the defence of non-insane automatism to be left to the jury even if one of the concurrent causes is self-induced intoxication.'

[98] (1990) 95 DLR (4th) 27.

blow can amount to a disease of the mind. In the Canadian case of *Rabey*,[99] which was considered by the Court of Appeal in *Burgess*, the majority of the Supreme Court of Canada approved the view of Martin J in the Ontario Court of Appeal that the mental impairment of a person, who acted under a dissociative state consequent on the psychological blow of his rejection by a girl with whom he was infatuated, was due to an internal cause; the psychological blow was not to be equated with an external cause such as concussion. The Court of Appeal in *Burgess* referred approvingly to Martin J's statement that:

> '[T]he ordinary stresses and disappointments of life which are the common lot of mankind do not constitute an external cause constituting an explanation for a malfunctioning of the mind which takes it out of the category of a disease of the mind.'

Martin J went on to say that the reason was that the exceptional effect which this ordinary event had on the defendant had to be considered as having its source primarily in the defendant's psychological make-up. Martin J did not say what would be the legal effect of an extraordinary event of such severity that it might reasonably be expected to cause a dissociative state in a reasonable person. The point was dealt with by the Crown Court in *T*,[100] where the judge held that a state of dissociation resulting (as post-traumatic stress) from being raped was due to an external cause, and was therefore not due to a disease of the mind. Clearly, the cause of the dissociative state here fell outside the ordinary stresses of life; it could not be said to have its source in the defendant's psychological make-up but, instead, its immediate cause was external, ie the rape.

Ignorance of nature and quality of act or that it is wrong

15.27 The defect of reason due to disease of the mind must affect legal responsibility,[101] something to which a person's capacity to appreciate what he was doing, and whether it was lawful is highly relevant, and **the defendant must go on to prove that because of his defect of reason due to disease of the mind either he did not know the nature and quality of his act or, if he did know this, he did not know he was doing wrong.**

15.28 *'Nature and quality'* The words 'nature and quality' in the *M'Naghten Rules* refer to **the physical character of the act.**[102] The jury must be satisfied that the defendant did not know what he was doing, or did not appreciate the effects of his conduct, or did not realise the material circumstances in which he was acting. An insane person who was acting in a state of automatism would not know the nature and quality of his act,[103] nor would someone who stabbed another with a knife without knowing that he was using the implement at all or under the insane delusion that he was about to be killed by him. The same would be the case where a person cut a sleeper's head off because 'it would be great

---

[99] (1977) 37 CCC (2d) 461. Also see *Hennessy* [1989] 2 All ER 9 at 14.
[100] [1990] Crim LR 256, Crown Ct.   [101] *Rivett* (1950) 34 Cr App Rep 87, CCA.
[102] *Codère* (1916) 12 Cr App Rep 21 at 28.   [103] *Sullivan* [1984] AC 156, HL.

fun to see him looking for it when he woke up'.[104] He would know he was engaged on the act of decapitation, but would be manifestly incapable of appreciating its physical effects. Similarly, if an insane person squeezes someone's throat, thinking that he is squeezing an orange, he does not know the nature and quality of his act. On the other hand, if he kills a boy, mistakenly believing the victim is a girl, he knows the nature and quality of his act since his mistake is not material.

15.29 *'Wrong'* Turning to the alternative limb of the test of responsibility, the jury must be asked whether, assuming the defendant knew what he was doing, he also knew that it was wrong. It was held in *Windle*[105] that **'wrong' in this context means prohibited by law, ie legally wrong**. In *Windle*, D induced his wife, who had frequently spoken of committing suicide, to consume 100 aspirins, because he thought it would be beneficial for her to die. On appeal, it was held that the trial judge was justified in withdrawing the case from the jury on the question of insanity. D had said that he would be hanged for what he had done, and there was no doubt that he knew it was contrary to law.

The High Court of Australia in *Stapleton v R*[106] and the Supreme Court of Canada in *Chaulk*[107] have declined to follow *Windle*, being of the opinion that 'wrong' in the *M'Naghten Rules* means contrary to the moral views of the majority of the members of society. According to this opinion, if Windle had believed his wife to be suffering from a painful incurable illness, and if he had also believed that euthanasia was approved by the bulk of ordinary Englishmen, he ought to have been acquitted even though he knew that mercy killing was prohibited by law.[108] Subsequently, the Supreme Court of Canada in *Oommen*[109] stated that:

> '[T]he inquiry focuses not on general capacity to know right from wrong, but rather on the ability to know that a particular act was wrong in the circumstances. The accused must possess the intellectual ability to know right from wrong in an abstract sense. But he or she must also possess the ability to apply that knowledge in a rational way to the alleged criminal act... Thus the question is not whether, assuming the delusions to be true, a reasonable person would have seen a threat to life and a need for death-threatening force. Rather, the real question is whether the accused should be exempted from criminal responsibility because a mental disorder at the time of the act deprived him of the capacity for rational perception and hence rational choice about the rightness or wrongness of the act.'

As Professor Mackay has commented, this reflects more accurately the true nature of the distorted thought process of those whose psychiatric disorder impacts on their capacity to know right from wrong.[110]

---

[104] Stephen *History of the Criminal Law* Vol II (1883), 166.
[105] [1952] 2 QB 826, CCA. Also see *Holmes* [1953] 2 All ER 324, CCA.
[106] (1952) 86 CLR 358, High Ct of Australia.   [107] (1990) 2 CR (4th) 1, SC of Canada.
[108] Norval Morris '"Wrong" in the M'Naghten Rules'(1953) 16 LR 435.
[109] [1994] 2 SCR 507, SC of Canada.
[110] Mackay 'Righting the Wrong? – Some Observations on the Second Limb of the M'Naghten Rules' [2009] Crim LR 80 at 85.

In *Johnson*,[111] the Court of Appeal stated in 2007 that, while there was room for reconsideration of *Windle*, reconsideration could not properly take place 'before us at this level'; the position in law in England and Wales remains as stated in *Windle*. The 'knowledge of wrong' test as interpreted in *Windle* provides a very narrow ground of exemption since even grossly disturbed persons generally know that murder, for instance, is a crime.[112]

15.30 It appears that *Windle* is not uncommonly ignored in practice by the judges and that little attempt is made in many cases to distinguish between ignorance of legal wrong and ignorance of moral wrong; indeed the 'wrongness' limb has also been interpreted to cover delusional beliefs about being possessed by a deity or the devil, or about the victim being possessed by the devil or the need for self-defence against evil.[113]

15.31 Stephen J, writing in an extra-judicial capacity, once said that the absence of the power of self-control would involve an incapacity to know right from wrong.[114] But this was at a time when it was not clear whether, according to English law, 'wrong' in the *M'Naghten Rules* meant legally wrong or morally wrong.

15.32 There is a significant difference between this limb and the previous one, since a person who did not know the nature and quality of his act for reasons other than a defect of reason due to a disease of the mind will often be entitled to a complete acquittal, and the defence of insanity in such a case merely results in a different verdict being returned in the Crown Court. On the other hand, ignorance of law is normally no excuse, but it becomes an excuse if it results from a defect of reason due to disease of the mind.

Medical evidence

15.33 It is for the jury, not medical witnesses, to determine whether the requirements for the defence of insanity have been satisfied after a proper direction from the judge,[115] but they may not acquit on the ground of insanity except on the evidence of two or more registered medical practitioners, at least one of whom is a specialist approved by the Secretary of State.[116]

The redundant statement in M'Naghten

15.34 In their advice in *M'Naghten's Case*,[117] the judges stated that, where someone commits a criminal act under an insane delusion, he is under the same degree of responsibility

---

[111] [2007] EWCA Crim 1978.

[112] *Report of the Committee on Mentally Abnormal Offenders* (the Butler Committee), Cmnd 6244 (1975), para 18.8.

[113] Mackay *Mental Condition Defences in the Criminal Law* (1995) 104; Mackay and Kearns 'More Fact(s) about the Insanity Defence' [1999] Crim LR 714 at 722–723; Mackay 'Righting the Wrong? – Some Observations on the Second Limb of the M'Naghten Rules' [2009] Crim LR 80 at 83.

[114] *History of the Criminal Law* Vol II (1883), 171.   [115] *Rivett* (1950) 34 Cr App Rep 87, CCA.

[116] Criminal Procedure (Insanity and Unfitness to Plead) Act 1991, s 1.

[117] (1843) 10 Cl & Fin 200.

as he would have been if the facts had been as he imagined them to be. To illustrate this the judges said:

> 'For example, if, under the influence of his delusion, the accused supposes another man to be in the act of attempting to take away his life, and he kills that man, as he supposes in self-defence, he would be exempt from punishment. If his delusion was that the deceased had inflicted a serious injury to his character and fortune, and he killed him in revenge for such supposed injury, he would be liable to punishment.'[118]

This statement is generally regarded as redundant since it merely restates a principle provided by the two tests (knowledge of nature and quality of the act and knowledge of wrong) just mentioned. The statement can also be criticised as defective in that it suggests that if the defendant kills his wife under the insane delusion that he is killing a cat he can be convicted of an offence in relation to a cat, since, said the judges, one who acts under an insane delusion is under the same degree of responsibility as he would have been if his delusion had been true. This clearly cannot be so since the defendant would not have committed any *actus reus* in relation to a cat. A study of the directions made in insanity cases shows that the statement is not referred to. It can safely be ignored.

Applicability

15.35 Traditionally, it has been assumed that the defence of insanity was available on a charge of any offence, with the isolated exception of a few offences, such as those referred to in para 6.6, which are truly ones of absolute liability. Consequently, the decision of the Divisional Court in *DPP v H*[119] in 1997 was a surprise. In that case D had been charged with driving with excess alcohol (contrary to the Road Traffic Act 1988, s 5) and had successfully pleaded the defence of insanity before a magistrates' court. The Divisional Court, however, held that he should have been convicted because that offence was one of strict liability, for which no *mens rea* had to be proved, and the defence of insanity could only succeed where *mens rea* was an essential element of the offence. The only authority relied on in support of this decision was *Horseferry Road Magistrates' Court, ex p K*,[120] where the Divisional Court accepted the proposition that the defence of insanity was based on the absence of *mens rea*. The decision in *DPP v H* involves at least two misconceptions.

First, the *M'Naghten Rules* are not limited to those who lack *mens rea* through a disease of the mind; the knowledge of wrong test is concerned with those who do not lack *mens rea*. Second, automatism is recognised as a defence in terms of offences generally,

---

[118] (1843) 10 Cl & Fin 200 at 211.

[119] [1997] 1 WLR 1406, DC. Discussed by Ward 'Magistrates, Insanity and the Criminal Law' [1997] Crim LR 796 at 800–802.   [120] [1997] QB 23, DC.

including driving offences.[121] The effect of *DPP v H* is that if the cause of automatism is a disease of the mind a defendant cannot plead the defence of insanity, if charged with a strict liability offence not requiring proof of *mens rea*, whereas if his automatism had some other cause he could – according to the present law – rely on the defence of non-insane automatism. The Divisional Court did not refer to either of these points. Perhaps that is why its decision is absurd. The Court failed to offer an adequate explanation for its distinction between strict liability offences requiring no *mens rea* and such offences requiring *mens rea* as to some of their elements (or, indeed, any offence requiring full *mens rea*).

Can the prosecution seek to prove insanity?

15.36 Although the *M'Naghten Rules* are described as the defence of insanity, this is somewhat misleading since it is sometimes possible for the prosecution to call evidence and seek to prove that a defendant who has not pleaded insanity is insane within the *M'Naghten Rules* and therefore not guilty by reason of insanity.

First, the Criminal Procedure (Insanity) Act 1964, s 6 provides that, where, on a trial for murder, the defendant pleads the defence of diminished responsibility, the prosecution may adduce or elicit evidence of insanity. It is for the prosecution to prove the requirements of the defence beyond reasonable doubt.[122]

Second, although the Court of Appeal doubted, obiter, in *Dickie*[123] that the prosecution could raise the issue of insanity, Lord Denning had previously stated the contrary, obiter, in *Bratty v A-G for Northern Ireland*,[124] which was not cited to the Court of Appeal in *Dickie* and which, it is submitted, represents the better view. **According to Lord Denning, if the defendant puts his state of mind in issue, eg by pleading non-insane automatism, it is open to the prosecution to show what his true state of mind was by raising the issue of insanity.**[125] In principle, the prosecution must prove its contention beyond reasonable doubt;[126] Lord Denning's statement in *Bratty*[127] that the prosecution need only prove the defendant's insanity on the balance of probabilities is questionable.

There is a certain paradox in the prosecution seeking an acquittal in the above types of case.

---

[121] See Automatism and other involuntary conduct, below.

[122] *Grant* [1960] Crim LR 424.

[123] [1984] 3 All ER 173, CA.   [124] [1963] AC 386 at 411.

[125] According to the Court of Appeal in *Dickie* [1984] 3 All ER 173, if the prosecution possesses evidence of insanity it must simply make it available to the defence, so that in its discretion the defence may make use of it.

[126] An analogy may be drawn with the rule that, where it alleges that the defendant is unfit to plead, the prosecution must prove this beyond reasonable doubt: *Robertson* [1968] 3 All ER 557, CA.

[127] [1963] AC 386 at 412.

Special verdict, orders and appeal

Special verdict

15.37 The Trial of Lunatics Act 1883, s 2, as amended by the Criminal Procedure (Insanity) Act 1964, s 1, provides that where at the trial of a person for an offence:

> 'it is given in evidence...that he was insane, so as not to be responsible, according to law, for his actions at the time when the act was done or omission made, then, if it appears to the jury...that he did the act or made the omission charged, but was insane as aforesaid when he did or made the same, the jury shall return a special verdict that the accused is not guilty by reason of insanity.'

The requirement that it should appear to the jury that the defendant 'did the act or made the omission charged' before he can be found not guilty by reason of insanity refers to the *actus reus* of the offence. On the other hand, the prosecution does not have to prove that the defendant acted or omitted to act with the requisite *mens rea*; apart from insanity the defendant's state of mind is irrelevant.[128] If the prosecution is unable to prove beyond reasonable doubt that the defendant has committed the *actus reus*, he is entitled to a simple not guilty verdict whether or not he was insane at the material time.[129] Unlike the position under the Criminal Procedure (Insanity) Act 1964, s 4A referred to in para 15.11, which also speaks of the jury being satisfied that the defendant 'did the act or omission charged', the prosecution does not have to disprove evidence that a defendant pleading insanity might have been acting by accident, under a mistake or involuntarily. These go to the heart of insanity under the *M'Naghten Rules*.

Orders

15.38 When the defendant is found not guilty by reason of insanity he does not necessarily go free. Until 1991, he had to be ordered to be detained in a hospital indefinitely until the Home Secretary was satisfied that this was no longer required for the protection of the public. This sometimes led persons accused of offences other than murder to choose to plead guilty if the prosecution raised the issue of insanity, or if the judge ruled that the defendant was raising the defence of insanity. However, the law on this matter was changed by the Criminal Procedure (Insanity and Unfitness to Plead) Act 1991, and then changed again by the Domestic Violence, Crime and Victims Act 2004.

The Criminal Procedure (Insanity) Act 1964, s 5, as substituted by the Domestic Violence, Crime and Victims Act 2004, s 24, now provides that, where a defendant is found not guilty by reason of insanity, the judge must make in respect of the defendant:

---

[128] *A-G's Reference (No 3 of 1998)* [2000] QB 401, CA.
[129] *A-G's Reference (No 3 of 1998)* [2000] QB 401 at 409.

- a hospital order (with or without a restriction order);
- a supervision order; or
- an order for his absolute discharge.[130]

Where the special verdict relates to a murder charge and the judge has power to make a hospital order, the judge has no choice; the judge must make a hospital order.[131] The reference to the power to make a hospital order is a reference to the power to do so under the Mental Health Act 1983, s 37. Section 37[132] provides that the judge has power to make such an order if the defendant *is* suffering from mental disorder (ie any disorder or disability of the mind) which makes detention in a hospital appropriate and the most suitable method for dealing with the defendant.

If a hospital order is made, the defendant is admitted to a hospital or hospital unit selected by the Secretary of State and detained there; it may be a special hospital, such as Broadmoor, or a Regional Secure Unit in a local NHS hospital, but it can be an ordinary mental hospital. If the order is made without restrictions on release, the decision about release is one for the hospital authorities (subject to review by the Mental Health Review Tribunal). However, if the judge considers it necessary in order to protect the public from serious harm, the judge can make an additional order imposing restrictions on discharge from hospital.[133] A restriction order may specify a minimum limit of time for the detention or it may be without limit of time. The Secretary of State and the Mental Health Review Tribunal each have power to terminate either type of restriction order. The effect of the latter type of restriction order is that the defendant will be detained until the Secretary of State or Mental Health Review Tribunal is satisfied that this is no longer required for the protection of the public. In the case of murder, a restriction order without limit of time must be made if a hospital order is made.

The most common orders have been hospital admission orders (now replaced by hospital orders) with a restriction order without limit of time and supervision and treatment orders (now replaced by supervision orders). In the period 1992–96 the former orders were made in 38.6 per cent of cases where a special verdict was returned (just under a quarter of the 38.6 per cent were cases involving a murder charge); the latter orders were made in 40.9 per cent of cases.[134] In the period 1997–2001 the disposals had a marked resemblance to those in the previous period; the former orders were made in 37.5 per cent of cases, and the latter in 41.7 per cent.[135]

---

[130] Criminal Procedure (Insanity) Act 1964, s 5, as substituted by the Domestic Violence, Crime and Victims Act 2004, s 24.

[131] Criminal Procedure (Insanity) Act 1964, s 5.

[132] As amended by the Mental Health Act 2007, Sch 1.

[133] Criminal Procedure (Insanity) Act 1964, s 5.

[134] Mackay and Kearns 'More Fact(s) about the Insanity Defence' [1999] Crim LR 714.

[135] Mackay, Mitchell and Howe 'Yet More Facts about the Insanity Defence' [2006] Crim LR 399. The article contains a number of other valuable statistical analyses about the operation of the insanity defence.

Appeal

15.39 The Criminal Appeal Act 1968, s 12 provides that there may be an appeal to the Court of Appeal against the special verdict of acquittal on the ground of insanity. The right of appeal is subject to the same conditions as apply to criminal appeals from the Crown Court generally.[136] The absence of this right of appeal could cause hardship, for example, in a case where the defendant's defence to a charge of murder, or other offence against the person, was accident, as well as insanity,[137] or in a case in which the defendant pleaded diminished responsibility in answer to a murder charge and was found to be insane.

Use of the M'Naghten Rules

15.40 Cases in which insanity has been expressly raised as a defence have been rare. Partly, this was a reaction until 1991 in respect of any offence in the Crown Court against the prospect of prolonged, even lifelong, detention in a hospital.[138] But it has also reflected the narrow test of legal responsibility under the *M'Naghten Rules* and the existence since the Homicide Act 1957 of the defence to murder of diminished responsibility.[139] Before that Act accused persons generally raised the defence of insanity only in murder cases, but since then a plea of the wider defence of diminished responsibility has traditionally been far more common in such cases[140] because, if that defence succeeds, the defendant may be given a determinate prison sentence (or some other 'normal' sentence).

In a 15-year period commencing in 1975, the special verdict of not guilty by reason of insanity was returned only in respect of 52 accused.[141] The removal by the Criminal Procedure (Insanity and Unfitness to Plead) Act 1991 of mandatory indefinite hospitalisation (except in murder) as a consequence of a verdict of not guilty by reason of insanity has led to an increase in such verdicts. In the first five years (1992–96), there were 44 special verdicts, four of them on murder charges, five attempted murder, 13 offences of wounding or grievous bodily harm contrary to the Offences Against the Person Act 1861, s 18 or s 20, and five of assault occasioning actual bodily harm contrary to the Offences Against the Person Act 1861, s 47.[142] In the second five years (1997–2001), the number of special verdicts rose to 72, seven on murder charges, 16 attempted murder, 13 wounding or grievous bodily harm, and eight assault occasioning actual bodily harm.[143]

---

[136] Criminal Appeal Act 1968, ss 12 and 13.

[137] *Duke* [1963] 1 QB 120, CCA.

[138] A survey published in 1990 revealed that, even when indefinite hospitalisation was mandatory whatever the offence, the consequences of a verdict of not guilty by reason of insanity had not been as severe in many cases as had been thought: Mackay *Mental Condition Defences in the Criminal Law* (1995) 104–105.

[139] Para 8.53.

[140] But see para 8.55 where a recent marked decline in successful pleas of diminished responsibility is noted.

[141] Mackay *Mental Condition Defences in the Criminal Law* (1995) 103.

[142] Mackay and Kearns 'More Fact(s) about the Insanity Defence' [1999] Crim LR 714.

[143] Mackay, Mitchell and Howe 'Yet More Facts about the Insanity Defence' [2006] Crim LR 399.

15.41 The defence of insanity may be raised indirectly by a defendant who has not expressly raised it as a defence. As stated in para 15.20, whether or not medical evidence of a mental condition amounts to evidence of a disease of the mind is a question of law for the judge to decide, and the danger is that, if the defendant pleads that he lacked the necessary *mens rea* (or was an automaton) and relies in support on medical evidence of a mental condition, he is liable to find that the judge rules that that evidence indicates a disease of the mind and that, there being medical evidence in support of all elements of the *M'Naghten Rules*, he is raising the defence of insanity, which alone must be left to the jury. Thus, the defendant cannot avoid the question of insanity being raised by simply describing the medical evidence as evidence of lack of *mens rea* (or of automatism).

An example is provided by *Sullivan*,[144] where the defendant, who was charged with inflicting grievous bodily harm, pleaded that he had acted as a non-insane automaton, adducing evidence that the attack in question had happened during the last stages of a minor epileptic seizure. The trial judge, correctly in the eyes of the House of Lords, ruled that on the evidence before him the defence amounted to one of insanity, rather than non-insane automatism, and that he would only leave the defence of insanity to the jury. At this point, the defendant changed his plea to guilty.

Summary trials

15.42 The *M'Naghten Rules* apply to cases tried in magistrates' courts. This was confirmed by the Divisional Court in *Horseferry Road Magistrates' Court, ex p K*.[145] However, the legislation concerning the special verdict of acquittal, and the results thereof, does not apply. It follows that, if a magistrates' court acquits the defendant on grounds of insanity, it must give an ordinary acquittal, in which case the defendant goes free. This is satisfactory if the interests of the defendant or society do not require protection, but some power is clearly necessary to deal with cases tried by magistrates where the public's or the defendant's interests demand further action. This need is met by the Mental Health Act 1983, s 37(3)[146] under which, when the offence is punishable with imprisonment and the defendant is suffering from mental disorder (ie any disorder or disability of the mind), the magistrates may make a hospital order or guardianship order without proceeding to trial or registering a conviction, if satisfied that the defendant 'did the act or made the omission charged'.[147] Section 37(3) can only apply when the defendant is mentally ill when he appears before the magistrates' court. It is limited to cases where the offence charged is triable only summarily or triable either way; it does not apply where the offence is only triable on indictment.[148]

---

[144] [1984] AC 156, HL.

[145] [1997] QB 23, DC. Discussed by White and Bowen 'Insanity Defences in Summary Trials' (1997) 61 JCL 198; Ward 'Magistrates, Insanity and the Common Law' [1997] Crim LR 796. The point has been confirmed in *DPP v H* (1996) 160 JP 441, DC and more recently in *R (on the application of Singh) v Stratford Magistrates' Court* [2007] EWHC 1582 (Admin), DC.

[146] As amended by the Mental Health Act 2007, Sch 1.   [147] See para 15.15.

[148] *Chippenham Magistrates' Court, ex p Thompson* (1996) 160 JP 207, DC.

Where insanity at the time of the offence (ie under the *M'Naghten Rules*) is in question, the defendant is not entitled to require that a summary trial proceeds and, if insanity is proved, that he be given an acquittal, although he is entitled to have fully considered a submission that there should be a trial.[149] Where a s 37(3) order is a possibility, the magistrates should start by determining whether the defendant has done the act or made the omission charged. If they are not satisfied of this, they must acquit the defendant, whatever concerns they may have about his mental state. If they are satisfied, the magistrates have a discretion whether to proceed to trial if there is good reason to do so; if they do, they have power in an appropriate case to pronounce a conclusion on the issue of insanity, without convicting or acquitting the defendant, provided that the conditions of s 37(3) are met.[150] If, however, it is clear that no s 37(3) order is going to be possible on the medical evidence whatsoever happens, as where the defendant has recovered mentally since the time of the offence, the case must proceed to trial, so that if it is proved that the defendant was insane at the time of the offence he is acquitted, and if he was not and the case is proved, he is convicted.[151]

No causal connection between the offence and the disorder need exist. Section 37(3) is not limited to insanity under the *M'Naghten Rules*, of course, but includes a wide range of mental disorders.

Defects with the *Rules*

15.43 A number of criticisms of the defence of insanity, which was formulated at a time when psychiatry was in its infancy, have been made above. Three more can be added; all of them doubtless relate to matters where policy considerations have predominated.

15.44 First, the *M'Naghten Rules* are limited to cognitive factors, excluding all matters concerning volition or the emotions, and thus make no allowance for so-called 'irresistible impulse', ie an impulse which is difficult, if not impossible to control. If someone knows the nature and quality of his act, and that it is wrong, but acts under an irresistible impulse due to a disease of the mind he has no defence under the *Rules*. It is a matter for debate whether it should be a defence for a person to show that, although he was aware of the nature and quality of his act and knew it to be wrong, he found, owing to insanity, that it was difficult, if not impossible, to prevent himself from doing what he did. Allowance is made for irresistible impulse in a number of Commonwealth and North American jurisdictions and the partial defence of diminished responsibility admits it on a charge of murder. A suggestion that a rule giving a defence to someone who acted under an irresistible impulse while suffering from a defect of reason due to disease of the mind should be grafted on to the *Rules* was repudiated in *Kopsch*.[152] According to his own

---

[149] *R (on the application of Singh) v Stratford Magistrates' Court* [2007] EWHC 1582 (Admin), DC.
[150] *R (on the application of Singh) v Stratford Magistrates' Court* [2007] EWHC 1582 (Admin), DC.
[151] *R (on the application of Singh) v Stratford Magistrates' Court* [2007] EWHC 1582 (Admin), DC.
[152] (1925) 19 Cr App Rep 50, CCA; see also *True* (1922) 16 Cr App Rep 164, CCA; *Flavell* (1926) 19 Cr App Rep 141, CCA; *Sodeman v R* [1936] 2 All ER 1138, PC.

admissions, D killed V by strangling her with his necktie; he said that he had done so at her request. There was evidence that he had acted under the direction of his subconscious mind, and it was argued that the judge should have directed the jury that a person who acts under an impulse which he cannot control is not criminally responsible. This was rejected by the Court of Criminal Appeal as 'a fantastic theory... which if it were to become part of our law would be merely subversive'.[153]

The Privy Council has held that the absence of the power of self-control is not *per se* evidence of incapacity to know the nature and quality of an act or that it is wrong. However, on the facts of a particular case, there may be medical evidence warranting the conclusion that a disease which impairs the defendant's power of self-control also impairs his ability to distinguish right from wrong.[154]

15.45 Second, although delusions which prevent the defendant knowing the nature and quality of his act fall within the *Rules*, other delusions which call into question whether he is a responsible person deserving punishment do not. Examples would be where the defendant believes his victim is persecuting him or is possessed by the devil. Society may need protection from such a defendant, but it seems odd to regard him as legally responsible.[155] As already stated, it appears that in practice this gap in the *Rules* is sometimes ignored and special verdicts are returned in such cases in the Crown Court.[156]

15.46 A third criticism is that it is objectionable that the label of insanity should be applied, and the consequences of the special verdict should follow, in cases (such as where the defendant acted during an epileptic fit or hyperglycaemic coma or while sleepwalking) where the defendant would not be regarded as insane in common – let alone medical – language. It is certainly odd that such people are labelled as insane by the law when the vast majority of people who are regarded medically (and in common parlance) as mentally ill or disordered are not. The incongruity of this has been recognised in the House of Lords and the Court of Appeal, but they have maintained that it does not lie within their power to alter the law in this respect.[157] What is needed is a new method of disposal to deal with people of the above type. While they do not deserve punishment for conduct committed when they were in a mentally impaired state through no fault of theirs, the fact remains that they pose a potential threat to others unless something is done. Until English law provides a satisfactory method of dealing with this threat the present state of the law in this respect can be justified on the basis that it does provide in the Crown Court a way, through the orders that can be made after verdict of not guilty by reason of insanity, of protecting others and of helping and supporting the defendant.

15.47 The law on the insanity defence appears to be out of line with the ECHR, Article 5(1)(e) where a hospital order is made. Article 5(1)(e) provides, as an exception to

---

[153] (1925) 19 Cr App Rep 50 at 51.

[154] *A-G for State of South Australia v Brown* [1960] AC 432, PC.

[155] See Howard 'Reform of the Insanity Defence: Theoretical Issues' (2003) 67 JCL 51.

[156] Para 15.30.

[157] *Sullivan* [1984] AC 156 at 173, per Lord Diplock; *Burgess* [1991] 2 QB 92 at 102.

the general prohibition on the deprivation of liberty in Article 5, that 'persons of unsound mind' may 'lawfully be detained in accordance with a procedure prescribed by law'. In *Winterwerp v Netherlands*,[158] the European Court of Human Rights interpreted this provision as involving three requirements:

- *There must be a strong correlation between the legal and medical criteria used to assess the issue of 'unsound mind'* This is not the case in respect of epilepsy, hyperglycaemia or sleepwalking.

- *The court's decision must be based on 'objective medical expertise'* Although an insanity verdict cannot be returned except on the evidence of two or more doctors,[159] that evidence only has to be considered by the jury; it does not have binding force.[160]

- *The court must decide that the mental disorder is 'of a kind or degree warranting compulsory confinement'* Under the law which applied before the substitution of the Criminal Procedure (Insanity) Act 1964, s 5 the judge had to make a hospital admission order (with a restriction order) in any case where the defendant was found to be not guilty of murder by reason of insanity. This was at odds with this requirement. As it now is s 5 is compatible with this requirement.[161]

Proposals for reform

15.48 The draft Criminal Code Bill[162] incorporates, with some adaptation, proposals for reform made by the Butler Committee on Mentally Abnormal Offenders.[163]

The draft Bill provides:

- a new special verdict, 'not guilty on evidence of mental disorder'. The power to give this verdict would be extended to magistrates' courts; and

- two alternative grounds (set out in cll 35 and 36) for the verdict of not guilty on evidence of mental disorder.

By cl 35, a mental disorder verdict could be returned if the defendant was proved to have committed an offence but it was proved on the balance of probabilities (whether by the prosecution or by the defendant) that the defendant was at the time suffering from severe mental illness or severe mental handicap. This would not apply if the jury or magistrates were satisfied beyond reasonable doubt that the offence was not attributable to the severe mental illness or severe mental handicap. This provision would extend the law considerably. It covers not only cases at present covered by the 'knowledge of wrong'

---

[158] (1979) 2 EHRR 387, ECtHR. Also see *Luberti v Italy* (1984) 6 EHRR 440, ECtHR.

[159] Para 15.33.   [160] Para 15.16.   [161] Para 15.38.

[162] Law Commission: *A Criminal Code for England and Wales* (1989), Law Com No 177; see para 1.73. These provisions are discussed by Mackay *Mental Condition Defences in the Criminal Law* (1995) 131–138.

[163] *Report of the Committee on Mentally Abnormal Offenders* (1975) Cmnd 6244, paras 18.1–18.50. For a discussion of the Committee's proposals, see Ashworth 'The Butler Committee and Criminal Responsibility' [1975] Crim LR 687.

test under the *M'Naghten Rules* but also any other case where, at the time of the act or omission charged, and proved, the defendant, although able to form intentions and carry them out, was suffering from severe mental illness or severe mental handicap. This ground would be of importance where the prosecution succeeded in proving the necessary *mens rea* for the offence charged. The definition of 'severe mental illness' is such that this defence would not exempt those who acted under an irresistible impulse, but it would exempt those who acted under a delusion – eg about being persecuted – which did not affect *mens rea*.

By cl 36, the mental disorder verdict could also be returned if the defendant was acquitted of an offence only because, by reason of mental disorder or a combination of mental disorder and intoxication, it was found that he acted or might have acted in a state of automatism, or without the fault required for the offence, or believing that an exempting circumstance existed, and it was proved on the balance of probabilities (whether by the defendant or the prosecution) that he was suffering from mental disorder at the time of the act. 'Mental disorder' is defined as severe mental illness, arrested or incomplete development of mind, or a state of automatism (not resulting only from intoxication) which is a feature of disorder, whether organic or functional and whether continuing or recurring, that may cause a similar state on another occasion. A diabetic in a hyperglycaemic coma as a result of not taking insulin or an epileptic having a fit would fall within 'mental disorder'. The present ground would work as follows: if, although the prosecution had proved the *actus reus*, it was found that the defendant acted or might have acted in a state of automatism, or without the fault required for the offence, or believing that an exempting circumstance existed, the defendant would be entitled to a complete acquittal unless the jury or magistrates were satisfied on the balance of probabilities that he was mentally disordered at the time of the offence.

Automatism and other involuntary conduct

> **Key points 15.5**
>
> Generally,[164] it is a defence that the act or omission or, even, event with which the defendant is charged was involuntary.[165] An act, omission to act or event on the part of the defendant is involuntary where it is beyond his control. Involuntary acts include those done under automatism.

---

[164] For exceptions, see paras 6.6, 15.55 and 15.64.

[165] *Woolmington v DPP* [1935] AC 462 at 482 per Viscount Sankey LC; *Bratty v A-G for Northern Ireland* [1963] AC 386 at 408–409, per Lord Denning; *Kilbride v Lake* [1962] NZLR 590, NZSC; *Ryan v R* (1967) 121 CLR 205, High Ct of Australia.

Involuntary act

15.49 One of the best known examples of an involuntary act is one done under compulsion, ie where it is compelled by external physical force. Hale gave the following example: 'If there be an actual forcing of a man, as if A by force take the arm of B and the weapon in his hand, and therewith stabs C whereof he dies, this is murder in A, and B is not guilty.'[166] In *Hill v Baxter*,[167] it was stated that a man could not be said to be driving where at the material time he was attacked by a swarm of bees and was prevented from exercising any directional control over the vehicle, any movements of his arms and legs being solely caused by the action of the bees. Another example of an involuntary act is where a motorist is suddenly deprived of control over his vehicle by a sudden blow-out or brake-failure.[168]

Automatism

15.50 Some involuntary acts are not directly caused by external physical force or the like but are done in a state of automatism. **An act is done in such a state if it is done by the muscles without any control by the mind (such as a reflex action, or a spasmodic or convulsive act) or if it is done during a state involving a loss of consciousness.**[169]

15.51 In law automatism is limited to cases where there is a total destruction of voluntary control; this is what is meant by 'loss of consciousness'.[170] **Impaired or reduced awareness will not do.** This was decided by the Court of Appeal in *A-G's Reference (No 2 of 1992)*[171] where the Court of Appeal resolved a conflict in the authorities. Prior to this decision the balance of authority indicated that a person was in law an automaton if his consciousness was impaired to such an extent that, while he exercised some control over his act, he was deprived of effective control over it. In cases like *Charlson*,[172] *Kemp*,[173] referred to in para 15.58, and *Quick*,[174] the defendant's acts of violence were treated as done in a state of automatism although they were probably done in a state of impaired consciousness in which it could not be said for sure that the defendant did not exercise any control over his acts. Moreover, in *Burgess*,[175] the facts of which were set out in para 15.25, the Court of Appeal appeared to have treated the defendant's acts of violence as done in a state of automatism where '[h]is mind was to some extent controlling his actions which were purposive rather than the result

---

166 Hale *Pleas of the Crown* Vol I, 434. Also see Hawkins *Pleas of the Crown* Vol I, Ch 29, s 3.
167 [1958] 1 QB 277, DC.   168 This example was given in *Bell* [1984] 3 All ER 842 at 846.
169 *Bratty v A-G for Northern Ireland* [1963] AC 386 at 409, per Lord Denning.
170 *A-G's Reference (No 2 of 1992)* [1994] QB 91, CA. Thus, the act of a driver who unintentionally presses the accelerator, intending to press the brake, is not done in a state of automatism. Despite the fact that in one sense he is not conscious of what he is doing, there is not a loss of consciousness in the required sense: *A-G's Reference (No 4 of 2000)* [2001] EWCA Crim 780.
171 [1994] QB 91, CA.   172 [1955] 1 All ER 859.   173 [1957] 1 QB 399.
174 [1973] QB 910, CA.   175 [1991] 2 QB 92, CA.

simply of muscular spasm, but without being consciously aware of what he was doing'. On the other hand, in *Broome v Perkins*,[176] where D drove five miles home, very erratically, in a hypoglycaemic state in which he might not have been conscious of what he was doing, the Divisional Court directed a conviction of driving without due care and attention, on the ground that D's impaired consciousness, if it existed, would not have constituted automatism because he must have reacted to stimuli, made decisions (eg to brake or steer) and given direction to his limbs, ie there was not a complete destruction of D's control over his acts.

In *A-G's Reference (No 2 of 1992)*, D, who was driving along a motorway, steered apparently deliberately on to the hard shoulder. He drove 700 yards along the hard shoulder before crashing into a stationary van whose hazard lights were flashing. The van was pushed forward, crushing to death two men who were standing between it and a recovery vehicle parked in front. D was charged with the now repealed offence of causing death by reckless driving. There was psychiatric evidence for the defence that D had been driving in a condition known as 'driving without awareness' and D argued that this amounted to driving in a state of automatism. The judge left to the jury the defence of automatism based on this evidence. The jury acquitted D.

The Attorney-General referred the case to the Court of Appeal on a point of law, viz whether the psychiatric evidence for the defence, taken at its highest, could amount to evidence of automatism fit to be left to the jury. The Court of Appeal answered: 'no'. The psychiatric evidence as to 'driving without awareness' was that, in that state, the driver's capacity to avoid a collision ceased to exist because repetitive stimuli experienced on a straight, flat, featureless motorway could induce a trancelike state in which the focal point for forward vision gradually came nearer and nearer until the driver was focusing just ahead of his windscreen, but that his peripheral vision would continue to send signals which were dealt with subconsciously and would enable the driver to steer within highway lanes. In this condition, the evidence continued, the driver's body would still be controlling the vehicle, there would be subconscious motivation to his steering, and, although largely unaware of what was happening ahead or of steering, D's unawareness would not be total. In other words, D would have retained some control over the vehicle. The Court of Appeal, relying on *Broome v Perkins* and similar cases, held that, for automatism, there had to be a total destruction of voluntary control on D's part; impaired control was not enough. Accordingly on the above evidence, the judge should not have left the issue of automatism to the jury. This decision constitutes a major restriction on the defence of automatism.

Under cl 33 of the draft Criminal Code Bill a defendant would be in a state of automatism if his act occurred while he was in a condition depriving him of effective control over it.

---

[176] (1987) 85 Cr App Rep 321, DC. Also see *Isitt* (1977) 67 Cr App Rep 44, CA (D's mind not in 'top gear' so that D unaware of moral inhibitions; no defence if acted purposefully).

Acts done under irresistible impulse or duress not involuntary

15.52 It is clear from the cases that the phrase 'automatism and other involuntary conduct' has a meaning limited to cases of unconscious or reflex actions and other actions beyond the control of the defendant. Thus, acts done under an irresistible impulse are not regarded as 'involuntary acts' because, although the person concerned may not be able to control the impulse which prompts his act, the doing of the act itself is not beyond his control.[177]

15.53 The narrow meaning given to 'involuntary conduct' also prevents that phrase covering acts done under duress (where there is a *threat* of physical force unless an act is done),[178] although the threat may provide an excuse, as seen later.[179]

Involuntary omission

15.54 An omission to act is involuntary (ie beyond the defendant's control) where he is physically restrained from acting or otherwise incapable of acting. Thus, in *Leicester v Pearson*,[180] which was concerned with the strict liability[181] offence of failing to accord precedence to a pedestrian on a zebra crossing, it was held that if the failure was beyond the control of a driver (eg because he had been pushed onto the crossing by a bump from a car behind) he would not be liable.

15.55 While it is generally the case that an involuntary omission is not culpable, the wording of the offence may lead to it being construed as one in which impossibility of complying with the duty in question is no excuse. An example of such an offence is provided by *Sparks v Worthington*.[182] In that case the Divisional Court held that the statutory offence of failing to produce a driving licence for examination had been committed, even though it was physically impossible for the licence holder to produce the licence because it had been sent to the Driver and Vehicle Licensing Centre at Swansea. Likewise, it has been held that a driver can be convicted of the statutory offence of failing to produce a vehicle test certificate notwithstanding that it was impossible for him to do so because it was in the possession of the vehicle's owner who refused to give it to the driver to produce.[183] Such an exceptional construction is likely to be limited to offences of a minor, regulatory nature. It is impossible to defend it where the impossibility of compliance with the duty is not due to the fault of the defendant.

---

[177] *Bratty v A-G for Northern Ireland* [1963] AC 386 at 409, per Lord Denning.

[178] Edwards 'Automatism and Criminal Responsibility' (1958) 21 MLR 375 at 381.

[179] Paras 16.37–16.61 and 16.67–16.83.

[180] [1952] 2 QB 668, DC. Also see *Burns v Bidder* [1967] 2 QB 227, DC (offence not committed if failure to accord precedence due to brake failure, resulting from unknown latent defect of which driver could not reasonably have known).

[181] *Hughes v Hall* [1960] 2 All ER 504, DC.   [182] [1986] RTR 64, DC.

[183] *Davey v Towle* [1973] RTR 328, DC.

Involuntary state of affairs

15.56 A state of affairs, eg possession of a prohibited thing, is involuntary where it is brought about by the physical compulsion of another or its occurrence is otherwise beyond the defendant's control. However, as stated (and criticised) in para 6.6, in status or situational offences it is liable to be held that a person can be convicted despite the fact that the relevant state of affairs was involuntary on his part.

The distinction between insane and non-insane automatism

Key points 15.6

Where the defendant was suffering from non-insane automatism he must be acquitted,[184] but if the case is one where the defendant was suffering from a 'defect of reason due to disease of the mind' the *M'Naghten Rules* apply and, if the trial is on indictment, he must be found not guilty by reason of insanity and an order will be made against him under the Criminal Procedure (Insanity) Act 1964, s 5 as explained in para 15.38.

15.57 The distinction between insane and non-insane automatism was established by the House of Lords in *Bratty v A-G for Northern Ireland*.[185] D was charged with the murder of a girl. It was not disputed that he had strangled her. D said that he had had a blackout and there was some evidence that he was suffering from psychomotor epilepsy, which is undoubtedly a disease of the mind. D relied on the defences of automatism and insanity, but the trial judge only directed the jury on the issue of insanity. D was convicted, and his appeals to the Northern Irish Court of Criminal Appeal and the House of Lords were dismissed. It was held that, where the only evidence of the cause of automatism is a disease of the mind, the case is one of insane automatism and the *M'Naghten Rules* apply. If, on the other hand, the evidence is that automatism was caused not by a disease of the mind (ie not by an internal cause) but by some other (external) cause, such as a blow on the head, the case is one of non-insane automatism.

15.58 **A defendant cannot, however, prevent his defence being treated as one of insanity if the medical evidence before the court, whether adduced by the defence or the prosecution, indicates that the alleged automatism arose from a disease of the mind, because it is for the judge to determine whether that evidence discloses a disease of the mind.**

What has just been said was denied by Barry J in *Charlson*,[186] where there was evidence that D had acted as an automaton as a result of a cerebral tumour. Barry J directed the

---

184 For a qualification, see para 15.64. 185 [1963] AC 386, HL. Also see *Quick* [1973] QB 910, CA.
186 [1955] 1 All ER 859.

jury that the case did not involve the defence of insanity, since that defence had not been raised by D who was alone competent to do so, and left the defence of non-insane automatism to them. However, in *Kemp*,[187] a contrary view was taken where it was not disputed that D had struck his wife with a hammer in a period of unawareness, caused by the effect on his brain of arteriosclerosis. Devlin J, as he then was, distinguished *Charlson* on the ground that in that case the doctors were apparently agreed that the defendant was not suffering from a 'disease of the mind', whereas in Kemp's case they were not so agreed. Devlin J accordingly held that Kemp's defence, if any, was one of insanity and directed the jury accordingly.

The two cases are not so easily reconciled since, as previously stated,[188] whether the alleged condition from which the defendant is suffering is a 'disease of the mind' is not a medical question to be decided by medical witnesses but a question of law for the judge. *Kemp* was approved, and *Charlson* doubted, in *Bratty's* case[189] by Lord Denning, who pointed out that the old notion that only the defence can raise insanity has gone, and it is now clear that the approach in *Kemp* represents the law.

15.59 An example of the approach taken in *Kemp* is *Hennessy*.[190] D, a diabetic, was charged with taking a conveyance without authority and with driving while disqualified. His defence was that he had failed to take his proper dose of insulin because of stress, anxiety and depression, and consequently was suffering from hyperglycaemia and in a state of automatism when the offences occurred. The trial judge ruled that, since D's alleged automatism was due to a disease of the mind, the defence (if any) was one of insanity. At this D changed his plea to guilty. The Court of Appeal held that the judge's ruling was correct since the hyperglycaemia caused by diabetes (a disease) not corrected by insulin was a disease of the mind and the stress, anxiety and depression, even if caused by external factors, were not in themselves external factors and could not override the effect of the diabetic shortage of insulin. *Hennessy* can be contrasted with *Bingham*,[191] where the Court of Appeal held that evidence that a diabetic had been suffering from hypoglycaemia (deficient blood sugar level caused by too much insulin or failing to eat properly after taking insulin to counteract it) was evidence of non-insane automatism.

15.60 The development of the law relating to insanity and automatism is such that many cases of automatism are, in law, of the insane type, although they would not be so described in common or medical parlance. An extreme example is provided by *Burgess*,[192] where the Court of Appeal held that the sleepwalking in issue constituted insane automatism because it was due to an internal cause. However, as pointed out in para 15.46, until English law provides a satisfactory method of dealing with defendants who, although lacking *mens rea*, have a condition which gives rise to a potential threat to others, the law

---

[187] [1957] 1 QB 399.   [188] Para 15.20.   [189] [1963] AC 386 at 411.
[190] [1989] 2 All ER 9, CA.   [191] [1991] Crim LR 433, CA.
[192] [1991] 2 QB 92, CA; para 15.25. Under the draft Criminal Code Bill, cl 33, sleepwalking would be classed as (non-insane) automatism.

in the present respect can be justified as giving the judge a power to make an order for the protection of the public as well as for the help and support of the defendant.[193]

15.61 Where there is more than one cause of automatism, the question is whether the immediate cause is an internal or external one. In *Roach*,[194] defence psychiatric witnesses at the defendant's trial for wounding with intent, contrary to the Offences Against the Person Act 1861, s 18, stated that at the time of his violent conduct the defendant had been suffering from 'insane automatism of psychogenic type'. They said that an underlying 'mixed personality disorder' had been acted on by prescribed drugs, a moderate quantity of alcohol and fatigue. The judge only left insane automatism to the jury. The Court of Appeal held that the judge had been wrong to do so. The psychiatrists had clearly attributed a causative role to the external factors (the drugs and the alcohol) as well as to the underlying personality disorder and fatigue. The Court of Appeal held that, whatever the correct psychiatric definition, and despite the psychiatrists' use of the term 'insane automatism', 'the legal definition of automatism allows for the fact that, if external factors are operative on an underlying condition which could not otherwise produce a state of automatism, then a defence of (non-insane) automatism should be left to the jury'. Where the immediate cause of alleged automatism is disputed on the evidence (so that it indicates that it may be internal or external), the judge will have to leave the defence of insanity (insane automatism) and the defence of non-insane automatism to the jury, directing them to consider which was the immediate cause. Because of the difference in the burden of proof, the judge's direction will unavoidably be complicated in such a case.

15.62 The distinction between insane and non-insane automatism is one of great importance because, in the case of non-insane automatism, the defendant simply bears the burden of adducing evidence;[195] once the issue is raised, the burden of disproving automatism is borne by the prosecution in accordance with the general principles enunciated in *Woolmington's* case. **If, however, the case is one of insane automatism the defendant bears the persuasive burden of proof as well as the burden of adducing evidence.[196]**

The defendant bears the burden of adducing evidence of non-insane automatism because there is a rebuttable presumption of law that everyone has sufficient mental capacity to be responsible for his crimes. If the prosecution had to adduce evidence of capacity in every case, its position would be intolerable. It is up to the defendant to indicate the nature of his alleged incapacity, and since, generally speaking, the mere statement 'I had a

---

[193] Wilson, Ebrahim, Fenwick and Marks 'Violence, Sleepwalking and the Criminal Law: (2) The Legal Aspects' [2005] Crim LR 614 at 623.

[194] [2001] EWCA Crim 2698. See also *Quick* [1973] QB 910, CA; *Burgess* [1991] 2 QB 92, CA.

[195] *Bratty v A-G for Northern Ireland* [1963] AC 386, HL; *Stripp* (1978) 69 Cr App Rep 318, CA; *Pullen* [1991] Crim LR 457, CA.   [196] Para 15.18.

black-out' or 'I can't remember what happened' will be totally insufficient,[197] the defendant's evidence will very rarely be sufficient unless it is supported by medical evidence.[198]

Self-induced automatism

> **Key points 15.7**
>
> In the case of an offence of 'basic intent' a defendant cannot always rely on self-induced
> automatism by way of defence.

15.63 Sometimes, non-insane automatism can be regarded as self-induced in that it
results from something done by the defendant or not done by him (as where a diabetic
becomes an automaton as a result of taking too much insulin or, having taken insulin,
failing to eat sufficient food so that the insulin reacts adversely).

15.64 In such a case, the position is as follows:

- As was held by the Court of Appeal in *Bailey*,[199] where the offence is one requiring
  proof of a 'specific intent', a term discussed in para 15.86, a defendant who was suffering from self-induced automatism at the material time cannot be convicted of that
  offence whatever the cause of the automatism. Examples of offences of specific intent
  are murder, wounding or causing grievous bodily harm with intent (contrary to the
  Offences Against the Person Act 1861, s 18) and attempt to commit an offence.
- Where the offence is one of 'basic intent', ie an offence other than one of specific intent,
  such as involuntary manslaughter or unlawful wounding or infliction of grievous
  bodily harm (contrary to the Offences Against the Person Act 1861, s 20), then:
  - If the automatism was due to voluntary intoxication, the defendant will be guilty[200]
    of the offence if at the material time he would have had the *mens rea* required for
    the offence charged, had he not been an intoxicated automaton (as will almost
    always be the case). In *Lipman*,[201] for example, the Court of Appeal upheld the
    conviction for manslaughter of D who had killed a girl while in a self-induced
    trance, during which he thought that he was fighting snakes whereas in fact he
    was stuffing a sheet into the girl's mouth and asphyxiating her. This is discussed
    in more detail in paras 15.74–15.77.
  - Where the automatism was due to some other cause, such as a failure by a diabetic
    to eat adequately after taking insulin, then, it was held by the Court of Appeal in

---

[197] *Cook v Atchison* [1968] Crim LR 266, DC.
[198] *Bratty v A-G for Northern Ireland* [1963] AC 386 at 413, per Lord Denning; *Moses v Winder* [1981] RTR 37,
DC. There cannot be a verdict of not guilty by reason of insanity except on the evidence of two or more registered
medical practitioners: para 15.33.   [199] [1983] 2 All ER 503, CA.
[200] This was recognised by the Court of Appeal in *Bailey* [1983] 2 All ER 503, CA.
[201] [1970] 1 QB 152, CA. See also *DPP v Majewski* [1977] AC 443, HL.

Bailey,[202] the defendant cannot, except in the case mentioned below, be convicted of an offence of basic intent. Within this category falls the situation where the defendant's automatism was caused by an occurrence which was brought about by his voluntary intoxication, as where, because of his intoxication, a person falls over, bangs his head and thereby becomes concussed; the blow on the head, and not the intoxication, is the immediate cause of the automatism.[203]

The exceptional case just referred to is where the defendant is proved to have been reckless in the following way: viz that, before he became an automaton, he appreciated the risk that something which he did or failed to do was likely to make him aggressive, unpredictable or uncontrollable with the result that he might endanger others (as opposed simply to becoming unconscious) and he deliberately ran the risk or otherwise disregarded it. In such a case, as the Court of Appeal held in *Bailey,*[204] the defendant can be convicted of an offence of basic intent, even though at the time of his conduct which constituted the *actus reus* of such an offence he lacked the *mens rea* normally required for it. Presumably, as in the case of voluntarily intoxicated automatism the defendant will not be guilty in the unlikely event that it is found that even if he had not been an automaton he would not have had the necessary *mens rea*.

15.65 In the case of dangerous driving or careless driving, a defendant who, for example, falls asleep at the wheel can be convicted *in relation to the time when he realised or should have realised the risk that he might become unconscious* but nevertheless continued to drive, if his continuing to do so before he became unconscious satisfies the relevant test of dangerousness or carelessness.[205]

Intoxication

15.66 Alcohol is a drug which is capable of altering mood, perception or consciousness, of loosening inhibitions and self-control, and of impairing movements, reactions, judgment and ability to foresee consequences. Certain other drugs and substances (including some glues) can also have such effects.

Unlike the other mental conditions referred to in this chapter, intoxication is not, and never has been, a defence in itself. Indeed, until the early nineteenth century voluntary intoxication was an aggravating factor warranting a punishment of more than ordinary severity. Sometimes, however, intoxication can be relied on in support of a claim that the defendant lacked the *mens rea* for the offence charged or had a defence which applies to that offence; in other cases it cannot.

---

[202] [1983] 2 All ER 503, CA, disapproving dicta in *Quick* [1973] QB 910, CA, on this point.

[203] *Stripp* (1978) 69 Cr App Rep 318 at 323. See also *Burns* [1970] 58 Cr App Rep 364, CA.

[204] [1983] 2 All ER 503, CA.

[205] *Kay v Butterworth* (1945) 173 LT 191, DC; *Henderson v Jones* (1955) 119 JP 305, DC. Cf *Moses v Winder* [1981] RTR 37, DC.

Voluntary intoxication

Key points 15.8

Voluntary intoxication is a factor relevant to criminal liability:

- if a specific intent is an essential element of the offence charged and the defendant's intoxication affords evidence that he lacked the *mens rea* for that offence;

- where statute expressly provides that a particular belief shall be a defence to the offence charged; and

- if it causes insanity under the *M'Naghten Rules* or alcoholism constituting an abnormality of mental functioning which satisfies the requirements of the partial defence of diminished responsibility.

15.67 Intoxication is voluntary where it results from the defendant knowingly taking alcohol or some other drug or intoxicating substance or a combination of these,[206] even though he does not know its precise nature or strength[207] (as where his beer has been laced with vodka), or even though the effect of the amount taken is much greater than would have been expected.

There are two exceptions. As shown in paras 15.105 and 15.106, intoxication is not voluntary in certain cases where it is caused by a drug taken under medical advice, or by a non-dangerous drug (ie a drug which is not normally liable to cause unpredictability or aggressiveness, such as a sedative or soporific drug).

15.68 It is no excuse that the defendant's power to judge between right and wrong was impaired so that he would not have acted as he did but for his intoxication, nor that his powers of self-control were relaxed so that he more readily gave way to temptation than if he were sober, nor even that, in his intoxicated condition, he found the impulse to act as he did irresistible.[208] Moreover, it is not always a defence in itself that the defendant's voluntary intoxication caused him to become an automaton.[209]

15.69 Voluntary intoxication is a factor relevant to criminal liability in three cases:

- if a specific intent (as opposed to a basic intent) is an essential element of the offence charged and the defendant's intoxication affords evidence that he lacked the *mens rea* for that offence. There are, however, qualifications to this;

- where statute expressly provides that a particular belief shall be a defence to the offence charged; and

---

[206] *Lipman* [1970] 1 QB 152, CA; *DPP v Majewski* [1977] AC 443, HL. Arguably, a drink whose alcohol level is so low that it does not require a licence for its sale, or something like a sherry trifle, should fall outside this definition. These are not commodities which one would consider capable of having an intoxicating effect.

[207] *Allen* [1988] Crim LR 698, CA.

[208] *DPP v Beard* [1920] AC 479, HL; *A-G for Northern Ireland v Gallagher* [1963] AC 349, HL.

[209] Para 15.64.

- if it causes insanity under the *M'Naghten Rules* or alcoholism constituting an abnormality of mental functioning which satisfies the requirements of the partial defence of diminished responsibility.

Voluntary intoxication as evidence of the absence of *mens rea* in offence of specific intent

15.70 Particularly in offences involving violence, the defendant may lack the necessary *mens rea* for the offence charged because of his intoxication, as where he kills another mistakenly believing in his drunken stupor that the other is a theatrical dummy or where because of his intoxication he is unable to appreciate that firing a gun at another is likely to harm him. In such a case a simple claim of lack of *mens rea* is extremely unlikely to succeed unless there is evidence of intoxication to support it. There is a mass of authority that the defendant may rely on voluntary intoxication as evidence that he lacked the necessary *mens rea* only if the offence is one requiring a specific intent (as opposed to a basic intent). This rule was affirmed by the House of Lords in 1976 in *DPP v Majewski*.[210] The House of Lords' decision in this case confirmed the view previously taken by the House in *DPP v Beard*,[211] although that decision was not free from ambiguity and some statements in it are no longer correct.

15.71 **It is important to emphasise that intoxication does not negative mens rea. All that the cases decide is that, where there is evidence of voluntary intoxication such as might have prevented the defendant having the necessary *mens rea* in a case involving a charge of an offence requiring specific intent, this evidence may be taken into account by the magistrates or jury along with all the other evidence in deciding whether the prosecution has proved that he did have that *mens rea*.** Normally, this evidence will have been adduced by the defendant, but it may come from some other source at the trial. In principle, if there is any evidence at a trial in the Crown Court, whatever its source and even though it is not relied on by counsel, on which a jury might conclude that the defendant did not have the relevant *mens rea*, because of intoxication, that evidence should be left to the jury since it relates to an essential element (*mens rea*) which the prosecution must prove.[212] It is therefore unfortunate that some recent cases have *suggested* that the defendant must provide specific evidence to show that he was intoxicated and lacked *mens rea* and that this requirement is not satisfied simply by evidence that he had consumed so much alcohol that he was intoxicated or that he could not remember what he was doing because he was drunk.[213]

In his direction in respect of an offence requiring specific intent, the judge must inform the jury that in deciding whether the defendant had the necessary *mens rea* they must

---

[210] [1977] AC 443, HL.   [211] [1920] AC 479, HL.

[212] *Bennett* [1995] Crim LR 877, CA; *Brown and Stratton* [1998] Crim LR 485, CA.

[213] *Sooklal v State of Trinidad and Tobago* [1999] 1 WLR 2011, PC; *McKnight* (2000) Times, 5 May, CA; *P* [2004] EWCA Crim 1043.

take into account the evidence that he was intoxicated and that if they consider that he did not have the necessary *mens rea* or might not have had it, he is entitled to be acquitted.[214] In other words, the judge must tell the jury that they can only convict the defendant of a specific intent offence if they are sure, having regard to all the evidence (including that of intoxication), that he had the necessary *mens rea*.[215]

15.72 At one time, the law was different. In *DPP v Beard*,[216] Lord Birkenhead LC, giving the judgment of the House, said that evidence of voluntary intoxication could be taken into consideration only if it rendered the defendant incapable of forming the specific intent essential to constitute the offence charged. This proposition had the following arbitrary result where, through intoxication, the defendant lacked the necessary specific intent: if the defendant's intoxication was such that he did not have the capacity to form the specific intent, he was exculpated; whereas if his intoxication did not render him incapable of forming that intent, although because of it he did not have that intent, he was criminally liable.

15.73 Fortunately, it is clear that, following the Criminal Justice Act 1967, s 8, Lord Birkenhead's requirement of incapacity to form the requisite specific intent exists no longer. As we have seen,[217] under s 8 a person is not to be presumed to intend the natural and probable consequences of his act; instead the question whether the defendant had the necessary *mens rea* is to be decided by the jury or magistrates on all the evidence. Thus, the jury in deciding whether the defendant had the necessary *mens rea* must take into account all the evidence, including that relating to intoxication, drawing such inferences from the evidence as appear proper in the circumstances. The strongest evidence, of course, is that the defendant was too intoxicated to be capable of forming the specific intent, but it is enough if, on all the evidence (including that relating to the defendant's intoxication), the jury find that while the defendant's intoxication was not such as to make him incapable of forming a specific intent, ie he could have intended, he did not in fact have that intent.[218]

A second change is that, contrary to dicta in *Beard*, it is now established that the burden is on the prosecution to establish that, despite the evidence of intoxication, the defendant had the necessary *mens rea*.[219]

Voluntary intoxication and offences of basic intent

15.74 The above amendments to the propositions of law in *Beard's* case do not remove the major limitation of the rule affirmed in *DPP v Majewski* that, **if the offence charged is**

---

[214] *Brown and Stratton* [1998] Crim LR 485, CA.   [215] *Groark* [1999] Crim LR 669, CA.
[216] [1920] AC 479, HL.   [217] Para 4.18.
[218] *Pordage* [1975] Crim LR 575, CA; *Sheehan* [1975] 2 All ER 960, CA; *Garlick* (1980) 72 Cr App Rep 291, CA; *Davies* [1991] Crim LR 469, CA; *Cole* [1993] Crim LR 300, CA; *Bowden* [1993] Crim LR 379, CA. Regrettably, the Court of Appeal still occasionally treats the question as being whether the defendant was capable of forming the specific intent: see, for example, *Brown and Stratton* [1998] Crim LR 485; *Groark* [1999] Crim LR 669; *McKnight* (2000) Times, 5 May. The same mistake was made in *Sooklal v State of Trinidad and Tobago* [1999] 1 WLR 2011.   [219] *Sheehan* [1975] 2 All ER 960, CA.

one of basic intent (ie does not require a specific intent), the defendant may be convicted of it if he was voluntarily intoxicated at the time of committing its *actus reus*, even though, through voluntary intoxication, he lacked the *mens rea* normally required for that offence (as where he made an intoxicated mistake, for instance), and even though he was then in a state of automatism. This part of the *Majewski* decision is open to at least three interpretations.

15.75 The first interpretation is that the intoxicated person has no defence because he was reckless as to the risk of becoming mentally impaired involved in taking the drink or drugs and recklessness is sufficient *mens rea* for the offence in question.[220] It is difficult to accept this theory. One reason is that it proceeds on the basis that one who takes drink or dangerous drugs is conclusively presumed to be reckless, which conflicts with the provisions of the Criminal Justice Act 1967, s 8.[221] Another reason is that *mens rea* must exist at the time of the defendant's prohibited conduct and in relation to the risks specified in the definition of the offence. To convict a defendant simply on the basis of recklessness at an earlier point of time (when he took the drink or drug) as to the risk involved in taking it is to base liability on a very different ground from that specified by the definition of the offence.

15.76 The second interpretation is that, where on a charge of a basic intent offence a claim of lack of *mens rea* is supported by evidence of voluntary intoxication, that evidence should be disregarded in deciding whether or not the defendant had that *mens rea*. This means that if the prosecution can prove facts from which (disregarding the intoxication evidence) the necessary *mens rea* can be inferred beyond reasonable doubt the defendant must be convicted. Although this second interpretation is easier to 'square' with principle than the first, it seems inconsistent with the requirement in the Criminal Justice Act 1967, s 8 that in deciding whether the defendant had the necessary intent or foresight the jury or magistrates should take into account 'all the evidence'. In *Majewski*, however, Lord Elwyn-Jones LC, with whom Lords Diplock, Simon and Salmon agreed, held that 'all the evidence' means all the legally relevant evidence. Nevertheless, it leads to the absurd proposition that a person can be convicted of an offence on an inference as to his *mens rea* which is false because it clearly disregards evidence (intoxication evidence) to the contrary.

15.77 The third interpretation is that, where on a charge of a basic intent offence, a claim of lack of *mens rea* is supported by evidence of voluntary intoxication, the prosecution does not have to prove the *mens rea* normally required for that offence (even though it is specified in the definition of the offence), because instead he can be convicted if he would have had that *mens rea* if he would have had it but for the fact that he was voluntarily intoxicated. The rule under this interpretation is one of substantive law and would therefore be

---

[220] See, for example, *DPP v Majewski* [1977] AC 443, per Lord Elwyn-Jones LC, with whom Lords Diplock and Kilbrandon agreed, and Lord Edmund-Davies; *Hardie* [1984] 3 All ER 848 at 853. This interpretation assumes that a crime where recklessness is sufficient *mens rea* is always one of basic intent, which may not necessarily be the case: see para 15.87. [221] Para 4.18.

unaffected by the provisions in the Criminal Justice Act 1967, s 8 about proof of intention or foresight, because the rule dispenses with the need for proof of intent or foresight if the defendant claims that he lacked *mens rea* through voluntary intoxication.

This interpretation is supported by appellate decisions in two cases concerning the offence of unlawfully inflicting grievous bodily harm contrary to the Offences Against the Person Act 1861 (OAPA 1861), s 20, where the *mens rea* is classified as a basic intent.

In *Aitken*,[222] the defendants set fire to the victim's flying suit, on which they had poured white spirit, during horseplay at an end-of-course celebration at a RAF station. The victim was severely burnt as a result. All involved had consumed a good deal of alcohol. The judge-advocate directed the court-martial that they had to be satisfied that each defendant:

> 'foresaw that he might cause some injury, albeit of a minor nature...or would have foreseen that the act might cause some injury, had he not been drinking.'

The Courts-Martial Appeal Court[223] held that this direction in regard to the defendant's intoxication was correct.

Aitken was applied by the Court of Appeal in *Richardson and Irwin*,[224] another case of horseplay, this time involving university students all of whom had consumed four or five pints of beer. During the horseplay, the defendants lifted the victim over the edge of a balcony. The victim slipped or was dropped to the ground and suffered grievous bodily harm. The Court of Appeal allowed the defendants' appeals against conviction under the OAPA 1861, s 20 on the ground that the trial judge had failed to tell the jury that they had to be sure that the defendants foresaw that the victim might slip or be dropped and suffer some bodily harm, or would have foreseen this risk had they not been drinking.

15.78 Voluntary intoxication evidence is obviously irrelevant in an offence of negligence because a reasonable person is not intoxicated.

Accidental act attributable to voluntary intoxication

15.79 The fact that an offence is one of basic intent does not prevent the defendant relying on evidence of his voluntary intoxication as evidence that his act (as opposed to its consequences) was an 'accident', as where the defendant stumbles into someone in an intoxicated state.[225]

In *Brady*,[226] D, who had voluntarily consumed drink and drugs, had climbed onto the balcony railings of a nightclub, stood on them and had fallen onto a dancer below. D was convicted of inflicting grievous bodily harm, contrary to the OAPA 1861, s 20 and appealed to the Court of Appeal. Because of the way that the case had been argued the Court had to consider the case on the basis of D's act of falling (*and not of the previous*

---

[222] [1992] 1 WLR 1006, C-MAC.   [223] As to this court, see para 2.32, n 91.
[224] [1999] 1 Cr App Rep 392, CA.
[225] The present point deals with a different meaning of 'accident' from that referred to in para 5.2.
[226] [2006] EWCA Crim 2413.

acts of climbing and perching, which were clearly reckless). Allowing D's appeal, the Court of Appeal held that the fall was an accident, not a deliberate act, and did not fall within the rule in *DPP v Majewski*.

Soon afterwards, the Court of Appeal expressed similar views in *Heard*.[227] During an incident at a hospital, D had exposed his penis, taken it in his hand and had rubbed it up and down the thigh of a police officer who was trying to stop D re-entering a hospital waiting area. D was heavily intoxicated at the time. D was charged with sexual assault, contrary to the Sexual Offences Act 2003, s 3, one element of which is that the defendant must intentionally touch another person. At his trial, D's case was that he could not remember anything about what had occurred. The judge directed the jury that the prosecution had to prove that D had 'intentionally, that is to say deliberately' touched the police officer, and that intoxication was not a defence to the charge. The jury convicted D who appealed unsuccessfully against conviction, arguing that, since only an intentional touching would do, the offence was one of specific intent with the result that voluntary intoxication was a relevant factor to consider in determining whether D had the necessary intention to touch.

Dismissing D's appeal, the Court of Appeal held that these issues were not relevant to the determination of the appeal because D plainly intended to touch the police officer with his penis. The Court went on to hold obiter that, although the intent in issue in the Sexual Offences Act 2003, s 3 was a basic intent, the judge's direction that the touching must be deliberate was correct; an accidental *act* attributable to voluntary intoxication would not suffice for liability. It stated:

> 'To flail about, stumble or barge around in an uncoordinated manner which results in an unintended touching, objectively sexual, is not this offence [ie the offence under the Sexual Offences Act 2003, s 3]. If to do so when sober is not this offence, then nor is it this offence to do so when intoxicated. . . . The intoxication, in such a situation, has not impacted on intention. Intention is simply not in question. What is in question is impairment of control of the limbs. . . . We would expect that in some cases where this was in issue the judge might well find it useful to add to the . . . direction that "a drunken intent is still an intent", the corollary that "a drunken accident is still an accident" . . . Whether, when a defendant claims accident, he is doing so truthfully, or as a means of disguising the reality that he intended to touch, will be what the jury has to decide on the facts of each such case.'[228]

The Court of Appeal's acceptance that the fact that an offence is one of basic intent does not prevent reliance on evidence that an act by an intoxicated person was accidental, provides some limit on the rigour of the law relating to basic intent offences. The situation after *Heard* can be illustrated as follows. If D deliberately extends his arm and touches V's genitals and then claims that he did not intend to touch another person because he was heavily intoxicated and did not know that V (or anyone else) was near him or thought he was touching a stuffed bear, the evidence of D's intoxication cannot be relied on at a trial

---

[227] [2007] EWCA Crim 125.   [228] [2007] EWCA Crim 125 at [23].

for an offence under SOA 2003, s 3 as evidence that D lacked the necessary intent. D's act of extending his arm was not accidental; it was the consequence (touching another person) which was. On the other hand, if D bumps into V accidentally while stumbling about in an intoxicated state he cannot be convicted under s 3. D's act of bumping into V when he stumbles is itself accidental. The distinction between these two situations is a fine one. So is the distinction between an accidental act done in a state of voluntary intoxication and an act done in a state of automatism induced by voluntary intoxication, which does not excuse the defendant.[229] These fine distinctions are unsupportable.

Cases where the normal rules do not apply

15.80 In one situation, at least, the rule that a person charged with an offence requiring a specific intent may rely on evidence of voluntary intoxication as evidence that he lacked the necessary *mens rea* is abrogated. This is the situation where under a mistake induced by voluntary intoxication the defendant mistakenly believes that he must act in self-defence or the like. Whether there are other exceptional situations is discussed in para 15.91.

We have seen that in the definitions of some offences against the person the words 'unlawful' or 'unlawfully' (which refer to the absence of elements of justification) are employed and that self-defence and the like are examples of such a justification. We have also seen that where they are used they are an element of the *actus reus* and that the defendant must be proved to have *mens rea* in relation to that element. For example, in murder the defendant must be proved to have intended *unlawfully* to kill or cause grievous bodily harm.

If a sober person kills another in the dark mistakenly believing that the other is a tailor's dummy, he is not guilty of murder because he lacks an intent unlawfully to kill or cause grievous bodily harm, and if he does so mistakenly believing that the person coming towards him is about to stab him, he is not guilty of murder (provided he uses force which is reasonable on the facts as he believes them to be) because he lacks an intent *unlawfully* to kill or cause grievous bodily harm.[230]

Except in two instances, the nature of the evidence adduced in support of the alleged mistake will not affect the outcome of a trial for a specific intent offence in either type of case if the alleged mistake is not disproved. The two exceptions are (a) where the defendant's plea in the Crown Court is in effect one of insanity,[231] and (b) where the evidence in support involves voluntary intoxication. This second exception arises as a result of the reasoning of the Court of Appeal in *O'Grady*.[232] According to that reasoning, if the defendant intended to kill but acted under a voluntarily intoxicated belief that he was

---

[229] Para 15.64. In *Heard* the Court of Appeal appears to have considered obiter that the act done in a state of automatism in *Lipman* (para 15.64) was accidental, but the act in that case would not normally be so described. The fact that Lipman was deprived of control over his acts did not mean that they were accidental.

[230] Paras 5.5–5.9.   [231] Paras 15.16–15.42.

[232] [1987] QB 995, CA; see MacDonald 'Intoxication, Mistake and Self-Defence' (1987) 137 NLJ 914 and Milgate 'Intoxication, Mistake and the Public Interest' (1987) 46 CLJ 381.

being attacked and had to kill to defend himself, he is guilty of murder even though, on the facts as he believed them the force used by him was reasonable, so that he did not intend *unlawfully* to kill or cause grievous bodily harm. The same rule would apply on a charge of any other offence requiring a specific intent unlawfully to cause some sort of harm or where an intoxicated mistaken belief related to some other public or private defence (eg defence of another or the prevention of crime).

15.81 The facts of *O'Grady* were that D and the deceased had fallen asleep after a day's heavy drinking. D woke to find the deceased hitting him and retaliated with what he thought were blows to defend himself. The fight subsided and D fell asleep again. When he awoke he found the deceased was dead, having suffered serious wounds consistent with blows from both blunt and sharp objects. D was charged with murder but convicted of involuntary manslaughter.

D appealed, arguing that the trial judge had been right to say that he should be judged according to his intoxicated mistaken belief that he was under attack, but wrong in not stating that the reasonableness of the force used should be judged according to D's understanding of the situation (the severity of the attack), and not objectively.

The Court of Appeal dismissed D's appeal. Indeed it took an even narrower view of the law than the trial judge, since it concluded that a defendant 'is not entitled to rely, so far as self-defence is concerned, upon a mistaken belief that one is under attack which has been induced by voluntary intoxication' and that this rule applied to specific intent offences, such as murder, as well as to basic intent offences, such as involuntary manslaughter.

The Court held that its decision in *Gladstone Williams*,[233] that a defendant who might have been labouring under a mistaken belief that it was necessary to use force to defend another (or in self-defence etc) must be judged according to his mistaken view of the facts, whether the mistake was reasonable or not, was irrelevant where the jury are satisfied that the mistake was caused by voluntary intoxication.

While the dismissal of D's appeal in *O'Grady* was correct under the present law, since involuntary manslaughter is an offence of basic intent, the reasoning behind *O'Grady* introduces additional complication and contradicts the rule affirmed in *Majewski*. We know that the *mens rea* for murder is an intention unlawfully to kill or do grievous bodily harm and that murder is an offence requiring specific intent, but apparently only in relation to the intention to kill or do grievous bodily harm to another human being, not in relation to the element of unlawfulness where a drunken mistaken belief that one is being attacked is involved. What is the difference in culpability between a drunk who kills another, thinking that he is a tailor's dummy, and someone who kills another, thinking that he is attacking him with a knife? The nonsensical state of the law derives from the view of the Court of Appeal that 'the question of mistake can and ought to be considered separately from the question of intent'. This view contradicts the clear statement to the contrary of the Court of Appeal in *Gladstone Williams* to the effect that the element of

---

[233] (1984) 78 Cr App Rep 276, CA.

unlawfulness is part of the *actus reus* of an offence against the person, in relation to which the defendant must be proved to have had *mens rea*.

O'Grady was applied by the Court of Appeal in *O'Connor*,[234] where the court confirmed that the approach in *O'Grady* applied to any claim of mistaken belief in self-defence, whether the offence was one of specific intent or basic intent. More recently, *O'Grady* was applied in *Hatton*,[235] where the Court of Appeal rejected the view[236] that what was said in *O'Grady* was obiter; the Court of Appeal was therefore bound by *O'Grady*.

15.82 *O'Grady* was clearly influenced by policy considerations, just as the rule affirmed in *Majewski* was. The Court of Appeal stated in *O'Grady*:

> 'There are two competing interests. On the one hand the interest of the defendant who has only acted according to what he believed to be necessary to protect himself, and on the other hand that of the public in general and the victim in particular who, probably through no fault of his own, has been injured or perhaps killed because of the defendant's drunken mistake. Reason recoils from the conclusion that in such circumstances a defendant is entitled to leave the court without a stain on his character. We find support for that view in the decision of the House of Lords in *Majewski*.'[237]

But here is another fallacy: the defendant would not leave court without a stain, because he could be convicted of involuntary manslaughter under the normal rules applicable to basic intent offences, so that the policy of the courts of protecting the public against voluntarily intoxicated offenders would be upheld.

15.83 Despite its oddity *as a matter of principle*, *O'Grady* was given statutory recognition in respect of a mistake relating to self-defence, defence of another, the prevention of crime or effecting or assisting in the lawful arrest of an offender by the Criminal Justice and Immigration Act 2008, s 76(5).[238] The effect of s 76(5) is that the normal rule[239] that whether the degree of force used by D against V was reasonable in the circumstances of self-defence, defence of another, prevention of crime or effecting or assisting in an arrest is to be decided by reference to the circumstances as D believed them to be, even if his belief was an unreasonably mistaken one, does not apply where D relies on a mistaken belief attributable to voluntary intoxication.

15.84 *O'Grady* appears even more odd as a matter of principle when contrasted with what was stated in *Aitken* and *Richardson and Irwin* about an intoxicated mistaken belief in the victim's consent on the defendant's part.

---

[234] [1991] Crim LR 135, CA.
[235] [2005] EWCA Crim 2951. For a critical analysis of this case, see Dingwall 'Intoxicated Mistakes about the Need for Self-Defence' (2007) 70 MLR 127.
[236] See JC Smith's commentary on *O'Grady* in [1987] Crim LR 706.
[237] [1987] QB 995 at 1000.   [238] Section 76(5) is set out in para 16.18.
[239] Paras 16.14 and 16.18.

Aitken[240] was concerned with an offence under the OAPA 1861, s 20. The *mens rea* for such an offence is an intention or recklessness as to some unlawful bodily harm resulting from one's act.[241] Bodily harm is not unlawful if it is validly consented to by the victim, as in the case of horseplay, consent being an element of justification.[242] In *Aitken* the Courts-Martial Appeal Court, having held that the judge-advocate at a court-martial had been correct to direct it that a person charged with an offence under the OAPA 1861, s 20 (a basic intent offence) could be convicted if he foresaw the risk of injury, or would have foreseen it, had he not been intoxicated, went on to hold that a mistaken belief, whether reasonable or not, on the part of that person that the victim was consenting to the horseplay in question would provide an excuse. The Court did not state that in assessing whether the defendant had this belief the evidence of voluntary intoxication had to be disregarded. In *Richardson and Irwin*[243] the Court of Appeal stated, obiter, that in relation to a case like *Aitken* or that before it, evidence of consumption of alcohol should be taken into account when considering whether the defendant realised that the victim did not consent. Thus, what *Aitken* and the obiter dicta in *Richardson and Irwin* appear to indicate is that, if a defendant to a charge of a non-fatal offence against the person claims that he lacked the requisite *mens rea* as to causing the specified degree of harm *unlawfully*, because of an intoxicated belief that he had the other's valid consent, evidence of voluntary intoxication may be taken into account in determining whether he had that *mens rea* as to *unlawfully* bringing about that harm, regardless of whether the offence is one of specific intent or of basic intent.

The above is difficult to accept, especially when compared with the situation[244] where D pleads that he lacked the necessary intent to cause the requisite degree of harm unlawfully in a specific intent offence against the person because, while he did intend to cause that harm, he was in a voluntarily intoxicated state and mistakenly believed that he was acting in self-defence; as stated above, D can nevertheless be convicted of the offence.

15.85 Thus, we seem to have the surprising situation where, in reversal of the normal principles:

- on a charge of a specific intent offence, such as murder, evidence of lack of the requisite *mens rea*, which is founded on voluntary intoxication and is based on a mistake as to the need to act in self-defence or the like, has the effect of enabling the defendant to be convicted of that offence regardless of the absence of proof of the *mens rea* normally required; whereas,

- even on a charge of a basic intent crime, such as an offence under the OAPA 1861, s 20, evidence of lack of the *mens rea* normally required, which is founded on voluntary intoxication and is based on a mistake as to the victim's valid consent, is relevant as evidence of lack of that *mens rea*.

---

[240] [1992] 1 WLR 1006, C-MAC.   [241] Para 7.87.   [242] Para 7.15.
[243] [1999] 1 Cr App Rep 392, CA.   [244] Paras 15.81–15.83.

Determining whether an offence is one of specific intent

Key points 15.9

Various definitions of 'specific intent' have been put forward by the judges and its meaning is unclear.

Where an offence has been classified by an appellate court as involving or not involving a specific intent the safe course is to follow it and not seek to classify it according to the various, inconsistent definitions.

15.86 The judges have put forward various definitions of 'specific intent', most of which are clearly incorrect. For example, in *DPP v Majewski*,[245] Lord Elwyn-Jones LC appears to have adopted the view that 'specific intent' was equivalent to 'ulterior intent'. However, murder, wounding causing grievous bodily harm with intent to cause such harm, handling stolen goods and various other offences which were recognised in *DPP v Majewski* itself and other cases to be ones of specific intent in the present context do not require an ulterior intent. This definition must therefore be rejected. In *DPP v Majewski* Lord Simon took the view that an ulterior intent was only one type of 'specific intent', which term he understood simply to mean (and require) 'direct intention'. This definition must also be rejected, since murder,[246] wounding or causing grievous bodily harm with intent to do grievous bodily harm[247] and handling stolen goods,[248] for example, do not require a direct intent.

15.87 The definition, which is generally reconcilable with the case law is that if intention and nothing less is required as to at least one element of the offence, the offence is one of specific intent, whereas if recklessness as to the elements of a particular offence suffices, that offence is one of basic intent. No decision has actually articulated this distinction. In *Comr of Metropolitan Police v Caldwell*,[249] the majority of the House of Lords held that voluntary intoxication is no defence to an offence in which recklessness is sufficient to constitute the necessary *mens rea* (ie that such an offence is one of basic intent), but they did not seek to define 'specific intent'. This part of the decision remains good law.

The decision of the Court of Appeal in *Heard*,[250] however, contains obiter dicta that the fact that intention (and nothing less) is required as to an element of the offence does not necessarily make that intent a specific intent. The Court held obiter that the rule, affirmed in *DPP v Majewski*, that voluntary intoxication cannot be relied on to negative *mens rea* in offences of basic intent is not limited to offences where recklessness suffices because an

---

[245] [1977] AC 443, HL.

[246] See *DPP v Beard* [1920] AC 479, HL; *A-G for Northern Ireland v Gallagher* [1963] AC 349, HL; *Sheehan* [1975] 2 All ER 960, CA.

[247] *Bryson* [1985] Crim LR 669, CA.   [248] *Durante* [1972] 3 All ER 962, CA.

[249] [1982] AC 341.   [250] [2007] EWCA Crim 125.

offence requiring proof of an intent can nevertheless involve a basic intent. In a passage not notable for its clarity the Court of Appeal dealt with the meaning of 'specific intent'. It appears that the Court of Appeal considered that 'specific intent' in the sense used in *DPP v Majewski* referred to two types of *mens rea*: a purposive (ie direct) intent, and a mental element required to be proved in relation to something beyond the *actus reus*, whether that element is expressed as an ulterior intent or other sort of *mens rea* relating to a matter ulterior to the *actus reus*, for example, criminal damage *being reckless as to endangering life* contrary to the Criminal Damage Act 1971, s 1(2).[251] The Court of Appeal held that since the intent to touch in the Sexual Offences Act 2003, s 3, was not of either of these types it was a 'basic intent' and not a 'specific intent'. As can be seen, neither of these meanings of 'specific intent' for present purposes can be reconciled with the pre-existing classification of offences.

15.88 The Court of Appeal's obiter pronouncement in *Heard* about the meaning of 'specific intent' involves a fundamental change to the previous understanding of *DPP v Majewski*. To what extent does it apply to other offences than that in issue in that case? Although *Heard* was concerned with the Sexual Offences Act 2003 (SOA 2003), s 3, the Court of Appeal's reinterpretation is clearly equally applicable to the offences under SOA 2006, ss 1, 2 and 5–7 (rape, sexual assault by penetration, rape of a girl under 13, sexual assault by penetration of such a girl and sexual assault of such a girl) and to other offences under SOA 2003 requiring an intentional touching, so that the requisite intent is not a specific intent, whereas the 'bolt on' ulterior *mens rea* required by other offences under the Act, eg 'for the purpose of obtaining sexual gratification' (offences of engaging in sexual activity in presence of child or other specified vulnerable person, contrary to SOA 2003, ss 11, 18, 32, 36 or 40, and offences of causing such a person to watch a sexual act contrary to ss 12, 19, 33, 37 or 41) or 'with the intent of committing a relevant sexual offence' (preparatory offences under ss 62 and 63), is a specific intent.

It remains to be seen whether the pronouncement in *Heard* will be applied to offences outside SOA 2003. Its extension to some other offences would be problematic because there is authority binding on the Court of Appeal to the effect that murder and a number of other offences are offences of specific intent, but they would not be if the view taken in *Heard* applied to them.

15.89 As the judges have not been consistent in their definition of 'specific intent', it is impossible to be certain, in advance of a judicial decision concerning a particular offence, whether or not it is one of 'specific intent'. Arguably, the courts grant or withhold the title of 'offence of specific intent' on grounds of policy and not principle. Where a decision has been made in respect of an offence, the safe course is to follow it and not to seek to divine whether or not it involves a specific intent.

---

[251] The Court of Appeal endorsed the view to this effect taken about the Criminal Damage Act 1971, s 1(2) by Lord Edmund-Davies (dissenting) in *Comr of Metropolitan Police v Caldwell* [1982] AC 341.

The following have been held to be offences of specific intent in the present context:

- murder;[252]
- wounding or causing grievous bodily harm with intent;[253]
- criminal damage contrary to the Criminal Damage Act 1971, s 1(1), where only intention to cause damage is alleged;[254]
- arson contrary to the Criminal Damage Act 1971, s 1(1) and (3), where only an intent to damage property is alleged;[255]
- criminal damage with intent to endanger life contrary to the Criminal Damage Act 1971, s 1(2);[256]
- arson with intent to endanger life; contrary to the Criminal Damage Act 1971, s 1(2) and (3);[257]
- theft;[258]
- robbery;[259]
- burglary with intent to steal;[260]
- handling stolen goods;[261] and
- attempt to commit an offence.[262]

Conversely, it is possible to draw up a list of those offences which are ones of basic intent, and not specific intent. The following can be included in this list:

- involuntary manslaughter;[263]
- sexual assault;[264]
- maliciously wounding or inflicting grievous bodily harm;[265]
- assault occasioning actual bodily harm;[266]

---

[252] See *DPP v Beard* [1920] AC 479, HL; *A-G for Northern Ireland v Gallagher* [1963] AC 349, HL; *Sheehan* [1975] 2 All ER 960, CA.

[253] *Bratty v A-G for Northern Ireland* [1963] AC 386 at 410, per Lord Denning; *Pordage* [1975] Crim LR 575, CA.

[254] *Comr of Metropolitan Police v Caldwell* [1982] AC 341, HL.

[255] *Comr of Metropolitan Police v Caldwell* [1982] AC 341, HL.

[256] *Comr of Metropolitan Police v Caldwell* [1982] AC 341, HL.

[257] *Comr of Metropolitan Police v Caldwell* [1982] AC 341, HL.

[258] *Ruse v Read* [1949] 1 KB 377, DC.

[259] This necessarily follows from the fact that a robbery involves a theft.

[260] For the same reason as in n 259.

[261] *Durante* [1972] 3 All ER 962, CA.

[262] *DPP v Majewski* [1977] AC 443, per Lord Salmon. Also see *Mohan* [1976] QB 1, CA.

[263] *Lipman* [1970] 1 QB 152, CA.   [264] *Heard* [2007] EWCA Crim 125.

[265] *Sullivan* [1981] Crim LR 46, CA.

[266] *Bolton v Crawley* [1972] Crim LR 222, DC; *DPP v Majewski* [1977] AC 443, HL. It follows that common assault or battery are offences of basic intent.

- assaulting a constable in the execution of his duty;[267]

- taking a conveyance without lawful authority;[268]

- criminal damage contrary to the CDA 1971, s 1(1), unless only an intention to damage property is alleged;

- arson contrary to the Criminal Damage Act 1971, s 1(1) and (3) unless only an intention to damage property is alleged;

- criminal damage being reckless as to endangering life contrary to the Criminal Damage Act 1971, s 1(2);

- arson being reckless as to endangering life contrary to the Criminal Damage Act 1971, s 1(2) and (3);[269] and

- false imprisonment and kidnapping.[270]

15.90 Liability as an accomplice depends on proof of an intent to assist, encourage or procure the commission of the principal offence. There is some authority to suggest that evidence of voluntary intoxication may be taken into account as evidence that an alleged accomplice to that offence – whether the principal offence was one of specific intent or basic intent – had the intent to assist, encourage or procure it. The authority referred to is *Clarkson*[271] decided at a time when the offence of rape was governed by the Sexual Offences Act 1956, s 1 (since repealed). In that case, the defendants were present as spectators at a gang-rape. They were convicted at a court-martial as accomplices to the rape. Quashing their convictions on the ground that the court-martial might have been left with the impression that mere continuing non-accidental presence was in itself enough, the Courts-Martial Appeal Court stated that not only must it be proved against a defendant that such presence actually encouraged the perpetrators of the rape but it must also be proved that the defendant intended to give encouragement. The Court continued that:

> 'it was essential that that element should be stressed, for there was here at least the possibility that a drunken man with his self-discipline loosened by drink...might not intend that his presence should offer encouragement to rapers;...he might not realise that he was giving encouragement'.[272]

If the suggestion in *Clarkson* is correct, any offence is one of specific intent insofar as liability as an accomplice is concerned. This is an area of the law where the relevant principles need to be established.

---

[267] *DPP v Majewski* [1977] AC 443, HL.

[268] *MacPherson* [1973] RTR 157, CA; criticised by White 'Taking the Joy out of Joy-Riding' [1980] Crim LR 609.

[269] *Comr of Metropolitan Police v Caldwell* [1982] AC 341, HL is the authority in respect of these instances under the 1971 Act. But see para 15.87 in relation to s 1(2).

[270] *Hutchins* [1988] Crim LR 379, CA.

[271] [1971] 3 All ER 344, C-MAC (as to this court, see para 2.32, n 91).   [272] [1971] 3 All ER 344 at 347.

15.91 The division of offences into those of specific intent and those of basic intent is over-simplistic where an offence requires more than one element of *mens rea* to be proved.

It is arguable that the mental elements in offences of specific intent can be divided into elements of specific intent and elements of *mens rea* which are not. If so, a defendant who had the specific intent element but lacked the other mental element because of voluntary intoxication can be convicted on the basis of a rule corresponding to the rule that, where the defendant is charged with an offence of basic intent and claims that he lacked the requisite *mens rea* because of voluntary intoxication, he can be convicted if he had that *mens rea* if he would have had it but for his intoxication. This can be explained by reference to the offence of wounding with intent to prevent the lawful apprehension of any person, contrary to the Offences Against the Person Act 1861, s 18. The *mens rea* for this offence is that the defendant must act 'maliciously', ie with intention or recklessness as to some unlawful physical harm resulting from his act, and with the ulterior intent to prevent lawful apprehension of any person. The ulterior intent is, of course, a specific intent.[273] Consequently, if the defendant is charged with this offence he may rely on evidence of voluntary intoxication as evidence that he lacked the intent to prevent lawful apprehension. On the other hand, it may be that in the event of a defendant admitting that he intended to prevent lawful apprehension but saying that in his intoxicated state he did not realise the risk that what he did to the police officer might cause physical harm, evidence of voluntary intoxication is irrelevant in relation to whether the defendant acted 'maliciously' because his intoxication evidence is not being used to deny a mental element which is a specific intent but to deny a mental element which, in other offences,[274] is a basic intent.[275] It is noteworthy that the case law on specific intent offences and voluntary intoxication has concerned defendants who alleged that they lacked the specific intent (and not any other *mens rea*) because of their intoxication.

If this argument is accepted, so may an argument that a basic intent offence may contain a specific intent element.

Views similar to those in this paragraph were expressed by the Court of Appeal in *Heard*,[276] where the Court stated, obiter, that it should not be supposed that every offence can be categorised simply as either one of specific intent or of basic intent. So to categorise might conceal the truth that different elements of it may require proof of different states of mind. The Court of Appeal added that: 'It is accordingly of very limited help to attempt to label the offence of sexual assault, as a whole, one of either basic or specific intent.'

If the above is correct, the sole function of the terms 'specific intent offence' and 'basic intent offence' is to refer to the nature of the predominant part of the *mens rea* required for them.

---

[273] *Pordage* [1975] Crim LR 575, CA.   [274] *Sullivan* [1981] Crim LR 46, CA.
[275] See White 'Offences of Basic and Specific Intent' [1989] Crim LR 271.
[276] [2007] EWCA Crim 125 at [15].

Basis of rules

15.92 The limited nature of the above rules relating to a plea of voluntary intoxication means that the rules are not exclusively based on the negation of *mens rea*, and are best explained as rules of judicial policy, based on a perception that it would not be acceptable to the public that voluntarily intoxicated offenders should secure an absolute acquittal, and aimed at maintaining law and order, while taking account of the effect on mental responsibility of intoxication.[277] Their consequence is that, while a person who lacked the requisite specific intent because of intoxication cannot be convicted of murder or wounding with intent, he can be convicted of the lesser offences of involuntary manslaughter or unlawful wounding if he would have had the requisite *basic intent* if he had not been intoxicated.[278] However, the application of this policy is imperfect because there are some specific intent offences, such as theft, for which there is generally no basic intent offence to fall back on.

Courts in a number of other Commonwealth jurisdictions have not adopted the approach confirmed in *Majewski*, holding that voluntary intoxication is always admissible to show that the defendant's act was involuntary or that he lacked the required *mens rea*.[279] There have, however, been some legislative retreats to *Majewski* and some legislative restrictions on this development in some jurisdictions.[280]

Voluntarily intoxicated belief and defences

Key points 15.10

Where a statutory defence is framed in terms of the defendant's belief, his voluntary intoxication can be taken into account to support a claim that he had that belief.

The defendant's voluntary intoxication cannot be used in support of an alleged mistaken belief in other defences.

15.93 It was explained in Chapter 5 that where a statutory excuse, specific to a particular offence, is framed in terms of the defendant's belief, it is no bar to the excuse succeeding that the defendant's belief was unreasonable. This is true even though the unreasonableness was due to his voluntary intoxication.

---

[277] This was admitted by Lord Mustill in *Kingston* [1995] 2 AC 355 at 369.
[278] For exceptions to these statements, see paras 15.80–15.85.
[279] Eg *Kamipeli* [1975] 2 NZLR 610, NZCA; *O'Connor* (1980) 146 CLR 64, High Ct of Australia. For a discussion of these cases, see Orchard 'Surviving without *Majewski* – a view from down under' [1993] Crim LR 426.
[280] See Gough 'Surviving without *Majewski*' [2000] Crim LR 719; also see [2001] Crim LR 258. For a description of the law on voluntary intoxication in Canada, Australia and New Zealand see Law Commission *Intoxication and Criminal Liability* (2009) Law Com No 314, Appendix C. Appendix C also describes briefly the law in the United States.

In *Jaggard v Dickinson*,[281] D was convicted by magistrates of intentional or reckless criminal damage to property (a basic intent offence), by breaking two windows and damaging a curtain in V's house. The incident occurred late at night and D, due to voluntary intoxication, mistakenly but honestly believed that she was damaging the property of X, a friend, and that he would have consented to her doing so. D's defence was that she had a lawful excuse within the Criminal Damage Act 1971, s 5. The Criminal Damage Act 1971, s 5(2) provides, inter alia, that a person charged with criminal damage is to be treated as having a lawful excuse if, at the material time, he believed that the person whom he believed to be entitled to consent to the destruction or damage had so consented, or would have so consented to it if he had known of the destruction or damage and its circumstances. The Criminal Damage Act 1971, s 5(3) adds that it is immaterial whether such a belief is justified or not if it is honestly held. The magistrates, being of the opinion that D could not rely on the defence under s 5(2) because her belief was induced by voluntary intoxication, convicted her.

Allowing D's appeal against conviction, **the Divisional Court held that the fact the offence charged was not one of specific intent was irrelevant because D was not relying on her intoxication to displace an inference of intention or recklessness, but was relying on it to give credibility to her alleged belief which, if honestly held, would give her a defence** under s 5(2). It was clear from s 5(3), said the Court, that if the belief was honestly held it was irrelevant that it was unreasonable; no exception was made by the Act for a mistake which was unreasonable because it was caused by voluntary intoxication and therefore the magistrates had been wrong to decide that D did not have the defence under s 5(2) because she was drunk at the time.[282]

The Court's reasoning seems applicable regardless of whether there is a statutory provision like s 5(3) which simply makes explicit that which is normally implicit.[283]

15.94 Sometimes evidence of voluntary intoxication is adduced to support a claim that the defendant mistakenly believed in facts which – if true – would give rise to an excuse, such as duress by threats or duress of circumstances, where the mistake must be reasonable to exculpate the defendant.[284] Since a voluntarily intoxicated mistake cannot be reasonable such a mistake as to such a matter of excuse cannot excuse.

15.95 The same applies in relation to the various 'no negligence' defences,[285] as shown by the decision of the Courts-Martial Appeal Court in *Young*.[286] In that case the defendant had undoubtedly been in possession of a controlled drug, namely LSD, with intent to supply it to another, and the only defence which might have been available to him was that under the Misuse of Drugs Act 1971, s 28. Section 28 provides that the defendant

---

[281] [1981] QB 527, DC.

[282] The defendant has an evidential burden in relation to such an excuse, which can pose problems for a defendant who was so intoxicated that he cannot clearly remember later what his belief was: see *Gannon* [1988] RTR 49, CA.

[283] Support for this can be found in *Young*, para 15.95, in relation to a defence based on a 'belief or suspicion', as opposed to 'reasonable suspicion'.

[284] Para 5.19.   [285] Para 6.46.   [286] [1984] 2 All ER 164, C-MAC (see para 2.32, n 91).

shall be acquitted if he 'proves' that he neither believed, nor suspected, nor had reason to suspect that the substance in question was a controlled drug. There was evidence that the defendant was voluntarily intoxicated at the material time. Dismissing his appeal against conviction, the Courts-Martial Appeal Court held that, although (for the same reasons as in para 15.93) evidence of voluntary intoxication was relevant to the question of belief or suspicion in s 28, it was irrelevant to the question of whether there was 'reason to suspect'. The question was not whether the defendant, with his intoxication, had reason to suspect that the substance was a controlled drug, but whether there was an objective reason to suspect that (to which question the defendant's intoxication was wholly irrelevant).

Voluntary intoxication causing insanity or alcoholism constituting an abnormality of mental functioning

> **Key points 15.11**
>
> If voluntary intoxication produces a distinct disease of the mind so as to bring the *M'Naghten Rules* into play the defendant can rely on the defence of insanity. On a murder charge, a plea of diminished responsibility can successfully be based on alcoholism in specified circumstances.

15.96 Another exception to the general rule that voluntary intoxication is irrelevant to criminal liability is where drinking or drug-taking produces a distinct disease of the mind so that the defendant is insane within the *M'Naghten Rules*. The defendant will have the defence of insanity if he proves that at the material time he was suffering from a defect of reason, due to the disease of the mind caused by intoxication, such that he did not know the nature and quality of his act or that it was wrong.[287] If the defendant proves this at a trial in the Crown Court he will be found not guilty by reason of insanity[288] by the jury; in a magistrates' court he will receive a complete acquittal if the case is tried there. The defence of insanity is, of course, of general application; it is not limited to offences requiring a specific intent.

Although mere malfunctioning of the mind due to intoxication does not constitute a 'disease of the mind',[289] habitual drinking or drug-taking can sometimes lead to such permanent changes in the brain tissues as to be accounted insanity, such as delirium tremens or alcoholic dementia. A plea of insanity based on intoxication is extremely rare but an old example is *Davis*.[290] At his trial for wounding with intent to murder (an offence which no longer exists in those words), D raised the defence of insanity. There

---

[287] If the prosecution has raised the issue of insanity, as it may, it will be for the prosecution – not the defendant – to prove these things; para 15.36.

[288] *Davis* (1881) 14 Cox CC 563; *DPP v Beard* [1920] AC 479, HL; *A-G for Northern Ireland v Gallagher* [1963] AC 349, HL.

[289] *Quick* [1973] QB 910, CA.   [290] (1881) 14 Cox CC 563.

was evidence that at the time, although sober, he was suffering from delirium tremens resulting from excessive drinking. Stephen J directed the jury that 'drunkenness is one thing and the diseases to which drunkenness leads are different things'.[291] He said that if a man by drink brought on a disease of the mind which caused a defect of reason, albeit temporarily, which would have relieved him from responsibility if it had been produced in any other way, he would not be criminally responsible. The jury were told to find a verdict of not guilty on the ground of insanity if they thought that D had been suffering from a distinct disease of the mind caused by drinking, but differing from drunkenness, and that by reason thereof he did not know that his act was wrong.

15.97 Two observations may be made about this exception to the general rule. First, it is only where it applies that the defendant's appreciation of the legal implications of his conduct becomes relevant; ignorance of the wrongfulness of conduct is irrelevant in the case of those who are sane but intoxicated, as has been stated above. Secondly, the distinction between temporary insanity caused by drink or drugs and simple intoxication is not easy to make. This is unfortunate since the distinction is important where the defendant alleges that because of drinking or drug-taking he did not know his conduct was wrong.

15.98 Stephen J's direction was approved by the House of Lords in both *DPP v Beard*[292] and *A-G for Northern Ireland v Gallagher*.[293] The latter case is particularly important in this context since the judgments emphasise that if the defendant was suffering from a disease of the mind which was insufficient to bring him within the *M'Naghten Rules*, eg because it would never induce anything more than lack of control, the fact that the disease was exacerbated by intoxication at the material time would not make the defence of insanity available to him. When sober, D formed the intention of killing his wife. He then purchased a bottle of whisky, and drank some of it before he in fact killed his wife with a knife. At D's trial he pleaded insanity and intoxication preventing him having specific intent. There was evidence that D was a psychopath, and that his psychopathy was a disease of the mind which would be aggravated by drink in such a way as to cause him the more readily to lose his self-control. The trial judge told the jury that, in considering whether the *M'Naghten Rules* applied to the case, they should have regard to D's state of mind just before he took the whisky. D was convicted. He successfully appealed to the Northern Irish Court of Criminal Appeal, but his conviction was subsequently reinstated by the House of Lords. The basis of the House of Lords' decision was that D's psychopathy was quiescent and, without the drink, could not have brought the *M'Naghten Rules* into play because it merely weakened his power of self-control, and the defence of insanity could not be made good by getting drunk on whisky. It would have been different, it was said, if D's psychopathy had been caused by drink and he had been insane within the *M'Naghten Rules*.

15.99 A plea of diminished responsibility on a murder charge cannot be based on an abnormality of mental functioning due to intoxication itself, but it can successfully be based on alcoholism in the circumstances described in Chapter 8.[294]

---

[291] (1881) 14 Cox CC 563 at 564.   [292] [1920] AC 479, HL.
[293] [1963] AC 349, HL.   [294] Para 8.69.

Dutch courage

15.100 A restriction on the exceptions to the general rule that voluntary intoxication is no defence was postulated by Lord Denning in *A-G for Northern Ireland v Gallagher*.[295] His Lordship dealt with the issues raised in that case in a way different from that of his colleagues and introduced what may be called the 'Dutch courage' rule, which is particularly important in the case of intoxication as evidence of the lack of a necessary specific intent.

Lord Denning said that the case had to be decided on the general rule that drunkenness is no defence to a criminal charge. He recognised that there were exceptions to this rule but held that they were inapplicable, because Gallagher had deliberately made himself drunk in order to give himself Dutch courage to commit the offence.

His Lordship said:

> 'If a man, whilst sane and sober, forms an intention to kill and makes preparation for it, knowing it is a wrong thing to do, and then gets himself drunk so as to give himself Dutch courage to do the thing, and whilst drunk carries out his intention, he cannot rely on this self-induced drunkenness as a defence to a charge of murder, nor even as reducing it to manslaughter. He cannot say that he got himself into such a stupid state that he was incapable of an intent to kill. So, also, when he is a psychopath, he cannot by drinking rely on his self-induced defect of reason as a defence of insanity. The wickedness of his mind before he got drunk is enough to condemn him, coupled with the act which he intended to do and did do. A psychopath who goes out intending to kill, knowing it is wrong, and does kill, cannot escape the consequences by making himself drunk before doing it.'[296]

Lord Denning suggested that the case would have been different if Gallagher had resiled from his intention to kill his wife before taking the drink. In that event, the question would have been whether the drunkenness was such as to bring the case within the first exception to the general rule (intoxication as evidence of the lack of a necessary specific intent). Although Lord Denning's formulation of the Dutch courage rule is to be welcomed as a matter of policy, it does provide an apparent exception to the rule that *mens rea* and conduct must be contemporaneous.[297]

Involuntary intoxication

Key points 15.12

Where the defendant was involuntarily intoxicated, evidence of his intoxication may be taken into account in deciding whether he had the *mens rea* for the offence (whether or not a specific intent is required).

---

[295] [1963] AC 349, HL; para 15.98.   [296] [1963] AC 349 at 382.   [297] Para 3.65.

15.101 The classic case of involuntary intoxication is where intoxication is induced by a third party, rather than being self-induced, as where the defendant's friends have slipped vodka into his lemonade or where he has been drugged by his enemies or he has taken an intoxicant under duress.

15.102 A person who is involuntarily intoxicated cannot, unlike a voluntarily intoxicated person, be said to be responsible for his condition. Consequently, it is not surprising that the law takes a more liberal view in his case and provides that the defendant has a defence if his involuntary intoxication causes automatism and that, where the defendant was involuntarily intoxicated, evidence of his intoxication may be taken into account in deciding whether he had the necessary *mens rea* for the offence (whether or not a specific intent is required).[298] However, involuntary intoxication is not in itself a defence. Provided he acted voluntarily with the requisite *mens rea*, the fact that involuntary intoxication led the defendant to have a blurred perception of morality or to commit an offence which he would not have committed when sober does not afford him a defence (although it may mitigate his punishment), and this is so even though because of his intoxication he acted under an irresistible impulse.

15.103 It was only in 1994 that these principles were authoritatively established, by the House of Lords in *Kingston*.[299] D, who had paedophiliac homosexual tendencies, was in dispute with a couple who arranged for X to obtain damaging information against D, which could be used against him. X invited a 15-year-old boy to his room. According to the prosecution, and the jury accepted this, the boy was drugged by X and fell asleep. While he was asleep D visited X's room and indulged in indecent acts on the boy. These were recorded by X. D was charged with the now repealed offence of indecent assault[300] on the boy. His defence was that he had been involuntarily intoxicated at the time because X had laced his drink. The trial judge directed the jury that it was not open to them to acquit D if they merely found that he had assaulted the boy pursuant to an intent induced by the influence of intoxication secretly induced by X nor was it open to them to find that such intoxication of itself negatived the *mens rea* required for the offence on D's part. The judge directed the jury that they should, on the other hand, acquit D if they found that he was involuntarily so intoxicated that he did not intend (or might not have intended) to commit the indecent assault (a basic intent offence) on the boy. The jury convicted D who appealed successfully to the Court of Appeal. The Crown then appealed successfully to the House of Lords, who held that the trial judge had correctly directed the jury and who stated the principles of law set out in the previous paragraph.

---

[298] Where the involuntary intoxication results in the defendant becoming an automaton, he will have the defence of non-insane automatism: paras 15.50 and 15.57–15.64.

[299] [1995] 2 AC 355, HL.

[300] By the Sexual Offences Act 2003. The offence would now be that of sexual assault contrary to the Sexual Offences Act 2003, s 3.

15.104 Intoxication is also involuntary in the following two cases, even though it is self-induced. It would appear that the law approaches both cases in the same way as the type of involuntary intoxication outlined above.

15.105 The first of the two cases is where the intoxication results from the taking of drugs administered or prescribed by a doctor or other qualified person. However, if the defendant has become intoxicated because he has not acted in accordance with the doctor's instructions, as where he has thereafter taken alcohol contrary to instructions or where he recklessly exceeds the prescribed dosage, his intoxication will be voluntary – not involuntary. The comment about recklessness made in para 15.107 is equally applicable in the latter instance.

15.106 The second case where self-induced intoxication is nevertheless involuntary (subject to the exception mentioned shortly) is where it is caused by a non-dangerous drug, even if the drug is taken in excessive quantities and is not taken under and in accordance with medical advice. A non-dangerous drug is one which is not normally liable to cause unpredictability or aggressiveness (eg a sedative or soporific drug, such as Valium). However, the intoxication will be voluntary, not involuntary, if the defendant was reckless when he took the non-dangerous drug.

The authority for all this is *Hardie*.[301] D's relationship with a woman with whom he was living in a flat broke down and she insisted that he must leave. He became distressed and took several of her Valium tablets to calm his nerves. Two of the tablets were taken in front of the woman, who had said 'Take as many as you like. They are old stock and will do you no harm.' Later D started a fire in the bedroom of the flat while the woman and the daughter were in the sitting room. He was charged with arson contrary to the Criminal Damage Act 1971, s 1(2) and (3), ie intentionally or recklessly damaging property by fire, intending to endanger the life of another thereby or being reckless as to whether another's life would thereby be endangered.[302] D argued that the effect of the drug was to prevent him having the relevant *mens rea*. The judge directed the jury that, because the intoxication was self-induced, it was irrelevant as a defence and its effects could not negative *mens rea*. In other words, he dealt with the case under the normal rule which applies to voluntary intoxication in a basic intent offence.

D was convicted but appealed successfully to the Court of Appeal, which held, although the offence was one of basic intent, that the normal rule did not apply where the intoxication was due to a non-dangerous drug, even if it had been taken in excessive quantities. Instead, the jury should have been told that, if they concluded that as a result of the Valium D had been unable to appreciate the risks from his actions, they should then consider whether the taking of Valium was itself reckless. Only if it was would D be guilty.

[301] [1984] 3 All ER 848, CA.
[302] It is now recognised that there are two offences of arson contrary to the Criminal Damage Act 1971, s 1(2) and (3): one involving an intent to endanger life, and the other recklessness in this respect. See para 13.25.

15.107 The Court of Appeal left a couple of points open in *Hardie*. First, it said that intoxication through a non-dangerous drug might in certain circumstances never be an answer; it gave the subsequently repealed offence of reckless driving, which has been replaced by that of dangerous driving, as an example. Second, it did not define what it meant by a 'reckless taking' of a drug but, clearly, it meant recklessness (ie awareness) as to the risk of becoming unpredictable or aggressive.[303]

Special statutory provision

15.108 The Public Order Act 1986, s 6(5) makes special provision for cases where the awareness of a person accused of riot, violent disorder, affray, threatening, abusive or insulting words or behaviour intended or likely to cause fear of, or to provoke violence, or threatening, abusive or insulting words or behaviour likely to cause harassment, alarm or distress, contrary to Pt I of the 1986 Act was impaired by intoxication. All the offences in question require an intention or awareness as to a specified factor. Section 6(5) provides that, for the purposes of an offence under Pt I:

> 'a person whose awareness is impaired by intoxication shall be taken to be aware of that of which he would be aware if not intoxicated, unless he shows[304] either that his intoxication was not self-induced or that it was caused solely by the taking or administration of a substance in the course of medical treatment.'

If one or other of these things is shown, this does not mean that the defendant is not guilty of the offence in question, but merely that, on a charge of riot, for example, he is not guilty unless it is proved that he actually intended to use violence or was aware that his conduct might be violent. The effect of s 6(5) is the same as would have resulted from an application of the common law rules on intoxication, except that the burden of showing involuntary intoxication is placed on the defendant and that those who become intoxicated after taking non-dangerous drugs (otherwise than in the course of medical treatment) are dealt with differently.

Proposals for reform

15.109 In 1975, the Butler Committee on Mentally Abnormal Offenders[305] proposed the creation of a new offence of dangerous intoxication, which would be committed by a person who, while voluntarily intoxicated, did an act, or failed to do an act, that would

---

[303] As in the case of self-induced automatism, see *Bailey* [1983] 2 All ER 503, CA; para 15.64.

[304] 'He shows' seems to place the persuasive burden of proof on the defendant. It is, however, arguable that, quite apart from the possibility of reading down the provision so as to impose only an evidential burden, the use of 'proves' in respect of the defendant elsewhere in the Public Order Act 1986 implies that the burden under s 6(5) is only an evidential one.

[305] *Report on Mentally Abnormal Offenders*, Cmnd 6244, paras 18.51–18.59.

amount to a 'dangerous offence' if he acted, or failed to act, with the requisite *mens rea* for that offence. This offence would not be charged in the first instance but would be available where the defendant was acquitted of a 'dangerous offence' (essentially an offence against the person) on the ground that he lacked the *mens rea* for the 'dangerous offence' because of his intoxication. The maximum punishment for the offence of dangerous intoxication would have been one year's imprisonment for a first offence, and three years' for a subsequent one.

15.110 In its Fourteenth Report, *Offences against the Person*,[306] published in 1980, the majority of the Criminal Law Revision Committee considered that the proposed offence was unsatisfactory since a record of a conviction would not indicate the nature of the act committed, for example whether it was an assault or a killing, and it would be unfair for a defendant who had committed a relatively minor offence while intoxicated to be labelled as having committed the same offence as one who had killed. It also thought that the proposed maximum sentence was inadequate for serious offences such as killings or rapes while intoxicated. The majority simply recommended that the common law rules based on *Majewski* should be replaced by provisions along similar lines.

15.111 In a consultation paper published in 1993,[307] the Law Commission provisionally proposed that the *Majewski* approach should be abolished and evidence of voluntary intoxication should always be admissible on the issue of whether the defendant had had *mens rea* or was an automaton. However, to prevent those who caused harm while intoxicated escaping social control, it provisionally proposed as an added option the creation of an offence of criminal intoxication. This offence would have been committed by a defendant who, while substantially intoxicated, caused the harm proscribed for a 'listed' offence, such as homicide, bodily harm, rape or criminal damage. It would have been irrelevant that the defendant did not have the *mens rea* for the 'listed' offence or was then an automaton.[308]

15.112 In the light of responses, the Law Commission abandoned this proposal and simply recommended in its report on intoxication,[309] published in 1995, the codification of the existing law with minor amendments and some clarification. Its attempts to do so, however, included a highly complicated draft Bill. Consequently, when preparing the draft Offences Against the Person Bill,[310] the Government did not incorporate the Law Commission's draft, but inserted a simpler provision which ensured that those who were voluntarily intoxicated could not rely on evidence of this to negative recklessness.

---

[306] Cmnd 7844, paras 257–261, 264–275.

[307] *Intoxication and Criminal Liability* (1993), Law Commission Consultation Paper No 127.

[308] For different views on the provisional proposal, see Virgo 'Reconciling Principle and Policy' [1993] Crim LR 415; S Gardner 'The Importance of *Majewski*' (1994) 14 OJLS 279.

[309] Law Commission: *Legislating the Criminal Code: Intoxication and Criminal Liability*, Law Com No 229. Discussed by Paton 'Re-formulating the Intoxication Rules: The Law Commission Report' [1995] Crim LR 382, Gough 'Intoxication and Criminal Liability: The Law Commission's Proposed Reforms' (1996) 112 LQR 335 and Horder 'Sobering Up' (1995) 58 MLR 534.

[310] Home Office: *Violence: Reforming the Offences against the Person Act 1861* (1998); para 7.131.

15.113 In 2009, the Law Commission issued another report on intoxication[311]: which, like its report on intoxication in 1995, recommends the codification of the present law relating to intoxication on the part of a perpetrator generally without any significant changes.

In addition, the Law Commission makes recommendations about the position of an intoxicated defendant who is a secondary party (ie an accomplice) to an offence, in relation to which the principles have not yet been developed by the judges.[312] The report also contains a recommendation to address the issue of intoxication where a person is charged with one of the inchoate offences of encouraging or assisting crime contrary to the Serious Crime Act 2007, Pt 2 (which offences do not require an offence to be encouraged or assisted to be committed).[313]

The draft Bill to give effect to the Commission's recommendations, which is included in the report, is much more straightforward than that attached to its 1995 report.

The Law Commission's recommendations in its report in respect of voluntary intoxication are as follows:

'RECOMMENDATION 1: [THE GENERAL RULE]

There should be a general rule that

(1) if D is charged with having committed an offence as a perpetrator;

(2) the fault element of the offence is not an integral fault element [see recommendation 3 below] (for example, because it merely requires proof of recklessness); and

(3) D was voluntarily intoxicated at the material time;

then, in determining whether or not D is liable for the offence, D should be treated as having been aware at the material time of anything which D would then have been aware of but for the intoxication.

RECOMMENDATION 2: THE RULE FOR INTEGRAL FAULT ELEMENTS

If the subjective fault element in the definition of the offence, as alleged [by the prosecution], is [an integral fault element], then the prosecution should have to prove that D acted with that relevant state of mind.

RECOMMENDATION 3: [THE INTEGRAL FAULT ELEMENTS]

The following subjective fault elements should be excluded from the application of the general rule and should, therefore, always be proved:

(1) intention as to a consequence;

(2) knowledge [which in this context clearly does not include wilful blindness] as to something;

---

[311] *Intoxication and Criminal Liability* (2009) Law Com No 314. For a review of the report, which criticises parts of it, see Child 'Drink, Drugs and Law Reform: A Review of Law Commission Report No 314' [2009] Crim LR 488.

[312] See para 15.90.   [313] Para 14.24.

(3) belief as to something (where the belief is equivalent to knowledge as to something);

(4) fraud; and

(5) dishonesty.'

These three recommendations retain the substance of the distinction between specific intent and basic intent. In view of the problems which the judges have had in defining these terms the re-casting of the law without them is to be welcomed.

'RECOMMENDATION 4: [DEFENCES AND MISTAKEN BELIEFS]

D should not be able to rely on a genuine mistake of fact arising from self-induced intoxication in support of a defence to which D's state of mind is relevant, regardless of the nature of the fault alleged. D's mistaken belief should be taken into account only if D would have held the same belief if D had not been intoxicated.'

This is intended to retain the present law as it relates to a voluntarily intoxicated mistaken belief in the need to act in self-defence or as to any other defence where the defendant's state of mind is relevant to the defence.

'RECOMMENDATION 5: ["HONEST BELIEF" PROVISIONS]

The rule governing mistakes of fact relied on in support of a defence [including self-defence or the prevention of crime and related defences] (recommendation 4) should apply equally to "honest belief" provisions which state how defences should be interpreted.'

Recommendation 5 reverses the principle in *Jaggard v Dickinson*.[314]

'RECOMMENDATION 6: [NEGLIGENCE AND NO-FAULT OFFENCES]

If the offence charged requires proof of a fault element of failure to comply with an objective standard of care, or requires no fault at all, D should be permitted to rely on a genuine but mistaken belief as to the existence of a fact, where D's state of mind is relevant to a defence, only if D would have made that mistake if he or she had not been voluntarily intoxicated.'

This recommendation would have the same effect as recommendation 4 where the offence was one of negligence or strict liability and the defendant acted under a voluntarily intoxicated mistake as to the need to act in self-defence or as to any other defence where the defendant's state of mind is relevant to the defence.

---

[314] Para 15.93.

The Law Commission's recommendations for principles to deal with voluntary intoxication in relation to secondary liability or liability under the Serious Crime Act 2007, Pt 2 are as follows:

> **'RECOMMENDATION 7: [SECONDARY LIABILITY GENERALLY]**
>
> For the doctrine of secondary liability generally (where no joint enterprise is alleged):
>
> (1) if the offence is one which always requires proof of an integral fault element, then the state of mind required for D to be secondarily liable for that offence should equally be regarded as an integral fault element;
>
> (2) if the offence does not always require proof of an integral fault element, then the [general] rule on voluntary intoxication should apply in determining D's secondary liability for the offence.
>
> **RECOMMENDATION 8: [SECONDARY LIABILITY – JOINT ENTERPRISES]**
>
> Our proposed rule [recommendation 7] on the relevance of voluntary intoxication to secondary liability generally should apply equally to cases of alleged joint enterprise.
>
> **RECOMMENDATION 9: [INCHOATE LIABILITY]**
>
> If D is charged under Part 2 of the Serious Crime Act 2007 with an offence of encouraging or assisting another person to commit a crime ("the crime"), then if the crime is one which would always require proof of an integral fault element for a perpetrator to be liable, and the allegation against D requires the prosecution to prove that D was "reckless" for the purposes of section 47(5) of the Act,[315] the state of mind of being "reckless" should be treated as an integral fault element.'

In relation to involuntary intoxication the Law Commission's recommendation simply gives effect to the principle established in *Kingston*.[316] The Commission rejected the idea of a new excuse of reduced inhibitions or blurred perception of morality where the defendant's condition was caused by involuntary intoxication.

If implemented, the Law Commission's recommendations would not affect the law relating to an issue of insanity or non-insane automatism.

FURTHER READING

Baker 'Human Rights, *M'Naghten* and the 1991 Act' [1994] Crim LR 84

Barlow 'Drug Intoxication and the Principle of *Capacitas Rationalis*' (1984) 100 LQR 639

Dell 'Wanted: An Insanity Defence that Can Be Used' [1984] Crim LR 431

Ebrahim, Wilson, Marks, Peacock and Fenwick 'Violence, Sleepwalking and the

---

[315] See para 14.24.   [316] Paras 15.102–15.103.

Criminal Law: (1) The Medical Aspects' [2005] Crim LR 601

Edwards 'Automatism and Criminal Responsibility' (1958) 21 MLR 375

S Gardner 'The Importance of *Majewski*' (1994) 14 OJLS 279

Hart *Punishment and Responsibility* (2nd edn, J Gardner (ed), 2008) 90

Horder 'Pleading Involuntary Lack of Capacity' (1993) 52 CLJ 298

Lederman 'Non-Insane and Insane Automatism: Reducing the Significance of a Problematic Distinction' (1983) 34 ICLQ 819

Mackay *Mental Condition Defences in the Criminal Law* (1995)

Mackay 'Righting the Wrong? Some Observations on the Second Limb of the M'Naghten Rules' [2009] Crim LR 80

Mackay and Kearns 'The Trial of the Facts and Unfitness to Plead' [1997] Crim LR 644

Mackay and Mitchell 'Sleepwalking, Automatism and Insanity' [2006] Crim LR 901

Mackay and Reuber 'Epilepsy and the Defence of Insanity – Time for Change?' [2007] Crim LR 782

Samuels 'Hospital Orders without Conviction' [1995] Crim LR 220

Simester 'Intoxication is Never a Defence' [2009] Crim LR 3

Smith and Clements 'Involuntary Intoxication, the Threshold of Inhibition and the Instigation of Crime' (1995) 46 NILQ 210

Sutherland and Gearty 'Insanity and the European Court of Human Rights' [1992] Crim LR 418

Ward 'Making Some Sense of Self-Induced Intoxication' (1986) 45 CLJ 247

Wells 'Whither Insanity?' [1983] Crim LR 787

White 'The Criminal Procedure (Insanity and Unfitness to Plead) Act' [1992] Crim LR 4

Wilson, Ebrahim, Fenwick and Marks 'Violence, Sleepwalking and the Criminal Law: (2) The Legal Aspects' [2005] Crim LR 614

16

Other general defences

OVERVIEW

This chapter deals with:

- the justifications of self-defence, prevention of crime and other 'public or private defences';
- the excuses of duress by threats and duress of circumstances;
- the excuse of marital coercion.

It concludes by considering when necessity can provide a justification for otherwise criminal conduct and whether superior orders can excuse a defendant.

Public or private defence

Key points 16.1

The term 'public or private defence' is used to describe cases where a defendant acts to protect one of the following public or private interests:

(a) to prevent the commission of a crime;[1]

(b) to effect a lawful arrest;[2]

(c) to prevent or terminate a breach of the peace;[3]

(d) to defend himself or another against an actual or imminent attack;[4]

---

[1] CLA 1967, s 3(1).   [2] CLA 1967, s 3(1).

[3] *King v Hodges* [1974] Crim LR 424, DC. See also *Albert v Lavin* [1982] AC 546 at 565, per Lord Diplock. A mere disturbance is not a breach of the peace; a breach of the peace requires that harm is actually done or is likely to be done to a person, or in his presence to his property, or that a person is in fear of being so harmed by an assault, riot or other disturbance: *Howell* [1982] QB 416, CA. Agitated or excited behaviour not involving any harm, or threat of harm, is not capable of amounting to a breach of the peace: *Jarrett v Chief Constable of the West Midlands* [2003] EWCA Civ 397. A breach of the peace may occur on private premises even if the only persons likely to be affected by the conduct are on those premises: *McConnell v Chief Constable of the Greater Manchester Police* [1990] 1 All ER 423, CA. A breach of the peace is not an offence in itself (*Williamson v Chief Constable of West Midlands Police* [2003] EWCA Civ 337), although the conduct involved in a particular breach of the peace may amount to an offence against the person or some other offence.

[4] *Duffy* [1967] 1 QB 63, CCA; *DPP v Bayer* [2003] EWHC 2567 (Admin), DC.

> (e) to defend his or another's property against such an attack;[5] or
>
> (f) to prevent or terminate the unlawful imprisonment of himself or another, or an imminent or actual trespass.[6]

16.1 An act for a purpose within (a) to (c) in the list in Key Points 16.1 is done in 'public defence', one for a purpose within (d) to (f) in 'private defence'. **These 'defences' are different from the excuses of duress by threats, duress of circumstances and marital coercion, discussed later in this chapter, because, if successfully pleaded, they render the defendant's conduct lawful; they justify it, as opposed simply to excusing the defendant from liability for conduct which is nevertheless unlawful.**[7] For this reason, inverted commas were placed round 'defences' in the last sentence.

It continues to be a requirement of (d) and (e) (self-defence, defence of another and defence of property) that what the defendant experiences or fears is criminal or unlawful (ie tortious). This was held by the Divisional Court in *DPP v Bayer*[8] where the defendants had chained themselves to tractors on private land in order to prevent genetically modified maize being drilled. They were held not to have the defence of property available to them as a defence on a charge of aggravated trespass[9] because they knew quite well that there was nothing criminal or unlawful about the drilling. One problem with *DPP v Bayer* is that a person does not normally commit an offence[10] or a tort[11] if he is an automaton at the time. It is inconceivable that one cannot use reasonable force to protect oneself against an attack by someone known to be an automaton.

16.2 Force used to damage or destroy *property to defend other property* is dealt with by the defence to criminal damage of 'lawful excuse', described in Chapter 13.

Statutory and common law defences

16.3 Until the Criminal Law Act 1967 (CLA 1967) the legal position of any person acting in public or private defence was governed by common law rules, but s 3(1) of that Act now provides that:

> 'A person may use such force as is reasonable in the circumstances in the prevention of crime,[12] or in effecting or assisting in the lawful arrest of offenders or suspected offenders or of persons unlawfully at large.'

---

[5] *Duffy* [1967] 1 QB 63, CCA; *DPP v Bayer* [2003] EWHC 2567 (Admin), DC.

[6] See, for example, *Weaver v Bush* (1798) 8 Term Rep 78 (trespass to land).

[7] Para 2.20. See also Williams 'The Theory of Excuses' [1982] Crim LR 732. Recognition that duress is an excuse was given in *Hasan* [2005] UKHL 22 at [18], per Lord Bingham.

[8] [2003] EWHC 2567 (Admin), DC.

[9] Contrary to the Criminal Justice and Public Order Act 1994, s 68.

[10] Key Points 15.5 and paras 15.50–15.64.

[11] *Morris v Marsden* [1952] 1 All ER 925; *Roberts v Ramsbottom* [1980] 1 All ER 7.

[12] 'Crime' in s 3(1) refers to an offence under domestic (ie English) law, and not to a crime only under international law: *Jones (Margaret)* [2006] UKHL 16.

The CLA 1967, s 3(1) permits anyone to use reasonable force for one of the specified purposes; it is not limited to police officers. In relation to the prevention of crime, the provision is not limited to serious offences (although in the case of the prevention of a minor offence it is likely that only a slight degree of force could be reasonable).

Section 3(1) is limited to the use of force. In *Blake v DPP*,[13] the Divisional Court held that s 3(1) could not apply where an anti-Gulf War demonstrator, charged with criminal damage, who had written a Biblical quotation with a felt-tip pen on a pillar, had argued, inter alia, that he had done so to prevent crimes being committed by the allies; his conduct was 'insufficient to amount to force within the section'. The fact that s 3(1) can excuse the use of force but not less serious conduct to prevent crime etc is puzzling.

The CLA 1967, s 3(2) provides that s 3(1) replaces the common law rules on when force used for the purposes mentioned in s 3(1) is justified by that purpose. Clearly, for example, s 3(1) has superseded the common law where force is used to prevent the commission of indecent exposure or to prevent a person making off without payment, but s 3(1) has not superseded the common law defences of self-defence, defence of another, defence of property, and prevention or termination of a breach of the peace, unlawful imprisonment or trespass.

16.4 A person acting in self-defence, defence of another or defence of property or to prevent or terminate a breach of the peace, unlawful imprisonment or trespass is usually engaged in the prevention of crime. In such a case it is arguable that the CLA 1967, s 3(1) alone now governs the situation. However, in *Cousins*,[14] the Court of Appeal was clearly of the opinion that **a person who used force to repel an attack could avail himself of the common law defence of self-defence and of the defence under s 3(1) of preventing the commission of the crime which such an attack would have involved**, provided in both cases that the force used was reasonable in the circumstances. In such a case then (and presumably in the case of defence of others and defence of property and the prevention or termination of a breach of the peace, unlawful imprisonment or trespass), the common law defence survives alongside the statutory one.

In some cases of self-defence and the like, only the common law defence will be available. One type of case is where the defendant uses force against an attacker who is a child under 10,[15] so that force cannot be said to have been used in the prevention of crime.[16] Other types of case are where force is used to prevent or terminate a breach of the peace or trespass not involving the commission of an offence, or where it is used against property

---

[13] [1993] Crim LR 586, DC. (This point does not appear in this brief report but is contained in the transcript.) Also see *Hutchinson v Newbury Magistrates' Court* (2000) Independent, 20 November, DC (cutting through a perimeter fence of an atomic weapons establishment held not to constitute 'force').

[14] [1982] QB 526, CA. See also *Devlin v Armstrong* [1971] NI 13, NICA.

[15] A child under 10 can commit the tort of battery (or any other tort) if it has the required state of mind for the tort: Murphy *Street on Torts* (12th edn, 2007) 622.

[16] *Re A (conjoined twins: surgical separation)* [2001] Fam 147 at 204, per Ward LJ.

for the purpose of self-protection or the protection of another (eg against a vicious attacking dog[17]).

16.5 The principles governing the common law defences are the same as apply in the case of the defences under s 3(1).[18] A number of restrictive rules which used to attach to the common law defences no longer apply. For example, old cases on self-defence established that a person attacked must retreat as far as he could before resorting to force. In *McInnes*,[19] decided in 1971, it was held that this is now simply a factor in deciding whether the force used was reasonable in the circumstances. (Indeed, the defendant need not even demonstrate his unwillingness to fight, although this is the best evidence that he was acting reasonably and in good faith in self-defence.)[20] Similarly, in the case of defence of property the test of reasonableness is applied by analogy to the exclusion of the old rules which can be deduced from some of the cases,[21] such as the rule that lethal force may always be used against a burglar or against someone seeking to evict a householder unlawfully and forcibly.

16.6 The statement above that the same principles apply to the common law defences as apply to the defences under s 3(1) is confirmed by the Criminal Justice and Immigration Act 2008 (CJIA 2008), s 76 in relation to *the common law defences of self-defence or defence of another and the defences under the CLA 1967, s 3(1) of use of force in the prevention of crime or making of a lawful arrest*. The CJIA 2008, s 76 is intended to clarify the operation of those defences.[22] It seeks to do so by putting into statutory form *four* of the principles established by the case law. Three of these principles are referred to in paras 16.18, 16.21 and 16.24 of this chapter; the fourth (defendant cannot rely on mistake attributable to voluntary intoxication in relation to question of whether force used was reasonable in the circumstances as he believed them to be) has been referred to in Chapter 15.[23] As will be seen, there are other principles established by the case law to which s 76 does not refer. To the extent that they apply, the provisions of s 76 supersede the common law.

Because of the partial coverage of s 76 in terms of the public and private defences to which it applies and of the principles to which it gives statutory form, it does not codify the existing law on public and private defences. It has rightly been criticised as pointless as far as criminal lawyers are concerned.[24]

Following the conviction in 2000 of Tony Martin, who fatally shot a burglar, there was much public discussion of the question of 'how much force may I use?' in self-defence or the prevention of crime or in pre-emptive action to deal with an anticipated situation requiring the use of force. At the Labour Party conference in 2007 the Secretary of

---

[17] Such an act would involve its keeper in tortious liability: see Murphy *Street on Torts* (12th edn, 2007) Ch 19.

[18] *McInnes* [1971] 3 All ER 295, CA; *Devlin v Armstrong* [1971] NI 13, NICA.

[19] [1971] 3 All ER 295, CA.

[20] *Bird* [1985] 2 All ER 513, CA, not following dicta in *Julien* [1969] 2 All ER 856, CA, that a demonstration of unwillingness to fight was required.

[21] Lanham 'Defence of Property in the Criminal Law' [1966] Crim LR 368, 426.

[22] CJIA 2008, s 76(2), (9) and (10)(b).   [23] Paras 15.80–15.83.

[24] [2008] Crim LR 507 (editorial).

State for Justice announced a review of the use of force in self-defence or the prevention of crime. Section 76 provides no clarification or guidance in answer to the above question. Perhaps this is inevitable as long as the test is that of 'reasonable force', because the reasonableness of force is always specific to the particular situation and surrounding circumstances, and the defendant's perception of them.

16.7 When references are made elsewhere in this chapter to the CJIA 2008, s 76 the reader should remember that, by s 76(1) and (2), s 76 only applies where in proceedings for an offence:

- an issue arises as to whether a person charged with the offence ('D') is entitled to rely on the common law defences of self-defence, or defence of another,[25] or the defences provided by the CLA 1967, s 3(1); and
- the question arises whether the degree of force[26] used by D against a person ('V') was reasonable in the circumstances.

Applicability of defences

16.8 Although a person who acts in self-defence or the like is normally actually being attacked, the defences of self-defence, defence of another or defence of property are not limited to this situation since it has been recognised that **they can apply to pre-emptive action against an imminent apprehended attack**.[27] Thus, provided he uses no more than reasonable force, the law permits a person to strike first to prevent an attack which he apprehends. Of course, what is reasonable force in a pre-emptive strike may well be less than what would be reasonable force against an actual attack.

16.9 **The application of the defences is not limited to offences against the person.** For example, in *Renouf*,[28] the Court of Appeal held that it was a defence to a charge of the now repealed offence of reckless driving that the use of force which constituted the reckless driving (edging another car off a road to assist in the arrest of its occupants) amounted to the use of reasonable force for the purpose of effecting the lawful arrest of an offender.[29] Another example would be the commission of criminal damage in self-defence against attack by someone's Rotweiler dog.

16.10 It has not yet been decided whether the defences discussed in this part can ever be pleaded successfully where the force is used against a *wholly* innocent person or his property, as where a police officer who is chasing a dangerous criminal knocks aside an innocent pedestrian who gets in his way or commandeers a car which he uses to ram the criminal's getaway vehicle.

---

[25] Although s 76(1) and (2) do not refer to defence of another person, references in s 76 to self-defence include references to acting in defence of another person: CJIA 2008, s 76(10)(b).

[26] References in s 76 to the degree of force used are to the type and amount of force used: CJIA 2008, s 76(10)(c).

[27] *Finch and Jardine* (1983) unreported, CA; *A-G's Reference (No 2 of 1983)* [1984] QB 456, CA; *Beckford v R* [1988] AC 130 at 144.

[28] [1986] 2 All ER 449, CA.   [29] Also see *A-G's Reference (No 2 of 1983)* [1984] QB 456, CA.

The operation of the defences

Key points 16.2

If there is sufficient evidence to raise an issue that, in using force, the defendant was acting in public or private defence, he will be acquitted unless the prosecution proves that,
on the basis of the circumstances and danger as the defendant believed them to be, the
defendant did not use such force as is reasonable in the circumstances in the prevention
of crime, self-defence or the protection of one of the other interests covered by public or
private defence.

16.11 The defendant does not have the burden of proof in relation to the defences under
the CLA 1967, s 3(1) or the common law defences. However, only if there is sufficient evidence to raise an issue that, in using force,[30] the defendant acted for a purpose covered
by one of these defences will the defence be left to the jury in the Crown Court, in which
case the prosecution must rebut it beyond reasonable doubt.[31] Normally, evidence of one
of these defences will come from the defendant but the issue of whether the defendant
has one of these defences may be raised by the prosecution's evidence or a co-defendant's
evidence. If there is sufficient evidence of self-defence or another of these defences, a
judge must leave the defence to the jury even though the defendant has not sought to rely
on it.[32]

16.12 If one of these defences has been raised as above, the question for the jury (or the
magistrates) is whether the prosecution has proved beyond reasonable doubt that the
defendant did not use such force as is reasonable in the circumstances as he believed
them to be in the prevention of crime, or (as the case may be) in effecting or assisting in a
lawful arrest, or in defence of himself etc.[33] A jury should be told that if the defence is not
disproved they should acquit the defendant, but that if it is the defence fails.

16.13 The question whether the force used was reasonable in the circumstances
involves two issues:

- Was the use of any force justified in the circumstances for one of the purposes
  described in Key Points 16.1 (ie was there a need to use any force for one of these
  purposes)?

- Was the force used excessive (ie objectively unreasonable) in the circumstances?

---

[30] The defendant need not have used the force personally; the use of a dog in self-defence, the effecting of
an arrest and so on is capable of amounting to the use of reasonable force: *Pollard v Chief Constable of West
Yorkshire* [1999] PIQR P219, CA (use of properly trained and handled police dog to effect an arrest).

[31] *Lobell* [1957] 1 QB 547, CCA; *Palmer v R* [1971] AC 814, PC; *Abraham* [1973] 3 All ER 694, CA; *Khan* [1995]
Crim LR 78, CA.

[32] *DPP (Jamaica) v Bailey* [1995] Crim LR 313, PC; *Owino* [1996] 2 Cr App Rep 128 at 132.

[33] See, for example, *Drane* [2008] EWCA Crim 1746.

Assessment on the basis of what defendant believed

16.14 Both of the above issues are answered on the basis of the circumstances as the defendant believed them to be. This is so even if his belief as to these facts was a mistaken one and (if so) even if his mistake was an unreasonable one.[34] This was decided by the Court of Appeal in *Gladstone Williams*,[35] possibly obiter, and by the Privy Council in *Beckford v R*,[36] in relation to the first issue, and, although it was implicit in those decisions, it was confirmed by the Court of Appeal in *Owino* [37] that this was so in relation to the second issue.

In *Scarlett*,[38] the Court of Appeal at one point used words which suggested a different approach, viz that a person who used force in public or private defence which, objectively viewed on the facts as he believed them to be was unreasonable, would not be liable if he mistakenly believed that the circumstances called for the degree of force used (ie if he believed that the force used was reasonable). Subsequently, the Court of Appeal in *Owino* [39] said that the words in question must be read in context, and did not mean what they seemed to mean; the law was as set out above. This must be correct. A completely subjective test of what constitutes reasonable force would excuse those too inclined to over-react. The law in this respect can be compared to the more liberal approach where the defendant destroys or damages property in defence of property. As seen in Chapter 13, in such a case the defendant has the defence of lawful excuse to a charge of criminal damage if he *believed* that the means employed were *reasonable*. The Law Commission has recommended that this rule should be brought into line with self-defence in this respect.[40]

16.15 By way of example of the principles just described, if V leaps out of a dark alley as a joke as D passes by late at night and D thinks that he is being attacked and hits V over the head with a heavy walking stick, the reasonableness of D's use of force must be assessed on the basis of his mistaken belief that he was being attacked by an armed and violent robber. Similarly, if D correctly believes that it is necessary to act in self-defence, prevention of crime or the like and uses force for this purpose, mistakenly believing that the assailant is armed, the reasonableness of the force used must be assessed on the basis of the facts as he believed them to be. In neither case would it be relevant that D believed the force used by him was reasonable. A further example is provided by *Faraj*[41] where D had been convicted of the false imprisonment of V. V was a gas engineer who had come to do a job at D's house, but D alleged that he mistakenly believed that V was a burglar and for this reason had threatened V with a knife and detained him. Allowing D's appeal against conviction, the Court of Appeal held that there was no reason why a householder should not be entitled to detain someone in his house whom he genuinely believed to be a burglar. He would be acting in defence of his property by doing so. Full effect could be

---

[34] But note the exception referred to at para 16.17.   [35] (1984) 78 Cr App Rep 276, CA.
[36] [1988] AC 130, PC. For a more recent authority, see *Faraj* [2007] EWCA Crim 1033.
[37] [1996] 2 Cr App Rep 128, CA.   [38] [1993] 4 All ER 629, CA.
[39] [1996] 2 Cr App Rep 128, CA. Also see *DPP v Armstrong-Braun* (1998) 163 JP 271, DC.
[40] See para 13.17.   [41] [2007] EWCA Crim 1033.

given to the defendant's belief however unreasonable it might be. But the householder had to believe honestly that he needed to detain the suspect and he had to do so in a way that was reasonable.

16.16 The fact that the defendant's mistaken belief is not required as a matter of law to be a reasonable one does not mean that the reasonableness of a mistake is entirely irrelevant. The reasonableness of the defendant's alleged mistake is of considerable evidential significance, because the more reasonable the mistake the more likely it is that the jury (or magistrates) will accept his story that he was acting under a mistake.[42]

16.17 As noted in paras 15.80 to 15.83, a defendant cannot rely for the above purposes on any mistaken belief attributable to voluntary intoxication.

16.18 The above points are given statutory form in relation to self-defence, the defence of another and the defences under the CLA 1967, s 3(1) by the CJIA 2008, s 76[43] as follows:

> '(3) The question whether the degree of force[44] used by D was reasonable in the circumstances is to be decided by reference to the circumstances as D believed them to be,...[45]
>
> (4) If D claims to have held a particular belief as regards the existence of any circumstances –
>   (a) the reasonableness or otherwise of that belief is relevant to the question whether D genuinely held it; but
>   (b) if it is determined that D did genuinely hold it, D is entitled to rely on it for the purposes of subsection (3), whether or not –
>   (i) it was mistaken, or
>   (ii) (if it was mistaken) the mistake was a reasonable one to have made.
>
> (5) But subsection (4)(b) does not enable D to rely on any mistaken belief attributable to intoxication that was voluntarily induced.'

16.19 Where the defendant alleges that he used force to prevent crime under the mistaken belief that the conduct in question was on the facts as he believed them to be criminal, he does not have the defence of prevention of crime.[46] His mistake is one of criminal law,[47] not of fact.

---

[42] This was recognised in *Gladstone Williams* (1984) 78 Cr App Rep 276, CA, and *Beckford v R* [1988] AC 130, PC.   [43] See para 16.7.

[44] References in s 76 to the degree of force used are to the type and amount of force used: CJIA 2008, s 76(10)(c).

[45] Section 76(4) to (8) (see paras 16.21 and 16.24) in respect of s 76(6)–(8) also apply in connection with deciding the question under s 76(3): s 76(3).

[46] *Hipperson v DPP* [1996] CLY 1445, DC (the present point does not clearly appear in the brief report, but is dealt with fully in the transcript); *Baker and Wilkins* [1997] Crim LR 497, CA (the brief report should be supplemented by reference to the transcript).   [47] Para 3.74.

16.20 The question of whether the defendant can rely successfully on a public or private defence if, although on the facts reasonable force could have been used in such a defence, he was not aware of any need to act in public or private defence was dealt with in para 2.24.

Reasonable force

16.21 **Except that it is based on the facts as the defendant believed them to be, the test of whether reasonable force has been used in the prevention of crime, self-defence etc is an objective one.** In other words, the question is whether, on the facts as the defendant believed them to be, a reasonable person would regard the force used as reasonable (ie proportionate) in self-defence etc. This test is given statutory form in respect of self-defence, defence of another and the defences under the CLA 1967, s 3(1) by the CJIA 2008, s 76(6),[48] which provides:

> 'The degree of force used by D is not to be regarded as having been reasonable in the circumstances as D believed them to be if it was disproportionate in those circumstances.'

Besides saying that references in s 76 to the degree of force used are to the type and amount of force used,[49] s 76 does not incorporate associated principles to be found in the case law, which are set out in paras 16.22 and 16.23.

16.22 In applying the present test, account should be taken of the purpose for which the force was used; force used to achieve one purpose may be reasonable, but it may be unreasonable to achieve another purpose covered by public or private defence.[50] All the immediate circumstances (as well as the danger) in which the defendant believed he was placed should also be taken into account, including in particular the type and amount of force used on each side, the relative strength (in terms both of physical power and of numbers) on each side, the seriousness of the evil to be prevented (or of the offence for which an arrest is being made) and the possibility of preventing it by other means (because the use of force can never be reasonable if it was unnecessary).[51]

16.23 In deciding whether the defendant used reasonable force account may be taken of his physical characteristics[52] but not (except in 'exceptional circumstances' – which were not explained – 'which would make the evidence especially probative') the fact that he was suffering from a psychiatric condition which would have made him perceive the circumstances as more dangerous than would a reasonable person. This was held by the

---

[48] See para 16.7.   [49] CJIA 2008, s 76(10)(c).   [50] *Kelbie* [1996] Crim LR 802, CA.

[51] See *Allen v Metropolitan Police Comr* [1980] Crim LR 441, DC. Also see Seventh Report of the Criminal Law Revision Committee (who proposed s 3 of the CLA 1967) (Cmnd 2659), para 23.

[52] For example, the fact that a defendant was physically handicapped (and therefore unable to escape a threatened attack which an able-bodied person could have escaped) can be taken into account, and vice versa.

Court of Appeal in the Tony Martin case, *Martin (Anthony Edward)*.[53] D, a farmer, had disturbed burglars in his isolated farmhouse and had fired a shotgun at them, killing one and wounding the others. There was psychiatric evidence that D would have perceived the circumstances as being more dangerous than would an ordinary person. The Court, in holding that this evidence was inadmissible, rejected an analogy with the defence of provocation[54] (where such evidence would have been admissible) on the ground that provocation is not a complete defence and only applies to murder. The Court held that it was inappropriate, except in exceptional circumstances which would make it especially probative, in deciding whether unreasonable force had been used, to take into account whether the defendant was suffering from a psychiatric condition. Thus, the Court did not say that psychiatric evidence would always be irrelevant in the present respect. To do so would be open to objection in the light of the approach taken in *Martin (David Paul)*[55] where psychiatric evidence was admitted as to the defendant's beliefs in respect of the defences of duress. This part of the decision in *Martin (Anthony Edward)* is unnecessarily restrictive. Psychiatric evidence may be of crucial importance in terms of what the defendant's belief was as to the circumstances and the danger. Quite apart from this, it appears to be inconsistent with the general statement referred to above, and repeated by the Privy Council in *Shaw v R*,[56] that the issues involved in determining 'reasonable force' are to be answered by taking into consideration not only the circumstances but also the danger as the defendant believed them to be. *Shaw v R* was not cited to the Court of Appeal in *Martin (Anthony Edward)*. It seems very odd that someone like the defendant in that case should be unable to rely on psychiatric evidence as to how he would have perceived the danger.

16.24 In assessing the reasonableness of the force, the jury or magistrates should take a liberal approach; they should 'not use jewellers' scales to measure reasonable force.'[57] In addition, and this goes even further in tempering with leniency the objectiveness of the test, there must be taken into account the time available to the defendant for reflection. A direction along the lines of the following statement by Lord Morris in *Palmer v R* should be given to the jury:

> 'If there has been an attack so that defence is reasonably necessary it will be recognised that a person defending himself cannot weigh to a nicety the exact measure of his necessary defensive action. If a jury thought that in a moment of unexpected anguish a person attacked had only done what he honestly and instinctively thought was necessary that would be most potent evidence that only reasonable defensive action had been taken.'[58]

---

[53] [2001] EWCA Crim 2245. The defendant's conviction for murder was quashed and a verdict of manslaughter on grounds of diminished responsibility was substituted.

[54] To be replaced by the defence of loss of control when the relevant provisions of the Coroners and Justice Act 2009 come into force on 4 October 2010.

[55] [2000] 2 Cr App Rep 42, CA; para 16.43.   [56] [2001] UKPC 26.

[57] *Reed v Wastie* [1972] Crim LR 221, per Geoffrey Lane J.   [58] [1971] AC 814 at 832.

Although this statement was made in relation to self-defence, the principle is equally applicable to the other defences at present under discussion. It was subsequently applied by the Court of Appeal in *Shannon*,[59] where the trial judge had left the defence of self-defence to the jury with the bald question: 'Are you satisfied that the appellant used more force than was necessary in the circumstances?' The Court of Appeal held that on its own this might have precluded the jury from considering Lord Morris's qualification that if they came to the conclusion that the defendant honestly thought, without having to weigh things to a nicety, that what he did was necessary to defend himself, they should regard that as 'most potent evidence' that it was actually reasonably necessary.

> 'In other words, if the jury concluded that the stabbing was the act of a desperate man in extreme difficulties, with his assailant dragging him down by the hair, they should consider very carefully before concluding that the stabbing was an offensive and not a defensive act, albeit it went beyond what an onlooker would regard as reasonably necessary'.[60]

Consequently, the conviction for murder was quashed.

The statement by Lord Morris in *Palmer v R* is given statutory form in relation to self-defence, defence of another and the defences under the CLA 1967, s 3(1) by the CJIA 2008, s 76(7) and (8),[61] which provides:

> '(7) In deciding the question [whether the degree of force used by D was reasonable in the circumstances as D believed them to be] the following considerations are to be taken into account (so far as relevant in the circumstances of the case) –
>   (a) that a person acting for a legitimate purpose may not be able to weigh to a nicety the exact measure of any necessary action; and
>   (b) that evidence of a person's having only done what the person honestly and instinctively thought was necessary for a legitimate purpose constitutes strong evidence that only reasonable action was taken by that person for that purpose.
>
> (8) Subsection (7) is not to be read as preventing other matters from being taken into account where they are relevant to deciding the question [whether the degree of force used by D was reasonable in the circumstances as D believed them to be].'

For these purposes, a 'legitimate purpose' means the purpose of self-defence or defence of another under the common law, or the prevention of crime or effecting or assisting in the lawful arrest of offenders or suspected offenders or of persons unlawfully at large.[62]

---

[59] (1980) 71 Cr App Rep 192, CA. Also see *Whyte* [1987] 3 All ER 416, CA.
[60] *Shannon* (1980) 71 Cr App Rep 192 at 196. Also see *Nugent* [1987] 3 NIJB 9, NICA.
[61] See para 16.7.   [62] CJIA 2008, s 76(10)(a), (b).

Use of fatal force and ECHR, Article 2

Key points 16.3

Subject to what is said below, English criminal law on public and private defence is consistent with the ECHR, Article 2 (right to life) where force is used with *fatal* effect in public or private defence.

16.25 The ECHR, Article 2 guarantees everybody's right to life. It is one of the most fundamental provisions in the ECHR.[63]

Article 2(1) provides that:

> 'Everyone's right to life shall be protected by law. No one shall be deprived of his life intentionally[64] save in the execution of a sentence of a court following his conviction of a crime for which this sentence is provided by law.'

However, Article 2(2) provides that:

> 'Deprivation of life shall not be regarded as inflicted in contravention of this Article when it results from the use of force which is no more than absolutely necessary:
>
> (a) in defence of any person from unlawful violence;
>
> (b) in order to effect a lawful arrest or to prevent the escape of a person lawfully detained;
>
> (c) in action lawfully taken for the purpose of quelling a riot or insurrection.'

Article 2(2) is concerned not only with acts intended to kill, but also the use of force which in fact kills, although death may not have been intended.[65] Although the discussion which follows centres on the use of fatal force by a police officer or member of the armed forces or security services, it must be borne in mind that the issue of the consistency of the criminal law on public and private defence with Article 2 also relates to the use of fatal force by a private individual because Article 2(2) also requires the State to take appropriate steps to safeguard people against its breach.[66]

---

[63] This was stated by the European Court of Human Rights in *McCann v United Kingdom* (1995) 21 EHRR 97 at [147].

[64] 'Intentionally' here refers to a direct intent; see para 16.95. A person who has decided to kill someone as a means to saving his own life or preventing crime, and so on, acts with a direct intent to kill, even though he also aims to achieve (and desires) the self-preservation or the prevention of crime, and so on: para 3.8.

[65] *Stewart v UK* [1985] 39 DR 162 at [15], E Comm of HR. As was pointed out by Collins J in *R (on the application of Bennett) v HM Coroner for Inner South London* [2006] EWHC 196 (Admin) at [22], it is not obvious that the absolute necessity requirement in Article 2(2) is appropriate where the death was neither intended nor foreseeable as an inevitable or even likely consequence of the force used.

[66] *Osman v United Kingdom* (2000) 29 EHRR 245, ECtHR; *Kilic v Turkey* (2001) 33 EHRR 58, ECtHR.

16.26 The United Kingdom would be in contravention of Article 2(1) where a State official, such as a police officer or member of the armed forces or security services, used force in circumstances not covered by the exhaustive list in Article 2(2). It will be noted that no specific exception is made for killing in defence of property or in the prevention of crime (unless unlawful violence to a person is threatened or the force is used to effect a lawful arrest), so that a killing for such a purpose by a State official could never satisfy Article 2, whereas, provided the force used was reasonable under the rules described above (and it would admittedly be an extreme case where this was so), a killing for one of these purposes would be justified under English law.

16.27 Although a killing by a State official in defence of any person from unlawful violence or for one of the other purposes listed in Article 2(2)(a)–(c) may not violate Article 2, this will only be so if the degree of force used is 'no more than absolutely necessary' for one of those purposes. In contrast, the CLA 1967, s 3(1) and the common law rules on self-defence and defence of another permit the use of 'such force as is reasonable in the circumstances' as those circumstances are believed by the defendant to be, whether reasonably or not. Is the English law on the fatal use of force incompatible with Article 2 in this respect?

16.28 In *McCann v United Kingdom*,[67] three members of the IRA were intercepted in Gibraltar by members of the SAS after they had parked a car. The soldiers shot and killed the IRA members because they believed that they had planted a radio controlled car bomb. The European Court of Human Rights held that 'absolutely necessary' in Article 2(2) means that the force used must be strictly proportionate to the achievement of the purposes set out in Article 2(2)(a)–(c). It stated that this test would be applied strictly and the Court would scrutinise not only the actions of the individuals but also all the surrounding circumstances, including the planning and control of the operation so as to minimise, to the greatest possible extent, recourse to fatal force.

In respect of the issue of the compatibility of the English law of self-defence or defence of another and Article 2, the Court noted that the difference between the standards under English law and under Article 2(2) were not sufficiently great that a violation of Article 2 could be found on this ground alone.[68] The Court accepted that the soldiers honestly believed, in the light of the information that they had been given, that it was necessary to shoot the suspects in order to prevent them from detonating a bomb and causing serious loss of life. The actions which they took were thus perceived by them as absolutely necessary in order to safeguard innocent lives. The Court stated that it:

'considers that the use of force by agents of the State in pursuit of one of the aims delineated in Article 2(2) of the Convention may be justified under this provision where it is based on an *honest belief* which is perceived, *for good reasons*, to be valid at the time but which subsequently turns out to be mistaken. To hold otherwise would be to impose an

---

[67] (1995) 21 EHRR 97, ECtHR.   [68] *McCann v United Kingdom* (1995) 21 EHRR 97 at [155].

unrealistic burden on the State and its law-enforcement personnel in the execution of their duty, perhaps to the detriment of their lives and those of others.

It follows that, having regard to the dilemma confronting the authorities in the circumstances of the case, the actions of the soldiers do not, in themselves, give rise to a violation of this provision.[69]

The Court went on to hold by a bare majority (10–9) that the planning of the operation as a whole was not controlled and organised in a way which showed the level of respect for life required by Article 2.

16.29 In a number of subsequent cases the European Court of Human Rights has returned to the requirements of Article 2(2). In *Andronicou v Cyprus*,[70] where a Cypriot special police unit attacked a house in which a hostage was being held, firing machine gun bullets in all directions and killing both the armed hostage-taker and the hostage, the Court held by a bare majority (5–4) that Article 2 had not been violated. It accepted that it had to consider the 'planning and control' of the operation, and determine whether the force used was 'strictly proportionate' to the purpose, on the facts as the police officers honestly believed, for good reasons, them to exist.

The decision in *Andronicou v Cyprus* seemed problematic because of the strictness of Article 2(2) and the liberality of its application to the facts. It was distinguished by the European Court of Human Rights in *Gül v Turkey*,[71] where the Court held that the action of Turkish police officers in firing approximately 55 bullets through the door of the deceased's apartment during a search, thereby killing him, contravened Article 2. The Court noted that in *Andronicou* the hostage-taker was known to be in possession of a gun, which he had already fired, whereas in the case before it there was not any reasonable belief on the part of the police officers that their lives were at risk.

16.30 Subsequently, in *Bubbins v United Kingdom*,[72] where an armed police officer (B) had shot dead a man whom he mistakenly believed to be an intruder who was pointing a gun at him and his colleagues, although in fact the gun was a replica, the European Court of Human Rights unanimously held that there had been no violation of Article 2. It noted that the man had appeared to aim a gun at one of the police officers present and had not responded to an order to drop it. It reiterated the requirement of an '*honest belief, for good reasons*', saying: 'the use of force by agents of the State in pursuit of one of the aims delineated in [Article 2(2)] may be justified under this provision where it is based on an *honest belief which is perceived, for good reasons, to be valid at the time but subsequently turns out to be mistaken*.'[73] However, it then weakened the requirement by saying that the Court could not substitute its own assessment of the situation for that of an officer who was required to react in the heat of the moment to avert an *honestly* perceived danger to his life, which is reminiscent of the 'heat of the moment' qualification, referred to in para 16.24.

---

[69] *McCann v United Kingdom* (1995) 21 EHRR 97 at [200].   [70] (1997) 25 EHRR 491, ECtHR.
[71] (1998) 25 EHRR 491, ECtHR.   [72] (2005) 41 EHRR 458, ECtHR.
[73] (2005) 41 EHRR 458 at [138]. Italics supplied.

It concluded that the use of fatal force had not been disproportionate and had not exceeded what was absolutely necessary to what was *honestly* perceived by officer B to be a real and immediate risk to him and his colleagues. Nor had Article 2 been infringed on account of the planning and control of the operation or on account of the authorities' failure to conduct an effective investigation.

16.31 The compatibility of the English law on self-defence and defence of another with Article 2 was considered by Collins J in *R (on the application of Bennett) v HM Coroner for Inner South London*.[74]

S was shot dead by a police officer (X). According to X, he believed that S was about to shoot him. It later transpired that what was believed by X to be a gun was in fact a cigarette lighter shaped like a gun. One of the points raised before Collins J was whether the coroner at the subsequent inquest had been correct to direct the jury in terms of the English law of self-defence, ie whether the force used by X was reasonable, having regard to the circumstances as X believed them to be. It was argued that this did not comply with Article 2 because under that Article the test when applied to State officials was that the force had to be absolutely necessary.

Having referred to *McCann v United Kingdom* and *Bubbins v UK*, Collins J held:

> 'It is thus clear that the European Court of Human Rights has considered what English law requires for self-defence, and has not suggested that there is any incompatibility with Art 2. In truth, if any officer reasonably decides that he must use lethal force, it will inevitably be because it is absolutely necessary to do so. *To kill when it is not absolutely necessary to do so is surely to act unreasonably. Thus, the reasonableness test does not in truth differ from the Art 2 test as applied in* McCann. *There is no support for the submission that the court has with hindsight to decide whether there was in fact absolute necessity. That* would be to ignore reality and to produce what the court in *McCann* indicated was an inappropriate fetter upon the actions of the police which would be detrimental not only to their own lives but to the lives of others.'[75]

Having added that Lord Morris's 'heat of the moment' qualification was worth bearing in mind, Collins J rejected the submission that Article 2 required a different test to be applied in the case of State officials from that applicable in general to the issue of self-defence.

This decision neatly deals with the issue: to kill in self-defence or the defence of another when it is not absolutely necessary is not the use of reasonable force, but the decision as to whether force was absolutely necessary is not to be made with hindsight but is to be based on the circumstances as the State official perceived them, in the heat of the moment, to be. Thus, an honest, mistaken belief can provide the 'good reasons' required by *McCann* and *Bubbins*, even if it turns out to have been unreasonable.

---

[74] [2006] EWHC 196 (Admin).   [75] [2006] EWHC 196 (Admin) at [25].

Is defence available where need to act created by defendant's own conduct?

16.32 It has been stated by the Northern Irish Court of Criminal Appeal in *Browne* that: 'The need to act must not have been created by the conduct of the defendant in the immediate context of the incident which was likely or intended to give rise to that need'.[76] It is clearly right that a person should not be able to invoke one of the defences under discussion if he has deliberately provoked an attack with a view to using force to prevent or terminate it, but what about other cases? The suggestion that a defence is available where an attack results from the defendant's conduct in defending someone else, even if the defendant knew that this was likely, has been approved obiter by the Court of Appeal.[77] In addition, a person who kills someone in a quarrel which he has started is not thereby precluded from relying on self-defence if the violent retaliation by the victim is disproportionate to his conduct.[78]

Excessive force and murder

Key points 16.4

The liability of someone who kills with the *mens rea* for murder by the use of excessive force in prevention of crime, self-defence etc is not reduced to manslaughter under the law relating to public or private defence. However, if the terms of the new defence of loss of control are satisfied the liability of someone who kills by using excessive force out of fear of serious violence from the victim against himself or another identified person is reduced to manslaughter.

16.33 Where the defendant uses an excessive degree of force (ie force which is unreasonable in the circumstances as he believed them to be) in prevention of crime or self-defence etc, he has no defence on grounds of public or private defence, even though he believes his force is reasonable in the circumstances. However, except in the case of murder, his error of judgement may be taken into account in mitigation of sentence.

It might have been expected that the fatal use of unreasonable force in public or private defence with the *mens rea* for murder would result *on that ground* in the liability of the defendant being reduced from murder to manslaughter,[79] but this is not the rule under the English law of public or private defence. Public or private defence is an all-or-nothing defence; there is no halfway house under the rules relating to it. In *Palmer v R*,[80] a case where the defendant had been convicted of murder, the Privy Council held that

---

[76] [1983] NI 96 at 107.   [77] *Balogun* (1999) unreported, CA.
[78] *Rashford* [2005] EWCA Crim 3377.
[79] This used to be the position in Australian law until it was reversed by the High Court of Australia in *Zecevic v DPP (Victoria)* (1987) 162 CLR 645.   [80] [1971] AC 814, PC.

'The defence of self-defence either succeeds so as to result in an acquittal or is disproved in which case as a defence it is rejected.'[81] *Palmer's* case was followed by the Court of Appeal in England by *McInnes*.[82] Subsequently, Viscount Dilhorne said, obiter, in *A-G for Northern Ireland's Reference (No 1 of 1975)*[83] that, where death results from the excessive use of force in the prevention of crime or in effecting an arrest, and the defendant intended to kill or do grievous bodily harm, the offence is likewise not reduced to manslaughter. This was affirmed in 1995 by the House of Lords in *Clegg* in respect of the excessive use of force in self-defence.[84] The House did so with some regret, but thought that any change in the law was a matter for Parliament.[85]

The decisions in *Palmer v R* and *Clegg* are open to the objection that it is improper to convict of murder someone who made an error of judgement as to the amount of force which he should use. However, it must be admitted that the 'heat of the moment' qualification, referred to in para 16.24 is liable to limit the number of cases in which a person who uses fatal force in self-defence etc will be found to have used excessive force.

16.34 The harshness of the law has been reduced to some extent in relation to the excessive, fatal use of force *in self-defence or defence of another* by the new defence of loss of control under the Coroners and Justice Act 2009, ss 54 and 55, which come into force at 4 October 2010. If the terms of those sections are satisfied, the liability of someone who uses such force for such a purpose is reduced to voluntary manslaughter. The details of ss 54 and 55 are set out in Chapter 8. Essentially, ss 54 and 55 will not be satisfied in the present context unless:

- the defendant's acts in doing the killing resulted from the defendant's *loss of self-control*;
- the loss of self-control was attributable to the defendant's *fear of serious violence from the victim against the defendant or another identified person*; and
- *a person of the defendant's sex and age, with a normal degree of tolerance and self-restraint and in the circumstances of the defendant, might have reacted in the same or in a similar way* to the defendant.

Resisting arrest

Key points 16.5

A person who is being lawfully arrested, and who knows that he is being arrested, is not entitled to use reasonable force to resist or escape; but a person who is being unlawfully arrested is so entitled, and so is someone who makes a mistake of fact and does not realise that he is being arrested.

---

[81] See articles by Morris [1960] Crim LR 468, Howard [1964] Crim LR 448, and Smith [1972] Crim LR 524.
[82] [1971] 3 All ER 295, CA.   [83] [1977] AC 105 at 148.   [84] [1995] 1 AC 482, HL.
[85] Para 1.36.

16.35 A person who is being lawfully arrested, and who knows he is being arrested, is not entitled to use reasonable force in order to resist or escape,[86] even if he believes that the arrest was unlawful because he thinks that the arrester (eg a police officer) is acting beyond his powers;[87] in such a case the mistake is one of criminal law.[88] So, it has been held,[89] is a mistaken belief which leads the defendant to think that the facts do not satisfy the requirements for a lawful arrest, as where he knows or believes he has not committed an offence. Although there are sound policy grounds for not permitting those who are lawfully arrested, but who think they are innocent, to challenge the arrest by a threat or use of force, it is doubtful that the mistake in this type of case is one of law. It looks like a mistake of fact which would prevent the defendant having the intent to resist lawful arrest.

On the other hand, a person who is being arrested or detained unlawfully is entitled to use reasonable force to resist or escape.[90] In addition, where the power of arrest would only be possessed by a police officer, a person is entitled to use reasonable force to resist or escape if he does not realise that he is being arrested by a police officer because he believes that the person concerned is not a police officer, as where he believes that he is being attacked by a robber or a thug.[91] Likewise a person, who believes that someone whom he knows is a police officer is violently attacking him, is entitled to use reasonable force to defend himself, even though in reality the officer is trying lawfully to arrest him.[92] In these two cases the mistake will be one of fact.

The same distinction applies where force is used to enable another person to resist or escape arrest.

Justification of conduct where force not actually used

16.36 The defences of self-defence, prevention of crime and the like are concerned with the use of force. However, the *terms* of the defences can also be relevant where, although no force has been used, a defendant has been charged with an offence whose definition excuses a person who acts for a lawful object or purpose or refers in some other way to lawfulness or unlawfulness, since they can be used to determine the question of lawfulness or unlawfulness in issue. One authority is *A-G's Reference (No 2 of 1983),*[93] which was concerned with the offence of making or possessing an explosive substance, under such circumstances as to give rise to a reasonable suspicion that the making or possession is not for a lawful object. The Court of Appeal held that the preparation of a petrol bomb for use in self-defence or in defence of another or of property against an imminent attack

---

[86] *Kenlin v Gardiner* [1967] 2 QB 510, DC.
[87] *Fennell* [1971] 1 QB 428, CA; *Albert v Lavin* [1982] AC 546, HL.
[88] *Bentley* (1850) 4 Cox CC 406.   [89] *Lee* [2001] 1 Cr App Rep 293, CA.
[90] *Pedro v Diss* [1981] 2 All ER 59 at 64.
[91] *Ryan* (1993) unreported, CA; *Blackburn v Bowering* [1994] 3 All ER 380, CA.
[92] *Burley* [2000] Crim LR 843, CA.
[93] [1984] QB 456, CA. See also *Georgiades* [1989] 1 WLR 759, CA.

would be a lawful object if the maker intended to use it in a way which was no more than reasonably necessary to meet the imminent attack. As the Court noted: 'In our judgment a defendant is not left in the paradoxical position of being able to justify acts carried out in self-defence but not acts immediately preparatory to it.'[94]

In the light of such authority a statement by the Court of Appeal in *Symonds*[95] is suspect. There D had driven off, dragging V (whose hand was trapped in the driver's window) some distance, allegedly to escape V. Dealing with D's conviction for careless driving, the Court of Appeal stated that there was some difficulty (more of theory than of substance) with the deployment of self-defence outside the area of offences where D is accused of using force on another. The substitute defence said to be appropriate in *Symonds*, duress of circumstances, would not assist in a case like *A-G's Reference (No 2 of 1983)* because it does not render conduct lawful.

Duress by threats

Key points 16.6

The excuse (ie defence) of duress by threats is concerned with the case where the defendant commits the *actus reus* of an offence with the relevant *mens rea*[96] but is impelled to do so because of a threat (or reasonable belief in a threat) by another person of imminent death or serious physical injury to him or a third person.

If the defendant was, or may have been, so impelled, the question arises as to whether a sober person of reasonable firmness, sharing the defendant's characteristics, would have responded to the threat (or perceived threat) and done as the defendant did. Unless the prosecution proves that the person of reasonable firmness would not have responded and done as the defendant did, the defence succeeds.

The excuse of duress by threats does not apply where the defendant voluntarily assumed the risk of threats of violence, nor does it apply to murder, attempted murder and perhaps certain types of treason.

16.37 The excuse (ie defence) of duress by threats is defined in strict terms. Reasons for this would seem to be that otherwise it would be a very easy defence to raise and very difficult for the prosecution to disprove, and that unlike self-defence, for example, the victim

---

[94] [1984] QB 456 at 471.   [95] [1998] Crim LR 280, CA.

[96] In *Bourne* (1952) 36 Cr App Rep 125, the Court of Criminal Appeal appears to have treated duress by threats as negativing *mens rea*. However, such a theory was rejected by the House of Lords in *DPP for Northern Ireland v Lynch* [1975] AC 653, according to whom the defence of duress by threats is something superimposed on the other ingredients of an offence, the *actus reus* and the *mens rea*, which by themselves would constitute the offence. See also *Howe* [1987] AC 417 at 428, 436, per Lords Hailsham LC and Bridge.

is morally innocent.[97] Those who act under a threat but who fall outside the defence can normally have this reflected in the sentence imposed.

Act done under duress not an 'involuntary act'

16.38 If the defence of duress by threats applies, a defendant who acted under it is excused from criminal liability for an offence which he has committed, but his act is nevertheless regarded as a voluntary one. This can be contrasted with the case where someone is made to act by an external physical force. There, the act is regarded as involuntary, cannot be imputed to him and cannot involve him in criminal liability. Thus, if someone is made to stab another by superior physical force exerted on his arm, it is not his act which does the stabbing, but that of the person who forces him.

Involuntary acts were dealt with in the last chapter.[98] The following paragraphs deal with a different question: the extent to which threats which do not have the effect of making the act of the defendant involuntary can afford an excuse.

The command associated with the threat

16.39 The defence of duress by threats is concerned with the case where the defendant commits the *actus reus* of an offence with the relevant *mens rea* but is induced to act by a threat made by another person (or a reasonable belief in such a threat) to the effect that unless the defendant commits the offence charged, harm will be done to him or a third person. The command associated with the threat may relate to the commission of the *actus reus* of an offence by the defendant or simply to something to which a ulterior intent must be established.[99] Thus, the defence of duress by threats could be available as a defence to a charge of possession of a controlled drug with intent unlawfully to supply where a person already in lawful possession of a drug forms the intent unlawfully to supply it as a result of a threat of serious physical injury if he does not, just as it would be available to a charge of unlawful supply if the drug was actually so supplied.

16.40 In *Cole*,[100] where D, his girlfriend and child had been threatened with violence by moneylenders, unless he paid his debts, the Court of Appeal held that **the defence of duress can only apply where the offence charged is 'the very offence' nominated by the person making the threat**. As the moneylenders had not nominated any offence as a means by which D should repay them, the Court upheld his conviction for robbery; duress by threats was not available as a defence. The phrase 'the very offence' suggests that the actual offence committed by D must have been nominated (so that, if D has robbed Lloyds Bank in the High Street, he must have been told 'rob Lloyds Bank in the High Street'). This seems to be an artificial limit on the defence, and an artificial distinction

---

[97] See the speech of Lord Bingham in *Hasan* [2005] UKHL 22 at [19]–[21].
[98] Key Points 15.5 and para 15.49.   [99] *Fisher* [2004] EWCA Crim 1190.
[100] [1994] Crim LR 582, CA; see, further, para 16.75.

between it and the analogous defence of duress of circumstances described later. In *Ali*,[101] the Court of Appeal seems to have assumed that the defence of duress by threats was available, although it failed for other reasons, where the instruction was to rob an unspecified bank or building society. It could be argued that this falls within the bounds of 'the very offence nominated' by the duressor. On the other hand, if the duressor simply says 'rob or else' and D robs someone, it becomes more difficult to do so. Whatever its extent, the present requirement seems to be an unnecessary one.

Nature of threat

16.41 Reference has been made in a number of cases[102] to the fact that the will of a person who acts under duress by threats has been 'overborne'. This simply means that the defendant would not have done as he did but for the threat (actual or reasonably believed).[103] However, it is not in itself enough that the defendant's will has been overborne since there are limitations on the type of threat which can amount to duress. **The threat, which may be express or implicit, must be of death or serious physical injury.**[104] 'Bodily harm' includes identifiable psychiatric injury for the purposes of offences against the person involving actual bodily harm or grievous bodily harm, and it might be thought that it could suffice for physical injury for duress.[105] In *Baker and Wilkins*,[106] however, the **Court of Appeal declined to hold that the defence of duress extended to a threat of serious psychological *injury*.** What it said was obiter because there was no evidence of such a threat, and in *DPP v Rogers*[107] the Divisional Court said, obiter, that there was 'a great deal of force' in criticism of this aspect of *Baker and Wilkins*.

In *Quayle and others; A-G's Reference (No 2 of 2004)*[108] the Court of Appeal held that a threat to cause severe pain not associated with an accompanying serious injury could not suffice for the defence of duress of circumstances (and by implication duress of threats). This is questionable, although it has to be admitted that measuring whether or not the pain would have been severe might be difficult. In *Singh*,[109] the Court of Appeal held that a 'blackmail threat' (ie a threat to expose something) could not give rise to the defence, and in *M'Growther*[110] it was ruled that the threat of harm to property was no excuse. In

---

[101] [1995] Crim LR 303, CA.

[102] Eg *Hudson and Taylor* [1971] 2 QB 202, CA; *Graham* [1982] 1 All ER 801 at 806.

[103] In *Hasan* [2005] UKHL 22 at [21], Lord Bingham, in summarising the law of duress, said that the defence of duress is available only where the criminal conduct has been directly caused by the threats relied on. See further n 119.

[104] *Hudson and Taylor* [1971] 2 QB 202, CA; *DPP for Northern Ireland v Lynch* [1975] AC 653, HL; *Williamson and Ellerton* (1977) 67 Cr App Rep 63, CA; *Hasan* [2005] UKHL 22 at [21], per Lord Bingham.

[105] Paras 7.59 and 7.79.

[106] [1997] Crim LR 497, CA. The brief report should be supplemented by reference to the transcript.

[107] [1998] Crim LR 202, DC.

[108] [2005] EWCA Crim 1415.

[109] [1973] 1 All ER 122, CA.

[110] (1746) Fost 13. A more modern authority is *DPP v Milcoy* [1993] COD 200, DC.

Steane,[111] Lord Goddard stated that a threat of 'violence or imprisonment' could amount to duress. This statement was an obiter dictum and it is inconceivable that the reference to threats of imprisonment would be adopted in view of the more restricted approach of the subsequent cases.

16.42 **The threat need not be to kill or cause serious physical injury to the defendant.** In *Wright*,[112] where D alleged that a threat had been made to kill her boyfriend, the Court of Appeal held that it was clear that a threat need not be made to harm the defendant himself or herself; it referred to the Judicial Studies Board's specimen direction which indicated that the threat could relate to a 'person for whom [the defendant] would reasonably regard himself as responsible'.[113] A similar statement was made by the Court of Appeal in *Shayler*, where it stated in relation to duress by threats and duress of circumstances:[114]

> 'The evil must be directed towards the defendant or a person or persons for whom he has responsibility or, we would add, persons for whom the situation makes him responsible... We make the addition to... cover, by way of example, the situation where the threat is made to set off a bomb unless the defendant performs the unlawful act. The defendant may not have had any previous connection with those who would be injured by the bomb but the threat itself creates the defendant's responsibility for those who will be at risk if he does not give way to the threat.'[115]

Expressed in this way, there is no limit to when a threat to kill or cause a third person or cause him serious physical injury can suffice for the defence. This is sensible because a person may well be more likely to be swayed by a threat seriously to injure a third person than by a threat of the same harm to himself. Fears about 'opening the floodgates' by allowing a threat to kill or seriously injure any third person without qualification can be answered by noting the strict requirements of the defence, especially the objective test, set out below.

Subjective and objective tests

16.43 The defence of duress by threats involves both a subjective and an objective test; the law requires a defendant to have the steadfastness reasonably to be expected of an ordinary citizen in his situation. If duress is raised on the evidence, the correct approach, which was laid down by the Court of Appeal in *Graham*,[116] and approved by the House of

---

[111] [1947] KB 997, CCA.   [112] [2000] Crim LR 510, CA.

[113] In his summary of the law in *Hasan* [2005] UKHL 22 at [21], Lord Bingham said that the threat must be against the defendant or his immediate family or someone for whom he is responsible.

[114] Para 16.67.

[115] [2001] EWCA Crim 1977 at [49]; affd without reference to this point ([2002] UKHL 11) on the ground that the facts of the case did not raise any question of duress of circumstances.

[116] [1982] 1 All ER 801, CA.

Lords in *Howe*[117] as well as being followed by the Court of Appeal in a number of cases on the related defence of duress of circumstances,[118] is as follows:

- *Subjective test: 'Was the defendant, or may he have been, impelled to act as he did because, as a result of what he reasonably believed [X] had said or done, he had good cause to fear that if he did not so act [X] would kill him or ... cause him serious physical injury?'*[119] The subjective test involves an objective element: the defendant's belief must have been a reasonable one and he must have good cause to fear death or serious physical injury. As the subjective test shows, there need not actually be a threat; it suffices that the defendant reasonably believed that there was a threat of death or serious physical injury.[120] In *Martin (David Paul)*,[121] the Court of Appeal stated that the defendant's belief as to such a threat need not be reasonable. This was clearly inconsistent with the approach approved in *Howe* but in line with the approach taken in self-defence and related defences.[122] However, in *Hasan*,[123] Lord Bingham, with whose reasoning Lords Steyn, Rodger and Brown concurred, rejected the suggestion that the defendant's belief need not be reasonable in the defence of duress, saying: 'It is, of course, essential that the defendant should genuinely, ie actually, believe in the efficacy of the threat by which he claims to have been compelled. But there is no warrant for relaxing the requirement that the belief must be reasonable as well as genuine.' **In respect of the *subjective* test, the defendant's psychiatric condition is relevant in relation to whether or not he had the necessary reasonable belief.** In *Martin (David Paul)*, psychiatric evidence was admitted that the defendant was suffering from a schizoid affective disorder making him more likely than an ordinary person to regard things said as threatening and to believe that the threats would be carried out. This can be contrasted with the approach taken in respect of self-defence and similar defences: para 16.23.

- *Objective test: 'If so, have the prosecution made the jury sure that a sober person of reasonable firmness, sharing the characteristics of the defendant, would not have responded to whatever he reasonably believed [X] had said or did [sic] [by acting as the defendant had done]?'*[124]

---

[117] [1987] AC 417, HL. Although, strictly, the approval of *Graham* in *Howe* was obiter, the fact that it was singled out for approval in *Howe* means that it should continue to be followed (*Safi* [2003] EWCA Crim 1809 at [16]), until the Supreme Court or Parliament chooses to change the law.   [118] Para 16.73.

[119] The defendant need not have acted as he did solely because of a threat of death or serious harm. It is enough that he would not have acted as he did but for such a threat, even though he also acted for some other reason (such as an additional threat to burn down his house or to expose his immorality): *Valderrama-Vega* [1985] Crim LR 220, CA. Also see *Ortiz* (1986) 83 Cr App Rep 173, CA.

[120] *Mackintosh* (1998) unreported, CA; *Safi* [2003] EWCA Crim 1809.

[121] [2000] 2 Cr App Rep 42, CA. See also, a similar decision, *DPP v Rogers* [1998] Crim LR 202, DC, in respect of duress of circumstances and criticism of it; para 16.73, n 217

[122] See paras 5.18, 16.14.   [123] [2005] UKHL 22 at [23].

[124] For criticism of this requirement, see KJM Smith 'Must Heroes Behave Heroically?' [1989] Crim LR 622 and 'Duress and Steadfastness: In Pursuit of the Unintelligible' [1999] Crim LR 363.

If the issue of duress is raised,[125] the defence succeeds unless the prosecution proves beyond reasonable doubt that at least one of these tests is not satisfied.[126]

In applying the two tests, all the circumstances of the threat, including the number, identity and status of those making it, are relevant.[127]

What characteristics of defendant can be invested in person of reasonable firmness?

16.44 In *Bowen*,[128] the Court of Appeal collected a number of principles from the cases about the characteristics of the defendant with which the ordinary person could be invested for the purposes of the *objective* test.

The question is whether an ordinary person of reasonable firmness sharing the defendant's characteristics would have been able to resist the threat. As a result **the ordinary person is not invested with a characteristic which did not make the defendant less able to resist the threat than an ordinary person of reasonable firmness. In addition, the ordinary person of reasonable firmness is not to be invested with a characteristic on the defendant's part such as pliancy, vulnerability to pressure,**[129] **timidity, or emotional instability,**[130] **since it would be a contradiction in terms to invest an ordinary person of reasonable firmness with these.**[131] No doubt for similar reasons, **characteristics due to self-induced abuse, eg addiction to drink or drugs, are irrelevant.**[132]

On the other hand, if the defendant is in a category of persons whom the jury might think less able to resist pressure than people outside that category, the characteristic which puts him or her in that category may be a relevant one.[133] In *Bowen*, the Court of Appeal said that:

> 'Obvious examples are age, where a young person may well not be so robust as a mature one; possibly sex, though many women would doubtless consider they had as much moral courage to resist pressure as men; pregnancy, where there is added fear for the unborn child; serious physical disability, which may inhibit self-protection; recognised mental illness or psychiatric condition, such as post-traumatic stress disorder leading to learned helplessness.'[134]

---

[125] *Gill* [1963] 2 All ER 688, CCA; *Bone* [1968] 2 All ER 644, CA, provide authority that the defendant only bears an evidential burden. In *Bianco* [2001] EWCA Crim 2516, it was held that this required evidence on which a jury could properly conclude that the defence of duress had not been negatived. This requires too much. In principle, it should suffice simply that there is evidence on which a jury could properly conclude that there had been an actual or believed threat of death or serious bodily harm. See para 4.10.

[126] *Mackintosh* (1998) unreported, CA; *Safi* [2003] EWCA Crim 1809.

[127] *Abdul-Hussain* [1999] Crim LR 570, CA (duress of circumstances).   [128] [1996] 4 All ER 837, CA.

[129] Also see *Horne* [1994] Crim LR 584, CA; *Hurst* [1995] 1 Cr App Rep 82, CA.

[130] *Hegarty* [1994] Crim LR 353, CA.

[131] *Hegarty* [1994] Crim LR 353, CA; *Horne* [1994] Crim LR 584, CA.

[132] Either because they do not affect a person's ability to resist threats or because they are not properly described as characteristics, being self-induced: *Flatt* [1996] Crim LR 576, CA.

[133] *Bowen* [1996] 4 All ER 837, CA. See also *Walker* [2003] EWCA Crim 1837; *Antar* [2004] EWCA Crim 2708.   [134] [1996] 4 All ER 837 at 844.

Attributing learned helplessness to a person of reasonable firmness seems to contradict the notion of such a person.

The existence of a characteristic of the type just referred to does not mean that the jury must invest the ordinary person of reasonable firmness with it: it simply means that it may be left to the jury. Whether or not the jury do so invest it will depend on whether they think that the characteristic made the defendant less able to resist the threat. Psychiatric evidence may be admissible to show that the defendant was suffering from some recognised mental illness or psychiatric condition which might make him more susceptible to pressure or threats,[135] but is not otherwise admissible in respect of the application of the objective test.[136] There is a fine line to be drawn sometimes between a recognised mental illness or psychiatric condition and vulnerability to pressure or emotional instability which is not imputable to the ordinary person.

16.45 *Bowen* provides an example of some of the above points. D was charged with a number of counts of obtaining services by deception, contrary to the Theft Act 1978, s 1 (since repealed), relating to a course of conduct over three years. At his trial he claimed that throughout he had acted under threats of serious harm if he did not obtain goods for those making the threats. It was alleged that D was abnormally suggestible and vulnerable, and had a low IQ, short of mental impairment or mental defectiveness. In the Court of Appeal D's counsel accepted that the judge had been correct in not telling the jury that the person of reasonable firmness shared the characteristics of abnormal suggestibility and vulnerability. However, she submitted that a low IQ was relevant since it might affect D's ability to withstand the threats. The Court of Appeal disagreed, saying 'We do not see how low IQ, short of mental impairment or mental defectiveness, can be said to be a characteristic which makes those who have it less courageous and less able to withstand threats and pressure.'

16.46 The courts have not yet had to decide whether a characteristic affecting the gravity of the threat to the defendant, as opposed to his ability to resist the threat, can be taken into account. In short, can the fact that the defendant who was threatened with 'kneecapping' was a top footballer whose career would be ruined thereby be taken into account? Presumably the answer is 'yes'.

Operative threat of imminent danger

16.47 The threat (or reasonably believed) threat must be of the *imminent* (ie liable to happen soon) peril of death or serious physical injury; the threat need not be one

---

[135] *Emery* (1992) 14 Cr App Rep (S) 394, CA. In *Emery*, the Court of Appeal held that evidence might be admitted to show that the defendant's failure to protect her child from a violent partner resulted from a condition of 'learned helplessness' as a result of her own long-term abuse. It stated that: 'the question for the doctors was whether a reasonable woman with the characteristics of Miss Emery, if abused in the manner which she said, would have had her will crushed so that she could not have protected the child'.

[136] *Hegarty* [1994] Crim LR 353, CA.

of immediate death or serious physical injury.[137] However, duress is not available as a defence if it is proved that the defendant failed to take advantage of an opportunity for evasive action to neutralise the effects of the threat of which he was aware which a reasonable person of a sort similar to the defendant[138] in his position would have taken.[139] The reason is that the objective test will not be satisfied.

The defence of duress by threats failed, for example, in *Heath*,[140] where D alleged that he had been pressured into transporting drugs, because D had more than one safe avenue of escape (going to the police, which he did not do because he was scared and because he was a drug addict, and going to his parents in Scotland, which he did not do because he did not want them to know about the position he was in).

Heath can be contrasted with *Hudson and Taylor*,[141] where two girls aged 19 and 17 gave false evidence at a criminal trial after a gang had threatened to 'cut them up' if they did not do so. The girls were charged with perjury. The trial judge told the jury that the defence of duress was not available because the defendants had not been subject to the threat of immediate physical violence when they gave the false evidence. The defendants were convicted but appealed successfully to the Court of Appeal. One of the grounds on which the Crown relied in support of the conviction was that the defendants should have removed the effect of the threat by seeking police protection either before or at the time of the former trial at which they had made the false statements. The Court of Appeal agreed that the defence of duress by threats could not be relied on if a defendant failed to take an opportunity which was reasonably open to him to render the threat ineffective. However, in deciding whether such an opportunity was reasonably open to the defendant, the jury should have regard to his age, and to the circumstances of the case and any risks which might be involved. Factors such as the period of time between the threat and the commission of the offence and the effectiveness of the protection which the police might be able to give would be relevant. The Court of Appeal rejected the prosecution's argument that the girls could have neutralised the threat by seeking police protection, on the ground that the police could not have provided effective protection. In *Hasan* Lord Bingham, with whom Lords Steyn, Rodger and Brown agreed, stated that this was too favourable to the defendants. He said:

> 'It should, however, be made clear to juries that if the retribution threatened against the defendant or his family or a person for whom he feels responsible is not such as he reasonably expects to follow immediately or almost immediately on his failure to comply with the threat, there may be little if any room for doubt that he could have taken evasive

---

[137] *Loughnan* [1981] VR 443, SC of Victoria; *Abdul-Hussain* [1999] Crim LR 570, CA (duress of circumstances); *Shayler* [2001] EWCA Crim 1977 (duress of circumstances: this point was not dealt with by the House of Lords on appeal ([2002] UKHL 11) on the ground that the facts of the case did not raise duress of circumstances); *Quayle and others; A-G's Reference (No 2 of 2004)* [2005] EWCA Crim 1415 at [77].

[138] *Baker and Ward* [1999] 2 Cr App Rep 335, CA. Ie a person sharing such characteristics of the defendant as may be attributed to the ordinary person in accordance with *Bowen*; para 16.44.

[139] *Baker and Ward* [1999] 2 Cr App Rep 335, CA; *McDonald* [2003] EWCA Crim 1170. Also see *Gill* [1963] 2 All ER 688, CCA; *Hudson and Taylor* [1971] 2 QB 202, CA.

[140] [2000] Crim LR 109, CA.   [141] [1971] 2 QB 202, CA.

action, whether by going to the police or in some other way, to avoid committing the
crime with which he is charged.'[142]

16.48 The threat (actual or reasonably believed) must have been operative and effective
at the time the offence was committed. Thus, the defendant is not excused if the threat
has ceased when he commits the offence.[143] If the defendant has embarked on the commission of a continuing offence and the threat is then withdrawn or becomes ineffective,
as a reasonable person would have known, he must desist from committing the offence
as soon as he reasonably can.[144] In deciding whether the defendant has acted reasonably,
regard must be had to the circumstances in which he finds himself.[145]

Of course, duress by threats is not available as a defence if the defendant commits a
criminal act which the compulsion does not oblige him to.[146]

Voluntary assumption of risk of threats of violence

16.49 The excuse of duress by threats is not available to someone who has voluntarily
put himself in a position in which he foresaw or ought reasonably to have foreseen the
risk of being subjected to any compulsion by threats of violence.[147] Thus, for example,
the defence is not available to a defendant who joins a criminal gang, knowing that other
members might use threats of violence to pressure him to rob someone, and who is an
active member of that gang when put under such pressure.[148] The rule was applied for
the first time in this country in *Sharp*,[149] where D had joined a gang which had used firearms to rob sub-post offices. During the last raid, the sub-postmaster was killed. D said
that he had not wanted to participate in this raid but that X had threatened to blow his
head off if he did not. D's conviction for manslaughter was upheld. The Court of Appeal
held that the trial judge had been correct to withdraw the issue of duress from the jury
because D had voluntarily joined the gang, whose violent nature he knew about. This is
an important rule because many allegations of duress involve threats by other members
of a gang etc.

The width of the present rule can be illustrated by reference to *Ali*[150] where D was
charged (inter alia) with the robbery of a building society. He alleged that he had acted
under duress. D was a drug addict. He had an arrangement with a supplier, X, whom he

---

[142] [2005] UKHL 22 at [28]. Also see *Hurst* [1995] 1 Cr App Rep 82 at 93: the defendant must 'know or believe
that the threat is one which will be carried out immediately or before the defendant or the other person threatened can obtain official protection'.

[143] *Stratton* (1779) 21 State Tr 1045 at 1231, per Lord Mansfield CJ; *Hudson and Taylor* [1971] 2 QB 202, CA;
Lynch v DPP for Northern Ireland [1975] AC 653, HL.

[144] *Pommell* [1995] 2 Cr App Rep 607, CA (a case concerned with duress of circumstances); para 16.77.

[145] *Pommell* [1995] 2 Cr App Rep 607 at 615.

[146] *Stratton* (1779) 21 State Tr 1045 at 1231, per Lord Mansfield CJ; *Hudson and Taylor* [1971] 2 QB 202, CA.

[147] *Hasan* [2005] UKHL 22.

[148] *Sharp* [1987] QB 853, CA; *Shepherd* (1988) 86 Cr App Rep 47, CA; *Ali* [1995] Crim LR 303, CA.

[149] [1987] QB 853, CA.   [150] [1995] Crim LR 303, CA.

knew to be very violent, whereby he would sell on drugs for X, taking a certain amount to use. One day, D used for his own use all the drugs supplied by X. That put him in debt to X. X told D that he wanted the money. He gave D a gun and told him to get it from a bank or building society, otherwise he would be killed. Dismissing D's appeal against conviction, the Court of Appeal held that the trial judge had correctly directed the jury about the present rule; if a defendant voluntarily participated in criminal offences (eg drug dealing) with someone whom he knew was violent and likely to require him to commit other offences, he could not rely on duress if that person did so.

16.50 The rule about voluntary assumption of the risk of threats does not require that the defendant foresaw or should have foreseen that there was a risk of being put under duress to commit the type of offence with which he is charged or, indeed, any offence[151] (although it is difficult to envisage circumstances where a party might be coerced to act lawfully). Instead, the rule applies if the defendant foresaw or ought to have foreseen that his voluntary association with known criminals involved a risk of being subjected to any compulsion by threats of violence, not necessarily compulsion to commit the offences of the kind with which he is charged. This was held by a majority (4–1) of the House of Lords in *Hasan*.[152] At his trial for aggravated burglary, D's defence was duress on the part of X, the boyfriend of Y, a prostitute, for whom D had been the minder and driver. D knew that X was a violent gangster and D said that X had impliedly threatened him with deadly consequences if he did not commit the burglary in question. The trial judge told the jury that the defence of duress was not open to D if he had voluntarily put himself in a position where he was likely to be subjected to threats. Allowing an appeal against conviction, the Court of Appeal held that this was a misdirection because it was not any kind of voluntary association with criminals that was relevant but only a voluntary association where the defendant could have anticipated pressure to commit an offence of the type with which he was charged.

Allowing the prosecution's appeal against the Court of Appeal's decision, the majority of the House of Lords held that the defence of duress was excluded where as a result of the defendant's voluntary association with others engaged in criminal activity he had foreseen or ought reasonably to have[153] foreseen the risk of being subjected to any compulsion by acts of violence. Although she also allowed the appeal, Baroness Hale took a different approach:

> 'I would say that it must be foreseeable that duress will be used to compel the person to commit crimes of some sort...The battered wife knows very well that she may be compelled to cook the dinner, wash the dishes, iron the shirts and submit to sexual

---

[151] *Hasan* [2005] UKHL 22. The statements in *Sharp* [1987] QB 853, CA, *Ali* [1995] Crim LR 303, CA, and *Baker and Ward* [1999] 2 Cr App Rep 335, CA, that such foresight was required are now wrong.

[152] [2005] UKHL 22.

[153] Because of the way that the certified point of law was framed the House of Lords did not have to reach a conclusion about whether the defence is only excluded if the defendant foresaw the risk or whether it is also excluded if he ought to have foreseen it. Lord Bingham favoured the latter, which would be in line with the restrictive nature of other parts of the defence.

intercourse. That should not deprive her of the defence of duress if she is obliged by the same threats to herself or her children to commit perjury or shoplift for food.'[154]

16.51 The case law on the voluntary assumption of the risk of threats rule has developed in terms of the person who has voluntarily associated with others engaged in criminal activity, where he foresaw or ought reasonably to have foreseen the risk of being subjected to compulsion by threats of violence. However, it was held in *Ali* in 2008 that the rule is not limited to that situation, although it will almost always be the situation in which the rule applies. The Court of Appeal stated:

'[I]n most cases where A subjects B to compulsion by threats of violence, A is engaged in criminal activity. But…, the core question is whether the defendant voluntarily put himself in the position in which he foresaw or ought reasonably to have foreseen the risk of being subjected to any compulsion by threats of violence. As a matter of fact, threats of violence will almost always be made by persons engaged in a criminal activity; but in our judgment it is the risk of being subjected to compulsion by threats of violence that must be foreseen or foreseeable that is relevant, rather than the nature of the activity in which the threatener is engaged.'[155]

Extent of the excuse

16.52 The excuse of duress by threats applies to offences in general,[156] including strict liability offences,[157] except murder,[158] attempted murder[159] and perhaps certain types of treason.[160] Since many offences have not been the subject of an authoritative decision as to the applicability of the defence, there is a risk that other exceptions may be established, should the occasion arise. We saw in para 6.6 that there are some rare offences whose wording seems to indicate that they are of absolute liability, in which case no defence is available.

Duress by threats and murder

16.53 The inapplicability to murder of the defence of duress by threats was settled by the House of Lords in 1987 in *Howe*.[161] Traditionally, the view of the courts and of writers of

---

[154] [2005] UKHL 22 at [77].   [155] [2008] EWCA Crim 716 at [12].

[156] *Hudson and Taylor* [1971] 2 QB 202 at 206. The defence has, for example, been held applicable to criminal damage (including arson) (*Shiartos* (1961) unreported); theft (*Gill* [1963] 2 All ER 688, CCA); robbery (*Baker and Ward* [1999] 2 Cr App Rep 335, CA); perjury (*Hudson and Taylor* [1971] 2 QB 202, CA); contempt of court (*K* (1983) 78 Cr App Rep 82, CA); possessing or supplying controlled drugs (*Ortiz* (1986) 83 Cr App Rep 173, CA; *Quayle and others; A-G's Reference (No 2 of 2004)* [2005] EWCA Crim 1415); possession of controlled drugs with intent to supply (*Panton* [2001] EWCA Crim 611) and being concerned in the importation of controlled drugs (*Valderrama-Vega* [1985] Crim LR 220, CA).

[157] *Eden District Council v Braid* [1999] RTR 329, DC.   [158] *Howe* [1987] AC 417, HL.

[159] *Gotts* [1992] 1 All ER 832, HL.   [160] Para 16.59.   [161] [1987] AC 417, HL.

authority[162] has been that the defence was not available on a charge of murder. However, in *DPP for Northern Ireland v Lynch*,[163] the majority (three–two) of the House of Lords held that the defence of duress was available to an accomplice to murder (such as a person who loads a rifle for someone who then fires a lethal shot or a person who drives a killer to the scene of the killing). On the other hand, in *Abbott v R*,[164] a majority (3–2) of the Privy Council, while accepting the decision in *Lynch*, refused to extend it to the perpetrator of murder. The resulting distinction in the present respect between perpetrators and accomplices of a murder was open to criticism, since the contribution of an accomplice to a killing may be no less significant (and occasionally may be greater) than that of the perpetrator.

16.54 In *Howe*, D1 and D2 participated with others in torturing, beating up and sexually abusing two men on different occasions. On the first occasion, D1 and D2 were accomplices to the murder of the man by O. On the second occasion, D1 and D2 had been the perpetrators of the murder by strangling the man with a shoelace. D1 and D2 said that they had acted under duress since on both occasions they had acted as they did on the directions of X, a powerful, violent and sadistic man who was participating in the events, and had been in fear that, if they disobeyed X's instructions, X would kill them or seriously injure them. In the light of *Lynch* and *Abbott*, the judge left the defence of duress by threats to the jury in relation to the first murder, but not in relation to the second. The Court of Appeal held that this was correct.

The House of Lords unanimously held that the defence of duress by threats should not have been left to the jury in relation to either murder. Among the reasons given by their Lordships for denying that duress by threats could be a defence for a perpetrator of murder, the most prominent was the supreme importance which the law attaches to the protection of the life of an innocent person. This was so important, said their Lordships, that a person should be required to sacrifice his own life rather than being permitted to choose who should live and who should die (but what if the threat is to kill the defendant's wife, parents and six children?). Their Lordships were unimpressed by the argument that it made no sense that a defendant who under duress wounded another with intent to do him grievous bodily harm, and who was therefore acquitted of that offence, should have no defence to a charge of murder on the basis of the same act committed under the same threats and with the same *mens rea* if the victim died of the original injury.

The House held that there was no valid distinction between a perpetrator of murder and an accomplice to it, and that the same rule should apply to both. Consequently, it overruled the decision to the contrary on this point in *Lynch*. Thus, duress by threats is no longer available as a defence to an accomplice to murder. (The overruling of *Lynch* on the present point does not affect the validity of statements in it on other points referred to in this and other chapters.)

---

[162] *Tyler and Price* (1838) 8 C & P 616; Hale *Pleas of the Crown* Vol 1, 51, 434; Blackstone *Commentaries* Vol 4 (1769), 30.

[163] [1975] AC 653, HL.   [164] [1977] AC 755, PC.

There are no exceptions to the rule that duress by threats is not a defence to murder. In *Wilson*,[165] a 13-year-old boy, who had participated as an accomplice in the murder of his mother, claimed that he had acted on the instructions of his violent father and had been motivated by fear and terror. Recognising that duress was no defence to murder, however susceptible the defendant might be to the duress, and whether the defendant was a perpetrator or an accomplice, the Court of Appeal observed that there might be grounds for criticising a principle of law that did not afford a 13-year-old boy any defence to a charge of murder on the ground that he was complying with his father's instructions which he was too frightened to disobey.

16.55 Lords Hailsham LC and Griffiths in *Howe* were happy to leave deserving cases of murder under duress to the executive discretion not to prosecute or, after conviction and mandatory sentence to life imprisonment, to order early release on licence or to exercise the royal prerogative to grant a pardon. These methods of mitigating the harshness of *Howe* are an unsatisfactory solution to the problem, since the outcome of the exercise of a discretion is always uncertain (whereas a person who has a defence is entitled to an acquittal) and, even if the discretion is exercised in the offender's favour, it does not remove the stigma of a guilty verdict at the trial. Mention may also be made of the view of Lord Wilberforce in *Lynch*:

'A law, which requires innocent victims of terrorist threats to be tried and convicted as murderers, is an unjust law even if the executive, resisting political pressures, may decide, after it all, and within the permissible limits of the prerogative, to release them. Moreover, if the defence is excluded in law, much of the evidence which would prove the duress would be inadmissible at the trial, not brought out in court, and not tested by cross-examination.'[166]

It is interesting to note that the availability of discretionary executive action after conviction for other offences, quite apart from the possibility of mitigation of sentence, has not prevented the development of the defence of duress by threats in relation to them. The fact that the judge cannot mitigate the sentence for murder provides a more pressing reason for duress to be a defence to murder than any reason which has resulted in it being a defence to other offences where mitigating factors can be taken into account in sentencing.

16.56 The effect of *Howe* is to require a person threatened with death or serious injury unless he kills another to be a hero, something which the law does not normally do. Where the threat relates to someone else the effect of the decision is to require the defendant to sacrifice that person or persons (to whom, as in the case of a parent-child relationship, he may owe a legal duty of care) in order to save another (the intended victim). An acceptable compromise solution to the problems posed in *Howe* might have been to treat

---

[165] [2007] EWCA Crim 1251.   [166] [1975] AC 653 at 685.

duress in murder as analogous to provocation,[167] with the result that the offence would be reduced to manslaughter in such a case, but the House of Lords rejected such an idea. This is open to criticism since, especially where the threat of death or serious harm relates to more than those killed, many people would think that the moral culpability of a person who kills under duress is less than that of one who kills under provocation. Moreover, as the Court of Appeal stated in *Graham*:

'Provocation and duress are analogous. In provocation the words or actions of one person break the self-control of another. In duress the words or actions of one person break the will of another.'[168]

The argument in favour of a compromise solution did not find favour with the Law Commission in the report referred to in para 16.61. The Commission considered that some instances of duress came close to being a justification for killing (just as self-defence is) rather than simply an excuse, and for this reason there was a compelling reason for distinguishing duress from provocation (or diminished responsibility).

16.57 The decision in *Howe* is bound to be controversial. Arguably, the decision was inevitable given the inflexibility of the defence of duress by threats. It is easier to accept that D should not have a defence if he intentionally kills P to save his own skin than that D should not have a defence if he acted to save the life of his wife, parents and six children, particularly since the threatener can be convicted of murder.[169] One consideration which affected several members of the House of Lords was the undesirability of the judges undertaking reform on such an important matter,[170] something which has not prevented the judicial invention of the defence of duress of circumstances in modern times. The view that it was for Parliament to come up with any relaxation in the law was reiterated in *Gotts*, referred to in para 16.58. In *Hasan*,[171] Lord Bingham said that the argument that duress should be available as a defence to murder was irresistible.

Duress by threats and attempted murder

16.58 The House of Lords in *Howe* did not decide whether duress by threats could be a defence to a charge of attempted murder, a point on which there was no direct authority. Lord Griffiths,[172] however, was of the view, obiter, that duress was not a defence to attempted murder because the prosecution had to prove an even more evil intent (an intent unlawfully to kill)[173] than in murder (where an intent unlawfully to cause grievous bodily harm can also suffice). The point was settled by the decision of a majority (by 3–2) of the House of Lords in 1992 in *Gotts*,[174] to the effect that duress is not a defence on an

---

[167] To be replaced by the defence of loss of control when the relevant provisions of the Coroners and Justice Act 2009 come into force on 4 October 2010. [168] [1982] 1 All ER 801 at 806.
[169] Para 16.66. [170] Para 1.36. [171] [2005] UKHL 22 at [21].
[172] [1987] AC 417 at 445. This reasoning appealed to the majority of the House of Lords in *Gotts* [1992] 2 AC 412. [173] Para 14.113.
[174] [1992] 2 AC 412, HL. See S Gardner 'Duress in the House of Lords' (1992) 108 LQR 349.

attempted murder charge, whether as perpetrator or accomplice. In *Gotts*, D, aged 16, attempted to kill his mother by stabbing her. His defence was that his father, a violent man, had ordered him to do so and had threatened to kill him if he did not comply. The House of Lords agreed with the Court of Appeal that the trial judge had been right to rule that duress was not a defence to attempted murder.

The decision in *Gotts* gives rise to an anomaly in that it appears that duress by threats is a defence to causing grievous bodily harm with intent to do grievous bodily harm,[175] the *mens rea* for which (like the *mens rea* for attempted murder) is the *mens rea* for murder, so that had the victim died the defendant would likewise have been guilty of murder. In both offences it may be mere chance that the victim does not die. Apart from the fact that the intent to kill required of an attempted murderer is more evil than the *mens rea* required for wounding with intent to do grievous bodily harm, there is nothing to distinguish between the two offences. Lord Jauncey, in *Gotts*, dismissed the risk of anomalies. He said:

'It is of course true that withholding the defence in any circumstances will create some anomalies but . . . nothing should be done to undermine in any way the highest duty of the law to protect the freedom and lives of those who live under it.'[176]

Duress by threats and treason

16.59 It seems that duress by threats can be a defence to some, if not all, types of treason. Lord Goddard CJ took a contrary view in *Steane*[177] but he must have overlooked cases such as *M'Growther*,[178] *Oldcastle's Case*,[179] *Stratton*[180] and *Purdy*[181] where the applicability of the defence to treason was recognised. It seems from these cases that only a threat of death will suffice, but the modern case law on the excuse in general suggests that if the point arose today a threat of serious bodily harm might be held sufficient.

Proposals for reform

16.60 Clause 25 of the draft Criminal Law Bill[182] deals with the excuse of duress by threats. It contains some major differences from the existing law.

Contrary to the present position, the defendant would have the persuasive burden of proof in that he would have to prove the defence. In addition, the defence would be

---

[175] Duress of circumstances has been held to be a defence to this offence (*Cairns* [1999] 2 Cr App Rep 137, CA) and there is no reason to doubt that the same applies to duress by threats.

[176] [1992] 2 AC 412 at 426.   [177] [1947] KB 997, CCA.   [178] (1746) Fost 13.

[179] (1419) 1 Hale PC 50.   [180] (1779) 21 State Tr 1045.   [181] (1946) 10 JCL 182.

[182] Law Commission: *Legislating the Criminal Code; Offences against the Person and General Principles* (1993), Law Com No 218; see para 7.131.

extended to all offences, including murder and attempted murder,[183] and would be based on what the defendant (as opposed to a reasonable person) knows or believes, and would provide a more generous approach by moving the focus away from whether the reasonable person would have resisted the threat to whether that threat was one which in all the circumstances (including any of his personal characteristics affecting its gravity) the defendant could not reasonably be expected to resist.

The proposed change in the burden of proof was intended to allay fears about the extension of the defence to murder and to give real effect to the proposed provision that the defence would not apply to a person who has knowingly and without reasonable excuse exposed himself to the risk of duress (since, for example, it can be particularly difficult to disprove a denial that the defendant had voluntarily joined a criminal group because of the risk of concoction by members of the group). In addition, the Commission considered that the excuse of duress by threats was exceptional, depending on factors unique to it which distinguish it from all others because it is much more likely than any other defence to depend on assertions which it is particularly difficult for the prosecution to investigate or disprove. In this respect, support can be found in the view of Lord Bingham in *Hasan*,[184] where his Lordship expressed the view that duress is 'peculiarly difficult for the prosecution to investigate and disprove beyond reasonable doubt'. Nevertheless, the reversal of the normal burden of proof would be unfortunate. There is a risk of concoction in all defences and the same problems of proof or disproof arise in respect of all defences. There is nothing special about duress, despite what the Law Commission and Lord Bingham have said. A defendant would not find it easy to discharge the burden of proof. Placing the burden of proof on the defendant is arguably incompatible with the ECHR, Article 6(2) (presumption of innocence),[185] although the Law Commission dismissed them in its report referred to in the next paragraph.[186] Moreover, subsequent changes to the law of criminal procedure mean that advance notice of the nature of a defence is now required, so that the prosecution are unlikely to be taken by surprise at the trial and will have time to scrutinise the defence and to investigate whether the defendant had voluntarily exposed himself to the risk of duress.

16.61 In a report published in 2006,[187] the Law Commission has indicated that it has not changed its mind about duress and murder and attempted murder. It recommended that duress (as currently defined) should be a full defence to the offences of first degree murder and second degree murder recommended by it[188] and to attempted murder. However, for duress to be a defence to these offences the threat would have to be one of death or life-threatening harm, and the defendant would have the persuasive burden of proving[189]

---

[183] For the Law Commission's more recent recommendations relating to murder and attempted murder, see para 16.61.

[184] [2005] UKHL 22 at [20] per Lord Bingham.   [185] But see para 15.18, n 70.

[186] As to the issue of compatibility of a reverse onus provision with the ECHR, Art 6(2), see para 4.8.

[187] Law Commission Report No 304 (2006): *Murder, Manslaughter and Infanticide*, Pt 6.

[188] Para 8.38.

[189] For a discussion of the above recommendation, see Ashworth 'Principles, Pragmatism and the Law Commission's Recommendations on Homicide Law Reform' [2007] Crim LR 333 at 340–342.

the requirements of the defence on the balance of probabilities. The Commission explained its recommendation in relation to murder on the ground that the law should not stigmatise a person who, on the basis of a genuine and reasonably[190] held belief, intentionally killed in fear of death or life-threatening injury in circumstances where a jury is satisfied that an ordinary person of reasonable fortitude might have acted in the same way.[191] If a reasonable person might have acted as the defendant did, the argument for withholding the complete defence was undermined. In addition, the Commission considered that its recommendation accorded with the effect of duress as a complete defence in other offences and was therefore conducive to coherence and consistency. The Commission repeated its commitment to placing the onus of proof on the defendant, referring to Lord Bingham's statement in *Hasan* that duress is 'peculiarly difficult for the prosecution to investigate and disprove beyond reasonable doubt'. It concluded that imposing a legal burden to prove duress on the balance of probabilities would be compatible with the ECHR, Article 6(2). The Commission was influenced in its proposal to place the burden of proof on the defendant by ECHR, Article 2 (guarantee of right to life) which requires not only that the State refrain from taking life intentionally but also that appropriate steps are taken by the State to safeguard it.[192] It considered that if those charged with murder on the basis of unjustifiably and intentionally killing could plead duress secure in the knowledge that the prosecution were unlikely to disprove the defence it would be questionable whether the State was effectively discharging its obligations under Article 2.

It is unfortunate that the Law Commission's recommendation has not been enacted. Some cases which would have been covered by the recommended defence may be covered by the partial defence of loss of self-control (via a fear of serious violence) introduced by the Coroners and Justice Act 2009, so as to reduce liability to manslaughter, but this defence does not apply to an attempted murder charge.

Marital coercion

> **Key points 16.7**
>
> A wife who commits any offence, other than murder or treason, has the excuse (ie defence) of marital coercion if she proves that she did so in the presence of her husband and under his coercion.

[190] It will be noted that the Law Commission has taken a different view, in requiring the defendant's belief to be reasonable, from that taken by it in its recommendations (see para 16.60) in respect of duress as a *general* defence.

[191] In deciding whether a person of reasonable firmness might have acted as the defendant did, the jury would be able to take into account all the circumstances of the defendant, including his or her age but not any other characteristics bearing on his capacity to withstand duress: Law Commission Report No 304, para 6.86.

[192] *Osman v United Kingdom* (2000) 29 EHRR 245, ECtHR; *Kilic v Turkey* (2001) 33 EHRR 58, ECtHR.

16.62 Before the Criminal Justice Act 1925 came into force, there was a rebuttable presumption of law that an offence, other than treason or murder or certain other offences, committed by a wife in the presence of her husband was committed under his coercion. Accordingly, the prosecution bore the burden of negativing coercion. The presumption was abolished by the Criminal Justice Act 1925, s 47 but this section goes on to provide:

> '...on a charge against a wife for any offence other than treason or murder it shall be a good defence to prove that the offence was committed in the presence of, and under the coercion of, the husband.'

It is important to note that the section places the persuasive burden of proving coercion on the wife, whereas in duress by threats the defendant merely bears an evidential burden.[193] Coercion is an excuse (ie defence) for a wife in addition to that of duress by threats, not in substitution for it.[194] Unlike duress by threats,[195] the defence of marital coercion is available on a charge of attempted murder.

The defence is only available to a wife; it is not available (vice versa) to a husband, nor is it available to an unmarried partner. Moreover, the Court of Appeal in *Ditta*[196] held that the defence is not available to a woman who mistakenly, but reasonably, believes that she is validly married to the man making the threat, as where that man was already married when she married him (although she had no reason to know that). The Court left open whether the defence of coercion could apply to a polygamous marriage. No corresponding defence is available to a civil partner who acts under the coercion of the other partner.

16.63 Proof of the defence requires proof that the offence was committed as a result of the wife's will being overborne by the husband, so that she was forced unwillingly to participate in the offence. Simply persuading a wife to act out of loyalty will not do.[197] This test seems to be wholly subjective; it makes an interesting comparison with the partly objective test in duress.

16.64 The defence of marital coercion is rarely pleaded and, because the Criminal Justice Act 1925, s 47 has not yet received much in the way of authoritative judicial interpretation, may give rise to difficulty in the future. One reason is that the nature of the conduct covered by marital coercion is not certain, although it is certainly wider than in the case of duress by threats. The Court of Appeal in *Shortland*[198] has held that the defence does not require proof of physical force or the threat of physical force. It approved a statement by a Circuit judge[199] that a 'moral threat' would suffice if it had the necessary effect. This leaves open the extent of a 'moral threat'. Threatening to deprive the wife of her children would be a moral

---

[193] Para 16.43, n 125.

[194] *DPP for Northern Ireland v Lynch* [1975] AC 653 at 684, 713, per Lords Wilberforce and Edmund-Davies; *Richman* [1982] Crim LR 507, Crown Ct.

[195] Para 16.58.   [196] [1988] Crim LR 43, CA.   [197] *Shortland* [1996] 1 Cr App Rep 116, CA.

[198] [1996] 1 Cr App Rep 116, CA. The point was repeated in *Cairns, Zaidi and Chaudhury* [2002] EWCA Crim 2838.   [199] *Richman* [1982] Crim LR 507, Crown Ct.

threat, but what about a threat to reveal her dishonesty to her employer? The answer must surely be 'no'. A threat to the wife's property would not seem to be a moral threat but it may be held that it can suffice if it has the requisite effect. A second reason why the defence may give rise to difficulty in the future is that the word 'presence', which is a limiting factor on the defence, has not yet been elucidated. It is, for instance, impossible to say whether s 47 would be held by the Court of Appeal to cover a case in which a husband induced his wife to enter a house for the purpose of stealing something, by threatening to leave her if she did not comply with his wishes, while he remained outside and kept watch.

16.65 The Law Commission has recommended the abolition of the defence of marital coercion on the grounds that it is not appropriate to modern conditions.[200] Under cl 36(2)(b) of the draft Criminal Law Bill, a wife would not have a separate defence of marital coercion.[201]

The person making the threat

16.66 Although the defences of duress by threats and marital coercion may be available to the person who actually performed the criminal act, the one who made the threats is liable for the offence committed. There is no doubt on this point, but we shall see in the next chapter[202] that the methods by which the result can be reached vary.

Duress of circumstances

> ### Key points 16.8
>
> The excuse (ie defence) of duress of circumstances is concerned with the case where the defendant commits the *actus reus* of an offence with the relevant *mens rea* but is impelled to do so to avoid a threat (or a reasonably believed threat) of imminent death or serious physical injury.
>
> If the defendant was, or may have been, so impelled, the question arises as to whether a sober person of reasonable firmness, sharing the defendant's characteristics, would have responded to the threat (or perceived threat) and done as the defendant did. Unless the prosecution proves that the person of reasonable firmness would not have responded and done as the defendant did, the defence succeeds.
>
> The excuse of duress of circumstances does not apply to murder, attempted murder and perhaps certain types of treason.

---

[200] *Defences of General Application* (1977), Law Com No 83.

[201] Law Commission: *Legislating the Criminal Code: Offences against the Person and General Principles* (1993), Law Com No 218.   [202] Paras 17.6 and 17.21–17.25.

16.67 Modern decisions of the Court of Appeal have established the excuse (ie defence) of duress by circumstances, which has a close affinity to the defence of duress by threats.[203] As with that defence, the defence of duress of circumstances has been developed by the courts on a case-by-case basis. The requirements of the defence are like that of duress by threats, save that:

- the threatening circumstances do not have to have a human source: they may alternatively come from a non-human cause, such as avalanche or wild animal;[204] and

- the threatening circumstances do not have to be accompanied by the instruction: 'Do this [ie commit this offence][205] or else...'

16.68 As in the excuse of duress by threats, the threatening circumstances must be extraneous to the defendant, ie they must come from some external agency, and be capable of objective scrutiny by judge and jury;[206] if those circumstances originate in the defendant it is insufficient. Thus, in *Rodger and Rose*,[207] the Court of Appeal held that the defendants' own suicidal thoughts (ie the threats which they made to themselves of suicide) could not afford a defence to the offence of prison breaking. Likewise, in *Quayle and others; A-G's Reference (No 2 of 2004)*,[208] the Court of Appeal, in holding that the relief of pain could not provide a defence to someone who committed a drugs offence in relation to cannabis for this purpose, gave as one of its reasons the absence of an extraneous circumstance capable of objective scrutiny. It stated that the requirement for such a circumstance rested on the pragmatic consideration that the defence, which the prosecution carries the onus to disprove, 'must be confined within narrowly defined limits or it will become an opportunity for almost untriable and certainly peculiarly difficult issues, not to mention abusive defences'.[209]

16.69 The defence has its origins in *Willer*,[210] where D was charged with reckless driving[211] after he had driven over the pavement into a shopping centre in order to escape a gang who were shouting out threats to kill him and his passenger. At his trial, D pleaded a defence of necessity but the judge refused to leave any such defence to the jury. D's conviction was quashed on appeal. The Court of Appeal held that it ought to have been left to the

---

[203] *Hasan* [2005] UKHL 22 at [19], per Lord Bingham.

[204] An obscure statement in *Jones (Margaret)* [2004] EWCA Crim 1981, not referred to by the House of Lords on appeal ([2006] UKHL 16), may be to the effect that the threatening circumstance must be the commission of an offence under domestic (ie English) law. There is no hint in any other case to this effect and such a rule would be inconsistent with the decision in *Martin (Colin)* referred to in para 16.71 where duress was held available where the threat was to commit suicide (suicide is not a crime under English law).

[205] See para 16.40 as to the particularity with which the offence must be specified in the excuse of duress by threats.

[206] *Rodger and Rose* [1998] 1 Cr App Rep 143, CA; *Abdul-Hussain* [1999] Crim LR 570, CA; *Shayler* [2001] EWCA Crim 1977 at [66]; affd without reference to this point [2002] UKHL 11; *Quayle and others; A-G's Reference (No 2 of 2004)* [2005] EWCA Crim 1415.

[207] [1998] 1 Cr App Rep 143, CA.　　[208] [2005] EWCA Crim 1415.

[209] [2005] EWCA Crim 1415 at [75]. See also [81].　　[210] (1986) 83 Cr App Rep 225, CA.

[211] This offence was abolished by the Road Traffic Act 1991.

jury to decide whether D drove 'under that form of compulsion, ie duress'. Although the Court seemed to treat the case simply as involving the defence of duress by threats, it was breaking new ground because the case did not involve a threat along the lines of 'Do this or else...' Indeed, the gang did not want D to drive onto the pavement to escape. Their wishes were quite to the contrary; they wanted him to stay to be dealt with.

16.70 Recognition of the true nature of the defence came soon afterwards in *Conway*,[212] where *Willer* was applied. X, a passenger in D's car, had been in a vehicle a few weeks before when another man was shot and had himself been chased and narrowly escaped. On the day in question, two plain-clothes police officers saw D in the driving seat of his parked car and X behind him. Wishing to interview X, they approached D's car, according to D at a run. At this, X shouted out to D to drive off. The police officers followed in an unmarked car. It was alleged that, during the car chase, D drove recklessly. At his trial for reckless driving, D alleged that he believed throughout the chase that the two men were out to kill X. Quashing D's conviction for reckless driving, the Court of Appeal held that the trial judge had been wrong not to direct the jury about the possibility of acquitting D on the ground of what it called 'duress of circumstances', which it distinguished from that of duress by threats and which it regarded as a species of necessity. The Court stated that, although a separate defence, duress of circumstances was like duress by threats, in that it was only available if from an objective standpoint the defendant could be said to have acted in order to avoid a threat of death or serious bodily harm.

16.71 The development of the law in *Willer* and *Conway* was continued by the Court of Appeal in *Martin (Colin)*.[213] According to D, his stepson overslept to such an extent that there was a reasonable prospect of him losing his job if D did not drive him to work. D's wife, who had suicidal tendencies, threatened suicide if D did not drive the stepson to work, and there was medical evidence that she would have carried out her threat. D, who was disqualified from driving, gave the stepson a lift. At his trial for driving while disqualified, he put forward a defence of necessity.[214] The judge ruled that necessity was not a defence to the offence charged. D's conviction was quashed by the Court of Appeal. The Court held that duress of circumstances, a species of necessity, was a defence to a charge of driving while disqualified and should have been left to the jury, however sceptically D's story might be regarded.

Nature of threat

16.72 It is clear that the defence of duress of circumstances is like that of duress by threats in that it is **limited to cases where the defendant acts to avert a threat of death or serious physical injury to himself or someone for whom he is responsible or for whom**

---

[212] [1989] QB 290, CA.   [213] [1989] 1 All ER 652, CA.

[214] It could be argued that duress by threats was the appropriate defence but this would raise two points not yet answered in relation to *that* defence: does it matter that the threat of harm is of harm to the threatener and does it matter that, as in the case of suicide, the threatened harm is not unlawful?

the situation makes him responsible,[215] and in that it involves a subjective test and an objective test along the same lines as in duress by threats. 'Serious physical injury' does not cover serious psychological injury. In *Baker and Wilkins*, referred to in para 16.41, the Court of Appeal declined to extend the defence to the aversion of such harm, and in *Quayle and others; A-G's Reference (No 2 of 2004)*, it declined to extend the defence to the aversion of severe pain because of the large element of subjectivity in the assessment of pain not directly associated with some current physical injury.[216]

Subjective and objective tests

16.73 In *Martin (Colin)* the Court of Appeal said this about the terms of the defence:

> '[A]ssuming the defence to be open to the accused on his account of the facts, the issue should be left to the jury who should be directed to determine these two questions: first, was the accused, or may he have been, impelled to act as he did because as a result of what he reasonably[217] believed to be the situation he had good cause to fear that otherwise death or serious physical injury would result; second, if so, would a sober person of reasonable firmness, sharing the characteristics of the accused, have responded to that situation by acting as the accused did? If the answer to both these questions was "Yes", then the jury would acquit; the defence of necessity would have been established.'[218]

If the issue of duress is raised and left to the jury, it succeeds unless the prosecution proves beyond reasonable doubt that the answer to one or both questions is 'No'.[219]

16.74 What is said about the subjective and objective tests for duress of threats in paras 16.43 to 16.46 is equally applicable to duress of circumstances. There is no difference between the elements of the two defences.[220] In addition, there can be no doubt that the defence is barred where the defendant has voluntarily exposed himself to the danger.

---

[215] Para 16.42.

[216] This decision was applied in *Altham* [2006] EWCA Crim 7, where, on a charge of possessing controlled drugs, D claimed that he was in possession for the purpose of alleviating pain. It was held that the ECHR, Article 3 (prohibition of inhuman or degrading treatment) was not engaged, and therefore did not entitle D to a defence, because the State had done nothing to subject him to such treatment.

[217] In *DPP v Rogers* [1998] Crim LR 202, DC, it was stated that the defendant's belief need not be reasonable. This was inconsistent with the approach taken in *Martin (Colin)* [1989] 1 All ER 652, (which the Court in *DPP v Rogers* referred to as stating the law accurately) and in all the other cases dealing with the point in respect of the defence of duress of circumstances (except *Safi* [2003] EWCA Crim 1809, where the Court of Appeal declined to decide the point). It was also inconsistent with the cases on duress by threats, including *Howe* [1987] AC 417, HL, except the later case of *Martin (David Paul)* [2000] 2 Cr App Rep 42, CA (see para 16.43). It was rejected by Lord Bingham, with whose reasoning Lords Steyn, Rodger and Brown concurred, in *Hasan* [2005] UKHL 22: see para 16.43.

[218] [1989] 1 All ER 652 at 653–654.   [219] *Cairns* [1999] 2 Cr App Rep 137, CA.

[220] *Abdul-Hussain* [1999] Crim LR 570, CA.

Operative threat of imminent danger

16.75 The requirements of the excuse of duress of circumstances were further explained by the Court of Appeal in *Cole*.[221] At D's trial for robbing two building societies, he pleaded that he had done so because of his inability to repay moneylenders who had threatened him and his girlfriend and child. The trial judge ruled that no defence of duress was open to D. Dismissing D's appeal against conviction, the Court of Appeal held that the defence of duress by threats was not open to D because the threateners had not nominated the offences which he had committed.[222] Nor, the Court held, was the defence of duress of circumstances available, because there was not the degree of directness and immediacy required of the link between the threatened peril and the offences charged. The connection between the threat and the offences was not as close and immediate as in *Willer, Conway* and *Martin*, where the offences had been virtually a spontaneous reaction to the threatening circumstances arising. The reference to immediacy by the Court of Appeal in *Cole* suggested that the law was stricter for duress of circumstances than for duress by threats, where the threat need not be of immediate death or serious physical injury.[223] The decision of the Court of Appeal in *Abdul-Hussain*, however, indicates that this is not so; 'immediate' in *Cole* was being used, it would seem, in a connexional sense between the threat and the offence and not in a temporal sense.

In *Abdul-Hussain*,[224] a group of Shiite Muslims who were fugitives from the Saddam Hussein regime and were living in Sudan boarded a plane bound for Jordan and hijacked it. They were arrested at Stansted Airport. At their trial for hijacking they said that they had acted out of fear that they would be deported from Sudan to Iraq, having overstayed their leave to be in Sudan, and that they would be killed. The trial judge ruled that the defence of duress of circumstances was not available to the defendants because there was at no time a sufficient connection between the danger feared by them and the act of hijacking; there was no immediate threat of death or serious physical injury. Referring to *Cole*, he held that there had to be a connection between the threat and the offence so close and immediate as to give rise to a virtually spontaneous reaction to the threat, and that the situation in question fell short of this requirement. The defendants were convicted of hijacking and appealed successfully to the Court of Appeal which held that, as in duress by threats, although the peril of death or serious physical injury must be imminent (ie liable to happen soon), the execution of the threat need not be immediately in prospect. To the extent that there was any conflict between *Hudson and Taylor* and *Cole*, it preferred *Hudson and Taylor* (which had been binding on the Court of Appeal in *Cole*, and was binding on the Court of Appeal in the instant case (ie *Abdul-Hussain*)). Consequently, the trial judge had been wrong in limiting the availability of the defence as he had by requiring a virtually spontaneous reaction. In *Hasan*,[225] a case on duress by threats, Lord Bingham considered that *Hudson and Taylor* and *Abdul-Hussain* had unduly weakened the limitation that there must have been no evasive action the defendant could reasonably

---

[221] [1994] Crim LR 582, CA.   [222] Para 16.40.   [223] Para 16.47.
[224] [1999] Crim LR 570, CA.   [225] [2005] UKHL 22.

have been expected to take. In subsequent cases on the defence of circumstances the Court of Appeal has continued to refer to an 'imminent or immediate' threat.[226]

16.76 In *S Ltd and L Ltd,* the Court of Appeal held that it is not necessary that the imminent or immediate threat of death or serious injury should be identifiable. It stated:

> '[I]t is possible to conceive of circumstances where a continuing threat to a certain area, for example the centre of London, was believed reasonably to be so imminent as to compel those responsible for the safety of that area to act in breach of the law. The nature of the threat, specific or general, may go to the gravity of the threat and in particular [to the issue of whether the threat caused the defendant to act], but, as a matter of law, the mere absence of a specific identifiable threat will not necessarily lead to the conclusion that it was not imminent nor immediate.'[227]

16.77 Duress of circumstances is also like duress by threats, in that **the threat must be operative at the time of the offence charged**. Where a person has embarked on committing a continuing offence and the threat then becomes ineffective, as a reasonable person would have known, he must stop committing the offence as soon as he reasonably can, otherwise the objective test will not be satisfied; in deciding whether he has acted reasonably, regard must be had to the circumstances in which he finds himself. This was held in *Pommell*.[228] When the police entered D's house at about 8 am to execute a search warrant, D was lying in bed holding a loaded sub-machine gun. He was charged (inter alia) with possessing a prohibited weapon without authority, contrary to the Firearms Act 1968, s 5. D claimed that someone had visited him during the night, threatening to kill some people, that he had persuaded him to give up the gun and that he (D) was waiting until the morning to give the gun to his brother for surrender to the police. The trial judge ruled that on these facts the defence of duress of circumstances was not available to D because D had failed to go to the police immediately. The Court of Appeal disagreed. It accepted that in some cases a delay, especially unexplained, might make it clear that the defendant had not ceased to commit the offence as soon as reasonably possible. In such a case the judge would be entitled to conclude that, even on the defendant's version of the facts, the defence was unavailable to the defendant (in which case he should not leave the defence to the jury). The Court of Appeal held, however, that in the case before it the facts were not sufficiently clear for the judge to take that step.[229]

Another example of the present principle is provided by *DPP v Mullaly,*[230] where D had driven with excess alcohol, contrary to the Road Traffic Act 1988, s 5, because she believed

---

[226] See *Quayle and others; A-G's Reference (No 2 of 2004)* [2005] EWCA Crim 1415; *S Ltd and L Ltd* [2009] EWCA Crim 85.

[227] [2009] EWCA Crim 85 at [8].   [228] [1995] 2 Cr App Rep 607, CA.

[229] It is not obvious from the facts that D had been 'impelled' to do as he did by the threat to kill, a matter not considered by the Court of Appeal.

[230] [2006] EWHC 3448 (Admin), DC. See also *DPP v Jones* [1990] RTR 33, DC; *DPP v Bell* [1992] RTR 335, DC; *DPP v Tomkinson* [2001] EWHC Admin 182, DC.

that this was necessary in order to escape imminent serious bodily harm which had been threatened against her. She had continued to drive even after, as D knew, the police were readily at hand and capable of affording her adequate protection. The Divisional Court directed the magistrates, who had acquitted D, to convict her. It held that, even if the driving off was initially reasonable (and covered by the defence of duress of circumstances), objectively viewed from the moment when D was aware that the police were on hand it ceased to be necessary for her to continue to drive with excess alcohol in order to avoid a serious assault.

Extent of the excuse

16.78 In *Pommell*,[231] the Court of Appeal confirmed that, although the defence of duress of circumstances had developed in relation to road traffic offences, it was **applicable to offences in general.**[232] It noted **three exceptions: murder (dealt with below), attempted murder and some forms of treason.** This was obiter, as was the repetition of both propositions by the Court of Appeal in *Abdul-Hussain*.[233] In *Hasan*, Lord Bingham listed the same three exceptions, adding 'perhaps' to the reference to 'some forms of treason'.[234] Strangely, the Court in *Abdul-Hussain* went on to suggest that duress of circumstances cannot afford a defence to conspiracy, the essence of which is agreement, not activity. If this was correct, it would be out of line with the assumption made in *Verrier*[235] that duress of threats applied on a charge of conspiracy, a conspiracy to defraud in that case. It would be odd if a person who would have a defence of duress of circumstances if charged with a particular offence would not have that defence if charged with conspiracy to commit it. As mentioned in para 6.6, there are some rare offences which may be ones of absolute liability, in which case duress of circumstances would not be available as a defence.

16.79 **The policy and scheme of a piece of legislation may be interpreted as excluding the defence of duress of circumstances in a particular context, even if the requirements of the defence are satisfied.** In *Quayle and others; A-G's Reference (No 2 of 2004)*,[236] the Court of Appeal held that to allow a defence of relief of pain in respect of the drug offences in issue would create a conflict with the purpose and effect of the legislative

---

[231] [1995] 2 Cr App Rep 607 at 615, CA.

[232] The defence has been held applicable, for example, to dangerous driving (*Symonds* [1998] Crim LR 280, CA; *Cairns* [1999] 2 Cr App Rep 137, CA); careless driving (*Symonds* [1998] Crim LR 280, CA; *Backshall* [1999] 1 Cr App Rep 35, CA); driving while disqualified (*Martin (Colin)* [1989] 1 All ER 652, 88 Cr App Rep 343, CA); drink-driving (*DPP v Davis* [1994] Crim LR 600, DC); possession of a prohibited weapon (*Pommell* [1995] 2 Cr App Rep 607, CA); causing grievous bodily harm with intent (*Cairns* [1999] 2 Cr App Rep 137, CA); possessing a firearm with intent to commit an indictable offence (*Fisher* [2004] EWCA Crim 1190); hijacking (*Abdul-Hussain* [1999] Crim LR 570, CA); offences under Official Secrets Act 1989 (*Shayler* [2001] EWCA Crim 1977. This was not discussed by the House of Lords on appeal on the ground that the facts of the case did not raise any question of duress of circumstances: [2002] UKHL 11).

[233] [1999] Crim LR 570, CA.   [234] [2005] UKHL 22 at [21].

[235] [1965] Crim LR 732, CCA; affd without reference to this point [1967] 2 AC 195, HL.

[236] [2005] EWCA Crim 1415; see para 16.72.

policy and scheme relating to cannabis; no use of it to relieve pain was permitted under the legislation, even on a doctor's prescription, and if there was a defence in such a case it would involve the proposition that it was lawful for unqualified individuals to assume the role of unqualified doctors by prescribing it for themselves or others. The Court left open whether the defence of duress of circumstances could be available in relation to a drugs offence where the policy and scheme of the drugs legislation was not in issue.

Duress of circumstances and murder

16.80 In relation to murder, reference may be made to *Dudley and Stephens*,[237] a case decided long before the term 'duress by circumstances' was coined but which was a case involving a situation of the duress by circumstances type. In *Dudley and Stephens* D1, D2, a third man and a cabin boy were shipwrecked seamen who had been adrift in an open boat with practically no food for 20 days, after which D1, abetted by D2, killed the cabin boy who was with them. D1, D2 and the third man then fed on the boy's body. Four days later they were picked up, and when they got back to England they were tried for murder. The jury returned a special verdict in which they found that the men would probably have died within four days if they had not killed the boy and fed on his body, that the boy would probably have died before the men, and that, at the time of the killing, there was every probability that all four would have died unless one of them was killed and eaten. On these findings the case was adjourned for argument before five judges who held D1 and D2 guilty of murder, although sentence of death was later commuted to six months' imprisonment. Although the decision could be interpreted as simply denying the application of what is now called the defence of duress of circumstances to the facts, the tenor of the Court's judgment, given by Lord Coleridge, suggests that duress of circumstances can never be a defence to a charge of murder. This is the view taken in modern cases where *Dudley and Stephens* has been interpreted as deciding that duress of circumstances can never be a defence to murder. In *Howe*,[238] Lord Hailsham LC was clearly of the opinion, obiter, that the Court in *Dudley and Stephens* had correctly decided that 'necessity' was never a defence to murder, and in *Pommell*,[239] the Court of Appeal stated, obiter, that *Dudley and Stephens* had decided that 'necessity' was not a defence to a charge of murder.

A point which concerned Lord Coleridge in *Dudley and Stephens* was the question of how the choice was to be made about who was to die:

> 'It is not needful to point out the awful danger of admitting the principle contended [that killing an innocent person to save one's own life could be justified by "necessity"]. Who is to be the judge of this sort of necessity? By what measure is the comparative value of lives to be measured? Is it to be strength, or intellect, or what? ... In this case the weakest, the

[237] (1884) 14 QBD 273. For a critical review of this decision, see Williams 'A Commentary on *R v Dudley and Stephens*' (1977) 8 Cambrian LR 91. For a masterly examination of the various aspects of this case, see Simpson *Cannibalism and the Common Law* (1984).

[238] [1987] AC 417 at 430–431.   [239] [1995] 2 Cr App Rep 607, CA.

> youngest, the most unresisting, was chosen. Was it more necessary to kill him than one of the grown men? The answer must be "No"…There is no safe path for judges to tread but to ascertain the law to the best of their ability and to declare it according to their judgment; and if in any case the law appears to be too severe on individuals, to leave it to the Sovereign to exercise that prerogative of mercy which the Constitution has intrusted to the hands fittest to dispense it.'[240]

Professor JC Smith (as he then was) suggested[241] that *Dudley and Stephens* could be distinguished in a case where there is no problem of choice. Suppose that D, a mountaineer, is roped to V, his companion who has fallen, a situation which neither can rectify, and D cuts the rope to avoid joining his companion in a virtually certain death. D is not choosing that V should die, unlike the choice made by D and E in *Dudley and Stephens*, because V is already doomed to an almost immediate death, barring a miracle. It cannot be the law that D in the example is guilty of murder because he chose to live and not join V in death.

   Professor Smith cited an example from the *Herald of Free Enterprise* disaster in 1987 (when a car ferry capsized). The route to safety of a dozen passengers in danger of drowning was blocked by another who stood petrified, unable to move, on a rope ladder for over 10 minutes. One of them pushed him off the ladder. He and the others were then able to escape to safety; the petrified passenger was never seen again. Professor Smith argued that in this example there was no question of choosing who had to die; the petrified passenger had chosen himself by his immobility on the ladder. He also argued a second ground for distinguishing *Dudley and Stephens* in that, unlike the cabin boy, the petrified passenger, although no way at fault, was preventing others going where they had a right, and urgent need to go, and was thereby unwittingly imperilling their lives.

16.81 Lord Coleridge's judgment in *Dudley and Stephens* prompts similar reflection concerning the proper sphere of the criminal law to that prompted by *Howe*. Is it right for the law to impose a higher standard than that to be expected of the average member of society? It can only be justified in the most exceptional cases, but *Dudley and Stephens* was just such a case. It is to be hoped that, when a case like the mountaineer's or the petrified passenger comes before the courts (although a prosecution in such a case is most unlikely), *Dudley and Stephens* will be distinguished on the lines just referred to.

Relationship between self-defence and defence of another and duress of circumstances

16.82 In *Symonds*, referred to in para 16.36, D had driven off, dragging V some distance, allegedly to escape V. D was convicted of inflicting grievous bodily harm and careless driving. The Court of Appeal pointed out that there were difficulties more of theory than of substance in deploying self-defence in offences (such as driving offences) outside the

---

[240] (1884) 14 QBD at 286–288.   [241] *Justification and Excuse in the Criminal Law* (1989) Ch 3.

area of offences where D is accused of using force on another. The Court stated that this did not affect the substance of the case because the matters on which D relied to demonstrate self-defence raised the excuse of duress of circumstances. It pointed out that the same matters relied on as self-defence in relation to the associated charge of inflicting grievous bodily harm also constituted a defence of duress of circumstances to driving offences. This cannot be correct as a general statement of law. In particular, self-defence etc is assessed on the basis of the facts as the defendant believed them to be; duress of circumstances on the basis of what a reasonable person would believe them to be.[242] Moreover, self-defence is not limited to cases where death or serious physical injury is feared; duress of circumstances is.

It is odd that as the law now stands, if *Symonds* is correct, those who commit offences involving force are treated more leniently in the present respect than those who commit an offence without the use of force.

The distinction between self-defence and duress of circumstances also means that those who act to prevent an actual or imminent attack are dealt with by more lenient rules than those who act under some other type of threat. Suppose that V attacks D with a machete, thereby threatening D with death or serious injury, and that D kills V in self-defence. The defence of self-defence is available (and will succeed if the relevant rules are satisfied). Suppose, instead, that V and D are shipwrecked and there is only one lifebelt. It cannot support them both. D realises that only if he kills V will he survive to be rescued, and that if he does not both will die, and therefore he kills V. D will not be acting to protect himself from actual or imminent attack; V is perfectly innocent. This is not a case of self-defence but one of duress of circumstances, which is inapplicable to murder: D has no defence.

Proposals for reform

16.83 Clause 26 of the draft Criminal Law Bill[243] provides for an excuse of duress of circumstances which corresponds to its cl 25 relating to duress by threats,[244] including placing the burden of proving the defence on the defendant. This is unfortunate, not only because it departs from general principles but also because there would be cases which might overlap with the justification of self-defence etc where the defendant does not bear the burden of proof. The jury could be confused if two possible defences were left to them, each of which was governed by a different burden of proof.

The reform proposals about duress and murder and attempted murder made by the Law Commission in 2006, referred to in para 16.61, also apply to duress of circumstances.

---

[242] See para 16.73.
[243] Law Commission *Legislating the Criminal Code: Offences against the Person and General Principles* (1993), Law Com No 218; see para 7.131.   [244] See para 16.60.

Necessity

> **Key points 16.9**
>
> The following paragraphs deal with the law relating to situations of 'pure necessity', where the defendant was not compelled to act as he does but chooses to act as he does in order to avert a greater evil.
>
> Many statutory provisions expressly or impliedly make allowance for such situations.
>
> In addition, it is clearly established that a common law justification of pure necessity applies to cases involving medical treatment.

16.84 Private defence and the limited excuses of duress by threats and duress of circumstances are often said to be (or probably to be) species of necessity.[245] Even more confusingly, the defence of duress of circumstances described above has been referred to by the Court of Appeal or Divisional Court on a number of occasions as the defence of 'necessity'[246] or as the defence of 'necessity or duress of circumstances'.[247] However, the better view is that there is a difference between private defence and duress, on the one hand, and another situation, which is described here as 'pure necessity'.

16.85 The difference between the situations is that in private defence the defendant has been *compelled* in an emergency to act as he does to protect himself or another against attack, and that in duress the defendant has been *compelled* to act as he does by the threat (human or otherwise) of imminent death or serious injury to which he or another person is subject. It is the effect of that threat on his freedom of choice as to his actions which can suffice to provide a defence. In comparison, **the principles of necessity are not concerned with whether the defendant was compelled to act as he did to resist an aggressor (unlike private defence) nor with whether he was compelled to act as he did by an extraneous threat of imminent death or serious injury (unlike duress, a concession to human frailty). Instead, they are concerned with where the defendant alleges that he chose to commit what would otherwise be an offence in order to avert a greater evil, and that this justifies his conduct.** This distinction was recognised by Brooke LJ in *Re A (conjoined twins: surgical separation)* as the distinction between 'pure necessity' and duress of circumstances which of all the other defences comes closest in context to 'pure necessity'.[248]

---

[245] See, for example, *Safi* [2003] EWCA Crim 1809.

[246] For example *DPP v Harris* [1995] 1 Cr App Rep 170, DC; *Backshall* [1999] 1 Cr App Rep 35, CA; *Quayle and others; A-G's Reference (No 2 of 2004)* [2005] EWCA Crim 1415.

[247] *Blake v DPP* [1993] Crim LR 586, DC; para 16.3; *Cairns* [1999] 2 Cr App Rep 137, CA; *Abdul-Hussain* [1999] Crim LR 570, CA (this point does not appear in this brief report but does appear in the transcript).

[248] [2001] Fam 147 at 236.

16.86 The case law on necessity is limited. This is partly because the courts have treated a defence of 'pure necessity' with caution on the ground that otherwise it would become a 'mask for anarchy',[249] and partly because those who act in a true situation of necessity are usually praised, not prosecuted. As a result of the limited case law, it is uncertain to what extent pure necessity is available as a defence to a criminal charge except in the case of certain statutory offences where there is express provision for circumstances of necessity.

Statutory provision for necessity

16.87 In the definition of many statutory offences allowance is made expressly or impliedly for the case where the defendant has acted under the stress of necessity. One example of the express justification of what would otherwise be criminal is the offence of child destruction, contrary to the Infant Life (Preservation) Act 1929, s 1, under which the prosecution must prove that the defendant was not acting in good faith in order to preserve the life of the mother.[250] Another example is provided by the Nurses, Midwives and Health Visitors Act 1997, s 16. Section 16(1) makes it a summary offence for someone other than a registered midwife or registered medical practitioner to attend a woman in childbirth, but s 16(2) states that this offence is not committed where the attention is given in a case of sudden or urgent necessity

16.88 Some statutes provide defences which cover necessity, as well as other circumstances. One example is the Abortion Act 1967, s 1, which was described in para 8.196. Another example is the Road Traffic Regulation Act 1984, s 87,[251] which dispenses with the need for fire and rescue service vehicles, police vehicles, Serious Organised Crime Agency vehicles and ambulances to observe the speed limit if the observance of the limit would be likely to hinder the use of the vehicle for the purpose for which it is being used. Regulation 36 of the Traffic Signs Regulations and General Directions 2002[252] permits police, Serious Organised Crime Agency or emergency services' vehicles to be driven through a red traffic light to avoid delay provided this is not likely to endanger anyone or to cause another driver crossing on green to have to avoid an accident. Lastly, by the Mental Health Act 1983, s 63, 'medical treatment', including force-feeding,[253] can be given, without his consent, to a patient compulsorily detained under the Act.[254]

---

[249] *Southwark London Borough Council v Williams* [1971] Ch 734 at 746, per Edmund Davies LJ.

[250] Para 8.201.

[251] As amended by the Fire and Rescue Services Act 2004, Sch 1, and the Serious Organised Crime and Police Act 2005, Sch 4.

[252] As amended by the Serious Organised Crime and Police Act 2005 (Consequential and Supplementary Amendments to Secondary Legislation) Order 2006, Sch 1.

[253] *B v Croydon Health Authority* [1995] Fam 133, CA. Also see *Collins, ex p Brady* [2000] Lloyd's Rep Med 355, DC.

[254] For further examples, see the Control of Pollution (Amendment) Act 1989, s 1(4)(a); the Merchant Shipping Act 1995, s 3(2); the Fire and Rescue Services Act 2004, s 44; and the Animal Welfare Act 2006, s 18.

16.89 An implied allowance for necessity, as well as other circumstances, would seem to be made by the wording of some statutory offences. For example, if D washed a hazardous chemical spillage down the drains in a street in order to prevent danger to those in the area and was charged with theft of the chemicals, a jury could, and no doubt would, find that he had not acted dishonestly.[255]

Pure necessity: a defence at common law?

16.90 There have been a number of cases over the last two centuries where the decision was based on principles of pure necessity but without express reference to a common law defence of necessity. It is arguable that they provide implicit recognition of the existence of such a defence.

For example, in *Vantandillo*,[256] it was held that the necessity for a mother to carry her infected child through the streets to seek medical attention 'might have been given in evidence as a matter of defence' to a charge of exposing a person with a contagious disease on the public highway. Another example is provided by *Bourne*,[257] where D, an obstetric surgeon, performed an abortion on a 14-year-old girl who had been violently raped. He was charged with unlawfully using an instrument with intent to procure a miscarriage, contrary to the Offences Against the Person Act 1861, s 58. The jury acquitted D after MacNaghten J had told the jury that D would not have acted unlawfully if he had acted in good faith to save the girl's life. Although the judge dealt with the matter from the point of view of the meaning of 'unlawfully' in s 58, and did not expressly refer to a defence of necessity, the case is clearly one where principles of necessity were implied into the meaning of 'unlawful', and it has subsequently been described by the Court of Appeal in *Southwark London Borough Council v Williams*[258] as being based on necessity.

16.91 Nevertheless, **a number of modern cases have indicated that, if there is a common law defence of pure necessity, it is very limited in its extent.** In *Martin (Colin)*,[259] the Court of Appeal, having said that 'English law does, in extreme circumstances, recognise a defence of necessity', regarded that defence as arising as duress by threats and duress of circumstances and, apparently, not otherwise. In *Pommell*, which was also concerned with duress of circumstances, the Court of Appeal stated:

> 'The strength of the argument that a person ought to be permitted to breach the letter of the criminal law in order to prevent a greater evil befalling himself or others has long been recognised, . . . but it has, in English law, not given rise to a recognised general defence of necessity . . .'.[260]

---

[255] Paras 10.73–10.75. For a contrary view, see Griew *Theft Acts 1968 and 1978* (7th edn, 1995) paras 2–140.

[256] (1815) 4 M & S 73. Also see *Johnson v Phillips* [1975] 3 All ER 682, DC.

[257] [1939] 1 KB 687. The facts of this case would now be governed by the provisions of the Abortion Act 1967; para 8.196. The decision in *Bourne* could be regarded as another example of an implied allowance for necessity by the words of the statute.

[258] [1971] Ch 734, CA.   [259] [1989] 1 All ER 652 at 653.   [260] [1995] 2 Cr App Rep 607 at 613.

In *Shayler*,[261] the Court of Appeal stated that 'apart from some of the medical cases like *Re F* [below] the law has tended to treat duress of circumstances and necessity as one and the same'. Lastly, in *Quayle and others; A-G's Reference (No 2 of 2004)*,[262] where the Court of Appeal was confronted with the question of whether necessity was available to a defendant in respect of offences of cultivating, producing, importing or possession with intent to supply cannabis or cannabis resin for the purpose of alleviating pain arising from a pre-existing illness, the Court proceeded on the basis that the only possible defence was duress of circumstances (which it referred to as 'necessity of circumstances'). The Court denied that there were wider 'over-arching principles applicable in all cases of necessity'.

A problem with discussing whether there is a separate defence of pure necessity is that some of the examples given in the past would now be covered by the defence of duress of circumstances (or by the defence of lawful excuse on a criminal damage charge).

16.92 Despite the above, **there is one type of case involving pure necessity for which there is express, strong authority that there is a justification of pure necessity which applies to cases not satisfying the requirements of duress of circumstances: that involving medical treatment. Apart from this it is doubtful, in the absence of positive authority and in the light of the negative approach referred to above, that currently a defence of pure necessity is available or would be extended.**

Express authority in terms of pure necessity and medical treatment is provided in particular by two House of Lords' decisions, *Re F*[263] and *Bournewood Community and Mental Health NHS Trust, ex p L*,[264] and by the decision of the Court of Appeal in *Re A (conjoined twins: surgical separation)*.[265] Although *Re F* and *Bournewood* were decided in the context of the law of tort, their recognition of a defence of necessity clearly extended to criminal liability. In *Bournewood* Lord Goff said:

> 'The concept of necessity has its role to play in all branches of our law of obligations: in contract,... in tort (see *F*'s case)... and in our criminal law. It is therefore a concept of great importance.'[266]

In *Re F*, the House of Lords held it to be lawful to carry out a sterilisation operation on a voluntary mental patient with serious mental disability who lacked the capacity to consent, in order to avert the risk of her becoming pregnant by a patient with whom she had formed a sexual relationship; pregnancy would have had disastrous psychiatric consequences for her. Lord Goff, with whose reasons Lords Bridge and Jauncey agreed, expressly based the decision on a 'principle of necessity'.

In *Bournewood Community and Mental Health NHS Trust, ex p L*, it was held that a hospital was entitled to give treatment and care which was in his best interests to an

---

261 [2001] EWCA Crim 1977; affd on different grounds ([2002] UKHL 11).

262 [2005] EWCA Crim 1415.

263 [1990] 2 AC 1, HL; discussed by S Gardner 'Necessity's Newest Inventions' (1991) 11 OJLS 125, 127–135

264 [1999] 1 AC 458, HL. Also see *Re MB* [1997] 2 FLR 426, CA.

265 [2001] Fam 147, CA.   266 [1999] 1 AC 458 at 490.

informal mentally disordered patient lacking any capacity to consent, and that the basis for this was the common law doctrine of necessity which had the effect of justifying actions which would otherwise be unlawful.[267]

Requirements

16.93 Reference to Lord Goff's speech in *Re F*,[268] indicates that the existence of an emergency in the normal sense of the word is not a requirement of the defence of necessity.

In *Re A (conjoined twins: surgical separation)*,[269] whose facts are in para 16.95, Brooke LJ adopted and applied the nineteenth century statement by Stephen that there were **three necessary requirements for the application of the defence of necessity:**

- **the act must be necessary to avoid inevitable and irreparable evil;**
- **no more should be done than is reasonably necessary for the purpose to be achieved; and**
- **the evil inflicted must not be disproportionate to the evil avoided.**[270]

To these requirements, there can no doubt be added one that the defendant must have been faced by an unavoidable choice between allowing some evil to occur or committing an offence (or what would otherwise be an offence).

Limits

16.94 There are two important limits on the defence of pure necessity applicable to medical treatment.

---

[267] In this case L, who was autistic, had a limited level of understanding and lacked the capacity to consent to medical treatment, became particularly agitated. He was admitted as an in-patient informally, and not under the compulsory detention powers under the Mental Health Act 1983. L brought civil proceedings claiming that he had been unlawfully detained. The House of Lords held that he had not been detained but that, in any case, detention would have been in his best interests and so justified by necessity. The European Court of Human Rights (*HL v United Kingdom* (2004) 17 BHRC 418) held that he had been deprived of his liberty during the period in which he was in hospital, and that the absence of procedural safeguards to protect against arbitrary deprivation of liberty on the ground of necessity after he had been compulsorily detained breached his right to liberty guaranteed by the ECHR, Art 5(1), and also breached his right to have the legality of his detention reviewed by a court, contrary to the ECHR, Art 5(4). The following provisions of the Mental Capacity Act 2005, inserted by the Mental Health Act 2007, represent Parliament's response to the decision of the European Court of Human Rights. The Mental Capacity Act 2005, s 4A provides that a person (D) may deprive a person (V) of his liberty if the deprivation is authorised by the Mental Capacity Act 2005, Sch A1. Schedule A1 applies to a mentally incapable patient accommodated in a hospital or care home, for the purposes of being given care or treatment, in circumstances amounting to deprivation of his liberty and provides safeguards in such a case which require a formal authorisation by the appropriate authority.

[268] [1990] 2 AC 1, HL. Also see *Re A (conjoined twins: surgical separation)* [2001] Fam 147 at 239, per Brooke LJ.

[269] [2001] Fam 147 at 240.   [270] *Digest of the Criminal Law* (4th edn, 1887) 2.

Necessity is not a defence where the victim of the defendant's conduct is a mentally competent adult patient who refuses to consent, provided that his conduct does not pose a threat to any other person or the property of another; individual autonomy is protected. Although this has not been expressly stated, it must follow from the Court of Appeal's decision in *St George's Healthcare NHS Trust v S*.[271] There the Court of Appeal held that to induce the delivery of a child, where the mother was mentally competent and refused to consent to that treatment, was unlawful because such a patient was entitled to refuse consent, even though in that case her life, and that of her unborn child, depended on the treatment. Likewise, necessity cannot be used to justify force-feeding a hunger-striking prisoner who is mentally competent, even if suicide is his intention.[272]

The second limit would seem to be that, consistent with the rule for duress of circumstances,[273] **the policy and scheme of a piece of legislation may be interpreted as excluding any justification of necessity.**

Pure necessity and murder

16.95 It was established by the Court of Appeal in *Re A (conjoined twins: surgical separation)*[274] that in one very limited set of circumstances pure necessity can be a defence to murder.

Re A was, like *Re F* and *Bournewood* referred to in para 16.92, a civil case in which matters relevant to the criminal law were discussed. In this case a Healthcare Trust sought a declaration that it would be lawful and in the best interest of conjoined ('Siamese') twins to separate them despite the fact that the parents withheld their consent (a matter dealt with in para 7.26) and despite the fact that this would inevitably lead to the death of Mary, the weaker of the two, who only lived because a common artery enabled the stronger twin, Jodie, to circulate life-sustaining oxygenated blood for both. There was evidence that the separation operation could be performed successfully and that it would give Jodie the opportunity of a separate good-quality life. On the other hand, if the operation was not carried out and the twins remained united, Jodie's heart would fail (and both would therefore die) in three to six months or so because of the strain of supporting two bodies.

The declaration sought having been granted, the parents appealed to the Court of Appeal. There were two issues before the Court, the first dependent on the second:

- whether, applying family law principles, the Court should overrule the parents' refusal of consent and give permission for the operation; and

---

[271] [1998] 3 All ER 673, CA.

[272] *Secretary of State for the Home Department v Robb* [1995] Fam 127, not following, on a number of grounds, *Leigh v Gladstone* (1909) 26 TLR 139 (where it was held that it was the duty of the prison authorities to force-feed a hunger-striking prisoner to save the prisoner's life).   [273] Para 16.79.

[274] [2001] Fam 147, CA. For a discussion of the issues in this case see the group of articles in (2001) 9 *Medical Law Review* 201–298; Rogers 'Necessity, Private Defence and the Killing of Mary' [2001] Crim LR 515; Huxtable 'Separation of Conjugal Twins: Where Next for English Law' [2002] Crim LR 459.

- whether the operation would be lawful, because the Court could not approve an unlawful course of action.

Given the conflict of interest between Jodie and Mary, and the Court's duty under family law to give paramount consideration to the welfare of each twin, the Court held that it had to choose the lesser of the two evils and decide whether to grant permission on the basis of the least detrimental alternative. It decided that the least detrimental choice, balancing the twins against each other, was to permit the operation to be performed. On this basis, it concluded, it would grant permission for the operation provided that such an operation would be lawful.

Would it be lawful? The Court pointed out that the separation operation would necessarily be invasive of Mary's body; it would involve acts which would kill her. Thus, it was not a case which could be covered under the rule about discontinuance of medical treatment established in *Airedale National Health Service Trust v Bland*.[275] Although the Court of Appeal was unanimous in reaching its conclusion that the operation would be lawful, it was not unanimous in the route which it took.

Brooke LJ rested his decision squarely on the defence of necessity. Having referred to the three necessary requirements of necessity given by Stephen (see para 16.93), he concluded: 'Given that the principles of modern family law point irresistibly to the conclusion that the interests of Jodie must be preferred to the conflicting interests of Mary, I consider that all three requirements are satisfied in this case'.[276] He did not think that the endorsement of *Dudley and Stephens* by the House of Lords in *Howe* prevented the defence of necessity applying to the situation in question, which was not in mind in *Howe*. *Dudley and Stephens* was distinguishable. Mary was self-designated for an early death; nobody could extend her life beyond a short span.

Like Brooke LJ, Ward LJ held that the operation would involve the intentional killing of Mary (see para 3.18). He held that the killing of Mary as a result of the operation would not be unlawful because the doctors were under a conflict of duty; they were under a duty to Mary not to operate because that would kill Mary, and under a duty to Jodie to operate because otherwise Jodie would die. They were under a duty to choose; they had to make the choice. The conflict of duty had to be resolved by the doctors by reference to the rightfulness of the choice, based on which was the lesser of two evils. Carrying out the operation would be justified as the lesser evil and no unlawful act would be committed. His Lordship added that to give the doctors the choice would not offend the 'sanctity of life principle' because there was no difference in essence between a resort to legitimate self-defence against a six-year-old shooting indiscriminately and the doctors coming to Jodie's defence and removing the fatal threat to Jodie posed by Mary. The availability, he said, of such a plea of 'quasi' self-defence made intervention by the doctors lawful.

---

[275] [1993] AC 789, HL; para 2.15.   [276] [2001] Fam 147 at 240.

Although it was not expressed as such, Ward LJ's reasoning as to resolving the conflict of duties is based on principles of necessity compatible with those adopted by Brooke LJ.

Robert Walker LJ, as he then was, based his decision on the lawfulness of the operation ultimately on 'intention'. In a statement which cannot be regarded as strictly representing the law (as explained in para 3.24) he said:

> 'The proposed operation would...be in the best interests of each of the twins. The decision does not require the Court to value one life above another.... The proposed operation would not be unlawful. It would involve the positive act of invasive surgery and Mary's death would be foreseen as an inevitable consequence of an operation which is intended, and is necessary, to save Jodie's life. But Mary's death would not be the purpose or intention of the surgery, and she would die because tragically her body, on its own, is not and never has been viable.'[277]

Earlier in his judgment, however, he said:

> 'I would extend it [the defence of necessity], if it needs to be extended, to cover this case. It is a case of doctors owing conflicting legal (and not merely social or moral) duties. It is a case where the test of proportionality is met, since it is a matter of life and death, and on the evidence Mary is bound to die soon in any event. It is not a case of evaluating the relative worth of two human lives, but of undertaking surgery without which neither life will have the bodily integrity (or wholeness) which is its due.'[278]

The Court of Appeal held that killing Mary was not a breach of the provision in the ECHR, Article 2(1) that: 'No one shall be deprived of his life intentionally save in the execution of a sentence of a court following his conviction for a crime for which this penalty is provided by law'. The reason was that 'intentionally' in Article 2(1) had an autonomous meaning, limited to a direct intention to kill, which the doctors did not have.

It is important to note the limits of *Re A*. It does not decide, for example, that a doctor who has decided that a patient cannot survive can take active steps to kill the patient. **The only circumstances in respect of which it can be regarded as authority that a killing by a doctor is lawful are where:**

- **it is impossible to preserve the life of some other patient (X) without bringing about the death of Y;**
- **Y by his or her continued existence will inevitably bring about X's death within a short period of time; and**
- **X is capable of living an independent life but Y is incapable under any circumstances (including all forms of medical intervention) of viable independent existence.**[279]

---

[277] [2001] Fam 147 at 259.   [278] [2001] Fam 147 at 255.   [279] [2001] Fam 147 at 205, per Ward LJ.

Other points

16.96 Necessity is like self-defence, and unlike duress, in that as Lord Goff's speech in *Re F*[280] indicates, **pure necessity justifies conduct which would otherwise be unlawful (ie it renders conduct lawful, as opposed simply to providing a defence to unlawful conduct)**. On this basis it is not strictly accurate, although it is convenient, to refer to it as a defence.

At one time the Law Commission was of the view that the 'defence' of necessity, to the extent that it existed at common law, should be abolished.[281] The Law Commission is now persuaded that the defence should be kept open to be developed by the courts. When the defence is sufficiently established, it may be confirmed by legislation.[282]

Superior orders

Key points 16.10

The criminal law does not recognise a defence of superior orders. Thus, a person who acts under the orders of a superior which are unlawful does not have a defence, even if he reasonably believes that the order is lawful. However, the unlawful orders of a superior may indirectly provide the defendant with a defence if they bring into operation some other rule of law which provides a defence.

16.97 Clearly, if a person acts on the lawful orders of a superior, as where a soldier is ordered by an officer to use reasonable force to resist attack, reasonable force by him to do so will be justified by the rules of public or private defence already mentioned.

The question of whether there is a separate general defence of superior orders is concerned with the situation where the superior's orders were in fact unlawful.

In South Africa,[283] it has been held that: 'if a soldier honestly believes he is doing his duty in obeying the commands of his superior, and if the orders are not so manifestly illegal that he must or ought to have known that they are unlawful, the private soldier would be protected by the orders of his superior officer'. Some Criminal Codes provide a defence of superior orders which is not limited to members of the armed forces. For example, the Italian Penal Code allows the defence if the order was not obviously illegal and the defendant has no way of ascertaining its legality.[284]

---

[280] [1990] 2 AC 1 at 74, HL.

[281] *Defences of General Application* (1977), Law Com No 83. For critical discussions of those proposals, see Williams [1978] Crim LR 128, and Huxley [1978] Crim LR 141.

[282] Law Commission: *Legislating the Criminal Code: Offences against the Persons and General Principles* (1993), Law Com No 218, paras 27.4 and 35.7; see para 7.131.

[283] *Smith* (1900) 17 SCR 561.

[284] This point is made by Walker 'On Excusing Colonel Priebke' (1997) 147 NLJ 720.

This is not, however, the position in English law. In *Lewis v Dickson*,[285] it was held that a civilian security officer, whose checking of vehicles in compliance with the instructions of his superior resulted in the obstruction of a road, was guilty of wilfully obstructing the highway without lawful authority or excuse; the fact that he was obeying his superior's instructions was no defence. In *Yip Chiu-cheung v R*,[286] the Privy Council held that there was no place in English law for a defence of superior orders (nor for a defence of executive authorisation of a breach of the criminal law). In *Clegg*,[287] Lord Lloyd, with whose speech the rest of the House of Lords agreed, stated, obiter, that there was no general defence of superior orders in English law. Obedience to superior orders can, of course, lead to a mitigation of sentence, except in the case of murder.

The rule that even a reasonably mistaken belief that the orders of a superior are lawful is no defence is an unrealistic one where the defendant is a member of the armed forces. The reason is that it requires an individual soldier etc who is trained to obey orders instantly to consider whether orders given to him are lawful and not to carry them out if they are in fact unlawful, whether manifestly or not.[288]

16.98 The unlawful orders of a superior, whether a civilian or member of the armed forces, may bring *other* rules of law into play, and thus indirectly provide the defendant with a defence. For example, such an order may induce in the defendant a mistake which results in him lacking the *mens rea* for the offence.[289] Suppose that a person is ordered to use a degree of force in a situation where that degree of force is unreasonable, so that the order is unlawful, he will not be guilty of an offence against the person when he uses that force if on the facts as he believed them to be (and the order may have contributed to that belief) the force used would have been reasonable. In such a case he will lack the necessary *mens rea*.[290] Likewise, suppose that a farm labourer removes a horse from V's field and takes it to his employer's stables pursuant to the latter's unlawful instructions. He may well believe that the horse belongs to the employer and that he is legally entitled to deprive V of it on the employer's behalf. If so, he is not guilty of theft because a person who believes that he has a legal right to deprive another of property on behalf of a third person lacks part of the *mens rea* for theft, dishonesty.[291]

Similarly, a superior order may induce in the defendant a mistake which results in him having a belief which is a statutory defence. For example, a person is not guilty of criminal damage if he believes that he has the owner's consent to do as he does, because he will have the defence provided by the Criminal Damage Act 1971, s 5. Consequently, if the farm labourer just referred to proceeds to dock the horse's tail pursuant to his employer's instructions, he may be not guilty of criminal damage.[292]

---

[285] [1976] RTR 431, DC.   [286] [1995] 1 AC 111, PC.   [287] [1995] 1 AC 482 at 498.

[288] For arguments in favour of a defence being available where military orders are not manifestly illegal, see Brownlee 'Superior Orders: Time for a New Realism' [1989] Crim LR 396. See also Nichols 'Untying the Soldier by Refurbishing the Common Law' [1976] Crim LR 181.

[289] *James* (1837) 8 C & P 131; *Trainer* (1864) 4 F & F 105.   [290] Paras 5.7 and 16.14.

[291] Para 10.69.   [292] *Denton* [1982] 1 All ER 65, CA; para 13.10.

FURTHER READING

Bohlander 'In Extremis – Hijacked Airplanes, "Collateral Damage" and the Limits of the Criminal Law' [2006] Crim LR 579

Bohlander 'Of Shipwrecked Sailors, Unborn Children, Conjoined Twins and Hijacked Aeroplanes – Taking Human Life and the Defence of Necessity' (2006) 70 JCL 147

Buchanan and Virgo 'Duress and Mental Abnormality' [1999] Crim LR 517

Colvin 'Exculpatory Defences in the Criminal Law' (1990) 10 OJLS 381

Elliott 'Necessity, Duress and Self-Defence' [1989] Crim LR 611

S Gardner 'Necessity: Newest Inventions' (1991) 11 OJLS 125

S Gardner 'Direct Action and the Defence of Necessity' [2005] Crim LR 371

Gearty 'Necessity: A Necessary Principle in English Law?' (1989) 48 CLJ 357

Horder *Excusing Crime* (2004) Ch 3

Leverick *Killing in Self-Defence* (2006)

Milgate 'Duress and the Criminal Law: Another About Turn by the House of Lords' (1988) 44 CLJ 61

Pace 'Marital Coercion – Anachronism or Modernism?' [1979] Crim LR 82

Rogers 'Have-a-Go Heroes' (2008) 158 NLJ 318

JC Smith *Justification and Excuse in the Criminal Law* (1989)

KJM Smith 'Duress and Steadfastness: In Pursuit of the Unintelligible' [1999] Crim LR 363

Walters 'Murder, Duress and Judicial Decision-Making in the House of Lords' (1988) 8 LS 61

Wasik 'Duress and Criminal Responsibility' [1977] Crim LR 453

Wilson 'The Structure of Criminal Defences' [2005] Crim LR 108

Yeo 'Killing in Defence of Property' (2000) 150 NLJ 730

17

Participation

OVERVIEW

So far this book has concentrated on the liability of the perpetrator of an offence. However, the commission of an offence may involve other people in criminal liability in various ways.

Most of this chapter is concerned with the liability of accomplices (secondary parties), ie those who aid, abet, counsel or procure the commission of an offence by a perpetrator, for example by encouraging the perpetrator or supplying him with equipment which he needs to commit it. An accomplice to an offence is liable for that offence. He is a party to it, just like the perpetrator.

A person who assists an offender after the commission of an offence is not liable as a party to it but he may commit one or more of a number of specific offences.

17.1 A perpetrator (sometimes described as a principal) is someone who directly brings about the *actus reus* of an offence[1] with the relevant *mens rea*. The crucial distinction between an accomplice (sometimes described as an accessory) and a perpetrator is that, although an accomplice has participated in the commission of an offence, he has not in law directly brought about its *actus reus*, even if his assistance or encouragement is a cause of the perpetrator acting as he does. This is true even of a result crime because, where D has assisted or encouraged E to do the act which is the immediate cause of the necessary consequence, eg firing the gun in murder, E's act is a free, deliberate and informed intervening act which breaks the chain of causation from D's assistance or encouragement; D is therefore not a joint perpetrator with E of the offence but an accomplice to it.

Professor Glanville Williams explained the matter as follows:

'Principals cause, accomplices encourage (or otherwise influence) or help. If the instigator were regarded as causing the result he would be a principal, and the conceptual division between principals (or, as I prefer to call them, perpetrators) and accessories would vanish. Indeed, it was because the instigator was not regarded as causing the crime that the notion of accessories had to be developed. This is the irrefragable argument for recognising the novus actus principle[2] as one of the bases of our criminal law. The final act is done

---

[1] This may be through the use of an innocent agent; para 17.6.
[2] Para 2.41.

> by the perpetrator, and his guilt pushes the accessories, conceptually speaking, into the background.'[3]

17.2 The liability of those who assist offenders after an offence is dealt with, for example, by the offences of assisting an offender, concealment of an offence for reward (both dealt with later in this chapter) and perverting the course of justice. The offence of handling stolen goods deals with those who help 'thieves' after the event,[4] as do offences of money laundering under the Proceeds of Crime Act 2002, Pt 7.

Perpetrators

17.3 Normally, it is clear who is the perpetrator: he is the one who, with the relevant *mens rea*, does the sufficient act for the *actus reus*, ie the one who fires the fatal shot in murder, or has sexual intercourse in rape, or appropriates the property in theft.

Joint perpetrators

17.4 There can be more than one perpetrator, as where two people by their joint and aggregate violence kill another.[5] Two or more people may also be joint perpetrators where each with the relevant *mens rea* does distinct acts which together constitute the sufficient act for the *actus reus* of an offence; for example, in an offence involving driving D1 and D2 have both been held to be driving where D1 was leaning across and steering while D2 operated the foot pedals and gears.[6] Another example can be provided by reference to the offence of robbery; D1 and D2 would be joint perpetrators of that offence if, with the requisite *mens rea*, D1 appropriated another's property while D2 used force to enable the appropriation to occur.

The distinction between a joint perpetrator and an accomplice who is present can be a fine one. Indeed, it appears to be the law in Australia that all those present at the time of the offence with a common purpose that it be committed are joint perpetrators, even though only one of them performed the acts constituting the offence.[7] A similar view was taken by the Court of Appeal in *Stewart and Schofield*,[8] but as indicated in para 17.53 it would not appear to represent the current state of English law.

17.5 Joint perpetrators are not necessarily liable for the same offence; the liability of each of them depends on the extent of his mens rea. Thus, if D1 and D2 both throw

---

[3] 'Finis for Novus Actus' (1989) 48 CLJ 391 at 398.
[4] Paras 11.33–11.56.
[5] *Macklin and Murphy* (1838) 2 Lew CC 225.
[6] *Tyler v Whatmore* [1976] RTR 83, DC.
[7] *Osland v R* (1998) 73 ALJR 173, HCt of Australia; discussed by Sir John Smith 'Joint Enterprise and Secondary Liability' (1999) 50 NILQ 153.
[8] [1995] 3 All ER 159, CA.

punches at V who, known to D1 but unknown to D2, has 'brittle bone disease' and suffers broken bones in consequence, D1 may be convicted of causing grievous bodily harm with intent, contrary to the Offences Against the Person Act 1861, s 18, if, as is likely, an intent to cause such harm could be proved. However, D2 could only be convicted of an offence of inflicting grievous bodily harm under the Offences Against the Person Act 1861, s 20 because of his ignorance of V's disease; he would neither aim to cause grievous bodily harm nor foresee that it would result from the punches. Joint perpetrators may also be liable for different offences, although they have the same *mens rea*, because one has a partial defence, as where D1 and D2 beat V, intending to kill him, and achieve that result by their combined efforts. If D2 successfully pleads diminished responsibility, he will be guilty of manslaughter, whereas D1 is guilty of murder.

Innocent agency

17.6 **If a person makes use of an innocent agent in order to procure the commission of an offence, that person, not the innocent agent, is the perpetrator, even though he is not present at the scene of the crime and does nothing with his own hands. An innocent agent is one who commits the *actus reus* of an offence but is himself devoid of responsibility, either by reason of incapacity (ie infancy[9] or insanity[10]) or because he lacks *mens rea* or has a defence such as duress by threats.** A striking example of innocent agency is where a daughter, acting on her mother's instructions, gave some powder to her father to relieve his cold. Unknown to the daughter it was a poison and her father died. It was held that the mother was the perpetrator of the crime of murder since the daughter, lacking *mens rea*, was an innocent agent by means of whom the mother had perpetrated the offence. Of course, if, as the report notes, the daughter had known that the powder was poison she would have been guilty as perpetrator and the mother as an accomplice.[11] A more modern, although more prosaic, example is provided by *Stringer*[12] where the business manager of a company signed false invoices, intending that innocent employees would automatically pass them for payment and that the company's bank account would be debited accordingly, which duly occurred. It was held that he could be convicted of theft of the sums paid on the false invoices, having appropriated them through innocent agents.

17.7 It is irrelevant that the actual innocent agent is not the person intended to be used. In *Michael*,[13] D, intending to kill her child, who was in the care of a nurse, gave the nurse a poison, telling her that it was medicine and should be given to the child. The nurse decided not to do so and put it on the mantelpiece. In her absence, one of her children, aged five, gave D's child a fatal dose. It was held that this administration by 'an innocent

---

9 *Michael* (1840) 9 C & P 356.
10 *Tyler and Price* (1838) 8 C & P 616.
11 *Anon* (1634) Kel 53. Also see *Manley* (1844) 3 LTOS 22.
12 (1991) 94 Cr App Rep 13, CA.
13 (1840) 9 C & P 356.

agent' was murder. To call the young child D's 'agent' seems to stretch the meaning of that term.[14]

Accomplices

17.8 A person who aids, abets, counsels or procures the commission of an offence (an accomplice) is liable to be tried and punished for that offence as a principal offender. This is provided by the Accessories and Abettors Act 1861, s 8 in relation to offences triable only on indictment and offences triable either way, and by the Magistrates' Courts Act 1980, s 44 in relation to summary offences. The liability of an accomplice is derived from his involvement in the principal offence and is often described as 'derivative liability' or 'secondary liability'.

So that a defendant may know whether he is alleged to have been a perpetrator or an accomplice, the particulars of the offence in the indictment should make it clear whether it is alleged that he was a perpetrator or an accomplice.[15] However, if the prosecution is advanced on the basis that the defendant was the perpetrator or an accomplice this does not prevent the prosecution from alleging this in a single count; it is not necessary to have separate counts.[16]

17.9 Five other introductory points may be made:

- A person can be convicted, as an accomplice, of an inchoate offence.[17] In relation to an attempt, the authority is *Dunnington*.[18] Here, the Court of Appeal held that a person who had driven would-be robbers to the scene of their intended crime could be convicted as an accomplice to attempted robbery when they were unsuccessful. There is no reason to doubt that a person can be convicted, as an accomplice, of one of the other inchoate offences if he satisfies the conditions necessary for conviction as an accomplice.[19]

- In *Jefferson*,[20] the Court of Appeal held that liability as an accomplice is of general application to all offences, unless expressly excluded by statute.[21] However, it may be that the wording of a statute can have the effect of implicitly excluding liability as an accomplice. In *Carmichael & Sons (Worcester) Ltd v Cottle*,[22] it was stated, obiter, that when a provision uses the words 'using, causing or permitting to be used' it may

---

[14] See Hart and Honoré *Causation in the Law* (2nd edn, 1985) 337.

[15] *DPP for Northern Ireland v Maxwell* [1978] 3 All ER 1140, HL; *Gaughan* (1991) 155 JP 235, CA; *Taylor* [1998] Crim LR 582, CA.

[16] *Gaughan* (1991) 155 JP 235, CA.

[17] Inchoate offences were discussed in Ch 14.

[18] [1984] QB 472, CA.

[19] Smith 'Secondary Participation and Inchoate Offences' in *Crime, Proof and Punishment* (1981) (Tapper (ed)) p 21.

[20] [1994] 1 All ER 270, CA.

[21] For an express exclusion in respect of an individual, but not a corporation, see the Corporate Manslaughter and Corporate Homicide Act 2007, s 18(1): para 8.157.

[22] [1971] RTR 11 at 14.

be that 'there is no room for the application of the principle relating to aiders and abettors'. Terms like 'cause or permit' clearly cover many of the types of conduct encompassed by 'aid, abet, counsel or procure' but the statement in the above case remains a suggestion, and no more, at present. The statement in *Carmichael v Cottle* can be compared with obiter dicta in *Brookes v Retail Credit Cards*,[23] to the effect that the words 'a breach of any requirement by...this Act shall incur no criminal sanction...', except to the extent provided by this Act' in the Consumer Credit Act 1974 did not exclude the normal liability of someone who was an accomplice to an offence under the Act.

- For the purpose of following the old cases, until the Criminal Law Act 1967 accomplices to the commission of a felony were described as 'principals in the second degree'[24] if they were present when it was committed, or as 'accessories before the fact' if absent. In either event they were properly described as 'principals' in offences other than felonies. They are now so described in respect of all offences.[25]

- A number of participants may also be guilty of conspiracy.

- In relation to people who aid, abet, counsel or procure abroad an offence committed in England and Wales it was established in *Robert Millar (Contractors) Ltd and Millar*[26] that they may be convicted in an English or Welsh court as accomplices to the principal offence, but people in England or Wales who aid, abet, counsel or procure the commission abroad of an offence may not,[27] unless that offence committed abroad is one over which an English or Welsh court has jurisdiction.

Key points 17.1

In order that a person may be convicted as an accomplice, it is not necessary that the perpetrator should have been brought to trial or convicted, or even that his identity should be known, but it is necessary for the prosecution to prove:

- that the defendant aided, abetted, counselled or procured the commission of the principal offence;

- that the principal offence was in fact committed; and

- that he had the *mens rea* required for liability as an accomplice.

---

[23] (1985) 150 JP 131, DC.

[24] The perpetrator of a felony was known as a 'principal in the first degree' until that Act.

[25] The serious offences created by the judges from the twelfth to the fourteenth century were called felonies, and the less serious came to be known as misdemeanours. The same distinction was subsequently drawn by Parliament in enacting statutory offences. All distinctions between felonies and misdemeanours were abolished by the Criminal Law Act 1967, s 1, which provides that, on all matters on which a distinction between felonies and misdemeanours had previously been made, the law applicable at the commencement of the Act to misdemeanours applies.

[26] [1970] 2 QB 54, CA.

[27] *Godfrey* [1923] 1 KB 24, CCA; *Ngan* [1998] 1 Cr App Rep 331, CA.

Aiding, abetting, counselling or procuring

17.10 If a defendant is alleged to have been an accomplice to the principal offence, the charge may allege that he aided, abetted, counselled or procured it, and he will be convicted if he is proved to have participated in one or more of these four ways.[28]

Although 'aiding' and 'abetting' have sometimes been regarded as synonymous,[29] there is a difference between them: **'aid' is used to describe the activity of a person who helps, supports or assists the perpetrator to commit the principal offence, and 'abet' to describe the activity of a person who incites, instigates or encourages the perpetrator to commit it, whether or not in either case he is present at the time of commission.**[30] Trivial encouragement can suffice. In *Giannetto* the Court of Appeal did not disagree with the judge's statement that a person could be convicted of murder where 'somebody came up to [him] and said "I'm going to kill your wife" [and] he played any part...in encouragement, as little as patting him on the back, nodding, saying "Oh, goody"'.[31] No doubt, trivial assistance can also suffice.

'Counsel' means 'advise', 'encourage' or the like.[32] It does not add anything strictly but is used to describe encouragement before the commission of the principal offence.

A person 'procures' the commission of an offence by setting out to see that it is committed and taking the appropriate steps to produce its commission; more succinctly, 'procure' means 'to produce by endeavour'. This was stated by the Court of Appeal in *A-G's Reference (No 1 of 1975)*.[33] The importance of this decision is illustrated by the facts on which it was based. D laced the drink of E, unknown to E, who was later charged with the offence of strict liability of driving with an excess of alcohol. In holding that D could be convicted as an accomplice to this offence, the Court of Appeal said:

> '[The principal offence] has been procured because, unknown to the driver and without his collaboration, he has been put in a position in which in fact he has committed an offence which he never would have committed otherwise'.[34]

It can be seen from the above that there are three ways of becoming an accomplice: by assisting in the commission of the principal offence, by encouraging its commission or by procuring its commission.

17.11 The assistance, encouragement or procuring which must be proved against an alleged accomplice may take a variety of forms. It may consist of active assistance

---

[28] *Re Smith* (1858) 3 H & N 227; *Ferguson v Weaving* [1951] 1 KB 814, DC.

[29] *DPP for Northern Ireland v Lynch* [1975] AC 653 at 678 and 698, per Lords Morris and Simon.

[30] *National Coal Board v Gamble* [1959] 1 QB 11, DC; *Thambiah v R* [1966] AC 37, PC; *Bentley v Mullen* [1986] RTR 7 at 10, per May LJ.

[31] [1997] 1 Cr App Rep 1 at 13.

[32] *Calhaem* [1985] QB 808, CA.

[33] [1975] QB 773 at 779.

[34] [1975] QB 773 at 780.

or encouragement in the criminal act, such as holding a woman down while she is raped,[35] or keeping watch,[36] or cheering and clapping an unlawful theatrical performance.[37] Alternatively, assistance or encouragement before the criminal act, such as driving the perpetrator to a location where he waits until the opportunity to commit the *actus reus* arises,[38] suffices. Assistance or encouragement in the preparation of an offence even at an early stage suffices, as where the defendant opens a bank account with the intention of facilitating the paying in of forged cheques by the perpetrator.[39]

Supplying the instrument or materials for use in the commission of the principal offence constitutes assistance in its commission,[40] and so does supplying information to enable the offence to be carried out.[41] A thing is supplied in this context if it is given, lent or sold, or if a right of property in it is otherwise transferred.[42] A person who gives to another for use in an offence a weapon of which the latter is owner aids in the commission of that offence as much as if he had sold or lent the weapon, but such conduct does not make him an accomplice.[43] This has been explained on the basis that, although the person who surrenders the weapon to its owner is physically performing a positive act, he is in law simply refraining from committing the civil wrong of conversion. It is unlikely that an action for the wrongful detention of a jemmy brought by a would-be burglar who owned it would succeed.[44] If E lends a gun to D, and later drags his wife before D, shouting 'Return my gun, I am going to kill this woman instantly with it', is it really the law that D incurs no liability, as accomplice, in respect of the murder of the wife if he meekly returns the gun with which she is instantly shot?

17.12 A person is not guilty of aiding, abetting or counselling the commission of a range of offences under the Sexual Offences Act 2003 against a child under 16, eg by giving contraceptives to the child or giving sex advice, if he acts for the purpose of protecting the child from sexually transmitted infection, protecting the physical safety of the child, preventing the child from becoming pregnant, or promoting the child's emotional well-being by the giving of advice, and not for the purpose of obtaining sexual gratification or for the purpose of causing or encouraging the activity constituting the offence or the child's participation in it.[45]

---

35 *Clarkson* [1971] 3 All ER 344, C-MAC (as to this court, see para 2.32, n 91).
36 *Betts and Ridley* (1930) 22 Cr App Rep 148, CCA.
37 *Wilcox v Jeffery* [1951] 1 All ER 464, DC.
38 *Bryce* [2004] EWCA Crim 1231.
39 *Thambiah v R* [1966] AC 37, PC.
40 *National Coal Board v Gamble* [1959] 1 QB 11, DC.
41 *Bullock* [1955] 1 All ER 15, CCA.
42 *National Coal Board v Gamble* [1959] 1 QB 11 at 20, per Devlin J.
43 *Lomas* (1913) 110 LT 239, CCA, as explained in *Bullock* [1955] 1 All ER 15, CCA.
44 *Garrett v Arthur Churchill (Glass) Ltd* [1970] 1 QB 92 at 99, per Lord Parker CJ.
45 Sexual Offences Act 2003, s 73; see paras 9.37, 9.44, 9.49, 9.58, 9.70, 9.77, 9.90, 9.106, n 206, 9.113, n 214, 9.117, n 218.

Can an omission suffice?

17.13 Normally, an act of assistance or encouragement is required. Thus, mere abstention from preventing an offence is generally not enough. However, if D has a right of control over E and deliberately fails to take an opportunity to prevent E committing an offence, and knows that this is capable of assisting or encouraging the commission of the principal offence, his omission will constitute aiding or abetting. In *Tuck v Robson*,[46] a publican, who deliberately made no effort to induce customers to leave his premises after closing time, was held properly convicted of aiding and abetting their consumption of liquor out of hours because of his failure to exercise his right of control. Similarly, the owner of a car, who sits in the passenger seat while another drives it dangerously, can be convicted, as an accomplice, of dangerous driving if he deliberately fails to take an opportunity to prevent it.[47]

The principle[48] that an omission to act can give rise to criminal liability if the defendant was under a duty to do the act in question is applicable to the liability of an accomplice. Consequently, for example, a parent who stands by and watches someone commit an offence against his young child which he could reasonably prevent may be convicted as an accomplice to that offence,[49] because he would be under a duty to take reasonable steps to intervene, whereas a stranger would not, and his deliberate abstention from action constitutes encouragement to the other's conduct.

The definition of procuring[50] is such as to preclude an omission sufficing for liability on the basis of procuring.

17.14 It follows from the above that a person cannot be convicted as an accomplice merely because he knows that the perpetrator is committing the principal offence. This is important, for example, where someone knows that his spouse or flatmate is committing an offence, and does nothing about it, one way or another. *Bland*[51] provides an example. D shared a room with her partner, a drugs dealer. D was charged, as an accomplice, with the offence of being in possession of controlled drugs with intent unlawfully to supply them. It could be inferred that D knew that her partner was dealing in drugs in the room but there was no direct evidence against her that she had assisted or encouraged him in drug-dealing there. Allowing D's appeal against conviction, the Court of Appeal held that the fact that D lived in the same room with her partner was not sufficient evidence from which an inference of assistance in his possession of the drugs with intent to supply could be drawn. As the Court of Appeal recognised, it would have been different if D had had a right of control over her partner and had failed to exercise it.

---

[46] [1970] 1 All ER 1171, DC. Also see *Cassady v Reg Morris (Transport) Ltd* [1975] RTR 470, DC; *J F Alford Transport Ltd* [1997] 2 Cr App Rep 326, CA.

[47] *Du Cros v Lambourne* [1907] 1 KB 40, DC; *Webster* [2006] EWCA Crim 415.

[48] Para 2.10.

[49] *Gibson and Gibson* (1984) 80 Cr App Rep 24, CA; *Russell and Russell* (1987) 85 Cr App Rep 388, CA.

[50] Para 17.10.

[51] (1987) 151 JP 857, CA.

The principal offence

The normal rule

17.15 Subject to an exceptional type of case dealt with in paras 17.21 to 17.25, a person cannot be convicted as an accomplice to an offence unless it is proved that that offence has been committed by someone else (the perpetrator). If D, for example, aids, abets, counsels or procures E to burgle a house but E never does so, perhaps because he 'gets cold feet' or because he dies, D cannot be convicted, as an accomplice, of burglary. In such cases, however, D may be guilty of an offence of encouragement or assistance of crime or of conspiracy[52] if the requirements for such an offence are proved.

17.16 The need for proof that the principal offence has been committed is shown by *Thornton v Mitchell*.[53] The driver of a bus had to reverse it. In order to do so, he relied on the signals of the conductor. The conductor gave the driver a signal to reverse, which he did, and two pedestrians were knocked down. The driver was summoned for driving without due care and attention and the conductor for abetting him. The case against the driver was dismissed on the basis that the *actus reus* of the principal offence consisted of careless driving (which had not been proved), and it was held by the Divisional Court that the conductor could not be convicted of aiding or abetting an offence which had not been committed.

Link between assistance, encouragement or procuring and principal offence

17.17 Although the commission of the principal offence must be proved, proof that the defendant's aiding, abetting or counselling was a cause of its commission by the perpetrator, in the sense that the perpetrator would not have committed the offence but for that assistance or encouragement, is not required.[54] If D encourages E to shoot at, and kill, V (and E does so) it is irrelevant that E had already decided to do so when he was encouraged to do so by D, and it is irrelevant that D knew this.[55] On the other hand, if the allegation against the defendant is necessarily one of procuring, such a causal link must be established. As was said in *A-G's Reference (No 1 of 1975)*:

'You cannot procure an offence unless there is a causal link between what you do and the commission of the offence, and here we are told that in consequence of the addition of

---

[52] Ch 14.

[53] [1940] 1 All ER 339, DC. Also see *Morris v Tolman* [1923] 1 KB 166, DC; *Pickford* [1995] QB 203 at 213; *Loukes* [1996] 1 Cr App Rep 444, CA (see para 17.25); *Roberts and George* [1997] RTR 462, CA.

[54] *Calhaem* [1985] QB 808, CA; *Luffman* [2008] EWCA Crim 1739. Contrast *Bryce* [2004] EWCA Crim 1231 where the Court of Appeal appeared to imply such a requirement, in relation to aiding at least.

[55] *Giannetto* [1977] 1 Cr App Rep 1; para 17.10.

> this alcohol the driver, when he drove home, drove with an excess quantity of alcohol in his body.'[56]

If the perpetrator required no persuading the defendant has not procured the principal offence.

17.18 Although proof is not required that the defendant's aiding, abetting or counselling was a cause of the commission of the principal offence, in the sense that the offence might not otherwise have been committed by the perpetrator, there must be proof that he has done something which assisted the perpetrator to commit it or that the perpetrator was aware that he has the defendant's encouragement (whether or not the perpetrator was influenced by it). For example, if D, knowing that E intends to kill V, leaves a loaded gun in E's coat pocket but E, unaware that D had done so, goes off without his coat and kills V by stabbing him, D is not an accomplice to the murder of V. Another example was given by the Court of Appeal in *Calhaem*, where the Court was dealing with counselling (although its remarks are equally applicable to abetting). The Court of Appeal said:

> 'There must clearly be, first, contact between the parties, and, secondly, a connection between the counselling and the murder. Equally, the act done must, we think, be done within the scope of the authority or advice,[57] and not, for example, accidentally when the mind of the final murderer did not go with his actions. For example, if the principal offender happened to be involved in a football riot in the course of which he laid about him with a weapon of some sort and killed someone who, unknown to him, was the person whom he had been counselled to kill, he would not, in our view, have been acting within the scope of his authority; he would have been acting entirely outside it, albeit what he had done was what he had been counselled to do.'[58]

What if the perpetrator is exempt from prosecution for offence?

17.19 It should be noted that, if the principal offence has been committed, there is no difficulty in convicting as an accomplice a person who assisted, encouraged or procured its commission, even though the perpetrator is exempt from prosecution for the offence in question. This is shown by *Austin*,[59] where D had assisted a father to snatch his young daughter from his estranged wife. The Court of Appeal held that, since the father had committed the offence of child stealing (contrary to the Offences Against the Person Act 1861, s 56, which has since been repealed), D could be convicted as an accomplice to that offence, even though the father could not have been prosecuted because of the proviso to the section, whereby a father was not liable to be prosecuted

---

[56] [1975] QB 773 at 780.
[57] See also *Luffman* [2008] EWCA Crim 1739.
[58] [1985] QB 808 at 813. See also *A-G's Reference (No 1 of 1975)* [1975] QB 773 at 779.
[59] [1981] 1 All ER 374, CA.

'on account of getting possession of the child'. The proviso merely meant that the father could not be prosecuted: it did not mean that he had not committed the offence.

An exceptional situation

17.20 Where the principal offence is proved, it is immaterial that it is one which the accomplice could not have committed as perpetrator, so that a woman may be guilty of rape as an accomplice.[60]

17.21 Difficulties, however, arise in cases where the *actus reus* of an offence is committed by someone to whom a defence is available, so that he cannot be said to have committed the offence. As we have seen,[61] normally it is possible to treat the person who does the act as the innocent agent of the person who has assisted, encouraged or procured him to do the act and to convict the latter as perpetrator. However, this is difficult where the offence is one which can be perpetrated personally only by a person of a particular description which only the innocent agent satisfies, or where the offence is defined in terms implying that the act must be committed personally by a perpetrator. Suppose, for example, that a bachelor exercises duress to induce a married woman to go through a ceremony of marriage with him. Logic might seem to require that he should be acquitted on a charge of being an accomplice to bigamy because, the woman being entitled to an acquittal on the ground of duress by threats, she cannot be convicted of perpetrating bigamy; and that, as a bachelor, not 'being married', cannot perpetrate bigamy, he should be acquitted on a charge of perpetrating bigamy through an innocent agent. However, there is authority against both of these suppositions, at least in relation to a case where the *actus reus* can be said to have been procured.

In *Bourne*,[62] D compelled his wife to have intercourse with a dog. Although his wife was not charged, it was accepted that she would have had the defence of duress by threats if she had been. Nevertheless, the indictment and conviction of D as an accomplice to the buggery were upheld as proper on appeal. Thus, this case shows that a person can be convicted as an accomplice despite the fact that no one else is liable as perpetrator and despite the fact that he could not personally perpetrate the offence. However, it was held in *Cogan and Leak*[63] that a husband, who was cohabiting with his wife and therefore could not at the time have been convicted of personally perpetrating the offence of rape against her,[64] could be convicted as the perpetrator of the rape of her through an innocent agent who lacked the necessary *mens rea* for rape and was acquitted.

17.22 The former solution (*Bourne*) is preferable since (quite apart from difficulties inherent in the idea that a person can have sexual intercourse through an innocent agent) the latter solution (the part of *Cogan and Leak* referred to above) involves convicting

---

[60] *Ram and Ram* (1893) 17 Cox CC 609.
[61] Para 17.6.
[62] (1952) 36 Cr App Rep 125, CCA.
[63] [1976] QB 217, CA.
[64] The law has since been changed in this respect: *R* [1992] 1 AC 599, HL; para 1.35.

someone as a perpetrator for something of which he could not be convicted had he done it personally. According to the latter solution, a woman who caused a man, who was innocent for some reason, to commit a rape would be guilty of rape as a perpetrator, notwithstanding that the definition of rape says that it can only be perpetrated personally by penetration by a person's penis. Such reasoning was not accepted by the Divisional Court in *DPP v K & B*,[65] where the particular point was in issue. Instead, the Divisional Court preferred the type of approach in *Bourne*, further discussed in the next paragraphs. It is unlikely that the above part of the decision in *Cogan and Leak* will be adopted in the future.

Elsewhere in its decision, the Court of Appeal in *Cogan and Leak* held that the husband could be convicted as an accomplice to rape even though the man who had intercourse lacked the necessary *mens rea*. **This, together with *Bourne*, shows that if D intends that the *actus reus* should be performed by E and induces E to perform it but E has some defence, such as duress by threats or lack of *mens rea*, D's *mens rea* may be added to E's *actus reus* so as to make D liable as an accomplice for an offence which he cannot personally perpetrate.** This approach was confirmed by the Court of Appeal in *Millward*.[66] E committed the *actus reus* of the offence of causing death by reckless driving, an offence subsequently abolished, which could only be committed by a person driving a motor vehicle on a road in a way giving rise to an obvious and serious risk of injury or damage to property. E had driven the vehicle on the road in a defective state and thereby caused death, and it was this that the Court of Appeal held constituted the *actus reus* of reckless driving causing death. The commission of that *actus reus* had been procured by D who had told E, his employee, to drive the vehicle. E lacked the *mens rea* for the offence in question because he did not know of the defect, but D did have the *mens rea* because he knew of the defect. E was acquitted of perpetrating the offence of causing death by reckless driving but D was convicted of being an accomplice to it.[67] D's appeal against conviction was unsuccessful on the ground that a person who with the relevant *mens rea* procured another to commit the *actus reus* of an offence, that other lacking the requisite *mens rea*, could be convicted as an accomplice to it. *Millward* was followed in *DPP v K & B*, where two girls, aged 14 and 11, had procured a boy, who was never traced, to rape a girl whom they had falsely imprisoned. It was established that the boy was at least 10 but there was evidence that he was under 14. The prosecution had been unable to rebut the presumption, which then applied, that the boy was incapable of committing an offence.[68] The Divisional Court held that this did not preclude the conviction of the two girls as procurers of the rape. The *actus reus* had been proved and the girls had the requisite *mens rea*.

---

[65] [1997] 1 Cr App Rep 36, DC.

[66] (1994) 158 JP 1091, CA.

[67] D could not have been convicted as perpetrator of the offence of causing death by reckless driving through the innocent agency of E because the definition of that offence implied that the act of driving must be committed personally by a perpetrator.

[68] Para 15.2.

17.23 The approach adopted in *Bourne*, the latter of the two parts of *Cogan and Leak* referred to above, *Millward* and *DPP v K & B* seems to be limited to cases of procuring. All four cases involved procuring and the Court of Appeal in *Millward* seems to have accepted that the approach is so limited. Analogy with the law on innocent agency[69] suggests this is correct.

17.24 In *DPP v K & B*, the Divisional Court stated that its decision would have been different if the boy had been under 10 because he could not have committed any offence. This would seem to be wrong; the doctrine of innocent agency applies where the *actus reus* has been physically committed by an innocent agent under 10, and there seems no reason why the present principle should not likewise apply where the *actus reus* has been so committed.

17.25 The approach taken in these cases depends on an analysis of the elements of an offence so as to see which of them are part of the *actus reus*. The question is then whether those *actus reus* elements are satisfied. How crucial this analysis can be is shown by *Thornton v Mitchell*[70] (para 17.16 above) and by *Loukes*,[71] where D, a haulage contractor, had been charged as an accomplice to causing death by dangerous driving, contrary to the Road Traffic Act 1988, s 1. The death had been caused by E, an employee, driving one of D's trucks in a dangerously defective condition. E was acquitted of perpetrating this offence, on the direction of the judge who had found there was no case to answer against him because there was insufficient evidence that he knew that the truck was dangerously defective or that it would have been obvious to him as a competent and careful driver. The prosecution case was that D had caused the truck to be driven in a dangerous condition when he knew or ought to have known of the dangerous defect. The jury convicted D as an accomplice to causing death by dangerous driving. Distinguishing *Millward* and allowing D's appeal against conviction, the Court of Appeal held that offences of dangerous driving were strict liability ones in which no *mens rea* was required, so that the acquittal of the driver must have meant that no *actus reus* had been committed to which D could have been an accomplice.

Acquittal of an alleged accomplice

17.26 As we have seen, the acquittal of the alleged perpetrator does not mean that another person cannot be convicted as accomplice. If D is charged with aiding or abetting the commission of an offence by E, with whom he is put up for trial, it would be logically absurd for D to be convicted and E acquitted if the evidence against each was identical. Nevertheless, it sometimes happens that there is stronger evidence against D than against E, or that evidence which is admissible against D is inadmissible against E, and in such an event the conviction of D is not logically incompatible with the acquittal of E.[72]

---

[69] Para 17.6.
[70] [1940] 1 All ER 339, DC.
[71] [1996] 1 Cr App Rep 444, CA.
[72] *Humphreys and Turner* [1965] 3 All ER 689; *Davis* [1977] Crim LR 542, CA.

Mens rea

Key points 17.2

The *mens rea* required of an accomplice is not the same as that required of the perpetrator of the principal offence. Instead, what is required to be proved is:

- an intent to assist, encourage or procure the commission by the perpetrator of the act which constitutes or results in the principal offence;
- knowledge of the facts essential to constitute the principal offence.

Intent to assist, encourage or procure

17.27 For a defendant who has encouraged or assisted the perpetrator to be convicted as an accomplice, it must be proved that his encouragement or assistance which constituted aiding, abetting etc was given:

- intentionally, in the sense that he gave it deliberately (and not accidentally), and
- with knowledge that it was capable of encouraging the commission of the principal offence.[73]

17.28 The defendant need not give his assistance or encouragement with the desire, aim or purpose that the principal offence be committed; he can be found to have intended to assist or encourage from evidence that he knew that his deliberate act of assistance or encouragement was capable of having that effect.[74] In *National Coal Board v Gamble*, Devlin J said:

'[A]n indifference to the result of the crime does not of itself negative abetting. If one man deliberately sells to another a gun to be used for murdering a third, he may be indifferent about whether the third lives or dies and interested only in the cash profit to be made out of the sale, but he can still be an aider and abettor.'[75]

This approach was affirmed by the House of Lords in *DPP for Northern Ireland v Lynch*,[76] where it was held that willingness to participate in the offence did not have to

---

[73] *JF Alford Transport Ltd* [1997] 2 Cr App Rep 326, CA; *Bryce* [2004] EWCA Crim 1231.

[74] *National Coal Board v Gamble* [1959] 1 QB 11, DC; *Bryce* [2004] EWCA Crim 1231. Cf *Fretwell* (1862) Le & Ca 161, CCR.

[75] [1959] 1 QB 11 at 23. Also see *A-G v Able* [1984] QB 795 at 810–811.

[76] [1975] AC 653, HL. This part of the decision was not overruled by the House of Lords in *Howe* [1987] AC 417; para 16.54. Cf *Fretwell* (1862) Le & Ca 161 where the defendant had reluctantly supplied a poison, with fatal consequences, after a woman had threatened suicide if he did not. It was held that he was not liable as an accomplice to the offence of homicide because he was unwilling that the poison should be used. In *A-G v Able* [1984]

be established. In consequence a person who knew of another's criminal purpose and voluntarily aided him in it could be held to have aided that offence, even though he regretted the plan or indeed was horrified by it. (Of course, if he was acting under compulsion sufficient to give rise to a defence of duress he would be not guilty on that ground unless that defence did not extend to the offence charged.)

Another example is provided by *J F Alford Transport Ltd*,[77] where a transport company's drivers had pleaded guilty to offences of making a false entry on a tachograph, contrary to the Transport Act 1968, s 99. The Court of Appeal stated that the managing director and transport manager of the company who (it had been alleged) had aided or abetted the offences by failing to exercise their right of control could only be guilty as accomplices of an offence if they had intended that acquiescence (ie had deliberately refrained from controlling the drivers' conduct), knowing that this was capable of assisting or encouraging the perpetration of the offence. It added that it would be irrelevant that a blind eye had been turned in order to keep the drivers happy rather than to encourage the production of false tachograph records.

17.29 What has been said above about absence of a requirement to prove a desire, aim or purpose to assist or encourage seems inconsistent with the view taken in *Gillick v West Norfolk and Wisbech Area Health Authority*,[78] a civil case, where a majority of the House of Lords held that a doctor who prescribed contraceptives for a girl under 16 for clinical reasons, knowing that this would encourage or facilitate sexual intercourse by the girl, which would be an offence by the man involved, would not be an accomplice to the man's offence.[79] Lord Scarman (with whom Lords Fraser and Bridge agreed) said:

> 'The bona fide exercise by a doctor of his clinical judgment must be a complete negation of the guilty mind which is an essential ingredient of the criminal offence of aiding and abetting the commission of unlawful sexual intercourse.'[80]

The view that the doctor did not intend to assist or encourage, despite the fact that he knew that prescribing the contraceptives would assist the commission of the offence, may have been based on the doctrine of double effect.[81]

17.30 The definition of 'procuring', given in *A-G's Reference (No 1 of 1975)*[82] – 'producing by endeavour; setting out to see that the thing happens and taking the appropriate steps to produce that happening' – means that it is meaningless to talk of anything other

QB 795 at 811, it was stated by Woolf J that this decision was 'confined to its own facts', ie was not to be regarded as laying down a general rule to be followed in the future.

[77] [1997] 2 Cr App Rep 326, CA.
[78] [1986] AC 112, HL.
[79] Express provision for this type of case is now made by the Sexual Offences Act 2003, s 73; paras 9.37 and 17.12.
[80] [1986] AC 112 at 190.
[81] The decision in *Gillick* can alternatively be explained as being based impliedly on principles of necessity.
[82] [1975] QB 773, CA.

than a direct intention that the principal offence be committed where only procuring is involved.[83]

Knowledge of the facts essential to constitute the principal offence

17.31 To be an accomplice, the defendant must also have knowledge of the facts essential to constitute the principal offence,[84] although of course he need not know that those facts constitute an offence.[85] The 'facts essential to constitute the principal offence' refers to any circumstances required for the *actus reus* of the principal offence, any consequence so required and any *mens rea* required on the part of the perpetrator. In *Ferguson v Weaving*,[86] for example, D, the licensee, was charged with aiding and abetting customers to commit the offence of consuming intoxicating liquor on licensed premises outside permitted hours, contrary to the Licensing Act 1921, s 4 (since repealed). D did not know that drinking was taking place after closing time. The Divisional Court held that on these facts D could not be convicted.

'Knowledge' in this context includes wilful blindness[87] or recklessness,[88] but not negligence.[89] Because wilful blindness or recklessness suffices, it is enough that an alleged accomplice is aware of the risk that the 'essential facts' may possibly exist.

Where the assistance or encouragement is given before the time of the principal offence, it is more appropriate to speak in terms of whether the defendant was aware that facts essential to the commission of the principal offence would, or might as a real possibility, exist or occur at the material time.[90]

17.32 An example of the present requirement of *mens rea* can be given by reference to murder, where it suffices for the purposes of the present requirement that the alleged accomplice contemplated as a real possibility that the perpetrator might unlawfully kill someone with intent to do so or to cause unlawful grievous bodily harm.[91] It is somewhat surprising that, while a person can only be convicted as a perpetrator of murder if he intended to kill or cause grievous bodily harm, someone who assists or encourages a person who kills with such an intention can be convicted of murder as an accomplice if he merely contemplated that the other might intentionally kill or cause grievous bodily harm. This anomaly was recognised by the House of Lords in *Powell and Daniels;*

---

[83] There is support for this in *Blakely and Sutton v DPP* [1991] RTR 405, DC.

[84] *Johnson v Youden* [1950] 1 KB 544, DC; *Ferguson v Weaving* [1951] 1 KB 814, DC; *DPP for Northern Ireland v Maxwell* [1978] 3 All ER 1140, HL.

[85] *Johnson v Youden* [1950] 1 KB 544, DC.

[86] [1951] 1 KB 814, DC.

[87] *Poultry World Ltd v Conder* [1957] Crim LR 803, DC; para 3.45.

[88] *Carter v Richardson* [1974] RTR 314, DC; para 3.33.

[89] *J F Alford Transport Ltd* [1997] 2 Cr App Rep 326, CA; *Roberts and George* [1997] RTR 462, CA; *Webster* [2006] EWCA Crim 415.

[90] *Powell and Daniels; English* [1999] 1 AC 1, HL; *Chan Wing-Siu v R* [1985] AC 168, PC; *Bryce* [2004] EWCA Crim 1231; *Webster* [2006] EWCA Crim 415.

[91] See the cases cited in n 90.

English[92] but explained on grounds of public policy, in particular that, where a person assists or encourages a criminal venture, aware that the perpetrator may act with the necessary *mens rea* for murder, he should not escape liability for murder simply because he did not intend death or serious bodily harm. According to Lord Steyn, if the law required proof of the necessary intent for murder, the utility of the law relating to accomplices would be seriously undermined because that intent would be difficult to prove and joint criminal ventures can all too readily escalate into more serious offences.[93]

If an alleged accomplice has thought about the possibility of the perpetrator committing an offence but has dismissed it as negligible, he will not have contemplated that offence as a real possibility.[94]

17.33 Provided that D is aware at the time that he does his act of assistance or encouragement that the perpetrator may act with the *mens rea* required for the principal offence it is irrelevant that the perpetrator has not formed the *mens rea* at that point of time.[95]

How much must be known?

17.34 **The defendant need not know the details of the principal offence; it is enough that he knows facts sufficient to indicate the particular type of offence which is committed.**[96] This rule is of particular relevance where assistance has been given. Thus, if someone supplies another with a jemmy with knowledge that there is a real possibility that it will be used to enter a building as a trespasser in order to steal (ie knowing the particular type of offence), he is guilty of aiding such a burglary committed with the jemmy and it makes no difference that he did not know which premises were going to be burgled or when the burglary was to take place. In *Bainbridge*,[97] D supplied thieves with oxygen cutting equipment purchased by him six weeks earlier. The equipment was used for breaking into a bank, and it was held that D was an accomplice to this offence if he knew, when supplying the equipment, that it was to be used for a 'breaking' offence. D would not have been an accomplice to the bank breaking if he had merely known that the equipment was to be used for some criminal purpose.

Bainbridge was approved and extended by the House of Lords in *DPP for Northern Ireland v Maxwell*.[98] In that case it was held that, where the alleged accomplice knows that one or more of a limited range of offences may be committed by the perpetrator, and one of them is actually committed by him, the alleged accomplice can be convicted as a party to it. In this case, D had guided a car containing terrorists to a public house; on arrival D had departed but shortly afterwards one of the terrorists had thrown a bomb into the building. Apparently, D did not know whether the attack would be by firing

---

[92] [1999] 1 AC 1, HL.   [93] [1999] 1 AC 1 at 14.

[94] *Chan Wing-Siu v R* [1985] AC 168, PC; *Ward* (1986) 85 Cr App Rep 71, CA; *Hyde* [1991] 1 QB 134, CA; *Roberts* [1993] 1 All ER 583, CA; *Powell and Daniels*; *English* [1999] 1 AC 1, HL.

[95] *Bryce* [2004] EWCA Crim 1231.

[96] *Bullock* [1955] 1 All ER 15 at 18; *Bainbridge* [1960] 1 QB 129, CCA; *Bryce* [2004] EWCA Crim 1231 at [49].

[97] [1960] 1 QB 129, CCA.

[98] [1978] 3 All ER 1140, HL. See also *Hamilton* [1987] NIJB 1, NICA.

guns, planting bombs or otherwise. The House of Lords held that D had properly been convicted, as an accomplice, of the statutory offences of doing an act with intent to cause an explosion likely to endanger life and of being in possession of a bomb with the same intent, since he knew that these offences were within the range of offences which the terrorists might perpetrate.

17.35 Two questions remain unresolved:

- Would *Bainbridge* have been liable, as accomplice, for a large number of breaking offences committed over a considerable period of time with the equipment?

- What is meant by a 'particular type of offence'? Suppose D lends E a jemmy, thinking that he is going to use it to enter a building as a trespasser in order to steal (burglary), but E uses it to enter a building in order to cause really serious harm to a woman therein. E's conduct would constitute burglary but would D have known the particular type of offence intended? Clearly, if E actually caused really serious harm to the woman, D could not be convicted as an accomplice to causing grievous bodily harm with intent[99] but could he be convicted as an accomplice to burglary? This depends on the definition of 'the particular type of offence'.

17.36 Although someone who aids, abets, counsels or procures another to commit an offence need not know the details and it suffices that he merely knows the type of offence, he is not liable if he has aided, abetted, counselled or procured the perpetrator to commit an offence against a particular person or thing and the perpetrator deliberately[100] commits that offence against another person or thing. Thus, if D encourages E to assault O with his fists but E deliberately attacks P, instead of O, with his fists, D cannot be convicted as an accomplice to the assault.[101] On the other hand, if the actual victim is unspecified, it is irrelevant that D does not know who is the intended victim or is mistaken as to the intended victim. In *Reardon*[102] E shot two men in a bar and then dragged them outside. He returned and said 'that [***] is still alive, [D], lend us your knife'. D gave E his knife. E went out and stabbed both victims fatally. D was charged with both murders as an accomplice on the basis of his lending of the knife. Rejecting his appeal against conviction for both murders, the Court of Appeal held that it was irrelevant that E's request only related to one of the victims (who was not specified). The question was whether the stabbing of both victims by E amounted to actions which D could reasonably, and did, foresee as the type of act which E might carry out. Whichever of the victims he stabbed first, clearly the killing of that victim was contemplated by D when he handed E the knife. Equally, it was open to the jury to conclude that D foresaw at least the strong possibility that, if E found the other victim still alive, he would also stab him. E's actions

---

[99] Para 17.32.

[100] As opposed to accidentally or mistakenly.

[101] Hawkins *Pleas of the Crown* c 29, s 21; *Leahy* [1985] Crim LR 99, Crown Ct. Nor is a person guilty as an accomplice if a perpetrator deliberately allows the intended offence to have effect on a person or property which was not the object of the unlawful enterprise: *Saunders and Archer* (1573) 2 Plowd 473.

[102] [1998] 5 Archbold News 2, CA.

were within the scope of D's contemplation and the fact that E used the knife in a foreseen manner twice rather than once was immaterial.

Strict liability offences

17.37 The above requirements of *mens rea* apply even though the offence which the defendant is alleged to have assisted, encouraged or procured is one of strict liability. Thus, a person cannot be convicted as an accomplice to an offence of strict liability if he is not proved to have known about a circumstance of the *actus reus* of the principal offence, even though such knowledge is not necessary so far as the perpetrator is concerned.[103]

Joint criminal ventures: unforeseen consequences of a joint criminal venture

> **Key points 17.3**
>
> Where two (or more) people engage in a joint criminal venture, each is liable to the same extent for the unforeseen consequences of the acts done by one of them in pursuance of the venture. A 'joint criminal venture' is sometimes referred to as a 'joint enterprise'.

17.38 A joint criminal venture exists where two (or more) people engage together with the common purpose that an offence be committed. A common purpose need not be express; it can be inferred from conduct, as where a number of people spontaneously join in an attack on someone.[104] It is not necessary to prove any specific act of assistance or encouragement; joining in the common purpose provides sufficient evidence of assistance or encouragement.

17.39 Sometimes a party to a joint criminal venture can be liable as an accomplice for the unforeseen consequences of the perpetrator's acts in carrying out the venture.

When two (or more) people engage in a joint criminal venture, each is liable to the same extent for the consequences, unforeseen by them, of the acts of one of them done in pursuance of that venture, and this includes liability for a consequence which results by accident or mistake from the execution of the joint criminal enterprise.[105] Thus, the fact that, because of a lack of skill or a mistake on the part of the perpetrator in trying to carry out the joint criminal venture, the intended offence takes place in relation to an unintended victim or property does not prevent a person being guilty as an accomplice to that offence.[106] (Of course, if E, who has been counselled by D to kill V, accidentally kills V in a riot not knowing that he is V, D will not be an accomplice to the homicide because

---

[103] *Callow v Tillstone* (1900) 83 LT 411, DC; *Johnson v Youden* [1950] 1 KB 544, DC.
[104] See, for example, *Uddin* [1999] QB 431, CA.
[105] *Baldessare* (1930) 22 Cr App Rep 70, CCA; *Swindall and Osborne* (1846) 2 Car & Kir 230 (see para 17.73); *Anderson and Morris* [1966] 2 QB 110, CCA.
[106] Foster *Crown Law* 370–371.

E will not have been involved in the execution of the joint criminal venture at the time of the killing, albeit that he has done what D counselled him to do.)[107]

17.40 In many cases where the perpetrator, in trying to carry out the joint criminal venture, accidentally commits the *actus reus* of an offence of a different type from that intended, neither he nor the accomplice is liable for that offence because they lack the necessary *mens rea* in relation to it. However, the situation is different in the case of offences which do not require foresight of their necessary consequence. Particularly relevant here are involuntary manslaughter and unlawfully wounding or inflicting grievous bodily harm, contrary to the Offences Against the Person Act 1861, s 20. We have seen, for example, that a person is guilty of involuntary manslaughter if death results from the commission by him of an unlawful act which risks harm to another, even though he did not foresee that death or grievous bodily harm was likely to result.[108] In the case of such an offence, the principle that both perpetrator and accomplice are liable to the same extent for an accidental consequence of their joint criminal venture produces the following results. If one person encourages another to assault a man with fists, and he unexpectedly dies in consequence of the blows received, they are each guilty of involuntary manslaughter. Similarly, someone who arranges for a criminal abortion to be performed is, like the perpetrator, guilty of involuntary manslaughter if the operation results in death.[109]

Joint criminal ventures: intentional perpetration of an offence which is not the common object of a joint criminal venture

---

Key points 17.4

Where a party to a joint criminal venture intentionally perpetrates an offence which is not the common object of the venture:

another party to the venture (D) is liable for that offence if D contemplates as a real possibility that another party to the venture may, in the course of carrying out the venture, do an act, with the requisite *mens rea*, constituting that offence, unless the act done by the perpetrator was fundamentally different from that foreseen by D.

Where a party to a joint criminal venture intentionally perpetrates an offence which shares the same actus reus *as another offence (the other offence) but is distinguishable from it by a higher degree of* mens rea *and D does not contemplate that another party may act with that higher degree of* mens rea:

D can be convicted of the other offence (ie the one with the lesser degree of *mens rea*) if he had the *mens rea* for that offence, unless the perpetrator's act was fundamentally different from that foreseen by D.

---

[107] *Calhaem* [1985] QB 808 at 813 and 817; para 17.18.
[108] Paras 8.97–8.118.
[109] *Creamer* [1966] 1 QB 72, CCA; *Buck and Buck* (1960) 44 Cr App Rep 213.

17.41 Cases of accidental departure from a joint criminal venture must be distinguished from those where, in carrying out a joint criminal venture with D, E intentionally perpetrates an offence (the 'collateral offence') which D has not assisted or encouraged E to commit. An example would be where D has set out with E to commit a burglary and has encouraged E to use his jemmy to frighten anyone who comes on him, and E, disturbed by the householder in the course of the burglary, intentionally kills the householder with the jemmy. The common purpose of the parties was the commission of an offence of burglary. E is undoubtedly guilty of murder, as well as of burglary. D is clearly guilty of burglary as an accomplice but is D also guilty of murder as an accomplice? Although the principles below which provide the answer to this question have been formulated in the context of homicide offences and of a pre-planned criminal venture, they are equally applicable to other offences[110] and to a case where two or more people spontaneously combine together in an attack assisting and encouraging each other. They apply so long as the joint venture continues and D remains a party to it.[111]

17.42 As indicated above, where the joint criminal venture involves more than two people, a person charged as accomplice to a 'collateral offence' need not have foreseen the identity of the perpetrator.[112] Thus, where one of a gang attacking someone murders him, it is irrelevant that the alleged accomplice (another member of the gang) did not foresee who would be the killer. The question is simply whether the relevant requirements set out below are satisfied.

The basic rule

17.43 A party to a joint criminal venture can be convicted of a 'collateral offence' if it is proved that he contemplated as a real possibility that the perpetrator might commit it but still participated in the venture. This is simply an application of the principles of *mens rea* dealt with above. In many cases where this test is satisfied, D will have expressly or tacitly[113] agreed to, or authorised the commission of the 'collateral offence', but this is not necessary in order for the test to be satisfied.[114] Thus, in the example given above, if it was proved that D contemplated as a real possibility that E might use his jemmy intentionally to kill or do grievous bodily harm to someone who came on him during the burglary D could be convicted as an accomplice to murder, even if it could not be proved that he had expressly or tacitly agreed to its use for that purpose and even though he had forbidden

---

[110] *Powell and Daniels; English* [1999] 1 AC 1 at 12, per Lord Steyn; *Rahman* [2008] UKHL 45 at 8.

[111] See, for example, *Mitchell and King* (1999) 163 JP 75, CA; *O'Flaherty, Ryan and Toussaint* [2004] EWCA Crim 526; *Mitchell and Ballantyne* [2008] EWCA Crim 2552. As to withdrawal from participation see paras 17.66–17.72.

[112] *Nelson* [1999] 6 Archbold News 2, CA; *Rahman* [2008] UKHL 45; *Smith* [2008] EWCA Crim 1342; *Yemoh* [2009] EWCA Crim 930.

[113] Depending on his knowledge of the facts, D may have tacitly agreed to, or authorised, the 'collateral offence' by taking part in the joint criminal venture: *Chan Wing-Siu v R* [1985] AC 168, PC; *Hyde* [1991] 1 QB 134, CA.

[114] *Smith* [1963] 3 All ER 597, CCA; *Hyde* [1991] 1 QB 134, CA; *Powell and Daniels; English* [1999] 1 AC 1, HL.

E to *use* violence on anyone. The leading authority for this rule, which applies whether or not D was present or absent from the scene of the crime,[115] is now the decision of the House of Lords in the consolidated appeals of *Powell and Daniels; English*.[116]

In *Powell and Daniels*, D1 and D2 went with E to a drug dealer's house to buy drugs. The drug dealer was shot when he came to the door. It was not clear which of the three men had fired the gun, but the prosecution argued that, if E had done so, D1 and D2 were guilty of murder because they knew that E was armed with a gun and might use it to kill or cause really serious injury to the drug dealer. D1 and D2 were convicted of murder on this basis. They appealed against conviction unsuccessfully to the Court of Appeal, and thence to the House of Lords who dismissed the appeals. The House of Lords held that, **where one party (D) to a joint criminal venture to commit an offence foresees as a real possibility that another party may, in the course of it, do an act, with the requisite *mens rea*, constituting another offence (and another party does so), D is liable for that offence.** This is so, it held, even if D has not expressly or tacitly agreed to that offence, and even though he has expressly forbidden it. As stated earlier, the requisite degree of foresight, 'foresight of real possibility', was described in *Powell and Daniels; English* as foresight of a risk which is not foreseen as so remote that the defendant 'dismissed it as altogether negligible'.[117]

The 'fundamentally different act' qualification

17.44 In *Powell and Daniels*, D1 and D2 knew that E was armed with a gun. Their case would have been dealt with differently if they had not known that E was armed with a gun or an equally dangerous weapon. This appears from the House of Lords' decision in *English*. Here, D and E participated in a joint attack on a police officer in which they both caused injury with wooden posts but the police officer died from stab wounds inflicted by E. D was convicted, as an accomplice, of murder after the trial judge had told the jury so to convict him if he had joined in the attack realising that there was a substantial risk that E might kill the officer or cause him really serious injury during the attack. D appealed against conviction unsuccessfully to the Court of Appeal, but his subsequent appeal to the House of Lords succeeded. **The House of Lords held that, even if an alleged accomplice (D) intended or foresaw that the perpetrator would or might act with in-tent to do grievous bodily harm, he could not be convicted as a party to that offence if the perpetrator's act was fundamentally different from the acts intended or foreseen by the alleged accomplice. On the other hand, if the perpetrator's act, though differ-ent, was as dangerous as that foreseen as a 'real possibility' by the accomplice, as where the actual act was stabbing with a knife to kill and that foreseen as a real possibility was shooting to kill, an alleged accomplice could not escape liability.** On this basis, D's appeal had to be allowed because the jury could have found on the evidence that D did

---

[115] *Rook* [1993] 2 All ER 955, CA.

[116] [1999] 1 AC 1, HL. Also, see *Uddin* [1999] QB 431, CA.

[117] Also see *Chan Wing-Siu v R* [1985] AC 168, PC; *Ward* (1986) 85 Cr App Rep 71, CA; *Hyde* [1991] 1 QB 134, CA; *Roberts* [1993] 1 All ER 583, CA.

not know that E had a knife (or equally dangerous weapon). This decision has much to commend it. However, when the defendant did not foresee the act in question as a real possibility, it is liable to result in fine distinctions as to whether what he did foresee as a real possibility was an equally dangerous act. In *Uddin*,[118] one of the issues on which the jury should have been told to focus was whether the use of a flick-knife was a more dangerous act than hitting the deceased with clubs or kicking him with shod feet; in *Greatrex and Bates*,[119] the Court of Appeal ordered a retrial so that the jury could decide whether hitting someone with a metal bar was a more dangerous act than kicking him with a shod foot. The problem of what is a 'fundamentally different act' is returned to in para 17.48.

17.45 The House of Lords' decision in *Rahman* provides two further explanations of the 'fundamentally different act' qualification, which are relevant only in the context of murder. These explanations are dealt with in paras 17.46 and 17.47.

17.46 In essence, the first of these further explanations is that **if E kills with intent to kill, but D only contemplated that another party to the joint criminal venture might intentionally cause grievous bodily harm, E's greater *mens rea* does not take the killing outside the scope of the common purpose to cause grievous bodily harm and does not render E's act fundamentally different from that contemplated by D.**

In *Rahman*,[120] the appellants (Ds) had been part of a group of men which chased and attacked V and his friends with weapons including baseball bats, metal bars and pieces of wood. V died from a deep knife wound in his back. The prosecution alleged that each of the Ds had been a party to a joint criminal venture to inflict serious bodily harm (ie grievous bodily harm) on V. There was no evidence that any of the Ds inflicted the fatal injury; the gang member who did (ie the perpetrator) probably escaped arrest. Each D said that he had joined the venture with at most an intent to cause serious harm (whereas the nature of the stab wound demonstrated an intent to kill on the part of the perpetrator), denied possession of the knife and also denied awareness that anyone else in the group intended to kill or had a knife. As a result, each D argued, the perpetrator acted outside the scope of a joint criminal venture to inflict serious bodily harm. Ds were convicted of murder after the judge had directed the jury that they could only convict a particular defendant if they were sure that he realised that one or more of the attackers might use a knife in the attack to kill with the intention of killing V or causing him serious harm. The Court of Appeal upheld the convictions but certified the following questions of law for the opinion of the House of Lords:

'If in the course of a joint enterprise to inflict unlawful violence the principal party kills with an intention to kill which is unknown to and unforeseen by a secondary party, is the principal's [ie perpetrator's] intention relevant, (i) to whether the killing was within the scope of a common purpose to which the secondary party was an accessory? (ii) to

[118] [1999] QB 431, CA.
[119] [1999] 1 Cr App Rep 126, CA.
[120] [2008] UKHL 45.

whether the principal's act was fundamentally different from the act or acts which the secondary party foresaw as part of the joint enterprise?'

Dismissing Ds' appeals, the House of Lords answered both questions in the negative.

Lord Bingham gave two reasons (with which Lords Brown, Scott, and Neuberger agreed) for rejecting Ds' submission that, since the evidence showed the fatal wound was inflicted with intent to kill, or at least raised the possibility of this, whereas they intended to cause grievous bodily harm and did not know that anyone else involved intended to kill, the perpetrator's intention to kill (if found by the jury) rendered the perpetrator's act of stabbing fundamentally different from anything Ds has foreseen; the trial judge had not directed the jury to this effect and that amounted to misdirection. Lord Bingham said:

> 'Authority apart, there are in my view two strong reasons, one practical, the other theoretical, for [rejecting Ds' submission]. The first is that the law of joint enterprise in a situation such as this is already very complex...; [Ds'] submission, if accepted, would introduce a new and highly undesirable level of complexity. Given the fluid, fast-moving course of events in incidents such as that which culminated in the killing of the deceased, incidents which are unhappily not rare, it must often be very hard for jurors to make a reliable assessment of what a particular defendant foresaw as likely or possible acts on the part of his associates. It would be even harder, and would border on speculation, to judge what a particular defendant foresaw as the intention with which his associates might perform such acts. It is safer to focus on the defendant's foresight of what an associate might do, an issue to which knowledge of the associate's possession of an obviously lethal weapon such as a gun or a knife would usually be very relevant.
>
> Secondly, [Ds'] submission, as it seems to me, undermines the principle on which...our law of murder is based. In the prosecution of a principal offender for murder, it is not necessary for the prosecution to prove or the jury to consider whether the defendant intended on the one hand to kill or on the other to cause really serious injury. That is legally irrelevant to guilt. The rationale of that principle plainly is that if a person unlawfully assaults another with intent to cause him really serious injury, and death results, he should be held criminally responsible for that fatality, even though he did not intend it. If he had not embarked on a course of deliberate violence, the fatality would not have occurred. This rationale may lack logical purity, but it is underpinned by a quality of earthy realism. To rule that an undisclosed and unforeseen intention to kill on the part of the primary offender may take a killing outside the scope of a common purpose to cause really serious injury, calling for a distinction irrelevant in the case of the primary offender, is in my view to subvert the rationale which underlies our law of murder.'[121]

As a result, the House of Lords held that if, in the course of a joint criminal venture to cause serious injury (eg jointly attacking V), one of the participants (the perpetrator) intentionally kills V, that intention being unknown to and unforeseen by another participant (D) who only contemplated that the perpetrator would act with the intention to cause serious harm, that intention to kill does not take the killing outside the scope of

---

[121] [2008] UKHL 45 at [24], [25].

the common purpose to cause serious harm and does not make the perpetrator's fatal act fundamentally different from the act which D foresaw as part of the joint venture for the purpose of the rule laid down in *English*.

The conclusion that Lord Bingham reached at the end of the second paragraph of the quotation seems right. The perpetrator in murder has *mens rea* if he intends unlawfully to kill or do grievous bodily harm. There is no reason in principle to draw a distinction between an intent to kill or an intent to do grievous bodily harm when one considers secondary liability.

17.47 In the Court of Appeal in *Rahman*, the Court held that, where a perpetrator killed someone by an act fundamentally different from that contemplated by the defendant, another party to a joint criminal venture, the defendant could not rely on the fundamentally different act qualification where he intended the perpetrator intentionally to kill or he foresaw that the perpetrator might kill with intent to kill; otherwise he could rely on the qualification.

In the House of Lords in *Rahman*, Lord Brown, obiter, restated the principles as they relate to murder as follows:

> 'If B realises (without agreeing to such conduct being used) that A may kill or intentionally inflict serious injury, but nevertheless continues to participate with A in the venture, that will amount to a sufficient mental element for B to be guilty of murder if A, with the requisite intent, kills in the course of the venture *unless (i) A suddenly produces and uses a weapon of which B knows nothing and which is more lethal than any weapon which B contemplates that A or any other participant may be carrying and (ii) for that reason A's act is to be regarded as fundamentally different from anything foreseen by B.* (The italicised words are designed to reflect the *English* qualification).'[122]

Lords Scott and Neuberger expressly agreed.[123] It follows from the statement that, although a defendant cannot rely on the qualification to *English* where he intended the perpetrator intentionally to kill, he can where he foresaw that the perpetrator might kill with intention to do so if (i) and (ii) above apply. This seems unduly generous to the defendant.

What is a fundamentally different act?

17.48 The answer to the question 'what is a fundamentally different act?' was complicated by statements made by various Law Lords in *Rahman*. As has been indicated, in the context of murder a difference in the perpetrator's (E's) *mens rea* from that contemplated by D does not suffice. On the other hand, a difference in E's conduct *may* suffice. While this is clear, it is not clear whether there are limits on when such a change *will* suffice. According to Lord Brown (see the passage in para 17.47), Lord Rodger[124] and

---

122 [2008] UKHL 45 at [68].
123 [2008] UKHL 45 at [31] and [72] respectively.
124 [2008] UKHL 45 at [47].

Lord Neuberger[125] only the use of a different and more deadly weapon than any weapon contemplated by D can render an act fundamentally different, although Lord Neuberger was prepared to accept that the facts of a future case might give rise to another ground justifying a finding of fundamental difference.[126] This approach of Lords Brown, Rodger and Neuberger does not reflect any previous judicial statements and, if it is correct, would impose an important limitation on the qualification to *English*, despite the fact that in the statement in the above passage Lord Brown said that was 'designed to reflect the *English* qualification'. It ignores the fact that the dangerousness of an act does not depend simply on the nature of the weapon used but also the way in which it is used and the circumstances in which it is used. In *English* Lord Hutton approved the decision in *Gamble*,[127] a Northern Irish case, where D1 and D2 entered a joint venture with two other defendants to give V a severe beating or to 'kneecap' him. In the course of the attack on V, the other two defendants murdered V by slitting his throat with a knife; they also fired bullets into his body, two of which would have been fatal had not V died from the slit throat. Carswell J (as he then was), sitting without a jury in the Northern Irish Crown Court, held that D1 and D2 were not guilty of murder; the fatal act had not been in their contemplation. In *Rahman* Lords Brown, Neuberger and Scott[128] had strong reservations about the decision in *Gamble* because, under the restated definition of what could constitute a fundamental difference, a knife was not more lethal than the gun which D1 and D2 contemplated being used. It is submitted that there is a critical difference between a gun being used to kneecap someone and a knife used to slit his throat; to view the dangerousness of an act solely by reference to the weapon used is artificial and unduly restricts the 'fundamentally different act' qualification.

None of the Law Lords in *Rahman* referred to *A-G's Reference (No 3 of 2004)*[129] where the Court of Appeal held that E's actual act of firing a firearm *at* V was fundamentally different from the act of firing that firearm *near to* V which D contemplated; on this basis, the dangerousness of an act depends on its circumstances.

Convicting accomplice of a less serious offence

17.49 Some offences, such as murder and manslaughter, and wounding with intent and unlawful wounding contrary to the Offences Against the Person Act 1861, ss 18 and 20, essentially share a common *actus reus* but are distinguished by the fact that a different state of mind is specified for each offence. A question raised by cases such as *Powell and Daniels; English* is **whether a defendant who is not guilty of being an accomplice to offence A (eg murder), because he did not contemplate that the perpetrator might act with the *mens rea* for that offence in carrying out the joint criminal venture, can nevertheless be convicted of offence B (eg manslaughter) if he had the *mens rea* for that**

---

[125] [2008] UKHL 45 at [88].
[126] [2008] UKHL 45 at [102].
[127] [1989] NI 268.
[128] [2008] UKHL 45 at [31], [68] and [93].
[129] See para 17.51.

offence. The answer is 'no' if the perpetrator's act was fundamentally different from that foreseen as a real possibility by D,[130] but 'yes' if the perpetrator's act was the one so foreseen by D, or was no more dangerous than the one so foreseen by D.[131] This distinction can be explained by contrasting *Anderson and Morris*[132] with *Gilmour*[133] and *Roberts, Day and Day*.[134]

In *Anderson and Morris*, approved in *Powell and Daniels; English*, D and E agreed to attack V. D began punching V. E then produced a knife and killed V with it. D said that he was unaware that E had the knife or was going to use it. E was convicted of murder and D of manslaughter. D's conviction was quashed. Clearly, E had departed from the contemplated joint venture and intentionally perpetrated a more dangerous act than that foreseen by D.

17.50 In *Gilmour*, D drove E, F and G, members of a Protestant terrorist organisation, to a housing estate. E and F threw a petrol bomb through a window of a house; the child occupants were killed. D knew a petrol bombing was planned but there was insufficient evidence that he knew that anyone would act with intent to kill or do grievous bodily harm; the most that could be attributed to him was that he realised that the perpetrators intended to cause a fire which might do some damage and put the occupants in fear. The Northern Ireland Court of Appeal, allowing D's appeal against conviction for murder on the basis of *Powell; English*, substituted a conviction for manslaughter on the basis that there was no reason 'why a person acting as an accomplice to a perpetrator who carries out the very deed contemplated by both should not be guilty of the degree of offence appropriate to the intent with which he had acted'.

The same principle as applied in *Gilmour* was applied by the Court of Appeal in *Roberts, Day and Day*, although the Court of Appeal did not refer to *Gilmour*. In *Roberts, Day and Day*, D went with E and F to 'look for' V. E punched V (who fell) and then kicked V on the head. V later died of his injuries. D was involved in fighting one of V's associates. E and F were convicted of the murder of V; D was convicted of the manslaughter of V. D appealed against conviction. The Court of Appeal dismissed the appeal on the ground that D must have foreseen the act of kicking V on the ground done by E and that a person who foresaw the fatal, dangerous act but who did not have the *mens rea* required to be a party to murder could be convicted of manslaughter as an accomplice.[135]

17.51 *Gilmour* and *Roberts, Day and Day* raise the question, already referred to in para 17.44, of whether the perpetrator's act is fundamentally different from, or equally

---

[130] *Anderson and Morris* [1966] 2 QB 110, CCA; *Lovesey and Peterson* [1970] 1 QB 352, CA; *Powell and Daniels; English* [1999] 1 AC 1, HL (HL in *English* did not substitute a conviction for manslaughter, presumably because it thought that there could not be liability for manslaughter in such a case); *Uddin* [1999] QB 431, CA; *Mitchell and King* (1999) 163 JP 75, CA; *Crooks* [1999] NI 266, NICA.

[131] *Stewart and Schofield* [1995] 1 Cr App Rep 441; *Gilmour* [2000] 2 Cr App Rep 407, NICA; *Roberts, Day and Day* [2001] EWCA Crim 1594.

[132] [1966] 2 QB 110, CCA.

[133] [2000] 2 Cr App Rep 407, NICA.

[134] [2001] EWCA Crim 1594.

[135] See also *Parsons* [2009] EWCA Crim 64.

dangerous to, that foreseen by the alleged accomplice.[136] *A-G's Reference (No 3 of 2004)*[137] provides authority that whether or not an act is fundamentally different from that contemplated by an alleged accomplice does not depend solely on the physical act done, eg squeezing the trigger of a firearm, but on the circumstances in which it is done. In that case, the judge had ruled at a preparatory hearing that, even if the prosecution could prove the facts it set out to prove, on the 'agreed basis of the prosecution's case for the purpose of legal argument' D could not be convicted (as an accomplice) of manslaughter. This was because, according to the 'agreed basis', the perpetrator's act which caused the death was the deliberate discharge of a firearm deliberately aimed *at* the victim (V), whereas the act contemplated by D was the deliberate discharge of a firearm *near* V in order to apply pressure on V, ie in circumstances which excluded the deliberate causing of physical injury, let alone death, by the use of the firearm, and that act was fundamentally different from the one actually done by the perpetrator. On a reference by the Attorney-General the Court of Appeal held that the conclusion reached by the judge was the right conclusion on the rather unrealistic assumed facts of the case: the act done by the perpetrator was of a fundamentally different character from any act contemplated by D. This case now needs to be assessed in the light of *Rahman*; see para 17.48.

17.52 We consider further in para 17.55 the issue of the differential liability of a perpetrator and accomplice.

A separate doctrine of joint criminal venture?

17.53 Views differ[138] about whether the rules relating to joint criminal venture in paras 17.38–17.52 are separate from those relating to accomplices in general. In *Stewart and Schofield*,[139] the Court of Appeal distinguished between cases of joint criminal venture where an accomplice was physically present when the offence was committed and those where the assistance or encouragement was given before its commission. It stated that:

> 'If the principal has committed the crime of murder, the liability of the secondary party can only be a liability for aiding and abetting murder. In contrast, where the allegation is joint enterprise, the allegation is that one defendant participated in the criminal act of another. This is a different principle.'[140]

---

[136] The fact that the perpetrator of murder intended to kill does not make the act fundamentally different for the purpose of determining the alleged accomplice's liability for manslaughter: *Yemoh* [2009] EWCA Crim 930.

[137] [2005] EWCA Crim 1882.

[138] Contrast Smith and Hogan *Criminal Law* (12th edn, 2008) (Ormerod (ed)) 206–208 and Simester and Sullivan *Criminal Law* (3rd edn, 2007) 228–230. Also see para 17.4.

[139] [1995] 3 All ER 159, CA.

[140] [1995] 3 All ER 159 at 165.

The approach taken in *Stewart and Schofield* is erroneous. The Court made no mention of the earlier decision of the Court of Appeal in *Rook*[141] where it was held that the rules about joint criminal venture (ie those in paras 17.38–17.52) apply whether the person who has lent assistance or encouragement has done so before the commission of the offence or is present when it is committed.[142] It is submitted that this is the correct view. The case law generally does not refer to any distinction of the type put forward in *Stewart and Schofield*. Moreover, although the matter was not considered in *Powell and Daniels; English* and *Rahman*, the House of Lords in both cases treated parties to a joint criminal venture as accomplices.

17.54 The law relating to the liability in a joint criminal venture of a party other than the perpetrator where there is intentional perpetration of an offence which is not the common object of that venture can be summarised as follows in the Table below.

Situation	Liability of party to venture other than perpetrator	Exception
Where a party (E) to a joint criminal venture intentionally perpetrates an offence which is not the common object of the venture:	Another party to the venture (D) is liable for that offence if D contemplates as a real possibility that E may, in the course of carrying out the venture, do an act, with the requisite *mens rea*, constituting that offence:	unless the act done by the perpetrator was fundamentally different from that foreseen by D
Where a party (E) to a joint criminal venture intentionally perpetrates an offence which shares the same actus reus as another offence (the other offence) but is distinguishable from it by a higher degree of mens rea:	Another party to the venture (D) can be convicted of the other offence (ie the one with the lesser degree of *mens rea*) if he had the *mens rea* for that offence and he does not contemplate that E may act with that higher degree of *mens rea*:	unless the act done by the perpetrator was fundamentally different from that foreseen by D

Differential liability

17.55 It was seen above[143] that sometimes the perpetrator and the accomplice can be convicted of offences of a different degree. There are the following further examples:

- The effect of the Homicide Act 1957, s 4(1) is that if there is a suicide pact between E and V and D assists E to kill V, E will be guilty of manslaughter but D will be guilty of murder; and that if there is a suicide pact between D and V and D assists E to kill V in pursuance of it D will be guilty of manslaughter and E of murder.

---

[141] [1993] 2 All ER 955, CA. Also see *Howe* [1987] AC 417, HL.
[142] The Court of Appeal implicitly proceeded on this basis in *Wan and Chan* [1995] Crim LR 296.
[143] Paras 17.49–17.51.

- A person who commits the *actus reus* of murder with malice aforethought, or who with the appropriate *mens rea* aids and abets another to do so, may have the partial defence of diminished responsibility or, when it comes into force, loss of control[144] which reduces his liability to manslaughter. However, the Homicide Act 1957, s 2(4) and the Coroners and Justice Act 2009, s 54(8) respectively provide that the fact that one party to the killing is not guilty of murder on account of his diminished responsibility or loss of control, as the case may be, does not affect the question whether the killing amounted to murder in the case of any other party to it.

- As stated above some offences essentially share a common *actus reus* but are distinguished by requiring different states of mind, and an accomplice can be convicted of one such offence and the perpetrator of another if they had different appropriate states of mind. This can result in an accomplice being convicted of a greater offence than the perpetrator if he had a greater degree of *mens rea*, whether or not he was present when the offence was committed.[145] Thus, if D, having decided to bring about V's death, hands a grenade to E informing him that it only contains a 'knockout gas' and telling him to go and throw it at V, but the grenade contains explosives (as D knows) and V is killed, D can be convicted of murder, even though E is guilty only of manslaughter.

Presence at the scene of the crime

Key points 17.5

A person who is a mere accidental spectator of the commission of an offence is not an accomplice to it, but non-accidental presence as a spectator is prima facie evidence of aiding or abetting.

17.56 Leaving aside the types of case outlined in para 17.13, where an omission to prevent an offence can constitute encouraging or assisting its commission, it is no offence to stand by, a mere accidental spectator of the commission of an offence; the ordinary citizen is not under a duty to take reasonable steps to prevent an offence and a failure to do so does not make him an accomplice to it.[146] On the other hand, there is no problem in convicting the defendant as an accomplice where he was present pursuant to an agreement that the principal offence be committed.[147] This provides the evidence of assistance

---

[144] Paras 8.77–8.94.

[145] The decision to the contrary (at least, if the defendant was not present) in *Richards* [1974] QB 776, CA was heavily criticised, although not expressly overruled, in *Howe* [1987] AC 417, HL, and it is submitted that *Richards* no longer represents the law on this point.

[146] *Coney* (1882) 8 QBD 534, CCR.

[147] *Smith v Reynolds* [1986] Crim LR 559, DC.

or encouragement. Nor is there a problem where the evidence clearly shows that he did a positive act of assistance or encouragement, such as shouting out 'fill him with lead' to a gunman who then fires a fatal shot.

17.57 Where the evidence does not go so far but merely shows that the defendant was present when the principal offence was committed and that his presence was not accidental (ie he was voluntarily and purposely present), as where someone deliberately leaves a pub to watch a fight outside, his non-accidental presence in such a case is not conclusive evidence of aiding or abetting, but only prima facie evidence. In *Coney*,[148] where the defendant had been voluntarily present at an illegal prize fight, his conviction as an accomplice to the battery of which the contestants were guilty was quashed because the direction of the judge could have been understood to mean that the defendant's voluntary presence was conclusive evidence of aiding and abetting. In such a case, it will be more difficult for the prosecution to prove the following two elements of liability:

- *That the defendant encouraged the perpetrator* Depending on the circumstances, presence alone is capable of demonstrating actual encouragement.[149]
- *That the defendant had the* mens rea *required to be an accomplice to the principal offence*.[150] This is the general requirement dealt with above; thus, where a defendant has unwittingly encouraged another, by his misinterpreted words or gestures, he cannot be convicted as an accomplice.[151]

Victims as accomplices

> **Key points 17.6**
>
> Where the purpose of a statutory offence is (wholly or in part) the protection of a certain class of people, it may be construed as excluding from liability as an accomplice any member of that class who is the willing victim of the offence in that he or she has assisted or encouraged its commission.

17.58 So far such a construction has only been given in respect of certain sexual offences designed to protect certain classes of people, such as the young or the mentally disordered, against exploitation to which they are peculiarly vulnerable.[152] It was held in

---

[148] (1882) 8 QBD 534, CCR.

[149] *Coney* (1882) 8 QBD 534 at 557 per Hawkins J; *Clarkson* [1971] 3 All ER 344, C-MAC.

[150] *Coney* (1882) 8 QBD 534, CCR; *Clarkson* [1971] 3 All ER 344, C-MAC.

[151] *Coney* (1882) 8 QBD 534 at 552 and 557, per Lopes and Hawkins JJ; *Jefferson* [1994] 1 All ER 270, CA.

[152] It has been argued that, even in the case of some of these offences, there is no clearly defined group of protected persons, or at least no coherent policy behind the legislation's classification as to who can be an offender and who can be a victim: Bohlander 'The Sexual Offences Act 2003 and the *Tyrrell* Principle – Criminalising the Victims?' [2005] Crim LR 701.

Tyrrell,[153] for example, that a girl under 16 could not be convicted of aiding, abetting, counselling or procuring a man to have sexual intercourse with her. More recently, a Crown Court judge has ruled that a prostitute could not be convicted of aiding, abetting, counselling or procuring a man to live off her immoral earnings, since the offence was created for the protection of prostitutes.[154] It must be emphasised that the rule acknowledged in *Tyrrell* is a rule of construction, and that it does not mean that the victim of an offence can never be convicted of aiding, abetting, counselling or procuring its commission, since it only applies to statutory offences designed to protect 'victims' who are peculiarly open to exploitation. Thus, a woman can be convicted as an accomplice to the commission of an unlawful abortion on herself.[155] It remains to be seen how far, if at all, the rule of construction will be applied outside the realm of sexual offences.[156] There are, for example, offences under the Asylum and Immigration (Treatment of Claimants, etc) Act 2004 designed in part to protect people who are trafficked for exploitation, and offences under the Gangmasters (Licensing) Act 2004 designed in part to protect certain types of workers. It would be unfortunate if the rule of construction did not extend to such protected persons, especially as the exemption for victims in respect of the inchoate offence of encouraging or assisting crime extends to any protective offence.

The above rule only applies to the offence of which the protected person is the victim. If, instead, that person assists or encourages the perpetration of an offence on another person he can be convicted as an accomplice to that offence.[157]

Entrapment and agents provocateurs

Key points 17.7

A law enforcement officer (or his agent) who provides the opportunity for the commission of an offence or who simply pretends to concur with, and participates in, a 'laid on' offence is not an accomplice to it if it is committed. On the other hand, a law enforcement officer (or his agent), who incites an offence which might not otherwise have been committed is an accomplice to it if it is committed.

It is no defence for a defendant that he was entrapped into committing an offence which he would not otherwise have committed. However, evidence obtained by entrapment may in some cases be excluded or, more likely, the proceedings may be stayed for abuse of process.

---

[153] [1894] 1 QB 710, CCR. Also see *Whitehouse* [1977] QB 868, CA.

[154] *Congdon* (1990), referred to in (1990) 140 NLJ 1221. The offence was repealed by the Sexual Offences Act 2003.

[155] *Sockett* (1908) 1 Cr App Rep 101, CCA.

[156] Williams argued that the 'victim rule' is only an example of a wider proposition that the courts may find that a person is excluded from liability as an accomplice to a statutory offence by implication as a matter of reasonable construction: 'Victims and Other Exempt Parties in Crime' (1990) 10 LS 245. This view is not yet supported by the available case law.

[157] *Cratchley* (1913) 9 Cr App Rep 232, CCA.

Liability of agent provocateur

17.59 A law enforcement officer or his agent (eg an informer or test purchaser) who, solely in order to entrap someone:

- provides the opportunity, and the temptation, for the commission of an offence (as in the case of a test purchase);[158] or
- participates in a criminal enterprise but goes no further than pretending to concur with the other parties and participating in an offence which has already been 'laid on' and which is going to be committed in any event,[159]

is not liable as an accomplice to that offence, and this is so even though that participation may have affected the time or other circumstances of the commission of the offence.[160] There must, however, be limits; the rule clearly could not apply to murder.

Some decisions may support the view that a law enforcement officer, who incites an offence which might not otherwise have been committed in order to entrap a criminal, is not liable as a party to the offence which the other commits,[161] but the view of Lord Salmon in *Sang*[162] to the effect that such a person would be so liable is more recent and, it is submitted, preferable.

In an effort to ensure that police and customs undercover operations are conducted with due propriety the Association of Chief Police Officers and HM Revenue and Customs have jointly issued a Code of Practice on such operations, including test purchases. The Code, which does not have any legal status, sets out authorisation procedures and criteria which the authorising officer must apply, as well as limits on what an undercover officer may do.

No defence of entrapment

17.60 Whereas in some jurisdictions in the United States a defendant has a defence if he commits an offence at the instigation of a law enforcement officer or his agent, unless he was already predisposed to do so,[163] there is no such defence of entrapment in our law.[164] Nor is it a defence that the entrapment was by someone other than a police officer or his agent, such as an investigative journalist.[165]

---

[158] *Williams v DPP* (1993) 98 Cr App Rep 209, DC.

[159] *Mullins* (1848) 12 JP 776; *McCann* (1971) 56 Cr App Rep 359, CA; *Clarke* (1984) 80 Cr App Rep 344, CA.

[160] *McEvilly and Lee* (1973) 60 Cr App Rep 150, CA.

[161] *Mullins* (1848) 12 JP 776; *Bickley* (1909) 73 JP 239, CCA. Contrast *Brannan v Peek* [1948] 1 KB 68, DC.

[162] [1980] AC 402 at 443. Lord Salmon's statement was versed in terms of a dishonest policeman who wanted to improve his detection rate but the reference to such a policeman seems to be superfluous.

[163] *Jacobson v US* 112 SC 1535 (1992), S Ct of US.

[164] *McEvilly* (1973) 60 Cr App Rep 150, CA; *Mealey and Sheridan* (1974) 60 Cr App Rep 59, CA; *Sang* [1980] AC 402, HL.

[165] *Morley* [1994] Crim LR 919, CA.

The fact of entrapment may, however, mitigate sentence if the offence would not have been committed but for the entrapment.[166]

In addition, to secure the defendant's right to a fair trial under the ECHR, Article 6, a judge may in some circumstances exercise the power to exclude evidence obtained by entrapment or the power to stay proceedings for abuse of process. These powers do not apply where what has been done may be described as providing an 'unexceptional opportunity to commit crime', as in the case of a test purchase by an undercover officer.[167]

Exclusion of evidence obtained by entrapment

17.61 Evidence obtained by entrapment which has gone beyond providing an unexceptional opportunity to commit a crime, whether by a law enforcement officer or his agent or a private citizen, may be excluded under the Police and Criminal Evidence Act 1984, s 78, which provides that a court may refuse to admit prosecution evidence if, having regard to all the circumstances, including the circumstances in which the evidence was obtained, the admission of the evidence would have such an adverse effect on the fairness of the proceedings that the court ought not to admit it.[168] It will be noted that under s 78 the exclusion of evidence obtained by entrapment depends ultimately on whether the fairness of the proceedings would be adversely affected by admitting that evidence, and not whether it is fair to bring the proceedings.

It appears that the courts will take a more restricted approach under s 78 to the exclusion of entrapment evidence where it has been obtained by a private citizen than where it has been obtained by a law enforcement officer or his agent.[169]

Stay of proceedings for abuse of process

17.62 In a case of entrapment by a law enforcement officer or his agent which has gone beyond providing an unexceptional opportunity to commit a crime, a court has power to stay the proceedings if it concludes that a fair trial is not possible or that, although a fair trial is possible, it would be contrary to the public interest in the integrity of the criminal justice system that a trial should take place. This was the view of the House of Lords in *Latif and Shahzad*,[170] which placed the emphasis on the latter ground. In reaching a decision on the latter ground, the court must, for example, weigh in the balance

---

[166] This was expressly recognised by the House of Lords in *Sang* [1980] AC 402.

[167] *DPP v Marshall* [1988] 3 All ER 683, DC; *Williams v DPP* (1994) 98 Cr App Rep 209, DC; *Jones (Ian Anthony)* [2007] EWCA Crim 1118 (para 17.65). See also *Looseley; A-G's Reference (No 3 of 2000)* [2001] UKHL 53 at [3], [54] and [65], per Lords Nicholls and Hoffmann.

[168] *Christou and Wright* [1992] QB 979, CA; *Smurthwaite and Gill* [1994] 1 All ER 898, CA; *Morley and Hutton* [1994] Crim LR 919, CA; *Shannon* [2001] 1 WLR 51, CA; *Looseley; A-G's Reference (No 3 of 2000)* [2001] UKHL 53.

[169] *Shannon* [2001] 1 WLR 51, CA. When this decision went to the European Court of Human Rights that Court confirmed that a prosecution based on entrapment by a private individual could infringe the ECHR, Art 6: *Shannon v UK* [2005] Crim LR 133, ECtHR.

[170] [1996] 1 All ER 353, HL.

the public interest in ensuring that people accused of grave offences should be tried and the competing interest in not conveying the impression that the court will adopt the approach that the end justifies any means.[171] That the emphasis is on the integrity of the criminal justice system, rather than fairness to the defendant, is also clear from the judgment of the House of Lords in the conjoined appeals in *Looseley; A-G's Reference (No 3 of 2000)*.[172] Here the House of Lords indicated that the main curb on excessive entrapment should be a stay of proceedings rather than ruling evidence inadmissible.

17.63 Although proceedings can be stayed on the ground of entrapment by an investigative journalist or someone else not acting as a law enforcement officer or his agent,[173] the court is much less likely to find it necessary to order a stay in such a case because the integrity of the criminal justice system is much less likely to be affected by entrapment by such a person.[174] The only reported case where a prosecution has been stayed for entrapment by a private person is *R (on the application of Dacre and Associated Newspapers) v City of Westminster Magistrates' Court*,[175] where the Divisional Court granted a stay of proceedings in respect of a private prosecution on the grounds of entrapment by the individual who was the private prosecutor. Latham LJ, with whose judgment Bennett J agreed, held that, whilst the considerations differed between public and private prosecutors (because of the particular dangers of state entrapment in the public context), there was no reason in principle why a private prosecution should not be considered an abuse of process if the crime which was the subject of the prosecution was one that had been encouraged by the private prosecutor or when in some other way the private prosecutor had essentially created the same mischief as that about which he or she complained.

17.64 It had been thought that an English court might regard the ECHR, Article 6 as requiring it to exclude evidence or stay proceedings where a defendant with no predisposition to commit an offence is lured into committing it by the incitement of an agent provocateur. The basis for this was that it is unfair for a court to entertain a prosecution in such a case, regardless of whether the trial as a whole was procedurally unfair or whether it would be contrary to the public interest for the trial to proceed. Indeed, it was thought that Article 6 might require the introduction of a defence of entrapment. This supposition was based on *Teixeira de Castro v Portugal*.[176] D, who had no criminal convictions and was unknown to the police, was introduced to undercover police officers. At their request, he bought heroin for them. He was convicted of drug dealing on their evidence

---

[171] *Latif and Shahzad* [1996] 1 All ER 353 at 361, per Lord Steyn; *Hardwicke and Thwaites* [2001] Crim LR 220, CA.

[172] [2001] UKHL 53. See Ashworth 'Redrawing the Boundaries of Entrapment' [2002] Crim LR 161.

[173] *Shannon* [2001] 1 WLR 51, CA; *Hardwicke and Thwaites* [2001] Crim LR 220, CA. Contrast *Paulssen* [2003] EWCA Crim 3109 at [45] where the Court of Appeal appears to have considered that entrapment by a private individual who was not an agent of the police could not constitute an abuse of process.

[174] *Hardwicke and Thwaites* [2001] Crim LR 220, CA.

[175] [2008] EWHC 1667 (Admin), DC.

[176] (1998) 28 EHRR 101, ECtHR; applied in *Eurofinancom v France* [2005] Crim LR 134, ECtHR.

and sentenced to six years' imprisonment. The European Court of Human Rights held that the officers had incited the offence and that there was nothing to suggest that without their intervention it would have been committed. It concluded that there had been a violation of Article 6 because D had been 'deprived of a fair trial from the outset' by the police officers' incitement; the public interest could not justify the use of evidence obtained as a result of police incitement. The words quoted suggested that Article 6 would be breached simply because the institution of the proceedings was unfair. The Court's reasoning did not refer to any balancing process such as that used under English law in deciding whether to exclude evidence or whether to stay proceedings.

In *Looseley; A-G's Reference (No 3 of 2000)*,[177] the House of Lords held that *Teixeira* did not require modification of the existing principles of English law.

Effect on police operations

17.65 The law on entrapment gives the law enforcement officers a good deal of freedom.

A recent example is provided by *Jones (Ian Anthony)*.[178] Following a complaint about graffiti on the door of a train toilet, seeking girls aged eight to 13 for sex in return for payment and requesting contact via a mobile telephone number, the police began an undercover operation using a woman police officer who pretended to be a girl aged 12. D was charged, inter alia, with attempting to cause or incite a child under 13 to engage in penetrative sexual activity. At trial, D applied to stay the proceedings as an abuse of process on the ground (inter alia) that he had been entrapped into committing the offence. The Court of Appeal held that the judge had been right not to order a stay on the above ground. The offence had not been instigated by the police but by D's own actions. The actions of the police were primarily to be seen in the context that the essence of D's criminality was the incitement. It was clear from D's conduct that he was looking for opportunities to incite a child to penetrative sexual activity; the police officer's conduct in relation to D followed on from those events and far from instigating the offence the police officer's conduct provided only the opportunity for D to attempt to commit a similar offence. The scope of the police officer's involvement had been essentially limited to providing an opportunity to attempt to commit the offence and to provide the evidence.

Withdrawal from participation

Key points 17.8

A person can excuse himself from liability as an accomplice to an offence by making an effective, voluntary withdrawal before it is committed.

---

177 [2001] UKHL 53.
178 [2007] EWCA Crim 1118.

17.66 There is no doubt that a person can excuse himself from liability for an offence which he has assisted, encouraged, counselled or procured by making an effective withdrawal from participation before it is committed. This can be justified on the grounds that a person who voluntarily withdraws before the commission of the offence which he has assisted or encouraged is significantly less blameworthy than someone who continues to support the offence up to its commission, and that it provides an incentive for withdrawal. An effective withdrawal from complicity by an accomplice does not, however, negative any liability for the inchoate offences of encouraging or assisting crime or conspiracy[179] since those offences[180] are committed and complete when the encouragement or assistance occurs or the conspiracy is made.

17.67 **The law takes a strict view about what will constitute an effective withdrawal. It is clear that mere repentance is not enough;**[181] **nor is merely failing to turn up at the scene of the crime as arranged;**[182] **nor is merely running away from the scene of the crime.**[183]

In *Whitehouse*,[184] a decision of the Court of Appeal of British Columbia approved by the Court of Appeal,[185] Soan JA stated that:

'[T]here must be, in my view, in the absence of exceptional circumstances, something more than a mere mental change of intention and physical change of location by those associated who wish to disassociate themselves from the consequences attendant upon their willing assistance up to the moment of the actual commission of that crime. I would not attempt to define too closely what must be done…That must depend upon the circumstances of each case but it seems to me that one essential element ought to be established in a case of this kind: Where practicable and reasonable there must be timely communication of the intention to abandon the common purpose from those who wish to dissociate themselves from the contemplated crime to those who desire to continue in it. What is "timely communication" must be determined by the facts of each case but where practicable and reasonable it ought to be such communication, verbal or otherwise, that will serve unequivocal notice upon the other party to the common unlawful cause that if he proceeds upon it he does so without the further aid and assistance of those who withdraw.'

In *O'Flaherty, Ryan and Toussaint*,[186] the Court of Appeal stated that whether or not a person has done enough to demonstrate that he is withdrawing is 'ultimately a question

---

[179] *Mogul Steamship Co Ltd v McGregor, Gow & Co* (1888) 21 QBD 544 at 549. Also see *Bennett* (1978) 68 Cr App Rep 168, CA.

[180] Ch 14.

[181] *Croft* [1944] 1 KB 295; *Fletcher* [1962] Crim LR 551, CCA; *Bryce* [2004] EWCA Crim 1231.

[182] *Rook* [1993] 2 All ER 955, CA.

[183] *Becerra and Cooper* (1975) 62 Cr App Rep 212, CA.

[184] (1941) 4 WWR 112 at 115.

[185] *Becerra and Cooper* (1975) 62 Cr App Rep 212, CA; *Whitefield* (1984) 79 Cr App Rep 36, CA.

[186] [2004] EWCA Crim 526 at [60].

of fact and degree for the jury. Account will be taken of inter alia the nature of the assistance and encouragement already given and how imminent the [principal offence] is, as well as the nature of the action said to constitute withdrawal.'

The requirement of timeliness means that a withdrawal of encouragement cannot be effective once the commission of the offence has commenced.[187] In relation to the requirement of unequivocality, it was held by the Court of Appeal in *Baker*[188] that it was not satisfied where D, a party to a joint criminal venture to kill V, had said, after starting the attack, 'I'm not doing it' and then moved a few feet away, whereupon the other parties stabbed V to death. The reason was that those words were far from being unequivocal notice that D was disassociating himself from the entire enterprise since they were quite capable of simply meaning 'I will not strike any more blows'.

17.68 **Where a person's participation has taken the form of assisting the commission of the principal offence by supplying the means for its commission, such as an article for use in its commission or information relevant to its commission or delivering the victim into a killer's hands, something more may be required.** This will vary depending on the circumstances. In some cases, for example, warning the police or the victim so that the offence can be prevented will suffice[189] but sometimes physical intervention in an attempt to prevent the commission of the offence will be required. In *Becerra and Cooper*,[190] D, E and F broke into a house to steal. D gave E a knife for use if necessary on anyone who interrupted them. V heard the noise and came downstairs. At this D said, 'There's a bloke coming. Let's go', and jumped out of the window. E then killed V with the knife. D's appeal against conviction for murder, as an accomplice, was dismissed because he had not done enough for his withdrawal from participation to be effective. The Court of Appeal commented that something 'different and vastly more effective' was required to relieve D of liability. It declined, however, to explain what would have been necessary on the facts of the case. So did the Northern Ireland Court of Appeal in *Graham*.[191] There, D, a member of a terrorist group, had transported a kidnap victim to a house where he realised the terrorists were, realising that they would kill the victim. D refused to render assistance to the terrorists further and asked them not to harm the victim. The terrorists took the victim to waste ground and shot him. The Northern Ireland Court of Appeal upheld D's conviction (as an accomplice) for murder. It stated:

> 'We consider that at the late stage which the murder plan had reached, and after the appellant had played such a significant part in assisting the killers to accomplish their aim, it could not be a sufficient withdrawal to indicate to them that he no longer supported their enterprise. Something more was required, and the judge was amply justified in holding

---

[187] *Whitefield* (1984) 79 Cr App Rep 36 at 39–40; *Robinson* (2000) unreported, CA.
[188] [1994] Crim LR 444, CA.
[189] *Becerra and Cooper* (1975) 62 Cr App Rep 212, CA.
[190] (1975) 62 Cr App Rep 212, CA.
[191] [1996] NI 157, NICA.

> that what the appellant did was not enough. His pleas were useless and the withholding of co-operation...was of minimal effect. We do not find it necessary to attempt to specify what acts would have been required of the appellant in the circumstances. It is sufficient for present purposes for us to say that the steps which he did take cannot be regarded as sufficient for withdrawal.'[192]

In *Becerra and Cooper* and in *Graham*, it is not easy to see what more D could have done to prevent the perpetration of the offence, other than to recover, or attempt to recover, the knife or rescue, or attempt to rescue, the victim, respectively, or some other form of physical intervention.

In *Rook*,[193] the Court of Appeal referred, obiter, to a situation where the assistance given took the form of the defendant supplying dynamite and a fuse. It said that it was not prepared to approve or disapprove the proposition that if the fuse had been set the defendant must step on it in order to withdraw from participation. It continued: 'It may be that this goes too far. It may be that it is enough that he should have done his best to step on the fuse'.

Thus, the statements in these cases suggested that in such situations reasonable steps to prevent the offence would have to be taken. However, in *O'Flaherty, Ryan and Toussaint*,[194] the Court of Appeal, without reference to those statements, stated obiter that such steps were not necessary. It did not distinguish between cases of assistance and cases of encouragement, and must be regarded as wrong in respect of the former.

The decisions in *Becerra and Cooper* and *Graham* can be contrasted with the decisions of the Court of Appeal in *Grundy*[195] and in *Whitefield*.[196] In *Grundy*, D gave burglars information which was of assistance in committing the burglary. D gave this information six weeks before the burglary. For two weeks before the burglary, D tried to dissuade the burglars from committing the burglary. The Court of Appeal held that there was evidence of an effective withdrawal, which should have been left to the jury. In *Whitefield* D gave E similar information to that in *Grundy*, and agreed to break into the building with E. There was evidence that, before the burglary, D had served unequivocal notice on E that, if E went on and committed the burglary, he would do so on his own. The Court of Appeal held that the jury should have been told that, if they accepted the evidence, D would have had the defence of withdrawal.

17.69 An unresolved question is whether, where there is more than one perpetrator, a withdrawal must be communicated unequivocally to all of them in order to be effective.

192 [1996] NI 157 at 169.
193 [1993] 2 All ER 955 at 962–963.
194 [2004] EWCA Crim 526 at [60].
195 [1977] Crim LR 543, CA.
196 (1984) 79 Cr App Rep 36, CA.

Spontaneous violence: an exception from need to communicate withdrawal?

17.70 In the above cases, the offence was pre-planned. In *Mitchell and King*,[197] the Court of Appeal held that communication of withdrawal was not necessary in cases of spontaneous violence. In that case, D1, D2 and E had engaged in a fight with F, a restaurant owner, and his two sons, G and H, after E had assaulted restaurant customers. There was evidence that, after leaving G (who had been subjected to a concerted attack involving beating, kicking and stamping on his head) prostrate on the ground, E had returned to administer a further beating to G's head. G died. The Court of Appeal allowed D1 and D2's appeals against conviction for murder and ordered a retrial. Its reason was that if G had been killed by E's blows administered after D1 and D2 had desisted and walked away, their desistance might have been sufficient to constitute withdrawal from the joint enterprise, leaving E solely liable for the murder. This possibility had not clearly been left to the jury and for this reason the Court of Appeal ruled D1 and D2's convictions unsafe. Having referred to Soan JA's statement in *Whitehouse*, referred to in para 17.67, it stated that in a case of spontaneous violence a direction about the requirement of communication of withdrawal was inappropriate; such communication was only necessary for withdrawal from pre-planned violence. This ruling was unduly favourable to accomplices. Quite apart from giving rise to issues about the dividing line between 'spontaneous' and 'pre-planned' violence, a distinction not drawn elsewhere in the law of secondary liability, it raises the question of why the distinction should be drawn. If a person would otherwise be liable for participating in spontaneous violence, why should he escape liability by simply repenting and stopping his attack if E goes on and kills? There is nothing on his part to countermand his previous assistance or encouragement, let alone a communication of this.

The effect of *Mitchell and King* was limited severely soon afterwards by the Court of Appeal in *Robinson*,[198] where it was held that *Mitchell and King* was exceptional. D and a gang had followed the victim, taunting him. The gang had encouraged D to hit the victim. D did so, whereupon the gang actively participated in the attack. D stood back while they did so, but, when he realised that the attack was going further than he had intended, he intervened and the attack ceased. D was convicted as a party to causing grievous bodily harm with intent. He appealed, arguing that the judge had been wrong to direct the jury that, in order to find that he had withdrawn from participation before the grievous bodily harm was caused, they had to find that he had or might have communicated such withdrawal. The Court of Appeal held that it was not truly a case of spontaneous violence and that, following *Becerra and Cooper*, communication of withdrawal was necessary. The Court added that, even where violence was spontaneous, withdrawal must be communicated to be effective 'unless it is not practicable or reasonable so to communicate'. This, of course, is wholly consistent with what was said in

---

[197] (1999) 163 JP 75, CA.
[198] [2005] 5 Archbold News 2, CA. Otton LJ presided in this case and in *Mitchell and King*.

Whitehouse. The Court of Appeal explained *Mitchell and King* as an exceptional case on the ground that it had not been practicable or reasonable for D1 and D2 to communicate with E because they had moved away before E returned to deliver his final blows.

Unfortunately, *Robinson* was not cited four years later in *O'Flaherty, Ryan and Toussaint*[199] where the Court of Appeal, obiter, referred to its decision in *Mitchell and King* with approval. Referring to *Mitchell and King*, it stated that in a case of spontaneous violence it is possible, in principle, to withdraw by ceasing to fight, throwing down one's weapon and walking away. Such differences of view do not assist in making the law certain.

Other points

17.71 Where it is not practicable and reasonable to communicate with the perpetrator in a pre-planned case, eg because he has disappeared after receiving assistance or encouragement from the defendant, it would presumably be sufficient for the accomplice to give the police timely notification of the proposed offence. Apart from this, it is difficult to offer guidance in a pre-planned case.

17.72 The mere fact that an accomplice is arrested before the principal offence is perpetrated does not prevent him being convicted of it.[200]

Uncertainty

> **Key points 17.9**
>
> The mere fact that it is not clear whether a defendant was the perpetrator or an accomplice does not prevent the conviction of the defendant if it can be proved beyond reasonable doubt that the defendant must have been either the perpetrator or an accomplice.

17.73 The above rule is of particular importance in cases where someone is killed or injured by one act when attacked by two or more people and it cannot be proved who perpetrated the act in question but it can be proved that each of the attackers must have been the perpetrator or an accomplice to the offence. It is not, however, limited to this situation. Thus, it was held in *Swindall and Osborne* in 1846[201] that, where either of two drivers, who indulged in unlawful racing in which each was encouraged by the other, might have run down the deceased, both could be convicted of manslaughter. More recently, in *Giannetto*[202] the prosecution case was that D was either the perpetrator of the murder

---

[199] [2004] EWCA Crim 526 at [61].
[200] *Johnson and Jones* (1841) Car & M 218.
[201] (1846) 2 Car & Kir 230.
[202] [1997] 1 Cr App Rep 1, CA. See also *Smith v Mellors and Soar* (1987) 84 Cr App Rep 279, DC; *Fitzgerald* [1992] Crim LR 660, CA.

of V or was an accomplice to that murder by hiring someone else to murder V. The Court of Appeal, upholding D's conviction for murder, held that it was open to the prosecution to invite the jury to find that at least D had encouraged the murder of V and that the jury were entitled to convict of murder if they were all satisfied that if D was not the perpetrator of murder he at least encouraged the murder.

On the other hand, if there is no evidence that each of the two or more possible perpetrators must either have perpetrated the offence or have assisted or encouraged the other(s) to do so,[203] with the appropriate *mens rea*, none of them can be convicted of the offence in question.[204] This has been a cause of particular concern in abuse cases where parents or other members of the household co-accused of an offence based on abuse have escaped conviction by remaining silent or blaming each other. The Domestic Violence, Crime and Victims Act 2004, s 5 closed this loophole where a child or vulnerable adult has died by creating an offence of causing or allowing the death of a child or vulnerable adult.[205]

Reform of the law of complicity

17.74 The account of the law given above discloses the technicalities involved in the law of complicity and the difficulties and uncertainties which it can produce. The technicalities result largely from the fact that the law of complicity, having been developed by the courts as new factual situations have arisen, lacks a coherent set of principles and from the fact that the liability of an accomplice is derived from his involvement in the commission of the principal offence by another.

Law Commission's Proposals

17.75 In 1993, the Law Commission produced a consultation paper which made provisional radical proposals for changes to the law relating to those who assist or encourage another to commit an offence.[206] Under the proposals the secondary liability for aiding, abetting, counselling or procuring the commission of an offence was to be abolished and replaced by two statutory inchoate offences of assisting and encouraging crime, respectively, which would have been committed whether or not the offence assisted or

---

[203] Whether by positive acts or by passive assistance or encouragement by failing to exercise a right or duty to control the acts of another: para 17.13.

[204] *Lane and Lane* (1985) 82 Cr App Rep 5, CA; *Russell and Russell* (1987) 85 Cr App Rep 388, CA; *Aston and Mason* (1991) 94 Cr App Rep 180, CA; *Petters and Parfitt* [1995] Crim LR 501, CA.

[205] See para 8.179.

[206] Law Commission: *Assisting and Encouraging Crime: A Consultation Paper* (1993), Law Commission Consultation Paper No 131. See Smith 'The Law Commission Consultation Paper on Complicity: A Blueprint for Rationalism' [1994] Crim LR 239; Sullivan 'The Law Commission Consultation Paper on Complicity: Fault Elements and Joint Enterprise' [1994] Crim LR 252; Smith 'Criminal Liability of Accessories: Law and Law Reform' (1997) 113 LQR 453.

encouraged was actually perpetrated. The proposed inchoate offences were different from those now contained in the Serious Crime Act 2007.[207]

17.76 The proposal to abolish secondary liability was extremely controversial. In particular, objections of principle were raised about the lack of adequate labelling and condemnation of those who had assisted or encouraged the principal offence.

These and other objections led the Law Commission in 2007 in its report *Participating in Crime*[208] to abandon the proposal and to make recommendations for reform which retain secondary liability for participation in an offence committed by a principal offender.[209] Although liability for complicity would continue to be derivative, the report makes various recommendations which would narrow the scope of the present law and deal with its uncertainty and incoherence. The Law Commission recommends that the Accessories and Abettors Act 1861, s 8, and the corresponding provisions in the Magistrates' Courts Act 1980, s 44,[210] should be repealed and replaced by a statutory provision which describes the requisite conduct as 'assisting or encouraging' (as opposed to 'aiding, abetting, counselling or procuring' as now), and therefore would narrow the law of complicity. This recommendation, and indeed the whole report, must be read together with the provisions of the Serious Crime Act 2007, Part 2, dealt with in Chapter 14.[211] The offences of encouraging or assisting crime therein would generally cover conduct caught by the present law of complicity which falls outside the recommendations in *Participating in Crime*.

Secondary liability

17.77 Under the recommendations in *Participating in Crime,* D would be liable for offences committed by another in two ways, which are set out in cll 1 and 2 of the draft Participating in Crime Bill attached to the report:

- assisting or encouraging an offence (cl 1); and

- participating in a joint criminal venture (cl 2).

17.78 *Assisting or encouraging crime* Under cl 1, D would be liable for the principal offence perpetrated by E if:

- D did an act with the intention that one or more of a number of acts would be done by E or someone else; and

- E's criminal act was one of those acts;

---

[207] Paras 14.1–14.44.

[208] Law Com No 305.

[209] For evaluation of the recommendations see Wilson 'A Rational Scheme of Liability for Participation in Crime' [2008] Crim LR 3; Sullivan 'Participating in Crime: Law Com No 305 – Joint Criminal Ventures' [2008] Crim LR 19; Taylor 'Procuring, Causation, Innocent Agency and the Law Commission' [2008] Crim LR 32; Buxton 'Joint Enterprise' [2009] Crim LR 233.

[210] Para 17.8.

[211] Paras 14.1–14.44.

- D's behaviour assisted or encouraged E to do his criminal act; and
- *either* D believed that a person doing the act would commit the offence (ie do the act with the relevant *mens rea*), *or* D's state of mind was such that, had he done the relevant act, he would have committed the offence.

Recklessness, or a belief, that E may commit the criminal act with D's assistance or encouragement would not suffice. Thus, a shopkeeper who sold E a crowbar, aware that E might use it to commit a burglary but not intending that E should commit that offence, would not be liable for it.

17.79 *Participating in a joint criminal venture*   Under cl 2 of the draft Bill, if one of the participants (E) in a joint criminal venture committed an offence, another participant (D) would also be guilty of the offence if E's criminal act fell within the scope of the venture. D would not escape liability under cl 2 for an offence committed by E at a time when D was a participant in the venture merely because D was at that time absent, against the venture being carried out, or indifferent as to whether it was carried out.

This is all that is said about 'joint criminal ventures'. It leaves that term undefined. In the body of the report the Law Commission makes recommendations about *mens rea* in joint criminal ventures but they do not appear in the draft Bill because the Law Commission wished to avoid the complexity of the provision which would result. The Commission expects those dealing with cl 2 to refer to the recommendations in its report to discover the *mens rea* required. This is hardly a satisfactory approach. The recommendations about *mens rea* are that, if D and E are parties to a joint criminal venture (eg to commit a burglary), D satisfies the *mens rea* requirement in relation to the conduct element of the principal offence or offences committed by E (eg burglary and/or unlawful wounding committed in addition to or instead of burglary) if: (a) D intended that E (or another party to the venture) should commit the conduct element; (b) D believed that E (or another party to the venture) would commit the conduct element; or (c) D believed that E (or another party to the venture) might commit the conduct element. The Commission recommends that, even if D intended or believed that E would or might commit the conduct element of the principal offence, D should nevertheless not be liable under the joint criminal venture provision for the principal offence if E's actions in committing the principal offence fell outside the scope of the joint venture. It further recommends that, if D and E are parties to a joint criminal venture, for D to be convicted of a principal offence that E commits, D must believe that E, in committing the conduct element of the offence, might be committing the offence.

Innocent agency

17.80 The doctrine of innocent agency is retained in the draft Bill.

Causing a no-fault offence

17.81 'Procuring' the commission of an offence as a mode of participation is replaced in the draft Bill by a new offence of 'causing a no-fault offence'.

Other points

17.82 The draft Bill also provides that:

- D would not be liable on any of the above bases for a protective offence if he falls in the protected class and he is the victim of the offence (ie the rule in *Tyrrell*[212] would be retained); and
- it would be a defence to liability for an offence as a secondary party if D proves on the balance of probabilities:

    (a) that he acted for the purpose of (i) preventing the commission of either the offence that he was encouraging or assisting or another offence, or (ii) preventing or limiting the occurrence of harm; and

    (b) that it was reasonable to act as D did in the circumstances.

Complicity in homicide: the Government's proposals

17.83 In its consultation paper, *Murder, Manslaughter and Infanticide: Proposals for Reform of the Law,*[213] the Government stated that it considered that the principles set out in the above Law Commission report[214] were a sound basis for reforming the law of complicity as it applied to homicide cases, and that it proposed to reform complicity to homicide with a view to reforming the law of complicity more generally at a later stage, guided by the same principles. However, there was a strong message from the consultation, which the Government accepted, that complicity in relation to homicide should not be reformed in isolation but only in the context of a review of the law of complicity in general. Consequently, the Government has not taken forward its proposals about complicity in homicide.

Key points 17.10

A person who assists an offender after the commission of an offence does not become an accomplice (ie party) to that offence but he will be guilty of the offence of assisting an offender if the terms of the Criminal Law Act 1967, s 4 are satisfied.

A person who conceals information relating to an offence in return for money or other consideration will be guilty of the offence of concealing an offence if the terms of the Criminal Law Act 1967, s 5 are satisfied.

---

[212] [1894] 1 QB 710, CCR; para 17.58.
[213] Ministry of Justice, Consultation Paper 19/08.
[214] And another Law Commission Report *Murder, Manslaughter and Infanticide* Law Com No 304, Pt 4.

Assisting an offender

17.84 The Criminal Law Act 1967, s 4(1)[215] provides that:

> 'Where a person has committed a relevant offence, any other person who, knowing or believing him to be guilty of the offence or of some other relevant offence does without lawful authority or reasonable excuse any act with intent to impede his apprehension or prosecution shall be guilty of an offence.'

An offence under s 4(1) is triable either way.[216] It is a separate offence to the 'relevant offence'. A person who satisfies the terms of s 4(1) does not thereby become a party to the 'relevant offence'. A prosecution can only be instituted by or with the consent of the Director of Public Prosecutions.[217] An offence under s 4(1) is limited to cases where the person assisted was guilty of a relevant offence, although a person who assists someone guilty of an offence which is not a relevant one may be convicted of perverting the course of justice or, in some cases, obstructing a constable in the execution of his duty.

Elements

17.85 In order to succeed on a charge of assisting an offender, the prosecution must prove four things:

- **The commission of a relevant offence by another ('the principal offender')** In the Criminal Law Act 1967, s 4 and s 5 below, 'relevant offence' means:

  - an offence for which the sentence is fixed by law, such as murder, or
  - an offence for which a person of 18 years or over (not previously convicted) may be sentenced to imprisonment for a term of five years (or, in the case of criminal damage, might be so sentenced but for the restrictions imposed by the Magistrates' Courts Act 1980, s 33[218]).[219]

In both s 4 and s 5, reference is made to a person who 'has committed a relevant offence'. There seems no reason why this should not cover an accomplice to the actual perpetration of an offence, as well as the perpetrator himself, and in the following account of ss 4 and 5 it should be remembered that the person 'who has committed a relevant offence' may have done so either as a perpetrator or an accomplice.

---

[215] As amended by the Serious Organised Crime and Police Act 2005, Sch 7.
[216] Magistrates' Courts Act 1980, s 17(1) and Sch 1.
[217] Criminal Law Act 1967, s 4(4).
[218] See para 13.2.
[219] Criminal Law Act 1967 s 4(1A) (as amended by the Serious Organised Crime and Police Act 2005, Sch 7).

Although the commission of the 'relevant offence' must be proved, no one need have been convicted of it,[220] and presumably even if there has been an acquittal that would not prevent a conviction for assisting the person acquitted at a separate trial on different evidence. The relevant offence alleged to have been committed must be specified in the indictment for assisting an offender. However, if the principal offender is not proved to be guilty of the specified offence, the defendant may still be convicted if the principal offender is proved guilty of another relevant offence of which he could be convicted on the indictment.[221]

- **The defendant's knowledge or belief that the principal offender is guilty of the actual relevant offence, or some other relevant offence** Wilful blindness in the present respect is not enough.[222] It is not necessary for the prosecution to prove that the defendant knew or believed the particular offence to be a relevant offence, or that he was aware of the identity of the person who committed it.[223]

- **An act done by the defendant with the intention of impeding the apprehension or prosecution of the principal offender** The principal offender need not actually be assisted (the definition of an offence under s 4(1) as assisting offenders is somewhat inaccurate) but the defendant must have done some act with intent to impede the prosecution or apprehension of the principal offender. An omission to act, even if accompanied by such intent, will not suffice. Thus, failure to report the principal offender to the police or to arrest him does not constitute assisting an offender. Authorities on the law relating to accessories after the fact, replaced by s 4, suggest that the requisite intent is a direct one.[224] Mere foresight that the offender will virtually certainly be assisted is insufficient, if the only direct intent of the defendant was the acquisition of money for himself or the protection of himself from prosecution.[225] The mere provision of accommodation in the ordinary way by the principal offender's family or landlord will not suffice, nor will mere efforts at persuasion not to prosecute. On the other hand, driving the principal offender away after the crime, hiding him from the police, destroying fingerprints or other evidence of the crime,[226] or telling the police lies in order to put them off the scent, do fall within the scope of the offence.[227]

- **The absence of lawful authority or reasonable excuse for the act of assistance** There would be lawful authority for impeding the prosecution if action were taken in consequence of an executive decision not to prosecute. An example of a case where,

---

[220] *Donald* (1986) 83 Cr App Rep 49, CA.

[221] *Morgan* [1972] 1 QB 436, CA.

[222] See para 3.46.

[223] *Brindley and Long* [1971] 2 QB 300, CA.

[224] This view was also taken by the Criminal Law Revision Committee who drafted the offence. See its Seventh Report, *Felonies and Misdemeanours* (Cmnd 2659), para 30.

[225] *Rose* (1961) 46 Cr App Rep 103, CCA; *Andrews and Craig* [1962] 3 All ER 961n, CCA.

[226] *Morgan* [1972] 1 QB 436, CA.

[227] *Brindley and Long* [1971] 2 QB 300, CA.

notwithstanding the intent to impede prosecution, there would be a reasonable excuse would be one in which a forged cheque was destroyed in pursuance of a lawful agreement[228] not to prosecute in consideration of the making good of the loss caused by the forgery.[229]

Punishment

17.86 Punishment varies according to the nature of the relevant offence which has been committed. In murder or any other offence whose punishment is fixed by law, the maximum punishment for acting with intent to impede its prosecution or the apprehension of the offender is 10 years' imprisonment; it is seven years' imprisonment if the maximum punishment for the principal offence is 14 years' imprisonment, five years' when the maximum punishment for the principal offence is 10 years' imprisonment, and three years' imprisonment in all other cases.[230]

The effect of the rule in *Courtie*[231] is that the Criminal Law Act 1967, s 4(1) creates four offences, punishable with ten, seven, five and three years' imprisonment respectively.

Concealing an offence for reward

17.87 The Criminal Law Act 1967, s 5(1)[232] provides that:

> 'Where a person has committed a relevant offence,[233] any other person who, knowing or believing that the offence or some other relevant offence has been committed, and that he has information which might be of material assistance in securing the prosecution or conviction of an offender for it, accepts or agrees to accept for not disclosing that information any consideration other than the making good of loss or injury caused by the offence, or the making of reasonable compensation for that loss or injury, [is guilty of an offence].'

The offence is triable either way.[234]

A prosecution for this offence may only be instituted by or with the consent of the Director of Public Prosecutions.[235] It is far less serious than assisting offenders, the maximum punishment being two years' imprisonment.[236]

---

[228] Para 17.87.

[229] *Seventh Report of the Criminal Law Revision Committee: Felonies and Misdemeanours*, (Cmnd 2659), para 28.

[230] Criminal Law Act 1967, s 4(3).

[231] Para 3.50, n 111.

[232] As amended by the Serious Organised Crime and Police Act 2005, Sch 7.

[233] See para 17.85.

[234] Magistrates' Courts Act 1980, s 17(1) and Sch 1.

[235] Criminal Law Act 1967, s 5(3).

[236] Criminal Law Act 1967, s 5(1).

17.88 The prosecution must prove three things:

- the commission of a relevant offence;
- the defendant's knowledge or belief that it, or some other relevant offence, has been committed and that he has information which might assist the prosecution; and
- the acceptance by the defendant of, or agreement by him to accept, some consideration (eg money or goods) other than the making good of loss or injury caused by the offence, or the making of reasonable compensation for that loss or injury, in return for not disclosing that information.

It follows from the above that the acceptance of any consideration for not reporting or prosecuting an offence which is not a relevant offence is not an offence under the Criminal Law Act 1967, s 5(1), nor does it constitute any other offence.[237] The same is true, with one exception, in the case of merely failing to inform the police of a relevant offence. The sole exception is failure to report a treason which still survives as the common law offence of misprision of treason, with a maximum punishment of life imprisonment.[238]

The related offence of advertising rewards for the return of stolen or lost goods with the promise that no questions will be asked etc has already been described.[239]

FURTHER READING

Alldridge 'The Doctrine of Innocent Agency' (1990) 2 Criminal Law Forum 45

Allen 'Entrapment: Time for Reconsideration' (1984) 13 Anglo-American LR 57

Ashworth 'Testing Fidelity to Legal Values: Official Involvement and Criminal Justice' (2000) 63 MLR 633

Ashworth 'Redrawing the Boundaries of Entrapment' [2002] Crim LR 161

Buxton 'Joint Enterprise' [2009] Crim LR 233

Clarkson 'Complicity, *Powell* and Manslaughter' [1998] Crim LR 556

Dennis 'The Mental Element for Accessories' in *Criminal Law: Essays in Honour of JC Smith* (1987) (Smith (ed)) 40

Dennis 'Intention and Complicity: A Reply' [1988] Crim LR 649

Griew 'Must Have Been One of Them?' [1989] Crim LR 129

Hogan 'Victims as Parties to Crime' [1962] Crim LR 683

Lanham 'Accomplices and Transferred Malice' (1980) 96 LQR 110

Lanham 'Accomplices and Withdrawal' (1981) 97 LQR 575

JC Smith 'Aid, Abet, Counsel or Procure' in *Reshaping the Criminal Law* (1978) (Glazebrook (ed)) 120

KJM Smith *A Modern Treatise on the Law of Complicity* (1991)

---

[237] This is the effect of the Criminal Law Act 1967, s 5(5).
[238] *Sykes v DPP* [1962] AC 528, HL.
[239] Para 11.57.

KJM Smith 'Withdrawal in Complicity: A Restatement of Principles' [2001] Crim LR 769

Sullivan 'Intent, Purpose and Complicity' [1988] Crim LR 641

Virgo 'Making Sense of Accessorial Liability' [2006] 6 Archbold News 6

Williams 'Victims as Parties to Crime – A Further Comment' [1964] Crim LR 686

Williams 'Evading Justice' [1975] Crim LR 430, 479, 608

Williams 'Which of You Did It?' (1989) 51 MLR 179

18

Vicarious liability, corporate liability and liability of unincorporated associations

OVERVIEW

In some cases, someone like an employer can be liable for an offence by another which he has not aided, abetted, counselled or procured. Such liability is known as vicarious liability. Companies and other corporate bodies can sometimes be convicted of an offence. A partnership or other unincorporated association can be convicted of some statutory offences.

Vicarious liability for the criminal acts of another

18.1 As we have seen, a person can be guilty under the law of complicity for the offence of another which he has aided, abetted, counselled or procured; if he has a right or duty to control the perpetrator, this includes the case where he has deliberately failed to prevent the offence.[1] However, it is a **general rule of the criminal law that one person is not vicariously liable for the acts of another which he has not aided, abetted, counselled or procured,** even if that other person is his employee acting in the course of his employment so that civil vicarious liability might arise. Thus, in the old case of *Huggins*[2] the warden of the Fleet prison was acquitted on a charge of murdering one of the inmates, as it appeared that death had been caused by confinement in an unhealthy cell by an employee of the defendant without any direction from him and without his knowledge.

---

[1] Para 17.13.
[2] (1730) 1 Barn KB 358, 396.

Exceptions to the general rule

Key points 18.1

Criminal vicarious liability is almost entirely limited to statutory offences of a regulatory nature.

   Most of the instances of vicarious liability for statutory offences have resulted not from the express wording of the statute but from judicial interpretation of it.

18.2 In certain limited cases a person can be criminally liable for the acts of others which he has not aided, abetted, counselled or procured, and of which he may have been ignorant. **Vicarious liability is only possible in respect of one common law offence: public nuisance.** An employer is criminally liable for a public nuisance committed on his property or on the highway by his employee, even if the latter was disobeying orders.[3] The common law offence of public nuisance is essentially civil in character.

18.3 It is, of course, possible (but rare) for a statute expressly to impose vicarious liability. An example is provided by the Property Misdescriptions Act 1991, s 1(1), which states that: 'Where a false or misleading statement about a prescribed matter is made in the course of an estate agency business... the person by whom the business is carried on shall be guilty of an offence', in addition to any employee to whose act or default the making of the statement is due.[4]

   The courts have used two principles of interpretation to impose vicarious liability for a large number of regulatory statutory offences:

- extensive construction; and
- delegation.

Extensive construction

18.4 It has become common[5] for the courts to give an extended construction to certain verbs used in statutory offences, such as 'sell' or 'use', so that the act of an employee is regarded as the act of his employer and thereby the employer is held to have committed the offence physically performed by his employee. Thus, an employer, as well as his driver, has been held guilty of 'using' a motor vehicle with a defective brake.[6] Similarly, an employer has been held guilty of 'exposing for sale' bags of coal containing short weight,

---

[3] *Stephens* (1866) LR 1 QB 702 at 710.

[4] Property Misdescriptions Act 1991, s 1(2). For another example, see the Transport and Works Act 1992, s 28.

[5] But not invariable: see, for example, *Haringey London BC v Marks and Spencer plc* [2004] EWHC (Admin) 1141, DC.

[6] *Green v Burnett* [1955] 1 QB 78, DC; *Mickleborough v BRS (Contracts)* [1977] RTR 389, DC.

although the short weight was due to the wrongdoing of the employee who exposed them for sale.[7] In *Coppen v Moore (No 2)*,[8] D owned a number of shops in one of which an assistant, contrary to instructions, sold an American ham as a 'Scotch ham'. D was held guilty of selling goods to which a false trade description had been applied.[9] Lastly, in *Anderton v Rodgers*,[10] all 11 members of the governing committee of an unincorporated social club were held vicariously liable for illegal sales of intoxicating liquor, unknown to them and contrary to their instructions, by their bar staff, since the staff were the employees of the committee.

18.5 The extensive construction principle is not limited to the relationship of employer and employee but has also been used to impose vicarious liability on a principal for the act of his agent or independent contractor acting under his instructions and control.[11] Moreover, a licensee has been held liable under the Licensing Act 1964 (since repealed) for illegal sales of alcohol by bar staff who were not his employees, but like him employed by the owner of the premises, since the act of selling could only be performed by virtue of the licence.[12] On the other hand, members of a board of directors, or of a governing committee, of a body corporate are not vicariously liable for the acts of an employee of the body corporate, even though they have the exclusive power to engage or dismiss that employee.[13] (The body corporate may, of course, be vicariously liable as an employer.) Similarly, the owner of a lorry which is used in a prohibited manner cannot be vicariously liable for that use, even if it is engaged on his business, if the driver is not his employee but that of a third party, such as an employment agency.[14] In contrast, the owner of a store has been held vicariously liable for the offence, contrary to the Consumer Protection Act 1987, s 20 (since repealed), of giving consumers 'in the course of any business of his' a misleading indication of the price of any goods where the indication was given by the employee of a concessionaire in the store. This decision seems to be an extreme application of the extensive construction principle based on the court's view that 'the misleading price indication had clearly been given in the course of the [store owner's] business'.[15]

---

[7] *Winter v Hinckley and District Industrial Co-operative Society Ltd* [1959] 1 All ER 403, DC.

[8] [1898] 2 QB 306, DC.

[9] Simester and Sullivan *Criminal Law: Theory and Doctrine* (3rd edn, 2007) 252 argue that this was not a case of vicarious liability because the sale in a legal sense was made by D, the employer, and no *mens rea* was required for the offence. Nevertheless, the physical acts involved in the sale were those of the employee, and were the immediate cause of the sale. The case is better explained as one of vicarious liability.

[10] [1981] Crim LR 404, DC.

[11] *Quality Dairies (York) Ltd v Pedley* [1952] 1 KB 275, DC; *FE Charman Ltd v Clow* [1974] 3 All ER 371, DC; *Hallett Silberman Ltd v Cheshire County Council* [1993] RTR 32, DC.

[12] *Goodfellow v Johnson* [1966] 1 QB 83, DC. The employer could also be vicariously liable for an unlawful sale by a member of the bar staff: *Nottingham City Justices v Wolverhampton and Dudley Breweries plc* [2003] EWHC 2847 (Admin), DC.

[13] *Phipps v Hoffman* [1976] Crim LR 315, DC.

[14] *Howard v GT Jones & Co Ltd* [1975] RTR 150, DC.

[15] *Surrey County Council v Burton Retail Ltd* (1997) 162 JP 545, DC.

18.6 The extensive construction principle cannot apply where the offence requires a prescribed physical act by the defendant, such as 'driving',[16] because, while someone like an employer can be said to 'sell' something or to 'use a vehicle' through an employee, he cannot be said to 'drive' a vehicle through an employee. It is the employee alone who drives the vehicle. A similar decision was reached in *A-G's Reference (No 2 of 2003)*,[17] where the question arose as to whether D, a consultant obstetrician and gynaecologist who was the 'person responsible' under the Human Fertilisation and Embryology Act 1990 for the supervision of authorised activities at two clinics licensed for the purposes of the Act, could be vicariously liable for offences of 'keeping' an embryo except in pursuance of a licence contrary to ss 3(1)(b) and 41(2)(a) of that Act when, unknown to D, the offences had been committed at one of the clinics by an embryologist employed there. The Court of Appeal answered 'no'. It was difficult to see how the language of the statutory provisions extended criminal liability for keeping an embryo except in pursuance of a licence to a person who, notwithstanding his statutory responsibilities, did not in fact keep the embryo at all. None of the relevant provisions of the 1990 Act suggested, let alone provided for, criminal liability on the part of the 'person responsible' solely by virtue of his appointment. That person was not 'deemed' to be the keeper of the embryo. This decision shows the importance of interpreting the offence in the context of the statute as a whole.

18.7 It seems that under the extensive construction principle only the act of the employee etc, and not his *mens rea*, can be imputed to the employer etc.[18] The result is that the principle is limited to offences of strict liability. Where, as is usually the case, a strict liability offence requires *mens rea* as to some of its elements, the employer (or, if the employer is a corporation, someone whose state of mind can be attributed to it)[19] must have *mens rea* as to those elements before the employer can be vicariously liable for the offence under the extensive construction principle.[20]

Delegation

18.8 This principle of interpretation appears to be limited to a small number of offences which can only be committed by a person of a specified type on whom statute

---

[16] *Richmond upon Thames LBC v Pinn & Wheeler Ltd* [1989] RTR 354, DC.

[17] [2004] EWCA Crim 785.

[18] *Vane v Yiannopoullos* [1965] AC 486, HL; *Winson* [1969] 1 QB 371 at 382; *Coupe v Guyett* [1973] 2 All ER 1058, DC. Contrast *Mousell Bros Ltd v London and North Western Rly Co Ltd* [1917] 2 KB 836, DC (employer convicted of statutory offence of falsifying the description of goods with intent to avoid payment of tolls). This is an obscure decision which is best explained as belonging 'to an intermediate stage in the development of corporate criminal responsibility' which would now be the basis of personal corporate liability on the facts (para 18.23), not vicarious liability: Williams *Criminal Law: The General Part* (2nd edn, 1961) 274. Also see Sir John Smith [2000] Crim LR 694–696.

[19] Para 18.27.

[20] See *Wings Ltd v Ellis* [1985] AC 272, HL.

places a duty. If a licensee, for example, delegates his responsibilities as licensee to another, and the delegate acts in breach of one of the delegated responsibilities, his acts *and state of mind* are imputed to the delegator for the purposes of such an offence. In *Allen v Whitehead*,[21] the licensee of a refreshment house delegated control of it to an employee who, in the licensee's absence and contrary to his express instructions, allowed prostitutes to enter. The licensee was convicted of 'knowingly suffering prostitutes to meet together in his house and remain therein', contrary to the Metropolitan Police Act 1839, s 44, the acts and *mens rea* of the delegate employee being imputed to him. The rationale behind the delegation principle is that without it the person of the specified type on whom a statutory responsibility is placed could render the offence relating to it nugatory by delegating his managerial functions and responsibilities to another.

18.9 Where the offence is one of strict liability, the extensive construction principle generally suffices to impose vicarious liability and the delegation principle normally comes into play only if the statute uses words which import a full requirement of *mens rea*.[22]

18.10 The delegation principle is not limited to cases where the delegate is the employee of the delegator. In *Linnett v Metropolitan Police Comr*,[23] it was held that one co-licensee was vicariously liable where his co-licensee, to whom he had delegated the management of a refreshment house owned by their employer, had knowingly permitted disorderly conduct there.

18.11 It is necessary that there should have been a complete delegation of managerial functions and responsibilities. Thus, the House of Lords held in *Vane v Yiannopoullos*[24] that a restaurateur, who was permitted to sell intoxicants only to customers consuming a meal, and who had told a waitress to serve such customers only, and then withdrawn to the basement, was not guilty of any infringement by the waitress of the Licensing Act 1964, s 161(1) (since repealed) (which penalised licensees who knowingly sold intoxicants to unpermitted persons). The restaurateur had retained control of the restaurant and had not delegated this to the waitress. On the other hand, if there has been a complete delegation of managerial functions and responsibilities, it is irrelevant that this only relates to part of the licensed premises or that the delegator licensee is still on the premises.[25]

18.12 In *Vane v Yiannopoullos*, Lords Morris and Donovan doubted the validity of the delegation principle, but in the light of its continued application it must still be regarded as part of the law.[26]

---

[21] [1930] 1 KB 211, DC.   [22] *Winson* [1969] 1 QB 371 at 382.   [23] [1946] KB 290, DC.
[24] [1965] AC 486, HL.   [25] *Howker v Robinson* [1973] QB 178, DC.
[26] See, for example, *Winson* [1969] 1 QB 371, CA; *Howker v Robinson* [1973] QB 178, DC.

Comments on vicarious liability

Within the scope of his employment or authority

18.13 Vicarious liability can arise only if the employee or delegate etc was acting within the scope of his employment or authority. Doing an authorised activity in an unauthorised way falls within such scope, but a wholly unauthorised activity does not. In *Coppen v Moore (No 2)*,[27] an employer was held vicariously liable for a sale effected by a sales assistant in an unauthorised manner, but in *Adams v Camfoni*,[28] the defendant licensee was acquitted of supplying intoxicants outside permitted hours because the supply had been effected by a messenger boy who had no authority to sell anything at all.

Liability of employee or delegate

18.14 The liability of the employee or delegate etc depends on the wording of the particular statute. If it specifies that only a person with a particular status can commit the offence, an employee or delegate who actually commits the act can be convicted only as an accomplice of that person, who is vicariously liable as perpetrator.[29] Where the statute does not specify a particular type of perpetrator, the employee etc can be convicted as perpetrator jointly with the person held vicariously liable.[30] This distinction is important because, if the offence in question is one of strict liability, the employee can be convicted in the first type of case only if he has *mens rea*, since a person can be convicted as an accomplice to an offence of strict liability only if he has *mens rea*.[31]

No vicarious liability as an accomplice or for attempt

18.15 A person cannot be vicariously liable for aiding or abetting[32] or for attempting to commit[33] an offence.

Statutory defences

18.16 There are several statutory defences which are open to employers and others who may be vicariously liable. The courts have refused to read into statutes, construed by them as imposing vicarious liability for offences, an exception protecting employers who show due diligence in the management of their business in cases where nothing which they

---

[27] [1898] 2 QB 306, DC. Also see *Police Comrs v Cartman* [1896] 1 QB 655, DC; *Allen v Whitehead* [1930] 1 KB 211, DC; *Anderton v Rodgers* [1981] Crim LR 404, DC.

[28] [1929] 1 KB 95, DC. Also see *Boyle v Smith* [1906] 1 KB 432, DC; *Phelon and Moore Ltd v Keel* [1914] 3 KB 165, DC; *Barker v Levinson* [1951] 1 KB 342, DC.

[29] *Griffiths v Studebakers Ltd* [1924] 1 KB 102, DC.

[30] *Green v Burnett* [1955] 1 QB 78, DC.

[31] Para 17.37.

[32] *Ferguson v Weaving* [1951] 1 KB 814, DC.

[33] *Gardner v Akeroyd* [1952] 2 QB 743, DC.

could reasonably be expected to do would have prevented the commission of the offence by the employee. Accordingly, some statutes contain an express provision for defences of this nature in relation to offences under them, of which examples are the Weights and Measures Act 1985, s 34 and the Trade Descriptions Act 1968, s 24.[34] There is much to be said for having a general defence of due diligence in all cases of vicarious criminal liability.

18.17 In a case concerning the statutory defence to an offence of supplying a video to a person under the appropriate age, provided by the Video Recordings Act 1984, s 11(2), viz that the defendant neither knew nor had reasonable grounds to believe that the buyer had not attained the appropriate age, the Divisional Court held that the state of mind of an employee whose act was imputed to the employer could also be attributed to the employer in relation to this defence. Consequently, if the employee knew and had reason to believe the above fact, the employer could not rely on the defence.[35] While this might be permissible where the delegation principle applies to impose vicarious liability, it would seem impermissible where (as in the case in question) vicarious liability is imposed under the extensive construction principle. Under that principle, an employee's *mens rea* cannot be attributed to the employer so as to make him vicariously liable where an offence requires *mens rea*; it is odd that an employee's state of mind can be attributed to the employer in relation to a defence.

Justification of vicarious liability

18.18 Criminal responsibility is generally regarded as essentially personal in nature. The exceptional principles, whereby a person can be convicted of an offence of which he was ignorant and which was actually committed by another, can be justified only on the basis of the need to enforce modern regulatory legislation, such as that governing the sale of food and drugs.[36] The courts consider that the most effective way of enforcing such legislation is to impose on the employer liability for contravention by employees in order to encourage the employer to prevent them infringing the legislation.[37] This justification calls for two comments. First, the assumption that the imposition of vicarious liability is the most effective method of securing compliance with the statute is unproved. Secondly, vicarious liability would be more acceptable if it were limited generally to employers who had been negligent in failing to prevent the contravention. Another justification put forward occasionally is that some offences can be committed only by a particular person, such as a licensee, and that without vicarious liability such an offence would be rendered nugatory where that person acted through others. The obvious answer is to amend the statute, not for the judges to impose vicarious liability.

---

[34] Para 6.47.
[35] *Tesco Stores Ltd v Brent London Borough Council* [1993] 2 All ER 718, DC; see further para 18.30.
[36] See, for example, *Gardner v Akeroyd* [1952] 2 QB 743 at 747–748, per Parker J.
[37] *Reynolds v GH Austin & Sons Ltd* [1951] 2 KB 135, DC; *Tesco Supermarkets Ltd v Nattrass* [1972] AC 153 at 194, per Lord Diplock; para 6.43.

Corporations

Key points 18.2

Corporations are legal persons.
A corporation can be criminally liable on one of four bases:

- vicarious liability;
- personal liability for an 'operational offence';
- personal liability for breach of statutory duty; or
- personal liability on the basis of attributing to the corporation the conduct and state of mind of an individual.

18.19 The general rule is that a corporation, such as an incorporated company, a limited liability partnership under the Limited Liability Partnership Act 2000 or a local authority, may be criminally liable to the same extent as a natural person.

In law a corporation is a separate person distinct from its members (eg the shareholders, limited liability partners or councillors, as the case may be). References to a 'person' in a statute include a corporation, unless the contrary intention appears.[38] There has never been any doubt that the members,[39] like the employees, of a corporation cannot shelter behind the corporation and may be successfully prosecuted for criminal acts performed or authorised by them; the problem with which we are concerned is the extent to which the corporate body itself may be criminally liable. The chief obstacle to the acceptance of the concept of the criminal liability of a corporation has been the combination of its artificiality with the traditional need for the proof of *mens rea* in crime: '…did you ever expect a corporation to have a conscience, when it has no soul to be damned and no body to be kicked?'[40] In 1700, a corporation was not indictable at all;[41] today a corporation can be liable on one of four bases:

- vicarious liability;
- personal liability for an 'operational offence';
- personal liability for breach of statutory duty; or
- personal liability on the basis of attributing to the corporation the conduct and state of mind of an individual.

---

[38] Interpretation Act 1978, ss 5, 22(1) and Schs 1 and 2, Pt I, para 4(5).
[39] In the case of an incorporated company, its members are normally its shareholders.
[40] Attributed to the second Baron Thurlow.
[41] *Anon* (1702) 12 Mod Rep 559.

Vicarious liability

18.20 There was little difficulty in holding a corporation vicariously liable for the acts of employees (however junior) and others in the same way as an individual.[42]

Operational offences

18.21 The courts have also held that a corporation can be personally liable for a strict liability offence which can be committed by the defendant's conduct of an operation of some kind without more on the defendant's part. An example is the offence of causing polluting matters to enter controlled waters, contrary to the Water Resources Act 1991, s 85, which may be committed (for example) simply by maintaining a tank containing a pollutant which escapes into a watercourse because of an unforeseeable (but not abnormal) act of a third party (such as a trespasser); it has been held that in such circumstances a corporation maintaining the tank causes the pollution and is guilty of the offence.[43]

Breach of statutory duty

18.22 The courts have had equally little difficulty in holding that a corporation can be guilty of breach of a statutory duty, such as the duty imposed on the 'occupier' of a factory to fence its machinery or on an 'employer' in respect of various health and safety matters. Since the middle of the nineteenth century it has been clear that, like anyone else, a corporation is liable if it is in breach of a statutory duty imposed on it as an occupier or employer or in some other similar capacity.[44] In *Evans & Co Ltd v LCC*,[45] the defendant company was charged that, being the occupier of a shop, it did not close it on the afternoon of an early closing day in breach of the duty imposed on the occupiers of shops by the Shops Act 1912 (since repealed). The Divisional Court held that the company was liable for breach of this statutory duty. A more recent example is provided by the decision of the House of Lords in *Associated Octel Co Ltd*,[46] which was concerned with the duty, under the Health and Safety at Work etc Act 1974, s 3(1), which is imposed on an employer to conduct an undertaking in such a way as to ensure that, so far as reasonably practicable, those who are not employees but who may be affected thereby are not exposed to risks to their health or safety. The Health and Safety at Work etc Act 1974, s 33(1) makes breach of this duty an offence which is triable either way and punishable with

---

[42] Paras 18.1–18.18. For an early example of corporate vicarious liability, see *Great North of England Rly Co* (1846) 2 Cox CC 70 (common law offence of public nuisance).

[43] *Environment Agency (formerly National Rivers Authority) v Empress Car Co (Abertillery) Ltd* [1999] 2 AC 22, HL.

[44] *Birmingham and Gloucester Rly Co* (1842) 3 QB 223.

[45] [1914] 3 KB 315, DC.

[46] [1996] 4 All ER 846, HL. See also *British Steel plc* [1995] 1 WLR 1356, CA; *Gateway Foodmarkets Ltd* [1997] 3 All ER 78, CA.

a maximum term of imprisonment of two years.[47] Upholding the defendant company's conviction under s 33(1), the House of Lords held that liability thereunder was not a vicarious liability but a personal liability which arose where an activity in question could be described as part of the employer's undertaking (and this could be so even where it was an independent contractor's activity) and had been carried out in a way which breached the employer's duty. In *A-G's Reference (No 2 of 1999),*[48] the Court of Appeal confirmed that the present principle is limited to cases where there has been a breach of a statutory duty imposed on a corporation to conduct its undertaking in a particular way. It refused to extend the principle to embrace a gross breach of the corporation's common law duty of care resulting in death, and therefore held that a corporation could not be guilty of manslaughter by gross negligence under the principle.

Liability on the basis of attributing the conduct and state of mind of an individual to the corporation: the identification principle

> **Key points 18.3**
>
> A corporation can generally be liable for an offence requiring proof of *mens rea* if the conduct and state of mind of an individual can be attributed to it. Whether there can be such attribution depends in common law offences and some statutory offences on the 'directing mind and will test' and in other statutory offences on the construction of the statute.

18.23 The three grounds of liability in paras 18.20 to 18.22 can render a corporation criminally liable only for a relatively small number of offences, essentially statutory offences of strict liability. Much more important is that, since 1944 at the latest,[49] it has been possible to impose criminal liability on a corporation, whether as a perpetrator or as an accomplice, for virtually any offence, notwithstanding that *mens rea* is required. **In such a case, liability is not vicarious, in that the corporation is not held responsible on the basis of liability for the acts of its agents; instead the corporation, as in the case of operational offences and breach of a statutory duty, is regarded as having committed the offence personally.**

Where *personal* liability is imposed on a corporation under the rules below on the basis that the individual identified with it has perpetrated an offence, it will be liable as a perpetrator. On the other hand, if the individual was an accomplice to the commission of an offence by another, the corporation's personal liability will be as an accomplice. Such

---

[47] Health and Safety at Work etc Act 1974, Sch 3A, inserted by the Health and Safety (Offences) Act 2008.

[48] [2000] QB 796, CA.

[49] Three cases reported in 1944 went far to establish the present law: *DPP v Kent and Sussex Contractors Ltd* [1944] KB 146, DC; *ICR Haulage Ltd* [1944] KB 551, CCA; *Moore v I Bresler Ltd* [1944] 2 All ER 515, DC.

liability may arise either through a positive act of aiding, abetting, counselling or procuring by an individual or through a failure by an individual to exercise a right or duty to control another, eg a junior employee, who perpetrates the offence.[50]

The imposition of liability in this way has been based on the 'identification principle' whereby not only the acts but also the state of mind of a person who can be identified with a corporation are attributed to the corporation.

Attribution via the 'directing mind and will test'

18.24 In the first case in which the identification principle was clearly recognised in the criminal law, *DPP v Kent and Sussex Contractors Ltd*,[51] D Ltd was charged with two offences requiring *mens rea*. The Divisional Court held that D Ltd could be convicted of both offences. The false documentation in question had been signed by an officer of D Ltd and he had the necessary *mens rea* and, the Court held, his *mens rea* could be attributed to D Ltd. Viscount Caldecote CJ stated that: 'a company is incapable of acting or speaking or even thinking except in so far as its officers have acted, spoken or thought'.[52]

18.25 The fact that a person is not a director or employee of a corporation is not a bar to him being identified with it.[53]

18.26 The nature of the 'directing mind and will test', and the clear distinction which exists between personal corporate liability resulting from it and the corporation's vicarious liability as an employer, is shown in the following passage from Lord Reid's speech in *Tesco Supermarkets Ltd v Nattrass*:

> 'A living person has a mind which can have knowledge or intention or be negligent and he has hands to carry out his intentions. A corporation has none of these: it must act through living persons, though not always one and the same person. Then the person who acts is not speaking or acting for the company. He is acting as the company and his mind which directs his acts is the mind of the company. There is no question of the company being vicariously liable. He is not acting as a servant, representative, agent or delegate. He is an embodiment of the company, or, one could say, he hears and speaks through the persona of the company, within his appropriate sphere, and his mind is the mind of the company. If it is a guilty mind then that guilt is the guilt of the company.'[54]

It is a question of law whether a person in doing (or failing to do) a particular thing is to be regarded as part of the corporation's directing mind and will or merely as the corporation's employee or agent. It follows that the judge should tell the jury that if they find

---

[50] Para 17.13.   [51] [1944] KB 146, DC.   [52] [1944] KB 146 at 155.
[53] *Worthy v Gordon Plant (Services) Ltd* [1989] RTR 7n, DC.   [54] [1972] AC 153 at 170.

certain facts proved then they must find that the acts (or omissions) and state of mind of that person are those of the corporation.[55]

18.27 An influential dictum on the distinction between those who form part of the directing mind and will of the corporation and those who do not is to be found in the civil case of *H L Bolton (Engineering) Co Ltd v T J Graham & Sons Ltd* where Denning LJ (as he then was) said:

> 'A company may in many ways be likened to a human body. It has a brain and nerve centre which controls what it does. It also has hands which hold the tools and act in accordance with directions from the centre. Some of the people in the company are mere servants and agents who are nothing more than hands to do the work and cannot be said to represent the mind or will. Others are directors and managers who represent the directing mind and will of the company, and control what it does. The state of mind of these managers is the state of mind of the company and is treated by the law as such.'[56]

This dictum was approved in *Tesco Supermarkets Ltd v Nattrass*[57] by Lords Reid, Dilhorne and Pearson who held that only those who constitute the 'directing mind and will' of the corporation can be identified with it.[58] These were people such as directors and others who manage the affairs of the corporation. In addition, they included a person to whom those responsible for the general management of the corporation had delegated some part of their functions of management, giving to that person full discretion to act independently of instructions from them.[59] Within the scope of the delegation, the delegate could act as the corporation. In assessing whether a particular person could be identified with the corporation, account should be taken of the constitution of the corporation but it is not decisive.[60]

On the above criteria, a manager to whom the directors have delegated full power in the running of its affairs[61] or part of its affairs has been regarded as the embodiment of the corporation.[62] For example, the traffic manager of a company has been identified with it in relation to the operation of its fleet of goods vehicles under an operator's licence.[63] On the other hand, a corporation has not been identified under the directing mind and will test with the branch manager of a company with a large number of branches who

---

[55] *Tesco Supermarkets Ltd v Nattrass* [1972] AC 153 at 170 and 173, per Lord Reid. See also *Andrews Weatherfoil Ltd* [1972] 1 All ER 65, CA.

[56] [1957] 1 QB 159 at 172.

[57] [1972] AC 153, HL.

[58] This rule is criticised by Wells 'Culture, Risk and Criminal Liability' [1993] Crim LR 551 at 558–561 and 563. See also Wells *Corporations and Criminal Responsibility* (2nd edn, 2001) 99–101.

[59] [1972] AC 153 at 192–193, per Lord Pearson.

[60] [1972] AC 153 at 199, per Lord Diplock. See also the speech of Lord Pearson [1972] AC 153 at 193.

[61] *Lennard's Carrying Co Ltd v Asiatic Petroleum Co Ltd* [1915] AC 705, HL.

[62] *Worthy v Gordon Plant (Services) Ltd* [1989] RTR 7n, DC.

[63] *Worthy v Gordon Plant (Services) Ltd* [1989] RTR 7n, DC; *Redhead Freight Ltd v Shulman* [1989] RTR 1, DC.

was required to comply with the general directions of the board of directors,[64] nor with a depot engineer,[65] nor with the operator of a weighbridge belonging to the corporation.[66]

18.28 It is important to remember that the application of the directing mind and will test does not depend on the title of a person's post but on whether or not the person is part of the directing mind and will of the corporation. The fact that a person with a particular title is held in one case to be part of a corporation's directing mind and will does not mean that someone with that title in another corporation will be so regarded. It will depend on the constitution and organisational structure of the corporation.

18.29 The 'directing mind and will test' is inappropriate where a statute provides a 'no-negligence' defence to a regulatory offence of strict liability. This is shown by the facts of *Tesco Supermarkets Ltd v Nattrass*,[67] which concerned the Trade Descriptions Act 1968, s 24(1). Under s 24(1) it is a defence for a defendant, who would otherwise be *vicariously* liable for a regulatory offence, to show that he has exercised all due diligence and that the commission of the offence was due to the act or default of 'another person'. Such a defence is known as a 'third party defence'. In *Tesco v Nattrass*, a local shop manager employed by a company running a chain of 800 supermarkets was not identified with the company. His faulty supervision had caused a shop assistant to sell goods in circumstances in which the company was prima facie guilty, under the principles of vicarious liability, of an offence under the Trade Descriptions Act 1968. A magistrates' court found that the company had set up a proper system and therefore had exercised all due diligence but it also found that the branch manager was not 'another person' for the purposes of the Trade Descriptions Act 1968, s 24(1), because his acts were those of the company. The House of Lords quashed this conviction. It held that the manager, though an employee, could not be equated with the company because he was not part of the directing mind and will of the company. Therefore, despite his default, the company could rely on the statutory defence under s 24(1). Thus, according to this decision the 'directing mind and will test' can apply not only to convict a corporation but also to establish a third party defence to a regulatory offence. The effect is, of course, to reduce the effectiveness of the Trade Descriptions Act 1968 where defendants are corporations because they will often be sheltered, as were Tesco, by the 'directing mind and will test'.

18.30 In relation to another 'no-negligence' defence whereby the defendant has a defence if he proves that he neither knew nor had reasonable ground to believe a particular fact the Divisional Court in *Tesco Stores Ltd v Brent London Borough Council*[68] refused to apply the 'directing mind and will test'. This case concerned the defence under the Video Recordings Act 1984, s 11(2), under which it is a defence to a charge of supplying a video recording of a classified work in breach of its age classification

---

[64] *Tesco Supermarkets Ltd v Nattrass* [1972] AC 153, HL; para 18.29.
[65] *Magna Plant v Mitchell* [1966] Crim LR 394, DC.
[66] *John Henshall (Quarries) Ltd v Harvey* [1965] 2 QB 233, DC.
[67] [1972] AC 153, HL.
[68] [1993] 2 All ER 718, DC.

(eg selling an '18' video to someone under that age) to prove that the defendant neither knew nor had reasonable grounds to believe that the person supplied had not reached the relevant age. In *Tesco v Brent* a sales assistant employed by Tesco, and clearly not part of the directing mind and will of Tesco, had sold a classified video recording to a customer below the relevant age, as the assistant had reasonable grounds to believe. The Divisional Court dismissed Tesco's appeal against conviction for supplying the video recording to an under-age person. It held that on the true interpretation of s 11(2) there was no distinction between the company accused of the offence in question and those under its control who physically supplied the video recording. Therefore, as the assistant had been under Tesco's control, the defence under s 11(2) was not available to Tesco. As Staughton LJ said in *Tesco v Brent*: 'Were it otherwise, the statute would be wholly ineffective in the case of a large company, unless by the merest chance a youthful purchaser were known to the board (sic) of directors. Yet Parliament contemplated that a company might commit the offence.'[69]

18.31 A further defect, of particular relevance to the directing mind and will test, is that the larger the corporation the less likely it is to be personally liable by virtue of the identification principle, since the larger the corporation the fewer (relatively) will be the activities and decisions of its controlling officers.

Another approach: attribution a matter of statutory construction

18.32 The 'directing mind and will test', affirmed in 2000 in respect of both common law offences and statutory offences by the Court of Appeal in *A-G's Reference (No 2 of 1999)*,[70] may not be determinative in all cases where a *statutory offence* is involved. According to the decision of the Privy Council in 1995 in *Meridian Global Funds Management Asia Ltd v Securities Commission*,[71] if the application of the directing mind and will test would defeat the purpose of the statute, attribution depends on the interpretation of the rule in question and its underlying policy (or purpose). This approach, which may be regarded as an extension of the identification principle, can result in the attribution to the corporation of the acts and state of mind of someone lower down the corporation than its directing mind and will.

Meridian was a Hong Kong investment management company. Two of its senior investment managers, who were not part of its 'directing mind and will', improperly used their authority to provide finance to buy into a publicly listed New Zealand company with a view to gaining control of it. Meridian thereby became a substantial security holder in the company. A New Zealand statute required a substantial security holder in a publicly listed company to give notice of the holding to that company and to the stock exchange, as soon as it knew or ought to know that it was such a holder. Those who were the directing mind and will of Meridian were ignorant of what had occurred and consequently Meridian failed to notify the New Zealand company and the stock exchange

---

[69] [1993] 2 All ER 718 at 721.   [70] [2000] QB 796, CA.   [71] [1995] 2 AC 500, PC.

that it had become a substantial security holder. Proceedings were brought by the New Zealand Securities Commission against Meridian and a civil order was made against it in favour of the Commission and of a shareholder in the New Zealand company.

The question before the Privy Council was whether the knowledge of one of the two senior investment managers, who was its chief investment manager, could be attributed to Meridian; if not, Meridian would not have known nor ought to have known of the relevant fact at the material time. The Privy Council held that the senior investment manager's knowledge could be attributed. **Lord Hoffmann, delivering the Privy Council's advice, stated that in attributing knowledge to a corporation the directing mind and will test was not always appropriate or necessary; sometimes the acts and state of mind of someone lower down in the organisation could be attributed. The answer to the question 'can this person's acts and state of mind be attributed to the corporation?' depended, said his Lordship, on the interpretation of the rule in question:**

> 'This is always a matter of interpretation: given that it was intended to apply to a company, how was it intended to apply? Whose act (or knowledge, or state of mind) was *for this purpose* intended to count as the act etc of the company? One finds the answer to this question by applying the usual canons of interpretation, taking into account the language of the rule (if it is a statute) and its content and policy.'[72]

That, said Lord Hoffmann, might indicate that the act and mind of someone outside the directing mind and will could be attributed to the company. The New Zealand statute's policy was to compel the immediate disclosure of the identity of a person who became a substantial security holder. Where that person was a corporation the relevant act and state of mind could include that of an individual who, within the scope of his authority, acquired the relevant interest; the statute's policy would be defeated if knowledge was required on the part of someone constituting part of the directing mind and will of the corporation.

18.33 The approach in *Meridian* has not yet been applied by an English court in a reported criminal case concerning a corporation's criminal liability. In *Re Odyssey (London) Ltd v OIC Run Off Ltd*,[73] referred to in para 18.40, however, the majority of the Court of Appeal held that the approach in *Meridian* is of general application and used it to *assist*[74] in determining whether perjured evidence was attributable in civil proceedings to the company on whose behalf it was given.

---

[72] [1995] 2 AC 500 at 507.

[73] (2000) 150 NLJ 430, CA (reported as *Sphere Drake Insurance plc v Orion Insurance Co plc*). This is a brief report. What is said in the text relies on the transcript.

[74] The Court did not apply the *Meridian* approach alone but combined it with what may be called the 'status and authority test' in *Andrews Weatherfoil Ltd* [1972] 1 All ER 65, CA. In that case it was held that not every 'responsible agent' could by his actions make the corporation criminally liable; it was necessary for the judge to invite the jury to consider whether or not there were established those facts which as a matter of law were required to identify the individual with the corporation.

Further support for the application of the *Meridian* approach in criminal cases was provided in *Ferguson v British Gas Trading Ltd*,[75] a civil case concerned with tortious liability for breach of the statutory prohibition of harassment under the Protection from Harassment Act 1997 referred to in paras 7.137 to 7.144. In *Ferguson v British Gas* the Court of Appeal rejected the view that attribution of the conduct and state of mind of an individual to a corporation was always limited to the conduct and state of mind of an individual who could be identified with the corporation as part of its 'directing mind and will'. It held that, whether or not the conduct of an employee of a corporation could be attributed to the corporation for the purposes of liability, including criminal liability, depended on the proper construction of the particular rule of law concerned. Referring to *Meridian*, the Court of Appeal held that the 'directing mind and will' approach in *Tesco Supermarkets Ltd v Nattrass* related to the specific statutory provisions in question: 'one cannot just jump from one Act to another and say the rule for one is the rule for another'.[76] The Court of Appeal declined, however, to decide what the test for attribution (and therefore corporate responsibility) was under the Protection from Harassment Act 1997 because the Court had not had a complete citation of relevant decided cases (the appeal was an interlocutory one). The point was left to be fully argued at the trial.

18.34 The extension of corporate criminal responsibility is generally regarded as desirable, but the approach taken in *Meridian* has the drawback that it is productive of uncertainty. The policy behind a statute may be difficult to discover. Moreover, the words of the statute are unlikely to indicate who constitutes the corporation for the purposes of the offence under it. Until a court had interpreted a particular offence it would not be possible to be certain whether someone below the directing mind and will of a corporation is to have his acts and state of mind attributed to it. In his dissenting speech in *Re Odyssey (London) Ltd v OIC Run Off Ltd*, Buxton LJ stated that *Meridian* was an imperfect guide to the rule for attribution of a crime. The approach in *Tesco v Nattrass* does, at least, have the merit of certainty despite its disadvantages.

Which of the two approaches applies to a particular offence?

18.35 The *Meridian* approach clearly does not apply to the small number of common law offences, such as conspiracy to defraud, because it is limited to the interpretation of statutory offences.[77] In these cases it is the directing mind and will test which applies.

In the absence of further authority giving guidance on the matter it is difficult to know in advance when the *Meridian* approach will be applied to a statutory offence in preference to the narrower approach in *Tesco v Nattrass*,[78] which subsequent to *Meridian* was regarded by the Divisional Court as applicable to a statutory offence of permitting breach of the rules about bus drivers' driving hours.[79]

---

[75] [2009] EWCA Civ 46. [76] [2009] EWCA Civ 46 at [34], per Jacob LJ.
[77] *A-G's Reference (No 2 of 1999)* [2000] QB 796, CA. [78] Para 18.26.
[79] *Yorkshire Traction Co Ltd v Vehicle Inspectorate* [2001] EWHC Admin 190, DC.

The Privy Council's emphasis in *Meridian* on the fact that the purpose of the statute would be defeated if the 'directing mind and will test' was applied suggests that the *Meridian* approach comes into play where the court considers that the application of that test would have that effect. This, however, is a somewhat loose restriction, but it may suggest that *Meridian* is more likely to be applied where the offence is a regulatory offence requiring *mens rea* than where the offence requiring *mens rea* is a 'real crime'.

The tenor of the *Odyssey v OIC* and *Ferguson v British Gas* decisions, however, is in favour of the *Meridian* approach being the normal approach to the application of the identification principle to statutory offences.

Acting within scope of authority

18.36 **A corporation is only criminally liable if the individual whose acts and state of mind are sought to be attributed to it acts within the scope of his authority.**[80] If the managing director of a company picks someone's pocket or causes death by his dangerous driving on his way to a business meeting, his acts and state of mind are not attributed to the company. However, the present requirement does not mean that activities contrary to the corporation's interests will exclude its liability. A corporation may be convicted even though it is itself defrauded, provided that the offence was committed by an individual (whose acts and state of mind are attributable to it) acting within the scope of his authority.[81]

Defects with the approaches

18.37 Attribution of a person's conduct and state of mind by either approach may work fairly well with small corporations but it fails to deal adequately with large or medium-sized corporations for two reasons:

- It is implicit in both approaches that they can only operate if there is a sufficient act (or omission) with sufficient *mens rea* on the part of a particular individual. **It is not possible to aggregate the acts and states of mind of two or more individuals (none of whom could be criminally liable) so as to render the corporation liable.**[82] This is unfortunate in the light of the fact that many corporate decisions or failures are constituted not by one individual but by the distinct contributions of a number of them or by a failure of its systems. As stated in para 8.140, this problem was manifested in a number of unsuccessful prosecutions of corporations for the common law offence of manslaughter by gross negligence.

---

[80] *DPP v Kent and Sussex Contractors Ltd* [1944] KB 146 at 168, per Macnaghten J; *Moore v I Bresler Ltd* [1944] 2 All ER 515, DC; *Meridian Global Funds Management Asta Ltd v Securities Commission* [1995] 2 AC 500 at 511.

[81] *Moore v I Bresler Ltd* [1944] 2 All ER 515, DC.

[82] *A-G's Reference (No 2 of 1999)* [2000] QB 796, CA. For earlier authority see *HM Coroner for East Kent, ex p Spooner* (1987) 88 Cr App Rep 10, DC; *P&O European Ferries (Dover) Ltd* (1990) 93 Cr App Rep 72, Crown Ct. This rule is criticised by Wells 'Culture, Risk and Criminal Liability' [1993] Crim LR 551 at 563–565.

- A further defect is the uncertainty about which of the two approaches a court will take when a particular statutory provision comes up for consideration.

18.38 The abolition of the non-aggregation rule and the introduction of a 'management failure' principle of liability would both make the law more effective and more appropriate to corporations in the twenty-first century.

Another approach, which might be complementary, would be to impose liability on a corporation which had caused or threatened a proscribed harm if, after the event, it had failed to take adequate steps to rectify what occurred (eg by compensating a victim), to prevent a recurrence and to discipline employees at fault. On this basis, the fault required for an offence physically committed under a corporation's auspices could be presumed, without the need to identify an individual employee of whatever level who was responsible for it, unless the corporation could establish that it had taken adequate steps of the above types.[83] In effect, the corporation would be being punished as much for what it did not do after the event as for what it did or did not do at the time. Not the least of the problems with this idea, however, is that the degree of 'after the event' fault required is left at large and that – since the offence to be charged may depend on which of a range of *mens rea* is alleged – there might be problems in the choice of the charge if actual *mens rea* did not have to be proved.[84]

Yet another approach is that contained in the Bribery Bill, before Parliament at the time of writing. Although the Bill assumes the application of the identification principle to offences under it, which of the two approaches under that principle would apply is not stated. It also provides an offence of failing to prevent a bribery offence under two of its provisions which could only be committed by a corporation or partnership carrying on a business. Under this provision, if a person associated with such a body committed one of these two bribery offences, that body would have a defence if it proved that it had in place adequate procedures designed to prevent persons associated with it committing such an offence.

Offences where liability cannot be based on the attribution of conduct and state of mind

18.39 In the *ICR Haulage Ltd* case,[85] although it was said that a corporation was prima facie criminally liable to the same extent as a natural person, two exceptions to this general rule were mentioned and it was recognised that there might be others.

18.40 The first exception was said to consist of 'cases where from its very nature, the offence cannot be committed by a corporation'.[86] The Court gave perjury and bigamy

---

[83] See Fisse and Braithwaite 'The Allocation of Responsibility for Corporate Crime: Individualism, Collectivism and Accountability' (1988) 11 Sydney LR 468.

[84] See, further, Simester and Sullivan *Criminal Law: Theory and Doctrine* (3rd edn, 2007) 263–264.

[85] [1944] KB 551, CCA.

[86] [1944] KB 551 at 554.

as examples, and sexual offences such as rape and familial sex offences also seem to fall within this category. In *Re Odyssey (London) Ltd v OIC Run Off Ltd*,[87] however, a civil case relating to perjured evidence given by a director and managing director of a limited company, the majority of the Court of Appeal held that the evidence of an individual given on behalf of a company is capable of being treated as the evidence of the company and that the company, as well as the individual, may be guilty of perjury if he gives false evidence. The latter part of this statement was an obiter dictum. The problem with this is that perjury requires that the false statement must be made by a person who has been lawfully sworn, and the corporation cannot be so described. However, if a governing body were to authorise the making of a false statement on oath in court, a corporation might be convicted, as an accomplice, of perjury. Similarly, although a corporation cannot commit bigamy as a perpetrator, if a marriage bureau is managed by a limited company, one of whose directors knowingly negotiates a bigamous marriage, it is difficult to see why the company should not be convicted of bigamy, as an accomplice, for a natural person may be convicted of aiding or abetting an offence which he could not commit himself as a perpetrator.[88] In *Re Odyssey (London) Ltd v OIC Run Off Ltd*,[89] the majority of the Court of Appeal stated that a company could be convicted of bigamy. Clearly, although a corporation cannot be convicted as a perpetrator of offences involving sexual intercourse, theoretically it could be convicted as an accomplice. It is, however, difficult to visualise a situation where someone whose conduct and state of mind were attributable to the corporation would be acting within the scope of his authority in respect of an offence of rape or a familial sex offence. On the other hand, it has been argued that: 'If Z, the managing director of X Co Ltd, a film company, supervises the filming of intercourse between M, an 18-year-old male, with N, a 15-year-old girl, there is no reason why Z and hence the film company should not be convicted as secondary parties to the [offence of sexual activity with a child under 16].'[90]

18.41 The second exception to the general rule of corporate liability for crime referred to in the *ICR Haulage Ltd* case **arises from the fact that 'the court will not stultify itself by embarking on a trial in which, if a verdict of guilty is returned, no effective order by way of sentence can be made'.**[91] This exception is now confined to murder for which the only punishment which the court can impose is imprisonment.

18.42 It was said obiter in several old cases that a corporation could not be indicted for a crime of violence.[92] These dicta were acted upon by Finlay J in *Cory Bros & Co*,[93] where he held that a company could not be indicted for manslaughter or the statutory offence of setting up an engine (in this case an electric fence) calculated to destroy life with intent to injure a trespasser. It is now clear that a corporation can be convicted of an offence despite the fact that it is one of violence. *Cory Bros & Co* was questioned in *ICR Haulage Ltd* and a corporation has since been convicted as an accomplice to causing death by dangerous

---

[87] See para 18.33, n 73. [88] Para 17.20. [89] Para 18.33, n 73.
[90] Reed and Fitzpatrick *Criminal Law* (3rd edn, 2006) 168. [91] [1944] KB 551 at 554.
[92] Eg *Birmingham and Gloucester Rly Co* (1842) 3 QB 223 at 232. [93] [1927] 1 KB 810.

driving[94] and a handful of corporations (all of them small companies) had been convicted of the common law offence of manslaughter by gross negligence before the enactment of the Corporate Manslaughter and Corporate Homicide Act 2007, dealt with in Chapter 8, s 20 of which prospectively abolished the common law offence of manslaughter by gross negligence in its application to corporations.

18.43 A third exception, not mentioned in *ICR Haulage Ltd* is that **statute may exclude liability for an offence based on attribution of the conduct and state of mind of an individual.** An example is the offence of corporate manslaughter introduced by the Corporate Manslaughter and Corporate Homicide Act 2007 to punish corporations if the way in which their activities are managed or organised causes death and amounts to gross negligence. Corporate manslaughter does not depend on the attribution of the act and state of mind of any individual.

Liability of directors and similar persons

18.44 The conviction of a corporation does not in itself involve any natural person in criminal liability. On the other hand, where a corporation is criminally liable for an offence, a natural person involved may also be convicted of it, as a joint perpetrator (if he is the person who physically committed the offence) or as an accomplice (if he aided, abetted, counselled or procured its commission). In addition, many statutes now provide for the guilt of controlling officers of the corporation who would not be criminally liable under ordinary principles, or whose guilt it would otherwise be hard to prove. This makes it easier to get at those who are really responsible for the corporation's offence.

An example of this type of provision contains the words italicised:

> 'Where an offence under this Act which has been *committed by a body corporate is proved to have been committed with the consent or connivance of, or to be attributable to any neglect on the part of, any director, manager* [ie someone managing in a governing role the affairs of the corporation, as opposed to someone with a day-to-day management function],[95] *secretary or other similar officer of the body corporate, or any person who was purporting to act in that capacity,* he, as well as the body corporate, shall be guilty of that offence.'

A provision of this type is contained in the Health and Safety at Work etc Act 1974. s 37, and is commonly to be found in other statutes.[96]

An individual who is liable under such a provision is by its express terms guilty of the same offence as that committed by the corporation; he does not commit, nor is he guilty

---

[94] *Robert Millar (Contractors) Ltd and Millar* [1970] 2 QB 54, CA.

[95] *Boal* [1992] QB 591, CA.

[96] Other examples of this type of provision are the Trade Descriptions Act 1968, s 20; the Insolvency Act 1986, s 432; the Consumer Protection Act 1987, s 40; the Children Act 1989, s 103; and the Food Safety Act 1990, s 36.

of, some separate offence created by the provision. An obiter dictum by the Court of Appeal in *Wilson*[97] that such a provision creates an offence ancillary to that committed by the corporation, and when it applies the individual is guilty of 'that offence', cannot be correct, given the unequivocal wording of the provision.

18.45 In *A-G's Reference (No 1 of 1995)*,[98] it was held that a person 'consents' to the commission of an offence by a corporation if he knows the material facts that constitute the offence by the corporation and agrees to the corporation's conduct of its business on the basis of those facts.[99] 'Connivance' is generally regarded as involving wilful blindness as to the commission of the offence,[100] which must no doubt be coupled in this context with acquiescence in it. A person who consents to, or connives at, an offence committed by a corporation (through another person's conduct) may be guilty of that offence as an accomplice; and this is so even in the case where he does nothing positive, if he had a right of control over that other person.[101] The importance of this part of the provision is that it makes the task of the prosecution less difficult, since it is enough for them to prove consent or connivance by a person of the specified type and they do not have to prove that it amounted to aiding, abetting, counselling or procuring.

By comparison, a person cannot be an accomplice to an offence simply because it is 'attributable to his neglect'. This phrase refers to the situation where a person of the specified type (D) fails to take steps within the functions of his office to prevent the offence being committed by a corporation through another person. D need not know about the commission of the offence, nor be wilfully blind as to it; it is enough that he should have been put on inquiry by reason of the surrounding circumstances so as to have made inquiries as to whether the offence is being committed.[102] Consequently, the words 'attributable to any neglect on the part of' are important since they considerably extend the ambit of the criminal law in this context, rendering a person of the specified type liable for his negligence in failing to prevent the offence committed by the corporation.[103] Unlike 'consent' or 'connivance' a causal link is required between the neglect and the commission of the offence. The commission of the offence must be attributable to some extent (but not necessarily wholly) to the neglect of the person in question of the specified type.

In *Chargot Ltd*,[104] where the House of Lords was concerned with the Health and Safety at Work etc Act 1974, s 37, Lord Hope (with whom the other Law Lords agreed) said this about the verbs discussed in this paragraph:

'No fixed rule can be laid down as to what the prosecution must identify and prove in order to establish that the officer's state of mind was such as to amount to consent, connivance or neglect. In some cases, as where the officer's place of activity was remote

[97] [1997] 1 All ER 119 at 121.   [98] *A-G's Reference (No 1 of 1995)* [1996] 2 Cr App Rep 320, CA.

[99] See also *Huckerby v Elliott* [1970] 1 All ER 189 at 194, per Ashworth J.

[100] *Somerset v Hart* (1884) 12 QBD 360, DC.   [101] Para 17.13.

[102] *P Ltd* [2007] EWCA Crim 1937.   [103] *Wilson* [1997] 1 All ER 119 at 121.

[104] [2008] UKHL 73.

from the work place or what was done there was not under his immediate direction and control, this may require the leading of quite detailed evidence of which fair notice may have to be given. In others, where the officer was in day to day contact with what was done there, very little more may be needed.... [T]he question, in the end of the day, will always be whether the officer in question should have been put on inquiry so as to have taken steps to determine whether or not the appropriate safety procedures were in place.'[105]

Referring to *A-G's Reference (No 1 of 1995)*, Lord Hope went on to say that he agreed with the statement in that case referred to at the start of this numbered paragraph. He said, however, that he

'would add that consent can be established by inference as well as by proof of an express agreement. The state of mind that the words "connivance" and "neglect" contemplate is one that may also be established by inference.... Where it is shown that the body corporate failed to achieve or prevent the [offence in question], it will be a relatively short step for the inference to be drawn that there was connivance or neglect on his part if the circumstances under which the risk arose were under the direction or control of the officer. The more remote his area of responsibility is from those circumstances, the harder it will be to draw that inference.'[106]

18.46 A similar type of provision to that just described is one whose wording is the same except that it omits any reference to 'attributable to neglect', so that a director, manager or other similar officer is only guilty (by virtue of it) of an offence committed by a corporation if he consented to it or connived at it.[107]

18.47 Often, provisions of either type go on to provide that where the affairs of a corporation are managed by its members, the provision applies in relation to the acts and default of a member in connection with his functions of management as if he were a director of the corporation.

18.48 In addition to any criminal liability, company directors and members of limited liability partnerships who are convicted of an indictable offence in connection with their management of a company can be disqualified for up to 15 years by a court[108] from acting as directors or members of limited liability partnerships under the Company Directors Disqualification Act 1986, s 2.[109]

---

[105] [2008] UKHL 73 at [33].

[106] [2008] UKHL 73 at [34].

[107] Theft Act 1968, s 18 (see para 12.47); Public Order Act 1986, ss 28 and 29M; Trade Marks Act 1994, s 101(5); Fraud Act 2006, s 12 (see para 12.47).

[108] When a conviction is in a magistrates' court the maximum period of disqualification is five years.

[109] Section 2 was extended to members of limited liability partnerships by the Limited Liability Partnerships Regulations 2001, reg 4(2).

Unincorporated associations

Key points 18.4

An unincorporated association cannot be convicted of a common law offence but may be convicted of a statutory offence where the statute expressly so provides or where the statutory offence is interpreted as capable of commission by an unincorporated association. However, this does not exempt the members of the association from criminal liability unless the statute in question provides otherwise.

18.49 Unlike a corporation, an unincorporated association, such as a partnership within the Partnership Act 1890 or a limited partnership registered under the Limited Partnerships Act 1907 (not to be confused with limited liability partnership under the Limited Liability Partnership Act 2000, which is a corporation), trade union or members' club, is not a separate legal person distinct from its members. As a result, a partnership or other unincorporated association cannot be convicted of a common law offence (although, of course, its individual members can be convicted if they are parties to an offence).

18.50 The situation is different in the case of statutory offences. First, but rarely, some statutes expressly provide that offences under them can be committed by an unincorporated association. An example is provided by the Corporate Manslaughter and Corporate Homicide Act 2007 (CMCHA 2007). The Act expressly provides that the offences of corporate manslaughter and of breach of a remedial order or of a publicity order may be committed by a partnership, or a trade union or employers' association, that is an employer.[110] CMCHA 2007, s 14(1) provides that, for the purposes of CMCHA 2007, a partnership is to be treated as owing whatever duties of care it would owe if it were a corporation. Proceedings for an offence under CMCHA 2007 alleged to have been committed by a partnership are to be brought in the name of the partnership (and not in that of any of its members).[111] A fine imposed on a partnership on its conviction of an offence under CMCHA 2007 is to be paid out of the funds of the partnership.[112]

18.51 Second, where a statute does not make express provision in relation to the criminal liability of an unincorporated association, a statutory offence may be interpreted as

---

[110] See paras 8.143, 8.144 and 8.156. For another example, under the Trade Union and Labour Relations (Consolidation) Act 1992, s 45, a trade union is guilty of an offence if it refuses or wilfully neglects to perform certain duties under that Act.

[111] CMCHA 2007, s 14(2).

[112] CMCHA 2007, s 14(3). CMCHA 2007, s 14 does not apply to a partnership that is a legal person under the law by which it is governed (eg a limited liability partnership under the Limited Liability Partnership Act 2000): CMCHA 2007, s 14(4).

capable of commission by such an association. The reason is that under the Interpretation Act 1978[113] 'person' in a statute passed after 1889 includes an unincorporated association unless the contrary intention appears. An increasing number of statutes[114] assume that offences under them can be committed by a partnership or by any type of unincorporated association by setting out one or more ancillary provisions relating to it. Examples are stipulating that where an offence is alleged to have been committed by such an entity it must be prosecuted in its own name (and not in that of any of its members), that a fine imposed on such an entity on *its* conviction for an offence shall be paid out of its funds and that an officer is liable for an offence committed by *it* where he consented to or connived in the commission of that offence or it was attributable to his neglect (ie an officer's liability clause corresponding to that described in para 18.44).

In *A-G v Able*,[115] Woolf J, as he then was, dealing with an alleged offence under the Suicide Act 1961, stated that an unincorporated association, the Voluntary Euthanasia Society, was incapable of committing an offence under the Act. On the other hand, in *W Stevenson and Sons (a partnership)*[116] the Court of Appeal recognised that post-1889 legislation could as a matter of statutory interpretation render a partnership criminally liable for a statutory offence as an entity separate from its members. The statutory provision in question contained an officers' liability clause referring to the liability of a partner of a partnership for offences committed by it. The Court of Appeal held that the regulatory offence in question (failing to submit an accurate note of fish sales) could be committed by a partnership; the officers' clause clearly contemplated that it could be prosecuted and bear criminal liability. The Court also held that any fine imposed on the partnership could only be levied against the assets of the partnership.

In *L*,[117] discussed below, the Court of Appeal recognised that other forms of unincorporated association can be criminally liable and that the offence in question could be committed by such an association.

Neither *W Stevenson* nor *L* provide much guidance about when a statutory offence applies to a partnership or unincorporated association. It is clear from these cases that the existence of one or more ancillary provisions of the type referred to above will be indicative that the offence applies to a partnership or unincorporated association, but it is also clear from *L* (where there were no such ancillary provisions) that the absence of such ancillary provisions is not determinative the other way.

The offences in issue in *W Stevenson* and *L* were ones of strict liability. In neither case did the Court of Appeal consider the situation where a statutory offence involved any

---

[113] See the Interpretation Act 1978, ss 5 and 22(1) and Schs 1 and 2, Pt I, para 4(1)(a).

[114] See, for example, the Transport Act 1968, s 120B, the Safeguarding of Vulnerable Groups Act 2006, s 18, the Health Act 2006, ss 76 and 77, and the Serious Crime Act 2007, s 70. For further examples see *L* [2008] EWCA Crim 1970 at [25].

[115] [1984] QB 795 at 810.

[116] [2008] EWCA Crim 273.

[117] [2008] EWCA Crim 1970.

element of *mens rea*. In *L*, the Court stated that if a statutory offence involved any element of *mens rea* that

'would be likely to raise quite different questions because of the personal and individual nature of a guilty mind. In such a case, it may well be that a contrary intention [for the purposes of the Interpretation Act 1978, s 5] appears. *A-G v Able* was a case in which the point which we have had to consider was not in any manner argued, and the 1978 Act was not mentioned. It is, however, not in the least surprising that Woolf J dealt with it on the assumed basis that "[i]t must be remembered that the [Voluntary Euthanasia] society is an unincorporated body and there can be no question of the society committing an offence", when that offence was of intentionally aiding, abetting, counselling or procuring the suicide of another, thus involving mens rea and indeed punishable with up to 14 years' imprisonment.'[118]

18.52 There can be no doubt that, in those offences which can be committed by it, an unincorporated association will not incur criminal liability simply because one of its members (or one of its employees) has committed an offence. Special rules described in Chapter 8 apply in the case of corporate manslaughter. In other offences, by analogy with the law relating to corporations, liability will arise if the general principles of vicarious liability are satisfied or if the unincorporated association can be said to be personally liable on the basis of committing an 'operational offence' or a breach of a statutory duty imposed on the association or (to the extent that it can be liable for an offence requiring *mens rea*) on the basis of the acts and state of mind of someone which can be attributed to the association in respect of the offence in question.

Liability of members of unincorporated association

18.53 The fact that an unincorporated association is criminally liable for a particular strict liability offence does not in itself exempt its members from liability, unless the statute in question provides otherwise.

The potential liability of the members of an unincorporated association was considered by the Court of Appeal in *L* referred to above. The case was concerned with the potential liability of members of an unincorporated association (a golf club with 900 members) for the strict liability offence committed by a person causing poisonous, noxious or polluting matter to enter controlled waters, contrary to the Water Resources Act 1991, s 85, after heating oil had escaped into a watercourse from the club's premises. A prosecution had been brought against two of the club's members (ie its Chairman and its Treasurer). The trial judge had ruled that this was wrong because the club could have been prosecuted as an unincorporated association and the two members were not personally at fault. The Court of Appeal agreed with the judge that, since the contrary intent did not appear, 'person' in s 85 of the 1991 Act included an unincorporated association; the judge had therefore been correct to rule that the club could have been prosecuted. However, the Court of Appeal disagreed with the second part of the judge's ruling.

[118] [2008] EWCA Crim 1970 at [30].

It held that not only the Chairman and Treasurer but all members of the club were liable for the strict liability offence in question. The judge had based the second part of his ruling on the fact that if the club had been a corporation the Chairman and Treasurer would not have been liable as officers of the corporation and had concluded from that that the liability of the officers of an unincorporated association should not be greater than their counterparts in a corporation. The Court of Appeal rejected the judge's view that there was no reason why the criminal liability of officers (or members) of an unincorporated association should exist on a different basis from that of the officers of a corporation. It went on:

> 'Although many statutes make it possible to prosecute an unincorporated association, and although we have held that this is perfectly possible under the Water Resources Act 1991, s 85, it does not follow that such an association is for all purposes the same as a company or other corporation. It is not. A corporation has, for all legal purposes, independent legal personality. It is also regulated, often heavily. It must have a registered address and registered directors and secretary. An unincorporated association may indeed look very like a corporation in some cases, and it may have standing and de facto independence, but equally it may not. A prosecution which could only be brought against an informal grouping of building workers, or sportsmen, or campaigners would be likely to be wholly ineffective. It is a necessary consequence of the different nature of an unincorporated association that all its members remain jointly and severally liable for its actions done within their authority. In the present case, the 900-odd members of the club were indeed all maintainers of the tank and all guilty of the strict liability offence of causing the leakage.
>
> This is not vicarious liability for the offence of the club... Vicarious liability, when it exists, arises out of the employment by the defendant of another person to act for him. There is no sense in which the chairman, treasurer, or any other member of this club employed the club to do anything for them. The criminal liability of the members of the club, including the chairman and the treasurer, is primary liability, not vicarious liability. It arises because each person jointly maintains the tank and has thus caused the leak.
>
> It follows that the correct position under the Water Resources Act 1991, s 85 is that a prosecution for the strict liability offence of causing polluting matter to enter controlled waters may be brought, on the facts of this case, against either the club in its own name, or against individual members. It is for the Crown in any individual case to determine the defendant(s) whom it seeks to prosecute. The court would interfere only in the very limited case of oppression involving abuse of process. No doubt relevant considerations will include the extent of the association's stability and assets and the nature of the act or omission said to constitute an offence. We have heard no argument on whether in exceptional circumstances it could be permissible for the Crown to seek to proceed against both the club and individuals, but there are no such exceptional circumstances here.'[119]

Despite the Court of Appeal's ruling, it concluded that a fresh trial would not be in the interests of justice, and it directed the acquittal of the two defendants.

---

[119] [2008] EWCA Crim 1970 at [33]–[35].

It follows from this decision that an ordinary member of an unincorporated association is personally liable for a strict liability offence committed by the association without any fault on his part simply because he is a member of that association. This compares oddly with the position of a shareholder in a company who is not criminally liable in corresponding circumstances.

FURTHER READING

Colvin 'Corporate Personality and Criminal Responsibility' (1995) 6 Criminal Law Forum 1

Fisse and Braithwaite *Corporations, Crime, and Accountability* (1993)

Glazebrook 'Situational Liability' in *Reshaping the Criminal Law* (1978) (Glazebrook (ed)) 108

Gobert 'Corporate Criminality: New Crimes for the Times' [1994] Crim LR 722

Gobert 'Corporate Criminal Liability: Four Models of Fault' (1994) 14 LS 393

Horder 'The Criminal Liability of Corporations' in *Halsbury's Laws of England: Centenary Essays 2007* (2007) (Hetherington (ed)) 103

Leigh *Strict and Vicarious Liability* (1982)

Pace 'Delegation – A Doctrine in Search of a Definition' [1982] Crim LR 627

Pinto and Evans *Corporate Criminal Liability* (2003)

Wells 'Corporations: Culture, Risk and Criminal Liability' [1993] Crim LR 551

Wells *Corporations and Criminal Responsibility* (2nd edn, 2001)

Index